SEVENTH EDITION

BUSINESS LAW TODAY

THE ESSENTIALS

TEXT & SUMMARIZED CASES

E-Commerce, Legal, Ethical, and International Environment

SEVENTH EDITION

BUSINESS LAW TODAY
THE ESSENTIALS

TEXT & SUMMARIZED CASES
E-Commerce, Legal, Ethical, and International Environment

ROGER LeROY MILLER
Institute for University Studies
Arlington, Texas

GAYLORD A. JENTZ
Herbert D. Kelleher
Emeritus Professor in Business Law
MSIS Department
University of Texas at Austin

THOMSON

SOUTH-WESTERN

WEST

Australia · Canada · Mexico · Singapore · Spain · United Kingdom · United States

THOMSON
WEST ™

SEVENTH EDITION
BUSINESS LAW TODAY
THE ESSENTIALS
TEXT & SUMMARIZED CASES
E-Commerce, Legal, Ethical, and International Environment

ROGER LeROY MILLER   GAYLORD A. JENTZ

Vice President and Editorial Director:
Jack Calhoun

Publisher, Business Law and Accounting:
Rob Dewey

Acquisition Editor:
Steve Silverstein

Senior Developmental Editor:
Jan Lamar

Executive Marketing Manager:
Lisa L. Lysne

Production Manager:
Bill Stryker

Technology Project Editor:
Christine A. Wittmer

Manufacturing Coordinator:
Charlene Taylor

Compositor:
Parkwood Composition
New Richmond, WI

Printer:
Quebecor World Versailles

Art Director:
Michelle Kunkler

Internal Designer:
Bill Stryker

Cover Designer:
Diane Gliebe/Design Matters

Web Coordinator:
Kelly Reid

Cover Images:
© Getty Images, Inc.; Gavel Illustration
by Lisa Ballard/Cincinnati, OH

For permission to use material from this
text or product, submit a request online
at **http://www.thomsonrights.com**.
For more information contact

Thomson Higher Education
5191 Natorp Boulevard
Mason, OH 45040
USA

Or you can visit our Internet site at:
http://www.westbuslaw.com

INTERNATIONAL LOCATIONS

ASIA (including India)
Thomson Learning
5 Shenton Way
#01-01 UIC Building
Singapore 068808

AUSTRALIA/NEW ZEALAND
Thomson Learning Australia
102 Dodds Street
Southbank, Victoria 3006
Australia

LATIN AMERICA
Thomson Learning
Seneca, 53
Colonia Polanco
11560 Mexico
D.F.Mexico

CANADA
Thomson Nelson
1120 Birchmount Road
Toronto, Ontario
Canada M1K 5G4

**UK/EUROPE/MIDDLE
EAST/AFRICA**
Thomson Learning
High Holborn House
50-51 Bedford Road
London WC1R 4LR
United Kingdom

SPAIN (includes Portugal)
Thomson Paraninfo
Calle Magallanes, 25
28015 Madrid, Spain

■ CONTENTS IN BRIEF

Appendices

◼ CONTENTS

Appendices

Preface
To the Instructor

We have always felt that business law and the legal environment should be an exciting, contemporary, and interesting course. We believe that *Business Law Today: The Essentials,* Seventh Edition, imparts this excitement to your students. We have spent a great deal of effort in giving this book a visual appeal that will encourage students to learn the law. We have also worked hard to make sure that *Business Law Today: The Essentials* continues its established tradition of being the most up-to-date text on the market. The law presented in the Seventh Edition includes new statutes, regulations, and cases, as well as the most recent developments in cyberlaw.

You will find that coverage of traditional business law has not been sacrificed in the process of creating this text. Additionally, *Business Law Today: The Essentials* explicitly addresses the American Assembly of Collegiate Schools of Business's (AACSB's) broad array of curriculum requirements. As you will see, many of the features and special pedagogical devices in this text focus on the global, political, ethical, social, environmental, technological, and cultural contexts of business law.

Emphasis on Internet Law

Business Law Today: The Essentials, Seventh Edition, is truly up to date and reflects current law to the fullest extent possible. Throughout the text, we have included sections discussing the most recent developments in the law as it is being applied to transactions and commerce conducted via the Internet. For example, in Chapter 5, which focuses on intellectual property, we point out how traditional laws—and some newly enacted laws—are being applied to online issues relating to *copyrights, trademarks, patents,* and *trade secrets.* Other chapters include sections on *privacy rights* in the online world, *jurisdictional issues* as they arise in cyberspace, *cyber torts* and *cyber crimes, online securities offerings,* and a number of other topics relating to the online legal environment. We also have devoted an entire chapter (Chapter 10) solely to the topic of *electronic contracts,* or e-contracts.

Emphasis on Ethics

For the Seventh Edition of *Business Law Today: The Essentials,* we have included a significantly revised and updated chapter on ethics and professional responsibility (Chapter 2). The chapter now presents a more practical approach to this topic, including a case study examining the scandal surrounding the actions of Enron Corporation in the early 2000s. We also discuss the Sarbanes-Oxley Act of 2002 and the corporate scandals that led to its passage. In addition to this chapter on ethics, nearly every chapter contains at least one *Ethical Issue* addressing an ethical dimension of a topic under discussion in the chapter. Also, many of the cases presented in the text conclude with *Ethical Consideration* sections that encourage students to probe the ethical ramifications of the courts' decisions. Moreover, for each chapter, a special case problem titled *A Question of Ethics* appears in the *Questions and Case Problems* section.

The Web Connection

In addition to incorporating cyberlaw throughout the basic text of the book, the Seventh Edition offers several other components focusing on technology.

BUSINESS LAW TODAY ON THE WEB

For this edition of *Business Law Today: The Essentials*, we have redesigned and streamlined the text's Web site so that users can easily locate the resources they seek. When you visit our Web site at **http://blt.westbuslaw.com**, you will find a broad array of teaching/learning resources, including the following:

- *Relevant Web sites* for all of the *Landmark in the Law* features and *Landmark and Classic Cases* that are presented in this text.
- *Sample answers* for each *Case Problem with Sample Answer*. This problem-answer set is designed to help your students learn how to answer case problems by acquainting them with model answers to selected case problems. Each chapter includes one of these special case problems.
- *Videos* referenced in the new video questions (discussed next) that have been added to selected chapters for this edition of *Business Law Today: The Essentials*.
- *Internet exercises* for every chapter in the text (at least two per chapter). These exercises, which are substantially new, help familarize students with online legal resources while introducing them to additional information on topics covered in the chapters.
- *Interactive quizzes* for every chapter in the text. At the end of each chapter, a *Before the Test* section directs students to the Web site, where they will find at least twenty questions relating to the topics covered in the chapter.
- *Court case updates* that present summaries of new cases from various West legal publications, all specifically keyed to chapters in this text.
- A *"Statutes" page* that offers links to the full text of selected statutes referenced in the text.
- *Links to other important legal resources* available for free on the Web.
- A *"Talk to Us" feature* that allows you and your students to e-mail us any questions you may have about *Business Law Today: The Essentials*.

WEST'S DIGITAL VIDEO LIBRARY

For this edition of *Business Law Today: The Essentials*, we have added special new *Video Questions* at the end of selected chapters. Each *Video Question* directs students to the text's Web site (at **http://blt.westbuslaw.com**) to view a video relevant to a topic covered in the chapter. This instruction is followed by a series of questions based on the video. The questions are repeated on the Web site, when the student accesses the video. The videos are part of West's Digital Video Library, a compendium of over sixty-five video scenarios and explanations. An access code for the videos can be packaged with each new copy of this textbook for no additional charge. If West's Digital Video Library access did not come packaged with the textbook, students can purchase it online at http://digitalvideolibrary.westbuslaw.com.

These videos can be used as homework assignments, discussion starters, or classroom demonstrations and are useful for generating student interest. Some of the videos are clips from actual movies, such as *The Money Pit* and *Bowfinger.* By watching a video and answering the questions, students will gain an understanding of how the legal concepts they have studied in the chapter apply to the real-life situation portrayed in the video. **Suggested answers for all of the video questions are given in both the *Instructor's Manual* and the *Answers Manual* that accompany this text.**

WESTLAW® CAMPUS

Westlaw® Campus is now available to students using West Legal Studies in Business texts. Westlaw Campus is derived from Westlaw®, the preferred computer-assisted legal research database of legal professionals. Access to Westlaw Campus can be bundled with the text at an outstanding discount. (Students who buy used books may purchase access to Westlaw Campus at http://campus.westbuslaw.com.)

In addition to primary legal materials (federal and state cases, statutes, and administrative law), Westlaw Campus offers secondary resources, such as *American Law Reports* (ALR), *American Jurisprudence 2d* (Am.Jur.2d), and law reviews. These materials can greatly enhance research assignments, critical-thinking exercises, and term papers.

ONLINE LEGAL RESEARCH GUIDE

With every new book, your students will receive a free copy of the *Online Legal Research Guide.* This is the most complete brief guide to using the Internet that exists today. Text co-author Roger LeRoy Miller developed and wrote this supplement, which has been updated for the Seventh Edition of *Business Law Today: The Essentials.* There is even an appendix on how to evaluate information obtained from the Internet.

■ Special Features and Pedagogy

In addition to the components of the *Business Law Today: The Essentials,* Seventh Edition, teaching/learning package described above, the text offers a number of other special features and pedagogy.

FEATURES

Virtually all of the chapters in this text have one or more of the following special features, which are designed both to instruct and to pique the interest of the student of business law and the legal environment.

- *Adapting the Law to the Online Environment*—Nearly every chapter in the Seventh Edition contains one of these special features. A concluding *For Critical Analysis* section asks the student to think critically about some aspect of the issue discussed in the feature. **Suggested answers to these questions are included in both the *Instructor's Manual* and the *Answers Manual* that accompany this text.**

- *Landmark in the Law*—This feature, which appears in most of the chapters in this edition, discusses a landmark case, statute, or other law that has had a significant effect on business law. Each of these features has a section titled *Application to Today's World,* which indicates how the law discussed in the feature affects the legal landscape of today's world. In addition, for the Seventh Edition we have added a *Relevant Web Sites* section that directs students to the book's companion Web site for links to additional information available online.

- *Application*—The majority of the chapters have an *Application* feature, which presents the student with some practical advice on how to apply the law discussed in the chapter to real-world business problems. Each *Application* ends with a "Checklist" for the future businessperson on how to avoid legal problems.

- *Letter of the Law*—This feature provides students with sometimes humorous, sometimes serious illustrations of how the letter of the law has been phrased, interpreted, or applied. Each feature concludes with a section called *The Bottom Line,* which summarizes the implications of the illustrated topic for businesspersons.

- *Ethical Issues*—In addition to a chapter on ethics, chapter-ending ethical questions, and the *Ethical Considerations* following many of the cases presented in this text, we have included special features called *Ethical Issues.* These features, which are closely integrated with the text, open with a question addressing an ethical dimension of the topic being discussed. Each *Ethical Issue* has been given a number so that it can be easily located for review or discussion.

CASE PRESENTATION

In each chapter, we present cases that illustrate the principles of law discussed in the text. The cases are numbered sequentially for easy referencing in class discussions, homework assignments, and examinations. In selecting the cases to be included in this edition, our goal has been to choose cases that reflect the most current law or represent a significant precedent in case law.

Each case is presented in a special format, beginning with the case title and citation (including parallel citations). Whenever possible, we also include a URL, just below the case citation, that can be used to access the case online (a footnote to the URL explains how to find the specific case at that Web site). We then briefly outline the facts of the dispute, the legal issue presented, and the court's decision. To enhance student understanding, we paraphrase the reason for the court's decision. Each case normally concludes with a *For Critical Analysis* section. For one case in each chapter, however, we have added a section titled *Why Is This Case Important?* This section clearly sets forth the importance of the court's decision for businesspersons today.

We give special emphasis to landmark and classic cases by setting them off with a special heading and logo. These cases also include a *Comments* section that stresses the significance of that particular decision for the evolution of the law in that area. For the Seventh Edition, we have added a section titled *Relevant Web Sites* at the conclusion of each landmark and classic case that directs students to additional online resources.

OTHER PEDAGOGICAL DEVICES WITHIN EACH CHAPTER

- Chapter-opening quotations.
- *Learning Objectives* (a series of brief questions at the beginning of each chapter designed to provide a framework for the student as he or she reads through the chapter).

■ *Chapter Outline* (an outline of the chapter's first-level headings).
■ **Margin definitions.**
■ **Margin *On the Web* features** (directing students to relevant Web sites where they will find online articles, statutes, or other legal or information sources concerning a topic being discussed in the text).
■ **Highlighted and numbered examples illustrating legal principles** (we have added more for this edition to better clarify legal concepts).
■ **URLs for cases** (whenever possible, we have included URLs that can be used to access the cases presented in the text; when a URL is available, it appears just below the case citation).
■ **Exhibits and forms** (including many new exhibits illustrating basic principles of contract law).
■ **Photographs** (with critical-thinking questions).

CHAPTER-ENDING PEDAGOGY

■ *Key Terms* (with appropriate page references).
■ *Chapter Summary* (in graphic format with page references).
■ *For Review* (the questions set forth in the chapter-opening *Learning Objectives* section are again presented to aid the student in reviewing the chapter; answers to the even-numbered questions for each chapter are provided in Appendix I).
■ *Questions and Case Problems* (including hypotheticals and case problems; many of the case problems are based on cases from the 2000s).
■ *Case Problem with Sample Answer* (as discussed earlier, each chapter contains one of these case problems; the answer for the problem is provided on the text's Web site at http://blt.westbuslaw.com).
■ *A Question of Ethics.*
■ *For Critical Analysis* (requiring students to think critically about some topic discussed in the chapter).
■ *Video Question* (in selected chapters).
■ *Online Activities* (including Internet exercises and interactive quizzes for each chapter).

APPENDICES

Because the majority of students keep their business law texts as a reference source, we have included at the end of the book the following set of appendices (Appendix I is new to the Seventh Edition):

A. The Constitution of the United States.

B. Articles 2 and 2A of the Uniform Commercial Code (including excerpts from the 2003 amendments to Article 2).

C. Securities Act of 1933 (Excerpts).

D. Securities Exchange Act of 1934 (Excerpts).

E. Title VII of the Civil Rights Act of 1964 (Excerpts).

F. Digital Millennium Copyright Act of 1998 (Excerpts).

G. Uniform Electronic Transactions Act (Excerpts).

H. Electronic Signatures in Global and National Commerce Act of 2000 (Excerpts).

I. Answers to Even-Numbered *For Review* Questions.

▦ A Flexible Teaching/Learning Package

We realize that different people have different teaching philosophies and learning goals. We believe that the Seventh Edition of *Business Law Today: The Essentials* and its extensive supplements offer business law instructors a flexible teaching/ learning package. For example, although we have attempted to make the materials flow from chapter to chapter, most of the chapters are self-contained. In other words, you can use the chapters in any order you wish. Additionally, the extensive number of supplements accompanying *Business Law Today: The Essentials* allows instructors to choose those supplements that will most effectively complement classroom instruction.

Suggestions on how you can adapt the *Business Law Today: The Essentials* teaching/learning package to fit your particular teaching and learning goals are given in the **Resource Integration Guide.** Furthermore, each chapter of the **Instructor's Manual** contains teaching suggestions, possible discussion questions, and additional information on key statutes or other legal sources that you may wish to use in your classroom. These and numerous other supplementary materials (including printed and multimedia supplements) all contribute to the goal of making *Business Law Today: The Essentials* the most flexible teaching/learning package on the market today.

▦ Supplemental Teaching Materials

This edition of *Business Law Today: The Essentials* is accompanied by an expansive group of teaching and learning supplements. Individually and in conjunction with a number of our colleagues, we have developed supplementary teaching materials that we believe are the best available today. Each component of the supplements package is listed below.

PRINTED SUPPLEMENTS

- *Online Legal Research Guide* (free with every new copy of the text; updated for the Seventh Edition).

- *Resource Integration Guide* (also available on the *Instructor's Resource CD-ROM,* or IRCD, to be discussed shortly).

- *Instructor's Manual* (includes additional cases on point with at least one such case summary per chapter, answers to all *For Critical Analysis* questions in the features, and answers for the *Video Questions* at the end of selected chapters; also available on the IRCD).

- *Study Guide.*

- A comprehensive *Test Bank* (also available on the IRCD).

- *Case Printouts* (includes printouts of cases referred to in selected features; also available on the IRCD).

- *Answers Manual* (includes answers to the *Questions and Case Problems,* answers to the *For Critical Analysis* questions in the features, and answers for

the *Video Questions* that conclude selected chapters; also available on the
IRCD).

■ *Instructor's Manual* for the *Drama of the Law* video series (also available on
the IRCD).

SOFTWARE, VIDEO, AND MULTIMEDIA SUPPLEMENTS

■ *Instructor's Resource CD-ROM* (IRCD)—Includes the following supplements:
Resource Integration Guide, Instructor's Manual, Answers Manual, Case-
Problem Cases, ExamView, PowerPoint slides, *Instructor's Manual* for the *Drama
of the Law* video series, Lecture Outline System, Test Bank, and Case Printouts.

■ **ExamView Testing Software.**

■ **WebTutor Advantage and WebTutor ToolBox**—Features chat, discussion
groups, testing, student progress tracking, and business law course materials.

■ **Lecture Outline System** (also available on the IRCD).

■ **PowerPoint slides.**

■ **Transparency acetates.**

■ **Westlaw®**—Ten free hours for qualified adopters.

■ **Westlaw® Campus** (previously described).

■ **West's Digital Video Library**—Provides access to over sixty-five videos, including
the *Drama of the Law* videos and video clips from actual Hollywood movies.
Access to West's Digital Library is available in an optional package with a new text
at no additional cost. If West's Digital Video Library access did not come packaged
with the textbook, students can purchase it online at **http://digitalvideolibrary.
westbuslaw.com**.

■ **VHS Videotapes**—Qualified adopters using this text have access to the entire
library of West videotapes, a vast selection covering most business law issues.
For more information about the videotapes, visit **http://video.westbuslaw.com**.

■ *Wall Street Journal*—Students and professors have the opportunity to subscribe
to the *Wall Street Journal* and access the *Journal's* Web site (**http://wsj.com**) at a
discount when bundled with the text. For students, the offer includes a fifteen-
week subscription and access to the Web site. Qualifying professors can receive a
fifty-two-week subscription, one-year access to the Web site, access to
ProfessorJournal.com, and a video instructing students on how to use the *Wall
Street Journal*.

■ For Users of the Sixth Edition

We thought that those of you who have been using *Business Law Today: The
Essentials* would like to know some of the major changes that have been made for
the Seventh Edition.

EXPANDED COVERAGE OF CYBERLAW

We have integrated coverage of Internet law throughout the text. We indicate below,
in the subsection describing significantly revised chapters, those chapters that now
include substantial coverage of cyberlaw. Additionally, as mentioned earlier, we
have devoted an entire chapter to e-contracts (Chapter 10) in the Seventh Edition.

Finally, most chapters in the book include an *Adapting the Law to the Online Environment* feature that focuses on a specific court case involving a dispute arising in the online environment.

AMENDMENTS TO ARTICLES 2 AND 2A

To ensure that *Business Law Today: The Essentials,* Seventh Edition, offers the most up-to-date coverage possible, we have rewritten portions of the chapters covering sales and lease contracts (Chapters 11 through 13) to incorporate the 2003 amendments to Articles 2 and 2A of the Uniform Commercial Code (UCC). These amendments were made largely to accommodate electronic commerce. At the time this book went to press, no state had yet adopted these amendments. Thus, instead of basing the text of these chapters on the amended version of Articles 2 and 2A, we refer in footnotes to any amendments that significantly change the UCC provisions currently in effect in most states. We include excerpts from these amendments in Appendix B.

NEW FEATURES AND SPECIAL PEDAGOGY

All of the features that have been retained from the Sixth Edition of *Business Law Today: The Essentials* have been updated or modified as necessary. A great number of them have been replaced with newly written features. In addition, we have added the following entirely new elements for the Seventh Edition:

- *Adapting the Law to the Online Environment.*
- A *Relevant Web Sites* section concluding each *Landmark in the Law* feature and each *Landmark and Classic Case.*
- A *Why Is This Case Important?* section concluding one case in each chapter.
- *Case Problem with Sample Answer* (in the *Questions and Case Problems* section).
- *Video Questions.*

SIGNIFICANTLY REVISED CHAPTERS

Every chapter of the Seventh Edition has been revised as necessary to incorporate new developments in the law or to streamline the presentations. A number of new trends in business law are also addressed in the cases and special features of the Seventh Edition. Other major changes and additions for this edition include the following:

- Chapter 1 (The Historical and Constitutional Foundations)—The section on constitutional law has been thoroughly revised and updated to incorporate recent United States Supreme Court decisions. A feature addressing the constitutionality of state laws regulating the Internet has also been added.
- Chapter 2 (Ethics and Professional Responsibility)—As noted earlier in this preface, this chapter has been extensively rewritten to present a more practical approach to business ethics and decision making. The chapter now includes sections on how to set an ethical tone in a business environment, the Enron scandal, the professional responsibilities of accountants and lawyers, and the requirements of the Sarbanes-Oxley Act of 2002.
- Chapter 3 (Traditional and Online Dispute Resolution)—A section (and a feature) on electronic evidence and discovery issues was added to this chapter. The sections on personal jurisdiction and Internet jurisdiction were revised to update

and clarify the law. Several new features were added to explore issues surrounding the use of unpublished decisions, secret settlement agreements, and mandatory arbitration clauses. The discussion of electronic filing systems and online dispute resolution has been updated.

■ Chapter 4 (Torts and Cyber Torts)—The section on cyber torts in this chapter now includes a discussion of the federal CAN-SPAM Act of 2003, as well as several new features on spamming and online defamation.

■ Chapter 5 (Intellectual Property)—The materials on intellectual property rights in the online environment have been thoroughly revised and updated. Several recent United States Supreme Court cases are discussed. The chapter now includes a new section (and a feature) on file-sharing, a discussion of registering trademarks abroad under the Madrid Protocol, and a feature offering practical advice on how to protect trade secrets.

■ Chapter 7 (Contracts: Nature, Classification, Agreement, and Consideration)— The section on types of contracts was reorganized, and three new exhibits that illustrate contract classifications were added to this opening chapter on contracts. Overall, ten exhibits were added to the contracts unit to demonstrate visually the legal principles discussed in the chapters.

■ Chapter 10 (E-Contracts)—This chapter has been thoroughly revised and now includes more numbered examples, expanded coverage of the Uniform Electronic Transactions Act (including a new exhibit on this topic), and a video question.

■ Chapters 11 through 13 (on sales and lease contracts)—As mentioned previously, throughout this unit, text or footnotes have been added, whenever relevant, to indicate how the 2003 amendments to Article 2 and 2A alter existing law. These chapters also include more numbered examples, new features, and video questions.

■ Chapter 14 (Negotiable Instruments)—This chapter has been revised to reflect the 2002 amendments to Articles 3 and 4 of the UCC.

■ Chapter 16 (Creditors' Rights and Bankruptcy)—This chapter now includes the updated dollar amounts of various provisions of the Bankruptcy Code and discusses the bankruptcy reform legislation that is pending in Congress.

■ Chapter 18 (Employment Law)—This chapter covering employment law has been thoroughly revised to include references to the latest developments and United States Supreme Court decisions in the areas of labor and employment law. Issues concerning employee privacy rights are explored, and a discussion of genetic testing has been added.

■ Chapter 21 (Financing, Investor Protection, and Online Securities Offerings)— This chapter now includes a section (and an exhibit) on the Sarbanes-Oxley Act of 2002, more coverage of penalties for violations, a discussion of the Uniform Securities Act of 2002, and an updated discussion of online securities offerings and fraud.

WHAT ELSE IS NEW?

In addition to the changes noted above, you will find a number of other new items or features in *Business Law Today: The Essentials,* Seventh Edition, as listed below.

New Cases and Case Problems   Most of the cases in this text are new, including many cases decided in 2003 or 2004. We have also added a number of new case problems and new video questions. Virtually every chapter in this edition now includes at least one problem based on a case decided in 2004.

New Exhibits   We have modified exhibits retained from the Sixth Edition whenever necessary to achieve greater clarity or accuracy. In addition, we have added several new exhibits for the Seventh Edition. New exhibits were added to the contracts unit, including an exhibit that helps students classify contracts based on contract formation and an exhibit helping them distinguish between enforceable, void, voidable, and unenforceable contracts. Additional contract exhibits cover mistakes of fact and contracts subject to the Statute of Frauds, third party beneficiaries and contract discharge, and remedies for breach of contracts. Other new exhibits include an exhibit comparing the electronic contracting provisions of the E-SIGN Act and the UETA and an exhibit summarizing the key provisions of the Sarbanes-Oxley Act of 2002 relating to corporate accountability.

NEW SUPPLEMENTS

- A greatly enhanced and streamlined Web site at <u>http://blt.westbuslaw.com</u>.
- A revised *Instructor's Resource CD-ROM* (IRCD).
- WebTutor ToolBox.
- West's Digital Video Library (at an additional cost).
- Westlaw® Campus (at an additional cost).
- *Wall Street Journal* subscription (at an additional cost).

Acknowledgments

Numerous careful and conscientious users of *Business Law Today: The Essentials* were kind enough to help us revise the book. In addition, the staff at West went out of its way to make sure that this edition came out early and in accurate form. In particular, we wish to thank Rob Dewey and Steve Silverstein for their countless new ideas, many of which have been incorporated into the Seventh Edition. Our production manager and designer, Bill Stryker, made sure that we came out with an error-free, visually attractive edition. We will always be in his debt. We are also indebted to the staff at Parkwood Composition. Their ability to generate the pages for this text quickly and accurately made it possible for us to meet our ambitious printing schedule. We also extend special thanks to Jan Lamar, our longtime developmental editor, for her many useful suggestions and for her efforts in coordinating reviews and ensuring the timely and accurate publication of all supplemental materials. We are particularly indebted to Lisa Lysne for her support and excellent marketing advice and to Christine Wittmer for her help in managing the Web site and working on the CD-ROMs.

We must especially thank Katherine Marie Silsbee and Lavina Leed Miller, who provided expert research, editing, and proofing services for this project. We also wish to thank William Eric Hollowell, co-author of the *Instructor's Manual, Study Guide, Test Bank,* and *Online Legal Research Guide,* for his excellent research efforts. The copyediting and proofreading services of Pat Lewis and Suzie Franklin DeFazio, respectively, will not go unnoticed. We also thank Vickie Reierson for her proofreading assistance and her role in coordinating the project, which helped to ensure an error-free text. Finally, our appreciation goes to Roxanne Lee and Suzanne Jasin for their many special efforts on the project.

ACKNOWLEDGMENTS FOR PREVIOUS EDITIONS

John J. Balek
Morton College, Illinois

Lorraine K. Bannai
Western Washington University

Marlene E. Barken
Ithaca College, New York

Daryl Barton
Eastern Michigan University

Merlin Bauer
Mid State Technical College, Wisconsin

Donna E. Becker
Frederick Community College, Maryland

Brad Botz
Garden City Community College, Kansas

Teresa Brady
Holy Family College, Philadelphia

Lee B. Burgunder
California Polytechnic University—San Luis Obispo

Dale Clark
Corning Community College, New York

Sandra J. Defebaugh
Eastern Michigan University

Patricia L. DeFrain
Glendale College, California

Julia G. Derrick
Brevard Community College, Florida

Joe D. Dillsaver
Northeastern State University, Oklahoma

Claude W. Dotson
Northwest College, Wyoming

Larry R. Edwards
Tarrant County Junior College, South Campus, Texas

Jacolin Eichelberger
Hillsborough Community College, Florida

George E. Eigsti
Kansas City, Kansas, Community College

Florence E. Elliott-Howard
Stephen F. Austin State University, Texas

Tony Enerva
Lakeland Community College, Ohio

Benjamin C. Fassberg
Prince George's Community College, Maryland

Jerry Furniss
University of Montana

Elizabeth J. Guerriero
Northeast Louisiana University

Phil Harmeson
University of South Dakota

Nancy L. Hart
Midland College, Texas

Janine S. Hiller
Virginia Polytechnic Institute & State University

Fred Ittner
College of Alameda, California

Susan S. Jarvis
University of Texas, Pan American, Texas

Jack E. Karns
East Carolina University, North Carolina

Sarah Weiner Keidan
Oakland Community College, Michigan

Richard N. Kleeberg
Solano Community College, California

Bradley T. Lutz
Hillsborough Community College, Florida

Darlene Mallick
Anne Arundel Community College, Maryland

John D. Mallonee
Manatee Community College, Florida

Joseph D. Marcus
Prince George's Community College, Maryland

Woodrow J. Maxwell
Hudson Valley Community College, New York

Beverly McCormick
Morehead State University, Kentucky

William J. McDevitt
Saint Joseph's University, Pennsylvania

John W. McGee
Aims Community College, Colorado

James K. Miersma
Milwaukee Area Technical Institute, Wisconsin

Susan J. Mitchell
Des Moines Area Community College, Iowa

Jim Lee Morgan
West Los Angeles College

Jack K. Morton
University of Montana

Solange North
Fox Valley Technical Institute, Wisconsin

Robert H. Orr
Florida Community College at Jacksonville

George Otto
Truman College, Illinois

Thomas L. Palmer
Northern Arizona University

Donald L. Petote
Genessee Community College, New York

Francis D. Polk
Ocean County College, New Jersey

Gregory Rabb
Jamestown Community College, New York

Hugh Rode
Utah Valley State College

William M. Rutledge
Macomb Community College, Michigan

Martha Wright Sartoris
North Hennepin Community College, Minnesota

Anne W. Schacherl
Madison Area Technical College, Wisconsin

Edward F. Shafer
Rochester Community College, Minnesota

Lou Ann Simpson
Drake University, Iowa

Denise Smith
Missouri Western State College

Hugh M. Spall
Central Washington University

James D. Van Tassel
Mission College, California

Frederick J. Walsh
Franklin Pierce College, New Hampshire

James E. Walsh, Jr.
Tidewater Community College, Virginia

Edward L. Welsh, Jr.
Phoenix College

Clark W. Wheeler
Santa Fe Community College, Florida

Kay O. Wilburn
The University of Alabama at Birmingham

James L. Wittenbach
University of Notre Dame

Joseph Zavaglia, Jr.
Brookdale Community College, New Jersey

ACKNOWLEDGMENTS FOR THE SEVENTH EDITION

Marlene E. Barken
Ithaca College

Bradley D. Childs
Belmont University

Karen A. Holmes
Hudson Valley Community College

Susan J. Mitchell
Des Moines Area Community College

Jamie L. O'Brien
South Dakota State University

David W. Pan
University of Tulsa

Maurice Tonissi
Quinsigamond Community College

Randy Waterman
Richland College

Jerry Wegman
University of Idaho

Lori Whisenant
University of Houston

We know that we are not perfect. If you or your students find something you don't like or want us to change, write to us or let us know via e-mail, using the "Talk to Us" feature on this text's Web site. That is how we can make *Business Law Today: The Essentials* an even better book in the future.

Roger LeRoy Miller
Gaylord A. Jentz

DEDICATION

To the Run Cycles team.
You clearly have the greatest
bike store in the world. And
I appreciate your continuing
assistance and guidance.

R.L.M.

To my wife, JoAnn; to my children,
Kathy, Gary, Lori, and Rory; and to
my grandchildren, Erin,
Megan, Eric, Emily, Michelle,
Javier, Carmen, and Steve.

G.A.J.

CHAPTER 1

The Historical and Constitutional Foundations

"The law is of as much interest
to the layman as it is to the lawyer."

Lord Balfour, 1848–1930
(British prime minister, 1902–1905)

CHAPTER OUTLINE

- **SOURCES OF AMERICAN LAW**

- **THE COMMON LAW TRADITION**

- **CLASSIFICATIONS OF LAW**

- **THE CONSTITUTIONAL POWERS OF GOVERNMENT**

- **BUSINESS AND THE BILL OF RIGHTS**

- **DUE PROCESS AND EQUAL PROTECTION**

- **PRIVACY RIGHTS**

LAW
A body of enforceable rules governing relationships among individuals and between individuals and their society.

LEARNING OBJECTIVES

After reading this chapter, you should be able to answer the following questions:

1 What is the common law tradition?

2 What is a precedent? When might a court depart from precedent?

3 What is the difference between remedies at law and remedies in equity?

4 What constitutional clause gives the federal government the power to regulate commercial activities among the various states?

5 What is the Bill of Rights? What freedoms are guaranteed by the First Amendment?

Lord Balfour's assertion in the quotation above emphasizes the underlying theme of every page in this book—that law is of interest to all persons, not just to lawyers. Those entering the world of business will find themselves subject to numerous laws and government regulations. A basic knowledge of these laws and regulations is beneficial—if not essential—to anyone contemplating a successful career in the business world of today.

There have been and will continue to be different definitions of law. Although the definitions vary in their particulars, they all are based on the general observation that, at a minimum, **law** consists of *enforceable rules governing relationships among individuals and between individuals and their society.* These "enforceable rules" may consist of unwritten principles of behavior established by a nomadic tribe. They may be set forth in an ancient or a contemporary law code. They may consist of

JURISPRUDENCE
The science or philosophy of law.

written laws and court decisions created by modern legislative and judicial bodies, as in the United States. Regardless of how such rules are created, they all have one thing in common: they establish rights, duties, and privileges that are consistent with the values and beliefs of their society or its ruling group. In the study of law, often referred to as **jurisprudence,** these broad statements provide a point of departure for all legal scholars and philosophers.

In this introductory chapter, we first look at the basic sources of American law, the common law tradition, and some general classifications of law. We then examine some important constitutional concepts and clauses and their significance for business. The chapter concludes with a discussion of how fundamental freedoms guaranteed by the Constitution affect businesspersons and the workplace.

▦ Sources of American Law

PRIMARY SOURCE OF LAW
A document that establishes the law on a particular issue, such as a constitution, a statute, an administrative rule, or a court decision.

There are numerous sources of American law. **Primary sources of law,** or sources that establish the law, include the following:

1 The U.S. Constitution and the constitutions of the various states.

2 Statutes, or laws, passed by Congress and by state legislatures.

3 Regulations created by administrative agencies, such as the federal Food and Drug Administration.

4 Case law (court decisions).

We describe each of these important primary sources of law in the following pages. (See the appendix at the end of this chapter for a discussion of how to find statutes, regulations, and case law.)

SECONDARY SOURCE OF LAW
A publication that summarizes or interprets the law, such as a legal encyclopedia, a legal treatise, or an article in a law review.

Secondary sources of law are books and articles that summarize and clarify the primary sources of law. Legal encyclopedias, compilations (such as *Restatements of the Law*, which summarize court decisions on a particular topic), official comments to statutes, treatises, articles in law reviews published by law schools, and articles in other legal journals are examples of secondary sources of law. Courts often refer to secondary sources of law for guidance in interpreting and applying the primary sources of law discussed here.

CONSTITUTIONAL LAW

CONSTITUTIONAL LAW
The body of law derived from the U.S. Constitution and the constitutions of the various states.

The federal government and the states have separate written constitutions that set forth the general organization, powers, and limits of their respective governments. **Constitutional law** is the law as expressed in these constitutions.

The U.S. Constitution is the supreme law of the land. As such, it is the basis of all law in the United States. A law in violation of the Constitution, if challenged, will be declared unconstitutional and will not be enforced no matter what its source. Because of its paramount importance in the American legal system, we discuss the U.S. Constitution later in this chapter and present the complete text of the Constitution in Appendix A.

The Tenth Amendment to the U.S. Constitution reserves to the states all powers not granted to the federal government. Each state in the union has its own constitution. Unless it conflicts with the U.S. Constitution or a federal law, a state constitution is supreme within the state's borders.

Young students view the U.S. Constitution on display in Washington, D.C. Can a law be in violation of the Constitution and still be enforced? Why or why not? (Michael Evans/ Corbis Sygma)

 To find state compilations (codes) of statutory laws, go to

http://findlaw.com/ casecode/state.html.

STATUTORY LAW
The body of law enacted by legislative bodies (as opposed to constitutional law, administrative law, or case law).

CITATION
A reference to a publication in which a legal authority—such as a statute or a court decision—or other source can be found.

ORDINANCE
A regulation enacted by a city or county legislative body that becomes part of that state's statutory law.

Statutory Law

Statutes enacted by legislative bodies at any level of government make up another source of law, which is generally referred to as **statutory law.**

Federal Statutes   Federal statutes are laws that are enacted by the U.S. Congress. Any federal statute that violates the U.S. Constitution will be held unconstitutional if it is challenged.

Federal statutes that affect business operations include laws regulating the purchase and sale of securities (corporate stocks and bonds—discussed in Chapter 21), consumer protection statutes (discussed in Chapter 13), and statutes prohibiting employment discrimination (discussed in Chapter 18). Whenever a particular statute is mentioned in this text, we usually provide a footnote showing its **citation** (a reference to a publication in which a legal authority—such as a statute or a court decision—or other source can be found). In the appendix following this chapter, we explain how you can use these citations to find statutory law.

State and Local Statutes and Ordinances   State statutes are laws enacted by state legislatures. Any state law that is found to conflict with the U.S. Constitution, with federal laws enacted by Congress, or with the state's constitution will be declared invalid if challenged. Statutory law also includes the **ordinances** passed by cities and counties, none of which can violate the U.S. Constitution, the relevant state constitution, or federal or state laws.

State statutes include state criminal statutes (discussed in Chapter 6), state corporation statutes (discussed in Chapter 20), and state versions of the Uniform Commercial Code (to be discussed shortly). Local ordinances include zoning ordinances and local laws regulating housing construction and such things as the overall appearance of a community.

A federal statute, of course, applies to all states. A state statute, in contrast, applies only within the state's borders. State laws thus vary from state to state.

Uniform Laws   The differences among state laws were particularly notable in the 1800s, when conflicting state statutes frequently created problems for the rapidly developing trade and commerce among the states. To counter these problems, a group of legal scholars and lawyers formed the National Conference of Commissioners on Uniform State Laws (NCCUSL) in 1892 to draft uniform ("model") statutes for adoption by the states. The NCCUSL still exists today and continues to issue uniform statutes.

Each state has the option of adopting or rejecting a uniform law. *Only if a state legislature adopts a uniform law does that law become part of the statutory law of that state.* Note that a state legislature may adopt all or part of a uniform law as it is written, or the legislature may rewrite the law however the legislature wishes. Hence, even when a uniform law is said to have been adopted in many states, those states' laws may not be entirely "uniform."

The earliest uniform law, the Uniform Negotiable Instruments Law, was completed by 1896 and was adopted in every state by the early 1920s (although not all states used exactly the same wording). Over the following decades, other acts were drawn up in a similar manner. In all, over two hundred uniform acts have been

You can find links to most uniform laws online at the Web site of the National Conference of Commissioners on Uniform State Laws. Go to

http://www.nccusl.org.

issued by the NCCUSL since its inception. The most ambitious uniform act of all, however, was the Uniform Commercial Code.

The Uniform Commercial Code (UCC)   The Uniform Commercial Code (UCC), which was created through the joint efforts of the NCCUSL and the American Law Institute,[1] was first issued in 1952. The UCC has been adopted in all fifty states,[2] the District of Columbia, and the Virgin Islands. The UCC facilitates commerce among the states by providing a uniform, yet flexible, set of rules governing commercial transactions. The UCC assures businesspersons that their contracts, if validly entered into, normally will be enforced.

Because of its importance in the area of commercial law, we cite the UCC frequently in this text. We also present excerpts from the version of the UCC that is currently in effect in most states in Appendix B. (For a discussion of the creation of the UCC, see the *Landmark in the Law* in Chapter 11.)

ADMINISTRATIVE LAW

ADMINISTRATIVE LAW
The body of law created by administrative agencies (in the form of rules, regulations, orders, and decisions) in order to carry out their duties and responsibilities.

ADMINISTRATIVE AGENCY
A federal or state government agency established to perform a specific function. Administrative agencies are authorized by legislative acts to make and enforce rules to administer and enforce the acts.

EXECUTIVE AGENCY
An administrative agency within the executive branch of government. At the federal level, executive agencies are those within the cabinet departments.

INDEPENDENT REGULATORY AGENCY
An administrative agency that is not considered part of the government's executive branch and is not subject to the authority of the president. Independent agency officials cannot be removed without cause.

Another important source of American law is **administrative law,** which consists of the rules, orders, and decisions of administrative agencies. An **administrative agency** is a federal, state, or local government agency established to perform a specific function. Rules issued by various administrative agencies now affect virtually every aspect of a business's operation, including the firm's capital structure and financing, its hiring and firing procedures, its relations with employees and unions, and the way it manufactures and markets its products.

At the national level, numerous **executive agencies** exist within the cabinet departments of the executive branch. For example, the Food and Drug Administration is within the Department of Health and Human Services. Executive agencies are subject to the authority of the president, who has the power to appoint and remove officers of federal agencies. There are also major **independent regulatory agencies** at the federal level, including the Federal Trade Commission, the Securities and Exchange Commission, and the Federal Communications Commission. The president's power is less pronounced in regard to independent agencies, whose officers serve for fixed terms and cannot be removed without just cause.

There are administrative agencies at the state and local levels as well. Commonly, a state agency (such as a state pollution-control agency) is created as a parallel to a federal agency (such as the Environmental Protection Agency). Just as federal statutes take precedence over conflicting state statutes, so do federal agency regulations take precedence over conflicting state regulations. Because the rules of state and local agencies vary widely, we focus here exclusively on federal administrative law.

ENABLING LEGISLATION
A statute enacted by Congress that authorizes the creation of an administrative agency and specifies the name, composition, purpose, and powers of the agency being created.

Agency Creation   Because Congress cannot possibly oversee the actual implementation of all the laws it enacts, it must delegate such tasks to others, particularly when the issues relate to highly technical areas, such as air and water pollution. Congress creates an administrative agency by enacting **enabling legislation,** which specifies the name, composition, purpose, and powers of the agency being created.

---

1. This institute was formed in the 1920s and consists of practicing attorneys, legal scholars, and judges.
2. Louisiana has adopted only Articles 1, 3, 4, 5, 7, 8, and 9.

ADJUDICATE
To render a judicial decision. In the administrative process, the proceeding in which an administrative law judge hears and decides issues that arise when an administrative agency charges a person or a firm with violating a law or regulation enforced by the agency.

ADMINISTRATIVE PROCESS
The procedure used by administrative agencies in the administration of law.

RULEMAKING
The process undertaken by an administrative agency when formally adopting a new regulation or amending an old one. Rulemaking involves notifying the public of a proposed rule or change and receiving and considering the public's comments.

 You can find proposed and final rules issued by administrative agencies by accessing the *Federal Register* online at **http://www.gpoaccess.gov/ fr/index.html**.

A suspicious stock transaction brought Martha Stewart to the attention of the Securities and Exchange Commission and resulted in criminal charges and sanctions, illustrating the investigation and enforcement powers of agencies. Should agencies have this much power? Why or why not? (EPA/Peter Foley)

■ **EXAMPLE 1.1** The Federal Trade Commission (FTC) was created in 1914 by the Federal Trade Commission Act.[3] This act prohibits unfair and deceptive trade practices. It also describes the procedures the agency must follow to charge persons or organizations with violations of the act, and it provides for judicial review (review by the courts) of agency orders. Other portions of the act grant the agency powers to "make rules and regulations for the purpose of carrying out the Act," to conduct investigations of business practices, to obtain reports from interstate corporations concerning their business practices, to investigate possible violations of the act, to publish findings of its investigations, and to recommend new legislation. The act also empowers the FTC to hold trial-like hearings and to **adjudicate** (resolve judicially) certain kinds of trade disputes that involve FTC regulations. ■

Note that the FTC's grant of power incorporates functions associated with the legislative branch of government (rulemaking), the executive branch (investigation and enforcement), and the judicial branch (adjudication). Taken together, these functions constitute **administrative process**, which is the administration of law by administrative agencies.

Rulemaking One of the major functions of an administrative agency is **rulemaking**— creating or modifying rules, or regulations, pursuant to its enabling legislation. The Administrative Procedure Act[4] of 1946 imposes strict procedural requirements that agencies must follow in their rulemaking and other functions.

The most common rulemaking procedure involves three steps. First, the agency must give public notice of the proposed rulemaking proceedings, where and when the proceedings will be held, the agency's legal authority for the proceedings, and the terms or subject matter of the proposed rule. The notice must be published in the *Federal Register,* a daily publication of the U.S. government. Second, following this notice, the agency must allow ample time for interested parties to comment in writing on the proposed rule. After the comments have been received and reviewed, the agency takes them into consideration when drafting the final version of the regulation. The third and last step is the drafting of the final rule and its publication in the *Federal Register.* (See the appendix following this chapter for an explanation of how to find agency regulations.)

Investigation and Enforcement Agencies have both investigatory and prosecutorial powers. An agency can request that individuals or organizations hand over specified books, papers, records, or other documents. In addition, agencies may conduct on-site inspections, although a search warrant is normally required for such inspections. Sometimes, a search of a home, an office, or a factory is the only means of obtaining evidence needed to prove a regulatory violation. Agencies investigate a wide range of activities, including coal mining, automobile manufacturing, and the industrial discharge of pollutants into the environment.

Adjudication After conducting its own investigation of a suspected rule violation, an agency may decide to take action against a specific party. The action may involve

---

3. 15 U.S.C. Sections 45–58.
4. 5 U.S.C. Sections 551–706.

ADMINISTRATIVE LAW JUDGE (ALJ)
One who presides over an administrative agency hearing and has the power to administer oaths, take testimony, rule on questions of evidence, and make determinations of fact.

a trial-like hearing before an **administrative law judge (ALJ)**. The ALJ may compel the charged party to pay a fine or may prohibit the party from carrying on some specified activity. Either side may appeal the ALJ's decision to the commission or board that governs the agency. If the party fails to get relief there, appeal can be made to a federal court.

CASE LAW AND COMMON LAW DOCTRINES

CASE LAW
The rules of law announced in court decisions. Case law includes the aggregate of reported cases that interpret judicial precedents, statutes, regulations, and constitutional provisions.

The rules of law announced in court decisions constitute another basic source of American law. These rules of law include interpretations of constitutional provisions, of statutes enacted by legislatures, and of regulations created by administrative agencies. Today, this body of judge-made law is referred to as **case law,** or the *common law*. The common law—the doctrines and principles embodied in case law—governs all areas not covered by statutory law or administrative law. Because of the importance of the common law in our legal system, we look at the origins and characteristics of the common law tradition in some detail in the pages that follow.

▦ The Common Law Tradition

Because of our colonial heritage, much of American law is based on the English legal system. A knowledge of this tradition is crucial to understanding our legal system today because judges in the United States still apply common law principles when deciding cases.

EARLY ENGLISH COURTS

COMMON LAW
That body of law developed from custom or judicial decisions in English and U.S. courts, not attributable to a legislature.

After the Normans conquered England in 1066, William the Conqueror and his successors began the process of unifying the country under their rule. One of the means they used to do this was the establishment of the king's courts, or *curiae regis*. Before the Norman Conquest, disputes had been settled according to the local legal customs and traditions in various regions of the country. The king's courts sought to establish a uniform set of rules for the country as a whole. What evolved in these courts was the beginning of the **common law**—a body of general rules that applied throughout the entire English realm. Eventually, the common law tradition became part of the heritage of all nations that were once British colonies, including the United States.

Courts developed the common law rules from the principles underlying judges' decisions in actual legal controversies. Judges attempted to be consistent, and whenever possible, they based their decisions on the principles suggested by earlier cases. They sought to decide similar cases in a similar way and considered new cases with care, because they knew that their decisions would make new law. Each interpretation became part of the law on the subject and served as a legal **precedent**—that is, a decision that furnished an example or authority for deciding subsequent cases involving similar legal principles or facts.

PRECEDENT
A court decision that furnishes an example or authority for deciding subsequent cases involving identical or similar facts.

In the early years of the common law, there was no single place or publication where court opinions, or written decisions, could be found. Beginning in the late thirteenth and early fourteenth centuries, however, each year portions of significant decisions of that year were gathered together and recorded in *Year Books*. The *Year Books* were useful references for lawyers and judges. In the sixteenth century, the *Year Books* were discontinued, and other reports of cases became available. (See the

The court of chancery in the reign of King George I. Early English court decisions formed the basis of what type of law? (From a painting by Benjamin Ferrers in the National Portrait Gallery, Photo Corbis Bettmann)

STARE DECISIS
A common law doctrine under which judges are obligated to follow the precedents established in prior decisions.

BINDING AUTHORITY
Any source of law that a court must follow when deciding a case. Binding authorities include constitutions, statutes, and regulations that govern the issue being decided, as well as court decisions that are controlling precedents within the jurisdiction.

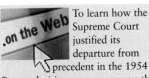

To learn how the Supreme Court justified its departure from precedent in the 1954 *Brown* decision, you can access the Court's opinion online by going to

http://findlaw.com/ casecode/supreme.html

and entering "347 U.S. 483" in the "Citation Search" box.

appendix following this chapter for a discussion of how cases are reported, or published, in the United States today.)

STARE DECISIS

The practice of deciding new cases with reference to former decisions, or precedents, eventually became a cornerstone of the English and American judicial systems. The practice forms a doctrine called *stare decisis*[5] ("to stand on decided cases").

The Importance of Precedents in Judicial Decision Making   The doctrine of *stare decisis* means that once a court has set forth a principle of law as being applicable to a certain set of facts, that court and courts of lower rank must adhere to that principle and apply it in future cases involving similar fact patterns.

■ **EXAMPLE 1.2** Suppose that the lower state courts in California have reached conflicting conclusions on whether drivers are liable for accidents they cause while merging into freeway traffic, even though the drivers looked and did not see any oncoming traffic and even though witnesses (passengers in their cars) testified to that effect. To settle the law on this issue, the California Supreme Court decides to review a case involving this fact pattern. The court rules that in such a situation, the driver who is merging into traffic is liable for any accidents caused by the driver's failure to yield to freeway traffic—even if the driver looked carefully and did not see an approaching vehicle. The California Supreme Court's decision on the matter will influence the outcome of all future cases on this issue brought before the California state courts. ■ Similarly, a decision on a given issue by the United States Supreme Court (the nation's highest court) is binding on all other courts.

Controlling precedents in a *jurisdiction* (an area in which a court or courts have the power to apply the law—see Chapter 3) are referred to as binding authorities. A **binding authority** is any source of law that a court must follow when deciding a case. Binding authorities include constitutions, statutes, and regulations that govern the issue being decided, as well as court decisions that are controlling precedents within the jurisdiction. Is a case precedent decided in 1875 still binding? For the answer to this question, see this chapter's *Letter of the Law* feature on the following page.

Stare Decisis **and Legal Stability**   The doctrine of *stare decisis* helps the courts to be more efficient, because if other courts have carefully reasoned through a similar case, their legal reasoning and opinions can serve as guides. *Stare decisis* also makes the law more stable and predictable. If the law on a given subject is well settled, someone bringing a case to court can usually rely on the court to make a decision based on what the law has been.

Departures from Precedent   Although courts are obligated to follow precedents, sometimes a court will depart from the rule of precedent if it decides that a given precedent should no longer be followed. If a court decides that a precedent is simply incorrect or that technological or social changes have rendered the precedent inapplicable, the court might rule contrary to the precedent. Cases that overturn precedent often receive a great deal of publicity.

---

5. Pronounced *ster*-ay dih-*si*-ses.

LETTER OF THE LAW Is an 1875 Case Precedent Still Binding?

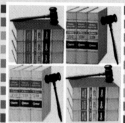

In a suit against the U.S. government for breach of contract, Boris Korczak sought compensation for services that he had allegedly performed for the Central Intelligence Agency (CIA) from 1973 to 1980. Korczak claimed that the government had failed to pay him an annuity and other compensation required by a secret *oral* agreement he had made with the CIA. The federal trial court dismissed Korczak's claim, and Korczak appealed the decision to the U.S. Court of Appeals for the Federal Circuit.

At issue on appeal was whether a Supreme Court case decided in 1875, *Totten v. United States,*[a] remained the controlling precedent in this area. In the *Totten* case, the plaintiff alleged that he had formed a secret contract with President Lincoln to collect information on the Confederate army during the Civil War. When the plaintiff sued the government for compensa-

tion for his services, the Supreme Court held that the agreement was unenforceable. According to the Court, to enforce such agreements could result in the disclosure of information that "might compromise or embarrass our government" or cause other "serious detriment" to the public. In Korczak's case, the federal appellate court held that the *Totten* case precedent was still "good law," and therefore Korczak, like the plaintiff in *Totten,* could not recover compensation for his services. Said the court, "*Totten,* despite its age, is the last pronouncement on this issue by the Supreme Court. . . . We are duty bound to follow the law given us by the Supreme Court unless and until it is changed."[b]

THE BOTTOM LINE

Supreme Court precedents, no matter how old, remain controlling until they are overruled by a subsequent decision of the Supreme Court, by a constitutional amendment, or by congressional legislation.

a. 92 U.S. 105 (1875).

b. *Korczak v. United States,* 124 F.3d 227 (Fed.Cir. 1997).

■ **EXAMPLE 1.3** In *Brown v. Board of Education of Topeka,*[6] the United States Supreme Court expressly overturned precedent when it concluded that separate educational facilities for whites and blacks, which had been upheld as constitutional in numerous previous cases,[7] were inherently unequal. The Supreme Court's departure from precedent in *Brown* received a tremendous amount of publicity as people began to realize the ramifications of this change in the law. ■

When There Is No Precedent   At times, courts hear cases for which there are no precedents within their jurisdictions on which to base their decisions. When hearing such cases, called "cases of first impression," courts often look to precedents set in other jurisdictions for guidance. Precedents from other jurisdictions, because they are not binding on the court, are referred to as **persuasive authorities**. A court may also consider a number of factors, including legal principles and policies underlying previous court decisions or existing statutes, fairness, social values and customs, public policy, and data and concepts drawn from the social sciences.

PERSUASIVE AUTHORITY
Any legal authority or source of law that a court may look to for guidance but on which it need not rely in making its decision. Persuasive authorities include cases from other jurisdictions and secondary sources of law.

ETHICAL ISSUE 1.1

Should the Supreme Court look to other nations' laws for guidance?   Over the last several years, justices on the United States Supreme Court have exhibited an increasing tendency to consider foreign law when deciding issues of national importance. For example, in 2003—for the first time ever—a majority opinion of the Supreme

6. 347 U.S. 483, 74 S.Ct. 686, 98 L.Ed. 873 (1954). See the appendix following this chapter for an explanation of how to read legal citations.

7. See *Plessy v. Ferguson,* 163 U.S. 537, 16 S.Ct. 1138, 41 L.Ed. 256 (1896).

Court cited foreign law (references to foreign law have appeared in footnotes and dissents on a few occasions in the past). The citation occurred in a controversial case in which the Court struck down laws that prohibit oral and anal sex between consenting adults of the same gender. In the majority opinion (an opinion that the majority of justices have signed), Justice Anthony Kennedy mentioned that the European Court of Human Rights and other foreign courts have consistently acknowledged that homosexuals have a right "to engage in intimate, consensual conduct."[8] This comment sparked debate in legal circles over whether the Supreme Court, or other U.S. courts, should ever consider world opinion or cite foreign law as persuasive authority. The practice has many critics, including Justice Antonin Scalia, who believes that foreign views are irrelevant to rulings on U.S. law. Several of the Supreme Court justices, however, believe that in our increasingly global community we should not ignore the opinions of courts in the rest of the world. ■

EQUITABLE REMEDIES AND COURTS OF EQUITY

REMEDY
The relief given to an innocent party to enforce a right or compensate for the violation of a right.

A **remedy** is the means given to a party to enforce a right or to compensate for the violation of a right. ■ **EXAMPLE 1.4** Suppose that Shem is injured because of Rowan's wrongdoing. A court may order Rowan to compensate Shem for the harm by paying Shem a certain amount of money. ■

In the early king's courts of England, the kinds of remedies that could be granted were severely restricted. If one person wronged another, the king's courts could award as compensation either money or property, including land. These courts became known as *courts of law,* and the remedies were called *remedies at law.* Even though this system introduced uniformity in the settling of disputes, when plaintiffs wanted a remedy other than economic compensation, the courts of law could do nothing, so "no remedy, no right."

Remedies in Equity *Equity* refers to a branch of the law, founded in justice and fair dealing, that seeks to supply a fair and adequate remedy when no remedy is available at law. In medieval England, when individuals could not obtain an adequate remedy in a court of law, they petitioned the king for relief. Most of these petitions were decided by an adviser to the king called the *chancellor.* The chancellor was said to be the "keeper of the king's conscience." When the chancellor thought that the claim was a fair one, new and unique remedies were granted. In this way, a new body of rules and remedies came into being, and eventually formal *chancery courts,* or *courts of equity,* were established. The remedies granted by these courts were called *remedies in equity.* Thus, two distinct court systems were created, each having a different set of judges and a different set of remedies.

PLAINTIFF
One who initiates a lawsuit.

DEFENDANT
One against whom a lawsuit is brought; the accused person in a criminal proceeding.

Plaintiffs (those bringing lawsuits) had to specify whether they were bringing an "action at law" or an "action in equity," and they chose their courts accordingly. ■ **EXAMPLE 1.5** A plaintiff might ask a court of equity to order a **defendant** (a person against whom a lawsuit is brought) to perform within the terms of a contract. A court of law could not issue such an order, because its remedies were limited to payment of money or property as compensation for damages. A court of equity, however, could issue a decree for *specific performance*—an order to perform what was

---

8. *Lawrence v. Texas,* 539 U.S. 558, 123 S.Ct. 2472, 156 L.Ed.2d 508 (2003). Other cases in which the Supreme Court has referenced foreign law include *Grutter v. Bollinger,* 539 U.S. 306, 123 S.Ct. 2325, 156 L.Ed.2d 304 (2003), in the dissent; and *Atkins v. Virginia,* 536 U.S. 304, 122 S.Ct. 2242, 153 L.Ed.2d 335 (2002), in footnote 21 to the majority opinion.

promised. A court of equity could also issue an *injunction,* directing a party to do or refrain from doing a particular act. In certain cases, a court of equity could allow for the *rescission* (cancellation) of the contract so that the parties would be returned to the positions that they held prior to the contract's formation. ■ Equitable remedies will be discussed in greater detail in Chapter 9.

The Merging of Law and Equity   Today, in most states the courts of law and equity have merged, and thus the distinction between the two courts has largely disappeared. A plaintiff may now request both legal and equitable remedies in the same action, and the trial court judge may grant either form—or both forms—of relief. The merging of law and equity, however, does not diminish the importance of distinguishing legal remedies from equitable remedies. To request the proper remedy, a businessperson (or her or his attorney) must know what remedies are available for the specific kinds of harms suffered. Today, as a rule, courts will grant an equitable remedy only when the remedy at law (money damages) is inadequate. Exhibit 1–1 summarizes the procedural differences (applicable in most states) between an action at law and an action in equity.

Equitable Principles and Maxims   Over time, a number of **equitable principles and maxims** evolved that have since guided the courts in deciding whether plaintiffs should be granted equitable relief. Because of their importance, both historically and in our judicial system today, these principles and maxims are set forth in this chapter's *Landmark in the Law* feature.

■ Classifications of Law

The huge body of the law may be broken down according to several classification systems. For example, one classification system divides law into **substantive law** (all laws that define, describe, regulate, and create legal rights and obligations) and **procedural law** (all laws that establish the methods of enforcing the rights established by substantive law). Other classification systems divide law into federal law and state law or private law (dealing with relationships between persons) and public law (addressing the relationship between persons and their governments).

Frequently, people use the term **cyberlaw** to refer to the emerging body of law that governs transactions conducted via the Internet. Cyberlaw is not really a classification of law, nor is it a new *type* of law. Rather, it is an informal term used to describe traditional legal principles that have been modified and adapted to fit situations that are unique to the online world. Of course, in some areas new statutes have been

REMEMBER Even though, in most states, courts of law and equity have merged, the principles of equity still apply.

EQUITABLE PRINCIPLES AND MAXIMS
General propositions or principles of law that have to do with fairness (equity).

SUBSTANTIVE LAW
Law that defines, describes, regulates, and creates legal rights and obligations.

PROCEDURAL LAW
Law that establishes the methods of enforcing the rights established by substantive law.

CYBERLAW
An informal term used to refer to all laws governing electronic communications and transactions, particularly those conducted via the Internet.

EXHIBIT 1–1 PROCEDURAL DIFFERENCES BETWEEN AN ACTION AT LAW AND AN ACTION IN EQUITY

PROCEDURE	ACTION AT LAW	ACTION IN EQUITY
Initiation of lawsuit	By filing a complaint	By filing a petition
Decision	By jury or judge	By judge (no jury)
Result	Judgment	Decree
Remedy	Monetary damages	Injunction, specific performance, or rescission

LANDMARK IN THE LAW

Equitable Principles and Maxims

In medieval England, courts of equity had the responsibility of using discretion in supplementing the common law. Even today, when the same court can award both legal and equitable remedies, it must exercise discretion. Courts often invoke equitable principles and maxims when making their decisions. Here are some of the most significant equitable principles and maxims:

1 *Whoever seeks equity must do equity.* (Anyone who wishes to be treated fairly must treat others fairly.)

2 *Where there is equal equity, the law must prevail.* (The law will determine the outcome of a controversy in which the merits of both sides are equal.)

3 *One seeking the aid of an equity court must come to the court with clean hands.* (Plaintiffs must have acted fairly and honestly.)

4 *Equity will not suffer a wrong to be without a remedy.* (Equitable relief will be awarded when there is a right to relief and there is no adequate remedy at law.)

5 *Equity regards substance rather than form.* (Equity is more concerned with fairness and justice than with legal technicalities.)

6 *Equity aids the vigilant, not those who rest on their rights.* (Equity will not help those who neglect their rights for an unreasonable period of time.)

The last maxim has become known as the *equitable doctrine of laches.* The doctrine arose to encourage people to bring lawsuits while the evidence was fresh; if they failed to do so, they would not be allowed to bring a lawsuit. What constitutes a reasonable time, of course, varies according to the circumstances of the case. Time periods for different types of cases are now usually fixed by **statutes of limitations.** After the time allowed under a statute of limitations has expired, no action can be brought, no matter how strong the case was originally.

APPLICATION TO TODAY'S WORLD

The equitable maxims listed above underlie many of the legal rules and principles that are commonly applied by the courts today—and that you will read about in this book. For example, in Chapter 7 you will read about the doctrine of promissory estoppel. *Under this doctrine, a person who has reasonably and substantially relied on the promise of another may be able to obtain some measure of recovery, even though no enforceable contract, or agreement, exists. The court will* estop *(bar, or impede) the one making the promise from asserting the lack of a valid contract as a defense. The rationale underlying the doctrine of promissory estoppel is similar to that expressed in the fourth and fifth maxims above.*

RELEVANT WEB SITES

To locate information on the Web concerning equitable principles, go to this text's Web site at **http://blt.westbuslaw.com***, select "Chapter 1," and click on "URLs for Landmarks."*

STATUTE OF LIMITATIONS
A federal or state statute setting the maximum time period during which a certain action can be brought or certain rights enforced.

enacted, at both the federal and state levels, to cover specific types of problems stemming from online communications. Throughout this book, you will read how the law in a given area is evolving to govern specific legal issues that arise in the online context.

CIVIL LAW AND CRIMINAL LAW

CIVIL LAW
The branch of law dealing with the definition and enforcement of all private or public rights, as opposed to criminal matters.

Civil law spells out the rights and duties that exist between persons and between persons and their governments, and the relief available when a person's rights are violated. Typically, in a civil case, a private party sues another private party (although the government can also sue a party for a civil law violation) to make that other party comply with a duty or pay for the damage caused by the failure to comply with a duty. Much of the law that we discuss in this text is civil law. Contract law, for example, which we discuss in Chapters 7 through 10, is civil law. The whole body of tort law (see Chapter 4) is civil law.

CRIMINAL LAW
Law that defines and governs actions that constitute crimes. Generally, criminal law has to do with wrongful actions committed against society for which society demands redress.

Criminal law has to do with wrongs committed against society for which society demands redress. Criminal acts are proscribed by local, state, or federal government statutes. Thus, criminal defendants are prosecuted by public officials, such as a district attorney (D.A.), on behalf of the state, not by their victims or other private parties. Whereas in a civil case the object is to obtain remedies (such as money damages) to compensate the injured party, in a criminal case the object is to punish the wrongdoer and to deter others from similar actions. Penalties for violations of criminal statutes consist of fines and/or imprisonment—and, in some cases, death. We will discuss the differences between civil and criminal law in greater detail in Chapter 6.

NATIONAL AND INTERNATIONAL LAW

The Library of Congress offers extensive information on national and international law at
http://www.loc.gov.

The law of a particular nation, such as the United States or Sweden, is **national law.** National law, of course, varies from country to country because each country's law reflects the interests, customs, activities, and values that are unique to that nation's culture. Even though the laws and legal systems of various countries differ substantially, broad similarities do exist.

NATIONAL LAW
Law that pertains to a particular nation (as opposed to international law).

In contrast to national law, international law applies to more than one nation. **International law** can be defined as a body of written and unwritten laws observed by independent nations and governing the acts of individuals as well as governments. International law is an intermingling of rules and constraints derived from a variety of sources, including the laws of individual nations, the customs that have evolved among nations in their relations with one another, and treaties and international organizations. In essence, international law is the result of centuries-old attempts to reconcile the traditional need of each nation to be the final authority over its own affairs with the desire of nations to benefit economically from trade and harmonious relations with one another.

INTERNATIONAL LAW
The law that governs relations among nations. National laws, customs, treaties, and international conferences and organizations are generally considered to be the most important sources of international law.

The key difference between national law and international law is that national law can be enforced by government authorities. If a nation violates an international law, however, the most that other countries or international organizations can do (if persuasive tactics fail) is to resort to coercive actions against the violating nation. Coercive actions range from the severance of diplomatic relations and boycotts to, at the last resort, war. We examine the laws governing international business transactions in Chapter 25.

◼️ The Constitutional Powers of Government

Laws that govern business have their origin in the lawmaking authority granted by the U.S. Constitution, which is the supreme law in this country. As mentioned earlier in this chapter, neither Congress nor any state can enact a law that is in conflict with the Constitution.

The U.S. Constitution created a **federal form of government** in which the national government and the states *share* sovereign power. The Constitution sets forth specific powers that can be exercised by the national government and provides that the national government has the implied power to undertake actions necessary to carry out its expressly designated powers. All other powers are "reserved" to the states. The broad language of the Constitution, though, has left much room for debate over the specific nature and scope of these powers. Generally, it has been the task of the courts to determine where the boundary line between state and national powers should lie—and that line changes over time.

FEDERAL FORM OF GOVERNMENT
A system of government in which the states form a union and the sovereign power is divided between the central government and the member states.

 You can find a copy of the U.S. Constitution online, as well as information about the document, including its history, at **http://www. constitutioncenter.org.**

COMMERCE CLAUSE
The provision in Article I, Section 8, of the U.S. Constitution that gives Congress the power to regulate interstate commerce.

THE COMMERCE CLAUSE

To prevent states from establishing laws and regulations that would interfere with trade and commerce among the states, the Constitution expressly delegated to the national government the power to regulate interstate commerce. Article I, Section 8, of the U.S. Constitution expressly permits Congress "[t]o regulate Commerce with foreign Nations, and among the several States, and with the Indian Tribes." This clause, referred to as the **commerce clause**, has had a greater impact on business than any other provision in the Constitution.

For some time, the commerce power was interpreted as being limited to *interstate* commerce (commerce among the states) and not applicable to *intrastate* commerce (commerce within a state). In 1824, however, in *Gibbons v. Ogden*,[9] the United States Supreme Court held that commerce within a state could also be regulated by the national government as long as the commerce *substantially affected* commerce involving more than one state.

The Commerce Clause and the Expansion of National Powers   As the nation grew and faced new kinds of problems, the commerce clause became a vehicle for the additional expansion of the national government's regulatory powers. Even activities that seemed purely local came under the regulatory reach of the national government if those activities were deemed to substantially affect interstate commerce. ◼️ **EXAMPLE 1.6** In 1942, in *Wickard v. Filburn*,[10] the Supreme Court held that wheat production by an individual farmer intended wholly for consumption on his own farm was subject to federal regulation. The Court reasoned that the home consumption of wheat reduced the demand for wheat and thus could have a substantial effect on interstate commerce. ◼️

The landmark case on the next page involved a challenge to the scope of the national government's constitutional authority to regulate local activities.

---

9. 22 U.S. (9 Wheat.) 1, 6 L.Ed. 23 (1824).
10. 317 U.S. 111, 63 S.Ct. 82, 87 L.Ed. 122 (1942).

LANDMARK AND CLASSIC CASES

CASE 1.1 ■ Heart of Atlanta Motel v. United States

Supreme Court of the United States, 1964.
379 U.S. 241,
85 S.Ct. 348,
13 L.Ed.2d 258.
http://supct.law.cornell.edu/supct/cases/name.htm[a]

HISTORICAL AND SOCIAL SETTING *In the first half of the twentieth century, state governments sanctioned segregation on the basis of race. In 1954, the United States Supreme Court decided that racially segregated school systems violated the Constitution. In the following decade, the Court ordered an end to racial segregation imposed by the states in other public facilities, such as beaches, golf courses, buses, parks, auditoriums, and courtroom seating. Privately owned facilities that excluded or segregated African Americans and others on the basis of race were not subject to the same constitutional restrictions, however. Congress passed the Civil Rights Act of 1964 to prohibit racial discrimination in "establishments affecting interstate commerce." These facilities included "places of public accommodation."*

FACTS The owner of the Heart of Atlanta Motel, in violation of the Civil Rights Act of 1964, refused to rent rooms to African Americans. The motel owner brought an action in a federal district court to have the Civil Rights Act declared unconstitutional, alleging that Congress had exceeded its constitutional authority to regulate commerce by enacting the act. The owner argued that his motel was not engaged in interstate commerce but was "of a purely local character." The motel, however, was accessible to state and interstate highways. The owner advertised nationally, maintained billboards throughout the state, and accepted convention trade from outside the state (75 percent of the guests were residents of other states). The court ruled that the act did not violate the Constitution and enjoined (prohibited) the owner from discriminating on the basis of race. The owner appealed. The case ultimately went to the United States Supreme Court.

ISSUE Did Congress exceed its constitutional power to regulate interstate commerce by enacting the Civil Rights Act of 1964?

DECISION No. The United States Supreme Court upheld the constitutionality of the act.

REASON The Court noted that the act was passed to correct "the deprivation of personal dignity" accompanying the denial of equal access to "public establishments." Testimony before Congress leading to the passage of the act indicated that African Americans in particular experienced substantial discrimination in attempting to secure lodging while traveling. This discrimination impeded interstate travel and thus impeded interstate commerce. As for the owner's argument that his motel was "of a purely local character," the Court said that even if this was true, the motel affected interstate commerce. According to the Court, "if it is interstate commerce that feels the pinch, it does not matter how local the operation that applies the squeeze." Therefore, under the commerce clause, "the power of Congress to promote interstate commerce also includes the power to regulate the local incidents thereof, including local activities."

COMMENTS *If the United States Supreme Court had invalidated the Civil Rights Act of 1964, the legal landscape of the United States would be much different today. The act prohibits discrimination based on race, color, national origin, religion, or gender in all "public accommodations," including hotels and restaurants. The act also prohibits discrimination in employment based on these criteria. Although state laws now prohibit many of these forms of discrimination as well, the protections available vary from state to state—and it is not certain when (and if) such laws would have been passed had the 1964 federal Civil Rights Act been deemed unconstitutional.*

RELEVANT WEB SITES *To locate information on the Web concerning the* Heart of Atlanta Motel *case, go to this text's Web site at* **http://blt.westbuslaw.com**, *select "Chapter 1," and click on "URLs for Landmarks."*

a. This is the "Historic Supreme Court Decisions—by Party Name" page within the "Caselists" collection of the Legal Information Institute available at its site on the Web. Click on the "H" link or scroll down the list of cases to the entry for the *Heart of Atlanta* case. Click on the case name. When the link opens, click on one of the choices to read the "Syllabus," the "Full Decision," or the "Edited Decision."

A physician examines the eyes of a woman who suffers from a brain tumor. The woman was partially paralyzed on the right side of her body until she started smoking marijuana. A significant issue today is whether the federal government can use its power under the commerce clause to prohibit the use of medical marijuana within a state's borders. Should the legality of using marijuana for medical purposes be determined by the federal government or by individual states? (AP Photo/Ben Margot)

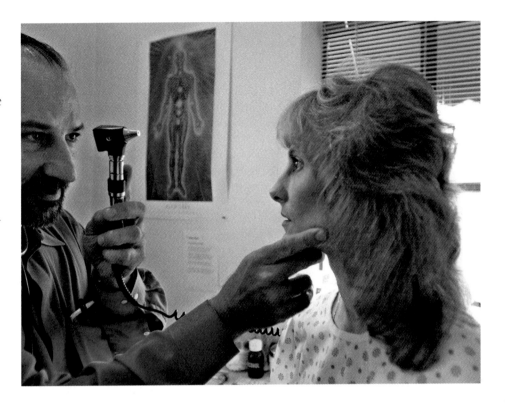

The Commerce Power Today   Today, at least theoretically, the power over commerce authorizes the national government to regulate every commercial enterprise in the United States. Federal (national) legislation governs virtually every major activity conducted by businesses—from hiring and firing decisions to workplace safety, competitive practices, and financing.

In the last decade or so, however, the Supreme Court has begun to curb somewhat the national government's regulatory authority under the commerce clause. In 1995, the Court held—for the first time in sixty years—that Congress had exceeded its regulatory authority under the commerce clause. The Court struck down an act that banned the possession of guns within one thousand feet of any school because the act attempted to regulate an area that had "nothing to do with commerce."[11] Subsequently, the Court invalidated other federal laws on the ground that they exceeded Congress's commerce clause authority.[12]

POLICE POWERS
Powers possessed by the states as part of their inherent sovereignty. These powers may be exercised to protect or promote the public order, health, safety, morals, and general welfare.

The Regulatory Powers of the States   As part of their inherent sovereignty, state governments have the authority to regulate affairs within their borders. This authority stems in part from the Tenth Amendment to the Constitution, which reserves all powers not delegated to the national government to the states. State regulatory powers are often referred to as **police powers**. The term encompasses not only the enforcement of

---

11. The United States Supreme Court held the Gun-Free School Zones Act of 1990 to be unconstitutional in *United States v. Lopez,* 514 U.S. 549, 115 S.Ct. 1624, 131 L.Ed.2d 626 (1995).

12. See, for example, *Printz v. United States,* 521 U.S. 898, 117 S.Ct. 2365, 138 L.Ed.2d 914 (1997), involving the Brady Handgun Violence Prevention Act of 1993; and *United States v. Morrison,* 529 U.S. 598, 120 S.Ct. 1740, 146 L.Ed.2d 658 (2000), concerning the federal Violence Against Women Act of 1994.

criminal law but also the right of state governments to regulate private activities to protect or promote the public order, health, safety, morals, and general welfare. Fire and building codes, antidiscrimination laws, parking regulations, zoning restrictions, licensing requirements, and thousands of other state statutes covering virtually every aspect of life have been enacted pursuant to a state's police powers. Local governments, including cities, also exercise police powers.[13] Generally, state laws enacted pursuant to a state's police powers carry a strong presumption of validity.

The "Dormant" Commerce Clause The United States Supreme Court has interpreted the commerce clause to mean that the national government has the *exclusive* authority to regulate commerce that substantially affects trade and commerce among the states. This express grant of authority to the national government, which is often referred to as the "positive" aspect of the commerce clause, implies a negative aspect— that the states do *not* have the authority to regulate interstate commerce. This negative aspect of the commerce clause is often referred to as the "dormant" (implied) commerce clause.

The dormant commerce clause comes into play when state regulations affect interstate commerce. In this situation, the courts normally weigh the state's interest in regulating a certain matter against the burden that the state's regulation places on interstate commerce. Because courts balance the interests involved, it can be extremely difficult to predict the outcome in a particular case.

■ EXAMPLE 1.7 A Michigan statute prohibited out-of-state wineries from shipping wine directly to Michigan residents but allowed in-state wineries to do so. The U.S. Court of Appeals for the Sixth Circuit ruled that the statute violated the dormant commerce clause. The court concluded that the regulations benefited in-state wineries and burdened out-of-state wineries, while failing to promote any legitimate local purpose.[14] Other appellate courts, however, have taken different positions on cases involving direct wine shipments. For instance, in 2004, the U.S. Court of Appeals for the Second Circuit upheld a similar statute on the ground that the state had a legitimate interest in monitoring the flow of alcohol into the state.[15] ■

What if a state law attempts to regulate the types of materials that may be distributed to state residents via the Internet? Would such a law violate the dormant commerce clause? See this chapter's *Adapting the Law to the Online Environment* feature for a discussion of that question.

THE SUPREMACY CLAUSE

Article VI of the Constitution provides that the Constitution, laws, and treaties of the United States are "the supreme Law of the Land." This article, commonly referred to as the **supremacy clause**, is important in the ordering of state and federal relationships. When there is a direct conflict between a federal law and a state law, the state law is rendered invalid. Because some powers are *concurrent* (shared by the federal government and the states), however, it is necessary to determine which law governs in a particular circumstance.

Preemption occurs when Congress chooses to act exclusively in a concurrent area. In this circumstance, a valid federal statute or regulation will take precedence over a conflicting state or local law or regulation on the same general subject. Often,

SUPREMACY CLAUSE
The provision in Article VI of the Constitution that provides that the Constitution, laws, and treaties of the United States are "the supreme Law of the Land." Under this clause, state and local laws that directly conflict with federal law will be rendered invalid.

PREEMPTION
A doctrine under which certain federal laws preempt, or take precedence over, conflicting state or local laws.

---

13. Local governments derive their authority to regulate their communities from the state, because they are creatures of the state. In other words, they cannot come into existence unless authorized by the state to do so.
14. *Heald v. Engler,* 342 F.3d 517 (6th Cir. 2003).
15. *Swedenburg v. Kelly,* 358 F.3d 223, 2004 WL 254401 (2d Cir. 2004).

ADAPTING THE LAW TO THE ONLINE ENVIRONMENT

Can States Regulate Internet Commerce?

The Constitution's commerce clause—and most of the United States Supreme Court's decisions interpreting that clause—were created long before the Internet became a reality. Prior to the advent of the Internet, "interstate commerce" typically meant commerce in goods or services that extended beyond a particular state's borders. In the online environment, however, physical boundaries do not exist. Thus, one of the difficulties facing the courts in the last several years has been how to apply this traditional body of law to online transactions.

TRADITIONAL COMMERCE CLAUSE ANALYSIS

The Constitution's commerce clause, as interpreted by the United States Supreme Court, gives the national government the *exclusive* power to regulate interstate commerce. That means, in effect, that states *cannot* regulate interstate commerce. As noted elsewhere in this chapter, this limitation on state powers is referred to as the negative, or "dormant," commerce clause. If a court finds that a state law places too great a burden on interstate commerce, the law will be deemed unconstitutional on the ground that it violates the dormant commerce clause.

By and large, the courts have applied traditional commerce clause analysis in cases challenging the constitutionality of state laws regulating the Internet. As in traditional commerce clause cases, the courts tend to invalidate state laws regulating the Internet if those laws extend to activities beyond their borders and place too great a burden on interstate commerce.

CAN VERMONT LIMIT MINORS' ACCESS TO WEB MATERIAL?

Consider a case that came before a federal appellate court in *American Booksellers Foundation v. Dean.*[a] The case

a. 342 F.3d 96 (2d Cir. 2003).

challenged the constitutionality of a Vermont law that prohibited the Internet distribution to minors of sexually explicit materials that are "harmful to minors."

The effect of this law on out-of-state residents was made clear in the argument put forth by one of the plaintiffs (those who brought the lawsuit), Sexual Health Network, Inc. (SHN). SHN, which was located in Connecticut, operated a Web site on which it posted information concerning a range of sex-related topics. SHN's aim was to provide access to sexuality-related information designed to assist persons with disabilities, illnesses, and changes in their lifestyles. Clearly, SHN could not prevent minors living in Vermont (or any other state—or nation) from accessing its Web site. To avoid possible prosecution for violating Vermont's law, SHN would virtually have to shut down its Web site. SHN and the other plaintiffs, including the American Civil Liberties Union, thus sought a court order barring the enforcement of the Vermont statute on the ground that, among other things, it violated the dormant commerce clause.

The court agreed with the plaintiffs. The court held that the Vermont law violated the dormant commerce clause because it "regulates Internet commerce occurring wholly outside Vermont's borders." The court noted that although Vermont aimed to protect only Vermont minors, in effect the rest of the nation was forced to comply with its regulation or risk prosecution under Vermont's law.

FOR CRITICAL ANALYSIS

In its opinion, the court pointed out that "at the same time that the Internet's geographic reach increases Vermont's interest in regulating out-of-state conduct, it makes state regulation impracticable." Analyze this statement.

it is not clear whether Congress, in passing a law, intended to preempt an entire subject area against state regulation. In these situations, it is left to the courts to determine whether Congress intended to exercise exclusive power over a given area. No single factor is decisive as to whether a court will find preemption. Generally, congressional intent to preempt will be found if a federal law regulating an activity is so pervasive, comprehensive, or detailed that the states have little or no room to regulate in that area. Also, when a federal statute creates an agency—such as the National Labor Relations Board—to enforce the law, matters that may come within the agency's jurisdiction will likely preempt state laws.

Business and the Bill of Rights

The importance of a written declaration of the rights of individuals eventually caused the first Congress of the United States to submit twelve amendments to the Constitution to the states for approval. The first ten of these amendments, commonly known as the **Bill of Rights,** were adopted in 1791 and embody a series of protections for the individual against various types of interference by the federal government.[16] Some constitutional protections apply to business entities as well. For example, corporations exist as separate legal entities, or legal persons, and enjoy many of the same rights and privileges as natural persons do. Summarized here are the protections guaranteed by these ten amendments (see the Constitution in Appendix A for the complete text of each amendment):

BILL OF RIGHTS
The first ten amendments to the U.S. Constitution.

BE CAREFUL Although most of these rights apply to actions of the states, some of them apply only to actions of the federal government.

1. The First Amendment guarantees the freedoms of religion, speech, and the press and the rights to assemble peaceably and to petition the government.

2. The Second Amendment guarantees the right to keep and bear arms.

3. The Third Amendment prohibits, in peacetime, the lodging of soldiers in any house without the owner's consent.

4. The Fourth Amendment prohibits unreasonable searches and seizures of persons or property.

5. The Fifth Amendment guarantees the rights to *indictment* (formal accusation—see Chapter 6) by grand jury, to due process of law, and to fair payment when private property is taken for public use. The Fifth Amendment also prohibits compulsory self-incrimination and double jeopardy (trial for the same crime twice).

6. The Sixth Amendment guarantees the accused in a criminal case the right to a speedy and public trial by an impartial jury and with counsel. The accused has the right to cross-examine witnesses against him or her and to solicit testimony from witnesses in his or her favor.

7. The Seventh Amendment guarantees the right to a trial by jury in a civil (noncriminal) case involving at least twenty dollars.[17]

8. The Eighth Amendment prohibits excessive bail and fines, as well as cruel and unusual punishment.

9. The Ninth Amendment establishes that the people have rights in addition to those specified in the Constitution.

10. The Tenth Amendment establishes that those powers neither delegated to the federal government nor denied to the states are reserved for the states.

As originally intended, the Bill of Rights limited only the powers of the national government. Over time, however, the Supreme Court "incorporated" most of these

---

16. One of these proposed amendments was ratified 203 years later (in 1992) and became the Twenty-seventh Amendment to the Constitution. See Appendix A.
17. Twenty dollars was forty days' pay for the average person when the Bill of Rights was written.

Police searching a crack house in Florida. Should the owners and occupants of such houses receive protection from unreasonable searches and seizures under the U.S. Constitution? Why or why not? (© Corbis. All rights reserved.)

rights into the protections against state actions afforded by the Fourteenth Amendment to the Constitution. That amendment, passed in 1868 after the Civil War, provides in part that "[n]o State shall . . . deprive any person of life, liberty, or property, without due process of law." Starting in 1925, the Supreme Court began to define various rights and liberties guaranteed in the national Constitution as constituting "due process of law," which was required of state governments under the Fourteenth Amendment. Today, most of the rights and liberties set forth in the Bill of Rights apply to state governments as well as the national government.

REMEMBER The First Amendment guarantee of freedom of speech applies only to *government* restrictions on speech.

We will look closely at several of the amendments included in the Bill of Rights in Chapter 6, in the context of criminal law and procedures. Here we examine two important guarantees of the First Amendment—freedom of speech and freedom of religion. These and other First Amendment freedoms (of the press, assembly, and petition) have all been applied to the states through the due process clause of the Fourteenth Amendment. As you read through the following pages, keep in mind that none of these (or other) constitutional freedoms confers an absolute right. Ultimately, it is the United States Supreme Court, as the final interpreter of the Constitution, that gives meaning to these rights and determines their boundaries.

THE FIRST AMENDMENT—FREEDOM OF SPEECH

Freedom of speech is the most prized freedom that Americans have. Indeed, it forms the basis for our democratic form of government, which could not exist if people were not allowed to express their political opinions freely and criticize government actions or policies. Because of its importance, the courts traditionally have protected this right to the fullest extent possible.

SYMBOLIC SPEECH
Nonverbal expressions of beliefs. Symbolic speech, which includes gestures, movements, and articles of clothing, is given substantial protection by the courts.

Speech often includes not only what we say but also what we do to express our political, social, and religious views. The courts generally protect **symbolic speech**—gestures, movements, articles of clothing, and other forms of nonverbal expressive conduct. ■ EXAMPLE 1.8 In 1989, the Supreme Court held that the burning of the American flag to protest government policies is a constitutionally protected form of expression.[18] Similarly, participating in a hunger strike or wearing a black armband would be protected as symbolic speech. ■

Expression—oral, written, or symbolized by conduct—is subject to reasonable restrictions. For example, on the campus of a public high school, certain rights may be circumscribed or denied, in part to protect minors from predatory adults and to protect adults and others from predatory minors. A balance must be struck, however, between a government's obligation to protect its citizens and those citizens' exercise of their rights. These competing interests were at issue in the following case.

18. See *Texas v. Johnson*, 491 U.S. 397, 109 S.Ct. 2533, 105 L.Ed.2d 342 (1989).

CASE 1.2 ▦ Hodgkins v. Peterson

United States Court of Appeals, Seventh Circuit, 2004.
355 F.3d 1048.

FACTS Shortly after 11 P.M. on August 26, 1999, sixteen-year-old Colin Hodgkins and three friends left a Steak 'n Shake restaurant in Indianapolis, Indiana, where they had stopped to eat after a school soccer game. At the time, an Indiana statute made it illegal for minors between fifteen and seventeen years old to be in a public place after 11 P.M. on weeknights unless accompanied by a parent or guardian, with a few exceptions. As Colin and his friends left the restaurant, police arrested and handcuffed them for violating this statute. Colin's mother, Nancy Hodgkins, and others filed a suit in a federal district court against Bart Peterson, the mayor of Indianapolis, and other local government officials, asking the court to order the defendants to stop enforcing the curfew on the ground that it violated the First Amendment. The court ruled in the defendants' favor, and the plaintiffs appealed to the U.S. Court of Appeals for the Seventh Circuit.

ISSUE Did the curfew violate the First Amendment rights of the minors?

DECISION Yes. The U.S. Court of Appeals for the Seventh Circuit reversed the lower court's judgment and ordered a permanent injunction against the enforcement of the curfew.

REASON The appellate court stated, "The strength of our democracy depends on a citizenry that knows and understands its freedoms, exercises them responsibly, and guards them vigilantly. Young adults are not suddenly granted the full panoply of constitutional rights on the day they attain the age of majority. We not only permit but expect youths to exercise those liberties—to learn to think for themselves, to give voice to their opinions, to hear and evaluate competing points of view—so that they might attain the right to vote at age eighteen with the tools to exercise that right. A juvenile's ability to worship, associate, and speak freely is therefore not simply a privilege that benefits her as an individual, but a necessary means of allowing her to become a fully enfranchised member of a democratic society." Many First Amendment activities can occur during curfew hours. The statute threatened the arrest of minors who were participating in these activities. "The chill that the prospect of arrest imposes on a minor's exercise of his or her First Amendment rights is patent [obvious]."

FOR CRITICAL ANALYSIS—Political Consideration
Can a curfew law be written to protect both the fundamental constitutional rights of minors and the safety of all citizens?

Corporate Political Speech Political speech by corporations also falls within the protection of the First Amendment. ■ EXAMPLE 1.9 In *First National Bank of Boston v. Bellotti*,[19] national banking associations and business corporations sought United States Supreme Court review of a Massachusetts statute that prohibited corporations from making political contributions or expenditures that individuals were permitted to make. The Court ruled that the Massachusetts law was unconstitutional because it violated the right of corporations to freedom of speech. ■ Similarly, the Court has held that a law prohibiting a corporation from using bill inserts to express its views on controversial issues violates the First Amendment.[20] Although a more conservative Supreme Court subsequently reversed this trend somewhat,[21] corporate political speech continues to be given significant protection under the First Amendment.

Commercial Speech The courts also give substantial protection to "commercial" speech, which consists of communications—primarily advertising and marketing—made by business firms that involve only their commercial interests. The protection given to commercial speech under the First Amendment is not as extensive as that afforded to noncommercial speech, however. A state may restrict certain kinds of advertising, for example, in the interest of protecting consumers from being misled by the advertising practices. States also have a legitimate interest in the beautification of roadsides, and this interest allows states to place restraints on billboard advertising.

 The law firm of Arent Fox offers extensive information relating to advertising law at **http://www. advertisinglaw.com**.

Generally, a restriction on commercial speech will be considered valid as long as it meets the following three criteria: (1) it must seek to implement a substantial government interest, (2) it must directly advance that interest, and (3) it must go no further than necessary to accomplish its objective. ■ EXAMPLE 1.10 The South Carolina Supreme Court held that a state statute banning ads for video gambling violated the First Amendment because the statute did not directly advance a substantial government interest. Although the court acknowledged that the state had a substantial interest in minimizing gambling, there was no evidence that a reduction in video gambling ads would result in a reduction in gambling.[22] ■

The court in the following case applied these principles to determine the constitutionality of a county ordinance that regulated video games based on their content—the ordinance applied only to "graphically violent" video games.

---

19. 435 U.S. 765, 98 S.Ct. 1407, 55 L.Ed.2d 707 (1978).
20. *Consolidated Edison Co. v. Public Service Commission,* 447 U.S. 530, 100 S.Ct. 2326, 65 L.Ed.2d 319 (1980).
21. See *Austin v. Michigan Chamber of Commerce,* 494 U.S. 652, 110 S.Ct. 1391, 108 L.Ed.2d 652 (1990), in which the Court upheld a state law prohibiting corporations from using general corporate funds for independent expenditures in state political campaigns.
22. *Evans v. State,* 344 S.C. 60, 543 S.E.2d 547 (2001).

 CASE 1.3 ■ **Interactive Digital Software Association v. St. Louis County, Missouri**

United States Court of Appeals, Eighth Circuit, 2003. 329 F.3d 954.

FACTS St. Louis County, Missouri, passed an ordinance that made it unlawful for any person knowingly to sell, rent, or make available "graphically violent" video games

(Continued)

CASE 1.3—Continued

to minors or to "permit the free play of" such games by minors, without a parent or guardian's consent.[a] Interactive Digital Software Association, and others that create or provide the public with video games and related software, filed a suit against the county in a federal district court. The plaintiffs asserted that the ordinance violated the First Amendment. The county argued that the ordinance promoted the compelling state interest of protecting the "psychological well-being of minors" by reducing the harm suffered by children who play violent video games. A psychologist, a high school principal, and other experts offered their conclusions that playing violent video games leads to aggressive behavior, but the county did not provide proof of a link between the games and any psychological harm. The court dismissed the case. The plaintiffs appealed to the U.S. Court of Appeals for the Eighth Circuit.

ISSUE Are video games entitled to the same First Amendment protection as other types of speech?

DECISION Yes. The U.S. Court of Appeals for the Eighth Circuit reversed the judgment of the lower court and remanded the case for the entry of an injunction against the county's enforcement of its ordinance. The defendants failed to present the evidence of harm required to uphold a law threatening protected speech.

a. St. Louis County Revised Ordinances Sections 602.425 through 602.460.

REASON The appellate court reasoned that "[i]f the first amendment is versatile enough to shield the painting of Jackson Pollock, music of Arnold Schoenberg, or Jabberwocky verse of Lewis Carroll, we see no reason why the pictures, graphic design, concept art, sounds, music, stories, and narrative present in video games are not entitled to a similar protection." The court noted that video games contain stories, imagery, age-old themes of literature, and messages, even ideologies, similar to books and movies. With video games, players may skip the expressive parts of the game and proceed straight to the player-controlled action. But the same could be said of action-packed movies, the court explained. There is no justification for disqualifying video games as speech simply because they are constructed to be interactive. The court also noted that some books, "in which the reader makes choices that determine the plot of the story, * * * can be every bit as interactive." Because video games are entitled to protection, the court held that the county must provide some objective evidence that violent video games cause psychological harm to minors. In this case, the county failed to present the substantial supporting evidence of harm as is required to uphold the ordinance.

WHY IS THIS CASE IMPORTANT? *Even though the courts allow more regulation of commercial speech than other types of speech, the state's power to regulate the speech is still limited. Proof that the message is violent or objectionable in some way does not justify regulating commercial speech. The government must establish that it has a substantial interest in regulating the speech and that the proposed regulation advances that interest.*

Unprotected Speech The United States Supreme Court has made it clear that certain types of speech will not be given any protection under the First Amendment. Speech that harms the good reputation of another, or defamatory speech (see Chapter 4), will not be protected. Speech that violates criminal laws (such as threatening speech) is not constitutionally protected. Other unprotected speech includes "fighting words," or words that are likely to incite others to respond violently.

The Supreme Court has also held that obscene speech is not protected by the First Amendment. The Court has grappled from time to time with the problem of trying to establish an objective definition of obscene speech. In a 1973 case, *Miller v. California*,[23] the Supreme Court created a test for legal obscenity, which involved a set of requirements that must be met for material to be legally obscene. Under this

---

23. 413 U.S. 15, 93 S.Ct. 2607, 37 L.Ed.2d 419 (1973).

test, material is obscene if (1) the average person finds that it violates contemporary community standards; (2) the work taken as a whole appeals to a prurient (arousing or obsessive) interest in sex; (3) the work shows patently offensive sexual conduct; and (4) the work lacks serious redeeming literary, artistic, political, or scientific merit.

Because community standards vary widely, the *Miller* test has had inconsistent applications, and obscenity remains a constitutionally unsettled issue. Numerous state and federal statutes make it a crime to disseminate obscene materials, however, and the Supreme Court has often upheld such laws, including laws prohibiting the sale and possession of child pornography.[24]

 To learn about issues involving free speech and cyberspace, go to the Web site of the American Civil Liberties Union at **http://www.aclu.org**. Click on one of the issues listed on the right side of the screen for links to ACLU articles on that issue.

Online Obscenity Congress first attempted to protect minors from pornographic materials on the Internet by passing the Communications Decency Act (CDA) of 1996. The CDA made it a crime to make available to minors online any "obscene or indecent" message that "depicts or describes, in terms patently offensive as measured by contemporary community standards, sexual or excretory activities or organs."[25] The act was challenged as an unconstitutional restraint on speech, and ultimately the United States Supreme Court ruled that portions of the act were unconstitutional. The Court held that the terms *indecent* and *patently offensive* covered large amounts of nonpornographic material with serious educational or other value.[26]

The Child's Online Protection Act (COPA)[27] of 1998, which banned material "harmful to minors" distributed without some kind of age-verification system to separate adult and minor users, also encountered constitutional stumbling blocks. The act has largely been tied up in the courts since its passage.[28] Another controversial act was the Children's Internet Protection Act (CIPA) of 2000,[29] which requires public schools and libraries to block adult content from access by children by installing **filtering software.** Such software is designed to prevent persons from viewing certain Web sites by responding to a site's Internet address or its key words. In 2003, however, the Supreme Court held that the act did not violate the First Amendment.[30]

FILTERING SOFTWARE
A computer program that includes a pattern through which data are passed. When designed to block access to certain Web sites, the pattern blocks the retrieval of a site whose URL or key words are on a list within the program.

ESTABLISHMENT CLAUSE
The provision in the First Amendment to the Constitution that prohibits the government from establishing any state-sponsored religion or enacting any law that promotes religion or favors one religion over another.

FREE EXERCISE CLAUSE
The provision in the First Amendment to the Constitution that prohibits the government from interfering with people's religious practices or forms of worship.

THE FIRST AMENDMENT—FREEDOM OF RELIGION

The First Amendment states that the government may neither establish any religion nor prohibit the free exercise of religious practices. The first part of this constitutional provision is referred to as the **establishment clause,** and the second part is known as the **free exercise clause.** Government action, both federal and state, must be consistent with this constitutional mandate.

The Establishment Clause The establishment clause prohibits the government from establishing a state-sponsored religion, as well as from passing laws that promote

---

24. For example, see *Osborne v. Ohio,* 495 U.S. 103, 110 S.Ct. 1691, 109 L.Ed.2d 98 (1990).
25. 47 U.S.C. Section 223(a)(1)(B)(ii).
26. *Reno v. American Civil Liberties Union,* 521 U.S. 844, 117 S.Ct. 2329, 138 L.Ed.2d 874 (1997).
27. 47 U.S.C. Section 231.
28. For the most recent court decision concerning the constitutionality of this act, see *American Civil Liberties Union v. Ashcroft,* ___ U.S. ___, 124 S.Ct. 2783, 157 L.Ed.2d 690 (2003).
29. 17 U.S.C. Sections 1701–1741.
30. *United States v. American Library Association,* 539 U.S. 194, 123 S.Ct. 2297, 156 L.Ed.2d 221 (2003).

(aid or endorse) religion or that show a preference for one religion over another. The establishment clause does not require a complete separation of church and state, though. On the contrary, it requires the government to accommodate religions.[31]

The establishment clause covers all conflicts about such matters as the legality of state and local government support for a particular religion, government aid to religious organizations and schools, the government's allowing or requiring school prayers, and the teaching of evolution versus fundamentalist theories of creation. The Supreme Court has held that for a government law or policy to be constitutional, it must be secular in aim, must not have the primary effect of advancing or inhibiting religions, and must not create "an excessive government entanglement with religion."[32] Generally, federal or state regulation that does not promote religion or place a significant burden on religion is constitutional even if it has some impact on religion.

■ EXAMPLE 1.11 "Sunday closing laws" make the performance of some commercial activities on Sunday illegal. These statutes, also known as "blue laws" (from the color of the paper on which an early Sunday law was written), have been upheld on the ground that it is a legitimate function of government to provide a day of rest. The United States Supreme Court has held that the closing laws, although originally of a religious character, have taken on the secular purpose of promoting the health and welfare of workers.[33] Even though Sunday closing laws admittedly make it easier for Christians to attend religious services, the Court has viewed this effect as an incidental, not a primary, purpose of Sunday closing laws. ■

ETHICAL ISSUE 1.2

Do religious displays on public property violate the establishment clause? The thorny issue of whether religious displays on public property violate the establishment clause often arises during the holiday season. Time and again, the courts have wrestled with this issue, but it has never been resolved in a way that satisfies everyone. In a 1984 case, the United States Supreme Court decided that a city's official Christmas display, which included a crèche (Nativity scene), did not violate the establishment clause because it was just one part of a larger holiday display that featured secular symbols, such as reindeer and candy canes.[34] In a later case, the Court held that the presence of a crèche within a county courthouse violated the establishment clause because it was not in close proximity to nonreligious symbols, including a Christmas tree, which were located outside, on the building's steps. The presence of a menorah (a nine-branched candelabrum used in celebrating Hanukkah) on the building's steps, however, did not violate the establishment clause because the menorah was situated in close proximity to the Christmas tree.[35] The courts continue to apply this reasoning in cases involving similar issues. For example, in 2004 a federal appellate court ruled that displaying a monument of the Ten Commandments in a city park in Nebraska violated the establishment clause.[36] ■

The Free Exercise Clause The free exercise clause guarantees that a person can hold any religious belief that she or he wants; or a person can have no religious belief. When religious *practices* work against public policy and the public welfare, however,

---

31. *Zorach v. Clauson,* 343 U.S. 306, 72 S.Ct. 679, 96 L.Ed. 954 (1952).

32. *Lemon v. Kurtzman,* 403 U.S. 602, 91 S.Ct. 2105, 29 L.Ed.2d 745 (1971).

33. *McGowan v. Maryland,* 366 U.S. 420, 81 S.Ct. 1101, 6 L.Ed.2d 393 (1961).

34. *Lynch v. Donnelly,* 465 U.S. 668, 104 S.Ct. 1355, 79 L.Ed.2d 604 (1984).

35. See, for example, *County of Allegheny v. American Civil Liberties Union,* 492 U.S. 573, 109 S.Ct. 3086, 106 L.Ed.2d 472 (1989).

36. *ACLU Nebraska Foundation v. City of Plattsmouth,* 2004 WL 298965 (8th Cir. 2004). This issue is now before the Supreme Court.

Sultana Freeman reads from the Qur'an, the holy book of the Islamic religion, to illustrate that her religious beliefs require her to keep her head and face covered. The woman is testifying that it is unconstitutional for the government to force her to remove her veil and be photographed to get a driver's license in Florida. By taking a photo of an Islamic woman without her face covered, does the state violate the woman's religious freedom? Why or why not? What state interests might justify such an intrusion? (Library of Congress)

DUE PROCESS CLAUSE
The provisions in the Fifth and Fourteenth Amendments to the Constitution that guarantee that no person shall be deprived of life, liberty, or property without due process of law. Similar clauses are found in most state constitutions.

the government can act. For example, regardless of a child's or parent's religious beliefs, the government can require certain types of vaccinations. Similarly, although children of Jehovah's Witnesses are not required to say the Pledge of Allegiance at school, their parents cannot prevent them from accepting medical treatment (such as blood transfusions) if in fact their lives are in danger. Additionally, public school students can be required to study from textbooks chosen by school authorities.

For business firms, an important issue involves the accommodation that businesses must make for the religious beliefs of their employees. For example, if an employee's religion prohibits him or her from working on a certain day of the week or at a certain type of job, the employer must make a reasonable attempt to accommodate these religious requirements. Employers must reasonably accommodate an employee's religious beliefs even if the beliefs are not based on the tenets or dogma of a particular church, sect, or denomination. The only requirement is that the belief be religious in nature and sincerely held by the employee. (We will look further at this issue in Chapter 18, in the context of employment discrimination.)

Due Process and Equal Protection

Two other constitutional guarantees of great significance to Americans are mandated by the due process clauses of the Fifth and Fourteenth Amendments and the equal protection clause of the Fourteenth Amendment.

DUE PROCESS

Both the Fifth and the Fourteenth Amendments provide that no person shall be deprived "of life, liberty, or property, without due process of law." The **due process clause** of each of these constitutional amendments has two aspects—procedural and substantive.

Procedural Due Process Procedural due process requires that any government decision to take life, liberty, or property must be made fairly. For example, fair procedures must be used in determining whether a person will be subjected to punishment or have some burden imposed on him or her. Fair procedure has been interpreted as requiring that the person have at least an opportunity to object to a proposed action before a fair, neutral decision maker (which need not be a judge). Thus, for example, if a driver's license is construed as a property interest, some sort of opportunity to object to its suspension or termination by the state must be provided.

Substantive Due Process Substantive due process focuses on the content, or substance, of legislation. If a law or other governmental action limits a *fundamental right*, it will be held to violate substantive due process unless it promotes a compelling or overriding state interest. Fundamental rights include interstate travel, privacy, voting, and all First Amendment rights. Compelling state interests could include, for example, the public's safety. ■ **EXAMPLE 1.12** Laws setting speed limits may be upheld even though they affect interstate travel, if they are shown to reduce highway fatalities. The courts uphold these laws because the state has a compelling interest in protecting the lives of its citizens. ■

In situations not involving fundamental rights, a law or action does not violate substantive due process if it rationally relates to any legitimate governmental end. It is almost impossible for a law or action to fail the "rationality" test. Under this test, virtually any business regulation will be upheld as reasonable—the United States Supreme Court has sustained insurance regulations, price and wage controls, banking limitations, and restrictions of unfair competition and trade practices against substantive due process challenges.

■ EXAMPLE 1.13 If a state legislature enacted a law imposing a fifteen-year term of imprisonment without a trial on all businesspersons who appeared in their own television commercials, the law would be unconstitutional on both substantive and procedural grounds. Substantive review would invalidate the legislation because it abridges freedom of speech. Procedurally, the law is unfair because it imposes the penalty without giving the accused a chance to defend her or his actions. ■ The lack of procedural due process will cause a court to invalidate any statute or prior court decision. Similarly, the courts will overrule any state or federal law that violates the Constitution by denying substantive due process.

EQUAL PROTECTION

Under the Fourteenth Amendment, a state may not "deny to any person within its jurisdiction the equal protection of the laws." The United States Supreme Court has used the due process clause of the Fifth Amendment to make the **equal protection clause** applicable to the federal government as well. Equal protection means that the government must treat similarly situated individuals in a similar manner.

Both substantive due process and equal protection require review of the substance of the law or other governmental action rather than review of the procedures used. When a law or action limits the liberty of all persons to do something, it may violate substantive due process; when a law or action limits the liberty of some persons but not others, it may violate the equal protection clause. ■ EXAMPLE 1.14 If a law prohibits all persons from buying contraceptive devices, it raises a substantive due process question. If a law prohibits only unmarried persons from buying the same devices, it raises an equal protection issue. ■

Basically, in determining whether a law or action violates the equal protection clause, a court will consider questions similar to those previously noted as applicable in a substantive due process review. Under an equal protection inquiry, when a law or action distinguishes between or among individuals, the basis for the distinction—that is, the classification—is examined. Depending on the classification, the courts apply one of the following three levels of scrutiny, or "tests," to determine whether the law or action violates the equal protection clause:

1 *Minimal Scrutiny—The "Rational Basis" Test.* Generally, laws regulating economic and social matters are presumed to be valid and are subject to only minimal scrutiny. A classification will be considered valid if there is any conceivable "rational basis" on which the classification might relate to any *legitimate government interest*. It is almost impossible for a law or action to fail the rational basis test.

2 *Intermediate Scrutiny.* This is a harder standard to meet and is applied in cases involving discrimination based on gender or legitimacy. Laws using these classifications must be substantially related to *important government objectives*.

3 *Strict Scrutiny.* This is the most difficult standard to meet. Very few cases survive strict-scrutiny analysis, which is applied when a law or action inhibits some persons' exercise of a fundamental right or is based on a suspect trait (such as race, national origin, or citizenship status). Strict scrutiny means that the court will examine the law or action involved very closely, and the law or action will

---

EQUAL PROTECTION CLAUSE
The provision in the Fourteenth Amendment to the Constitution that guarantees that no state will "deny to any person within its jurisdiction the equal protection of the laws." This clause mandates that the state governments treat similarly situated individuals in a similar manner.

be allowed to stand only if it is necessary to promote a *compelling government interest.*

Privacy Rights

In the past, privacy issues typically related to personal information that government agencies, including the Federal Bureau of Investigation, might obtain and keep about an individual. Since the 1990s, one of the major concerns of individuals has been how to protect privacy rights in cyberspace and to safeguard private information that may be revealed online (including credit-card numbers and financial information).

Today, individuals face additional concerns about government intrusions into their privacy. Legislation passed by Congress in the wake of the terrorist attacks of September 11, 2001, gave increased authority to government officials to monitor Internet activities (such as e-mail and Web site visits) and to gain access to personal financial data and student information.[37] The government must certify that the information likely to be obtained is relevant to an ongoing criminal investigation, but it does not need to provide proof of any wrongdoing to gain access to this information. Privacy advocates argue that this law has adversely affected the constitutional rights of all Americans, and it has been widely criticized in the media, fueling the public debate over how to secure privacy rights in an electronic age.

In this section, we look at the protection of privacy rights under the U.S. Constitution and various federal statutes. Note that state constitutions and statutes also protect individuals' privacy rights, often to a significant degree. Privacy rights are also protected under tort law (see Chapter 4). Additionally, the Federal Trade Commission has played an active role in protecting the privacy rights of online consumers (see Chapter 13). The protection of employees' privacy rights, particularly with respect to electronic monitoring practices, is another area of growing concern (see Chapter 18).

CONSTITUTIONAL PROTECTION OF PRIVACY RIGHTS

The U.S. Constitution does not explicitly mention a general right to privacy, and only relatively recently have the courts regarded the right to privacy as a constitutional right. In a landmark 1965 case, *Griswold v. Connecticut,*[38] the Supreme Court invalidated a Connecticut law that effectively prohibited the use of contraceptives. The Court held that the law violated the right to privacy. Justice William O. Douglas formulated a unique way of reading this right into the Bill of Rights. He claimed that "emanations" from the rights guaranteed by the First, Third, Fourth, Fifth, and Ninth Amendments formed and gave "life and substance" to "penumbras" (partial shadows) around these guaranteed rights. These penumbras included an implied constitutional right to privacy.

When we read these amendments, we can see the foundation for Justice Douglas's reasoning. Consider the Fourth Amendment. By prohibiting unreasonable searches and seizures, the amendment effectively protects individuals' privacy. Consider also the words of the Ninth Amendment: "The enumeration in the Constitution of certain rights, shall not be construed to deny or disparage others retained by the people." In other words, although neither the Constitution nor its amendments mentions the right to privacy, this right does exist.

---

37. Uniting and Strengthening America by Providing Appropriate Tools Required to Intercept and Obstruct Terrorism Act of 2001, also known as the USA Patriot Act, was enacted as Pub. L. No. 107-56 (2001).
38. 381 U.S. 479, 85 S.Ct. 1678, 14 L.Ed.2d 510 (1965).

FEDERAL STATUTES PROTECTING PRIVACY RIGHTS

In the last several decades, Congress has enacted a number of statutes that protect the privacy of individuals in various areas of concern. In 1966, Congress enacted the Freedom of Information Act, which allows any person to request copies of any information on her or him contained in federal government files. The Privacy Act of 1974 also gives persons the right to access such information. These and other major federal laws protecting privacy rights are listed and described in Exhibit 1–2.

Responding to the growing need to protect the privacy of individuals' health records—particularly computerized records—Congress passed the Health Insurance Portability and Accountability Act (HIPAA)[39] of 1996. This act, which took effect on April 14, 2003, defines and limits the circumstances in which an individual's "protected health information" may be used or disclosed.

---

39. The HIPAA was enacted as Pub. L. No. 104-191 (1996) and is codified in 29 U.S.C.A. Sections 1181 *et seq.*

EXHIBIT 1–2   FEDERAL LEGISLATION RELATING TO PRIVACY

TITLE	PROVISIONS CONCERNING PRIVACY
Freedom of Information Act (1966)	Provides that individuals have a right to obtain access to information about them collected in government files.
Family and Educational Rights and Privacy Act (1974)	Limits access to computer-stored records of education-related evaluations and grades in private and public colleges and universities.
Privacy Act (1974)	Protects the privacy of individuals about whom the federal government has information. Under this act, agencies that use or disclose personal information must make sure that the information is reliable and guard against its misuse. Individuals must be able to find out what data concerning them the agency is compiling and how the data will be used. In addition, the agency must give individuals a means to correct inaccurate data and must obtain their consent before using the data for any other purpose.
Tax Reform Act (1976)	Preserves the privacy of personal financial information.
Right to Financial Privacy Act (1978)	Prohibits financial institutions from providing the federal government with access to customers' records unless a customer authorizes the disclosure.
Electronic Communications Privacy Act (1986)	Prohibits the interception of information communicated by electronic means.
Driver's Privacy Protection Act (1994)	Prevents states from disclosing or selling a driver's personal information without the driver's consent.
Health Insurance Portability and Accountability Act (1996)	Prohibits the use of a consumer's medical information for any purpose other than that for which such information was provided, unless the consumer expressly consents to the use. Final rules became effective on April 14, 2003.
Financial Services Modernization Act (Gramm-Leach-Bliley Act) (1999)	Prohibits the disclosure of nonpublic personal information about a consumer to an unaffiliated third party unless strict disclosure and opt-out requirements are met. Final rules became mandatory on July 1, 2001.

APPLICATION ▪ How Can You Choose and Use a Lawyer?*

If you are contemplating a career in the business world, sooner or later you will probably face the question, "Do I need a lawyer?" The answer to this question will likely be "Yes," at least at some time during your career. Even businesspersons who have gone to law school often hire an outside lawyer to help them with their legal problems. Today, it is virtually impossible for nonexperts to keep up with the myriad rules and regulations that govern the conduct of business in the United States. It is also increasingly possible for businesspersons to incur penalties for violating laws or regulations of which they are totally unaware.

Although lawyers may seem expensive—anywhere from $100 to $500 or more per hour—cautious businesspersons will make sure that they are not "penny wise and pound foolish." The consultation fee paid to an attorney may be insignificant compared with the potential liability facing a businessperson.

SELECTING AN ATTORNEY

In selecting an attorney, you can ask friends, relatives, or business associates to recommend someone. Alternatively, you can call the local or state bar association to obtain the names of several lawyers. West Group has an online database containing biographies of attorneys throughout the country, listed by area of specialty and state. You can find attorneys in your area by accessing West's Legal Directory online at <u>http://directory.findlaw.com</u>. Some legal aid programs have staff attorneys, and others may refer you to volunteers. You might also investigate legal clinics and prepaid legal service plans.

For your initial meeting with the attorney you have selected, you should prepare a written list of your questions and perhaps a summary of the problem for which you need legal advice. Attach to your list copies of any relevant documents that you can leave with the lawyer. While at the meeting, ask about legal fees, discuss the legal problem you are facing (remember that virtually everything you say to your attorney is protected by the attorney-client privilege of confidentiality), and clarify the scope of what you want the lawyer to do for you.

EVALUATING YOUR ATTORNEY

Ask yourself the following questions after your first meeting: Did the attorney seem knowledgeable about what is needed to address your concerns? Did he or she seem willing to investigate the law and the facts further to ensure an accurate understanding of your legal situation? Did you communicate well with each other? Did the attorney perceive what issues were of foremost concern to you and address those issues to your satisfaction? Did the attorney "speak your language" when explaining the legal implications of those issues?

Continue to evaluate the relationship over time. For many businesspersons, relationships with attorneys last for decades. Make sure that your relationship with your attorney will be a fruitful one.

CHECKLIST FOR CHOOSING AND USING A LAWYER

1. If you ever think that you need legal advice, you probably do.
2. When choosing an attorney, try to get recommendations from friends, relatives, or business associates who have had long-standing relationships with their attorneys. If that fails, check with your local or state bar association or check West Group's online directory.
3. When you initially consult with an attorney, bring a written list of questions to which you want answers, perhaps a summary of your problem, and copies of relevant documents.
4. Do not hesitate to ask about the legal fees that your attorney will charge, and be sure to clarify the scope of the work to be undertaken by the attorney. Ask whatever questions are necessary to ensure that you understand what your legal options are. Do not worry about appearing foolish.

* With appreciation to James D. Van Tassel at Mission College, California, for his helpful suggestions on this topic.

▦ KEY TERMS

adjudicate 5	due process clause 25	plaintiff 9
administrative agency 4	enabling legislation 4	police powers 15
administrative law 4	equal protection clause 26	precedent 6
administrative law judge (ALJ) 6	equitable principles and maxims 10	preemption 16
administrative process 5	establishment clause 23	primary source of law 2
Bill of Rights 18	executive agency 4	procedural law 10
binding authority 7	federal form of government 13	remedy 9
case law 6	filtering software 23	rulemaking 5
citation 3	free exercise clause 23	secondary source of law 2
civil law 12	independent regulatory agency 4	*stare decisis* 7
commerce clause 13	international law 12	statute of limitations 11
common law 6	jurisprudence 2	statutory law 3
constitutional law 2	law 1	substantive law 10
criminal law 12	national law 12	supremacy clause 16
cyberlaw 10	ordinance 3	symbolic speech 20
defendant 9	persuasive authority 8	

CHAPTER SUMMARY ▦ The Historical and Constitutional Foundations

Sources of American Law
(See pages 2–6.)

1. *Constitutional law*—The law as expressed in the U.S. Constitution and the various state constitutions. The U.S. Constitution is the supreme law of the land. State constitutions are supreme within state borders to the extent that they do not violate the U.S. Constitution or a federal law.

2. *Statutory law*—Laws or ordinances created by federal, state, and local legislatures and governing bodies. None of these laws can violate the U.S. Constitution or the relevant state constitutions. Uniform laws, when adopted by a state legislature, become statutory law in that state.

3. *Administrative law*—The rules, orders, and decisions of federal or state government administrative agencies. Federal administrative agencies are created by enabling legislation enacted by the U.S. Congress. Agency functions include rulemaking, investigation and enforcement, and adjudication.

4. *Case law and common law doctrines*—Judge-made law, including interpretations of constitutional provisions, of statutes enacted by legislatures, and of regulations created by administrative agencies. The common law—the doctrines and principles embodied in case law—governs all areas not covered by statutory law (or agency regulations issued to implement various statutes).

The Common Law Tradition
(See pages 6–10.)

1. *Common law*—Law that originated in medieval England with the creation of the king's courts, or *curiae regis,* and the development of a body of rules that were common to (or applied throughout) the land.

2. *Stare decisis*—A doctrine under which judges "stand on decided cases"—or follow the rule of precedent—in deciding cases. *Stare decisis* is the cornerstone of the common law tradition.

3. *Remedies*—

   a. Remedies at law—Money or something else of value.

CHAPTER SUMMARY ▪ The Historical and Constitutional Foundations—Continued

The Common Law Tradition—Continued	b. *Remedies in equity*—Remedies that are granted when the remedies at law are unavailable or inadequate. Equitable remedies include specific performance, an injunction, and contract rescission (cancellation).
Classifications of Law (See pages 10–12.)	The law may be broken down according to several classification systems, such as substantive or procedural law, federal or state law, and private or public law. Two broad classifications are civil and criminal law, and national and international law. Cyberlaw is not really a classification of law but a term that is applied to the growing body of case law and statutory law that applies to Internet transactions.
The Constitutional Powers of Government (See page 13.)	The U.S. Constitution established a federal form of government, in which government powers are shared by the national government and the state governments. At the national level, government powers are divided among the legislative, executive, and judicial branches.
The Commerce Clause (See pages 13–16.)	1. *The expansion of national powers*—The commerce clause expressly permits Congress to regulate commerce. Over time, courts expansively interpreted this clause, thereby enabling the national government to wield extensive powers over the economic life of the nation.
	2. *The commerce power today*—Today, the commerce power authorizes the national government, at least theoretically, to regulate every commercial enterprise in the United States. In recent years, the Supreme Court has reined in somewhat the national government's regulatory powers under the commerce clause.
	3. *The regulatory powers of the states*—The Tenth Amendment reserves all powers not expressly delegated to the national government to the states. Under their police powers, state governments may regulate private activities to protect or promote the public order, health, safety, morals, and general welfare.
	4. *The "dormant" commerce clause*—If state regulations substantially interfere with interstate commerce, they will be held to violate the "dormant" commerce clause of the U.S. Constitution. The positive aspect of the commerce clause, which gives the national government the exclusive authority to regulate interstate commerce, implies a "dormant" aspect—that the states do *not* have this power.
The Supremacy Clause (See pages 16–18.)	The U.S. Constitution provides that the Constitution, laws, and treaties of the United States are "the supreme Law of the Land." Whenever a state law directly conflicts with a federal law, the state law is rendered invalid.
Business and the Bill of Rights (See pages 18–25.)	The Bill of Rights, which consists of the first ten amendments to the U.S. Constitution, was adopted in 1791 and embodies a series of protections for individuals—and, in some instances, business entities—against various types of interference by the federal government. Freedoms guaranteed by the First Amendment that affect businesses include the following:
	1. *Freedom of speech*—Speech, including symbolic speech, is given the fullest possible protection by the courts. Corporate political speech and commercial speech also receive substantial protection under the First Amendment. Certain types of speech, such as defamatory speech and lewd or obscene speech, are not protected under the First Amendment. Government attempts to regulate unprotected forms of speech in the online environment have, to date, met with numerous challenges.
	2. *Freedom of religion*—Under the First Amendment, the government may neither establish any religion (the establishment clause) nor prohibit the free exercise of religion (the free exercise clause).

(Continued)

CHAPTER SUMMARY ▪ The Historical and Constitutional Foundations—Continued

Due Process and Equal Protection (See pages 25–27.)	1. *Due process*—Both the Fifth and the Fourteenth Amendments provide that no person shall be deprived of "life, liberty, or property, without due process of law." Procedural due process requires that any government decision to take life, liberty, or property must be made fairly, using fair procedures. Substantive due process focuses on the content of legislation. Generally, a law that is not compatible with the Constitution violates substantive due process unless the law promotes a compelling state interest, such as public safety.
	2. *Equal protection*—Under the Fourteenth Amendment, a state may not "deny to any person within its jurisdiction the equal protection of the laws." A law or action that limits the liberty of some persons but not others may violate the equal protection clause. Such a law may be deemed valid, however, if there is a rational basis for the discriminatory treatment of a given group or if the law substantially relates to an important government objective.
Privacy Rights (See pages 27–28.)	Americans are increasingly becoming concerned over privacy issues raised by Internet-related technology. The Constitution does not contain a specific guarantee of a right to privacy, but such a right has been derived from guarantees found in several constitutional amendments. A number of federal statutes protect privacy rights. Privacy rights are also protected by many state constitutions and statutes, as well as under tort law.

▪ FOR REVIEW

Answers for the even-numbered questions in this For Review *section can be found in Appendix I at the end of this text.*

1 What is the common law tradition?

2 What is a precedent? When might a court depart from precedent?

3 What is the difference between remedies at law and remedies in equity?

4 What constitutional clause gives the federal government the power to regulate commercial activities among the various states?

5 What is the Bill of Rights? What freedoms are guaranteed by the First Amendment?

▪ QUESTIONS AND CASE PROBLEMS

1–1. Reading Citations. Assume that you want to read the entire court opinion in the case of *Thompson v. Altheimer & Gray,* 248 F.3d 621 (7th Cir. 2001). The case deals with whether an attorney may dismiss "for cause" a prospective juror in a case involving racial discrimination. Read the section entitled "Finding Case Law" in the appendix that follows this chapter, and then explain specifically where you would find the court's opinion.

1–2. Sources of American Law. This chapter discussed a number of sources of American law. Which source of law takes priority in each of the following situations, and why?

(a) A federal statute conflicts with the U.S. Constitution.

(b) A federal statute conflicts with a state constitution.

(c) A state statute conflicts with the common law of that state.

(d) A state constitutional amendment conflicts with the U.S. Constitution.

(e) A federal administrative regulation conflicts with a state constitution.

1–3. *Stare Decisis.* In the text of this chapter, we stated that the doctrine of *stare decisis* "became a cornerstone of the English and American judicial systems." What does *stare decisis* mean, and why has this doctrine been so fundamental to the development of our legal tradition?

1–4. Commercial Speech. A mayoral election is about to be held in a large U.S. city. One of the candidates is Luis Delgado, and his campaign supporters wish to post campaign signs on lampposts and utility posts throughout the city. A city ordinance, however, prohibits the posting of any signs on public property. Delgado's supporters contend that the city ordinance is unconstitutional because it violates their rights to free speech. What factors might a court consider in determining the constitutionality of this ordinance?

1–5. Commerce Clause. Suppose that Georgia enacts a law requiring the use of contoured rear-fender mudguards on trucks and trailers operating within its state lines. The statute further makes it illegal for trucks and trailers to use straight mudguards. In thirty-five other states, straight mudguards are legal. Moreover, in the neighboring state of Florida, straight mudguards are explicitly required by law. There is some evidence suggesting that contoured mudguards might be a little safer than straight mudguards. Discuss whether this Georgia statute would violate the commerce clause of the U.S. Constitution.

CASE PROBLEM WITH SAMPLE ANSWER

1–6. In February 1999, Carl Adler mailed a driver's license renewal application form and a check for $28 to the New York Department of Motor Vehicles (DMV). The form required Adler's Social Security number, which he intentionally omitted. The DMV returned the application and check and told Adler to supply his Social Security number or send proof that the Social Security Administration could not give him a number. Claiming a right to privacy, Adler refused to comply. The DMV responded that federal law authorizes the states to obtain Social Security numbers from individuals in the context of administering certain state programs, including driver's license programs, and that Adler's application would not be processed until he supplied the number. Adler filed a suit in a New York state court against the DMV, asserting in part that it was in violation of the federal Privacy Act of 1974. Adler asked the court to, among other things, order the DMV to renew his license. Should the court grant Adler's request? Why or why not? [*Adler v. Jackson*, 712 N.Y.S.2d 240 (Sup. 2000)]

After you have answered this problem, compare your answer with the sample answer given on the Web site that accompanies this text. Go to http://blt.westbuslaw.com, select "Chapter 1," and click on "Case Problem with Sample Answer."

1–7. Free Speech. Henry Mishkoff is a Web designer whose firm does business as "Webfeats." When Taubman Co. began building a mall called "The Shops at Willow Bend" near Mishkoff's home, Mishkoff registered the domain name "shopsatwillowbend.com" and created a Web site with that address. The site featured information about the mall, a disclaimer indicating that Mishkoff's site was unofficial, and a link to the mall's official site. Taubman discovered Mishkoff's site and filed a suit in a federal district

court against him. Mishkoff then registered other names, including "taubmansucks.com," with links to a site documenting his battle with Taubman. (A Web name with a "sucks.com" moniker attached to it is known as a "complaint name," and the process of registering and using such names is known as "cybergriping.") Taubman asked the court to order Mishkoff to stop using all of these names. Should the court grant Taubman's request? On what basis might the court protect Mishkoff's use of the names? [*Taubman Co. v. Webfeats*, 319 F.3d 770 (6th Cir. 2003)]

1–8. Due Process. In 1994, the Board of County Commissioners of Yellowstone County, Montana, created Zoning District 17 in a rural area of the county and a Planning and Zoning Commission for the district. The commission adopted zoning regulations, which provided, among other things, that "dwelling units" could be built only through "on-site construction." Later, county officials could not identify any health or safety concerns that the on-site construction provision addressed, and there was no indication that homes built off-site would affect property values or any other general welfare interest of the community. In December 1999, Francis and Anita Yurczyk bought two forty-acre tracts in District 17. The Yurczyks also bought a modular home and moved it onto the property the following spring. Within days, the county advised the Yurczyks that the home violated the on-site construction regulation and would have to be removed. The Yurczyks filed a suit in a Montana state court against the county, alleging in part that the regulation violated the Yurczyks' due process rights. Should the court rule in the plaintiffs' favor? Explain. [*Yurczyk v. Yellowstone County*, 2004 MT 3, 319 Mont. 169, 83 P.3d 266 (2004)]

A QUESTION OF ETHICS

1–9. In 1999, in an effort to reduce smoking by children, the attorney general of Massachusetts issued comprehensive regulations governing the advertising and sale of tobacco products. Among other things, the regulations banned cigarette advertisements within one thousand feet of any elementary school, secondary school, or public playground and required retailers to post any advertising in their stores at least five feet off the floor, out of the immediate sight of young children. A group of tobacco manufacturers and retailers filed suit against the state, claiming that the regulations were preempted by the federal Cigarette Labeling and Advertising Act of 1965, as amended. That act sets uniform labeling requirements and bans broadcast advertising for cigarettes. Ultimately, the case reached the United States Supreme Court, which held that the federal law on cigarette ads preempted the cigarette advertising restrictions adopted by Massachusetts. The only portion of the Massachusetts regulatory package to survive was the requirement that retailers had to place tobacco products in an area accessible only by the sales staff. In view of these facts, consider the following questions.

[*Lorillard Tobacco Co. v. Reilly,* 533 U.S. 525, 121 S.Ct. 2404, 69 L.Ed.2d 532 (2001)]

1. Some argue that having a national standard for tobacco regulation is more important than allowing states to set their own standards for tobacco regulation. Do you agree? Why or why not?
2. According to the Court in this case, the federal law does not restrict the ability of state and local governments to adopt general zoning restrictions that apply to cigarettes, so long as those restrictions are "on equal terms with other products." How would you argue in support of this reasoning? How would you argue against it?

FOR CRITICAL ANALYSIS

 1–10. In recent years, many people have criticized the film and entertainment industries for promoting violence by exposing the American public, and particularly American youth, to extremely violent films and song lyrics. Do you think that the right to free speech can (or should) be traded off in an attempt to reduce violence in the United States? Generally, in the wake of the September 11, 2001, terrorist attack on the World Trade Center towers and the Pentagon, should Americans trade off some of their civil liberties for (possibly) more protection against violence and terrorism?

ONLINE ACTIVITIES

INTERNET EXERCISES

Go to the *Business Law Today: The Essentials* home page at <u>http://blt.westbuslaw.com,</u> select "Chapter 1," and click on "Internet Exercises." There you will find the following Internet research exercises that you can perform to learn more about topics covered in this chapter.

Activity 1–1: LEGAL PERSPECTIVE—Commercial Speech

Activity 1–2: MANAGEMENT PERSPECTIVE—Privacy Rights in Cyberspace

Activity 1–3: SOCIAL PERSPECTIVE—The Case of the Speluncean Explorers

BEFORE THE TEST

Go to the *Business Law Today: The Essentials* home page at <u>http://blt.westbuslaw.com,</u> select "Chapter 1," and click on "Interactive Quizzes." You will find at least twenty interactive questions relating to this chapter.

CHAPTER 1

Appendix

The statutes, agency regulations, and case law referred to in this text establish the rights and duties of businesspersons engaged in various types of activities. The cases presented in the following chapters provide you with concise, real-life illustrations of how the courts interpret and apply these laws. Because of the importance of knowing how to find statutory, administrative, and case law, this appendix offers a brief introduction to how these laws are published and to the legal "shorthand" employed in referencing these legal sources.

■ Finding Statutory and Administrative Law

When Congress passes laws, they are collected in a publication titled *United States Statutes at Large*. When state legislatures pass laws, they are collected in similar state publications. Most frequently, however, laws are referred to in their codified form—that is, the form in which they appear in the federal and state codes. In these codes, laws are compiled by subject.

UNITED STATES CODE

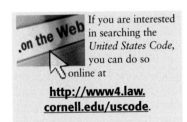

If you are interested in searching the *United States Code,* you can do so online at

http://www4.law. cornell.edu/uscode.

The *United States Code* (U.S.C.) arranges all existing federal laws of a public and permanent nature by subject. Each of the fifty subjects into which the U.S.C. arranges the laws is given a title and a title number. For example, laws relating to commerce and trade are collected in "Title 15, Commerce and Trade." Titles are subdivided by sections. A citation to the U.S.C. includes title and section numbers. Thus, a reference to "15 U.S.C. Section 1" means that the statute can be found in Section 1 of Title 15. ("Section" may also be designated by the symbol §, and "Sections" by §§.)

Sometimes a citation includes the abbreviation *et seq.*—as in "15 U.S.C. Sections 1 *et seq.*" The term is an abbreviated form of *et sequitur,* which in Latin means "and the following"; when used in a citation, it refers to sections that concern the same subject as the numbered section and follow it in sequence.

Commercial publications of these laws and regulations are available and are widely used. For example, West Group publishes the *United States Code Annotated* (U.S.C.A.). The U.S.C.A. contains the complete text of laws included in the U.S.C., as well as notes of court decisions that interpret and apply specific sections of the statutes, plus the text of presidential proclamations and executive orders. The U.S.C.A. also includes research aids, such as cross-references to related statutes, historical notes, and library references. A citation to the U.S.C.A. is similar to a citation to the U.S.C.: "15 U.S.C.A. Section 1."

STATE CODES

State codes follow the U.S.C. pattern of arranging law by subject. The state codes may be called codes, revisions, compilations, consolidations, general statutes, or statutes, depending on the preferences of the states. In some codes, subjects are designated by number. In others, they are designated by name. For example, "13 Pennsylvania Consolidated Statutes Section 1101" means that the statute can be found in Title 13, Section 1101, of the Pennsylvania code. "California Commercial Code Section 1101" means the statute can be found under the subject heading "Commercial Code" of the California code in Section 1101. Abbreviations may be used. For example, "13 Pennsylvania Consolidated Statutes Section 1101" may be abbreviated "13 Pa. C.S. § 1101," and "California Commercial Code Section 1101" may be abbreviated "Cal. Com. Code § 1101."

ADMINISTRATIVE RULES

The *Code of Federal Regulations* is online at **http://www. gpoaccess.gov/cfr/index.html**.

Rules and regulations adopted by federal administrative agencies are compiled in the *Code of Federal Regulations* (C.F.R.). Like the U.S.C., the C.F.R. is divided into fifty titles. Rules within each title are assigned section numbers. A full citation to the C.F.R. includes title and section numbers. For example, a reference to "17 C.F.R. Section 230.504" means that the rule can be found in Section 230.504 of Title 17.

▉ Finding Case Law

Before discussing the case reporting system, we need to look briefly at the court system (which will be discussed in detail in Chapter 3). There are two types of courts in the United States, federal courts and state courts. Both the federal and state court systems consist of several levels, or tiers, of courts. *Trial courts,* in which evidence is presented and testimony given, are on the bottom tier (which also includes lower courts handling specialized issues). Decisions from a trial court can be appealed to a higher court, which commonly would be an intermediate *court of appeals,* or an *appellate court.* Decisions from these intermediate courts of appeals may be appealed to an even higher court, such as a state supreme court or the United States Supreme Court.

STATE COURT DECISIONS

Most state trial court decisions are not published. Except in New York and a few other states that publish selected opinions of their trial courts, decisions from state trial courts are merely filed in the office of the clerk of the court, where the decisions are available for public inspection. (Sometimes, they can be found online as well.) Written decisions of the appellate, or reviewing, courts, however, are published and distributed. As you will note, most of the state court cases presented in this book are from state appellate courts. The reported appellate decisions are published in volumes called *reports* or *reporters,* which are numbered consecutively. State appellate court decisions are found in the state reporters of that particular state.

Additionally, state court opinions appear in regional units of the *National Reporter System,* published by West Group. Most lawyers and libraries have the West reporters because they report cases more quickly and are distributed more widely than the state-published reports. In fact, many states have eliminated their own reporters in favor of West's National Reporter System. The National Reporter System divides the states into the following geographic areas: *Atlantic* (A. or A.2d), *South Eastern* (S.E. or S.E.2d), *South Western* (S.W., S.W.2d, or S.W.3d), *North Western* (N.W. or N.W.2d), *North Eastern* (N.E. or N.E.2d), *Southern* (So. or So.2d), and *Pacific* (P., P.2d, or P.3d). (The *2d* and *3d* in the abbreviations refer to *Second Series* and *Third Series,* respectively.) The states included in each of these regional divisions are indicated in Exhibit 1A–1, which illustrates West's National Reporter System.

EXHIBIT 1A–1 NATIONAL REPORTER SYSTEM—REGIONAL/FEDERAL

Regional Reporters	Coverage Beginning	Coverage
Atlantic Reporter (A. or A.2d)	1885	Connecticut, Delaware, Maine, Maryland, New Hampshire, New Jersey, Pennsylvania, Rhode Island, Vermont, and District of Columbia.
North Eastern Reporter (N.E. or N.E.2d)	1885	Illinois, Indiana, Massachusetts, New York, and Ohio.
North Western Reporter (N.W. or N.W.2d)	1879	Iowa, Michigan, Minnesota, Nebraska, North Dakota, South Dakota, and Wisconsin.
Pacific Reporter (P., P.2d, or P.3d)	1883	Alaska, Arizona, California, Colorado, Hawaii, Idaho, Kansas, Montana, Nevada, New Mexico, Oklahoma, Oregon, Utah, Washington, and Wyoming.
South Eastern Reporter (S.E. or S.E.2d)	1887	Georgia, North Carolina, South Carolina, Virginia, and West Virginia.
South Western Reporter (S.W., S.W.2d, or S.W.3d)	1886	Arkansas, Kentucky, Missouri, Tennessee, and Texas.
Southern Reporter (So. or So.2d)	1887	Alabama, Florida, Louisiana, and Mississippi.
Federal Reporters		
Federal Reporter (F., F.2d, or F.3d)	1880	U.S. Circuit Courts from 1880 to 1912; U.S. Commerce Court from 1911 to 1913; U.S. District Courts from 1880 to 1932; U.S. Court of Claims (now called U.S. Court of Federal Claims) from 1929 to 1932 and since 1960; U.S. Courts of Appeals since 1891; U.S. Court of Customs and Patent Appeals since 1929; U.S. Emergency Court of Appeals since 1943.
Federal Supplement (F.Supp. or F.Supp.2d)	1932	U.S. Court of Claims from 1932 to 1960; U.S. District Courts since 1932; and U.S. Customs Court since 1956.
Federal Rules Decisions (F.R.D.)	1939	U.S. District Courts involving the Federal Rules of Civil Procedure since 1939 and Federal Rules of Criminal Procedure since 1946.
Supreme Court Reporter (S.Ct.)	1882	U.S. Supreme Court since the October term of 1882.
Bankruptcy Reporter (Bankr.)	1980	Bankruptcy decisions of U.S. Bankruptcy Courts, U.S. District Courts, U.S. Courts of Appeals, and U.S. Supreme Court.
Military Justice Reporter (M.J.)	1978	U.S. Court of Military Appeals and Courts of Military Review for the Army, Navy, Air Force, and Coast Guard.

NATIONAL REPORTER SYSTEM MAP

After appellate decisions have been published, they are normally referred to (cited) by the name of the case; the volume, name, and page number of the state's official reporter (if different from West's National Reporter System); the volume, name, and page number of the *National Reporter;* and the volume, name, and page number of any other selected reporter. This information is included in the *citation.* (Citing a reporter by volume number, name, and page number, in that order, is common to all citations.) When more than one reporter is cited for the same case, each reference is called a *parallel citation.* For example, consider the following case: *Yale Diagnostic Radiology v. Estate of Harun Foundation,* 267 Conn. 351, 838 A.2d 179 (2004). We see that the opinion in this case may be found in Volume 267 of the official *Connecticut Reports,* on page 351. The parallel citation is to Volume 838 of the *Atlantic Reporter, Second Series,* page 179. In presenting appellate opinions in this text, in addition to the reporter, we give the name of the court hearing the case and the year of the court's decision.

A few states—including those with intermediate appellate courts, such as California, Illinois, and New York—have more than one reporter for opinions issued by their courts. Sample citations from these courts, as well as others, are listed and explained in Exhibit 1A–2.

FEDERAL COURT DECISIONS

Federal district court decisions are published unofficially in West's *Federal Supplement* (F.Supp. or F.Supp.2d), and opinions from the circuit courts of appeals (federal reviewing courts) are reported unofficially in West's *Federal Reporter* (F., F.2d, or F.3d). Cases concerning federal bankruptcy law are published unofficially in West's *Bankruptcy Reporter* (Bankr.). The official edition of United States Supreme Court decisions is the *United States Reports* (U.S.), which is published by the federal government. Unofficial editions of Supreme Court cases include West's *Supreme Court Reporter* (S.Ct.) and the *Lawyers' Edition of the Supreme Court Reports* (L.Ed. or L.Ed.2d). Sample citations for federal court decisions are also listed and explained in Exhibit 1A–2.

UNPUBLISHED OPINIONS AND OLD CASES

Many court opinions that are not yet published or that are not intended for publication can be accessed through Westlaw® (abbreviated in citations as "WL"), an online legal database maintained by West Group. When no citation to a published reporter is available for cases cited in this text, we give the WL citation (see Exhibit 1A–2 for an example).

On a few occasions, this text cites opinions from old, classic cases dating to the nineteenth century or earlier; some of these are from the English courts. The citations to these cases may not conform to the descriptions given above because the reporters in which they were published have since been replaced.

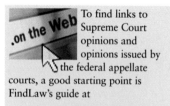

To find links to Supreme Court opinions and opinions issued by the federal appellate courts, a good starting point is FindLaw's guide at

http://findlaw.com/ 10fedgov/judicial.

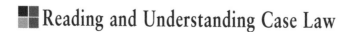

Reading and Understanding Case Law

The cases in this text have been condensed from the full text of the courts' opinions and paraphrased by the authors. For those wishing to review court cases for future research projects or to gain additional legal information, the following sections will provide useful insights into how to read and understand case law.

EXHIBIT 1A-2 HOW TO READ CITATIONS

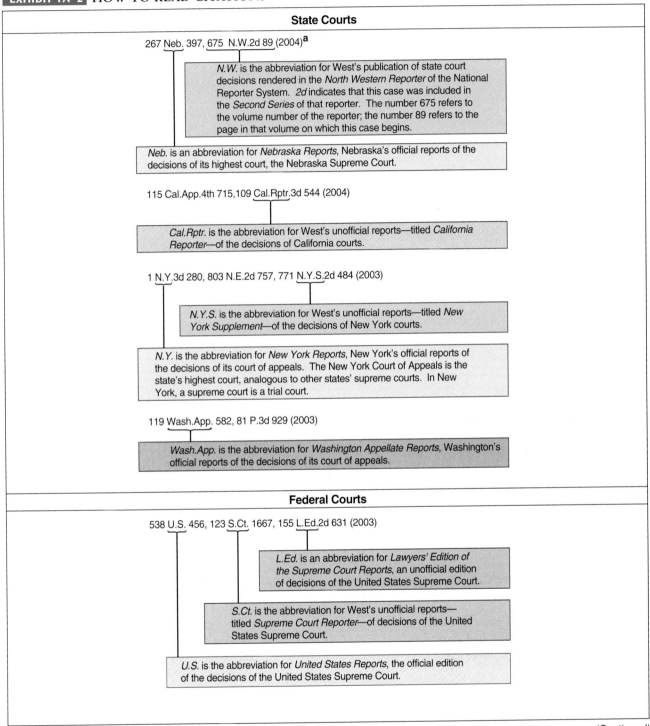

a. The case names have been deleted from these citations to emphasize the publications. It should be kept in mind, however, that the name of a case is as important as the specific page numbers in the volumes in which it is found. If a citation is incorrect, the correct citation may be found in a publication's index of case names. In addition to providing a check on errors in citations, the date of a case is important because the value of a recent case as an authority is likely to be greater than that of older cases.

EXHIBIT 1A–2 HOW TO READ CITATIONS—CONTINUED

Federal Courts (Continued)

354 F.3d 508 (5th Cir. 2004)

> *5th Cir.* is an abbreviation denoting that this case was decided in the United States Court of Appeals for the Fifth Circuit.

298 F.Supp. 2d 276 (D. Conn. 2004)

> *D. Conn.* is an abbreviation indicating that the United States District Court for the District of Connecticut decided this case.

English Courts

9 Exch. 341, 156 Eng.Rep. 145 (1854)

> *Eng.Rep.* is an abbreviation for *English Reports, Full Reprint,* a series of reports containing selected decisions made in English courts between 1378 and 1865.

> *Exch.* is an abbreviation for *English Exchequer Reports,* which included the original reports of cases decided in England's Court of Exchequer.

Statutory and Other Citations

18 U.S.C. Section 1961(1)(A)

> *U.S.C.* denotes *United States Code,* the codification of *United States Statutes at Large.* The number 18 refers to the statute's U.S.C. title number and 1961 to its section number within that title. The number 1 refers to a subsection within the section and the letter A to a subdivision within the subsection.

UCC 2–206(1)(b)

> *UCC* is an abbreviation for *Uniform Commercial Code.* The first number 2 is a reference to an article of the UCC and 206 to a section within that article. The number 1 refers to a subsection within the section and the letter b to a subdivision within the subsection.

Restatement (Second) of Torts, Section 568

> *Restatement (Second) of Torts* refers to the second edition of the American Law Institute's *Restatement of the Law of Torts.* The number 568 refers to a specific section.

17 C.F.R. Section 230.505

> *C.F.R.* is an abbreviation for *Code of Federal Regulations,* a compilation of federal administrative regulations. The number 17 designates the regulation's title number, and 230.505 designates a specific section within that title.

EXHIBIT 1A–2 HOW TO READ CITATIONS—CONTINUED

Westlaw® Citations

2005 WL 405961

WL is an abbreviation for Westlaw®. The number 2005 is the year of the document that can be found with this citation in the Westlaw® database. The number 405961 is a number assigned to a specific document. A higher number indicates that a document was added to the Westlaw® database later in the year.

Uniform Resource Locators[b]

www.westlaw.com

The suffix *com* is the top level domain (TLD) for this Web site. The TLD *com* is an abbreviation for "commercial," which usually means that a for-profit entity hosts (maintains) this Web site.

westlaw is the host name—the part of the domain name selected by the organization that registered the name. In this case, West Group registered the name. This Internet site is the Westlaw database on the Web.

www is an abbreviation for "World Wide Web." The Web is a system of Internet servers[c] that support documents formatted in *HTML* (hypertext markup language). HTML supports links to text, graphics, and audio and video files.

www.uscourts.gov

This is "The Federal Judiciary Home Page." The host is the Administrative Office of the U.S. Courts. The TLD *gov* is an abbreviation for "government." This Web site includes information and links from, and about, the federal courts.

www.law.cornell.edu/index.html

This part of a URL points to a Web page or file at a specific location within the host's domain. This page, at this Web site, is a menu with links to documents within the domain and to other Internet resources.

This is the host name for a Web site that contains the Internet publications of the Legal Information Institute (LII), which is a part of Cornell Law School. The LII site includes a variety of legal materials and links to other legal resources on the Internet. The TLD *edu* is an abbreviation for "educational institution" (a school or a university).

www.ipl.org.ref/RR

RR is an abbreviation for this Web site's "Ready Reference Collection," which contains links to a variety of Internet resources.

ref is an abbreviation for "Internet Public Library Reference Center," which is a map of the topics into which the links at this Web site have been categorized.

ipl is an abbreviation for Internet Public Library, which is an online service that provides reference resources and links to other information services on the Web. The IPL is supported chiefly by the School of Information at the University of Michigan. The TLD *org* is an abbreviation for "organization" (usually nonprofit).

b. The basic form for a URL is "service://hostname/path." The Internet service for all of the URLs in this text is *http* (hypertext transfer protocol). Most Web browsers will add this prefix automatically when a user enters a host name or a hostname/path.

c. A *server* is hardware that manages the resources on a network. For example, a network server is a computer that manages the traffic on the network, and a print server is a computer that manages several printers.

CASE TITLES AND TERMINOLOGY

The title of a case, such as *Adams v. Jones,* indicates the names of the parties to the lawsuit. The *v.* in the case title stands for *versus,* which means "against." In the trial court, Adams was the plaintiff—the person who filed the suit. Jones was the defendant. If the case is appealed, however, the appellate court will sometimes place the name of the party appealing the decision first, so the case may be called *Jones v. Adams.* Because some reviewing courts retain the trial court order of names, it is often impossible to distinguish the plaintiff from the defendant in the title of a reported appellate court decision. You must carefully read the facts of each case to identify the parties.

The following terms and phrases are frequently encountered in court opinions and legal publications. Because it is important to understand what these terms and phrases mean, we define and discuss them here.

Plaintiffs and Defendants   As mentioned in Chapter 1, the plaintiff in a lawsuit is the party that initiates the action. The defendant is the party against which a lawsuit is brought. Lawsuits frequently involve more than one plaintiff and/or defendant.

Appellants and Appellees   The *appellant* is the party that appeals a case to another court or jurisdiction from the court or jurisdiction in which the case was originally brought. Sometimes, an appellant is referred to as the *petitioner.* The *appellee* is the party against which the appeal is taken. Sometimes, the appellee is referred to as the *respondent.*

Judges and Justices   The terms *judge* and *justice* are usually synonymous and represent two designations given to judges in various courts. All members of the United States Supreme Court, for example, are referred to as justices. And justice is the formal title usually given to judges of appellate courts, although this is not always the case. In New York, a justice is a judge of the trial court (which is called the Supreme Court), and a member of the Court of Appeals (the state's highest court) is called a judge. The term *justice* is commonly abbreviated to J., and *justices* to JJ. A Supreme Court case might refer to Justice O'Connor as O'Connor, J., or to Chief Justice Rehnquist as Rehnquist, C.J.

Decisions and Opinions   Most decisions reached by reviewing, or appellate, courts are explained in written *opinions.* The opinion contains the court's reasons for its decision, the rules of law that apply, and the judgment. When all judges or justices unanimously agree on an opinion, the opinion is written for the entire court and can be deemed a *unanimous opinion.* When there is not unanimous agreement, a *majority opinion* is written, outlining the views of the majority of the judges or justices deciding the case.

Often, a judge or justice who feels strongly about making or emphasizing a point that was not made or emphasized in the unanimous or majority opinion will write a *concurring opinion.* That means the judge or justice agrees (concurs) with the judgment given in the unanimous or majority opinion but for different reasons. When there is not a unanimous opinion, a *dissenting opinion* is usually written by a judge or justice who does not agree with the majority. The dissenting opinion is important because it may form the basis of the arguments used years later in overruling the precedential majority opinion. Occasionally, a court issues a *per curiam*

(Latin for "of the court") opinion, which does not indicate which judge or justice authored the opinion.

A Sample Court Case

Knowing how to read and analyze a court opinion is an essential step in undertaking accurate legal research. A further step involves "briefing" the case. Legal researchers routinely brief cases by summarizing and reducing the texts of the opinions to their essential elements. The cases contained within the chapters of this text have already been analyzed and briefed by the authors, and the essential aspects of each case are presented in a convenient format consisting of four basic sections: *Facts, Issue, Decision,* and *Reason,* as shown in Exhibit 1A–3 on the following page, which has also been annotated to illustrate the kind of information that is contained in each section.

Throughout this text, in addition to this basic format, we sometimes include a special introductory section entitled *Historical and Social [Economic, Technological, Political, or other] Setting.* In some instances, a *Company Profile* is included in place of the introductory setting. These profiles provide a background on one of the parties to the lawsuit. Each case is followed by either a brief *For Critical Analysis* section, which, as in Exhibit 1A–3, presents a question regarding some issue raised by the case, or a *Why Is This Case Important?* section, which explains the significance of the case.

The Supreme Court building in Washington, D.C. In what reporters are Supreme Court opinions published? (PhotoDisc)

EXHIBIT 1A-3   A SAMPLE COURT CASE

1   UMG RECORDINGS, INC. v. SINNOTT

2   United States District Court,
Eastern District of California, 2004.

3   300 F.Supp.2d 993.

4   **FACTS**   Richard Sinnott owns and operates the Marysville Flea Market (MFM) in Marysville, California. The MFM is open every Sunday and has the capacity to accommodate about two hundred vendor booths. Each vendor, or seller, pays Sinnott a fee to rent a booth to sell merchandise. Sinnott provides security personnel, utilities, restrooms, and other amenities. On September 3, 2000, investigators with the Recording Industry Association of America (RIAA) found MFM vendors offering counterfeit CDs and cassettes for sale and asked Sinnott to help stop the illegal activity. The investigators told Sinnott that he could be liable for the sales and offered to train MFM employees to detect counterfeit recordings. Sinnott refused and ordered the investigators out of his office. Over the next two years, the investigators visited six more times and found vendors offering as many as 20,000 counterfeit items for sale. The RIAA wrote Sinnott four letters, repeatedly advising him of the illegal activity, his potential liability, and their offer to train MFM employees. When Sinnott failed to cooperate, UMG Recordings, Inc., and other owners of the rights to the pirated music filed a suit in a federal district court against Sinnott, seeking to hold him responsible. The plaintiffs filed a motion for summary judgment.

5   **ISSUE**   Can a flea market owner be held liable for a vendor's infringement of another's copyright?

6   **DECISION**   Yes. In the first federal court decision on the issue, the court held a flea market owner contributorily liable for the copyright infringement by the owner's vendors. The court granted a summary judgment in the plaintiffs' favor.

7   **REASON**   The court explained that the Copyright Act does not impose secondary liability for copyright infringement, but "courts have long recognized that in certain circumstances, vicarious or contributory liability will be imposed. * * * To hold Sinnott liable for contributory infringement, Plaintiffs must show that Sinnott knew or had reason to know of direct infringement" and that he materially contributed to that infringement. "RIAA investigators personally told him of the infringement * * *. Sinnott claims this is insufficient to establish actual knowledge because he did not know who or what RIAA was, and claims to have felt threatened by the investigators. What he does not claim, however, is that he did not receive and understand the message the investigators delivered. * * * The fact that he was not personally acquainted with the messenger does not mean that he can ignore the message and claim ignorance of its contents." Finally, "[o]perating a flea market or swap meet involves providing vendors with support services such as the provision of space, utilities, parking, advertising, plumbing, and customers. This is all that is required to satisfy the requirement of material contribution."

8   **FOR CRITICAL ANALYSIS—Social Consideration**   *What should flea market owners, and others similarly situated, do to prevent sales of pirated music on their property?*

REVIEW OF SAMPLE COURT CASE

1 The name of the case is *UMG Recordings, Inc. v. Sinnott*. One of the owners of the copyrighted music at the center of this case is the identified plaintiff; the owner of the flea market is the defendant.

2 The court deciding this case is the U.S. District Court for the Eastern District of California.

3 The case citation includes a citation to the official *Federal Supplement, Second Series*. The case can be found in Volume 300 of this reporter, on page 993.

4 The *Facts* section identifies the plaintiff and the defendant, describes the events leading up to this suit, and explains what the plaintiff sought to obtain by bringing this action. If this were a case before an appellate court, the rulings of the lower court and the appellant's contention on appeal would also be included here.

5 The *Issue* section presents the central issue (or issues) to be decided by the court. This case involves copyright infringement. Under the Copyright Act, persons who author original works in music or literature, for example, can bring a copyright infringement action against anyone who makes unauthorized copies (see Chapter 5). In this case, the issue is whether to extend that liability to other persons who indirectly but knowingly contribute to that infringement. Most cases concern more than one issue, but the authors of this textbook have edited each case to focus on just one issue.

6 The *Decision* section, as the name indicates, contains the court's decision on the issue or issues before the court. The decision reflects the opinion of the judge, or the majority of the judges or justices, hearing the case. In this particular case, the court granted the plaintiffs' motion for summary judgment (a summary judgment for one party can be entered by the judge before the case proceeds to trial—see Chapter 3). In other words, the court decided that the flea market owner was liable because he knew about the infringing activities of the vendors and did nothing to stop them, thereby contributing to the infringement. Decisions by appellate courts are frequently phrased in reference to the lower court's decision; that is, the appellate court may "affirm" the lower court's ruling or "reverse" it. In either situation, the appellate court may "remand," or send back, the case for further proceedings.

7 The *Reason* section indicates what relevant laws and judicial principles were applied in forming the particular conclusion arrived at in the case at bar ("before the court"). In this case, the relevant statute was the Copyright Act, which governs the rights of authors and others to certain literary or artistic productions. The court determined that a flea market owner who had reason to know about a vendor's infringement of another's copyright may be held liable under the Copyright Act when the vendor offers for sale counterfeit CDs or cassettes.

8 The *For Critical Analysis—Social Consideration* section raises a question to be considered in relation to the case just presented. Here the question involves a "social" consideration. In other cases presented in this text, the "consideration" may involve a cultural, economic, environmental, ethical, international, political, social, or technological consideration.

CHAPTER 2

Ethics and Professional Responsibility

"New occasions teach new duties."

James Russell Lowell, 1819–1891
(American editor, poet, and diplomat)

■■ LEARNING OBJECTIVES

After reading this chapter, you should be able to answer the following questions:

1 What is ethics? What is business ethics? Why is business ethics important?

2 How can business leaders encourage their companies to act ethically?

3 How do duty-based ethical standards differ from outcome-based ethical standards?

4 What duties do professionals owe to those who rely on their services?

5 What types of ethical issues might arise in the context of international business transactions?

During the early part of the 2000s, the American public was shocked as one business ethics scandal after another became headline news. Each scandal involved serious consequences. Certainly, those responsible for grossly inflating the reported profits at WorldCom, Inc., ended up not only destroying shareholder value in a great company but also facing possible prison terms. Those officers and directors at Enron Corporation who utilized a system of complicated off-the-books transactions to inflate current earnings saw their company go bankrupt— one of the largest bankruptcies in U.S. history. They harmed not only their employees and shareholders but also the communities in which they worked—and themselves (some of them have since received prison sentences, and others have been indicted). The officers and directors of Tyco International who used corporate funds to pay for lavish personal lifestyles also ended up in court. The shareholders of that company suffered dearly, too.

In response to the public's outrage over these scandals, Congress passed the Sarbanes-Oxley Act of 2002. This act imposed requirements on corporations that are designed to deter similar unethical and illegal business behavior in the future. As the chapter-opening quotation states, "New occasions teach new duties." Indeed, the ethics scandals of the early 2000s taught businesses throughout the country that corporate governance is not to be taken lightly.

Business ethics, the focus of this chapter, is not just theory. It is practical, useful, and essential. Although a good understanding of business law and the legal environment is critical, it is not enough. Understanding how one should act in her or his business dealings is equally—if not more—important in today's business arena.

Business Ethics

Before we look at business ethics, we need to discuss what is meant by ethics generally. **Ethics** can be defined as the study of what constitutes right or wrong behavior. It is the branch of philosophy that focuses on morality and the way in which moral principles are derived or the way in which a given set of moral principles applies to one's conduct in daily life. Ethics has to do with questions relating to the fairness, justness, rightness, or wrongness of an action. What is fair? What is just? What is the right thing to do in this situation? These are essentially ethical questions.

ETHICS
Moral principles and values applied to social behavior.

WHAT IS BUSINESS ETHICS?

Business ethics focuses on what constitutes right or wrong behavior in the business world and on how moral and ethical principles are applied by businesspersons to situations that arise in their daily activities in the workplace. Note that business ethics is not a separate *kind* of ethics. The ethical standards that guide our behavior as, say, mothers, fathers, or students apply equally well to our activities as businesspersons. Business decision makers, though, must often address more complex ethical issues and conflicts in the workplace than they face in their personal lives.

BUSINESS ETHICS
Ethics in a business context; a consensus of what constitutes right or wrong behavior in the world of business and the application of moral principles to situations that arise in a business setting.

WHY IS BUSINESS ETHICS IMPORTANT?

Why is business ethics important? The answer to this question is clear from this chapter's introduction. A keen and in-depth understanding of business ethics is important to the long-run viability of a corporation. A thorough knowledge of business ethics is also important to the well-being of the individual officers and directors of the corporation, as well as to the welfare of the firm's employees and various "stakeholders" in the entity's well-being. Certainly, corporate decisions and activities can significantly affect not only those who own, operate, or work for the company but also such groups as suppliers, the community, and society as a whole.

Note that questions concerning ethical and responsible behavior are not confined to the corporate context. Business ethics applies to *all* businesses, regardless of their organizational forms. In a business partnership, for example, partners owe a *fiduciary duty* (a duty of trust and loyalty) to each other and to their firm. This duty can sometimes conflict with what a partner sees as his or her own best interest. Partners who act solely in their own interests may violate their duties to the other partners and the firm, however. By violating this duty, they may end up paying steep penalties—as the following case illustrates.

CASE 2.1 ■ Time Warner Entertainment Co. v. Six Flags Over Georgia, L.L.C.

Georgia Court of Appeals, 2002.
254 Ga.App. 598,
563 S.E.2d 178.
http://www.ganet.org/appeals/opinions/index.cgi[a]

FACTS The Six Flags Over Georgia theme park in Atlanta, Georgia, was developed in 1967 as a limited partnership known as Six Flags Over Georgia, L.L.C. (Flags). The sole limited partner was Six Flags Fund, Limited (Fund). The general partner was Six Flags Over Georgia, Inc. (SFOG). In 1991, Time Warner Entertainment Company (TWE) became the majority shareholder of SFOG. The next year, TWE secretly bought 13.7 acres of land next to the park, limiting the park's expansion opportunities. Over the next couple of years, using confidential business information from the park, TWE began plans to develop a competing park. Meanwhile, TWE installed no major new attractions at the park, deferred basic maintenance, withheld financial information from Fund (the limited partner), and began signing future employment contracts with SFOG officers. TWE also charged Flags for unrelated expenses, including over $4 million for lunches in New York City and luxury automobiles for TWE officers. Flags and Fund filed a suit in a Georgia state court against TWE and SFOG, alleging, among other things, breach of fiduciary duty. A jury awarded the plaintiffs $197,296,000 in compensatory damages and $257,000,000 in punitive damages. TWE appealed to a state intermediate appellate court, alleging in part that the amount of the punitive damages was excessive.

a. This Web site is sponsored by the state of Georgia. At the search screen, click on "Search Court of Appeals Opinions." On the appellate court's screen, set the search year to "all." You can go to a case most directly if you use as key words the full name of a party—for example, "Time Warner Entertainment Co."

ISSUE Was the amount of punitive damages excessive?

DECISION No. The state intermediate appellate court affirmed the judgment of the lower court.

REASON The appellate court held that the award of punitive damages was not excessive, considering the amount of compensatory damages ("the ratio of compensatory to punitive damages is 1 to 1.3"), the defendants' financial status "with collective assets measured in billions of dollars," and their "reprehensible" (blameworthy) conduct toward the plaintiffs. The appellate court stated, "In examining the degree of reprehensibility of a defendant's conduct, [there are] a number of aggravating factors [to consider], including whether the harm was more than purely economic in nature, and whether the defendant's behavior evinced [showed] indifference to or reckless disregard for the health and safety of others. Here, although the harm to Flags and Fund was primarily economic, it was caused by conduct we find especially reprehensible. Appellants' intentional breach of its fiduciary duty revealed a callous indifference to the financial well-being of its limited partners and their individual investors." The court concluded that "[a]ppellants' conduct was, in short, the kind of behavior we find deserving of reproof, rebuke, or censure; blameworthy—the very definition of reprehensible. *   *   * Trickery and deceit are reprehensible wrongs, especially when done intentionally through affirmative acts of misconduct."

FOR CRITICAL ANALYSIS—Ethical Consideration *If TWE had proceeded with its plans to build a competing park but had not otherwise acted "reprehensibly" toward Flags and Fund, how might the decision in this case have been different?*

■ Setting the Right Ethical Tone

Many unethical business decisions are made simply because they *can* be made. In other words, the decision makers not only have the opportunity to make such decisions but also are not too concerned about being seriously sanctioned for their unethical actions. Perhaps one of the most difficult challenges for business leaders today is to create the right "ethical tone" in their workplaces so as to deter unethical conduct.

THE IMPORTANCE OF ETHICAL LEADERSHIP

Talking about ethical business decision making means nothing if management does not set standards. Moreover, managers must apply those standards to themselves and to the employees in the company. The *Application* feature at the end of this chapter provides additional suggestions on how management can create an ethical workplace.

Attitude of Top Management   One of the most important factors in creating and maintaining an ethical workplace is the attitude of top management. Managers who are not totally committed to maintaining an ethical workplace will rarely succeed in creating one. Surveys of business executives indicate that management's behavior, more than anything else, sets the ethical tone of a firm. In other words, employees take their cue from management. If a firm's managers adhere to obvious ethical norms in their business dealings, employees will likely follow their example. In contrast, if managers act unethically, employees will see no reason not to do so themselves. ■ **EXAMPLE 2.1** An employee observes a manager cheating on her expense account. That employee quickly understands that such behavior is acceptable. ■

Looking the Other Way   A manager who looks the other way when he knows about an employee's unethical behavior also sets an example—one indicating that ethical transgressions will be accepted. Managers must show that they will not tolerate unethical business behavior. Although this may seem harsh, managers have found that discharging even one employee for ethical reasons has a tremendous impact as a deterrent to unethical behavior in the workplace. The following case illustrates what can happen when managers look the other way.

CASE 2.2 ■ In re the *Exxon Valdez*

United States District Court,
District of Alaska, 2004.
296 F.Supp.2d 1071.

FACTS Exxon Shipping Company owned the *Exxon Valdez,* an oil supertanker as long as three football fields with the capacity to hold 53 million gallons of crude oil. The captain of the *Valdez* was Joseph Hazelwood, an alcoholic, who had sought treatment in 1985 but had relapsed before the next spring. Exxon knew that Hazelwood had relapsed and that he drank while onboard ship, but nevertheless allowed him to command the *Valdez.* On March 24, 1989, the *Valdez* ran aground on Bligh Reef in Prince William Sound, Alaska. About 11 million gallons of crude oil leaked from the ship and spread around the sound. Commercial fisheries closed for the rest of the year. Subsistence fishing and shore-based businesses dependent on the fishing industry were disrupted. Exxon spent $2.1 billion to clean up the spilled oil and paid $303 million to those whose livelihoods were disrupted. Thousands of claims were consolidated into a single case tried in a federal district court. The jury awarded, in part, $5 billion in punitive damages against

Exxon. Exxon appealed to the U.S. Court of Appeals for the Ninth Circuit, which remanded the case for reconsideration of this award, according to the reprehensibility of the defendant's conduct and other factors. The court also instructed the lower court to reduce the amount if the award was upheld.

ISSUE Did the $5 billion punitive damages award against Exxon constitute grossly excessive or arbitrary punishment?

DECISION No. The court determined that Exxon's conduct was "intentionally malicious" and "highly reprehensible." Concluding that "[p]unitive damages should reflect the enormity of the defendant's offense," the court upheld the award but reduced the amount to $4.5 billion "as the means of resolving the conflict between its conclusion and the directions of the court of appeals."

REASON The court pointed out that "Exxon's conduct did not simply cause economic harm to the plaintiffs. Exxon's decision to leave Captain Hazelwood in command

(Continued)

CASE 2.2—Continued

of the *Exxon Valdez* demonstrated reckless disregard for a broad range of legitimate Alaska concerns: the livelihood, health, and safety of the residents of Prince William Sound, the crew of the *Exxon Valdez,* and others. Exxon's conduct targeted some financially vulnerable individuals, namely subsistence fishermen [those who make their living by fishing]. Plaintiffs' harm was not the result of an isolated incident but was the result of Exxon's repeated decisions, over a period of approximately three years, to allow Captain Hazelwood to remain in command despite Exxon's knowledge that he was drinking and driving again." The court compared Exxon's conduct to other cases in which punitive damages were awarded and concluded that "Exxon's conduct was many degrees of magnitude more egregious [conspicuously wrongful]. For approximately three years, Exxon management, with knowledge that Captain Hazelwood had fallen off the wagon, willfully permitted him to operate a fully loaded, crude oil tanker in and out of Prince William Sound—a body of water which Exxon knew to be highly valuable for its fisheries resources. Exxon's argument that its conduct in permitting a relapsed alcoholic to operate an oil tanker should be characterized as less reprehensible *   *   * suggests that Exxon, even today, has not come to grips with the opprobrium [disgrace, contempt] which society rightly attaches to drunk driving."

WHY IS THIS CASE IMPORTANT?   *This case is an excellent illustration of the consequences that a business may face when it ignores a serious risk that has been created by its action (or inaction). By allowing Captain Hazelwood, a relapsed alcoholic, to remain in charge of the* Exxon Valdez, *Exxon created serious risks to the environment and the residents of Prince William Sound. These risks led to severe harms. The consequences for Exxon—$4.5 billion in punitive damages—were also severe.*

Setting Realistic Goals Helps   Managers can reduce the probability that employees will act unethically by setting realistic production or sales goals. ■ EXAMPLE 2.2 Suppose that a sales quota can be met only through high-pressure and unethical sales tactics. Employees trying to act "in the best interests of the firm" may think that management is implicitly asking them to behave unethically. ■

Periodic Evaluation   Some companies require their managers to meet individually with employees and to grade them on their ethical (or unethical) behavior. ■ EXAMPLE 2.3 One company asks its employees to fill out ethical checklists each month and return them to their supervisors. This practice serves two purposes: First, it demonstrates to employees that ethics matters. Second, employees have an opportunity to reflect on how well they have measured up in terms of ethical performance. ■

CREATING ETHICAL CODES OF CONDUCT

One of the most effective ways of setting a tone of ethical behavior within an organization is to create an ethical code of conduct. A well-written code of ethics explicitly states a company's ethical priorities.

Costco—An Example   This chapter includes a foldout exhibit showing a code of ethics created by Costco Wholesale Corporation, a large warehouse-club retailer with over 45 million "members." This code of conduct indicates Costco's commitment to legal compliance, as well as to the welfare of its members (those who purchase its goods), its employees, and its suppliers. The code also details some specific ways in which the interests and welfare of these different groups will be protected. If you look closely at this exhibit, you will also see that Costco acknowledges that by protecting these groups' interests, it will realize its "ultimate goal"—rewarding its shareholders with maximum shareholder value.

Another Necessity—Clear Communication to Employees   For an ethical code to be effective, its provisions must be clearly communicated to employees. Most large companies have implemented ethics training programs, in which managers discuss with employees on a face-to-face basis the firm's policies and the importance of ethical conduct. Some firms hold periodic ethics seminars during which employees can openly discuss any ethical problems that they may be experiencing and learn how the firm's ethical policies apply to those specific problems.

Johnson & Johnson—An Example of Web-Based Ethics Training   Creating a code of conduct and implementing it are two different activities. In many companies, codes of conduct are simply documents that have very little relevance to day-to-day operations. When Johnson & Johnson wanted to "do better" than other companies with respect to ethical business decision making, it created a Center for Legal and Credo Awareness. (Its code of ethical conduct is called its credo.)

The center created a Web-based set of instructions designed to enhance the corporation's efforts to train employees in the importance of its code of conduct. Given that Johnson & Johnson has over 110,000 employees in fifty-seven countries around the world, reinforcing its code of conduct and its values has not been easy, but Web-based training has helped. The company established a Web-based legal and compliance center, which uses a set of interactive modules to train employees in areas of law and ethics.

For an example of a company that provides online ethics and compliance training to companies nationwide, go to the Web site of Interactive Corporation at

http://www. integrity-interactive.com/ welcome.htm.

CORPORATE COMPLIANCE PROGRAMS

In large corporations, ethical codes of conduct are usually just one part of a comprehensive corporate compliance program. Other components of such a program, some of which were already mentioned, include a corporation's ethics committee, ethical training programs, and internal audits to monitor compliance with applicable laws and the company's standards of ethical conduct.

The Sarbanes-Oxley Act and Web-Based Reporting Systems   The Sarbanes-Oxley Act of 2002[1] requires companies to set up confidential systems so that employees and others may "raise red flags" about suspected illegal or unethical auditing and accounting practices. The act required publicly traded companies to have such systems in place by April 2003.

Some companies have implemented online reporting systems. In one Web-based reporting system, employees can click on an icon on their computers that anonymously links them with Ethicspoint, an organization based in Vancouver, Washington. Through Ethicspoint, employees may report suspicious accounting practices, sexual harassment, and other possibly unethical behavior. Ethicspoint, in turn, alerts management personnel or the audit committee at the designated company to the possible problem. Those who have used the system say that it is less inhibiting than calling a company's 800 number.

Compliance Programs Must Be Integrated   To be effective, a compliance program must be integrated throughout the firm. For large corporations, such integration is essential. Ethical policies and programs need to be coordinated and monitored by a committee that is separate from various corporate departments. Otherwise, unethical behavior in one department can easily escape the attention of those in control of

---

1. 15 U.S.C. Sections 7201 *et seq.*

the corporation or the corporate officials responsible for implementing and monitoring the company's compliance program.

ETHICAL ISSUE 2.1

Should companies hire chief governance officers? According to a survey released by the Ethics Resource Center and the Society for Human Resource Management in April 2003, ethical conduct is not rewarded in today's business world. Indeed, 24 percent of the human resources (HR) managers surveyed felt pressure to compromise ethical standards either all of the time, fairly often, or periodically. In 1997, only 13 percent of the same class of respondents felt the same way. This finding is significant because HR personnel are often caught in the middle between employees who come to them with ethical complaints and company officers who may or may not agree with the HR manager's recommendations as to how the company should respond to specific complaints.

What can companies do to ensure ethical compliance? Should they hire specially trained legal executives, known as chief governance officers (CGOs), to oversee corporate compliance? According to some business ethicists, having a CGO can help a company prevent future governance problems that could be costly. In 1992, pharmaceutical manufacturer Pfizer, Inc., became the first company to hire a CGO. Since then, about sixty other companies have done so. In the wake of the business scandals of the early 2000s and the requirements imposed under the subsequent Sarbanes-Oxley Act of 2002, the number of companies that have CGOs is expected to grow rapidly.[2] ■

CONFLICTS AND TRADE-OFFS

Management constantly faces ethical trade-offs, some of which may lead to legal problems. As mentioned earlier, firms have implied ethical (and legal) duties to a number of groups, including shareholders and employees.

When a company decides to reduce costs by downsizing and restructuring, the decision may benefit shareholders, but it will harm those employees who are laid off or fired. When downsizing occurs, which employees should be laid off first? Cost-cutting considerations might dictate firing the most senior employees, who generally have higher salaries, and retaining less senior employees, whose salaries are much lower. A company does not necessarily act illegally when it does so. Yet the decision to be made by management clearly involves an important ethical question: Which group's interests—those of the shareholders or those of employees who have been loyal to the firm for a long period of time—should take priority in this situation?

You can find articles on issues relating to corporate governance and accountability at the Corporate Governance Web site. Go to

http://www.corpgov.net.

■ **EXAMPLE 2.4** In one case, an employer facing a dwindling market and decreasing sales decided to reduce its costs by eliminating some of its obligations to its employees. It did this by establishing a subsidiary corporation and then transferring some of its employees, and the administration of their retirement benefits, to that entity. The company expected the subsidiary to fail, and when it did, some employees and retirees who were left with no retirement benefits sued the company. The plaintiffs claimed that the company had breached a fiduciary duty under a federal law governing employer-provided pensions. Ultimately, the United States Supreme Court agreed with the plaintiffs, stating, among other things, that "[l]ying is inconsistent with the duty of loyalty owed by all fiduciaries."[3] ■

---

2. Tamara Loomis, "Companies Are Hiring Chief Governance Officers," *The National Law Journal,* May 5, 2003, p. A15.
3. *Varity Corp. v. Howe,* 516 U.S. 489, 116 S.Ct. 1065, 134 L.Ed.2d 130 (1996).

▪▪ Business Ethics and the Law

Today, legal compliance is regarded as a **moral minimum**—the minimum acceptable standard for ethical business behavior. Had Enron Corporation strictly complied with existing laws and generally accepted accounting practices, very likely the "Enron scandal," which came to light in the early 2000s, would never have happened. Simply obeying the law does not fulfill all business ethics obligations, however. In the interests of preserving personal freedom, as well as for practical reasons, the law does not—and cannot—codify all ethical requirements. No law says, for example, that it is illegal to lie to one's family, but it may be unethical to do so.

It might seem that determining the legality of a given action should be simple. Either something is legal or it is not. In fact, one of the major challenges businesspersons face is that the legality of a particular action is not always clear. In part, this is because business is regulated by so many laws that it is possible to violate one of them without realizing it. The law also contains numerous "gray areas," making it difficult to predict how a court will apply a given law to a particular action. This is especially true when technological developments have raised new types of questions. For example, if a business's trademark is used in a domain name followed by "fraud" or "sucks," is this an infringement of the owner's trademark? For a discussion of this question, see this chapter's *Adapting the Law to the Online Environment* feature on the next page.

LAWS REGULATING BUSINESS

Today's business firms are subject to extensive government regulation. As mentioned in Chapter 1, virtually every action a firm undertakes—from the initial act of going into business, to hiring and firing personnel, to selling products in the marketplace—is subject to statutory law and to numerous rules and regulations issued by administrative agencies. Furthermore, these rules and regulations are changed or supplemented frequently.

Determining whether a planned action is legal thus requires that decision makers keep abreast of the law. Normally, large business firms have attorneys on their staffs to assist them in making key decisions. Small firms must also seek legal advice before making important business decisions because the consequences of just one violation of a regulatory rule may be costly.

Ignorance of the law will not excuse a business owner or manager from liability for violating a statute or regulation. ▪ EXAMPLE 2.5 In one case, the court imposed criminal fines, as well as imprisonment, on a company's supervisory employee for violating a federal environmental act. This punishment was imposed even though the employee was completely unaware of what was required under the provisions of that act.[4] ▪

"GRAY AREAS" IN THE LAW

In many situations, business firms can predict with a fair amount of certainty whether a given action would be legal. For instance, firing an employee solely because of that person's race or gender would clearly violate federal laws prohibiting employment discrimination. In some situations, though, the legality of a particular action may be less clear.

▪ EXAMPLE 2.6 Suppose that a firm decides to launch a new advertising campaign. How far can the firm go in making claims for its products or services? Federal and

---

4. *United States v. Hanousek*, 176 F.3d 1116 (9th Cir. 1999)—see Case 6.1 in Chapter 6.

ADAPTING THE LAW TO THE ONLINE ENVIRONMENT

"Sucks" Sites—Can They Be Shut Down?

In today's online environment, a recurring challenge for businesses is how to deal with cybergripers—those who complain in cyberspace about corporate products, services, or activities. For trademark owners, the issue becomes particularly thorny when cybergriping sites add "sucks," "fraud," "scam," "ripoff," or some other disparaging term as a suffix to the domain name of a particular company. These sites, sometimes collectively referred to as "sucks" sites, are established solely for the purpose of criticizing the products or services sold by the companies that own the marks. In some cases, they have been used maliciously to harm the reputation of a competitor. Can businesses do anything to ward off these cyber attacks on their reputations and goodwill?

THE TRADEMARK ISSUE

A number of companies have sued the owners of "sucks" sites for trademark infringement in the hope that a court or an arbitrating panel will order the owner of that site to cease using the domain name. To date, however, companies have had little success pursuing this alternative. In one case, Bear Stearns Companies, Inc., sued a cybergriper, Nye Lavalle, alleging that Lavalle infringed its trademark by creating Web sites including "Bear Stearns" in the domain names. Some of these sites were called "BearStearnsFrauds.com," "BearStearnsCriminals.com," and "BearStearnsComplaints.com."

As will be discussed in Chapter 5, one of the tests for trademark infringement is whether consumers would be confused by the use of a similar or identical trademark. Would consumers mistakenly believe that Lavalle's sites were operated by Bear Stearns? In the court's eyes, no. The court concluded that Lavalle's "Frauds.com" and "Criminals.com" sites were "unmistakenly critical" of the target company and that no Internet user would conclude that Bear Stearns sponsored the sites. As to the "Complaints.com" site, however, the court concluded that consumers might be confused—because Bear Stearns could have a "complaints" page on its Web site. Therefore, the "Complaints.com" site violated trademark law, but the other two sites did not.[a]

FOR CYBERGRIPERS, THE MORE OUTRAGEOUS THE SUFFIX, THE BETTER

For cybergripers, the message seems to be clear: the more outrageous or obnoxious the suffix added to a target company's trademark, the less likely it is that the use will constitute trademark infringement. This point is underscored in decisions reached by other courts as well. In *Taubman Co. v. Webfeats*,[b] for example, a cybergriping case decided by the U.S. Court of Appeals for the Sixth Circuit, the court stressed that Internet users were unlikely be confused by "sucks" sites using the Taubman Company name. Because the allegedly infringing domain names all ended with "sucks.com," the court concluded that they were unlikely to mislead Web site visitors into believing that the trademark owner was the source or sponsor of the complaint. The court also noted in its opinion that, generally, the more vicious an attack site's domain name, the less likely that a cybergriper will be found liable for trademark infringement.

FOR CRITICAL ANALYSIS

How might cybergriping sites help to improve the ethical performance of the businesses they criticize? What can business owners do to prevent the use of their marks in "sucks" sites?

a. *Bear Stearns Companies, Inc. v. Lavalle*, 2002 WL 31757771 (N.D.Tex. 2002).
b. 319 F.3d 770 (6th Cir. 2003).

state laws prohibit firms from engaging in "deceptive advertising." At the federal level, the test for deceptive advertising normally used by the Federal Trade Commission is whether an advertising claim would deceive a "reasonable consumer."[5] At what point, though, would a reasonable consumer be deceived by a particular ad? ■

5. See Chapter 13 for a discussion of the Federal Trade Commission's role in regulating deceptive trade practices, including misleading advertising.

In short, business decision makers need to proceed with caution and evaluate an action and its consequences from an ethical perspective. Generally, if a company can demonstrate that it acted in good faith and responsibly in the circumstances, it has a better chance of successfully defending its action in court or before an administrative law judge.

ETHICAL ISSUE 2.2

How can a business decide whether a warning is "adequate"? One of the "gray areas" in the law has to do with product misuse. As you will read in Chapter 13, product liability laws require manufacturers and sellers to warn consumers of the kind of injuries that might result from the foreseeable misuse of their products. An exception to this rule is made when a risk associated with a product is "open and obvious." Sharp knives, for example, can obviously injure their users. Sometimes, however, a business has no way of predicting how a court might rule in deciding whether a particular risk is open and obvious or whether consumers should be warned of the risk. If consumers should be warned, a further question arises: What constitutes an adequate warning? Even the courts often disagree on such matters.

In one case, for example, a company sold small aerosol cans of butane, a fuel for cigarette lighters. On each can was the warning "DO NOT BREATHE SPRAY." Nonetheless, twenty-year-old Stephen Pavlik died from *intentionally* inhaling the contents of one of the cans. In the lawsuit that followed, brought by Pavlik's father, the trial court and the appellate court came to different conclusions. The trial court reasoned that Pavlik must have been aware of the dangers of inhaling butane and that a more specific warning would not have affected his conduct. The appellate court, though, concluded that the warning gave Pavlik "no notice of the serious nature of the danger posed by inhalation, intentional or otherwise."[6] Cases such as this send a clear message to businesspersons: never assume that a risk that may seem open and obvious to you will necessarily be open and obvious to a court. ■

TECHNOLOGICAL DEVELOPMENTS AND LEGAL UNCERTAINTIES

Uncertainties concerning how particular laws may apply to specific factual situations have been compounded in the cyber age. As noted in earlier chapters, the widespread use of the Internet has given rise to situations never before faced by the courts.

The case presented next is illustrative. The case involved an airline pilot who claimed that defamatory, gender-based messages made by her co-workers in an online forum created a hostile working environment. As will be discussed in Chapter 18, federal law prohibits harassment in the workplace, including "hostile-environment harassment," which occurs when an employee is subjected to sexual conduct or comments that he or she perceives as offensive. Generally, employers are expected to take immediate and appropriate corrective action in response to employees' complaints of sexual harassment or abuse. Otherwise, they may be held liable for the harassing actions of an employee's co-workers or supervisors. At issue in the case was whether the online forum could be considered part of the "workplace" over which the employer had control.

---

6. *Pavlik v. Lane Ltd./Tobacco Exporters International,* 135 F.3d 876 (3d Cir. 1998).

CASE 2.3 Blakey v. Continental Airlines, Inc.

New Jersey Supreme Court, 2000.
751 A.2d 538.
http://lawlibrary.rutgers.edu/search.shtml[a]

HISTORICAL AND TECHNOLOGICAL SETTING *CompuServe, Inc., which is now a wholly owned subsidiary of America Online, Inc., is the Internet service provider for Continental Airlines, Inc. CompuServe provides Continental's pilots and other crew members with online access to their flight schedules. As part of the service, CompuServe makes a "Crew Members Forum" available for the exchange of ideas and information. Through customized software, any individual with a Continental pilot or crew member identification number can access the forum. This includes chief pilots and assistant chief pilots, who are considered management at Continental. Technical assistance is provided by system operators, who are volunteer crew members.*

FACTS Tammy Blakey, a pilot for Continental Airlines since 1984, was the airline's first female captain—and one of only five Continental pilots—to fly an Airbus aircraft. Shortly after qualifying to be a captain on the Airbus A300, Blakey complained about pornographic photos and vulgar gender-based comments directed at her in her plane's cockpit and other work areas by her male co-employees. Blakey pursued claims against Continental with the Equal Employment Opportunity Commission, the agency that administers federal laws prohibiting employment discrimination, and in a federal district court.[b] Meanwhile, Continental pilots published a series of harassing, gender-based, defamatory messages about Blakey on the Internet forum. When the court refused to consider these messages, Blakey filed a complaint against Continental and others in a New Jersey state court. She alleged, in part, gender-based harassment arising from a hostile work environment. Continental filed a motion for summary judgment on this claim, which the court granted. A state intermediate appellate court upheld the summary judgment, and Blakey appealed to the New Jersey Supreme Court.

ISSUE Can an employees' online forum be such an integral part of the workplace that harassment on it may be regarded as an extension of a pattern of harassment in the workplace?

DECISION Yes. The New Jersey Supreme Court reversed the judgment of the lower court and remanded the case for further proceedings. The state supreme court indicated that the trial court was to determine, among other things, which messages were harassing, whether Continental had notice of those messages, and the severity or pervasiveness of the harassing conduct.

REASON The state supreme court explained that "[o]ur common experience tells us how important are the extensions of the workplace where the relations among employees are cemented or sometimes sundered. If an 'old boys' network' continued, in an after-hours setting, the belittling conduct that edges over into harassment, what exactly is the outsider (whether black, Latino, or woman) to do? Keep swallowing the abuse or give up the chance to make the team? We believe that severe or pervasive harassment in a work-related setting that continues a pattern of harassment on the job is sufficiently related to the workplace that an informed employer who takes no effective measures to stop it, sends the harassed employee the message that the harassment is acceptable and that the management supports the harasser." The court compared CompuServe's role to "that of a company that builds an old-fashioned bulletin board. If the maker of an old-fashioned bulletin board provided a better bulletin board by setting aside space on it for employees to post messages, we would have little doubt that messages on the company bulletin board would be part of the workplace setting."

FOR CRITICAL ANALYSIS—Technological Consideration *Does the holding in the* Blakey *case mean that employers have a duty to monitor their employees' e-mail and other online communications? Why or why not?*

---

a. In the "Search the N.J. Courts Decisions" box, type "Blakey" and click on the "Search" link. When the results appear, scroll down the list and click on the *Blakey* case name to access the opinion. This Web site is maintained by Rutgers School of Law in Camden, New Jersey.
b. In 1997, the federal court ruled in favor of Blakey on a claim of gender-based harassment, awarding her a total of $495,000 in forgone pay and $250,000 for emotional distress, pain, and suffering. The court also found that Blakey had failed to mitigate damages (reduce her damages—by finding other work, for example) and subtracted $120,000 from her back pay award.

■ Approaches to Ethical Reasoning

ETHICAL REASONING
A reasoning process in which an individual links his or her moral convictions or ethical standards to the particular situation at hand.

Each individual, when faced with a particular ethical dilemma, engages in **ethical reasoning**—that is, a reasoning process in which the individual examines the situation at hand in light of her or his moral convictions or ethical standards. Businesspersons do likewise when making decisions with ethical implications.

How do business decision makers decide whether a given action is the "right" one for their firms? What ethical standards should they apply? Broadly speaking, ethical reasoning relating to business traditionally has been characterized by two fundamental approaches. One approach defines ethical behavior in terms of duty, which also implies certain rights. The other approach determines what is ethical in terms of the consequences, or outcome, of any given action. We examine each of these approaches here.

DUTY-BASED ETHICS

Duty-based ethical standards are often derived from revealed truths, such as religious precepts. They can also be derived through philosophical reasoning.

Religious Ethical Standards In the Judeo-Christian tradition, which is the dominant religious tradition in the United States, the Ten Commandments of the Old Testament establish fundamental rules for moral action. Other religions have their own sources of revealed truth. Religious rules generally are absolute with respect to the behavior of their adherents. ■ **EXAMPLE 2.7** The commandment "Thou shalt not steal" is an absolute mandate for a person, such as a Jew or a Christian, who believes that the Ten Commandments reflect revealed truth. Even a benevolent motive for stealing (such as Robin Hood's) cannot justify the act because the act itself is inherently immoral and thus wrong. ■

Ethical standards based on religious teachings also involve an element of *compassion*. ■ **EXAMPLE 2.8** Even though it might be profitable for a firm to lay off a less productive employee, if that employee would find it difficult to find employment elsewhere and his or her family would suffer as a result, this potential suffering would be given substantial weight by the decision makers. ■ Compassionate treatment of others is also mandated—to a certain extent, at least—by the Golden Rule of the ancients ("Do unto others as you would have them do unto you"), which has been adopted by most religions.

Kantian Ethics Duty-based ethical standards may also be derived solely from philosophical reasoning. The German philosopher Immanuel Kant (1724–1804), for example, identified some general guiding principles for moral behavior based on what he believed to be the fundamental nature of human beings. Kant held that it is rational to assume that human beings are qualitatively different from other physical objects occupying space. Persons are endowed with moral integrity and the capacity to reason and conduct their affairs rationally. Therefore, their thoughts and actions should be respected. When human beings are treated merely as a means to an end, they are being viewed as the equivalent of objects and are being denied their basic humanity.

A central postulate in Kantian ethics is that individuals should evaluate their actions in light of the consequences that would follow if *everyone* in society acted in the same way. This **categorical imperative** can be applied to any action. ■ **EXAMPLE 2.9** Suppose that you are deciding whether to cheat on an examination. If you have adopted Kant's categorical imperative, you will decide not to cheat because if everyone cheated, the examination would be meaningless. ■

The Principle of Rights   The principle that human beings have certain fundamental rights (to life, freedom, and the pursuit of happiness, for example) is deeply embedded in Western culture. Those who adhere to this **principle of rights,** or "rights theory," believe that a key factor in determining whether a business decision is ethical is how that decision affects the rights of others. These others include the firm's owners, its employees, the consumers of its products or services, its suppliers, the community in which it does business, and society as a whole.

A potential dilemma for those who support rights theory, however, is that they may disagree on which rights are most important. When considering all those affected by a business decision, for example, how much weight should be given to employees relative to shareholders, customers relative to the community, or employees relative to society as a whole?

In general, rights theorists believe that whichever right is stronger in a particular circumstance takes precedence. ■ **EXAMPLE 2.10** Suppose that a firm can either shut down a plant to avoid dumping pollutants into a river that would negatively affect the health of thousands of people or save the jobs of the twelve workers in the plant. In this situation, a rights theorist can easily choose which group to favor. (Not all choices are so clear-cut, however.) ■

OUTCOME-BASED ETHICS: UTILITARIANISM

"Thou shalt act so as to generate the greatest good for the greatest number." This is a paraphrase of the major premise of the utilitarian approach to ethics. **Utilitarianism** is a philosophical theory developed by Jeremy Bentham (1748–1832) and then advanced, with some modifications, by John Stuart Mill (1806–1873)—both British philosophers. In contrast to duty-based ethics, utilitarianism is outcome oriented. It focuses on the consequences of an action, not on the nature of the action itself or on any set of preestablished moral values or religious beliefs.

Under a utilitarian model of ethics, an action is morally correct, or "right," when, among the people it affects, it produces the greatest amount of good for the greatest number. When an action affects the majority adversely, it is morally wrong. Applying the utilitarian theory thus requires (1) a determination of which individuals will be affected by the action in question; (2) a **cost-benefit analysis,** which involves an assessment of the negative and positive effects of alternative actions on these individuals; and (3) a choice among alternative actions that will produce maximum societal utility (the greatest positive net benefits for the greatest number of individuals).

The utilitarian approach to decision making commonly is employed by businesses, as well as by individuals. Weighing the consequences of a decision in terms of its costs and benefits for everyone affected by it is a useful analytical tool in the decision-making process. At the same time, utilitarianism is often criticized because its objective, calculated approach to problems tends to reduce the welfare of human beings to plus and minus signs on a cost-benefit worksheet and to "justify" human costs that many find totally unacceptable.

A lab worker conducts research for the development of a drug. If the drug proves beneficial to most people but adverse to a few, would it, under a utilitarian model of ethics, be marketed? Why or why not? (© Ted Horowitz, Getty Images)

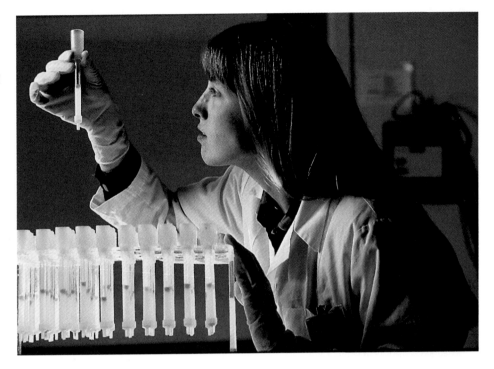

◨ Professional Responsibility

Business ethics goes hand in hand with professional responsibility. As you will learn in Chapter 4, all individuals, including businesspersons, owe a duty of care to others. Professionals—those who have knowledge or skills in a specific area such as accounting or law—are expected to perform their work in a manner consistent with that status. Generally, professionals are required to deliver competent services and are obligated to adhere to standards of performance commonly accepted within their professions. A professional who fails to abide by professional standards may be sued for malpractice. If the action also constitutes a statutory violation, the professional may face liability (or even criminal penalties) under the relevant statute.

Here we examine some of the duties owed by two groups of professionals—accountants and attorneys—whose work can significantly affect business decision making. Certainly, the dizzying collapse of Enron Corporation and the failure of other major companies, including WorldCom, Inc., in the early 2000s called attention to the importance of abiding by professional accounting standards. Arthur Andersen, LLP, one of the world's leading public accounting firms, also closed its doors after being convicted on criminal charges for allegedly thwarting the government's investigation into Enron's accounting practices.

After examining the duties owed by accountants and attorneys, we present a case study of Enron's defiance of established accounting rules. Following that, we look at some of the duties subsequently imposed on accountants by the Sarbanes-Oxley Act of 2002.

ACCOUNTANTS' DUTY OF CARE

Accountants play a major role in a business's financial system. Accountants have the necessary expertise and experience in establishing and maintaining accurate financial records to design, control, and audit record-keeping systems; to prepare reliable statements that reflect an individual's or a business's financial status; and to give tax advice and prepare tax returns.

An *audit* is a systematic inspection, by analyses and tests, of a business's financial records. The purpose of an audit is to provide the auditor with evidence to support an opinion on the fairness of the business's financial statements. A normal audit is not intended to uncover fraud or other misconduct. An accountant may be liable for failing to detect misconduct, however, if a normal audit would have revealed it or if the auditor agreed to examine the records for evidence of fraud or other misconduct that should have been obvious.

Standard of Care   Generally, an accountant must possess the skills that an ordinarily prudent accountant would have and must exercise the degree of care that an ordinarily prudent accountant would exercise. The level of skill expected of accountants and the degree of care that they should exercise in performing their services are reflected in what are known as **generally accepted accounting principles (GAAP)** and **generally accepted auditing standards (GAAS)**. The Financial Accounting Standards Board (FASB, usually pronounced "faz-bee") determines what accounting conventions, rules, and procedures constitute GAAP at a given point in time. GAAS are standards concerning an auditor's professional qualities and the judgment that he or she exercises in auditing financial records. GAAS are established by the American Institute of Certified Public Accountants. GAAP and GAAS are also reflected in the rules established by the Securities and Exchange Commission (see Chapter 21).

GENERALLY ACCEPTED ACCOUNTING PRINCIPLES (GAAP)
The conventions, rules, and procedures necessary to define accepted accounting practices at a particular time. The source of the principles is the Financial Accounting Standards Board (FASB).

GENERALLY ACCEPTED AUDITING STANDARDS (GAAS)
Standards concerning an auditor's professional qualities and the judgment exercised by him or her in the performance of an examination and report. The source of the standards is the American Institute of Certified Public Accountants.

Violations of GAAP and GAAS   A violation of GAAP and GAAS will be considered *prima facie* (on its face) evidence of negligence on the part of the accountant. Compliance with GAAP and GAAS, however, does not necessarily relieve an accountant from potential legal liability. An accountant may be held to a higher standard of conduct established by state or federal statute and by judicial decisions. If an accountant is found to have been negligent in the performance of accounting services for a client, the client may collect damages for any losses that arose from the accountant's negligence. An accountant may also be liable to third parties, such as investors or corporate managers, who rely on the opinions of accountants when making decisions.

ATTORNEYS' DUTY OF CARE

The conduct of attorneys is governed by rules established by each state and by the American Bar Association's Model Rules of Professional Conduct. All attorneys owe a duty to provide competent and diligent representation. Attorneys are required to be familiar with well-settled principles of law applicable to a case and to discover law that can be found through a reasonable amount of research. The lawyer must also investigate and discover facts that could materially affect the client's legal rights.

Standard of Care   In judging an attorney's performance, the standard used will normally be that of a reasonably competent general practitioner of ordinary skill, experience, and capacity. If an attorney holds himself or herself out as having expertise in a special area of law (for example, corporate taxation), then the attorney's standard of care in that area is higher than for attorneys without such expertise.

Liability for Malpractice   When an attorney fails to exercise reasonable care and professional judgment, she or he breaches the duty of care and can be held liable for *malpractice* (professional negligence). In malpractice cases—as in all cases involving allegations of negligence—the plaintiff must prove that the attorney's breach of the duty of care actually caused the plaintiff to suffer some injury. ■ EXAMPLE 2.11 Suppose an attorney allows the statute of limitations (a statute that establishes the time period within which a lawsuit may be brought) to lapse on a client's claim. The attorney can be held liable for malpractice because the client can no longer file a cause of action in this case and has lost a potential award of damages. ■

Traditionally, to establish causation, the client normally had to show that "but for" the attorney's negligence, the client would not have suffered the injury. In recent years, however, several courts have held that plaintiffs in malpractice cases need only show that the defendant's negligence was a "substantial factor" in causing the plaintiff's injury.

STATUTORY DUTIES OF ACCOUNTANTS

Both civil and criminal liability may be imposed on accountants under securities laws. Accountants are also subject to criminal liability under the Internal Revenue Code.

You can read a variety of articles concerning accounting and business ethics at Questia's online library, at

http://www.questia.com/ Index.jsp?CRID=business_ ethics&OFFID=se2.

The Duty of Accountants under Securities Laws   Securities laws are designed to promote disclosure and prevent fraud in the purchase and sale of *securities*—corporate stocks and bonds. As you will read in Chapter 21, the Securities Act of 1933 governs initial sales of stock by businesses. The act requires that all essential information concerning the issuance of securities be made available to the investing public when the securities are registered with the Securities and Exchange Commission (SEC). The SEC is the federal agency that administers and enforces securities laws. The Securities Exchange Act of 1934 regulates the markets in which securities are sold by maintaining a continuous disclosure system for all corporations with securities on the securities exchanges.

Accountants frequently prepare and certify the issuer's financial statements that are included in the registration statement that is filed with the SEC. If a financial statement contains a misstatement or omission of a material fact, the accountant may be liable to any purchasers of the security. To avoid liability under the 1933 act, accountants must show that they used *due diligence*—a standard of care that accountants must meet—in the preparation of the financial statements. Among other things, due diligence requires that the accountant follow GAAP and GAAS. Accountants may also face liability for false or deceptive statements, reports, or other documents under the antifraud provisions of the Securities Exchange Act of 1934.

Potential Criminal Liability of Accountants   Criminal penalties may also be imposed on accountants for violating securities laws. For *willful* violations of the 1933 act, accountants may be imprisoned for up to five years and/or be subject to a fine of up to $10,000. For willful violations of the 1934 act, an accountant may be imprisoned for up to ten years and fined up to $100,000. The Sarbanes-Oxley Act of 2002, which will be discussed later in this chapter, provides that for a securities filing that is accompanied by an accountant's false or misleading certified audit statement, the accountant may be fined up to $5 million, imprisoned for up to twenty years, or both.

Accountants are also subject to criminal liability under the Internal Revenue Code, as well as under both state and federal criminal codes. The Internal Revenue Code makes aiding or assisting in the preparation of a false tax return a felony punishable by a fine of $100,000 ($500,000 for a corporation) and imprisonment for up to three years. This provision does not apply solely to accountants but to anyone who prepares tax returns for others for compensation. A penalty of $250 per tax return is levied on tax preparers for negligent understatement of the client's tax liability, and a penalty of $1,000 is imposed for willful understatement of tax liability or the reckless or intentional disregard of rules or regulations. In addition, those who prepare tax returns for others may be fined $1,000 per document for aiding and abetting another's understatement of tax liability (the penalty is increased to $10,000 in corporate cases).

■ Defying the Rules: The Enron Case

Deceptive accounting practices were at the heart of the Enron debacle—one of the largest bankruptcies in the history of U.S. business. For years to come, the Enron scandal will remain a symbol of the cost of unethical behavior to management, employees, suppliers, shareholders, the community, society, and indeed the world. Shareholders lost $62 billion of value in a very short period of time in the early 2000s. This case study of "cooking the books," conflicts of interest, and deviation from accepted ethical standards of business has all of the trappings of an epic novel. Unfortunately, for the thousands of employees who lost millions of dollars and for the millions of shareholders who lost billions of dollars, the Enron story was not fiction.

Both CNN and *Time* magazine have published numerous articles on the Enron scandal. See, for example, the articles available at

http://www.time.com/time/ business/article/ 0,8599,193520,00.html

and

http://archives.cnn.com/ 2002/ALLPOLITICS/07/07/ senate.enron.

THE GROWTH OF ENRON IN A NUTSHELL

In the 1990s, two gas-pipeline companies, Houston Natural Gas Corporation and InterNorth, Inc., merged to create a very large energy trading company, Enron Corporation. It was a "first mover" in a deregulated electricity market and enjoyed impressive growth. By 1998, Enron was the largest energy trader in the world. Then it entered the *online* energy trading market. By December 2000, its shares were selling at $85. Most Enron employees had a large part or even all of their retirement packages tied up in the company's stock.

When competition in energy trading increased, Enron diversified into water, power plants in Brazil and India, and finally fiber optics and high-speed Internet transmission.

ACCOUNTING ISSUES

According to the rules of the Financial Accounting Standards Board, energy traders such as Enron could include in *current* earnings profits that they *anticipated* on energy contracts. Herein lay the beginning of a type of accounting "fudging" that increased over time as the company struggled to improve its reported current earnings. By 2000, 50 percent of Enron's $1.4 billion of reported pretax profits consisted of "anticipated" future earnings on energy contracts.

Because Enron's managers received bonuses based on whether they met earnings goals, they had an incentive to inflate the anticipated earnings on such contracts. Some of the contracts extended as long as twenty years in the future. In retrospect, the temptation to management was too great, and common norms of both ethical and legal business decision making were violated as managers overestimated future earnings in order to inflate current earnings.

OFF-THE-BOOKS TRANSACTIONS

To artificially maintain and even increase its reported earnings, Enron also created a complex network of subsidiaries that enabled it to move losses from the core company to the subsidiaries—companies that did not show up on Enron's books. When it created the subsidiaries, Enron transferred assets to them, assigning a value to the assets that was much greater than their actual market value. The effect was to increase Enron's apparent net worth. Consider one example: Enron sold its unused fiber-optic cable capacity to a subsidiary for $30 million in cash and a $70 million promissory note. This transaction added $53 million to Enron's reported earnings for just one quarter. The value of the unused fiber-optic cable would soon be negligible, however.

For several years, Enron transferred assets from its books, along with the accompanying debt, to partnerships outside the main corporation. Many of these transactions were carried out in the Cayman Islands, a haven for those seeking corporate secrecy as well as a means for avoiding federal income taxes.

SELF-DEALING

Enron's chief executive officer (CEO) frequently did business with companies owned by his son and his daughter. The son created a company that was later bought by Enron. The son was then hired as an executive with a guaranteed pay package of $1 million over three years as well as 20,000 Enron stock options. The CEO's daughter owned a Houston travel agency that received over $10 million—50 percent of the agency's total revenues—from Enron during a three-year period.

THE CORPORATE CULTURE

The many transgressions just described could not have happened without a corporate culture that fostered unethical and, in many instances, illegal business decision making. This case study of unethical behavior is sufficiently important that West Legal Studies in Business has created a project titled "Inside Look" that is accessible on the Web at **http://insidelook.westbuslaw.com**. There you will discover how, on numerous occasions, Enron management was apprised, by both insiders and outsiders, that a "house of cards" had been created. Nonetheless, upper management more often than not refused to investigate and reveal to the public (or to its shareholders and employees) the financial improprieties that had occurred over the previous three years.

■ The Sarbanes-Oxley Act of 2002

As mentioned earlier, in response to the business scandals of the early 2000s, including the Enron debacle, Congress enacted the Sarbanes-Oxley Act of 2002. The act imposes a number of strict requirements on both domestic and foreign public

Kenneth Lay, a former executive of Enron Corporation, is sworn in during a congressional hearing on Enron's financial affairs in 2002. What legislation did Congress pass in 2002 in an attempt to curb unethical and deceptive accounting practices? (AP Photo/ Ron Edmonds)

accounting firms that provide auditing services to companies, or "issuers," whose securities are sold to public investors. (Provisions of the act that are more directly concerned with corporate fraud and the responsibilities of corporate officers and directors will be listed and described in Exhibit 21–4 in Chapter 21.)

THE PUBLIC COMPANY ACCOUNTING OVERSIGHT BOARD

Among other things, the Sarbanes-Oxley Act calls for a greater degree of government oversight over public accounting practices. To this end, the act created the Public Company Accounting Oversight Board, which reports to the Securities and Exchange Commission. The board consists of a chair and four other members.

Generally, the duties of the board are to oversee the audit of companies ("issuers") whose securities are sold to public investors in order to protect the interests of investors and the public interest and to register public accounting firms that prepare audit reports for issuers. The board was also asked to establish or adopt standards relating to the preparation of audit reports for issuers. To enforce compliance with the Sarbanes-Oxley Act, the board is required to inspect registered public accounting firms, investigate firms that violate the act's provisions, and discipline those firms by imposing sanctions. Sanctions range from temporary or permanent suspension to civil penalties that can be as high as $15 million for intentional violations.

APPLICABILITY TO PUBLIC ACCOUNTING FIRMS

Titles I and II of the act set forth the key provisions relating to the duties of the new oversight board and the requirements relating to public accounting firms—defined by the act as firms and associated persons that are "engaged in the practice of public accounting or preparing or issuing audit reports."

Auditor Independence   To help ensure that auditors remain independent of the firms that they audit, Title II of the Sarbanes-Oxley Act does the following:

1. Makes it unlawful for registered public accounting firms to contemporaneously perform both audit services and nonaudit services (such as management functions).

2. Requires preapproval for most auditing services from the issuer's audit committee.

3. Prohibits registered public accounting firms from providing audit services to an issuer if either the lead audit partner or the audit partner responsible for reviewing the audit has provided such services to the issuer in each of the prior five years.

4. Requires registered public accounting firms to make timely reports to the audit committees of the issuers, indicating all critical accounting policies and practices to be used; all alternative treatments of financial information within generally accepted accounting principles that have been discussed with the issuer's management officials, the ramifications of the use of such alternative treatments, and the treatment preferred by the auditor; and other material written communications between the auditor and the issuer's management.

5. Makes it unlawful for a registered public accounting firm to provide auditing services to an issuer if the issuer's chief executive officer, chief financial officer, chief accounting officer, or controller was previously employed by the auditor and participated in any capacity in the audit of the issuer during the one-year period preceding the date that the audit began.

 For information on the accounting profession, including links to the Sarbanes-Oxley Act of 2002 and articles concerning the act's impact on the accounting profession, go to the Web site for the American Institute of Certified Public Accountants (AICPA) at

http://www.aicpa.org/ index.htm.

Document Destruction   The Sarbanes-Oxley Act also prohibits the destruction or falsification of records with the intent to obstruct or influence a federal investigation or in relation to bankruptcy proceedings. Violation of this provision can result in a fine, imprisonment for up to twenty years, or both.

■ Business Ethics on a Global Level

Given the various cultures and religions throughout the world, it is not surprising that conflicts in ethics frequently arise between foreign and U.S. businesspersons. ■ EXAMPLE 2.12 In certain countries, the consumption of alcohol and specific foods is forbidden for religious reasons. Under such circumstances, it would be thoughtless and imprudent for a U.S. businessperson to invite a local business contact out for a drink. ■

The role played by women in other countries may also present some difficult ethical problems for firms doing business internationally. Equal employment opportunity is a fundamental public policy in the United States, and Title VII of the Civil Rights Act of 1964 prohibits discrimination against women in the employment context (see Chapter 18). Some other countries, however, offer little protection for women against gender discrimination in the workplace, including sexual harassment.

We look here at how laws governing workers in other countries, particularly developing countries, have created some especially difficult ethical problems for U.S. sellers of goods manufactured in foreign countries. We also examine some of the ethical ramifications of a U.S. law that prohibits U.S. businesspersons from bribing foreign officials to obtain favorable business contracts.

MONITORING THE EMPLOYMENT PRACTICES OF FOREIGN SUPPLIERS

Many U.S. businesses now contract with companies in developing nations to produce goods, such as shoes and clothing, because the wage rates in those nations are significantly lower than wages in the United States. Yet what if a foreign company exploits its workers—by hiring women and children at below-minimum-wage rates, for example, or by requiring its employees to work long hours in a workplace full of health hazards? What if the company's supervisors routinely engage in workplace conduct that is offensive to women?

Given today's global communications network, few companies can assume that their actions in other nations will go unnoticed by "corporate watch" groups that discover and publicize unethical corporate behavior. As a result, U.S. businesses today usually take steps to avoid such adverse publicity—either by refusing to deal with certain suppliers or by arranging to monitor their suppliers' workplaces to make sure that the employees are not being mistreated.

Global Exchange offers information on global business activities, including some of the ethical issues stemming from those activities, at

http://www. globalexchange.org.

THE FOREIGN CORRUPT PRACTICES ACT

Another ethical problem in international business dealings has to do with the legitimacy of certain side payments to government officials. In the United States, the majority of contracts are formed within the private sector. In many foreign countries, however, decisions on most major construction and manufacturing contracts

Workers at their sewing machines in a garment plant in Micronesia. How might cultural differences affect what businesspersons consider ethical conduct? If, for example, employees in a particular region typically work twelve-hour days, is it unethical for an American business operating in that region to require the same number of hours? Why or why not? Would it be any more ethical if the American company subcontracted with another company whose employees were required to work twelve-hour days? (AP Photo/Charles Hanley)

are made by government officials because of extensive government regulation and control over trade and industry. Side payments to government officials in exchange for favorable business contracts are not unusual in such countries, nor are they considered to be unethical. In the past, U.S. corporations doing business in these countries largely followed the dictum, "When in Rome, do as the Romans do."

In the 1970s, however, the U.S. press, and government officials as well, uncovered a number of business scandals involving large side payments by U.S. corporations—such as Lockheed Aircraft—to foreign representatives for the purpose of securing advantageous international trade contracts. In response to this unethical behavior, in 1977 Congress passed the Foreign Corrupt Practices Act (FCPA), which prohibits U.S. businesspersons from bribing foreign officials to secure advantageous contracts.

Prohibition against the Bribery of Foreign Officials   The first part of the FCPA applies to all U.S. companies and their directors, officers, shareholders, employees, and agents. This part prohibits the bribery of most officials of foreign governments if the purpose of the payment is to get the officials to act in their official capacity to provide business opportunities.

The FCPA does not prohibit payment of substantial sums to minor officials whose duties are ministerial. These payments are often referred to as "grease," or facilitating payments. They are meant to accelerate the performance of administrative services that might otherwise be carried out at a slow pace. Thus, for example, if a firm makes a payment to a minor official to speed up an import licensing process, the firm has not violated the FCPA.

Generally, the act, as amended, permits payments to foreign officials if such payments are lawful within the foreign country. The act also does not prohibit payments to private foreign companies or other third parties unless the U.S. firm knows that the payments will be passed on to a foreign government in violation of the FCPA.

Accounting Requirements In the past, bribes were often concealed in corporate financial records. Thus, the second part of the FCPA is directed toward accountants. All companies must keep detailed records that "accurately and fairly" reflect the company's financial activities. In addition, all companies must have an accounting system that provides "reasonable assurance" that all transactions entered into by the company are accounted for and legal. These requirements assist in detecting illegal bribes. The FCPA further prohibits any person from making false statements to accountants or false entries in any record or account.

Penalties for Violations In 1988, the FCPA was amended to provide that business firms that violate the act may be fined up to $2 million. Individual officers or directors who violate the FCPA may be fined up to $100,000 (the fine cannot be paid by the company) and may be imprisoned for up to five years.

OTHER NATIONS DENOUNCE BRIBERY

For twenty years, the Foreign Corrupt Practices Act (FCPA) of 1977 was the only law of its kind in the world, despite attempts by U.S. political leaders to convince other nations to pass similar legislation. Clearly, U.S. companies, as they often complained, were at a disadvantage relative to companies from other countries that faced no such constraint. That situation is now changing.

In 1997, the Organization for Economic Cooperation and Development created a convention (treaty) that made the bribery of foreign public officials a serious crime. By 2004, at least thirty-five nations had adopted the convention, which obligates them to enact legislation within their own nations in accordance with the convention. In addition, other international institutions, including the European Union, the Organization of American States, and the United Nations, have either passed or are in the process of negotiating rules against bribery in business transactions.

Many are hopeful that these global efforts will go far in preventing corruption and bribery in the awarding of contracts. Others, however, point out that despite antibribery laws, it is often impossible to prosecute bribery cases because of lack of evidence. Evidence of bribery is difficult to discover because, typically, both the party giving the bribe and the party receiving it have a strong incentive to cover it up. That may be one reason why there were less than fifty prosecutions of U.S. companies under the FCPA during the nearly thirty years since its passage. Gathering evidence against foreign parties who take bribes will likely be even more difficult.

APPLICATION ■ How Can You Create an Ethical Workplace?*

If you are a manager, rest assured that unless you are totally committed to the goal of creating and maintaining an ethical workplace, you will not succeed in achieving it. In addition to your attitude toward ethics and your conduct, two other factors help to create an ethical workplace environment: a written code of ethics, or policy statement, and the effective communication of the firm's ethical policies to employees. Finally, you should provide employees with a means by which they can anonymously complain about unethical behavior on the part of their co-workers or supervisors.

THE ROLE OF MANAGEMENT

As mentioned in this chapter, management's behavior is crucial in establishing the ethical tone of a firm. Managers must make it clear, both in their words and by their conduct, that unethical behavior is not acceptable. If an employee persists in unethical behavior, you should consider discharging the employee as a clear example to other employees that you will not tolerate unethical actions. Studies have shown that employees quickly adapt to the "rules" of their workplace environments, but it is up to the company managers to let employees know what those rules are—and to enforce them.

INSTRUCT EMPLOYEES IN ETHICAL STANDARDS

A written ethics code or policy statement helps to make clear to employees how they are expected to relate to their supervisors or managers, to consumers, to suppliers, and to other employees. Above all, it is important to state

* This *Application* is not meant to substitute for the services of an attorney who is licensed to practice law in your state.

explicitly what your firm's ethical priorities are and make sure that the firm's employees are aware of those priorities.

A good way to communicate these priorities to employees is by implementing an ethics training program, in which managers discuss with employees—face to face—the firm's policies and the importance of ethical conduct. Ethics seminars should be held at routine intervals so that employees have an opportunity to discuss ethical problems as they arise. Another effective technique is to evaluate periodically the ethical performance of each employee.

Employees should also be instructed in how they can anonymously report unethical behavior. For publicly traded systems, federal law now requires the establishment of confidential reporting systems for this purpose. This can be accomplished through a Web-based reporting system, as described earlier in this chapter, or by using a company "hot line" installed for this purpose.

CHECKLIST FOR THE BUSINESS MANAGER

1. Make sure that management is committed to ethical behavior and sets an ethical example.
2. Create, print, and distribute an ethical code clearly stating your firm's ethical goals and priorities, as well as what behavior is expected of employees in their areas of responsibility.
3. Implement an ethics training program to communicate your firm's ethical policies to employees.
4. Devise a method, such as an ethical checklist, for evaluating the ethical performance of each individual employee.
5. Provide a mechanism through which employees can anonymously complain about unethical behavior in the workplace.

■ KEY TERMS

CHAPTER SUMMARY ▦ Ethics and Professional Responsibility

Business Ethics (See pages 47–48.)	Ethics can be defined as the study of what constitutes right or wrong behavior. Business ethics focuses on how moral and ethical principles are applied in the business context.
Setting the Right Ethical Tone (See pages 48–52.)	1. *Role of management*—Management's commitment and behavior are essential in creating an ethical workplace. Most large firms have ethical codes or policies and corporate compliance programs to help employees determine whether certain actions are ethical. 2. *Ethical trade-offs*—Management constantly faces ethical trade-offs because firms have ethical and legal duties to a number of groups, including shareholders and employees.
Business Ethics and the Law (See pages 53–56.)	1. *The moral minimum*—Lawful behavior is a moral minimum. The law has its limits, though, and some actions may be legal but not ethical. 2. *Legal uncertainties*—It may be difficult to predict with certainty whether particular actions are legal given the numerous and frequent changes in the laws regulating business and the "gray areas" in the law. 3. *Technological developments and legal uncertainties*—Technological developments can also lead to legal uncertainties until it is clear how the law will be applied to the questions raised by these developments.
Approaches to Ethical Reasoning (See pages 57–58.)	1. *Duty-based ethics*—Ethics based on religious beliefs; philosophical reasoning, such as that of Immanuel Kant; and the basic rights of human beings (the principle of rights). 2. *Outcome-based ethics (utilitarianism)*—Ethics based on philosophical reasoning, such as that of John Stuart Mill.
Professional Responsibility (See pages 59–62.)	1. *Duty of care*—Accountants and attorneys are held to standards of care established by their respective professions. Failure to meet the required standard of care may result in liability for negligence. The standard of care expected of accountants is reflected in generally accepted accounting principles (GAAP) and generally accepted auditing standards (GAAS). The standard of care expected of attorneys is reflected in rules established in each state and by the American Bar Association's Model Rules of Professional Conduct. 2. *Statutory duties of accountants*—Accountants are subject to requirements established by securities laws. Violations of these requirements may result in both civil and criminal penalties. Accountants are also subject to criminal liability under the Internal Revenue Code.
Defying the Rules: The Enron Case (See pages 62–63.)	The Enron scandal—involving one of the largest bankruptcies in U.S. history—can serve as a case study of a corporate culture that fostered unethical and, in part, illegal business decision making.
The Sarbanes-Oxley Act of 2002 (See pages 63–65.)	Imposes strict requirements on domestic and foreign public accounting firms that provide auditing services to companies selling securities to the public. Establishes an oversight board and rules to keep auditors independent and prevent the destruction or falsification of records.
Business Ethics on a Global Level (See pages 65–67.)	Businesses must take account of the many cultural, religious, and legal differences among nations. Notable differences relate to the role of women in society, employment laws governing workplace conditions, and the practice of giving side payments to foreign officials to secure favorable contracts.

▦ FOR REVIEW

Answers for the even-numbered questions in this For Review *section can be found in Appendix I at the end of this text.*

1 What is ethics? What is business ethics? Why is business ethics important?

2 How can business leaders encourage their companies to act ethically?

3 How do duty-based ethical standards differ from outcome-based ethical standards?

4 What duties do professionals owe to those who rely on their services?

5 What types of ethical issues might arise in the context of international business transactions?

■ QUESTIONS AND CASE PROBLEMS

2–1. Business Ethics. Some business ethicists maintain that whereas personal ethics has to do with right or wrong behavior, business ethics is concerned with appropriate behavior. In other words, ethical behavior in business has less to do with moral principles than with what society deems to be appropriate behavior in the business context. Do you agree with this distinction? Do personal and business ethics ever overlap? Should personal ethics play any role in business ethical decision making?

2–2. Business Ethics and Public Opinion. Assume that you are a high-level manager for a shoe manufacturer. You know that your firm could increase its profit margin by producing shoes in Indonesia, where you could hire women for $100 a month to assemble them. You also know, however, that a competing shoe manufacturer recently was accused by human rights advocates of engaging in exploitative labor practices because the manufacturer sold shoes made by Indonesian women for similarly low wages. You personally do not believe that paying $100 a month to Indonesian women is unethical because you know that in their country, $100 a month is a better-than-average wage rate. Assuming that the decision is yours to make, should you have the shoes manufactured in Indonesia and make higher profits for your company? Should you instead avoid the risk of negative publicity and the consequences of that publicity for the firm's reputation and subsequent profits? Are there other alternatives? Discuss fully.

2–3. Business Ethics and Public Opinion. Human rights groups, environmental activists, and other interest groups concerned with unethical business practices have often conducted publicity campaigns against various corporations that those groups feel have engaged in unethical practices. Do you believe that a small group of well-organized activists should dictate how a major corporation conducts its affairs? Discuss fully.

2–4. Ethical Decision Making. Shokun Steel Co. owns many steel plants. One of its plants is much older than the others. Equipment at that plant is outdated and inefficient, and the costs of production at that plant are now twice as high as at any of Shokun's other plants. The company cannot raise the price of steel because of competition, both domestic and international. The plant is located in Twin Firs, Pennsylvania, which has a population of about 45,000, and currently employs over a thousand workers. Shokun is contemplating whether to close the plant. What factors should the firm consider in making its decision? Will the firm violate any ethical duties if it closes the plant? Analyze these questions from the two basic perspectives on ethical reasoning discussed in this chapter.

2–5. Ethical Conduct. Richard and Suzanne Weinstein owned Elm City Cheese Co. Elm City sold its products to three major customers that used the cheese as a "filler" to blend into their cheeses. In 1982, Mark Federico, a certified public accountant, became Elm City's accountant and the Weinsteins' personal accountant. The Weinsteins had known Federico since he was seven years old, and even before he became their accountant, he knew the details of Elm City's business. Federico's duties went beyond typical accounting work, and when the Weinsteins were absent, Federico was put in charge of operations. In 1992, Federico was made a vice president of the company, and a year later he was placed in charge of day-to-day operations. He also continued to serve as Elm City's accountant. The relationship between Federico and the Weinsteins deteriorated, and in 1995, he resigned as Elm City's employee and as its accountant. Less than two years later, Federico opened Lomar Foods, Inc., to make the same products as Elm City by the same process and to sell the products to the same customers. Federico located Lomar closer to Elm City's suppliers. Elm City filed a suit in a Connecticut state court against Federico and Lomar, alleging, among other things, misappropriation of trade secrets. Elm City argued that it was entitled to punitive damages because Federico's conduct was "willful and malicious." Federico responded in part that he did not act willfully and maliciously because he did not know that Elm City's business details were trade secrets. Were Federico's actions "willful and malicious"? Were they ethical? Explain. [*Elm City Cheese Co. v. Federico,* 251 Conn. 59, 752 A.2d 1037 (1999)]

CASE PROBLEM WITH SAMPLE ANSWER

 2–6. Richard Fraser was an "exclusive career insurance agent" under a contract with Nationwide Mutual Insurance Co. Fraser leased computer hardware and software from Nationwide for his business. During a dispute between Nationwide and the Nationwide Insurance Independent Contractors Association, an organization representing Fraser and other exclusive career agents, Fraser prepared a letter to Nationwide's competitors asking whether they were interested in acquiring the represented agents' policyholders. Nationwide obtained a copy of the letter and searched its electronic file server for e-mail indicating that the letter had been sent. It found a stored e-mail that Fraser had sent to a co-worker indicating that the letter had been sent to at least one competitor. The e-mail was retrieved from the co-worker's file of already received and discarded messages stored on the receiver. When Nationwide canceled its contract with Fraser, he filed a suit in a federal district court against the firm, alleging, among other things, violations of various federal laws that prohibit the interception of electronic communications during transmission. In whose favor should the court rule, and why? In any case, did Nationwide act ethically in retrieving the e-mail? [*Fraser v. Nationwide Mutual Insurance Co.*, 135 F.Supp.2d 623 (E.D.Pa. 2001)]

After you have answered this problem, compare your answer with the sample answer given on the Web site that accompanies this text. Go to http://blt.westbuslaw.com, select "Chapter 2," and click on "Case Problem with Sample Answer."

2–7. Ethical Conduct. Unable to pay more than $1.2 billion in debt, Big Rivers Electric Corp. filed a petition to declare bankruptcy in a federal bankruptcy court in September 1996. Big Rivers' creditors included Bank of New York (BONY), Chase Manhattan Bank, Mapco Equities, and others. The court appointed J. Baxter Schilling to work as a "disinterested" (neutral) party with Big Rivers and the creditors to resolve their disputes; the court set an hourly fee as Schilling's compensation. Schilling told Chase, BONY, and Mapco that he wanted them to pay him an additional percentage fee based on the "success" he attained in finding "new value" to pay Big Rivers' debts. He said that without such a deal, he would not perform his mediation duties. Chase agreed; the others disputed the deal, but no one told the court. In October 1998, Schilling asked the court for nearly $4.5 million in compensation, including the hourly fees, which totaled about $531,000, and the percentage fees. Big Rivers and others asked the court to deny Schilling any fees on the basis that he had improperly negotiated "secret side agreements." How did Schilling violate his duties as a "disinterested" party? Should he be denied compensation? Why or why not? [*In re Big Rivers Electric Corp.*, 355 F.3d 415 (6th Cir. 2004)]

A QUESTION OF ETHICS

2–8. Hazen Paper Co. manufactured paper and paperboard for use in such products as cosmetic wrap, lottery tickets, and pressure-sensitive items. Walter Biggins, a chemist hired by Hazen in 1977, developed a water-based paper coating that was both environmentally safe and of superior quality. By the mid-1980s, the company's sales had increased dramatically as a result of its extensive use of "Biggins Acrylic." Because of this, Biggins thought he deserved a substantial raise in salary, and from 1984 to 1986, Biggins's persistent requests for a raise became a bone of contention between him and his employers. Biggins ran a business on the side, which involved cleaning up hazardous wastes for various companies. Hazen told Biggins that unless he signed a "confidentiality agreement" promising to restrict his outside activities during the time he was employed by Hazen and for a limited time afterward, he would be fired. Biggins said he would sign the agreement only if Hazen raised his salary to

$100,000. Hazen refused to do so, fired Biggins, and hired a younger man to replace him. At the time of his discharge in 1986, Biggins was sixty-two years old, had worked for the company nearly ten years, and was just a few weeks away from being entitled to pension rights worth about $93,000. In view of these circumstances, evaluate and answer the following questions. [*Hazen Paper Co. v. Biggins*, 507 U.S. 604, 113 S.Ct. 1701, 123 L.Ed.2d 338 (1993)]

1. Did the company owe an ethical duty to Biggins to increase his salary, given that its sales increased dramatically as a result of Biggins's efforts and ingenuity in developing the coating? If you were one of the company's executives, would you have raised Biggins's salary? Why or why not?

2. Generally, what public policies come into conflict in cases involving employers who, for reasons of cost and efficiency of operations, fire older, higher-paid workers and replace them with younger, lower-paid workers? If you were an employer facing the need to cut back on personnel to save costs, what would you do, and on what ethical premises would you justify your decision?

FOR CRITICAL ANALYSIS

2–9. If a firm engages in "ethically responsible" behavior solely for the purpose of gaining profits from the goodwill it generates, the "ethical" behavior is essentially a means toward a self-serving end (profits and the accumulation of wealth). In this situation, is the firm acting unethically in any way? Should motive or conduct carry greater weight on the ethical scales in this situation?

VIDEO QUESTION

2–10. Go to this text's Web site at **http://blt. westbuslaw.com** and select "Chapter 2." Click on "Video Questions" and view the video titled *Ethics: Business Ethics an Oxymoron?* Then answer the following questions.

1. According to the instructor in the video, what is the primary reason why businesses act ethically?

2. Which of the two approaches to ethical reasoning that were discussed in the chapter seems to have had more influence on the instructor in the discussion of how business activities are related to societies? Explain your answer.

3. The instructor asserts that "[i]n the end, it is the unethical behavior that becomes costly, and conversely ethical behavior creates its own competitive advantage." Do you agree with this statement? Why or why not?

INTERNET EXERCISES

Go to the *Business Law Today: The Essentials* home page at **http://blt.westbuslaw.com**, select "Chapter 2," and click on "Internet Exercises." There you will find the following Internet research exercises that you can perform to learn more about topics covered in this chapter.

Activity 2–1: LEGAL PERSPECTIVE—Ethics in Business

Activity 2–2: MANAGEMENT PERSPECTIVE—Environmental Self-Audits

BEFORE THE TEST

Go to the *Business Law Today: The Essentials* home page at **http://blt.westbuslaw.com**, select "Chapter 2," and click on "Interactive Quizzes." You will find at least twenty interactive questions relating to this chapter.

CHAPTER 3

Traditional and Online Dispute Resolution

"The Judicial Department comes home in its effects to every man's fireside: it passes on his property, his reputation, his life, his all."

John Marshall, 1755–1835
(Chief justice of the United States Supreme Court, 1801–1835)

CHAPTER OUTLINE

- **THE JUDICIARY'S ROLE IN AMERICAN GOVERNMENT**

- **BASIC JUDICIAL REQUIREMENTS**

- **THE STATE AND FEDERAL COURT SYSTEMS**

- **FOLLOWING A STATE COURT CASE**

- **THE COURTS ADAPT TO THE ONLINE WORLD**

- **ALTERNATIVE DISPUTE RESOLUTION**

- **ONLINE DISPUTE RESOLUTION**

LEARNING OBJECTIVES

After reading this chapter, you should be able to answer the following questions:

1 What is judicial review? How and when was the power of judicial review established?

2 Before a court can hear a case, it must have jurisdiction. Over what must it have jurisdiction? How are the courts applying traditional jurisdictional concepts to cases involving Internet transactions?

3 What is the difference between a trial court and an appellate court?

4 In a lawsuit, what are the pleadings? What is discovery, and how does electronic discovery differ? What is electronic filing?

5 How are online forums being used to resolve disputes?

As Chief Justice John Marshall remarked in the above quotation, ultimately, we are all affected by what the courts say and do. This is particularly true in the business world—nearly every businessperson will face either a potential or an actual lawsuit at some time or another. For this reason, anyone contemplating a career in business will benefit from an understanding of American court systems, including the mechanics of lawsuits.

In this chapter, after examining the judiciary's overall role in the American governmental scheme, we discuss some basic requirements that must be met before a party may bring a lawsuit before a particular court. We then look at the court systems of the United States in some detail and, to clarify judicial procedures, follow a hypothetical case through a state court system. Even though there are fifty-two court systems—one for each of the fifty states, one for the District of Columbia, plus a federal system—similarities abound. Keep in mind that the federal courts are not superior to the state courts; they are simply an independent system of courts, which derives its authority from Article III, Sections 1 and 2, of the U.S. Constitution. The chapter concludes with an overview of some alternative methods of settling disputes, including methods for settling disputes in online forums.

Note that technological developments are affecting court procedures just as they are affecting all other areas of the law. In this chapter, we will also indicate how court doctrines and procedures, as well as alternative methods of dispute settlement, are being adapted to the needs of a cyber age.

The Judiciary's Role in American Government

As you learned in Chapter 1, the body of American law includes the federal and state constitutions, statutes passed by legislative bodies, administrative law, and the case decisions and legal principles that form the common law. These laws would be meaningless, however, without the courts to interpret and apply them. This is the essential role of the judiciary—the courts—in the American governmental system: to interpret and apply the law.

JUDICIAL REVIEW

JUDICIAL REVIEW
The process by which a court decides on the constitutionality of legislative enactments and actions of the executive branch.

As the branch of government entrusted with interpreting the laws, the judiciary can decide, among other things, whether the laws or actions of the other two branches are constitutional. The process for making such a determination is known as **judicial review.** The power of judicial review enables the judicial branch to act as a check on the other two branches of government, in line with the checks-and-balances system established by the U.S. Constitution.

THE ORIGINS OF JUDICIAL REVIEW IN THE UNITED STATES

The power of judicial review was not mentioned in the Constitution, but the concept was not new at the time the nation was founded. Indeed, prior to 1789 state courts had already overturned state legislative acts that conflicted with state constitutions. Additionally, many of the founders expected the United States Supreme Court to assume a similar role with respect to the federal Constitution. Alexander Hamilton and James Madison both emphasized the importance of judicial review in their essays urging the adoption of the new Constitution. When was the doctrine of judicial review established? See this chapter's *Landmark in the Law* feature for the answer.

Basic Judicial Requirements

Before a court can hear a lawsuit, certain requirements must first be met. These requirements relate to jurisdiction, venue, and standing to sue. We examine each of these important concepts here.

JURISDICTION

JURISDICTION
The authority of a court to hear and decide a specific action.

In Latin, *juris* means "law," and *diction* means "to speak." Thus, "the power to speak the law" is the literal meaning of the term **jurisdiction.** Before any court can hear a case, it must have jurisdiction over the person against whom the suit is brought or over the property involved in the suit. The court must also have jurisdiction over the subject matter.

LANDMARK IN THE LAW *Marbury v. Madison* (1803)

In the edifice of American law, the *Marbury v. Madison*[a] decision in 1803 can be viewed as the keystone of the constitutional arch. The facts of the case were as follows. John Adams, who had lost his bid for reelection to the presidency to Thomas Jefferson in 1800, feared the Jeffersonians' antipathy toward business and toward a strong central government. Adams thus worked feverishly to "pack" the judiciary with loyal Federalists (those who believed in a strong national government) by appointing what came to be called "midnight judges" just before Jefferson took office. All of the fifty-nine judicial appointment letters had to be certified and delivered, but Adams's secretary of state (John Marshall) had succeeded in delivering only forty-two of them by the time Jefferson took over as president. Jefferson, of course, refused to order his secretary of state, James Madison, to deliver the remaining commissions.

MARSHALL'S DILEMMA William Marbury and three others to whom the commissions had not been delivered sought a writ of *mandamus* (an order directing a government official to fulfill a duty) from the United States Supreme Court, as authorized by Section 13 of the Judiciary Act of 1789. As fate would have it, John Marshall had stepped down as Adams's secretary of state only to become chief justice of the Supreme Court. Marshall faced a dilemma: If he ordered the commissions delivered, the new secretary of state (Madison) could simply refuse to deliver them—and the Court had no way to compel action, because it had no police force. At the same time, if Marshall simply allowed the new administration to do as it wished, the Court's power would be severely eroded.

MARSHALL'S DECISION Marshall masterfully fashioned his decision. On the one hand, he enlarged the power of the Supreme Court by affirming the Court's power of judicial review. He stated, "It is emphatically the province and duty of the Judicial Department to say what the law is. . . . If two laws conflict with each other, the courts must decide on the operation of each. . . . So if the law be in opposition to the Constitution . . . [t]he Court must determine which of these conflicting rules governs the case. This is the very essence of judicial duty."

On the other hand, his decision did not require anyone to do anything. He stated that the highest court did not have the power to issue a writ of *mandamus* in this particular case. Marshall pointed out that although the Judiciary Act of 1789 specified that the Supreme Court could issue writs of *mandamus* as part of its original jurisdiction, Article III of the Constitution, which spelled out the Court's original jurisdiction, did not mention writs of *mandamus*. Because Congress did not have the right to expand the Supreme Court's jurisdiction, this section of the Judiciary Act of 1789 was unconstitutional—and thus void. The decision still stands today as a judicial and political masterpiece.

APPLICATION TO TODAY'S WORLD

Since the Marbury v. Madison *decision, the power of judicial review has remained unchallenged. Today, this power is exercised by both federal and state courts. For example, as you read in Chapter 1, some of the laws that Congress has passed in*

a. 5 U.S. (1 Cranch) 137, 2 L.Ed. 60 (1803).

(Continued)

LANDMARK IN THE LAW—Continued

an attempt to protect minors from Internet pornography have been held unconstitutional by the courts. If the courts did not have the power of judicial review, the constitutionality of these acts of Congress could not be challenged in court—a congressional statute would remain law until changed by Congress. Because of the importance of Marbury v. Madison *in our legal system, the courts of other countries that have adopted a constitutional democracy often cite this decision as a justification for judicial review.*

RELEVANT WEB SITES

To locate information on the Web concerning the Marbury v. Madison *decision, go to this text's Web site at* <u>http://blt.westbuslaw.com</u>, *select "Chapter 3," and click on "URLs for Landmarks."*

James Madison. If Madison had delivered the commissions of the Federalist judges, would the United States Supreme Court today have the power of judicial review? Why did the Court not force Madison to deliver the commissions? (Library of Congress)

LONG ARM STATUTE
A state statute that permits a state to obtain personal jurisdiction over nonresident defendants. A defendant must have certain "minimum contacts" with that state for the statute to apply.

Jurisdiction over Persons   Generally, a court can exercise personal jurisdiction (*in personam* jurisdiction) over any person or business that resides in a certain geographic area. A state trial court, for example, normally has jurisdictional authority over residents (including businesses) in a particular area of the state, such as a county or district. A state's highest court (often called the state supreme court)[1] has jurisdiction over all residents of that state.

In addition, under the authority of a state **long arm statute,** a court can exercise personal jurisdiction over certain out-of-state defendants based on activities that took place within the state. Before exercising long arm jurisdiction over a nonresident, however, the court must be convinced that the defendant had sufficient contacts, or *minimum contacts,* with the state to justify the jurisdiction.[2] Generally, this means that the defendant must have enough of a connection to the state for the judge to conclude that it is fair for the state to exercise power over the defendant. ■ **EXAMPLE 3.1**   If an out-of-state defendant caused an automobile accident or sold defective goods within the state, a court will usually find that minimum contacts exist to exercise jurisdiction over that defendant. Similarly, a state may exercise personal jurisdiction over a nonresident defendant who is sued for breaching a contract that was formed within the state. ■

In regard to corporations,[3] the minimum-contacts requirement is usually met if the corporation does business within the state. ■ **EXAMPLE 3.2** Suppose that a Maine corporation has a branch office or a manufacturing plant in Georgia. Does this Maine corporation have sufficient minimum contacts with the state of Georgia to allow a Georgia court to exercise jurisdiction over it? Yes, it does. If the Maine corporation advertises and sells its products in Georgia, those activities will also likely suffice to meet the minimum-contacts requirement, even if the corporate headquarters are located in a different state. ■

In the following case, the issue was whether phone calls and letters constituted sufficient minimum contacts to give a court jurisdiction over a nonresident defendant.

---

1. As will be discussed shortly, a state's highest court is frequently referred to as the state supreme court, but there are exceptions. For example, in New York, the supreme court is a trial court.
2. The minimum-contacts standard was established in *International Shoe Co. v. State of Washington,* 326 U.S. 310, 66 S.Ct. 154, 90 L.Ed. 95 (1945).
3. In the eyes of the law, corporations are "legal persons"—entities that can sue and be sued. See Chapter 20.

CASE 3.1 Cole v. Mileti

United States Court of Appeals,
Sixth Circuit, 1998.
133 F.3d 433.
http://www.law.emory.edu/6circuit/jan98/index.html[a]

FACTS Nick Mileti, a resident of California, co-produced a movie called *Streamers* and organized a corporation, Streamers International Distributors, Inc., to distribute the film. Joseph Cole, a resident of Ohio, bought two hundred shares of Streamers stock. Cole also lent the firm $475,000, which he borrowed from Equitable Bank of Baltimore. The film was unsuccessful. Mileti agreed to repay Cole's loan in a contract arranged through phone calls and correspondence between California and Ohio. When Mileti did not repay the loan, the bank sued Cole, who in turn filed a suit against Mileti in a federal district court in Ohio. The court entered a judgment against Mileti. He appealed to the U.S. Court of Appeals for the Sixth Circuit, arguing in part that the district court's exercise of jurisdiction over him was unfair.

ISSUE Can a federal district court in Ohio[b] exercise personal jurisdiction over a resident of California who does business in Ohio via phone calls and letters?

a. This is a page, at the Web site of the Emory University School of Law, that lists the published opinions of the U.S. Court of Appeals for the Sixth Circuit for January 1998. Scroll down the list of cases to the *Cole* case. To access the opinion, click on the case name.
b. As will be discussed shortly, federal district courts can exercise jurisdiction over disputes between parties living in different states. This is called *diversity-of-citizenship* jurisdiction. When a federal district court exercises diversity jurisdiction, the court normally applies the law of the state in which the court sits—in this case, the law of Ohio.

DECISION Yes. The U.S. Court of Appeals for the Sixth Circuit held that the district court could exercise personal jurisdiction over Mileti.

REASON The appellate court set out a three-part test to determine whether a court has jurisdiction over a nonresident defendant. A defendant must conduct activities in the state in which the suit is filed, the cause of action must arise from those activities, and those activities or their consequences must have a substantial connection to the state. The court reasoned that a nonresident who does business by "negotiating and executing a contract via telephone calls and letters to an Ohio resident" has conducted sufficient activities in the state. A cause of action arises from those activities if it is for breach of that contract. Finally, under those circumstances, the activities have a substantial connection to the state, and "the assertion of personal jurisdiction was proper."

FOR CRITICAL ANALYSIS—Economic Consideration *Why might a defendant prefer to be sued in one state rather than in another?*

Jurisdiction over Property A court can also exercise jurisdiction over property that is located within its boundaries. This kind of jurisdiction is known as *in rem* jurisdiction, or "jurisdiction over the thing." ■ **EXAMPLE 3.3** Suppose that a dispute arises over the ownership of a boat in dry dock in Fort Lauderdale, Florida. The boat is owned by an Ohio resident, over whom a Florida court normally cannot exercise personal jurisdiction. The other party to the dispute is a resident of Nebraska. In this situation, a lawsuit concerning the boat could be brought in a Florida state court on the basis of the court's *in rem* jurisdiction. ■

Jurisdiction over Subject Matter Jurisdiction over subject matter is a limitation on the types of cases a court can hear. In both the federal and state court systems, there are courts of *general* (unlimited) *jurisdiction* and courts of *limited jurisdiction*. An example of a court of general jurisdiction is a state trial court or a federal district

PROBATE COURT
A state court of limited jurisdiction that conducts proceedings relating to the settlement of a deceased person's estate.

BANKRUPTCY COURT
A federal court of limited jurisdiction that handles only bankruptcy proceedings. Bankruptcy proceedings are governed by federal bankruptcy law.

court. An example of a state court of limited jurisdiction is a probate court. **Probate courts** are state courts that handle only matters relating to the transfer of a person's assets and obligations after that person's death, including matters relating to the custody and guardianship of children. An example of a federal court of limited subject-matter jurisdiction is a bankruptcy court. **Bankruptcy courts** handle only bankruptcy proceedings, which are governed by federal bankruptcy law (discussed in Chapter 16). In contrast, a court of general jurisdiction can decide a broad array of cases.

A court's jurisdiction over subject matter is usually defined in the statute or constitution creating the court. In both the federal and state court systems, a court's subject-matter jurisdiction can be limited not only by the subject of the lawsuit but also by the amount in controversy, by whether a case is a felony (a more serious type of crime) or a misdemeanor (a less serious type of crime), or by whether the proceeding is a trial or an appeal.

Original and Appellate Jurisdiction The distinction between courts of original jurisdiction and courts of appellate jurisdiction normally lies in whether the case is being heard for the first time. Courts having original jurisdiction are courts of the first instance, or trial courts—that is, courts in which lawsuits begin, trials take place, and evidence is presented. In the federal court system, the *district courts* are trial courts. In the various state court systems, the trial courts are known by various names, as will be discussed shortly.

The key point here is that, normally, any court having original jurisdiction is known as a trial court. Courts having appellate jurisdiction act as reviewing courts, or appellate courts. In general, cases can be brought before appellate courts only on appeal from an order or a judgment of a trial court or other lower court.

Jurisdiction of the Federal Courts Because the federal government is a government of limited powers, the jurisdiction of the federal courts is limited. Article III of the U.S. Constitution establishes the boundaries of federal judicial power. Section 2 of Article III states that "[t]he judicial Power shall extend to all Cases, in Law and Equity, arising under this Constitution, the Laws of the United States, and Treaties made, or which shall be made, under their Authority."

FEDERAL QUESTION
A question that pertains to the U.S. Constitution, acts of Congress, or treaties. A federal question provides a basis for federal jurisdiction.

Whenever a plaintiff's cause of action is based, at least in part, on the U.S. Constitution, a treaty, or a federal law, then a **federal question** arises, and the case comes under the judicial power of the federal courts. Any lawsuit involving a federal question can originate in a federal court. People who claim that their rights under the U.S. Constitution have been violated can begin their suits in a federal court.

DIVERSITY OF CITIZENSHIP
Under Article III, Section 2, of the Constitution, a basis for federal district court jurisdiction over a lawsuit between (1) citizens of different states, (2) a foreign country and citizens of a state or of different states, or (3) citizens of a state and citizens or subjects of a foreign country. The amount in controversy must be more than $75,000 before a federal district court can take jurisdiction in such cases.

Federal district courts can also exercise original jurisdiction over cases involving **diversity of citizenship.** Such cases may arise between (1) citizens of different states, (2) a foreign country and citizens of a state or of different states, or (3) citizens of a state and citizens or subjects of a foreign country. The amount in controversy must be more than $75,000 before a federal court can take jurisdiction in such cases. For purposes of diversity jurisdiction, a corporation is a citizen of both the state in which it is incorporated and the state in which its principal place of business is located. A case involving diversity of citizenship can be filed in the appropriate federal district court, or, if the case starts in a state court, it can sometimes be transferred to a federal court. A large percentage of the cases filed in federal courts each year are based on diversity of citizenship.

Note that in a case based on a federal question, a federal court will apply federal law. In a case based on diversity of citizenship, however, a federal court will apply the relevant state law (which is often the law of the state in which the court sits).

Exclusive versus Concurrent Jurisdiction   When both federal and state courts have the power to hear a case, as is true in suits involving diversity of citizenship, **concurrent jurisdiction** exists. When cases can be tried only in federal courts or only in state courts, exclusive jurisdiction exists. Federal courts have **exclusive jurisdiction** in cases involving federal crimes, bankruptcy, patents, and copyrights; in suits against the United States; and in some areas of admiralty law (law governing transportation on the seas and ocean waters). States also have exclusive jurisdiction over certain subject matters—for example, divorce and adoption. The concepts of exclusive and concurrent jurisdiction are illustrated in Exhibit 3–1.

When concurrent jurisdiction exists, a party has a choice of whether to bring a suit in, for example, a federal or a state court. The party's lawyer will consider several factors in counseling the party as to which choice is preferable. The lawyer may prefer to litigate the case in a state court because he or she is more familiar with the state court's procedures, or perhaps the attorney believes that the state's judge or jury would be more sympathetic to the client and the case. Alternatively, the lawyer may advise the client to sue in federal court. Perhaps the state court's **docket** (the court's schedule listing the cases to be heard) is crowded, and the case could be brought to trial sooner in a federal court. Perhaps some feature of federal practice or procedure could offer an advantage in the client's case. Other important considerations include the law in the particular jurisdiction, how that law has been applied in the jurisdiction's courts, and what the results in similar cases have been in that jurisdiction.

JURISDICTION IN CYBERSPACE

The Internet's capacity to bypass political and geographic boundaries undercuts the traditional basic limitations on a court's authority to exercise jurisdiction. These

CONCURRENT JURISDICTION
Jurisdiction that exists when two different courts have the power to hear a case. For example, some cases can be heard in a federal or a state court.

EXCLUSIVE JURISDICTION
Jurisdiction that exists when a case can be heard only in a particular court or type of court.

DOCKET
The list of cases entered on a court's calendar and thus scheduled to be heard by the court.

EXHIBIT 3–1 EXCLUSIVE AND CONCURRENT JURISDICTION

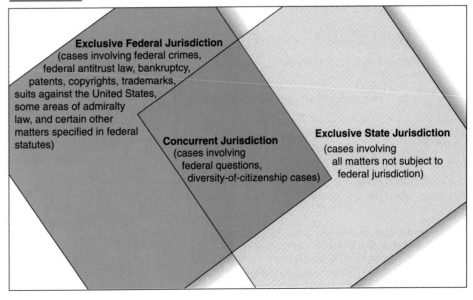

Exclusive Federal Jurisdiction
(cases involving federal crimes, federal antitrust law, bankruptcy, patents, copyrights, trademarks, suits against the United States, some areas of admiralty law, and certain other matters specified in federal statutes)

Concurrent Jurisdiction
(cases involving federal questions, diversity-of-citizenship cases)

Exclusive State Jurisdiction
(cases involving all matters not subject to federal jurisdiction)

limits include a party's contacts with a court's geographic jurisdiction. As already discussed, for a court to compel a defendant to come before it, there must be at least minimum contacts—the presence of a salesperson within the state, for example. Are there sufficient minimum contacts if the only connection to a jurisdiction is an ad on the Web originating from a remote location?

The "Sliding-Scale" Standard Gradually, the courts are developing a standard—called a "sliding-scale" standard—for determining when the exercise of jurisdiction over an out-of-state defendant is proper. In developing this standard, the courts have identified three types of Internet business contacts: (1) substantial business conducted over the Internet (with contracts and sales, for example); (2) some interactivity through a Web site; and (3) passive advertising. Jurisdiction is proper for the first category, improper for the third, and may or may not be appropriate for the second.[4] An Internet communication is typically considered passive if people have to voluntarily access it to read the message and active if it is sent to specific individuals.

In certain situations, even a single contact can satisfy the minimum-contacts requirement. ■ EXAMPLE 3.4 A Texas resident, Davis, sent an unsolicited e-mail message to numerous Mississippi residents advertising a pornographic Web site. Davis falsified the "from" header in the e-mail so that it appeared that Internet Doorway had sent the mail. Internet Doorway filed a lawsuit against Davis in Mississippi claiming that its reputation and goodwill in the community had been harmed. The U.S. district court in Mississippi held that Davis's single e-mail to Mississippi residents satisfied the minimum-contacts requirement for jurisdiction. The court concluded that Davis, by sending the e-mail solicitation, should reasonably have expected that she could be "haled into court in a distant jurisdiction to answer for the ramifications."[5] ■ In the following case, the court considered whether jurisdiction could be exercised over defendants whose only contacts with the jurisdiction were through their Web site.

---

4. For a leading case on this issue, see *Zippo Manufacturing Co. v. Zippo Dot Com, Inc.,* 952 F.Supp. 1119 (W.D.Pa. 1997).

5. *Internet Doorway, Inc. v. Parks,* 138 F.Supp.2d 773 (S.D.Miss. 2001).

CASE 3.2 ▪ Bird v. Parsons

United States Court of Appeals,
Sixth Circuit, 2002.
289 F.3d 865.
http://pacer.ca6.uscourts.gov/opinions/main.php[a]

HISTORICAL AND TECHNOLOGICAL
SETTING *The creation of a Web site requires the reservation of a location, called an Internet Protocol (IP) address, and a computer to host the contents of the site. To make using the Internet easier, a domain name is*

---

a. This is a page within the Web site of the U.S. Court of Appeals for the Sixth Circuit. In the left-hand column, click on "Opinions Search." In the "Short Title contains" box, type "Parsons" and click on "Submit Query." In the "Opinion" box corresponding to the name of the case, click on the number to access the opinion.

assigned to correspond to an IP address. A person who wants a specific domain name must apply for the name with a domain name registrar. To access a Web site, a user enters in a browser a domain name corresponding to an IP address and then is routed electronically to the computer that hosts the site at that address. Because not every person who establishes a site hosts it on his or her own computer, surrogate hosts license space on their computers to site owners.

FACTS Darrell Bird, a citizen of Ohio, has operated Financia, Inc., a national computer software business, since 1983. Financia, Inc., owns the domain name financia.com. Dotster, Inc., a domain name registrar incorporated in Washington, operates its registry at

CASE 3.2—Continued

http://www.dotster.com.[b] Dotster allows registrants who lack an Internet server to which a name can be assigned to park their names on Dotster's "Futurehome" page. Marshall Parsons registered the name efinancia.com on Dotster's site in 2000 and "parked" the name on the Futurehome page with the address **http://www. efinancia.com**. George DeCarlo and Steven Vincent, on behalf of Dotster, activated Parsons's site. The name efinancia.com was soon offered for sale at **http://www. afternic.com**, an auction site for the sale of domain names. Bird filed a suit against Dotster and others in a federal district court, alleging, in part, trademark infringement, copyright infringement, and cybersquatting.[c] Dotster, DeCarlo, and Vincent (the "Dotster defendants") asked the court to dismiss the complaint against them for, among other reasons, lack of personal jurisdiction. The court dismissed the suit. Alleging that Dotster sold 4,666 registrations to Ohio residents, Bird appealed to the U.S. Court of Appeals for the Sixth Circuit.

ISSUE Could the state of Ohio assert personal jurisdiction over out-of-state defendants whose only contact with Ohio was through a Web site?

b. Dotster's registration process is in conjunction with the Domain Registration of Internet Assigned Names and Numbers, which is maintained by Network Solutions, Inc. (owned by VeriSign), and regulated by the Internet Corporation for Assigned Names and Numbers (ICANN). Dotster is an ICANN–accredited registrar.
c. *Cybersquatting* is registering another person's trademark as a domain name and offering it for sale. This is a violation of the Anticybersquatting Consumer Protection Act of 1999. Cybersquatting and trademark and copyright infringement are discussed in more detail in Chapter 5.

DECISION Yes. The U.S. Court of Appeals for the Sixth Circuit concluded that the lower court erred in granting the Dotster defendants' motion to dismiss for lack of personal jurisdiction. Bird had established that the court's exercise of jurisdiction over the Dotster defendants was proper.

REASON To be subject to jurisdiction "[f]irst, the defendant must purposefully avail himself of the privilege of acting in the forum state (the state in which a lawsuit is initiated) or causing a consequence in the forum state. Second, the cause of action must arise from the defendant's activities there. Finally, the acts of the defendant or consequences caused by the defendant must have a substantial enough connection with the forum state to make the exercise of jurisdiction over the defendant reasonable." All of these factors were present. Dotster "maintain[s] a website on which Ohio residents can register domain names" and "allegedly accept[ed] the business of 4,666 Ohio residents." Dotster's contacts with Ohio and Bird's claims "stem from [the] defendants' operation of the Dotster website." Also, among other things, "Ohio has a legitimate interest in protecting the business interests of its citizens, even though all of Bird's claims involve federal law." The court ruled against Bird on the substance of his claims, however, and ultimately affirmed the lower court's dismissal of the suit on this ground.

WHY IS THIS CASE IMPORTANT? *This case illustrates how defendants can be sued in states in which they may never have been physically present, provided they have had sufficient contact with that state's residents over the Internet.*

International Jurisdictional Issues Because the Internet is international in scope, international jurisdictional issues understandably have come to the fore. What seems to be emerging in the world's courts is a standard that echoes the "minimum-contacts" requirement applied by the U.S. courts. Most courts are indicating that minimum contacts—doing business within the jurisdiction, for example—are enough to compel a defendant to appear and that a physical presence is not necessary. The effect of this standard is that a business firm has to comply with the laws in any jurisdiction in which it targets customers for its products.

VENUE

VENUE
The geographic district in which an action is tried and from which the jury is selected.

Jurisdiction has to do with whether a court has authority to hear a case involving specific persons, property, or subject matter. **Venue**[6] is concerned with the most appropriate location for a trial. Two state courts (or two federal courts) may have

---

6. Pronounced *ven*-yoo.

the authority to exercise jurisdiction over a case, but it may be more appropriate or convenient to hear the case in one court than in the other.

Basically, the concept of venue reflects the policy that a court trying a suit should be in the geographic neighborhood (usually the county) where the incident leading to the lawsuit occurred or where the parties involved in the lawsuit reside. Venue in a civil case typically is where the defendant resides, whereas venue in a criminal case is normally where the crime occurred. Pretrial publicity or other factors, though, may require a change of venue to another community, especially in criminal cases when the defendant's right to a fair and impartial jury has been impaired. ■ **EXAMPLE 3.5** A change of venue from Oklahoma City to Denver, Colorado, was ordered for the trials of Timothy McVeigh and Terry Nichols, who had been indicted in connection with the 1995 bombing of the Alfred P. Murrah Federal Building in Oklahoma City. (At trial, both McVeigh and Nichols were convicted. McVeigh received the death penalty and was put to death by lethal injection in early 2001. Nichols was sentenced to life imprisonment.) ■

STANDING TO SUE

STANDING TO SUE
The requirement that an individual must have a sufficient stake in a controversy before he or she can bring a lawsuit. The plaintiff must demonstrate that he or she has been either injured or threatened with injury.

Before a person can bring a lawsuit before a court, the party must have **standing to sue,** or a sufficient "stake" in a matter to justify seeking relief through the court system. In other words, to have standing, a party must have a legally protected and tangible interest at stake in the litigation. The party bringing the lawsuit must have suffered a harm, or have been threatened by a harm, as a result of the action about which she or he has complained. At times, a person will have standing to sue on behalf of another person. ■ **EXAMPLE 3.6** Suppose that a child suffered serious injuries as a result of a defectively manufactured toy. Because the child is a minor, a lawsuit could be brought on his or her behalf by another person, such as the child's parent or legal guardian. ■

JUSTICIABLE CONTROVERSY
A controversy that is not hypothetical or academic but real and substantial; a requirement that must be satisfied before a court will hear a case.

Standing to sue also requires that the controversy at issue be a **justiciable**[7] **controversy**—a controversy that is real and substantial, as opposed to hypothetical or academic. ■ **EXAMPLE 3.7** In the above example, the child's parent could not sue the toy manufacturer merely on the ground that the toy was defective. The issue would become justiciable only if the child had actually been injured due to the defect in the toy as marketed. In other words, the parent normally could not ask the court to determine, for example, what damages might be obtained if the child had been injured, because this would be merely a hypothetical question. ■

■■ The State and Federal Court Systems

As mentioned earlier in this chapter, each state has its own court system. Additionally, there is a system of federal courts. Although state court systems differ, Exhibit 3–2 illustrates the basic organizational structure characteristic of the court systems in many states. The exhibit also shows how the federal court system is structured. We turn now to an examination of these court systems, beginning with the state courts.

---

7. Pronounced jus-*tish*-uh-bul.

EXHIBIT 3–2 FEDERAL COURTS AND STATE COURT SYSTEMS

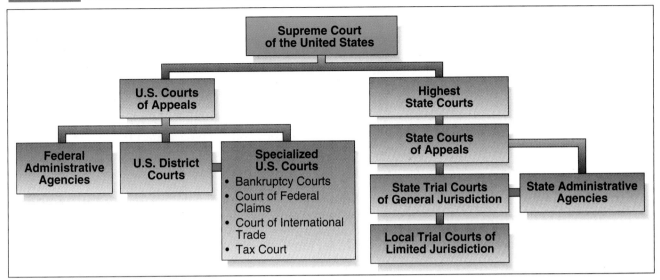

STATE COURT SYSTEMS

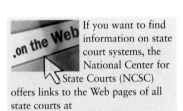
A mother talks with a social worker after a court awarded the mother custody of her child. Are child-custody matters decided by federal or state courts? (Albuquerque Journal, Mark Holm/AP Photo)

Typically, a state court system will include several levels, or tiers, of courts. As indicated in Exhibit 3–2, state courts may include (1) trial courts of limited jurisdiction, (2) trial courts of general jurisdiction, (3) appellate courts, and (4) the state's highest court (often called the state supreme court). Generally, any person who is a party to a lawsuit has the opportunity to plead the case before a trial court and then, if he or she loses, before at least one level of appellate court. Finally, if a federal statute or federal constitutional issue is involved in the decision of the state supreme court, that decision may be further appealed to the United States Supreme Court.

Judges in the state court system are usually elected by the voters for a specified term. State judicial elections or appointments vary significantly, however, from state to state. For example, in Iowa the governor appoints judges, and then the general population decides whether to confirm their appointment in the next general election. The states usually specify the number of years that the judge will serve. In contrast, as you will read shortly, judges in the federal court system are appointed by the president of the United States and, if they are confirmed by the Senate, hold office for life—unless they engage in blatantly illegal conduct.

Trial Courts   Trial courts are exactly what their name implies—courts in which trials are held and testimony taken. State trial courts have either general or limited jurisdiction. Trial courts that have general jurisdiction as to subject matter may be called county, district, superior, or circuit courts.[8] The jurisdiction of these courts is often determined by the size of the county in which the court sits. State trial courts of general jurisdiction have jurisdiction over a wide variety of subjects, including both civil disputes and criminal prosecutions. (In some states, trial courts of general jurisdiction may hear appeals from courts of limited jurisdiction.)

---

8. The name in Ohio is court of common pleas; the name in New York is supreme court.

SMALL CLAIMS COURT
A special court in which parties may litigate small claims (such as $5,000 or less). Attorneys are not required in small claims courts and, in some states, are not allowed to represent the parties.

Some courts of limited jurisdiction are called special inferior trial courts or minor judiciary courts. **Small claims courts** are inferior trial courts that hear only civil cases involving claims of less than a certain amount, such as $5,000 (the amount varies from state to state). Suits brought in small claims courts are generally conducted informally, and lawyers are not required. In a minority of states, lawyers are not even allowed to represent people in small claims courts for most purposes. Another example of an inferior trial court is a local municipal court that hears mainly traffic cases. Decisions of small claims courts and municipal courts may sometimes be appealed to a state trial court of general jurisdiction.

Other courts of limited jurisdiction as to subject matter include domestic relations courts, which handle primarily divorce actions and child-custody disputes, and probate courts, as mentioned earlier.

Appellate, or Reviewing, Courts   Every state has at least one court of appeals (appellate court, or reviewing court), which may be an intermediate appellate court or the state's highest court. About three-fourths of the states have intermediate appellate courts. Generally, courts of appeals do not conduct new trials, in which evidence is submitted to the court and witnesses are examined. Rather, an appellate court panel of three or more judges reviews the record of the case on appeal, which includes a transcript of the trial proceedings, and determines whether the trial court committed an error.

Usually, appellate courts do not look at questions of *fact* (such as whether a party did, in fact, commit a certain action, such as burning a flag) but at questions of *law* (such as whether the act of flag-burning is a form of speech protected by the First Amendment to the Constitution). Only a judge, not a jury, can rule on questions of law. Appellate courts normally defer to a trial court's findings on questions of fact because the trial court judge and jury were in a better position to evaluate testimony—by directly observing witnesses' gestures, demeanor, and nonverbal behavior during the trial. At the appellate level, the judges review the written transcript of the trial, which does not include these nonverbal elements.

An appellate court will challenge a trial court's finding of fact only when the finding is clearly erroneous (that is, when it is contrary to the evidence presented at trial) or when there is no evidence to support the finding. ■ **EXAMPLE 3.8** Suppose that a jury concluded that a manufacturer's product harmed the plaintiff but no evidence was submitted to the court to support that conclusion. In that situation, the appellate court would hold that the trial court's decision was erroneous. The options exercised by appellate courts will be further discussed later in this chapter. ■

BE CAREFUL   The decisions of a state's highest court are final on questions of state law.

Highest State Courts   The highest appellate court in a state is usually called the supreme court but may be called by some other name. For example, in both New York and Maryland, the highest state court is called the court of appeals. The decisions of each state's highest court are final on all questions of state law. Only when issues of federal law are involved can a decision made by a state's highest court be overruled by the United States Supreme Court.

THE FEDERAL COURT SYSTEM

The federal court system is basically a three-tiered model consisting of (1) U.S. district courts (trial courts of general jurisdiction) and various courts of limited jurisdiction, (2) U.S. courts of appeals (intermediate courts of appeals), and (3) the United States Supreme Court.

To find information about the federal court system and links to all federal courts, go to the home page of the federal judiciary at **http://www.uscourts.gov**.

Unlike state court judges, who are usually elected, federal court judges—including the justices of the Supreme Court—are appointed by the president of the United States and confirmed by the U.S. Senate. All federal judges receive lifetime appointments (because under Article III they "hold their offices during Good Behavior").

U.S. District Courts   At the federal level, the equivalent of a state trial court of general jurisdiction is the district court. There is at least one federal district court in every state. The number of judicial districts can vary over time, primarily owing to population changes and corresponding caseloads. Currently, there are ninety-four federal judicial districts.

U.S. district courts have original jurisdiction in federal matters. Federal cases typically originate in district courts. There are other courts with original, but special (or limited), jurisdiction, such as the federal bankruptcy courts and others shown in Exhibit 3–2 on page 83.

U.S. Courts of Appeals   In the federal court system, there are thirteen U.S. courts of appeals—also referred to as U.S. circuit courts of appeals. The federal courts of appeals for twelve of the circuits, including the U.S. Court of Appeals for the District of Columbia Circuit, hear appeals from the federal district courts located within their respective judicial circuits. The Court of Appeals for the Thirteenth Circuit, called the Federal Circuit, has national appellate jurisdiction over certain types of cases, such as cases involving patent law and cases in which the U.S. government is a defendant.

The decisions of the circuit courts of appeals are final in most cases, but appeal to the United States Supreme Court is possible. Exhibit 3–3 on the following page shows the geographic boundaries of the U.S. circuit courts of appeals and the boundaries of the U.S. district courts within each circuit.

The United States Supreme Court   The highest level of the three-tiered model of the federal court system is the United States Supreme Court. According to the language of Article III of the U.S. Constitution, there is only one national Supreme Court. All other courts in the federal system are considered "inferior." Congress is empowered to create other inferior courts as it deems necessary. The inferior courts that Congress has created include the second tier in our model—the U.S. courts of appeals—as well as the district courts and any other courts of limited, or specialized, jurisdiction.

The United States Supreme Court consists of nine justices. Although the Supreme Court has original, or trial, jurisdiction in rare instances (set forth in Article III, Section 2), most of its work is as an appeals court. The Supreme Court can review any case decided by any of the federal courts of appeals, and it also has appellate authority over some cases decided in the state courts.

Appeals to the Supreme Court.   To bring a case before the Supreme Court, a party requests the Court to issue a writ of *certiorari*. A **writ of *certiorari***[9] is an order issued by the Supreme Court to a lower court requiring the latter to send it the record of the case for review. The Court will not issue a writ unless at least four of the nine justices approve of it. This is called the **rule of four.** Whether the Court will issue a writ of *certiorari* is entirely within its discretion. The Court is not required

 .on the Web   The decisions of all of the U.S. courts of appeals, as well as those of the United States Supreme Court, are now published online shortly after the decisions are rendered. You can find these decisions and obtain information about the federal court system by accessing the Federal Court Locator at

http://www.law.vill.edu/ library/researchguides/ fedcourtlocator.asp.

WRIT OF *CERTIORARI*
A writ from a higher court asking the lower court for the record of a case.

RULE OF FOUR
A rule of the United States Supreme Court under which the Court will not issue a writ of *certiorari* unless at least four justices approve of the decision to issue the writ.

---

9. Pronounced sur-shee-uh-*rah*-ree.

EXHIBIT 3-3 BOUNDARIES OF THE U.S. COURTS OF APPEALS AND U.S. DISTRICT COURTS

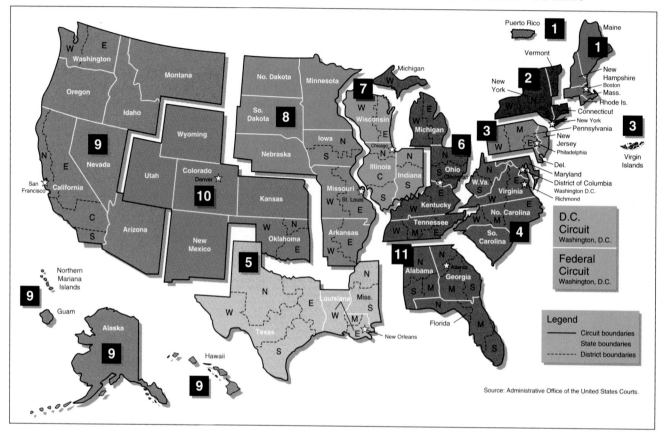

Source: Administrative Office of the United States Courts.

Legend
— Circuit boundaries
— State boundaries
--- District boundaries

to issue one, and most petitions for writs are denied. (Thousands of cases are filed with the Supreme Court each year; yet it hears, on average, fewer than one hundred of these cases.)[10] A denial is not a decision on the merits of a case, nor does it indicate agreement with the lower court's opinion. Furthermore, a denial of the writ has no value as a precedent.

Petitions Granted by the Court. Typically, the Court grants petitions when cases raise important constitutional questions or conflict with other state or federal court decisions. Similarly, if federal appellate courts are rendering inconsistent opinions on an important issue, the Supreme Court may review the case and issue a decision to define the law on the matter. The justices, however, never explain their reasons for hearing certain cases and not others, so it is difficult to predict which type of case the Court might select.

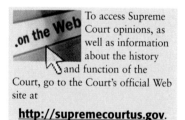

.on the Web To access Supreme Court opinions, as well as information about the history and function of the Court, go to the Court's official Web site at
http://supremecourtus.gov.

---

10. From the mid-1950s through the early 1990s, the Supreme Court reviewed more cases per year than it has in the last few years. In the Court's 1982–1983 term, for example, the Court issued opinions in 151 cases. In contrast, in its 2002–2003 term, the Court issued opinions in only 80 cases.

The justices of the United States Supreme Court (as of 2004) are, seated left to right, Antonin Scalia, John Paul Stevens, Chief Justice William H. Rehnquist, Sandra Day O'Connor, and Anthony M. Kennedy; and standing left to right, Ruth Bader Ginsburg, David H. Souter, Clarence Thomas, and Stephen Breyer. Does the fact that these justices are appointed for life have any effect on the decisions they reach in the cases they hear? Explain. (Photo by Richard Strauss, Smithsonian Institution, Collection of the Supreme Court of the United States)

Following a State Court Case

To illustrate the procedures that would be followed in a civil lawsuit brought in a state court, we present a hypothetical case and follow it through the state court system. The case involves an automobile accident in which Kevin Anderson, driving a Mercedes, struck Lisa Marconi, driving a Ford Taurus. The accident occurred at the intersection of Wilshire Boulevard and Rodeo Drive in Beverly Hills, California. Marconi suffered personal injuries, incurring medical and hospital expenses as well as lost wages for four months. Anderson and Marconi are unable to agree on a settlement, and Marconi sues Anderson. Marconi is the plaintiff, and Anderson is the defendant. Both are represented by lawyers.

During each phase of the **litigation** (the process of working a lawsuit through the court system), Marconi and Anderson will be required to observe strict procedural requirements. A large body of law—procedural law—establishes the rules and standards for determining disputes in courts. Procedural rules are very complex, and they vary from court to court and from state to state. There is a set of federal rules of procedure as well as various sets of rules for state courts. Additionally, the applicable procedures will depend on whether the case is a civil or criminal proceeding. Generally, the Marconi-Anderson civil lawsuit will involve the procedures discussed in the following subsections. Keep in mind that attempts to settle the case may be ongoing throughout the trial.

THE PLEADINGS

The complaint and answer (and the counterclaim and reply)—all of which are discussed below—taken together are called the **pleadings.** The pleadings inform each party of the other's claims and specify the issues (disputed questions) involved in the case. Because the rules of procedure vary depending on the jurisdiction of the court, the style and form of the pleadings may look quite different in different states.

LITIGATION
The process of resolving a dispute through the court system.

PLEADINGS
Statements made by the plaintiff and the defendant in a lawsuit that detail the facts, charges, and defenses involved in the litigation. The complaint and answer are part of the pleadings.

The Plaintiff's Complaint　Marconi's suit against Anderson commences when her lawyer files a **complaint** with the appropriate court. The complaint contains a statement alleging (asserting to the court, in a pleading) the facts necessary for the court to take jurisdiction, a brief summary of the facts necessary to show that the plaintiff is entitled to a remedy, and a statement of the remedy the plaintiff is seeking. Exhibit 3–4 illustrates how the complaint might read in the Marconi-Anderson case.

COMPLAINT
The pleading made by a plaintiff alleging wrongdoing on the part of the defendant; the document that, when filed with a court, initiates a lawsuit.

EXHIBIT 3–4 EXAMPLE OF A TYPICAL COMPLAINT

IN THE LOS ANGELES SUPERIOR COURT
COUNTY OF LOS ANGELES, STATE OF CALIFORNIA

Lisa Marconi
　　　　Plaintiff,

　　　　v.

Kevin Anderson
　　　　Defendant.

CIVIL NO. 8–1026

COMPLAINT

Comes now the plaintiff and for her cause of action against the defendant alleges and states as follows:

1. The jurisdiction of this court is based on Section 86 of the California Civil Code.
2. This action is between plaintiff, a California resident living at 1434 Palm Drive, Anaheim, California, and defendant, a California resident living at 6950 Garrison Avenue, Los Angeles, California.
3. On September 10, 2005, plaintiff, Lisa Marconi, was exercising good driving habits and reasonable care in driving her car through the intersection of Rodeo Drive and Wilshire Boulevard when defendant, Kevin Anderson, negligently drove his vehicle through a red light at the intersection and collided with plaintiff's vehicle. Defendant was negligent in the operation of the vehicle as to:

　　a. Speed,
　　b. Lookout,
　　c. Management and control.

4. As a result of the collision plaintiff suffered severe physical injury that prevented her from working and property damage to her car. The costs she incurred included $10,000 in medical bills, $9,000 in lost wages, and $5,000 for automobile repairs.

WHEREFORE, plaintiff demands judgment against the defendant for the sum of $24,000 plus interest at the maximum legal rate and the costs of this action.

By *Roger Harrington*
Roger Harrington
Attorney for the Plaintiff
800 Orange Avenue
Anaheim, CA 91426

Complaints may be lengthy or brief, depending on the complexity of the case and the rules of the jurisdiction.

After the complaint has been filed, the sheriff, a deputy of the county, or another *process server* (one who delivers a complaint and summons) serves a **summons** and a copy of the complaint on defendant Anderson. The summons notifies Anderson that he must file an answer to the complaint with both the court and the plaintiff's attorney within a specified time period (usually twenty to thirty days). The summons also informs Anderson that failure to answer may result in a **default judgment** for the plaintiff, meaning the plaintiff will be awarded the damages alleged in her complaint.

The Defendant's Answer   The defendant's **answer** either admits the statements or allegations set forth in the complaint or denies them and outlines any defenses that the defendant may have. If Anderson admits to all of Marconi's allegations in his answer, the court will enter a judgment for Marconi. If Anderson denies any of Marconi's allegations, the litigation will go forward.

Anderson can deny Marconi's allegations and set forth his own claim that Marconi was in fact negligent and therefore owes him money for damages to his Mercedes. This is appropriately called a **counterclaim**. If Anderson files a counterclaim, Marconi will have to answer it with a pleading, normally called a **reply**, which has the same characteristics as an answer.

Anderson can also admit the truth of Marconi's complaint but raise new facts that may result in dismissal of the action. This is called raising an affirmative defense. For example, Anderson could assert the expiration of the time period under the relevant statute of limitations (a state or federal statute that sets the maximum time period during which a certain action can be brought or rights enforced) as an affirmative defense.

Motion to Dismiss   A **motion to dismiss** requests the court to dismiss the case for stated reasons. A defendant often makes a motion to dismiss before filing an answer to the plaintiff's complaint. Grounds for dismissal of a case include improper delivery of the complaint and summons, improper venue, and the plaintiff's failure to state a claim for which a court could grant relief (a remedy). For example, if Marconi had suffered no injuries or losses as a result of Anderson's negligence, Anderson could move to have the case dismissed because Marconi had not stated a claim for which relief could be granted.

If the judge grants the motion to dismiss, the plaintiff generally is given time to file an amended complaint. If the judge denies the motion, the suit will go forward, and the defendant must then file an answer. Note that if Marconi wishes to discontinue the suit because, for example, an out-of-court settlement has been reached, she can likewise move for dismissal. The court can also dismiss the case on its own motion.

PRETRIAL MOTIONS

Either party may attempt to get the case dismissed before trial through the use of various pretrial motions. We have already mentioned the motion to dismiss. Two other important pretrial motions are the motion for judgment on the pleadings and the motion for summary judgment.

At the close of the pleadings, either party may make a **motion for judgment on the pleadings,** or on the merits of the case. The judge will grant the motion only when there is no dispute over the facts of the case and the sole issue to be resolved

---

SUMMONS
A document informing a defendant that a legal action has been commenced against him or her and that the defendant must appear in court on a certain date to answer the plaintiff's complaint. The document is delivered by a sheriff or any other person so authorized.

DEFAULT JUDGMENT
A judgment entered by a court against a defendant who has failed to appear in court to answer or defend against the plaintiff's claim.

ANSWER
Procedurally, a defendant's response to the plaintiff's complaint.

COUNTERCLAIM
A claim made by a defendant in a civil lawsuit against the plaintiff. In effect, the defendant is suing the plaintiff.

REPLY
Procedurally, a plaintiff's response to a defendant's answer.

MOTION TO DISMISS
A pleading in which a defendant asserts that the plaintiff's claim fails to state a cause of action (that is, has no basis in law) or that there are other grounds on which a suit should be dismissed.

MOTION FOR JUDGMENT ON THE PLEADINGS
A motion by either party to a lawsuit at the close of the pleadings requesting the court to decide the issue solely on the pleadings without proceeding to trial. The motion will be granted only if no facts are in dispute.

MOTION FOR SUMMARY JUDGMENT
A motion requesting the court to enter a judgment without proceeding to trial. The motion can be based on evidence outside the pleadings and will be granted only if no facts are in dispute.

is a question of law. In deciding on the motion, the judge may consider only the evidence contained in the pleadings.

In contrast, in a **motion for summary judgment** the court may consider evidence outside the pleadings, such as sworn statements (affidavits) by parties or witnesses or other documents relating to the case. A motion for summary judgment can be made by either party. As with the motion for judgment on the pleadings, a motion for summary judgment will be granted only if there are no genuine questions of fact and the sole question is a question of law.

DISCOVERY

DISCOVERY
A phase in the litigation process during which the opposing parties may obtain information from each other and from third parties prior to trial.

Before a trial begins, each party can use a number of procedural devices to obtain information and gather evidence about the case from the other party or from third parties. The process of obtaining such information is known as **discovery**. Discovery includes gaining access to witnesses, documents, records, and other types of evidence.

The Federal Rules of Civil Procedure and similar rules in the states set forth the guidelines for discovery activity. The rules governing discovery are designed to make sure that a witness or a party is not unduly harassed, that privileged material (communications that need not be presented in court) is safeguarded, and that only matters relevant to the case at hand are discoverable.

Discovery prevents surprises at trial by giving parties access to evidence that might otherwise be hidden. This allows both parties to learn as much as they can about what to expect at a trial before they reach the courtroom. It also serves to narrow the issues so that trial time is spent on the main questions in the case.

DEPOSITION
The testimony of a party to a lawsuit or a witness taken under oath before a trial.

Depositions and Interrogatories   Discovery can involve the use of depositions or interrogatories, or both. **Depositions** are sworn testimony by a party to the lawsuit or any witness. The person being deposed (the deponent) answers questions asked by the attorneys, and the questions and answers are recorded by an authorized court official and sworn to and signed by the deponent. (Occasionally, written depositions are taken when witnesses are unable to appear in person.) The answers given to depositions will, of course, help the attorneys prepare their cases. They can also be used in court to impeach (challenge the credibility of) a party or a witness who changes testimony at the trial. In addition, the answers given in a deposition can be used as testimony if the witness is not available at trial.

INTERROGATORIES
A series of written questions for which written answers are prepared, usually with the assistance of the party's attorney, and then signed under oath by a party to a lawsuit.

Interrogatories are written questions for which written answers are prepared and then signed under oath. The main difference between interrogatories and written depositions is that interrogatories are directed to a party to the lawsuit (the plaintiff or the defendant), not to a witness, and the party can prepare answers with the aid of an attorney. The scope of interrogatories is broader because parties are obligated to answer questions, even if that means disclosing information from their records and files.

Other Information   A party can serve a written request on the other party for an admission of the truth of matters relating to the trial. Any matter admitted under such a request is conclusively established for the trial. For example, Marconi can ask Anderson to admit that he was driving at a speed of forty-five miles an hour. A request for admission saves time at trial because the parties will not have to spend time proving facts on which they already agree.

A party can also gain access to documents and other items not in her or his possession in order to inspect and examine them. Likewise, a party can gain "entry on land" to inspect the premises. Anderson's attorney, for example, normally can gain permission to inspect and duplicate Marconi's car repair bills.

When the physical or mental condition of one party is in question, the opposing party can ask the court to order a physical or mental examination. If the court is willing to make the order, which it will do only if the need for the information outweighs the right to privacy of the person to be examined, the opposing party can obtain the results of the examination.

Electronic Discovery   Any relevant material, including information stored electronically, can be the object of a discovery request. Electronic evidence, or **e-evidence**, consists of all types of computer-generated or electronically recorded information, including e-mail, voice mail, spreadsheets, word processing documents, and other data. E-evidence is important because it can reveal significant facts that are not discoverable by other means. For example, whenever a person is working on a computer, information is being recorded on the hard drive disk without ever being saved by the user. This information includes the file's location, path, creator, date created, date last accessed, concealed notes, earlier versions, passwords, and formatting. It reveals information about how, when, and by whom a document was created, accessed, modified, and transmitted. This information can be obtained from the file only in its electronic format—not from printed-out versions.

The federal rules and most state rules (as well as court decisions) now specifically allow parties to obtain discovery of electronic "data compilations" (or e-evidence). Although traditional means, such as interrogatories and depositions, may still be used to find out about the e-evidence, the parties must usually hire an expert to retrieve the evidence in its electronic format. Using special software, the expert can reconstruct e-mail exchanges to establish who knew what and when they knew it. The expert can even recover files from a computer that the user thought had been deleted. Reviewing back-up copies of documents and e-mail can provide useful—and often quite damaging—information about how a particular matter progressed over several weeks or months.

Although electronic discovery has significant advantages over paper discovery, it is also time consuming and expensive. Who should pay the costs associated with electronic discovery? This chapter's *Adapting the Law to the Online Environment* feature on the next page discusses how the law is evolving to address this issue.

PRETRIAL CONFERENCE

Either party or the court can request a pretrial conference, or hearing. Usually, the hearing consists of an informal discussion between the judge and the opposing attorneys after discovery has taken place. The purpose of the hearing is to explore the possibility of a settlement without trial and, if this is not possible, to identify the matters that are in dispute and to plan the course of the trial.

JURY SELECTION

A trial can be held with or without a jury. The Seventh Amendment to the U.S. Constitution guarantees the right to a jury trial for cases in federal courts when the amount in controversy exceeds $20. Most states have similar guarantees in their own constitutions (although the threshold dollar amount is higher than $20). The right to a trial by jury does not have to be exercised, and many cases are tried without a jury. In most states and in federal courts, one of the parties must request a jury, or the right is presumed to be waived.

E-EVIDENCE
A type of evidence that consists of computer-generated or electronically recorded information, including e-mail, voice mail, spreadsheets, word processing documents, and other data.

Picking the "right" jury is often an important aspect of litigation strategy, and a number of firms now specialize in jury consulting services. You can learn more about these services by going to the Web site of the Jury Research Institute at **http://www.jri-inc.com**.

ADAPTING THE LAW TO THE ONLINE ENVIRONMENT

Who Bears the Costs of Electronic Discovery?

Traditionally, the party responding to a discovery request must pay the expenses involved in obtaining the requested materials. If compliance would be too burdensome or too costly, however, the judge can either limit the scope of the request or shift some or all of the costs to the requesting party. How do these traditional rules governing discovery apply to requests for electronic evidence?

WHY COURTS MIGHT SHIFT THE COSTS OF ELECTRONIC DISCOVERY

Electronic discovery has dramatically increased the costs associated with complying with discovery requests. It is no longer simply a matter of photocopying paper documents. Now the responding party may need to hire computer forensics experts to make "image" copies of desktop, laptop, and server hard drives, as well as removable storage media (including CD-ROMs, DVDs, and Zip drives), back-up tapes, voice mail, cell phones, and any other device that digitally stores data.

In cases involving multiple parties or large corporations with many offices and employees, the electronic discovery process can easily run into hundreds of thousands—if not millions—of dollars. For example, in one case concert promoters alleged that thirty separate defendant companies had engaged in discriminatory practices. The federal district court hearing the case found that the complete restoration of the back-up tapes of just one of those defendants would cost $9.75 million. Acquiring 200,000 e-mail messages from another defendant would cost between $43,000 and $84,000, with an additional $247,000 to have an attorney review the retrieved documents. Restoring the 523 back-up tapes of a third defendant would cost $395,000 and another $120,000 for the attorney to review them. The judge hearing the case decided that

both plaintiffs and defendants would share in these discovery costs.[a]

WHAT FACTORS DO COURTS CONSIDER IN DECIDING WHETHER TO SHIFT COSTS?

Increasingly, the courts are shifting part of the costs of obtaining electronic discovery to the party requesting it (which is usually the plaintiff). At what point, however, should this cost-shifting occur? In *Zubulake v. UBS Warburg LLC,*[b] the court identified a three-step analysis for deciding disputes over discovery costs. First, if the data are kept in an accessible format, the usual rules of discovery apply: the responding party should pay the costs of producing responsive data. A court should consider cost-shifting *only* when electronic data are in a relatively inaccessible form, such as in back-up tapes or deleted files. Second, the court should determine what data may be found on the inaccessible media. Requiring the responding party to restore and produce responsive documents from a small sample of the requested medium is a sensible approach in most cases. Third, the court should consider a series of other factors, including, for example, the availability of the information from other sources, the total cost of production compared to the amount in controversy, and each party's ability to pay these costs.

FOR CRITICAL ANALYSIS

The court in the Zubulake *case noted that "as large companies increasingly move to entirely paper-free environments, the frequent use of cost-shifting will have the effect of crippling discovery," especially in cases in which private parties are suing large corporations. Why might cost-shifting thwart discovery? Who would benefit if courts considered cost-shifting in every case involving electronic discovery?*

a. *Rowe Entertainment Inc. v. William Morris Agency,* 2002 WL 975713 (S.D.N.Y.).
b. 2003 WL 21087884 (S.D.N.Y.).

VOIR DIRE
An old French phrase meaning "to speak the truth." In legal language, the phrase refers to the process in which the attorneys question prospective jurors to learn about their backgrounds, attitudes, biases, and other characteristics that may affect their ability to serve as impartial jurors.

Before a jury trial commences, a jury must be selected. The jury selection process is known as *voir dire.*[11] During *voir dire* in most jurisdictions, attorneys for the plaintiff and the defendant ask prospective jurors oral questions to determine whether a potential jury member is biased or has any connection with a party to the action or with a prospective witness. In some jurisdictions, the judge may do all or part of the questioning based on written inquiries submitted by counsel for the parties.

---

11. Pronounced vwahr *deehr.*

During *voir dire*, a party may challenge a certain number of prospective jurors *peremptorily*—that is, ask that an individual not be sworn in as a juror without providing any reason. Alternatively, a party may challenge a prospective juror *for cause*—that is, provide a reason why an individual should not be sworn in as a juror. If the judge grants the challenge, the individual is asked to step down. A prospective juror may not be excluded from the jury by the use of discriminatory challenges, however, such as those based on racial criteria[12] or gender.[13]

AT THE TRIAL

At the beginning of the trial, the attorneys present their opening arguments, setting forth the facts that they expect to provide during the trial. Then the plaintiff's case is presented. In our hypothetical case, Marconi's lawyer would introduce evidence (relevant documents, exhibits, and the testimony of witnesses) to support Marconi's position. The defendant has the opportunity to challenge any evidence introduced and to cross-examine any of the plaintiff's witnesses.

At the end of the plaintiff's case, the defendant's attorney has the opportunity to ask the judge to direct a verdict for the defendant on the ground that the plaintiff has presented no evidence that would justify the granting of the plaintiff's remedy. This is called a **motion for a directed verdict** (known in federal courts as a *motion for judgment as a matter of law*). If the motion is not granted (it seldom is), the defendant's attorney then presents the evidence and witnesses for the defendant's case. At the conclusion of the defendant's case, the defendant's attorney has another opportunity to make a motion for a directed verdict. The plaintiff's attorney can challenge any evidence introduced and cross-examine the defendant's witnesses.

After the defense concludes its presentation, the attorneys present their closing arguments, each urging a verdict in favor of her or his client. The judge instructs the jury in the law that applies to the case (these instructions are often called *charges*), and the jury retires to the jury room to deliberate a verdict. In the Marconi-Anderson case, the jury will not only decide for the plaintiff or for the defendant but, if it finds for the plaintiff, will also decide on the amount of the **award** (the money to be paid to her).

POSTTRIAL MOTIONS

After the jury has rendered its verdict, either party may make a posttrial motion. If Marconi wins, and Anderson's attorney has previously moved for a directed verdict, Anderson's attorney may make a **motion for judgment n.o.v.** (from the Latin *non obstante veredicto*, which means "notwithstanding the verdict"—called a *motion for judgment as a matter of law* in the federal courts) in Anderson's favor on the ground that the jury's verdict in favor of Marconi was unreasonable and erroneous. If the judge decides that the jury's verdict was reasonable in light of the evidence presented at trial, the motion will be denied. If the judge agrees with Anderson's attorney, then he or she will set the jury's verdict aside and enter a judgment in favor of Anderson.

Alternatively, Anderson could make a **motion for a new trial**, requesting the judge to set aside the adverse verdict and to hold a new trial. The motion will be granted if the judge is convinced, after looking at all the evidence, that the jury was in error

TAKE NOTE A prospective juror cannot be excluded solely on the basis of his or her race or gender.

MOTION FOR A DIRECTED VERDICT
In a jury trial, a motion for the judge to take the decision out of the hands of the jury and to direct a verdict for the party who filed the motion on the ground that the other party has not produced sufficient evidence to support her or his claim.

AWARD
In litigation, the amount of money awarded to a plaintiff in a civil lawsuit as damages. In the context of alternative dispute resolution, the decision rendered by an arbitrator.

MOTION FOR JUDGMENT N.O.V.
A motion requesting the court to grant judgment in favor of the party making the motion on the ground that the jury's verdict against him or her was unreasonable and erroneous.

MOTION FOR A NEW TRIAL
A motion asserting that the trial was so fundamentally flawed (because of error, newly discovered evidence, prejudice, or other reason) that a new trial is necessary to prevent a miscarriage of justice.

---

12. *Batson v. Kentucky,* 476 U.S. 79, 106 S.Ct. 1712, 90 L.Ed.2d 69 (1986).
13. *J.E.B. v. Alabama ex rel. T.B.,* 511 U.S. 127, 114 S.Ct. 1419, 128 L.Ed.2d 89 (1994). (*Ex rel.* is Latin for *ex relatione.* The phrase refers to an action brought on behalf of the state, by the attorney general, at the instigation of an individual who has a private interest in the matter.)

but does not feel it is appropriate to grant judgment for the other side. A new trial may also be granted on the ground of newly discovered evidence, misconduct by the participants or the jury during the trial, or error by the judge.

THE APPEAL

Assume here that any posttrial motion is denied and that Anderson appeals the case. (If Marconi wins but receives a smaller money award than she sought, she can appeal also.) A notice of appeal must be filed with the clerk of the trial court within a prescribed time. Anderson now becomes the appellant, or petitioner, and Marconi becomes the appellee, or respondent.

Filing the Appeal   Anderson's attorney files with the appellate court the record on appeal, which includes the pleadings, the trial transcript, the judge's rulings on motions made by the parties, and other trial-related documents. Anderson's attorney will also provide a condensation of the record, known as an *abstract*, which is filed with the reviewing court along with the brief. The **brief** is a formal legal document outlining the facts and issues of the case, the judge's rulings or jury's findings that should be reversed or modified, the applicable law, and arguments on Anderson's behalf (citing applicable statutes and relevant cases as precedents).

Marconi's attorney will file an answering brief. Anderson's attorney can file a reply to Marconi's brief, although it is not required. The reviewing court then considers the case.

Appellate Review   As mentioned earlier, a court of appeals does not hear evidence. Rather, it reviews the record for errors of law. Its decision concerning a case is based on the record on appeal, the abstracts, and the attorneys' briefs. The attorneys can present oral arguments, after which the case is taken under advisement. In general, appellate courts do not reverse findings of fact unless the findings are unsupported or contradicted by the evidence.

If the reviewing court believes that an error was committed during the trial or that the jury was improperly instructed, the judgment will be *reversed*. Sometimes the case will be *remanded* (sent back to the court that originally heard the case) for a new trial. Even when a case is remanded to a trial court for further proceedings, however, the appellate court normally spells out how the relevant law should be interpreted and applied to the case.

■ EXAMPLE 3.9 A case may be remanded for several reasons. For instance, if the appellate court decides that a judge improperly granted summary judgment, the case will be remanded for a trial. If the appellate court decides that the trial judge erroneously applied the law, the case will be remanded for a new trial, with instructions to the trial court to apply the law as clarified by the appellate court. If the appellate court decides that the trial jury's award of damages was too high, the case will be remanded with instructions to reduce the damages award. ■ In most cases, the judgment of the lower court is *affirmed*, resulting in the enforcement of the court's judgment or decree.

Appeal to a Higher Appellate Court   If the reviewing court is an intermediate appellate court, the losing party normally may appeal to the state supreme court (the highest state court). Such a petition corresponds to a petition for a writ of

BRIEF
A formal legal document submitted by the attorney for the appellant or the appellee (in answer to the appellant's brief) to an appellate court when a case is appealed. The appellant's brief outlines the facts and issues of the case, the judge's rulings or jury's findings that should be reversed or modified, the applicable law, and the arguments on the client's behalf.

certiorari from the United States Supreme Court. If the petition is granted (in some states, a petition is automatically granted), new briefs must be filed before the state supreme court, and the attorneys may be allowed or requested to present oral arguments. Like the intermediate appellate court, the supreme court may reverse or affirm the appellate court's decision or remand the case. At this point, unless a federal question is at issue, the case has reached its end.

ENFORCING THE JUDGMENT

The uncertainties of the litigation process are compounded by the lack of guarantees that any judgment will be enforceable. Even if a plaintiff wins an award of damages in court, the defendant may not have sufficient assets or insurance to cover that amount. Usually, one of the factors considered before a lawsuit is initiated is whether the defendant has sufficient assets to cover the amount of damages sought, should the plaintiff win the case. What other factors should be considered when deciding whether to initiate a lawsuit? See the *Application* at the end of this chapter for answers to this question.

 For links to every trial-level court in the United States that currently has a Web site, go to the Web site of the Nation's Courts Directory at

http://www.courts.net.

■ The Courts Adapt to the Online World

We have already mentioned that the courts have attempted to adapt traditional jurisdictional concepts to the online world. Not surprisingly, the Internet has also brought about changes in court procedures and practices, including new methods for filing pleadings and other documents and issuing decisions and opinions. Several courts are experimenting with electronic delivery, such as via the Internet or CD-ROM. Some jurisdictions are exploring the possibility of cyber courts, in which legal proceedings could be conducted totally online.

ELECTRONIC FILING

The federal court system first experimented with an electronic filing system in January 1996, in an asbestos case heard by the U.S. District Court for the Northern District of Ohio. Currently, a number of federal courts permit attorneys to file documents electronically in certain types of cases. At last count, more than 130,000 documents in approximately 10,000 cases had been filed electronically in federal courts. The Administrative Office of the U.S. Courts is considering permitting electronic filing in all U.S. district courts nationwide.

State and local courts are also setting up electronic filing systems. Since the late 1990s, the court system in Pima County, Arizona, has been accepting pleadings via e-mail. The supreme court of the state of Washington also now accepts online filings of litigation documents. In addition, electronic filing projects are being developed in other states, including California, Idaho, Kansas, Maryland, Michigan, Texas, Utah, and Virginia. The state of Colorado implemented the first statewide court e-filing system and currently allows e-filing in over sixty courts. Generally, when electronic filing is made available, it is optional. In early 2001, however, a trial court judge in the District of Columbia launched a pilot project that *required* attorneys to use electronic filing for all documents relating to certain types of civil cases.

The expenses associated with an appeal can be considerable, and e-filing can add substantially to the cost. In some cases, appellants who successfully appeal a judgment are entitled to be awarded their costs, including an amount for printing the copies of the record on appeal and the briefs. In the following case, the appellants spent $16,112 for the paper copies and an additional $16,065 to prepare and submit briefs and other documents in an electronic format. Should the appellants be reimbursed for these expenses?

CASE 3.3 Phansalkar v. Andersen, Weinroth & Co.

United States Court of Appeals,
Second Circuit, 2004.
356 F.3d 188.

FACTS Andersen, Weinroth & Company (AW) is a small firm that finds and creates investment opportunities for itself, its partners, and other investors. AW's income includes returns on its investments, fees paid by its investors, and the compensation and other benefits earned by its employees for their service on boards of directors of the companies with which AW does business. Some AW employees receive stock and "investment opportunities" rather than salaries. Rohit Phansalkar worked for AW from February 1998 until June 2000, when he became the chairman and chief executive officer of Osicom Technologies, Inc. After Phansalkar left, AW refused to pay him the returns on certain "investment opportunities" that he had been given while at AW. Phansalkar filed a suit in a federal district court against AW, alleging in part breach of contract. The court awarded Phansalkar more than $4.4 million. AW appealed to the U.S. Court of Appeals for the Second Circuit, which reversed this judgment on the ground that Phansalkar had acted with disloyalty during his employment with AW by failing to disclose compensation and benefits that he received for serving on various boards. AW then asked for an award of the amount that it spent to create copies of the briefs and other documents involved in the appeal in hyperlinked CD-ROM format.

ISSUE Could AW recover the costs associated with preparing and submitting electronic copies of the appeal documents?

DECISION No. The U.S. Court of Appeals for the Second Circuit ruled that AW could not recover these costs.

REASON The court recognized that it had been one of the first courts to encourage the submission of electronic briefs. "The submission of an electronic version of a paper brief very likely entails small incremental costs. CD-ROM submissions that hyperlink briefs to relevant sections of the appellate record are more versatile, more useful, and considerably more expensive," however. The court could find "no local rule or holding * * * that allocates CD-ROM costs," and "[n]o guidance" in the *Federal Rules of Civil Procedure,* which authorize an award of costs incurred to produce "necessary" copies of briefs and other costs of an appeal. Factors that are important in determining if a cost is authorized by the rules include "whether the party seeking disallowance has clearly consented to the expense; whether a court has previously approved the expense; and whether the alternative arrangement costs less than the expense specifically authorized." None of these factors was present in this case. In fact, because AW "incurred costs both to produce hard copies of their appellate materials *and* to produce hyperlinked CD-ROM copies, * * * the CD-ROM costs in this case were duplicative." The court also noted that "there is no written stipulation or understanding between the parties concerning the allocation of the incremental costs of this useful technology."

FOR CRITICAL ANALYSIS—Social Consideration
How might the result in this case have been different if the court had required, rather than merely encouraged, the submission of electronic copies of the appeal documents?

COURTS ONLINE

Most courts today have sites on the Web. Of course, each court decides what to make available at its site. Some courts display only the names of court personnel and office phone numbers. Others add court rules and forms. Many include judicial decisions, although generally the sites do not feature archives of old decisions. Instead, decisions usually are available online for a limited time. For example, California keeps opinions online for only sixty days. In addition, in some states, such as California and Florida, court clerks offer docket information and other searchable databases online.

Appellate court decisions are often posted online immediately after they are rendered. Recent decisions of the U.S. courts of appeals, for example, are available online at their Web sites. The United States Supreme Court also has an official Web site and publishes its opinions there immediately after they are announced to the public. (These Web sites are listed elsewhere in this chapter in the *On the Web* features.) In fact, even decisions that are designated as unpublished opinions by the appellate courts are often published online. What is the value of an unpublished decision in today's courts? See this chapter's *Letter of the Law* feature for a discussion of this issue.

LETTER OF THE LAW Should "Unpublished" Opinions Be Law?

Appellate courts churn out thousands of decisions that are labeled "unpublished" and are not included in appellate reporters. Typically, these decisions do not contain the same detailed recital of facts or comprehensive legal analysis as published opinions. The idea is that by designating the opinion as unpublished, the judges will be able to spend less time writing and editing the decision. Traditionally, the rules of many courts banned the citation of unpublished decisions.

The rules regarding unpublished decisions may be changing, however. As a 2000 opinion by the U.S. Court of Appeals for the Eighth Circuit pointed out, it goes against the doctrine of precedent *not* to allow these unpublished decisions to affect later court decisions, and it may even be unconstitutional.[a] After all,

the role of the judge is not to invent new law but to interpret the law in a particular context by looking at previous court decisions. This opinion—as well as the online posting of unpublished decisions—has influenced judges' views around the nation. Some courts now permit unpublished decisions to be cited, though usually as persuasive rather than binding authority. In 2002, for example, the U.S. Court of Appeals for the D.C. Circuit adopted new rules that allow unpublished decisions to be cited as precedent. Some state courts, such as those in Texas, are also beginning to allow unpublished opinions to be cited.

THE BOTTOM LINE
Increasingly, judges are allowing unpublished opinions to be cited as authority in their courtrooms and permitting the reasoning used in those cases to persuade their way of thinking.

a. *Anastasoff v. United States,* 223 F.3d 898 (8th Cir. 2000); opinion withdrawn on rehearing *en banc,* 235 F.3d 1054 (8th Cir. 2000). This opinion involved a woman who sought a tax refund for overpaid taxes. When the Internal Revenue Service refunded the taxes, the decision was withdrawn because the tax issue was resolved.

CYBER COURTS AND PROCEEDINGS

Smith & Johnson, P.C., a Michigan law firm, offers a summary of Michigan's cyber court legislation on its Web page at

http://www. smith-johnson.com/ businesslaw/cybercourt.htm.

Someday, litigants may be able to use cyber courts, in which judicial proceedings take place only on the Internet. The parties to a case could meet online to make their arguments and present their evidence. This might be done with e-mail submissions, through video cameras, in designated "chat" rooms, at closed sites, or through the use of other Internet facilities. These courtrooms could be efficient and economical. We might also see the use of virtual lawyers, judges, and juries—and possibly the replacement of court personnel with computer software. Already the state of Michigan has passed legislation creating cyber courts that will hear cases involving technology issues and high-tech businesses. Many lawyers predict that other states will follow suit.

The courts may also use the Internet in other ways. In a groundbreaking decision in early 2001, for example, a Florida county court granted "virtual" visitation rights in a couple's divorce proceeding. Although the court granted custody of the couple's ten-year-old daughter to the father, the court also ordered each parent to buy a computer and a videoconferencing system so that the mother could "visit" with her child via the Internet at any time.[14]

ETHICAL ISSUE 3.1

How will online access to courts affect privacy? From a practical perspective, trial court records, although normally available to the public, remain obscure. Because the decisions of most state trial courts (and some federal courts) are not published, someone must be strongly motivated to go to the trouble of traveling to the relevant courthouse in person to access the documents. As online access to court records increases and electronic filing becomes the norm, this "practical obscurity," as lawyers call it, may soon disappear. Electronic filing on a nationwide basis would open up all court documents to anyone with an Internet connection and a Web browser. Utilizing special "data-mining" software, anyone could go online and within just a few minutes access information—ranging from personal health records to financial reports to criminal violations—from dozens of courts. This means that serious privacy issues are at stake. Should the courts restrict public access to certain types of documents, such as bankruptcy records or documents containing personal information that is not directly related to the legal issue being decided? Many courts are struggling with these questions and have taken a myriad of different approaches. Some courts make civil case information available but restrict Internet access to criminal case information. Other courts, such as those in Florida, have deemed certain types of documents and court proceedings confidential and no longer post this information online. ■[15]

■ Alternative Dispute Resolution

ALTERNATIVE DISPUTE RESOLUTION (ADR)
The resolution of disputes in ways other than those involved in the traditional judicial process. Negotiation, mediation, and arbitration are forms of ADR.

Litigation is expensive. It is also time consuming. Because of the backlog of cases pending in many courts, several years may pass before a case is actually tried. For these and other reasons, more and more businesspersons are turning to **alternative dispute resolution (ADR)** as a means of settling their disputes.

---

14. For a discussion of this case, see Shelley Emling, "After the Divorce, Internet Visits?" *Austin American-Statesman,* January 30, 2001, pp. A1 and A10.
15. *In re Report of Supreme Court Workgroup on Public Records,* 825 So.2d 889 (Fla. 2002).

Methods of ADR range from neighbors sitting down over a cup of coffee in an attempt to work out their differences to huge multinational corporations agreeing to resolve a dispute through a formal hearing before a panel of experts. The great advantage of ADR is its flexibility. Normally, the parties themselves can control how the dispute will be settled, what procedures will be used, and whether the decision reached (either by themselves or by a neutral third party) will be legally binding or nonbinding.

Today, approximately 95 percent of cases are settled before trial through some form of ADR. Indeed, most states either require or encourage parties to undertake ADR prior to trial. Several federal courts have instituted ADR programs as well. In the following pages, we examine various forms of ADR. Keep in mind, though, that new methods of ADR—and new combinations of existing methods—are constantly being devised and employed. In addition, ADR services are now being offered via the Internet. After looking at traditional forms of ADR, we examine some of the ways in which disputes are being resolved in various online forums.

ETHICAL ISSUE 3.2

Should "secret" settlements be allowed?   Perhaps one of the greatest incentives for settling a case is to avoid the publicity of a trial. Often an individual or business defendant is willing to pay a significant amount of money in return for the plaintiff's silence about the terms of the settlement. This practice, however, is increasingly coming under fire, particularly when the lawsuit involves a potential public safety or health hazard. For example, suppose that you are seriously injured by a defective product and sue the manufacturer of that product (product liability will be discussed in Chapter 13). Rather than proceed to trial, the manufacturer offers to pay you several million dollars provided that you agree to keep the terms of the settlement confidential. Many plaintiffs would find it difficult to refuse such an offer.

In most states, confidential or sealed settlement agreements are perfectly legal, even when they may not be perceived as ethical. A few states, such as South Carolina and New York, have passed laws attempting to prohibit—or at least limit—the use of secrecy provisions in settlement agreements. Several federal jurisdictions have also attempted to address the problem. So far, however, there is no uniform approach to resolving this issue, and many critics argue that limiting secrecy will only reduce the number of cases that settle. ∎

NEGOTIATION

NEGOTIATION
A process in which parties attempt to settle their dispute informally, with or without attorneys to represent them.

One of the simplest forms of ADR is **negotiation,** a process in which the parties attempt to settle their dispute informally, with or without attorneys to represent them. Attorneys frequently advise their clients to negotiate a settlement voluntarily before they proceed to trial.

Negotiation traditionally involves just the parties themselves and (typically) their attorneys. The attorneys, though, are advocates—they are obligated to put their clients' interests first. Often parties find it helpful to have the opinion and guidance of a neutral (unbiased) third party when deciding whether or how to negotiate a settlement of their dispute. The methods of ADR discussed next all involve neutral third parties.

MEDIATION

MEDIATION
A method of settling disputes outside of court by using the services of a neutral third party, who acts as a communicating agent between the parties and assists them in negotiating a settlement.

In the **mediation** process, the parties themselves attempt to negotiate an agreement, but with the assistance of a neutral third party, a mediator. In mediation, the mediator talks with the parties separately as well as jointly. The mediator emphasizes points of agreement, helps the parties evaluate their positions, and proposes solutions. The mediator, however, does not make a decision on the matter being disputed. The mediator, who need not be a lawyer, usually charges a fee for his or her services (which can be split between the parties). States that require parties to undergo ADR before trial often offer mediation as one of the ADR options or (as in Florida) the only option.

Mediation is not adversarial in nature, as lawsuits are. In litigation, the parties "do battle" with each other in the courtroom, while the judge is the neutral party. Because of its nonadversarial nature, the mediation process tends to reduce the antagonism between the disputants and to allow them to resume their former relationship. For this reason, mediation is often the preferred form of ADR for disputes involving business partners, employers and employees, or other parties involved in long-term relationships. ■ **EXAMPLE 3.10** Suppose that two business partners have a dispute over how the profits of their firm should be distributed. If the dispute is litigated, the parties will be adversaries, and their respective attorneys will emphasize how the parties' positions differ, not what they have in common. In contrast, when a dispute is mediated, the mediator emphasizes the common ground shared by the parties and helps them work toward agreement. ■

Today, characteristics of mediation are being combined with those of arbitration (to be discussed next). In *binding mediation,* for example, the parties agree that if they cannot resolve the dispute, the mediator can make a legally binding decision on the issue. In *mediation-arbitration,* or "med-arb," the parties agree to first attempt to settle their dispute through mediation. If no settlement is reached, the dispute will be arbitrated.

ARBITRATION

A more formal method of ADR is **arbitration,** in which an arbitrator (a neutral third party or a panel of experts) hears a dispute and renders a decision. The key difference between arbitration and the forms of ADR just discussed is that in arbitration, the third party hearing the dispute makes the decision for the parties. Usually, the parties in arbitration agree that the third party's decision will be *legally binding,* although the parties can also agree to *nonbinding* arbitration. Additionally, arbitration that is mandated by the courts often is not binding on the parties. If the parties do not agree with the arbitrator's decision, they can go forward with the lawsuit.

In some respects, formal arbitration resembles a trial, although usually the procedural rules are much less restrictive than those governing litigation. In the typical hearing format, the parties present opening arguments to the arbitrator and state what remedies should or should not be granted. Evidence is then presented, and witnesses may be called and examined by both sides. The arbitrator then renders a decision, which is called an *award.*

An arbitrator's award is usually the final word on the matter. Although the parties may appeal an arbitrator's decision, a court's review of the decision will be much more restricted in scope than an appellate court's review of a trial court's decision. The general view is that because the parties were free to frame the issues and set the powers of the arbitrator at the outset, they cannot complain about the results. The award will be set aside only if the arbitrator's conduct or "bad faith" substantially prejudiced the rights of one of the parties, if the award violates an established public policy, or if the arbitrator exceeded her or his powers (arbitrated issues that the parties did not agree to submit to arbitration).

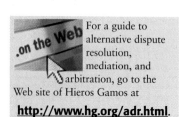

For a guide to alternative dispute resolution, mediation, and arbitration, go to the Web site of Hieros Gamos at **http://www.hg.org/adr.html**.

ARBITRATION
The settling of a dispute by submitting it to a disinterested third party (other than a court), who renders a decision that is (most often) legally binding.

KEEP IN MIND Litigation—even of a dispute over whether a particular matter should be submitted to arbitration—can be time consuming and expensive.

ARBITRATION CLAUSE
A clause in a contract that provides that, in the event of a dispute, the parties will submit the dispute to arbitration rather than litigate the dispute in court.

Arbitration Clauses and Statutes   Virtually any commercial matter can be submitted to arbitration. Frequently, parties include an **arbitration clause** in a contract (a written agreement—see Chapter 7); the clause provides that any dispute that arises under the contract will be resolved through arbitration rather than through the court system. Parties can also agree to arbitrate a dispute after a dispute arises.

Most states have statutes (often based in part on the Uniform Arbitration Act of 1955) under which arbitration clauses will be enforced, and some state statutes compel arbitration of certain types of disputes, such as those involving public employees. At the federal level, the Federal Arbitration Act (FAA), enacted in 1925, enforces arbitration clauses in contracts involving maritime activity and interstate commerce (though its applicability to employment contracts has been controversial, as discussed in a later subsection). Because of the breadth of the commerce clause (see Chapter 1), arbitration agreements involving transactions only slightly connected to the flow of interstate commerce may fall under the FAA.

The Issue of Arbitrability   When a dispute arises as to whether the parties have agreed in an arbitration clause to submit a particular matter to arbitration, one party may file suit to compel arbitration. The court before which the suit is brought will decide *not* the basic controversy but rather the issue of arbitrability—that is, whether the matter is one that must be resolved through arbitration. If the court finds that the subject matter in controversy is covered by the agreement to arbitrate, then a party may be compelled to arbitrate the dispute. Even when a claim involves a violation of a statute passed to protect a certain class of people, such as employees, a court may determine that the parties must nonetheless abide by their agreement to arbitrate the dispute. Usually, a court will allow the claim to be arbitrated if the court, in interpreting the statute, can find no legislative intent to the contrary.

No party, however, will be ordered to submit a particular dispute to arbitration unless the court is convinced that the party consented to do so.[16] Additionally, the courts will not compel arbitration if it is clear that the prescribed arbitration rules and procedures are inherently unfair to one of the parties. ■ **EXAMPLE 3.11** In one case, an employer asked a court to issue an order compelling a former employee to submit to arbitration in accordance with an arbitration agreement that the parties had signed. Under that agreement, the employer was to establish the procedure and the rules for the arbitration. The court held that the employee did not have to submit her claim to arbitration because "the rules were so one-sided that their only possible purpose is to undermine the neutrality of the proceeding." According to the court, the biased rules created "a sham system unworthy even of the name of arbitration" in violation of the parties' contract to arbitrate.[17] ■

Mandatory Arbitration in the Employment Context   A significant question in the last several years has concerned mandatory arbitration clauses in employment contracts. Many claim that employees' rights are not sufficiently protected when they are forced, as a condition of hiring, to agree to arbitrate all disputes and thus waive their rights under statutes specifically designed to protect employees. The United States Supreme Court, however, has generally held that mandatory arbitration clauses in employment contracts are enforceable.

---

16. See, for example, *Wright v. Universal Maritime Service Corp.,* 525 U.S. 70, 119 S.Ct. 391, 142 L.Ed.2d 361 (1998).
17. *Hooters of America, Inc. v. Phillips,* 173 F.3d 933 (4th Cir. 1999).

■ **EXAMPLE 3.12** In a landmark 1991 decision, *Gilmer v. Interstate/Johnson Lane Corp.*,[18] the Supreme Court held that a claim brought under a federal statute prohibiting age discrimination (see Chapter 18) could be subject to arbitration. The Court concluded that the employee had waived his right to sue when he agreed, as part of a required registration application to be a securities representative with the New York Stock Exchange, to arbitrate "any dispute, claim, or controversy" relating to his employment. ■ The *Gilmer* decision was controversial and generated much discussion during the 1990s. By the early 2000s, some lower courts had begun to question whether Congress intended the Federal Arbitration Act (FAA)—which expressly excludes the employment contracts of seamen, railroad employees, or any other class of workers engaged in foreign or interstate commerce—to apply to any employment contracts.

In 2001, the United States Supreme Court addressed this issue in *Circuit City Stores, Inc. v. Adams*.[19] In that case, as part of the application process, a sales employee was required to sign an arbitration clause. Two years later, the employee, Adams, filed suit against Circuit City for violating state employment-discrimination laws, and the employer asked the court to compel arbitration. Adams argued that the FAA did not apply to employment contracts, and the U.S. Court of Appeals for the Ninth Circuit agreed. The Supreme Court reversed, however, holding that the act applied to most employment contracts, except those that involve interstate transportation workers.

ETHICAL ISSUE 3.3   *Should the courts enforce mandatory arbitration clauses that inherently favor the employer?*   The Supreme Court's holding in *Circuit City* permits employers to require employees (and prospective employees) to sign arbitration agreements as a condition of their employment. Is this fair? Should the courts enforce arbitration clauses even when they appear to be disproportionately weighted in favor of the employer? Some courts are finding reasons not to enforce such clauses.

For example, the federal appellate court that reviewed the *Circuit City* case on remand declined to enforce the arbitration agreement on the ground that it was unconscionable. (An unconscionable contract or clause is one that is so one sided and unfair as to "shock the conscience" of the court—see Chapter 8.) The court noted that Circuit City drafted the agreement and required the plaintiff to sign it without modification as a prerequisite to employment. Under the terms of the agreement, only the employees were required to arbitrate their disputes, while Circuit City remained free to litigate in court any claims it had against its employees. Moreover, Circuit City's contract severely limited the relief that was available to employees, required employees to split the arbitrator's fee, and imposed a strict one-year statute of limitations on claims. For all of these reasons, the court held the entire arbitration agreement unenforceable.[20] Other courts have cited similar reasons for deciding not to enforce one-sided arbitration clauses.[21] ■

OTHER TYPES OF ADR

The three forms of ADR just discussed are the oldest and traditionally the most commonly used. In recent years, a variety of new types of ADR have emerged, some of which were mentioned earlier in the discussion of mediation. Other ADR forms

---

18. 500 U.S. 20, 111 S.Ct. 1647, 114 L.Ed.2d 26 (1991).
19. 532 U.S. 105, 121 S.Ct. 1302, 149 L.Ed.2d 234 (2001).
20. *Circuit City Stores, Inc. v. Adams*, 279 F.3d 889 (9th Cir. 2002).
21. See, for example, *Hardwick v. Sherwin Williams Co.*, 2002 WL 31992364 (Ohio App. 8 Dist. 2003).

EARLY NEUTRAL CASE EVALUATION
A form of alternative dispute resolution in which a neutral third party evaluates the strengths and weaknesses of the disputing parties' positions. The evaluator's opinion then forms the basis for negotiating a settlement.

MINI-TRIAL
A private proceeding in which each party to a dispute argues its position before the other side and vice versa. A neutral third party may be present as an adviser and may render an opinion if the parties fail to reach an agreement.

SUMMARY JURY TRIAL (SJT)
A method of settling disputes, used in many federal courts, in which a trial is held, but the jury's verdict is not binding. The verdict acts only as a guide to both sides in reaching an agreement during the mandatory negotiations that immediately follow the summary jury trial.

.on the Web To obtain information on the services offered by the American Arbitration Association (AAA), as well as forms that are used to submit a case for arbitration, go to the AAA's Web site at

http://www.adr.org.

ONLINE DISPUTE RESOLUTION (ODR)
The resolution of disputes with the assistance of organizations that offer dispute-resolution services via the Internet.

that are used today are sometimes referred to as "assisted negotiation" because they involve a third party in what is essentially a negotiation process. For example, in **early neutral case evaluation**, the parties select a neutral third party (generally an expert in the subject matter of the dispute) to evaluate their respective positions. The parties explain their positions to the case evaluator in any manner they choose. The case evaluator then assesses the strengths and weaknesses of the parties' positions, and this evaluation forms the basis for negotiating a settlement.

Another form of assisted negotiation that is often used by business parties is the **mini-trial**, in which each party's attorney briefly argues the party's case before representatives of each firm who have the authority to settle the dispute. Typically, a neutral third party (usually an expert in the area being disputed) acts as an adviser. If the parties fail to reach an agreement, the adviser renders an opinion as to how a court would likely decide the issue. The proceeding assists the parties in determining whether they should negotiate a settlement or take the dispute to court.

Today's courts are also experimenting with a variety of ADR alternatives to speed up (and reduce the cost of) justice. Numerous federal courts now hold **summary jury trials (SJTs)**, in which the parties present their arguments and evidence and the jury renders a verdict. The jury's verdict is not binding, but it does act as a guide to both sides in reaching an agreement during the mandatory negotiations that immediately follow the trial. Other alternatives being employed by the courts include summary procedures for commercial litigation and the appointment of special masters to assist judges in deciding complex issues.

PROVIDERS OF ADR SERVICES

ADR services are provided by both government agencies and private organizations. A major provider of ADR services is the American Arbitration Association (AAA), which was founded in 1926 and now handles over 200,000 claims a year in its numerous offices around the country. Most of the largest U.S. law firms are members of this nonprofit association.

Cases brought before the AAA are heard by an expert or a panel of experts in the area relating to the dispute and are usually settled quickly. Generally, about half of the panel members are lawyers. To cover its costs, the AAA charges a fee, paid by the party filing the claim. In addition, each party to the dispute pays a specified amount for each hearing day, as well as a special additional fee for cases involving personal injuries or property loss.

Hundreds of for-profit firms around the country also provide various forms of dispute-resolution services. Typically, these firms hire retired judges to conduct arbitration hearings or otherwise assist parties in settling their disputes. The judges follow procedures similar to those of the federal courts and use similar rules. Usually, each party to the dispute pays a filing fee and a designated fee for a hearing session or conference.

■ Online Dispute Resolution

An increasing number of companies and organizations offer dispute-resolution services using the Internet. The settlement of disputes in these online forums is known as **online dispute resolution (ODR)**. To date, the disputes resolved in these forums have most commonly involved disagreements over the rights to domain names (Web site addresses—see Chapter 5) and disagreements over the quality of goods sold via the Internet, including goods sold through Internet auction sites.

Currently, ODR may be best for resolving small- to medium-sized business liability claims, which may not be worth the expense of litigation or traditional ADR methods. Rules being developed in online forums, however, may ultimately become a code of conduct for all of those who do business in cyberspace. Most online forums do not automatically apply the law of any specific jurisdiction. Instead, results are often based on general, universal legal principles. As with offline methods of dispute resolution, any party may appeal to a court at any time.

NEGOTIATION AND MEDIATION SERVICES

The online negotiation of a dispute is generally simpler and more practical than litigation. Typically, one party files a complaint, and the other party is notified by e-mail. Password-protected access is possible twenty-four hours a day, seven days a week. Fees are generally low (often 2 to 4 percent, or less, of the disputed amount).

CyberSettle.com, clickNsettle.com, U.S. Settlement Corporation (ussettle.com), and other Web-based firms offer online forums for negotiating monetary settlements. The parties to a dispute may agree to submit offers; if the offers fall within a previously agreed-on range, they will end the dispute, and the parties will split the difference. Special software keeps secret any offers that are not within the range. If there is no agreed-on range, typically an offer includes a deadline within which the other party must respond before the offer expires. The parties can drop the negotiations at any time.

Mediation providers have also tried resolving disputes online. SquareTrade, for example, has provided mediation services for the online auction site eBay and also resolves disputes among other parties. SquareTrade uses Web-based software that walks participants through a five-step e-resolution process. Negotiation between the parties occurs on a secure page within SquareTrade's Web site. The parties may consult a mediator. The entire process takes as little as ten to fourteen days, and at present no fee is charged unless the parties use a mediator.

ARBITRATION PROGRAMS

A number of organizations, including the American Arbitration Association, offer online arbitration programs. The Internet Corporation for Assigned Names and Numbers (ICANN), a nonprofit corporation that the federal government set up to oversee the distribution of domain names, has issued special rules for the resolution of domain name disputes.[22] ICANN has also authorized several organizations to arbitrate domain name disputes in accordance with ICANN's rules.

Resolution Forum, Inc. (RFI), a nonprofit organization associated with the Center for Legal Responsibility at South Texas College of Law, offers arbitration services through its CAN-WIN conferencing system. Using standard browser software and an RFI password, the parties to a dispute access an online conference room. When multiple parties are involved, private communications and breakout sessions are possible via private messaging facilities. RFI also offers mediation services.

The Virtual Magistrate Project (VMAG) is affiliated with the American Arbitration Association, Chicago-Kent College of Law, Cyberspace Law Institute, National Center for Automated Information Research, and other organizations. VMAG offers arbitration for disputes involving users of online systems; victims of wrongful messages, postings, and files; and system operators subject to complaints or similar

To read about the policies and goals of the Virtual Magistrate Project, go to **http://www.vmag.org/docs/ concept.html**.

---

22. ICANN's Rules for Uniform Domain Name Dispute Resolution Policy are online at **http://www.icann. org/udrp/udrp-rules-24oct99.htm**. Domain names will be discussed in more detail in Chapter 5, in the context of trademark law.

demands. VMAG also arbitrates intellectual property, personal property, real property, and tort disputes related to online contracts. VMAG attempts to resolve a dispute within seventy-two hours. The proceedings occur in a password-protected online newsgroup setting, and private e-mail among the participants is possible. A VMAG arbitrator's decision is issued in a written opinion. A party may appeal the outcome to a court.

APPLICATION ▪▪ To Sue or Not to Sue?

Wrongs are committed every minute of every day in the United States. These wrongs may be committed inadvertently or intentionally. Sometimes businesspersons believe that wrongs have been committed against them by other businesspersons, by consumers, or by the local, state, or federal government. If you are deciding whether or not to sue for a wrong that has been committed against you or your business, you must consider many issues.

THE QUESTION OF COST

Competent legal advice is not inexpensive. Good commercial business law attorneys charge $100 to $500 an hour, plus expenses. It is almost always worthwhile to make an initial visit to an attorney who has skills in the area in which you are going to sue to get an estimate of the expected costs of pursuing a redress for your grievance. You may be charged for the initial visit as well.

Note that less than 10 percent of all corporate lawsuits end up in trial—the rest are settled beforehand. You may end up settling for far less than you think you are "owed" simply because of the length of time it takes your attorney to bring your case to trial and to finish the trial. And then you might not win, anyway!

Basically, therefore, you must do a cost-benefit analysis to determine whether you should sue. Your attorney can give you an estimate of the dollar costs involved in litigating the dispute. Realize, though, that litigation also involves nondollar costs. These costs include time away from your business, stress, inconvenience, and publicity—to name but a few. You need to weigh all of these costs against the benefits. You can "guesstimate" the benefits by multiplying the probable size of the award by the probability of obtaining that award.

THE ALTERNATIVES BEFORE YOU

Another method of settling your grievance is by alternative dispute resolution (ADR). Negotiation, mediation, arbitration, and other ADR forms are becoming increasingly attractive alternatives to court litigation because they usually yield quick results at a comparatively low cost. Most disputes relating to business can be mediated or arbitrated through the American Arbitration Association (AAA), which can be accessed online at http://www.adr.org.

There are numerous other ADR centers as well. You can obtain information on ADR from the AAA, courthouses, chambers of commerce, law firms, state bar associations, or the American Bar Association. The latter's Web site can be accessed at http://www.abanet.org. The Yellow Pages in large metropolitan areas usually list agencies and firms that can help you settle your dispute out of court; look under "Mediation" or "Social Service Agencies."

Depending on the nature of the dispute and the amount of damages you seek, you might wish to contact an organization that offers online dispute-resolution services, such as one of those discussed in this chapter.

CHECKLIST FOR DECIDING WHETHER TO SUE

1. Are you prepared to pay for going to court? Make this decision only after you have consulted an attorney to get an estimate of the costs of litigating the dispute.
2. Do you have the patience to follow a court case through the judicial system, even if it takes several years?
3. Is there a way for you to settle your grievance without going to court? Even if the settlement is less than you think you are owed—in net terms corrected for future expenses, lost time, and frustration—you may be better off settling now for the smaller figure.
4. Can you use some form of alternative dispute resolution? Before you say no, investigate these alternatives—they are usually cheaper and quicker to use than the standard judicial process.

* This *Application* is not meant to substitute for the services of an attorney who is licensed to practice law in your state.

■■ KEY TERMS

alternative dispute
   resolution (ADR) 98
answer 89
arbitration 100
arbitration clause 101
award 93
bankruptcy court 78
brief 94
complaint 88
concurrent jurisdiction 79
counterclaim 89
default judgment 89
deposition 90
discovery 90
diversity of citizenship 78
docket 79
early neutral case evaluation 103

e-evidence 91
exclusive jurisdiction 79
federal question 78
interrogatories 90
judicial review 74
jurisdiction 74
justiciable controversy 82
litigation 87
long arm statute 76
mediation 99
mini-trial 103
motion for a directed verdict 93
motion for a new trial 93
motion for judgment *n.o.v.* 93
motion for judgment on the
   pleadings 89
motion for summary judgment 90

motion to dismiss 89
negotiation 99
online dispute
   resolution (ODR) 103
pleadings 87
probate court 78
reply 89
rule of four 85
small claims court 84
standing to sue 82
summary jury trial (SJT) 103
summons 89
venue 81
voir dire 92
writ of *certiorari* 85

CHAPTER SUMMARY Traditional and Online Dispute Resolution

The Judiciary's Role in American Government (See page 74.)	The role of the judiciary—the courts—in the American governmental system is to interpret and apply the law. Through the process of judicial review—determining the constitutionality of laws—the judicial branch acts as a check on the executive and legislative branches of government.

Basic Judicial Requirements (See pages 74–82.)	1. *Jurisdiction*—Before a court can hear a case, it must have jurisdiction over the person against whom the suit is brought or the property involved in the suit, as well as jurisdiction over the subject matter.
	
	   a. Limited versus general jurisdiction—Limited jurisdiction exists when a court is limited to a specific subject matter, such as probate or divorce. General jurisdiction exists when a court can hear any kind of case.
	
	   b. Original versus appellate jurisdiction—Original jurisdiction exists with courts that have authority to hear a case for the first time (trial courts). Appellate jurisdiction exists with courts of appeals, or reviewing courts; generally, appellate courts do not have original jurisdiction.
	
	   c. Federal jurisdiction—Arises (1) when a federal question is involved (when the plaintiff's cause of action is based, at least in part, on the U.S. Constitution, a treaty, or a federal law) or (2) when a case involves diversity of citizenship (citizens of different states, for example) and the amount in controversy exceeds $75,000.
	
	   d. Concurrent versus exclusive jurisdiction—Concurrent jurisdiction exists when two different courts have authority to hear the same case. Exclusive jurisdiction exists when only state courts or only federal courts have authority to hear a case.
	
	2. *Jurisdiction in cyberspace*—Because the Internet does not have physical boundaries, traditional jurisdictional concepts have been difficult to apply in cases involving activities

CHAPTER SUMMARY Traditional and Online Dispute Resolution—Continued

Basic Judicial Requirements— Continued	conducted via the Web. Gradually, the courts are developing standards to use in determining when jurisdiction over a Web owner or operator in another state is proper.
	3. *Venue*—Venue has to do with the most appropriate location for a trial, which is usually the geographic area where the event leading to the dispute took place or where the parties reside.
	4. *Standing to sue*—A requirement that a party must have a legally protected and tangible interest at stake sufficient to justify seeking relief through the court system. The controversy at issue must also be a justiciable controversy—one that is real and substantial, as opposed to hypothetical or academic.
The State and Federal Court Systems (See pages 82–86.)	1. *Trial courts*—Courts of original jurisdiction, in which legal actions are initiated.
	a. State—Courts of general jurisdiction can hear any case; courts of limited jurisdiction include divorce courts, probate courts, traffic courts, small claims courts, and so on.
	b. Federal—The federal district court is the equivalent of the state trial court. Federal courts of limited jurisdiction include the U.S. Tax Court, the U.S. Bankruptcy Court, and the U.S. Court of Federal Claims.
	2. *Intermediate appellate courts*—Courts of appeals, or reviewing courts; generally without original jurisdiction. Many states have an intermediate appellate court; in the federal court system, the U.S. circuit courts of appeals are the intermediate appellate courts.
	3. *Supreme (highest) courts*—Each state has a supreme court, although it may be called by some other name; appeal from the state supreme court to the United States Supreme Court is possible only if a federal question is involved. The United States Supreme Court is the highest court in the federal court system and the final arbiter of the Constitution and federal law.
Following a State Court Case (See pages 87–95.)	Rules of procedure prescribe the way in which disputes are handled in the courts. Rules differ from court to court, and separate sets of rules exist for federal and state courts, as well as for criminal and civil cases. A sample civil court case in a state court would involve the following procedures:
	1. *The pleadings*—
	a. Complaint—Filed by the plaintiff with the court to initiate the lawsuit; served with a summons on the defendant.
	b. Answer—Admits or denies allegations made by the plaintiff; may assert a counterclaim or an affirmative defense.
	c. Motion to dismiss—A request to the court to dismiss the case for stated reasons, such as the plaintiff's failure to state a claim for which relief can be granted.
	2. *Pretrial motions (in addition to the motion to dismiss)*—
	a. Motion for judgment on the pleadings—May be made by either party; will be granted if the parties agree on the facts and the only question is how the law applies to the facts. The judge bases the decision solely on the pleadings.
	b. Motion for summary judgment—May be made by either party; will be granted if the parties agree on the facts. The judge applies the law in rendering a judgment. The judge can consider evidence outside the pleadings when evaluating the motion.
	3. *Discovery*—The process of gathering evidence concerning the case. Discovery involves depositions (sworn testimony by a party to the lawsuit or any witness), interrogatories (written questions and answers to these questions made by parties to the action with the aid of their attorneys), and various requests (for admissions, documents, and medical examinations, for example). Discovery may also involve electronically recorded information, such as e-mail, voice mail, word processing documents, and other data compilations.

(Continued)

CHAPTER SUMMARY Traditional and Online Dispute Resolution—Continued

Following a State Court Case—Continued	Although electronic discovery has significant advantages over paper discovery, it is also more time consuming and expensive and often requires the parties to hire experts.
	4. *Pretrial conference*—Either party or the court can request a pretrial conference to identify the matters in dispute after discovery has taken place and to plan the course of the trial.
	5. *Trial*—Following jury selection *(voir dire),* the trial begins with opening statements from both parties' attorneys. The following events then occur:
	a. The plaintiff's introduction of evidence (including the testimony of witnesses) supporting the plaintiff's position. The defendant's attorney can challenge evidence and cross-examine witnesses.
	b. The defendant's introduction of evidence (including the testimony of witnesses) supporting the defendant's position. The plaintiff's attorney can challenge evidence and cross-examine witnesses.
	c. Closing arguments by the attorneys in favor of their respective clients, the judge's instructions to the jury, and the jury's verdict.
	6. *Posttrial motions*—
	a. Motion for judgment *n.o.v.* ("notwithstanding the verdict")—Will be granted if the judge is convinced that the jury was in error.
	b. Motion for a new trial—Will be granted if the judge is convinced that the jury was in error; can also be granted on the grounds of newly discovered evidence, misconduct by the participants during the trial, or error by the judge.
	7. *Appeal*—Either party can appeal the trial court's judgment to an appropriate court of appeals. After reviewing the record on appeal, the abstracts, and the attorneys' briefs, the appellate court holds a hearing and renders its opinion.
The Courts Adapt to the Online World (See pages 95–98.)	A number of state and federal courts now allow parties to file litigation-related documents with the courts via the Internet or other electronic means. The federal courts are considering the implementation of electronic filing systems in all federal district courts. Virtually every court now has a Web page offering information about the court and its procedures, and increasingly courts are publishing their opinions online. In the future, we may see "cyber courts," in which all trial proceedings are conducted online.
Alternative Dispute Resolution (See pages 98–103.)	1. *Negotiation*—The parties come together, with or without attorneys to represent them, and try to reach a settlement without the involvement of a third party.
	2. *Mediation*—The parties themselves reach an agreement with the help of a neutral third party, called a mediator, who proposes solutions. At the parties' request, a mediator may make a legally binding decision.
	3. *Arbitration*—A more formal method of ADR in which the parties submit their dispute to a neutral third party, the arbitrator, who renders a decision. The decision may or may not be legally binding, depending on the circumstances.
	4. *Other types of ADR*—These include early neutral case evaluation, mini-trials, and summary jury trials (SJTs); generally, these are forms of "assisted negotiation."
	5. *Providers of ADR services*—The leading nonprofit provider of ADR services is the American Arbitration Association. Hundreds of for-profit firms also provide ADR services.
Online Dispute Resolution (See pages 103–105.)	A number of organizations and firms are now offering negotiation, mediation, and arbitration services through online forums. To date, these forums have been a practical alternative for the resolution of domain name disputes and e-commerce disputes in which the amount in controversy is relatively small.

▣ FOR REVIEW

Answers for the even-numbered questions in this For Review *section can be found in Appendix I at the end of this text.*

1 What is judicial review? How and when was the power of judicial review established?

2 Before a court can hear a case, it must have jurisdiction. Over what must it have jurisdiction? How are the courts applying traditional jurisdictional concepts to cases involving Internet transactions?

3 What is the difference between a trial court and an appellate court?

4 In a lawsuit, what are the pleadings? What is discovery, and how does electronic discovery differ? What is electronic filing?

5 How are online forums being used to resolve disputes?

▣ QUESTIONS AND CASE PROBLEMS

3–1. Arbitration. In an arbitration proceeding, the arbitrator need not be a judge or even a lawyer. How, then, can the arbitrator's decision have the force of law and be binding on the parties involved?

3–2. Jurisdiction. Marya Callais, a citizen of Florida, was walking near a busy street in Tallahassee one day when a large crate flew off a passing truck and hit her, resulting in numerous injuries to Callais. She incurred a great deal of pain and suffering plus numerous medical expenses, and she could not work for six months. She wishes to sue the trucking firm for $300,000 in damages. The firm's headquarters are in Georgia, although the company does business in Florida. In what court may Callais bring suit—a Florida state court, a Georgia state court, or a federal court? What factors might influence her decision?

3–3. Standing. Blue Cross and Blue Shield insurance companies (the Blues) provide 68 million Americans with health-care financing. The Blues have paid billions of dollars for care attributable to illnesses related to tobacco use. In an attempt to recover some of this amount, the Blues filed a suit in a federal district court against tobacco companies and others, alleging fraud, among other things. The Blues claimed that beginning in 1953, the defendants conspired to addict millions of Americans, including members of Blue Cross plans, to cigarettes and other tobacco products. The conspiracy involved misrepresentation about the safety of nicotine and its addictive properties, marketing efforts targeting children, and agreements not to produce or market safer cigarettes. As a result of the defendants' efforts, many tobacco users developed lung, throat, and other cancers, as well as heart disease, stroke, emphysema, and other illnesses. The defendants asked the court to dismiss the case on the ground that the plaintiffs did not have standing to sue. Do the Blues have standing in this case? Why or why not? [*Blue Cross and Blue Shield of New Jersey, Inc. v. Philip Morris, Inc.,* 36 F.Supp.2d 560 (E.D.N.Y. 1999)]

3–4. Jurisdiction. George Noonan, a Boston police detective and a devoted nonsmoker, has spent most of his career educating Bostonians about the health risks of tobacco use. In 1992, an ad for Winston cigarettes featuring Noonan's image appeared in several French magazines. Some of the magazines were on sale at newsstands in Boston. Noonan filed a suit in a federal district court against The Winston Co., Lintas:Paris (the French ad agency that created the ads), and others. Lintas:Paris and the other French defendants claimed that they did not know the magazines would be sold in Boston and filed a motion to dismiss the suit for lack of personal jurisdiction. Does the court have jurisdiction? Why or why not? [*Noonan v. The Winston Co.,* 135 F.3d 85 (1st Cir. 1998)]

CASE PROBLEM WITH SAMPLE ANSWER

3–5. Ms. Thompson filed a suit in a federal district court against her employer, Altheimer & Gray, seeking damages for alleged racial discrimination in violation of federal law. During *voir dire,* the judge asked the prospective jurors whether "there is something about this kind of lawsuit for money damages that would start any of you leaning for or against a particular party." Ms. Leiter, one of the prospective jurors, raised her hand and explained that she had "been an owner of a couple of businesses and am currently an owner of a business, and I feel that as an employer and owner of a business that will definitely sway my judgment in this case." She explained, "I am constantly faced with people that want various benefits or different positions in the company or better contacts or, you know, a myriad of issues that employers face on a regular basis, and I have to decide whether or not that person should get them." Asked by Thompson's lawyer whether "you believe that people file lawsuits just because they don't get something they want," Leiter answered, "I believe there are some people that do." In answer to another question, she said, "I think I bring a lot of background to this case, and I can't say that it's not going to cloud my judgment. I can try to be as fair as I can, as I do every day." Thompson filed a motion to strike Leiter for cause. Should the judge grant the motion? Explain. [*Thompson v. Altheimer & Gray*, 248 F.3d 621 (7th Cir. 2001)]

After you have answered this problem, compare your answer with the sample answer given on the Web site that accompanies this text. Go to http://blt.westbuslaw.com, select "Chapter 3," and click on "Case Problem with Sample Answer."

3–6. Arbitration. Alexander Little worked for Auto Stiegler, Inc., an automobile dealership in Los Angeles County, California, eventually becoming the service manager. While employed, Little signed an arbitration agreement that required all employment-related disputes to be submitted to arbitration. The agreement also provided that any award over $50,000 could be appealed to a second arbitrator. Little was later demoted and terminated. Alleging that these actions were in retaliation for investigating and reporting warranty fraud and thus were in violation of public policy, Little filed a suit in a California state court against Auto Stiegler. The defendant filed a motion with the court to compel arbitration. Little responded that the arbitration agreement should not be enforced in part because the appeal provision was unfairly one sided. Is this provision enforceable? Should the court grant Auto Stiegler's motion? Why or why not? [*Little v. Auto Stiegler, Inc.*, 29 Cal.4th 1064, 63 P.3d 979, 130 Cal.Rptr.2d 892 (2003)]

3–7. Standing to Sue. Lamar Advertising of Penn, LLC, an outdoor advertising business, wanted to erect billboards of varying sizes in a multiphase operation throughout the town of Orchard Park, New York. An Orchard Park ordinance restricted the signs to certain sizes in certain areas, to advertising products and services available for sale only on the premises, and to other limits. Lamar asked Orchard Park for permission to build signs in some areas larger than the ordinance allowed in those locations (but not as large as allowed in other areas). When the town refused, Lamar filed a suit in a federal district court, claiming that the ordinance violated the First Amendment. Did Lamar have standing to challenge the ordinance? If the court could sever the provisions of the ordinance restricting a sign's content from the provisions limiting a sign's size, would your answer be the same? Explain. [*Lamar Advertising of Penn, LLC v. Town of Orchard Park, New York*, 356 F.3d 365 (2d Cir. 2004)]

A QUESTION OF ETHICS

3–8. Linda Bender brought an action in a federal court against her supervisor at A. G. Edwards & Sons, Inc., a stockbrokerage firm (the defendants). Bender alleged sexual harassment in violation of

Title VII of the Civil Rights Act of 1964, which prohibits, among other things, employment discrimination based on gender. In her application for registration as a stockbroker, Bender had agreed to arbitrate any disputes with her employer. The defendants moved to compel arbitration. The district court judge denied the motion, holding that Bender could not be forced to waive her right to adjudicate Title VII claims in federal court. The appellate court reversed, ruling that Title VII claims are arbitrable. The court held that compelling Bender to submit her claim for arbitration did not deprive her of the right to a judicial forum, because if the arbitration proceedings were somehow legally deficient, she could still take her case to a federal court for review. [*Bender v. A. G. Edwards & Sons, Inc.*, 971 F.2d 698 (11th Cir. 1992)]

1. Does the right to a postarbitration judicial forum equate to the right to initial access to a judicial forum in employment disputes?
2. Should the fact that reviewing courts rarely set aside arbitrators' awards have any bearing on the arbitrability of certain types of claims, such as those brought under Title VII?

FOR CRITICAL ANALYSIS

3–9. American courts are forums for adversarial justice, in which attorneys defend the interests of their respective clients before the court. This means that an attorney may end up claiming in court that his or her client is innocent, even though the attorney knows that the client acted wrongfully. Is it ethical for attorneys to try to "deceive" the court in these situations? Can the adversarial system of justice really lead to "truth"?

VIDEO QUESTION

3–10. Go to this text's Web site at http://blt.westbuslaw.com and select "Chapter 3." Click on "Video Questions" and view the video titled *Jurisdiction in Cyberspace*. Then answer the following questions.

1. What standard would a court apply to determine whether it has jurisdiction over the out-of-state computer firm in the video?
2. What factors is a court likely to consider in assessing whether sufficient contacts existed when the only connection to the jurisdiction is through a Web site?
3. How do you think the court would resolve the issue in this case?

INTERNET EXERCISES

Go to the *Business Law Today: The Essentials* home page at <u>http://blt.westbuslaw.com</u>, select "Chapter 3," and click on "Internet Exercises." There you will find the following Internet research exercises that you can perform to learn more about topics covered in this chapter.

Activity 3–1: LEGAL PERSPECTIVE—The Judiciary's Role in American Government

Activity 3–2: MANAGEMENT PERSPECTIVE—Alternative Dispute Resolution

Activity 3–3: SOCIAL PERSPECTIVE—Resolve a Dispute Online

BEFORE THE TEST

Go to the *Business Law Today: The Essentials* home page at <u>http://blt.westbuslaw.com</u>, select "Chapter 3," and click on "Interactive Quizzes." You will find at least twenty interactive questions relating to this chapter.

CHAPTER 4

Torts and Cyber Torts

" 'Tort' more or less means 'wrong' . . . .
One of my friends [in law school]
said that Torts is the course which proves
that your mother was right."

Scott Turow, 1949–
(American lawyer and author)

CHAPTER OUTLINE

- ■ THE BASIS OF TORT LAW

- ■ INTENTIONAL TORTS
  AGAINST PERSONS

- ■ INTENTIONAL TORTS
  AGAINST PROPERTY

- ■ UNINTENTIONAL TORTS
  (NEGLIGENCE)

- ■ STRICT LIABILITY

- ■ CYBER TORTS

▦ LEARNING OBJECTIVES

After reading this chapter, you should be able to answer the following questions:

1 What is a tort?

2 What is the purpose of tort law? What are two basic categories of torts?

3 What are the four elements of negligence?

4 What is meant by strict liability? In what circumstances is strict liability applied?

5 What is a cyber tort, and how are tort theories being applied in cyberspace?

TORT
A civil wrong not arising from a breach of contract. A breach of a legal duty that proximately causes harm or injury to another.

As Scott Turow's statement in the above quotation indicates, **torts** are wrongful actions.[1] Through tort law, society compensates those who have suffered injuries as a result of the wrongful conduct of others. Although some torts, such as assault and trespass, originated in the English common law, the field of tort law continues to expand. As new ways to commit wrongs are discovered, such as the use of the Internet to commit wrongful acts, the courts are extending tort law to cover these wrongs.

As you will see in later chapters of this book, many of the lawsuits brought by or against business firms are based on the tort theories discussed in this chapter. Some of the torts examined here can occur in any context, including the business environment.

---

1. The word *tort* is French for "wrong."

BUSINESS TORT
Wrongful interference with another's business rights.

Others traditionally have been referred to as **business torts,** which are defined as wrongful interferences with the business rights of others. Included in business torts are such vague concepts as *unfair competition* and *wrongfully interfering with the business relations of others.*

The Basis of Tort Law

Two notions serve as the basis of all torts: wrongs and compensation. Tort law is designed to compensate those who have suffered a loss or injury due to another person's wrongful act. In a tort action, one person or group brings a personal suit against another person or group to obtain compensation (money **damages**) or other relief for the harm suffered.

DAMAGES
Money sought as a remedy for a breach of contract or a tortious action.

THE PURPOSE OF TORT LAW

Generally, the purpose of tort law is to provide remedies for the invasion of various *protected interests.* Society recognizes an interest in personal physical safety, and tort law provides remedies for acts that cause physical injury or that interfere with physical security and freedom of movement. Society recognizes an interest in protecting real and personal property, and tort law provides remedies for acts that cause destruction or damage to property. Society also recognizes an interest in protecting certain intangible interests, such as personal privacy, family relations, reputation, and dignity, and tort law provides remedies for invasion of these protected interests.

CLASSIFICATIONS OF TORTS

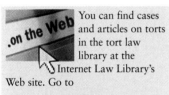 You can find cases and articles on torts in the tort law library at the Internet Law Library's Web site. Go to
http://www.lawguru.com/ ilawlib.

There are two broad classifications of torts: *intentional torts* and *unintentional torts* (torts involving negligence). The classification of a particular tort depends largely on how the tort occurs (intentionally or negligently) and the surrounding circumstances. In the following pages, you will read about these two classifications of torts.

Torts committed via the Internet are sometimes referred to as **cyber torts.** We look at how the courts have applied traditional tort law to wrongful actions in the online environment in the concluding pages of this chapter.

CYBER TORT
A tort committed in cyberspace.

Intentional Torts against Persons

INTENTIONAL TORT
A wrongful act knowingly committed.

TORTFEASOR
One who commits a tort.

An **intentional tort,** as the term implies, requires *intent.* The **tortfeasor** (the one committing the tort) must intend to commit an act, the consequences of which interfere with the personal or business interests of another in a way not permitted by law. An evil or harmful motive is not required—in fact, the actor may even have a beneficial motive for committing what turns out to be a tortious act. In tort law, intent means only that the actor intended the consequences of his or her act or knew with substantial certainty that certain consequences would result from the act. The law generally assumes that individuals intend the *normal* consequences of their actions. Thus, forcefully pushing another—even if done in jest and without any evil motive—is an intentional tort (if injury results), because the object of a strong push can ordinarily be expected to fall down.

This section discusses intentional torts against persons, which include assault and battery, false imprisonment, infliction of emotional distress, defamation, invasion of the right to privacy, appropriation, misrepresentation, and wrongful interference.

ASSAULT AND BATTERY

ASSAULT
Any word or action intended to make another person fearful of immediate physical harm; a reasonably believable threat.

Any intentional, unexcused act that creates in another person a reasonable apprehension or fear of immediate harmful or offensive contact is an **assault.** Apprehension is not the same as fear. If a contact is such that a reasonable person would want to avoid it, and if there is a reasonable basis for believing that the contact will occur, then the plaintiff suffers apprehension whether or not he or she is afraid. The interest protected by tort law concerning assault is the freedom from having to expect harmful or offensive contact. The occurrence of apprehension is enough to justify compensation.

The *completion* of the act that caused the apprehension, if it results in harm to the plaintiff, is a **battery,** which is defined as an unexcused and harmful or offensive physical contact *intentionally* performed. For example, suppose that Ivan threatens Jean with a gun, then shoots her. The pointing of the gun at Jean is an assault; the firing of the gun (if the bullet hits Jean) is a battery. The interest protected by tort law concerning battery is the right to personal security and safety. The contact can be harmful, or it can be merely offensive (such as an unwelcome kiss). Physical injury need not occur. The contact can involve any part of the body or anything attached to it—for example, a hat or other item of clothing, a purse, or a chair or an automobile in which one is sitting. Whether the contact is offensive or not is determined by the *reasonable person standard.*[2] The contact can be made by the defendant or by some force the defendant sets in motion—for example, a rock thrown, food poisoned, or a stick swung.

BATTERY
The unprivileged, intentional touching of another.

Compensation   If the plaintiff shows that there was contact, and the jury agrees that the contact was offensive, the plaintiff has a right to compensation. There is no need to show that the defendant acted out of **malice;** the person could have just been joking or playing around. The underlying motive does not matter, only the intent to bring about the harmful or offensive contact to the plaintiff. In fact, proving a motive is never necessary (but is sometimes relevant). A plaintiff may be compensated for the emotional harm or loss of reputation resulting from a battery, as well as for physical harm.

MALICE
A desire to cause pain, injury, or distress to another.

Defenses to Assault and Battery   A number of legally recognized **defenses** (reasons why plaintiffs should not obtain what they are seeking) can be raised by a defendant who is sued for assault or battery, or both:

DEFENSE
A reason offered and alleged by a defendant in an action or suit as to why the plaintiff should not recover or establish what she or he seeks.

BE AWARE Some of these same four defenses can be raised by a defendant who is sued for other torts.

1. *Consent.* When a person consents to the act that damages her or him, there is generally no liability (legal responsibility) for the damage done.
2. *Self-defense.* An individual who is defending his or her life or physical well-being can claim self-defense. In situations of both *real* and *apparent* danger, a person may use whatever force is *reasonably* necessary to prevent harmful contact.
3. *Defense of others.* An individual can act in a reasonable manner to protect others who are in real or apparent danger.
4. *Defense of property.* Reasonable force may be used in attempting to remove intruders from one's home, although force that is likely to cause death or great bodily injury can never be used just to protect property.

---

2. The *reasonable person standard* is an objective test of how a reasonable person would have acted under the same circumstances. See "The Duty of Care and Its Breach" later in this chapter.

FALSE IMPRISONMENT

False imprisonment is the intentional confinement or restraint of another person's activities without justification. False imprisonment interferes with the freedom to move without restraint. The confinement can be accomplished through the use of physical barriers, physical restraint, or threats of physical force. Moral pressure or threats of future harm do not constitute false imprisonment. It is essential that the person being restrained not comply with the restraint willingly.

Businesspersons are often confronted with suits for false imprisonment after they have attempted to confine a suspected shoplifter for questioning. Under the "privilege to detain" granted to merchants in some states, a merchant can use the defense of *probable cause* to justify delaying a suspected shoplifter. Probable cause exists when there is sufficient evidence to support the belief that a person is guilty. Although laws governing false imprisonment vary from state to state, generally they require that any detention be conducted in a *reasonable* manner and for only a *reasonable* length of time.

INTENTIONAL INFLICTION OF EMOTIONAL DISTRESS

The tort of *intentional infliction of emotional distress* can be defined as an intentional act that amounts to extreme and outrageous conduct resulting in severe emotional distress to another. ■ **EXAMPLE 4.1** A prankster telephones an individual and says that the individual's spouse has just been in a horrible accident. As a result, the individual suffers intense mental pain or anxiety. The caller's behavior is deemed to be extreme and outrageous conduct that exceeds the bounds of decency accepted by society and is therefore **actionable** (capable of serving as the ground for a lawsuit). ■

The tort of intentional infliction of emotional distress poses several problems for the courts. One problem is the difficulty of proving the existence of emotional suffering. For this reason, courts in some jurisdictions require that the emotional distress be evidenced by some physical symptom or illness or some emotional disturbance that can be documented by a psychiatric consultant or other medical professional.

Another problem is that emotional distress claims must be subject to some limitation, or they could flood the courts with lawsuits. A society in which individuals are rewarded if they are unable to endure the normal emotional stresses of day-to-day living is obviously undesirable. Therefore, the law usually holds that indignity or annoyance alone is not enough to support a lawsuit based on the intentional infliction of emotional distress. Repeated annoyances (such as those experienced by a person who is being stalked), however, coupled with threats, are enough. In the business context, the repeated use of extreme methods to collect a delinquent account may be actionable.

DEFAMATION

Defamation of character involves wrongfully hurting a person's good reputation. The law has imposed a general duty on all persons to refrain from making false, defamatory statements about others. Breaching this duty orally involves the tort of **slander;** breaching it in writing involves the tort of **libel.** The tort of defamation also arises when a false statement is made about a person's product, business, or title to property. We deal with these torts later in the chapter.

The Publication Requirement   The basis of the tort of defamation is the publication of a statement or statements that hold an individual up to contempt, ridicule,

ACTIONABLE
Capable of serving as the basis of a lawsuit. An actionable claim can be pursued in a lawsuit or other court action.

DEFAMATION
Anything published or publicly spoken that causes injury to another's good name, reputation, or character.

SLANDER
Defamation in oral form.

LIBEL
Defamation in writing or other permanent form (such as a digital recording) having the quality of permanence.

or hatred. *Publication* here means that the defamatory statements are communicated to persons other than the defamed party. ■ **EXAMPLE 4.2** If Thompson writes Andrews a private letter accusing him of embezzling funds, the action does not constitute libel. If Peters calls Gordon dishonest, unattractive, and incompetent when no one else is around, the action does not constitute slander. In neither case was the message communicated to a third party. ■

The courts have generally held that even dictating a letter to a secretary constitutes publication, although the publication may be *privileged* (privileged communications will be discussed shortly). Moreover, if a third party overhears defamatory statements by chance, the courts usually hold that this also constitutes publication. Defamatory statements made via the Internet are also actionable, as you will read later in this chapter. Note further that any individual who republishes or repeats defamatory statements is liable even if that person reveals the source of such statements.

Damages for Defamation   Generally, in a case alleging slander, the plaintiff must prove "special damages" to establish the defendant's liability. The plaintiff must show that the slanderous statement caused her or him to suffer actual economic or monetary losses. This requirement is imposed in cases involving slander because slanderous statements have a temporary quality. In contrast, a libelous (written) statement has the quality of permanence, can be circulated widely, and usually results from some degree of deliberation on the part of the author. For that reason, a plaintiff can recover "general damages" for libel and need not prove any special damages.

Exceptions to the burden of proving special damages in cases alleging slander are made for certain types of slanderous statements. If a false statement constitutes "slander *per se*," no proof of special damages is required for it to be actionable. The following four types of utterances are considered to be slander *per se*:

1. A statement that another has a loathsome communicable disease.
2. A statement that another has committed improprieties while engaging in a profession or trade.
3. A statement that another has committed or has been imprisoned for a serious crime.
4. A statement that a woman is unchaste or has engaged in serious sexual misconduct.

Defenses against Defamation   Truth is normally an absolute defense against a defamation charge. In other words, if the defendant in a defamation suit can prove that his or her allegedly defamatory statements were true, the defendant will not be liable.

PRIVILEGE
A legal right, exemption, or immunity granted to a person or a class of persons. In the context of defamation, an absolute privilege immunizes the actor from suit, regardless of whether the actor's statements were malicious. A qualified privilege immunizes an actor from suit only when the privilege is properly exercised in the performance of a legal or moral duty.

Privileged Communications.   Another defense that is sometimes raised is that the statements were **privileged** communications, and thus the defendant is immune from liability. Privileged communications are of two types: absolute and qualified. Only in judicial proceedings and certain government proceedings is *absolute* privilege granted. For example, statements made in the courtroom by attorneys and judges during a trial are absolutely privileged. So are statements made by government officials during legislative debate, even if the officials make such statements maliciously—that is, knowing them to be untrue. An absolute privilege is granted in these situations because government personnel deal with matters that are so much in the public interest that the parties involved should be able to speak out fully and freely without restriction.

A *qualified,* or *conditional,* privilege applies when a statement is related to a matter of public interest or when the statement is necessary to protect a person's private interest and is made to another person with an interest in the same subject matter. ■ EXAMPLE 4.3 Jorge applies for membership at the local country club. After the country club's board rejects his application, Jorge sues the club's office manager for making allegedly defamatory statements to the board concerning a conversation she had with Jorge. Assuming that the office manager had simply relayed what she thought was her duty to convey to the club's board, her statements would likely be protected by a qualified privilege.[3] ■

Public Figures.   In general, false and defamatory statements that are made about *public figures* (public officials who exercise substantial governmental power and any persons in the public limelight) and that are published in the press are privileged if they are made without **actual malice**.[4] To be made with actual malice, a statement must be made *with either knowledge of falsity or a reckless disregard of the truth*. Statements made about public figures, especially when they are made via a public medium, are usually related to matters of general interest; they are made about people who substantially affect all of us. Furthermore, public figures generally have some access to a public medium for answering disparaging (belittling, discrediting) falsehoods about themselves; private individuals do not. For these reasons, public figures have a greater burden of proof in defamation cases (they must prove actual malice) than do private individuals.

INVASION OF THE RIGHT TO PRIVACY

A person has a right to solitude and freedom from prying public eyes—in other words, to privacy. As discussed in Chapter 1, the Supreme Court has held that a fundamental right to privacy is also implied by various amendments to the U.S. Constitution. Some state constitutions explicitly provide for privacy rights. In addition, a number of federal and state statutes have been enacted to protect individual rights in specific areas. Tort law also safeguards these rights through the tort of *invasion of privacy.* Four acts qualify as an invasion of privacy:

1 *The use of a person's name, picture, or other likeness for commercial purposes without permission.* This tort, which is usually referred to as the tort of appropriation, will be examined shortly.

2 *Intrusion into an individual's affairs or seclusion.* For example, invading someone's home or illegally searching someone's briefcase is an invasion of privacy. The tort has been held to extend to eavesdropping by wiretap, the unauthorized scanning of a bank account, compulsory blood testing, and window peeping.

3 *Publication of information that places a person in a false light.* This could be a story attributing to the person ideas not held or actions not taken by the person. (Publishing such a story could involve the tort of defamation as well.)

4 *Public disclosure of private facts about an individual that an ordinary person would find objectionable.* A newspaper account of a private citizen's sex life or financial affairs could be an actionable invasion of privacy.

ACTUAL MALICE
In a defamation suit, a statement made about a public figure normally must be made with actual malice (with either knowledge of its falsity or a reckless disregard of the truth) for liability to be incurred.

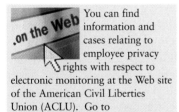 You can find information and cases relating to employee privacy rights with respect to electronic monitoring at the Web site of the American Civil Liberties Union (ACLU). Go to

http://www.aclu.org/library/ pbr2.html.

---

3. For a case involving a qualified privilege, see *Hickson Corp. v. Northern Crossarm Co.,* 235 F.Supp.2d 1352 (N.D.Ga. 2002).
4. *New York Times Co. v. Sullivan,* 376 U.S. 254, 84 S.Ct. 710, 11 L.Ed.2d 686 (1964).

APPROPRIATION

The use by one person of another person's name, likeness, or other identifying characteristic, without permission and for the benefit of the user, constitutes the tort of **appropriation.** Under the law, an individual's right to privacy normally includes the right to the exclusive use of her or his identity.

■ **EXAMPLE 4.4**   Vanna White, the hostess of the popular television game show *Wheel of Fortune,* brought a case against Samsung Electronics America, Inc. Without White's permission, Samsung included in an advertisement for its videocassette recorders (VCRs) a depiction of a robot dressed in a wig, gown, and jewelry, posed in a scene that resembled the *Wheel of Fortune* set, in a stance for which White is famous. The court held in White's favor, holding that the tort of appropriation does not require the use of a celebrity's name or likeness. The court stated that Samsung's robot ad left "little doubt" as to the identity of the celebrity whom the ad was meant to depict.[5] ■

Cases of wrongful appropriation, or misappropriation, may also involve the rights of those who invest time and funds in the creation of a special system, such as a method of broadcasting sports events. Commercial misappropriation may also occur when a person takes and uses the property of another for the sole purpose of capitalizing unfairly on the goodwill or reputation of the property owner.

MISREPRESENTATION (FRAUD)

A misrepresentation leads another to believe in a condition that is different from the condition that actually exists. This is often accomplished through a false or incorrect statement. Misrepresentations may be innocently made by someone who is unaware of the existing facts, but the tort of **fraudulent misrepresentation,** or fraud, involves intentional deceit for personal gain. The tort includes several elements:

1 The misrepresentation of facts or conditions with knowledge that they are false or with reckless disregard for the truth.

2 An intent to induce another to rely on the misrepresentation.

3 Justifiable reliance by the deceived party.

4 Damages suffered as a result of the reliance.

5 A causal connection between the misrepresentation and the injury suffered.

For fraud to occur, more than mere **puffery,** or *seller's talk,* must be involved. Fraud exists only when a person represents as a fact something he or she knows is untrue. For example, it is fraud to claim that a building does not leak when one knows it does. Facts are objectively ascertainable, whereas seller's talk is not. "I am the best accountant in town" is seller's talk. The speaker is not trying to represent something as fact because the term *best* is a subjective, not an objective, term.[6]

Normally, the tort of misrepresentation or fraud occurs only when there is reliance on a *statement of fact.* Sometimes, however, reliance on a *statement of opinion* may involve the tort of misrepresentation if the individual making the statement of opinion has a superior knowledge of the subject matter. For example, when a lawyer makes a statement of opinion about the law in a state in which the lawyer

---

5. *White v. Samsung Electronics America, Inc.,* 971 F.2d 1395 (9th Cir. 1992).
6. In contracts for the sale of goods, Article 2 of the Uniform Commercial Code distinguishes, for warranty purposes, between statements of opinion ("puffery") and statements of fact. See Chapter 13 for a further discussion of this issue.

The 'Lectric Law Library's Legal Lexicon includes an informative discussion of the elements of fraud, as well as different types of fraud. To access this page, go to

http://www.lectlaw.com/def/1079.htm.

is licensed to practice, a court would construe reliance on such a statement to be equivalent to reliance on a statement of fact. We examine fraudulent misrepresentation in further detail in Chapter 8, in the context of contract law.

WRONGFUL INTERFERENCE

Business torts involving wrongful interference are generally divided into two categories: wrongful interference with a contractual relationship and wrongful interference with a business relationship.

Wrongful Interference with a Contractual Relationship　The body of tort law relating to *intentional interference with a contractual relationship* has expanded greatly in recent years. A landmark case involved an opera singer, Joanna Wagner, who was under contract to sing for a man named Lumley for a specified period of years. A man named Gye, who knew of this contract, nonetheless "enticed" Wagner to refuse to carry out the agreement, and Wagner began to sing for Gye. Gye's action constituted a tort because it wrongfully interfered with the contractual relationship between Wagner and Lumley.[7] (Of course, Wagner's refusal to carry out the agreement also entitled Lumley to sue Wagner for breach of contract.)

Three elements are necessary for wrongful interference with a contractual relationship to occur:

1 A valid, enforceable contract must exist between two parties.

2 A third party must know that this contract exists.

3 The third party must *intentionally* cause either of the two parties to breach the contract.

The contract may be between a firm and its employees or a firm and its customers. Sometimes a competitor of a firm draws away one of the firm's key employees. If the original employer can show that the competitor induced the breach—that is, that the former employee would not otherwise have broken the contract—damages can be recovered from the competitor.

It is the intent to do an act that is important in tort law, not the motive behind the intent.

Wrongful Interference with a Business Relationship　Businesspersons devise countless schemes to attract customers, but they are forbidden by the courts to interfere unreasonably with another's business in their attempts to gain a share of the market. There is a difference between competitive methods and **predatory behavior**—actions undertaken with the intention of unlawfully driving competitors completely out of the market.

The distinction usually depends on whether a business is attempting to attract customers in general or to solicit only those customers who have shown an interest in a similar product or service of a specific competitor. If a shopping center contains two shoe stores, an employee of Store A cannot be positioned at the entrance of Store B for the purpose of diverting customers to Store A. This type of activity constitutes the tort of wrongful interference with a business relationship, which is commonly considered to be an unfair trade practice. If this type of activity were permitted, Store A would reap the benefits of Store B's advertising.

PREDATORY BEHAVIOR
Business behavior that is undertaken with the intention of unlawfully driving competitors out of the market.

Defenses to Wrongful Interference　A person will not be liable for the tort of wrongful interference with a contractual or business relationship if it can be shown that the

---

7. *Lumley v. Gye,* 118 Eng.Rep. 749 (1853).

interference was justified, or permissible. Bona fide competitive behavior is a permissible interference even if it results in the breaking of a contract. ■ **EXAMPLE 4.5** If Antonio's Meats advertises so effectively that it induces Beverly's Restaurant Chain to break its contract with Otis Meat Company, Otis Meat Company will be unable to recover against Antonio's Meats on a wrongful interference theory. After all, the public policy that favors free competition in advertising outweighs any possible instability that such competitive activity might cause in contractual relations. ■

Intentional Torts against Property

Intentional torts against property include trespass to land, trespass to personal property, conversion, and disparagement of property. These torts are wrongful actions that interfere with individuals' legally recognized rights with regard to their land or personal property. The law distinguishes real property from personal property (see Chapters 23 and 24). *Real property* is land and things "permanently" attached to the land. *Personal property* consists of all other items, which are basically movable. Thus, a house and lot are real property, whereas the furniture inside a house is personal property. Money and stocks and bonds are also personal property.

TRESPASS TO LAND

A **trespass to land** occurs whenever a person, without permission, enters onto, above, or below the surface of land that is owned by another; causes anything to enter onto the land; remains on the land; or permits anything to remain on it. Actual harm to the land is not an essential element of this tort because the tort is designed to protect the right of an owner to exclusive possession of his or her property. Common types of trespass to land include walking or driving on someone else's land, shooting a gun over the land, throwing rocks at a building that belongs to someone else, building a dam across a river and thereby causing water to back up on someone else's land, and constructing a building so that part of it is on an adjoining landowner's property.

TRESPASS TO LAND
The entry onto, above, or below the surface of land owned by another without the owner's permission or legal authorization.

Trespass Criteria, Rights, and Duties Before a person can be a trespasser, the owner of the real property (or other person in actual and exclusive possession of the property) must establish that person as a trespasser. For example, "posted" trespass signs expressly establish as a trespasser a person who ignores these signs and enters onto the property. A guest in your home is not a trespasser—unless she or he has been asked to leave but refuses. Any person who enters onto your property to commit an illegal act (such as a thief entering a lumberyard at night to steal lumber) is established impliedly as a trespasser, without posted signs.

At common law, a trespasser is liable for damages caused to the property and generally cannot hold the owner liable for injuries sustained on the premises. This common law rule is being abandoned in many jurisdictions in favor of a "reasonable duty of care" rule that varies depending on the status of the parties; for example, a landowner may have a duty to post a notice that the property is patrolled by guard dogs. Furthermore, under the "attractive nuisance" doctrine, children do not assume the risks of the premises if they are attracted to the property by some object, such as a swimming pool, an abandoned building, or a sand pile. Trespassers normally can be removed from the premises through the use of reasonable force without the owner's being liable for assault and battery.

A sign warns trespassers. Should the law allow a trespasser to recover from a landowner for injuries sustained on the premises? Why or why not? (Frederick D. Bodling/Stock Boston)

Defenses against Trespass to Land Trespass to land involves wrongful interference with another person's real property rights. One defense against a trespass claim is to show that the trespass was warranted, as when a trespasser enters to assist someone in danger. Another defense exists when the trespasser can show that he or she had a license to come onto the land. A *licensee* is one who is invited (or allowed to enter) onto the property of another for the licensee's benefit. A person who enters another's property to read an electric meter, for example, is a licensee. When you purchase a ticket to attend a movie or sporting event, you are licensed to go onto the property of another to view that movie or event. Note that licenses to enter on another's property are *revocable* by the property owner. If a property owner asks a meter reader to leave and the meter reader refuses to do so, the meter reader at that point becomes a trespasser.

TRESPASS TO PERSONAL PROPERTY

TRESPASS TO PERSONAL PROPERTY
The unlawful taking or harming of another's personal property; interference with another's right to the exclusive possession of his or her personal property.

Whenever an individual unlawfully harms the personal property of another or otherwise interferes with the personal property owner's right to exclusive possession and enjoyment of that property, **trespass to personal property**—also called *trespass to personalty*[8]—occurs. If a student takes a classmate's business law book as a practical joke and hides it so that the owner is unable to find it for several days prior to the final examination, the student has engaged in a trespass to personal property.

If it can be shown that the trespass to personal property was warranted, then a complete defense exists. Most states, for example, allow automobile repair shops to hold a customer's car (under what is called an *artisan's lien*, discussed in Chapter 16) when the customer refuses to pay for repairs already completed. Trespass to personal property was one of the allegations in the following case. (For a discussion of whether spamming constitutes trespass to personal property, see the examination of cyber torts later in this chapter.)

---

8. Pronounced *per*-sun-ul-tee.

CASE 4.1 Register.com, Inc. v. Verio, Inc.

United States Court of Appeals,
Second Circuit, 2004.
356 F.3d 393.

FACTS The Internet Corporation for Assigned Names and Numbers (ICANN) administers the Internet domain name system. (Domain names will be discussed in detail in Chapter 5.) ICANN appoints registrars to issue the names to persons preparing to establish Web sites on the Internet. An applicant for a name must provide certain information, including an e-mail address. An agreement between ICANN and its registrars refers to this information as "WHOIS information" and requires the registrars to provide public access to it through the Internet "for any lawful purposes" except "the transmission of mass unsolicited, commercial advertising or solicitations via email (spam)." A party who wishes to obtain this information must also agree not to use it for this purpose. Register.com, Inc., is an ICANN registrar. Verio, Inc., sells

Web site design and other services. Verio devised an automated software program (robot, or bot) to submit daily queries for Register's WHOIS data. Verio would then send ads by e-mail and other methods to the identified parties. Despite Register's request, Verio refused to stop. Register filed a suit in a federal district court against Verio, alleging in part trespass to personal property. The court ordered Verio to, among other things, stop accessing Register's computers by bot. Verio appealed to the U.S. Court of Appeals for the Second Circuit.

ISSUE Did Verio's use of its search bot constitute trespass to personal property?

DECISION Yes. The U.S. Court of Appeals for the Second Circuit affirmed the lower court's order. Trespass

(Continued)

CASE 4.1—Continued

to personal property occurs when one party impairs the condition, quality, or value of another's computer.

REASON The court explained that trespass to personal property is committed when one intentionally uses or interferes with a chattel [an item of personal property] in the possession of another in such a way as to impair its condition, quality, or value. In this case, Verio used search robots, which are software programs that perform multiple automated successive queries. Verio's use of these robots consumed a significant portion of the capacity of Register's computer systems. While Verio's robots alone might not incapacitate Register's systems, the court found that "if Verio were permitted to continue to access

Register's computers through such robots, it was highly probable that other Internet service providers would devise similar programs to access Register's data, and that the system would be overtaxed and would crash." The court dismissed Verio's argument that it could not be liable for trespass because Register had never instructed it not to use its robot programs. Register had requested Verio to stop and this, in the court's view, was sufficient to advise Verio that its use of robots was not authorized and could cause harm to Register's systems.

FOR CRITICAL ANALYSIS—Technological Consideration *Why should the use of a bot to initiate "multiple automated successive queries" have a different legal effect than typing and submitting queries manually?*

CONVERSION

CONVERSION
Wrongfully taking or retaining possession of an individual's personal property and placing it in the service of another.

Whenever personal property is wrongfully taken from its rightful owner or possessor and placed in the service of another, the act of **conversion** occurs. Conversion is defined as any act depriving an owner of personal property without that owner's permission and without just cause. When conversion occurs, the tort of trespass to personal property usually occurs as well. If the initial taking of the property was unlawful, there is trespass; retention of that property is conversion. If the initial taking of the property was permitted by the owner or for some other reason is not a trespass, failure to return it may still be conversion. Conversion is the civil side of crimes related to theft. A store clerk who steals merchandise from the store commits a crime and engages in the tort of conversion at the same time.

Even if a person mistakenly believed that she or he was entitled to the goods, the tort of conversion may occur. In other words, good intentions are not a defense against conversion; in fact, conversion can be an entirely innocent act. Someone who buys stolen goods, for example, is guilty of conversion even if he or she did not know that the goods were stolen. If the true owner brings a tort action against the buyer, the buyer must either return the property to the owner or pay the owner the full value of the property, despite having already paid the thief.

A successful defense against the charge of conversion is that the purported owner does not in fact own the property or does not have a right to possess it that is superior to the right of the holder. Necessity is another possible defense against conversion. ■ **EXAMPLE 4.6** If Abrams takes Mendoza's cat, Abrams is guilty of conversion. If Mendoza sues Abrams, Abrams must return the cat or pay damages. If, however, the cat has rabies and Abrams took the cat to protect the public, Abrams has a valid defense—necessity (and perhaps even self-defense, if he can prove that he was in danger because of the cat). ■

DISPARAGEMENT OF PROPERTY

DISPARAGEMENT OF PROPERTY
An economically injurious falsehood made about another's product or property. A general term for torts that are more specifically referred to as slander of quality or slander of title.

Disparagement of property occurs when economically injurious falsehoods are made about another's product or property, not about another's reputation. Disparagement of property is a general term for torts that can be more specifically referred to as *slander of quality* or *slander of title*.

SLANDER OF QUALITY (TRADE LIBEL)
The publication of false information about another's product, alleging that it is not what its seller claims.

Slander of Quality   Publication of false information about another's product, alleging that it is not what its seller claims, constitutes the tort of **slander of quality,** or **trade libel.** The plaintiff must prove that actual damages proximately resulted from the slander of quality. In other words, the plaintiff must show not only that a third person refrained from dealing with the plaintiff because of the improper publication but also that there were associated damages. The economic calculation of such damages—they are, after all, conjectural—is often extremely difficult.

An improper publication may be both a slander of quality and a defamation. For example, a statement that disparages the quality of a product may also, by implication, disparage the character of the person who would sell such a product.

SLANDER OF TITLE
The publication of a statement that denies or casts doubt on another's legal ownership of any property, causing financial loss to that property's owner.

Slander of Title   When a publication denies or casts doubt on another's legal ownership of any property, and this results in financial loss to that property's owner, the tort of **slander of title** may exist. Usually, this is an intentional tort in which someone knowingly publishes an untrue statement about property with the intent of discouraging a third person from dealing with the person slandered. For example, it would be difficult for a car dealer to attract customers after competitors published a notice that the dealer's stock consisted of stolen autos.

◼ Unintentional Torts (Negligence)

NEGLIGENCE
The failure to exercise the standard of care that a reasonable person would exercise in similar circumstances.

The tort of **negligence** occurs when someone suffers injury because of another's failure to live up to a required *duty of care*. In contrast to intentional torts, in torts involving negligence, the tortfeasor neither wishes to bring about the consequences of the act nor believes that they will occur. The actor's conduct merely creates a *risk* of such consequences. If no risk is created, there is no negligence.

Many of the actions discussed in the section on intentional torts constitute negligence if the element of intent is missing. ◼ **EXAMPLE 4.7** Suppose that Juarez walks up to Natsuyo and intentionally shoves her. Natsuyo falls and breaks an arm as a result. In this situation, Juarez will have committed the intentional tort of assault and battery. If Juarez carelessly bumps into Natsuyo, however, and she falls and breaks an arm as a result, Juarez's action will constitute negligence. In either situation, Juarez has committed a tort. ◼

In examining a question of negligence, one should ask the following four questions (each of these elements of negligence will be discussed below):

1 Did the defendant owe a duty of care to the plaintiff?
2 Did the defendant breach that duty?
3 Did the plaintiff suffer a legally recognizable injury as a result of the defendant's breach of the duty of care?
4 Did the defendant's breach cause the plaintiff's injury?

THE DUTY OF CARE AND ITS BREACH

DUTY OF CARE
The duty of all persons, as established by tort law, to exercise a reasonable amount of care in their dealings with others. Failure to exercise due care, which is normally determined by the "reasonable person standard," constitutes the tort of negligence.

The concept of a **duty of care** arises from the notion that if we are to live in society with other people, some actions can be tolerated and some cannot; some actions are right and some are wrong; and some actions are reasonable and some are not. The basic principle underlying the duty of care is that people are free to act as they please so long as their actions do not infringe on the interests of others.

When someone fails to comply with the duty to exercise reasonable care, a potentially tortious act may have been committed. Failure to live up to a standard of care may be an act (setting fire to a building) or an omission (neglecting to put out a

Drawing by Maslin; © 1990 The New Yorker Magazine, Inc.

"To answer your question. Yes, if you shoot an arrow into the air and it falls to earth you should know not where, you could be liable for any damage it may cause."

campfire). It may be a careless act or a carefully performed but nevertheless dangerous act that results in injury. Courts consider the nature of the act (whether it is outrageous or commonplace), the manner in which the act is performed (cautiously versus heedlessly), and the nature of the injury (whether it is serious or slight) in determining whether the duty of care has been breached.

REASONABLE PERSON STANDARD
The standard of behavior expected of a hypothetical "reasonable person"; the standard against which negligence is measured and that must be observed to avoid liability for negligence.

The Reasonable Person Standard   Tort law measures duty by the **reasonable person standard.** In determining whether a duty of care has been breached, the courts ask how a reasonable person would have acted in the same circumstances. The reasonable person standard is said to be (though in an absolute sense it cannot be) objective. It is not necessarily how a particular person would act. It is society's judgment on how people *should* act. If the so-called reasonable person existed, he or she would be careful, conscientious, even tempered, and honest. The courts frequently use this hypothetical reasonable person in decisions relating to other areas of law as well.

That individuals are required to exercise a reasonable standard of care in their activities is a pervasive concept in business law, and many of the issues discussed in subsequent chapters of this text have to do with this duty. What constitutes reasonable care varies, of course, with the circumstances.

ETHICAL ISSUE 4.1

Does a person's duty of care include a duty to come to the aid of a stranger in peril? Suppose that you are walking down a city street and notice that a pedestrian is about to step directly in front of an oncoming bus. Do you have a legal duty to warn that individual? No. Although most people would probably concede that the observer has an *ethical* or moral duty to warn the other in this situation, tort law does not impose a general duty to rescue others in peril. People involved in special relationships, however, have been held to have a duty to rescue other parties within the relationship. A person has a duty to rescue his or her child or spouse if either is in danger, for example. Other special relationships, such as those between teachers and students or hiking and hunting partners, may also give rise to a duty to rescue. In addition, if a person who has no duty to rescue undertakes to rescue another, then the rescuer is charged with a duty to follow through with due care in the rescue attempt. ■

The Duty of Landowners   Landowners are expected to exercise reasonable care to protect persons coming onto their property from harm. As mentioned earlier, in some jurisdictions, landowners are held to owe a duty to protect even trespassers against certain risks. Landowners who rent or lease premises to tenants (see Chapter 24) are expected to exercise reasonable care to ensure that the tenants and their guests are not harmed in common areas, such as stairways, entryways, laundry rooms, and the like.

Retailers and other firms that explicitly or implicitly invite persons to come onto their premises are usually charged with a duty to exercise reasonable care to protect those persons, who are considered **business invitees.** For example, if you entered a supermarket, slipped on a wet floor, and sustained injuries as a result, the owner of the supermarket would be liable for damages if when you slipped there was no sign warning that the floor was wet. A court would hold that the business owner was negligent because the owner failed to exercise a reasonable degree of care in protecting the store's customers against foreseeable risks about which the owner knew or *should have known.* That a patron might slip on the wet floor and be injured as a result was a foreseeable risk, and the owner should have taken care to avoid this risk or to warn the customer of it. The landowner also has a duty to discover and remove any hidden dangers that might injure a customer or other invitee.

Some risks, of course, are so obvious that the owner need not warn of them. For instance, a business owner does not need to warn customers to open a door before attempting to walk through it. Other risks, however, even though they may seem obvious to a business owner, may not be so in the eyes of another, such as a child. For example, a hardware store owner may not think it is necessary to warn customers not to climb a stepladder leaning against the back wall of the store. It is possible, though, that a child could climb up and tip the ladder over and be hurt as a result and that the store could be held liable.

In the following case, the court had to decide whether a store owner should be held liable for a customer's injury on the premises. The question was whether the owner had notice of the condition that led to the customer's injury.

BUSINESS INVITEE
A person, such as a customer or a client, who is invited onto business premises by the owner of those premises for business purposes.

CASE 4.2 ■ Martin v. Wal-Mart Stores, Inc.

United States Court of Appeals,
Eighth Circuit, 1999.
183 F.3d 770.
**http://guide.lp.findlaw.com/casecode/courts/
8th.html[a]**

a. This URL will take you to a Web site maintained by FindLaw, which is now a part of West Group. When you access the site, enter "Wal-Mart" in the "Party Name Search" box and then click on "Search." Scroll down the list on the page that opens and select the link to "Harold Martin v. Wal-Mart Stores."

FACTS Harold Martin was shopping in the sporting goods department of a Wal-Mart store. There was one employee in the department at that time. In front of the sporting goods section, in the store's main aisle (which the employees referred to as "action alley"), there was a large display of stacked cases of shotgun shells. On top of the cases were individual boxes of shells. Shortly after the sporting

(Continued)

CASE 4.2—Continued

goods employee walked past the display, Martin did so, but Martin slipped on some loose shotgun shell pellets and fell to the floor. He immediately lost feeling in, and control of, his legs. Sensation and control returned, but during the next week, he lost the use of his legs several times for periods of ten to fifteen minutes. Eventually, sensation and control did not return to the front half of his left foot. Doctors diagnosed the condition as permanent. Martin filed a suit against Wal-Mart in a federal district court, seeking damages for his injury. The jury found in his favor, and the court denied Wal-Mart's motion for a directed verdict. Wal-Mart appealed to the U.S. Court of Appeals for the Eighth Circuit.

ISSUE   Should Wal-Mart be held liable for Martin's injury?

DECISION   Yes. The U.S. Court of Appeals for the Eighth Circuit affirmed the judgment of the lower court.

REASON   The appellate court stated, "The traditional rule * * * required a plaintiff in a slip and fall case to establish that the defendant store had either actual or constructive notice[b] of the dangerous condition." The court, however, explained that this case involved the self-service store exception to the traditional slip-and-fall rule. A self-service store has notice that certain dangers arising through customer involvement are likely to occur and has a duty to anticipate them. Part of this duty is to "warn customers or protect them from the danger." Here, Wal-Mart had constructive notice of the pellets on the floor in the main aisle. Martin slipped on pellets next to a large display of shotgun shells immediately abutting the sporting goods department. The chance that merchandise will wind up on the floor (or merchandise will be spilled on the floor) in the department in which that merchandise is sold or displayed is "exactly the type of foreseeable risk" that is part of the self-service store exception.

FOR CRITICAL ANALYSIS—Ethical Consideration
Why do the courts impose constructive notice requirements on owners of self-service stores but not on owners of other stores?

b. *Constructive notice* is notice that is implied by law, in view of the circumstances.

You can locate the professional standards for various organizations at **http://www.lib.uwaterloo.ca/ society/standards.html**.

MALPRACTICE
Professional misconduct or the lack of the requisite degree of skill as a professional. Negligence—the failure to exercise due care—on the part of a professional, such as a physician, is commonly referred to as malpractice.

The Duty of Professionals   If an individual has knowledge, skill, or intelligence superior to that of an ordinary person, the individual's conduct must be consistent with that status. Professionals—including physicians, dentists, architects, engineers, accountants, lawyers, and others—are required to have a standard minimum level of special knowledge and ability. Therefore, in determining what constitutes reasonable care in the case of professionals, their training and expertise are taken into account. In other words, an accountant cannot defend against a lawsuit for negligence by stating, "But I was not familiar with that principle of accounting."

If a professional violates her or his duty of care toward a client, the professional may be sued for **malpractice**. For example, a patient might sue a physician for *medical malpractice*. A client might sue an attorney for *legal malpractice*.

THE INJURY REQUIREMENT AND DAMAGES

For a tort to have been committed, the plaintiff must have suffered a *legally recognizable* injury. To recover damages (receive compensation), the plaintiff must have suffered some loss, harm, wrong, or invasion of a protected interest. Essentially, the purpose of tort law is to compensate for legally recognized injuries resulting from wrongful acts. If no harm or injury results from a given negligent action, there is nothing to compensate—and no tort exists. ■ EXAMPLE 4.8 If you carelessly bump into a passerby, who stumbles and falls as a result, you may be liable in tort if the passerby is injured in the fall. If the person is unharmed, however, there normally could be no suit for damages, because no injury was suffered. ■

As already mentioned, the purpose of tort law is not to punish people for tortious acts but to compensate the injured parties for harm suffered by awarding damages.

COMPENSATORY DAMAGES
A money award equivalent to the actual value of injuries or damages sustained by the aggrieved party.

PUNITIVE DAMAGES
Money damages that may be awarded to a plaintiff to punish the defendant and deter future similar conduct.

Compensatory damages are intended to reimburse a plaintiff for actual losses—to make the plaintiff whole. Occasionally, **punitive damages** are also awarded to punish the wrongdoer and deter others from similar wrongdoing. Punitive damages are rarely awarded in lawsuits for ordinary negligence and usually are given only in cases involving intentional torts. They may be awarded, however, in suits involving *gross negligence*, which can be defined as an intentional failure to perform a manifest duty in reckless disregard of the consequences of such a failure for the life or property of another.

In *State Farm Mutual Automobile Insurance Co. v. Campbell,*[9] the United States Supreme Court held that to the extent an award of punitive damages is grossly excessive, it furthers no legitimate purpose and violates due process requirements (discussed in Chapter 1). While this case dealt with intentional torts (fraud and intentional infliction of emotional distress), the Court's holding applies equally to punitive damages awards in gross negligence cases.

CAUSATION

Another element necessary to a tort is *causation.* If a person fails in a duty of care and someone suffers injury, the wrongful activity must have caused the harm for a tort to have been committed. In deciding whether there is causation, the court must address two questions:

1 *Is there causation in fact?* Did the injury occur because of the defendant's act, or would it have occurred anyway? If an injury would not have occurred without the defendant's act, then there is causation in fact. **Causation in fact** can usually be determined by the use of the *but for* test: "but for" the wrongful act, the injury would not have occurred. Theoretically, causation in fact is limitless. One could claim, for example, that "but for" the creation of the world, a particular injury would not have occurred. Thus, as a practical matter, the law has to establish limits, and it does so through the concept of proximate cause.

CAUSATION IN FACT
An act or omission without which an event would not have occurred.

PROXIMATE CAUSE
Legal cause; exists when the connection between an act and an injury is strong enough to justify imposing liability.

2 *Was the act the proximate cause of the injury?* **Proximate cause,** or legal cause, exists when the connection between an act and an injury is strong enough to justify imposing liability. ■ **EXAMPLE 4.9** Ackerman carelessly leaves a campfire burning. The fire not only burns down the forest but also sets off an explosion in a nearby chemical plant that spills chemicals into a river, killing all the fish for a hundred miles downstream and ruining the economy of a tourist resort. Should Ackerman be liable to the resort owners? To the tourists whose vacations were ruined? These are questions of proximate cause that a court must decide. ■

Probably the most cited case on proximate cause is the *Palsgraf* case, discussed in this chapter's *Landmark in the Law* feature on the next page. In determining the issue of proximate cause, the court addressed the following question: Does a defendant's duty of care extend only to those who may be injured as a result of a foreseeable risk, or does it extend also to a person whose injury could not reasonably be foreseen?

NOTE Proximate cause can be thought of as a question of social policy. Should the defendant be made to bear the loss instead of the plaintiff?

DEFENSES TO NEGLIGENCE

Defendants often defend against negligence claims by asserting that the plaintiffs failed to prove the existence of one or more of the required elements for negligence. Additionally, there are three basic *affirmative* defenses in negligence cases (defenses that defendants can use to avoid liability even if the facts are as the plaintiffs state):

9. 538 U.S. 408, 123 S.Ct. 1513, 155 L.Ed.2d 585 (2003).

LANDMARK IN THE LAW

Palsgraf v. Long Island Railroad Co. (1928)

In 1928, the New York Court of Appeals (that state's highest court) issued its decision in *Palsgraf v. Long Island Railroad Co.,*[a] a case that has become a landmark in negligence law with respect to proximate cause.

THE FACTS OF THE CASE

The plaintiff, Palsgraf, was waiting for a train on a station platform. A man carrying a small package wrapped in newspaper was rushing to catch a train that had begun to move away from the platform. As the man attempted to jump aboard the moving train, he seemed unsteady and about to fall. A railroad guard on the train car reached forward to grab him, and another guard on the platform pushed him from behind to help him board the train. In the process, the man's package fell on the railroad tracks and exploded, because it contained fireworks. The repercussions of the explosion caused scales at the other end of the train platform to fall on Palsgraf, who was injured as a result. She sued the railroad company for damages in a New York state court.

THE QUESTION OF PROXIMATE CAUSE

At the trial, the jury found that the railroad guards were negligent in their conduct. On appeal, the question before the New York Court of Appeals was whether the conduct of the railroad guards was the proximate cause of Palsgraf's injuries. In other words, did the guards' duty of care extend to Palsgraf, who was outside the zone of danger and whose injury could not reasonably have been foreseen?

The court stated that the question of whether the guards were negligent *with respect to Palsgraf* depended on whether her injury was *reasonably foreseeable* to the railroad guards. Although the guards may have acted negligently with respect to the man boarding the train, this had no bearing on the question of their negligence with respect to Palsgraf. This was not a situation in which a person committed an act so potentially harmful (for example, firing a gun at a building) that he or she would be held responsible for any harm that resulted. The court stated that here "there was nothing in the situation to suggest to the most cautious mind that the parcel wrapped in newspaper would spread wreckage through the station." The court thus concluded that the railroad guards were not negligent with respect to Palsgraf because her injury was not reasonably foreseeable.

APPLICATION TO TODAY'S WORLD

The Palsgraf *case established* foreseeability *as the test for proximate cause. Today, the courts continue to apply this test in determining proximate cause—and thus tort liability for injuries. Generally, if the victim of a harm or the consequences of a harm done are unforeseeable, there is no proximate cause. Note, though, that in the online environment, distinctions based on physical proximity, such as the "zone of danger" cited by the court in this case, are largely inapplicable.*

RELEVANT WEB SITES

To locate information on the Web concerning the Palsgraf *decision, go to this text's Web site at* **http://blt.westbuslaw.com**, *select "Chapter 4," and click on "URLs for Landmarks."*

a. 248 N.Y. 339, 162 N.E. 99 (1928).

(1) assumption of risk, (2) superseding cause, and (3) contributory and comparative negligence.

Assumption of Risk   A plaintiff who voluntarily enters into a risky situation, knowing the risk involved, will not be allowed to recover. This is the defense of **assumption of risk.** The requirements of this defense are (1) knowledge of the risk and (2) voluntary assumption of the risk.

The risk can be assumed by express agreement, or the assumption of risk can be implied by the plaintiff's knowledge of the risk and subsequent conduct. For example, a driver entering a race knows that there is a risk of being killed or injured in a crash. Of course, the plaintiff does not assume a risk different from or greater than the risk normally carried by the activity. In our example, the race driver would not assume the risk that the banking in the curves of the racetrack will give way during the race because of a construction defect.

Risks are not deemed to be assumed in situations involving emergencies. Neither are they assumed when a statute protects a class of people from harm and a member of the class is injured by the harm. For example, employees are protected by statute from harmful working conditions and therefore do not assume the risks associated with the workplace. An employee who is injured will generally be compensated regardless of fault under state workers' compensation statutes (discussed in Chapter 18).

Superseding Cause   An unforeseeable intervening event may break the connection between a wrongful act and an injury to another. If so, the event acts as a *superseding cause*—that is, it relieves a defendant of liability for injuries caused by the intervening event. ■ **EXAMPLE 4.10** Suppose that Derrick keeps a can of gasoline in the trunk of his car. The presence of the gasoline creates a foreseeable risk and is thus a negligent act. If Derrick's car skids and crashes into a tree, causing the gasoline can to explode, Derrick would be liable for injuries sustained by passing pedestrians because of his negligence. If the explosion had been caused by lightning striking the car, however, the lightning would supersede Derrick's original negligence as a cause of the damage, because the lightning was not foreseeable. ■

Contributory and Comparative Negligence   All individuals are expected to exercise a reasonable degree of care in looking out for themselves. In the past, under the common law doctrine of **contributory negligence,** a plaintiff who was also negligent (failed to exercise a reasonable degree of care) could not recover anything from the defendant. Under this rule, no matter how insignificant the plaintiff's negligence was relative to the defendant's negligence, the plaintiff would be precluded from recovering any damages. Today, only a few jurisdictions still hold to this doctrine. In the majority of states, the doctrine of contributory negligence has been replaced by a **comparative negligence** standard.

Under the comparative negligence standard, both the plaintiff's and the defendant's negligence are computed, and the liability for damages is distributed accordingly. Some jurisdictions have adopted a "pure" form of comparative negligence that allows the plaintiff to recover, even if the extent of his or her fault is greater than that of the defendant. For example, if the plaintiff was 80 percent at fault and the defendant 20 percent at fault, the plaintiff may recover 20 percent of his or her damages. Many states' comparative negligence statutes, however, contain a "50 percent" rule that precludes the plaintiff from any recovery if she or he was more than 50 percent at fault.

ASSUMPTION OF RISK
A doctrine under which a plaintiff may not recover for injuries or damages suffered from risks he or she knows of and has voluntarily assumed.

CONTRIBUTORY NEGLIGENCE
A rule in tort law that completely bars the plaintiff from recovering any damages if the damage suffered is partly the plaintiff's own fault; used in a minority of states.

COMPARATIVE NEGLIGENCE
A rule in tort law that reduces the plaintiff's recovery in proportion to the plaintiff's degree of fault, rather than barring recovery completely; used in the majority of states.

A bungee jumper leaps from a platform. If the jumper is injured and sues the operator of the jump for negligence, what defenses might the operator use to avoid liability? (Paul Thompson/Image State)

SPECIAL NEGLIGENCE DOCTRINES AND STATUTES

There are a number of special doctrines and statutes relating to negligence. We examine a few of them here.

Res Ipsa Loquitur   Generally, in lawsuits involving negligence, the plaintiff has the burden of proving that the defendant was negligent. In certain situations, however, when negligence is very difficult or impossible to prove, the courts may infer that negligence has occurred; then the burden of proof rests on the defendant—to prove he or she was *not* negligent. The inference of the defendant's negligence is known as the doctrine of *res ipsa loquitur*,[10] which translates as "the facts speak for themselves."

This doctrine is applied only when the event creating the damage or injury is one that ordinarily would occur only as a result of negligence. ■ **EXAMPLE 4.11** If a person undergoes knee surgery and following the surgery has a severed nerve in the knee area, that person can sue the surgeon under a theory of *res ipsa loquitur*. In this instance, the injury would never occur in the absence of the surgeon's negligence.[11] ■ For the doctrine of *res ipsa loquitur* to apply, the event must have been within the defendant's power to control, and it must not have been due to any voluntary action or contribution on the part of the plaintiff.

RES IPSA LOQUITUR
A doctrine under which negligence may be inferred simply because an event occurred, if it is the type of event that would never occur in the absence of negligence. Literally, the term means "the facts speak for themselves."

Negligence *Per Se*   Certain conduct, whether it consists of an action or a failure to act, may be treated as **negligence *per se*** (*per se* means "in or of itself"). Negligence *per se* may occur if an individual violates a statute or an ordinance providing for a criminal penalty and that violation causes another to be injured. The injured person must prove (1) that the statute clearly sets out what standard of conduct is expected, when and where it is expected, and of whom it is expected; (2) that he or she is in the class intended to be protected by the statute; and (3) that the statute was designed to prevent the type of injury that he or she suffered. The standard of conduct required by the statute is the duty that the defendant owes to the plaintiff, and a violation of the statute is the breach of that duty.

NEGLIGENCE *PER SE*
An action or failure to act in violation of a statutory requirement.

■ **EXAMPLE 4.12** A statute may require a landowner to maintain a building in safe condition and may also subject the owner to a criminal penalty, such as a fine, if the building is not kept safe. The statute is meant to protect those who are rightfully in the building. Thus, if the owner, without a sufficient excuse, violates the statute and a tenant is thereby injured, then a majority of courts will hold that the owner's unexcused violation of the statute conclusively establishes a breach of a duty of care—that is, that the owner's violation is negligence *per se*. ■

"Danger Invites Rescue" Doctrine   Typically, if an individual takes a defensive action, such as swerving to avoid an oncoming car, the original wrongdoer will not be relieved of liability even if the injury actually resulted from the attempt to escape harm. The same is true under the "danger invites rescue" doctrine. ■ **EXAMPLE 4.13** If Lemming commits an act that endangers Salter, and Yokem sustains an injury trying to protect Salter, then Lemming will be liable for Yokem's injury. Lemming will also be liable for any injuries Salter may sustain. ■ Rescuers can injure themselves, or the person rescued, or even a stranger, but the original wrongdoer will still be liable.

---

10. Pronounced *rehz ihp*-suh *low*-kwuh-tuhr.
11. *Edwards v. Boland*, 41 Mass.App.Ct. 375, 670 N.E.2d 404 (1996).

GOOD SAMARITAN STATUTE
A state statute stipulating that persons who provide emergency services to, or rescue, someone in peril cannot be sued for negligence, unless they act recklessly, thereby causing further harm.

DRAM SHOP ACT
A state statute that imposes liability on the owners of bars and taverns, as well as those who serve alcoholic drinks to the public, for injuries resulting from accidents caused by intoxicated persons when the sellers or servers of alcoholic drinks contributed to the intoxication.

STRICT LIABILITY
Liability regardless of fault. In tort law, strict liability is imposed on a manufacturer or seller that introduces into commerce a good that is unreasonably dangerous when in a defective condition.

Special Negligence Statutes   A number of states have enacted statutes prescribing duties and responsibilities in certain circumstances. For example, most states now have what are called **Good Samaritan statutes.** Under these statutes, someone who is aided voluntarily by others cannot turn around and sue the "Good Samaritans" for negligence. These laws were passed largely to protect physicians and medical personnel who voluntarily render services in emergency situations to those in need, such as individuals hurt in car accidents.

Many states have also passed **dram shop acts,** under which a tavern owner or bartender may be held liable for injuries caused by a person who became intoxicated while drinking at the bar or who was already intoxicated when served by the bartender. In some states, statutes impose liability on *social hosts* (persons hosting parties) for injuries caused by guests who became intoxicated at the hosts' homes. Under these statutes, it is unnecessary to prove that the tavern owner, bartender, or social host was negligent.

Strict Liability

Another category of torts is called **strict liability,** or *liability without fault.* Intentional torts and torts of negligence involve acts that depart from a reasonable standard of care and cause injuries. Under the doctrine of strict liability, liability for injury is imposed for reasons other than fault. Strict liability for damages proximately caused by an abnormally dangerous or exceptional activity is one application of this doctrine. Courts apply the doctrine of strict liability in such cases because of the extreme risk of the activity. Even if blasting with dynamite is performed with all reasonable care, there is still a risk of injury. Balancing that risk against the potential for harm, it seems reasonable to ask the person engaged in the activity to pay for injuries caused by that activity. Although there is no fault, there is still responsibility because of the dangerous nature of the undertaking.

There are other applications of the strict liability principle. Persons who keep dangerous animals, for example, are strictly liable for any harm inflicted by the animals. A significant application of strict liability is in the area of *product liability*—liability of manufacturers and sellers for harmful or defective products. Liability here is a matter of social policy and is based on two factors: (1) the manufacturer or seller can better bear the cost of injury because it can spread the cost throughout society by increasing prices of goods and services, and (2) the manufacturer or seller is making a profit from its activities and therefore should bear the cost of injury as an operating expense. We will discuss product liability in greater detail in Chapter 13.

Cyber Torts

It should come as no surprise that torts can also be committed in the online environment. Torts committed via the Internet are often called *cyber torts.* Over the last ten years, the courts have had to decide how to apply traditional tort law to torts committed in cyberspace. Consider, for example, issues of proof. How can it be proved that an online defamatory remark was "published" (which requires that a third party see or hear it)? How can the identity of the person who made the remark be discovered? Can an Internet service provider (ISP), such as AOL, be forced to reveal the source of an anonymous comment made by one of its subscribers? We explore some of these questions in this section, as well as some of the legal questions that have arisen with respect to bulk e-mail advertising.

DEFAMATION ONLINE

Recall from the discussion of defamation earlier in this chapter that one who repeats or otherwise republishes a defamatory statement can be subject to liability as if he or she had originally published it. Thus, publishers generally can be held liable for defamatory contents in the books and periodicals that they publish. Now consider online forums. These forums allow anyone—customers, employees, or crackpots— to complain about a firm's personnel, policies, practices, or products. Whatever the truth of the complaint is, it might have an impact on the business of the firm. One of the early questions in the online legal arena was whether the providers of such forums could be held liable, as publishers, for defamatory statements made in those forums.

For an interesting article discussing the increasing number of online defamation cases and the associated costs, go to the Web site of Computer Times at

http://computertimes.asia1. com/issues/story/ 0,5104,1577,00.html.

Liability of Internet Service Providers   Prior to the passage of the Communications Decency Act (CDA) of 1996, the courts grappled on several occasions with the question of whether ISPs should be regarded as publishers and thus be held liable for defamatory messages made by users of their services. The CDA resolved the issue by stating that "[n]o provider or user of an interactive computer service shall be treated as the publisher or speaker of any information provided by another information content provider."[12] In a number of key cases, the ISP provisions of the CDA have been invoked to shield ISPs from liability for defamatory postings on their bulletin boards.

◼ **EXAMPLE 4.14** In a leading case on this issue, decided the year after the CDA was enacted, America Online, Inc. (AOL, now part of Time Warner, Inc.), was not held liable even though it did not promptly remove defamatory messages of which it had been made aware. In upholding a U.S. district court's ruling in AOL's favor, a federal appellate court stated that the CDA "plainly immunizes computer service providers like AOL from liability for information that originates with third parties." The court explained that the purpose of the statute is "to maintain the robust nature of Internet communication and, accordingly, to keep government interference in the medium to a minimum."[13] ◼

In subsequent cases, the courts have reached similar conclusions.[14] The courts have also extended the immunity to liability provided by the CDA to auction houses, such as eBay.[15] At issue in the following case was whether the CDA also shields secondary publishers, or distributors, from liability.

---

12. 47 U.S.C. Section 230.

13. *Zeran v. America Online, Inc.,* 129 F.3d 327 (4th Cir. 1997); *cert.* denied, 524 U.S. 934, 118 S.Ct. 2341, 141 L.Ed.2d 712 (1998).

14. See, for example, *Noah v. AOL Time Warner, Inc.,* 261 F.Supp.2d 532 (E.D.Va. 2003).

15. *Stoner v. eBay, Inc.,* 2000 WL 1705637 (Cal.Super.Ct. 2000).

CASE 4.3 ■ Barrett v. Rosenthal

California Court of Appeal,
First District,
Division 2, 2004.
9 Cal.Rptr.3d 142.

FACTS Stephen Barrett and Terry Polevoy are physicians engaged in combating illegal or unsubstantiated alternative health-care practices and products. Each maintains Web sites that expose "health frauds and quackery" and provide guides to help consumers make intelligent health-care decisions. Ilena Rosenthal directs the Humantics Foundation for Women and participates in Usenet newsgroups that focus on alternative medicine. Among her postings, Rosenthal distributed an e-mail message that she received from another individual, Timothy Bolen, accusing Polevoy of stalking women. Polevoy informed Rosenthal that the message was not true and asked her to withdraw it, but she refused and reposted the message many times, referring to Barrett and Polevoy as "quacks." She also posted statements that the two physicians were "a power-hungry, misguided bunch of pseudoscientific socialist bigots" and were "being sued by many doctors and health organizations." Barrett and Polevoy filed a suit in a California state court against Rosenthal and others, alleging libel and other torts. The court ruled in part that under the CDA, Rosenthal was immune from liability for the reposting of Bolen's statements. The plaintiffs appealed to a state intermediate appellate court.

ISSUE Is a secondary publisher, or distributor, of another's libelous statements immune from liability under the CDA?

DECISION No. The state intermediate appellate court vacated the lower court's ruling on this issue and remanded the case for further proceedings.[a]

a. The lower court's decision on remand was not available at the time this book went to press, but it may be by the time you read this. If you have purchased access to Westlaw Campus, you might be able to locate the remanded decision using that database. Alternatively, you may be able to find the case online at some other site. (See this text's inside front cover for information on Westlaw Campus and URLs for online court decisions.)

REASON The court reasoned: "It is true that defamation requires a publication, and that every repetition is a publication, whether it is effectuated by a primary publisher or by a distributor; this is why distributors are sometimes referred to as 'secondary publishers.' However, the common law subjects the two types of publishers to distinctly different standards of liability for the transmission of the defamation of a third person. Because primary publishers ordinarily exercise control over content, they have a duty to monitor content; distributors, who have no such control, therefore have no such duty. It is entirely reasonable to assume Congress was aware of this significant and very well-established distinction, and that if it intended [the CDA] to immunize providers and users not merely from primary publisher liability but also from distributor liability it would have made this clear, as, for example, by adding the word 'distributor,' and not merely barring liability 'as the publisher or speaker' of information provided by another. * * * Legislative use of the legally uncertain word 'publisher' is simply too flimsy a basis upon which to grant providers and users of interactive computer services what amounts to an absolute protection requiring the total sacrifice of the competing value served by the law of defamation and the subordination of a concept at the root of any decent system of ordered liberty."

WHY IS THIS CASE IMPORTANT? *In this case, the court refused to extend to secondary publishers (distributors) the immunity that the CDA gives to primary publishers. The court concluded that if Congress had intended to protect providers and users from distributor liability, Congress would have made that intent clear. This ruling establishes that, on some level, secondary publishers can be held responsible for the libelous materials that they distribute.*

Piercing the Veil of Anonymity A threshold barrier to anyone who seeks to bring an action for online defamation is discovering the identity of the person who posted the defamatory message online. ISPs can disclose personal information about their customers only when ordered to do so by a court. Consequently, businesses and individuals are increasingly resorting to lawsuits against "John Does." Then, using the authority of the courts, they can obtain from the ISPs the identities of the persons responsible for the messages.

■ **EXAMPLE 4.15** In one case, Eric Hvide, a former chief executive of a company called Hvide Marine, sued a number of "John Does" who had posted allegedly defamatory statements about his company on various online message boards. Hvide, who eventually lost his job, sued the John Does for libel in a Florida court. The court ruled that Yahoo and AOL had to reveal the identities of the defendant Does.[16] ■

In other cases, however, the courts have refused to order an ISP to disclose the identity of subscribers.[17] Generally, in these cases the courts must decide which right should take priority: the right to free (anonymous) speech under the First Amendment or the right not to be defamed.

Spam

Bulk, unsolicited e-mail ("junk" e-mail) sent to all of the users on a particular e-mailing list is often called **spam**.[18] Typically, spam consists of a product ad sent to all of the users on an e-mailing list or all of the members of a newsgroup.

SPAM
Bulk, unsolicited ("junk") e-mail.

Spam wastes user time and network bandwidth (the amount of data that can be transmitted within a certain time). It also imposes a burden on an ISP's equipment as well as on e-mail recipients' computer systems. Does this mean that spamming may constitute a form of trespass to personal property? For a discussion of this question, see this chapter's *Adapting the Law to the Online Environment.*

In the last few years, the number of e-mail ads traveling through cyberspace has escalated significantly, and today spam accounts for an estimated 60 percent of all e-mail. Indeed, many contend that unwanted e-mail is threatening the viability of e-mail as a communications tool and an instrument of commerce. Because of the problems associated with spam, a majority of the states now have laws regulating spam. In 2003, the U.S. Congress also enacted a law to regulate the use of spam.

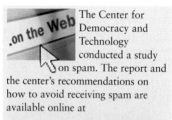 The Center for Democracy and Technology conducted a study on spam. The report and the center's recommendations on how to avoid receiving spam are available online at

http://www.cdt.org/speech/ spam/030319spamreport. shtml.

State Regulation of Spam   Because of the problems associated with spam, thirty-six states have enacted laws that prohibit or regulate its use. A few states, such as Washington, prohibit unsolicited e-mail that is promoting goods, services, or real estate for sale or lease. In some other states, including Minnesota, an unsolicited e-mail ad must state in its subject line that it is an ad ("ADV:"). Many state laws regulating spam require the senders of e-mail ads to instruct the recipients on how they can "opt out" of further e-mail ads from the same sources. For instance, in some states an unsolicited e-mail ad must include a toll-free phone number or return e-mail address through which the recipient can contact the sender to request that no more ads be e-mailed.

The most stringent state law is California's antispam law, which went into effect on January 1, 2004. That law follows the "opt-in" model favored by consumer groups and antispam advocates. In other words, the law prohibits any person or business from sending e-mail ads to or from any e-mail address in California unless

---

16. *Does v. Hvide,* 770 So.2d 1237 (Fla.App.3d 2000).
17. See, for example, *Graham v. Oppenheimer,* 2000 WL 33381418 (E.D.Va. 2000).
18. The term *spam* is said to come from a Monty Python song with the lyrics, "Spam spam spam spam, spam spam spam spam, lovely spam, wonderful spam." Like these lyrics, spam online is often considered to be a repetition of worthless text.

ADAPTING THE LAW TO THE ONLINE ENVIRONMENT

Can Spamming Constitute a Tort?

Spam-related issues are, of course, unique to the cyber age. Can traditional tort law apply to such issues? For example, when spam overloads a business's computer system or impairs its computer equipment, can the recipient of the spam bring an action under tort law? Since the latter half of the 1990s, a number of plaintiffs have done so, with some success, by claiming that spamming constitutes a trespass to personal property, or *chattels*—a term used under the common law to denote all forms of personal property. The term *trespass to chattels* is usually defined as any unauthorized interference with the use of the personal property of another.

SPAMMING AS A FORM OF TRESPASS

In a leading case on this issue, decided in 1997, Cyber Promotions, Inc., sent bulk e-mail to subscribers of CompuServe, Inc., an ISP. CompuServe subscribers complained to the service about the ads, and many canceled their subscriptions. Handling the ads also placed a tremendous burden on CompuServe's equipment.

CompuServe told Cyber Promotions to stop using CompuServe's equipment to process and store the ads—in effect, to stop sending the ads to CompuServe subscribers. Ignoring the demand, Cyber Promotions stepped up the volume of its ads. After CompuServe attempted unsuccessfully to block the flow with screening software, it filed a suit against Cyber Promotions in a federal district court, seeking an injunction on the ground that the ads constituted trespass to personal property. The court agreed and ordered Cyber Promotions to stop sending its ads to e-mail addresses maintained by CompuServe.[a]

NEW DIRECTIONS IN CALIFORNIA

A 2003 decision by the California Supreme Court may make it more difficult for plaintiffs in that state's courts to combat spammers using tort law. The case was brought by Intel Corporation against one of its former employees, Ken Hamidi. After he was fired, Hamidi sent a series of six e-mail messages to 35,000 Intel employees over a twenty-one-month period. In the messages, Hamidi criticized the company's labor practices and urged employees to leave the company.

Intel sought a court order to stop the e-mail campaign, arguing that Hamidi's actions constituted a trespass to chattels because the e-mail significantly interfered with productivity, thus causing economic damage. When the case reached the California Supreme Court, the court held that under California law, the tort of trespass to chattels requires some evidence of injury to the plaintiff's personal property. Because Hamidi's e-mail had neither damaged Intel's computer system nor impaired its functioning, Hamidi's actions did not amount to a trespass to chattels.

The court distinguished Intel's case from cases in which spamming actually interfered with a computer system or threatened to do so. The court did not reject the idea that trespass theory could apply to cyberspace. Rather, the court simply held that to succeed in a lawsuit for trespass to chattels, a plaintiff must demonstrate that some concrete harm resulted from the unwanted e-mail. Although Hamidi's e-mail messages may have diverted employees' time and attention, thereby interfering with their productivity, the e-mails did not overburden Intel's computer systems—and thus did not amount to a concrete harm in the eyes of the court.[b]

FOR CRITICAL ANALYSIS

Three dissenting justices in the California case maintained that intruding on private property, regardless of injury, should be sufficient to demonstrate trespass to chattels. Do you agree? Why or why not?

a. *CompuServe, Inc. v. Cyber Promotions, Inc.,* 962 F.Supp. 1015 (S.D. Ohio 1997).

b. *Intel Corp. v. Hamidi,* 30 Cal.4th 1342, 71 P.3d 296, 1 Cal.Rptr.3d 32 (2003).

the recipient has expressly agreed to receive e-mails from the sender. An exemption is made for e-mail sent to consumers with whom the advertiser has a "preexisting or current business relationship."

The Federal CAN-SPAM Act   In 2003, Congress enacted the Controlling the Assault of Non-Solicited Pornography and Marketing (CAN-SPAM) Act, which took effect on January 1, 2004. The legislation applies to any "commercial electronic mail messages" that are sent to promote a commercial product or service. Significantly, the statute preempts state antispam laws except for those provisions in state laws that prohibit false and deceptive e-mailing practices.

Generally, the act permits the use of unsolicited commercial e-mail but prohibits certain types of spamming activities, including the use of a false return address and the use of false, misleading, or deceptive information when sending e-mail. The statute also prohibits the use of "dictionary attacks"—sending messages to randomly generated e-mail addresses—and the "harvesting" of e-mail addresses from Web sites through the use of specialized software. Additionally, the law requires senders of commercial e-mail to do the following:

1 Include a return address on the e-mail.

2 Include a clear notification that the message is an ad and provide a valid physical postal address.

3 Provide a mechanism that allows recipients to "opt out" of further e-mail ads from the same source.

4 Take action on a recipient's "opt-out" request within ten days.

5 Label any sexually oriented materials as such.

ETHICAL ISSUE 4.2

Who benefits from the CAN-SPAM Act?   Some of the stricter state laws regulating spam, such as California's law, favor the members of the public who are not engaged in e-mail advertising. Through its "opt-in" provisions requiring e-mail advertisers to obtain the recipient's consent before sending ads, California's law would have significantly curbed Internet advertising campaigns. The federal CAN-SPAM Act, however, preempts state laws, except for certain provisions relating to deceptive e-mailing practices. This means that these stricter provisions in state laws will no longer be effective.

Clearly, the federal act reflects Congress's intent to protect the e-mail marketing industry against state laws, such as California's, that would make e-mail advertising extremely difficult. The federal government also sought to eliminate advertising by peddlers of financial scams and pornography. Yet critics point out that the new law will do little to reduce the amount of unsolicited e-mail flowing through cyberspace. For one thing, many of the Internet ads being sent today already meet the requirements of the CAN-SPAM Act. For another, because the federal act uses an "opt-out" approach, it places the burden on e-mail recipients to prevent the delivery of further ads from the same source. Additionally, the act cannot regulate spam sent from foreign servers. Indeed, a survey showed that during the first two months after the act became effective, 56 percent of the respondents saw no noticeable reduction in the amount of spam received through e-mail, and 16 percent reported that they had received more spam since the law went into effect.[19] ■

19. Pew Internet and American Life Project survey conducted from February 3 to March 1, 2004.

◼ KEY TERMS

actionable   115
actual malice   117
appropriation   118
assault   114
assumption of risk   129
battery   114
business invitee   125
business tort   113
causation in fact   127
comparative negligence   129
compensatory damages   127
contributory negligence   129
conversion   122
cyber tort   113
damages   113

defamation   115
defense   114
disparagement of property   122
dram shop act   131
duty of care   123
fraudulent misrepresentation   118
Good Samaritan statute   131
intentional tort   113
libel   115
malice   114
malpractice   126
negligence   123
negligence *per se*   130
predatory behavior   119
privilege   116

proximate cause   127
puffery   118
punitive damages   127
reasonable person standard   124
res ipsa loquitur   130
slander   115
slander of quality   123
slander of title   123
spam   134
strict liability   131
tort   112
tortfeasor   113
trade libel   123
trespass to land   120
trespass to personal property   121

CHAPTER SUMMARY ◼ Torts and Cyber Torts

Intentional Torts against Persons
(See pages 113–120.)

1. *Assault and battery*—An assault is an unexcused and intentional act that causes another person to be apprehensive of immediate harm. A battery is an assault that results in physical contact.

2. *False imprisonment*—The intentional confinement or restraint of another person's movement without justification.

3. *Intentional infliction of emotional distress*—An intentional act that amounts to extreme and outrageous conduct resulting in severe emotional distress to another.

4. *Defamation (libel or slander)*—A false statement of fact, not made under privilege, that is communicated to a third person and that causes damage to a person's reputation. For public figures, the plaintiff must also prove actual malice.

5. *Invasion of the right to privacy*—The use of a person's name or likeness for commercial purposes without permission, wrongful intrusion into a person's private activities, publication of information that places a person in a false light, or disclosure of private facts that an ordinary person would find objectionable.

6. *Appropriation*—The use of another person's name, likeness, or other identifying characteristic, without permission and for the benefit of the user.

7. *Misrepresentation (fraud)*—A false representation made by one party, through misstatement of facts or through conduct, with the intention of deceiving another and on which the other reasonably relies to his or her detriment.

8. *Wrongful interference*—The knowing, intentional interference by a third party with an enforceable contractual relationship or an established business relationship between other parties for the purpose of advancing the economic interests of the third party.

(Continued)

CHAPTER SUMMARY ▪ Torts and Cyber Torts—Continued

Intentional Torts against Property (See pages 120–123.)	1. *Trespass to land*—The invasion of another's real property without consent or privilege. Specific rights and duties apply once a person is expressly or impliedly established as a trespasser. 2. *Trespass to personal property*—Unlawfully damaging or interfering with the owner's right to use, possess, or enjoy her or his personal property. 3. *Conversion*—Wrongfully taking personal property from its rightful owner or possessor and placing it in the service of another. 4. *Disparagement of property*—Any economically injurious falsehood that is made about another's product or property; an inclusive term for the torts of *slander of quality* and *slander of title*.

Unintentional Torts (Negligence) (See pages 123–131.)	1. *Negligence*—The careless performance of a legally required duty or the failure to perform a legally required act. Elements that must be proved are that a legal duty of care exists, that the defendant breached that duty, and that the breach caused damage or injury to another.
	
	 2. *Defenses to negligence*—The basic affirmative defenses in negligence cases are (a) assumption of risk, (b) superseding cause, and (c) contributory or comparative negligence.
	
	 3. *Special negligence doctrines and statutes*—
	
	   a. *Res ipsa loquitur*—A doctrine under which a plaintiff need not prove negligence on the part of the defendant because "the facts speak for themselves."
	
	   b. Negligence *per se*—A type of negligence that may occur if a person violates a statute or an ordinance providing for a criminal penalty and the violation causes another to be injured.
	
	   c. Special negligence statutes—State statutes that prescribe duties and responsibilities in certain circumstances, the violation of which will impose civil liability. Dram shop acts and Good Samaritan statutes are examples of special negligence statutes.

Strict Liability (See page 131.)	Under the doctrine of strict liability, a person may be held liable, regardless of the degree of care exercised, for damages or injuries caused by her or his product or activity. Strict liability includes liability for harms caused by abnormally dangerous activities, by dangerous animals, and by defective products (product liability).
Cyber Torts (See pages 131–136.)	General tort principles are being extended to cover cyber torts, or torts that occur in cyberspace, such as online defamation and spamming (which may constitute trespass to personal property). Federal and state statutes may also apply to certain forms of cyber torts. For example, under the federal Communications Decency Act of 1996, Internet service providers (ISPs) are not liable for defamatory messages posted by their subscribers. A majority of the states and the federal government now regulate unwanted e-mail ads (spam).

▪ FOR REVIEW

Answers for the even-numbered questions in this For Review *section can be found in Appendix I at the end of this text.*

1 What is a tort?

2 What is the purpose of tort law? What are two basic categories of torts?

3 What are the four elements of negligence?

4 What is meant by strict liability? In what circumstances is strict liability applied?

5 What is a cyber tort, and how are tort theories being applied in cyberspace?

■ QUESTIONS AND CASE PROBLEMS

4–1. Defenses to Negligence. Corinna was riding her bike on a city street. While she was riding, she frequently looked back to verify that the books that she had fastened to the rear part of her bike were still attached. On one occasion while she was looking behind her, she failed to notice a car that was entering an intersection just as she was crossing it. The car hit her, causing her to sustain numerous injuries. Three eyewitnesses stated that the driver of the car had failed to stop at the stop sign before entering the intersection. Corinna sued the driver of the car for negligence. What defenses might the defendant driver raise in this lawsuit? Discuss fully.

4–2. Liability to Business Invitees. Kim went to Ling's Market to pick up a few items for dinner. It was a rainy, windy day, and the wind had blown water through the door of Ling's Market each time the door opened. As Kim entered through the door, she slipped and fell in the approximately one-half inch of rainwater that had accumulated on the floor. The manager knew of the weather conditions but had not posted any sign to warn customers of the water hazard. Kim injured her back as a result of the fall and sued Ling's for damages. Can Ling's be held liable for negligence in this situation? Discuss.

4–3. Negligence. In which of the following situations will the acting party be liable for the tort of negligence? Explain fully.

(a) Mary goes to the golf course on Sunday morning, eager to try out a new set of golf clubs she has just purchased. As she tees off on the first hole, the head of her club flies off and injures a nearby golfer.

(b) Mary's doctor gives her some pain medication and tells her not to drive after she takes it, as the medication induces drowsiness. In spite of the doctor's warning, Mary decides to drive to the store while on the medication. Owing to her lack of alertness, she fails to stop at a traffic light and crashes into another vehicle, injuring a passenger.

4–4. Causation. Ruth carelessly parks her car on a steep hill, leaving the car in neutral and failing to engage the parking brake. The car rolls down the hill, knocking down an electric line. The sparks from the broken line ignite a grass fire. The fire spreads until it reaches a barn one mile away. The barn houses dynamite, and the burning barn explodes, causing part of the roof to fall on and injure a passing motorist, Jim. Can Jim recover from Ruth? Why or why not?

4–5. Duty of Care. As pedestrians exited at the close of an arts and crafts show, Jason Davis, an employee of the show's producer, stood near the exit. Suddenly and without warning, Davis turned around and collided with Yvonne Esposito, an eighty-year-old woman. Esposito was knocked to the ground, fracturing her hip. After hip-replacement surgery, she was left with a permanent physical impairment. Esposito filed a suit in a federal district court against Davis and others, alleging negligence. What are the factors that indicate whether Davis owed Esposito a duty of care? What do those factors indicate in these circumstances? [*Esposito v. Davis*, 47 F.3d 164 (5th Cir. 1995)]

CASE PROBLEM WITH SAMPLE ANSWER

4–6. During the spring and summer of 1999, Edward and Geneva Irvine received numerous "hang up" phone calls, including three calls in the middle of the night. With the help of their local phone company, the Irvines learned that many of the calls were from the telemarketing department of the *Akron Beacon Journal* in Akron, Ohio. The *Beacon*'s sales force was equipped with an automatic dialing machine. During business hours, the dialer was used to maximize productivity by calling multiple phone numbers at once and connecting a call to a sales representative only after it was answered. After business hours, the dialer was used to dial a list of disconnected numbers to determine whether they had been reconnected. If the dialer detected a ring, it recorded the information and dropped the call. If the automated dialing system crashed, which it did frequently, it redialed the entire list. The Irvines filed a suit in an Ohio state court against the *Beacon* and others, alleging in part invasion of privacy. In whose favor should the court rule, and why? [*Irvine v. Akron Beacon Journal*, 147 Ohio App.3d 428, 770 N.E.2d 1105 (9 Dist. 2002)]

After you have answered this problem, compare your answer with the sample answer given on the Web site that accompanies this text. Go to http://blt.westbuslaw.com, select "Chapter 4," and click on "Case Problem with Sample Answer."

4–7. Defamation. Lydia Hagberg went to her bank, California Federal Bank, FSB, to cash a check made out to her by Smith Barney (SB), an investment services firm. Nolene Showalter, a bank employee, suspected that the check was counterfeit. Showalter phoned SB and was told that the check was not valid. As she phoned the police, Gary Wood, a bank security officer, contacted SB again and was told that its earlier statement was "erroneous" and that the check was valid. Meanwhile, a police officer arrived, drew Hagberg away from the teller's window, spread her legs, patted her down, and handcuffed her. The officer searched her purse, asked her whether she had any weapons or stolen property and whether she was driving a stolen vehicle, and arrested her. Hagberg filed a suit in a California state court against the bank and others, alleging, among other things, slander. Should the absolute privilege for communications made in judicial or other official proceedings apply to statements made when a citizen contacts the police to report suspected criminal activity? Why or why not? [*Hagberg v. California Federal Bank, FSB*, 32 Cal.4th 39, 81 P.3d 244, 7 Cal.Rptr.3d 803 (2004)]

A QUESTION OF ETHICS

4–8. Patsy Slone, while a guest at the Dollar Inn, a hotel, was stabbed in the thumb by a hypodermic needle concealed in the tube of a roll of toilet paper. Slone, fearing that she might have been exposed to the virus that causes acquired immune deficiency syndrome (AIDS), sued the hotel for damages to compensate her for the emotional distress she suffered after the needle stab. An Indiana trial court held for Slone and awarded her $250,000 in damages. The hotel appealed, and one of the issues before the court was whether Slone had to prove that she was actually exposed to AIDS to recover for emotional distress. The appellate court held that she did not and that her fear of getting AIDS was reasonable in these circumstances. [*Slone v. Dollar Inn, Inc.,* 695 N.E.2d 185 (Ind.App. 1998)]

1. Should the plaintiff in this case have been required to show that she was actually exposed to the AIDS virus in order to recover for emotional distress? Should she have been required to show that she actually acquired the AIDS virus as a result of the needle stab?

2. In some states, plaintiffs are barred from recovery in emotional distress cases unless the distress is evidenced by some kind of physical symptoms. Is this fair?

FOR CRITICAL ANALYSIS

4–9. What general principle underlies the common law doctrine that business owners have a duty of care toward their customers? Does the duty of care unfairly burden business owners? Why or why not?

VIDEO QUESTION

4–10. Go to this text's Web site at **http://blt. westbuslaw.com** and select "Chapter 4." Click on "Video Questions" and view the video titled *Jaws.* Then answer the following questions.

1. In the video, the mayor (Murray Hamilton) and a few other men try to persuade Chief Brody (Roy Scheider) not to close the town's beaches. If Brody keeps the beaches open and a swimmer is injured or killed because he failed to warn swimmers about the potential shark danger, has Brody committed a tort? If so, what kind of tort (intentional tort against persons, intentional tort against property, negligence)? Explain your answer.

2. Can Chief Brody be held liable for any injuries or deaths to swimmers under the doctrine of strict liability? Why or why not?

3. If Chief Brody goes against the mayor's instructions and warns swimmers to stay off the beach, and the town suffers economic damages as a result, has he committed the tort of disparagement of property? Why or why not?

INTERNET EXERCISES

Go to the *Business Law Today: The Essentials* home page at **http://blt.westbuslaw.com**, select "Chapter 4," and click on "Internet Exercises." There you will find the following Internet research exercises that you can perform to learn more about topics covered in this chapter.

Activity 4–1: LEGAL PERSPECTIVE—Negligence and the *Titanic*

Activity 4–2: MANAGEMENT PERSPECTIVE—Legal and Illegal Uses of Spam

BEFORE THE TEST

Go to the *Business Law Today: The Essentials* home page at **http://blt.westbuslaw.com**, select "Chapter 4," and click on "Interactive Quizzes." You will find at least twenty interactive questions relating to this chapter.

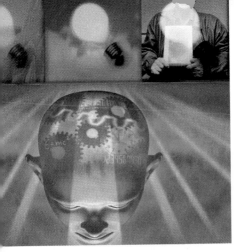

CHAPTER 5
Intellectual Property

"The Internet, by virtue of its ability to
~sh what will be hundreds of millions of
~ople together, . . . is . . . a profoundly
~erent capability that by and large human
beings have not had before."

Tony Rutkowski, 1943–
(Executive director of the Internet Society, 1994–1996)

CHAPTER OUTLINE

- **TRADEMARKS AND RELATED PROPERTY**

- **CYBER MARKS**

- **PATENTS**

- **COPYRIGHTS**

- **TRADE SECRETS**

- **INTERNATIONAL PROTECTION FOR INTELLECTUAL PROPERTY**

INTELLECTUAL PROPERTY
Property resulting from intellectual, creative processes.

■■ LEARNING OBJECTIVES

After reading this chapter, you should be able to answer the following questions:

1 What is intellectual property?

2 Why are trademarks and patents protected by the law?

3 What laws protect authors' rights in the works they generate?

4 What are trade secrets, and what laws offer protection for this form of intellectual property?

5 What steps have been taken to protect intellectual property rights in today's digital age?

O f significant concern to businesspersons today is the need to protect their rights in intellectual property. **Intellectual property** is any property resulting from intellectual, creative processes—the products of an individual's mind. Although it is an abstract term for an abstract concept, intellectual property is nonetheless wholly familiar to virtually everyone. The information contained in books and computer files is intellectual property. The software you use, the movies you see, and the music you listen to are all forms of intellectual property. In fact, in today's information age, it should come as no surprise that the value of the world's intellectual property now exceeds the value of physical property, such as machines and houses.

The need to protect creative works was voiced by the framers of the U.S. Constitution over two hundred years ago: Article I, Section 8, of the Constitution authorized Congress "[t]o promote the Progress of Science and useful Arts, by securing for limited Times to Authors and Inventors the exclusive Right to their respective Writings and Discoveries." Laws protecting patents, trademarks, and copyrights are explicitly designed to protect and reward inventive and artistic creativity. Exhibit 5–1 offers a comprehensive summary of these forms of intellectual property, as well as intellectual property that consists of *trade secrets*.

EXHIBIT 5–1   FORMS OF INTELLECTUAL PROPERTY

	DEFINITION	HOW ACQUIRED	DURATION	REMEDY FOR INFRINGEMENT
Patent	A grant from the government that gives an inventor exclusive rights to an invention.	By filing a patent application with the U.S. Patent and Trademark Office and receiving its approval.	Twenty years from the date of the application; for design patents, fourteen years.	Money damages, including royalties and lost profits, *plus* attorneys' fees. Damages may be tripled for intentional infringements.
Copyright	The right of an author or originator of a literary or artistic work, or other production that falls within a specified category, to have the exclusive use of that work for a given period of time.	Automatic (once the work or creation is put in tangible form). Only the *expression* of an idea (and not the idea itself) can be protected by copyright.	For authors: the life of the author plus 70 years. For publishers: 95 years after the date of publication or 120 years after creation.	Actual damages plus profits received by the party who infringed *or* statutory damages under the Copyright Act, *plus* costs and attorneys' fees in either situation.
Trademark (Service Mark and Trade Dress)	Any distinctive word, name, symbol, or device (image or appearance), or combination thereof, that an entity uses to distinguish its goods or services from those of others. The owner has the exclusive right to use that mark or trade dress.	1. At common law, ownership created by use of the mark. 2. Registration with the appropriate federal or state office gives notice and is permitted if the mark is currently in use or will be within the next six months.	Unlimited, as long as it is in use. To continue notice by registration, owner must renew by filing between the fifth and sixth years, and thereafter, every ten years.	1. Injunction prohibiting the future use of the mark. 2. Actual damages plus profits received by the party who infringed (can be increased under the Lanham Act). 3. Destruction of articles that infringed. 4. *Plus* costs and attorneys' fees.
Trade Secret	Any information that a business possesses and that gives the business an advantage over competitors (including formulas, lists, patterns, plans, processes, and programs).	Through the originality and development of the information and processes that constitute the business secret and are unknown to others.	Unlimited, so long as not revealed to others. Once revealed to others, they are no longer trade secrets.	Money damages for misappropriation (the Uniform Trade Secrets Act also permits punitive damages if willful), *plus* costs and attorneys' fees.

An understanding of intellectual property law is important because intellectual property has taken on increasing significance, not only in the United States but globally as well. Today, ownership rights in intangible intellectual property are more important to the prosperity of many U.S. companies than are their tangible assets. As you will read in this chapter, protecting these assets in today's online world has proved particularly challenging. This is because, as indicated in the chapter-opening quotation, the Internet's capability is "profoundly different" from anything we have had in the past.

▚ Trademarks and Related Property

TRADEMARK
A distinctive mark, motto, device, or emblem that a manufacturer stamps, prints, or otherwise affixes to the goods it produces so that they may be identified on the market and their origins made known. Once a trademark is established (under the common law or through registration), the owner is entitled to its exclusive use.

A **trademark** is a distinctive mark, motto, device, or emblem that a manufacturer stamps, prints, or otherwise affixes to the goods it produces so that they can be identified on the market and their origin vouched for. At common law, the person who used a symbol or mark to identify a business or product was protected in the use of that trademark. Clearly, by using another's trademark, a business could lead consumers to believe that its goods were made by the other business. The law seeks to avoid this kind of confusion. In the following classic case concerning Coca-Cola, the defendants argued that the Coca-Cola trademark was entitled to no protection under the law because the term did not accurately represent the product.

LANDMARK AND CLASSIC CASES

CASE 5.1 ▧ The Coca-Cola Co. v. Koke Co. of America

Supreme Court of the United States, 1920.
254 U.S. 143,
41 S.Ct. 113,
65 L.Ed. 189.
http://www.findlaw.com/casecode/supreme.html[a]

COMPANY PROFILE *John Pemberton, an Atlanta pharmacist, invented a caramel-colored, carbonated soft drink in 1886. His bookkeeper, Frank Robinson, named the beverage Coca-Cola after two of the ingredients, coca leaves and kola nuts. Asa Candler bought the Coca-Cola Company in 1891, and within seven years, he made the soft drink available in all of the United States, as well as in parts of Canada and Mexico. Candler continued to sell Coke aggressively and to open up new markets, reaching Europe before 1910. In doing so, however, he attracted*

numerous competitors, some of whom tried to capitalize directly on the Coke name.

FACTS The Coca-Cola Company brought an action in a federal district court to enjoin other beverage companies from using the words "Koke" and "Dope" for the defendants' products. The defendants contended that the Coca-Cola trademark was a fraudulent representation and that Coca-Cola was therefore not entitled to any help from the courts. By use of the Coca-Cola name, the defendants alleged, the Coca-Cola Company represented that the beverage contained cocaine (from coca leaves). The district court granted the injunction, but the federal appellate court reversed. The Coca-Cola Company appealed to the United States Supreme Court.

ISSUE Did the marketing of products called Koke and Dope by the Koke Company of America and other firms constitute an infringement on Coca-Cola's trademark?

DECISION Yes for Koke, but no for Dope. The Supreme Court enjoined the competing beverage companies from calling their products Koke but did not prevent them from calling their products Dope.

a. This is the "U.S. Supreme Court Opinions" page within the Web site of the "FindLaw Internet Legal Resources" database. This page provides several options for accessing an opinion. Because you know the citation for this case, you can go to the "Citation Search" box, type in the appropriate volume and page numbers for the *United States Reports* ("254" and "143," respectively, for the *Coca-Cola* case), and click on "Get It."

(Continued)

CASE 5.1—Continued

REASON The Court noted that, to be sure, prior to 1900 the Coca-Cola beverage had contained a small amount of cocaine, but this ingredient had been deleted from the formula by 1906 at the latest, and the Coca-Cola Company had advertised to the public that no cocaine was present in its drink. Coca-Cola was a widely popular drink "to be had at almost any soda fountain." Because of the public's widespread familiarity with Coca-Cola, the retention of the name of the beverage (referring to coca leaves and kola nuts) was not misleading: "Coca-Cola probably means to most persons the plaintiff's familiar product to be had everywhere rather than a compound of particular substances." The name "Coke" was found to be so common a term for the trademarked product Coca-Cola that the defendants' use of the similar-sounding "Koke" as a name for their beverages was disallowed. The Court could find no reason to restrain the defendants from using the name "Dope," however.

COMMENTS *In this classic case, the United States Supreme Court made it clear that trademarks and trade names (and nicknames for those marks and names, such as the nickname "Coke" for "Coca-Cola") that are in common use receive protection under the common law. This holding is significant historically because the federal statute later passed to protect trademark rights (the Lanham Act of 1946, to be discussed shortly) in many ways represented a codification of common law principles governing trademarks.*

RELEVANT WEB SITES *To locate information on the Web concerning the Coca-Cola Co. decision, go to this text's Web site at* **http://blt.westbuslaw.com**, *select "Chapter 5," and click on "URLs for Landmarks."*

STATUTORY PROTECTION OF TRADEMARKS

Statutory protection of trademarks and related property is provided at the federal level by the Lanham Act of 1946.[1] The Lanham Act was enacted in part to protect manufacturers from losing business to rival companies that used confusingly similar trademarks. The Lanham Act incorporates the common law of trademarks and provides remedies for owners of trademarks who wish to enforce their claims in federal court. Many states also have trademark statutes.

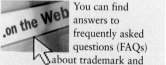 You can find answers to frequently asked questions (FAQs) about trademark and patent law, as well as a host of other information, at the Web site of the U.S. Patent and Trademark Office. Go to

http://www.uspto.gov.

Trademark Dilution   In 1995, Congress amended the Lanham Act by passing the Federal Trademark Dilution Act,[2] which extended the protection available to trademark owners by creating a federal cause of action for trademark *dilution*. Until the passage of this amendment, federal trademark law only prohibited the unauthorized use of the same mark on competing—or on noncompeting but "related"—goods or services when such use would likely confuse consumers as to the origin of those goods and services. Trademark dilution laws protect "distinctive" or "famous" trademarks (such as Jergens, McDonald's, RCA, and Macintosh) from certain unauthorized uses of the marks *regardless* of a showing of competition or a likelihood of confusion. More than half of the states have also enacted trademark dilution laws.

Although Congress passed the Federal Trademark Dilution Act in an effort to create uniformity and consistency in dilution cases, until recently, the federal courts were split on the level of proof required to show dilution. Some courts required proof that the defendant's use would cause an "actual lessening" of selling power, whereas other courts required only a showing of a "likelihood of dilution."

---

1. 15 U.S.C. Sections 1051–1128.
2. 15 U.S.C. Section 1125.

In 2003, the United States Supreme Court resolved this issue in favor of the higher standard in the case of *Moseley v. V Secret Catalogue, Inc.*[3] In that case, famous lingerie maker Victoria's Secret brought a trademark dilution action against "Victor's Little Secret," a small retail store that sold adult videos, lingerie, and other items. The lower courts had granted Victoria's Secret an injunction prohibiting the adult store from diluting the trademark. The Supreme Court, however, concluded that likelihood of dilution is not enough and reversed the lower court's decision. The Court held that to establish dilution under the federal act, some evidence must establish that the allegedly infringing user's mark actually reduces the value of the famous mark or lessens its capacity to identify goods and services.

Use of a Similar Mark May Constitute Trademark Dilution A famous mark may be diluted not only by the use of an *identical* mark but also by the use of a *similar* mark. ■ EXAMPLE 5.1 Ringling Bros.–Barnum & Bailey, Combined Shows, Inc., brought a suit against the state of Utah, claiming that Utah's use of the slogan "The Greatest Snow on Earth"—to attract visitors to the state's recreational and scenic resorts—diluted the distinctiveness of the circus's famous trademark, "The Greatest Show on Earth." Utah moved to dismiss the suit, arguing that the 1995 provisions protect owners of famous trademarks only against the unauthorized use of identical marks. A federal court disagreed and refused to grant Utah's motion to dismiss the case.[4] ■

TRADEMARK REGISTRATION

Trademarks may be registered with the state or with the federal government. To register for protection under federal trademark law, a person must file an application with the U.S. Patent and Trademark Office in Washington, D.C. Under current law, a mark can be registered (1) if it is currently in commerce or (2) if the applicant intends to put the mark into commerce within six months.

In special circumstances, the six-month period can be extended by thirty months, giving the applicant a total of three years from the date of notice of trademark approval to make use of the mark and file the required use statement. Registration is postponed until the mark is actually used. Nonetheless, during this waiting period, any applicant can legally protect his or her trademark against a third party who previously has neither used the mark nor filed an application for it. Registration is renewable between the fifth and sixth years after the initial registration and every ten years thereafter (every twenty years for trademarks registered before 1990).

To access the federal database of registered trademarks, go to

http://www.uspto.gov/main/trademarks.htm.

ETHICAL ISSUE 5.1

Should the courts cancel existing trademarks that are disparaging? The Lanham Act prohibits the U.S. Patent and Trademark Office from registering trademarks that are immoral, scandalous, or disparaging. Trademark examiners review applications and reject any proposed trademarks that are disparaging (demeaning) by today's standards. But what if a trademark that was registered some time ago is perceived as disparaging to a group of people today? Can that registration be canceled? According to a federal district court in 2003, the answer is no. The case involved the Washington Redskins, a professional football team, and six Native Americans

---

3. 537 U.S. 418, 123 S.Ct. 1115, 155 L.Ed.2d 1 (2003).
4. *Ringling Bros.–Barnum & Bailey, Combined Shows, Inc. v. Utah Division of Travel Development,* 935 F.Supp. 763 (E.D.Va. 1996).

Various billboards in New York City's Times Square. Why are trademarks protected by the law? (Photo by Bill Stryker)

(the plaintiffs) who argued that the trademark should be canceled because the term *Redskins* is the most derogatory one used for native people.

The federal district court held that the plaintiffs had not presented enough evidence to prove the mark was disparaging. According to the court, the test is not whether the trademark is disparaging to Native Americans today but whether it was disparaging at the time it was originally registered. Here, the plaintiffs presented evidence that a number of Native Americans found the term insulting today. The plaintiffs also presented some evidence, including survey results and the testimony of historians and linguists, suggesting that the mark was disparaging when it was first registered in 1967. The court found that evidence insufficient, however, and held that the plaintiffs had waited too long to complain about the trademark.[5] Some contend that this ruling is unfair because what is considered disparaging may change over time. ■

TRADEMARK INFRINGEMENT

Registration of a trademark with the U.S. Patent and Trademark Office gives notice on a nationwide basis that the trademark belongs exclusively to the registrant. The registrant is also allowed to use the symbol ® to indicate that the mark has been registered. Whenever that trademark is copied to a substantial degree or used in its entirety by another, intentionally or unintentionally, the trademark has been *infringed* (used without authorization). When a trademark has been infringed, the owner of the mark has a cause of action against the infringer. A person need not have registered a trademark in order to sue for trademark infringement, but registration does furnish proof of the date of inception of the trademark's use.

Only those trademarks that are deemed sufficiently distinctive from all competing trademarks will be protected, however. The trademarks must be sufficiently distinct to enable consumers to identify the manufacturer of the goods easily and to differentiate among competing products.

Strong Marks   Fanciful, arbitrary, or suggestive trademarks are generally considered to be the most distinctive (strongest) trademarks because they are normally taken from outside the context of the particular product and thus provide the best means of distinguishing one product from another.

■ **EXAMPLE 5.2** Fanciful trademarks include invented words, such as "Xerox" for one manufacturer's copiers and "Kodak" for another company's photographic products. Arbitrary trademarks include actual words that have no literal connection to the product, such as "English Leather" used as a name for an aftershave lotion (and not for leather processed in England). Suggestive trademarks are those that suggest something about a product without describing the product directly. For instance, "Dairy Queen" suggests an association between its products and milk, but it does not directly describe ice cream. ■

Secondary Meaning   Descriptive terms, geographic terms, and personal names are not inherently distinctive and do not receive protection under the law *until* they acquire a secondary meaning. A secondary meaning may arise when customers begin to associate a specific term or phrase, such as "London Fog," with specific trademarked items (coats with "London Fog" labels). Whether a secondary meaning becomes attached to a term or name usually depends on how extensively the

5. *Pro-Football, Inc. v. Harjo*, 284 F.Supp.2d 96 (D.D.C. 2003).

product is advertised, the market for the product, the number of sales, and other factors. The United States Supreme Court has held that even a color can qualify for trademark protection.[6] Once a secondary meaning is attached to a term or name, a trademark is considered distinctive and is protected.

Generic Terms   Generic terms (general, commonly used terms that refer to an entire class of products, such as *bicycle* or *computer*) receive no protection, even if they acquire secondary meanings. A particularly thorny problem arises when a trademark acquires generic use. For instance, *aspirin* and *thermos* were originally trademarked products, but today the words are used generically. Other examples are *escalator, trampoline, raisin bran, dry ice, lanolin, linoleum, nylon,* and *corn flakes.*

Note that a generic term will not be protected under trademark law even if the term has acquired a secondary meaning. ■ **EXAMPLE 5.3** In one case, America Online, Inc. (AOL), sued AT&T Corporation, claiming that AT&T's use of "You Have Mail" on its WorldNet Service infringed AOL's trademark rights in the same phrase. The court ruled, however, that because each of the three words in the phrase was a generic term, the phrase as a whole was generic. Although the phrase had become widely associated with AOL's e-mail notification service, and thus may have acquired a secondary meaning, this issue was of no significance in this case. The court stated that it would not consider whether the mark had acquired any secondary meaning because "generic marks with secondary meaning are still not entitled to protection."[7] ■

---

6. *Qualitex Co. v. Jacobson Products Co.,* 514 U.S. 159, 115 S.Ct. 1300, 131 L.Ed.2d 248 (1995).
7. *America Online, Inc. v. AT&T Corp.,* 243 F.3d 812 (4th Cir. 2001).

The purple and orange colors displayed on FedEx envelopes, packets, and delivery vehicles, including this airplane, are a distinctive feature of that company. If a start-up company specializing in courier delivery services used those same colors, would the new company be infringing on FedEx's trademark? (Photo Courtesy of Federal Express)

A "UL" certification mark. How does a certification mark differ from a trademark?

SERVICE, CERTIFICATION, AND COLLECTIVE MARKS

A **service mark** is similar to a trademark but is used to distinguish the services of one person or company from those of another. For instance, each airline has a particular mark or symbol associated with its name. Titles and character names used in radio and television are frequently registered as service marks.

Other marks protected by law include certification marks and collective marks. A *certification mark* is used by one or more persons other than the owner to certify the region, materials, mode of manufacture, quality, or accuracy of the owner's goods or services. When used by members of a cooperative, association, or other organization, it is referred to as a *collective mark*. ■ **EXAMPLE 5.4** Certification marks include such marks as "Good Housekeeping Seal of Approval" and "UL Tested." Collective marks appear at the ends of the credits of movies to indicate the various associations and organizations that participated in making the movie. The union marks found on the tags of certain products are also collective marks. ■

TRADE NAMES

Trademarks apply to *products*. The term **trade name** is used to indicate part or all of a business's name, whether the business is a sole proprietorship, a partnership, or a corporation. Generally, a trade name is directly related to a business and its goodwill. Trade names may be protected as trademarks if the trade name is the same as the company's trademarked product—for example, Coca-Cola. Unless also used as a trademark or service mark, a trade name cannot be registered with the federal government. Trade names are protected under the common law, however. As with trademarks, words must be unusual or fancifully used if they are to be protected as trade names. The word *Safeway*, for instance, was held by the courts to be sufficiently fanciful to obtain protection as a trade name for a grocery chain.[8]

TRADE DRESS

The term **trade dress** refers to the image and overall appearance of a product. Basically, trade dress is subject to the same protection as trademarks. ■ **EXAMPLE 5.5** The distinctive decor, menu, layout, and style of service of a particular restaurant may be regarded as the restaurant's trade dress. Similarly, if a golf course is distinguished from other golf courses by prominent features, such as a golf hole designed to look like a lighthouse, those features may be considered the golf course's trade dress. ■ In cases involving trade dress infringement, as in trademark infringement cases, a major consideration is whether consumers are likely to be confused by the allegedly infringing use. Also, features that enhance a product's function will not be protected as trade dress.

◼ Cyber Marks

In cyberspace, trademarks are sometimes referred to as **cyber marks.** We turn now to a discussion of trademark-related issues in cyberspace and how new laws and the courts are addressing these issues. One concern relates to the rights of a trademark's owner to use the mark as part of a domain name (Internet address). Other issues have to do with cybersquatting, meta tags, and trademark dilution on the Web. The use of licensing as a way to avoid liability for infringing on another's intellectual property rights in cyberspace will also be discussed.

SERVICE MARK
A mark used in the sale or the advertising of services to distinguish the services of one person from those of others. Titles, character names, and other distinctive features of radio and television programs may be registered as service marks.

TRADE NAME
A term that is used to indicate part or all of a business's name and that is directly related to the business's reputation and goodwill. Trade names are protected under the common law (and under trademark law, if the name is the same as the firm's trademarked property).

TRADE DRESS
The image and overall appearance of a product—for example, the distinctive decor, menu, layout, and style of service of a particular restaurant. Basically, trade dress is subject to the same protection as trademarks.

CYBER MARK
A trademark in cyberspace.

---

8. *Safeway Stores v. Suburban Foods,* 130 F.Supp. 249 (E.D.Va. 1955).

DOMAIN NAMES

In the real world, one business can often use the same name as another without causing any conflict, particularly if the businesses are small, their goods or services are different, and the areas where they do business are separate. In the online world, however, there is only one area of business—cyberspace. Thus, disputes between parties over which one has the right to use a particular domain name have become common. A **domain name** is part of an Internet address, such as "westlaw.com." The top level domain (TLD) is the part of the name to the right of the period and indicates the type of entity that operates the site (for example, "com" is an abbreviation for "commercial"). The second level (the part of the name to the left of the period) is chosen by the business entity or individual registering the domain name.

Conflicts over rights to domain names emerged during the 1990s as e-commerce expanded on a worldwide scale. As e-commerce grew, the *.com* TLD came to be widely used by businesses on the Web. Competition among firms with similar names and products preceding the *.com* TLD led, understandably, to numerous disputes over domain name rights. By using the same, or a similar, domain name, parties have attempted to profit from the goodwill of a competitor, to sell pornography, to offer for sale another party's domain name, and to otherwise infringe on others' trademarks.

As noted in Chapter 3, the federal government set up the Internet Corporation for Assigned Names and Numbers (ICANN), a nonprofit corporation, to oversee the distribution of domain names. ICANN has also played a leading role in facilitating the settlement of domain name disputes worldwide. Since January 2000, ICANN has been operating an online arbitration system to resolve domain name disputes and approve dispute-resolution providers. By 2003, ICANN–approved online arbitration providers were handling over one thousand disputes annually.

ANTICYBERSQUATTING LEGISLATION

In the late 1990s, Congress passed legislation prohibiting another practice that had given rise to numerous disputes over domain names: cybersquatting. **Cybersquatting** occurs when a person registers a domain name that is the same as, or confusingly similar to, the trademark of another and then offers to sell the domain name back to the trademark owner. During the 1990s, cybersquatting became a contentious issue and led to much litigation. Although it was not always easy for the courts to separate cybersquatting from legitimate business activity, many cases held that cybersquatting violated trademark law.[9]

In 1999, Congress addressed this issue by passing the Anticybersquatting Consumer Protection Act (ACPA), which amended the Lanham Act—the federal law protecting trademarks, discussed earlier in this chapter. The ACPA makes it illegal for a person to "register, traffic in, or use" a domain name (1) if the name is identical or confusingly similar to the trademark of another and (2) if the one registering, trafficking in, or using the domain name has a "bad faith intent" to profit from that trademark. The act does not define what constitutes bad faith. Instead, it lists several factors that courts can consider in deciding whether bad faith exists. Some of these factors are the trademark rights of the other person, whether there is an intent to divert consumers in a way that could harm the goodwill represented by the trademark, whether there is an offer to transfer or sell the domain name to the

DOMAIN NAME
The last part of an Internet address, such as "westlaw.com." The top level (the part of the name to the right of the period) indicates the type of entity that operates the site ("com" is an abbreviation for "commercial"). The second level (the part of the name to the left of the period) is chosen by the entity.

CYBERSQUATTING
The act of registering a domain name that is the same as, or confusingly similar to, the trademark of another and then offering to sell that domain name back to the trademark owner.

---

9. See, for example, *Panavision International, L.P. v. Toeppen*, 141 F.3d 1316 (9th Cir. 1998).

trademark owner, and whether there is an intent to use the domain name to offer goods and services.

The ACPA applies to all domain name registrations of trademarks, even domain names registered before the passage of the act. Successful plaintiffs in suits brought under the act can collect actual damages and profits, or elect to receive statutory damages of from $1,000 to $100,000.

META TAGS

META TAGS
Words inserted into a Web site's key-word field to increase the site's inclusion in search engine results.

Search engines compile their results by looking through a Web site's key-word field. **Meta tags,** or key words, may be inserted into this field to increase the site's inclusion in search engine results, even though the site may have nothing to do with the inserted words. Using this same technique, one site may appropriate the key words of other sites with more frequent hits, so that the appropriating site appears in the same search engine results as the more popular sites. Using another's trademark in a meta tag without the owner's permission, however, constitutes trademark infringement. One use of meta tags was at issue in the following case.

CASE 5.2   Playboy Enterprises, Inc. v. Welles

United States Court of Appeals,
Ninth Circuit, 2002.
279 F.3d 796.

FACTS Playboy Enterprises, Inc. (PEI), maintains Web sites to promote *Playboy* magazine and PEI models. PEI's trademarks include the terms "Playboy," "Playmate," and "Playmate of the Year." Terri Welles is a self-employed model and spokesperson, who was featured as the "Playmate of the Year" in June 1981. Welles maintains a Web site titled "Terri Welles—Playmate of the Year 1981." As meta tags, Welles's site uses the terms "Playboy" and "Playmate," among others. PEI asked Welles to stop using these terms, but she refused. PEI filed a suit in a federal district court against Welles, asking the court to order her to, among other things, stop using those terms as meta tags. On this issue, the court granted a summary judgment in Welles's favor. PEI appealed to the U.S. Court of Appeals for the Ninth Circuit.

ISSUE Did Welles's use of PEI's meta tags to direct users to her Web site constitute trademark infringement?

DECISION No. The U.S. Court of Appeals for the Ninth Circuit concluded that Welles's use of PEI's trademarks as meta tags was a permissible, nominative use.[a]

REASON The U.S. Court of Appeals for the Ninth Circuit explained that the test for nominative use is "[f]irst, the product or service in question must be one not readily identifiable without use of the trademark; second, only so much of the mark or marks may be used as is reasonably necessary to identify the product or service; and third, the user must do nothing that would, in conjunction with the mark, suggest sponsorship or endorsement by the trademark holder." The court reasoned that "[t]here is simply no descriptive substitute for the trademarks used in Welles' meta tags. Precluding their use would have the unwanted effect of hindering the free flow of information on the Internet, something which is certainly not a goal of trademark law." Also, "[t]he meta tags use only so much of the marks as reasonably necessary and nothing is done in conjunction with them to suggest sponsorship or endorsement by the trademark holder."

WHY IS THIS CASE IMPORTANT? *This case illustrates how some uses of another's trademark are permissible and not infringing, provided that the user does not suggest that the trademark owner authorized or sponsored the use.*

---

a. A *nominative use* of a trademark is one that does not imply sponsorship or endorsement of a product because the product's mark is used only to describe the thing, rather than to identify its source. See *New Kids on the Block v. News America Publishing, Inc.,* 971 F.2d 302 (9th Cir. 1992).

DILUTION IN THE ONLINE WORLD

As discussed earlier, trademark *dilution* occurs when a trademark is used, without authorization, in a way that diminishes the distinctive quality of the mark. Unlike trademark infringement, a dilution cause of action does not require proof that consumers are likely to be confused by a connection between the unauthorized use and the mark. For this reason, the products involved do not have to be similar. In the first case alleging dilution on the Web, a court precluded the use of "candyland.com" as the URL for an adult site. The suit was brought by the maker of the "Candyland" children's game and owner of the "Candyland" mark.[10]

In another case, a court issued an injunction on the ground that spamming under another's logo is trademark dilution. In that case, Hotmail, Inc., provided e-mail services and worked to dissociate itself from spam. Van$ Money Pie, Inc., and others spammed thousands of e-mail customers, using the free e-mail Hotmail as a return address. The court ordered the defendants to stop.[11]

LICENSING

One of the ways to make use of another's trademark or other form of intellectual property, while avoiding litigation, is to obtain a license to do so. A license in this context is essentially an agreement permitting the use of a trademark, copyright, patent, or trade secret for certain purposes. For instance, a licensee (the party obtaining the license) might be allowed to use the trademark of the licensor (the party issuing the license) as part of the name of its company, or as part of its domain name, without otherwise using the mark on any products or services. (Like all contracts, contracts granting licenses must be carefully drafted—see, for example, the problems faced by the parties in the case discussed in this chapter's *Letter of the Law* feature on the following page.)

◼ Patents

PATENT
A government grant that gives an inventor the exclusive right or privilege to make, use, or sell his or her invention for a limited time period.

A **patent** is a grant from the government that gives an inventor the exclusive right to make, use, and sell an invention for a period of twenty years from the date of filing the application for a patent. Patents for designs, as opposed to inventions, are given for a fourteen-year period. For either a regular patent or a design patent, the applicant must demonstrate to the satisfaction of the U.S. Patent and Trademark Office that the invention, discovery, process, or design is genuine, novel, useful, and not obvious in light of current technology. A patent holder gives notice to all that an article or design is patented by placing on it the word *Patent* or *Pat.* plus the patent number. In contrast to patent law in other countries, in the United States patent protection is given to the first person to invent a product or process, even though someone else may have been the first to file for a patent on that product or process.

At one time, it was difficult for developers and manufacturers of software to obtain patent protection because many software products simply automate procedures that can be performed manually. In other words, the computer programs do not meet the "novel" and "not obvious" requirements previously mentioned. Also,

---

10. *Hasbro, Inc. v. Internet Entertainment Group, Ltd.,* 1996 WL 84853 (W.D.Wash. 1996).
11. *Hotmail Corp. v. Van$ Money Pie, Inc.,* 47 U.S.P.Q.2d 1020 (N.D.Cal. 1998).

LETTER OF THE LAW   A Book Is a Book Is a Book—But Is It an "E-Book"?

One of the significant issues raised by the cyber age has to do with whether copyrights in printed materials extend to the same materials presented in digital form over the Internet. A related issue involving licensing agreements came before a federal district court in 2001. The case was brought by the well-known publishing firm Random House, Inc., against Rosetta Books, LLC,[a] with which several authors had arranged to publish works electronically. At issue in the case was the following question: Did contracts in which the authors had licensed Random House to "print, publish and sell" their works in "book form" include the right to publish their works in electronic formats (as "e-books") as well?

In evaluating the issue, the court looked to the letter of the law, as decided by other court cases, but found little guidance. Hence, it looked to the words of the contract and to the definition of the term *book* given by the *Random House Webster's Unabridged Dictionary*. That dictionary defines a "book" as "a written or printed work of fiction or nonfiction, usually on sheets of paper fastened or bound together within covers." The court ultimately concluded that a book is not an e-book and therefore refused to grant Random House's motion to enjoin (prohibit) Rosetta Books from publishing the authors' works as e-books.[b]

THE BOTTOM LINE

To avoid litigation, anyone signing a licensing contract should make sure that the specific wording in the contract makes very clear what rights are or are not being conveyed.

a. *LLC* stands for "Limited Liability Company," a form of business organization that will be discussed in Chapter 19.

b. *Random House, Inc. v. Rosetta Books, LLC,* 150 F.Supp.2d 613 (S.D.N.Y. 2001).

---

the basis for software is often a mathematical equation or formula, which is not patentable. In 1981, however, the United States Supreme Court held that it is possible to obtain a patent for a process that incorporates a computer program—providing, of course, that the process itself is patentable.[12] Subsequently, many patents have been issued for software-related inventions.

A significant development relating to patents is the availability online of the world's patent databases. The Web site of the U.S. Patent and Trademark Office provides searchable databases covering U.S. patents granted since 1976. The Web site of the European Patent Office maintains databases covering all patent documents in sixty-five nations and the legal status of patents in twenty-two of those countries.

PATENT INFRINGEMENT

If a firm makes, uses, or sells another's patented design, product, or process without the patent owner's permission, it commits the tort of patent infringement. Patent infringement may exist even though the patent owner has not put the patented product in commerce. Patent infringement may also occur even though not all features or parts of an invention are copied. (With respect to a patented process, however, all steps or their equivalent must be copied for infringement to exist.)

Often, litigation for patent infringement is so costly that the patent holder will instead offer to sell to the infringer a license to use the patented design, product, or process. Indeed, in many cases the costs of detection, prosecution, and monitoring

---

12. *Diamond v. Diehr,* 450 U.S. 175, 101 S.Ct. 1048, 67 L.Ed.2d 155 (1981).

Should a software program that allows consumers to make offers for vacation packages via the Internet be considered a "new and useful" process that can be the subject of a business process patent? Why or why not?

are so high that patents are valueless to their owners; the owners cannot afford to protect them.

BUSINESS PROCESS PATENTS

Traditionally, patents have been granted for inventions that are "new and useful processes, machines, manufactures, or compositions of matter, or any new and useful improvements thereof." The U.S. Patent and Trademark Office routinely rejected computer systems and software applications because they were deemed not to be useful processes, machines, articles of manufacture, or compositions of matter. They were simply considered to be mathematical algorithms, abstract ideas, or "methods of doing business." In a landmark 1998 case, however, *State Street Bank & Trust Co. v. Signature Financial Group, Inc.,*[13] the U.S. Court of Appeals for the Federal Circuit ruled that only three categories of subject matter will always remain unpatentable: (1) the laws of nature, (2) natural phenomena, and (3) abstract ideas. This decision meant, among other things, that business processes were patentable.

After this decision, numerous technology firms applied for business process patents. Walker Digital applied for a business process patent for its "Dutch auction" system, which allowed consumers to make offers for airline tickets on the Internet and led to the creation of Priceline.com. Amazon.com obtained a business process patent for its "one-click" ordering system, a method of processing credit-card orders securely. Indeed, since the *State Street* decision, the number of Internet-related patents issued by the U.S. Patent and Trademark Office has increased more than 800 percent.

Ease of interactivity is a key ingredient in the success of the Internet. From the user's perspective, easily communicating via e-mail and accessing information on the Web are among the benefits of current computer technology. The Web browsers of the early 1990s, however, had limited capability for interactivity. Now, interactivity seems nearly effortless because of the patented device at the center of the following case.

---

13. 149 F.3d 1368 (Fed. Cir. 1998).

CASE 5.3 ■ **Eolas Technologies, Inc. v. Microsoft Corp.**

United States District Court,
Northern District of Illinois,
Eastern Division, 2004.
__ F.Supp.2d __.

FACTS In 1994, at the University of California, Michael Doyle, David Martin, and Cheong Ang invented a method for building a Web browser that could display interactive objects embedded in a single Web page and could use other applications to enable interactivity, allowing users to manipulate images and other data in a single window. They obtained a patent for this method and licensed its use exclusively to Eolas Technologies, Inc. Without Eolas's permission, Microsoft Corporation included the method's

features in its Internet Explorer browser, which was bundled with the Windows operating system. Eolas filed a suit in a federal district court against Microsoft, alleging patent infringement. A jury found Microsoft liable to Eolas and assessed $512 million in damages. Eolas filed a motion to enjoin (prevent) Microsoft from continuing to use the patented method. Microsoft responded that the Explorer and Windows bundled product "is in such widespread use that a broad injunction would impose unacceptably high costs on the product's users. These costs will include not only dollars but also other irreparable injuries such as loss of time and interruption of work. * * * Moreover, Web-based business will be affected because Web pages may

(Continued)

CASE 5.3—Continued

have to be redesigned. The redesign may, in some cases, require upgrades to millions of older Windows systems."

ISSUE Should Microsoft be barred from distributing versions of Explorer that include the features of Eolas's patented method?

DECISION Yes. The court upheld the jury's verdict and granted the injunction. The court stayed (postponed) the injunction, however, while Microsoft appealed the judgment.

REASON The court explained that inventors have a right to keep their invention to themselves, to share it with whom they choose, or to completely prevent others from using it. According to the court, "It is the loss of these rights that cause the irreparable injury that can be vindicated only by an injunction, not by damages." Thus, the court found that Eolas was entitled to an injunction but further held that the injunction should be limited in scope so as to minimize the harm to Microsoft and to the public.

The court stated, "The injunction should be carefully crafted to preclude [prevent] infringement only with respect to future conduct by Microsoft; infringements in the past are to be remedied by damages." The court noted that it is important to distinguish between past and future infringements here because the infringement occurs many times each day when Windows users display interactive objects embedded in Web pages. These infringements, in the court's view, belong in the category of past infringements because the operating system (the device used to infringe) was made and sold long before the judgment in this case was rendered. "The future infringement is limited to new versions of Microsoft's Windows operating system or any major service pack [updates] of any existing versions of the Windows operating system containing Internet Explorer that Microsoft releases to manufacturing."

FOR CRITICAL ANALYSIS—Technological Consideration *If Microsoft loses on appeal, should the firm be given time to devise and release noninfringing technology before being held in violation of the injunction? Why or why not?*

▪▪ Copyrights

COPYRIGHT
The exclusive right of "authors" to publish, print, or sell an intellectual production for a statutory period of time. A copyright has the same monopolistic nature as a patent or trademark, but it differs in that it applies exclusively to works of art, literature, and other works of authorship (including computer programs).

A **copyright** is an intangible property right granted by federal statute to the author or originator of certain literary or artistic productions. Currently, copyrights are governed by the Copyright Act of 1976,[14] as amended. Works created after January 1, 1978, are automatically given statutory copyright protection for the life of the author plus 70 years. For copyrights owned by publishing houses, the copyright expires 95 years from the date of publication or 120 years from the date of creation, whichever is first. For works by more than one author, the copyright expires 70 years after the death of the last surviving author.

These time periods reflect the extensions of the length of copyright protection enacted by Congress in the Copyright Term Extension Act of 1998.[15] Critics challenged this act as overstepping the bounds of Congress's power and violating the constitutional requirement that copyrights endure for only a limited time. In 2003, however, the United States Supreme Court upheld the act in *Eldred v. Ashcroft*.[16] This ruling obviously favored copyright holders by preventing copyrighted works from the 1920s and 1930s from losing protection and falling into the public domain for an additional two decades.

Copyrights can be registered with the U.S. Copyright Office in Washington, D.C. A copyright owner no longer needs to place a © or *Copr.* or *Copyright* on the work, however, to have the work protected against infringement. Chances are that if somebody created it, somebody owns it.

For information on copyrights, go to the U.S. Copyright Office at

http://lcweb.loc.gov/ copyright.

---

14. 17 U.S.C. Sections 101 *et seq.*

15. 17 U.S.C.A. Section 302.

16. 537 U.S. 186, 123 S.Ct. 769, 154 L.Ed.2d 683 (2003).

WHAT IS PROTECTED EXPRESSION?

Works that are copyrightable include books, records, films, artworks, architectural plans, menus, music videos, product packaging, and computer software. To obtain protection under the Copyright Act, a work must be original and fall into one of the following categories: (1) literary works; (2) musical works; (3) dramatic works; (4) pantomimes and choreographic works; (5) pictorial, graphic, and sculptural works; (6) films and other audiovisual works; and (7) sound recordings. To be protected, a work must be "fixed in a durable medium" from which it can be perceived, reproduced, or communicated. Protection is automatic. Registration is not required.

BE CAREFUL If a creative work does not fall into a certain category, it may not be copyrighted, but it may be protected by other intellectual property law.

Section 102 Exclusions   Section 102 of the Copyright Act specifically excludes copyright protection for any "idea, procedure, process, system, method of operation, concept, principle, or discovery, regardless of the form in which it is described, explained, illustrated, or embodied." Note that it is not possible to copyright an *idea*. The underlying ideas embodied in a work may be freely used by others. What is copyrightable is the particular way in which an idea is *expressed*. Whenever an idea and an expression are inseparable, the expression cannot be copyrighted. Generally, anything that is not an original expression will not qualify for copyright protection. Facts widely known to the public are not copyrightable. Page numbers are not copyrightable because they follow a sequence known to everyone. Mathematical calculations are not copyrightable.

Compilations of Facts   *Compilations* of facts, however, are copyrightable. Section 103 of the Copyright Act defines a compilation as "a work formed by the collection and assembling of preexisting materials of data that are selected, coordinated, or arranged in such a way that the resulting work as a whole constitutes an original work of authorship." The key requirement for the copyrightability of a compilation is originality. ■ **EXAMPLE 5.6** The white pages of a telephone directory do not qualify for copyright protection when the information that makes up the directory (names, addresses, and telephone numbers) is not selected, coordinated, or arranged in an original way.[17] In one case, even the Yellow Pages of a telephone directory did not qualify for copyright protection.[18] ■

COPYRIGHT INFRINGEMENT

You can find a host of information on copyright law, including the Copyright Act and significant United States Supreme Court cases in the area of copyright law, at

http://supct.law.cornell.edu/ supct/cases/copyrt.htm.

Whenever the form or expression of an idea is copied, an infringement of copyright occurs. The reproduction does not have to be exactly the same as the original, nor does it have to reproduce the original in its entirety. If a substantial part of the original is reproduced, there is copyright infringement.

Damages for Copyright Infringement   Those who infringe copyrights may be liable for damages or criminal penalties. These range from actual damages or statutory damages, imposed at the court's discretion, to criminal proceedings for willful violations. Actual damages are based on the harm caused to the copyright holder by

17. *Feist Publications, Inc. v. Rural Telephone Service Co.*, 499 U.S. 340, 111 S.Ct. 1282, 113 L.Ed.2d 358 (1991).
18. *Bellsouth Advertising & Publishing Corp. v. Donnelley Information Publishing, Inc.*, 999 F.2d 1436 (11th Cir. 1993).

the infringement, while statutory damages, not to exceed $150,000, are provided for under the Copyright Act. In addition, criminal proceedings may result in fines and/or imprisonment.

The "Fair Use" Exception An exception to liability for copyright infringement is made under the "fair use" doctrine. In certain circumstances, a person or organization can reproduce copyrighted material without paying royalties (fees paid to the copyright holder for the privilege of reproducing the copyrighted material). Section 107 of the Copyright Act provides as follows:

> [T]he fair use of a copyrighted work, including such use by reproduction in copies or phonorecords or by any other means specified by [Section 106 of the Copyright Act,] for purposes such as criticism, comment, news reporting, teaching (including multiple copies for classroom use), scholarship, or research, is not an infringement of copyright. In determining whether the use made of a work in any particular case is a fair use the factors to be considered shall include—
>
> (1) the purpose and character of the use, including whether such use is of a commercial nature or is for nonprofit educational purposes;
> (2) the nature of the copyrighted work;
> (3) the amount and substantiality of the portion used in relation to the copyrighted work as a whole; and
> (4) the effect of the use upon the potential market for or value of the copyrighted work.

Because these guidelines are very broad, the courts determine whether a particular use is fair on a case-by-case basis. Thus, anyone reproducing copyrighted material may be committing a violation. In determining whether a use is fair, courts have often considered the fourth factor to be the most important.

COPYRIGHT PROTECTION FOR SOFTWARE

In 1980, Congress passed the Computer Software Copyright Act, which amended the Copyright Act of 1976 to include computer programs in the list of creative works protected by federal copyright law. The 1980 statute, which classifies computer programs as "literary works," defines a computer program as a "set of statements or instructions to be used directly or indirectly in a computer in order to bring about a certain result."

Because of the unique nature of computer programs, the courts have had many problems applying and interpreting the 1980 act. Generally, though, the courts have held that copyright protection extends not only to those parts of a computer program that can be read by humans, such as the high-level language of a source code, but also to the binary-language object code of a computer program, which is readable only by the computer.[19] Additionally, such elements as the overall structure, sequence, and organization of a program were deemed copyrightable.[20] The courts have disagreed as to whether the "look and feel"—the general appearance, command structure, video images, menus, windows, and other screen displays—of computer programs should also be protected by copyright. The courts have tended, however, not to extend copyright protection to look-and-feel aspects of computer programs.

---

19. See *Stern Electronics, Inc. v. Kaufman,* 669 F.2d 852 (2d Cir. 1982); and *Apple Computer, Inc. v. Franklin Computer Corp.,* 714 F.2d 1240 (3d Cir. 1983).
20. *Whelan Associates, Inc. v. Jaslow Dental Laboratory, Inc.,* 797 F.2d 1222 (3d Cir. 1986).

COPYRIGHTS IN DIGITAL INFORMATION

Copyright law is probably the most important form of intellectual property protection on the Internet. This is because much of the material on the Internet consists of works of authorship (including multimedia presentations, software, and database information), which are the traditional focus of copyright law. Copyright law is also important because the nature of the Internet requires that data be "copied" to be transferred online. Copies are a significant part of the traditional controversies arising in this area of the law.

The Copyright Act of 1976 When Congress drafted the principal U.S. law governing copyrights, the Copyright Act of 1976, cyberspace did not exist for most of us. The threat to copyright owners was posed not by computer technology but by unauthorized *tangible* copies of works and the sale of rights to movies, television, and other media.

Some issues that were unimagined when the Copyright Act was drafted have posed thorny questions for the courts. For instance, to sell a copy of a work, permission of the copyright holder is necessary. Because of the nature of cyberspace, however, one of the early controversies involved determining at what point an intangible, electronic "copy" of a work has been made. The courts have held that loading a file or program into a computer's random access memory, or RAM, constitutes the making of a "copy" for purposes of copyright law.[21] RAM is a portion of a computer's memory into which a file, for instance, is loaded so that it can be accessed (read or written over). Thus, a copyright is infringed when a party downloads

The University of Michigan provides information on copyrights generally and copyrights in digital information at

http://www.copyright.umich. edu/law.html.

---

21. *MAI Systems Corp. v. Peak Computer, Inc.,* 991 F.2d 511 (9th Cir. 1993).

software into RAM without owning the software or otherwise having a right to download it.[22]

Other rights, including those relating to the revision of "collective works" such as magazines, were acknowledged thirty years ago but were considered to have only limited economic value. Today, technology has made some of those rights vastly more significant. How does the old law apply to these rights? That was one of the questions in the following case.

22. *DSC Communications Corp. v. Pulse Communications, Inc.,* 170 F.3d 1354 (Fed. Cir. 1999).

CASE 5.4 ▪ New York Times Co. v. Tasini

Supreme Court of the United States, 2001.
533 U.S. 483,
121 S.Ct. 2381,
150 L.Ed.2d 500.
http://supct.law.cornell.edu/supct[a]

FACTS Magazines and newspapers, including the *New York Times,* buy and publish articles written by freelance writers. Besides circulating hard copies of their periodicals, these publishers sell the contents to e-publishers for inclusion in online and other electronic databases. Jonathan Tasini and other freelance writers filed a suit in a federal district court against the New York Times Company and other publishers, including the e-publishers, contending that the e-publication of the articles violated the Copyright Act. The publishers responded that, among other things, the Copyright Act gave them a right to produce "revisions" of their publications. The writers argued that the Copyright Act did not cover electronic "revisions." The court granted a summary judgment in the publishers' favor, which was reversed on the writers' appeal to the U.S. Court of Appeals for the Second Circuit. The publishers appealed to the United States Supreme Court.

ISSUE To put the contents of periodicals into e-databases and onto CD-ROMs, do publishers need to obtain the per-

mission of the writers whose contributions are included in the periodicals?

DECISION Yes. The United States Supreme Court affirmed the lower court's judgment. The Supreme Court remanded the case for a determination as to how the writers should be compensated.

REASON The Court pointed out that databases are "vast domain[s] of diverse texts," consisting of "thousands or millions of files containing individual articles from thousands of collective works." The Court found that these databases have little relationship to the articles' original publication. The databases are not "revisions," as the publishers argued, because the databases reproduce and distribute articles "clear of the context provided by the original periodical editions"—not "as part of that particular collective work" to which the author contributed, not "as part of * * * any revision," and not "as part of * * * any later collective work in the same series," as the Copyright Act provides. The Court reasoned that a database composed of such articles was no more a revision of an original work than "a 400-page novel quoting a sonnet in passing would represent a 'revision' of that poem."

FOR CRITICAL ANALYSIS—Economic Consideration   *When rights such as those in this case become more valuable as a result of new technology, should the law be changed to redistribute the economic benefit of those rights? Explain.*

a.   In the "Search" box at the top of the page, enter "Tasini." Click on "submit." In the result, scroll to the case name and select the appropriate link to access the opinion.

Further Developments in Copyright Law   In the last several years, Congress has enacted legislation designed specifically to protect copyright holders in a digital age. Prior to 1997, criminal penalties under copyright law could be imposed only if unauthorized copies were exchanged for financial gain. Yet much piracy of copyrighted materials was "altruistic" in nature; that is, unauthorized copies were made and distributed not for financial gain but simply for reasons of generosity—to share the copies with others.

Cary Sherman, president of the Recording Industry Association of America (RIAA). Sherman is talking with reporters after announcing that the RIAA was filing hundreds of lawsuits against individuals who shared copyrighted music files via the Internet. Under what theories can a company that distributes file-sharing software also be held liable if individuals use the software to exchange copyrighted music? (AP Photo/George Nikitin)

PEER-TO-PEER (P2P) NETWORKING
The sharing of resources (such as files, hard drives, and processing styles) among multiple computers without necessarily requiring a central network server.

DISTRIBUTED NETWORK
A network that can be used by persons located (distributed) around the country or the globe to share computer files.

To combat altruistic piracy and for other reasons, Congress passed the No Electronic Theft (NET) Act of 1997. This act extends criminal liability for the piracy of copyrighted materials to persons who exchange unauthorized copies of copyrighted works, such as software, even though they realize no profit from the exchange. The act also imposes penalties on those who make unauthorized electronic copies of books, magazines, movies, or music for *personal* use, thus altering the traditional "fair use" doctrine. The criminal penalties for violating the act are steep; they include fines as high as $250,000 and incarceration for up to five years.

In 1998, Congress passed further legislation to protect copyright holders—the Digital Millennium Copyright Act. Because of its significance in protecting against the piracy of copyrighted materials in the online environment, this act is presented as this chapter's *Landmark in the Law* feature on pages 160 and 161.

MP3 AND FILE-SHARING TECHNOLOGY

At one time, music fans swapped compact discs (CDs) and recorded the songs that they liked from others' CDs onto their own cassettes. This type of "file-sharing" was awkward at best. Soon after the Internet became popular, a few enterprising programmers created software to compress large data files, particularly those associated with music. The reduced file sizes make transmitting music over the Internet feasible. The most widely known compression and decompression system is MP3, which enables music fans to download songs or entire CDs onto their computers or onto a portable listening device, such as Rio or iPod. The MP3 system also made it possible for music fans to access other music fans' files by engaging in file-sharing via the Internet.

Peer-to-Peer (P2P) Networking   File-sharing via the Internet is accomplished through what is called **peer-to-peer (P2P) networking.** The concept is simple. Rather than going through a central Web server, P2P involves numerous personal computers (PCs) that are connected to the Internet. Files stored on one PC can be accessed by others who are members of the same network. Sometimes this is called a **distributed network.** In other words, parts of the network are distributed all over the country or the world. File-sharing offers an unlimited number of uses for distributed networks. Currently, for instance, many researchers allow their home computers' computing power to be accessed through file-sharing software so that very large mathematical problems can be solved quickly. Additionally, persons scattered throughout the country or the world can work together on the same project by using file-sharing programs.

Sharing Stored Music Files   When file-sharing is used to download others' stored music files, copyright issues arise. Recording artists and their labels stand to lose large amounts of royalties and revenues if relatively few CDs are purchased and then made available on distributed networks, from which everyone can get them for free. The issue of file-sharing infringement has been the subject of an ongoing debate over the last few years.

■ **EXAMPLE 5.7** In the highly publicized case of *A&M Records, Inc. v. Napster, Inc.*,[23] several firms in the recording industry sued Napster, Inc., the owner of the

23. 239 F.3d 1004 (9th Cir. 2001).

LANDMARK IN THE LAW

The Digital Millennium Copyright Act of 1998

The United States leads the world in the production of creative products, including books, films, videos, recordings, and software. In fact, as indicated earlier in this chapter, the creative industries are more important to the U.S. economy than the traditional product industries are. Exports of U.S. creative products, for example, surpass those of every other U.S. industry in value. Creative industries are growing at nearly three times the rate of the economy as a whole.

Steps have been taken, both nationally and internationally, to protect ownership rights in intellectual property, including copyrights. As you will read later in this chapter, to curb unauthorized copying of copyrighted materials, the World Intellectual Property Organization (WIPO) enacted a treaty in 1996 to upgrade global standards of copyright protection, particularly for the Internet.

IMPLEMENTING THE WIPO TREATY In 1998, Congress implemented the provisions of the WIPO treaty by updating U.S. copyright law. The new law—the Digital Millennium Copyright Act of 1998—is a landmark step in the protection of copyright owners and, because of the leading position of the United States in the creative industries, serves as a model for other nations. Among other things, the act established civil and criminal penalties for anyone who circumvents (bypasses, or gets around—through clever maneuvering, for example) encryption software or other technological antipiracy protection. Also prohibited are the manufacture, import, sale, and distribution of devices or services for circumvention.

The act provides for exceptions to fit the needs of libraries, scientists, universities, and others. In general, the law does not restrict the "fair use" of circumvention methods for educational and other noncommercial purposes. For example, circumvention is allowed to test computer security, conduct encryption research, protect personal privacy, and enable parents to monitor their children's use of the Internet. The exceptions are to be reconsidered every three years.

then-popular Napster Web site. The Napster site provided registered users with free software that enabled them to transfer exact copies of the contents of MP3 files from one computer to another via the Internet. Napster also maintained centralized search indices so that users could locate specific titles or artists' recordings on the computers of other members. The firms argued that Napster should be liable for contributory and vicarious[24] copyright infringement because it assisted others in obtaining copies of copyrighted music without the copyright owners' permission. Both the federal district court and the U.S. Court of Appeals for the Ninth Circuit agreed and held Napster liable for violating copyright laws. ∎

Since the 2001 *Napster* decision, the recording industry has filed and won numerous lawsuits against companies that distribute online file-sharing software. The courts have held these Napsterlike companies liable based on two theories: contributory infringement, which applies if the company had reason to know about a user's infringement and failed to stop it; and vicarious liability, which exists if the company was able to control the users' activities and stood to benefit financially from

---

24. Vicarious (indirect) liability exists when one person is subject to liability for another's actions. A common example occurs in the employment context, when an employer is held vicariously liable by third parties for torts committed by employees in the course of their employment.

LANDMARK IN THE LAW The Digital Millennium Copyright Act of 1998—Continued

LIMITING THE LIABILITY OF INTERNET SERVICE PROVIDERS   The 1998 act also limited the liability of Internet service providers (ISPs). Under the act, an ISP is not liable for any copyright infringement by its customer *unless* the ISP is aware of the subscriber's violation. An ISP may be held liable only if it fails to take action to shut the subscriber down after learning of the violation. A copyright holder has to act promptly, however, by pursuing a claim in court, or the subscriber has the right to be restored to online access.

APPLICATION TO TODAY'S WORLD

The application of the Digital Millennium Copyright Act of 1998 to today's world is fairly self-evident. If Congress had not enacted this legislation, copyright owners would have a far more difficult time obtaining legal redress against those who, without authorization, decrypt and/or copy copyrighted materials. Of course, problems remain, particularly because of the global nature of the Internet. From a practical standpoint, the degree of protection afforded to copyright holders depends on the extent to which other nations that have signed the WIPO treaty actually implement its provisions and agree on the interpretation of terms, such as what constitutes an electronic copy.

RELEVANT WEB SITES

To locate information on the Web concerning the Digital Millennium Copyright Act of 1998, go to this text's Web site at http://blt.westbuslaw.com, *select "Chapter 5," and click on "URLs for Landmarks."*

---

their infringement. In the *Napster* case, the court held the company liable under both doctrines, largely because the technology that Napster had used was centralized and gave it "the ability to locate infringing material listed on its search indices, and the right to terminate users' access to the system."

New File-Sharing Technologies   In the wake of the *Napster* decision, other companies developed new technologies that allow P2P network users to share stored music files, without paying a fee, more quickly and efficiently than ever. Today's file-sharing software is decentralized and does not use search indices. Thus, the companies have no ability to supervise or control which music (or other media files) their users are exchanging. Unlike the Napster system, in which the company played a role in connecting people who were downloading and uploading songs, the new systems are designed to work without the company's input.

Software such as Morpheus and KaZaA, for example, provides users with an interface that is similar to a Web browser. This technology is different from that used by Napster. Instead of the company locating songs for users on other members' computers, the software automatically annotates files with descriptive information so that the music can easily be categorized and cross-referenced (by artist and title, for instance). When a user performs a search, the software is able to locate a list of peers that have the file available for downloading. Also, to expedite the P2P transfer and ensure that the complete file is received, the software distributes the download task over the entire list of peers simultaneously. By downloading even one file, the user becomes a point of distribution for that file, which is then automatically shared with others on the network.

How will the courts decide the legality of these new digital technologies? See this chapter's *Adapting the Law to the Online Environment* feature for a discussion of this issue.

ADAPTING THE LAW TO THE ONLINE ENVIRONMENT

 # New File-Sharing Technology and Copyright Law

Over 18 million Americans downloaded music from the Internet in 2004. It is not known what percentage of those downloaded copies were unauthorized, or "pirated." Clearly, any person who downloads copyrighted music without permission from the copyright holder is liable for copyright infringement. But what about the companies that provide the software that enables users to swap copyrighted music? In what circumstances will the companies be held liable? It has been difficult for the courts to apply traditional doctrines of contributory and vicarious copyright liability to new file-sharing technologies.

THE *GROKSTER* CASE

Consider the situation faced by the court in *Metro-Goldwyn-Mayer Studios, Inc. v. Grokster, Ltd.*[a] In that case, organizations in the music and film industry (the plaintiffs) sued several companies that distribute file-sharing software used in P2P networks, including Grokster, Ltd., and StreamCast Networks, Inc. (the defendants). The plaintiffs claimed that the companies were contributorily and vicariously liable for the infringement of their end users.

The federal district court examined the technology involved and concluded that the defendants were not liable for contributory infringement because they lacked the requisite level of knowledge. It was not enough that the defendants *generally* knew that the software they provided might be used to infringe on copyrights; they also had to have *specific knowledge* of the infringement "at a time when they can use that knowledge to stop the particular infringement." Here, the companies had merely distributed free software. They had no knowledge of whether users were swapping copyrighted files and no

ability to stop users from infringing activities. Further, the two defendants could not be held vicariously liable for the infringement because it was not possible for the companies to supervise or control their users' conduct.

A SIGNIFICANT DEFEAT FOR THE ENTERTAINMENT INDUSTRY

The *Grokster* case represents a significant defeat for the entertainment and recording industries. The district court's decision was appealed to the U.S. Court of Appeals for the Ninth Circuit—the same court that decided the *Napster* case—and was affirmed. The appellate court noted that "we live in a quicksilver technological environment with courts ill suited to fix the flow of Internet innovation." The court went on to find that "it is prudent for courts to exercise caution before restructuring liability theories for the purpose of addressing specific market abuses, despite their apparent present magnitude." The court also acknowledged that according to the United States Supreme Court, such matters should be left to Congress. After all, Congress has the power to promote the progress of science and the arts, and the sign of how far Congress has chosen to go with respect to this protection can come only from Congress.[b]

FOR CRITICAL ANALYSIS

On appeal, the defense compared distributing file-sharing software to selling copy machines, arguing that the courts would not hold Xerox Corporation liable simply because people frequently use its machines to make infringing copies of copyrighted material. Should different rules apply to providers of file-sharing software than to makers of copy machines or videocassette recorders, both of which can be used to infringe on copyrights? Why or why not?

a. 243 F.Supp.2d 1073 (C.D.Cal. 2003).

b. *Metro-Goldwyn-Mayer Studios, Inc. v. Grokster, Ltd.*, 380 F.3d 1154 (9th Cir. 2004).

■■ Trade Secrets

TRADE SECRET
Information or processes that give a business an advantage over competitors that do not know the information or processes.

Some business processes and information that are not or cannot be patented, copyrighted, or trademarked are nevertheless protected against appropriation by a competitor as trade secrets. **Trade secrets** consist of customer lists, plans, research and development, pricing information, marketing techniques, production methods, and generally anything that makes an individual company unique and that would have value to a competitor.

Unlike copyright and trademark protection, protection of trade secrets extends both to ideas and to their expression. (For this reason, and because a trade secret involves no registration or filing requirements, trade secret protection may be well suited for software.) Of course, the secret formula, method, or other information must be disclosed to some persons, particularly to key employees. Businesses generally attempt to protect their trade secrets by having all employees who use the process or information agree in their contracts, or in confidentiality agreements, never to divulge it. For further information on how trade secrets can be protected, see the *Application* feature at the end of this chapter.

STATE AND FEDERAL LAW ON TRADE SECRETS

Under Section 757 of the *Restatement of Torts,* those who disclose or use another's trade secret, without authorization, are liable to that other party if (1) they discovered the secret by improper means, or (2) their disclosure or use constitutes a breach of a duty owed to the other party. The theft of confidential business data by industrial espionage, as when a business taps into a competitor's computer, is a theft of trade secrets without any contractual violation and is actionable in itself.

Until twenty years ago, virtually all law with respect to trade secrets was common law. In an effort to reduce the unpredictability of the common law in this area, a model act, the Uniform Trade Secrets Act, was presented to the states for adoption in 1979. Parts of this act have been adopted in more than thirty states. Typically, a state that has adopted parts of the act has adopted only those parts that encompass its own existing common law. Additionally, in 1996 Congress passed the Economic Espionage Act, which made the theft of trade secrets a federal crime. We will examine the provisions and significance of this act in Chapter 6, in the context of crimes related to business.

 The Cyberspace Law Institute offers articles and information on such topics as trade secrets at **http://www.cli.org**.

TRADE SECRETS IN CYBERSPACE

The nature of new computer technology undercuts a business firm's ability to protect its confidential information, including trade secrets.[25] For instance, a dishonest employee could e-mail trade secrets in a company's computer to a competitor or a future employer. If e-mail is not an option, the employee might walk out with the information on a computer disk.

 **ETHICAL ISSUE 5.2**

Does preventing a Web site from posting computer codes that reveal trade secrets violate free speech rights? An ongoing issue with ethical dimensions is the point at which free speech rights come into conflict with the right of copyright holders to protect their property by using encryption technology. This issue came before the California Supreme Court in 2003 in the case of *DVD Copy Control Association v. Bunner.*[26] Trade associations in the movie industry (the plaintiffs) sued an Internet Web site operator (the defendant) who had posted the code of a computer program

25. Note that the courts have even found that customers' e-mail addresses may constitute trade secrets. See *T-N-T Motorsports, Inc. v. Hennessey Motorsports, Inc.,* 965 S.W.2d 18 (Tex.App.–Hous. [1 Dist.] 1998); rehearing overruled (1998); petition dismissed (1998).
26. 31 Cal.4th 864, 75 P.3d 1, 4 Cal.Rptr.3d 69 (2003).

that cracked technology used to encrypt DVDs. This posed a significant threat to the plaintiffs because, by using the code-cracking software, users would be able to duplicate the copyrighted movies stored on the DVDs. In their suit, the plaintiffs claimed that the defendant had misappropriated trade secrets. The defendant argued that software programs designed to break encryption programs were a form of constitutionally protected speech. When the case reached the California Supreme Court, the court held that although the First Amendment applies to computer code, computer code is not a form of "pure speech" and the courts can therefore protect it to a lesser extent. The court reinstated the trial court's order that enjoined (prevented) the defendant from continuing to post the code. ■

■ International Protection for Intellectual Property

For many years, the United States has been a party to various international agreements relating to intellectual property rights. For example, the Paris Convention of 1883, to which about ninety countries are signatory, allows parties in one country to file for patent and trademark protection in any of the other member countries. Other international agreements include the Berne Convention and the TRIPS agreement.

THE BERNE CONVENTION

Under the Berne Convention of 1886, an international copyright agreement, if an American writes a book, every country that has signed the convention must recognize the American author's copyright in the book. Also, if a citizen of a country that has not signed the convention first publishes a book in a country that has signed, all other countries that have signed the convention must recognize that author's copyright. Copyright notice is not needed to gain protection under the Berne Convention for works published after March 1, 1989.

    This convention and other international agreements have given some protection to intellectual property on a worldwide level. None of them, however, has been as significant and far reaching in scope as the agreement on Trade-Related Aspects of Intellectual Property Rights, or, more simply, TRIPS.

The Web site of Cornell University's Legal Information Institute includes the texts of the Berne Convention and other international treaties on copyright issues at

http://www.law.cornell.edu/ topics/copyright.html.

THE TRIPS AGREEMENT

Representatives from over one hundred nations signed the TRIPS agreement in 1994. The agreement established, for the first time, standards for the international protection of intellectual property rights, including patents, trademarks, and copyrights for movies, computer programs, books, and music. Prior to the agreement, U.S. sellers of intellectual property in the international market faced difficulties because many other countries had no laws protecting intellectual property rights or failed to enforce existing laws. To address this problem, the TRIPS agreement provides that each member country must include in its domestic laws broad intellectual property rights and effective remedies (including civil and criminal penalties) for violations of those rights.

    Generally, the TRIPS agreement provides that each member nation must not discriminate (in the administration, regulation, or adjudication of intellectual property rights) against foreign owners of such rights. In other words, a member nation cannot give its own nationals (citizens) favorable treatment without offering the same treatment to nationals of all member countries. For instance, if a U.S. software manufacturer brings a suit for the infringement of intellectual property rights under a member nation's national laws, the U.S. manufacturer is entitled to receive the same treatment as a domestic manufacturer. Each member nation must also ensure that legal procedures are available for parties who wish to bring actions for infringement of intellectual property rights. Additionally, a related document established a mechanism for settling disputes among member nations.

Particular provisions of the TRIPS agreement relate to patent, trademark, and copyright protection for intellectual property. The agreement specifically provides copyright protection for computer programs by stating that compilations of data, databases, and other materials are "intellectual creations" and that they are to be protected as copyrightable works. Other provisions relate to trade secrets and the rental of computer programs and cinematographic works.

APPLICATION ▪ How Can You Protect Your Trade Secrets?*

Most successful businesses have trade secrets. The law protects trade secrets indefinitely, provided that the information is not generally known, is kept a secret, and has commercial value. Sometimes, of course, a business needs to disclose secret information to a party in the course of conducting business. For example, a company may need to hire a consultant to revamp a computer system, an engineer to design a manufacturing system, or a marketing firm to implement a sales program. All of these individuals may need access to some of the company's trade secrets. One way to protect against the unauthorized disclosure of such information is through confidentiality agreements.

CONFIDENTIALITY AGREEMENTS

In a confidentiality agreement, one party promises not to divulge information about the other party to anyone else or to use the other party's confidential information for his or her own benefit. Confidentiality agreements are often included in licensing and employment contracts, but they can also be separate contracts. The key is to make sure that the agreement adequately protects the trade secrets and applies to any related transactions between the parties. For instance, if you execute a separate confidentiality agreement with a marketing firm, you need to make sure that it refers to any other contracts you have made with that firm prior to the confidentiality agreement. Also, subsequent contracts with the firm should either refer back to the confidentiality agreement or include a new confidentiality provision.

DEFINING THE SCOPE OF THE AGREEMENT

Confidentiality agreements must be reasonable. Businesspersons should consider what information needs to be pro-

tected and for how long. Make certain to define what you mean by *confidential information* in the agreement. Do you want to protect just your customer list or all financial, technical, and other business information? Think ahead, cover the bases, and be specific.

The duration of the agreement usually depends on the nature of the information. Very important secret information should remain confidential for a longer time than less important secrets. Sometimes, as with an advertising campaign, the time period for confidentiality may be self-evident (if the campaign ends in six months, for example). Tailor the agreement to your needs as much as possible. If the party to whom you are disclosing information will no longer need the information after a certain date—such as when the project is completed—include a provision requiring the return of confidential information after that date. This will alleviate concerns that your confidential trade secrets might later fall into the hands of a stranger.

CHECKLIST FOR THE OWNER OF TRADE SECRETS

1. Determine what your trade secrets are and who may need access to them.
2. Make sure that confidentiality agreements define, in an all-inclusive manner, what information should be considered confidential.
3. Specify a time period that is reasonable under the circumstances.
4. Identify the agreements to which the confidentiality provisions apply.
5. Require that the confidential materials be returned to you.

* This *Application* is not meant to substitute for the services of an attorney who is licensed to practice law in your state.

▣ KEY TERMS

copyright   154
cyber mark   148
cybersquatting   149
distributed network   159
domain name   149

intellectual property   141
meta tags   150
patent   151
peer-to-peer (P2P) networking   159
service mark   148

trade dress   148
trade name   148
trade secret   163
trademark   143

CHAPTER SUMMARY ▣ Intellectual Property

Trademarks and Related Property (See pages 143–148.)	1. A *trademark* is a distinctive mark, motto, device, or emblem that a manufacturer stamps, prints, or otherwise affixes to the goods it produces so that they can be identified on the market and their origin vouched for.
	2. The major federal statutes protecting trademarks and related property are the Lanham Act of 1946 and the Federal Trademark Dilution Act of 1995. Generally, to be protected, a trademark must be sufficiently distinctive from all competing trademarks.
	3. *Trademark infringement* occurs when one uses a mark that is the same as, or confusingly similar to, the protected trademark, service mark, trade name, or trade dress of another without permission when marketing goods or services.
Cyber Marks (See pages 148–151.)	A *cyber mark* is a trademark in cyberspace. Trademark infringement in cyberspace occurs when one person uses, in a domain name or in meta tags, a name that is the same as, or confusingly similar to, the protected mark of another.
Patents (See pages 151–154.)	1. A *patent* is a grant from the government that gives an inventor the exclusive right to make, use, and sell an invention for a period of twenty years from the date of filing the application for a patent. To be patentable, an invention (or a discovery, process, or design) must be genuine, novel, useful, and not obvious in light of current technology. Computer software may be patented.
	2. *Patent infringement* occurs when one uses or sells another's patented design, product, or process without the patent owner's permission.
Copyrights (See pages 154–162.)	1. A *copyright* is an intangible property right granted by federal statute to the author or originator of certain literary or artistic productions. Computer software may be copyrighted.
	2. *Copyright infringement* occurs whenever the form or expression of an idea is copied without the permission of the copyright holder. An exception applies if the copying is deemed a "fair use."
	3. Copyrights are governed by the Copyright Act of 1976, as amended. To protect copyrights in digital information, Congress passed the No Electronic Theft Act of 1997 and the Digital Millennium Copyright Act of 1998.
	4. Technology that allows users to share files via the Internet on distributed networks often raises copyright infringement issues. Companies that provide file-sharing software to users have been held liable in the past for contributory and vicarious copyright liability. The courts, however, are having difficulty applying these doctrines of liability to new file-sharing technologies.
Trade Secrets (See pages 163–164.)	*Trade secrets* include customer lists, plans, research and development, and pricing information, for example. Trade secrets are protected under the common law and, in some states, under statutory law against misappropriation by competitors. The Economic Espionage Act of 1996 made the theft of trade secrets a federal crime (see Chapter 6).

CHAPTER SUMMARY ▦ Intellectual Property—Continued

International Protection for Intellectual Property (See pages 164–165.)	Various international agreements provide international protection for intellectual property. A landmark agreement is the 1994 agreement on Trade-Related Aspects of Intellectual Property Rights (TRIPS), which provides for enforcement procedures in all countries signatory to the agreement.

▦ FOR REVIEW

Answers for the even-numbered questions in this For Review *section can be found in Appendix I at the end of this text.*

1 What is intellectual property?

2 Why are trademarks and patents protected by the law?

3 What laws protect authors' rights in the works they generate?

4 What are trade secrets, and what laws offer protection for this form of intellectual property?

5 What steps have been taken to protect intellectual property rights in today's digital age?

▦ QUESTIONS AND CASE PROBLEMS

5–1. Copyright Infringement. In which of the following situations would a court likely hold Maruta liable for copyright infringement?

(a) At the library, Maruta photocopies ten pages from a scholarly journal relating to a topic on which she is writing a term paper.

(b) Maruta makes leather handbags and sells them in her small leather shop. She advertises her handbags as "Vutton handbags," hoping that customers might mistakenly assume that they were made by Vuitton, the well-known maker of high-quality luggage and handbags.

(c) Maruta owns a video store. She purchases one copy of all the latest videos from various video manufacturers. Then, using blank videotapes, she makes copies to rent or sell to her customers.

(d) Maruta teaches Latin American history at a small university. She has a videocassette recorder and frequently tapes television programs relating to Latin America. She then takes the videos to her classroom so that her students can watch them.

5–2. Patent Infringement. John and Andrew Doney invented a hard-bearing device for balancing rotors. Although they registered their invention with the U.S. Patent and Trademark Office, it was never used as an automobile wheel balancer. Some time later, Exetron Corp. produced an automobile wheel balancer that used a hard-bearing device with a support plate similar to that of the Doneys. Given that the Doneys had not used their device for automobile wheel balancing, does Exetron's use of a similar hard-bearing device infringe on the Doneys' patent?

5–3. Trademark Infringement. Elvis Presley Enterprises, Inc. (EPE), owns all of the trademarks of the Elvis Presley estate.

None of these marks is registered for use in the restaurant business. Barry Capece registered "The Velvet Elvis" as a service mark for a restaurant and tavern with the U.S. Patent and Trademark Office. Capece opened a nightclub called "The Velvet Elvis" with a menu, decor, advertising, and promotional events that evoked Elvis Presley and his music. EPE filed a suit in a federal district court against Capece and others, claiming, among other things, that "The Velvet Elvis" service mark infringed on EPE's trademarks. During the trial, witnesses testified that they thought the bar was associated with Elvis Presley. Should Capece be ordered to stop using "The Velvet Elvis" mark? Why or why not? [*Elvis Presley Enterprises, Inc. v. Capece,* 141 F.3d 188 (5th Cir. 1998)]

5–4. Trademark Infringement. A&H Sportswear, Inc., a swimsuit maker, obtained a trademark for its MIRACLESUIT in 1992. The MIRACLESUIT design makes the wearer appear slimmer. The MIRACLESUIT was widely advertised and discussed in the media. The MIRACLESUIT was also sold for a brief time in the Victoria's Secret (VS) catalogue, which is published by Victoria's Secret Catalogue, Inc. In 1993, Victoria's Secret Stores, Inc., began selling a cleavage-enhancing bra, which was named THE MIRACLE BRA and for which a trademark was obtained. The next year, THE MIRACLE BRA swimwear debuted in the VS catalogue and stores. A&H filed a suit in a federal district court against VS Stores and VS Catalogue, alleging in part that THE MIRACLE BRA mark, when applied to swimwear, infringed on the MIRACLESUIT mark. A&H argued that there was a "possibility of confusion" between the marks. The VS entities contended that the appropriate standard was "likelihood of confusion" and that, in this case, there was no likelihood of confusion. In whose favor will the court rule, and why? [*A&H Sportswear, Inc. v. Victoria's Secret Stores, Inc.,* 166 F.3d 197 (3d Cir. 1999)]

CASE PROBLEM WITH SAMPLE ANSWER

5–5. In 1999, Steve and Pierce Thumann and their father, Fred, created Spider Webs, Ltd., a partnership, to, according to Steve, "develop Internet address names." Spider Webs registered nearly two thousand Internet domain names for an average of $70 each, including the names of cities, the names of buildings, names related to a business or trade (such as air conditioning or plumbing), and the names of famous companies. It offered many of the names for sale on its Web site and through eBay.com. Spider Webs registered the domain name "ERNESTANDJULIOGALLO.COM" in Spider Webs' name. E. and J. Gallo Winery filed a suit against Spider Webs, alleging, in part, violations of the Anticybersquatting Consumer Protection Act. Gallo asked the court for, among other things, statutory damages. Gallo also sought to have the domain name at issue transferred to Gallo. During the suit, Spider Webs published anticorporate articles and opinions, and discussions of the suit, at the URL "ERNESTANDJULIOGALLO.COM." Should the court rule in Gallo's favor? Why or why not? [*E. & J. Gallo Winery v. Spider Webs, Ltd.,* 129 F.Supp.2d 1033 (S.D.Tex. 2001)]

After you have answered this problem, compare your answer with the sample answer given on the Web site that accompanies this text. Go to http://blt.westbuslaw.com, select "Chapter 5," and click on "Case Problem with Sample Answer."

5–6. Trade Secrets. Four Pillars Enterprise Co. is a Taiwanese company owned by Pin Yen Yang. Avery Dennison, Inc., a U.S. corporation, is one of Four Pillars' chief competitors in the manufacture of adhesives. In 1989, Victor Lee, an Avery employee, met Yang and Yang's daughter Hwei Chen. They agreed to pay Lee $25,000 a year to serve as a consultant to Four Pillars. Over the next eight years, Lee supplied the Yangs with confidential Avery reports, including information that Four Pillars used to make a new adhesive that had been developed by Avery. The Federal Bureau of Investigation (FBI) confronted Lee, and he agreed to cooperate in an operation to catch the Yangs. When Lee next met the Yangs, he showed them documents provided by the FBI. The documents bore "confidential" stamps, and Lee said that they were Avery's confidential property. The FBI arrested the Yangs with the documents in their possession. The Yangs and Four Pillars were charged with, among other crimes, the attempted theft of trade secrets. The defendants argued in part that it was impossible for them to have committed this crime because the documents were not actually trade secrets. Should the court acquit them? Why or why not? [*United States v. Yang,* 281 F.3d 534 (6th Cir. 2002)]

5–7. Patent Infringement. As a cattle rancher in Nebraska, Gerald Gohl used handheld searchlights to find and help calving animals (animals giving birth) in harsh blizzard conditions. Gohl thought that it would be more helpful to have a portable searchlight mounted on the outside of a vehicle and remotely controlled. He and Al Gebhardt developed and patented practical applications of this idea—the Golight and the wireless, remote-controlled Radio Ray, which could rotate 360 degrees—and formed Golight, Inc., to make and market these products. In 1997, Wal-Mart Stores, Inc., began selling a portable, wireless, remote-controlled searchlight that was identical to the Radio Ray except for a stop piece that prevented the light from rotating more than 351 degrees. Golight sent Wal-Mart a letter, claiming that its device infringed Golight's patent. Wal-Mart sold its remaining inventory of the devices and stopped carrying the product. Golight filed a suit in a federal district court against Wal-Mart, alleging patent infringement. How should the court rule? Explain. [*Golight, Inc. v. Wal-Mart Stores, Inc.,* 355 F.3d 1327 (Fed. Cir. 2004)]

A QUESTION OF ETHICS

5–8. Texaco, Inc., conducts research to develop new products and technology in the petroleum industry. As part of the research, Texaco employees routinely photocopy articles from scientific and medical journals without the permission of the copyright holders. The publishers of the journals brought a copyright infringement action against Texaco in a federal district court. The court ruled that the copying was not a fair use. The U.S. Court of Appeals for the Second Circuit affirmed this ruling "primarily because the dominant purpose of the use is 'archival'—to assemble a set of papers for future reference, thereby serving the same purpose for which additional subscriptions are normally sold, or . . . for which photocopying licenses may be obtained." [*American Geophysical Union v. Texaco, Inc.,* 37 F.3d 881 (2d Cir. 1994)]

1. Do you agree with the court's decision that the copying was not a fair use? Why or why not?
2. Do you think that the law should impose a duty on every person to obtain permission to photocopy or reproduce any article under any circumstance? What would be some of the implications of such a duty for society? Discuss fully.

FOR CRITICAL ANALYSIS

5–9. Patent protection in the United States is granted to the first person to invent a given product or process, even though another person may be the first to file for a patent on the same product or process. What are the advantages of this patenting procedure? Can you think of any disadvantages? Explain.

VIDEO QUESTION

5–10. Go to this text's Web site at **http://blt. westbuslaw.com** and select "Chapter 5." Click on "Video Questions" and view the video titled *Jerk.* Then answer the following questions.

1. In the video, Navin (Steve Martin) creates a special handle for Mr. Fox's (Bill Macy's) glasses. Can Navin obtain

a patent or a copyright protecting his invention? Explain your answer.

2. Suppose that after Navin legally protects his idea, Fox steals it and decides to develop it for himself, without Navin's permission. Has Fox committed infringement? If so, what kind: trademark, patent, or copyright?

3. Suppose that after Navin legally protects his idea, he realizes he doesn't have the funds to mass-produce the special glasses handle. Navin therefore agrees to allow Fox to manufacture the product. Has Navin granted Fox a license? Explain.

4. Assume that Navin is able to manufacture his invention. What might Navin do to ensure that his product is identifiable and can be distinguished from other products on the market?

INTERNET EXERCISES

Go to the *Business Law Today: The Essentials* home page at **http://blt.westbuslaw.com**, select "Chapter 5," and click on "Internet Exercises." There you will find the following Internet research exercises that you can perform to learn more about topics covered in this chapter.

Activity 5–1: LEGAL PERSPECTIVE—Unwarranted Legal Threats

Activity 5–2: TECHNOLOGICAL PERSPECTIVE—File-Sharing

Activity 5–3: MANAGEMENT PERSPECTIVE—Protecting Intellectual Property across Borders

BEFORE THE TEST

Go to the *Business Law Today: The Essentials* home page at **http://blt.westbuslaw.com**, select "Chapter 5," and click on "Interactive Quizzes." You will find at least twenty interactive questions relating to this chapter.

CHAPTER 6

Criminal Law and Cyber Crimes

"No State shall . . . deprive any person of life, liberty, or property without due process of law, nor deny to any person within its jurisdiction the equal protection of the laws."

Fourteenth Amendment to the U.S. Constitution, July 28, 1868

CHAPTER OUTLINE

- CIVIL LAW AND CRIMINAL LAW
- CLASSIFICATION OF CRIMES
- CRIMINAL LIABILITY
- CORPORATE CRIMINAL LIABILITY
- TYPES OF CRIMES
- DEFENSES TO CRIMINAL LIABILITY
- CONSTITUTIONAL SAFEGUARDS AND CRIMINAL PROCEDURES
- CYBER CRIME

LEARNING OBJECTIVES

After reading this chapter, you should be able to answer the following questions:

1 What two elements must exist before a person can be held liable for a crime? Can a corporation commit crimes?

2 What are five broad categories of crimes? What is white-collar crime?

3 What defenses might be raised by criminal defendants to avoid liability for criminal acts?

4 What constitutional safeguards exist to protect persons accused of crimes? What are the basic steps in the criminal process?

5 What is cyber crime? What laws apply to crimes committed in cyberspace?

Various sanctions are used to bring about a society in which individuals engaging in business can compete and flourish. These sanctions include damages for various types of tortious conduct (as discussed in Chapter 4), damages for breach of contract (to be discussed in Chapter 9), and the equitable remedies discussed in Chapter 1. Additional sanctions are imposed under criminal law. Many statutes regulating business provide for criminal as well as civil sanctions. Therefore, criminal law joins civil law as an important element in the legal environment of business.

In this chapter, following a brief summary of the major differences between criminal and civil law, we look at how crimes are classified and what elements must be present for criminal liability to exist. We then examine various categories of crime, the defenses that can be raised to avoid liability for criminal actions, and criminal procedural law. Criminal procedural law attempts to ensure that a criminal defendant's right to "due process of law" is enforced. This right is guaranteed by the Fourteenth Amendment to the U.S. Constitution, as stated in the chapter-opening quotation.

Since the advent of computer networks and, more recently, the Internet, new types of crimes or new variations of traditional crimes have been committed in cyberspace. For that reason, they are often referred to as **cyber crime**. Generally, cyber crime refers more to the way particular crimes are committed than to a new category of crimes. We devote the concluding pages of this chapter to a discussion of this increasingly significant area of criminal activity.

CYBER CRIME
A crime that occurs online, in the virtual community of the Internet, as opposed to the physical world.

■ Civil Law and Criminal Law

Remember from Chapter 1 that *civil law* spells out the duties that exist between persons or between persons and their governments, excluding the duty not to commit crimes. Contract law, for example, is part of civil law. The whole body of tort law, which deals with the infringement by one person on the legally recognized rights of another, is also an area of civil law.

Criminal law, in contrast, has to do with crime. A **crime** can be defined as a wrong against society proclaimed in a statute and, if committed, punishable by society through fines and/or imprisonment—and, in some cases, death. As mentioned in Chapter 1, because crimes are *offenses against society as a whole*, they are prosecuted by a public official, such as a district attorney (D.A.), not by victims.

CRIME
A wrong against society proclaimed in a statute and, if committed, punishable by society through fines and/or imprisonment—and, in some cases, death.

KEY DIFFERENCES BETWEEN CIVIL LAW AND CRIMINAL LAW

Because the state has extensive resources at its disposal when prosecuting criminal cases, there are numerous procedural safeguards to protect the rights of defendants. One of these safeguards is the higher burden of proof that applies in a criminal case. As you can see in Exhibit 6–1 on the next page, which summarizes some of the key differences between civil law and criminal law, in a civil case the plaintiff usually must prove his or her case by a *preponderance of the evidence*. Under this standard, the plaintiff must convince the court that, based on the evidence presented by both parties, it is more likely than not that the plaintiff's allegation is true.

In a criminal case, however, the state must prove its case **beyond a reasonable doubt.** For the defendant to be convicted, *every* juror in a criminal case must be convinced, beyond a reasonable doubt, that the defendant has committed each essential element of the offense with which she or he is charged. In contrast, in civil cases typically only three-fourths of the jurors need to agree that it is more likely than not that the defendant caused the plaintiff's harm. In a criminal case, the verdict normally must be unanimous. The higher burden of proof in criminal cases reflects a fundamental social value—the belief that it is worse to convict an innocent individual than to let a guilty person go free. We will look at other safeguards later in the chapter, in the context of criminal procedure.

BEYOND A REASONABLE DOUBT
The burden of proof used in criminal cases. If there is any reasonable doubt that a criminal defendant did not commit the crime with which she or he has been charged, then the verdict must be "not guilty."

EXHIBIT 6–1 KEY DIFFERENCES BETWEEN CIVIL AND CRIMINAL LAW

ISSUE	CIVIL LAW	CRIMINAL LAW
Party who brings suit	Person who suffered harm	The state
Burden of proof	Preponderance of the evidence	Beyond a reasonable doubt
Verdict	Three-fourths majority (typically)	Unanimous
Remedy	Damages to compensate for the harm or a decree to achieve an equitable result	Punishment (fine, imprisonment, or death)

CIVIL LIABILITY FOR CRIMINAL ACTS

Those who commit crimes may be subject to both civil and criminal liability. ■ **EXAMPLE 6.1** Joe is walking down the street, minding his own business, when suddenly a person attacks him. In the ensuing struggle, the attacker stabs Joe several times, seriously injuring him. A police officer restrains and arrests the wrongdoer. In this situation, the attacker may be subject both to criminal prosecution by the state and to a tort lawsuit brought by Joe. ■ Exhibit 6–2 illustrates how the same act can result in both a tort action and a criminal action against the wrongdoer.

■ Classification of Crimes

Depending on their degree of seriousness, crimes are classified as felonies or misdemeanors. **Felonies** are serious crimes punishable by death or by imprisonment in a federal or state penitentiary for more than a year. The Model Penal Code[1] provides for four degrees of felony: (1) capital offenses, for which the maximum penalty is death; (2) first degree felonies, punishable by a maximum penalty of life imprisonment; (3) second degree felonies, punishable by a maximum of ten years' imprisonment; and (4) third degree felonies, punishable by a maximum of five years' imprisonment.

Under federal law and in most states, any crime that is not a felony is considered a **misdemeanor.** Misdemeanors are crimes punishable by a fine or by confinement for up to a year. If incarcerated (imprisoned), the guilty party goes to a local jail instead of a prison. Disorderly conduct and trespass are common misdemeanors. Some states have different classes of misdemeanors. For example, in Illinois misdemeanors are either Class A (confinement for up to a year), Class B (not more than six months), or Class C (not more than thirty days). Whether a crime is a felony or a misdemeanor can also determine whether the case is tried in a magistrate's court (for example, by a justice of the peace) or in a general trial court.

FELONY
A crime—such as arson, murder, rape, or robbery—that carries the most severe sanctions, which range from more than one year in a state or federal prison to the death penalty.

MISDEMEANOR
A lesser crime than a felony, punishable by a fine or incarceration in jail for up to one year.

---

1. The American Law Institute issued the Official Draft of the Model Penal Code in 1962. The Model Penal Code is not a uniform code. Uniformity of criminal law among the states is not as important as uniformity in other areas of the law. Types of crimes vary with local circumstances, and it is appropriate that punishments vary accordingly. The Model Penal Code contains four parts: (1) general provisions, (2) definitions of special crimes, (3) provisions concerning treatment and corrections (such as incarceration in a prison or a jail), and (4) provisions on the organization of corrections.

EXHIBIT 6–2 TORT LAWSUIT AND CRIMINAL PROSECUTION FOR THE SAME ACT

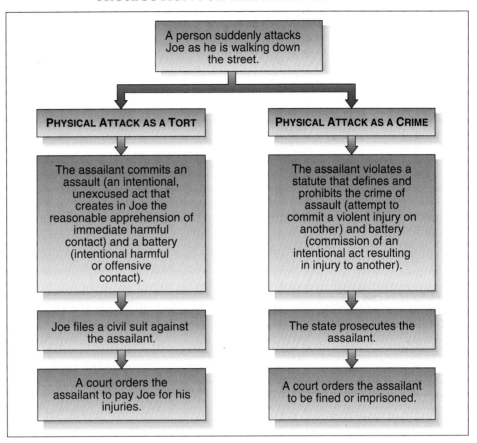

PETTY OFFENSE
In criminal law, the least serious kind of criminal offense, such as a traffic or building-code violation.

In most jurisdictions, **petty offenses** are considered to be a subset of misdemeanors. Petty offenses are minor violations, such as jaywalking or violations of building codes. Even for petty offenses, however, a guilty party can be put in jail for a few days, fined, or both, depending on state or local law.

Criminal Liability

Two elements must exist simultaneously for a person to be convicted of a crime: (1) the performance of a prohibited act and (2) a specified state of mind or intent on the part of the actor. Every criminal statute prohibits certain behavior. Most crimes require an act of *commission;* that is, a person must *do* something in order to be accused of a crime.[2] In some instances, an act of *omission* can be a crime, but only when a person has a legal duty to perform the omitted act. Failure to file a tax return is an example of an omission that is a crime.

The *guilty act* requirement is based on one of the premises of criminal law—that a person is punished for harm done to society. Thinking about killing someone or about

---

2. Called the *actus reus* (pronounced *ak*-tuhs *ray*-uhs), or "guilty act."

stealing a car may be wrong, but the thoughts do no harm until they are translated into action. Of course, a person can be punished for attempting murder or robbery, but normally only if he or she took substantial steps toward the criminal objective.

A *wrongful mental state*[3] is generally required to establish criminal liability. What constitutes such a mental state varies according to the wrongful action. For murder, the act is the taking of a life, and the mental state is the intent to take life. For theft, the guilty act is the taking of another person's property, and the mental state involves both the knowledge that the property belongs to another and the intent to deprive the owner of it.

Criminal liability typically arises for actions that violate state criminal statutes. Federal criminal jurisdiction is normally limited to crimes that occur outside the jurisdiction of any state, crimes involving interstate commerce or communications, crimes that interfere with the operation of the federal government or its agents, and crimes directed at citizens or property located outside the United States. Federal jurisdiction also exists if a federal law or a federal government agency (such as the U.S. Department of Justice or the federal Environmental Protection Agency) defines a certain type of action as a crime. Today, businesspersons are subject to criminal penalties under numerous federal laws and regulations. We will examine many of these laws in later chapters of this text.

Many state criminal codes are now online. To find your state's code, go to

http://www.findlaw.com

and select "State" under the link to "US Laws: Cases and Codes."

Corporate Criminal Liability

At one time, it was thought that a corporation could not incur criminal liability because, although a corporation is a legal person, it can act only through its agents (corporate directors, officers, and employees). Therefore, the corporate entity itself could not "intend" to commit a crime. Under modern criminal law, however, a corporation may be held liable for crimes. Obviously, corporations cannot be imprisoned, but they can be fined or denied certain legal privileges (such as a license). Today, corporations are normally liable for the crimes committed by their agents and employees within the course and scope of their employment.

Corporate directors and officers are personally liable for the crimes they commit, regardless of whether the crimes were committed for their personal benefit or on the corporation's behalf. Additionally, corporate directors and officers may be held liable for the actions of employees under their supervision. Under what has become known as the "responsible corporate officer" doctrine, a court may impose criminal liability on a corporate officer regardless of whether she or he participated in, directed, or even knew about a given criminal violation.

■ **EXAMPLE 6.2** In *United States v. Park,*[4] the chief executive officer of a national supermarket chain was held personally liable for sanitation violations in corporate warehouses, in which the food was exposed to contamination by rodents. The United States Supreme Court imposed personal liability on the corporate officer not because he intended the crime or even knew about it but because he was in a "responsible relationship" to the corporation and had the power to prevent the violation. ■ Since the *Park* decision, courts have applied this "responsible corporate officer" doctrine on a number of occasions to hold corporate officers liable for their employees' statutory violations. The following case illustrates that corporate offi-

---

3. Called the *mens rea* (pronounced mehns *ray*-uh), or "evil intent."
4. 421 U.S. 658, 95 S.Ct. 1903, 44 L.Ed.2d 489 (1975).

cers and supervisors who oversee operations causing environmental harm may be held liable under the criminal provisions of environmental statutes.

CASE 6.1 ■ United States v. Hanousek

United States Court of Appeals,
Ninth Circuit, 1999.
176 F.3d 1116.
http://www.ca9.uscourts.gov/ca9/newopinions.nsf[a]

FACTS Edward Hanousek worked for Pacific & Arctic Railway and Navigation Company (P&A) as a roadmaster of the White Pass & Yukon Railroad in Alaska. Hanousek was responsible "for every detail of the safe and efficient maintenance and construction of track, structures and marine facilities of the entire railroad," including special projects. One project was a rock quarry, known as "6-mile," above the Skagway River. Next to the quarry, and just beneath the surface, ran a high-pressure oil pipeline owned by Pacific & Arctic Pipeline, Inc., P&A's sister company. When the quarry's backhoe operator punctured the pipeline, an estimated 1,000 to 5,000 gallons of oil were discharged into the river. Hanousek was charged with, among other things, negligently discharging a harmful quantity of oil into a navigable water of the United States in violation of the criminal provisions of the Clean Water Act (CWA). After a trial in a federal district court, a jury convicted Hanousek, and the court imposed a sentence of six months' imprisonment, six months in a halfway house, six months' supervised release, and a fine of $5,000. Hanousek appealed to the U.S. Court of Appeals for the Ninth Circuit, arguing in part that the statute under which he was convicted violated his right to due process because he was not aware of what the CWA required.

a. The U.S. Court of Appeals for the Ninth Circuit maintains this Web site. Click on the "OPINIONS BY DATE" link. From that page, click on the "1999" icon, and when the menu opens, click on "March." Scroll down and click on "USA V HANOUSEK" to access the case.

ISSUE Were Hanousek's due process rights violated?

DECISION No. The U.S. Court of Appeals for the Ninth Circuit affirmed Hanousek's conviction.

REASON A corporate manager who has responsibility for operations with the potential to cause harm can be held criminally liable for harm that results even if he or she does not actually know of the specific statute under which liability may be imposed. The CWA is public-welfare legislation, which "is designed to protect the public from potentially harmful or injurious items and may render criminal a type of conduct that a reasonable person should know is subject to stringent public regulation." The court stated, "[I]t is well established that a public welfare statute may subject a person to criminal liability for his or her ordinary negligence without violating due process." When "dangerous or deleterious [harmful] devices or products or obnoxious waste materials are involved, the probability of regulation is so great that anyone who is aware that he is in possession of them or dealing with them must be presumed to be aware of the regulation." Hanousek knew about the pipeline and the danger that a puncture would pose. "Therefore, Hanousek should have been alerted to the probability of strict regulation."

WHY IS THIS CASE IMPORTANT? *This case illustrates the liability that corporate managers and others who take responsibility for corporate operations might face if those operations cause harm to others or, as in this case, to the environment. It underscores the need for corporate managers to become aware of the laws that might come into play during any operations for which the managers assume responsibility.*

■ Types of Crimes

The number of acts that are defined as criminal is nearly endless. Federal, state, and local laws provide for the classification and punishment of hundreds of thousands of different criminal acts. Traditionally, though, crimes have been grouped into five broad categories, or types: violent crime (crimes against persons), property crime, public order crime, white-collar crime, and organized crime. Cyber crime—which consists of crimes committed in cyberspace with the use of computers—is, as mentioned earlier in this chapter, less a category of crime than a new way to commit crime. We will examine cyber crime later in this chapter.

VIOLENT CRIME

Crimes against persons, because they cause others to suffer harm or death, are referred to as *violent crimes*. Murder is a violent crime. So is sexual assault, or rape. Assault and battery, which were discussed in Chapter 4 in the context of tort law, are also classified as violent crimes. **Robbery**—defined as the taking of money, personal property, or any other article of value from a person by means of force or fear—is also a violent crime. Typically, states have more severe penalties for *aggravated robbery*—robbery with the use of a deadly weapon.

Each of these violent crimes is further classified by degree, depending on the circumstances surrounding the criminal act. These circumstances include the intent of the person committing the crime, whether a weapon was used, and (in cases other than murder) the level of pain and suffering experienced by the victim.

PROPERTY CRIME

The most common type of criminal activity is property crime—crimes in which the goal of the offender is some form of economic gain or the damaging of property. Robbery is a form of property crime, as well as a violent crime, because the offender seeks to gain the property of another. We look here at a number of other crimes that fall within the general category of property crime.

Burglary   Traditionally, **burglary** was defined under the common law as breaking and entering the dwelling of another at night with the intent to commit a felony. Originally, the definition was aimed at protecting an individual's home and its occupants. Most state statutes have eliminated some of the requirements found in the common law definition. The time at which the breaking and entering occurs, for example, is usually immaterial. State statutes frequently omit the element of breaking, and some states do not require that the building be a dwelling. Aggravated burglary, which is defined as burglary with the use of a deadly weapon, burglary of a dwelling, or both, incurs a greater penalty.

Larceny   Any person who wrongfully or fraudulently takes and carries away another person's personal property is guilty of **larceny**. Larceny includes the fraudulent intent to deprive an owner permanently of property. Many business-related larcenies entail fraudulent conduct. Whereas robbery involves force or fear, larceny does not. Therefore, picking pockets is larceny. Similarly, taking company products and supplies home for personal use, if one is not authorized to do so, is larceny.

In most states, the definition of property that is subject to larceny statutes has expanded. Stealing computer programs may constitute larceny even though the "property" consists of magnetic impulses. Stealing computer time can also constitute larceny. So, too, can the theft of natural gas. Trade secrets can be subject to larceny statutes. Obtaining another's phone-card number and then using that number, without authorization, to place long-distance calls is a form of property theft. These types of larceny are covered by "theft of services" statutes in many jurisdictions.

The common law distinguishes between grand and petit larceny depending on the value of the property taken. Many states have abolished this distinction, but in those that have not, grand larceny is a felony and petit larceny, a misdemeanor.

ROBBERY
The act of forcefully and unlawfully taking personal property of any value from another. Force or intimidation is usually necessary for an act of theft to be considered a robbery.

BURGLARY
The unlawful entry or breaking into a building with the intent to commit a felony. (Some state statutes expand this to include the intent to commit any crime.)

LARCENY
The wrongful taking and carrying away of another person's personal property with the intent to permanently deprive the owner of the property. Some states classify larceny as either grand or petit, depending on the property's value.

Obtaining Goods by False Pretenses   It is a criminal act to obtain goods by means of false pretenses—for example, buying groceries with a check, knowing that one has insufficient funds to cover it. Statutes dealing with such illegal activities vary widely from state to state.

Receiving Stolen Goods   It is a crime to receive stolen goods. The recipient of such goods need not know the true identity of the owner or the thief. All that is necessary is that the recipient knows or should have known that the goods are stolen, which implies an intent to deprive the owner of those goods.

ARSON
The intentional burning of another's dwelling. Some statutes have expanded this to include any real property regardless of ownership and the destruction of property by other means—for example, by explosion.

Arson   The willful and malicious burning of a building (and in some states, personal property) owned by another is the crime of **arson**. At common law, arson traditionally applied only to burning down another person's house. The law was designed to protect human life. Today, arson statutes have been extended to cover the destruction of any building, regardless of ownership, by fire or explosion.

Every state has a special statute that covers a person's burning a building for the purpose of collecting insurance. ■ EXAMPLE 6.3 If Smith owns an insured apartment building that is falling apart and sets fire to it himself or pays someone else to do so, he is guilty not only of arson but also of defrauding insurers, which is an attempted larceny. ■ Of course, the insurer need not pay the claim when insurance fraud is proved.

FORGERY
The fraudulent making or altering of any writing in a way that changes the legal rights and liabilities of another.

Forgery   The fraudulent making or altering of any writing in a way that changes the legal rights and liabilities of another is **forgery**. If, without authorization, Severson signs Bennett's name to the back of a check made out to Bennett, Severson is committing forgery. Forgery also includes changing trademarks, falsifying public records, counterfeiting, and altering a legal document.

PUBLIC ORDER CRIME

Historically, societies have always outlawed activities that are considered to be contrary to public values and morals. Today, the most common public order crimes include public drunkenness, prostitution, gambling, and illegal drug use. These crimes are sometimes referred to as victimless crimes because they normally harm only the offender. From a broader perspective, however, they are deemed detrimental to society as a whole because they might create an environment that gives rise to property and violent crimes. (Is swearing in public a crime? See this chapter's *Letter of the Law* feature on the next page for a discussion of this question.)

WHITE-COLLAR CRIME

WHITE-COLLAR CRIME
Nonviolent crime committed by individuals or corporations to obtain a personal or business advantage.

Crimes that typically occur only in the business context are commonly referred to as **white-collar crimes**. Although there is no official definition of white-collar crime, the term is popularly used to mean an illegal act or series of acts committed by an individual or business entity using some nonviolent means. Usually, this kind of crime is committed in the course of a legitimate occupation. Corporate crimes fall into this category.

EMBEZZLEMENT
The fraudulent appropriation of funds or other property by a person to whom the funds or property has been entrusted.

Embezzlement   When a person entrusted with another person's property or money fraudulently appropriates it, **embezzlement** occurs. Typically, embezzlement involves an employee who steals funds. Banks face this problem, and so do a number of businesses in which corporate officers or accountants "jimmy" the books to cover up

LETTER OF THE LAW   The Case of the "Cussing Canoeist"

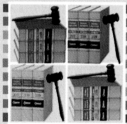

Timothy Boomer, then a twenty-eight-year-old engineer, went on a swearing rampage when his canoe tipped over on the Rifle River in Michigan. Others heard the swearing, including a couple and their two children, and a sheriff, who wrote him a ticket for violating an 1897 Michigan law that banned cursing in front of women and children. Specifically, the law made it illegal for anyone to use indecent, immoral, obscene, vulgar, or insulting language near children and women. Boomer was convicted and ordered to pay a fine of $75 and volunteer four days in a child-care program. Boomer, with the assistance of the American Civil Liberties Union, appealed the decision, arguing that the law was unconstitutionally vague. After all, what might be considered "vulgar" or "obscene" by one person might not be by another. A Michigan appellate court agreed and struck down the law.[a]

THE BOTTOM LINE

Eight other states—Louisiana, New Mexico, Oklahoma, South Carolina, South Dakota, Texas, Virginia, and Wisconsin—also have "swearing laws." Whether these laws will survive challenges remains to be seen.

a. *Michigan v. Boomer*, 250 Mich.App. 534, 655 N.W.2d 255 (2002). This case is also discussed in Tresa Baldas, "A 'Cussing Canoeist' Cans a Controversial Michigan Law," *The National Law Journal*, May 6, 2002, p. A6.

---

the fraudulent conversion of funds for their own benefit. Embezzlement is not larceny, because the wrongdoer does not physically take the property from the possession of another, and it is not robbery, because force or fear is not used.

It does not matter whether the accused takes the funds from the victim or from a third person. If, as the financial officer of a large corporation, Saunders pockets a certain number of checks from third parties that were given to her to deposit into the corporate account, she is embezzling.

Ordinarily, an embezzler who returns what has been taken will not be prosecuted because the owner usually will not take the time to make a complaint, give depositions, and appear in court. That the accused intended eventually to return the embezzled property, however, does not constitute a sufficient defense to the crime of embezzlement.

Mail and Wire Fraud   One of the most potent weapons against white-collar criminals is the Mail Fraud Act of 1990.[5] Under this act, it is a federal crime (mail fraud) to use the mails to defraud the public. Illegal use of the mails must involve (1) mailing or causing someone else to mail a writing—something written, printed, or photocopied—for the purpose of executing a scheme to defraud and (2) a contemplated or an organized scheme to defraud by false pretenses. If, for example, Johnson advertises by mail the sale of a cure for cancer that he knows to be fraudulent because it has no medical validity, he can be prosecuted for fraudulent use of the mails.

Federal law also makes it a crime to use wire (for example, the telephone), radio, or television transmissions to defraud.[6] Violators may be fined up to $1,000, imprisoned for up to five years, or both. If the violation affects a financial institution, the violator may be fined up to $1 million, imprisoned for up to thirty years, or both.

---

5. 18 U.S.C. Sections 1341–1342.
6. 18 U.S.C. Section 1343.

Bribery   Basically, three types of bribery are considered crimes: bribery of public officials, commercial bribery, and bribery of foreign officials. The attempt to influence a public official to act in a way that serves a private interest is a crime. As an element of this crime, intent must be present and proved. The bribe can be anything the recipient considers to be valuable. Realize that *the crime of bribery occurs when the bribe is offered.* It does not matter whether the person to whom the bribe is offered accepts the bribe or agrees to perform whatever action is desired by the person offering the bribe. *Accepting a bribe* is a separate crime.

Typically, people make commercial bribes to obtain proprietary information, cover up an inferior product, or secure new business. Industrial espionage sometimes involves commercial bribes. For example, a person in one firm may offer an employee in a competing firm some type of payoff in exchange for trade secrets or pricing schedules. So-called kickbacks, or payoffs for special favors or services, are a form of commercial bribery in some situations.

Bribing foreign officials to obtain favorable business contracts is a crime. The Foreign Corrupt Practices Act of 1977, which was discussed in Chapter 2, was passed to curb the use of bribery by American businesspersons in securing foreign contracts.

Bankruptcy Fraud   Today, federal bankruptcy law (see Chapter 16) allows individuals and businesses to be relieved of oppressive debt through bankruptcy proceedings. Numerous white-collar crimes may be committed during the many phases of a bankruptcy proceeding. A creditor, for example, may file a false claim against the debtor, which is a crime. Also, a debtor may fraudulently transfer assets to favored parties before or after the petition for bankruptcy is filed. For example, a company-owned automobile may be "sold" at a bargain price to a trusted friend or relative. Closely related to the crime of fraudulent transfer of property is the crime of fraudulent concealment of property, such as hiding gold coins.

The Theft of Trade Secrets   As discussed in Chapter 5, trade secrets constitute a form of intellectual property that for many businesses can be extremely valuable. The Economic Espionage Act of 1996[7] made the theft of trade secrets a federal crime. The act also made it a federal crime to buy or possess trade secrets of another person, knowing that the trade secrets were stolen or otherwise acquired without the owner's authorization.

Violations of the act can result in steep penalties. An individual who violates the act can be imprisoned for up to ten years and fined up to $500,000. If a corporation or other organization violates the act, it can be fined up to $5 million. Additionally, the law provides that any property acquired as a result of the violation and any property used in the commission of the violation are subject to criminal *forfeiture*—meaning that the government can take the property. A theft of trade secrets conducted via the Internet, for example, could result in the forfeiture of every computer, printer, or other device used to commit or facilitate the violation.

Insider Trading   An individual who obtains "inside information" about the plans of a publicly listed corporation can often make stock-trading profits by using the information to guide decisions relating to the purchase or sale of corporate securities.

---

7. 18 U.S.C. Sections 1831–1839.

Insider trading is a violation of securities law and will be considered more fully in Chapter 21. Generally, the rule is that a person who possesses inside information and has a duty not to disclose it to outsiders may not profit from the purchase or sale of securities based on that information until the information is available to the public.

ORGANIZED CRIME

As mentioned, white-collar crime takes place within the confines of the legitimate business world. *Organized crime*, in contrast, operates *illegitimately* by, among other things, providing illegal goods and services. For organized crime, the traditional preferred markets are gambling, prostitution, illegal narcotics, and loan sharking (lending funds at higher than legal maximum interest rates), along with more recent ventures into counterfeiting and credit-card scams.

Money Laundering   The profits from illegal activities amount to billions of dollars a year, particularly the profits from illegal drug transactions and, to a lesser extent, from racketeering, prostitution, and gambling. Under federal law, banks, savings and loan associations, and other financial institutions are required to report currency transactions involving more than $10,000. Consequently, those who engage in illegal activities face difficulties in depositing their cash profits from illegal transactions.

As an alternative to simply storing cash from illegal transactions in a safe-deposit box, wrongdoers and racketeers have invented ways to launder "dirty" money to make it "clean." This **money laundering** is done through legitimate businesses.

■ **EXAMPLE 6.4** Matt, a successful drug dealer, becomes a partner with a restaurateur. Little by little, the restaurant shows an increasing profit. As a partner in the restaurant, Matt is able to report the "profits" of the restaurant as legitimate income on which he pays federal and state income taxes. He can then spend those after-tax funds without worrying that his lifestyle may exceed the level possible with his reported income. ■

Jeffrey Skilling, former chief executive officer (CEO) of Enron Corporation, testifies before a congressional committee concerning allegations that Enron insiders profited at the company's expense while improperly concealing losses and inflating earnings. About a month after Skilling resigned as CEO, he sold nearly $60 million of his stock in Enron. This led prosecutors to believe that he sold those shares knowing of the bankruptcy that Enron was facing. Skilling was subsequently indicted on numerous counts of fraud and insider trading. If Skilling knew that the company was on the brink of bankruptcy at the time that he sold his stock, is he guilty of a crime? Explain your answer. (AP Photo/Kenneth Lambert)

The Federal Bureau of Investigation estimates that organized crime has invested tens of billions of dollars in as many as a hundred thousand business establishments in the United States for the purpose of money laundering. Globally, it is estimated that more than $500 billion in illegal money moves through the world banking system every year.

The Racketeer Influenced and Corrupt Organizations Act   In 1970, in an effort to curb the apparently increasing entry of organized crime into the legitimate business world, Congress passed the Racketeer Influenced and Corrupt Organizations Act (RICO).[8] The act, which was enacted as part of the Organized Crime Control Act, makes it a federal crime to (1) use income obtained from racketeering activity to purchase any interest in an enterprise, (2) acquire or maintain an interest in an enterprise through racketeering activity, (3) conduct or participate in the affairs of an enterprise through racketeering activity, or (4) conspire to do any of the preceding activities.

Racketeering activity is not a new type of substantive crime created by RICO; rather, RICO incorporates by reference twenty-six separate types of federal crimes and nine types of state felonies[9] and declares that if a person commits two of these offenses, he or she is guilty of "racketeering activity." Additionally, RICO is more often used today to attack white-collar crimes than organized crime.

In the event of a violation, the statute permits the government to seek civil penalties, including the divestiture of a defendant's interest in a business (called forfeiture) or the dissolution of the business. Perhaps the most controversial aspect of RICO is that, in some cases, private individuals are allowed to recover three times their actual losses (treble damages), plus attorneys' fees, for business injuries caused by a violation of the statute. Under criminal provisions of RICO, any individual found guilty of a violation is subject to a fine of up to $25,000 per violation, imprisonment for up to twenty years, or both. Additionally, the statute provides that those who violate RICO may be required to forfeit (give up) any assets, in the form of property or cash, that were acquired as a result of the illegal activity or that were "involved in" or an "instrumentality of" the activity.

 You can gain insights into criminal law and procedures, including a number of the defenses that can be raised to avoid criminal liability, by looking at some of the famous criminal law cases included on Court TV's Web site. Go to

http://www.courttv.com/ index.html.

Defenses to Criminal Liability

Among the most important defenses to criminal liability are infancy, intoxication, insanity, mistake, consent, duress, justifiable use of force, entrapment, and the statute of limitations. Many of these defenses involve assertions that the intent requirement for criminal liability is lacking. Also, in some cases, defendants are given immunity and thus relieved, at least in part, of criminal liability for crimes they committed. We look at each of these defenses here.

Note that procedural violations, such as obtaining evidence without a valid search warrant, may also operate as defenses. As you will read later in this chapter, evidence obtained in violation of a defendant's constitutional rights normally may not be admitted in court. If the evidence is suppressed, then there may be no basis for prosecuting the defendant.

---

8. 18 U.S.C. Sections 1961–1968.
9. See 18 U.S.C. Section 1961(1)(A).

INFANCY

The term *infant*, as used in the law, refers to any person who has not yet reached the age of majority (see Chapter 8). In all states, certain courts handle cases involving children who are alleged to have violated the law. In some states, juvenile courts handle children's cases exclusively. In other states, however, courts that handle children's cases may also have jurisdiction over additional matters.

Originally, juvenile court hearings were informal, and lawyers were rarely present. Since 1967, however, when the United States Supreme Court ruled that a child charged with delinquency must be allowed to consult with an attorney before being committed to a state institution,[10] juvenile court hearings have become more formal. In some states, a child may be treated as an adult and tried in a regular court if she or he is above a certain age (usually fourteen) and is charged with a felony, such as rape or murder.

INTOXICATION

The law recognizes two types of intoxication, whether from drugs or from alcohol: *involuntary* and *voluntary*. Involuntary intoxication occurs when a person either is physically forced to ingest or inject an intoxicating substance or is unaware that a substance contains drugs or alcohol. Involuntary intoxication is a defense to a crime if its effect was to make a person incapable of obeying the law or incapable of understanding that the act committed was wrong. Voluntary intoxication is rarely a defense, but it may be effective in cases in which the defendant was *extremely* intoxicated when committing the wrong.

INSANITY

Someone suffering from a mental illness may be judged incapable of having the state of mind required to commit a crime. Thus, insanity may be a defense to a criminal charge. The courts have had difficulty deciding what the test for legal insanity should be, however, and psychiatrists as well as lawyers are critical of the tests used. Almost all federal courts and some states use the relatively liberal standard set forth in the Model Penal Code:

> A person is not responsible for criminal conduct if at the time of such conduct as a result of mental disease or defect he [or she] lacks substantial capacity either to appreciate the wrongfulness of his [or her] conduct or to conform his [or her] conduct to the requirements of the law.

Some states use the *M'Naghten* test,[11] under which a criminal defendant is not responsible if, at the time of the offense, he or she did not know the nature and quality of the act or did not know that the act was wrong. Other states use the irresistible-impulse test. A person operating under an irresistible impulse may know an act is wrong but cannot refrain from doing it.

MISTAKE

Everyone has heard the saying, "Ignorance of the law is no excuse." Ordinarily, ignorance of the law or a mistaken idea about what the law requires is not a valid defense. In some states, however, that rule has been modified. Criminal defendants who claim that they honestly did not know that they were breaking a law may have a valid

---

10. *In re Gault,* 387 U.S. 1, 87 S.Ct. 1428, 18 L.Ed.2d 527 (1967).
11. A rule derived from *M'Naghten's* case, 8 Eng.Rep. 718 (1843).

Three suspects were charged with assaulting Matthew Shepard, a gay University of Wyoming student. Shepard was beaten, burned, and tied to a fence like a scarecrow. Should the court allow the defendants to claim that they were temporarily insane because of "homosexual rage"? Why or why not? (AP Photo/Ed Andrieski)

defense if (1) the law was not published or reasonably made known to the public or (2) the defendant relied on an official statement of the law that was erroneous.

A *mistake of fact,* as opposed to a *mistake of law,* operates as a defense if it negates the mental state necessary to commit a crime. ■ **EXAMPLE 6.5** If Oliver Wheaton mistakenly walks off with Julie Cabrera's briefcase because he thinks it is his, there is no theft. Theft requires knowledge that the property belongs to another. (If Wheaton's act causes Cabrera to incur damages, however, Wheaton may be subject to liability for trespass to personal property or conversion, torts that were discussed in Chapter 4.) ■

CONSENT

What if a victim consents to a crime or even encourages the person intending a criminal act to commit it? Ordinarily, **consent** does not operate as a bar to criminal liability. In some rare circumstances, however, the law may allow consent to be used as a defense. In each case, the question is whether the law forbids an act that was committed against the victim's will or forbids the act without regard to the victim's wish. The law forbids murder, prostitution, and drug use regardless of whether the victim consents to it. Also, if the act causes harm to a third person who has not consented, there is no escape from criminal liability. Consent or forgiveness given after a crime has been committed is not really a defense, though it can affect the likelihood of prosecution or the severity of the sentence. Consent operates most successfully as a defense in crimes against property.

■ **EXAMPLE 6.6** Barry gives Phong permission to hunt for deer on Barry's land while staying in Barry's lakeside cabin. After observing Phong carrying a gun into the cabin at night, a neighbor calls the police, and an officer subsequently arrests Phong. If charged with burglary (or aggravated burglary, because he had a weapon), Phong can assert the defense of consent. He had obtained Barry's consent to enter the premises. ■

COMPARE "Ignorance" is a lack of information. "Mistake" is a confusion of information.

CONSENT
The voluntary agreement to a proposition or an act of another; a concurrence of wills.

DURESS

Duress exists when the *wrongful threat* of one person induces another person to perform an act that she or he would not otherwise perform. In such a situation, duress is said to negate the mental state necessary to commit a crime. For duress to qualify as a defense, the following requirements must be met:

1. The threat must be of serious bodily harm or death.
2. The harm threatened must be greater than the harm caused by the crime.
3. The threat must be immediate and inescapable.
4. The defendant must have been involved in the situation through no fault of his or her own.

JUSTIFIABLE USE OF FORCE

Probably the best-known defense to criminal liability is **self-defense.** Other situations, however, also justify the use of force: the defense of one's dwelling, the defense of other property, and the prevention of a crime. In all of these situations, it is important to distinguish between deadly and nondeadly force. *Deadly force* is likely to result in death or serious bodily harm. *Nondeadly force* is force that reasonably appears necessary to prevent the imminent use of criminal force.

Generally speaking, people can use the amount of nondeadly force that seems necessary to protect themselves, their dwellings, or other property or to prevent the commission of a crime. Deadly force can be used in self-defense if there is a *reasonable belief* that imminent death or grievous bodily harm will otherwise result, if the attacker is using unlawful force (an example of lawful force is that exerted by a police officer), and if the defender has not initiated or provoked the attack. Deadly force normally can be used to defend a dwelling only if the unlawful entry is violent and the person believes deadly force is necessary to prevent imminent death or great bodily harm or—in some jurisdictions—if the person believes deadly force is necessary to prevent the commission of a felony (such as arson) in the dwelling.

ENTRAPMENT

Entrapment is a defense designed to prevent police officers or other government agents from encouraging crimes in order to apprehend persons wanted for criminal acts. In the typical entrapment case, an undercover agent *suggests* that a crime be committed and somehow pressures or induces an individual to commit it. The agent then arrests the individual for the crime.

For entrapment to be considered a defense, both the suggestion and the inducement must take place. The defense is intended not to prevent law enforcement agents from setting a trap for an unwary criminal but rather to prevent them from pushing the individual into it. The crucial issue is whether the person who committed a crime was predisposed to do so or acted because the agent induced it.

STATUTE OF LIMITATIONS

With some exceptions, such as for the crime of murder, statutes of limitations apply to crimes just as they do to civil wrongs. In other words, criminal cases must be prosecuted within a certain number of years. If a criminal action is brought after the statutory time period has expired, the accused person can raise the statute of limitations as a defense.

IMMUNITY

At times, the state may wish to obtain information from a person accused of a crime. Accused persons are understandably reluctant to give information if it will be used to prosecute them, and they cannot be forced to do so. The privilege against self-incrimination is granted by the Fifth Amendment to the Constitution, which reads, in part, "nor shall [any person] be compelled in any criminal case to be a witness against himself." In cases in which the state wishes to obtain information from a person accused of a crime, the state can grant *immunity* from prosecution or agree to prosecute for a less serious offense in exchange for the information. Once immunity is given, the person can no longer refuse to testify on Fifth Amendment grounds, because he or she now has an absolute privilege against self-incrimination.

Often, a grant of immunity from prosecution for a serious crime is part of the **plea bargaining** between the defendant and the prosecuting attorney. The defendant may be convicted of a lesser offense, while the state uses the defendant's testimony to prosecute accomplices for serious crimes carrying heavy penalties.

Constitutional Safeguards and Criminal Procedures

Criminal law brings the power of the state, with all its resources, to bear against the individual. Criminal procedures are designed to protect the constitutional rights of individuals and to prevent the arbitrary use of power on the part of the government.

The U.S. Constitution provides specific safeguards for those accused of crimes. Most of these safeguards protect individuals against state government actions, as well as federal government actions, by virtue of the due process clause of the Fourteenth Amendment. These safeguards are set forth in the Fourth, Fifth, Sixth, and Eighth Amendments.

FOURTH AMENDMENT PROTECTIONS

The Fourth Amendment protects the "right of the people to be secure in their persons, houses, papers, and effects." Before searching or seizing private property, law enforcement officers must obtain a **search warrant**—an order from a judge or other public official authorizing the search or seizure. To obtain a search warrant, the officers must convince a judge that they have reasonable grounds, or **probable cause,** to believe a search will reveal a specific illegality. Probable cause requires law enforcement officials to have trustworthy evidence that would convince a reasonable person that the proposed search or seizure is more likely justified than not. Furthermore, the Fourth Amendment prohibits general warrants. It requires a particular description of what is to be searched or seized. General searches through a person's belongings are impermissible. The search cannot extend beyond what is described in the warrant.

There are exceptions to the requirement of a search warrant, as when it is likely that the items sought will be removed before a warrant can be obtained. For example, if a police officer has probable cause to believe an automobile contains evidence of a crime and the vehicle is likely to be unavailable by the time a warrant is obtained, the officer can search the vehicle without a warrant.

Constitutional protection against unreasonable searches and seizures is important to businesses and professionals. As federal and state regulation of commercial activities increased, frequent and unannounced government inspections were conducted to ensure compliance with the regulations. Such inspections were extremely

PLEA BARGAINING
The process by which a defendant and the prosecutor in a criminal case work out a mutually satisfactory disposition of the case, subject to court approval; usually involves the defendant's pleading guilty to a lesser offense in return for a lighter sentence.

SEARCH WARRANT
An order granted by a public authority, such as a judge, that authorizes law enforcement personnel to search particular premises or property.

PROBABLE CAUSE
Reasonable grounds for believing that a person should be arrested or searched.

 You can learn about some of the constitutional questions raised by various criminal laws and procedures by going to the Web site of the American Civil Liberties Union at

http://www.aclu.org.

disruptive at times. In *Marshall v. Barlow's, Inc.,*[12] the United States Supreme Court held that government inspectors do not have the right to enter business premises without a warrant, although the standard of probable cause is not the same as that required in nonbusiness contexts. The existence of a general and neutral enforcement plan will justify issuance of the warrant.

FIFTH AMENDMENT PROTECTIONS

BE AWARE The Fifth Amendment protection against self-incrimination does not cover partnerships or corporations.

DOUBLE JEOPARDY
A situation occurring when a person is tried twice for the same criminal offense; prohibited by the Fifth Amendment to the Constitution.

The Fifth Amendment offers significant protections for accused persons. One is the guarantee that no one can be deprived of "life, liberty, or property without due process of law" (see Chapter 1 for a discussion of the due process clause). The Fifth Amendment also protects persons from **double jeopardy** (being tried twice for the same criminal offense). The prohibition against double jeopardy means that once a criminal defendant is acquitted (found "not guilty") of a particular crime, the government may not reindict the person and retry him or her for the same crime.

Additionally, the Fifth Amendment guarantees that no person "shall be compelled in any criminal case to be a witness against himself." Thus, in any criminal proceeding, an accused person cannot be compelled to give testimony that might subject her or him to any criminal prosecution. The Fifth Amendment's guarantee against **self-incrimination** extends only to natural persons. Protection against self-incrimination does not apply to corporations or partnerships.[13]

SELF-INCRIMINATION
The giving of testimony that may subject the testifier to criminal prosecution. The Fifth Amendment to the Constitution protects against self-incrimination by providing that no person "shall be compelled in any criminal case to be a witness against himself."

PROTECTIONS UNDER THE SIXTH AND EIGHTH AMENDMENTS

The Sixth Amendment guarantees several important rights for criminal defendants: the right to a speedy trial, the right to a jury trial, the right to a public trial, the right to confront witnesses, and the right to counsel. The Eighth Amendment prohibits excessive bail and fines, and cruel and unusual punishment.

The Sixth Amendment right to counsel is one of the rights of which a suspect must be advised when he or she is arrested under the *Miranda* rule (discussed later in this chapter). In many cases, a statement that a criminal suspect makes in the absence of counsel is not admissible at trial unless the suspect has knowingly and voluntarily waived this right. Is this right to counsel triggered when judicial proceedings are initiated through any preliminary step? Or is this right triggered only when a suspect is "interrogated" by the police? In the following case, the Supreme Court considered these questions.

---

12. 436 U.S. 307, 98 S.Ct. 1816, 56 L.Ed.2d 305 (1978).

13. The privilege has been applied to some small family partnerships. See *United States v. Slutsky,* 352 F.Supp. 1105 (S.D.N.Y. 1972).

CASE 6.2 ■ Fellers v. United States

Supreme Court of the United States, 2004.
540 U.S. 519,
124 S.Ct. 1019,
157 L.Ed.2d 1016.
http://supct.law.cornell.edu/supct[a]

a. In the "Search" box, type "Fellers," select "Current decisions only," and click on "submit." In the result, scroll to the name of the case, and click on it to access the opinion. The Legal Information Institute of Cornell Law School in Ithaca, New York, maintains this Web site.

FACTS In February 2000, an indictment was issued charging John Fellers, a resident of Lincoln, Nebraska, with conspiracy to distribute methamphetamine. Police officers Michael Garnett and Jeff Bliemeister went to Fellers's home to arrest him. They told Fellers that the purpose of their visit was to discuss his use and distribution of methamphetamine. They said that they had a warrant for his arrest and that the charges referred to his involvement with four indi-

CASE 6.2–Continued

viduals. Fellers responded that he knew the persons and had used methamphetamine with them. The officers took Fellers to jail and advised him for the first time of his right to counsel. He waived this right and repeated his earlier statements. Before Fellers's trial, the court ruled that his "jailhouse statements" could be admitted at his trial because he had waived his right to counsel before making them. After Fellers's conviction, he appealed to the U.S. Court of Appeals for the Eighth Circuit, arguing that the officers had elicited his incriminating "home statements" without advising him of his right to counsel and that his "jailhouse statements" should thus have been excluded from his trial as "fruits" of his earlier statements. The appellate court affirmed the lower court's judgment, holding that Fellers had not had a right to counsel at his home because he had not been subject to police "interrogation." Fellers appealed to the United States Supreme Court.

ISSUE Did Garnett and Bliemeister violate Fellers's right to counsel by deliberately eliciting information from him during their visit to his home without advising him of his right to counsel?

DECISION Yes. The United States Supreme Court reversed the lower court's decision and remanded the case for the determination of a different issue.[b] The

b. The lower court's decision on remand was not available at the time this book went to press, but it may be by the time you read this book. If you have purchased access to Westlaw Campus, you may be able to locate the remanded decision using that database. Alternatively, you might be able to find the case online at some other site. (See this text's inside front cover for information on Westlaw Campus and URLs for online court decisions.)

Supreme Court held that the Sixth Amendment bars the use at trial of a suspect's incriminating words, deliberately elicited by police after an indictment, in the absence of either counsel or a waiver of the right to counsel, regardless of whether police conduct constitutes an "interrogation."

REASON The Court explained, "The Sixth Amendment right to counsel is triggered at or after the time that judicial proceedings have been initiated * * *. [A]n accused is denied the basic protections of the Sixth Amendment when there is used against him at his trial evidence of his own incriminating words, which federal agents * * * deliberately elicited from him after he had been indicted and in the absence of his counsel." In this case, "there is no question that the officers * * * deliberately elicited information from petitioner [Fellers]. Indeed, the officers, upon arriving at petitioner's house, informed him that their purpose in coming was to discuss his involvement in the distribution of methamphetamine and his association with certain charged co-conspirators. * * * [T]he ensuing discussion took place after petitioner had been indicted, outside the presence of counsel, and in the absence of any waiver of petitioner's Sixth Amendment rights."

FOR CRITICAL ANALYSIS—Social Consideration
Should Fellers's "jailhouse statements" also have been excluded from his trial? Why or why not?

THE EXCLUSIONARY RULE AND THE *MIRANDA* RULE

Two other procedural protections for criminal defendants are the exclusionary rule and the *Miranda* rule.

EXCLUSIONARY RULE
In criminal procedure, a rule under which any evidence that is obtained in violation of the accused's constitutional rights guaranteed by the Fourth, Fifth, and Sixth Amendments, as well as any evidence derived from illegally obtained evidence, will not be admissible in court.

The Exclusionary Rule Under what is known as the **exclusionary rule,** all evidence obtained in violation of the constitutional rights spelled out in the Fourth, Fifth, and Sixth Amendments, as well as all evidence derived from the illegally obtained evidence, normally must be excluded from the trial. Evidence derived from illegally obtained evidence is known as the "fruit of the poisonous tree." For example, if a confession is obtained after an illegal arrest, the arrest is "the poisonous tree," and the confession, if "tainted" by the arrest, is the "fruit."

The purpose of the exclusionary rule is to deter police from conducting warrantless searches and from engaging in other misconduct. The rule is sometimes criticized because it can lead to injustice. Many a defendant has "gotten off on a technicality" because law enforcement personnel failed to observe procedural requirements. Even though a defendant may be obviously guilty, if the evidence of that guilt was obtained improperly (without a valid search warrant, for example), it normally cannot be used against the defendant in court. In the following case, the court had to decide whether a lost computer printout should cause evidence to be excluded.

CASE 6.3 People v. McFarlan

New York Supreme Court, 2002.[a]
191 Misc.2d 531,
744 N.Y.S.2d 287.

FACTS In May 2001, Lisa Kordes saw two men picking pockets on a Lexington Avenue bus in Manhattan, in New York City. Based on Kordes's description of the men, a police department computer produced a six-photo array of possible suspects. Kordes selected a photo of Kevin McFarlan as one of the men she had seen. Five days later, on a bus, Neal Ariano, a police officer, arrested McFarlan after seeing him bump an elderly woman while placing his hand near her pocketbook. At the police station, Kordes viewed a lineup including McFarlan and identified him as the man she had seen on the Lexington Avenue bus. McFarlan was charged in a New York state court with various crimes. The printout of the computer-generated photo array that Kordes had been shown was lost, but the "People" (the state of New York) introduced into evidence a second printout to show what Kordes had seen. McFarlan argued, among other things, that the first printout was the original photo array and that because that printout had been lost, the court should presume the photo-array procedure had been illegal. Thus, McFarlan's arrest and Kordes's identification of him in the lineup should be excluded as "fruit of the poisonous tree."

ISSUE Should the second printout of the photo array be considered "fruit of the poisonous tree" and thus inadmissible?

a. In New York, a supreme court is a trial court.

DECISION No. The New York state court held that the second printout of the photo array was not "fruit of the poisonous tree" and could be properly accepted into evidence.

REASON The court concluded that because both printouts were generated in the same format, there could be no prejudice from the fact that the defendant was selected from the first printout and that a second identical printout was later introduced into evidence. Because the printouts were identical and conveyed the full recoverable information, the court held that to decide otherwise would be absurd. "Where, for example, a witness is shown only the screen display, what must the People [public prosecutor] keep? For on such an analysis the printout of the screen could not be the 'original.'" The court pointed out that the purpose of requiring the preservation of a record was clear. According to the court, concern for the integrity of information has always led the courts to prefer the original and has led to many rules to bar or limit the use of nonoriginal material. "Here," said the court, "the original array was in electronic form in the computer memory, the testimony was unequivocal that [both] printout[s] * * * were generated in the same manner. * * * [A]s a result, defendant's argument crumbles."

FOR CRITICAL ANALYSIS—Technological Consideration *When a record is stored on a computer, which should be considered the "original" record—the version on the computer or a printout of the computer version? Why?*

The *Miranda* Rule In *Miranda v. Arizona*,[14] a case decided in 1966, the United States Supreme Court established the rule that individuals who are arrested must be informed of certain constitutional rights, including their Fifth Amendment right to remain silent and their Sixth Amendment right to counsel. If the arresting officers fail to inform a criminal suspect of these constitutional rights, any statements the suspect makes normally will not be admissible in court.

REMEMBER Once a suspect has been informed of his or her rights, anything that person says can be used as evidence in a trial.

14. 384 U.S. 436, 86 S.Ct. 1602, 16 L.Ed.2d 694 (1966).

If you are interested in reading the Supreme Court's opinion in *Miranda v. Arizona*, go to

http://supct.law.cornell. edu:8080/supct/ cases/name.htm.

Select "M" from the menu at the top of the page, and scroll down the page that opens to the *Miranda v. Arizona* case.

The Supreme Court's *Miranda* decision was controversial, and Congress subsequently attempted to overrule it by enacting Section 3501 of the Omnibus Crime Control Act[15] of 1968. Essentially, Section 3501 reinstated the rule that had been in effect for 180 years before *Miranda*—namely, that statements by defendants can be used against them as long as the statements are made voluntarily. Section 3501, however, was never enforced. The Supreme Court has held that the *Miranda* rights enunciated by the Court in the 1966 case were constitutionally based and thus could not be overruled by a legislative act.[16]

Exceptions to the *Miranda* Rule   Over time, as part of a continuing attempt to balance the rights of accused persons against the rights of society, the United States Supreme Court has carved out numerous exceptions to the *Miranda* rule. In 1984, for example, the Court recognized a "public safety" exception to the *Miranda* rule. The need to protect the public warranted the admissibility of statements made by the defendant (in this case, indicating where he placed the gun) as evidence at trial, even though the defendant had not been informed of his *Miranda* rights.[17]

In 1985, the Supreme Court further held that a confession need not be excluded even though the police failed to inform a suspect in custody that his attorney had tried to reach him by telephone.[18] In an important 1991 decision, the Court stated that a suspect's conviction will not be automatically overturned if the suspect was coerced into making a confession. If other, legally obtained evidence admitted at trial is strong enough to justify the conviction without the confession, then the fact that the confession was obtained illegally can, in effect, be ignored.[19]

---

15. 42 U.S.C. Section 3789d.
16. *Dickerson v. United States,* 530 U.S. 428, 120 S.Ct. 2326, 147 L.Ed.2d 405 (2000).
17. *New York v. Quarles,* 467 U.S. 649, 104 S.Ct. 2626, 81 L.Ed.2d 550 (1984).
18. *Moran v. Burbine,* 475 U.S. 412, 106 S.Ct. 1135, 89 L.Ed.2d 410 (1985).
19. *Arizona v. Fulminante,* 499 U.S. 279, 111 S.Ct. 1246, 113 L.Ed.2d 302 (1991).

Police officers take a suspect into custody. Why must a criminal suspect be informed of his or her legal rights? (© Corbis. All rights reserved.)

In yet another case, in 1994, the Supreme Court ruled that a suspect must unequivocally and assertively request to exercise his or her right to counsel in order to stop police questioning. Saying, "Maybe I should talk to a lawyer" during an interrogation after being taken into custody is not enough. The Court held that police officers are not required to decipher the suspect's intentions in such situations.[20]

CRIMINAL PROCEDURES AND SENTENCING

As mentioned, a criminal prosecution differs significantly from a civil case in several respects. These differences reflect the desire to safeguard the rights of the individual against the state. Exhibit 6–3 summarizes the major procedural steps in processing a criminal case.

Traditionally, persons who committed the same crime might receive very different sentences, depending on the judge hearing the case, the jurisdiction in which it was heard, and many other factors. Today, however, court judges typically must follow state or federal guidelines when sentencing convicted persons.

At the federal level, the Sentencing Reform Act created the U.S. Sentencing Commission, which was charged with the task of standardizing sentences for federal crimes. The commission fulfilled its task, and since 1987 its sentencing guidelines for all federal crimes have been applied by federal court judges. The guidelines establish a range of possible penalties for each federal crime. Depending on the defendant's criminal record, the seriousness of the offense, and other factors specified in the guidelines, federal judges must select a sentence from within this range.

The commission also created specific guidelines for the punishment of crimes committed by corporate employees (white-collar crimes). These guidelines established stiffer penalties for criminal violations of securities laws (see Chapter 21), antitrust laws (see Chapter 22), employment laws (see Chapter 18), mail and wire fraud, commercial bribery, and kickbacks and money laundering.[21] The guidelines allow federal judges to take into consideration a number of factors when selecting from the range of possible penalties for a specified crime. These factors include the defendant company's history of past violations, the extent of management's cooperation with federal investigators, and the extent to which the firm has undertaken specific programs and procedures to prevent criminal activities by its employees.

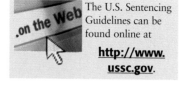

.on the Web To learn more about criminal procedures, access the following site and select "Anatomy of a Murder: A Trip through Our Nation's Legal Justice System": **http://library.thinkquest.org/ 2760/home.htm**.

.on the Web The U.S. Sentencing Guidelines can be found online at **http://www. ussc.gov**.

■■ Cyber Crime

COMPUTER CRIME
Any act that is directed against computers and computer parts, that uses computers as instruments of crime, or that involves computers and constitutes abuse.

Some years ago, the American Bar Association defined **computer crime** as any act that is directed against computers and computer parts, that uses computers as instruments of crime, or that involves computers and constitutes abuse. Today, because much of the crime committed with the use of computers occurs in cyberspace, many computer crimes fall under the broad label of cyber crime. Here we look at several types of activity that constitute cyber crimes against persons or property. Other cyber crimes will be discussed in later chapters of this text as they relate to particular topics, such as banking or consumer law.

---

20. *Davis v. United States,* 512 U.S. 452, 114 S.Ct. 2350, 129 L.Ed.2d 362 (1994).
21. The sentencing guidelines were amended in 2003, as required under the Sarbanes-Oxley Act of 2002, to impose stiffer penalties for corporate securities fraud—see Chapter 21.

EXHIBIT 6–3 MAJOR PROCEDURAL STEPS IN A CRIMINAL CASE

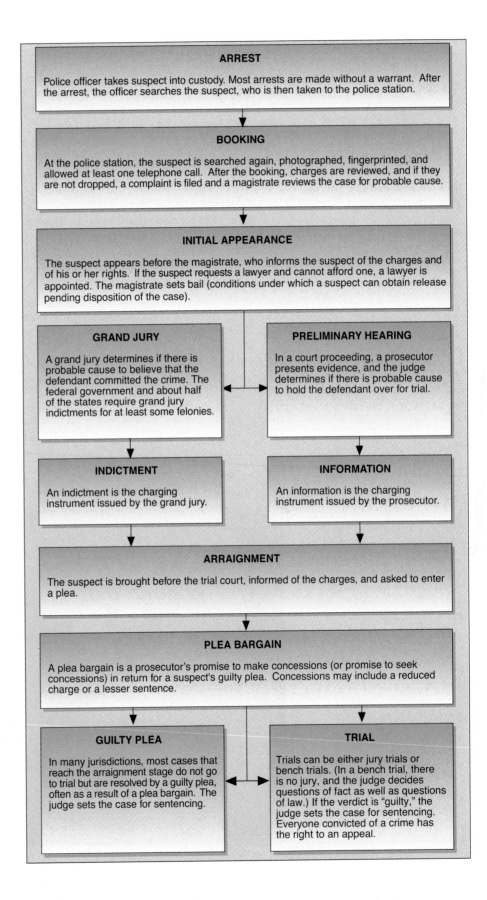

ARREST

Police officer takes suspect into custody. Most arrests are made without a warrant. After the arrest, the officer searches the suspect, who is then taken to the police station.

BOOKING

At the police station, the suspect is searched again, photographed, fingerprinted, and allowed at least one telephone call. After the booking, charges are reviewed, and if they are not dropped, a complaint is filed and a magistrate reviews the case for probable cause.

INITIAL APPEARANCE

The suspect appears before the magistrate, who informs the suspect of the charges and of his or her rights. If the suspect requests a lawyer and cannot afford one, a lawyer is appointed. The magistrate sets bail (conditions under which a suspect can obtain release pending disposition of the case).

GRAND JURY

A grand jury determines if there is probable cause to believe that the defendant committed the crime. The federal government and about half of the states require grand jury indictments for at least some felonies.

PRELIMINARY HEARING

In a court proceeding, a prosecutor presents evidence, and the judge determines if there is probable cause to hold the defendant over for trial.

INDICTMENT

An indictment is the charging instrument issued by the grand jury.

INFORMATION

An information is the charging instrument issued by the prosecutor.

ARRAIGNMENT

The suspect is brought before the trial court, informed of the charges, and asked to enter a plea.

PLEA BARGAIN

A plea bargain is a prosecutor's promise to make concessions (or promise to seek concessions) in return for a suspect's guilty plea. Concessions may include a reduced charge or a lesser sentence.

GUILTY PLEA

In many jurisdictions, most cases that reach the arraignment stage do not go to trial but are resolved by a guilty plea, often as a result of a plea bargain. The judge sets the case for sentencing.

TRIAL

Trials can be either jury trials or bench trials. (In a bench trial, there is no jury, and the judge decides questions of fact as well as questions of law.) If the verdict is "guilty," the judge sets the case for sentencing. Everyone convicted of a crime has the right to an appeal.

CYBER THEFT

Computer networks also provide opportunities for employees to commit crimes that can involve serious economic losses. For example, employees of a company's accounting department can transfer funds among accounts with little effort and often with less risk than would be involved in transactions evidenced by paperwork. Generally, the dependence of businesses on computer operations has left firms vulnerable to sabotage, fraud, embezzlement, and the theft of proprietary data, such as trade secrets or other intellectual property. As noted in Chapter 5, the piracy of intellectual property via the Internet is one of the most serious legal challenges facing lawmakers and the courts today.

A form of cyber theft that has become particularly troublesome in recent years is **identity theft.** Identity theft occurs when the wrongdoer steals a form of identification—such as a name, date of birth, or Social Security number—and uses the information to access the victim's financial resources. This crime existed to a certain extent before the widespread use of the Internet. The Internet, however, has turned identity theft into perhaps the fastest-growing financial crime in the United States. An estimated 10 million Americans are victims of identity theft each year, and annual losses are estimated to exceed $50 billion.

CYBER-STALKING

California enacted the first stalking law in 1990, in response to the murders of six women—including Rebecca Schaeffer, a television star—by men who had harassed them. The law made it a crime to harass or follow a person while making a "credible threat" that puts that person in reasonable fear for his or her safety or the safety of

The U.S. Department of Justice offers an impressive collection of statistics on crime, including cyber crime, at the following Web site:

http://www.ojp.usdoj.gov/bjs.

IDENTITY THEFT
The act of stealing another's identifying information—such as a name, date of birth, or Social Security number—and using that information to access the victim's financial resources.

BE AWARE Technological change is one of the primary factors that lead to new types of crime.

An Arkansas man, Rick Woody, holds a picture of his thirteen-year-old daughter, Kacie, who was kidnapped and murdered by a man she met through an Internet chat room. How do cyber-stalking laws differ from traditional stalking laws? (AP Photo/Mike Wintroath)

CYBER STALKER
A person who commits the crime of stalking in cyberspace. Generally, stalking consists of harassing a person and putting that person in reasonable fear for his or her safety or the safety of the person's immediate family.

the person's immediate family.[22] Since then, all other states have enacted some form of stalking laws. In about half of the states, these laws require a physical act such as following the victim.

Cyber stalkers (stalkers who commit their crimes in cyberspace), however, find their victims through Internet chat rooms, Usenet newsgroups or other bulletin boards, or e-mail. To close this "loophole" in existing stalking laws, more than three-fourths of the states now have laws specifically designed to combat cyber-stalking and other forms of online harassment.

Note that cyber-stalking can be even more threatening than physical stalking in some respects. While it takes a great deal of effort to physically stalk someone, it is relatively easy to harass a victim with electronic messages. Furthermore, the possibility of personal confrontation may discourage a stalker from actually following a victim. This disincentive is removed in cyberspace. Also, there is always the possibility that a cyber stalker will eventually pose a physical threat to her or his target. Finally, the Internet makes it easier to obtain information about the victim, such as where he or she lives or works. (Can Internet sellers of personal information be held responsible for crimes by stalkers who use that information to locate their victims? For a discussion of this issue, see this chapter's *Adapting the Law to the Online Environment* feature on the following page.)

HACKING AND CYBER TERRORISM

HACKER
A person who uses one computer to break into another. Professional computer programmers refer to such persons as "crackers."

CYBER TERRORIST
A hacker whose purpose is to exploit a target computer for a serious impact, such as corrupting a program to sabotage a business.

Persons who use one computer to break into another are sometimes referred to as **hackers.** Hackers who break into computers without authorization often commit cyber theft. Sometimes, however, their principal aim is to prove how smart they are by gaining access to others' password-protected computers and causing random data errors or making unpaid-for telephone calls.[23] **Cyber terrorists** are hackers who, rather than trying to attract attention, strive to remain undetected so that they can exploit computers for a serious impact. Just as "real" terrorists destroyed the World Trade Center towers and a portion of the Pentagon in September 2001, cyber terrorists might explode "logic bombs" to shut down central computers. Such activities can pose a danger to national security.

Businesses may be targeted by cyber terrorists as well as hackers. The goals of a hacking operation might include a wholesale theft of data, such as a merchant's customer files, or the monitoring of a computer to discover a business firm's plans and transactions. A cyber terrorist might also want to insert false codes or data. For example, the processing control system of a food manufacturer could be changed to alter the levels of ingredients so that consumers of the food would become ill.

A cyber terrorist attack on a major financial institution such as the New York Stock Exchange or a large bank could leave securities or money markets in flux and seriously affect the daily lives of millions of citizens. Similarly, any prolonged disruption of computer, cable, satellite, or telecommunications systems due to the actions of expert hackers would have serious repercussions on business operations—and national security—on a global level. Computer viruses are another tool that can be used by cyber terrorists to cripple communications networks.

 The Computer Crime Research Center is a nonprofit organization that provides up-to-date information and articles on cyber crime and cyber terrorism at **http://www. crime-research.org.**

---

22. See, for example, Cal. Penal Code Section 646.9.
23. The total cost of crime on the Internet is estimated to be several billion dollars annually, but two-thirds of that total is said to consist of unpaid-for toll calls.

ADAPTING THE LAW TO THE ONLINE ENVIRONMENT

Stalking and Internet Data Brokers

A cutting-edge issue coming before today's courts has to do with stalking and Internet data brokers—those in the business of selling personal information via the Internet. Suppose that a stalker purchases personal information (such as a home address) from a Web broker and then uses that information to commit a crime (such as murder). The stalker, of course, can be prosecuted under criminal law for the crime of murder. At issue is the broker's responsibility for the crime. Can the broker be sued under tort law (see Chapter 4) for damages?

ONE COURT WEIGHS IN

At least one court has weighed in on this issue. In *Remsburg v. Docusearch, Inc.,*[a] the Supreme Court of New Hampshire concluded that an Internet data broker had a duty to exercise reasonable care when selling personal information online. The case involved Liam Youens, a New Hampshire resident, and Docusearch, Inc., an Internet-based investigation and information service. Youens contacted Docusearch through its Web site and requested information about Amy Boyer. Youens provided his name, address, and phone number and paid Docusearch's fee by credit card. In return, Docusearch provided Boyer's home address, birth date, and Social Security number. Youens also asked for Boyer's workplace address, which Docusearch obtained for him. After Youens had obtained the address of Boyer's place of employment, he drove to the workplace, fatally shot her, and then shot and killed himself.

a. 149 N.H. 148, 816 A.2d 1001 (2003).

Helen Remsburg, Boyer's mother, sued Docusearch, claiming that the defendant had acted wrongfully. The federal district court referred the case to the New Hampshire Supreme Court for a determination of the parties' duties under the state's common law. The state supreme court held that an information broker who sells information about a third person to a client has a duty to exercise reasonable care in disclosing the information.

A FORESEEABLE RISK?

One of the key issues for the court was whether the crime committed by Youens was a foreseeable risk to Docusearch. Remember from Chapter 4 that under tort law, the test for proximate cause—and the extent of a defendant's duty of care—is the foreseeability of a risk of harm. If certain consequences of an action are not foreseeable, there is no proximate cause.

In determining whether a risk of criminal misconduct was foreseeable to Docusearch, the Supreme Court of New Hampshire found that Docusearch's information disclosure presented two foreseeable risks: stalking and identity theft. Therefore, the company had a duty to exercise reasonable care in disclosing personal information about Boyer to Youens. Because Docusearch had not exercised reasonable care (taken steps to find out if Youens's requests were for a legitimate purpose), Docusearch could be sued for damages for breaching this duty.

FOR CRITICAL ANALYSIS

What other crimes can you think of, in addition to stalking and identity theft, that might qualify as "foreseeable risks" created by the online sale of personal data by information brokers?

ETHICAL ISSUE 6.1

Is it possible to control cyber crime without sacrificing some civil liberties? Governments in some countries, such as China, have succeeded in controlling Internet crime to a certain extent by monitoring the e-mail and other electronic transmissions of users of specific Internet service providers. In the United States, however, Americans have been reluctant to allow the government to monitor Internet use to detect criminal conspiracies or terrorist activities. The traditional attitude has been that civil liberties must be safeguarded to the greatest extent feasible.

As noted in Chapter 1, however, after the terrorist attacks on the World Trade Center and the Pentagon in September 2001, Congress enacted legislation, including the USA Patriot Act, to give law enforcement personnel more authority to conduct electronic surveillance, such as monitoring Web sites and e-mail exchanges. For a time, it seemed that the terrorist attacks might have made Americans more willing to trade off some of their civil liberties for greater national security. Today, however, many complain that this legislation has gone too far in curbing traditional civil liberties guaranteed by the U.S. Constitution. ■

PROSECUTING CYBER CRIMES

The "location" of cyber crime (cyberspace) has raised new issues in the investigation of crimes and the prosecution of offenders. A threshold issue is, of course, jurisdiction. A person who commits an act against a business in California, where the act is a cyber crime, might never have set foot in California but might instead reside in New York, or even in Canada, where the act may not be a crime. If the crime was committed via e-mail, the question arises as to whether the e-mail would constitute sufficient "minimum contacts" (see Chapter 3) for the victim's state to exercise jurisdiction over the perpetrator.

Identifying the wrongdoers can also be difficult. Cyber criminals do not leave physical traces, such as fingerprints or DNA samples, as evidence of their crimes. Even electronic "footprints" can be hard to find and follow. For example, e-mail may be sent through a remailer, an online service that guarantees that a message cannot be traced to its source.

For these reasons, laws written to protect physical property are difficult to apply in cyberspace. Nonetheless, governments at both the state and federal levels have taken significant steps toward controlling cyber crime, both by applying existing criminal statutes and by enacting new laws that specifically address wrongs committed in cyberspace. For suggestions on how to protect your business from losses caused by cyber crime, see the *Application* at the end of this chapter.

The Computer Fraud and Abuse Act   Perhaps the most significant federal statute specifically addressing cyber crime is the Counterfeit Access Device and Computer Fraud and Abuse Act of 1984 (commonly known as the Computer Fraud and Abuse Act, or CFAA). This act, as amended by the National Information Infrastructure Protection Act of 1996,[24] provides, among other things, that a person who accesses a computer online, without authority, to obtain classified, restricted, or protected data, or attempts to do so, is subject to criminal prosecution. Such data could include financial and credit records, medical records, legal files, military and national security files, and other confidential information in government or private computers. The crime has two elements: accessing a computer without authority and taking the data.

This theft is a felony if it is committed for a commercial purpose or for private financial gain, or if the value of the stolen data (or computer time) exceeds $5,000. Penalties include fines and imprisonment for up to twenty years. A victim of computer theft can also bring a civil suit against the violator to obtain damages, an injunction, and other relief.

Other Federal Statutes   The federal wire fraud statute, the Economic Espionage Act of 1996, and RICO, all of which were discussed earlier in this chapter, extend to crimes committed in cyberspace as well. Other federal statutes that may apply include the Electronic Fund Transfer Act of 1978, which makes the unauthorized

Professor Brenner at the University of Dayton Law School posts numerous articles on combating cyber crime, as well as information and links to the relevant laws of other nations, the policies of the European Council, and the United Nations' approach. You can access the site at

http://www.cybercrimes.net/ International/IntLinks.html.

The U.S. Department of Justice maintains a site dedicated to cyber crime at

http://www.usdoj.gov/ criminal/cybercrime.

---

24. 18 U.S.C. Section 1030.

access to an electronic fund transfer system a crime; the Anticounterfeiting Consumer Protection Act of 1996, which increased penalties for stealing copyrighted or trademarked property; and the National Stolen Property Act of 1988, which concerns the interstate transport of stolen property. Recall from Chapter 1 that the federal government has also enacted laws (many of which have been challenged on constitutional grounds) to protect minors from online pornographic materials. In later chapters of this text, you will read about other federal statutes and regulations that are designed to address wrongs committed in cyberspace in specific areas of the law.

APPLICATION ■■ How Can You Protect against Cyber Crime?*

In addition to protecting their physical property, business owners today also are concerned about protecting their intangible property—such as computer data or files—from unauthorized access. U.S. business firms lose millions of dollars to industrial espionage and sabotage every year. Once a computer system has been corrupted, it can be difficult to recover. To prevent losses through computer systems, some firms hire experts to improve the security of the systems.

COMPUTER SYSTEM SAFEGUARDS

Many sources of software offer security programs that can easily be used to protect computers that are connected to an internal network or to the Internet. For example, most word processing programs include a "password" function. To gain access to information within the program, a user must know the password. A document that can be unlocked only with the password can be e-mailed as an attachment, providing some security.

Cryptography also provides increased protection for computer data and files. Encryption hardware is available in the form of computer chips and is commonly used in automated teller machines. These chips quickly encrypt or decrypt information. The same results can be achieved using encryption software.

Additionally, effective "firewalls" can be installed at the interface between computers and the Internet to protect against unwanted intruders. Firewall software can also be used to keep internal network segments secure.

EMPLOYMENT POLICIES

Although outside hackers are a threat, employees, former employees, and other "insiders" are responsible for most computer abuse, including breaches of information security. Generally, employees should be given access only to information that they need to know. Additionally, employees and other insiders should be instructed in what constitutes proper and improper use of your company's computer systems. They should also be told that any form of computer abuse is against company policy, is illegal, and will be the basis for termination of employment and even criminal prosecution.

Another safeguard is to have employees agree, in a written confidentiality agreement (see the *Application* feature in Chapter 5), not to disclose confidential information during or after employment without the employer's consent. Monitoring certain computer-related employee activities may be appropriate, but if monitoring is to take place, employees should be informed (see Chapter 18). Still other security measures include the use of digital signatures (see Chapter 10), facility lockups, visitor screenings, and announced briefcase checks.

CHECKLIST FOR THE BUSINESS OWNER

1. Consider protecting your computer security and documents through the use of passwords, encryption, and firewalls.
2. Instruct your employees in how computers and computer information are to be used and not used.
3. Consider using confidentiality agreements, monitoring, and digital signatures to protect your computer system and data against unauthorized use.

* This *Application* is not meant to substitute for the services of an attorney who is licensed to practice law in your state.

■ KEY TERMS

CHAPTER SUMMARY ■ Criminal Law and Cyber Crimes

Civil Law and Criminal Law (See pages 171–172.)	1. *Civil law*—Spells out the duties that exist between persons or between citizens and their governments, excluding the duty not to commit crimes.
	2. *Criminal law*—Has to do with crimes, which are defined as wrongs against society proclaimed in statutes and, if committed, punishable by society through fines, and/or imprisonment—and, in some cases, death. Because crimes are *offenses against society as a whole,* they are prosecuted by a public official, not by victims.
	3. *Key differences*—An important difference between civil and criminal law is that the burden of proof is higher in criminal cases (see Exhibit 6–1 on page 172 for other differences between criminal and civil law).
	4. *Civil liability for criminal acts*—A criminal act may give rise to both criminal liability and tort liability (see Exhibit 6–2 on page 173 for an example of criminal and tort liability for the same act).
Classification of Crimes (See pages 172–173.)	1. *Felonies*—Serious crimes punishable by death or by imprisonment in a penitentiary for more than one year.
	2. *Misdemeanors*—Under federal law and in most states, any crimes that are not felonies.
Criminal Liability (See pages 173–174.)	1. *Guilty act*—In general, some form of harmful act must be committed for a crime to exist.
	2. *Intent*—An intent to commit a crime, or a wrongful mental state, is generally required for a crime to exist.
Corporate Criminal Liability (See pages 174–175.)	1. *Liability of corporations*—Corporations normally are liable for the crimes committed by their agents and employees within the course and scope of their employment. Corporations cannot be imprisoned, but they can be fined or denied certain legal privileges.
	2. *Liability of corporate officers and directors*—Corporate directors and officers are personally liable for the crimes they commit and may be held liable for the actions of employees under their supervision.
Types of Crimes (See pages 175–181.)	Crimes fall into five general categories: violent crime, property crime, public order crime, white-collar crime, and organized crime.

(Continued)

CHAPTER SUMMARY ▦ Criminal Law and Cyber Crimes—Continued

Defenses to Criminal Liability (See pages 181–185.)	Defenses to criminal liability include infancy, intoxication, insanity, mistake, consent, duress, justifiable use of force, entrapment, and the statute of limitations. Also, in some cases defendants may be relieved of criminal liability, at least in part, if they are given immunity.
Constitutional Safeguards and Criminal Procedures (See pages 185–190.)	1. *Fourth Amendment*—Provides protection against unreasonable searches and seizures and requires that probable cause exist before a warrant for a search or an arrest can be issued. 2. *Fifth Amendment*—Requires due process of law, prohibits double jeopardy, and protects against self-incrimination. 3. *Sixth Amendment*—Provides guarantees of a speedy trial, a trial by jury, a public trial, the right to confront witnesses, and the right to counsel. 4. *Eighth Amendment*—Prohibits excessive bail and fines, and cruel and unusual punishment. 5. *Exclusionary rule*—A criminal procedural rule that prohibits the introduction at trial of all evidence obtained in violation of constitutional rights, as well as any evidence derived from the illegally obtained evidence. 6. *Miranda rule*—A rule set forth by the Supreme Court in *Miranda v. Arizona* that individuals who are arrested must be informed of certain constitutional rights, including their right to counsel. 7. *Arrest, indictment, and trial*—Procedures governing arrest, indictment, and trial for a crime are designed to safeguard the rights of the individual against the state. See Exhibit 6–3 for a summary of the procedural steps involved in prosecuting a criminal case. 8. *Sentencing guidelines*—Both the federal government and the states have established sentencing laws or guidelines. The federal sentencing guidelines indicate a range of penalties for each federal crime; federal judges must abide by these guidelines when imposing sentences on those convicted of federal crimes.
Cyber Crime (See pages 190–196.)	Cyber crime is any crime that occurs in cyberspace. Examples include cyber theft (financial crimes committed with the aid of computers, as well as identity theft), cyber-stalking, hacking, and cyber terrorism. Significant federal statutes addressing cyber crimes include the Electronic Fund Transfer Act of 1978 and the Counterfeit Access Device and Computer Fraud and Abuse Act of 1984, as amended by the National Information Infrastructure Protection Act of 1996.

▦ FOR REVIEW

Answers for the even-numbered questions in this For Review *section can be found in Appendix I at the end of this text.*

1 What two elements must exist before a person can be held liable for a crime? Can a corporation commit crimes?

2 What are five broad categories of crimes? What is white-collar crime?

3 What defenses might be raised by criminal defendants to avoid liability for criminal acts?

4 What constitutional safeguards exist to protect persons accused of crimes? What are the basic steps in the criminal process?

5 What is cyber crime? What laws apply to crimes committed in cyberspace?

QUESTIONS AND CASE PROBLEMS

6–1. Criminal versus Civil Trials. In criminal trials, the defendant must be proved guilty beyond a reasonable doubt, whereas in civil trials, the defendant need only be proved guilty by a preponderance of the evidence. Discuss why a higher burden of proof is required in criminal trials.

6–2. Types of Crimes. The following situations are similar (all involve the theft of Makoto's television set), yet they represent three different crimes. Identify the three crimes, noting the differences among them.

(a) While passing Makoto's house one night, Sarah sees a portable television set left unattended on Makoto's lawn. Sarah takes the television set, carries it home, and tells everyone she owns it.

(b) While passing Makoto's house one night, Sarah sees Makoto outside with a portable television set. Holding Makoto at gunpoint, Sarah forces him to give up the set. Then Sarah runs away with it.

(c) While passing Makoto's house one night, Sarah sees a portable television set in a window. Sarah breaks the front-door lock, enters, and leaves with the set.

6–3. Types of Crimes. Which, if any, of the following crimes necessarily involve illegal activity on the part of more than one person?

(a) Bribery.

(b) Forgery.

(c) Embezzlement.

(d) Larceny.

(e) Receiving stolen property.

6–4. Double Jeopardy. Armington, while robbing a drugstore, shot and seriously injured Jennings, a drugstore clerk. Armington was subsequently convicted in a criminal trial of armed robbery and assault and battery. Jennings later brought a civil tort suit against Armington for damages. Armington contended that he could not be tried again for the same crime, as that would constitute double jeopardy, which is prohibited by the Fifth Amendment to the Constitution. Is Armington correct? Explain.

6–5. Fifth Amendment. The federal government was investigating a corporation and its employees. The alleged criminal wrongdoing, which included the falsification of corporate books and records, occurred between 1993 and 1996 in one division of the corporation. In 1999, the corporation pleaded guilty and agreed to cooperate in an investigation of the individuals who might have been involved in the improper corporate activities. "Doe I," "Doe II," and "Doe III" were officers of the corporation during the period when the illegal activities occurred and worked in the division where the wrongdoing took place. They were no longer working for the corporation, however, when, as part of the subsequent investigation, the government asked them to provide specific corporate documents in their possession. All three asserted the Fifth Amendment privilege against self-incrimination. The government asked a federal district court to order the three

to produce the records. Corporate employees can be compelled to produce corporate records in a criminal proceeding because they hold the records as representatives of the corporation, to which the Fifth Amendment privilege against self-incrimination does not apply. Should *former* employees also be compelled to produce corporate records in their possession? Why or why not? [*In re Three Grand Jury Subpoenas* Duces Tecum *Dated January 29, 1999*, 191 F.3d 173 (2d Cir. 1999)]

CASE PROBLEM WITH SAMPLE ANSWER

6–6. The District of Columbia Lottery Board licensed Soo Young Bae, a Washington, D.C., merchant, to operate a terminal that prints and dispenses lottery tickets for sale. Bae used the terminal to generate tickets with a face value of $525,586, for which he did not pay. The winning tickets among these had a total redemption value of $296,153, of which Bae successfully obtained all but $72,000. Bae pleaded guilty to computer fraud, and the court sentenced him to eighteen months in prison. In sentencing a defendant for fraud, a federal court must make a reasonable estimate of the victim's loss. The court determined that the value of the loss due to the fraud was $503,650—the market value of the tickets less the commission Bae would have received from the lottery board had he sold those tickets. Bae appealed, arguing that "[a]t the instant any lottery ticket is printed," it is worth whatever value the lottery drawing later assigns to it; that is, losing tickets have no value. Bae thus calculated the loss at $296,153, the value of his winning tickets. Should the U.S. Court of Appeals for the District of Columbia Circuit affirm or reverse Bae's sentence? Why? [*United States v. Bae*, 250 F.3d 774 (C.A.D.C. 2001)]

After you have answered this problem, compare your answer with the sample answer given on the Web site that accompanies this text. Go to http://blt.westbuslaw.com, select "Chapter 6," and click on "Case Problem with Sample Answer."

6–7. Larceny. In February 2001, a homeowner hired Jimmy Smith, a contractor claiming to employ a crew of thirty workers, to build a garage. The homeowner paid Smith $7,950 and agreed to make additional payments as needed to complete the project, up to $15,900. Smith promised to start the next day and finish within eight weeks. Nearly a month passed with no work, while Smith lied to the homeowner that materials were on "back order." During a second month, footings were created for the foundation, and a subcontractor poured the concrete slab, but Smith did not return the homeowner's phone calls. After eight weeks, the homeowner confronted Smith, who promised to complete the job, worked on the site that day until lunch, and never returned. Three months later, the homeowner again confronted Smith, who promised to "pay [him] off" later that day but did not do so. In March 2002, the state of Georgia filed criminal charges against Smith. While his trial was pending, he promised to pay the homeowner "next week," but again failed to refund any money. The value of the labor performed before Smith abandoned the project was between $800 and $1,000, the value of the materials was $367, and the subcontractor was paid $2,270. Did Smith commit larceny? Explain. [*Smith v. State of Georgia*, __ S.E.2d __ (Ga.App. 2004)]

A QUESTION OF ETHICS

6–8. A troublesome issue concerning the constitutional privilege against self-incrimination has to do with "jail plants"—that is, undercover police officers placed in cells with criminal suspects to gain information from the suspects. For example, in one case the police placed an undercover agent, Parisi, in a jail cell block with Lloyd Perkins, who had been imprisoned on charges unrelated to the murder that Parisi was investigating. When Parisi asked Perkins if he had ever killed anyone, Perkins made statements implicating himself in the murder. Perkins was then charged with the murder. [*Illinois v. Perkins*, 496 U.S. 292, 110 S.Ct. 2394, 110 L.Ed.2d 243 (1990)]

1. Review the discussion of *Miranda v. Arizona* in this chapter. Should Perkins's statements be suppressed—that is, not be admissible as evidence at trial—because he was not "read his rights," as required by the *Miranda* decision, prior to making his self-incriminating statements? Does *Miranda* apply to Perkins's situation?

2. Do you think that it is fair for the police to resort to trickery and deception to bring those who have committed crimes to justice? Why or why not? What rights or public policies must be balanced in deciding this issue?

FOR CRITICAL ANALYSIS

6–9. Do you think that criminal procedure in this country is weighted too heavily in favor of accused persons? Can you think of a fairer way to balance the constitutional rights of accused persons against the right of society to be protected against criminal behavior? Should different criminal procedures be used when terrorism is involved? Explain.

VIDEO QUESTION

6–10. Go to this text's Web site at **http://blt. westbuslaw.com** and select "Chapter 6." Click on "Video Questions" and view the video titled *Casino*. Then answer the following questions.

1. In the video, a casino manager, Ace (Robert DeNiro), discusses how politicians "won their 'comp life' when they got elected." "Comps" are the free gifts that casinos give to high-stakes gamblers to keep their business. If an elected official accepts comps, is he or she committing a crime? If so, what type of crime? Explain your answers.

2. Assume that Ace committed a crime by giving politicians comps. Can the casino, Tangiers Corporation, be held liable for that crime? Why or why not? How could a court punish the corporation?

3. Suppose that the Federal Bureau of Investigation (FBI) wants to search the premises of Tangiers for evidence of criminal activity. If casino management refuses to consent to the search, what constitutional safeguards and criminal procedures, if any, protect Tangiers?

INTERNET EXERCISES

Go to the *Business Law Today: The Essentials* home page at **http://blt.westbuslaw.com**, select "Chapter 6," and click on "Internet Exercises." There you will find the following Internet research exercises that you can perform to learn more about topics covered in this chapter.

Activity 6–1: LEGAL PERSPECTIVE—Revisiting *Miranda*

Activity 6–2: MANAGEMENT PERSPECTIVE—Hackers

Activity 6–3: INTERNATIONAL PERSPECTIVE—Fighting Cyber Crime Worldwide

BEFORE THE TEST

Go to the *Business Law Today: The Essentials* home page at **http://blt.westbuslaw.com**, select "Chapter 6," and click on "Interactive Quizzes." You will find at least twenty interactive questions relating to this chapter.

CHAPTER 7

Contracts: Nature, Classification, Agreement, and Consideration

"The social order rests upon the stability and predictability of conduct, of which keeping promises is a large item."

Roscoe Pound, 1870–1964
(American jurist)

CHAPTER OUTLINE

■ THE NATURE AND FUNCTION OF CONTRACTS

■ TYPES OF CONTRACTS

■ AGREEMENT

■ CONSIDERATION

▪▪ LEARNING OBJECTIVES

After reading this chapter, you should be able to answer the following questions:

1 What is a contract? What are the four elements necessary to the formation of a valid contract?

2 What are the various types of contracts?

3 What are the requirements of an offer?

4 How can an offer be accepted?

5 What are the elements of consideration?

PROMISE
An assertion that something either will or will not happen in the future.

A s Roscoe Pound—an eminent jurist—observed in the above quotation, "keeping promises" is important to a stable social order. Contract law deals with, among other things, the formation and keeping of promises. A **promise** is an assertion that something either will or will not happen in the future.

Like other types of law, contract law reflects our social values, interests, and expectations at a given point in time. It shows, for example, what kinds of promises our society thinks should be legally binding. It shows what excuses our society accepts for breaking such promises. Additionally, it shows what promises are considered to be contrary to public policy, or against the interests of society, and therefore legally void. If a promise goes against the interests of society as a whole, it will be invalid. Also, if it was made by a child or a mentally incompetent person, or on the basis of false information, a question will arise as to whether the promise should be enforced. Resolving such questions is the essence of contract law.

In this chapter, we first discuss the nature and function of contracts and the various types of contracts that exist. We also consider the basic requirements for a valid and enforceable contract. We then look closely at two of these requirements—*agreement* and *consideration*.

■ The Nature and Function of Contracts

No aspect of modern life is entirely free of contractual relationships. You acquire rights and obligations, for example, when you borrow funds, when you buy or lease a house, when you procure insurance, when you form a business, and when you purchase goods or services. Contract law is designed to provide stability and predictability for both buyers and sellers in the marketplace.

Contract law assures the parties to private agreements that the promises they make will be enforceable. Clearly, many promises are kept because the parties involved feel a moral obligation to do so or because keeping a promise is in their mutual self-interest, not because the **promisor** (the person making the promise) or the **promisee** (the person to whom the promise is made) is conscious of the rules of contract law. Nevertheless, the rules of contract law are often followed in business agreements to avoid potential problems.

By supplying procedures for enforcing private agreements, contract law provides an essential condition for the existence of a market economy. Without a legal framework of reasonably assured expectations within which to plan and venture, businesspersons would be able to rely only on the good faith of others. Duty and good faith are usually sufficient, but when dramatic price changes or adverse economic conditions make it costly to comply with a promise, these elements may not be enough. Contract law is necessary to ensure compliance with a promise or to entitle the innocent party to some form of relief.

THE LAW GOVERNING CONTRACTS

Although aspects of contract law vary from state to state, much of it is based on the common law. In 1932, the American Law Institute compiled the *Restatement of the Law of Contracts*. This work is a nonstatutory, authoritative exposition of the present law on the subject of contracts and is currently in its second edition (a third edition is in the process of being drafted). Throughout the following chapters on contracts, we will refer to the second edition of the *Restatement of the Law of Contracts* as simply the *Restatement (Second) of Contracts*.

The Uniform Commercial Code (UCC), which governs contracts and other transactions relating to the sale and lease of goods, occasionally departs from common law contract rules. Generally, the different treatment of contracts falling under the UCC stems from the general policy of encouraging commerce. The ways in which the UCC changes common law contract rules will be discussed in later chapters. When discussing the common law of contracts, we indicate only briefly or in footnotes those common law rules that have been altered significantly by the UCC for sales and lease contracts.[1]

PROMISOR
A person who makes a promise.

PROMISEE
A person to whom a promise is made.

You can keep abreast of recent and planned revisions of the *Restatements of the Law* by accessing the American Law Institute's Web site at

http://www.ali.org.

---

1. Note that throughout the chapters on the common law of contracts, we cite in the footnotes the section numbers of the UCC that are used in the UCC version that is currently in effect in most states. As you will read in later chapters covering sales contracts, the UCC was amended in 2003, and thus some of the section numbers may have been changed by those amendments.

DEFINITION OF A CONTRACT

CONTRACT
An agreement that can be enforced in court; formed by two or more competent parties who agree, for consideration, to perform or to refrain from performing some legal act now or in the future.

A **contract** is an agreement that can be enforced in court. It is formed by two or more parties who agree to perform or to refrain from performing some act now or in the future. Generally, contract disputes arise when there is a promise of future performance. If the contractual promise is not fulfilled, the party who made it is subject to the sanctions of a court (see Chapter 9). That party may be required to pay money damages for failing to perform the contractual promise; in limited instances, the party may be required to perform the promised act.

REQUIREMENTS OF A CONTRACT

The following list describes the four requirements that must be met for a valid contract to exist. Each item will be explained more fully in the chapter indicated.

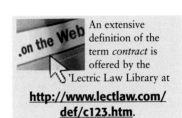
An extensive definition of the term *contract* is offered by the 'Lectric Law Library at **http://www.lectlaw.com/ def/c123.htm.**

1 *Agreement.* An agreement includes an offer and an acceptance. One party must offer to enter into a legal agreement, and another party must accept the terms of the offer (this chapter).

2 *Consideration.* Any promises made by parties must be supported by legally sufficient and bargained-for consideration (something of value received or promised, to convince a person to make a deal) (this chapter).

3 *Contractual capacity.* Both parties entering into the contract must have the contractual capacity to do so; the law must recognize them as possessing characteristics that qualify them as competent parties (Chapter 8).

4 *Legality.* The contract's purpose must be to accomplish some goal that is legal and not against public policy (Chapter 8).

If any of these four elements is lacking, no contract will have been formed. Even if all of these elements exist, however, a contract may be unenforceable if the following requirements are not met. These requirements typically are raised as *defenses* to the enforceability of an otherwise valid contract.

1 *Genuineness of assent.* The apparent consent of both parties must be genuine (Chapter 8).

2 *Form.* The contract must be in whatever form the law requires; for example, some contracts must be in writing to be enforceable (Chapter 8).

FREEDOM OF CONTRACT AND FREEDOM FROM CONTRACT

As a general rule, the law recognizes everyone's ability to enter freely into contractual arrangements. This recognition is called *freedom of contract,* a freedom protected by the U.S. Constitution in Article I, Section 10. Because freedom of contract is a fundamental public policy of the United States, courts rarely interfere with contracts that have been voluntarily made.

Of course, as in other areas of the law, there are many exceptions to the general rule that contracts voluntarily negotiated will be enforced. For example, illegal bargains, agreements that unreasonably restrain trade, and certain unfair contracts made between one party with a great amount of bargaining power and another with little power are generally not enforced. In addition, as you will read in Chapter 8, certain contracts and clauses may not be enforceable if they are contrary to public policy, fairness, and justice. These exceptions provide freedom from contract for persons who may have been forced into making contracts unfavorable to themselves.

For an excellent overview of the basic principles of contract law, go to **http://profs.lp. findlaw.com/contracts/ index.html**.

OFFEROR
A person who makes an offer.

OFFEREE
A person to whom an offer is made.

BILATERAL CONTRACT
A type of contract that arises when a promise is given in exchange for a return promise.

UNILATERAL CONTRACT
A contract that results when an offer can be accepted only by the offeree's performance.

Types of Contracts

There are numerous types of contracts. They are categorized based on legal distinctions as to their formation, performance, and enforceability. Exhibit 7–1 illustrates three classifications, or categories, of contracts based on their mode of formation.

CONTRACT FORMATION

As you can see in Exhibit 7–1, three classifications, or categories, of contracts are based on how and when a contract is formed. The best way to explain each type of contract is to compare one type with another, as we do in the following pages.

Bilateral versus Unilateral Contracts   Every contract involves at least two parties. The **offeror** is the party making the offer. The **offeree** is the party to whom the offer is made. The offeror always promises to do or not to do something and thus is also a promisor. Whether the contract is classified as *bilateral* or *unilateral* depends on what the offeree must do to accept the offer and bind the offeror to a contract.

Bilateral Contracts.   If to accept the offer the offeree must only promise to perform, the contract is a **bilateral contract.** Hence, a bilateral contract is a "promise for a promise." An example of a bilateral contract is a contract in which one person agrees to buy another person's automobile for a specified price. No performance, such as the payment of money or delivery of goods, need take place for a bilateral contract to be formed. The contract comes into existence at the moment the promises are exchanged.

Unilateral Contracts.   If the offer is phrased so that the offeree can accept only by completing the contract performance, the contract is a **unilateral contract.** Hence, a unilateral contract is a "promise for an act." In other words, the contract is formed not at the moment when promises are exchanged but rather when the contract is *performed.* ■ **EXAMPLE 7.1** Joe says to Celia, "If you drive my car from New York to Los Angeles, I'll give you $1,000." Only on Celia's completion of the act—bringing the car to Los Angeles—does she fully accept Joe's offer to pay $1,000. If she chooses not to accept the offer to drive the car to Los Angeles, there are no legal consequences. ■

EXHIBIT 7–1 CLASSIFICATIONS BASED ON CONTRACT FORMATION

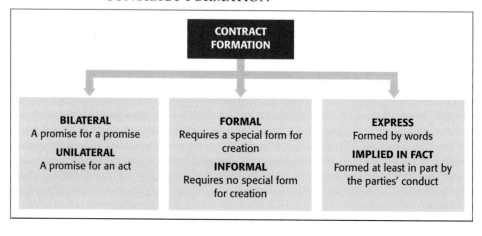

CONTRACT FORMATION

BILATERAL	**FORMAL**	**EXPRESS**
A promise for a promise	Requires a special form for creation	Formed by words
UNILATERAL	**INFORMAL**	**IMPLIED IN FACT**
A promise for an act	Requires no special form for creation	Formed at least in part by the parties' conduct

Contests, lotteries, and other competitions offering prizes are also examples of offers for unilateral contracts. If a person complies with the rules of the contest—such as by submitting the right lottery number at the right place and time—a unilateral contract is formed, binding the organization offering the prize to a contract to perform as promised in the offer.

Can a school's, or an employer's, letter of tentative acceptance to a prospective student, or a possible employee, qualify as a unilateral contract? That was the issue in the following case.

CASE 7.1 ▌ Ardito v. City of Providence

United States District Court,
District of Rhode Island, 2003.
263 F.Supp.2d 358.

FACTS In 2001, the city of Providence, Rhode Island, decided to begin hiring police officers to fill vacancies in its police department. Because only individuals who had graduated from the Providence Police Academy were eligible, the city also decided to conduct two training sessions, the "60th and 61st Police Academies." To be admitted, an applicant had to pass a series of tests and be deemed qualified by members of the department after an interview. The applicants judged most qualified were sent a letter informing them that they had been selected to attend the academy if they successfully completed a medical checkup and a psychological examination. The letter for the applicants to the 61st Academy, dated October 15, stated that it was "a conditional offer of employment." Meanwhile, a new chief of police, Dean Esserman, decided to revise the selection process, which caused some of those who had received the letter to be rejected. Derek Ardito and thirteen other newly rejected applicants filed a suit in a federal district court against the city, seeking a halt to the 61st Academy unless they were allowed to attend. They alleged in part that the city was in breach of contract.

ISSUE Was the October 15 letter a unilateral offer that the plaintiffs had accepted by passing the required medical and psychological examinations?

DECISION Yes. The court issued an injunction to prohibit the city from conducting the 61st Police Academy unless the plaintiffs were included.

REASON The court found the October 15 letter to be "a classic example of an offer to enter into a unilateral contract. The October 15 letter expressly stated that it was a 'conditional offer of employment' and the message that it conveyed was that the recipient would be admitted into the 61st Academy if he or she successfully completed the medical and psychological examinations." The court contrasted the letter with "notices sent to applicants by the City at earlier stages of the selection process. Those notices merely informed applicants that they had completed a step in the process and remained eligible to be considered for admission into the Academy. Unlike the October 15 letter, the prior notices did not purport to extend a 'conditional offer' of admission." The court concluded that "[t]he plaintiffs accepted the City's offer of admission into the Academy by satisfying the specified conditions. Each of the plaintiffs submitted to and passed lengthy and intrusive medical and psychological examinations."

FOR CRITICAL ANALYSIS—Social Consideration
How might the city have phrased the October 15 letter to avoid its being considered a unilateral contract?

Revocation of Offers for Unilateral Contracts. A problem arises in unilateral contracts when the promisor attempts to *revoke* (cancel) the offer after the promisee has begun performance but before the act has been completed. ▌ **EXAMPLE 7.2** Suppose that Roberta offers to buy Ed's sailboat, moored in San Francisco, on delivery of the boat to Roberta's dock in Newport Beach, three hundred miles south of San Francisco. Ed rigs the boat and sets sail. Shortly before his arrival at Newport Beach, Ed receives a radio message from Roberta withdrawing her offer. Roberta's offer is an offer for a unilateral contract, and only Ed's delivery of the sailboat at her dock is an acceptance. ▌

For easy-to-understand definitions of legal terms and concepts, including terms and concepts relating to contract law, go to

http://dictionary.law.com

and key in a term, such as "contract" or "consideration."

FORMAL CONTRACT
A contract that by law requires a specific form, such as being executed under seal, for its validity.

KEEP IN MIND Not every contract is a document with "Contract" printed in block letters at the top. A contract can be expressed in a letter, a memo, or another document.

INFORMAL CONTRACT
A contract that does not require a specified form or formality to be valid.

EXPRESS CONTRACT
A contract in which the terms of the agreement are stated in words, oral or written.

IMPLIED-IN-FACT CONTRACT
A contract formed in whole or in part from the conduct of the parties (as opposed to an express contract).

In contract law, offers are normally *revocable* (capable of being taken back, or canceled) until accepted. Under the traditional view of unilateral contracts, Roberta's revocation would terminate the offer. Because of the harsh effect on the offeree of the revocation of an offer to form a unilateral contract, the modern-day view is that once performance has been *substantially* undertaken, the offeror cannot revoke the offer. Thus, in our example, even though Ed has not yet accepted the offer by complete performance, Roberta is prohibited from revoking it. Ed can deliver the boat and bind Roberta to the contract.

Formal versus Informal Contracts　Contracts that require a special form or method of creation (formation) to be enforceable are known as **formal contracts.** Formal contracts include (1) contracts under seal, (2) recognizances, (3) negotiable instruments, and (4) letters of credit.[2]

Contracts under seal are formalized writings with a special seal attached.[3] The significance of the seal has lessened, although about ten states require no consideration for formation of a valid contract when a contract is under seal. A *recognizance* is an acknowledgment in court by a person that he or she will perform some specified obligation or pay a certain sum if he or she fails to perform. One form of recognizance is the surety bond.[4] Another is the personal recognizance bond used as bail in a criminal matter. As will be discussed at length in subsequent chapters, *negotiable instruments* include checks, notes, drafts, and certificates of deposit; letters of credit are agreements to pay contingent on the purchaser's receipt of invoices and bills of lading (documents evidencing receipt of, and title to, goods shipped).

Informal contracts (also called *simple contracts*) include all other contracts. No special form is required (except for certain types of contracts that must be in writing), as the contracts are usually based on their substance rather than their form. Typically, businesspersons put their contracts in writing to ensure that there is some proof of a contract's existence should problems arise.

Express versus Implied Contracts　Contracts may also be formed and categorized as express or implied by the conduct of the parties. We look here at the differences between these two types of contracts.

Express Contracts.　An **express contract** is one in which the terms of the agreement are fully and explicitly stated in words, oral or written. A signed lease for an apartment or a house is an express written contract. If a classmate accepts your offer to sell your textbooks from last semester for $75, an express oral contract has been made.

Implied Contracts.　A contract that is implied from the conduct of the parties is called an **implied-in-fact contract,** or an implied contract. This type of contract differs from an express contract in that the *conduct* of the parties, rather than their words, creates and defines at least some of the terms of the contract.

■ EXAMPLE 7.3　Suppose that you need an accountant to fill out your tax return this year. You look through the Yellow Pages and find an accounting firm located in

---

2. *Restatement (Second) of Contracts,* Section 6.
3. A seal may be actual (made of wax or some other durable substance), impressed on the paper, or indicated simply by the word *seal* or the letters *L.S.* at the end of the document. *L.S.* stands for *locus sigilli,* which means "the place for the seal."
4. An obligation of a party who guarantees that he or she will pay a second party if a third party does not perform.

What determines whether a contract for accounting, tax preparation, or any other service is an express contract or an implied-in-fact contract? (© Getty Images)

your neighborhood. You drop by the firm's office, explain your problem to an accountant, and learn what fees will be charged. The next day you return and give the receptionist all of the necessary information and documents, such as canceled checks, W-2 forms, and so on. Then you walk out the door without saying anything expressly to the receptionist. In this situation, you have entered into an implied-in-fact contract to pay the accountant the usual and reasonable fees for the accounting services. The contract is implied by your conduct. The accountant expects to be paid for completing your tax return. By bringing in the records the accountant will need to do the work, you have implied an intent to pay for the services. ■ (For another example of how an implied-in-fact contract can arise, see this chapter's *Application* feature at the end of this chapter.)

Requirements for an Implied-in-Fact Contract.   For an implied-in-fact contract to arise, certain requirements must be met. Normally, if the following conditions exist, a court will hold that an implied contract was formed:

1 The plaintiff furnished some service or property.
2 The plaintiff expected to be paid for that service or property, and the defendant knew or should have known that payment was expected.
3 The defendant had a chance to reject the services or property and did not.

EXECUTED CONTRACT
A contract that has been completely performed by both parties.

EXECUTORY CONTRACT
A contract that has not as yet been fully performed.

CONTRACT PERFORMANCE

Contracts are also classified according to their state of performance. A contract that has been fully performed on both sides is called an **executed contract.** A contract that has not been fully performed on either side is called an **executory contract.** If one party has fully performed but the other has not, the contract is said to be executed on the one side and executory on the other, but the contract is still classified as executory.

■ EXAMPLE 7.4 Assume that you agree to buy ten tons of coal from Western Coal Company. Further assume that Western has delivered the coal to your steel mill, where it is now being burned. At this point, the contract is an executory contract—it is executed on the part of Western and executory on your part. After you pay Western for the coal, the contract will be executed on both sides. ■

CONTRACT ENFORCEABILITY

VALID CONTRACT
A contract that results when the elements necessary for contract formation (agreement, consideration, legal purpose, and contractual capacity) are present.

A **valid contract** has the four elements necessary for contract formation: (1) an agreement (offer and acceptance) (2) supported by legally sufficient consideration (3) for a legal purpose and (4) made by parties who have the legal capacity to enter into the contract. As mentioned, we will discuss each of these elements in this chapter and the one that follows.

As you can see in Exhibit 7–2, valid contracts may be enforceable, voidable, or unenforceable. Additionally, a contract may be referred to as a *void contract*. We look next at the meaning of the terms *voidable*, *unenforceable*, and *void* in relation to contract enforceability.

VOIDABLE CONTRACT
A contract that may be legally avoided (canceled, or annulled) at the option of one or both of the parties.

Voidable Contracts   A **voidable contract** is a *valid* contract but one that can be avoided at the option of one or both of the parties. The party having the option can elect either to avoid any duty to perform or to *ratify* (make valid) the contract. If the contract is avoided, both parties are released from it. If it is ratified, both parties must fully perform their respective legal obligations.

EXHIBIT 7–2 ENFORCEABLE, VOID, VOIDABLE, AND UNENFORCEABLE CONTRACTS

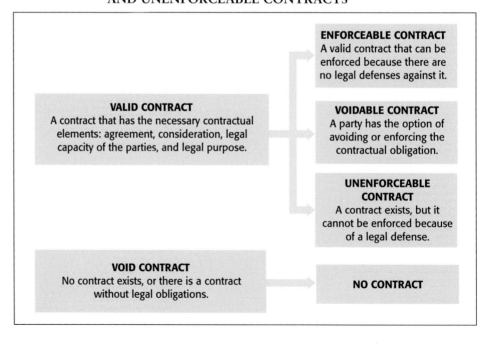

VALID CONTRACT
A contract that has the necessary contractual elements: agreement, consideration, legal capacity of the parties, and legal purpose.

ENFORCEABLE CONTRACT
A valid contract that can be enforced because there are no legal defenses against it.

VOIDABLE CONTRACT
A party has the option of avoiding or enforcing the contractual obligation.

UNENFORCEABLE CONTRACT
A contract exists, but it cannot be enforced because of a legal defense.

VOID CONTRACT
No contract exists, or there is a contract without legal obligations.

NO CONTRACT

As you will read in Chapter 8, contracts made by minors, insane persons, and intoxicated persons may be voidable. As a general rule, for example, contracts made by minors are voidable at the option of the minor. Additionally, contracts entered into under fraudulent conditions are voidable at the option of the defrauded party. Contracts entered into under legally defined duress or undue influence are voidable (see Chapter 8).

UNENFORCEABLE CONTRACT
A valid contract rendered unenforceable by some statute or law.

Unenforceable Contracts   An **unenforceable contract** is one that cannot be enforced because of certain legal defenses against it. It is not unenforceable because a party failed to satisfy a legal requirement of the contract; rather, it is a valid contract rendered unenforceable by some statute or law. For example, some contracts must be in writing (see Chapter 8), and if they are not, they will not be enforceable except in certain exceptional circumstances.

VOID CONTRACT
A contract having no legal force or binding effect.

Void Contracts   A **void contract** is no contract at all. The terms *void* and *contract* are contradictory. None of the parties has any legal obligations if a contract is void. A contract can be void because, for example, one of the parties was previously determined by a court to be legally insane (and thus lacked the legal capacity to enter into a contract) or because the purpose of the contract was illegal.

QUASI CONTRACTS

QUASI CONTRACT
A fictional contract imposed on parties by a court in the interests of fairness and justice; usually imposed to avoid the unjust enrichment of one party at the expense of another.

Quasi contracts, or contracts *implied in law,* are wholly different from actual contracts. Express contracts and implied-in-fact contracts are actual, or true, contracts. The word *quasi* is Latin for "as if" or "analogous to." Quasi contracts are thus not true contracts. They do not arise from any agreement, express or implied, between the parties themselves. Rather, quasi contracts are fictional contracts imposed on parties by courts "as if" the parties had entered into an actual contract. Usually, quasi contracts are imposed to avoid the *unjust enrichment* of one party at the expense of another. The doctrine of unjust enrichment is based on the theory that individuals should not be allowed to profit or enrich themselves inequitably at the expense of others.

■ **EXAMPLE 7.5** Suppose that a vacationing physician is driving down the highway and encounters Emerson, who is lying unconscious on the side of the road. The physician renders medical aid that saves Emerson's life. Although the injured, unconscious Emerson did not solicit the medical aid and was not aware that the aid had been rendered, Emerson received a valuable benefit, and the requirements for a quasi contract were fulfilled. In such a situation, the law normally will impose a quasi contract, and Emerson will have to pay the physician for the reasonable value of the medical services provided. ■

ETHICAL ISSUE 7.1

When does enrichment qualify as "unjust enrichment"? Sometimes a party is enriched by (benefits from) the actions of another, yet the benefits do not necessarily constitute unjust enrichment. For example, in one case the owner of a building (the lessor) leased the building to a commercial tenant (the lessee) for five years. The lessee, which assumed all responsibility for repairs, maintenance, and alterations, hired DCB Construction Company to make alterations to the premises that cost about $300,000. The lessor told DCB that it would not be responsible for any of the costs. Nonetheless, when the lessee quit paying rent, was evicted, and failed to pay DCB for the completed work, DCB sued the lessor for the amount still owing ($280,000). In this case, clearly the lessor had benefited from DCB's work. Yet did this benefit amount to unjust enrichment under the law? No, stated the court. The

A worker takes apart machinery. If the worker, without a contract, makes a design modification that the manufacturer incorporates into later models of the machine, should the worker be compensated? Why or why not? (Billy E. Barnes, PhotoEdit)

AGREEMENT
A meeting of two or more minds in regard to the terms of a contract; usually broken down into two events—an offer by one party to form a contract, and an acceptance of the offer by the person to whom the offer is made.

OFFER
A promise or commitment to perform or refrain from performing some specified act in the future.

court pointed out that DCB did the work for the lessee and was notified by the lessor that it would not be held liable for the costs of the work. Further, no fraud or mistake was involved. The court noted that the courts almost always reject unjust enrichment claims such as this one.[5] ■

Limitations on Quasi-Contractual Recovery Although quasi contracts exist to prevent unjust enrichment, in some situations the party who obtains a benefit will not be deemed to have been unjustly enriched. Basically, the quasi-contractual principle cannot be invoked by a party who has conferred a benefit on someone else unnecessarily or as a result of misconduct or negligence.

■ **EXAMPLE 7.6** You take your car to the local car wash and ask to have it run through the washer and to have the gas tank filled. While your car is being washed, you go to a nearby shopping center for two hours. In the meantime, one of the workers at the car wash mistakenly assumes that your car is the one that he is supposed to hand wax. When you come back, you are presented with a bill for a full tank of gas, a wash job, and a hand wax. Clearly, you have received a benefit, but this benefit was conferred because of a mistake by the car wash employee. You have not been *unjustly* enriched under these circumstances. People normally cannot be forced to pay for benefits "thrust" on them. ■

When a Contract Already Exists The doctrine of quasi contract generally cannot be used when an actual contract covers the area in controversy. This is because a remedy already exists if a party is unjustly enriched as a result of a breach of contract: the nonbreaching party can sue the breaching party for breach of contract. In this instance, a court does not need to impose a quasi contract to achieve justice.

■■ Agreement

An essential element for contract formation is **agreement**—the parties must agree on the terms of the contract. Ordinarily, agreement is evidenced by two events: an *offer* and an *acceptance*. One party offers a certain bargain to another party, who then accepts that bargain.

Because words often fail to convey the precise meaning intended, the law of contracts generally adheres to the *objective theory of contracts*. Under this theory, a party's words and conduct are held to mean whatever a reasonable person in the offeree's position would think they meant. The court will give words their usual meanings even if "it were proved by twenty bishops that [the] party . . . intended something else."[6]

REQUIREMENTS OF THE OFFER

An **offer** is a promise or commitment to perform or refrain from performing some specified act in the future. As discussed earlier, the party making an offer is called the *offeror*, and the party to whom the offer is made is called the *offeree*.

---

5. *DCB Construction Co. v. Central City Development Co.*, 940 P.2d 958 (Colo.App. 1997).
6. Judge Learned Hand in *Hotchkiss v. National City Bank of New York*, 200 F. 287 (2d Cir. 1911); aff'd 231 U.S. 50, 34 S.Ct. 20, 58 L.Ed. 115 (1913). (The term *aff'd* is an abbreviation for *affirmed*; an appellate court can affirm a lower court's judgment, decree, or order, thereby declaring that it is valid and must stand as rendered.)

Three elements are necessary for an offer to be effective:

1 There must be a serious, objective intention by the offeror.

2 The terms of the offer must be reasonably certain, or definite, so that the parties and the court can ascertain the terms of the contract.

3 The offer must be communicated to the offeree.

Once an effective offer has been made, the offeree's acceptance of that offer creates a legally binding contract (providing the other essential elements for a valid and enforceable contract are present).

In today's e-commerce world, offers are frequently made online. Essentially, the requirements for traditional offers apply to online offers as well, as you will read in Chapter 10.

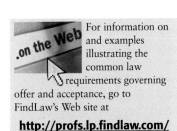 For information on and examples illustrating the common law requirements governing offer and acceptance, go to FindLaw's Web site at **http://profs.lp.findlaw.com/ contracts/index.html**.

Intention   The first requirement for an effective offer to exist is a serious, objective intention on the part of the offeror. Intent is not determined by the *subjective* intentions, beliefs, or assumptions of the offeror. Rather, it is determined by what a reasonable person in the offeree's position would conclude the offeror's words and actions meant. Offers made in obvious anger, jest, or undue excitement do not meet the serious-and-objective-intent test. Because these offers are not effective, an offeree's acceptance does not create an agreement.

■ **EXAMPLE 7.7** You and three classmates ride to school each day in Julio's new automobile, which has a market value of $18,000. One cold morning the four of you get into the car, but Julio cannot get it started. He yells in anger, "I'll sell this car to anyone for $500!" You drop $500 in his lap. A reasonable person, taking into consideration Julio's frustration and the obvious difference in value between the car's market price and the purchase price, would declare that Julio's offer was not made with serious and objective intent and that you do not have an agreement. ■ In the subsections that follow, we further examine the concept of intention as we look at the distinctions between offers and nonoffers.

Lucy v. Zehmer, presented next, is a classic case in the area of contractual agreement. The case involved a business transaction in which boasts, brags, and dares "after a few drinks" resulted in a contract to sell certain property. The sellers claimed that the offer had been made in jest and that, in any event, the contract was voidable at their option because they were intoxicated when the offer was made and thus lacked contractual capacity (see Chapter 8). The court, however, looked to the words and actions of the parties—not their secret intentions—to determine whether a contract had been formed.

LANDMARK AND CLASSIC CASES
CASE 7.2 ■ Lucy v. Zehmer

Supreme Court of Appeals of Virginia, 1954.
196 Va. 493,
84 S.E.2d 516.

FACTS   Lucy and Zehmer had known each other for fifteen to twenty years. For some time, Lucy had been wanting to buy Zehmer's farm. Zehmer had always told Lucy that he was not interested in selling. One night, Lucy stopped in to visit with the Zehmers at a restaurant they operated. Lucy said to Zehmer, "I bet you wouldn't take $50,000 for that place." Zehmer replied, "Yes, I would, too; you wouldn't give fifty." Throughout the evening, the conversation returned to the sale of the farm. At the same time, the parties were drinking whiskey. Eventually, Zehmer wrote up an agreement, on the back of a restaurant check, for the sale of the farm, and he asked his wife

(Continued)

CASE 7.2—Continued

to sign it—which she did. When Lucy brought an action in a Virginia state court to enforce the agreement, Zehmer argued that he had been "high as a Georgia pine" at the time and that the offer had been made in jest: "two dog-goned drunks bluffing to see who could talk the biggest and say the most." Lucy claimed that he had not been intoxicated and did not think Zehmer had been, either, given the way Zehmer handled the transaction. The trial court ruled in favor of the Zehmers, and Lucy appealed.

ISSUE   Can the agreement be avoided on the basis of intoxication?

DECISION   No. The agreement to sell the farm was binding.

REASON   The opinion of the court was that the evidence given about the nature of the conversation, the appearance and completeness of the agreement, and the signing all tended to show that a serious business transaction, not a casual jest, was intended. The court had to look into the objective meaning of the words and acts of the Zehmers: "An agreement or mutual assent is of course essential to a valid contract, but the law imputes to a person an intention corresponding to the reasonable meaning of his words and acts. If his words and acts, judged by a reasonable standard, manifest an intention to agree, it is immaterial what may be the real but unexpressed state of mind."

COMMENTS   *This is a classic case in contract law because it illustrates so clearly the objective theory of contracts with respect to determining whether an offer was intended. Today, the objective theory of contracts continues to be applied by the courts, and* Lucy v. Zehmer *is routinely cited as a significant precedent in this area. Note that in cases involving contracts formed online, the issue of contractual intent rarely arises. Perhaps this is because an online offer is, by definition, "objective" in the sense that it consists of words only—the offeror's physical actions and behavior are not evidenced.*

RELEVANT WEB SITES   *To locate information on the Web concerning* Lucy v. Zehmer, *go to this text's Web site at* **http://blt.westbuslaw.com**, *select "Chapter 7," and click on "URLs for Landmarks."*

Expressions of Opinion.   An expression of opinion is not an offer. It does not evidence an intention to enter into a binding agreement. ■ **EXAMPLE 7.8** In *Hawkins v. McGee,*[7] Hawkins took his son to McGee, a doctor, and asked McGee to operate on the son's hand. McGee said that the boy would be in the hospital three or four days and that the hand would *probably* heal a few days later. The son's hand did not heal for a month, but nonetheless the father did not win a suit for breach of contract. The court held that McGee did not make an offer to heal the son's hand in three or four days. He merely expressed an opinion as to when the hand would heal. ■

Statements of Intention.   A statement of an *intention* to do something in the future is not an offer. ■ **EXAMPLE 7.9** If Ari says, "I *plan* to sell my stock in Novation, Inc., for $150 per share," a contract is not created if John "accepts" and tenders $150 per share for the stock. Ari has merely expressed his intention to enter into a future contract for the sale of the stock. If John accepts and tenders the $150 per share, no contract is formed because a reasonable person would conclude that Ari was only *thinking about* selling his stock, not promising to sell it. ■

BE CAREFUL   An opinion is not an offer and not a contract term. Goods or services can be "perfect" in one party's opinion and "poor" in another's.

Preliminary Negotiations.   A request or invitation to negotiate is not an offer; it only expresses a willingness to discuss the possibility of entering into a contract. Examples are statements such as "Will you sell Forest Acres?" and "I wouldn't sell my car for less than $1,000." A reasonable person in the offeree's position would

---

7. 84 N.H. 114, 146 A. 641 (1929).

not conclude that such a statement evidenced an intention to enter into a binding obligation. Likewise, when the government and private firms need to have construction work done, contractors are invited to submit bids. The *invitation* to submit bids is not an offer, and a contractor does not bind the government or private firm by submitting a bid. (The bids that the contractors submit are offers, however, and the government or private firm can bind the contractor by accepting the bid.)

Advertisements, Catalogues, and Circulars. In general, advertisements, mail-order catalogues, price lists, and circular letters (meant for the general public) are treated as invitations to negotiate, not as offers to form a contract.[8] ▪ **EXAMPLE 7.10** Suppose that you put an ad in the classified section of your local newspaper offering to sell your guitar for $75. Seven people call and "accept" your "offer" before you can remove the ad from the newspaper. If the ad were truly an offer, you would be bound by seven contracts to sell your guitar. Because advertisements are treated as *invitations* to make offers rather than offers, however, you will have seven offers to choose from, and you can accept the best one without incurring any liability for the six you reject. ▪ On some occasions, though, courts have construed advertisements to be offers because the ads contained definite terms that invited acceptance (such as an ad offering a reward for the return of a lost dog).[9]

> **KEEP IN MIND** Advertisements are not binding, but they cannot be deceptive.

Price lists are another form of invitation to negotiate or trade. A seller's price list is not an offer to sell at that price; it merely invites the buyer to offer to buy at that price. In fact, the seller usually puts "prices subject to change" on the price list. Only in rare circumstances will a price quotation be construed as an offer.[10]

ETHICAL ISSUE 7.2

Should promises of prizes made in ads and circulars always be enforced? Businesses and other organizations commonly promote their products or services by offering prizes, rewards, and the like for certain performance. Ordinarily, these ads for prizes present few problems. At times, though, people perform whatever is necessary to win advertised prizes only to learn that the offers were made in jest—that is, the ads' sponsors had no real intention of giving anyone the prizes. Consider an example. PepsiCo launched an ad campaign in which consumers could use "Pepsi Points"—which could be found on specially marked packages of Pepsi or purchased for ten cents each—to obtain T-shirts and other merchandise with the Pepsi logo. One of the ads featured a Harrier fighter jet, which was listed at 7,000,000 Pepsi Points. When a consumer, John Leonard, raised $700,000, purchased 7,000,000 Pepsi Points, and laid claim to the prize, however, PepsiCo contended that the Harrier jet in the commercial was "fanciful" and that the offer was made in jest.

In the lawsuit that followed, the court agreed, stating that "no objective person could reasonably have concluded that the commercial actually offered consumers a Harrier jet."[11] Yet Leonard obviously did draw that conclusion, and in a number of other cases, individuals have undertaken serious efforts to win nonexistent prizes. Some claim that not enforcing such promises is unfair to individuals who rely on the promises, as John Leonard did in the *PepsiCo* case. ▪

---

8. *Restatement (Second) of Contracts,* Section 26, Comment b.

9. The classic example is *Lefkowitz v. Great Minneapolis Surplus Store, Inc.,* 251 Minn. 188, 86 N.W.2d 689 (1957).

10. See, for example, *Fairmount Glass Works v. Grunden-Martin Woodenware Co.,* 106 Ky. 659, 51 S.W. 196 (1899).

11. *Leonard v. PepsiCo,* 88 F.Supp.2d 116 (S.D.N.Y. 1999); aff'd 210 F.3d 88 (2d Cir. 2000).

Auctions.   In an auction, a seller "offers" goods for sale through an auctioneer. This is not, however, an offer to form a contract. Rather, it is an invitation asking bidders to submit offers. In the context of an auction, a bidder is the offeror, and the auctioneer is the offeree. The offer is accepted when the auctioneer strikes the hammer. Before the fall of the hammer, a bidder may revoke (take back) her or his bid, or the auctioneer may reject that bid or all bids. Typically, an auctioneer will reject a bid that is below the price the seller is willing to accept.

When the auctioneer accepts a higher bid, he or she rejects all previous bids. Because rejection terminates an offer (as will be discussed later), those bids represent offers that have been terminated. Thus, if the highest bidder withdraws his or her bid before the hammer falls, none of the previous bids is reinstated. If the bid is not withdrawn or rejected, the contract is formed when the auctioneer announces, "Going once, going twice, sold!" (or something similar) and lets the hammer fall.

Traditionally, auctions have been either "with reserve" or "without reserve." In an auction with reserve, the seller (through the auctioneer) may withdraw the goods at any time before the auctioneer closes the sale by announcement or by the fall of the hammer. All auctions are assumed to be auctions with reserve unless the terms of the auction are explicitly stated to be *without reserve*. In an auction without reserve, the goods cannot be withdrawn by the seller and must be sold to the highest bidder. In auctions with reserve, the seller may reserve the right to confirm or reject the sale even after "the hammer has fallen." In this situation, the seller is obligated to notify those attending the auction that sales of goods made during the auction are not final until confirmed by the seller.[12]

How do these rules apply to an online auction of rights to a domain name? For a discussion of a case involving this issue, see this chapter's *Adapting the Law to the Online Environment* feature.

Agreements to Agree.   Traditionally, agreements to agree—that is, agreements to agree to the material terms of a contract at some future date—were not considered

---

12. These rules apply under both the common law of contracts and the Uniform Commercial Code, or UCC. See UCC 2–328.

In an auction, such as this one in Booneville, Missouri, is the party selling the goods the "offeror" for purposes of contract law? Why or why not? (AP Photo/L.G. Patterson)

ADAPTING THE LAW TO THE ONLINE ENVIRONMENT

Can an Online Bid Constitute an Acceptance?

Under the Uniform Commercial Code, or UCC (see Chapter 11), a bid at an auction constitutes an offer. The offer (the highest bid) is accepted when the auctioneer's hammer falls. The UCC also states that auctions are "with reserve" unless the seller specifies otherwise. As just noted, in an auction with reserve, the seller reserves the right not to sell the goods to the highest bidder. Hence, even after the hammer falls, the contract for sale remains conditioned on the seller's approval. The question of how these rules should be applied to an online auction of a domain name, in which no hammer falls, came before a California court.

THE BID (OR OFFER?)

The case involved an online auction conducted by The.TV Corporation International (DotTV) on its Web site. DotTV posted an announcement on its Web site asking for bids for rights to the "Golf.tv" domain name and stating that the name would go to the highest bidder. Je Ho Lim submitted a bid for $1,010 and authorized DotTV to charge that amount to his credit card if his bid was the highest. Later, DotTV sent Lim an e-mail message stating that he had "won the auction" and charged the bid price of $1,010 to Lim's credit card. When DotTV subsequently refused to transfer the name, Lim sued DotTV for, among other things, breach of contract. Lim argued that his bid constituted an acceptance of DotTV's offer to sell the name. DotTV contended that Lim's bid was an offer, which it had not accepted. Furthermore, even if it had accepted Lim's offer, because the auction was "with reserve," DotTV could withdraw the domain name from the auction even after acceptance. The trial court held for DotTV, and Lim appealed.

THE COURT'S ANALYSIS

The appellate court first looked at the UCC's provisions concerning auctions but noted that the UCC did not apply in this case because the UCC applies only to "goods" and domain names are not goods. The court then looked at common law principles as codified in the *Restatement (Second) of Contracts.* The rules under the *Restatement* are similar to those of the UCC: a bid in an auction is an offer that is accepted when the "hammer falls," and an auction is with reserve unless otherwise specified by the seller.

The court also pointed out, however, that DotTV's charging of the bid price to Lim's credit card was inconsistent with DotTV's claim that it could withdraw the domain name from the bidding because the auction was with reserve. Furthermore, stated the court, even if it concluded that Lim's bid was an offer and not an acceptance, DotTV had accepted the offer by its e-mail to Lim stating that he had won the auction. In all, held the court, there was no evidence that a contract between DotTV and Lim had *not* been formed, and Lim had stated a valid claim against DotTV for breach of contract. The court thus reversed the lower court's decision and remanded the case for further deliberation consistent with the appellate court's opinion.[a]

FOR CRITICAL ANALYSIS

Should the UCC rules governing auctions apply to items sold on online auction sites, such as eBay? Why or why not? How can you know whether eBay's auctions are "with reserve" or "without reserve"?

a. *Lim v. The.TV Corp. International,* 99 Cal.App.4th 684, 121 Cal.Rptr.2d 333 (2d Dist. 2002).

to be binding contracts. The modern view, however, is that agreements to agree may be enforceable agreements (contracts) if it is clear that the parties intend to be bound by the agreements. In other words, under the modern view the emphasis is on the parties' intent rather than on form.

■ EXAMPLE 7.11 When the Pennzoil Company discussed with the Getty Oil Company the possible purchase of Getty's stock, a memorandum of agreement was drafted to reflect the terms of the conversations. After more negotiations over the price, both companies issued press releases announcing an agreement in principle on the terms of the memorandum. The next day, Texaco, Inc., offered to buy all of

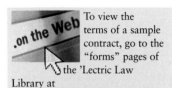

To view the terms of a sample contract, go to the "forms" pages of the 'Lectric Law Library at

http://www.lectlaw.com/ formb.htm

and select one of the types of contracts listed there to review.

Getty's stock at a higher price. The day after that, Getty's board of directors voted to accept Texaco's offer, and Texaco and Getty signed a merger agreement. When Pennzoil sued Texaco for tortious interference with its "contractual" relationship with Getty, a jury concluded that Getty and Pennzoil had intended to form a binding contract, with only the details left to be worked out, before Texaco made its offer. Texaco was held liable for wrongfully interfering with this contract.[13] ■

Definiteness   The second requirement for an effective offer involves the definiteness of its terms. An offer must have reasonably definite terms so that a court can determine if a breach has occurred and give an appropriate remedy.[14]

An offer may invite an acceptance to be worded in such specific terms that the contract is made definite. ■ **EXAMPLE 7.12** Suppose that Marcus Business Machines contacts your corporation and offers to sell "from one to ten MacCool copying machines for $1,600 each; state number desired in acceptance." Your corporation agrees to buy two copiers. Because the quantity is specified in the acceptance, the terms are definite, and the contract is enforceable. ■

Communication   A third requirement for an effective offer is communication— the offer must be communicated to the offeree. ■ **EXAMPLE 7.13** Suppose that Tolson advertises a reward for the return of her lost cat. Dirlik, not knowing of the reward, finds the cat and returns it to Tolson. Ordinarily, Dirlik cannot recover the reward because an essential element of a reward contract is that the one who claims the reward must have known it was offered. A few states would allow recovery of the reward, but not on contract principles—Dirlik would be allowed to recover on the basis that it would be unfair to deny him the reward just because he did not know about it. ■

TERMINATION OF THE OFFER

The communication of an effective offer to an offeree gives the offeree the power to transform the offer into a binding, legal obligation (a contract) by an acceptance. This power of acceptance, however, does not continue forever. It can be terminated by action of the parties or by operation of law.

Termination by Action of the Parties   An offer can be terminated by the action of the parties in any of three ways: by revocation, by rejection, or by counteroffer.

Revocation of the Offer.   The offeror's act of withdrawing an offer is referred to as **revocation.** Unless an offer is irrevocable, the offeror usually can revoke the offer (even if he or she has promised to keep the offer open), as long as the revocation is communicated to the offeree before the offeree accepts. Revocation may be accomplished by an express repudiation of the offer (for example, with a statement such as "I withdraw my previous offer of October 17") or by the performance of acts that are inconsistent with the existence of the offer and that are made known to the offeree.

REVOCATION
In contract law, the withdrawal of an offer by an offeror. Unless the offer is irrevocable, it can be revoked at any time prior to acceptance without liability.

---

13. *Texaco, Inc. v. Pennzoil Co.,* 729 S.W.2d 768 (Tex.App.–Houston [1st Dist.] 1987, writ ref'd n.r.e.). (Generally, a complete Texas Court of Appeals citation includes the writ-of-error history showing the Texas Supreme Court's disposition of the case. In this case, *writ ref'd n.r.e.* is an abbreviation for "writ refused, no reversible error," which means that Texas's highest court refused to grant the appellant's request to review the case, because the court did not think there was any reversible error.)
14. *Restatement (Second) of Contracts,* Section 33. The UCC has relaxed the requirements regarding the definiteness of terms in contracts for the sale of goods. See UCC 2–204(3).

■ EXAMPLE 7.14 Geraldine offers to sell some land to Gary. A week passes, and Gary, who has not yet accepted the offer, learns from his friend Konstantine that Geraldine has in the meantime sold the property to Nunan. Gary's knowledge of Geraldine's sale of the land to Nunan, even though he learned of it through a third party, effectively revokes Geraldine's offer to sell the land to Gary. Geraldine's sale of the land to Nunan is inconsistent with the continued existence of the offer to Gary, and thus the offer to Gary is revoked. ■

The general rule followed by most states is that a revocation becomes effective when the offeree or the offeree's agent (a person who acts on behalf of another) actually receives it. Therefore, a letter of revocation mailed on April 1 and delivered at the offeree's residence or place of business on April 3 becomes effective on April 3.

An offer made to the general public can be revoked in the same manner in which the offer was originally communicated. ■ EXAMPLE 7.15 Suppose that a department store offers a $10,000 reward to anyone giving information leading to the apprehension of the persons who burglarized its downtown store. The offer is published in three local papers and in four papers in neighboring communities. To revoke the offer, the store must publish the revocation in all seven papers for the same number of days it published the offer. The revocation is then accessible to the general public, and the offer is revoked even if some particular offeree does not know about the revocation. ■

Irrevocable Offers.   Although most offers are revocable, some can be made irrevocable. Increasingly, courts refuse to allow an offeror to revoke an offer when the offeree has changed position because of justifiable reliance on the offer (under the doctrine of detrimental reliance, or promissory estoppel, discussed later in this chapter). In some circumstances, "firm offers" made by merchants may also be considered irrevocable. We discuss these offers in Chapter 11.

A poster offers a reward for a missing seven-year-old girl. How can this offer be revoked? (AP Photo/Denis Poroy)

OPTION CONTRACT
A contract under which the offeror cannot revoke his or her offer for a stipulated time period, and the offeree can accept or reject the offer during this period without fear that the offer will be made to another person. The offeree must give consideration for the option (the irrevocable offer) to be enforceable.

Another form of irrevocable offer is an option contract. An **option contract** is created when an offeror promises to hold an offer open for a specified period of time in return for a payment (consideration) given by the offeree. An option contract takes away the offeror's power to revoke an offer for the period of time specified in the option. If no time is specified, then a reasonable period of time is implied. ■ **EXAMPLE 7.16** Suppose that you are in the business of writing movie scripts. Your agent contacts the head of development at New Line Cinema and offers to sell New Line your most recent movie script. New Line likes your script and agrees to pay you $5,000 for a six-month option. In this situation, you (through your agent) are the offeror, and New Line is the offeree. You cannot revoke your offer to sell New Line your script for the next six months. If after six months no contract has been formed, however, New Line loses the $5,000, and you are free to sell your movie script to another firm. ■

Option contracts are also frequently used in conjunction with the sale of real estate. ■ **EXAMPLE 7.17** You might agree with a landowner to lease a home and include in the lease contract a clause stating that you will pay $2,000 for an option to purchase the home within a specified period of time. If you decide not to purchase the home after the specified period has lapsed, you lose the $2,000, and the landlord is free to sell the property to another buyer. ■

BE CARFUL The way in which a response to an offer is phrased can determine whether the offer has legally been accepted or rejected.

Rejection of the Offer by the Offeree.   If the offeree rejects the offer, the offer is terminated. Any subsequent attempt by the offeree to accept will be construed as a new offer, giving the original offeror (now the offeree) the power of acceptance. A rejection is ordinarily accomplished by words or by conduct evidencing an intent not to accept the offer.

As with revocation, rejection of an offer is effective only when it is actually received by the offeror or the offeror's agent. ■ **EXAMPLE 7.18** Suppose that Growgood Farms mails a letter to Campbell Soup Company offering to sell carrots at ten cents a pound. (Of course, today, such offers tend to be sent electronically rather than by mail, as will be discussed in Chapter 10.) Campbell Soup Company could reject the offer by mailing, faxing, or e-mailing a letter to Growgood Farms expressly rejecting the offer, or by returning the offer back to Growgood, evidencing an intent to reject it. Alternatively, Campbell could offer to buy the carrots at eight cents per pound (a counteroffer), necessarily rejecting the original offer. ■

Merely inquiring about an offer does not constitute rejection. ■ **EXAMPLE 7.19** A friend offers to buy your CD-ROM library for $300. You respond, "Is this your best offer?" or "Will you pay me $375 for it?" A reasonable person would conclude that you did not reject the offer but merely made an inquiry for further consideration of the offer. You can still accept and bind your friend to the $300 purchase price. When the offeree merely inquires as to the firmness of the offer, there is no reason to presume that she or he intends to reject it. ■

COUNTEROFFER
An offeree's response to an offer in which the offeree rejects the original offer and at the same time makes a new offer.

Counteroffer by the Offeree.   A **counteroffer** is a rejection of the original offer and the simultaneous making of a new offer. ■ **EXAMPLE 7.20** Suppose that Burke offers to sell his home to Lang for $170,000. Lang responds, "Your price is too high. I'll offer to purchase your house for $165,000." Lang's response is called a counteroffer because it rejects Burke's offer to sell at $170,000 and creates a new offer by Lang to purchase the home at a price of $165,000. ■

MIRROR IMAGE RULE
A common law rule that requires that the terms of the offeree's acceptance adhere exactly to the terms of the offeror's offer for a valid contract to be formed.

At common law, the **mirror image rule** requires that the offeree's acceptance match the offeror's offer exactly. In other words, the terms of the acceptance must "mirror" those of the offer. If the acceptance materially changes or adds to the terms of the original offer, it will be considered not an acceptance but a counteroffer—which, of course, need not be accepted. The original offeror can, however, accept the terms of the counteroffer and create a valid contract.[15]

Termination by Operation of Law   The offeree's power to transform an offer into a binding, legal obligation can be terminated by operation of law if any of four conditions occur: lapse of time, destruction of the specific subject matter, death or incompetence of the offeror or offeree, or supervening illegality of the proposed contract.

Lapse of Time.   An offer terminates automatically by law when the period of time *specified in the offer* has passed. If the offer states that it will be left open until a particular date, then the offer will terminate at midnight on that day. If the offer states that it will be left open for a number of days, such as ten days, this time period normally begins to run when the offer is actually received by the offeree, not when it is formed or sent. When the offer is delayed (through the misdelivery of mail, for example), the period begins to run from the date the offeree would have received the offer, but only if the offeree knows or should know that the offer is delayed.[16]

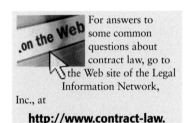

For answers to some common questions about contract law, go to the Web site of the Legal Information Network, Inc., at

http://www.contract-law. com/TheLaw.htm.

■ **EXAMPLE 7.21** Suppose that Beth offers to sell her boat to Jonah, stating that the offer will remain open until May 20. Unless Jonah accepts the offer by midnight on May 20, the offer will lapse (terminate). Now suppose that Beth writes a letter to Jonah, offering to sell him her boat if Jonah accepts the offer within twenty days of the letter's date, which is May 1. Jonah must accept within twenty days after May 1, or the offer will terminate. The same rule would apply even if Beth had used improper postage when mailing the offer, and Jonah received the letter ten days after May 1, not knowing of the improper mailing. If, however, Jonah knew about the improper mailing, the offer would lapse twenty days after the day Jonah ordinarily would have received the offer had Beth used proper postage. ■

If the offer does not specify a time for acceptance, the offer terminates at the end of a *reasonable* period of time. A reasonable period of time is determined by the subject matter of the contract, business and market conditions, and other relevant circumstances. An offer to sell farm produce, for example, will terminate sooner than an offer to sell farm equipment because farm produce is perishable and subject to greater fluctuations in market value.

Destruction of the Subject Matter.   An offer is automatically terminated if the specific subject matter of the offer is destroyed before the offer is accepted. For example, if Bekins offers to sell his prize cow to Yatsen, but the cow is struck by lightning and dies before Yatsen can accept, the offer is automatically terminated. (Note that if Yatsen accepted the offer just before lightning struck the cow, a contract would have been formed, but, because of the cow's death, a court would likely excuse Bekins's obligation to perform the contract on the basis of impossibility of performance—see Chapter 9.)

Death or Incompetence of the Offeror or Offeree.   An offeree's power of acceptance is terminated when the offeror or offeree dies or is deprived of legal capacity to enter

---

15. The mirror image rule has been greatly modified in regard to sales contracts. Section 2–207 [Section 2–206(3) in the 2003 amendments] of the UCC provides that a contract is formed if the offeree makes a definite expression of acceptance (such as signing the form in the appropriate location), even though the terms of the acceptance modify or add to the terms of the original offer (see Chapter 11).
16. *Restatement (Second) of Contracts,* Section 49.

into the proposed contract, *unless the offer is irrevocable.*[17] An offer is personal to both parties and normally cannot pass to the decedent's heirs, guardian, or estate. This rule applies whether or not one party had notice of the death or incompetence of the other party. ■ **EXAMPLE 7.22** Kapola, who is quite ill, writes to her friend Amanda, offering to sell Amanda her grand piano for only $400. That night, Kapola dies. The next day, Amanda, not knowing of Kapola's death, writes a letter to Kapola accepting the offer and enclosing a check for $400. Is there a contract? No. There is no contract because the offer automatically terminated on Kapola's death. ■

Supervening Illegality of the Proposed Contract. A statute or court decision that makes an offer illegal automatically terminates the offer. ■ **EXAMPLE 7.23** If Acme Finance Corporation offers to lend Jack $20,000 at 15 percent annually, and the state legislature enacts a statute prohibiting loans at interest rates greater than 12 percent before Jack can accept, the offer is automatically terminated. (If the statute is enacted after Jack accepts the offer, a valid contract is formed, but the contract may still be unenforceable—see Chapter 8.) ■

ACCEPTANCE

An **acceptance** is a voluntary act by the offeree that shows assent, or agreement, to the terms of an offer. The offeree's act may consist of words or conduct. The acceptance must be unequivocal and must be communicated to the offeror.

Who Can Accept? Generally, a third person cannot substitute for the offeree and effectively accept the offer. After all, the identity of the offeree is as much a condition of a bargaining offer as any other term contained therein. Thus, except in special circumstances, only the person to whom the offer is made or that person's agent can accept the offer and create a binding contract. For example, Lottie makes an offer to Paul. Paul is not interested, but Paul's friend José accepts the offer. No contract is formed.

Unequivocal Acceptance To exercise the power of acceptance effectively, the offeree must accept unequivocally. This is the *mirror image rule* previously discussed. If the acceptance is subject to new conditions or if the terms of the acceptance materially change the original offer, the acceptance may be deemed a counteroffer that implicitly rejects the original offer.

Certain terms, when added to an acceptance, will not qualify the acceptance sufficiently to constitute rejection of the offer. ■ **EXAMPLE 7.24** Suppose that in response to a person offering to sell a painting by a well-known artist, the offeree replies, "I accept; please send a written contract." The offeree is requesting a written contract but is not making it a condition for acceptance. Therefore, the acceptance is effective without the written contract. If the offeree replies, "I accept *if* you send a written contract," however, the acceptance is expressly conditioned on the request for a writing, and the statement is not an acceptance but a counteroffer. (Notice how important each word is!)[18] ■

---

17. *Restatement (Second) of Contracts,* Section 48. If the offer is irrevocable, it is not terminated when the offeror dies. Also, if the offer is such that it can be accepted by the performance of a series of acts, and those acts began before the offeror died, the offeree's power of acceptance is not terminated.

18. As noted in footnote 15, in regard to sales contracts, the UCC provides that an acceptance may still be effective even if some terms are added. The new terms are simply treated as proposals for additions to the contract, unless both parties are merchants—in which case the additional terms (with some exceptions) become part of the contract [UCC 2–207(2)].

ACCEPTANCE
A voluntary act by the offeree that shows assent, or agreement, to the terms of an offer; may consist of words or conduct.

DON'T FORGET When an offer is rejected, it is terminated.

Silence as Acceptance   Ordinarily, silence cannot constitute acceptance, even if the offeror states, "By your silence and inaction, you will be deemed to have accepted this offer." This general rule applies because an offeree should not be put under a burden of liability to act affirmatively in order to reject an offer. No consideration— that is, nothing of value—has passed to the offeree to impose such a liability.

In some instances, however, the offeree does have a duty to speak; if so, his or her silence or inaction will operate as an acceptance. Silence may be an acceptance when an offeree takes the benefit of offered services even though he or she had an opportunity to reject them and knew that they were offered with the expectation of compensation. ■ EXAMPLE 7.25 Suppose that John, a college student who earns extra income by washing store windows, taps on the window of a store and catches the attention of the store's manager. John points to the window and raises his cleaner, signaling that he will be washing the window. The manager does nothing to stop him. Here, the store manager's silence constitutes an acceptance, and an implied-in-fact contract is created. The store is bound to pay a reasonable value for John's work. ■

Silence can also operate as an acceptance when the offeree has had prior dealings with the offeror. If a merchant, for example, routinely receives shipments from a supplier and in the past has always notified the supplier when defective goods are rejected, then silence constitutes acceptance. Also, if a buyer solicits an offer specifying that certain terms and conditions are acceptable, and the seller makes the offer in response to the solicitation, the buyer has a duty to reject—that is, a duty to tell the seller that the offer is not acceptable. Failure to reject (silence) would operate as an acceptance.

Communication of Acceptance   Whether the offeror must be notified of the acceptance depends on the nature of the contract. In a bilateral contract, communication of acceptance is necessary because acceptance is in the form of a promise (not performance), and the contract is formed when the promise is made (rather than when the act is performed). Communication of acceptance is not necessary, however, if the offer dispenses with the requirement. Also, if the offer can be accepted by silence, no communication is necessary.[19]

REMEMBER A bilateral contract is a promise for a promise, and a unilateral contract is performance for a promise.

---

19. Under the UCC, an order or other offer to buy goods that are to be promptly shipped may be treated as either a bilateral or a unilateral offer and can be accepted by a promise to ship or by actual shipment. See UCC 2–206(1)(b).

This photo shows a letter from a DVD club that was sent to a club member. If the recipient (offeree) does nothing, has he or she accepted the offer? Why or why not?

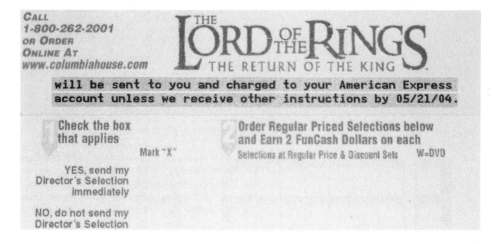

CALL
1-800-262-2001
OR ORDER
ONLINE AT
www.columbiahouse.com

THE LORD OF THE RINGS
THE RETURN OF THE KING

will be sent to you and charged to your American Express
account unless we receive other instructions by 05/21/04.

Check the box
that applies   Order Regular Priced Selections below
                                      and Earn 2 FunCash Dollars on each
                    Mark "X"   Selections at Regular Price & Discount Sets   W=DVD

YES, send my
Director's Selection
immediately

NO, do not send my
Director's Selection

In a unilateral contract, the full performance of some act is called for; therefore, acceptance is usually evident, and notification is unnecessary. Exceptions do exist, however. When the offeror requests notice of acceptance or has no adequate means of determining whether the requested act has been performed, or when the law (such as Article 2 of the UCC) requires notice of acceptance, then notice is necessary.[20]

Mode and Timeliness of Acceptance   The general rule is that acceptance in a bilateral contract is timely if it is effected within the duration of the offer. Problems arise, however, when the parties involved are not dealing face to face. In such situations, the offeree may use an authorized mode of communication.

The Mailbox Rule.   Acceptance takes effect, thus completing formation of the contract, at the time the offeree sends or delivers the communication via the mode expressly or impliedly authorized by the offeror. This is the so-called **mailbox rule**, also called the "deposited acceptance rule," which the majority of courts uphold. Under this rule, if the authorized mode of communication is the mail, then an acceptance becomes valid when it is dispatched (placed in the control of the U.S. Postal Service)—*not* when it is received by the offeror.

The mailbox rule was formed to prevent the confusion that arises when an offeror sends a letter of revocation but, before it arrives, the offeree sends a letter of acceptance. Thus, whereas a revocation becomes effective only when it is *received* by the offeree, an acceptance becomes effective on *dispatch* (even if it is never received), provided that an *authorized* means of communication is used.

Authorized Means of Communication.   Authorized means of communicating an acceptance can be either expressly authorized—that is, expressly stipulated in the offer—or impliedly authorized by facts or law.[21] An acceptance sent by means not expressly or impliedly authorized is normally not effective until it is received by the offeror.

When an offeror specifies how acceptance should be made (for example, by first class mail or express delivery), *express authorization* is said to exist. Moreover, both the offeror and the offeree are bound in contract the moment that such means of acceptance are employed. Most offerors do not expressly specify the means by which the offeree is to accept. Thus, the common law recognizes the following implied authorized means of acceptance:[22]

1 The offeror's choice of a particular means in making the offer implies that the offeree is authorized to use the same *or a faster* means for acceptance.

2 When two parties are at a distance, mailing is impliedly authorized.

Exceptions.   There are three basic exceptions to the rule that a contract is formed when acceptance is sent by authorized means:

---

20. UCC 2–206(2).

21. *Restatement (Second) of Contracts,* Section 30, provides that an offer invites acceptance "by any medium reasonable in the circumstances," unless the offer is specific about the means of acceptance. Under Section 65, a medium is reasonable if it is one used by the offeror or one customary in similar transactions, unless the offeree knows of circumstances that would argue against the reasonableness of a particular medium (the need for speed because of rapid price changes, for example).

22. Note that UCC 2–206(1)(a) states specifically that an acceptance of an offer for the sale of goods can be made by any medium that is *reasonable* under the circumstances.

MAILBOX RULE
A rule providing that an acceptance of an offer becomes effective on dispatch (on being placed in an official mailbox), if mail is, expressly or impliedly, an authorized means of communication of acceptance to the offeror.

If an offer expressly authorizes acceptance of the offer by first-class mail or express delivery, can the offeree accept by a faster means, such as by fax or e-mail? Why or why not? (© Michael Newman, PhotoEdit)

CONSIDERATION
Generally, the value given in return for a promise. The consideration must result in a detriment to the promisee (something of legally sufficient value and bargained for) or a benefit to the promisor.

FORBEARANCE
The act of refraining from an action that one has a legal right to undertake.

1 If the acceptance is not properly dispatched (if a letter is incorrectly addressed, for example, or lacks the proper postage), in most states it will not be effective until it is received by the offeror.

2 The offeror can stipulate in the offer that an acceptance will not be effective until it is received (usually by a specified time) by the offeror.

3 Sometimes an offeree sends a rejection first, then later changes his or her mind and sends an acceptance. Obviously, this chain of events could cause confusion and even detriment to the offeror, depending on whether the rejection or the acceptance arrived first. In such situations, the law cancels the rule of acceptance on dispatch, and the first communication received by the offeror determines whether a contract is formed. If the rejection arrives first, there is no contract.[23]

Technology and Acceptances Technology, and particularly the Internet, has all but eliminated the need for the mailbox rule because online acceptances typically are communicated instantaneously to the offeror. As you will learn in Chapter 10, while online offers are not significantly different from traditional offers contained in paper documents, online acceptances have posed some unusual problems.

▣ Consideration

In every legal system, some promises will be enforced, and other promises will not be enforced. The simple fact that a party has made a promise, then, does not mean the promise is enforceable. Under the common law, a primary basis for the enforcement of promises is consideration. **Consideration** is usually defined as the value given in return for a promise. We look here at the basic elements of consideration and then at some other contract doctrines relating to consideration.

ELEMENTS OF CONSIDERATION

Often, consideration is broken down into two parts: (1) something of *legally sufficient value* must be given in exchange for the promise, and (2) there must be a *bargained-for exchange*.

Legal Value The "something of legally sufficient value" may consist of (1) a promise to do something that one has no prior legal duty to do (to pay money on receipt of certain goods, for example), (2) the performance of an action that one is otherwise not obligated to undertake (such as providing accounting services), or (3) the refraining from an action that one has a legal right to undertake (called a **forbearance**).

---

23. *Restatement (Second) of Contracts*, Section 40.

Consideration in bilateral contracts normally consists of a promise in return for a promise, as explained earlier in this chapter. ■ **EXAMPLE 7.26** Suppose that in a contract for the sale of goods, the seller promises to ship specific goods to the buyer, and the buyer promises to pay for those goods when they are received. Each of these promises constitutes consideration for the contract. ■ In contrast, unilateral contracts involve a promise in return for a performance. ■ **EXAMPLE 7.27** Suppose that Anita says to her neighbor, "If you paint my garage, I will pay you $100." Anita's neighbor paints the garage. The act of painting the garage is the consideration that creates Anita's contractual obligation to pay her neighbor $100. ■

What if, in return for a promise to pay, a person forbears to pursue harmful habits, such as the use of tobacco and alcohol? Does such forbearance create consideration for the contract? This was the issue before the court in *Hamer v. Sidway*, a classic case concerning consideration that we present as this chapter's *Landmark in the Law* feature.

Bargained-for Exchange The second element of consideration is that it must provide the basis for the bargain struck between the contracting parties. The promise given by the promisor must induce the promisee to incur a legal detriment either now or in the future, and the detriment incurred must induce the promisor to make the promise. This element of bargained-for exchange distinguishes contracts from gifts.

■ **EXAMPLE 7.28** Suppose that Roberto says to his son, "In consideration of the fact that you are not as wealthy as your brothers, I will pay you $500." This promise is not enforceable because Roberto's son has not given any return consideration for the $500 promised.[24] The son (the promisee) incurs no legal detriment; he does not have to promise anything or undertake (or refrain from undertaking) any action to receive the $500. Here, Roberto has simply stated his motive for giving his son a gift. The fact that the word *consideration* is used does not, by itself, mean that consideration has been given. ■

LEGAL SUFFICIENCY AND ADEQUACY OF CONSIDERATION

Legal sufficiency of consideration involves the requirement that consideration be something of value in the eyes of the law. Adequacy of consideration involves "how much" consideration is given. Essentially, adequacy of consideration concerns the fairness of the bargain. On the surface, fairness would appear to be an issue when the items exchanged are of unequal value. In general, however, courts do not question the adequacy of consideration if the consideration is legally sufficient. Under the doctrine of freedom of contract, parties are usually free to bargain as they wish. If people could sue merely because they had entered into an unwise contract, the courts would be overloaded with frivolous suits.

In extreme cases, however, a court of law may look to the amount or value (the adequacy) of the consideration because apparently inadequate consideration can indicate that fraud, duress, or undue influence was involved or that a gift was made (if a father "sells" a $100,000 house to his daughter for only $1, for example). Additionally, when the consideration is grossly inadequate, the courts may declare the contract unenforceable on the ground that it is *unconscionable*,[25] meaning that, generally speaking, it is so one sided under the circumstances as to be clearly unfair. (Unconscionability will be discussed further in Chapter 8.)

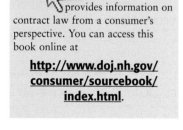

.on the Web The New Hampshire Consumer's Sourcebook provides information on contract law from a consumer's perspective. You can access this book online at **http://www.doj.nh.gov/ consumer/sourcebook/ index.html**.

BE AWARE A consumer's signature on a contract does not always guarantee that the contract will be enforced. Ultimately, the terms must be fair.

---

24. See *Fink v. Cox*, 18 Johns. 145, 9 Am.Dec. 191 (N.Y. 1820).
25. Pronounced un-*kon*-shun-uh-bul.

LANDMARK IN THE LAW   *Hamer v. Sidway* (1891)

In *Hamer v. Sidway,*[a] the issue before the court arose from a contract created in 1869 between William Story, Sr., and his nephew, William Story II. The uncle promised his nephew that if the nephew refrained from drinking alcohol, using tobacco, and playing billiards and cards for money until he reached the age of twenty-one, the uncle would pay him $5,000 (about $75,000 in today's dollars). The nephew, who indulged occasionally in all of these "vices," agreed to refrain from them and did so for the next six years. Following his twenty-first birthday in 1875, the nephew wrote to his uncle that he had performed his part of the bargain and was thus entitled to the promised $5,000. A few days later, the uncle wrote the nephew a letter stating, "[Y]ou shall have the five thousand dollars, as I promised you." The uncle said that the money was in the bank and that the nephew could "consider this money on interest."

THE ISSUE OF CONSIDERATION   The nephew left the funds in the care of his uncle, who held it for the next twelve years. When the uncle died in 1887, however, the executor of the uncle's estate refused to pay the $5,000 claim brought by Hamer, a third party to whom the promise had been *assigned*. (The law allows parties to assign, or transfer, rights in contracts to third parties; see Chapter 9.) The executor, Sidway, contended that the contract was invalid because there was insufficient consideration to support it. The uncle had received nothing, and the nephew had actually benefited by fulfilling the uncle's wishes. Therefore, no contract existed.

THE COURT'S CONCLUSION   Although a lower court upheld Sidway's position, the New York Court of Appeals reversed and ruled in favor of the plaintiff, Hamer. "The promisee used tobacco, occasionally drank liquor, and he had a legal right to do so," the court stated. "That right he abandoned for a period of years upon the strength of the promise of the testator [one who makes a will] that for such forbearance he would give him $5,000. We need not speculate on the effort which may have been required to give up the use of those stimulants. It is sufficient that he restricted his lawful freedom of action within certain prescribed limits upon the faith of his uncle's agreement."

APPLICATION TO TODAY'S WORLD

Although this case was decided over a century ago, the principles enunciated by the court remain applicable to contracts formed today, including online contracts. For a contract to be valid and binding, consideration must be given, and that consideration must be something of legally sufficient value.

RELEVANT WEB SITES

To locate information on the Web concerning the Hamer v. Sidway *decision, go to this text's Web site at* **http://blt.westbuslaw.com,** *select "Chapter 7," and click on "URLs for Landmarks."*

a. 124 N.Y. 538, 27 N.E. 256 (1891).

In the following case, the issue was whether consideration existed in a contract to accept lower payments for medical services than the maximum fees allowed under state regulations.

CASE 7.3 Seaview Orthopaedics v. National Healthcare Resources, Inc.

Superior Court of New Jersey,
Appellate Division, 2004.
366 N.J.Super. 501, 841 A.2d 917.
http://lawlibrary.rutgers.edu/search.shtml [a]

FACTS Consumer Health Network (CHN) is a large medical-insurance preferred provider organization (PPO) in New Jersey. CHN provides medical services providers (its clients) with a PPO network in three distinct areas: workers' compensation, group health benefits, and auto insurance. The network includes over 11,000 physicians and nearly 14,000 medical services providers (which include physicians, laboratories, and hospitals). By entering into a contract with CHN, a medical services provider gains potential access to 950,000 enrollees in exchange for accepting reimbursement at rates lower than the maximum rates permitted by New Jersey state regulations. Seaview Orthopaedics is a CHN client that renders services to auto accident victims insured by Allstate Indemnity Company. Allstate pays the CHN rates for Seaview's services through Allstate's claims administrator, National Healthcare Resources (NHR). Seaview and others filed a suit in a New Jersey state court against NHR and others to recover the difference between the CHN rates and the state's maximum rates. The court issued a summary judgment in favor of the defendants. The plaintiffs appealed to a state intermediate appellate court, claiming that the CHN contract was not enforceable, in part because it lacked consideration.

ISSUE Did the CHN contract lack consideration?

a. Click on "Search by Party Name." On that page, select "Appellate Division" as the court, and type "Seaview Orthopaedics" in the "First Name" box. Click on "Submit Form" to view a synopsis of the case, and then "click here to get this case" to read the opinion. Rutgers University School of Law in Camden, New Jersey, maintains this Web site.

DECISION No. The state intermediate appellate court affirmed the lower court's summary judgment.

REASON The court acknowledged that contracts are not enforceable in the absence of consideration—that is, both sides must get something out of the exchange. The court explained, however, that the determination of whether consideration exists does not depend on the comparative value of the things exchanged. Instead, stated the court, the consideration must merely be valuable in the sense that it is something that is bargained for in fact. The court noted, "Here, the contract provided benefits to plaintiffs in a variety of ways which either collectively or separately constituted valuable consideration for plaintiffs' promise to accept the CHN rates for reimbursement from auto accident victims (and other types of patients) and not the maximum rate permitted by the [state's] schedule. Plaintiffs, for example, obtained the benefit of marketing their businesses in a directory of providers utilized by numerous payors in the workers' compensation and health benefits markets and many thousands of potential patients. Payors make the list available to the largest PPO membership network in New Jersey and, in the health and workers' compensation settings, are generally offered substantial financial incentives when those patients use the providers on the list." The court concluded that it is the totality of the exchange of promises and benefits that must be considered, and in this case, the exchange was sufficient to create an enforceable contract.

WHY IS THIS CASE IMPORTANT? *As this case illustrates, something need not be of direct economic or financial value to be considered legally sufficient consideration. In many situations, as here, the exchange of promises and potential benefits is deemed sufficient as consideration.*

CONTRACTS THAT LACK CONSIDERATION

Sometimes, one or both of the parties to a contract may think that they have exchanged consideration when in fact they have not. Here we look at some situations in which the parties' promises or actions do not qualify as contractual consideration.

Preexisting Duty Under most circumstances, a promise to do what one already has a legal duty to do does not constitute legally sufficient consideration because no legal detriment is incurred.[26] The preexisting legal duty may be imposed by law or may arise out of a previous contract. A sheriff, for example, cannot collect a reward for information leading to the capture of a criminal if the sheriff already has a legal duty to capture the criminal. Likewise, if a party is already bound by contract to perform a certain duty, that duty cannot serve as consideration for a second contract.

■ **EXAMPLE 7.29** Suppose that Bauman-Bache, Inc., begins construction on a seven-story office building and after three months demands an extra $75,000 on its contract. If the extra $75,000 is not paid, it will stop working. The owner of the land, having no one else to complete construction, agrees to pay the extra $75,000. The agreement is not enforceable because it is not supported by legally sufficient consideration; Bauman-Bache had a preexisting contractual duty to complete the building. ■

Unforeseen Difficulties.   The rule regarding preexisting duty is meant to prevent extortion and the so-called holdup game. What happens, though, when an honest contractor, who has contracted with a landowner to build a house, runs into extraordinary difficulties that were totally unforeseen at the time the contract was formed? In the interests of fairness and equity, the courts sometimes allow exceptions to the preexisting duty rule. In the example just mentioned, if the landowner agrees to pay extra compensation to the contractor for overcoming the unforeseen difficulties (such as having to use dynamite and special equipment to remove an unexpected rock formation to excavate for a basement), the court may refrain from applying the preexisting duty rule and enforce the agreement. When the "unforeseen difficulties" that give rise to a contract modification are the types of risks ordinarily assumed in business, however, the courts will usually assert the preexisting duty rule.[27]

Rescission and New Contract.   The law recognizes that two parties can mutually agree to rescind their contract, at least to the extent that it is executory (still to be carried out). **Rescission**[28] is defined as the unmaking of a contract so as to return the parties to the positions they occupied before the contract was made. When rescission and the making of a new contract take place at the same time, the courts frequently are given a choice of applying the preexisting duty rule or allowing rescission and letting the new contract stand.

Past Consideration   Promises made in return for actions or events that have already taken place are unenforceable. These promises lack consideration in that the element of bargained-for exchange is missing. In short, you can bargain for something to take place now or in the future but not for something that has already taken place. Therefore, **past consideration** is no consideration.

■ **EXAMPLE 7.30** Suppose that Elsie, a real estate agent, does her friend Judy a favor by selling Judy's house and not charging any commission. Later, Judy says to Elsie, "In return for your generous act, I will pay you $3,000." This promise is made in return for past consideration and is thus unenforceable; in effect, Judy is stating her intention to give Elsie a gift. ■

To learn more about how the courts decide such issues as whether consideration was lacking for a particular contract, look at relevant case law, which can be accessed through the Web site of Cornell University's School of Law at

http://www.law.cornell.edu/ topics/contracts.html.

RESCISSION
A remedy whereby a contract is canceled and the parties are returned to the positions they occupied before the contract was made; may be effected through the mutual consent of the parties, by the parties' conduct, or by court decree.

PAST CONSIDERATION
An act that takes place before the contract is made and that ordinarily, by itself, cannot be consideration for a later promise to pay for the act.

---

26. See *Foakes v. Beer*, 9 App.Cas. 605 (1884).

27. Note that under the UCC, any agreement modifying a contract within Article 2 on Sales needs no consideration to be binding. See UCC 2–209(1).

28. Pronounced reh-*sih*-zhen.

Illusory Promises   If the terms of the contract express such uncertainty of performance that the promisor has not definitely promised to do anything, the promise is said to be *illusory*—without consideration and unenforceable. ■ **EXAMPLE 7.31** The president of Tuscan Corporation says to his employees, "All of you have worked hard, and if profits remain high, a 10 percent bonus at the end of the year will be given—if management thinks it is warranted." This is an *illusory promise,* or no promise at all, because performance depends solely on the discretion of the president (the management). There is no bargained-for consideration. The statement declares merely that management may or may not do something in the future. ■

Option-to-cancel clauses in contracts for specified time periods sometimes present problems in regard to consideration. ■ **EXAMPLE 7.32** Abe contracts to hire Chris for one year at $5,000 per month, reserving the right to cancel the contract at any time. On close examination of these words, you can see that Abe has not actually agreed to hire Chris, as Abe could cancel without liability before Chris started performance. Abe has not given up the opportunity of hiring someone else. This contract is therefore illusory. Now suppose that Abe contracts to hire Chris for a one-year period at $5,000 per month, reserving the right to cancel the contract at any time after Chris has begun performance by giving Chris thirty days' notice. Abe, by saying that he will give Chris thirty days' notice, is relinquishing the opportunity (legal right) to hire someone else instead of Chris for a thirty-day period. If Chris works for one month, at the end of which Abe gives him thirty days' notice, Chris has a valid and enforceable contractual claim for $10,000 in salary. ■

SETTLEMENT OF CLAIMS

Businesspersons or others can settle legal claims in several ways. It is important to understand the nature of the consideration given in these settlement agreements, or contracts. Claims are commonly settled through an *accord and satisfaction,* in which a debtor offers to pay a lesser amount than the creditor purports to be owed. Two other methods that are also often used to settle claims are the *release* and the *covenant not to sue.*

ACCORD AND SATISFACTION
A common means of settling a disputed claim, in which a debtor offers to pay a lesser amount than the creditor purports to be owed. The creditor's acceptance of the offer creates an accord (agreement), and when the accord is executed, satisfaction occurs.

REMEMBER Businesspersons should consider settling potential legal disputes to save both their own time and resources and those of the courts.

Accord and Satisfaction   In an **accord and satisfaction,** a debtor offers to pay, and a creditor accepts, a lesser amount than the creditor originally claimed was owed. Thus, in an accord and satisfaction, the debtor attempts to terminate an existing obligation. The *accord* is the settlement agreement. In an accord, the debtor offers to give or perform something less than the parties originally agreed on, and the creditor accepts that offer in satisfaction of the claim. *Satisfaction* is the performance (usually payment), which takes place after the accord is executed. A basic rule is that there can be no satisfaction unless there is first an accord.

For accord and satisfaction to occur, the amount of the debt *must be in dispute.* If a debt is *liquidated,* accord and satisfaction cannot take place. A debt is liquidated if its amount has been ascertained, fixed, agreed on, settled, or exactly determined. An example of a liquidated debt is a loan contract in which the borrower agrees to pay a stipulated amount every month until the amount of the loan is paid. In the majority of states, acceptance of (an accord for) a lesser sum than the entire amount of a liquidated debt is not satisfaction, and the balance of the debt is still legally owed. The rationale for this rule is that the debtor has given no consideration to satisfy the obligation of paying the balance to the creditor—because the debtor has a preexisting legal obligation to pay the entire debt.

An *unliquidated debt* is the opposite of a liquidated debt. Here, reasonable persons may differ over the amount owed. It is not settled, fixed, agreed on, ascertained, or determined. In these circumstances, acceptance of payment of the lesser sum operates as a satisfaction, or discharge, of the debt. One argument to support this rule is that the parties give up a legal right to contest the amount in dispute, and thus consideration is given.

RELEASE
A contract in which one party forfeits the right to pursue a legal claim against the other party.

Release   A **release** is a contract in which one party forfeits the right to pursue a legal claim against the other party. Releases will generally be binding if they are (1) given in good faith, (2) stated in a signed writing (required by many states), and (3) accompanied by consideration.[29] Clearly, parties are better off if they know the extent of their injuries or damages before signing releases.

■ EXAMPLE 7.33 Suppose that you are involved in an automobile accident caused by Raoul's negligence. Raoul offers to give you $1,000 if you will release him from further liability resulting from the accident. You believe that this amount will cover your damages, so you agree to and sign the release. Later you discover that the repairs to your car will cost $1,200. Can you collect the balance from Raoul? The answer is normally no; you are limited to the $1,000 in the release. Why? The reason is that a valid contract existed. You and Raoul both assented to the bargain (hence, agreement existed), and sufficient consideration was present. Your consideration for the contract was the legal detriment you suffered (by releasing Raoul from liability, you forfeited your right to sue to recover damages, should they be more than $1,000). This legal detriment was induced by Raoul's promise to give you the $1,000. Raoul's promise was, in turn, induced by your promise not to pursue your legal right to sue him for damages. ■

 You can find a copy of a release form and the information that should be included in a release by going to

http://www.nolo.com/ category/cm_home.html

and clicking on "Release from Legal Claims" in the right-hand column of the page.

Covenant Not to Sue   Unlike a release, a **covenant not to sue** does not always bar further recovery. The parties simply substitute a contractual obligation for some other type of legal action based on a valid claim. Suppose (following the earlier example) that you agree with Raoul not to sue for damages in a tort action if he will pay for the damage to your car. If Raoul fails to pay, you can bring an action for breach of contract.

COVENANT NOT TO SUE
An agreement to substitute a contractual obligation for some other type of legal action based on a valid claim.

PROMISSORY ESTOPPEL

Sometimes individuals rely on promises, and such reliance may form a basis for contract rights and duties. Under the doctrine of **promissory estoppel** (also called *detrimental reliance*), a person who has reasonably relied on the promise of another can often obtain some measure of recovery. When the doctrine of promissory estoppel is applied, the promisor (the offeror) is **estopped** (barred, or impeded) from revoking the promise. For the doctrine of promissory estoppel to be applied, the following elements are required:

PROMISSORY ESTOPPEL
A doctrine that applies when a promisor makes a clear and definite promise on which the promisee justifiably relies; such a promise is binding if justice will be better served by the enforcement of the promise.

ESTOPPED
Barred, impeded, or precluded.

■ There must be a clear and definite promise.

■ The promisee must justifiably rely on the promise.

■ The reliance normally must be of a substantial and definite character.

■ Justice will be better served by the enforcement of the promise.

---

29. Under the UCC, a written, signed waiver or renunciation by an aggrieved party discharges any further liability for a breach, even without consideration [UCC 1–107].

■ **EXAMPLE 7.34** Your uncle tells you, "I'll pay you $150 a week so you won't have to work anymore." In reliance on your uncle's promise, you quit your job, but your uncle refuses to pay you. Under the doctrine of promissory estoppel, you may be able to enforce his promise.[30] Now your uncle makes a promise to give you $10,000 to buy a car. If you buy the car with your own funds and he does not pay you, you may once again be able to enforce the promise under this doctrine. ■

---

30. A classic example is *Ricketts v. Scothorn,* 57 Neb. 51, 77 N.W. 365 (1898).

APPLICATION ■ How Can You Avoid Unintended Employment Contracts?*

Employers have learned many lessons from court decisions. In recent years, for example, the message has been clear that employers should be cautious about what they say in their employment manuals.

EMPLOYMENT MANUALS AND IMPLIED-IN-FACT CONTRACTS

Promises made in an employment manual may create an implied-in-fact employment contract. If an employment handbook states that employees will be fired only for specific causes, the employer may be held to that "promise." Even if, by state law, employment is "at will"—that is, the employer is allowed to hire and fire employees at will, with or without cause (see Chapter 18)—the at-will doctrine will not apply if the terms of employment are subject to a contract between the employer and the employee. If a court holds that an implied employment contract exists—on the basis of promises made in an employment manual—the employment is no longer at will. The employer will be bound by the contract and liable for damages for breaching the contract.

TAKING PRECAUTIONS

Employers who wish to avoid potential liability for breaching unintended employment contracts should therefore make it clear to employees that the policies expressed in an employment manual are not to be interpreted as contractual promises. An effective way to do this is to inform employees, when initially giving them the handbook or discussing its contents with them, that the handbook is not intended as

a contract and to include a disclaimer to that effect in the employment manual. The disclaimer might read as follows: "This policy manual describes the basic personnel policies and practices of our Company. You should understand that the manual does not modify our Company's 'at will' employment doctrine or provide employees with any kind of contractual rights."

The employer should make the disclaimer clear and prominent so that the applicant cannot later claim that it was the employer's fault that the employee did not see the disclaimer. A disclaimer will be clear and prominent if it is set off from the surrounding text by the use of larger type, a different color, all capital letters, or some other device that calls the reader's attention to it.

In the handbook, the employer should also avoid making definite promises that employees will be fired only for cause, that after they have worked for a certain length of time they will not be fired except for specific reasons, or the like. The handbook itself should include a clear and prominent disclaimer of contractual liability for its contents.

CHECKLIST FOR THE EMPLOYER

1. Inform new employees that statements in an employment handbook are not intended as contractual terms.
2. Include a clear and prominent disclaimer to this effect in employment applications.
3. Avoid including in the handbook any definite promises relating to job security, and include a clear and prominent disclaimer of contractual liability for any statements made within the handbook.

* This *Application* is not meant to substitute for the services of an attorney who is licensed to practice law in your state.

▦ KEY TERMS

CHAPTER SUMMARY ▦ Contracts: Nature, Classification, Agreement, and Consideration

The Nature and Function of Contracts (See pages 202–203.)	Contract law establishes what kinds of promises will be legally binding and supplies procedures for enforcing legally binding promises, or agreements. A contract is defined as an agreement that can be enforced in court. It is formed by two or more competent parties who agree to perform or to refrain from performing some act now or in the future. For a contract to exist, the following requirements must be met: 1. *Elements of a valid contract*—Agreement, consideration, contractual capacity, and legality. 2. *Possible defenses to the enforcement of a contract*—Genuineness of assent and form.
Types of Contracts (See pages 204–210.)	1. *Bilateral*—A promise for a promise. 2. *Unilateral*—A promise for an act (acceptance is the completed—or substantial—performance of the contract by the offeree). 3. *Formal*—Requires a special form for contract formation. 4. *Informal*—Requires no special form for contract formation. 5. *Express*—Formed by words (oral, written, or a combination). 6. *Implied in fact*—Formed at least in part by the conduct of the parties. 7. *Executed*—A fully performed contract. 8. *Executory*—A contract not yet fully performed. 9. *Valid*—A contract that has the necessary contractual elements of offer and acceptance, consideration, parties with legal capacity, and having been made for a legal purpose. 10. *Voidable*—A contract in which a party has the option of avoiding or enforcing the contractual obligation. 11. *Unenforceable*—A valid contract that cannot be enforced because of a legal defense. 12. *Void*—No contract exists, or there is a contract without legal obligations. 13. *Quasi contract*—A quasi contract, or a contract implied in law, is a contract that is imposed by law to prevent unjust enrichment.

(Continued)

CHAPTER SUMMARY ▣ Contracts: Nature, Classification, Agreement, and Consideration—Continued

Requirements of the Offer (See pages 210–216.)	1. *Intent*—There must be a serious, objective intention by the offeror to become bound by the offer. Nonoffer situations include (a) expressions of opinion; (b) statements of intention; (c) preliminary negotiations; (d) generally, advertisements, catalogues, price lists, and circulars; (e) solicitations for bids made by an auctioneer; and (f) traditionally, agreements to agree in the future. 2. *Definiteness*—The terms of the offer must be sufficiently definite to be ascertainable by the parties or by a court. 3. *Communication*—The offer must be communicated to the offeree.

Termination of the Offer (See pages 216–220.)	1. *By action of the parties*—
	
	  a. Revocation—Unless the offer is irrevocable, it can be revoked at any time before acceptance without liability. Revocation is not effective until received by the offeree or the offeree's agent. Some offers, such as a merchant's firm offer and option contracts, are irrevocable.
	
	  b. Rejection—Accomplished by words or actions that demonstrate a clear intent not to accept the offer; not effective until received by the offeror or the offeror's agent.
	
	  c. Counteroffer—A rejection of the original offer and the making of a new offer.
	
	2. *By operation of law*—
	
	  a. Lapse of time—The offer terminates (1) at the end of the time period specified in the offer or (2) if no time period is stated in the offer, at the end of a reasonable time period.
	
	  b. Destruction of the specific subject matter of the offer—Automatically terminates the offer.
	
	  c. Death or incompetence—Terminates the offer unless the offer is irrevocable.
	
	  d. Illegality—Supervening illegality terminates the offer.

Acceptance (See pages 220–223.)	1. Can be made only by the offeree or the offeree's agent.
	
	2. Must be unequivocal. Under the common law (mirror image rule), if new terms or conditions are added to the acceptance, it will be considered a counteroffer.
	
	3. Acceptance of a unilateral offer is effective on full performance of the requested act. Generally, no communication is necessary.
	
	4. Acceptance of a bilateral offer can be communicated by the offeree by any authorized mode of communication and is effective on dispatch. Unless the mode of communication is expressly specified by the offeror, the following methods are impliedly authorized:
	
	  a. The same mode used by the offeror or a faster mode.
	
	  b. Mail, when the two parties are at a distance.
	
	  c. In sales contracts, by any reasonable medium.

Elements of Consideration (See pages 223–224.)	Consideration is broken down into two parts: (1) something of *legally sufficient value* must be given in exchange for the promise, and (2) there must be a *bargained-for exchange*.
Adequacy of Consideration (See pages 224–226.)	Legal sufficiency of consideration relates to the first element of consideration—something of legal value must be given in exchange for a promise. Adequacy of consideration relates to "how much" consideration is given and whether a fair bargain was reached. Courts will inquire into the adequacy of consideration (whether the consideration is legally sufficient) only when fraud, undue influence, duress, or unconscionability may be involved.

CHAPTER SUMMARY ▦ Contracts: Nature, Classification, Agreement, and Consideration—Continued

Contracts That Lack Consideration (See pages 226–228.)	Consideration is lacking in the following situations: 1. *Preexisting duty*—Consideration is not legally sufficient if one is either by law or by contract under a *preexisting duty* to perform the action being offered as consideration for a new contract. 2. *Past consideration*—Actions or events that have already taken place do not constitute legally sufficient consideration. 3. *Illusory promises*—When the nature or extent of performance is too uncertain, the promise is rendered illusory (without consideration and unenforceable).
Settlement of Claims (See pages 228–229.)	1. *Accord and satisfaction*—An *accord* is an agreement in which a debtor offers to pay a lesser amount than the creditor purports to be owed. *Satisfaction* may take place when the accord is executed. 2. *Release*—An agreement in which, for consideration, a party forfeits the right to seek further recovery beyond the terms specified in the release. 3. *Covenant not to sue*—An agreement not to sue on a present, valid claim.
Promissory Estoppel (See pages 229–230.)	The equitable doctrine of promissory estoppel applies when a promisor reasonably expects a promise to induce definite and substantial action or forbearance by the promisee, and the promisee does act in reliance on the promise. Such a promise is binding if injustice can be avoided only by enforcement of the promise. Also known as the doctrine of detrimental reliance.

▦ FOR REVIEW

Answers for the even-numbered questions in this For Review *section can be found in Appendix I at the end of this text.*

1 What is a contract? What are the four elements necessary to the formation of a valid contract?

2 What are the various types of contracts?

3 What are the requirements of an offer?

4 How can an offer be accepted?

5 What are the elements of consideration?

▦ QUESTIONS AND CASE PROBLEMS

7–1. Express versus Implied Contracts. Suppose that a local businessperson, McDougal, is a good friend of Krunch, the owner of a local candy store. Every day on his lunch hour McDougal goes into Krunch's candy store and spends about five minutes looking at the candy. After examining Krunch's candy and talking with Krunch, McDougal usually buys one or two candy bars. One afternoon, McDougal goes into Krunch's candy shop, looks at the candy, and picks up a $1 candy bar. Seeing that Krunch is very busy, he catches Krunch's eye, waves the candy bar at Krunch without saying a word, and walks out. Is there a contract? If so, classify it within the categories presented in this chapter.

7–2. Contract Classification. High-Flying Advertising, Inc., contracted with Big Burger Restaurants to fly an advertisement above the Connecticut beaches. The advertisement offered $5,000 to any person who could swim from the Connecticut beaches to Long Island across Long Island Sound in less than a day. McElfresh saw the streamer and accepted the challenge. He started his marathon swim that same day at 10 A.M. After he had been swimming for four hours and was about halfway across the sound, McElfresh saw another plane pulling a streamer that read, "Big Burger revokes." Is there a contract between McElfresh and Big Burger? If there is a contract, what type(s) of contract is (are) formed?

7–3. Offers versus Nonoffers. On June 1, Jason placed an ad in a local newspaper, to be run on the following Sunday, June 5, offering a reward of $100 to anyone who found his wallet. When his wallet had not been returned by June 12, he purchased another wallet and took steps to obtain duplicates of his driver's license, credit cards, and other items that he had lost. He also placed another ad in the same newspaper revoking his offer. The second ad was the same size as the original. On June 15, Sharith, who had seen Jason's first ad in the paper, found Jason's wallet, returned it to Jason, and asked for the $100. Is Jason obligated to pay Sharith the $100? Why or why not?

7–4. Consideration. Ben hired Lewis to drive his racing car in a race. Tuan, a friend of Lewis, promised to pay Lewis $3,000 if he won the race. Lewis won the race, but Tuan refused to pay the $3,000. Tuan contended that no legally binding contract had been formed because he had received no consideration from Lewis for his promise to pay the $3,000. Lewis sued Tuan for breach of contract, arguing that winning the race was the consideration given in exchange for Tuan's promise to pay the $3,000. What rule of law discussed in this chapter supports Tuan's claim? Explain.

CASE PROBLEM WITH SAMPLE ANSWER

7–5. Professor Dixon was an adjunct professor at Tulsa Community College (TCC) in Tulsa, Oklahoma. Each semester, near the beginning of the term, the parties executed a written contract that always included the following provision: "It is agreed that this agreement may be cancelled by the Administration or the instructor at anytime before the first class session." In the spring semester of Dixon's seventh year, he filed a complaint with TCC alleging that one of his students, Meredith Bhuiyan, had engaged in disruptive classroom conduct. He gave her an incomplete grade and asked TCC to require her to apologize as a condition of receiving a final grade. TCC later claimed, and Dixon denied, that he was told to assign Bhuiyan a grade if he wanted to teach in the fall. Toward the end of the semester, Dixon was told which classes he would teach in the fall, but the parties did not sign a written contract. The Friday before classes began, TCC terminated him. Dixon filed a suit in an Oklahoma state court against TCC and others, alleging breach of contract. Did the parties have a contract? If so, did TCC breach it? Explain. [*Dixon v. Bhuiyan*, 10 P.3d 888 (Okla. 2000)]

After you have answered this problem, compare your answer with the sample answer given on the Web site that accompanies this text. Go to http://blt.westbuslaw.com, select "Chapter 7," and click on "Case Problem with Sample Answer."

7–6. Bilateral versus Unilateral Contracts. D.L. Peoples Group (D.L.) placed an ad in a Missouri newspaper to recruit admissions representatives, who were hired to recruit Missouri residents to attend D.L.'s college in Florida. Donald Hawley responded to the ad, his interviewer recommended him for the job, and he signed, in Missouri, an "Admissions Representative Agreement," which was mailed to D.L.'s president, who signed it in his office in Florida. The agreement provided in part that Hawley would devote exclusive time and effort to the business in his assigned territory in Missouri and that D.L. would pay Hawley a commission if he successfully recruited students for the school. While attempting to make one of his first calls on his new job, Hawley was accidentally shot and killed. On the basis of his death, a claim was filed in Florida for workers' compensation. (Under Florida law, when an accident occurs outside Florida, workers' compensation benefits are payable only if the employment contract was made in Florida.) Is this admissions representative agreement a bilateral or a unilateral contract? What are the consequences of the distinction in this case? Explain. [*D.L. Peoples Group, Inc. v. Hawley*, 804 So.2d 561 (Fla.App. 1 Dist. 2002)]

7–7. Intention. Music that is distributed on compact discs and similar media generates income in the form of "mechanical" royalties. Music that is publicly performed, such as when a song is played on the radio, included in a movie or commercial, or sampled in another song, produces "performance" royalties. Both types of royalties are divided between the songwriter and the song's publisher. Vincent Cusano is a musician and songwriter who performed under the name "Vinnie Vincent" as a guitarist with the group KISS in the early 1980s. Cusano co-wrote three songs entitled "Killer," "I Love It Loud," and "I Still Love You," which KISS recorded and released in 1982 on an album titled *Creatures of the Night*. Cusano left KISS in 1984. Eight years later, Cusano sold to Horipro Entertainment Group "one hundred (100%) percent undivided interest" of his rights in the songs "other than Songwriter's share of performance income." Later, Cusano filed a suit in a federal district court against Horipro, claiming in part that he never intended to sell the writer's share of the mechanical royalties. Horipro filed a motion for summary judgment. Should the court grant the motion? Explain. [*Cusano v. Horipro Entertainment Group*, 301 F.Supp.2d 272 (S.D.N.Y. 2004)]

A QUESTION OF ETHICS

7–8. When LeRoy McIlravy began working for Kerr-McGee Corp., he was given an employee handbook that listed examples of misconduct that could result in discipline or discharge and spelled out specific procedures that would be used in those instances. When McIlravy was later laid off, he and other former employees filed a suit against Kerr-McGee, contending, among other things, that the handbook constituted an implied contract that Kerr-McGee had breached, because the handbook implied that employees would not be dismissed without "cause." In view of these facts, consider the following questions. [*McIlravy v. Kerr-McGee Corp.*, 119 F.3d 876 (10th Cir. 1997)]

1. Would it be fair to the employer for the court to hold that an implied contract had been created in this case, given that the employer did not *intend* to create a contract? Would it be fair to the employees to hold that no contract was created? If the decision were up to you, how would you decide this issue?

2. Suppose that the handbook contained a disclaimer stating that the handbook was not to be construed as a contract. How would this affect your answers to the above questions? From an ethical perspective, would it ever be fair to hold that an implied contract exists *notwithstanding* such a disclaimer?

FOR CRITICAL ANALYSIS

7–9. Review the list of basic requirements for contract formation given at the beginning of this chapter. In view of those requirements, analyze the relationship entered into when a student enrolls in a college or university. Has a contract been formed? If so, is it a bilateral contract or a unilateral contract? Discuss.

VIDEO QUESTION

7–10. Go to this text's Web site at **http://blt. westbuslaw.com** and select "Chapter 7." Click on "Video Questions" and view the video titled *Bowfinger*. Then answer the following questions.

1. In the video, Renfro (Robert Downey, Jr.) says to Bowfinger (Steve Martin), "You bring me this script and Kit Ramsey and you've got yourself a 'go' picture." Assume for the purposes of this question that their agreement is a contract. Is the contract bilateral or unilateral? Is it express or implied? Is it formal or informal? Is it executed or executory? Explain your answers.

2. What criteria would a court rely on to interpret the terms of the contract?

3. Recall from the video that the contract between Bowfinger and the producer was oral. Suppose that a statute requires contracts of this type to be in writing. In that situation, would the contract be void, voidable, or unenforceable? Explain.

INTERNET EXERCISES

Go to the *Business Law Today: The Essentials* home page at **http://blt.westbuslaw.com**, select "Chapter 7," and click on "Internet Exercises." There you will find the following Internet research exercises that you can perform to learn more about topics covered in this chapter.

Activity 7–1: LEGAL PERSPECTIVE—Contract Terms

Activity 7–2: MANAGEMENT PERSPECTIVE—Implied Employment Contracts

Activity 7–3: HISTORICAL PERSPECTIVE—Contracts in Ancient Mesopotamia

BEFORE THE TEST

Go to the *Business Law Today: The Essentials* home page at **http://blt.westbuslaw.com**, select "Chapter 7," and click on "Interactive Quizzes." You will find at least twenty interactive questions relating to this chapter.

CHAPTER 8

Contracts: Capacity, Legality, Assent, and Form

> "Liberty of contract is not an absolute concept. It is relative to many conditions of time and place and circumstance."
>
> Benjamin Cardozo, 1870–1938
> (Associate justice of the United States Supreme Court, 1932–1938)

CHAPTER OUTLINE

- **CONTRACTUAL CAPACITY**

- **LEGALITY**

- **GENUINENESS OF ASSENT**

- **THE STATUTE OF FRAUDS—REQUIREMENT OF A WRITING**

- **THE STATUTE OF FRAUDS—SUFFICIENCY OF THE WRITING**

■■ LEARNING OBJECTIVES

After reading this chapter, you should be able to answer the following questions:

1 What are some exceptions to the rule that a minor can disaffirm (avoid) any contract?

2 Does an intoxicated person have the capacity to enter into an enforceable contract?

3 In what types of situations might genuineness of assent to a contract's terms be lacking?

4 What elements must exist for fraudulent misrepresentation to occur?

5 What contracts must be in writing to be enforceable?

Courts generally want contracts to be enforceable, and much of the law is devoted to aiding the enforceability of contracts. Nonetheless, as indicated in the opening quotation, "liberty of contract" is not absolute. In other words, not all people can make legally binding contracts at all times. Contracts entered into by persons lacking the capacity to do so may be voidable. Similarly, contracts calling for the performance of an illegal act are illegal and thus void—they are not contracts at all.

In this chapter, we first examine contractual capacity and some aspects of illegal bargains. We then look at genuineness of assent. An otherwise valid contract may still be unenforceable if the parties have not genuinely assented to its terms. As mentioned in Chapter 7, lack of genuine assent is a *defense* to the enforcement of a contract. A contract that is otherwise valid may also be unenforceable if it is not in the proper form. For example, if a contract is required by law to be in writing and there is no written evidence of the contract, it may not be enforceable. In the concluding section of this chapter, we examine the kinds of contracts that require a writing under what is called the *Statute of Frauds*.

▉ Contractual Capacity

CONTRACTUAL CAPACITY
The threshold mental capacity required by law for a party who enters into a contract to be bound by that contract.

Contractual capacity is the legal ability to enter into a contractual relationship. Courts generally presume the existence of contractual capacity, but in some situations, capacity is lacking or may be questionable. A person *adjudged by a court* to be mentally incompetent, for example, cannot form a legally binding contract with another party. In other situations, a party may have the capacity to enter into a valid contract but also have the right to avoid liability under it. For example, minors—or *infants*, as they are commonly referred to legally—usually are not legally bound by contracts. In this section, we look at the effect of youth, intoxication, and mental incompetence on contractual capacity.

MINORS

Today, in virtually all states, the *age of majority* (when a person is no longer a minor) for contractual purposes is eighteen years—the so-called coming of age. (The age of majority may still be twenty-one for other purposes, however, such as the purchase and consumption of alcohol.) In addition, some states provide for the termination of minority on marriage. Subject to certain exceptions, the contracts entered into by a minor are voidable at the option of that minor.

The general rule is that a minor can enter into any contract an adult can, provided that the contract is not one prohibited by law for minors (for example, the sale of alcoholic beverages or tobacco). Although minors have the right to avoid their contracts, there are exceptions (to be discussed shortly).

Disaffirmance   The legal avoidance, or setting aside, of a contractual obligation is referred to as **disaffirmance**. To disaffirm, a minor must express his or her intent, through words or conduct, not to be bound to the contract. The minor must disaffirm the entire contract, not merely a portion of it. For instance, a minor cannot decide to keep part of the goods purchased under a contract and return the remaining goods. When a minor disaffirms a contract, the minor can recover any property that he or she transferred to the adult as consideration for the contract, even if it is then in the possession of a third party.[1]

DISAFFIRMANCE
The legal avoidance, or setting aside, of a contractual obligation.

A contract can ordinarily be disaffirmed at any time during minority[2] or for a reasonable time after the minor comes of age. While two months would probably be considered reasonable, a court may not consider it reasonable to wait a year or more after coming of age to disaffirm, depending on the circumstances. If an individual fails to disaffirm an executed contract within a reasonable time after reaching the age of majority, a court will likely hold that the contract has been ratified (ratification will be discussed shortly).

Note that an adult who enters into a contract with a minor cannot avoid his or her contractual duties on the ground that the minor can do so. Unless the minor exercises the option to disaffirm the contract, the adult party normally is bound by it.

---

1. The Uniform Commercial Code, in Section 2–403(1), allows an exception if the third party is a "good faith purchaser for value."

2. In some states, however, a minor who enters into a contract for the sale of land cannot disaffirm the contract until she or he reaches the age of majority.

A Minor's Obligations on Disaffirmance. Although all states' laws permit minors to disaffirm contracts (with certain exceptions), including executed contracts, state laws differ on the extent of a minor's obligations on disaffirmance. Courts in a majority of states hold that the minor need only return the goods (or other consideration) subject to the contract, provided the goods are in the minor's possession or control. ■ **EXAMPLE 8.1** Jim Garrison, a seventeen-year-old, purchases a computer from Radio Shack. While transporting the computer to his home, Garrison, through no fault of his own, is involved in a car accident. As a result of the accident, the plastic casing of the computer is broken. The next day, he returns the computer to Radio Shack and disaffirms the contract. Under the majority view, this return fulfills Garrison's duty even though the computer is now damaged. Garrison is entitled to receive a refund of the purchase price (if paid in cash) or to be relieved of any further obligations under an agreement to purchase the computer on credit. ■

A growing number of states, either by statute or by court decision, place an additional duty on the minor—the duty to restore the adult party to the position she or he held before the contract was made. ■ **EXAMPLE 8.2** Sixteen-year-old Joseph Dodson bought a pickup truck for $4,900 from a used-car dealer. Although the truck developed mechanical problems nine months later, Dodson continued to drive it until the engine blew up and it stopped running. Then Dodson disaffirmed the contract and attempted to return the truck to the dealer for a refund of the full purchase price. The dealer refused to accept the pickup or refund the money. Dodson filed suit. Ultimately, the Tennessee Supreme Court allowed Dodson to disaffirm the contract but required the seller to be compensated for the depreciated value—not the purchase price—of the pickup.[3] ■ This example illustrates the trend among

---

3. *Dodson v. Shrader*, 824 S.W.2d 545 (1992).

Two young men discuss the sale of a car. When a minor disaffirms a contract, such as a contract to buy a car, most states require the minor to return whatever he or she purchased, if it is within his or her control. Why do some states require more? (© Michael Newman, PhotoEdit)

today's courts to hold a minor responsible for damage, ordinary wear and tear, and depreciation of goods that the minor used prior to disaffirmance.

Misrepresentation of Age. Suppose that a minor tells a seller she is twenty-one years old when she is really seventeen. Ordinarily, the minor can disaffirm the contract even though she has misrepresented her age. Moreover, in some jurisdictions the minor is not liable for the tort of fraudulent misrepresentation, the rationale being that such a tort judgment might indirectly force the minor to perform the contract.

In many jurisdictions, however, a minor who has misrepresented his or her age can be bound by a contract under certain circumstances. First, several states have enacted statutes for precisely this purpose. In these states, misrepresentation of age is enough to prohibit disaffirmance. Other statutes prohibit disaffirmance by a minor who has engaged in business as an adult. Second, some courts refuse to allow minors to disaffirm executed (fully performed) contracts unless they can return the consideration received. The combination of the minors' misrepresentations and their unjust enrichment has persuaded these courts to *estop* (prevent) the minors from asserting contractual incapacity.

Finally, some courts allow a misrepresenting minor to disaffirm the contract, but they hold the minor liable for damages in tort. Here, the defrauded party may sue the minor for misrepresentation or fraud. Authority is split on this point because some courts, as previously noted, have recognized that allowing a suit in tort is equivalent to indirectly enforcing the minor's contract.

Contracts for Necessaries, Insurance, and Loans. A minor who enters into a contract for necessaries may disaffirm the contract but remains liable for the reasonable value of the goods used. **Necessaries** are basic needs, such as food, clothing, shelter, and medical services, at a level of value required to maintain the minor's standard of living or financial and social status. Thus, what will be considered a necessary for one person may be a luxury for another. Additionally, what is considered a necessary depends on whether the minor is under the care or control of his or her parents, who are required by law to provide necessaries for the minor. If a minor's parents provide the minor with shelter, for example, then a contract to lease shelter (such as an apartment) normally will not be considered as a contract for necessaries.

Generally, then, to qualify as a contract for necessaries, (1) the item contracted for must be necessary to the minor's existence, (2) the value of the necessary item may be up to a level required to maintain the minor's standard of living or financial and social status, and (3) the minor must not be under the care of a parent or guardian who is required to supply this item. Unless these three criteria are met, the minor can normally disaffirm the contract *without* being liable for the reasonable value of the goods used.

Traditionally, insurance has not been viewed as a necessary, so minors can ordinarily disaffirm their insurance contracts and recover all premiums paid. Some jurisdictions, however, prohibit the disaffirmance of insurance contracts—for example, when minors contract for life insurance on their own lives. Financial loans are seldom considered to be necessaries, even if the minor spends the funds borrowed on necessaries. If, however, a lender makes a loan to a minor for the express purpose of enabling the minor to purchase necessaries, and the lender personally makes sure the funds are so spent, the minor normally is obligated to repay the loan. The issue in the following case was whether a medical service provider could collect from a minor the cost of emergency services rendered to the minor when his mother did not pay.

NECESSARIES
Necessities required for life, such as food, shelter, clothing, and medical attention; may include whatever is believed to be necessary to maintain a person's standard of living or financial and social status.

BE AWARE A minor's station in life (including financial and social status and lifestyle) is important in determining whether an item is a necessary or a luxury. For example, clothing is a necessary, but if a minor from a low-income family contracts for the purchase of a $2,000 leather coat, a court may deem the coat a luxury. In this situation, the contract would not be for "necessaries."

CASE 8.1 ■ Yale Diagnostic Radiology v. Estate of Harun Fountain

Supreme Court of Connecticut, 2004.
267 Conn. 351,
838 A.2d 179.

FACTS In March 1996, Harun Fountain was shot in the back of the head at point-blank range by a playmate. Fountain required extensive lifesaving medical services from a variety of providers, including Yale Diagnostic Radiology. Yale billed Fountain's mother, Vernetta Turner-Tucker, for the cost of its services, $17,694, but she did not pay. Instead, in January 2001, Turner-Tucker filed for bankruptcy (see Chapter 16), and all of her debts, including the amount owed to Yale, were discharged. Meanwhile, she filed a suit in a Connecticut state court against the boy who shot Fountain and obtained money for Fountain's medical care. These funds were deposited in an account—sometimes referred to as an "estate"—established on Fountain's behalf. Yale filed a suit against Fountain's estate, asking the court to order the estate to pay Yale's bill, but the court refused to grant the order. Yale appealed to a state intermediate appellate court, which reversed this ruling and ordered the payment. The estate appealed to the state supreme court.

ISSUE Can a party who provides emergency medical services to a minor collect for those services from the minor if his or her parents do not pay?

DECISION Yes. The Connecticut Supreme Court affirmed the judgment of the lower court. Yale could col-

lect from Fountain's estate for the cost of its services under the doctrine of necessaries.

REASON The state supreme court explained that while Connecticut has long recognized the rule that a minor's contracts are voidable, a minor cannot avoid a contract for goods or services necessary for the minor's health. The court reasoned that this principle is based on the theory of quasi contract (also known as implied-in-law contracts—see Chapter 7). According to the court, two contracts arise when a necessary medical service is provided to a minor. The primary contract is between the provider and the minor's parents and is based on the parents' duty to pay for the child's necessary health expenses. A secondary contract is implied in law between the provider and the minor to prevent unjust enrichment. "Therefore," stated the court, "where necessary medical services are rendered to a minor whose parents do not pay for them, equity and justice demand that a secondary implied-in-law contract arise between the medical services provider and the minor who has received the benefits of those services."

FOR CRITICAL ANALYSIS—Social Consideration
What might have happened in future cases if the court had held that there was no implied-in-law contract between Fountain and Yale?

RATIFICATION
The act of accepting and giving legal force to an obligation that previously was not enforceable.

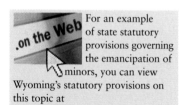

For an example of state statutory provisions governing the emancipation of minors, you can view Wyoming's statutory provisions on this topic at

http://legisweb.state.wy.us/ statutes/sub14.htm.

Ratification In contract law, **ratification** is the act of accepting and giving legal force to an obligation that previously was not enforceable. A minor who has reached the age of majority can ratify a contract expressly or impliedly. Express ratification occurs when the minor expressly states, orally or in writing, that she or he intends to be bound by the contract. Implied ratification exists when the conduct of the minor indicates an intention to be bound by the contract. Ratification will be implied if the minor's conduct is inconsistent with disaffirmance (as when the minor enjoys the benefits of the contract) or if the minor fails to disaffirm an executed (fully performed) contract within a reasonable time after reaching the age of majority. If the contract is still executory (not yet performed or only partially performed), however, failure to disaffirm the contract will not necessarily imply ratification.

■ **EXAMPLE 8.3** Lin enters a contract to sell her laptop to Arturo, a minor. If Arturo does not disaffirm the contract and, on reaching the age of majority, writes a letter to Lin stating that he still agrees to buy the laptop, he has expressly ratified the contract. If, instead, Arturo takes possession of the laptop as a minor and continues to use it well after reaching the age of majority, he has impliedly ratified the contract. ■

In determining whether implied ratification has occurred, the courts generally look at whether the minor, after reaching the age of majority, has had ample opportunity to consider the nature of the contractual obligations he or she entered into as a minor and at the extent to which the adult party to the contract has performed.

INTOXICATED PERSONS

Contractual capacity also becomes an issue when a party to a contract was intoxicated at the time the contract was made. Intoxication is a condition in which a person's normal capacity to act or think is inhibited by alcohol or some other drug. If the person was sufficiently intoxicated to lack mental capacity, the contract may be voidable even if the intoxication was purely voluntary. For the contract to be voidable, however, the person must prove that the intoxication impaired her or his reason and judgment so severely that she or he did not comprehend the legal consequences of entering into the contract. In addition, to avoid the contract in the majority of states, the person claiming intoxication must be able to return all consideration received.

If, despite intoxication, the person understood the legal consequences of the agreement, the contract is enforceable. The fact that the terms of the contract are foolish or obviously favor the other party does not make the contract voidable (unless the other party fraudulently induced the person to become intoxicated). As a practical matter, courts rarely permit contracts to be avoided on the ground of intoxication because it is difficult to determine whether a party was sufficiently intoxicated to avoid legal duties. Rather than inquire into the intoxicated person's mental state, many courts instead focus on objective indications of capacity to determine whether the contract is voidable.[4]

MENTALLY INCOMPETENT PERSONS

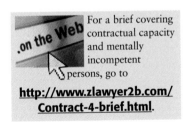

For a brief covering contractual capacity and mentally incompetent persons, go to **http://www.zlawyer2b.com/ Contract-4-brief.html**.

Contracts made by mentally incompetent persons can be void, voidable, or valid. If a court has previously determined that a person is mentally incompetent and has appointed a guardian to represent the person, any contract made by that mentally incompetent person is *void*—no contract exists. Only the guardian can enter into a binding contract on behalf of the mentally incompetent person.

If a court has not previously judged a person to be mentally incompetent but in fact the person was incompetent at the time, the contract may be *voidable*. A contract is voidable if the person did not know he or she was entering into the contract or lacked the mental capacity to comprehend its nature, purpose, and consequences. In such situations, the contract is voidable at the option of the mentally incompetent person but not the other party. The contract may then be disaffirmed or ratified (if the person regains mental competence). Like intoxicated persons, mentally incompetent persons must return any consideration and pay for the reasonable value of any necessaries they receive.

A contract entered into by a mentally incompetent person (whom a court has not previously declared incompetent) may also be deemed *valid* if the person had capacity *at the time the contract was formed*. For instance, a person may be able to understand the nature and effect of entering into a certain contract yet simultaneously lack capacity to engage in other activities. In such cases, the contract ordinarily will be valid because the person is not legally mentally incompetent for contractual

---

4. See, for example, the court's decision in *Lucy v. Zehmer*, presented as Case 7.2 in Chapter 7.

purposes.[5] Similarly, an otherwise mentally incompetent person may have a *lucid interval*—a temporary restoration of sufficient intelligence, judgment, and will to enter into contracts—during which he or she will be considered to have full legal capacity.

▣ Legality

To this point, we have discussed three of the requirements for a valid contract to exist—agreement, consideration, and contractual capacity. Now we examine a fourth—legality. For a contract to be valid and enforceable, it must be formed for a legal purpose. A contract to do something that is prohibited by federal or state statutory law is illegal and, as such, void from the outset and thus unenforceable. Additionally, a contract to commit a tortious act or to commit an action that is contrary to public policy is illegal and unenforceable.

CONTRACTS CONTRARY TO STATUTE

Statutes often set forth rules specifying which terms and clauses may be included in contracts and which are prohibited. We examine here several ways in which contracts may be contrary to a statute and thus illegal.

Usury Virtually every state has a statute that sets the maximum rate of interest that can be charged for different types of transactions, including ordinary loans. A lender who makes a loan at an interest rate above the lawful maximum commits **usury**. The maximum rate of interest varies from state to state.

USURY
Charging an illegal rate of interest.

Although usury statutes place a ceiling on allowable rates of interest, exceptions are made to facilitate business transactions. For example, many states exempt corporate loans from the usury laws. In addition, almost all states have special statutes allowing much higher interest rates on small loans to help those borrowers who need funds and could not otherwise obtain loans.

The consequences for lenders who make usurious loans vary from state to state. A number of states allow the lender to recover only the principal of a loan along with interest up to the legal maximum. In effect, the lender is denied recovery of the excess interest. In other states, the lender can recover the principal amount of the loan but no interest. In a few states, a usurious loan is a void transaction, and the lender cannot recover either the principal or the interest.

Gambling All states have statutes that regulate gambling—defined as any scheme that involves the distribution of property by chance among persons who have paid valuable consideration for the opportunity (chance) to receive the property.[6] Gambling is the creation of risk for the purpose of assuming it. Traditionally, the states have deemed gambling contracts illegal and thus void.

In several states, however, including Louisiana, Nevada, and New Jersey, casino gambling is legal. In other states, certain other forms of gambling are legal. California, for example, has not defined draw poker as a crime, although criminal statutes prohibit numerous other types of gambling games. A number of states allow gambling on horse races, and the majority of states have legalized state-operated lot-

---

5. Modern courts no longer require a person to be completely incompetent to disaffirm contracts on the basis of mental incompetence. A contract may be voidable if, by reason of a mental illness or defect, an individual was unable to act reasonably with respect to the transaction and the other party had reason to know of the condition.

6. See *Wishing Well Club v. Akron*, 66 Ohio Law Abs. 406, 112 N.E.2d 41 (1951).

teries, as well as lotteries (such as bingo) conducted for charitable purposes. Many states also allow gambling on Indian reservations.

Sometimes it is difficult to distinguish a gambling contract from the risk sharing inherent in almost all contracts. ■ EXAMPLE 8.4 In one case, five co-workers each received a free lottery ticket from a customer and agreed to split the winnings if one of the tickets turned out to be the winning one. At first glance, this may seem entirely legal. The court, however, noted that the oral contract in this case "was an exchange of promises to share winnings from the parties' individually owned lottery tickets upon the happening of the uncertain event" that one of the tickets would win. Consequently, concluded the court, the agreement at issue was "founded on a gambling consideration" and therefore was void.[7] ■

ETHICAL ISSUE 8.1

How can states enforce gambling laws in the age of the Internet? One of the threshold issues in regulating online gambling is jurisdictional in nature. For example, in those states that do not allow casino gambling or offtrack betting, what can a state government do if residents of the state place bets online? After all, as you read in Chapter 1, states have no constitutional authority to regulate activities that occur in other states. Another threshold issue in regulating online gambling involves determining where the physical act of placing a bet on the Internet occurs. Is it where the gambler is located or where the gambling site is based? For example, suppose that a resident of New York places bets via the Internet at a gambling site located in Antigua. Is the actual act of "gambling" taking place in New York or in Antigua?

When this exact question came before a New York court, the court, in a precedent-setting decision, concluded that the act of gambling occurred in New York, because under New York law a bet has to be legal in both the jurisdiction where the bet is placed and the jurisdiction where it is received. According to the court, "if the person engaged in gambling is located in New York, then New York is the location where the gambling occurred." Significantly, the U.S. Court of Appeals for the Second Circuit upheld the New York court's decision.[8] ■

Sabbath (Sunday) Laws   Statutes referred to as Sabbath (Sunday) laws prohibit the formation or performance of certain contracts on a Sunday. Under the common law, such contracts are legal in the absence of this statutory prohibition. According to some state and local laws, all contracts entered into on a Sunday are illegal. Laws in other states or municipalities prohibit only the sale of certain types of merchandise, such as alcoholic beverages, on a Sunday.

As noted in Chapter 1, these laws, which date back to colonial times, are often called **blue laws.** Blue laws get their name from the blue paper on which New Haven, Connecticut, printed its new town ordinance in 1781. The ordinance prohibited all work on Sunday and required all shops to close on the "Lord's Day." A number of states and municipalities enacted laws forbidding the carrying on of "all secular labor and business on the Lord's Day." Exceptions to Sunday laws permit contracts for necessities (such as food) and works of charity. Additionally, a fully performed (executed) contract that was entered into on a Sunday normally cannot be rescinded (canceled).

Sunday laws are often not enforced, and some of these laws have been held to be unconstitutional on the ground that they are contrary to the freedom of religion. Nonetheless, as a precaution, business owners contemplating doing business in a particular locality should check to see if any Sunday statutes or ordinances will affect their business activities.

BLUE LAWS
State or local laws that prohibit the performance of certain types of commercial activities on Sunday.

 If you are interested in reading the earliest legislation regulating activities on the Sabbath in colonial America (and about some of the punishments meted out for failing to obey these regulations), go to

http://www.natreformassn. org/statesman/99/ charactr.html.

---

7. *Dickerson v. Deno,* 770 So.2d 63 (Ala. 2000).
8. *United States v. Cohen,* 260 F.3d. 68 (2d Cir. 2001).

Adults gamble at a casino. Would this same activity be illegal if it were conducted online? If so, could it be prevented? How? (© M. Borchi/Photo Researchers)

Licensing Statutes   All states require that members of certain professions obtain licenses allowing them to practice. Physicians, lawyers, real estate brokers, architects, electricians, and stockbrokers are but a few of the people who must be licensed. Some licenses are obtained only after extensive schooling and examinations, which indicate to the public that a special skill has been acquired. Others require only that the particular person be of good moral character and pay a fee.

The Purpose of Licensing Statutes. Generally, business licenses provide a means of regulating and taxing certain businesses and protecting the public against actions that could threaten the general welfare. For example, in nearly all states, a stockbroker must be licensed and must file a bond with the state to protect the public from fraudulent transactions in stock. Similarly, a plumber must be licensed and bonded to protect the public against incompetent plumbers and to protect the public health. Only persons or businesses possessing the qualifications and complying with the conditions required by statute are entitled to licenses. For instance, the owner of a tavern can be required to sell food as a condition of obtaining a license to serve liquor.

Contracts with Unlicensed Practitioners. A contract with an unlicensed practitioner may still be enforceable, depending on the nature of the licensing statute. Some states expressly provide that the lack of a license in certain occupations bars the enforcement of work-related contracts. If the statute does not expressly state this, one must look to the underlying purpose of the licensing requirements for a particular occupation. If the purpose is to protect the public from unauthorized practitioners, a contract involving an unlicensed individual is illegal and unenforceable. If, however, the underlying purpose of the statute is to raise government revenues, a contract with an unlicensed practitioner is enforceable—although the unlicensed person is usually fined.

CONTRACTS CONTRARY TO PUBLIC POLICY

Although contracts involve private parties, some are not enforceable because of the negative impact they would have on society. These contracts are said to be *contrary to public policy.* Examples include a contract to commit an immoral act, such as selling a child (see, for example, the case discussed in this chapter's *Letter of the Law* feature), and a contract that prohibits marriage. ■ **EXAMPLE 8.5** Everett offers a young man $10,000 if he refrains from marrying Everett's daughter. If the young man accepts, no contract is formed (the contract is void) because it is contrary to public policy. Thus, if the man marries Everett's daughter, Everett cannot sue him for breach of contract. ■ Business contracts that may be contrary to public policy include contracts in restraint of trade and unconscionable contracts or clauses.

EMPLOYMENT CONTRACT
A contract between an employer and an employee in which the terms and conditions of employment are stated.

COVENANT NOT TO COMPETE
A contractual promise of one party to refrain from conducting business similar to that of another party for a certain period of time and within a specified geographic area. Courts commonly enforce such covenants if they are reasonable in terms of time and geographic area and part of, or supplemental to, an employment contract or a contract for the sale of a business.

Contracts in Restraint of Trade   Contracts in restraint of trade (anticompetitive agreements) usually adversely affect the public policy that favors competition in the economy. Typically, such contracts also violate one or more federal or state statutes.[9] An exception is recognized when the restraint is reasonable and is part of, or supplemental to, a contract for the sale of a business or an **employment contract** (a contract stating the terms and conditions of employment). Many such exceptions involve a type of restraint called a **covenant not to compete,** or a restrictive covenant.

---

9. Federal statutes prohibiting anticompetitive agreements include the Sherman Antitrust Act, the Clayton Act, and the Federal Trade Commission Act (see Chapter 22).

LETTER OF THE LAW For Sale: "The Most Beautiful Baby in the World"

Lawrence Schaub, a former windshield repairman in Detroit, Michigan, was facing financial problems. He was out of work. He was behind in his mobile home payments. He had three children to feed. Desperate to obtain funds, he decided to sell the youngest of his three children. To that end, he created a videotape titled "The Most Beautiful Baby in the World" to show to prospective buyers. Unfortunately for Schaub, his children's babysitter informed the police of his plan, and he was caught in a "sting" operation when undercover police officers posed as a would-be adoptive family. Schaub accepted $10,000 from the officers as a down payment on the $60,000 contract price.

If a case involving a similar contract came before a civil court, the court would likely deem the contract void as against public policy. Schaub's was a criminal case, however, and a significant question immediately arose: What statute had Schaub violated? Until September 1, 2000, Michigan was one of about twenty-five states that did not explicitly outlaw the sale of children. Shortly after Schaub's arrest drew attention to this "oversight" in state law, the Michigan legislature passed a bill making trafficking in humans punishable by up to twenty years in prison and a $100,000 fine. At the time Schaub tried to sell his daughter, however, the law did not exist. At worst, the only state crime that Schaub committed was attempting to profit from an adoption, which is subject to a penalty of ninety days in jail.[a]

THE BOTTOM LINE
Occasionally, bizarre cases such as this one alert state legislatures to loopholes in their laws. Note, though, that the prosecutors in Schaub's case found other ways to keep Schaub in jail for a while—at least until his former wife claimed custody of the children. The prosecutors charged Schaub with child abandonment, driving with a suspended license, and violating his probation stemming from an earlier drug case.

a. For a summary of Schaub's actions and the prosecution's case against him, see M. L. Elrick, "Baby for Sale," *The National Law Journal,* September 11, 2000, pp. A1–A2.

Covenants Not to Compete and the Sale of an Ongoing Business.   Covenants not to compete are often contained in contracts concerning the sale of an ongoing business. A covenant not to compete is created when a seller agrees not to open a new store in a certain geographic area surrounding the old store. Such an agreement, when it is ancillary to a sales contract and reasonable in terms of time and geographic area, enables the seller to sell, and the purchaser to buy, the "goodwill" and "reputation" of an ongoing business. If, for example, a well-known merchant sells his or her store and opens a competing business a block away, many of the merchant's customers will likely do business at the new store. This renders valueless the good name and reputation sold to the other merchant for a price. If a covenant not to compete is not ancillary to a sales agreement, however, it will be void because it unreasonably restrains trade and is contrary to public policy.

Covenants Not to Compete in Employment Contracts.   Agreements not to compete can also be included in employment contracts. People in middle-level and upper-level management positions commonly agree not to work for competitors or not to start a competing business for a specified period of time after terminating employment. Such agreements are generally legal so long as the specified period of time is not excessive in duration and the geographic restriction is reasonable. Basically, the restriction on competition must be reasonable—that is, not any greater than necessary to protect a legitimate business interest. While a time restriction of one year may be upheld by a court as reasonable, a time restriction of two, three, or five years may not be.

For more information on restrictive covenants in employment contracts, you can access an article written by attorneys at Loose Brown & Associates, P.C., at

http://www.loosebrown. com/articles/art009.pdf.

Determining what constitute "reasonable" time and geographic restrictions in the online environment is a more difficult issue being addressed by the courts. The Internet environment has no physical borders, so geographic restrictions are no longer relevant. Also, a reasonable time period in the online environment may be less than what is reasonable in conventional employment contracts because the restrictions would apply worldwide.

■ **EXAMPLE 8.6** Mark Schlack worked as a Web site manager and vice president for EarthWeb, Inc., a company in the information technology industry. At the time he was hired, Schlack signed a covenant not to compete. It stated that, on termination of his employment, he would not work for any competing company for one year. When Schlack later accepted an offer from another company to design a Web site, EarthWeb sued to enforce the covenant not to compete. The federal district court hearing the case decided that the covenant was unreasonable because it prohibited Schlack from working for a competing company located anywhere in the world for one year. According to that court, "in the Internet environment, a one-year hiatus [break] from the work force is several generations, if not an eternity."[10] ■

Enforcement Problems.   The laws governing the enforceability of covenants not to compete vary significantly from state to state. In some states, such as Texas, such a covenant will not be enforced unless the employee has received some benefit in return for signing the noncompete agreement. This is true even if the covenant is reasonable as to time and area. If the employee receives no benefit, the covenant will be deemed void. California prohibits the enforcement of covenants not to compete altogether.

Occasionally, depending on the jurisdiction, courts will *reform* covenants not to compete. If a covenant is found to be unreasonable in time or geographic area, the

---

10. *EarthWeb, Inc. v. Schlack,* 71 F.Supp.2d 299 (S.D.N.Y. 1999).

court may convert the terms into reasonable ones and then enforce the reformed covenant. This presents a problem, however, in that the judge, implicitly, has become a party to the contract. Consequently, courts usually resort to contract **reformation** only when necessary to prevent undue burdens or hardships.

Unconscionable Contracts or Clauses   Ordinarily, a court does not look at the fairness or equity of a contract; for example, a court normally will not inquire into the adequacy of consideration. Persons are assumed to be reasonably intelligent, and the court does not come to their aid just because they have made unwise or foolish bargains. In certain circumstances, however, bargains are so oppressive that the courts relieve innocent parties of part or all of their duties. Such a bargain is called an **unconscionable contract** (or **unconscionable clause**). Both the Uniform Commercial Code (UCC) and the Uniform Consumer Credit Code (UCCC) embody the unconscionability concept—the former with regard to the sale of goods and the latter with regard to consumer loans and the waiver of rights.[11] A contract can be unconscionable on either procedural or substantive grounds, as discussed in the following subsections.

Procedural Unconscionability.   Procedural unconscionability has to do with how a term becomes part of a contract and relates to factors bearing on a party's lack of knowledge or understanding of the contract terms because of inconspicuous print, unintelligible language ("legalese"), lack of opportunity to read the contract, lack of opportunity to ask questions about the contract's meaning, and other factors. Procedural unconscionability sometimes relates to purported lack of voluntariness because of a disparity in bargaining power between the two parties. Contracts entered into because of one party's vastly superior bargaining power may be deemed unconscionable. These situations usually involve an **adhesion contract**, which is a contract drafted by the dominant party and then presented to the other—the adhering party—on a "take-it-or-leave-it" basis.[12]

Substantive Unconscionability.   Substantive unconscionability characterizes those contracts, or portions of contracts, that are oppressive or overly harsh. Courts generally focus on provisions that deprive one party of the benefits of the agreement or leave that party without remedy for nonperformance by the other. For example, suppose that a person with little income and only a fourth-grade education agrees to purchase a refrigerator for $3,000 and signs a two-year installment contract. The same type of refrigerator usually sells for $600 on the market. Despite the general rule that the courts will not inquire into the adequacy of the consideration, some courts hold that this type of contract is unconscionable because the contract terms are so oppressive as to "shock the conscience" of the court.[13] Is a contract to prescribe medications via the Internet unconscionable? For a discussion of this issue, see this chapter's *Adapting the Law to the Online Environment* feature on the next page.

Exculpatory Clauses   Often closely related to the concept of unconscionability are **exculpatory clauses**, which release a party from liability in the event of monetary or physical injury, *no matter who is at fault*. Indeed, some courts refer to such clauses

REFORMATION
A court-ordered correction of a written contract so that it reflects the true intentions of the parties.

UNCONSCIONABLE CONTRACT (OR UNCONSCIONABLE CLAUSE)
A contract or clause that is void on the basis of public policy because one party, as a result of disproportionate bargaining power, is forced to accept terms that are unfairly burdensome and that unfairly benefit the dominating party.

ADHESION CONTRACT
A "standard-form" contract, such as that between a large retailer and a consumer, in which the stronger party dictates the terms.

EXCULPATORY CLAUSE
A clause that releases a contractual party from liability in the event of monetary or physical injury, no matter who is at fault.

---

11. See, for example, UCC Sections 2–302 and 2–719.
12. See, for example, *Henningsen v. Bloomfield Motors, Inc.,* 32 N.J. 358, 161 A.2d 69 (1960).
13. See, for example, *Jones v. Star Credit Corp.,* 59 Misc.2d 189, 298 N.Y.S.2d 264 (1969). This case is presented in Chapter 11 as Case 11.2.

ADAPTING THE LAW TO THE ONLINE ENVIRONMENT

Is It Unconscionable for Physicians to Prescribe Medication Online?

Anyone with an e-mail address has undoubtedly received scores of messages offering to sell prescription medications, such as Viagra, online. In the past, someone who wanted a prescription for a certain medication—whether it was for allergies, weight loss, or sexual enhancement—had to see a physician and, normally, undergo a physical examination to see if that medication was appropriate. Today, however, it is possible to enter into a contract to obtain a prescription for, and order, many medications via the Internet without ever setting foot in a physician's office. Contracting with a physician online to receive prescription drugs may be ill advised, but are such contracts unconscionable?

A VIRTUAL DIAGNOSIS

The hallmark of an unconscionable contract is that its terms are so oppressive, one sided, or unfair as to "shock the conscience" of the court. Thus, the issue is whether Internet prescription contracts are so unfair that they "shock the conscience" of the court. After all, physicians are trained to examine patients, diagnose medical conditions, and evaluate possible treatments. A physician who is prescribing medication for a person online, however, has no objective way to determine the person's health status or whether the person understands the risks involved. For example, in the online context, a physician cannot tell if a person is truthfully reporting his or her age and weight, which can significantly affect whether a medication is recommended. In addition, physicians who prescribe drugs online cannot monitor the use of these drugs and evaluate their effectiveness.

AN EMERGING ISSUE

To date, only a few courts have addressed this issue, and no court as yet has held that prescribing drugs online is unconscionable. For example, in 2003, in a case before the Kansas Supreme Court, the state attorney general claimed that it was unconscionable for an out-of-state physician to contract with residents to prescribe drugs via the Internet. The case involved three Kansas residents, including a minor, who entered into contracts on the Web to obtain prescription weight loss drugs (Meridia and phentermine).[a]

The court held that the physician's conduct and the resulting contracts were not unconscionable because there was no evidence that the physician had deceived, oppressed, or misused superior bargaining power. The Web site used by the physician had included a great deal of general information about the specific drugs and their side effects, online questionnaires to obtain medical histories, and waivers of the physician's liability for the prescriptions. The Web site had also provided an online calculator for body weight so that a person could determine if she or he was twenty-five pounds overweight, as required to obtain a prescription for Meridia. Because the court found that the individuals had gotten exactly what they bargained for—the prescription medications they sought—the court refused to step in and declare the contracts unconscionable.

FOR CRITICAL ANALYSIS

If the physicians are not deceptive, should the courts allow all types of medications to be prescribed over the Internet? Why or why not? Explain whether the practice of prescribing medications via the Internet might reach the point at which it "shocks the conscience" of the court.

a. *State ex rel. Stovall v. DVM Enterprises, Inc.,* 275 Kan. 243, 62 P.3d 653 (2003); see also *State ex rel. Stovall v. Confimed.com, L.L.C.,* 272 Kan. 1313, 38 P.3d 707 (2002). (The Latin phrase *ex rel.* means "by or on the relation of" and is used in case names when the suit is brought by the government on the application of a private party who is interested in the matter.)

in terms of unconscionability. ■ **EXAMPLE 8.7** Suppose, for example, that Madison Manufacturing Company hires a laborer and has him sign a contract containing the following clause:

> Said employee hereby agrees with employer, in consideration of such employment, that he will take upon himself all risks incident to his position and will in no case hold the company liable for any injury or damage he may sustain, in his person or otherwise, by accidents or injuries in the factory, or which may result from defective machinery or carelessness or misconduct of himself or any other employee in service of the employer.

This contract provision attempts to remove Madison's potential liability for injuries occurring to the employee, and it would usually be held contrary to public policy.[14] ■ Additionally, exculpatory clauses found in agreements to lease commercial property are normally held to be contrary to public policy. Such clauses are almost universally held to be illegal and unenforceable when they are included in residential property leases.

Exculpatory clauses may be enforced, however, when the parties seeking their enforcement are not involved in businesses considered important to the public interest. Businesses such as health clubs, amusement parks, horse-rental concessions, golf-cart concessions, and skydiving organizations frequently use exculpatory clauses to limit their liability for patrons' injuries. Because these services are not essential, the firms offering them are sometimes considered to have no relative advantage in bargaining strength, and anyone contracting for their services is considered to do so voluntarily.

THE EFFECT OF ILLEGALITY

In general, an illegal contract is void; that is, the contract is deemed never to have existed, and the courts will not aid either party. In most illegal contracts, both parties are considered to be equally at fault—*in pari delicto*. If the contract is executory (not yet fulfilled), neither party can enforce it. If it has been executed, there can be neither contractual nor quasi-contractual recovery.

That one wrongdoer in an illegal contract is unjustly enriched at the expense of the other is of no concern to the law—except under certain circumstances (to be discussed shortly). The major justification for this hands-off attitude is that it is improper to place the machinery of justice at the disposal of a plaintiff who has broken the law by entering into an illegal bargain. Another justification is the hoped-for deterrent effect of this general rule. A plaintiff who suffers a loss because of an illegal bargain will presumably be deterred from entering into similar illegal bargains in the future.

There are exceptions to the general rule that neither party to an illegal bargain can sue for breach and neither party can recover for performance rendered. We look at these exceptions here.

Justifiable Ignorance of the Facts   When one of the parties to a contract is relatively innocent (has no reason to know that the contract is illegal), that party can often recover any benefits conferred in a partially executed contract. In this situation, the courts will not enforce the contract but will allow the parties to return to their original positions.

A court may sometimes permit an innocent party who has fully performed under a contract to enforce the contract against the guilty party. ■ EXAMPLE 8.8 A trucking company contracts with Gillespie to carry crated goods to a specific destination for a normal fee of $500. The trucker delivers the crates and later finds out that they contained illegal goods. Although the shipment, use, and sale of the goods are illegal under the law, the trucker, being an innocent party, can normally still legally collect the $500 from Gillespie. ■

---

14. For a case with similar facts, see *Little Rock & Fort Smith Railway Co. v. Eubanks,* 48 Ark. 460, 3 S.W. 808 (1887). In such a case, the exculpatory clause may also be illegal because it violates a state workers' compensation law.

Members of Protected Classes   When a statute protects a certain class of people, a member of that class can enforce an illegal contract even though the other party cannot. ■ **EXAMPLE 8.9** Statutes prohibit certain employees (such as flight attendants) from working more than a specified number of hours per month. These employees thus constitute a class protected by statute. An employee who is required to work more than the maximum can recover for those extra hours of service. ■

BLUE SKY LAWS
State laws that regulate the offer and sale of securities.

Other examples of statutes designed to protect a particular class of people are **blue sky laws**—state laws that regulate and supervise investment companies for the protection of the public (see Chapter 21)—and state statutes regulating the sale of insurance. If an insurance company violates a statute when selling insurance, the purchaser can nevertheless enforce the policy and recover from the insurer.

Withdrawal from an Illegal Agreement   If the illegal part of a bargain has not yet been performed, the party rendering performance can withdraw from the contract and recover the performance or its value. ■ **EXAMPLE 8.10** Suppose that Marta and Amil decide to wager (illegally) on the outcome of a boxing match. Each deposits money with a stakeholder, who agrees to pay the winner of the bet. At this point, each party has performed part of the agreement, but the illegal part of the agreement will not occur until the money is paid to the winner. Before such payment occurs, either party is entitled to withdraw from the agreement by giving notice to the stakeholder of his or her withdrawal. ■

Severable, or Divisible, Contracts   A contract that is *severable,* or divisible, consists of distinct parts that can be performed separately, with separate consideration provided for each part. With an *indivisible* contract, in contrast, the parties intended that complete performance by each party would be essential, even if the contract contains a number of seemingly separate provisions.

If a contract is divisible into legal and illegal portions, a court may enforce the legal portion but not the illegal one, so long as the illegal portion does not affect the essence of the bargain. This approach is consistent with the basic policy of enforcing the legal intentions of the contracting parties whenever possible. ■ **EXAMPLE 8.11** If an employment contract includes an overly broad and thus illegal covenant not to compete, the court might allow the employment contract to be enforceable but reform the unreasonably broad covenant by converting its terms into reasonable ones. Alternatively, the court could declare the covenant illegal (and thus void) and enforce the remaining employment terms. ■

Contracts Illegal through Fraud, Duress, or Undue Influence   Often, one party to an illegal contract is more at fault than the other. When a party has been induced to enter into an illegal bargain through fraud, duress, or undue influence on the part of the other party to the agreement, the first party will be allowed to recover for the performance or its value.

▉ Genuineness of Assent

Genuineness of assent may be lacking because of mistake, fraudulent misrepresentation, undue influence, or duress. Generally, a party who demonstrates that he or she did not genuinely assent to the terms of a contract can choose either to carry out the contract or to rescind (cancel) it and thus avoid the entire transaction.

MISTAKES

We all make mistakes, so it is not surprising that mistakes are made when contracts are created. In certain circumstances, contract law allows a contract to be avoided on the basis of mistake. Realize, though, that the concept of mistake in contract law has to do with mistaken assumptions relating to contract formation. For example, the error you make when you send your monthly bank loan payment to your plumber "by mistake" is totally different from the kind of mistake that we are discussing here. In contract law, a mistake may be a defense to the enforcement of a contract if it can be proved that the parties entered into the contract, each having different assumptions relating to the subject matter of the contract.

Courts have considerable difficulty in specifying the circumstances that justify allowing a mistake to invalidate a contract. Generally, though, courts distinguish between *mistakes as to judgment of market value or conditions* and *mistakes as to fact*. Only the latter normally have legal significance.

■ **EXAMPLE 8.12** Jud Wheeler contracts to buy ten acres of land because he believes that he can resell the land at a profit to Bart. Can Jud escape his contractual obligations if it later turns out that he was mistaken? Not likely. Jud's overestimation of the value of the land or of Bart's interest in it is an ordinary risk of business for which a court normally will not provide relief. Now suppose that Jud purchases a painting of a landscape from Roth's Gallery. Both Jud and Roth believe that the painting is by the artist Van Gogh. Jud later discovers that the painting is a very clever fake. Because neither Jud nor Roth was aware of this fact when they made their deal, Jud can normally rescind the contract and recover the purchase price of the painting. ■

Mistakes occur in two forms—*unilateral* and *bilateral* (mutual). A unilateral mistake is made by only one of the contracting parties; a mutual mistake is made by both. We look next at these two types of mistakes and illustrate them graphically in Exhibit 8–1.

Unilateral Mistakes   A unilateral mistake occurs when only one party is mistaken as to a *material fact*—that is, a fact important to the subject matter of the contract. Generally, a unilateral mistake does not give the mistaken party any right to relief from the contract. In other words, the contract normally is enforceable against the

EXHIBIT 8–1 MISTAKES OF FACT

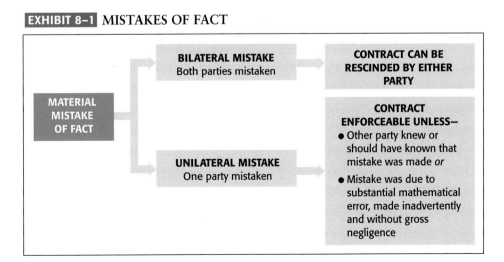

mistaken party. ■ **EXAMPLE 8.13** Elena intends to sell her motor home for $17,500. When she learns that Chin is interested in buying a used motor home, she types a letter offering to sell her vehicle to him. When typing the letter, however, she mistakenly keys in the price of $15,700. Chin writes back, accepting Elena's offer. Even though Elena intended to sell her motor home for $17,500, she has made a unilateral mistake and is bound by contract to sell the vehicle to Chin for $15,700. ■

There are at least two exceptions to this rule.[15] First, if the *other* party to the contract knows or should have known that a mistake of fact was made, the contract may not be enforceable. In the above example, if Chin knew that Elena intended to sell her motor home for $17,500, then Elena's unilateral mistake (stating $15,700 in her offer) may render the resulting contract unenforceable. The second exception arises when a unilateral mistake of fact was due to a mathematical error in addition, subtraction, division, or multiplication and was made inadvertently and without gross (extreme) negligence. If a contractor's bid was significantly low because he or she made a mistake in addition when totaling the estimated costs, any contract resulting from the bid normally may be rescinded. Of course, in both situations, the mistake must still involve some *material fact*.

Bilateral (Mutual) Mistakes   When both parties are mistaken about the same material fact, the contract can be rescinded by either party.[16] Note that, as with unilateral mistakes, the mistake must be about a *material fact* (one that is important and central to the contract—as was the "Van Gogh" painting in Example 8.12). If, instead, a mutual mistake concerns the future market value or quality of the object of the contract, the contract normally can be enforced by either party. This rule is based on the theory that both parties assume certain risks when they enter into a contract. Without this rule, almost any party who did not receive what she or he considered a fair bargain could argue bilateral mistake.

A word or term in a contract may be subject to more than one reasonable interpretation. In that situation, if the parties to the contract attach materially different meanings to the term, their mutual misunderstanding may allow the contract to be rescinded.

■ **EXAMPLE 8.14** In *Raffles v. Wichelhaus*,[17] a classic case involving a mutual mistake, Wichelhaus purchased a shipment of cotton from Raffles to arrive on a ship called the *Peerless* from Bombay, India. Wichelhaus meant a ship called the *Peerless* sailing from Bombay in October; Raffles meant another ship called the *Peerless* sailing from Bombay in December. When the goods arrived on the December *Peerless*, Raffles delivered them to Wichelhaus. By that time, however, Wichelhaus was no longer willing to accept them. The British court hearing the case stated, "There is nothing on the face of the contract to show that any particular ship called the 'Peerless' was meant; but the moment it appears that two ships called the 'Peerless' were about to sail from Bombay there is a latent ambiguity. . . . That being so, there was no consensus . . . and therefore no binding contract." ■

In the following case, an injured worker sought to set aside a settlement agreement entered into with his employer, arguing that the agreement was based on a mutual mistake of fact—a physician's mistaken diagnosis of the worker's injury.

BE CAREFUL   What a party to a contract knows or should know can determine whether the contract is enforceable.

---

15. The *Restatement (Second) of Contracts,* Section 153, liberalizes the general rule to take into account the modern trend of allowing avoidance in some circumstances even though only one party has been mistaken.

16. *Restatement (Second) of Contracts,* Section 152.

17. 159 Eng.Rep. 375 (1864).

CASE 8.2 Roberts v. Century Contractors, Inc.

Court of Appeals of North Carolina, 2004.
592 S.E.2d 215.
http://www.aoc.state.nc.us/www/public/html/
opinions.htm[a]

FACTS Bobby Roberts was an employee of Century Contractors, Inc., when a pipe struck him in a work-related accident in July 1993, causing trauma to his neck and back. Dr. James Markworth of Southeastern Orthopaedic Clinic diagnosed Roberts's injuries. After surgery and treatment, Markworth concluded that Roberts was at maximum medical improvement (MMI) and stopped treating him. Roberts agreed with Century to accept $125,000 and payment of related medical expenses, and to waive any right to make further claims in regard to his injury. In June 1998, still experiencing pain, Roberts saw Dr. Allen Friedman, who determined that Roberts was not at MMI. Markworth then admitted that his diagnosis was a mistake. Roberts filed a claim for workers' compensation (see Chapter 18), seeking compensation and medical benefits for his injury. He alleged that his agreement with Century should be set aside due to a mutual mistake of fact. The North Carolina state administrative agency authorized to rule on workers' compensation claims awarded Roberts what he sought. Century appealed to a state intermediate appellate court.

ISSUE Should the agreement between Roberts and Century be set aside on the basis of a mutual mistake of fact?

a. In the "Keywords" box, type "Roberts." In the "What" pull-down menu, select "Title." In the "Additional Search Options" section, choose "Court of Appeals Opinions Only." Click on "Search." In the result, scroll to the name of the case and click on it to access the opinion. The North Carolina Administrative Office of the Courts maintains this Web site.

DECISION Yes. The state intermediate appellate court affirmed the award of compensation and medical benefits to Roberts.

REASON The court explained that compromise settlement agreements, including settlement agreements in workers' compensation cases, are governed by general principles of contract law. The court stated that it is a well-settled principle of contract law that a valid contract exists only where there has been a meeting of the minds as to all essential terms of the agreement. "Therefore," said the court, "where a mistake is common to both parties and concerns a material past or presently existing fact, such that there is no meeting of the minds, a contract may be avoided." The mistake "must be as to a fact which enters into and forms the basis of the contract * * * and must be such that it animates and controls the conduct of the parties." Also, "relief from a contract due to mistake of fact will be had only where *both* parties to an agreement are mistaken." The court pointed out that Markworth's MMI diagnosis was "material to the settlement of this claim" and that both parties relied on this information in entering into settlement negotiations. Later, however, "Dr. Friedman testified, and the [state agency found] as fact, that plaintiff was not at maximum medical improvement." Thus, the court concluded that there was a mutual mistake with regard to the plaintiff's medical condition at the time of the signing of the settlement agreement.

FOR CRITICAL ANALYSIS—Social Consideration
Why did the court consider Markworth's misdiagnosis a bilateral mistake rather than a unilateral mistake?

FRAUDULENT MISREPRESENTATION

Although fraud is a tort, the presence of fraud also affects the genuineness of the innocent party's consent to a contract. When an innocent party consents to a contract with fraudulent terms, the contract usually can be avoided because he or she has not *voluntarily* consented to the terms.[18] Normally, the innocent party can either rescind (cancel) the contract and be restored to his or her original position or enforce the contract and seek damages for injuries resulting from the fraud.

---

18. *Restatement (Second) of Contracts,* Sections 163 and 164.

Typically, fraud involves three elements:

1 A misrepresentation of a material fact must occur.

2 There must be an intent to deceive.

3 The innocent party must justifiably rely on the misrepresentation.

Additionally, to collect damages, a party must have been injured as a result of the misrepresentation.

Fraudulent misrepresentation can also occur in the online environment. Indeed, a major challenge today is how to curb Internet fraud—a topic that will be explored further in Chapter 13, in the context of consumer law.

Misrepresentation Must Occur   The first element of proving fraud is to show that misrepresentation of a material fact has occurred. This misrepresentation can take the form of words or actions. For example, an art gallery owner's statement, "This painting is a Picasso" is a misrepresentation of fact if the painting was done by another artist.

A statement of opinion is generally not subject to a claim of fraud. For example, claims such as "This computer will never break down" and "This car will last for years and years" are statements of opinion, not fact, and contracting parties should recognize them as such and not rely on them. A fact is objective and verifiable; an opinion is usually subject to debate. Therefore, a seller is allowed to "huff and puff his [or her] wares" without being liable for fraud. In certain cases, however, particularly when a naïve purchaser relies on an expert's opinion, the innocent party may be entitled to rescission or reformation (an equitable remedy granted by a court in which the terms of a contract are altered to reflect the true intentions of the parties).

Intent to Deceive   The second element of fraud is knowledge on the part of the misrepresenting party that facts have been misrepresented. This element, normally

REMEMBER To collect damages in almost any lawsuit, there must be some sort of injury.

Workers excavate a site and bury a sewer line. Would the party who contracted for this work be liable for fraud if the party knew, or should have known, that subsoil conditions could greatly increase the expense of the work and failed to disclose this to the bidders? Why or why not? (© Mark Mellett, Stock Boston)

SCIENTER
Knowledge by the misrepresenting party that material facts have been falsely represented or omitted with an intent to deceive.

called *scienter,*[19] or "guilty knowledge," generally signifies that there was an intent to deceive. *Scienter* clearly exists if a party knows that a fact is not as stated. *Scienter* also exists if a party makes a statement that he or she believes not to be true or makes a statement recklessly, without regard to whether it is true or false. Finally, this element is met if a party says or implies that a statement is made on some basis, such as personal knowledge or personal investigation, when it is not.

■ **EXAMPLE 8.15** Suppose that Alicia Rolando, when selling a house to Cariton, tells Cariton that the plumbing pipe is of a certain quality. Rolando knows nothing about the quality of the pipe but does not believe it to be what she is representing it to be (and in fact it is not what she says it is). Rolando's statement induces Cariton to buy the house. Rolando's statement is a fraudulent misrepresentation because she does not believe that what she says is true and because she knows that she does not have any basis for making the statement. Cariton can avoid the contract. ■

Can an employer avoid liability for the breach of a contract that was induced by an employee's fraud during the hiring process? That was the question in the following case.

---

19. Pronounced sy-*en*-ter.

CASE 8.3 ⬛ **Sarvis v. Vermont State Colleges**

Supreme Court of Vermont, 2001.
772 A.2d 494.

FACTS In 1995, Robert Sarvis was convicted of bank fraud, ordered to pay more than $12 million in restitution, and sentenced to forty-six months in prison. While incarcerated, he worked in the prison's electrical department. Two weeks after his release in 1998, he applied for an adjunct professor position at Community College of Vermont (CCV). On his résumé, he stated that during "1984–1998" he was "President and Chairman of the Board" of "CMI International Inc., Boston, Massachusetts," where he was "[r]esponsible for all operations and financial matters." For a position as CCV's Coordinator of Academic Services, he submitted a second résumé, on which he added, "1998–present. Semi-retired. Adjunct Instructor of Business at Colby-Sawyer College and Franklin Pierce College." He stated that he was "well equipped to teach" business law and business ethics, that he had "a great interest and knowledge of business law," and that he believed he would do "an excellent job" teaching a business ethics class because this subject was "of particular concern" to him. CCV hired him as academic coordinator, teacher, and independent studies instructor. After he began work, his probation officer alerted CCV to Sarvis's criminal history, and CCV terminated his employment. Sarvis filed a suit in a Vermont state court against CCV, alleging, among other things, breach of contract. CCV filed a motion for summary judgment, in part on the ground of fraud, seeking rescission. The court granted

CCV's motion, and Sarvis appealed to the Vermont Supreme Court.

ISSUE Can a partial disclosure during the preemployment process, with an intent to deceive, support the termination of an employment contract?

DECISION Yes. The Vermont Supreme Court affirmed the lower court's judgment and rescinded the contract between Sarvis and CCV.

REASON The state supreme court explained that "[t]he misrepresentation in this case occurred through plaintiff's partial disclosure of his past work history and references and his effort to limit defendant's inquiry into his past." The court emphasized that Sarvis "was not silent; he carefully drafted his résumés and supplemental materials to lead defendant to believe he had made a full disclosure about his past and his qualifications. He listed classes in business ethics and law in which he claimed he had the highest level of capability and knowledge but failed to mention his felony bank fraud conviction. Plaintiff assured defendant that making additional inquiries into his background would have revealed 'more of the same' type of information * * * . This was not true. Contact with plaintiff's probation officer or supervisor at the * * * prison would have notified defendant of plaintiff's fraud convictions, period of incarceration, and work history at the prison."

(Continued)

CASE 8.3—Continued

WHY IS THIS CASE IMPORTANT? *This case illustrates the long-applied legal principle that when a contract is formed as a result of fraudulent misrepre-* sentation, the defrauded party can avoid the contract. *From the facts in this case, CCV clearly would not have hired Sarvis had he fully disclosed information about his past and his qualifications.*

Reliance on the Misrepresentation   The third element of fraud is *justifiable reliance* on the misrepresentation of fact. The deceived party must have a justifiable reason for relying on the misrepresentation, and the misrepresentation must be an important factor (but not necessarily the sole factor) in inducing the party to enter into the contract.

Reliance is not justified if the innocent party knows the true facts or relies on obviously extravagant statements. ■ **EXAMPLE 8.16** If a used-car dealer tells you, "This old Cadillac will get over sixty miles to the gallon," you normally would not be justified in relying on this statement. Suppose, however, that Merkel, a bank director, induces O'Connell, a co-director, to sign a statement that the bank's assets will satisfy its liabilities by telling O'Connell, "We have plenty of assets to satisfy our creditors." This statement is false. If O'Connell knows the true facts or, as a bank director, should know the true facts, he is not justified in relying on Merkel's statement. If O'Connell does not know the true facts, however, *and has no way of finding them out*, he may be justified in relying on the statement. ■

REMEMBER An opinion is neither a contract offer, nor a contract term, nor fraud.

ETHICAL ISSUE 8.2

How much information must employers disclose to prospective employees? One of the problems employers face is that it is not always clear what information they should disclose to prospective employees. To lure qualified workers, employers are often tempted to "promise the moon" to prospective employees and paint their companies' prospects as bright. Employers must be careful, though, to avoid any conduct that could be interpreted by a court as intentionally deceptive. In particular, they must avoid making any statements about their companies' future prospects or financial health that they know to be false. If they do make a false statement on which a prospective employee relies to her or his detriment, they may be sued for fraudulent misrepresentation.

In one case, for example, an employee accepted a job with a brokerage firm, relying on assurances that the firm was not about to be sold. In fact, as the employee was able to prove in his later lawsuit against the firm for fraud, negotiations to sell the firm were under way at the time he was hired. The trial court awarded the employee over $6 million in damages, a decision that was affirmed on appeal.[20] Generally, employers must be truthful in their hiring to avoid possible lawsuits for fraudulent misrepresentation. ■

Injury to the Innocent Party   Most courts do not require a showing of injury when the action is to *rescind* (cancel) the contract—these courts hold that because rescission returns the parties to the positions they held before the contract was made, a showing of injury to the innocent party is unnecessary.[21]

---

20. *McConkey v. Aon Corp.,* 804 A.2d 572 (N.J.Super.A.D. 2002).
21. For a leading case on this issue, see *Kaufman v. Jaffe,* 244 App.Div. 344, 279 N.Y.S. 392 (1935).

To recover damages caused by fraud, however, proof of an injury is universally required. The measure of damages is ordinarily equal to the property's value had it been delivered as represented, less the actual price paid for the property. In actions based on fraud, courts often award *punitive,* or *exemplary, damages,* which are granted to a plaintiff over and above the compensation for the actual loss. As pointed out in Chapter 4, punitive damages are based on the public-policy consideration of punishing the defendant or setting an example to deter similar wrongdoing by others.

UNDUE INFLUENCE

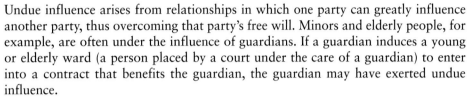

To read more about contesting contracts on the grounds of fraud and duress, go to

http://www.lawyers.com/ lawyers/A~1001073~LDC/ CONTESTING+CONTRACT.html.

Undue influence arises from relationships in which one party can greatly influence another party, thus overcoming that party's free will. Minors and elderly people, for example, are often under the influence of guardians. If a guardian induces a young or elderly ward (a person placed by a court under the care of a guardian) to enter into a contract that benefits the guardian, the guardian may have exerted undue influence.

Undue influence can arise from a number of confidential or fiduciary relationships, including attorney-client, physician-patient, guardian-ward, parent-child, husband-wife, and trustee-beneficiary relationships. The essential feature of undue influence is that the party being taken advantage of does not, in reality, exercise free will in entering into a contract. A contract entered into under excessive or undue influence lacks genuine assent and is therefore voidable.[22]

DURESS

Assent to the terms of a contract is not genuine if one of the parties is forced into the agreement. Forcing a party to enter into a contract because of the fear created by threats is referred to as *duress.*[23] Inducing consent to a contract through blackmail or extortion also constitutes duress. Duress is both a defense to the enforcement of a contract and a ground for rescission, or cancellation, of a contract. Therefore, a party who signs a contract under duress can choose to carry out the contract or to avoid the entire transaction. (The wronged party usually has this choice in cases in which assent is not real or genuine.)

Economic need is generally not sufficient to constitute duress, even when one party exacts a very high price for an item the other party needs. If the party exacting the price also creates the need, however, economic duress may be found. ■ **EXAMPLE 8.17** The Internal Revenue Service (IRS) assessed a large tax and penalty against Weller. Weller retained Eyman to resist the assessment. Two days before the deadline for filing a reply with the IRS, Eyman declined to represent Weller unless he agreed to pay a very high fee for Eyman's services. The agreement was held to be unenforceable.[24] Although Eyman had threatened only to withdraw his services, something that he was legally entitled to do, he was responsible for delaying his withdrawal until the last two days. Because Weller was forced into either signing the contract or losing his right to challenge the IRS assessment, the agreement was secured under duress. ■

---

22. *Restatement (Second) of Contracts,* Section 177.
23. *Restatement (Second) of Contracts,* Sections 174 and 175.
24. *Thompson Crane & Trucking Co. v. Eyman,* 123 Cal.App.2d 904, 267 P.2d 1043 (1954).

The Statute of Frauds—Requirement of a Writing

Today, every state has a statute that stipulates what types of contracts must be in writing. In this text, we refer to such statutes as the **Statute of Frauds.** The primary purpose of the statute is to ensure that, for certain types of contracts, there is reliable evidence of the contracts and their terms. These types of contracts are those deemed historically to be important or complex. Although the statutes vary slightly from state to state, the following types of contracts are normally required to be in writing or evidenced by a written memorandum:

1 Contracts involving interests in land.

2 Contracts that cannot by their terms be performed within one year from the date of formation.

3 Collateral contracts, such as promises to answer for the debt or duty of another.

4 Promises made in consideration of marriage.

5 Contracts for the sale of goods priced at $500 or more ($5,000 or more under the 2003 amendments to the Uniform Commercial Code, or UCC—see Chapter 11).

Agreements or promises that fit into one or more of these categories are said to "fall under" or "fall within" the Statute of Frauds. (Certain exceptions are made to the applicability of the Statute of Frauds in some circumstances, however, as you will read later in this section.)

The actual name of the Statute of Frauds is misleading because it does not apply to fraud. Rather, the statute denies enforceability to certain contracts that do not comply with its requirements. The name derives from an English act passed in 1677, which is presented as this chapter's *Landmark in the Law* feature.

CONTRACTS INVOLVING INTERESTS IN LAND

Land is a form of *real property,* or real estate, which includes not only land but all physical objects that are permanently attached to the soil, such as buildings, plants, trees, and the soil itself. Under the Statute of Frauds, a contract involving an interest in land must be evidenced by a writing to be enforceable.[25] If Carol, for example, contracts orally to sell Seaside Shelter to Axel but later decides not to sell, Axel cannot enforce the contract. Similarly, if Axel refuses to close the deal, Carol cannot force Axel to pay for the land by bringing a lawsuit. The Statute of Frauds is a *defense* to the enforcement of this type of oral contract.

A contract for the sale of land ordinarily involves the entire interest in the real property, including buildings, growing crops, vegetation, minerals, timber, and anything else affixed to the land. Therefore, a *fixture* (personal property so affixed or so used as to become a part of the realty—see Chapter 24) is treated as real property.

The Statute of Frauds requires written contracts not just for the sale of land but also for the transfer of other interests in land, such as mortgages and leases. We describe these other interests in Chapter 24.

THE ONE-YEAR RULE

Contracts that cannot, *by their own terms,* be performed within one year from the day after the contract is formed must be in writing to be enforceable. Because disputes

STATUTE OF FRAUDS
A state statute under which certain types of contracts must be in writing to be enforceable.

KEEP IN MIND Although only certain types of contracts must be in writing to be enforceable, it is good practice to put other contracts in writing as well to prevent disputes over contract terms.

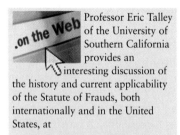

Professor Eric Talley of the University of Southern California provides an interesting discussion of the history and current applicability of the Statute of Frauds, both internationally and in the United States, at

http://www.bcf.usc.edu/ ~etalley/frauds.html.

---

25. In some states, the contract will be enforced, however, if each party admits to the existence of the oral contract in court or admits to its existence during discovery before trial (see Chapter 3).

LANDMARK IN THE LAW The Statute of Frauds

On April 12, 1677, the English Parliament passed "An Act for the Prevention of Frauds and Perjuries." Four days later, the act was signed by King Charles II and became the law of the land. The act contained twenty-five sections and stipulated that if certain types of contracts were to be enforceable by the courts, they would henceforth have to be in writing or evidenced by a written memorandum.[a]

ENFORCEMENT OF ORAL PROMISES   The English act was enacted specifically to prevent the many frauds that were being perpetrated through the perjured testimony of witnesses in cases involving breached oral agreements for which no written evidence existed. During the early history of the common law in England, oral contracts were generally not enforced by the courts, but in the fourteenth century, they began to be enforced in certain *assumpsit* actions.[b] These actions, to which the origins of modern contract law are traced, allowed a party to sue and obtain relief when a promise or contract had been breached. During the next two centuries, the king's courts commonly enforced oral promises in actions in *assumpsit*.

PROBLEMS WITH ORAL CONTRACTS   Because the courts enforced oral contracts on the strength of oral testimony by witnesses, it was not too difficult to evade justice by alleging that a contract had been breached and then procuring "convincing" witnesses to support the claim. The possibility of fraud in such actions was enhanced by the fact that seventeenth-century English courts did not allow oral testimony to be given by the parties to a lawsuit—or by any parties with an interest in the litigation, such as husbands or wives. Defense against actions for breach of contract was thus limited to written evidence and the testimony of third parties. The Statute of Frauds was enacted to minimize the possibility of fraud in oral contracts relating to certain types of transactions.

APPLICATION TO TODAY'S WORLD

Essentially, the Statute of Frauds offers a defense against contracts that fall under the statute. Indeed, the statute has been criticized by some because, although it was created to protect the innocent, it can also be used as a technical defense by a party who has breached a genuine, mutually agreed-on oral contract—if the contract falls within the Statute of Frauds. For this reason, some legal scholars believe the act has caused more fraud than it has prevented. Nonetheless, U.S. courts continue to apply the Statute of Frauds to disputes involving oral contracts. The definitions of such terms as writing *and* signature, *however, are changing as we move further into an electronic age—as you will read in Chapter 10, which covers e-contracts.*

RELEVANT WEB SITES

To locate information on the Web concerning the Statute of Frauds, go to this text's Web site at **http://blt.westbuslaw.com**, *select "Chapter 8," and click on "URLs for Landmarks."*

a. These contracts are discussed in the text of this chapter.
b. *Assumpsit* is Latin for "he undertook" or "she promised." The emergence of remedies given on the basis of breached promises and duties dates to these actions. One of the earliest occurred in 1370, when the court allowed an individual to sue a person who, in trying to cure the plaintiff's horse, had acted so negligently that the horse died. Another such action was permitted in 1375, when a plaintiff obtained relief for having been maimed by a surgeon hired to cure him.

over such contracts are unlikely to occur until some time after the contracts are made, resolution of these disputes is difficult unless the contract terms have been put in writing. The one-year period begins to run *the day after the contract is made.*

■ **EXAMPLE 8.18** Suppose that Superior University forms a contract with Kimi San, stating that San will teach three courses in history during the coming academic year (September 15 through June 15). If the contract is formed in March, it must be in writing to be enforceable—because it cannot be performed within one year. If the contract is not formed until July, however, it will not have to be in writing to be enforceable—because it can be performed within one year. ■ Exhibit 8–2 graphically illustrates the one-year rule.

Normally, the test for determining whether an oral contract is enforceable under the one-year rule of the Statute of Frauds is not whether the agreement is *likely* to be performed within one year from the day after the date of contract formation but whether performance within a year is *possible.* When performance of a contract is objectively impossible during the one-year period, the oral contract will be unenforceable.

COLLATERAL PROMISES

COLLATERAL PROMISE
A secondary promise that is ancillary (subsidiary) to a principal transaction or primary contractual relationship, such as a promise made by one person to pay the debts of another if the latter fails to perform. A collateral promise normally must be in writing to be enforceable.

A **collateral promise,** or secondary promise, is one that is ancillary (subsidiary) to a principal transaction or primary contractual relationship. In other words, a collateral promise is one made by a third party to assume the debts or obligations of a primary party to a contract if that party does not perform. Any collateral promise of this nature falls under the Statute of Frauds and therefore must be in writing to be enforceable. To understand this concept, it is important to distinguish between primary and secondary promises and obligations.

Primary versus Secondary Obligations   As a general rule, a contract in which a party assumes a primary obligation does not need to be in writing to be enforceable. ■ **EXAMPLE 8.19** Suppose that Kenneth orally contracts with Joanne's Floral

EXHIBIT 8–2 THE ONE-YEAR RULE

Under the Statute of Frauds, contracts that by their terms are impossible to perform within one year from the day after the date of contract formation must be in writing to be enforceable. Put another way, if it is at all possible to perform an oral contract within one year from the day after the contract is made, the contract will fall outside the Statute of Frauds and be enforceable.

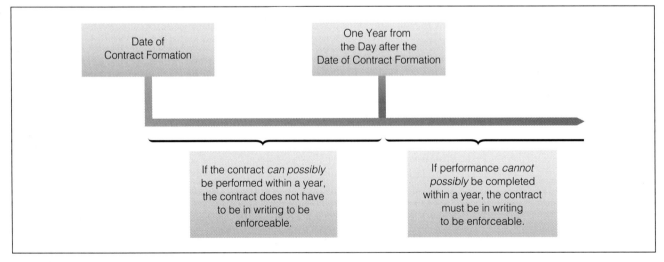

Boutique to send his mother a dozen roses for Mother's Day. Kenneth promises to pay the boutique when he receives the bill for the flowers. Kenneth is a direct party to this contract and has incurred a *primary* obligation under the contract. Because he is a party to the contract and has a primary obligation to Joanne's Floral Boutique, this contract does not fall under the Statute of Frauds and does not have to be in writing to be enforceable. If Kenneth fails to pay the florist and the florist sues him for payment, Kenneth cannot raise the Statute of Frauds as a defense. He cannot claim that the contract is unenforceable because it was not in writing. ■

In contrast, a contract in which a party assumes a secondary obligation does have to be in writing to be enforceable. ■ EXAMPLE 8.20 Suppose that Kenneth's mother borrows $1,000 from the Medford Trust Company on a promissory note payable six months later. Kenneth promises the bank officer handling the loan that he will pay the $1,000 *if his mother does not pay the loan on time.* Kenneth, in this situation, becomes what is known as a *guarantor* on the loan; that is, he is guaranteeing to the bank (the creditor) that he will pay the loan if his mother fails to do so. This kind of collateral promise, in which the guarantor states that he or she will become responsible only if the primary party does not perform, must be in writing to be enforceable. ■ We return to the concept of guaranty and the distinction between primary and secondary obligations in Chapter 16, in the context of creditors' rights.

An Exception—The "Main Purpose" Rule   An oral promise to answer for the debt of another is covered by the Statute of Frauds *unless* the guarantor's purpose in accepting secondary liability is to secure a personal benefit. Under the "main purpose" rule, this type of contract need not be in writing.[26] The assumption is that a court can infer from the circumstances of a case whether a "leading objective" of the promisor was to secure a personal benefit.

■ EXAMPLE 8.21 Carrie Oswald contracts with Machine Manufacturing Company to have some machines custom-made for her factory. To ensure that Machine Manufacturing will have the supplies it needs to make the machines, Oswald promises Allrite Materials Supply Company, Machine Manufacturing's supplier, that if Allrite continues to deliver materials to Machine Manufacturing, she will guarantee payment. This promise need not be in writing, even though the effect may be to pay the debt of another, because Oswald's main purpose is to secure a benefit for herself. ■

Another typical application of the so-called main purpose doctrine occurs when one creditor guarantees the debtor's debt to another creditor to forestall litigation. This allows the debtor to remain in business long enough to generate profits sufficient to pay *both* creditors. In this situation, the guaranty does not need to be in writing to be enforceable.

PROMISES MADE IN CONSIDERATION OF MARRIAGE

A unilateral promise to pay a sum of money or to give property in consideration of marriage must be in writing. If Mr. Baumann promises to pay Joe Villard $10,000 if Villard marries Baumann's daughter, the promise must be in writing to be enforceable. The same rule applies to **prenuptial agreements**—agreements made before marriage (also called *antenuptial agreements*) that define each partner's ownership rights in the other partner's property. For example, a prospective wife or husband

PRENUPTIAL AGREEMENT
An agreement made before marriage that defines each partner's ownership rights in the other partner's property. Prenuptial agreements must be in writing to be enforceable.

26. *Restatement (Second) of Contracts,* Section 116.

may wish to limit the amount the prospective spouse can obtain if the marriage ends in divorce. Prenuptial agreements made in consideration of marriage must be in writing to be enforceable.

CONTRACTS FOR THE SALE OF GOODS

The Uniform Commercial Code (UCC) contains Statute of Frauds provisions that require written evidence of a contract. Section 2–201 contains the major provision, which generally requires a writing or memorandum for the sale of goods priced at $500 or more ($5,000 or more under the 2003 amendments to the UCC—see Chapter 11). A writing that will satisfy the UCC requirement need only state the quantity term; other terms agreed on need not be stated "accurately" in the writing, as long as they adequately reflect both parties' intentions. The contract will not be enforceable, however, for any quantity greater than that set forth in the writing. In addition, the writing must be signed by the person against whom enforcement is sought. Beyond these two requirements, the writing need not designate the buyer or the seller, the terms of payment, or the price.

EXCEPTIONS TO THE STATUTE OF FRAUDS

Exceptions to the applicability of the Statute of Frauds are made in certain situations. We describe those situations here.

Partial Performance   In cases involving oral contracts for the transfer of interests in land, if the purchaser has paid part of the price, taken possession, and made valuable improvements to the property, and if the parties cannot be returned to their status quo prior to the contract, a court may grant *specific performance* (performance of the contract according to its precise terms). Whether a court will enforce an oral contract for an interest in land when partial performance has taken place is usually determined by the degree of injury that would be suffered if the court chose *not* to enforce the oral contract. In some states, mere reliance on certain types of oral contracts is enough to remove them from the Statute of Frauds.

Under the UCC, an oral contract for goods priced at $500 or more ($5,000 or more under the 2003 amendments) is enforceable to the extent that a seller accepts payment or a buyer accepts delivery of the goods.[27] For example, if Ajax Corporation orders by telephone twenty crates of bleach from Cloney, Inc., and repudiates the contract after ten crates have been delivered and accepted, Cloney can enforce the contract to the extent of the ten crates accepted by Ajax.

Admissions   In some states, if a party against whom enforcement of an oral contract is sought admits in pleadings, testimony, or otherwise in court proceedings that a contract for sale was made, the contract will be enforceable.[28] A contract subject to the UCC will be enforceable, but only to the extent of the quantity admitted.[29] Thus, if the president of Ajax Corporation admits under oath that an oral agreement was made with Cloney, Inc., for the twenty crates of bleach, the agreement will be enforceable to that extent.

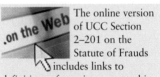
The online version of UCC Section 2–201 on the Statute of Frauds includes links to definitions of certain terms used in the section. To access this site, go to

http://www.law.cornell.edu/ ucc/2/2-201.html.

---

27. UCC 2–201(3)(c). See Chapter 11.
28. *Restatement (Second) of Contracts,* Section 133.
29. UCC 2–201(3)(b). See Chapter 11.

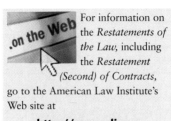

For information on the *Restatements of the Law,* including the *Restatement (Second) of Contracts,* go to the American Law Institute's Web site at

http://www.ali.org.

Promissory Estoppel   In some states, an oral contract that would otherwise be unenforceable under the Statute of Frauds may be enforced under the doctrine of promissory estoppel, or detrimental reliance. Recall from Chapter 7 that if a promisor makes a promise on which the promisee justifiably relies to her or his detriment, a court may *estop* (prevent) the promisor from denying that a contract exists. Section 139 of the *Restatement (Second) of Contracts* provides that in these circumstances, an oral promise can be enforceable, notwithstanding the Statute of Frauds, if the reliance was foreseeable to the person making the promise and if injustice can be avoided only by enforcing the promise.

Special Exceptions under the UCC   Special exceptions to the applicability of the Statute of Frauds exist for sales contracts. Oral contracts for customized goods may be enforced in certain circumstances. Another exception has to do with oral contracts between merchants that have been confirmed in writing. We will examine these exceptions in Chapter 11. Exhibit 8–3 graphically summarizes the types of contracts that fall under the Statute of Frauds and the various exceptions that apply.

■ The Statute of Frauds—Sufficiency of the Writing

A written contract will satisfy the writing requirement of the Statute of Frauds. A *written memorandum* (written evidence of the oral contract) signed by the party against whom enforcement is sought will also satisfy the writing requirement.[30]

---

30. As mentioned earlier, under the UCC Statute of Frauds, a writing is required only for contracts for the sale of goods priced at $500 or more ($5,000 or more under the 2003 amendments to UCC Article 2). See Chapter 11.

EXHIBIT 8–3 CONTRACTS SUBJECT TO THE STATUTE OF FRAUDS

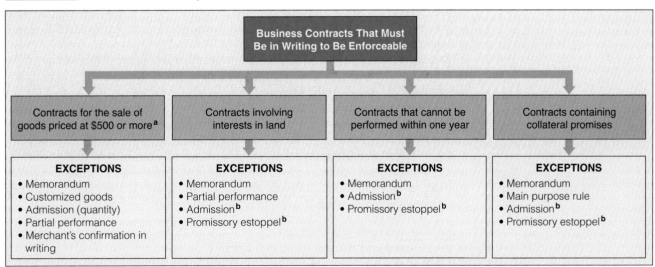

a. Under a 2003 amendment to the UCC, a contract for a sale of goods must involve goods priced at $5,000 or more to be subject to the writing requirement of the Statute of Frauds (see Chapter 11). This amendment also exempts contracts for the sale of goods from the one-year rule.
b. Some states follow Section 133 (on admissions) and Section 139 (on promissory estoppel) of the *Restatement (Second) of Contracts.*

The signature need not be placed at the end of the document but can be anywhere in the writing; it can even be initials rather than the full name. (See the *Application* feature for suggestions on how to prevent problems with oral contracts.)

A significant issue in today's business world has to do with how "signatures" can be created and verified on electronic contracts and other documents. We will examine electronic signatures in Chapter 10.

WHAT CONSTITUTES A WRITING?

A writing can consist of any confirmation, invoice, sales slip, check, or fax—or such items in combination. The written contract need not consist of a single document to constitute an enforceable contract. One document may incorporate another document by expressly referring to it. Several documents may form a single contract if they are physically attached, such as by staple, paper clip, or glue. Several documents may form a single contract even if they are only placed in the same envelope. ■ **EXAMPLE 8.22** Sam orally agrees to sell some land next to a shopping mall to Terry. Sam gives Terry an unsigned memo that contains a legal description of the property, and Terry gives Sam an unsigned first draft of their contract. Sam sends Terry a signed letter that refers to the memo and to the first and final drafts of the contract. Terry sends Sam an unsigned copy of the final draft of the contract with a signed check stapled to it. Together, the documents can constitute a writing sufficient to satisfy the Statute of Frauds and bind both parties to the terms of the contract as evidenced by the writings. ■

WHAT MUST BE CONTAINED IN THE WRITING?

A memorandum evidencing the oral contract need only contain the essential terms of the contract. Under most provisions of the Statute of Frauds, the writing must name the parties, subject matter, consideration, and quantity. With respect to contracts for the sale of land, some states require that the memorandum also set forth the essential terms of the contract, such as location and price, with sufficient clarity to allow the terms to be determined from the memo itself, without reference to any outside sources.[31] Under the UCC, in regard to the sale of goods, the writing need only name the quantity term and be signed by the party against whom enforcement is sought.

Because only the party against whom enforcement is sought need have signed the writing, a contract may be enforceable by one of its parties but not by the other. ■ **EXAMPLE 8.23** Rock orally agrees to buy Betty Devlin's lake house and lot for $150,000. Devlin writes Rock a letter confirming the sale by identifying the parties and the essential terms of the sales contract—price, method of payment, and legal address—and signs the letter. Devlin has made a written memorandum of the oral land contract. Because she signed the letter, she normally can be held to the oral contract by Rock. Rock, however, because he has not signed or entered into a written contract or memorandum, can plead the Statute of Frauds as a defense, and Devlin cannot enforce the contract against him. ■

---

31. *Rhodes v. Wilkins*, 83 N.M. 782, 498 P.2d 311 (1972).

APPLICATION ▪ How Can You Prevent Problems with Oral Contracts?*

As a general rule, most business contracts should be in writing even when they fall outside the Statute of Frauds. Businesspersons frequently make oral contracts over the telephone, however, particularly when the parties have done business with each other in the past.

CONFIRM THE AGREEMENT IN WRITING

Any time an oral contract is made, it is advisable for one of the parties to send either a written memorandum or a confirmation of the oral agreement by fax or e-mail to the other party. This accomplishes two purposes: (1) it demonstrates the party's clear intention to form a contract, and (2) it provides the terms of the contract as that party understood them. If the party receiving the memorandum or confirmation then disagrees with the terms as described, the issue can be addressed before performance begins.

SPECIAL RULES FOR CONTRACTS BETWEEN MERCHANTS

What about the sale of goods between merchants? Under the UCC, written confirmation received by one merchant removes the Statute of Frauds requirement of a writing unless the merchant receiving the confirmation objects in writing within ten days of its receipt. This law (discussed in Chapter 11) clearly points out the need for the merchant receiving the confirmation to review it carefully to ascertain that the confirmation conforms to the oral contract. If the writing does not so conform, the merchant can object in writing (the Statute of Frauds still applies), and the parties can resolve misunderstandings without legal liability. If the merchant fails to object, the written confirmation can be used as evidence to prove the terms of the oral contract. Note, however, that this ten-day rule does not apply to contracts for interests in realty or for services, to which the UCC does not apply.

CHECKLIST FOR THE BUSINESSPERSON

1. When feasible, use written contracts.
2. If you enter into an oral contract over the telephone, fax or e-mail a written confirmation outlining your understanding of the oral contract.
3. If you receive the other party's written confirmation, read it carefully to make sure that it states the terms already agreed to in the oral contract, as you understand them.
4. If you have any objections, notify the other party of these objections, in writing, within ten days.

* This *Application* is not meant to substitute for the services of an attorney who is licensed to practice law in your state.

▪ KEY TERMS

adhesion contract   247
blue laws   243
blue sky laws   250
collateral promise   260
contractual capacity   237
covenant not to compete   245

disaffirmance   237
employment contract   245
exculpatory clause   247
necessaries   239
prenuptial agreement   261
ratification   240

reformation   247
scienter   255
Statute of Frauds   258
unconscionable contract
    or unconscionable clause   247
usury   242

CHAPTER SUMMARY ▦ Contracts: Capacity, Legality, Assent, and Form

	CONTRACTUAL CAPACITY

Minors
(See pages 237–241.)
	A minor is a person who has not yet reached the age of majority. In most states, the age of majority is eighteen for contract purposes. Contracts with minors are voidable at the option of the minor.
	
	1. *Disaffirmance*—The legal avoidance of a contractual obligation.
	
	  a. Disaffirmance can take place (in most states) at any time during minority and within a reasonable time after the minor has reached the age of majority.
	
	  b. If a minor disaffirms part of a contract, the entire contract must be disaffirmed.
	
	  c. When disaffirming executed contracts, the minor has a duty to return received goods if they are still in the minor's control or (in some states) to pay their reasonable value.
	
	  d. A minor who has committed an act of fraud (such as misrepresentation of age) will be denied the right to disaffirm by some courts.
	
	  e. A minor may disaffirm a contract for necessaries but remains liable for the reasonable value of the goods.
	
	2. *Ratification*—The acceptance, or affirmation, of a legal obligation; may be express or implied.
	
	  a. Express ratification—Exists when the minor, through a writing or an oral agreement, explicitly assumes the obligations imposed by the contract.
	
	  b. Implied ratification—Exists when the conduct of the minor is inconsistent with disaffirmance or when the minor fails to disaffirm an executed contract within a reasonable time after reaching the age of majority.

Intoxicated Persons (See page 241.)	1. A contract entered into by an intoxicated person is voidable at the option of the intoxicated person if the person was sufficiently intoxicated to lack mental capacity, even if the intoxication was voluntary. 2. A contract with an intoxicated person is enforceable if, despite being intoxicated, the person understood the legal consequences of entering into the contract.
Mentally Incompetent Persons (See pages 241–242.)	1. A contract made by a person adjudged by a court to be mentally incompetent is void. 2. A contract made by a mentally incompetent person not adjudged by a court to be mentally incompetent is voidable at the option of the mentally incompetent person.
	LEGALITY
Contracts Contrary to Statute (See pages 242–244.)	1. *Usury*—Usury occurs when a lender makes a loan at an interest rate above the lawful maximum. The maximum rate of interest varies from state to state. 2. *Gambling*—Gambling contracts that contravene (go against) state statutes are deemed illegal and thus void. 3. *Sabbath (Sunday) laws*—These laws prohibit the formation or the performance of certain contracts on Sunday. Such laws vary widely from state to state, and many states do not enforce them. 4. *Licensing statutes*—Contracts entered into by persons who do not have a license, when one is required by statute, will not be enforceable *unless* the underlying purpose of the statute is to raise government revenues (and not to protect the public from unauthorized practitioners).
Contracts Contrary to Public Policy (See pages 245–249.)	1. *Contracts in restraint of trade*—Contracts to reduce or restrain free competition are illegal. Most such contracts are now prohibited by statutes. An exception is a *covenant not to compete*. It is usually enforced by the courts if the terms are ancillary to a contract (such as a

CHAPTER SUMMARY Contracts: Capacity, Legality, Assent, and Form—Continued

Contracts Contrary to Public Policy— Continued	contract for the sale of a business or an employment contract) and are reasonable as to time and area of restraint. Courts tend to scrutinize covenants not to compete closely. If a covenant is overbroad, a court may either reform the covenant to make the restraints more reasonable and then enforce the reformed contract or declare the covenant void and thus unenforceable. 2. *Unconscionable contracts and clauses*—When a contract or contract clause is so unfair that it is oppressive to one party, it can be deemed unconscionable; as such, it is illegal and cannot be enforced. 3. *Exculpatory clauses*—An exculpatory clause is a clause that releases a party from liability in the event of monetary or physical injury, no matter who is at fault. In certain situations, exculpatory clauses may be contrary to public policy and thus unenforceable.
Effect of Illegality (See pages 249–250.)	In general, an illegal contract is void, and the courts will not aid either party when both parties are considered to be equally at fault *(in pari delicto)*. If the contract is executory, neither party can enforce it. If the contract is executed, there can be neither contractual nor quasi-contractual recovery. Several exceptions exist to the general rule that neither party to an illegal bargain will be able to recover. In the following situations, the court may grant recovery: 1. *Justifiable ignorance of the facts*—When one party to the contract is relatively innocent. 2. *Members of protected classes*—When one party to the contract is a member of a group of persons protected by statute, such as employees. 3. *Withdrawal from an illegal agreement*—When either party seeks to recover consideration given for an illegal contract before the illegal act is performed. 4. *Severable, or divisible, contracts*—When the court can divide the contract into illegal and legal portions and the illegal portion is not essential to the bargain. 5. *Fraud, duress, or undue influence*—When one party was induced to enter into an illegal bargain through fraud, duress, or undue influence.
	GENUINENESS OF ASSENT
Mistakes (See pages 251–253.)	1. *Unilateral*—Generally, the mistaken party is bound by the contract *unless* (a) the other party knows or should have known of the mistake or (b) the mistake is an inadvertent mathematical error—such as an error in addition or subtraction—committed without gross negligence. 2. *Bilateral* (mutual)—When both parties are mistaken about the same material fact, such as identity, either party can avoid the contract. If the mistake concerns value or quality, either party can enforce the contract.
Fraudulent Misrepresentation (See pages 253–257.)	When fraud occurs, usually the innocent party can enforce or avoid the contract. The elements necessary to establish fraud are as follows: 1. A misrepresentation of a material fact must occur. 2. There must be an intent to deceive. 3. The innocent party must justifiably rely on the misrepresentation.
Undue Influence (See page 257.)	Undue influence arises from special relationships, such as fiduciary or confidential relationships, in which one party's free will has been overcome by the undue influence exerted by the other party. Usually, the contract is voidable.
Duress (See page 257.)	Duress is the tactic of forcing a party to enter a contract under the fear of a threat—for example, the threat of violence or serious economic loss. The party forced to enter the contract can rescind the contract.

(Continued)

CHAPTER SUMMARY ▦ Contracts: Capacity, Legality, Assent, and Form—Continued

	FORM
The Statute of Frauds— Requirement of a Writing (See pages 258–263.)	*Applicability*—The following types of contracts fall under the Statute of Frauds and must be in writing to be enforceable: 1. *Contracts involving interests in land*—The statute applies to any contract for an interest in realty, such as a sale, a lease, or a mortgage. 2. *Contracts whose terms cannot be performed within one year*—The statute applies only to contracts objectively impossible to perform fully within one year from the day after the contract's formation. 3. *Collateral promises*—The statute applies only to express contracts made between the guarantor and the creditor whose terms make the guarantor secondarily liable. Exception: the "main purpose" rule. 4. *Promises made in consideration of marriage*—The statute applies to promises to pay money or give property in consideration of a promise to marry and to prenuptial agreements made in consideration of marriage. 5. *Contracts for the sale of goods priced at $500 or more*—Under the UCC Statute of Frauds provision in UCC 2–201. (Under a 2003 amendment to that UCC section, the threshold amount is raised from $500 to $5,000.) *Exceptions*—Partial performance, admissions, and promissory estoppel.
The Statute of Frauds—Sufficiency of the Writing (See pages 263–264.)	To constitute an enforceable contract under the Statute of Frauds, a writing must be signed by the party against whom enforcement is sought, must name the parties, must identify the subject matter, and must state with reasonable certainty the essential terms of the contract. In a sale of land, the price and a description of the property may need to be stated with sufficient clarity to allow them to be determined without reference to outside sources. Under the UCC, a contract for a sale of goods is not enforceable beyond the quantity of goods shown in the contract.

▦ FOR REVIEW

Answers for the even-numbered questions in this For Review *section can be found in Appendix I at the end of this text.*

1 What are some exceptions to the rule that a minor can disaffirm (avoid) any contract?

2 Does an intoxicated person have the capacity to enter into an enforceable contract?

3 In what types of situations might genuineness of assent to a contract's terms be lacking?

4 What elements must exist for fraudulent misrepresentation to occur?

5 What contracts must be in writing to be enforceable?

▦ QUESTIONS AND CASE PROBLEMS

8–1. Contracts by Minors. Kalen is a seventeen-year-old minor who has just graduated from high school. He is attending a university two hundred miles from home and has contracted to rent an apartment near the university for one year at $500 per month. He is working at a convenience store to earn enough income to be self-supporting. After living in the apartment and paying monthly rent for four months, he becomes involved in a dispute with his landlord. Kalen, still a minor, moves out and returns the key to the landlord. The landlord wants to hold Kalen liable for the balance of the payments due under the lease. Discuss fully Kalen's liability in this situation.

8–2. Licensing Statutes. State X requires that persons who prepare and serve liquor in the form of drinks at commercial establishments be licensed by the state to do so. The only requirement for obtaining a yearly license is that the person be at least twenty-one years old. Mickey, aged thirty-five, is hired as a bartender for the Southtown Restaurant. Gerald, a staunch alumnus of a nearby university, brings twenty of his friends to the restaurant to celebrate a football victory one afternoon. Gerald orders four rounds of drinks, and the bill is nearly $200. On learning that Mickey has failed to renew his bartender's license, Gerald refuses to pay, claiming that the contract is unenforceable. Discuss whether Gerald is correct.

8–3. Fraudulent Misrepresentation. Larry offered to sell Stanley his car and told Stanley that the car had been driven only 25,000 miles and had never been in an accident. Stanley hired Cohen, a mechanic, to appraise the condition of the car, and Cohen said that the car probably had at least 50,000 miles on it and probably had been in an accident. In spite of this information, Stanley still thought the car would be a good buy for the price, so he purchased it. Later, when the car developed numerous mechanical problems, Stanley sought to rescind the contract on the basis of Larry's fraudulent misrepresentation of the auto's condition. Will Stanley be able to rescind his contract? Discuss.

8–4. Exculpatory Clause. Norbert Eelbode applied for a job with Travelers Inn in the state of Washington. As part of the application process, Eelbode was sent to Laura Grothe, a physical therapist at Chec Medical Centers, Inc., for a preemployment physical exam. Before the exam, Eelbode signed a document that stated in part, "I hereby release Chec and the Washington Readicare Medical Group and its physicians from all liability arising from any injury to me resulting from my participation in the exam." During the exam, Grothe asked Eelbode to lift an item while bending from the waist using only his back with his knees locked. Eelbode experienced immediate sharp and burning pain in his lower back and down the back of his right leg. Eelbode filed a suit in a Washington state court against Grothe and Chec, claiming that he was injured because of an improperly administered back torso strength test. Citing the document that Eelbode signed, Grothe and Chec filed a motion for summary judgment. Should the court grant the motion? Why or why not? [*Eelbode v. Chec Medical Centers, Inc.*, 984 P.2d 436 (Wash.App. 1999)]

8–5. Oral Contracts. Robert Pinto, doing business as Pinto Associates, hired Richard MacDonald as an independent contractor in March 1992. The parties orally agreed on the terms of employment, including payment to MacDonald of a share of the company's income, but they did not put anything in writing. In March 1995, MacDonald quit. Pinto then told MacDonald that he was entitled to $9,602.17—25 percent of the difference between the accounts receivable and the accounts payable as of

MacDonald's last day. MacDonald disagreed and demanded more than $83,500—25 percent of the revenue from all invoices, less the cost of materials and outside processing, for each of the years that he worked for Pinto. Pinto refused. MacDonald filed a suit in a Connecticut state court against Pinto, alleging breach of contract. In Pinto's response and at the trial, he testified that the parties had an oral contract under which MacDonald was entitled to 25 percent of the difference between accounts receivable and payable as of the date of MacDonald's termination. Did the parties have an enforceable contract? How should the court rule, and why? [*MacDonald v. Pinto*, 62 Conn.App. 317, 771 A.2d 156 (2001)]

CASE PROBLEM WITH SAMPLE ANSWER

8–6. In 1993, Mutual Service Casualty Insurance Co. and its affiliates (collectively, MSI) hired Thomas Brass as an insurance agent. Three years later, Brass entered into a career agent's contract with MSI. This contract contained provisions regarding Brass's activities after termination. These provisions stated that, for a period of not less than one year, Brass could not solicit any MSI customers to "lapse, cancel, or replace" any insurance contract in force with MSI in an effort to take that business to a competitor. If he did, MSI could at any time refuse to pay the commissions that it otherwise owed him. The contract also restricted Brass from working for American National Insurance Co. for three years after termination. In 1998, Brass quit MSI and immediately went to work for American National, soliciting MSI customers. MSI filed a suit in a Wisconsin state court against Brass, claiming that he had violated the noncompete terms of his MSI contract. Should the court enforce the covenant not to compete? Why or why not? [*Mutual Service Casualty Insurance Co. v. Brass*, 625 N.W.2d 648 (Wis.App. 2001)]

After you have answered this problem, compare your answer with the sample answer given on the Web site that accompanies this text. Go to <u>http://blt.westbuslaw.com</u>, select "Chapter 8," and click on "Case Problem with Sample Answer."

8–7. Covenant Not to Compete. Gary Forsee was an executive officer with responsibility for the U.S. operations of BellSouth Corp., a company providing global telecommunications services. Under a covenant not to compete, Forsee agreed that for a period of eighteen months after termination from employment, he would not "provide services * * * in competition with [BellSouth] * * * to any person or entity which provides products or services identical or similar to products and services provided by [BellSouth] * * * within the territory." *Territory* was defined to include the geographic area in which Forsee provided services to BellSouth. The *services* included "management, strategic planning, business planning, administration, or other participation in or providing advice with respect to the communications services business." Forsee announced his intent to resign and accept a position as chief executive officer of Sprint Corp., a competitor of BellSouth. BellSouth filed a suit in a Georgia state court against Forsee, claiming in part that his acceptance of employment with Sprint would violate the covenant not to compete. Is the covenant legal? Should it be enforced? Why or why not? [*BellSouth Corp. v. Forsee*, 595 S.E.2d 99 (Ga.App. 2004)]

A QUESTION OF ETHICS

8–8. Nancy Levy worked for Health Care Financial Enterprises, Inc., and signed a noncompete agreement in June 1992. When Levy left Health Care and opened her own similar business in 1993, Health Care brought a court action in a Florida state court to enforce the covenant not to compete. The trial court concluded that the noncompete agreement prevented Levy from working in too broad a geographic area and thus refused to enforce the agreement. A Florida appellate court, however, reversed the trial court's ruling and remanded the case with instructions that the trial court modify the geographic area to make it reasonable and then enforce the covenant. [*Health Care Financial Enterprises, Inc. v. Levy*, 715 So.2d 341 (Fla.App.4th 1998)]

1. At one time in Florida, under the common law, non-compete covenants were illegal, although modern Florida statutory law now allows such covenants to be enforced. Generally, what interests are served by refusing to enforce covenants not to compete? What interests are served by allowing them to be enforced?

2. What argument could be made in support of reforming (and then enforcing) illegal covenants not to compete? What argument could be made against this practice?

FOR CRITICAL ANALYSIS

8–9. Do you think that the advent of legalized forms of gambling, such as state-operated lotteries, is consistent with a continued public policy against the enforcement of gambling contracts? Why or why not?

VIDEO QUESTION

8–10. Go to this text's Web site at **http://blt.westbuslaw.com** and select "Chapter 8." Click on "Video Questions" and view the video titled *Money Pit*. Then answer the following questions.

1. Assume that a valid contract exists between Walter (Tom Hanks) and the plumber. Recall from the video that the plumber had at least two drinks before agreeing to take on the plumbing job. If the plumber was intoxicated, is the contract voidable? Why or why not?

2. Suppose that state law requires plumbers in Walter's state to have a plumber's license and that this plumber does not have a license. Would the contract be enforceable? Why or why not?

3. In the video, the plumber suggests that Walter has been "turned down by every other plumber in the valley." Although the plumber does not even look at the house's plumbing, he agrees to do the repairs if Walter gives him a check for $5,000 right now "before he changes his mind." If Walter later seeks to void the contract because it is contrary to public policy, what should he argue?

ONLINE ACTIVITIES

INTERNET EXERCISES

Go to the *Business Law Today: The Essentials* home page at **http://blt.westbuslaw.com**, select "Chapter 8," and click on "Internet Exercises." There you will find the following Internet research exercises that you can perform to learn more about topics covered in this chapter.

Activity 8–1: LEGAL PERSPECTIVE—Covenants Not to Compete

Activity 8–2: MANAGEMENT PERSPECTIVE—Minors and the Law

Activity 8–3: HISTORICAL PERSPECTIVE—The English Act for the Prevention of Frauds and Perjuries

BEFORE THE TEST

Go to the *Business Law Today: The Essentials* home page at **http://blt.westbuslaw.com**, select "Chapter 8," and click on "Interactive Quizzes." You will find at least twenty interactive questions relating to this chapter.

CHAPTER 9

Contracts: Third Party Rights, Discharge, Breach, and Remedies

"The laws of a state change with the changing times."
Aeschylus, 525–456 B.C.E.
(Greek dramatist)

CHAPTER OUTLINE

■ ASSIGNMENTS AND DELEGATIONS

■ THIRD PARTY BENEFICIARIES

■ CONTRACT DISCHARGE

■ DAMAGES

■ EQUITABLE REMEDIES

■ RECOVERY BASED ON QUASI CONTRACT

■ ELECTION OF REMEDIES

PRIVITY OF CONTRACT
The relationship that exists between the promisor and the promisee of a contract.

■■ LEARNING OBJECTIVES

After reading this chapter, you should be able to answer the following questions:

1 What is the difference between an assignment and a delegation?

2 What factors indicate that a third party beneficiary is an intended beneficiary?

3 What is the difference between compensatory damages and consequential damages? What are nominal damages, and when do courts award nominal damages?

4 Under what circumstances will equitable remedies be available?

5 What is the rationale underlying the doctrine of election of remedies?

Because a contract is a private agreement between the parties who have entered into it, it is fitting that these parties alone should have rights and liabilities under the contract. This concept is referred to as **privity of contract**, and it establishes the basic principle that third parties have no rights in contracts to which they are not parties.

You may be convinced by now that for every rule of contract law, there is an exception. As times change, so must the laws, as indicated in the opening quotation. When justice cannot be served by adherence to a rule of law, exceptions to the rule must be made. In this chapter, we look at some exceptions to the rule of privity of contract. We also examine how contractual obligations can be *discharged*. Normally, contract discharge is accomplished when both parties have performed the acts promised in the contract. In the latter part of this chapter, we look at the degree of

271

BREACH OF CONTRACT
The failure, without legal excuse, of a promisor to perform the obligations of a contract.

performance required to discharge a contractual obligation, as well as at some other ways in which contract discharge can occur.

When it is no longer advantageous for a party to fulfill her or his contractual obligations, that party may breach the contract. A **breach of contract** occurs when a party fails to perform part or all of the required duties under a contract.[1] Once a party fails to perform or performs inadequately, the other party—the nonbreaching party—can choose one or more of several remedies.

▉▉ Assignments and Delegations

When third parties acquire rights or assume duties arising from contracts, the rights are transferred to them by *assignment*, and the duties are transferred by *delegation*.

ASSIGNMENTS

ASSIGNMENT
The act of transferring to another all or part of one's rights arising under a contract.

ASSIGNOR
A party who transfers (assigns) his or her rights under a contract to another party (called the assignee).

ASSIGNEE
A party to whom the rights under a contract are transferred, or assigned.

OBLIGEE
One to whom an obligation is owed.

OBLIGOR
One who owes an obligation to another.

In a bilateral contract, normally one party has a right to require the other to perform some task, and the other has a duty to perform it. The transfer of contract *rights* to a third person is known as an **assignment.** The party assigning the rights to a third party is known as the **assignor,** and the party receiving the rights is the **assignee.** Other traditional terminology used to describe the parties in assignment relationships are the **obligee** (the person to whom a duty, or obligation, is owed) and the **obligor** (the person who is obligated to perform the duty).

When rights under a contract are assigned unconditionally, the rights of the *assignor* (the party making the assignment) are extinguished.[2] The third party (the *assignee,* or the party receiving the assignment) has a right to demand performance from the other original party to the contract (the *obligor,* the person who is obligated to perform). ▉ **EXAMPLE 9.1** Brent owes Alex $1,000, and Alex, the assignor, assigns to Carmen the right to receive the $1,000. Here, a valid assignment of a debt exists. Carmen, the assignee, can enforce the contract against Brent, the obligor, if Brent fails to perform. ▉ Exhibit 9–1 illustrates assignment relationships.

The assignee takes only those rights that the assignor originally had. Furthermore, the assignee's rights are subject to the defenses that the obligor has against the assignor. ▉ **EXAMPLE 9.2** Brent owes Alex $1,000 under a contract in which Brent agreed to buy Alex's computer work station. Alex assigns his right to receive the $1,000 to Carmen. Brent, in deciding to purchase the work station, relied on Alex's fraudulent misrepresentation that the computer's hard drive had a storage capacity of 120 gigabytes. When Brent discovers that the computer can store only 20 gigabytes, he tells Alex that he is going to return the work station and cancel the contract. Even though Alex has assigned his "right" to receive the $1,000 to Carmen, Brent need not pay Carmen the $1,000—Brent can raise the defense of Alex's fraudulent misrepresentation to avoid payment. ▉

The Importance of Assignments in the Business Context   Assignments are important because they are utilized in much business financing. Lending institutions, such as banks, frequently assign the rights to receive payments under their loan contracts to other firms, which pay for those rights. If you obtain a loan from your local bank to purchase a car, you may later receive in the mail a notice stating that your bank has transferred (assigned) its rights to receive payments on the loan to another firm

---

1. *Restatement (Second) of Contracts,* Section 235(2).
2. *Restatement (Second) of Contracts,* Section 317.

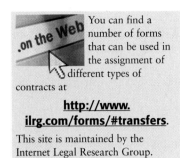

You can find a number of forms that can be used in the assignment of different types of contracts at

http://www. ilrg.com/forms/#transfers.

This site is maintained by the Internet Legal Research Group.

and that, when the time comes to repay your loan, you must make the payments to that other firm.

Lenders that make *mortgage loans* (loans to allow prospective home buyers to purchase land or a home) often assign their rights to collect the mortgage payments to a third party, such as GMAC Mortgage Corporation. Following an assignment, the home buyer is notified that future payments must be made not to the lender that loaned the funds but to the third party. Millions of dollars change hands daily in the business world in the form of assignments of rights in contracts. If it were not possible to transfer (assign) contractual rights, many businesses could not continue to operate.

Rights That Cannot Be Assigned   As a general rule, all rights can be assigned. Exceptions are made, however, in the following special circumstances.

When a Statute Expressly Prohibits Assignment. If a statute expressly prohibits assignment, the particular right in question cannot be assigned. ■ EXAMPLE 9.3 Marn is a new employee of CompuFuture, Inc. CompuFuture is an employer under workers' compensation statutes (see Chapter 18) in this state, and thus Marn is a covered employee. Marn has a relatively high-risk job. In need of a loan, she borrows some funds from Stark, assigning to Stark all workers' compensation benefits due her should she be injured on the job. A state statute prohibits the assignment of *future* workers' compensation benefits, and thus such rights cannot be assigned. ■

When a Contract Is Personal in Nature.   When a contract is for personal services, the rights under the contract normally cannot be assigned unless all that remains is a

EXHIBIT 9–1 ASSIGNMENT RELATIONSHIPS

In the assignment relationship illustrated here, Alex assigns his *rights* under a contract that he made with Brent to a third party, Carmen. Alex thus becomes the *assignor* and Carmen the *assignee* of the contractual rights. Brent, the *obligor* (the party owing performance under the contract), now owes performance to Carmen instead of Alex. Alex's original contract rights are extinguished after assignment.

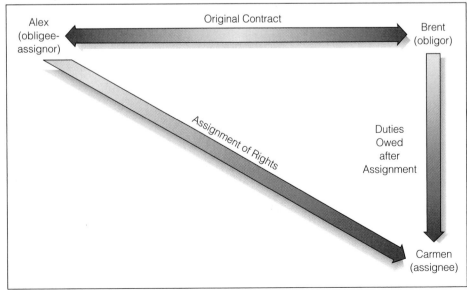

money payment.[3] ■ **EXAMPLE 9.4** Brent signs a contract to be a tutor for Alex's children. Alex then attempts to assign to Carmen his right to Brent's services. Carmen cannot enforce the contract against Brent. Brent may not like Carmen's children or may for some other reason not want to tutor them. Because personal services are unique to the person rendering them, rights to receive personal services cannot be assigned. ■

When an Assignment Will Increase or Alter the Risk or Duties of the Obligor. A right cannot be assigned if assignment will materially increase or alter the risk or duties of the obligor.[4] ■ **EXAMPLE 9.5** Alex has a hotel, and to insure it, he takes out a policy with Northwest Insurance Company. The policy insures against fire, theft, floods, and vandalism. Alex attempts to assign the insurance policy to Carmen, who also owns a hotel. The assignment is ineffective because it may substantially alter the insurance company's duty of performance and the risk that the company undertakes. An insurance company evaluates the particular risk of a certain party and tailors its policy to fit that risk. If the policy is assigned to a third party, the insurance risk is materially altered. ■

When the Contract Prohibits Assignment. If a contract stipulates that the right cannot be assigned, then *ordinarily* it cannot be assigned. ■ **EXAMPLE 9.6** Brent agrees to build a house for Alex. The contract between Brent and Alex states, "This contract cannot be assigned by Alex without Brent's consent. Any assignment without such consent renders this contract void, and all rights hereunder will thereupon terminate." Alex then assigns his rights to Carmen, without first obtaining Brent's consent. Carmen cannot enforce the contract against Brent. ■ This rule has several exceptions:

1 A contract cannot prevent an assignment of the right to receive money. This exception exists to encourage the free flow of funds and credit in modern business settings.

---

3. *Restatement (Second) of Contracts,* Sections 317 and 318.
4. See Section 2–210(2) of the Uniform Commercial Code (UCC).

A music teacher instructs her pupil. Assuming that the boy's parent contracted with the instructor for her services, can the parent assign the right to receive music lessons to another party? Why or why not? (AP Photo/ Fort Collins Coloradoan, Sherri Barber)

ALIENATION
The process of transferring land out of one's possession (thus "alienating" the land from oneself).

2 The assignment of ownership rights in real estate often cannot be prohibited because such a prohibition is contrary to public policy in most states. Prohibitions of this kind are called restraints against **alienation** (the voluntary transfer of land ownership).

3 The assignment of negotiable instruments (see Chapter 14) cannot be prohibited.

4 In a contract for the sale of goods, the right to receive damages for breach of contract or for payment of an account owed may be assigned even though the sales contract prohibits such assignment.[5]

In the following case, both parties had violated an antiassignment clause. The question before the court was how one party's violation affected that party's recovery for the other party's violation.

5. UCC 2–210(2).

CASE 9.1 Forest Commodity Corp. v. Lone Star Industries, Inc.

Court of Appeals of Georgia, 2002.
564 S.E.2d 755.

FACTS Forest Commodity Corporation (FCC) owns an ocean terminal facility where ships unload and store bulk cargo. FCC, which has no employees or equipment, leases the facility to Woodchips Export Corporation (WEC). Construction Aggregates, Limited, owned by Lone Star Industries, Inc. (jointly referred to as CAL), mines and ships aggregate stone. FCC and CAL entered into a three-year contract under which FCC agreed to provide terminal space for unloading aggregate stone, which FCC would then store, reload onto trucks, and weigh for further shipment. CAL promised to unload a minimum of 150,000 tons per year or pay a higher price. The contract prohibited its assignment without the other party's consent. FCC transferred its obligations under this contract to WEC without CAL's consent. About a year later, after CAL had shipped nearly 200,000 tons, Martin Marietta Materials, Inc., acquired CAL and offered to accept its obligations under the contract with FCC, but FCC refused. At the same time, FCC and Martin Marietta entered into a separate, but substantially similar, contract. The total aggregate shipped under both contracts over a three-year period was 484,868 tons. FCC filed a suit in a Georgia state court against CAL for breach of contract, alleging that CAL had failed to ship the agreed minimum. The court issued a summary judgment in CAL's favor. FCC appealed to a state intermediate appellate court.

ISSUE Was FCC's breach of the antiassignment clause a material breach of the agreement with CAL, which would prevent FCC from holding CAL to the contract?

DECISION Yes. The state intermediate appellate court affirmed the lower court's judgment. FCC breached its con-

tract with CAL by violating the antiassignment clause, and this breach precluded FCC from enforcing the contract.

REASON The court explained that a party's refusal to abide by a contract provision prohibiting assignment amounted to an anticipatory repudiation of the contract.[a] The court stated that "[s]uch a repudiation of the agreement estops [prevents] FCC from seeking to enforce other provisions of the agreement." FCC claimed that any breach of the antiassignment clause was not material, because "the fundamental purpose of the agreement—to provide CAL with a place to discharge and store its aggregate cargo [stone]—was satisfied." The court responded, "FCC's own refusal of CAL's request for consent to an assignment of the agreement to Martin Marietta * * * shows that FCC thought the identity of the parties to the agreement was important or it would have accepted CAL's proposed assignment. In addition, the agreement creates a bailment relationship between FCC and CAL, wherein CAL entrusts aggregate to FCC's safekeeping.[b] Certainly, the uniqueness and identity of the parties is a material term in such a relationship."

FOR CRITICAL ANALYSIS—Social Consideration
Would the result in this case have been different if FCC had not entered into a substantially similar contract with Martin Marietta? Why or why not?

a. As will be discussed later in this chapter, an anticipatory repudiation of a contract occurs when one party, before the time for performance, indicates by words or actions that the party will not perform the contract.
b. In a bailment relationship, the property of one party is entrusted to another, who is obligated to return the property or otherwise dispose of it as instructed. See Chapter 23.

DELEGATIONS

DELEGATION OF DUTIES
The act of transferring to another all or part of one's duties arising under a contract.

DELEGATOR
A party who transfers (delegates) her or his obligations under a contract to another party (called the delegatee).

DELEGATEE
A party to whom contractual obligations are transferred, or delegated.

Just as a party can transfer rights to a third party through an assignment, a party can also transfer duties. Duties are not assigned, however; they are *delegated*. Normally, a **delegation of duties** does not relieve the party making the delegation (the **delegator**) of the obligation to perform in the event that the party to whom the duty has been delegated (the **delegatee**) fails to perform. No special form is required to create a valid delegation of duties. As long as the delegator expresses an intention to make the delegation, it is effective; the delegator need not even use the word *delegate*. Exhibit 9–2 graphically illustrates delegation relationships.

Duties That Cannot Be Delegated   As a general rule, any duty can be delegated. This rule has some exceptions, however. Delegation is prohibited in the following circumstances:

1 When performance depends on the personal skill or talents of the obligor.

2 When special trust has been placed in the obligor.

3 When performance by a third party will vary materially from that expected by the obligee (the one to whom performance is owed) under the contract.

4 When the contract expressly prohibits delegation.

The following examples will help to clarify the kinds of duties that can and cannot be delegated:

1 Brent contracts with Alex to tutor Alex in various aspects of financial underwriting and investment banking. Brent, an experienced businessperson known for his expertise in finance, delegates his duties to a third party, Carmen. This

EXHIBIT 9–2 DELEGATION RELATIONSHIPS

In the delegation relationship illustrated here, Brent delegates his *duties* under a contract that he made with Alex to a third party, Carmen. Brent thus becomes the *delegator* and Carmen the *delegatee* of the contractual duties. Carmen now owes performance of the contractual duties to Alex. Note that a delegation of duties normally does not relieve the delegator (Brent) of liability if the delegatee (Carmen) fails to perform the contractual duties.

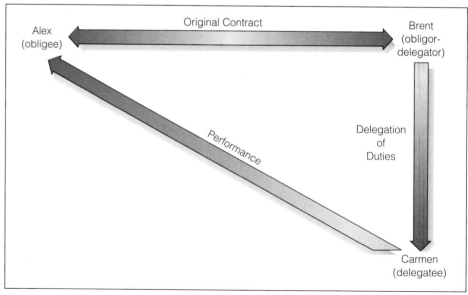

delegation is ineffective because Brent contracted to render a service that is founded on Brent's *expertise*, and the delegation changes Alex's expectancy under the contract.

2 Brent contracts with Alex to *personally* mow Alex's lawn during June, July, and August. Then Brent decides that he would rather spend the summer at the beach. Brent delegates his lawn-mowing duties to Carmen, who is in the business of mowing lawns and doing other landscaping work to earn income to pay for college. No matter how competent Carmen is, the delegation is not effective without Alex's consent. The contract was for *personal* performance.

3 Brent contracts with Alex to pick up and deliver heavy construction machinery to Alex's property. Brent delegates this duty to Carmen, who is in the business of delivering heavy machinery. This delegation is effective. The performance required is of a routine and nonpersonal nature, and the delegation does not change Alex's expectations under the contract.

Effect of a Delegation   If a delegation of duties is enforceable, the *obligee* (the one to whom performance is owed) must accept performance from the delegatee (the one to whom the duties are delegated). ■ EXAMPLE 9.7   In the third example in the above list, Brent delegates his duty (to pick up and deliver heavy construction machinery to Alex's property) to Carmen. In that situation, Alex (the obligee) must accept performance from Carmen (the delegatee) because the delegation was effective. The obligee can legally refuse performance from the delegatee only if the duty is one that cannot be delegated. ■

A valid delegation of duties does not relieve the delegator of obligations under the contract.[6] In the above example, if Carmen (the delegatee) fails to perform, Brent (the delegator) is still liable to Alex (the obligee). The obligee can also hold the delegatee liable if the delegatee made a promise of performance that will directly benefit the obligee. In this situation, there is an "assumption of duty" on the part of the delegatee, and breach of this duty makes the delegatee liable to the obligee. For example, if Carmen (the delegatee) promises Brent (the delegator), in a contract, to pick up and deliver the construction equipment to Alex's property but fails to do so, Alex (the obligee) can sue Brent, Carmen, or both. Although there are many exceptions, the general rule today is that the obligee can sue both the delegatee and the delegator.

COMPARE In an assignment, the assignor's original contract rights are extinguished after assignment. In a delegation, the delegator remains liable for performance under the contract if the delegatee fails to perform.

"Assignment of All Rights"   Sometimes, a contract provides for an "assignment of all rights." The traditional view was that under this type of assignment, the assignee did not assume any duties. This view was based on the theory that the assignee's agreement to accept the benefits of the contract was not sufficient to imply a promise to assume the duties of the contract.

Modern authorities, however, take the view that the probable intent in using such general words is to create both an assignment of rights and an assumption of duties.[7] Therefore, when general words are used (for example, "I assign the contract" or "all my rights under the contract"), the contract is construed as implying both an assignment of rights and an assumption of duties.

---

6. For a classic case on this issue, see *Crane Ice Cream Co. v. Terminal Freezing & Heating Co.,* 147 Md. 588, 128 A. 280 (1925).

7. See UCC 2–210(1), (4); *Restatement (Second) of Contracts,* Section 328.

▪▪ Third Party Beneficiaries

As mentioned earlier in this chapter, to have contractual rights, a person normally must be a party to the contract. In other words, privity of contract must exist. An exception to the doctrine of privity exists when the original parties to the contract intend, at the time of contracting, that the contract performance directly benefit a third person. In this situation, the third person becomes a **third party beneficiary** of the contract. As an **intended beneficiary** of the contract, the third party has legal rights and can sue the promisor directly for breach of the contract.

THIRD PARTY BENEFICIARY
One for whose benefit a promise is made in a contract but who is not a party to the contract.

INTENDED BENEFICIARY
A third party for whose benefit a contract is formed. An intended beneficiary can sue the promisor if such a contract is breached.

TYPES OF INTENDED BENEFICIARIES

The law distinguishes between *intended* beneficiaries and *incidental* beneficiaries. Only intended beneficiaries acquire legal rights in a contract. One type of intended beneficiary is a *creditor beneficiary*. A creditor beneficiary benefits from a contract in which one party (the promisor) promises another party (the promisee) to pay a debt that the promisee owes to a third party (the creditor beneficiary). As an intended beneficiary, the creditor beneficiary can sue the promisor directly to enforce the contract.

Another type of intended beneficiary is a *donee* beneficiary. When a contract is made for the express purpose of giving a *gift* to a third party, the third party (the donee beneficiary) can sue the promisor directly to enforce the promise.[8] The most common donee beneficiary contract is a life insurance contract. ▪ **EXAMPLE 9.8** Akins (the promisee) pays premiums to Standard Life, a life insurance company, and Standard Life (the promisor) promises to pay a certain amount on Akins's death to anyone Akins designates as a beneficiary. The designated beneficiary is a donee beneficiary under the life insurance policy and can enforce the promise made by the insurance company to pay him or her on Akins's death. ▪

As the law concerning third party beneficiaries evolved, numerous cases arose in which the third party beneficiary did not fit readily into either category—creditor beneficiary or donee beneficiary. Thus, the modern view, and the one adopted by the *Restatement (Second) of Contracts*, does not draw such clear lines and distinguishes only between intended beneficiaries (who can sue to enforce contracts made for their benefit) and incidental beneficiaries (who cannot sue, as will be discussed shortly).

ETHICAL ISSUE 9.1

Should third party beneficiaries be able to recover from attorneys on the basis of negligence? Periodically, the courts are asked to decide whether a designated beneficiary under a legal document, such as a will, can sue the attorney who drafted the document to recover for benefits that were lost as a result of the attorney's negligence. This is a significant issue for the beneficiaries of a will because normally the question does not arise until the party who signed the will has died—and thus cannot rectify the problem. Traditionally, the rule was that third party beneficiaries could not sue the attorney in these situations because they were not in privity of contract with the attorney—that is, an attorney's duty of care extends only to her or his client, and thus third parties do not have standing to sue the attorney for negligence.

Clearly, restricting suits against attorneys in these situations can have harsh results for intended beneficiaries. Although some courts continue to adhere to the traditional rule, increasingly courts are allowing third party beneficiaries to sue attorneys in these circumstances.[9] ▪

---

8. This principle was first enunciated in *Seaver v. Ransom,* 224 N.Y. 233, 120 N.E. 639 (1918).
9. See, for example, *Leak-Gilbert v. Fahle,* 55 P.3d 1054 (Okla. 2002).

WHEN THE RIGHTS OF AN INTENDED BENEFICIARY VEST

An intended third party beneficiary cannot enforce a contract against the original parties until the rights of the third party have *vested,* meaning that the rights have taken effect and cannot be taken away. Until these rights have vested, the original parties to the contract—the promisor and the promisee—can modify or rescind the contract without the consent of the third party. When do the rights of third parties vest? Generally, the rights vest when one of the following occurs:

1. When the third party demonstrates manifest assent to the contract, such as sending a letter or note acknowledging awareness of and consent to a contract formed for her or his benefit.

2. When the third party materially alters his or her position in detrimental reliance on the contract, such as when a donee beneficiary contracts to have a home built in reliance on the receipt of funds promised to him or her in a donee beneficiary contract.

3. When the conditions for vesting are satisfied. For example, the rights of a beneficiary under a life insurance policy vest when the insured person dies.

If the contract expressly reserves to the contracting parties the right to cancel, rescind, or modify the contract, the rights of the third party beneficiary are subject to any changes that result. In such a situation, the vesting of the third party's rights does not terminate the power of the original contracting parties to alter their legal relationships.[10]

INCIDENTAL BENEFICIARIES

INCIDENTAL BENEFICIARY
A third party who incidentally benefits from a contract but whose benefit was not the reason the contract was formed. An incidental beneficiary has no rights in a contract and cannot sue to have the contract enforced.

The benefit that an **incidental beneficiary** receives from a contract between two parties is unintentional. Therefore, an incidental beneficiary cannot enforce a contract to which he or she is not a party.

■ **EXAMPLE 9.9** In one case, spectators at a Mike Tyson boxing match in which Tyson was disqualified for biting his opponent's ear sued Tyson and the fight's promoters for a refund of their money on the basis of breach of contract. The spectators claimed that they had standing to sue the defendants as third party beneficiaries of the contract between Tyson and the fight's promoters. The court, however, held that the spectators did not have standing to sue because they were not in contractual privity with any of the defendants. Furthermore, any benefits they received from the contract were incidental to the contract. The court noted that the spectators got what they paid for: "the right to view whatever event transpired."[11] ■

Is a person who benefits from a contract between another party and a government entity an incidental beneficiary or an intended beneficiary? For a discussion of a case raising this question, see this chapter's *Adapting the Law to the Online Environment* feature on the following page.

INTENDED VERSUS INCIDENTAL BENEFICIARIES

In determining whether a third party beneficiary is an intended or an incidental beneficiary, the courts generally use the *reasonable person* test—that is, a beneficiary

---

10. Defenses raised against third party beneficiaries are given in the *Restatement (Second) of Contracts,* Section 309.
11. *Castillo v. Tyson,* 268 A.D.2d 336, 701 N.Y.S.2d 423 (Sup.Ct.App.Div. 2000).

ADAPTING THE LAW TO THE ONLINE ENVIRONMENT

Government Contracts and Third Party Beneficiaries

Government entities often contract with private organizations to provide certain services to the public. Are those who benefit under such contracts intended beneficiaries? This question came before the court in a case involving a person who had registered a domain name with an organization that had contracted with the federal government to provide domain name registration services.

THE DOMAIN NAME CONFLICT

In 1994, in the early days of the Internet (as a public surfing/shopping vehicle), domain names were free for the asking. At that time, Network Solutions, Inc. (NSI), was the sole registrar of domain names. NSI had a contract with a federal government agency stating that NSI had the primary responsibility for "ensuring the quality, timeliness, and effective management" of domain name registration services.

Gary Kremen, seeing what he felt was a great opportunity, registered the name "sex.com" with NSI. Unfortunately for Kremen, Stephen Cohen also saw the potential of that domain name. Cohen, who had just gotten out of prison for impersonating a bankruptcy lawyer, knew that Kremen had already registered the name. That fact, however, in the words of the court, "was only a minor impediment for a man of Cohen's boundless resource and bounded integrity." Through forgery and deceit, Cohen succeeded in having NSI transfer the domain name to his company. When Kremen later contacted NSI, he was told that it was too late to undo the transfer. Kremen then turned to the courts for assistance.

THE LEGAL ISSUES

Kremen sued Cohen, seeking as damages the substantial profits that Cohen had made by using the name. The court

held in Kremen's favor and awarded him millions of dollars in damages. Kremen could not collect the judgment, however, because Cohen had disappeared—after first transferring large sums to offshore accounts. Kremen then tried to hold NSI responsible for his losses by alleging, among other things, that he was an intended third party beneficiary of NSI's contract with the government. He claimed that because NSI had not "effectively managed" its duties, as it was obligated to do under the contract, his domain name had been wrongfully transferred.

Was Kremen an intended third party beneficiary of the contract? When the case ultimately reached the Court of Appeals for the Ninth Circuit, the court held that Kremen was not an intended third party beneficiary of the contract. The court noted that a third party can enforce a contract if the contract reflects an "express or implied intention of the parties to the contract to benefit the third party." The court emphasized, however, that when a contract is with a government entity, a more stringent test applies: for a third party to be an intended beneficiary, *the contract must express a clear intent to benefit the third party.* If it does not express this clear intent, then anyone who benefits under the contract is regarded as an incidental beneficiary and, as such, cannot sue to enforce the contract.[a]

FOR CRITICAL ANALYSIS

Kremen also alleged that NSI had breached an implied-in-fact contract with him, but the court dismissed this claim. Why would the court hold that no contract existed between Kremen and NSI? Was a required element for a valid contract lacking?

a. *Kremen v. Cohen*, 337 F.3d 1024 (9th Cir. 2003).

will be considered an intended beneficiary if a reasonable person in the position of the beneficiary would believe that the promisee *intended* to confer on the beneficiary the right to bring suit to enforce the contract. In determining whether a party is an intended or an incidental beneficiary, the courts also look at a number of other factors. The presence of one or more of the following factors strongly indicates that the third party is an intended (rather than an incidental) beneficiary to the contract:

1 Performance is rendered directly to the third party.

2 The third party has the right to control the details of performance.

3 The third party is expressly designated as a beneficiary in the contract.

Contract Discharge

DISCHARGE
The termination of an obligation. In contract law, discharge occurs when the parties have fully performed their contractual obligations or when events, conduct of the parties, or operation of law releases the parties from performance.

PERFORMANCE
In contract law, the fulfillment of one's duties arising under a contract with another; the normal way of discharging one's contractual obligations.

The most common way to **discharge,** or terminate, one's contractual duties is by the **performance** of those duties. The duty to perform under a contract may be *conditioned* on the occurrence or nonoccurrence of a certain event, or the duty may be *absolute*. As you can see in Exhibit 9–3, in addition to performance, a contract can be discharged in numerous other ways, including discharge by agreement of the parties and discharge by operation of law.

CONDITIONS OF PERFORMANCE

In most contracts, promises of performance are not expressly conditioned or qualified. Instead, they are *absolute promises*. They must be performed, or the party

EXHIBIT 9-3 CONTRACT DISCHARGE

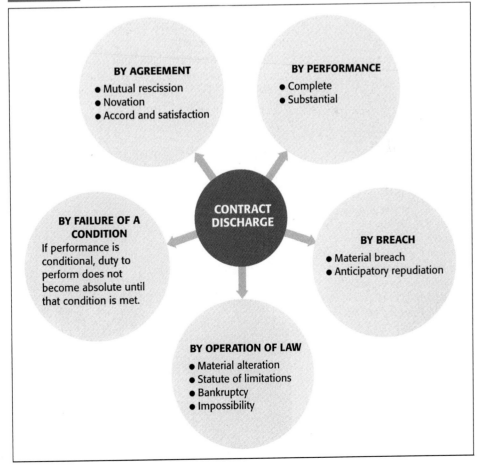

promising the act will be in breach of contract. ■ **EXAMPLE 9.10** JoAnne contracts to sell Alfonso a painting for $10,000. The parties' promises are unconditional: JoAnne's transfer of the painting to Alfonso and Alfonso's payment of $10,000 to JoAnne. The payment does not have to be made if the painting is not transferred. ■

In some situations, however, contractual promises are conditioned. A **condition** is a possible future event, the occurrence or nonoccurrence of which will trigger the performance of a legal obligation or terminate an existing obligation under a contract. If the condition is not satisfied, the obligations of the parties are discharged. ■ **EXAMPLE 9.11** Suppose that Alfonso, in the above example, offers to purchase JoAnne's painting only if an independent appraisal indicates that it is worth at least $10,000. JoAnne accepts Alfonso's offer. Their obligations (promises) are conditioned on the outcome of the appraisal. Should this condition not be satisfied (for example, if the appraiser deems the value of the painting to be only $5,000), their obligations to each other are discharged and cannot be enforced. ■

DISCHARGE BY PERFORMANCE

The contract comes to an end when both parties fulfill their respective duties by performing the acts they have promised. Performance can also be accomplished by tender. **Tender** is an unconditional offer to perform by a person who is ready, willing, and able to do so. Therefore, a seller who places goods at the disposal of a buyer has tendered delivery and can demand payment according to the terms of the agreement. A buyer who offers to pay for goods has tendered payment and can demand delivery of the goods.

Once performance has been tendered, the party making the tender has done everything possible to carry out the terms of the contract. If the other party then refuses to perform, the party making the tender can consider the duty discharged and sue for breach of contract.

CONDITION
A qualification, provision, or clause in a contractual agreement, the occurrence or nonoccurrence of which creates, suspends, or terminates the obligations of the contracting parties.

TENDER
An unconditional offer to perform an obligation by a person who is ready, willing, and able to do so.

A couple negotiates with a salesperson to purchase a car. Suppose that the parties reach an agreement on the sale, which is conditioned on the dealer's servicing the car's air conditioner. When the couple returns to the lot the following day, they discover that the air conditioner has not been serviced. Are they still obligated to buy the car? Why or why not? What type of condition is this? (© Getty Images)

Different brands of construction supplies displayed at a site. If a contract for the construction of a building or house specifies a particular brand, can a product of a different brand of comparable quality be substituted? Why or why not? (© Tony Freeman, PhotoEdit)

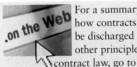

For a summary of how contracts may be discharged and other principles of contract law, go to

http://www.lawyers.com/ legal_topics/browse_by_ topic/index.php?.

Click on "Business Needs." Then, under the heading "General Business," click on "Contracts" and select the appropriate links.

Complete versus Substantial Performance   Normally, conditions expressly stated in the contract must fully occur in all aspects for *complete performance* (strict performance) of the contract to occur. Any deviation breaches the contract and discharges the other party's obligations to perform. Although in most contracts the parties fully discharge their obligations by complete performance, sometimes a party fails to fulfill all of the duties or completes the duties in a manner contrary to the terms of the contract. The issue then arises as to whether the performance was nonetheless sufficiently substantial to discharge the contractual obligations.

To qualify as *substantial performance,* the performance must not vary greatly from the performance promised in the contract, and it must create substantially the same benefits as those promised in the contract. If performance is substantial, the other party's duty to perform remains absolute (less damages, if any, for the minor deviations).

■ **EXAMPLE 9.12** A couple contracts with a construction company to build a house. The contract specifies that Brand X plasterboard be used for the walls. The builder cannot obtain Brand X plasterboard, and the buyers are on holiday in the mountains of Peru and virtually unreachable. The builder decides to install Brand Y instead, which he knows is identical in quality and durability to Brand X plasterboard. All other aspects of construction conform to the contract. Does this deviation constitute a breach of contract? Can the buyers avoid their contractual obligation to pay the builder because Brand Y plasterboard was used instead of Brand X? Very likely, a court would hold that the builder had substantially performed his end of the bargain, and therefore the couple will be obligated to pay the builder.

What if the plasterboard substituted for Brand X was not of the same quality as Brand X, and the value of the house was reduced by $10,000? Again, a court would likely hold that the contract had been substantially performed and that the contractor should be paid the price agreed on in the contract, less that $10,000. ■

Performance to the Satisfaction of Another   Contracts often state that completed work must personally satisfy one of the parties or a third person. The question is whether this satisfaction becomes a contract *condition*, requiring actual personal satisfaction or approval for discharge, or whether the test of satisfaction is performance that would satisfy a *reasonable person* (substantial performance).

When the subject matter of the contract is personal, a contract to be performed to the satisfaction of one of the parties is conditioned, and performance must actually satisfy that party. For example, contracts for portraits, works of art, and tailoring are considered personal. Therefore, only the personal satisfaction of the party fulfills the condition—unless a court finds the party is expressing dissatisfaction only to avoid payment or otherwise is not acting in good faith.

Contracts that involve mechanical fitness, utility, or marketability need be performed only to the satisfaction of a reasonable person unless they *expressly state otherwise.* When such contracts require performance to the satisfaction of a third party (for example, "to the satisfaction of Robert Ames, the supervising engineer"), the courts are divided. A majority of courts require the work to be satisfactory to a reasonable person, but some courts hold that the personal satisfaction of the third party designated in the contract (Robert Ames, in this example) must be met. Again, the personal judgment must be made honestly, or the condition will be excused.

Material Breach of Contract　　When a breach of contract is *material*[12]—that is, when performance is not deemed substantial—the nonbreaching party is excused from the performance of contractual duties and has a cause of action to sue for damages caused by the breach. If the breach is *minor* (not material), the nonbreaching party's duty to perform may sometimes be suspended until the breach is remedied, but the duty is not entirely excused. Once the minor breach is cured, the nonbreaching party must resume performance of the contractual obligations that had been undertaken.

A breach entitles the nonbreaching party to sue for damages, but only a material breach discharges the nonbreaching party from the contract. The policy underlying these rules is that contracts should go forward when only minor problems occur, but contracts should be terminated if major problems arise.[13]

Did a seller's failure to repair the plumbing in an apartment building within the eight-month period specified in a contract with the buyers constitute a material breach of the parties' contract? That was the issue in the following case.

---

12. *Restatement (Second) of Contracts,* Section 241.
13. See UCC 2–612, which deals with installment contracts for the sale of goods.

CASE 9.2　■　Kim v. Park

Court of Appeals of Oregon, 2004.
192 Or.App. 365,
86 P.3d 63.
http://www.publications.ojd.state.or.us/appeals.htm[a]

FACTS　Su Yong Kim sold an apartment building in Portland, Oregon, to Chon Sik Park, Bok Soon Park, Johan Cen, William Itzineag, Johnny Perea, and Patricia Maldonado. At the time, the building's plumbing violated the Portland Housing Code. The contract provided the following: "Seller shall correct the plumbing code violation　*　*　* within eight months　*　*　* . Buyer shall cooperate with seller in　*　*　* providing access to the premises to complete repairs." Kim did not make the repairs within eight months, but twelve months after the date of the contract, Kim cut holes in the walls of the apartments to expose the plumbing. Seven weeks later, early one morning, Kim sent plumbers to the building without notice to the owners, apparently in an attempt to make repairs. The owners ordered the plumbers to leave, refused to allow Kim to send others, and stopped making payments under the contract. Kim filed a suit in an

Oregon state court against the buyers, seeking the amount due. The buyers asserted that Kim's failure to repair the plumbing was a material breach that excused the performance of their obligations and counterclaimed for damages for the breach. The court concluded that Kim's breach was not material and ordered relief in his favor. The buyers appealed to a state intermediate appellate court.

ISSUE　Was the seller's failure to repair the plumbing according to the parties' contract a material breach excusing the buyers' performance?

DECISION　Yes. The state intermediate appellate court reversed the decision of the lower court on this issue and remanded the case for a determination of the amount of damages.[b]

---

a. Click on "March" under "Cases decided in 2004." In the result, scroll to the name of the case under 3/3/04 and click on it to access the opinion. The state of Oregon's judicial branch maintains this Web site.

b. The lower court's decision on remand was not available at the time this book went to press, but it may be by the time you read this. If you have purchased access to Westlaw Campus, you may be able to locate the remanded decision using that database. Alternatively, you may be able to find the case online at some other site. (See this text's inside front cover for information on Westlaw Campus and URLs for online court decisions.)

CASE 9.2—Continued

REASON The appellate court reasoned that a breach is material if it "goes to the very substance of the contract and defeats the object of the parties entering into the contract." In this case, as a result of the code violations, "the City of Portland continued to assess fines against defendants and defendants lost some tenants." The court pointed out that the requirement that the seller repair the plumbing within eight months was intended to ensure that the building's plumbing would satisfy the city code within a reasonable time after the sale. Also, the buyers had purchased the building from the seller so that they could rent out the apartments in it. According to the court, "[a]lthough the repairs to the plumbing in the building would have caused some temporary inconvenience to the tenants, the failure of plaintiff to make the repairs in accordance with the contract ultimately prevented defen-dants from using the building as intended by the parties' agreement. In light of that evidence, we hold that as a matter of law the plaintiff's [seller's] failure to perform as promised was a material breach of the contract." The court added that because the seller's breach was material, the buyers were not obligated to continue to perform their obligation to make the payments under the contract.

WHY IS THIS CASE IMPORTANT? *This case emphasizes that when one party's failure to perform a contractual obligation causes another to suffer significant harm, the other party normally is entitled to a remedy. Recall from Chapter 7 that even when no contract exists, if a party justifiably relies to his or her detriment on the promise of another, the party may be able to obtain relief under the doctrine of quasi contract or promissory estoppel.*

ANTICIPATORY REPUDIATION
An assertion or action by a party indicating that he or she will not perform an obligation that the party is contractually obligated to perform at a future time.

Anticipatory Repudiation of a Contract Before either party to a contract has a duty to perform, one of the parties may refuse to perform her or his contractual obligations. This is called **anticipatory repudiation.**[14] When anticipatory repudiation occurs, it is treated as a material breach of contract, and the nonbreaching party is permitted to bring an action for damages immediately, even though the scheduled time for performance under the contract may still be in the future.[15] Until the nonbreaching party treats this early repudiation as a breach, however, the breaching party can retract the anticipatory repudiation by proper notice and restore the parties to their original obligations.[16]

An anticipatory repudiation is treated as a present, material breach for two reasons. First, the nonbreaching party should not be required to remain ready and willing to perform when the other party has already repudiated the contract. Second, the nonbreaching party should have the opportunity to seek a similar contract elsewhere and may have the duty to do so to minimize his or her loss.

REMEMBER The risks that prices will fluctuate and values will change are ordinary business risks for which the law does not provide relief.

Quite often, an anticipatory repudiation occurs when a sharp fluctuation in market prices creates a situation in which performance of the contract would be extremely unfavorable to one of the parties. ■ EXAMPLE 9.13 Shasta Manufacturing Company contracts to manufacture and sell 100,000 personal computers to New Age, Inc., a computer retailer with 500 outlet stores. Delivery is to be made two months from the date of the contract. One month later, three suppliers of computer parts raise their prices to Shasta. Because of these higher prices, Shasta stands to lose $500,000 if it sells the computers to New Age at the contract price. Shasta writes to New Age, stating that it cannot deliver the 100,000 computers at the agreed-on contract price. Even though you might sympathize with Shasta, its letter is an anticipatory repudiation of the contract, allowing New Age the option of treating the

---

14. *Restatement (Second) of Contracts,* Section 253, and UCC 2–610.

15. The doctrine of anticipatory repudiation first arose in the landmark case of *Hochster v. De La Tour,* 2 Ellis and Blackburn Reports 678 (1853), when the English court recognized the delay and expense inherent in a rule requiring a nonbreaching party to wait until the time of performance before suing on an anticipatory repudiation.

16. See UCC 2–611.

repudiation as a material breach and proceeding immediately to pursue remedies, even though the contract delivery date is still a month away. ■

DISCHARGE BY AGREEMENT

Any contract can be discharged by agreement of the parties. The agreement can be contained in the original contract, or the parties can form a new contract for the express purpose of discharging the original contract.

Discharge by Rescission As discussed in Chapter 7, rescission is the process in which the parties cancel the contract and are returned to the positions they occupied prior to the contract's formation. For *mutual rescission* to take place, the parties must make another agreement that also satisfies the legal requirements for a contract—there must be an *offer,* an *acceptance,* and *consideration.* Ordinarily, if the parties agree to rescind the original contract, their promises not to perform those acts promised in the original contract will be legal consideration for the second contract.

Mutual rescission can occur in this manner when the original contract is executory on both sides (that is, neither party has completed performance). The agreement to rescind an executory contract is generally enforceable, even if it is made orally and even if the original agreement was in writing.[17] When one party has fully performed, however, an agreement to rescind the original contract usually is not enforceable unless additional consideration or restitution is made.[18]

NOVATION
The substitution, by agreement, of a new contract for an old one, with the rights under the old one being terminated. Typically, novation involves the substitution of a new person who is responsible for the contract and the removal of the original party's rights and duties under the contract.

Discharge by Novation The process of **novation** substitutes a third party for one of the original parties. Essentially, the parties to the original contract and one or more new parties all get together and agree to the substitution. The requirements of a novation are as follows:

1. The existence of a previous, valid obligation.
2. Agreement by all of the parties to a new contract.
3. The extinguishing of the old obligation (discharge of the prior party).
4. A new, valid contract.

A novation may appear similar to an assignment or delegation. There is an important distinction, however: a novation involves a new contract, and an assignment or delegation involves the old contract.

■ **EXAMPLE 9.14** Suppose that you contract with Logan Enterprises to sell it your office equipment business. Logan later learns that it should not expand at this time but knows of another party, MBI Corporation, that is interested in purchasing your business. All three of you get together and agree to a novation. As long as the new contract is supported by consideration, the novation discharges the original contract between you and Logan and replaces it with the new contract between you and MBI Corporation. Logan prefers the novation because it discharges its liabilities under the contract with you. If the original contract had been an installment sales contract requiring twelve monthly payments, and Logan had merely assigned the contract (assigned its rights and delegated its duties under the contract) to MBI Corporation,

---

17. Agreements to rescind contracts involving transfers of realty, however, must be evidenced by a writing. Another exception has to do with the sale of goods under the UCC, when the sales contract requires written rescission.
18. Under UCC 2–209(1), however, no consideration is needed to modify a contract for a sale of goods. See Chapter 11. Also see UCC 1–107.

Logan would have remained liable to you for the payments if MBI Corporation defaulted. ■

Discharge by Accord and Satisfaction   As discussed in Chapter 7, in an *accord and satisfaction*, the parties agree to accept performance different from the performance originally promised. An *accord* is an executory contract (one that has not yet been performed) to perform some act in order to satisfy an existing contractual duty that is not yet discharged.[19] A *satisfaction* is the performance of the accord agreement. An *accord* and its *satisfaction* discharge the original contractual obligation.

Once the accord has been made, the original obligation is merely suspended until the accord agreement is fully performed. If it is not performed, the party to whom performance is owed can bring an action on the original obligation or for breach of the accord. ■ **EXAMPLE 9.15** Shea obtains a judgment against Marla for $4,000. Later, both parties agree that the judgment can be satisfied by Marla's transfer of her automobile to Shea. This agreement to accept the auto in lieu of $4,000 in cash is the accord. If Marla transfers her automobile to Shea, the accord agreement is fully performed, and the $4,000 debt is discharged. If Marla refuses to transfer her car, the accord is breached. Because the original obligation is merely suspended, Shea can bring an action to enforce the judgment for $4,000 in cash or bring an action for breach of the accord. ■

DISCHARGE BY OPERATION OF LAW

Under some circumstances, contractual duties may be discharged by operation of law. These circumstances include material alteration of the contract, the running of the relevant statute of limitations, bankruptcy, and impossibility of performance.

Contract Alteration   To discourage parties from altering written contracts, the law allows an innocent party to be discharged when one party has materially altered a written contract without the knowledge or consent of the other party. For example, if a party alters a material term of the contract—such as the quantity term or the price term—without the knowledge or consent of the other party, the party who was unaware of the alteration can treat the contract as discharged or terminated.

Statutes of Limitations   As mentioned earlier in this text, statutes of limitations limit the period during which a party can sue on a particular cause of action. After the applicable limitations period has passed, a suit can no longer be brought. For example, the limitations period for bringing suits for breach of oral contracts is usually two to three years; for written contracts, four to five years; and for recovery of amounts awarded in judgment, ten to twenty years, depending on state law. Suits for breach of a contract for the sale of goods must be brought within four years after the cause of action has accrued. By original agreement, the parties can reduce this four-year period to a one-year period. They cannot, however, extend it beyond the four-year limitations period.

Bankruptcy   A proceeding in bankruptcy attempts to allocate the debtor's assets to the creditors in a fair and equitable fashion. Once the assets have been allocated, the debtor receives a *discharge in bankruptcy* (see Chapter 16). A discharge in bankruptcy ordinarily bars enforcement of most of a debtor's contracts by the creditors.

---

19. *Restatement (Second) of Contracts,* Section 281.

IMPOSSIBILITY OF PERFORMANCE
A doctrine under which a party to a contract is relieved of his or her duty to perform when performance becomes objectively impossible or totally impracticable (through no fault of either party).

NOTE The doctrine of commercial impracticability does not provide relief from such events as ordinary price increases or easily predictable changes in the weather.

When Performance Is Impossible   After a contract has been made, performance may become impossible in an objective sense. This is known as **impossibility of performance** and may discharge the contract.[20]

Objective Impossibility.   *Objective impossibility* ("It can't be done") must be distinguished from subjective impossibility ("I'm sorry, I simply can't do it"). An example of subjective impossibility is the inability to pay funds on time because the bank is closed.[21] In effect, the nonperforming party is saying, "It is impossible for *me* to perform," rather than "It is impossible for *anyone* to perform." Accordingly, such excuses do not discharge a contract, and the nonperforming party is normally held in breach of contract. Four basic types of situations will generally qualify as grounds for the discharge of contractual obligations based on impossibility of performance:[22]

1. *When a party whose personal performance is essential to the completion of the contract dies or becomes incapacitated prior to performance.* ■ **EXAMPLE 9.16** Fred, a famous dancer, contracts with Ethereal Dancing Guild to play a leading role in its new ballet. Before the ballet can be performed, Fred becomes ill and dies. His personal performance was essential to the completion of the contract. Thus, his death discharges the contract and his estate's liability for his nonperformance. ■

2. *When the specific subject matter of the contract is destroyed.* ■ **EXAMPLE 9.17** A-1 Farm Equipment agrees to sell Gudgel the green tractor on its lot and promises to have the tractor ready for Gudgel to pick up on Saturday. On Friday night, however, a truck veers off the nearby highway and smashes into the tractor, destroying it beyond repair. Because the contract was for this specific tractor, A-1's performance is rendered impossible owing to the accident. ■

3. *When a change in the law renders performance illegal.* An example is a contract to build an apartment building, when the zoning laws are changed to prohibit the construction of residential rental property at this location. This change renders the contract impossible to perform.

4. *When performance becomes commercially impracticable.* The inclusion of this type of "impossibility" as a basis for contract discharge results from a growing trend to allow parties to discharge contracts when the originally contemplated performance turns out to be much more difficult or expensive than anticipated. In such situations, courts may excuse parties from their performance obligations under the doctrine of *commercial impracticability.* For example, in one case, a court held that a contract could be discharged because a party would have to pay ten times more than the original estimate to excavate a certain amount of gravel.[23]

Temporary Impossibility.   An occurrence or event that makes performance temporarily impossible operates to suspend performance until the impossibility ceases. Then, ordinarily, the parties must perform the contract as originally planned. If, however, the lapse of time and the change in circumstances surrounding the contract make it substantially more burdensome for the parties to perform the promised acts, the contract is discharged.

---

20. *Restatement (Second) of Contracts,* Section 261.
21. *Ingham Lumber Co. v. Ingersoll & Co.,* 93 Ark. 447, 125 S.W. 139 (1910).
22. *Restatement (Second) of Contracts,* Sections 262–266, and UCC 2–615.
23. *Mineral Park Land Co. v. Howard,* 172 Cal. 289, 156 P. 458 (1916).

A production line in a commercial bakery. If a fire incapacitated the bakery's oven, would the bakery be excused from performing its contracts until the oven was fixed? If a contract involved a special holiday order and the oven could not be fixed until after the holiday, would the contract be discharged? Why or why not? (© Dick Luria, Getty Images)

REMEMBER The terms of a contract must be sufficiently definite for a court to determine the amount of damages to award.

■ **EXAMPLE 9.18** The leading case on the subject, *Autry v. Republic Productions,*[24] involved an actor who was drafted into the army in 1942. Being drafted rendered the actor's contract temporarily impossible to perform, and it was suspended until the end of the war. When the actor got out of the army, the purchasing power of the dollar had so changed that performance of the contract would have been substantially burdensome to him. Therefore, the contract was discharged. ■ Review the *Application* feature at the end of this chapter for more on what to do when a contract cannot be performed.

◨ Damages

A breach of contract entitles the nonbreaching party to sue for money damages. As you read in Chapter 4, damages are designed to compensate a party for harm suffered as a result of another's wrongful act. In the context of contract law, damages are designed to compensate the nonbreaching party for the loss of the bargain. Often, courts say that innocent parties are to be placed in the position they would have occupied had the contract been fully performed.[25]

TYPES OF DAMAGES

There are basically four broad categories of damages:

1 Compensatory (to cover direct losses and costs).

2 Consequential (to cover indirect and foreseeable losses).

3 Punitive (to punish and deter wrongdoing).

4 Nominal (to recognize wrongdoing when no monetary loss is shown).

Compensatory and punitive damages were discussed in Chapter 4 in the context of tort law. Here, we look at these types of damages, as well as consequential and nominal damages, in the context of contract law.

Compensatory Damages   Damages compensating the nonbreaching party for the *loss of the bargain* are known as *compensatory damages*. These damages compensate the injured party only for damages actually sustained and proved to have arisen directly from the loss of the bargain caused by the breach of contract. They simply replace what was lost because of the wrong or damage.

The standard measure of compensatory damages is the difference between the value of the breaching party's promised performance under the contract and the value of her or his actual performance. This amount is reduced by any loss that the injured party has avoided, however.

■ **EXAMPLE 9.19** You contract with Marinot Industries to perform certain personal services exclusively for Marinot during August for a payment of $3,500. Marinot cancels the contract and is in breach. You are able to find another job during August but can earn only $1,000. You normally can sue Marinot for breach and recover $2,500 as compensatory damages. You may also recover from Marinot the amount that you spent to find the other job. ■ Expenses that are directly incurred because of a breach of contract—such as those incurred to obtain performance from another source—are called *incidental damages*.

24. 30 Cal.2d 144, 180 P.2d 888 (1947).
25. *Restatement (Second) of Contracts,* Section 347; and Section 1–106(1) of the Uniform Commercial Code (UCC).

The measurement of compensatory damages varies by type of contract. Certain types of contracts deserve special mention—contracts for the sale of goods, contracts for the sale of land, and construction contracts.

Sale of Goods.   In a contract for the sale of goods, the usual measure of compensatory damages is the difference between the contract price and the market price.[26] ■ **EXAMPLE 9.20** MediQuick Laboratories contracts with Cal Computer Industries to purchase ten model UTS 400 network servers for $8,000 each. If Cal Computer fails to deliver the ten servers, and the current market price of the servers is $8,150, MediQuick's measure of damages is $1,500 (10 × $150) plus any incidental damages (expenses) caused by the breach. ■ If the buyer breaches and the seller has not yet produced the goods, compensatory damages normally equal the seller's lost profits on the sale rather than the difference between the contract price and the market price.

Sale of Land.   Ordinarily, because each parcel of land is unique, the remedy for a seller's breach of a contract for a sale of real estate is specific performance—that is, the buyer is awarded the parcel of property for which he or she bargained (specific performance is discussed more fully later in this chapter). When this remedy is unavailable (because the property has been sold, for example) or when the buyer is the party in breach, the measure of damages is typically the difference between the contract price and the market price of the land. The majority of states follow this rule.

Construction Contracts.   The measure of damages in a building or construction contract varies depending on which party breaches and when the breach occurs. The owner can breach at three different stages of the construction:

1 Before performance has begun.

2 During performance.

3 After performance has been completed.

If the owner breaches *before performance has begun,* the contractor can recover only the profits that would have been made on the contract (that is, the total contract price less the cost of materials and labor). If the owner breaches *during performance,* the contractor can recover the profits plus the costs incurred in partially constructing the building. If the owner breaches *after the construction has been completed,* the contractor can recover the entire contract price plus interest.

When the contractor breaches the construction contract—either by failing to begin construction or by stopping work partway through the project—the measure of damages is the cost of completion, which includes reasonable compensation for any delay in performance. If the contractor finishes late, the measure of damages is the loss of use. Exhibit 9–4 summarizes the rules concerning the measurement of damages in breached construction contracts.

Consequential Damages   Foreseeable damages that result from a party's breach of contract are referred to as **consequential damages,** or *special damages.* Consequential damages differ from compensatory damages in that they are caused by special cir-

on the Web

For a summary of how contracts may be breached and other information on contract law, go to

**http://www.lawyers.com/
lawyers/A~1001075~LDC/
TERMINATING+A+
CONTRACT.html.**

CONSEQUENTIAL DAMAGES
Special damages that compensate for a loss that does not directly or immediately result from the breach (for example, lost profits). For the plaintiff to collect consequential damages, they must have been reasonably foreseeable at the time the breach or injury occurred.

---

26. That is, the difference between the contract price and the market price at the time and place at which the goods were to be delivered or tendered. [See UCC 2–708, 2–713, and 2–715(1), discussed in Chapter 12.]

EXHIBIT 9–4	MEASUREMENT OF DAMAGES—BREACH OF CONSTRUCTION CONTRACTS	

PARTY IN BREACH	TIME OF BREACH	MEASUREMENT OF DAMAGES
Owner	Before construction has begun	Profits (contract price less cost of materials and labor)
Owner	During construction	Profits plus costs incurred up to time of breach
Owner	After construction is completed	Contract price plus interest
Contractor	Before construction has begun	Cost above contract price to complete work
Contractor	Before construction is completed	Generally, all costs incurred by owner to complete work

cumstances beyond the contract itself. They flow from the consequences, or results, of a breach. When a seller fails to deliver goods, knowing that the buyer is planning to use or resell those goods immediately, consequential damages are awarded for the loss of profits from the planned resale.

■ EXAMPLE 9.21 Gilmore contracts to have a specific item shipped to her—one that she desperately needs to repair her printing press. In her contract with the shipper, Gilmore states that she must receive the item by Monday or she will not be able to print her paper and will lose $950. If the shipper is late, Gilmore normally can recover the consequential damages caused by the delay (that is, the $950 in losses). ■

NOTE A seller who does not wish to take on the risk of consequential damages can limit the buyer's remedies via contract.

To recover consequential damages, the breaching party must know (or have reason to know) that special circumstances will cause the nonbreaching party to suffer an additional loss.[27] When was this rule first enunciated? See this chapter's *Landmark in the Law* feature on the following pages for a discussion of *Hadley v. Baxendale,* a case decided in England in 1854.

Punitive Damages   Recall from Chapter 4 that punitive damages are designed to punish a wrongdoer and set an example to deter similar conduct in the future. Punitive damages, or *exemplary damages,* are generally not awarded in an action for breach of contract. Such damages have no legitimate place in contract law because they are, in essence, penalties, and a breach of contract is not unlawful in a criminal sense. A contract is simply a civil relationship between the parties. The law may compensate one party for the loss of the bargain—no more and no less.

In a few situations, a person's actions can cause both a breach of contract and a tort. ■ EXAMPLE 9.22 Two parties establish by contract a certain reasonable standard or duty of care. Failure to live up to that standard is a breach of the contract. The same act that breached the contract may also constitute negligence, or it may be an intentional tort if, for example, the breaching party committed fraud. In such a situation, it is possible for the nonbreaching party to recover punitive damages for the tort in addition to compensatory and consequential damages for the breach of contract. ■

NOMINAL DAMAGES
A small monetary award (often one dollar) granted to a plaintiff when no actual damage was suffered.

Nominal Damages   When no actual damage or financial loss results from a breach of contract and only a technical injury is involved, the court may award **nominal damages** to the innocent party. Nominal damage awards are often small, such as one dollar, but they do establish that the defendant acted wrongfully. Most lawsuits for nominal damages are brought as a matter of principle under the theory that a breach has occurred and some damages must be imposed regardless of actual loss.

---

27. UCC 2–715(2). See Chapter 12.

LANDMARK IN THE LAW

Hadley v. Baxendale (1854)

The rule that notice of special ("consequential") circumstances must be given if consequential damages are to be recovered was first enunciated in *Hadley v. Baxendale*,[a] a landmark case decided in 1854.

CASE BACKGROUND   This case involved a broken crankshaft used in a flour mill run by the Hadley family in Gloucester, England. The crankshaft attached to the steam engine in the mill broke, and the shaft had to be sent to a foundry located in Greenwich so that a new shaft could be made to fit the other parts of the engine.

The Hadleys hired Baxendale, a common carrier, to transport the shaft from Gloucester to Greenwich. Baxendale received payment in advance and promised to deliver the shaft the following day. It was not delivered for several days, however. As a consequence, the mill was closed during those days because the Hadleys had no extra crankshaft on hand to use. The Hadleys sued Baxendale to recover the profits they lost during that time. Baxendale contended that the loss of profits was "too remote."

In the mid-1800s, it was common knowledge that large mills, such as that run by the Hadleys, normally had more than one crankshaft in case the main one broke and had to be repaired, as happened in this case. It is against this background that the parties argued their respective positions on whether the damages resulting from loss of profits while the crankshaft was out for repair were "too remote" to be recoverable.

THE ISSUE BEFORE THE COURT AND THE COURT'S RULING   The crucial issue before the court was whether the Hadleys had informed the carrier, Baxendale, of the special circumstances surrounding the crankshaft's repair, particularly that the mill would have to shut down while the crankshaft was being repaired. If Baxendale had been notified of this circumstance at the time the contract was formed, then the

a. 9 Exch. 341, 156 Eng.Rep. 145 (1854).

■ EXAMPLE 9.23   Hernandez contracts to buy potatoes at fifty cents a pound from Lentz. Lentz breaches the contract and does not deliver the potatoes. Meanwhile, the price of potatoes falls. Hernandez is able to buy them in the open market at half the price he agreed to pay Lentz. Hernandez is clearly better off because of Lentz's breach. Thus, in a suit for breach of contract, Hernandez may be awarded only nominal damages for the technical injury he sustained, as no monetary loss was involved. ■

(Note that nominal damages may take on greater significance in tort cases involving defamation or trade libel. If a false statement made by a competing firm calls into question a business's integrity or good reputation, the business may find it desirable to establish the falsity of the statement in public court proceedings. If the business wins in court, the court may award nominal damages because actual damages in such cases are difficult to estimate.)

MITIGATION OF DAMAGES

MITIGATION OF DAMAGES
A rule requiring a plaintiff to do whatever is reasonable to minimize the damages caused by the defendant.

In most situations, when a breach of contract occurs, the injured party is held to a duty to mitigate, or reduce, the damages that he or she suffers. Under this doctrine of **mitigation of damages,** the required action depends on the nature of the situation.

LANDMARK IN THE LAW —Continued

remedy for breaching the contract would have been the amount of damages that would reasonably follow from the breach—including the Hadleys' lost profits.

In the court's opinion, however, the only circumstances communicated by the Hadleys to Baxendale at the time the contract was made were that the item to be transported was a broken crankshaft of a mill and that the Hadleys were the owners and operators of that mill. The court concluded that these circumstances did not reasonably indicate that the mill would have to stop operations if the delivery of the crankshaft was delayed.

APPLICATION TO TODAY'S WORLD

Today, the rule enunciated by the court in this case still applies. When damages are awarded, compensation is given only for those injuries that the defendant could reasonably have foreseen as a probable result of the usual course of events following a breach. If the injury complained of is outside the usual and foreseeable course of events, the plaintiff must show specifically that the defendant had reason to know the facts and foresee the injury. This rule applies to contracts in the online environment as well. For example, suppose that a Web merchant loses business (and profits) due to a computer system's failure. If the failure was caused by malfunctioning software, the merchant normally may recover the lost profits from the software maker if these consequential damages were foreseeable.

RELEVANT WEB SITES

To locate information on the Web concerning Hadley v. Baxendale, *go to this text's Web site at* <u>http://blt.westbuslaw.com</u>, *select "Chapter 9," and click on "URLs for Landmarks."*

■ EXAMPLE 9.24 Some states require a landlord to use reasonable means to find a new tenant if a tenant abandons the premises and fails to pay rent. If an acceptable tenant becomes available, the landlord is required to lease the premises to this tenant to mitigate the damages recoverable from the former tenant. The former tenant is still liable for the difference between the amount of the rent under the original lease and the rent received from the new tenant. If the landlord has not used the reasonable means necessary to find a new tenant, a court will likely reduce any award by the amount of rent the landlord could have received had such reasonable means been used. ■

In the majority of states, a person whose employment has been wrongfully terminated has a duty to mitigate damages incurred because of the employer's breach of the employment contract. In other words, wrongfully terminated employees have a duty to take similar jobs if they are available. If the employees fail to do this, the damages they receive will be equivalent to their salaries less the incomes they would have received in similar jobs obtained by reasonable means. The employer has the burden of proving that such jobs existed and that the employee could have been hired. Normally, the employee is under no duty to take a job that is not of the same type and rank.

LIQUIDATED DAMAGES VERSUS PENALTIES

LIQUIDATED DAMAGES
An amount, stipulated in a contract, that the parties to the contract believe to be a reasonable estimation of the damages that will occur in the event of a breach.

PENALTY
A contractual clause that states that a certain amount of money damages will be paid in the event of a future default or breach of contract. The damages are not a measure of compensation for the contract's breach but rather a punishment for a default. The agreement as to the amount will not be enforced, and recovery will be limited to actual damages.

A **liquidated damages** provision in a contract specifies that a certain dollar amount is to be paid in the event of a future default or breach of contract. (*Liquidated* means determined, settled, or fixed.) Liquidated damages differ from penalties. A **penalty** specifies a certain amount to be paid in the event of a default or breach of contract and is designed to penalize the breaching party. Liquidated damages provisions normally are enforceable. In contrast, if a court finds that a provision calls for a penalty, the agreement as to the amount will not be enforced, and recovery will be limited to actual damages.[28]

To determine whether a particular provision is for liquidated damages or for a penalty, the court must answer two questions:

1. At the time the contract was formed, was it apparent that damages would be difficult to estimate in the event of a breach?

2. Was the amount set as damages a reasonable estimate of those potential damages and not excessive?[29]

If the answers to both questions are yes, the provision normally will be enforced. If either answer is no, the provision will normally not be enforced. In a construction contract, it is difficult to estimate the amount of damages that might be caused by a delay in completing construction, so liquidated damages clauses are often used.

The court in the following case addressed the liquidated damages questions just referred to in evaluating a provision in an agreement for the lease of a hotel.

---

28. This is also the rule under the UCC. See UCC 2–718(1).
29. *Restatement (Second) of Contracts,* Section 356(1).

CASE 9.3 ▪▪ Green Park Inn, Inc. v. Moore

North Carolina Court of Appeals, 2002.
562 S.E.2d 53.
http://www.aoc.state.nc.us/www/public/html/opinions.htma

COMPANY PROFILE *Green Park Inn*
(**http://www.greenparkinn.com**) *is one of the oldest hotels in the United States. Established in 1882 and listed on the National Register of Historic Places, it is located in the Blue Ridge Mountains near Blowing Rock, North Carolina. Eminent guests have included Annie Oakley, Herbert Hoover, Eleanor Roosevelt, Margaret Mitchell, Calvin Coolidge, and John D. Rockefeller. Green Park Inn is a full-service, first class hotel and restaurant.*

a. In the "Court of Appeals Opinions" section, click on "2002." On the next page, scroll to the "2 April 2002" section and click on the name of the case to access the opinion. The North Carolina Appellate Division Reporter maintains this Web site.

FACTS Allen and Pat McCain own Green Park Inn, Inc., which operates the Green Park Inn. In 1996, they leased the Inn to GMAFCO, LLC, which is owned by Gary and Gail Moore. The lease agreement provided that, in case of a default by GMAFCO, Green Park Inn, Inc., would be entitled to $500,000 as "liquidated damages." GMAFCO defaulted on the February 2000 rent. Green Park Inn, Inc., gave GMAFCO an opportunity to cure the default, but GMAFCO made no further payments and returned possession of the property to the lessor. When Green Park Inn, Inc., sought the "liquidated damages," the Moores refused to pay. Green Park Inn, Inc., filed a suit in a North Carolina state court against the Moores, GMAFCO, and their bank to obtain the $500,000. The defendants contended in part that the lease clause requiring payment of "liquidated damages" was an unenforceable penalty provision. The court ordered the defendants to pay Green Park Inn, Inc. The defendants appealed to a state intermediate appellate court.

CASE 9.3—Continued

ISSUE Did the liquidated damages provision in the lease agreement constitute an unenforceable penalty clause?

DECISION No. The state intermediate appellate court affirmed the decision of the lower court.

REASON The appellate court quoted from the lease agreement's liquidated damages clause, which listed such items to be included in the lessor's damages as "restoration of the physical plant," "lost lease payments," and "harm to the reputation of the hotel." The clause also stated that the McCains had retired to Florida and would have to relocate back to Blowing Rock if they were "forced out of retirement to take over the operation of the hotel." The parties had agreed in the lease that $500,000 was a fair and reasonable estimate of the damages the McCains would suffer in the event of a default. The court held that these provisions satisfied the two-part test for liquidated damages: the amount of the damages would have been difficult to determine at the time the lease was signed, and the estimate of the damages was reasonable. The court noted that while some of the items listed in the clause could be determined, "others, such as the harm to the hotel's reputation or the cost to the McCains of being forced out of retirement, clearly would have been difficult to ascertain at the time the Lease Agreement was signed." The court also pointed out that after McCain and his wife came out of retirement and were again operating the hotel, he testified that $500,000 was "a fair and reasonable estimate to measure the damages" and that the Moores did not attempt to show that this amount was unreasonable.

FOR CRITICAL ANALYSIS—Economic Consideration *If the lease had specified $3 million in damages, would the result in this case have been different? Why or why not?*

ETHICAL ISSUE 9.2

Should liquidated damages clauses be enforced when no actual damages are incurred? An issue involving liquidated damages clauses that occasionally comes before the courts has to do with deposits on the purchase price of a home or other real estate. For example, in one case a couple signed a contract to buy a home and paid a nonrefundable deposit of $18,000 toward the purchase price. The full agreement was contingent on the buyers' sale of their current home. Because the couple was unable to sell their existing home, they had to back out of the agreement. Shortly thereafter, another buyer agreed to purchase the home for a higher price than the initial buyers had agreed to pay. Thus, the seller incurred no actual damages and, in fact, reaped higher profits as a result of the buyers' inability to perform. In such situations, does a clause requiring the buyers to forgo their deposit constitute a penalty clause rather than a liquidated damages clause?

Not in most cases. The courts routinely hold that such clauses are enforceable liquidated damages clauses. Although this may seem unfair to home buyers who cannot perform due to events beyond their control, consider the alternative: if the courts refused to enforce liquidated damages clauses in these circumstances, it would, in the words of one court, undermine "the peace of mind and certainty of result the parties sought when they contracted for liquidated damages."[30] ■

■ Equitable Remedies

In some situations, damages are an inadequate remedy for a breach of contract. In these cases, the nonbreaching party may ask the court for an equitable remedy. Equitable remedies include rescission and restitution, specific performance, and reformation.

---

30. *Kelly v. Marx,* 705 N.E.2d 1114 (Mass. 1999).

RESCISSION AND RESTITUTION

As discussed earlier, *rescission* is essentially an action to undo, or cancel, a contract—to return nonbreaching parties to the positions that they occupied prior to the transaction. When fraud, mistake, duress, or failure of consideration is present, rescission is available. The failure of one party to perform under a contract entitles the other party to rescind the contract.[31] The rescinding party must give prompt notice to the breaching party.

Restitution   To rescind a contract, both parties generally must make **restitution** to each other by returning goods, property, or money previously conveyed.[32] If the physical property or goods can be returned, they must be. If the property or goods have been consumed, restitution must be made in an equivalent dollar amount.

Essentially, restitution involves the recapture of a benefit conferred on the defendant that has unjustly enriched her or him. ■ **EXAMPLE 9.25** Andrea pays $12,000 to Myles in return for his promise to design a house for her. The next day, Myles calls Andrea and tells her that he has taken a position with a large architectural firm in another state and cannot design the house. Andrea decides to hire another architect that afternoon. Andrea can require restitution of $12,000 because Myles has received an unjust benefit of $12,000. ■

Restitution Is Not Limited to Rescission Cases   Restitution may be required when a contract is rescinded, but the right to restitution is not limited to rescission cases. Restitution may be sought in actions for breach of contract, tort actions, and other actions at law or in equity. Usually, restitution can be obtained when funds or property has been transferred by mistake or because of fraud. An award in a case may include restitution of money or property obtained through embezzlement, conversion, theft, copyright infringement, or misconduct by a party in a confidential or other special relationship.

SPECIFIC PERFORMANCE

The equitable remedy of **specific performance** calls for the performance of the act promised in the contract. This remedy is often attractive to a nonbreaching party because it provides the exact bargain promised in the contract. It also avoids some of the problems inherent in a suit for money damages. First, the nonbreaching party need not worry about collecting the judgment.[33] Second, the nonbreaching party need not look around for another contract. Third, the actual performance may be more valuable than the money damages.

Normally, however, specific performance will not be granted unless the party's legal remedy (money damages) is inadequate.[34] For this reason, contracts for the

RESTITUTION
An equitable remedy under which a person is restored to his or her original position prior to loss or injury, or placed in the position he or she would have been in had the breach not occurred.

CONTRAST   Restitution offers several advantages over traditional damages. First, restitution may be available in situations when damages cannot be proved or are difficult to prove. Second, restitution can be used to recover specific property. Third, restitution sometimes results in a greater overall award.

SPECIFIC PERFORMANCE
An equitable remedy requiring exactly the performance that was specified in a contract; usually granted only when money damages would be an inadequate remedy and the subject matter of the contract is unique (for example, real property).

---

31. The rescission discussed here refers to *unilateral* rescission, in which only one party wants to undo the contract. In *mutual* rescission, both parties agree to undo the contract. Mutual rescission discharges the contract; unilateral rescission is generally available as a remedy for breach of contract.

32. *Restatement (Second) of Contracts,* Section 370.

33. Courts dispose of cases, after trials, by entering judgments. A judgment may order the losing party to pay money damages to the winning party. Collecting a judgment, however, can pose problems. For example, the judgment debtor may be insolvent (cannot pay his or her bills when they come due) or have only a small net worth, or exemption laws may prevent a creditor from seizing the debtor's assets to satisfy a debt (see Chapter 16).

34. *Restatement (Second) of Contracts,* Section 359.

sale of goods rarely qualify for specific performance. Money damages ordinarily are adequate in such situations because substantially identical goods can be bought or sold in the market. Only if the goods are unique will a court of equity grant specific performance. For instance, paintings, sculptures, and rare books and coins are often unique, and money damages will not enable a buyer to obtain substantially identical substitutes in the market.

Sale of Land   A court will grant specific performance to a buyer in a contract for the sale of land. The legal remedy for breach of a land sales contract is inadequate because every parcel of land is considered to be unique. Money damages will not compensate a buyer adequately because the same land in the same location obviously cannot be obtained elsewhere. Only when specific performance is unavailable (for example, when the seller has sold the property to someone else) will money damages be awarded instead.

Contracts for Personal Services   Personal-service contracts require one party to work personally for another party. Courts normally refuse to grant specific performance of contracts for personal services. This is because to order a party to perform personal services against his or her will amounts to a type of involuntary servitude, which is contrary to the public policy expressed in the Thirteenth Amendment to the Constitution. Moreover, the courts do not want to monitor contracts for personal services.

■ EXAMPLE 9.26 If you contract with a brain surgeon to perform brain surgery on you and the surgeon refuses to perform, the court will not compel (and you certainly would not want) the surgeon to perform under these circumstances. There is no way the court can assure meaningful performance in such a situation.[35] ■

---

35. Similarly, courts often refuse to order specific performance of construction contracts because courts are not set up to operate as construction supervisors or engineers.

Suppose that a seller contracts to sell some valuable coins to a buyer. If the seller breaches the contract, would specific performance be an appropriate remedy for the buyer to seek? Why or why not? (Elizabeth Simpson, Getty Images)

REFORMATION

Reformation is an equitable remedy used when the parties have *imperfectly* expressed their agreement in writing. Reformation allows the contract to be rewritten to reflect the parties' true intentions. It applies most often when fraud or mutual mistake is present. ■ **EXAMPLE 9.27** If Keshan contracts to buy a forklift from Shelley but the written contract refers to a crane, a mutual mistake has occurred. Accordingly, a court could reform the contract so that the writing conforms to the parties' original intention as to which piece of equipment is being sold. ■

Courts frequently reform contracts in two other situations. The first occurs when two parties who have made a binding oral contract agree to put the oral contract in writing but, in doing so, make an error in stating the terms. Universally, the courts allow into evidence the correct terms of the oral contract, thereby reforming the written contract. The second situation occurs when the parties have executed a written covenant not to compete (see Chapter 8). If the covenant not to compete is for a valid and legitimate purpose (such as the sale of a business) but the area or time restraints are unreasonable, some courts will reform the restraints by making them reasonable and will enforce the entire contract as reformed. Other courts, however, will throw the entire restrictive covenant out as illegal. Exhibit 9–5 summarizes the remedies, including reformation, that are available to the nonbreaching party.

◼ Recovery Based on Quasi Contract

Recall from Chapter 7 that a quasi contract is not a true contract but rather a fictional contract that a court imposes on the parties to prevent unjust enrichment. Hence, quasi contract provides a basis for relief when no enforceable contract exists. The legal obligation arises because the law considers that a promise to pay for benefits received is implied by the party accepting the benefits. Generally, when one party confers a benefit on another party, justice requires that the party receiving the benefit pay a reasonable value for it.

DON'T FORGET The function of a quasi contract is to impose a legal obligation on a party who made no actual promise.

WHEN QUASI CONTRACTS ARE USED

Quasi contract is a legal theory under which an obligation is imposed in the absence of an agreement. It allows the courts to act as if a contract exists when there is no actual contract or agreement between the parties. The courts can also use this theory when the parties have a contract, but it is unenforceable for some reason.

EXHIBIT 9–5 REMEDIES FOR BREACH OF CONTRACT

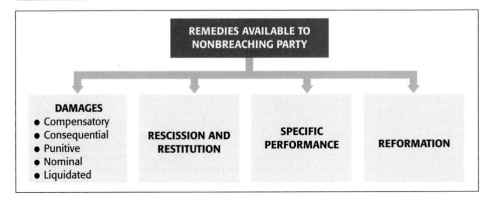

Quasi-contractual recovery is often granted when one party has partially performed under a contract that is unenforceable. It provides an alternative to suing for damages and allows the party to recover the reasonable value of the partial performance. ■ **EXAMPLE 9.28** Ericson contracts to build two oil derricks for Petro Industries. The derricks are to be built over a period of three years, but the parties do not create a written contract. Therefore, the Statute of Frauds will bar the enforcement of the contract.[36] After Ericson completes one derrick, Petro Industries informs him that it will not pay for the derrick. Ericson can sue Petro Industries under the theory of quasi contract. ■

THE REQUIREMENTS OF QUASI CONTRACT

To recover on quasi contract, the party seeking recovery must show the following:

1 The party conferred a benefit on the other party.

2 The party conferred the benefit with the reasonable expectation of being paid.

3 The party did not act as a volunteer in conferring the benefit.

4 The party receiving the benefit would be unjustly enriched by retaining the benefit without paying for it.

In the example just given, Ericson can sue in quasi contract because all of the conditions for quasi-contractual recovery have been fulfilled. Ericson built the oil derrick with the expectation of being paid. The derrick conferred an obvious benefit on Petro Industries, and Petro Industries would be unjustly enriched if it was allowed to keep the derrick without paying Ericson for the work. Therefore, Ericson should be able to recover the reasonable value of the oil derrick that was built (under the theory of *quantum meruit*[37]—"as much as he deserves"). The reasonable value is ordinarily equal to the fair market value.

■■ Election of Remedies

In many cases, a nonbreaching party has several remedies available. Because the remedies may be inconsistent with one another, the common law of contracts requires the party to choose which remedy to pursue. This is called *election of remedies*. The purpose of the doctrine of election of remedies is to prevent double recovery. ■ **EXAMPLE 9.29** Suppose that Jefferson agrees to sell his land to Adams. Then Jefferson changes his mind and repudiates the contract. Adams can sue for compensatory damages or for specific performance. If Adams receives damages as a result of the breach, she should not also be granted specific performance of the sales contract because that would mean she would unfairly end up with both the land and the damages. The doctrine of election of remedies requires Adams to choose the remedy she wants, and it eliminates any possibility of double recovery. ■

In contrast, remedies under the UCC are cumulative. They include all of the remedies available under the UCC for breach of a sales or lease contract.[38] We will examine the UCC provisions on limited remedies in Chapter 12, in the context of the remedies available on the breach of a contract for the sale or lease of goods.

BE AWARE Which remedy a plaintiff elects depends on the subject of the contract, the defenses of the breaching party, the advantages that might be gained in terms of tactics against the defendant, and what the plaintiff can prove with respect to the remedy sought.

---

36. Contracts that by their terms cannot be performed within one year from the day after the date of contract formation must be in writing to be enforceable. See Chapter 8. (Under the 2003 amendments to the Uniform Commercial Code, the one-year rule will no longer apply to sales contracts. See Chapter 11.)

37. Pronounced *kwahn*-tuhm *mehr*-oo-wuht.

38. See UCC 2–703 and 2–711.

APPLICATION ▪▪ What Do You Do When You Cannot Perform?*

Not every contract can be performed. If you are a contractor, you may take on a job that, for one reason or another, you cannot or do not wish to perform. Simply walking away from the job and hoping for the best normally is not the most effective way to avoid litigation—which can be costly, time consuming, and emotionally draining. Instead, you should consider different options that may reduce the likelihood of litigation.

For example, suppose that you are a building contractor and you sign a contract to build a home for the Andersons. Performance is to begin on June 15. On June 1, Central Enterprises offers you a position that will yield you two and a half times the amount of net income you could earn as an independent builder. To take the job, you have to start on June 15. You cannot be in two places at the same time, so to accept the new position, you must breach the contract with the Andersons.

CONSIDER YOUR OPTIONS

What can you do in this situation? One option is to subcontract the work to another builder and oversee the work yourself to make sure it conforms to the contract. Another option is to negotiate with the Andersons for a release. You can offer to find another qualified builder who will build a house of the same quality at the same price. Alternatively,

you can offer to pay any additional costs if another builder takes the job and is more expensive. In any event, this additional cost would be the measure of damages that a court would impose on you if the Andersons prevailed in a suit for breach of contract. Thus, by making the offer, you might be able to avoid the expense of litigation—if the Andersons accept your offer.

SETTLEMENT OFFERS

Often, parties are reluctant to propose compromise settlements because they fear that what they say will be used against them in court if litigation ensues. The general rule, however, is that offers for settlement cannot be used in court to prove that you are liable for a breach of contract.

* This *Application* is not meant to substitute for the services of an attorney who is licensed to practice law in your state.

CHECKLIST FOR THE CONTRACTOR WHO CANNOT PERFORM

1. Consider a compromise.
2. Subcontract out the work and oversee it.
3. Offer to find an alternative contractor to fulfill your obligation.
4. Make a cash offer to "buy" a release from your contract. If anything other than an insignificant amount of money is involved, however, work with an attorney in making the offer.

▪▪ KEY TERMS

CHAPTER SUMMARY Contracts: Third Party Rights, Discharge, Breach, and Remedies

THIRD PARTY RIGHTS

Assignments
(See pages 272–275.)
	1. An assignment is the transfer of rights under a contract to a third party. The person assigning the rights is the *assignor,* and the party to whom the rights are assigned is the *assignee.* The assignee has a right to demand performance from the other original party to the contract.
	
	2. Generally, all rights can be assigned, except in the following circumstances:
	   a. When assignment is expressly prohibited by statute (for example, workers' compensation benefits).
	   b. When a contract calls for the performance of personal services.
	   c. When the assignment will materially increase or alter the risks or duties of the *obligor* (the party that is obligated to perform).
	   d. When the contract itself stipulates that the rights cannot be assigned (with some exceptions).

Delegations
(See pages 276–277.)
	1. A delegation is the transfer of duties under a contract to a third party (the *delegatee*), who then assumes the obligation of performing the contractual duties previously held by the one making the delegation (the *delegator*).
	
	2. As a general rule, any duty can be delegated, except in the following circumstances:
	   a. When performance depends on the personal skill or talents of the obligor.
	   b. When special trust has been placed in the obligor.
	   c. When performance by a third party will vary materially from that expected by the obligee (the one to whom the duty is owed) under the contract.
	   d. When the contract expressly prohibits delegation.
	
	3. A valid delegation of duties does not relieve the delegator of obligations under the contract. If the delegatee fails to perform, the delegator is still liable to the obligee.
	
	4. An "assignment of all rights" or an "assignment of the contract" is often construed to mean that both the rights and the duties arising under the contract are transferred to a third party.

Third Party Beneficiaries (See pages 278–281.)	A third party beneficiary contract is one made for the purpose of benefiting a third party. 1. *Intended beneficiary*—One for whose benefit a contract is created. When the promisor (the one making the contractual promise that benefits a third party) fails to perform as promised, the third party can sue the promisor directly. Examples of third party beneficiaries are creditor and donee beneficiaries. 2. *Incidental beneficiary*—A third party who indirectly (incidentally) benefits from a contract but for whose benefit the contract was not specifically intended. Incidental beneficiaries have no rights to the benefits received and cannot sue to have the contract enforced.

CONTRACT DISCHARGE

Discharge by Performance (See pages 282–286.)	A contract may be discharged by complete (strict) performance or by substantial performance. In some cases, performance must be to the satisfaction of another. Totally inadequate performance constitutes a material breach of contract. An anticipatory repudiation of a contract allows the other party to sue immediately for breach of contract.
Discharge by Agreement (See pages 286–287.)	Parties may agree to discharge their contractual obligations in several ways: 1. *By rescission*—The parties mutually agree to rescind (cancel) the contract. 2. *By novation*—A new party is substituted for one of the primary parties to a contract. 3. *By accord and satisfaction*—The parties agree to render and accept performance different from that on which they originally agreed.

(Continued)

CHAPTER SUMMARY ▣ Contracts: Third Party Rights, Discharge, Breach, and Remedies—Continued

Discharge by Operation of Law (See pages 287–289.)	Parties' obligations under contracts may be discharged by operation of law owing to one of the following: 1. Contract alteration. 2. Statutes of limitations. 3. Bankruptcy. 4. Impossibility of performance.
	COMMON REMEDIES AVAILABLE TO NONBREACHING PARTY

Damages (See pages 289–295.)	The legal remedy designed to compensate the nonbreaching party for the loss of the bargain. By awarding money damages, the court tries to place the parties in the positions that they would have occupied had the contract been fully performed. The nonbreaching party frequently has a duty to *mitigate* (lessen or reduce) the damages incurred as a result of the contract's breach. There are five broad categories of damages:
	
	1. *Compensatory damages*—Damages that compensate the nonbreaching party for injuries actually sustained and proved to have arisen directly from the loss of the bargain resulting from the breach of contract.
	
	    a. In breached contracts for the sale of goods, the usual measure of compensatory damages is the difference between the contract price and the market price.
	
	    b. In breached contracts for the sale of land, the measure of damages is ordinarily the same as in contracts for the sale of goods.
	
	    c. In breached construction contracts, the measure of damages depends on which party breaches and at what stage of construction the breach occurs.
	
	2. *Consequential damages*—Damages resulting from special circumstances beyond the contract itself; the damages flow only from the consequences of a breach. For a party to recover consequential damages, the damages must be the foreseeable result of a breach of contract, and the breaching party must have known at the time the contract was formed that special circumstances existed that would cause the nonbreaching party to incur additional loss on breach of the contract. Also called *special damages.*
	
	3. *Punitive damages*—Damages awarded to punish the breaching party. Usually not awarded in an action for breach of contract unless a tort is involved.
	
	4. *Nominal damages*—Damages small in amount (such as one dollar) that are awarded when a breach has occurred but no actual damages have been suffered. Awarded only to establish that the defendant acted wrongfully.
	
	5. *Liquidated damages*—Damages that may be specified in a contract as the amount to be paid to the nonbreaching party in the event the contract is breached in the future. Clauses providing for liquidated damages are enforced if the damages were difficult to estimate at the time the contract was formed and if the amount stipulated is reasonable. If the amount is construed to be a penalty, the clause will not be enforced.

Rescission and Restitution (See page 296.)	1. *Rescission*—A remedy whereby a contract is canceled and the parties are restored to the original positions that they occupied prior to the transaction. Available when fraud, a mistake, duress, or failure of consideration is present. The rescinding party must give prompt notice of the rescission to the breaching party. 2. *Restitution*—When a contract is rescinded, both parties must make restitution to each other by returning the goods, property, or funds previously conveyed. Restitution prevents the unjust enrichment of the parties.

CHAPTER SUMMARY Contracts: Third Party Rights, Discharge, Breach, and Remedies—Continued	
Specific Performance (See pages 296–297.)	An equitable remedy calling for the performance of the act promised in the contract. This remedy is available only in special situations—such as those involving contracts for the sale of unique goods or land—and when monetary damages would be an inadequate remedy. Specific performance is not available as a remedy in breached contracts for personal services.
Reformation (See page 298.)	An equitable remedy allowing a contract to be "reformed," or rewritten, to reflect the parties' true intentions. Available when an agreement is imperfectly expressed in writing.
Recovery Based on Quasi Contract (See pages 298–299.)	An equitable theory imposed by the courts to obtain justice and prevent unjust enrichment in a situation in which no enforceable contract exists. The party seeking recovery must show the following: 1. A benefit was conferred on the other party. 2. The party conferring the benefit did so with the expectation of being paid. 3. The benefit was not volunteered. 4. Retaining the benefit without paying for it would result in the unjust enrichment of the party receiving the benefit.
CONTRACT DOCTRINE RELATING TO REMEDIES	
Election of Remedies (See page 299.)	A common law doctrine under which a nonbreaching party must choose one remedy from those available. This doctrine prevents double recovery. Under the UCC, remedies are cumulative for the breach of a contract for the sale of goods.

FOR REVIEW

Answers for the even-numbered questions in this For Review *section can be found in Appendix I at the end of this text.*

1 What is the difference between an assignment and a delegation?

2 What factors indicate that a third party beneficiary is an intended beneficiary?

3 What is the difference between compensatory damages and consequential damages? What are nominal damages, and when do courts award nominal damages?

4 Under what circumstances will equitable remedies be available?

5 What is the rationale underlying the doctrine of election of remedies?

QUESTIONS AND CASE PROBLEMS

9–1. Third Party Beneficiaries. Wilken owes Rivera $2,000. Howie promises Wilken that he will pay Rivera the $2,000 in return for Wilken's promise to give Howie's children guitar lessons. Is Rivera an intended beneficiary of the Howie-Wilken contract? Explain.

9–2. Assignments. Aron, a college student, signs a one-year lease agreement that runs from September 1 to August 31. The lease agreement specifies that the lease cannot be assigned without the landlord's consent. In late May, Aron decides not to go to summer school and assigns the balance of the lease (three months) to a close friend, Erica. The landlord objects to the assignment and denies Erica access to the apartment. Aron claims that Erica is financially sound and should be allowed the full rights and privileges of an assignee. Discuss fully whether the landlord or Aron is correct.

9–3. Impossibility of Performance. Millie contracted to sell Frank 1,000 bushels of corn to be grown on Millie's farm. Owing to a drought during the growing season, Millie's yield was much less than anticipated, and she could deliver only 250 bushels to Frank. Frank accepted the lesser amount but sued Millie for breach of contract. Can Millie defend successfully on the basis of objective impossibility of performance? Explain.

9–4. Measure of Damages. Ben owns and operates a famous candy store. He makes most of the candy sold in the store, and business is particularly heavy during the Christmas season. Ben contracts with Sweet, Inc., to purchase ten thousand pounds of sugar, to be delivered on or before November 15. Ben informs Sweet that this particular order is to be used for the Christmas season business. Because of production problems, the sugar is not tendered to Ben until December 10, at which time Ben refuses the order because it is so late. Ben has been unable to purchase the quantity of sugar needed to meet the Christmas orders and has had to turn down numerous regular customers, some of whom have indicated that they will purchase candy elsewhere in the future. The sugar that Ben has been able to purchase has cost him ten cents per pound above Sweet's price. Ben sues Sweet for breach of contract, claiming as damages the higher price paid for the sugar from other suppliers, lost profits from this year's lost Christmas sales, future lost profits from customers who have indicated that they will discontinue doing business with him, and punitive damages for failure to meet the contracted-for delivery date. Sweet claims Ben is limited to compensatory damages only. Discuss who is correct, and why.

CASE PROBLEM WITH SAMPLE ANSWER

9–5. In May 1996, O'Brien-Shiepe Funeral Home, Inc., in Hempstead, New York, hired Teramo & Co. to build an addition to O'Brien's funeral home. The parties' contract did not specify a date for the completion of the work. The city of Hempstead issued a building permit for the project on June 14, and Teramo began work about two weeks later. There was some delay in construction because O'Brien asked that no work be done during funeral services, but by the end of March 1997, the work was substantially complete. The city of Hempstead issued a "Certificate of Completion" on April 15. During the construction, O'Brien made periodic payments to Teramo, but there was a balance due of $17,950, which O'Brien did not pay. To recover this amount, Teramo filed a suit in a New York state court against O'Brien. O'Brien filed a counterclaim to recover lost profits for business allegedly lost due to the time Teramo took to build the addition, and for $6,180 spent to correct problems caused by poor work. Which, if any, party is entitled to an award in this

case? Explain. [*Teramo & Co. v. O'Brien-Shiepe Funeral Home, Inc.,* 725 N.Y.S.2d 87 (A.D. 2 Dept. 2001)]

After you have answered this problem, compare your answer with the sample answer given on the Web site that accompanies this text. Go to http://blt.westbuslaw.com, select "Chapter 9," and click on "Case Problem with Sample Answer."

9–6. Third Party Beneficiaries. Action Steel, Inc., entered into a contract with Systems Builders, Inc., a general contractor, to construct an addition to a commercial building in Indianapolis, Indiana. The contract provided that after the addition's completion, Action Steel would obtain insurance, which "shall include the interest of . . . subcontractors." The parties would then "waive all rights against . . . any of their subcontractors." Varco-Pruden Building, a subcontractor, designed the addition, which was completed in the summer of 1995. Action Steel obtained an insurance policy from Midwestern Indemnity Co. In January 1996, a snowstorm hit the Indianapolis area, and the new addition collapsed. Midwestern paid over $1.3 million to Action Steel for the loss. Because Midwestern paid for the loss, it stood in Action Steel's place in a suit filed in an Indiana state court against Varco-Pruden and others to recover this amount. Varco-Pruden filed a motion for summary judgment, arguing in part that it was a third party beneficiary of the waiver clause in the contract between Action Steel and Systems Builders. Should the court grant this motion? Why or why not? [*Midwestern Indemnity Co. v. Systems Builders, Inc.,* 801 N.E.2d 661 (Ind.App. 2004)]

9–7. Liquidated Damages versus Penalties. Every homeowner in the Putnam County, Indiana, subdivision of Stardust Hills must be a member of the Stardust Hills Owners Association, Inc., and must pay annual dues of $200 for the maintenance of common areas and other community services. Under the Association's rules, dues paid more than ten days late "shall bear a delinquent fee at a rate of $2.00 per day." Phyllis Gaddis failed to pay the dues on a Stardust Hills lot that she owned. Late fees began to accrue. Nearly two months later, the Association filed a suit in an Indiana state court to collect the unpaid dues and the late fees. Gaddis argued in response that the delinquent fee was an unenforceable penalty. What questions should be considered in determining the status of this fee? Should the Association's rule regarding assessment of the fee be enforced? Explain. [*Gaddis v. Stardust Hills Owners Association, Inc.,* 804 N.E.2d 231 (Ind.App. 2004)]

A QUESTION OF ETHICS

9–8. Bath Iron Works (BIW) offered a job to Thomas Devine, contingent on Devine's passing a drug test. The testing was conducted by NorDx, a subcontractor of Roche Biomedical Laboratories. When NorDx found that Devine's urinalysis showed the presence of opiates, a result confirmed by Roche, BIW refused to offer Devine permanent employment. Devine claimed that the ingestion of poppy seeds can lead to a positive result and that he tested positive for opiates only because of his daily consumption of poppy seed muffins. In Devine's suit against Roche, Devine argued, among other things, that he was a third party beneficiary of the contract between his employer (BIW) and NorDx (Roche). Given this factual background, consider the following questions. [*Devine v. Roche Biomedical Laboratories*, 659 A.2d 868 (Me. 1995)]

1. Is Devine an intended third party beneficiary of the BIW–NorDx contract? In deciding this issue, should the court focus on the nature of the promises made in the contract itself or on the consequences of the contract for Devine, a third party?

2. Should employees whose job security and reputation have suffered as a result of false test results be allowed to sue drug-testing labs for the tort of negligence? In such situations, do drug-testing labs have a duty to the employees to exercise reasonable care in conducting the tests?

FOR CRITICAL ANALYSIS

 9–9. The concept of substantial performance permits a party to be discharged from a contract even though the party has not fully performed his or her obligations according to the contract's terms. Is this fair? What policy interests are at issue here?

VIDEO QUESTION

 9–10. Go to this text's Web site at **http://blt. westbuslaw.com** and select "Chapter 9." Click on "Video Questions" and view the video titled *Midnight Run*. Then answer the following questions.

1. In the video, Eddie (Joe Pantoliano) and Jack (Robert DeNiro) negotiate a contract for Jack to find the Duke, a mob accountant who embezzled funds, and bring him back for trial. Assume that the contract is valid. If Jack breaches the contract by failing to bring in the Duke, what kinds of remedies, if any, can Eddie seek? Explain your answer.

2. Would the equitable remedy of specific performance be available to either Jack or Eddie in the event of a breach? Why or why not?

3. Now assume the contract between Eddie and Jack is unenforceable. Nevertheless, Jack performs his side of the bargain (brings in the Duke). Is any remedy available to him? Why or why not?

INTERNET EXERCISES

Go to the *Business Law Today: The Essentials* home page at **http://blt.westbuslaw.com**, select "Chapter 9," and click on "Internet Exercises." There you will find the following Internet research exercises that you can perform to learn more about topics covered in this chapter.

Activity 9–1: LEGAL PERSPECTIVE—Anticipatory Repudiation

Activity 9–2: MANAGEMENT PERSPECTIVE—Commercial Impracticability

Activity 9–3: MANAGEMENT PERSPECTIVE—The Duty to Mitigate

BEFORE THE TEST

Go to the *Business Law Today: The Essentials* home page at **http://blt.westbuslaw.com**, select "Chapter 9," and click on "Interactive Quizzes." You will find at least twenty interactive questions relating to this chapter.

CHAPTER 10

E-Contracts

"[B]usiness models and methods for doing business have evolved to take advantage of the speed, efficiencies, and cost benefits of electronic technologies."

Prefatory Note, Uniform Electronic Transactions Act

CHAPTER OUTLINE

- **FORMING CONTRACTS ONLINE**

- **E-SIGNATURES**

- **PARTNERING AGREEMENTS**

- **THE UNIFORM ELECTRONIC TRANSACTIONS ACT**

- **THE UNIFORM COMPUTER INFORMATION TRANSACTIONS ACT**

E-CONTRACT
A contract that is formed electronically.

■■ LEARNING OBJECTIVES

After reading this chapter, you should be able to answer the following questions:

1 What are some important clauses to include when making offers to form electronic contracts, or e-contracts?

2 How do shrink-wrap and click-on agreements differ from other contracts? How have traditional laws been applied to these agreements?

3 What is an electronic signature? Are electronic signatures valid?

4 What is a partnering agreement? What purpose does it serve?

5 What is the Uniform Electronic Transactions Act (UETA)? What are some of the major provisions of this act?

As the chapter-opening quotation indicates, electronic technology offers businesses several advantages, including speed, efficiency, and lower costs. In the 1990s, many observers argued that the development of cyberspace was revolutionary. Therefore, new legal theories, and new laws, would be needed to govern **e-contracts,** or contracts entered into electronically. To date, however, most courts have adapted traditional contract law principles and, when applicable, provisions of the Uniform Commercial Code to cases involving e-contract disputes.

In the first part of this chapter, we look at how traditional laws are being applied to contracts formed online. We then examine some new laws that have been created to apply in situations in which traditional laws governing contracts have sometimes been thought inadequate. For example, traditional laws governing signature and writing requirements are not easily adapted to contracts formed in the online environment. Thus, new laws have been created to address these issues.

◼️ Forming Contracts Online

Today, numerous contracts are being formed online. Although the medium through which these contracts are generated has changed, the age-old problems attending contract formation have not. Disputes concerning contracts formed online continue to center around contract terms and whether the parties voluntarily assented to those terms.

Note that online contracts may be formed not only for the sale of goods and services but also for *licensing.* ◼️ **EXAMPLE 10.1** The "sale" of software generally involves a license, or a right to use the software, rather than the passage of title (ownership rights) from the seller to the buyer. ◼️ As you read through the following pages, keep in mind that although we typically refer to the offeror and the offeree as a *seller* and a *buyer,* in many transactions these parties would be more accurately described as a *licensor* and a *licensee.*

ONLINE OFFERS

Sellers doing business via the Internet can protect themselves against contract disputes and legal liability by creating offers that clearly spell out the terms that will govern their transactions if the offers are accepted. All important terms should be conspicuous and easily viewed by potential buyers.

An important rule to keep in mind is that the offeror controls the offer and thus the resulting contract. The seller should therefore anticipate the terms he or she wants to include in a contract and provide for them in the offer. In some instances, a standardized contract form may suffice—the *Application* at the end of this chapter offers suggestions on how to find and use online contract forms.

At a minimum, an online offer should include the following provisions:

1. A provision specifying the remedies available to the buyer if the goods are found to be defective or if the contract is otherwise breached. Any limitation of remedies should be clearly spelled out.

2. A clause that clearly indicates what constitutes the buyer's agreement to the terms of the offer.

3. A provision specifying how payment for the goods and of any applicable taxes must be made.

4. A statement of the seller's refund and return policies.

5. Disclaimers of liability for certain uses of the goods. For example, an online seller of business forms may add a disclaimer that the seller does not accept responsibility for the buyer's reliance on the forms rather than on an attorney's advice.

6. A statement indicating how the seller will use the information gathered about the buyer.

Dispute-Settlement Provisions   In addition to the above provisions, many online offers include provisions relating to dispute settlement. For example, the offer might include an arbitration clause specifying that any dispute arising under the contract will be arbitrated in a designated forum.

FORUM-SELECTION CLAUSE
A provision in a contract designating the court, jurisdiction, or tribunal that will decide any disputes arising under the contract.

Many online contracts also contain a **forum-selection clause** (indicating the forum, or location, for the resolution of any dispute arising under the contract). As discussed in Chapter 3, significant jurisdictional issues may occur when parties are at a great distance, as they often are when they form contracts via the Internet. A forum-selection clause will help to avert future jurisdictional problems and also help to ensure that the seller will not be required to appear in court in a distant state.

ETHICAL ISSUE 10.1

Are forum-selection clauses fair to online purchasers? One of the issues that has come before the courts over the last several years has to do with forum-selection clauses included in online contracts. Online businesses typically include such clauses so that they will not have to travel to other states to defend against lawsuits brought by dissatisfied customers. This seems fair to businesses, but is it fair to consumers? Should the courts always enforce these clauses? Generally, the courts do enforce forum-selection clauses that are freely and voluntarily entered into by the parties.[1]

If, however, the enforcement of a forum-selection clause would significantly deprive a plaintiff of her or his rights under state law, a court may refuse to enforce the clause. In one case, for example, a group of Florida subscribers of America Online, Inc. (AOL), brought a suit in a Florida state court, claiming that AOL had continued to debit their credit cards for monthly service fees, without authorization, for some time after they had terminated their subscriptions. AOL sought to enforce its forum-selection clause, which was included in its "Terms of Service" agreement with its subscribers. The clause provided that all lawsuits under the agreement had to be brought in Virginia, AOL's home state. In this case, a Florida court refused to enforce the clause because the "purpose and effectiveness" of the Florida consumer statutes would be "seriously undermined" if the plaintiffs were required to bring their suit in Virginia.[2] ■

Displaying the Offer   The seller's Web site should include a hypertext link to a page containing the full contract so that potential buyers are made aware of the terms to which they are assenting. The contract generally must be displayed online in a readable format such as a twelve-point typeface. All provisions should be reasonably clear. ■ EXAMPLE 10.2 Suppose that Netquip sells a variety of heavy equipment, such as trucks and trailers, online at its Web site. Because Netquip's pricing schedule is very complex, the schedule must be fully provided and explained on the Web site. ■

Indicating How the Offer Can Be Accepted   An online offer should also include some mechanism by which the customer may accept the offer. Typically, online sellers include boxes containing the words "I agree" or "I accept the terms of the offer" that offerees can click on to indicate acceptance. The contract resulting from such an acceptance is often called a **click-on agreement.**

ONLINE ACCEPTANCES

In many ways, click-on agreements are the Internet equivalents of **shrink-wrap agreements** (or *shrink-wrap licenses*, as they are sometimes called). A *shrink-wrap agreement* is an agreement whose terms are expressed inside a box in which the goods are packaged. (The term *shrink-wrap* refers to the plastic that covers the box.) Usually, the party who opens the box is told that she or he agrees to the terms by keeping whatever is in the box. Similarly, when the purchaser opens a software package, he or she agrees to abide by the terms of the limited license agreement.

■ EXAMPLE 10.3 John orders a new computer from a national company, which ships the computer to him. Along with the computer, the box contains an agreement setting forth the terms of the sale, including what remedies are available. The

CLICK-ON AGREEMENT
An agreement that arises when a buyer, engaging in a transaction on a computer, indicates his or her assent to be bound by the terms of an offer by clicking on a button that says, for example, "I agree"; sometimes referred to as a *click-on license* or a *click-wrap agreement.*

SHRINK-WRAP AGREEMENT
An agreement whose terms are expressed in a document located inside a box in which goods (usually software) are packaged; sometimes called a *shrink-wrap license.*

---

1. See, for example, *Freedman v. America Online, Inc.,* 294 F.Supp.2d 238 (D.Conn. 2003).
2. *America Online, Inc. v. Pasieka,* 870 So.2d 170 (Fla.App.—1st Dist. 2004).

document also states that John's retention of the computer for longer than thirty days will be construed as an acceptance of the terms. ■

In most cases, a shrink-wrap agreement is not between a retailer and a buyer, but between the manufacturer of the hardware or software and the ultimate buyer-user of the product. The terms generally concern warranties, remedies, and other issues associated with the use of the product.

We look next at how the law has been applied to both shrink-wrap and click-on agreements.

Shrink-Wrap Agreements—Enforceable Contract Terms   The *Restatement (Second) of Contracts*—a compilation of common law contract principles—states that parties may agree to a contract "by written or spoken words or by other action or by failure to act."[3] The Uniform Commercial Code (UCC)—the law governing sales contracts—has a similar provision. Section 2–204 of the UCC states that any contract for the sale of goods "may be made in any manner sufficient to show agreement, including conduct by both parties which recognizes the existence of such a contract." The courts have used these provisions to conclude that a binding contract can be created by conduct, including conduct accepting the terms in either a shrink-wrap agreement or a click-on agreement. Thus, a buyer's failure to object to terms contained within a shrink-wrapped software package (or an online offer) may constitute an acceptance of the terms by conduct.[4]

In many cases, the courts have enforced the terms of shrink-wrap agreements the same as the terms of other contracts. Some courts have reasoned that by including the terms with the product, the seller proposed a contract that the buyer could accept by using the product after having an opportunity to read the terms. Also, it seems practical from a business's point of view to enclose a full statement of the legal terms of a sale with the product rather than to read the statement over the phone, for example, when a buyer calls in an order for the product.

Shrink-Wrap Terms That May Not Be Enforced   Not all of the terms included in shrink-wrap agreements have been enforced, however. One important consideration is whether the parties form their contract before or after the seller communicates the terms of the shrink-wrap agreement to the buyer. If a court finds that the buyer learned of the shrink-wrap terms *after* the parties entered into a contract, the court may conclude that those terms were proposals for additional terms and were not part of the contract unless the buyer expressly agreed to them.[5] Could any other problems arise with shrink-wrap agreements? For a discussion of a case involving an issue that arose for one firm, see this chapter's *Adapting the Law to the Online Environment* feature on the following two pages.

Click-On Agreements   As described earlier, a click-on agreement (also sometimes called a *click-on license* or *click-wrap agreement*) arises when a buyer, completing a transaction on a computer, indicates his or her assent to be bound by the terms of an offer by clicking on a button that says, for example, "I agree." The terms may be contained on a Web site through which the buyer is obtaining goods or services, or they may appear on a computer screen when software is loaded. Exhibit 10–1 on the next page contains the language of a click-on agreement that accompanies a package of software made and marketed by Microsoft.

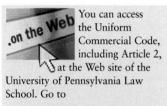

You can access the Uniform Commercial Code, including Article 2, at the Web site of the University of Pennsylvania Law School. Go to

http://www.law.upenn.edu/ bll/ulc/ulc.htm.

---

3. *Restatement (Second) of Contracts,* Section 19.

4. For a leading case on this issue, see *ProCD, Inc. v. Zeidenberg,* 86 F.3d 1447 (7th Cir. 1996).

5. See, for example, *Klocek v. Gateway, Inc.,* 104 F.Supp.2d 1332 (D.Kan. 2000).

EXHIBIT 10–1 A CLICK-ON AGREEMENT

This exhibit illustrates an online offer to form a contract. To accept the offer, the user simply scrolls down the page and clicks on the "Accept" box.

License

Microsoft Windows Media Player 9 Series for Mac OS X
END-USER LICENSE AGREEMENT FOR MICROSOFT SOFTWARE

IMPORTANT—READ CAREFULLY: This Microsoft End-User License Agreement ("EULA") is a legal agreement between you (either an individual or a single entity) and Microsoft Corporation ("Microsoft") for the Microsoft software identified above, which includes computer software and may include associated media, printed materials, and "online" or electronic documentation (collectively, "SOFTWARE"). By installing, copying, or otherwise using the SOFTWARE, you agree to be bound by the terms of this EULA. If you do not agree to the terms of this EULA, do not install, copy, or otherwise use the SOFTWARE.

SOFTWARE LICENSE
The SOFTWARE is protected by copyright laws and international copyright treaties, as well as other intellectual property laws and treaties. The SOFTWARE is licensed, not sold.
1.   GRANT OF LICENSE. This EULA grants you the following limited, non-exclusive rights:
.   Installation and Use.
SOFTWARE. You may install and use a reasonable number of copies of the SOFTWARE on computers at your premises.
.   Reserved Rights. Microsoft and its suppliers retain title and all ownership rights to the SOFTWARE. All rights not expressly granted are reserved to Microsoft.

| English ▼ | | Print... | Save As... | Decline | Accept |

ADAPTING THE LAW TO THE ONLINE ENVIRONMENT

Avoiding Deception in Software Sales

Sometimes, businesspersons who include shrink-wrap licenses with their products may have some terms elsewhere, such as on a disk or on a download page of the Internet. Not including all of the terms in the shrink-wrap agreement, however, can lead to problems—as one software producer learned when the state of New York brought an action against its company for fraud.

THE LAWSUIT AGAINST NETWORK ASSOCIATES, INC.

Network Associates, Inc. (NA), develops and sells software, including Gauntlet, a software firewall product, via the Internet. NA included on its disks and on its Internet download page—but not in its license agreement that accompanied its products—a restrictive clause.

The restrictive clause provided that anyone installing the Gauntlet software accepted the terms and conditions of the license agreement in the box and urged users to read the license before installing the software. The clause also stated, among other things, that the customer "will not publish reviews of this product without prior consent from Network Associates." The problem was that the license agreement in the box stated that the agreement contained all of the rights and duties of the parties. How, then, did the restrictive clause apply to the sale?

When *Network World Fusion*, an online magazine, published a comparative review of firewall software products, including NA's Gauntlet, without NA's permission, NA protested. Ultimately, the state attorney general of New York brought an action against NA for fraud.

THE FRAUD ISSUE

According to the New York court hearing the case, NA's restrictive clause misled customers and was thus deceptive. First, the license agreement stated that it contained all of the terms of the agreement. Therefore, the rules and regulations listed in the restrictive clause appeared to be

ADAPTING THE LAW TO THE ONLINE ENVIRONMENT—Continued

Avoiding Deception in Software Sales—Continued

independent of the license contract. This could mislead purchasers of the software because they might believe that the restriction was created by some other entity, such as the federal government.

For these reasons, the court concluded that the restrictive clause was deceptive and constituted fraud. The court ordered NA to stop including the clause in its software. The court also ordered NA to reveal "the number of instances in which software was sold on disks or

through the Internet containing the above-mentioned language in order for the court to determine what, if any, penalties and costs should be ordered."[a]

FOR CRITICAL ANALYSIS

What is the difference, if any, between reading a restrictive clause in a shrink-wrap agreement and accessing it through a link as part of a click-on agreement?

a. *People v. Network Associates, Inc.,* 195 Misc.2d 384, 758 N.Y.S.2d 466 (2003).

Generally, under the law governing contracts, including sales and lease contracts under the UCC, there is no requirement that all of the terms in a contract must actually have been read by all of the parties to be effective. For example, clicking on a button or box that states "I accept" to certain terms can be enough.

In the following case, the court considered the enforceability of a click-on (click-wrap) agreement under Article 2 of the UCC.

CASE 10.1 ▪ i.LAN Systems, Inc. v. NetScout Service Level Corp.

United States District Court,
District of Massachusetts, 2002.
183 F.Supp.2d 328.

COMPANY PROFILE *i.LAN Systems, Inc.* (**http://www.ilan.com**)*, helps companies monitor their computer networks. Based in Los Angeles, California, with a staff that includes approximately forty technicians, i.LAN can troubleshoot network problems almost anywhere in the world. Over the Internet, many problems can be solved remotely using the software tools already built into a network. These tools include software designed and sold by NetScout Service Level Corporation, formerly known as NextPoint Networks, Inc.*

FACTS A click-wrap provision in the NextPoint software states that the seller's liability is limited to the price paid for the software unless a different term is "specifically accepted by NextPoint in writing." In 1998, i.LAN and NextPoint signed an agreement under which i.LAN agreed to resell the software. In 1999, under a different purchase order, i.LAN bought what it thought was the unlimited

right to rent, rather than sell, the software, complete with perpetual upgrades and technical support. When NextPoint disputed this interpretation, i.LAN filed a suit in a federal district court, alleging, among other things, breach of contract. i.LAN sought specific performance (a remedy in which a court orders the breaching party to perform as specified in the contract—see Chapter 9) that included unlimited upgrades and support. The defendant argued that even if the allegations were true, the click-wrap provision limited its liability to the price paid for the software. Both parties filed motions for summary judgment.

ISSUE Was the click-wrap agreement enforceable?

DECISION Yes. The court denied the plaintiff's motion for summary judgment and instead issued a summary judgment in favor of the defendant (NextPoint).

REASON The court reasoned that the plaintiff agreed to the click-wrap terms when it clicked on the "I agree"

(Continued)

CASE 10.1—Continued

box. Those terms effectively limited the defendant's liability. In the words of the court, "pursuant to UCC 2–204, the analysis is simple: i.LAN manifested assent to the click-wrap license agreement when it clicked on the box stating 'I agree,' so the agreement is enforceable."[a] The court reasoned that "money now, terms later" forms a contract when the purchaser receives the box of software,

a. As pointed out earlier, under UCC 2–204 a contract "may be made in any manner sufficient to show agreement, including conduct by both parties which recognizes the existence of such a contract."

sees the license agreement, and does not return the software. The court noted that "money now, terms later" is a practical way to form contracts, especially with purchasers of software. The court concluded that if it is "correct to enforce a shrink-wrap license agreement, where any assent is implicit, then it must also be correct to enforce a click-wrap license agreement, where the assent is explicit."

FOR CRITICAL ANALYSIS—Economic Consideration *If click-wrap agreements were not enforceable, what would be the effect on the software industry?*

BROWSE-WRAP TERMS
Terms and conditions of use that are presented to an Internet user at the time certain products, such as software, are being downloaded but that need not be agreed to (by clicking "I agree," for example) before the user is able to install or use the product.

Browse-Wrap Terms Like the terms of a click-on agreement, **browse-wrap terms** can occur in a transaction conducted over the Internet. Unlike a click-on agreement, however, browse-wrap terms do not require an Internet user to assent to the terms before, say, downloading or using certain software. In other words, a person can install the software without clicking "I agree" to the terms of a license. Offerors of browse-wrap terms generally assert that the terms are binding without the user's active consent.

Critics contend that browse-wrap terms are not enforceable because they do not satisfy the basic elements of contract formation. It has been suggested that to form a valid contract online, a user must at least be presented with the terms before indicating assent.[6] With respect to a browse-wrap term, this would require that a user navigate past it and agree to it before being able to obtain whatever is being granted to the user.

The following case involved the enforceability of a clause in an agreement that the court characterized as a browse-wrap license.

6. American Bar Association Committee on the Law of Cyberspace, "Click-Through Agreements: Strategies for Avoiding Disputes on the Validity of Assent" (document presented at the annual American Bar Association meeting in August 2001).

CASE 10.2 ■ Specht v. Netscape Communications Corp.

United States District Court,
Southern District of New York, 2001.
150 F.Supp.2d 585.

FACTS Netscape Communications Corporation's "SmartDownload" software makes it easier for users to download files from the Internet without losing progress if they pause to do some other task or their Internet connection is interrupted. Netscape offers SmartDownload free of charge on its Web site to those who indicate, by clicking the mouse in a designated box, that they wish to obtain it. John Gibson clicked in the box and downloaded the software. On the Web site's download page is a reference to a license agreement that is visible only by scrolling to the next screen. Affirmatively indicating assent to the agreement is not required to download the software. The agreement provides that any disputes arising from use of the software are to be submitted to arbitration in California.

Believing that the use of SmartDownload transmits private information about its users, Gibson and others filed a suit in a federal district court in New York against Netscape, alleging violations of federal law. Netscape asked the court to order the parties to arbitration in California, according to the license agreement.

ISSUE Was the arbitration clause in the license agreement enforceable?

DECISION No. The court denied the motion to compel arbitration.

REASON The court applied UCC Article 2 because "[a]lthough in this case the product was provided free of charge, the roles are essentially the same as when an individual uses the Internet to purchase software from a

CASE 10.2—Continued

company: here, the Plaintiff requested Defendant's product by clicking on an icon marked 'Download,' and Defendant then tendered the product." The court emphasized that unless the plaintiffs agreed to the license contract, they could not be bound by the arbitration clause. The court discussed the forms of license agreements that accompany sales of software (shrink-wrap, click-on, and browse-wrap licenses) and their enforceability, and characterized Netscape's license in this case as a browse-wrap license. According to the court, Netscape's SmartDownload "allows a user to download and use the software without taking any action that plainly manifests assent to the terms of the associated license or indicates an understanding that a contract is being formed." The court pointed out that "the individual obtaining SmartDownload is not made aware

that he is entering into a contract * * *. [T]he user need not view any license agreement terms or even any reference to a license agreement, and need not do anything to manifest assent." The court reasoned that the plaintiffs did not assent to the license agreement, and thus they were not subject to the arbitration clause.

WHY IS THIS CASE IMPORTANT? *The ruling in this case is significant because it marks an application of traditional contract principles to a type of dispute that can arise only in the online context. In the case, the court clearly applied a long-standing principle of contract law: a person will not be bound to an agreement to which he or she did not assent.*

▪ E-Signatures

E-SIGNATURE
As defined by the Uniform Electronic Transactions Act, "an electronic sound, symbol, or process attached to or logically associated with a record and executed or adopted by a person with the intent to sign the record."

In many instances, a contract cannot be enforced unless it is signed by the party against whom enforcement is sought. A significant issue in the context of e-commerce has to do with how electronic signatures, or **e-signatures**, can be created and verified on e-contracts.

In the days when many people could not write, they signed documents with an "X." Then handwritten signatures become common, followed by typed signatures, printed signatures, and, most recently, digital signatures that are transmitted electronically. Throughout the evolution of signature technology, the question of what constitutes a valid signature has arisen again and again, and with good reason—without some consensus on what constitutes a valid signature, less business or legal work could be accomplished.

E-Signature Technologies

Today, numerous technologies allow electronic documents to be signed. These include digital signatures and alternative technologies.

Digital Signatures The most prevalent e-signature technology is the *asymmetric cryptosystem*, which creates a digital signature using two different (asymmetric) cryptographic "keys." With this system, a person attaches a digital signature to a document using a private key, or code. The key has a publicly available counterpart. Anyone with the appropriate software can use the public key to verify that the digital signature was made using the private key. A **cybernotary**, or legally recognized certification authority, issues the key pair, identifies the owner of the keys, and certifies the validity of the public key. The cybernotary also serves as a repository for public keys.

CYBERNOTARY
A legally recognized authority that can certify the validity of digital signatures.

Signature Dynamics With another type of signature technology, known as *signature dynamics,* a sender's signature is captured using a stylus and an electronic digitizer pad. A computer program takes the signature's measurements, the sender's identity,

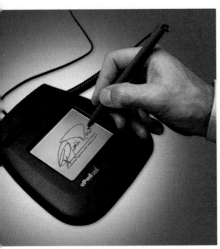

The ePad-Ink is an electronic signature pad that can be used to insert handwritten signatures into electronic documents. What type of e-signature technology does this device utilize? What procedure is used to verify the authenticity of a signature created using this ePad? (Photo courtesy of Interlink Electronics)

the time and date of the signature, and the identity of the hardware. This information is then placed in an encrypted *biometric token* attached to the document being transmitted. To verify the authenticity of the signature, the recipient of the document compares the measurements of the signature with the measurements in the token. When this type of e-signature is used, it is not necessary to have a third party verify the signatory's identity.

Other E-Signature Forms   Other forms of e-signatures have been—or are now being—developed as well. ■ EXAMPLE 10.4 Some e-signatures use "smart cards." As you will read in Chapter 15, a smart card is a device the size of a credit card that is embedded with code and other data. Like credit and debit cards, a smart card can be inserted into computers to transfer information. Unlike those other cards, however, a smart card can be used to establish a person's identity as validly as a signature on a piece of paper. ■ In addition, technological innovations now under way will allow an e-signature to be evidenced by an image of a person's retina, fingerprint, or face that is scanned by a computer and then matched to a numeric code. The scanned image and the numeric code are registered with security companies that maintain files on an accessible server that can be used to authenticate a transaction.

STATE LAWS GOVERNING E-SIGNATURES

Most states have laws governing e-signatures. The problem is that the state e-signature laws are not uniform. Some states—California is a notable example—provide that many types of documents cannot be signed with e-signatures, while other states are more permissive. Additionally, some states recognize only digital signatures as valid, while others permit other types of e-signatures.

The National Conference of Commissioners on Uniform State Laws, in an attempt to create more uniformity among the states, promulgated the Uniform Electronic Transactions Act (UETA) in 1999. To date, the UETA has been adopted, at least in part, by more than forty states. The UETA provides, among other things, that a signature may not be denied legal effect or enforceability solely because it is in electronic form. (Other aspects of the UETA will be discussed shortly.)

FEDERAL LAW ON E-SIGNATURES AND E-DOCUMENTS

In 2000, Congress enacted the Electronic Signatures in Global and National Commerce Act (E-SIGN Act) to provide that no contract, record, or signature may be "denied legal effect" solely because it is in an electronic form. In other words, under this law, an electronic signature is as valid as a signature on paper, and an electronic document can be as enforceable as a paper one.

For an electronic signature to be enforceable, the contracting parties must have agreed to use electronic signatures. For an electronic document to be valid, it must be in a form that can be retained and accurately reproduced.

The E-SIGN Act does not apply to all types of documents, however. Contracts and documents that are exempt include court papers, divorce decrees, evictions, foreclosures, health-insurance terminations, prenuptial agreements, and wills. Also, the only agreements governed by the UCC that fall under this law are those covered by Articles 2 and 2A and UCC 1–107 and 1–206.

Despite these limitations, the E-SIGN Act greatly expands the possibilities for contracting online. ■ EXAMPLE 10.5 From a remote location, anyone can now open an account with a financial institution, obtain a mortgage or other loan, buy insurance,

You can find many good resources online about the E-SIGN Act of 2000, including articles available at

http://archives.cnn.com/ 2000/ALLPOLITICS/ stories/06/30/clinton. e.signatures.04/index.html

and

http://www.bizjournals.com/ albany/stories/2000/09/11/ editorial5.html.

and purchase real estate over the Internet. Payments and transfers of funds can be done entirely online. Thus, using e-contracts can avoid the time and costs associated with producing, delivering, signing, and returning paper documents. ■

At issue in the following case was whether an exchange of e-mail between the representatives of a seller and its buyers constituted a "writing."

CASE 10.3 In re Cafeteria Operators, L.P.[a]

United States Bankruptcy Court,
Northern District of Texas, 2003.
299 Bankr. 411.

FACTS Under the Perishable Agricultural Commodities Act (PACA) of 1930, a seller of fruits and vegetables has a right to the proceeds from their sale but loses this right if he or she agrees in *writing* to extend the time for payment beyond thirty days. Cafeteria Operators, L.P., operates cafeterias primarily in the Southwest. In 2002, Cafeteria Operators and other buyers ordered cherries from Cherrco, Inc., a wholesale food distributor, through Tim Dent of George E. Dent Sales, Inc. Cherrco bought the fruit from Peterson Farms, Inc., and others and delivered it as specified in invoices that required payment within thirty days. When the buyers failed to pay, Dent and Gene Baldwin, the buyers' representative, tried to negotiate a new payment schedule via e-mail. In January 2003, with $25,269.12 still owed, the buyers filed a petition in a federal bankruptcy court, seeking permission to pay less than this amount. Cherrco objected, asserting that it had a right to the full amount under PACA. The buyers claimed that Cherrco had waived this right in the e-mail exchanged between Dent and Baldwin. Cherrco argued in part that this e-mail was not a "writing."

ISSUE Did the e-mail exchanged between Dent and Baldwin constitute a "writing"?

DECISION Yes. The court rejected Cherrco's argument, holding that the e-mail constituted a "writing" under the

a. *L.P.* stands for "limited partnership," a special form of business organization discussed in Chapter 19.

E-SIGN Act. The court also held, however, that Cherrco had not waived its PACA right and awarded the seller the full amount of its claim.

REASON The court noted that an e-mail message to Dent from Sarah Peterson-Schlukebir, a Peterson Farms representative, stated, "[B]oth Peterson Farms and Cherrco are not willing to sign" a release of the original payment terms. "If we sign the release, we are no longer covered by PACA." Dent e-mailed this message to Baldwin, who, after further negotiations, e-mailed the last note between the parties, "[W]e do not need a formal [contract]. We will just start making the payments starting today. All we really want is the agreement from them that the payment plan is ok." The court quoted from the E-SIGN Act, which provides that "with respect to any transaction in or affecting interstate or foreign commerce * * * a contract * * * may not be denied legal effect, validity, or enforceability solely because an electronic signature or electronic record was used in its formation." In other words, in a transaction involving interstate commerce, e-mail can constitute a "writing." The court concluded, "The transactions between Cherrco and the Debtor[s] occurred in 2002, and clearly qualify for the requirement that the transaction is in or affects interstate commerce." Thus, the court concluded that the e-mails between the parties satisfied the writing requirement under PACA.

FOR CRITICAL ANALYSIS—Social Consideration
Did the e-mail between Dent and Baldwin constitute an agreement between the parties to extend the original payment terms beyond thirty days? Why or why not?

PARTNERING AGREEMENT
An agreement between a seller and a buyer who frequently do business with each other concerning the terms and conditions that will apply to all subsequently formed electronic contracts.

■ Partnering Agreements

One way that online sellers and buyers can prevent disputes over signatures in their e-contracts, as well as disputes over the terms and conditions of those contracts, is to form partnering agreements. In a **partnering agreement,** a seller and a buyer who frequently do business with each other agree in advance on the terms and conditions that will apply to all transactions subsequently conducted electronically. The partnering agreement can also establish special access and identification codes to be used by the parties when transacting business electronically.

A partnering agreement reduces the likelihood that disputes will arise under the contract because the buyer and the seller have agreed in advance to the terms and conditions that will accompany each sale. Furthermore, if a dispute does arise, a court or arbitration forum will be able to refer to the partnering agreement when determining the parties' intent with respect to subsequent contracts. Of course, even with a partnering agreement fraud remains a possibility. If an unauthorized person uses a purchaser's designated access number and identification code, it may be some time before the problem is discovered.

The Uniform Electronic Transactions Act

As noted earlier, the Uniform Electronic Transactions Act (UETA) was promulgated in 1999. The UETA represents one of the first comprehensive efforts to create uniform laws pertaining to e-commerce.

The primary purpose of the UETA is to remove barriers to e-commerce by giving the same legal effect to electronic records and signatures as is currently given to paper documents and signatures. The UETA broadly defines an *e-signature* as "an electronic sound, symbol, or process attached to or logically associated with a record and executed or adopted by a person with the intent to sign the record."[7] An e-signature includes encrypted digital signatures, names (intended as signatures) at the ends of e-mail messages, and "clicks" on a Web page if the click includes the identification of the person. A **record** is "information that is inscribed on a tangible medium or that is stored in an electronic or other medium and is retrievable in perceivable [visual] form."[8]

THE SCOPE AND APPLICABILITY OF THE UETA

The UETA does not create new rules for electronic contracts but rather establishes that records, signatures, and contracts may not be denied enforceability solely due to their electronic form. The UETA does not apply to all writings and signatures but only to electronic records and electronic signatures *relating to a transaction*. A *transaction* is defined as an interaction between two or more people relating to business, commercial, or governmental activities.[9]

The act specifically does not apply to laws governing wills or testamentary trusts, to the UCC (other than Articles 2 and 2A), or to the Uniform Computer Information Transactions Act (discussed later in this chapter).[10] In addition, the provisions of the UETA allow the states to exclude its application to other areas of law.

As described earlier, Congress passed the E-SIGN Act in 2000, a year after the UETA was presented to the states for adoption. Thus, a significant issue is whether and to what extent the federal E-SIGN Act preempts the UETA as adopted by the states.

THE FEDERAL E-SIGN ACT AND THE UETA

The E-SIGN Act refers explicitly to the UETA and provides that if a state has enacted the uniform version of the UETA, it is not preempted by the E-SIGN Act.[11]

RECORD
According to the Uniform Electronic Transactions Act, information that is either inscribed on a tangible medium or stored in an electronic or other medium and that is retrievable. The Uniform Computer Information Transactions Act also uses the term *record* instead of *writing*.

The Web site of the National Conference of Commissioners on Uniform State Laws includes an update of the list of states that have adopted the UETA or considered it for adoption. The site also contains a summary of the act and "Question and Answer" sections concerning this law. Go to

http://www.nccusl.org.

---

7. UETA 102(8).
8. UETA 102(15).
9. UETA 2(12) and 3.
10. UETA 3(b).
11. 15 U.S.C. Section 7002(2)(A)(i).

In other words, if the state has enacted the UETA *without modification*, state law will govern. The problem is that many states have enacted nonuniform (modified) versions of the UETA, largely for the purpose of excluding other areas of state law from the UETA's terms. The E-SIGN Act specifies that those exclusions will be preempted to the extent that they are inconsistent with the E-SIGN Act's provisions.

The E-SIGN Act, however, explicitly allows the states to enact alternative requirements for the use of electronic records or electronic signatures. Generally, though, the requirements must be consistent with the provisions of the E-SIGN Act, and the state must not give greater legal status or effect to one specific type of technology. Additionally, if a state has enacted alternative requirements *after* the E-SIGN Act was adopted, the state law must specifically refer to the E-SIGN Act. The relationship between the UETA and the E-SIGN Act is illustrated in Exhibit 10–2.

HIGHLIGHTS OF THE UETA

We look next at selected provisions of the UETA. Our discussion is, of course, based on the act's uniform provisions. Keep in mind that the states that have enacted the UETA may have adopted slightly different versions.

The Parties Must Agree to Conduct Transactions Electronically   The UETA will not apply to a transaction unless each of the parties has previously agreed to conduct transactions by electronic means. The agreement need not be explicit, however, and it may be implied by the conduct of the parties and the surrounding circumstances.[12] In the comments that accompany the UETA, the drafters stated that it may be reasonable to infer that a person who gives out a business card with an

---

12. UETA 5(b).

EXHIBIT 10–2 THE E-SIGN ACT AND THE UETA

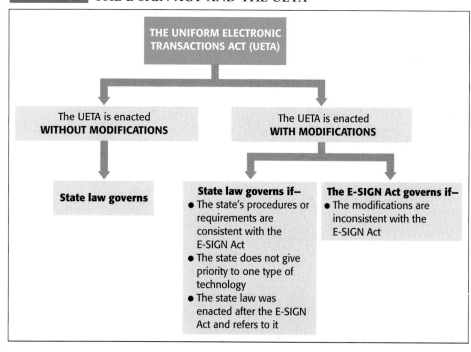

e-mail address on it has consented to transact business electronically.[13] The parties' agreement may also be inferred from a letter or other writing, as well as from some verbal communications.

A person who has previously agreed to an electronic transaction can also withdraw his or her consent and refuse to conduct further business electronically. Additionally, the act expressly gives parties the power to vary the UETA's provisions by contract. In other words, *parties can opt out of all or some of the terms of the UETA.* If the parties do not opt out of the terms of the UETA, however, the UETA will govern their electronic transactions.

Attribution   In the context of electronic transactions, the term *attribution* refers to the procedures that may be used to ensure that the person sending an electronic record is the same person whose e-signature accompanies the record. Under the UETA, if an electronic record or signature is the act of a particular person, the record or signature may be attributed to that person. If a person types her or his name at the bottom of an e-mail purchase order, that name would qualify as a "signature" and be attributed to the person whose name appeared. Just as in paper contracts, one may use any relevant evidence to prove that the record or signature is or is not the act of the person.[14]

Note that even if an individual's name does not appear on a record, the UETA states that the effect of the record is to be determined from the context and surrounding circumstances. In other words, a record may have legal effect even if no one has signed it. ■ **EXAMPLE 10.6** Suppose that Darby sends a fax to Corina. The fax contains a letterhead identifying Darby as the sender, but the document is not signed by Darby. Depending on the circumstances, the fax may be attributed to Darby. ■

The UETA does not contain any express provisions about what constitutes fraud or whether an agent (a person who acts on behalf of another—see Chapter 17) is authorized to enter into a contract. Under the UETA, other state laws control if any issues relating to agency, authority, forgery, or contract formation arise.

Notarization   If a document is required to be notarized under existing state law, the UETA provides that this requirement is satisfied by the electronic signature of a notary public or other person authorized to verify signatures. ■ **EXAMPLE 10.7** Suppose that Joel intends to accept an offer to purchase real estate via e-mail. Under the UETA, the requirement is satisfied if a notary public is present to verify Joel's identity and to affix an electronic signature to the e-mail acceptance. ■

The Effect of Errors   The UETA encourages, but does not require, the use of security procedures (such as encryption) to verify changes to electronic documents and to correct errors. Section 10 of the UETA provides that if the parties have agreed to a security procedure and one party does not detect an error because he or she did not follow the procedure, the conforming party can legally avoid the effect of the change or error. If the parties have not agreed to use a security procedure, then other state laws (including contract law governing mistakes—see Chapter 9) will determine the effect of the error on the parties' agreement.

To avoid the effect of errors, a party must take certain steps. First, the party must promptly notify the other party of the error and of her or his intent not to be bound by the error. Second, the party must take reasonable steps to return any benefit or

At the Web site of the Consumers Union, you can read an article discussing some concerns that consumer groups have about many of the provisions in the UETA. Go to

http://www.consumersunion.org/finance/899nclcwc.htm.

13. UETA 5, Comment 4B.
14. UETA 9.

consideration received. Parties cannot avoid a transaction from which they have benefited. ■ **EXAMPLE 10.8** Suppose that Marissa, as the result of an error, received access to valuable information. Because she cannot "give back" or make restitution for the valuable information she now knows, the transaction may be unavoidable. ■ In all other situations in which a change or error occurs in an electronic record (and the parties' agreement does not specifically address errors), the UETA states that the traditional law governing mistakes will apply.

Timing Section 15 of the UETA sets forth provisions relating to the sending and receiving of electronic records. These provisions apply unless the parties agree to different terms. Under Section 15, an electronic record is considered *sent* when it is properly directed to the intended recipient in a form readable by the recipient's computer system. Once the electronic record leaves the control of the sender or comes under the control of the recipient, the UETA deems it to have been sent. An electronic record is considered *received* when it enters the recipient's processing system in a readable form—*even if no individual is aware of its receipt.*

Additionally, the UETA provides that, unless otherwise agreed, an electronic record is to be sent from or received at the party's principal place of business. If a party has no place of business, the provision then authorizes the place of sending or receipt to be the party's residence. If a party has multiple places of business, the record should be sent from or received at the location that has the closest relationship to the underlying transaction.

▪ The Uniform Computer Information Transactions Act

COMPUTER INFORMATION
As defined by the Uniform Computer Information Transactions Act, "information in an electronic form obtained from or through use of a computer, or that is in digital or an equivalent form capable of being processed by a computer."

The National Conference of Commissioners on Uniform State Laws (NCCUSL) promulgated the Uniform Computer Information Transactions Act (UCITA) in 1999. The primary purpose of the UCITA is to validate e-contracts to license or purchase software, or contracts that give access to—or allow the distribution of—**computer information.** The UCITA is controversial, and only two states (Maryland and Virginia) have adopted it, while four states (Iowa, North Carolina, Vermont, and West Virginia) have passed anti–UCITA provisions. In 2003, the NCCUSL withdrew its support of the UCITA. Although the UCITA remains a legal resource, the NCCUSL will no longer seek its adoption by the states, which are thus unlikely to consider it further.

APPLICATION ▪ How Can You Find and Use Online Contract Forms?*

Before the printing press, every contract form had to be handwritten. Since the advent of printing, however, most standard contract forms have been readily available at low cost. Now the Internet has made available an even larger variety of contract forms, as well as other legal and business forms.

* This *Application* is not meant to substitute for the services of an attorney who is licensed to practice law in your state.

WHERE TO OBTAIN ONLINE CONTRACT FORMS

The 'Lectric Law Library has a collection of forms at **http://www.lectlaw.com/form.html**. The site includes forms for the assignment of a contract, a contract for the sale of a motor vehicle, and many others. In addition to actual forms, there are comments on how the forms should be used and filled out. Another excellent online resource for

(Continued)

APPLICATION ▪ How Can You Find and Use Online Contract Forms?—Continued

various types of forms is FindForms, at http://www. findforms.com.

Other online forms collections can be found at LegalWiz. com (go to http://www.legalwiz.com/forms.htm), a Web site that provides free legal forms, including a form that can be used to sell personal property. At http://www. legaldocs.com, you will find an electronic forms book that offers hundreds of standardized legal forms, some of which are free. Washburn University School of Law has a Web page containing links to an extensive number of forms archives at http://www.washlaw.edu/legalforms.

A special Web site for small-business owners is http:// www.lawvantage.com/index.shtml. Some documents are free; others require a fee or an annual subscription. Many law firms post legal forms, including contract forms, on their Web sites. For example, see the Web site of Bornstein & Naylor (at http://lbnlaw.com/Freedownload2.htm).

Finally, a number of forms are available from FindLaw. Go to http://forms.lp.findlaw.com and scroll down the

screen to "Other Form Resources." FindLaw is now a part of West Group.

CHECKLIST FOR THE ONLINE SELLER

1. When looking for a contract form appropriate to your business, "shop around" for a form that most closely meets your needs.
2. Consider customizing any standardized contract form that you use to ensure that it will cover all of the contingencies that you deem important.
3. When using a standardized contract form, make sure that you provide for a means of acceptance—for example, by including a box stating "I accept" or "I agree."
4. Consider posting your own customized contract forms on your Web site for prospective customers or others to use.

▪ KEY TERMS

browse-wrap terms   312
click-on agreement   308
computer information   319
cybernotary   313

e-contract   306
e-signature   313
forum-selection clause   307
partnering agreement   315

record   316
shrink-wrap agreement   308

CHAPTER SUMMARY ▪ E-Contracts

Online Offers (See pages 307–308.)	Businesspersons who present contract offers via the Internet should keep in mind that the terms of the offer should be just as inclusive as the terms in an offer made in a written (paper) document. All possible contingencies should be anticipated and provided for in the offer. Because jurisdictional issues frequently arise with online transactions, it is particularly important to include dispute-settlement provisions in the offer, as well as a forum-selection clause. The offer should be displayed in an easily readable and clear format. An online offer should also include some mechanism, such as an "I agree" or "I accept" box, by which the customer may accept the offer.

CHAPTER SUMMARY ▦ E-Contracts—Continued

Online Acceptances
(See pages 308–313.)
	1. *Shrink-wrap agreement—*
	
	   a. Definition—An agreement whose terms are expressed inside a box in which the goods are packaged. The party who opens the box is informed that, by keeping the goods that are in the box, he or she agrees to the terms of the shrink-wrap agreement.
	
	   b. Enforceability—The courts have often enforced shrink-wrap agreements, even if the purchaser-user of the goods did not read the terms of the agreement. A court may deem a shrink-wrap agreement unenforceable, however, if the buyer learns of the shrink-wrap terms *after* the parties entered into the agreement.
	
	2. *Click-on agreement—*
	
	   a. Definition—An agreement created when a buyer, completing a transaction on a computer, is required to indicate her or his assent to be bound by the terms of an offer by clicking on a button that says, for example, "I agree." The terms of the agreement may appear on the Web site through which the buyer is obtaining goods or services, or they may appear on a computer screen when software is downloaded.
	
	   b. Enforceability—The courts have enforced click-on agreements, holding that by clicking "I agree," the offeree has indicated acceptance by conduct. Browse-wrap terms, however (terms in a license that an Internet user does not have to read prior to downloading the product, such as software), may not be enforced on the ground that the user is not made aware that he or she is entering into a contract.

E-Signatures (See pages 313–315.)	1. *Definition*—The Uniform Electronic Transactions Act (UETA) defines the term *e-signature* as "an electronic sound, symbol, or process attached to or logically associated with a record and executed or adopted by a person with the intent to sign the record." 2. *E-signature technologies*—These include the *asymmetric cryptosystem* (which creates a digital signature using two different cryptographic "keys"); *signature dynamics* (which involves capturing a sender's signature using a stylus and an electronic digitizer pad); a *smart card* (a device the size of a credit card that is embedded with code and other data); and, probably in the near future, scanned images of retinas, fingerprints, or other physical characteristics that are linked to numeric codes. 3. *State laws governing e-signatures*—Although most states have laws governing e-signatures, these laws are not uniform. The UETA provides for the validity of e-signatures and may ultimately create more uniformity among the states in this respect. 4. *Federal law on e-signatures and e-documents*—The Electronic Signatures in Global and National Commerce Act (E-SIGN Act) of 2000 gave validity to e-signatures by providing that no contract, record, or signature may be "denied legal effect" solely because it is in an electronic form.
Partnering Agreements (See pages 315–316.)	To reduce the likelihood that disputes will arise under their e-contracts, parties who frequently do business with each other may form a *partnering agreement*. In effect, the parties agree in advance on the terms and conditions that will apply to all transactions subsequently conducted electronically. The agreement can also establish access and identification codes to be used by the parties when transacting business electronically.
The Uniform Electronic Transactions Act (UETA) (See pages 316–319.)	1. *Definition*—A uniform act submitted to the states for adoption by the National Conference of Commissioners on Uniform State Laws (NCCUSL). 2. *Purpose*—To create rules to support the enforcement of e-contracts. Under the UETA, contracts entered into online, as well as other documents, are presumed to be valid. The UETA does not apply to transactions governed by the UCC or to wills or testamentary trusts.

(Continued)

CHAPTER SUMMARY ▪ E-Contracts—Continued

| **The Uniform Computer Information Transactions Act** (See page 319.) | 1. *Definition*—A uniform act previously submitted to the states for adoption by the NCCUSL. The NCCUSL withdrew its support in 2003. |
| | 2. *Purpose*—To validate e-contracts to license or purchase software, or contracts that give access to—or allow the distribution of—computer information. |

▪ FOR REVIEW

Answers for the even-numbered questions in this For Review *section can be found in Appendix I at the end of this text.*

1 What are some important clauses to include when making offers to form electronic contracts, or e-contracts?

2 How do shrink-wrap and click-on agreements differ from other contracts? How have traditional laws been applied to these agreements?

3 What is an electronic signature? Are electronic signatures valid?

4 What is a partnering agreement? What purpose does it serve?

5 What is the Uniform Electronic Transactions Act (UETA)? What are some of the major provisions of this act?

▪ QUESTIONS AND CASE PROBLEMS

10–1. Click-On Agreements. Paul is a financial analyst for King Investments, Inc., a brokerage firm. He uses the Internet to investigate the background and activities of companies that might be good investments for King's customers. While visiting the Web site of Business Research, Inc., Paul sees on his screen a message that reads, "Welcome to businessresearch.com. By visiting our site, you have been entered as a subscriber to our e-publication, *Companies Unlimited*. This publication will be sent to you daily at a cost of $7.50 per week. An invoice will be included with *Companies Unlimited* every four weeks. You may cancel your subscription at any time." Has Paul entered into an enforceable contract to pay for *Companies Unlimited*? Why or why not?

10–2. Click-On Agreements. Anne is a reporter for *Daily Business Journal*, a print publication consulted by investors and other businesspersons. She often uses the Internet to perform research for the articles that she writes for the publication. While visiting the Web site of Cyberspace Investments Corp., Anne reads a pop-up window that states, "Our business newsletter, *E-Commerce Weekly*, is available at a one-year subscription rate of $5 per issue. To subscribe, enter your e-mail address below and click 'SUBSCRIBE.' By subscribing, you agree to the terms of the subscriber's agreement. To read this agreement, click 'AGREEMENT.' " Anne enters her e-mail address, but does not click on "AGREEMENT" to read the terms. Has Anne entered into an enforceable contract to pay for *E-Commerce Weekly*? Explain.

10–3. Online Acceptance. Bob, a sales representative for Central Computer Co., occasionally uses the Internet to obtain information about his customers and to look for new sales leads. While visiting the Web site of Marketing World, Inc., Bob is presented with an on-screen message that offers, "To improve your ability to make deals, read our monthly online magazine, *Sales Genius*, available at a subscription rate of $15 a month. To subscribe, fill in your name, company name, and e-mail address below, and click 'YES!' By clicking 'YES!' you agree to the terms of the subscription contract. To read this contract, click 'TERMS.' " Among those terms is a clause that allows Marketing World to charge interest for subscription bills not paid within a certain time. The terms also prohibit subscribers from copying or distributing part or all of *Sales Genius* in any form. Bob subscribes without reading the terms. Marketing World later files a suit against Bob, based on his failure to pay for his subscription. Should the court hold that Bob is obligated to pay interest on the amount? Explain.

10–4. Shrink-Wrap/Click-On Agreements. 1-A Equipment Co. signed a sales order to lease Accware 10 User NT software, which is made and marketed by ICode, Inc. Just above the signature line, the order stated: "Thank you for your order. No returns or refunds will be issued for software license and/or services. All sales are final. Please read the End User License and Service Agreement." The software was delivered in a sealed envelope inside a box. On the outside of the envelope, an "End

User Agreement" provided in part, "BY OPENING THIS PACKAGING, CLICKING YOUR ACCEPTANCE OF THE AGREEMENT DURING DOWNLOAD OR INSTALLATION OF THIS PRODUCT, OR BY USING ANY PART OF THIS PRODUCT, YOU AGREE TO BE LEGALLY BOUND BY THE TERMS OF THE AGREEMENT. . . . This agreement will be governed by the laws in force in the Commonwealth of Virginia . . . and exclusive venue for any litigation shall be in Virginia." Later, dissatisfied with the software, 1-A filed a suit in a Massachusetts state court against ICode, alleging breach of contract and misrepresentation. ICode asked the court to dismiss the case on the basis of the "End User Agreement." Is the agreement enforceable? Should the court dismiss the suit? Why or why not? [*1-A Equipment Co. v. ICode, Inc.*, 43 UCC Rep.Serv.2d 807 (Mass.Dist. 2000)]

CASE PROBLEM WITH SAMPLE ANSWER

10–5. Peerless Wall & Window Coverings, Inc., is a small business in Pennsylvania. To run the cash registers in its stores, manage inventory, and link the stores electronically, in 1994 Peerless installed Point of Sale V6.5 software produced by Synchronics, Inc., a small corporation in Tennessee that develops and markets business software. Point of Sale V6.5 was written with code that used only a two-digit year field—for example, 1999 was stored as "99." This meant that all dates were interpreted as falling within the twentieth century (2001, stored as "01," would be mistaken for 1901). In other words, Point of Sale V6.5 was not "Year 2000" (Y2K) compliant. The software was licensed under a shrink-wrap agreement printed on the envelopes containing the disks. The agreement included a clause that, among other things, limited remedies to replacement within ninety days if there was a defect in the disks and stated, "The entire risk as to the quality and performance of the Software is with you." In 1995, Synchronics stopped selling and supporting Point of Sale V6.5. Two years later, Synchronics told Peerless that the software was not Y2K compliant and should be replaced. Peerless sued Synchronics in a federal district court, alleging, in part, breach of contract. Synchronics filed a motion for summary judgment. Who is more likely to bear the cost of replacing the software? Why? [*Peerless Wall & Window Coverings, Inc. v. Synchronics, Inc.*, 85 F.Supp.2d 519 (W.D.Pa. 2000), aff'd 234 F.3d 1265 (3d Cir. 2000)]

After you have answered this problem, compare your answer with the sample answer given on the Web site that accompanies this text. Go to http://blt.westbuslaw.com, select "Chapter 10," and click on "Case Problem with Sample Answer."

10–6. Click-On Agreements. America Online, Inc. (AOL), provided e-mail service to Walter Hughes and other members under a click-on agreement titled "Terms of Service." This agreement consisted of three parts: a "Member Agreement," "Community Guidelines," and a "Privacy Policy." The "Member Agreement" included a forum-selection clause that read, "You expressly agree that exclusive jurisdiction for any claim or dispute with AOL or relating in any way to your membership or your use of AOL resides in the courts of Virginia." When Officer Thomas McMenamon of the Methuen, Massachusetts, Police Department received threatening e-mail sent from an AOL account, he requested and obtained from AOL Hughes's name and other personal information. Hughes filed a suit in a federal district court against AOL, which filed a motion to dismiss on the basis of the forum-selection clause. Considering that the clause was a click-on provision, is it enforceable? Explain. [*Hughes v. McMenamon*, 204 F.Supp.2d 178 (D.Mass. 2002)]

10–7. Shrink-Wrap Agreements/Browse-Wrap Terms. Mary DeFontes bought a computer and a service contract from Dell Computers Corp. DeFontes was charged $950.51, of which $13.51 was identified on the invoice as "tax." This amount was paid to the state of Rhode Island. DeFontes and other Dell customers filed a suit in a Rhode Island state court against Dell, claiming that Dell was overcharging its customers by collecting a tax on service contracts and transportation costs. Dell asked the court to order DeFontes to submit the dispute to arbitration. Dell cited its "Terms and Conditions Agreement," which provides in part that by accepting delivery of Dell's products or services, a customer agrees to submit any dispute to arbitration. Customers can view this agreement through an *inconspicuous* link at the bottom of Dell's Web site, and Dell encloses a copy with an order when it is shipped. Dell argued that DeFontes accepted these terms by failing to return her purchase within thirty days, although the agreement did not state this. Is DeFontes bound to the "Terms and Conditions Agreement"? Should the court grant Dell's request? Why or why not? [*DeFontes v. Dell Computers Corp.*, __ A.2d __ (R.I. 2004)]

A QUESTION OF ETHICS

10–8. Over the phone, Rich and Enza Hill ordered a computer from Gateway 2000, Inc. Inside the box were the computer and a list of contract terms, which provided that the terms governed the transaction unless the customers returned the computer within thirty days. Among those terms was a clause that required any claims to be submitted to arbitration. The Hills kept the computer for more than thirty days before complaining to Gateway about the computer's components and its performance. When the matter was not resolved to their satisfaction, the Hills filed a suit in a federal district court against Gateway, arguing, among other things, that the computer was defective. Gateway asked the court to enforce the arbitration clause. The Hills claimed that this term was not part of a contract to buy the computer because the list on which it appeared had been in the box and they did not see the list until after the computer was delivered. In view of these facts, consider the following questions. [*Hill v. Gateway 2000, Inc.*, 105 F.3d 1147 (7th Cir. 1997)]

1. Should the court enforce the arbitration clause in this case? If you were the judge, how would you rule on this issue?
2. In your opinion, do shrink-wrap agreements impose too great a burden on purchasers? Why or why not?

3. An ongoing complaint about shrink-wrap and click-wrap agreements is that all too often the terms of these agreements go unread. Should purchasers be bound in contract by terms that they have not even read? Why or why not?

FOR CRITICAL ANALYSIS

10–9. Would you say that, on balance, most of the legal issues presented by e-commerce and e-contracting are unique to the cyber age or simply old legal issues in a new form?

VIDEO QUESTION

10–10. Go to this text's Web site at **http://blt. westbuslaw.com** and select "Chapter 10." Click on "Video Questions" and view the video titled *E-Contracts: Agreeing Online.* Then answer the following questions.

1. According to the instructor in the video, what is the key factor in determining whether a particular term in an online agreement is enforceable?

2. Suppose that you click on "I accept" in order to download software from the Internet. You do not read the terms of the agreement before accepting it, even though you know that such agreements often contain forum-selection and arbitration clauses. The software later causes irreparable harm to your computer system, and you want to sue. When you go to the Web site and view the agreement, however, you discover that a choice-of-law clause in the contract specified that the law of Nigeria controls. Is this term enforceable? Is it a term that should reasonably be expected in an online contract?

3. Does it matter what the term actually says if it is a type of term that one could reasonably expect to be in the contract? What arguments can be made for and against enforcing a choice-of-law clause in an online contract?

INTERNET EXERCISES

Go to the *Business Law Today: The Essentials* home page at **http://blt.westbuslaw.com**, select "Chapter 10," and click on "Internet Exercises." There you will find the following Internet research exercises that you can perform to learn more about topics covered in this chapter.

Activity 10–1: LEGAL PERSPECTIVE—E-Contract Formation

Activity 10–2: MANAGEMENT PERSPECTIVE—E-Signatures

BEFORE THE TEST

Go to the *Business Law Today: The Essentials* home page at **http://blt.westbuslaw.com**, select "Chapter 10," and click on "Interactive Quizzes." You will find at least twenty interactive questions relating to this chapter.

CHAPTER 11

Sales and Leases: Formation, Title, and Risk

"The great object of the law is to encourage commerce."

J. Chambre, 1739–1823
(British jurist)

CHAPTER OUTLINE

■ THE SCOPE OF THE UCC

■ THE SCOPE OF
ARTICLE 2—SALES

■ THE SCOPE OF
ARTICLE 2A—LEASES

■ THE FORMATION
OF SALES AND LEASE
CONTRACTS

■ TITLE, RISK, AND
INSURABLE INTEREST

■■ LEARNING OBJECTIVES

After reading this chapter, you should be able to answer the following questions:

1 How do Article 2 and Article 2A of the UCC differ? What types of transactions does each article cover?

2 If an offeree includes additional or different terms in an acceptance, will a contract result? If so, what happens to these terms?

3 If the parties to a contract do not expressly agree on when title to goods passes, what determines when title passes?

4 Risk of loss does not necessarily pass with title. If the parties to a contract do not expressly agree when risk passes and the goods are to be delivered without movement by the seller, when does risk pass?

5 At what point does the buyer acquire an insurable interest in goods subject to a sales contract? Can both the buyer and the seller have an insurable interest in the goods simultaneously?

The opening quotation states that the object of the law is to encourage commerce. This is particularly true with respect to the Uniform Commercial Code (UCC). The UCC facilitates commercial transactions by making the laws governing sales and lease contracts uniform, clearer, simpler, and more readily applicable to the numerous difficulties that can arise during such transactions. Recall from Chapter 1 that the UCC is one of many uniform (model) acts drafted by the National Conference of Commissioners on Uniform State Laws and submitted to the states for adoption. Once a state legislature has adopted a uniform act, the act becomes statutory law in that state. Thus, when we turn to sales and lease contracts, we move away from common law principles and into the area of statutory law.

We open this chapter with a discussion of the general coverage of the UCC and its significance as a legal landmark. We then look at the scope of the UCC's Article 2 (on sales) and Article 2A (on leases) as a background to the focus of this chapter, which is the formation of contracts for the sale and lease of goods.

A sale of goods transfers ownership rights in (title to) the goods from the seller to the buyer. Often, a sales contract is signed before the actual goods are available. For example, a sales contract for oranges might be signed in May, but the oranges may not be ready for picking and shipment until October. Any number of things can happen between the time the sales contract is signed and the time the goods are actually transferred into the buyer's possession. Fire, flood, or frost may destroy the orange groves, or the oranges may be lost or damaged in transit. In the latter part of this chapter, we look at the rights and liabilities of the parties between the time the contract is formed and the time the goods are actually received by the buyer (or the lessee, if the goods are being leased).

The UCC was amended in 2003 to update its provisions to accommodate electronic commerce. As of 2005, the amendments to Articles 2 and 2A had not been adopted by any state. Throughout this chapter and the chapters that follow, however, any amendments that significantly change the UCC provisions currently in effect in most states will be discussed in footnotes. Note, though, that even when the changes are not substantive, some of the section and subsection numbers may be slightly different under the amended Article 2 due to the addition of new provisions. (Excerpts from the 2003 amendments appear in Appendix B.)

◼️ The Scope of the UCC

The UCC attempts to provide a consistent and integrated framework of rules to deal with all phases ordinarily arising in a commercial sales transaction from start to finish. For example, consider the following events, all of which occur during a single sales transaction:

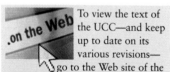

To view the text of the UCC—and keep up to date on its various revisions— go to the Web site of the National Conference of Commissioners on Uniform State Laws (NCCUSL) at

http://www.nccusl.org.

Cornell University's Legal Information Institute also offers the full text of the UCC at

http://www.law.cornell.edu/ uniform/ucc.html.

1 *A contract for the sale or lease of goods is formed and executed.* Article 2 and Article 2A of the UCC provide rules governing all facets of this transaction.

2 *The transaction may involve a payment—by check, electronic fund transfer, or other means.* Article 3 (on negotiable instruments), Article 4 (on bank deposits and collections), Article 4A (on fund transfers), and Article 5 (on letters of credit) cover this part of the transaction.

3 *The transaction may involve a bill of lading or a warehouse receipt that covers goods when they are shipped or stored.* Article 7 (on documents of title) deals with this subject.

4 *The transaction may involve the demand by a seller or lender for some form of security for a remaining balance owed.* Article 9 (on secured transactions) covers this part of the transaction.

Two articles of the UCC seemingly do not address the "ordinary" commercial sales transaction. Article 6, on bulk transfers, has to do with merchants who sell off the major part of their inventory. Such bulk sales are not part of the ordinary course of business. Article 8, which covers investment securities, deals with transactions involving negotiable securities (stocks and bonds)—transactions that do not involve

BE CAREFUL Although the UCC has been widely adopted without many changes, states have modified some of the details to suit their particular needs.

SALES CONTRACT
A contract for the sale of goods under which the ownership of goods is transferred from a seller to a buyer for a price.

the sale of goods. The UCC's drafters, however, considered the subject matter of Articles 6 and 8 to be *sufficiently* related to commercial transactions to warrant its inclusion in the UCC.

The UCC has been adopted in whole or in part by all of the states.[1] Because of its importance in the area of commercial transactions, we present the UCC as this chapter's *Landmark in the Law* feature on the following page.

■ The Scope of Article 2—Sales

Article 2 of the UCC governs **sales contracts,** or contracts for the sale of goods. To facilitate commercial transactions, Article 2 modifies some of the common law contract requirements that were discussed in detail in Chapters 7 through 9. To the extent that it has not been modified by the UCC, however, the common law of contracts also applies to sales contracts. In general, the rule is that when a UCC provision addresses a certain issue, the UCC governs; when the UCC is silent, the common law governs.

In regard to Article 2, you should keep in mind two things. First, Article 2 deals with the sale of *goods;* it does not deal with real property (real estate), services, or intangible property such as stocks and bonds. Thus, if the subject matter of a dispute is goods, the UCC governs. If it is real estate or services, the common law applies. The relationship between general contract law and the law governing sales of goods is illustrated in Exhibit 11–1. Second, in some cases, the rules may vary quite a bit, depending on whether the buyer or the seller is a merchant. We look now at how the UCC defines three important terms: *sale, goods,* and *merchant status.*

---

1. Louisiana has not adopted Articles 2 and 2A, however.

EXHIBIT 11–1 LAW GOVERNING CONTRACTS

This exhibit graphically illustrates the relationship between general contract law and the law governing contracts for the sale of goods. Contracts for the sale of goods are not governed exclusively by Article 2 of the Uniform Commercial Code but are also governed by general contract law whenever it is relevant and has not been modified by the UCC.

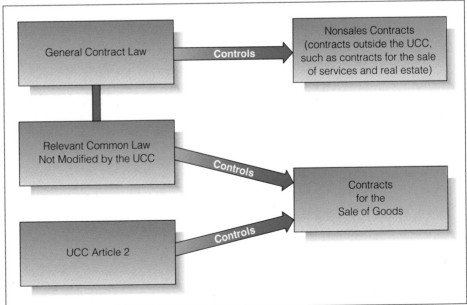

LANDMARK IN THE LAW

The Uniform Commercial Code

Of all the attempts in the United States to produce a uniform body of laws relating to commercial transactions, none has been as comprehensive or successful as the Uniform Commercial Code (UCC).

THE ORIGINS OF THE UCC   The UCC was the brainchild of William A. Schnader, president of the National Conference of Commissioners on Uniform State Laws (NCCUSL). The drafting of the UCC began in 1945. The most significant individual involved in the project was its chief editor, Karl N. Llewellyn of the Columbia University Law School. Llewellyn's intellect, continuous efforts, and ability to compromise made the first version of the UCC (1949) a legal landmark. Over the next several years, the UCC was substantially accepted by virtually every state in the nation.

PERIODIC CHANGES AND UPDATES   Various articles and sections of the UCC are periodically changed or supplemented to clarify certain rules or to establish new rules when changes in business customs render the existing UCC provisions inapplicable. For example, because of the increasing importance of leases of goods in the commercial context, Article 2A governing leases was added to the UCC. To clarify the rights of parties to commercial fund transfers, particularly electronic fund transfers, Article 4A was issued. Articles 3 and 4, on negotiable instruments and banking relationships, underwent a significant revision in the 1990s. Because of other changes in business and in the law, the NCCUSL has recommended the repeal of Article 6 (on bulk transfers), offering a revised Article 6 to those states that prefer not to repeal it. The NCCUSL also revised Article 9, covering secured transactions. The revised Article 9, which has been adopted by all of the states, will be discussed in Chapter 16. In 2003, the NCCUSL approved amendments to Articles 2 and 2A, which have now been proposed to the states for adoption. These amendments were made largely to accommodate electronic commerce. For example, throughout the amendments, the word *writing* has been replaced with the word *record,* and the definition of *sign* has been modified to include electronic signatures.

APPLICATION TO TODAY'S WORLD

By periodically revising the UCC's articles, the NCCUSL has been able to adapt its provisions to changing business customs and practices. UCC provisions governing sales and lease contracts have also been extended to contracts formed in the online environment. Note, though, that it can take some time for individual states to decide whether to adopt the updated UCC provisions. Therefore, the 2003 amendments to Articles 2 and 2A may not be adopted in the majority of the states for some time.

RELEVANT WEB SITES

To locate information on the Web concerning the Uniform Commercial Code, go go to this text's Web site at **http://blt.westbuslaw.com,** *select "Chapter 11," and click on "URLs for Landmarks."*

WHAT IS A SALE?

The UCC defines a **sale** as "the passing of title from the seller to the buyer for a price" [UCC 2–106(1)]. The price may be payable in money or in other goods or services.

WHAT ARE GOODS?

To be characterized as a *good*, the item of property must be *tangible*, and it must be *movable*.[2] **Tangible property** has physical existence—it can be touched or seen. **Intangible property**—such as corporate stocks and bonds, patents and copyrights, and ordinary contract rights—has only conceptual existence and thus does not come under Article 2.[3] A movable item can be carried from place to place. Hence, real estate is excluded from Article 2.

Two areas of dispute arise in determining whether the object of a contract is goods and thus whether Article 2 is applicable. One problem has to do with *goods associated with real estate,* such as crops or timber, and the other concerns contracts involving a combination of *goods and services.*

Goods Associated with Real Estate   Goods associated with real estate often fall within the scope of Article 2. Section 2–107 provides the following rules:

1 A contract for the sale of minerals or the like (including oil and gas) or a structure (such as a building) is a contract for the sale of goods if *severance,* or *separation,* is to be made by the *seller.* If the *buyer* is to sever (separate) the minerals or structure from the land, the contract is considered to be a sale of real estate governed by the principles of real property law, not the UCC.

2 A sale of growing crops[4] (such as potatoes, carrots, wheat, and the like) or timber to be cut is considered to be a contract for the sale of goods *regardless of who severs them.*

3 Other "things attached" to realty but capable of severance without material harm to the land are considered goods *regardless of who severs them.*[5] "Things attached" that are severable without harm to realty could include such items as a heater, a window air conditioner in a house, and stools in a restaurant. Thus, removal of one of these things would be considered a sale of goods. The test is whether removal will cause substantial harm to the real property to which the item is attached.

Goods and Services Combined   In cases in which goods and services are combined, courts disagree. For instance, is the blood furnished to a patient during an operation a "sale of goods" or the "performance of a medical service"? Some courts say it is a good; others say it is a service. Because the UCC does not provide the answers to such

---

2. The 2003 amendments to Article 2 change the phrasing of this section slightly. The new section states that "goods must be both *existing* and *identified* before any interest in them may pass" [Amended UCC 2–105(1)].
3. The 2003 amendments to Article 2 specifically exclude "information" that is not associated with goods [Amended UCC 2–103(1)(k)]. Nevertheless, Article 2 *may* apply to transactions involving both goods and information when a sale involves "smart goods" (for example, a toy or an automobile that contains computer programs). The courts must determine whether and to what extent the article should be applied to such transactions.
4. Note that the 2003 amendments moved the definition of goods to UCC 2–103(k), but growing crops are expressly included within the definition of *goods.* Contracts to sell timber, minerals, or structures to be removed from the land will continue to be controlled by UCC 2–107(1).
5. The UCC avoids the term *fixtures* here because of the numerous definitions of the word. A fixture is anything so firmly or permanently attached to land or to a building as to become a part of it. Once personal property becomes a fixture, it is governed by real estate law. See Chapter 24.

(margin notes)

SALE
The passing of title to property from the seller to the buyer for a price.

TANGIBLE PROPERTY
Property that has physical existence and can be distinguished by the senses of touch, sight, and so on. A car is tangible property; a patent right is intangible property.

INTANGIBLE PROPERTY
Property that cannot be seen or touched but exists only conceptually, such as corporate stocks and bonds, patents and copyrights, and ordinary contract rights. Article 2 of the UCC does not govern intangible property.

Sunflowers in bloom. Does Article 2 apply to the sale of sunflower seeds to a snack-foods company? Why or why not? (Telegraph Colour Library, Getty Images)

questions, the courts generally try to determine which factor is predominant—the good or the service. The UCC does stipulate, however, that serving food or drink to be consumed either on or off restaurant premises is a "sale of goods," at least for the purpose of an implied warranty of merchantability (to be explained in Chapter 13) [UCC 2–314(1)]. Other special transactions, including sales of unborn animals and rare coins, are also explicitly characterized as sales of goods by the UCC.

Whether the transaction in question involves the sale of goods or services is important because the majority of courts treat services as being excluded by the UCC. If the transaction is not covered by the UCC, then UCC provisions, including those relating to implied warranties, will not apply. ■ **EXAMPLE 11.1** An Indiana company contracts to purchase customized software from Dharma Systems. The contract states that half of the purchase price is for Dharma Systems' professional services and the other half is for the goods (the software). If the court determines that the contract is predominantly for the software, rather than the services to customize the software, the court will hold that the transaction falls under Article 2.[6] ■

The court in the following case applied the **predominant-factor test** to determine whether Article 2 applied to a contract that involved goods and services.

PREDOMINANT-FACTOR TEST
A test courts use to determine whether a contract is primarily for the sale of goods or for the sale of services.

6. See *Micro Data Base Systems, Inc. v. Dharma Systems, Inc.,* 148 F.3d 649 (7th Cir.1998).

CASE 11.1 ■ Mécanique C.N.C., Inc. v. Durr Environmental, Inc.

United States District Court,
Southern District of Ohio, 2004.
304 F.Supp.2d 971.

FACTS Durr Environmental, Inc., contracted with GE Quartz, Inc. (GE), to design, make, install, and test a selective catalytic reduction system at GE's plant in Hebron, Ohio. The system was to control the emission of nitrogen oxides. On August 3, 2000, Mécanique C.N.C., Inc. (CNC), sent a bid to Durr offering to make and install the ductwork necessary for the system and itemizing the price. Durr

responded with a signed contract. CNC also signed the contract, added three handwritten terms in an attempt to avoid certain costs, and returned it. Durr revised the contract to include only one of the terms and sent it back to CNC. Durr also sent the project's specifications, which CNC met. When problems with the ductwork developed at GE's site, Durr submitted new specifications, which CNC also met, though at substantial added expense and with some delay. Nevertheless, CNC was on schedule to complete the work when, in March 2001, Durr terminated CNC. CNC filed a

CASE 11.1–Continued

suit in a federal district court against Durr and others, alleging in part breach of contract. One of the questions was whether Article 2 applied to the CNC contract. The defendants (Durr and others) filed a motion for summary judgment on this point.

ISSUE Was the contract between Durr and CNC predominantly a contract for a sale of goods?

DECISION Yes. The court held that the contract was predominantly for a sale of goods, with services only incidentally involved. The court granted the defendants' motion for summary judgment.

REASON The court reasoned that "virtually all commercial goods involve some type of service, whether design, assembly, installation, or manufacture," but this does not transform every contract for goods into a contract for services. That a manufacturer uses its effort and expertise to make a good does not mean that the buyer is buying the service instead of the good. The question is whether a buyer's goal is to acquire a product or procure a service. The court con-

cluded that CNC's service, "though extensive," was incidental to Durr's purpose of acquiring the ductwork. CNC's "compensation was tied to the goods produced rather than the labor provided. There was no separate price for installation. * * * CNC played no role in the design of the product." The court added, "Even more significantly, the parties did not contemplate that CNC would be involved in any ongoing servicing or testing of the ductwork once it was installed. CNC's job was to provide a product in accordance with certain specifications. Once that product was created and installed, CNC had no further role."

WHY IS THIS CASE IMPORTANT? *This case illustrates how important it is to anticipate the factors that courts consider in determining whether Article 2 of the UCC applies. For example, even though the purchase of software may appear to be a purchase of goods, if the contract also provides for installing and modifying the software, a court might construe the contract as predominantly for services. For the buyer, this would mean that the UCC does not apply, which may be a very important consideration in some transactions.*

WHO IS A MERCHANT?

Article 2 governs the sale of goods in general. It applies to sales transactions between all buyers and sellers. In a limited number of instances, however, the UCC presumes that certain special business standards ought to be imposed on merchants because they possess a relatively high degree of commercial expertise.[7] Such standards do not apply to the casual or inexperienced seller or buyer ("consumer"). Section 2–104 defines three ways in which merchant status can arise:

Cornell University's Legal Information Institute offers online access to the UCC as enacted in several of the states at

http://www.law.cornell.edu/ statutes.html#state.

1. A merchant is a person who *deals in goods of the kind* involved in the sales contract. Thus, a retailer, a wholesaler, or a manufacturer is a merchant of those goods sold in the business. A merchant for one type of goods is not necessarily a merchant for another type. For example, a sporting equipment retailer is a merchant when selling tennis equipment but not when selling a used computer.

2. A merchant is a person who, by occupation, holds himself or herself out as having knowledge and skill unique to the practices or goods involved in the transaction. Note that this broad definition may include banks or universities as merchants.

3. A person who *employs a merchant as a broker, agent, or other intermediary* has the status of merchant in that transaction. Hence, if a "gentleman farmer" who ordinarily does not run the farm hires a broker to purchase or sell livestock, the farmer is considered a merchant in the transaction.

---

7. The provisions that apply only to merchants deal principally with the Statute of Frauds, firm offers, confirmatory memoranda, and contract modification. These special rules reflect expedient business practices commonly known to merchants in the commercial setting. They will be discussed later in this chapter.

MERCHANT
A person who is engaged in the purchase and sale of goods. Under the UCC, a person who deals in goods of the kind involved in the sales contract or who holds herself or himself out as having skill or knowledge peculiar to the practices or use of the goods being purchased or sold. For definitions, see UCC 2–104.

In summary, a person is a **merchant** when she or he, acting in a mercantile capacity, possesses or uses an expertise specifically related to the goods being sold. This basic distinction is not always clear-cut. For example, courts in most states have determined that farmers may be merchants if they sell products or livestock on a regular basis, but courts in other states have held that the drafters of the UCC did not intend to include farmers as merchants.

The Scope of Article 2A—Leases

In the past few decades, leases of personal property (goods) have become increasingly common. Article 2A of the UCC was created to fill the need for uniform guidelines in this area. Article 2A covers any transaction that creates a lease of goods, as well as subleases of goods [UCC 2A–102, 2A–103(1)(k)]. Except that it applies to leases of goods, rather than sales of goods, Article 2A is essentially a repetition of Article 2 and varies only to reflect differences between sale and lease transactions. (Note that Article 2A is not concerned with leases of real property, such as land or buildings. The laws governing these types of transactions will be examined in Chapter 24.) As previously mentioned, Article 2A was also amended in 2003, and these amendments have been recommended to the states for adoption.

DEFINITION OF A LEASE

LEASE AGREEMENT
In regard to the lease of goods, an agreement in which one person (the lessor) agrees to transfer the right to the possession and use of property to another person (the lessee) in exchange for rental payments.

LESSOR
A person who sells the right to the possession and use of goods to another in exchange for rental payments.

LESSEE
A person who acquires the right to the possession and use of another's goods in exchange for rental payments.

Article 2A defines a **lease agreement** as a lessor and lessee's bargain with respect to the lease of goods, as found in their language and as implied by other circumstances, including course of dealing and usage of trade or course of performance [UCC 2A–103(1)(k)]. A **lessor** is one who sells the right to the possession and use of goods under a lease [UCC 2A–103(1)(p)]. A **lessee** is one who acquires the right to the temporary possession and use of goods under a lease [UCC 2A–103(1)(o)]. In other words, the lessee is the party who is leasing the goods from the lessor. Article 2A applies to all types of leases of goods, including commercial leases and consumer leases. Special rules apply to certain types of leases, however, including consumer leases and finance leases.

CONSUMER LEASES

A *consumer lease* involves three elements: (1) a lessor who regularly engages in the business of leasing or selling; (2) a lessee (except an organization) who leases the goods "primarily for a personal, family, or household purpose"; and (3) total lease payments that are less than a dollar amount set by state statute [UCC 2A–103(1)(e)].[8] In the interest of providing special protection for consumers, certain provisions of Article 2A apply only to consumer leases. For example, one provision states that a consumer may recover attorneys' fees if a court finds that a term in a consumer lease contract is unconscionable [UCC 2A–108(4)(a)].

FINANCE LEASES

A *finance lease* involves a lessor, a lessee, and a supplier. The lessor buys or leases goods from a supplier and leases or subleases them to the lessee [UCC 2A–103(1)(g)].[9]

---

8. The 2003 amendments to Article 2A define a consumer lease in UCC 2A–103(1)(f). The amended section leaves it up to the states to decide whether to place a dollar limitation on the total lease payments.
9. Finance leases are defined in UCC 2A–103(1)(g) of the amended Article 2A.

Typically, in a finance lease, the lessor is simply financing the transaction. ■ EXAMPLE 11.2 Suppose that Marlin Corporation wants to lease a crane for use in its construction business. Marlin's bank agrees to purchase the equipment from Jennco, Inc., and lease the equipment to Marlin. In this situation, the bank is the lessor-financer, Marlin is the lessee, and Jennco is the supplier. ■

Article 2A, unlike ordinary contract law, makes the lessee's obligations under a commercial finance lease irrevocable and independent from the financer's obligations [UCC 2A–407]. In other words, the lessee must perform and continue to make lease payments even if the leased equipment turns out to be defective. (See this chapter's *Letter of the Law* feature on the next page for a case discussing this aspect of finance leases.) The lessee must look almost entirely to the supplier for warranties.

■■ The Formation of Sales and Lease Contracts

In regard to the formation of sales and lease contracts, the UCC modifies the common law in several ways. We look here at how Article 2 and Article 2A of the UCC modify common law contract rules. Remember, though, that parties to sales contracts are free to establish whatever terms they wish. The UCC comes into play only when the parties have failed to provide in their contract for a contingency that later gives rise to a dispute. The UCC makes this clear time and again by using such phrases as "unless the parties otherwise agree" or "absent a contrary agreement by the parties."

OFFER

NOTE Under the UCC, it is the actions of the parties that determine whether they intended to form a contract.

In general contract law, the moment a definite offer is met by an unqualified acceptance, a binding contract is formed. In commercial sales transactions, the verbal exchanges, correspondence, and actions of the parties may not reveal exactly when a binding contractual obligation arises. The UCC states that an agreement sufficient to constitute a contract can exist even if the moment of its making is undetermined [UCC 2–204(2), 2A–204(2)].

Open Terms Remember from Chapter 7 that under the common law of contracts, an offer must be definite enough for the parties (and the courts) to ascertain its essential terms when it is accepted. In contrast, the UCC states that a sales or lease contract will not fail for indefiniteness even if one or more terms are left open as long as (1) the parties intended to make a contract and (2) there is a reasonably certain basis for the court to grant an appropriate remedy [UCC 2–204(3), 2A–204(3)].

■ EXAMPLE 11.3 Mike agrees to lease from CompuQuik a highly specialized computer work station. Mike and one of CompuQuik's sales representatives sign a lease agreement that leaves some of the details blank, to be "worked out" the following week, when the leasing manager will be back from her vacation. In the meantime, CompuQuik obtains the necessary equipment from one of its suppliers and spends several days modifying the equipment to suit Mike's needs. When the leasing manager returns, she calls Mike and tells him that his work station is ready. Mike says he is no longer interested in the work station, as he has arranged to lease the same type of equipment for a lower price from another firm. CompuQuik sues Mike to recover its costs in obtaining and modifying the equipment, and one of the issues before the court is whether the parties had an enforceable contract. The court will likely hold that they did, based on their intent and conduct, despite the "blanks" in their written agreement. ■

LETTER OF THE LAW Finance Leases and the "Hell or High Water" Payment Term

As mentioned elsewhere, in a finance lease, the lessee is obligated to pay the lessor, or financer, no matter what, or—as some say—come hell or high water. Typically, this "hell or high water" payment obligation is specified in the lease agreement. For example, in one finance lease, a provision stated that the lessee could not "withhold, set off, or reduce such payments for any reason." Yet what if a lessee arranges to lease equipment under a finance lease and the equipment turns out to be defective? Must the lessee still make the payments? Yes. Even if the lease contract does not expressly state the payment obligation, the lessee will have to pay—because Article 2A makes it clear that the lessee is obligated to pay the financer/lessor regardless of problems with the leased goods.

To illustrate: In one case, American Transit Insurance Company (ATIC) arranged to lease telephone equipment through a finance lease. The manufacturer of the equipment transferred the equipment to Siemens Credit Corporation, which then leased the equipment to ATIC for a five-year term at $2,314 per month. When the equipment turned out to be defective, ATIC stopped making the lease payments. Siemens subsequently sued ATIC for the lease payments due. ATIC alleged, among other things, that it was unconscionable to require it to make payments on defective equipment. The court, though, viewed the matter differently. The lease clearly qualified as a finance lease under Article 2A, and the letter of the law was clear: the insurance company was obligated to "make all payments due under the lease regardless of the condition or performance of the leased equipment."[a]

THE BOTTOM LINE

The fact that ATIC was obligated to make the lease payments regardless of the condition of the equipment does not mean that ATIC was without a remedy. As the court noted in this case, "ATIC has raised triable issues of fact [issues that could go to trial] as to its equipment problems, but * * * they are properly brought only against the manufacturer," not against the lessor (Siemens).

a. *Siemens Credit Corp. v. American Transit Insurance Co.,* 2001 WL 40775 (S.D.N.Y. 2001).

Relative to the common law of contracts, the UCC has radically lessened the requirement of definiteness of terms. Keep in mind, though, that the more terms left open, the less likely it is that a court will find that the parties intended to form a contract.

Open Price Term. If the parties have not agreed on a price, the court will determine a "reasonable price at the time for delivery" [UCC 2–305(1)]. If either the buyer or the seller is to determine the price, the price is to be fixed (set) in good faith [UCC 2–305(2)]. Under the UCC, good faith means honesty in fact and the observance of reasonable commercial standards of fair dealing in the trade [UCC 2–103(1)(b)]. The concepts of *good faith* and *commercial reasonableness* permeate the UCC.

Sometimes the price fails to be fixed through the fault of one of the parties. In that situation, the other party can treat the contract as canceled or fix a reasonable price. ■ **EXAMPLE 11.4** Perez and Merrick enter into a contract for the sale of unfinished doors and agree that Perez will determine the price. Perez refuses to fix the price. Merrick can either treat the contract as canceled or set a reasonable price [UCC 2–305(3)]. ■

Open Payment Term. When parties do not specify payment terms, payment is due at the time and place at which the buyer is to receive the goods [UCC 2–310(a)]. The buyer can tender payment using any commercially normal or acceptable means,

CONTRAST The common law requires that the parties make their terms definite before they have a contract. The UCC applies general commercial standards to make the terms of a contract definite.

such as a check or credit card. If the seller demands payment in cash, however, the buyer must be given a reasonable time to obtain it [UCC 2–511(2)]. This is especially important when the contract states a definite and final time for performance.

ETHICAL ISSUE 11.1

Is it fair for the UCC to impose payment terms when the parties did not agree to these terms? Many people buy and sell goods all the time in their daily lives without knowing what the UCC is or how it may apply to their transactions. Is it fair for the UCC to impose terms that the parties never discussed when forming their contract?

Consider, for example, a simple transaction that took place on a farm. Max Alexander agreed to purchase hay from Wagner's farm. Alexander left his truck and trailer at the farm for the seller to load the hay. Nothing was said about when payment was due, and the parties were unaware of the UCC's rules. When Alexander came back to get the hay, a dispute broke out. Alexander claimed that he was not given the quantity of hay that he had ordered and argued that he did not have to pay at that time. Wagner refused to release the hay (or the vehicles on which the hay was loaded) until Alexander paid for it.

Eventually, Alexander jumped into his truck and drove off without paying for the hay. When Alexander was later prosecuted for the crime of theft (see Chapter 6), he claimed that he could not be guilty of taking the property of another because he had bought the hay and was the rightful owner. The court, however, disagreed. Because the parties had failed to specify when payment was due, the court held that UCC 2–310(a) controlled: payment was due at the time Alexander picked up the hay. Thus, Alexander's theft conviction was affirmed.[10] ■

Open Delivery Term. When no delivery terms are specified, the buyer normally takes delivery at the seller's place of business [UCC 2–308(a)]. If the seller has no place of business, the seller's residence is used. When goods are located in some other place and both parties know it, delivery is made there. If the time for shipment or delivery is not clearly specified in the sales contract, the court will infer a "reasonable" time for performance [UCC 2–309(1)].

Duration of an Ongoing Contract. A single contract might specify successive performances but not indicate how long the parties are required to deal with each other. In this situation, either party may terminate the ongoing contractual relationship. Principles of good faith and sound commercial practice call for reasonable notification before termination, however, to give the other party reasonable time to seek a substitute arrangement [UCC 2–309(2), (3)].

Options and Cooperation regarding Performance. When the contract contemplates shipment of the goods but does not specify the shipping arrangements, the *seller* has the right to make these arrangements in good faith, using commercial reasonableness in the situation [UCC 2–311].

When a sales contract omits terms relating to the assortment of goods, the *buyer* can specify the assortment. ■ **EXAMPLE 11.5** Petry Drugs, Inc., agrees to purchase one thousand toothbrushes from Marconi's Dental Supply. The toothbrushes come in a variety of colors, but the contract does not specify color. Petry, the buyer, has the right to take six hundred blue toothbrushes and four hundred green ones if it

10. *State v. Alexander,* 186 Or.App. 600, 64 P.3d 1148 (2003).

wishes. Petry, however, must exercise good faith and commercial reasonableness in making its selection [UCC 2–311]. ■

Open Quantity Term.   Normally, if the parties do not specify a quantity, a court will have no basis for determining a remedy. The UCC recognizes two exceptions, however, in requirements and output contracts [UCC 2–306(1)].

In a **requirements contract,** the buyer agrees to purchase and the seller agrees to sell all or up to a stated amount of what the buyer *needs* or *requires*. ■ **EXAMPLE 11.6** Umpqua Cannery forms a contract with Al Garcia. The cannery agrees to purchase from Garcia, and Garcia agrees to sell to the cannery, all of the green beans that the cannery needs or requires during the summer of 2005. ■ There is implicit consideration in a requirements contract because the buyer (the cannery, in this situation) gives up the right to buy green beans from any other seller, and this forfeited right creates a legal detriment (that is, consideration). Requirements contracts are common in the business world and are normally enforceable. If, however, the buyer promises to purchase only if the buyer *wishes* to do so, or if the buyer reserves the right to buy the goods from someone other than the seller, the promise is illusory (without consideration) and unenforceable by either party.

In an **output contract,** the seller agrees to sell and the buyer agrees to buy all or up to a stated amount of what the seller *produces*. ■ **EXAMPLE 11.7** Al Garcia forms a contract with Umpqua Cannery. Garcia agrees to sell to the cannery, and the cannery agrees to purchase from Garcia, all of the beans that Garcia produces on his farm during the summer of 2005. ■ Again, because the seller essentially forfeits the right to sell goods to another buyer, there is implicit consideration in an output contract.

The UCC imposes a *good faith limitation* on requirements and output contracts. The quantity under such contracts is the amount of requirements or the amount of output that occurs during a *normal* production year. The actual quantity purchased or sold cannot be unreasonably disproportionate to normal or comparable prior requirements or output [UCC 2–306].

Merchant's Firm Offer   Under regular contract principles, an offer can be revoked at any time before acceptance. The major common law exception is an *option contract* (discussed in Chapter 7), in which the offeree pays consideration for the offeror's irrevocable promise to keep the offer open for a stated period. The UCC creates a second exception for firm offers made by a merchant to sell, buy, or lease goods.

A **firm offer** arises when a merchant-offeror gives *assurances* in a *signed writing* that the offer will remain open. The merchant's firm offer is irrevocable without the necessity of consideration[11] for the stated period or, if no definite period is stated, a reasonable period (neither period to exceed three months) [UCC 2–205, 2A–205]. ■ **EXAMPLE 11.8** Osaka, a used-car dealer, writes a letter to Saucedo on January 1 stating, "I have a 2002 Camry on the lot that I'll sell you for $8,500 any time between now and January 31." This writing creates a firm offer, and Osaka will be liable for breach if he sells the Camry to someone other than Saucedo before January 31. ■

It is necessary that the offer be both *written* and *signed* by the offeror.[12] When a firm offer is contained in a form contract prepared by the offeree, the offeror must

---

REQUIREMENTS CONTRACT
An agreement in which a buyer agrees to purchase and the seller agrees to sell all or up to a stated amount of what the buyer needs or requires.

OUTPUT CONTRACT
An agreement in which a seller agrees to sell and a buyer agrees to buy all or up to a stated amount of what the seller produces.

FIRM OFFER
An offer (by a merchant) that is irrevocable without consideration for a stated period of time or, if no definite period is stated, for a reasonable time (neither period to exceed three months). A firm offer by a merchant must be in writing and must be signed by the offeror.

---

11. If the offeree pays consideration, then an option contract (not a merchant's firm offer) is formed.
12. "Signed" includes any symbol executed or adopted by a party with a present intention to authenticate a writing [UCC 1–201(39)]. A complete signature is not required. Therefore, initials, a thumbprint, a trade name, or any mark used in lieu of a written signature will suffice, regardless of its location on the document.

also sign a separate firm offer assurance. This requirement ensures that the offeror is aware of the offer. If the firm offer is buried amid copious language in one of the pages of the offeree's form contract, the offeror may inadvertently sign the contract without realizing that it contains a firm offer, thus defeating the purpose of the rule—which is to give effect to a merchant's deliberate intent to be bound to a firm offer.

ACCEPTANCE

The following subsections examine the UCC's provisions governing acceptance. As you will see, acceptance of an offer to buy, sell, or lease goods generally may be made in any reasonable manner and by any reasonable means.

BE AWARE The UCC's rules on means of acceptance illustrate the UCC's flexibility. The rules have been adapted to new forms of communication, such as faxes and online communications.

Methods of Acceptance   The general common law rule is that an offeror can specify, or authorize, a particular means of acceptance, making that means the only one effective for contract formation. Even an unauthorized means of communication is effective, however, as long as the acceptance is received by the specified deadline. ■ **EXAMPLE 11.9** Janel offers to sell her Humvee to Arik for $48,000. The offer states, "Answer by fax within five days." If Arik sends a letter, and Janel receives it within five days, a valid contract is formed, nonetheless. ■

Any Reasonable Means.   When the offeror does not specify a means of acceptance, the UCC provides that acceptance can be made by any means of communication reasonable under the circumstances [UCC 2–206(1), 2A–206(1)]. This broadens the common law rules concerning authorized means of acceptance. (For a review of the requirements relating to mode and timeliness of acceptance, see Chapter 7.)

■ **EXAMPLE 11.10** Anodyne Corporation writes Bethlehem Industries a letter offering to lease $1,000 worth of postage meters. The offer states that Anodyne will keep the offer open for only ten days from the date of the letter. Before the ten days elapse, Bethlehem sends Anodyne an acceptance by fax. Is a valid contract formed? The answer is yes, because acceptance by fax is a commercially reasonable medium of acceptance under the circumstances. Acceptance is effective on Bethlehem's transmission of the fax, which occurred before the offer lapsed. ■

Promise to Ship or Prompt Shipment.   The UCC permits a seller to accept an offer to buy goods "either by a prompt *promise* to ship or by the prompt or current shipment of conforming or nonconforming goods" [UCC 2–206(1)(b)]. *Conforming* goods are goods that accord with the contract's terms; *nonconforming* goods do not. The seller's prompt shipment of *nonconforming goods* in response to the offer constitutes both an acceptance (a contract) and a *breach* of that contract.

SEASONABLY
Within a specified time period or, if no period is specified, within a reasonable time.

This rule does not apply if the seller **seasonably** (within a reasonable amount of time) notifies the buyer that the nonconforming shipment is offered only as an *accommodation,* or as a favor. The notice of accommodation must clearly indicate to the buyer that the shipment does not constitute an acceptance and that, therefore, no contract has been formed.

■ **EXAMPLE 11.11** McFarrell Pharmacy orders five cases of Johnson & Johnson 3-by-5-inch gauze pads from Halderson Medical Supply, Inc. If Halderson ships five cases of Xeroform 3-by-5-inch gauze pads instead, the shipment acts as both an acceptance of McFarrell's offer and a breach of the resulting contract. McFarrell may sue Halderson for any appropriate damages. If, however, Halderson notifies McFarrell that the Xeroform gauze pads are being shipped *as an accommodation—* because Halderson has only Xeroform pads in stock—the shipment will constitute a counteroffer, not an acceptance. A contract will be formed only if McFarrell accepts the Xeroform gauze pads. ■

Communication of Acceptance   Under the common law, because acceptance of a unilateral contract is usually evident by performance, the offeree normally is not required to notify the offeror of the acceptance (see Chapter 7). The UCC changes this common law rule. According to the UCC, when "the beginning of requested performance is a reasonable mode of acceptance, an offeror who is not notified of acceptance within a reasonable time may treat the offer as having lapsed before acceptance" [UCC 2–206(2), 2A–206(2)].

■ EXAMPLE 11.12 Lee writes to Pickwick Bookstore on Monday, "Please send me a copy of *Webster's New College Dictionary* for $55.55, C.O.D.," and signs it, "Lee." Pickwick receives the request but does not ship the book for four weeks. When the book arrives, Lee rejects it, claiming that it has arrived too late to be of value. In this situation, because Lee had heard nothing from Pickwick for a month, he was justified in assuming that the store did not intend to deliver the book. Lee could consider that the offer had lapsed because of the length of time Pickwick delayed shipment. ■

Additional Terms   Under the common law, if Alderman makes an offer to Beale, and Beale in turn accepts but in the acceptance makes some slight modification to the terms of the offer, there is no contract. Recall from Chapter 7 that the so-called *mirror image rule* requires that the terms of the acceptance exactly match those of the offer. The UCC, however, dispenses with the mirror image rule. The UCC generally takes the position that if the offeree's response indicates a *definite* acceptance of the offer, a contract is formed even if the acceptance includes additional or different terms from those contained in the offer [UCC 2–207(1)]. What happens to these additional terms? The answer to this question depends, in part, on whether the parties are nonmerchants or merchants.[13]

Rules When One Party or Both Parties Are Nonmerchants.   If one (or both) of the parties is a *nonmerchant,* the contract is formed according to the terms of the original offer submitted by the original offeror and not according to the additional terms of the acceptance [UCC 2–207(2)]. ■ EXAMPLE 11.13 Tolsen offers in writing to sell his personal computer, printer, and scanner to Valdez for $1,500. Valdez faxes a reply to Tolsen stating, "I accept your offer to purchase your computer, printer, and scanner for $1,500. I would like a box of laser printer paper and two extra toner cartridges to be included in the purchase price." Valdez has given Tolsen a definite expression of acceptance (creating a contract), even though the acceptance also suggests an added term for the offer. Because Tolsen is not a merchant, the additional term is merely a proposal (suggestion), and Tolsen is not legally obligated to comply with that term. ■

Rules When Both Parties Are Merchants.   In contracts *between merchants*, the additional terms automatically become part of the contract unless (1) the original

DON'T FORGET   The UCC recognizes that a proposed deal is a contract if, in commercial understanding, the deal has been closed.

---

13. The 2003 amendments to Article 2 do not distinguish between merchants and others in setting out rules for the effect of additional terms in sales contracts. Instead, a court is directed to determine whether (1) the terms appear in the records of both parties, (2) both parties agree to the terms even if they are not in a record, or (3) they are supplied or incorporated under another provision of Article 2 [Amended UCC 2–207]. Basically, the amendments give the courts more discretion to include or exclude certain additional terms.

offer expressly limits acceptance to the terms of the offer, (2) the new or changed terms *materially* alter the contract, or (3) the offeror objects to the new or changed terms within a reasonable period of time [UCC 2–207(2)].

What constitutes a material alteration is frequently a question that only a court can decide. Generally, if the modification involves no unreasonable element of surprise or hardship for the offeror, the court will hold that the modification did not materially alter the contract.

■ EXAMPLE 11.14 Woolf has ordered meat from Tupman sixty-four times over a two-year period. Each time, Woolf placed the order over the phone, and Tupman mailed a confirmation form, and then an invoice, to Woolf. Tupman's confirmation form and invoice have always included an arbitration clause. If Woolf places another order and fails to pay for the meat, the court will likely hold that the additional term—the arbitration provision—did not materially alter the contract because Woolf should not have been surprised by the term. ■

Conditioned on Offeror's Assent.   Regardless of merchant status, the UCC provides that the offeree's expression cannot be construed as an acceptance if it contains additional or different terms that are explicitly conditioned on the offeror's assent to those terms [UCC 2–207(1)]. ■ EXAMPLE 11.15 Philips offers to sell Hundert 650 pounds of turkey thighs at a specified price and with specified delivery terms. Hundert responds, "I accept your offer for 650 pounds of turkey thighs *on the condition that you give me ninety days to pay for them.*" Hundert's response will be construed not as an acceptance but as a counteroffer, which Philips may or may not accept. ■

Additional Terms May Be Stricken.   The UCC provides yet another option for dealing with conflicting terms in the parties' writings. Section 2–207(3) states that conduct by both parties that recognizes the existence of a contract is sufficient to establish a contract for the sale of goods even though the writings of the parties do not otherwise establish a contract. In this situation, "the terms of the particular contract will consist of those terms on which the writings of the parties agree, together with any supplementary terms incorporated under any other provisions of this Act." In a dispute over contract terms, this provision allows a court simply to strike from the contract those terms on which the parties do not agree.

■ EXAMPLE 11.16 AAA Marketing orders goods over the phone from Brigg Sales, Inc., which ships the goods with an acknowledgment form (confirming the order) to AAA. AAA accepts and pays for the goods. The parties' writings do not establish a contract, but there is no question that a contract exists. If a dispute arises over the terms, such as the extent of any warranties, UCC 2–207(3) provides the governing rule. ■

CONSIDERATION

The common law rule that a contract requires consideration also applies to sales and lease contracts. Unlike the common law, however, the UCC does not require a contract modification to be supported by new consideration. An agreement modifying a contract for the sale or lease of goods "needs no consideration to be binding" [UCC 2–209(1), 2A–208(1)].

Modifications Must Be Made in Good Faith   Of course, contract modification must be sought in good faith [UCC 1–203]. ■ EXAMPLE 11.17 Allied, Inc., agrees to lease a new recreational vehicle (RV) to Louise for a stated monthly payment. Subsequently, a sudden shift in the market makes it difficult for Allied to lease the new RV to Louise at the contract price without suffering a loss. Allied tells Louise of the situation, and she agrees to pay an additional sum for the lease of the RV. Later Louise reconsiders and refuses to pay more than the original price. Under the UCC, Louise's promise to modify the contract needs no consideration to be binding. Hence, she is bound by the modified contract. ■

In this example, a shift in the market is a *good faith* reason for contract modification. What if there really was no shift in the market, however, and Allied knew that Louise needed to lease the new RV immediately but refused to deliver it unless she agreed to pay an additional sum of money? This attempt at extortion through modification without a legitimate commercial reason would be ineffective because it would violate the duty of good faith. Allied would not be permitted to enforce the higher price.

When Modification without Consideration Requires a Writing   In some situations, modification of a sales or lease contract without consideration must be in writing to be enforceable. If the contract itself prohibits any changes to the contract unless they are in a signed writing, for instance, then only those changes agreed to in a signed writing are enforceable. If a consumer (nonmerchant buyer) is dealing with a merchant and the merchant supplies the form that contains a prohibition against oral modification, the consumer must sign a separate acknowledgment of such a clause [UCC 2–209(2), 2A–208(2)].

Also, under Article 2, any modification that brings a sales contract under the Statute of Frauds must usually be in writing to be enforceable. Thus, if an oral contract for the sale of goods priced at $400 is modified so that the contract goods are now priced at $600, the modification must be in writing—because sales contracts for goods priced at $500 or more must be in writing to be enforceable, as you will read shortly. If, however, the buyer accepts delivery of the goods after the modification, he or she is bound to the $600 price [UCC 2–201(3)(c)].

STATUTE OF FRAUDS

The UCC contains Statute of Frauds provisions covering sales and lease contracts. Under these provisions, sales contracts for goods priced at $500 or more and lease contracts requiring payments of $1,000 or more must be in writing to be enforceable [UCC 2–201(1), 2A–201(1)].[14]

BE AWARE It has been proposed that the UCC be revised to eliminate the Statute of Frauds.

Sufficiency of the Writing   The UCC has greatly relaxed the requirements for the sufficiency of a writing to satisfy the Statute of Frauds. A writing or a memorandum will be sufficient as long as it indicates that the parties intended to form a contract and as long as it is signed by the party (or agent of the party) against whom enforcement is sought. The contract normally will not be enforceable beyond the quantity of goods shown in the writing, however. All other terms can be proved in court by oral testimony. For leases, the writing must reasonably identify and describe the goods leased and the lease term.

Special Rules for Contracts between Merchants   Once again, the UCC provides a special rule for merchants. Merchants can satisfy the requirements of a writing for the Statute of Frauds if, after the parties have agreed orally, one of the merchants sends a signed written confirmation to the other merchant within a reasonable time after the oral agreement was reached. The communication must indicate the terms

---

14. Note that a 2003 amendment significantly increased the price of goods that will cause a sales contract to fall under the Statute of Frauds. Under the amended UCC 2–201(1), goods must be priced at $5,000 or more for a sales contract to be subject to the record (writing) requirement.

of the agreement, and the merchant receiving the confirmation must have reason to know of its contents. Unless the merchant who receives the confirmation gives written notice of objection to its contents within ten days after receipt, the writing is sufficient against the receiving merchant, even though she or he has not signed anything [UCC 2–201(2)].[15] What happens if a merchant sends a written confirmation of an order that was never placed? For a discussion of this issue, see this chapter's *Adapting the Law to the Online Environment* feature.

---

15. According to the comments accompanying UCC 2A–201 (Article 2A's Statute of Frauds), the "between merchants" provision was not included because the number of such transactions involving leases, as opposed to sales, was thought to be modest.

ADAPTING THE LAW TO THE ONLINE ENVIRONMENT

Can an Employee's E-Mail Constitute a Waiver of Contract Terms?

Under UCC 2–209, an agreement that excludes modification except by a signed writing cannot be otherwise modified. If the written-modification requirement is contained in a form supplied by one merchant to another, the other party must separately sign the form for it to be binding. This rule has an exception, though, which can be significant in the online environment. Under the UCC, *an attempt at modification that does not meet the writing requirement may operate as a waiver* [UCC 2–209(4)]. In other words, the parties can waive, or give up, the right to require that contract modifications be in a signed writing. Can an employee's e-mail communications form a waiver of a contract's written-modification requirement? This issue arose in *Cloud Corp. v. Hasbro, Inc.*[a]

THE CONTRACT TERMS AND THE PARTIES' RELATIONSHIP

Cloud Corporation contracted to supply packets of a special powder to Hasbro, Inc., for use in Hasbro's new "Wonder World Aquarium." At the time of their initial agreement, Hasbro sent a letter to Cloud containing a "terms and conditions" form, which stated that Cloud, the supplier, could not deviate from a purchase order without Hasbro's written consent. Cloud signed and returned that form to Hasbro as requested, and Hasbro began placing orders. Each time Hasbro ordered packets, Cloud sent back an "order acknowledgment" form confirming the quantity ordered.

After placing several orders, Hasbro told Cloud to change the formula in the packets. As a result, Cloud was able to produce three times as many packets using the same amount of material that it already had on hand

a. 314 F.3d 289 (7th Cir. 2002).

to fill Hasbro's previous orders. Although Hasbro had not ordered any additional packets, Cloud sent Hasbro an order acknowledgment for extra packets at a lower price. Hasbro did not explicitly respond to Cloud's acknowledgment form. One of Hasbro's employees, however, referred to the additional quantities of packets at some point in her e-mail exchanges with Cloud. Several months later, after Cloud had produced the additional packets, Hasbro quit making the Wonder World Aquarium and refused to pay for the packets that it did not order. Cloud then sued Hasbro for breach of contract.

WAS THE EMPLOYEE'S E-MAIL A WAIVER?

Ultimately, a federal appellate court held that because Hasbro's employee had referred to the additional packets in at least one e-mail, Hasbro must pay for them. According to the court, the employee's e-mail alone could be sufficient to satisfy the requirement of written consent to modify the contract. Even if it did not, however, the court held that it operated as a waiver. The court stated that for the e-mail to operate as a waiver, Cloud "must show either that it reasonably relied on the other party's having waived the requirement of a writing, or that the waiver was clear and unequivocal." Here, the employee's e-mail had not clearly waived the writing requirement but there was *reasonable reliance*. According to the court, Hasbro should have advised Cloud if it did not want to be committed to buying the additional quantity rather than "leading Cloud down the primrose path."

FOR CRITICAL ANALYSIS

How might the parties to a sales contract prevent their subsequent e-mail communications from waiving the contract's explicit modification requirements? (Hint: How can the parties prevent contract disputes generally?)

An artisan creates a specially designed "bowl within a bowl" out of one piece of clay. If a restaurant orally contracted with the artisan to create twenty of the specially designed bowls for use in its business, at a price of $450, would the contract have to be in writing to be enforceable? Explain. (AP/Wide World Photos)

REMEMBER An admission can be made in documents, including internal memos and employee reports, that may be obtained during discovery prior to trial.

■ **EXAMPLE 11.18** Alfonso is a merchant-buyer in Cleveland. He contracts over the telephone to purchase $4,000 worth of spare aircraft parts from Goldstein, a New York City merchant-seller. Two days later, Goldstein sends written confirmation detailing the terms of the oral contract, and Alfonso subsequently receives it. If Alfonso does not notify Goldstein in writing of his objection to the contents of the confirmation within ten days of receipt, Alfonso cannot raise the Statute of Frauds as a defense against the enforcement of the oral contract. ■

Exceptions   In addition to the special rules for merchants, the UCC defines three exceptions to the writing requirements of the Statute of Frauds. An oral contract for the sale of goods priced at $500 or more ($5,000 or more under the 2003 amendments to Article 2 of the UCC) or the lease of goods involving total payments of $1,000 or more will be enforceable despite the absence of a writing in the circumstances discussed in the following subsections [UCC 2–201(3), 2A–201(4)].

Specially Manufactured Goods.   An oral contract is enforceable if (1) it is for goods that are specially manufactured for a particular buyer or specially manufactured or obtained for a particular lessee, (2) these goods are not suitable for resale or lease to others in the ordinary course of the seller's or lessor's business, and (3) the seller or lessor has substantially started to manufacture the goods or has made commitments for their manufacture or procurement. In this situation, once the seller or lessor has taken action, the buyer or lessee cannot repudiate the agreement claiming the Statute of Frauds as a defense.

Admissions.   An oral contract for the sale or lease of goods is enforceable if the party against whom enforcement of the contract is sought admits in pleadings, testimony, or other court proceedings that a contract for sale was made.[16] In this situation, the contract will be enforceable even though it was oral, but enforceability will be limited to the quantity of goods admitted.

Partial Performance.   An oral contract for the sale or lease of goods is enforceable if payment has been made and accepted or goods have been received and accepted. This is the "partial performance" exception. The oral contract will be enforced at least to the extent that performance *actually* took place.

UNCONSCIONABILITY

As discussed in Chapter 8, an unconscionable contract is one that is so unfair and one sided that it would be unreasonable to enforce it. The UCC allows the court to evaluate a contract or any clause in a contract, and if the court deems it to have been unconscionable at the time it was made, the court can (1) refuse to enforce the contract, (2) enforce the remainder of the contract without the unconscionable clause, or (3) limit the application of any unconscionable clauses to avoid an unconscionable result [UCC 2–302, 2A–108].[17] The following landmark case illustrates an early application of the UCC's unconscionability provisions.

---

16. Any admission made under oath, including one not made in a court, satisfies UCC 2–201(3)(b) and 2A–201(4)(b) under the 2003 amendments to Articles 2 and 2A.

17. The 2003 amendments to this section changed the word *clause* to *term,* recognizing that even a single term (word) in a contract can be unconscionable and authorizing the court to strike any single term that it finds unconscionable.

LANDMARK AND CLASSIC CASES
CASE 11.2   Jones v. Star Credit Corp.

Supreme Court of New York, Nassau County, 1969.
59 Misc.2d 189,
298 N.Y.S.2d 264.

HISTORICAL AND ECONOMIC SETTING *In the sixth century, Roman civil law allowed the courts to rescind a contract if the market value of the goods that were the subject of the contract equaled less than half the contract price. This same ratio has appeared over the last thirty years in many cases in which courts have found contract clauses to be unconscionable under UCC 2–302 on the ground that the price was excessive. In a Connecticut case, for example, the court held that a contract requiring a person who was poor to make payments totaling $1,248 for a television set that retailed for $499 was unconscionable.*[a] *The seller had not told the buyer the full purchase price. Most of the litigants who have used UCC 2–302 successfully have been consumers who are poor or otherwise at a disadvantage. In one New York case, for example, the court held that a contract requiring a Spanish-speaking consumer to make payments totaling nearly $1,150 for a freezer that wholesaled for less than $350 was unconscionable.*[b] *The contract was in English, and the salesperson did not translate or explain it.*

FACTS The Joneses, the plaintiffs, agreed to purchase a freezer for $900 as the result of a salesperson's visit to their home. Tax and financing charges raised the total price to $1,234.80. At trial, the freezer was found to have a maximum retail value of approximately $300. The plaintiffs, who had made payments totaling $619.88, brought a suit in a New York state court to have the purchase contract declared unconscionable under the UCC.

a. *Murphy v. McNamara,* 36 Conn.Supp. 183, 416 A.2d 170 (1979).
b. *Frostifresh Corp. v. Reynoso,* 52 Misc.2d 26, 274 N.Y.S.2d 757 (1966), rev'd on issue of damages, 54 Misc.2d 119, 281 N.Y.S.2d 946 (1967).

ISSUE Can this contract be denied enforcement on the ground of unconscionability?

DECISION Yes. The court held that the contract was not enforceable as it stood, and the contract was reformed so that no further payments were required.

REASON The court relied on UCC 2–302(1), which states that if "the court as a matter of law finds the contract or any clause of the contract to have been unconscionable at the time it was made, the court may * * * so limit the application of any unconscionable clause as to avoid any unconscionable result." The court then examined the disparity between the $900 purchase price and the $300 retail value, as well as the fact that the credit charges alone exceeded the retail value. These excessive charges were exacted despite the seller's knowledge of the plaintiffs' limited resources. The court reformed the contract so that the plaintiffs' payments, amounting to more than $600, were regarded as payment in full.

COMMENTS *Classical contract theory holds that a contract is a bargain in which the terms have been worked out freely between the parties. In many modern commercial transactions, this may not be true. For example, standard-form contracts and leases are often signed by consumer-buyers who understand few of the terms used and who often do not even read them. The inclusion of Sections 2–302 and 2A–108 in the UCC gave the courts a means of policing such transactions, and the courts continue to use this means to prevent injustice.*

RELEVANT WEB SITES *To locate information on the Web concerning* Jones v. Star Credit Corp.*, go to this text's Web site at* **http://blt.westbuslaw.com**, *select "Chapter 11," and click on "URLs for Landmarks."*

■ Title, Risk, and Insurable Interest

Before the creation of the Uniform Commercial Code (UCC), *title*—the right of ownership—was the central concept in sales law, controlling all issues of rights and remedies of the parties to a sales contract. In some situations, title is still relevant under the UCC, and the UCC has special rules for determining who has title. These rules will be discussed in the sections that follow. In most situations, however, the UCC has replaced the concept of title with three other concepts: (1) identification,

(2) risk of loss, and (3) insurable interest. By breaking down the transfer of ownership into these three components, the drafters of the UCC created greater precision in the law governing sales—leaving as few points of law as possible to the decision of the courts.

In lease contracts, of course, title to the goods is retained by the lessor-owner of the goods. Hence, the UCC's provisions relating to passage of title do not apply to leased goods. Other concepts discussed in this chapter, though, including identification, risk of loss, and insurable interest, relate to lease contracts as well as to sales contracts.

IDENTIFICATION

Before any interest in specific goods can pass from the seller or lessor to the buyer or lessee, two conditions must prevail: (1) the goods must be in existence, and (2) they must be identified as the specific goods designated in the contract. **Identification** takes place when specific goods are designated as the subject matter of a sales or lease contract. Title and risk of loss cannot pass from seller to buyer unless the goods are identified to the contract. (As mentioned, title to leased goods remains with the lessor—or, if the owner is a third party, with that party. The lessee does not acquire title to leased goods.) Identification is significant because it gives the buyer or lessee the right to insure (or to have an insurable interest in) the goods and the right to recover from third parties who damage the goods.

PASSAGE OF TITLE

Once goods exist and are identified, the provisions of UCC 2–401 apply to the passage of title. In virtually all subsections of UCC 2–401, the words "unless otherwise explicitly agreed" appear, meaning that any explicit understanding between the buyer and the seller determines when title passes. Without an explicit agreement to the contrary, title passes to the buyer at the time and the place the seller performs by delivering the goods [UCC 2–401(2)].

Shipment and Destination Contracts   Unless otherwise agreed, delivery arrangements can determine when title passes from the seller to the buyer. In a **shipment contract,** the seller is required or authorized to ship goods by carrier, such as a trucking company. Under a shipment contract, the seller is required only to deliver conforming goods into the hands of a carrier, and title passes to the buyer at the time and place of shipment [UCC 2–401(2)(a)]. Generally, *all contracts are assumed to be shipment contracts if nothing to the contrary is stated in the contract.*

In a **destination contract,** the seller is required to deliver the goods to a particular destination, usually directly to the buyer, but sometimes the buyer designates that the goods should be delivered to another party. Title passes to the buyer when the goods are *tendered* at that destination [UCC 2–401(2)(b)]. A tender of delivery is the seller's placing or holding of conforming goods at the buyer's disposition (with any necessary notice), enabling the buyer to take delivery [UCC 2–503(1)].

Delivery without Movement of the Goods   When the sales contract does not call for the seller to ship or deliver the goods (when the buyer is to pick up the goods), the passage of title depends on whether the seller must deliver a **document of title,** such as a bill of lading or a warehouse receipt, to the buyer. A *bill of lading* is a receipt for goods that is signed by a carrier and that serves as a contract for the transportation of the goods. A *warehouse receipt* is a receipt issued by a warehouser for goods stored in a warehouse.

IDENTIFICATION
In a sale of goods, the express designation of the goods provided for in the contract.

SHIPMENT CONTRACT
A contract for the sale of goods in which the seller is required or authorized to ship the goods by carrier. The seller assumes liability for any losses or damage to the goods until they are delivered to the carrier.

DESTINATION CONTRACT
A contract for the sale of goods in which the seller is required or authorized to ship the goods by carrier and tender delivery of the goods at a particular destination. The seller assumes liability for any losses or damage to the goods until they are tendered at the destination specified in the contract.

DOCUMENT OF TITLE
Paper exchanged in the regular course of business that evidences the right to possession of goods (for example, a bill of lading or a warehouse receipt).

This train derailed in Oklahoma while hauling wheat across the country. How would a court decide who held title to the goods at the time they were destroyed? (Reuters/Jerry Laizure/Landov)

When a document of title is required, title passes to the buyer *when and where the document is delivered.* Thus, if the goods are stored in a warehouse, title passes to the buyer when the appropriate documents are delivered to the buyer. The goods never move. In fact, the buyer can choose to leave the goods at the same warehouse for a period of time, and the buyer's title to those goods will be unaffected.

When no documents of title are required and delivery is made without moving the goods, title passes at the time and place the sales contract is made, if the goods have already been identified. If the goods have not been identified, title does not pass until identification occurs. ■ EXAMPLE 11.19 Juan sells lumber to Bodan. They agree that Bodan will pick up the lumber at the lumberyard. If the lumber has been identified (segregated, marked, or in any other way distinguished from all other lumber), title passes to Bodan when the contract is signed. If the lumber is still in storage bins at the lumberyard, title does not pass to Bodan until the particular pieces of lumber to be sold under this contract are identified [UCC 2–401(3)]. ■

RISK OF LOSS

Under the UCC, risk of loss does not necessarily pass with title. When risk of loss passes from a seller or lessor to a buyer or lessee is generally determined by the contract between the parties. Sometimes, the contract states expressly when the risk of loss passes. At other times, it does not, and a court must interpret the performance and delivery terms of the contract to determine whether the risk has passed.

Delivery with Movement of the Goods—Carrier Cases   When the agreement does not state when risk of loss passes, the courts apply the following rules to cases involving movement of the goods (carrier cases).

Contract Terms.   Specific delivery terms in the contract can determine when risk of loss passes to the buyer. These terms, which are defined in Exhibit 11–2, relate generally to the determination of which party will bear the costs of delivery. *Unless otherwise agreed,* these terms also determine who has the risk of loss.

The 2003 amendments to UCC Article 2 omit these terms because they are "inconsistent with modern commercial practice." The Official Comments to the

---

EXHIBIT 11–2 CONTRACT TERMS—DEFINITIONS

The contract terms listed and defined in this exhibit help to determine which party will bear the costs of delivery and when risk of loss will pass from the seller to the buyer.

F.O.B. (free on board)—Indicates that the selling price of goods includes transportation costs to the specific F.O.B. place named in the contract. The seller pays the expenses and carries the risk of loss to the F.O.B. place named [UCC 2–319(1)]. If the named place is the place from which the goods are shipped (for example, the seller's city or place of business), the contract is a shipment contract. If the named place is the place to which the goods are to be shipped (for example, the buyer's city or place of business), the contract is a destination contract.

F.A.S. (free alongside)—Requires that the seller, at his or her own expense and risk, deliver the goods alongside the carrier before risk passes to the buyer [UCC 2–319(2)].

C.I.F. or **C.&F.** (cost, insurance, and freight or just cost and freight)—Requires, among other things, that the seller "put the goods in the possession of a carrier" before risk passes to the buyer [UCC 2–320(2)]. (These are basically pricing terms, and the contracts remain shipment contracts, not destination contracts.)

Delivery ex-ship (delivery from the carrying vessel)—Means that risk of loss does not pass to the buyer until the goods are properly unloaded from the ship or other carrier [UCC 2–322].

amendments, however, state that if the parties use these shipping terms without expressly agreeing on the meaning of the terms, the terms "must be interpreted in light of any appropriate usage of trade and any course of performance or course of dealing between the parties." Thus, the effect of these terms may be the same even after a state has adopted the amendments to Article 2.

Shipment Contracts. In a shipment contract, if the seller or lessor is required or authorized to ship goods by carrier (but not required to deliver them to a particular final destination), risk of loss passes to the buyer or lessee when the goods are duly delivered to the carrier [UCC 2–319(1)(a), 2–509(1)(a), 2A–219(2)(a)].

■ **EXAMPLE 11.20** A seller in Texas sells five hundred cases of grapefruit to a buyer in New York, F.O.B. Houston (free on board in Houston—that is, the buyer pays the transportation charges from Houston). The contract authorizes shipment by carrier; it does not require that the seller tender the grapefruit in New York. Risk passes to the buyer when conforming goods are properly placed in the possession of the carrier. If the goods are damaged in transit, the loss is the buyer's. (Actually, buyers have recourse against carriers, subject to certain limitations, and buyers usually insure the goods from the time the goods leave the seller.) ■

Destination Contracts. In a destination contract, the risk of loss passes to the buyer or lessee when the goods are tendered to the buyer or lessee at the specified destination [UCC 2–319(1)(b), 2–509(1)(b), 2A–219(2)(b)]. In Example 11.20, if the contract had been F.O.B. New York, the risk of loss during transit to New York would have been the seller's.

Delivery without Movement of the Goods The UCC also addresses situations in which the seller or lessor is required neither to ship nor to deliver the goods. Frequently, the buyer or lessee is to pick up the goods from the seller or lessor, or the goods are held by a bailee. Under the UCC, a **bailee** is a party who, by a bill of lading, warehouse receipt, or other document of title, acknowledges possession of goods and/or contracts to deliver them. A warehousing company, for example, or a trucking company that normally issues documents of title for the goods it receives is a bailee.[18]

BAILEE
Under the UCC, a party who, by a bill of lading, warehouse receipt, or other document of title, acknowledges possession of goods and/or contracts to deliver them.

Goods Held by the Seller. If the goods are held by the seller, a document of title is usually not used. If the seller is a merchant, risk of loss to goods held by the seller passes to the buyer when the buyer *actually takes physical possession of the goods* [UCC 2–509(3)]. If the seller is not a merchant, the risk of loss to goods held by the seller passes to the buyer on *tender of delivery* [UCC 2–509(3)]. (As you will read in Chapter 12, tender of delivery occurs when the seller places conforming goods at the disposal of the buyer and gives the buyer whatever notification is reasonably necessary to enable the buyer to take possession.) With respect to leases, the risk of loss passes to the lessee on the lessee's receipt of the goods if the lessor—or supplier, in a finance lease—is a merchant. Otherwise, the risk passes to the lessee on tender of delivery [UCC 2A–219(c)].[19]

The following case illustrates the consequences of passing the risk of loss under these principles.

---

18. Bailments will be discussed in Chapter 23.
19. Under the 2003 amendments to UCC 2–509(3) and 2A–219(c), the risk of loss passes to the buyer or the lessee on that party's receipt of the goods regardless of whether the seller or the lessor is a merchant.

CASE 11.3 Ganno v. Lanoga Corp.

Court of Appeals of Washington,
Division 2, 2003.
119 Wash.App. 310,
80 P.3d 180.
http://www.legalwa.org[a]

FACTS Henry Ganno went to the Lumbermen's Building Center store in Fife, Washington, where he bought a 12-foot beam weighing 100 pounds. In the lumberyard, a store employee approached Ganno, took his receipt, and used a forklift to place the beam in the open bed of Ganno's truck. The beam projected about 4 feet from the end of the truck. The employee asked Ganno if he wanted the beam flagged, Ganno said, "Yes," and the employee flagged the beam. The employee did not tie down or otherwise secure the beam, however. A sign in the lumberyard stated that it was Lumbermen's policy *not* to secure loads for customers. Ganno, who did not get out of the truck or check the load to make sure that it was secure, drove out of the lumberyard onto a public street. When he turned a corner, the beam fell off the truck. As Ganno attempted to retrieve the beam, another vehicle hit it, causing it to strike Ganno's leg and shatter his kneecap. Ganno filed a suit in a Washington state court against Lanoga Corporation, which owned the Fife Lumbermen's store, alleging negligence in failing to secure the beam.

a. Click on the "Washington State Supreme Court and Appellate Court Decisions" link. Type "Ganno" in the search box, choose "Search case titles only," select "Washington Appellate Reports" (and NOT "Washington Reports") in the "Limit search to:" column, and click on "Search." In the result, click on the name of the case to access the opinion. Municipal Research & Services Center of Washington maintains this Web site.

The court granted a judgment in Lanoga's favor. Ganno appealed to a state intermediate appellate court.

ISSUE Had the risk passed to the buyer before the loss?

DECISION Yes. The state intermediate appellate court affirmed the lower court's judgment, holding that it was Ganno's duty, not Lumbermen's, to make sure his load was secure before driving onto the public streets.

REASON The appellate court noted that Lumbermen's is a merchant under UCC 2–104(1), which defines a merchant as "a person who deals in goods of the kind or otherwise by his occupation holds himself out as having knowledge or skill peculiar to the practices or goods involved in the transaction." Under UCC 2–509(3), "where the seller is a merchant, the risk of loss passes to the buyer on receipt of goods." Here, Ganno received the beam from Lumbermen's at its place of business. The risk of loss passed to Ganno when Lumbermen's loaded the beam onto his truck. "In the absence of a legal duty to secure a customer's load, as here, there is no liability to a customer once he is in possession of the goods." Thus, the court concluded, "Lumbermen's is not liable for the ensuing damage after Ganno took possession and left Lumbermen's property."

WHY IS THIS CASE IMPORTANT? *This case clearly illustrates how the passage of risk of loss can affect a seller's or a buyer's potential liability. The UCC's rules on passage of risk of loss vary, depending on the nature of the transaction.*

COMPARE A business that is to make delivery at its own place has control of the goods and can be expected to insure its interest in them. The buyer has no control of the goods and will likely not carry insurance on goods that he or she does not possess.

Goods Held by a Bailee. When a bailee is holding goods for a person who has contracted to sell them and the goods are to be delivered without being moved, the goods are usually represented by a negotiable or nonnegotiable document of title (a bill of lading or a warehouse receipt). Risk of loss passes to the buyer when (1) the buyer receives a negotiable document of title for the goods, (2) the bailee acknowledges the buyer's right to possess the goods, or (3) the buyer receives a nonnegotiable document of title *and* has had a *reasonable time* to present the document to the bailee and demand the goods. Obviously, if the bailee refuses to honor the document, the risk of loss remains with the seller [UCC 2–503(4)(b), 2–509(2)].

In respect to leases, if goods held by a bailee are to be delivered without being moved, the risk of loss passes to the lessee on acknowledgment by the bailee of the lessee's right to possession of the goods [UCC 2A–219(2)(b)].

Conditional Sales Buyers and sellers sometimes form sales contracts that are conditioned either on the buyer's approval of the goods or on the buyer's resale of the goods. Under such contracts, the buyer is in possession of the goods. Sometimes, however, questions arise as to whether the buyer or seller should bear the loss if, for example, the goods are damaged or stolen while in the possession of the buyer.

Sale or Return. A **sale or return** (sometimes called a *sale and return*) is a type of contract by which the seller sells a quantity of goods to the buyer with the understanding that the buyer can void the sale by returning the goods or any portion of them. The buyer is required to pay for any goods *not* returned. When the buyer receives possession of the goods under a sale-or-return contract, the title and risk of loss pass to the buyer. Title and risk of loss remain with the buyer until the buyer returns the goods to the seller within the time period specified. If the buyer fails to return the goods within this time period, the sale is finalized. The goods are returned at the buyer's risk and expense. Goods held under a sale-or-return contract are subject to the claims of the buyer's creditors while they are in the buyer's possession (even if the buyer has not paid for the goods) [UCC 2–326, 2–327].

The UCC treats a **consignment** as a sale or return. Under a consignment, the owner of goods (the *consignor*) delivers them to another (the *consignee*) for the consignee to sell. If the consignee sells the goods, the consignee must pay the consignor for them. If the consignee does not sell the goods, they may simply be returned to the consignor. While the goods are in the possession of the consignee, the consignee holds title to them, and creditors of the consignee will prevail over the consignor in any action to repossess the goods [UCC 2–326(3)].[20]

---

20. Although the 2003 amendments to UCC Article 2 retain the provisions concerning sale on approval and sale or return, the portion of this section relating to consignments is omitted. Consignments are to be covered by UCC Article 9.

SALE OR RETURN
A type of conditional sale in which title and possession pass from the seller to the buyer, but the buyer retains the option to return the goods during a specified period even though the goods conform to the contract.

CONSIGNMENT
A transaction in which an owner of goods (the consignor) delivers the goods to another (the consignee) for the consignee to sell. The consignee pays the consignor only for the goods that are sold by the consignee.

Some forklifts move freight around in a warehouse, which is holding the goods as bailee. Suppose that Versatile Products, Inc., contracts with a seller to purchase goods that are held at this warehouse. When does the risk of loss pass to the buyer in a bailment situation? (Tannen Maury/Bloomberg News/Landov)

SALE ON APPROVAL
A type of conditional sale in which
the buyer may take the goods on a
trial basis. The sale becomes
absolute only when the buyer
approves of (or is satisfied with) the
goods being sold.

Sale on Approval.   When a seller offers to sell goods to a buyer and permits the buyer to take the goods on a trial basis, a **sale on approval** is usually made. The term *sale* here is a misnomer, as only an *offer* to sell has been made, along with a *bailment* created by the buyer's possession. (A bailment is a temporary delivery of personal property into the care of another—see Chapter 23.)

Therefore, title and risk of loss (from causes beyond the buyer's control) remain with the seller until the buyer accepts (approves) the offer. Acceptance can be made expressly, by any act inconsistent with the *trial* purpose or the seller's ownership, or by the buyer's election not to return the goods within the trial period. If the buyer does not wish to accept, the buyer may notify the seller of that fact within the trial period, and the return is made at the seller's expense and risk [UCC 2–327(1)]. Goods held on approval are not subject to the claims of the buyer's creditors until acceptance.

It is often difficult to determine whether a particular transaction involves a contract for a sale on approval, a contract for a sale or return, or a contract for sale. The UCC states that (unless otherwise agreed) "if the goods are delivered primarily for use," the transaction is a sale on approval; "if the goods are delivered primarily for resale," the transaction is a sale or return [UCC 2–326(1)].

Risk of Loss When a Sales or Lease Contract Is Breached   A sales or lease contract can be breached in many ways, and the transfer of risk operates differently depending on which party breaches. Generally, the party in breach bears the risk of loss.

When the Seller or Lessor Breaches.   If the goods are so nonconforming that the buyer has the right to reject them, the risk of loss does not pass to the buyer until the defects are **cured** (that is, until the goods are repaired, replaced, or discounted in price by the seller) or until the buyer accepts the goods in spite of their defects (thus waiving the right to reject). ■ **EXAMPLE 11.21** A buyer orders ten white refrigerators from a seller, F.O.B. the seller's plant. The seller ships amber refrigerators instead. The amber refrigerators (nonconforming goods) are damaged in transit. The risk of loss falls on the seller. Had the seller shipped white refrigerators (conforming goods) instead, the risk would have fallen on the buyer [UCC 2–510(2)]. ■

CURE
The right of a party who tenders
nonconforming performance to
correct that performance within the
contract period [UCC 2–508(1)].

If a buyer accepts a shipment of goods and later discovers a defect, acceptance can be revoked. Revocation allows the buyer to pass the risk of loss back to the seller, at least to the extent that the buyer's insurance does not cover the loss [UCC 2–510(2)].

In regard to leases, Article 2A states a similar rule. If the lessor or supplier tenders goods that are so nonconforming that the lessee has the right to reject them, the risk of loss remains with the lessor or the supplier until cure or acceptance [UCC 2A–220(1)(a)]. If the lessee, after acceptance, revokes his or her acceptance of nonconforming goods, the revocation passes the risk of loss back to the seller or supplier, to the extent that the lessee's insurance does not cover the loss [UCC 2A–220(1)(b)].

When the Buyer or Lessee Breaches.   The general rule is that when a buyer or lessee breaches a contract, the risk of loss immediately shifts to the buyer or lessee. This rule has three important limitations:

1 The seller or lessor must already have identified the contract goods.

2 The buyer or lessee bears the risk for only a commercially reasonable time after the seller has learned of the breach.

3 The buyer or lessee is liable only to the extent of any deficiency in the seller's insurance coverage [UCC 2–510(3), 2A–220(2)].

INSURABLE INTEREST

Parties to sales and lease contracts often obtain insurance coverage to protect against damage, loss, or destruction of goods. Any party purchasing insurance, however, must have a sufficient interest in the insured item to obtain a valid policy. Insurance laws—not the UCC—determine sufficiency. The UCC is helpful, however, because it contains certain rules regarding insurable interests in goods.

INSURABLE INTEREST
In regard to the sale or lease of goods, a property interest in the goods that is sufficiently substantial to permit a party to insure against damage to the goods.

Insurable Interest of the Buyer or Lessee   A buyer or lessee has an **insurable interest** in identified goods. The moment the contract goods are identified by the seller or lessor, the buyer or lessee has a special property interest that allows the buyer or lessee to obtain necessary insurance coverage for those goods even before the risk of loss has passed [UCC 2–501(1), 2A–218(1)].

The rule stated in UCC 2–501(1)(c) is that buyers obtain an insurable interest in crops by identification, which occurs when the crops are planted or otherwise become growing crops, provided that the contract is for "the sale of crops to be harvested within twelve months or the next normal harvest season after contracting, whichever is longer." ■ **EXAMPLE 11.22** In March, a farmer sells a cotton crop he hopes to harvest in October. When the crop is planted, the buyer acquires an insurable interest in it because those goods (the cotton crop) are identified to the sales contract between the seller and the buyer. ■

Insurable Interest of the Seller or Lessor   A seller has an insurable interest in goods if she or he retains title to the goods. Even after title passes to the buyer, a seller who has a security interest in the goods (a right to secure payment—see Chapter 16) still has an insurable interest and can insure the goods [UCC 2–501(2)]. Hence,

A freeze can destroy an orange grove. In a contract for a sale of the oranges, when does the buyer obtain an insurable interest? (© Wayne Eastep, Getty Images)

both a buyer and a seller can have an insurable interest in identical goods at the same time. Of course, the buyer or seller must sustain an actual loss to have the right to recover from an insurance company. In regard to leases, the lessor retains an insurable interest in leased goods until the lessee exercises an option to buy and the risk of loss has passed to the lessee [UCC 2A–218(3)].

APPLICATION ◧ Who Bears the Risk of Loss—the Seller or the Buyer?*

The shipment of goods is a major aspect of commercial transactions. Many issues arise when an unforeseen event, such as fire or theft, causes damage to goods in transit. At the time of contract negotiation, both the seller and the buyer should determine the importance of risk of loss. In some circumstances, risk is relatively unimportant (such as when ten boxes of copier paper are being sold), and the delivery terms should simply reflect costs and price. In other circumstances, risk is extremely important (such as when a fragile piece of pharmaceutical testing equipment is being sold), and the parties will need an express agreement as to the moment risk is to pass so that they can insure the goods accordingly. The point is that risk should be considered before the loss occurs, not after.

A major consideration relating to risk is when to insure goods against possible losses. Buyers and sellers should determine the point at which they have an insurable interest in the goods and obtain insurance coverage to protect them against loss from that point.

CHECKLIST TO DETERMINE RISK OF LOSS

The UCC uses a three-part checklist to determine risk of loss:

1. If the contract includes terms allocating risk of loss, those terms are binding and must be applied.
2. If the contract is silent as to risk, and either party breaches the contract, the breaching party is liable for risk of loss.
3. When a contract makes no reference to risk, and neither party breaches, risk of loss is borne by the party having control over the goods (delivery terms).

IF YOU ARE THE SELLER

If you are a seller of goods to be shipped, realize that as long as you have control over the goods, you are liable for any loss unless the buyer is in breach or the contract contains an explicit agreement to the contrary. When there is no explicit agreement, the UCC uses the delivery terms in your contract as a basis for determining control. Thus, "F.O.B. buyer's business" is a destination-delivery term, and risk of loss for goods shipped under these terms does not pass to the buyer until there is a tender of delivery at the point of destination. Any loss or damage in transit falls on the seller because the seller has control until proper tender has been made.

IF YOU ARE THE BUYER

From the buyer's point of view, it is important to remember that most sellers prefer "F.O.B. seller's business" as a delivery term. Under these terms, once the goods are delivered to the carrier, the buyer bears the risk of loss. Thus, if conforming goods are completely destroyed or lost in transit, the buyer not only suffers the loss but is obligated to pay the seller the contract price.

CHECKLIST FOR THE SHIPMENT OF GOODS

1. Prior to entering a contract, determine the importance of risk of loss for a given sale.
2. If risk is extremely important, the contract should expressly state the moment risk of loss will pass from the seller to the buyer. This clause could even provide that risk will not pass until the goods are "delivered, installed, inspected, and tested (or in running order for a period of time)."
3. If an express clause is not agreed on, delivery terms determine passage of risk of loss.
4. When appropriate, either party or both parties should consider procuring insurance.

*This *Application* is not meant to substitute for the services of an attorney who is licensed to practice law in your state.

▦ KEY TERMS

CHAPTER SUMMARY Sales and Leases: Formation, Title, and Risk

THE FORMATION OF SALES AND LEASE CONTRACTS

The Scope of the UCC (See pages 326–327.)	The UCC attempts to provide a consistent, uniform, and integrated framework of rules to deal with all phases *ordinarily arising* in a commercial sales or lease transaction, including contract formation, passage of title and risk of loss, performance, remedies, payment for goods, warehoused goods, and secured transactions.
The Scope of Article 2—Sales (See pages 327–332.)	Article 2 governs contracts for the sale of goods (tangible, movable personal property). The common law of contracts also applies to sales contracts to the extent that the common law has not been modified by the UCC. If there is a conflict between a common law rule and the UCC, the UCC controls.
The Scope of Article 2A—Leases (See pages 332–333.)	Article 2A governs contracts for the lease of goods. Except that it applies to leases, instead of sales, of goods, Article 2A is essentially a repetition of Article 2 and varies only to reflect differences between sale and lease transactions.
Offer and Acceptance (See pages 333–339.)	1. *Offer—* a. Not all terms have to be included for a contract to be formed (only the subject matter and quantity term must be specified). b. The price does not have to be included for a contract to be formed. c. Particulars of performance can be left open. d. A written and signed offer by a *merchant,* covering a period of three months or less, is irrevocable without payment of consideration. 2. *Acceptance—* a. Acceptance may be made by any reasonable means of communication; it is effective when dispatched. b. The acceptance of a unilateral offer can be made by a promise to ship or by prompt shipment of conforming goods, or by prompt shipment of nonconforming goods if not accompanied by a notice of accommodation. c. Acceptance by performance requires notice within a reasonable time; otherwise, the offer can be treated as lapsed. d. A definite expression of acceptance creates a contract even if the terms of the acceptance vary from those of the offer unless the varied terms in the acceptance are expressly conditioned on the offeror's assent to the varied terms.

CHAPTER SUMMARY Sales and Leases: Formation, Title, and Risk—Continued

Consideration (See pages 339–340.)	A modification of a contract for the sale of goods does not require consideration.

Requirements under the Statute of Frauds
(See pages 340–342.)
	1. All contracts for the sale of goods priced at $500 or more must be in writing. A writing is sufficient as long as it indicates a contract between the parties and is signed by the party against whom enforcement is sought. A contract is not enforceable beyond the quantity shown in the writing.
	
	2. When written confirmation of an oral contract *between merchants* is not objected to in writing by the receiver within ten days, the contract is enforceable.
	
	3. Exceptions to the requirement of a writing exist in the following situations:
	   a. When the oral contract is for specially manufactured goods not suitable for resale to others, and the seller has substantially started to manufacture the goods.
	   b. When the defendant admits in pleadings, testimony, or other court proceedings that an oral contract for the sale of goods was made. In this case, the contract will be enforceable to the extent of the quantity of goods admitted.
	   c. The oral agreement will be enforceable to the extent that payment has been received and accepted by the seller or to the extent that the goods have been received and accepted by the buyer.

Unconscionability (See pages 342–343.)	An unconscionable contract is one that is so unfair and one sided that it would be unreasonable to enforce it. If the court deems a contract to have been unconscionable at the time it was made, the court can (1) refuse to enforce the contract, (2) refuse to enforce the unconscionable clause of the contract, or (3) limit the application of any unconscionable clauses to avoid an unconscionable result.

TITLE, RISK, AND INSURABLE INTEREST

Shipment Contracts (See page 344.)	In the absence of an agreement, title and risk pass on the seller's or lessor's delivery of conforming goods to the carrier [UCC 2–319(1)(a), 2–401(2)(a), 2–509(1)(a), 2A–219(2)(a)].
Destination Contracts (See page 344.)	In the absence of an agreement, title and risk pass on the seller's or lessor's *tender* of delivery of conforming goods to the buyer or lessee at the point of destination [UCC 2–401(2)(b), 2–319(1)(b), 2–509(1)(b), 2A–219(2)(b)].

Delivery without Movement of the Goods
(See pages 344–347.)
	1. In the absence of an agreement, if the goods are not represented by a document of title:
	   a. Title passes on the formation of the contract [UCC 2–401(3)(b)].
	   b. Risk passes to the buyer or lessee, if the seller or lessor (or supplier, in a finance lease) is a merchant, when the buyer or lessee receives the goods or, if the seller or lessor is a nonmerchant, when the seller or lessor *tenders* delivery of the goods [UCC 2–509(3), 2A–219(c)].
	
	2. In the absence of an agreement, if the goods are represented by a document of title:
	   a. If the document is negotiable and the goods are held by a bailee, title and risk pass on the buyer's *receipt* of the document [UCC 2–401(3)(a), 2–509(2)(a)].
	   b. If the document is nonnegotiable and the goods are held by a bailee, title passes on the buyer's receipt of the document, but risk does *not* pass until the buyer, after receipt of the document, has had a reasonable time to present the document to demand the goods [UCC 2–401(3)(a), 2–509(2)(c), 2–503(4)(b)].
	
	3. In the absence of an agreement, if the goods are held by a bailee and no document of title is transferred, risk passes to the buyer when the bailee acknowledges the buyer's right to the possession of the goods [UCC 2–509(2)(b)].
	
	4. In respect to leases, if goods held by a bailee are to be delivered without being moved, the risk of loss passes to the lessee on acknowledgment by the bailee of the lessee's right to possession of the goods [UCC 2A–219(2)(b)].

(Continued)

CHAPTER SUMMARY ▦ Sales and Leases: Formation, Title, and Risk—Continued

Sale-or-Return Contracts (See page 348.)	When the buyer receives possession of the goods, title and risk of loss pass to the buyer, but the buyer has the option of returning the goods to the seller. If the buyer returns the goods to the seller, title and risk of loss pass back to the seller [UCC 2–327(2)].
Sale-on-Approval Contracts (See page 349.)	Title and risk of loss (from causes beyond the buyer's control) remain with the seller until the buyer approves (accepts) the offer [UCC 2–327(1)].
Risk of Loss When a Sales or Lease Contract Is Breached (See page 349.)	1. If the seller or lessor breaches by tendering nonconforming goods that are rejected by the buyer or lessee, the risk of loss does not pass to the buyer or lessee until the defects are cured (unless the buyer or lessee accepts the goods in spite of their defects, thus waiving the right to reject) [UCC 2–510(1), 2A–220(1)]. 2. If the buyer or lessee breaches the contract, the risk of loss immediately shifts to the buyer or lessee. Limitations to this rule are as follows [UCC 2–510(3), 2A–220(2)]: a. The seller or lessor must already have identified the contract goods. b. The buyer or lessee bears the risk for only a commercially reasonable time after the seller or lessor has learned of the breach. c. The buyer or lessee is liable only to the extent of any deficiency in the seller's or lessor's insurance coverage.
Insurable Interest (See pages 350–351.)	1. Buyers and lessees have an insurable interest in goods the moment the goods are identified to the contract by the seller or the lessor [UCC 2–501(1), 2A–218(1)]. 2. Sellers have an insurable interest in goods as long as they have (1) title to the goods or (2) a security interest in the goods [UCC 2–501(2)]. Lessors have an insurable interest in leased goods until the lessee exercises an option to buy and the risk of loss has passed to the lessee [UCC 2A–218(3)].

▦ FOR REVIEW

Answers for the even-numbered questions in this For Review *section can be found in Appendix I at the end of this text.*

1 How do Article 2 and Article 2A of the UCC differ? What types of transactions does each article cover?

2 If an offeree includes additional or different terms in an acceptance, will a contract result? If so, what happens to these terms?

3 If the parties to a contract do not expressly agree on when title to goods passes, what determines when title passes?

4 Risk of loss does not necessarily pass with title. If the parties to a contract do not expressly agree when risk passes and the goods are to be delivered without movement by the seller, when does risk pass?

5 At what point does the buyer acquire an insurable interest in goods subject to a sales contract? Can both the buyer and the seller have an insurable interest in the goods simultaneously?

▦ QUESTIONS AND CASE PROBLEMS

11–1. Statute of Frauds. Fresher Foods, Inc., orally agreed to purchase from Dale Vernon, a farmer, one thousand bushels of corn for $1.25 per bushel. Fresher Foods paid $125 down and agreed to pay the remainder of the purchase price on delivery, which was scheduled for one week later. When Fresher Foods tendered the balance of $1,125 on the scheduled day of delivery and requested the corn, Vernon refused to deliver it. Fresher Foods sued Vernon for damages, claiming that Vernon had breached their oral contract. Can Fresher Foods recover? If so, to what extent?

11–2. Merchant's Firm Offer. On September 1, Jennings, a used-car dealer, wrote a letter to Wheeler in which he stated, "I have a 1955 Thunderbird convertible in mint condition that I will sell you for $13,500 at any time before October 9. [signed] Peter Jennings." By September 15, having heard nothing from Wheeler, Jennings sold the Thunderbird to another party. On September 29, Wheeler accepted Jennings's offer and tendered the $13,500. When Jennings told Wheeler he had sold the car to another party, Wheeler claimed Jennings had breached their contract. Is Jennings in breach? Explain.

11–3. Risk of Loss. When will risk of loss pass from the seller to the buyer under each of the following contracts, assuming the parties have not expressly agreed on when risk of loss would pass?

(a) A New York seller contracts with a San Francisco buyer to ship goods to the buyer F.O.B. San Francisco.

(b) A New York seller contracts with a San Francisco buyer to ship goods to the buyer in San Francisco. There is no indication as to whether the shipment will be F.O.B. New York or F.O.B. San Francisco.

(c) A seller contracts with a buyer to sell goods located on the seller's premises. The buyer pays for the goods and arranges to pick them up the next week at the seller's place of business.

(d) A seller contracts with a buyer to sell goods located in a warehouse.

11–4. Sale on Approval. Chi Moy, a student, contracts to buy a television set from Ted's Electronics. Under the terms of the contract, Moy is to try out the set for thirty days, and if he likes it, he is to pay for the set at the end of the thirty-day period. If he does not want to purchase the set after thirty days, he can return the TV to Ted's Electronics with no obligation. Ten days after Moy takes the set home, it is stolen from his apartment, although he was not negligent in his care of the set in any way. Ted's Electronics claims that Moy must pay for the stolen set. Moy argues that the risk of loss falls on Ted's Electronics. Which party will prevail?

11–5. Risk of Loss. H.S.A. II, Inc., made parts for motor vehicles. Under an agreement with Ford Motor Co., Ford provided steel to H.S.A. to make Ford parts. Ford's purchase orders for the parts contained the term "FOB Carrier Supplier's [Plant]." GMAC Business Credit, L.L.C., loaned money to H.S.A. under terms that guaranteed payment would be made, if the funds were not otherwise available, from H.S.A.'s inventory, raw materials, and finished goods. H.S.A. filed for bankruptcy on February 2, 2000, and ceased operations on June 20, when it had in its plant more than $1 million in finished goods for Ford. Ford sent six trucks to H.S.A. to pick up the goods. GMAC halted the removal. The parties asked the bankruptcy court to determine whose interest had priority. GMAC contended in part that Ford did not have an interest in the goods because there had not yet been a sale. Ford responded that under its purchase orders, title and risk of loss transferred on completion of the parts. In whose favor should the court rule, and why? [*In re H.S.A. II, Inc.*, 271 Bankr. 534 (E.D.Mich. 2002)]

CASE PROBLEM WITH SAMPLE ANSWER

11–6. In 1988, International Business Machines Corp. (IBM) and American Shizuki Corp. (ASC) signed an agreement for "future purchase by IBM" of plastic film capacitors made by ASC to be used in IBM computers. The agreement stated that IBM was not obligated to buy from ASC and that future purchase orders "shall be [ASC]'s only authorization to manufacture Items." In February 1989, IBM wrote to ASC about "the possibility of IBM purchasing 15,000,000 Plastic Capacitors per two consecutive twelve (12) month periods. . . . This quantity is a forecast only, and represents no commitment by IBM to purchase these quantities during or after this time period." ASC said that it wanted greater assurances. In a second letter, IBM reexpressed its "intent to order" from ASC 30 million capacitors over a minimum period of two years, contingent on the condition "[t]hat IBM's requirements for these capacitors continue." ASC spent about $2.6 million on equipment to make the capacitors. By 1997, the need for plastic capacitors had dissipated with the advent of new technology, and IBM told ASC that it would no longer buy them. ASC filed a suit in a federal district court against IBM, seeking $8.5 million in damages. On what basis might the court rule in favor of IBM? Explain fully. [*American Shizuki Corp. v. International Business Machines Corp.*, 251 F.3d 1206 (8th Cir. 2001)]

After you have answered this problem, compare your answer with the sample answer given on the Web site that accompanies this text. Go to http://blt.westbuslaw.com, select "Chapter 11," and click on "Case Problem with Sample Answer."

11–7. Statute of Frauds. Quality Pork International is a Nebraska firm that makes and sells custom pork products. Rupari Food Services, Inc., buys and sells food products among retail operations and food brokers. In November 1999, Midwest Brokerage arranged an oral contract between Quality and Rupari, under which Quality would ship three orders to Star Food Processing, Inc., and Rupari would pay for the products. Quality shipped the goods to Star and sent invoices to Rupari. In turn, Rupari billed Star for all three orders, but paid Quality only for the first two (for $43,736.84 and $47,467.80, respectively), not for the third. Quality filed a suit in a Nebraska state court against Rupari, alleging breach of contract, to recover $44,051.98, the cost of the third order. Rupari argued that there was nothing in writing, as required by Section 2–201 of the Uniform Commercial Code (UCC), and thus there was no contract. What are the exceptions to the UCC's writing requirement? Do any of those exceptions apply here? Explain. [*Quality Pork International v. Rupari Food Services, Inc.*, 267 Neb. 474, 675 N.W.2d 642 (2004)]

A QUESTION OF ETHICS

11–8. John Schwanbeck entered into negotiations with Federal-Mogul Corp. to purchase Federal-Mogul's Vellumoid Division. The two parties drew up a letter of intent stating that "[n]o further obligation will arise until a definitive agreement is reduced to writing" and that it was the parties' intention "to proceed in good faith in the negotiation of such binding definitive agreement." At another place in the letter of intent were the following words: "Of course, this letter is not intended to create, nor do you or we presently have any binding legal obligation whatever in any way relating to such sale and purchase." Federal-Mogul eventually sold the Vellumoid Division to another party. Schwanbeck sued Federal-Mogul, alleging, among other things, that Federal-Mogul had breached an agreement to negotiate in good faith the proposed contract with Schwanbeck. Given these facts, consider the following questions. [*Schwanbeck v. Federal-Mogul Corp.*, 412 Mass. 703, 592 N.E.2d 1289 (1992)]

1. Did the letter of intent create a legally binding obligation, or was the letter merely an "agreement to agree" in the future? (You may wish to review the section on "Agreements to Agree" in Chapter 9 before you answer this question.)
2. Regardless of its legal duties, did Federal-Mogul have an ethical duty to proceed in negotiating a contract with Schwanbeck? Discuss.

FOR CRITICAL ANALYSIS

11–9. Why is the designation "merchant" or "nonmerchant" important?

VIDEO QUESTION

11–10. Go to this text's Web site at **http://blt.westbuslaw.com** and select "Chapter 11." Click on "Video Questions" and view the video titled *Sales and Lease Contracts: Price as a Term*. Then answer the following questions.

1. Is Anna correct in assuming that a contract can exist even though the sales price for the computer equipment was not specified? Explain.
2. According to the Uniform Commercial Code (UCC), what conditions must be satisfied in order for a contract to be formed when certain terms are left open? What terms (in addition to price) can be left open?
3. Are the e-mail messages that Anna refers to sufficient proof of the contract?
4. How do proposed changes to Article 2 of the UCC improve Anna's position?

ONLINE ACTIVITIES

INTERNET EXERCISES

Go to the *Business Law Today: The Essentials* home page at **http://blt.westbuslaw.com**, select "Chapter 11," and click on "Internet Exercises." There you will find the following Internet research exercises that you can perform to learn more about topics covered in this chapter.

Activity 11–1: LEGAL PERSPECTIVE—Is It a Contract?

Activity 11–2: MANAGEMENT PERSPECTIVE—A Checklist for Sales Contracts

Activity 11–3: MANAGEMENT PERSPECTIVE—Passage of Title

BEFORE THE TEST

Go to the *Business Law Today: The Essentials* home page at **http://blt.westbuslaw.com**, select "Chapter 11," and click on "Interactive Quizzes." You will find at least twenty interactive questions relating to this chapter.

CHAPTER 12

Sales and Leases: Performance and Breach

"It has been uniformly laid down . . . ,
as far back as we can remember,
that good faith is the basis of all
mercantile transactions."

J. Buller, 1746–1800
(British jurist)

CHAPTER OUTLINE

- **PERFORMANCE OBLIGATIONS**

- **OBLIGATIONS OF THE SELLER OR LESSOR**

- **OBLIGATIONS OF THE BUYER OR LESSEE**

- **ANTICIPATORY REPUDIATION**

- **REMEDIES OF THE SELLER OR LESSOR**

- **REMEDIES OF THE BUYER OR LESSEE**

- **LIMITATION OF REMEDIES**

■□ LEARNING OBJECTIVES

After reading this chapter, you should be able to answer the following questions:

1 What are the respective obligations of the parties under a contract for the sale or lease of goods?

2 What is the perfect tender rule? What are some important exceptions to this rule that apply to sales and lease contracts?

3 What options are available to the nonbreaching party when the other party to a sales or lease contract repudiates the contract prior to the time for performance?

4 What remedies are available to a seller or lessor when the buyer or lessee breaches the contract? What remedies are available to a buyer or lessee if the seller or lessor breaches the contract?

5 In contracts subject to the UCC, are parties free to limit the remedies available to the nonbreaching party on a breach of contract? If so, in what ways?

The performance that is required of the parties under a sales or lease contract consists of the duties and obligations each party has under the terms of the contract. Keep in mind that "duties and obligations" under the terms of the contract include those specified by the agreement, by custom, and by the Uniform Commercial Code (UCC). In this chapter, we examine the basic performance obligations of the parties under a sales or lease contract.

Sometimes, circumstances make it difficult for a person to carry out the promised performance, in which case the contract may be breached. When breach occurs, the aggrieved party looks for remedies—which we deal with in the second half of the chapter.

Performance Obligations

As discussed in previous chapters and stressed in the opening quotation to this chapter, the standards of good faith and commercial reasonableness are read into every contract. These standards provide a framework in which the parties can specify particulars of performance. Thus, when one party delays specifying particulars of performance for an unreasonable period of time or fails to cooperate with the other party, the innocent party is excused from any resulting delay in performance. The innocent party can proceed to perform in any reasonable manner, and the other party's failure to specify particulars or to cooperate can be treated as a breach of contract. Good faith is a question of fact for the jury.

In the performance of a sales or lease contract, the basic obligation of the seller or lessor is to *transfer and deliver conforming goods*. The basic obligation of the buyer or lessee is to *accept and pay for conforming goods* in accordance with the contract [UCC 2–301, 2A–516(1)]. Overall performance of a sales or lease contract is controlled by the agreement between the parties. When the contract is unclear and disputes arise, the courts look to the UCC.

Obligations of the Seller or Lessor

The major obligation of the seller or lessor under a sales or lease contract is to tender conforming goods to the buyer or lessee.

TENDER OF DELIVERY

Tender of delivery requires that the seller or lessor have and hold *conforming goods* at the disposal of the buyer or lessee and give the buyer or lessee whatever notification is reasonably necessary to enable the buyer or lessee to take delivery [UCC 2–503(1), 2A–508(1)].

Tender must occur at a *reasonable hour* and in a *reasonable manner*. In other words, a seller cannot call the buyer at 2:00 A.M. and say, "The goods are ready. I'll give you twenty minutes to get them." Unless the parties have agreed otherwise, the goods must be tendered for delivery at a reasonable time and kept available for a reasonable period of time to enable the buyer to take possession of them [UCC 2–503(1)(a)].

All goods called for by a contract must be tendered in a single delivery unless the parties agree otherwise or the circumstances are such that either party can rightfully request delivery in lots [UCC 2–307, 2–612, 2A–510]. Hence, an order for 1,000 shirts cannot be delivered 2 shirts at a time. If, however, the seller and the buyer contemplate that the shirts will be delivered in four orders of 250 each, as they are produced (for summer, fall, winter, and spring stock), and the price can be apportioned accordingly, it may be commercially reasonable to deliver the shirts in this way.

PLACE OF DELIVERY

The UCC provides for the place of delivery pursuant to a contract if the contract does not. Of course, the parties may agree on a particular destination, or their contract's terms or the circumstances may indicate the place of delivery.

Noncarrier Cases   If the contract does not designate the place of delivery for the goods, and the buyer is expected to pick them up, the place of delivery is the *seller's place of business* or, if the seller has none, the seller's residence [UCC 2–308]. If the contract involves the sale of *identified goods,* and the parties know when they enter into the contract that these goods are located somewhere other than at the seller's place of business (such as at a warehouse), then the *location of the goods* is the place for their delivery [UCC 2–308].

■ **EXAMPLE 12.1** Rogers and Aguirre live in San Francisco. In San Francisco, Rogers contracts to sell Aguirre five used trucks, which both parties know are located in a Chicago warehouse. If nothing more is specified in the contract, the place of delivery for the trucks is Chicago. ■ The seller may tender delivery either by giving the buyer a *negotiable or nonnegotiable document of title* or by obtaining the *bailee's (warehouser's) acknowledgment* that the buyer is entitled to possession.[1]

Carrier Cases   In many instances, attendant circumstances or delivery terms in the contract make it apparent that the parties intend that a carrier be used to move the goods. In carrier cases, a seller can complete performance of the obligation to deliver the goods in two ways—through a shipment contract or through a destination contract.

Shipment Contracts.   Recall from Chapter 11 that a shipment contract requires or authorizes the seller to ship goods by a carrier. The contract does not require that the seller deliver the goods at a particular destination [UCC 2–319, 2–509].[2] Under a shipment contract, unless otherwise agreed, the seller must do the following:

1 Put the goods into the hands of the carrier.

2 Make a contract for their transportation that is reasonable according to the nature of the goods and their value. (For example, certain types of goods need refrigeration in transit.)

3 Obtain and promptly deliver or tender to the buyer any documents necessary to enable the buyer to obtain possession of the goods from the carrier.

4 Promptly notify the buyer that shipment has been made [UCC 2–504].

If the seller fails to notify the buyer that shipment has been made or fails to make a proper contract for transportation, the buyer can treat the contract as breached and reject the goods, but only if a *material loss* of the goods or a significant *delay* results. Of course, the parties can agree that a lesser amount of loss or that any delay will be grounds for rejection.

Destination Contracts.   Under a *destination contract,* the seller agrees to see that conforming goods will be duly tendered to the buyer at a particular destination. The goods must be tendered at a reasonable hour and held at the buyer's disposal for a reasonable length of time. The seller must also give the buyer any appropriate notice that is necessary to enable the buyer to take delivery. In addition, the seller must provide the buyer with any documents of title necessary to enable the buyer to obtain delivery from the carrier [UCC 2–503].

KEEP IN MIND If goods never arrive, the buyer or seller usually has at least some recourse against the carrier. Also, a buyer normally insures the goods from the time they leave the seller's possession.

DON'T FORGET Documents of title include bills of lading, warehouse receipts, and any other documents that, in the regular course of business, entitle a person holding these documents to obtain possession of, and title to, the goods covered.

---

1. If the seller delivers a nonnegotiable document of title or merely writes instructions to the bailee to release the goods to the buyer without the bailee's *acknowledgment* of the buyer's rights, this is also a sufficient tender, unless the buyer objects [UCC 2–503(4)]. Risk of loss, however, does not pass until the buyer has a reasonable amount of time in which to present the document or to give the bailee instructions for delivery.

2. As mentioned in Chapter 11, UCC 2–319 was omitted from the 2003 amendments to Article 2.

THE PERFECT TENDER RULE

As previously noted, the seller or lessor has an obligation to ship or tender *conforming goods,* and the buyer or lessee is required to accept and pay for the goods according to the terms of the contract. Under the common law, the seller was obligated to deliver goods in conformity with the terms of the contract in every detail. This was called the *perfect tender* doctrine. The UCC preserves the perfect tender doctrine by stating that if goods or tender of delivery fail *in any respect* to conform to the contract, the buyer or lessee has the right to accept the goods, reject the entire shipment, or accept part and reject part [UCC 2–601, 2A–509].

■ **EXAMPLE 12.2** A lessor contracts to lease fifty Vericlear monitors to be delivered at the lessee's place of business on or before October 1. On September 28, the lessor discovers that it has only thirty Vericlear monitors in inventory but that it will have another forty Vericlear monitors within the next two weeks. The lessor tenders delivery of the thirty Vericlear monitors on October 1, with the promise that the other monitors will be delivered within three weeks. Because the lessor failed to make a perfect tender of fifty Vericlear monitors, the lessee has the right to reject the entire shipment and hold the lessor in breach. ■

EXCEPTIONS TO PERFECT TENDER

Because of the rigidity of the perfect tender rule, several exceptions to the rule have been created, some of which are discussed here.

Agreement of the Parties   Exceptions to the perfect tender rule may be established by agreement. If the parties have agreed, for example, that defective goods or parts will not be rejected if the seller or lessor is able to repair or replace them within a reasonable period of time, the perfect tender rule does not apply.

Cure   The UCC does not specifically define the term *cure,* but it refers to the right of the seller or lessor to repair, adjust, or replace defective or nonconforming goods [UCC 2–508, 2A–513]. When any tender of delivery is rejected because of nonconforming goods and the time for performance has not yet expired, the seller or lessor can notify the buyer or lessee promptly of the intention to cure and can then do so *within the contract time for performance* [UCC 2–508(1), 2A–513(1)]. Once the time for performance has expired, the seller or lessor can still, for a reasonable time, exercise the right to cure with respect to the rejected goods if he or she had, at the time of delivery, *reasonable grounds to believe that the nonconforming tender would be acceptable to the buyer or lessee* [UCC 2–508(2), 2A–513(2)].[3]

Sometimes, a seller or lessor will tender nonconforming goods with some type of price allowance. The allowance serves as the "reasonable grounds" for the seller or lessor to believe that the nonconforming tender will be acceptable to the buyer or lessee. A seller or lessor might also have other reasons for assuming that a buyer or lessee will accept a nonconforming tender. ■ **EXAMPLE 12.3** Suppose that in the past the buyer, an office supply store, frequently accepted blue pens when the seller

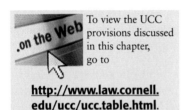

To view the UCC provisions discussed in this chapter, go to

http://www.law.cornell.edu/ucc/ucc.table.html.

3. The 2003 amendments to UCC Articles 2 and 2A expressly exempt "consumer contracts" and "consumer leases" from these provisions [Amended UCC 2–508, 2A–508]. In other words, cure is not available as a matter of right after a justifiable revocation of acceptance under a consumer contract or lease. Also, the new provisions abandon the "reasonable grounds to believe" test, thus expanding the seller's right to cure after the time for performance has expired. Although this test has been abandoned, the requirement that the initial tender be made in good faith prevents a seller from deliberately tendering goods that the seller knows the buyer cannot use.

did not have black pens in stock. In this context, the seller has reasonable grounds to believe the store will again accept such a substitute. If the store rejects the substituted goods (blue pens) on a particular occasion, the seller nonetheless had reasonable grounds to believe that the blue pens would be acceptable. Therefore, the seller can cure within a reasonable time, even though the delivery of black pens will occur after the time limit for performance allowed under the contract. ■

The right to cure means that, to reject goods, the buyer or lessee must give notice to the seller or lessor of a particular defect. For example, if a lessee refuses a tender of goods as nonconforming but does not disclose the nature of the defect to the lessor, the lessee cannot later assert the defect as a defense if the defect is one that the lessor could have cured. Generally, buyers and lessees must act in good faith and state specific reasons for refusing to accept goods [UCC 2–605, 2A–514].[4]

Substitution of Carriers When an agreed-on manner of delivery (such as which carrier will be used to transport the goods) becomes impracticable or unavailable through no fault of either party, but a commercially reasonable substitute is available, the seller must use this substitute performance, which is sufficient tender to the buyer [UCC 2–614(1)]. ■ EXAMPLE 12.4 A sales contract calls for the delivery of a large generator to be shipped by Roadway Trucking Corporation on or before June 1. The contract terms clearly state the importance of the delivery date. The employees of Roadway Trucking go on strike. The seller is required to make a reasonable substitute tender, perhaps by rail if that is available. Note that the seller will normally be responsible for any additional shipping costs, unless other arrangements have been made in the sales contract. ■

---

4. The 2003 amendments to UCC 2–605 and 2A–514 change this restriction in three ways. First, a buyer's or lessee's failure to disclose the nature of the defect affects only the right to reject or revoke acceptance, not the right to establish a breach of contract. Second, the new sections expressly require that the seller or lessor must have had a right to cure, as well as the ability to cure. Finally, these sections extend to include not only rejection but also revocation of acceptance.

Competitors' trucks travel the same route. When is it acceptable to substitute one carrier for another specified in a contract? (Sandy Huffaker/Bloomberg News/Landov)

INSTALLMENT CONTRACT
Under the UCC, a contract that requires or authorizes delivery in two or more separate lots to be accepted and paid for separately.

Installment Contracts   An **installment contract** is a single contract that requires or authorizes delivery in two or more separate lots to be accepted and paid for separately. In an installment contract, a buyer or lessee can reject an installment *only if the nonconformity substantially impairs the value* of the installment and cannot be cured [UCC 2–612(2), 2–307, 2A–510(1)].[5]

Unless the contract provides otherwise, the entire installment contract is breached only when one or more nonconforming installments *substantially* impair the value of the *whole contract*. If the buyer or lessee subsequently accepts a nonconforming installment and fails to notify the seller or lessor of cancellation, however, the contract is reinstated [UCC 2–612(3), 2A–510(2)].

A major issue to be determined is what constitutes substantial impairment of the "value of the whole contract." ■ **EXAMPLE 12.5** Consider an installment contract for the sale of twenty carloads of plywood. The first carload does not conform to the contract because 9 percent of the plywood deviates from the thickness specifications. The buyer cancels the contract, and immediately thereafter the second and third carloads of conforming plywood arrive at the buyer's place of business. If a lawsuit ensues, the court will have to grapple with the question of whether the 9 percent of nonconforming plywood substantially impaired the value of the whole. ■

The point to remember is that the UCC significantly alters the right of the buyer or lessee to reject the entire contract if the contract requires delivery to be made in several installments. The UCC strictly limits rejection to cases of *substantial* nonconformity.

Commercial Impracticability   As mentioned in Chapter 9, occurrences that were not foreseeable by either party when a contract was made may make performance commercially impracticable. When this occurs, the rule of perfect tender no longer holds. According to UCC 2–615(a) and 2A–405(a), delay in delivery or nondelivery in whole or in part is not a breach when performance has been made impracticable "by the occurrence of a contingency the nonoccurrence of which was a basic assumption on which the contract was made." The seller or lessor must, however, notify the buyer or lessee as soon as practicable that there will be a delay or nondelivery.

Foreseeable versus Unforeseeable Contingencies.   An increase in cost resulting from inflation does not in itself excuse performance, as a seller or lessor ordinarily assumes this kind of risk when conducting business. The unforeseen contingency must be one that would have been impossible to contemplate in a given business situation. ■ **EXAMPLE 12.6** A major oil company that receives its supplies from the Middle East has a contract to supply a buyer with 100,000 gallons of oil. Because of an oil embargo by the Organization of Petroleum Exporting Countries, the seller is prevented from securing oil supplies to meet the terms of the contract. Because of the same embargo, the seller cannot secure oil from any other source. This situation comes fully under the commercial impracticability exception to the perfect tender doctrine. ■

Can unanticipated increases in a seller's costs, which make performance "impracticable," constitute a valid defense to performance on the basis of commercial impracticability? The court dealt with this question in the following case.

---

5. The 2003 amendments to Articles 2 and 2A make it clear that the buyer's or lessee's right to reject an installment depends on whether the value of the installment to the buyer or lessee is substantially impaired and not on whether the seller or lessor is able to cure [Amended UCC 2–612(2), 2A–510(2)].

LANDMARK AND CLASSIC CASES

CASE 12.1 ■ Maple Farms, Inc. v. City School District of Elmira

Supreme Court of New York, 1974.
76 Misc.2d 1080,
352 N.Y.S.2d 784.

FACTS On June 15, 1973, Maple Farms, Inc., formed an agreement with the city school district of Elmira, New York, to supply the school district with milk for the 1973–1974 school year. The agreement was in the form of a requirements contract, under which Maple Farms would sell to the school district all the milk the district required at a fixed price—which was the June market price of milk. By December 1973, the price of raw milk had increased by 23 percent over the price specified in the contract. This meant that if the terms of the contract were fulfilled, Maple Farms would lose $7,350. Because it had similar contracts with other school districts, Maple Farms stood to lose a great deal if it was held to the price stated in the contracts. When the school district would not agree to release Maple Farms from its contract, Maple Farms brought an action in a New York state court for a declaratory judgment (a determination of the parties' rights under a contract). Maple Farms contended that the substantial increase in the price of raw milk was an event not contemplated by the parties when the contract was formed and that, given the increased price, performance of the contract was commercially impracticable.

ISSUE Can Maple Farms be released from the contract on the ground of commercial impracticability?

DECISION No. The court ruled that performance in this case was not impracticable.

REASON The court reasoned that commercial impracticability arises when an event occurs that is totally unexpected and unforeseeable by the parties. The increased price of raw milk was not totally unexpected, given that in the previous year the price of milk had risen 10 percent and that the price of milk had traditionally varied. Additionally, the general inflation of prices in the United States should have been anticipated. Maple Farms had reason to know these facts and could have included a clause in its contract with the school district to protect itself from its present situation. The court also noted that the primary purpose of the contract, on the part of the school district, was to protect itself (for budgeting purposes) against price fluctuations.

COMMENTS *This case is a classic illustration of the UCC's commercial impracticability doctrine. Under this doctrine, parties who freely enter into contracts normally will not be excused from their contractual obligations simply because changed circumstances make performance difficult or very costly. Rather, to be excused from performance, a party must show that the changed circumstances were impossible to foresee at the time the contract was formed. This principle continues to be applied today.*

RELEVANT WEB SITES *To locate information on the Web concerning* Maple Farms, Inc. v. City School District of Elmira, *go to this text's Web site at* **http://blt.westbuslaw.com**, *select "Chapter 12," and click on "URLs for Landmarks."*

Partial Performance. Sometimes, an unforeseen event only *partially* affects the capacity of the seller or lessor to perform, and the seller or lessor is thus able to fulfill the contract *partially* but cannot tender total performance. In this event, the seller or lessor is required to allocate in a fair and reasonable manner any remaining production and deliveries among those to whom it is contractually obligated to deliver the goods, and this allocation may take into account its regular customers [UCC 2–615(b), 2A–405(b)]. The buyer or lessee must receive notice of the allocation and has the right to accept or reject the allocation [UCC 2–615(c), 2A–405(c)].

■ **EXAMPLE 12.7** A Florida orange grower, Best Citrus, Inc., contracts to sell this season's crop to a number of customers, including Martin's grocery chain. Martin's contracts to purchase two thousand crates of oranges. Best Citrus has sprayed some of its orange groves with a chemical called Karmoxin. The Department of Agriculture discovers that persons who eat products sprayed with Karmoxin may develop cancer. The department issues an order prohibiting the sale of these products. Best Citrus picks all of the oranges not sprayed with Karmoxin, but the quantity does not fully meet all the contracted-for deliveries. In this situation, Best Citrus is required to allocate its production, and it notifies Martin's that it cannot deliver the full quantity agreed on in the contract and specifies the amount it will be able to deliver under the circumstances. Martin's can either accept or reject the allocation, but Best Citrus has no further contractual liability. ■

Destruction of Identified Goods   The UCC provides that when an unexpected event, such as a fire, totally destroys *goods identified at the time the contract is formed* through no fault of either party and *before risk passes to the buyer or lessee,* the parties are excused from performance [UCC 2–613, 2A–221]. If the goods are only partially destroyed, however, the buyer or lessee can inspect them and either treat the contract as void or accept the goods with a reduction of the contract price.

■ EXAMPLE 12.8 Atlas Sporting Equipment agrees to lease to River Bicycles sixty bicycles of a particular model that has been discontinued. No other bicycles of that model are available. River specifies that it needs the bicycles to rent to tourists. Before Atlas can deliver the bikes, they are destroyed by a fire. In this situation, Atlas is not liable to River for failing to deliver the bikes. The goods were destroyed through no fault of either party, before the risk of loss passed to the lessee. The loss was total, so the contract is avoided. Clearly, Atlas has no obligation to tender the bicycles, and River has no obligation to pay for them. ■

Assurance and Cooperation   Two other exceptions to the perfect tender doctrine apply equally to parties to sales and lease contracts: the right of assurance and the duty of cooperation.

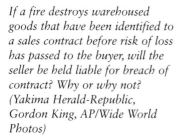

If a fire destroys warehoused goods that have been identified to a sales contract before risk of loss has passed to the buyer, will the seller be held liable for breach of contract? Why or why not? (Yakima Herald-Republic, Gordon King, AP/Wide World Photos)

The Right of Assurance. The UCC provides that if one party to a contract has "reasonable grounds" to believe that the other party will not perform as contracted, he or she may *in writing* "demand adequate assurance of due performance" from the other party. Until such assurance is received, he or she may "suspend" further performance (such as payments due under the contract) without liability. What constitutes "reasonable grounds" is determined by commercial standards. If such assurances are not forthcoming within a reasonable time (not to exceed thirty days), the failure to respond may be treated as a *repudiation* of the contract [UCC 2–609, 2A–401]. The following case illustrates this principle.

CASE 12.2 ▦ Koch Materials Co. v. Shore Slurry Seal, Inc.

United States District Court,
District of New Jersey, 2002.
205 F.Supp.2d 324.
http://lawlibrary.rutgers.edu/fed/search.html[a]

FACTS Koch Materials Company is a manufacturer of road surfacing materials. In February 1998, Koch agreed to pay $5 million, payable in three installments, to Shore Slurry Seal, Inc., for an asphalt plant in New Jersey and the rights to license a specialty road surfacing substance, known as Novachip. Shore also agreed that for seven years following the sale, it would buy all of its asphalt requirements from Koch, or at least 2 million gallons of asphalt per year (the Exclusive Supply Agreement). Shore promised to use at least 2.5 million square yards of Novachip annually and to pay royalties to Koch accordingly (the Sublicense Agreement). Midway through the term of the contract, Shore told Koch that it planned to sell its assets to Asphalt Paving Systems, Inc. Koch sought assurances that Asphalt Paving would continue the original deal. Shore refused to provide any more information. Koch filed a suit in a federal district court against Shore, asking in part for the right to treat Shore's failure to give assurances as a repudiation of their contract. Koch filed a motion for summary judgment on this issue.

ISSUE Did Shore in effect repudiate the contract?

DECISION Yes. The court issued a summary judgment in Koch's favor. The court concluded that Shore's failure to provide assurances to Koch constituted a repudiation of

its contract, authorizing Koch to terminate the contract and seek damages.

REASON The court concluded that Koch had a commercially reasonable basis for demanding assurances. Shore planned to sell all of its assets but retain the licensing agreement. The court stated that "any reasonable person would wonder how Shore planned to sell anything with no telephones, no computers, and no office furniture." Also, as for leasing these items, a party might ask, "Would Shore have had the financial capacity to obtain leases and hire a sales staff?" As for the requirements supply contract, the court pointed out that "[s]tart-up construction businesses * * * begin unbonded, unable to win any bid for their first year, and unable to secure sufficient bonding for large construction bids for several years.[b] Koch had no way of knowing whether Asphalt was already a going business, and, if not, whether it would be able to win sufficient subcontracting bids even to meet the minimum requirements, let alone approach the potential upside of an established enterprise like Shore."

WHY IS THIS CASE IMPORTANT? *This case clearly illustrates how the UCC comes to the aid of a party who has reasonable grounds to suspect that the other party to a contract will not perform as promised. Rather than having to "wait and see" (and possibly incur significant losses as a result), the party with such suspicions may seek adequate assurance of performance from the other party. The failure to give such assurance can be treated as an anticipatory repudiation (breach) of the contract, thus entitling the nonbreaching party to seek damages.*

a. In the "Find Decisions by Docket Number" section, select "Civil Case," type "01-2059" in the "Enter Docket Number" box, and click on "Submit Form." From the results, click on "ca01-2059-1.html" to access the opinion. Rutgers University School of Law in Camden, New Jersey, maintains this Web site.

b. In this context, a *bond* is a guaranty to complete or to pay the cost of a construction contract if the contractor defaults.

The Duty of Cooperation.   Sometimes, the performance of one party depends on the cooperation of the other. The UCC provides that when such cooperation is not forthcoming, the other party can suspend her or his own performance without liability and hold the uncooperative party in breach or proceed to perform the contract in any reasonable manner [UCC 2–311(3)(b)].

■■ Obligations of the Buyer or Lessee

Once the seller or lessor has adequately tendered delivery, the buyer or lessee is obligated to accept the goods and pay for them according to the terms of the contract. In the absence of any specific agreements, the buyer or lessee must make payment at the time and place the goods are received [UCC 2–310(a), 2A–516(1)].

PAYMENT

When a sale is made on credit, the buyer is obliged to pay according to the specified credit terms (for example, 60, 90, or 120 days), not when the goods are received. The credit period usually begins on the *date of shipment* [UCC 2–310(d)]. Under a lease contract, a lessee must pay the lease payment that was specified in the contract [UCC 2A–516(1)].

Payment can be made by any means agreed on by the parties—cash or any other method generally acceptable in the commercial world. If the seller demands cash when the buyer offers a check, credit card, or the like, the seller must permit the buyer reasonable time to obtain legal tender [UCC 2–511].

RIGHT OF INSPECTION

Unless otherwise agreed, or for C.O.D. (collect on delivery) transactions, the buyer or lessee has an absolute right to inspect the goods. This right allows the buyer or lessee to verify, before making payment, that the goods tendered or delivered are what were contracted for or ordered. If the goods are not what were ordered, the buyer or lessee has no duty to pay. *An opportunity for inspection is therefore a condition precedent to the right of the seller or lessor to enforce payment* [UCC 2–513(1), 2A–515(1)].

Unless otherwise agreed, inspection can take place at any reasonable place and time and in any reasonable manner. Generally, what is reasonable is determined by custom of the trade, past practices of the parties, and the like. Costs of inspecting conforming goods are borne by the buyer unless otherwise agreed [UCC 2–513(2)].

C.O.D. Shipments   If a seller ships goods to a buyer C.O.D. (or under similar terms) and the buyer has not agreed to a C.O.D. shipment in the contract, the buyer can rightfully *reject* the goods. This is because a C.O.D. shipment cannot be inspected before payment, which is a denial of the buyer's right of inspection. When the buyer has agreed to a C.O.D. shipment in the contract, however, or has agreed to pay for the goods on the presentation of a bill of lading, no right of inspection exists because it was negated by the agreement [UCC 2–513(3)].[6]

RECALL A bill of lading is a receipt for goods that is signed by a carrier and serves as a contract for the transportation of goods.

---

6. References to "C.O.D." and similar terms that represent commercial shorthand (such as F.O.B., C.&F., and other terms discussed in Chapter 11) have been deleted in the 2003 amendments to UCC Article 2. See, for example, Amended UCC 2–513(3)(a).

Payment Due—Documents of Title   Under certain contracts, payment is due on the receipt of the required documents of title even though the goods themselves may not have arrived at their destination. With C.I.F. and C.&F. contracts (see Exhibit 11–2 in Chapter 11), payment is required on receipt of the documents unless the parties have agreed otherwise. Thus, payment may be required prior to inspection and must be made unless the buyer knows that the goods are nonconforming [UCC 2–310(b), 2–513(3)].

ACCEPTANCE

A buyer or lessee can manifest assent to the delivered goods in the following ways, each of which constitutes acceptance:

■ The buyer or lessee can expressly accept the shipment by words or conduct. For example, there is an acceptance if the buyer or lessee, after having had a reasonable opportunity to inspect the goods, signifies agreement to the seller or lessor that the goods are either conforming or are acceptable despite their nonconformity [UCC 2–606(1)(a), 2A–515(1)(a)].

■ Acceptance is presumed if the buyer or lessee has had a reasonable opportunity to inspect the goods and has failed to reject them within a reasonable period of time [UCC 2–606(1)(b), 2–602(1), 2A–515(1)(b)].

Additionally, in sales contracts, the buyer will be deemed to have accepted the goods if he or she performs any act that would indicate that the seller no longer owns the goods. For example, any use or resale of the goods generally constitutes an acceptance. Limited use for the sole purpose of testing or inspecting the goods is not an acceptance, however [UCC 2–606(1)(c)].

If some of the goods delivered do not conform to the contract and the seller or lessor has failed to cure, the buyer or lessee can make a *partial* acceptance [UCC 2–601(c), 2A–509(1)]. The same is true if the nonconformity was not reasonably discoverable before acceptance. (In the latter situation, the buyer or lessee may be able to revoke the acceptance, as will be discussed later in this chapter.) A buyer or lessee cannot accept less than a single commercial unit, however. The UCC defines a *commercial unit* as a unit of goods that, by commercial usage, is viewed as a "single whole" for purposes of sale, division of which would materially impair the character of the unit, its market value, or its use [UCC 2–105(6), 2A–103(1)(c)]. A commercial unit can be a single article (such as a machine), a set of articles (such as a suite of furniture or an assortment of sizes), a quantity (such as a bale, a gross, or a carload), or any other unit treated in the trade as a single whole.

■ Anticipatory Repudiation

What if, before the time for contract performance, one party clearly communicates to the other the intention not to perform? As discussed in Chapter 9, such an action is a breach of the contract by anticipatory repudiation.[7] When anticipatory repudiation occurs, the nonbreaching party has a choice of two responses: (1) treat the repudiation as a final breach by pursuing a remedy or (2) wait to see if the repudiating party will decide to honor the contract despite the avowed intention to renege [UCC 2–610, 2A–402]. In either situation, the nonbreaching party may suspend performance.

---

7. This doctrine was first enunciated in an English case decided in 1853, *Hochster v. De La Tour*, 2 Ellis and Blackburn Reports 678 (1853).

Should the latter course be pursued, the UCC permits the breaching party (subject to some limitations) to "retract" her or his repudiation. This can be done by any method that clearly indicates an intent to perform. Once retraction is made, the rights of the repudiating party under the contract are reinstated [UCC 2–611, 2A–403].

▚ Remedies of the Seller or Lessor

When the buyer or lessee is in breach, the seller or lessor has numerous remedies available under the UCC. Generally, the remedies available to the seller or lessor depend on the circumstances at the time of the breach, such as which party has possession of the goods, whether the goods are in transit, and whether the buyer or lessee has rejected or accepted the goods, for example.

WHEN THE GOODS ARE IN THE POSSESSION OF THE SELLER OR LESSOR

Under the UCC, if the buyer or lessee breaches the contract before the goods have been delivered to her or him, the seller or lessor has the right to pursue the remedies discussed here.

NOTE A buyer or lessee breaches a contract by wrongfully rejecting the goods, wrongfully revoking acceptance, refusing to pay, or repudiating the contract.

The Right to Cancel the Contract One of the options available to a seller or lessor when the buyer or lessee breaches the contract is simply to cancel (rescind) the contract [UCC 2–703(f), 2A–523(1)(a)]. The seller must notify the buyer or lessee of the cancellation, and at that point all remaining obligations of the seller or lessor are discharged. The buyer or lessee is not discharged from all remaining obligations, however; he or she is in breach, and the seller or lessor can pursue remedies available under the UCC for breach.

The Right to Withhold Delivery In general, sellers and lessors can withhold or discontinue performance of their obligations under sales or lease contracts when the buyers or lessees are in breach. If a buyer or lessee has wrongfully rejected or revoked acceptance of contract goods (rejection and revocation of acceptance will be discussed later), failed to make proper and timely payment, or repudiated a part of the contract, the seller or lessor can withhold delivery of the goods in question [UCC 2–703(a), 2A–523(1)(c)]. If the breach results from the buyer's or the lessee's insolvency (inability to pay debts as they become due), the seller or lessor can refuse to deliver the goods unless the buyer or lessee pays in cash [UCC 2–702(1), 2A–525(1)].

The Right to Resell or Dispose of the Goods When a buyer or lessee breaches or repudiates a sales contract while the seller or lessor is still in possession of the goods, the seller or lessor can resell or dispose of the goods. The seller can retain any profits made as a result of the sale and can hold the buyer or lessee liable for any loss [UCC 2–703(d), 2–706(1), 2A–523(1)(e), 2A–527(1)].[8]

When the goods contracted for are unfinished at the time of breach, the seller or lessor can do one of two things: (1) cease manufacturing the goods and resell them

---

8. Under the 2003 amendments to UCC Articles 2 and 2A, this loss includes consequential damages, except that a seller or lessor cannot recover consequential damages from a consumer under a consumer contract or lease [Amended UCC 2–706(1), 2–710, 2A–527(2), 2A–530]. Consequential damages may also be recovered, except from a consumer under a consumer contract or lease, when a seller or lessor has a right to recover the purchase price or lease payments due or to recover other damages [Amended UCC 2–708(1), 2–709(1), 2–710, 2A–528(1), 2A–529(1), 2A–530]. Subtracted from these amounts, of course, would be any expenses saved as a consequence of the buyer's or lessee's breach.

369

for scrap or salvage value or (2) complete the manufacture and resell or dispose of them, holding the buyer or lessee liable for any deficiency. In choosing between these two alternatives, the seller or lessor must exercise reasonable commercial judgment to mitigate the loss and obtain maximum value from the unfinished goods [UCC 2–704(2), 2A–524(2)]. Any resale of the goods must be made in good faith and in a commercially reasonable manner.

In sales transactions, the seller can recover any deficiency between the resale price and the contract price, along with **incidental damages,** defined as those costs to the seller resulting from the breach [UCC 2–706(1), 2–710]. The resale can be private or public, and the goods can be sold as a unit or in parcels. The seller must give the original buyer reasonable notice of the resale, unless the goods are perishable or will rapidly decline in value [UCC 2–706(2), (3)]. A good faith purchaser in a resale takes the goods free of any of the rights of the original buyer, even if the seller fails to comply with these requirements of the UCC [UCC 2–706(5)].

In lease transactions, the lessor may lease the goods to another party and recover from the original lessee, as damages, any unpaid lease payments up to the beginning date of the lease term under the new lease. The lessor can also recover any deficiency between the lease payments due under the original lease contract and under the new lease contract, along with incidental damages [UCC 2A–527(2)].

The Right to Recover the Purchase Price or the Lease Payments Due Under the UCC, an unpaid seller or lessor can bring an action to recover the purchase price or payments due under the lease contract, plus incidental damages, if the seller or lessor is unable to resell or dispose of the goods [UCC 2–709(1), 2A–529(1)].

■ **EXAMPLE 12.9** Suppose that Southern Realty contracts with Gem Point, Inc., to purchase one thousand pens with Southern Realty's name inscribed on them. Gem Point tenders delivery of the one thousand pens, but Southern Realty wrongfully refuses to accept them. In this situation, Gem Point has, as a proper remedy, an action for the purchase price. Gem Point tendered delivery of conforming goods, and Southern Realty, by failing to accept the goods, is in breach. Gem Point obviously cannot sell to anyone else the pens inscribed with the buyer's business name, so this situation falls under UCC 2–709. ■

If a seller or lessor is unable to resell or dispose of goods and sues for the contract price or lease payments due, the goods must be held for the buyer or lessee. The seller or lessor can resell or dispose of the goods at any time prior to collection (of the judgment) from the buyer or lessee but must credit the net proceeds from the sale to the buyer or lessee. This is an example of the duty to mitigate damages.

The Right to Recover Damages If a buyer or lessee repudiates a contract or wrongfully refuses to accept the goods, a seller or lessor can maintain an action to recover the damages that were sustained. Ordinarily, the amount of damages equals the difference between the contract price or lease payments and the market price or lease payments (at the time and place of tender of the goods), plus incidental damages [UCC 2–708(1), 2A–528(1)]. The time and place of tender are frequently given by such terms as F.O.B., F.A.S., C.I.F., and the like, which determine whether there is a shipment or destination contract.[9]

In the following case, the court had to determine the proper measure of damages after a buyer breached a sales contract.

INCIDENTAL DAMAGES
All costs resulting from a breach of contract, including all reasonable expenses incurred because of the breach.

---

9. See Exhibit 11–2 for a definition of these contract terms, which are omitted from the 2003 amendments to Article 2 [Amended UCC 2–319 through 2–324].

CASE 12.3 ■ Utica Alloys, Inc. v. Alcoa, Inc.

United States District Court,
Northern District of New York, 2004.
303 F.Supp.2d 247.

FACTS Alcoa, Inc., through its business, generates scrap metal. Utica Alloys, Inc., buys and processes this type of scrap and sells it to its only user, General Electric Company (GE), which uses it in land-based power turbines. In July 2001, Utica agreed to buy all of Alcoa's scrap through August 2003. Their contract indexed the monthly price of the scrap to the monthly market price of nickel but contemplated that the parties would review this price semiannually. In November 2001, GE reduced its production of turbines, which lowered the market value of the scrap. This change was not reflected in Alcoa's arrangement with Utica, however, because the price in their contract was based on the market value of nickel. In January 2002, the opportunity arose to review the price of the scrap, and the parties began to negotiate while they continued to ship and process the scrap. In May, when the parties were unable to agree on a price, Alcoa stated that the contract was over, retrieved the scrap processed after January, and sold it to another party. Utica filed a suit in a federal district court against Alcoa, alleging in part unjust enrichment. Alcoa counterclaimed for breach of contract. The court entered a judgment in Alcoa's favor, holding that Utica breached the agreement by failing to pay for the scrap received after January. Alcoa asked for damages based on the difference between the contract price for the *unprocessed* scrap and the price at which the *processed* scrap sold after it was retrieved.

ISSUE Was Alcoa entitled to the amount of damages that it requested?

DECISION No. The court held that the proper measure of Alcoa's damages was the difference between the contract's monthly price for the *unprocessed* scrap and the monthly fair market value of *unprocessed* scrap.

REASON The court reasoned that the amount Alcoa sought "would serve as a double penalty to Utica Alloys, Inc. for processing the scrap." The court explained that without the contract with Utica, Alcoa would have sold the unprocessed scrap at the market price for unprocessed scrap. In other words, whether the scrap was processed after its sale to Utica was not part of the parties' contract. The court acknowledged that processing the scrap actually decreased its value in this case because of the reduction in demand for processed scrap. But the court pointed out that when Alcoa chose to end the contract in May, it accepted the processed scrap from Utica without paying for the cost of the processing. Alcoa "cannot be permitted in one breath to denounce processing as irrelevant to the contractual relationship, while in another embrace the market change of processed scrap as the yardstick for measuring its damages under the contract."

FOR CRITICAL ANALYSIS—Economic Consideration *How, specifically, should the amount of damages in this case be determined, considering that the contract called for monthly shipments and prices?*

WHEN THE GOODS ARE IN TRANSIT

If the seller or lessor has delivered the goods to a carrier or a bailee but the buyer or lessee has not as yet received them, the goods are said to be in transit. If, while the goods are in transit, the seller or lessor learns that the buyer or lessee is insolvent, the seller or lessor can stop the carrier or bailee from delivering the goods, regardless of the quantity of goods shipped.

    ■ **EXAMPLE 12.10** Suppose that Arturo Ortega orders a truckload of lumber from Timber Products, Inc., to be shipped to Ortega six weeks later. Ortega, who owes Timber Products for a past shipment, promises to pay the debt immediately and to pay for the current shipment as soon as it is received. After the lumber has been shipped, Timber Products is notified by a bankruptcy court judge that Ortega has filed a petition in bankruptcy and listed Timber Products as one of his creditors (see Chapter 16). If the goods are still in transit, Timber Products can stop the carrier from delivering the lumber to Ortega. ■ If the buyer or lessee is in breach but is not insolvent, the seller or lessor can stop the goods in transit only if the quantity shipped is at least a carload, a truckload, a planeload, or a larger shipment [UCC 2–705(1), 2A–526(1)].[10]

Requirements for Stopping Delivery　To stop delivery, the seller or lessor must *timely notify* the carrier or other bailee that the goods are to be returned or held for the seller or lessor. If the carrier has sufficient time to stop delivery, it must hold and deliver the goods according to the instructions of the seller or lessor, who is liable to the carrier for any additional costs incurred [UCC 2–705(3), 2A–526(3)].

Exceptions　UCC 2–705(2) and 2A–526(2) provide that the seller or lessor loses the right to stop delivery of goods in transit when any of the following events occur:

1 The buyer or lessee obtains possession of the goods.

2 The carrier acknowledges the rights of the buyer or lessee by reshipping or storing the goods for the buyer or lessee.

3 A bailee of the goods other than a carrier acknowledges that he or she is holding the goods for the buyer or lessee.

Additionally, in sales transactions, the seller loses the right to stop delivery of goods in transit when a negotiable document of title covering the goods has been negotiated (properly transferred, giving the buyer ownership rights in the goods) to the buyer [UCC 2–705(2)].

Once the seller or lessor reclaims the goods in transit, she or he can pursue the remedies allowed to sellers and lessors when the goods are in their possession. In other words, the seller or lessor who has reclaimed goods may do the following:

1 Cancel (rescind) the contract.

2 Resell the goods and recover any deficiency.

3 Sue for any deficiency between the contract price (or lease payments due) and the market price (or market lease payments), plus incidental damages.

4 Sue to recover the purchase price or lease payments due if the goods cannot be resold, plus incidental damages.

5 Sue to recover damages.

WHEN THE GOODS ARE IN THE POSSESSION OF THE BUYER OR LESSEE

When the buyer or lessee breaches a sales or lease contract and the goods are in the buyer's or lessee's possession, the UCC gives the seller or lessor the following limited remedies.

The Right to Recover the Purchase Price or Payments Due under the Lease Contract
If the buyer or lessee has accepted the goods but refuses to pay for them, the seller or lessor can sue for the purchase price of the goods or the lease payments due, plus incidental damages [UCC 2–709(1), 2A–529(1)].

The Right to Reclaim the Goods　In regard to sales contracts, if the buyer has received goods on credit and the seller discovers that the buyer is insolvent, the seller

RECALL Incidental damages include all reasonable expenses incurred because of a breach of contract.

---

10. The 2003 amendments to UCC Articles 2 and 2A omit the restriction that prohibited the stoppage of less than "a carload, truckload, planeload, or larger shipment" because carriers can now identify a shipment as small as a single package [Amended UCC 2–705(1), 2A–526(1)].

can demand return of the goods if the demand is made within ten days of the buyer's receipt of the goods. The seller can demand and reclaim the goods at any time if the buyer misrepresented his or her solvency in writing within three months prior to the delivery of the goods [UCC 2–702(2)].[11] The seller's right to reclaim the goods, however, is subject to the rights of a good faith purchaser or other subsequent buyer in the ordinary course of business who purchases the goods from the buyer before the seller reclaims them.

Under the UCC, a seller seeking to exercise the right to reclaim goods receives preferential treatment over the buyer's other creditors—the seller need only demand the return of the goods within ten days after the buyer has received them.[12] Because of this preferential treatment, the UCC provides that reclamation *bars* the seller from pursuing any other remedy as to these goods [UCC 2–702(3)].

In regard to lease contracts, if the lessee defaults (fails to make payments that are due, for example), the lessor may reclaim the leased goods that are in the lessee's possession [UCC 2A–525(2)].

◼ Remedies of the Buyer or Lessee

When the seller or lessor breaches the contract, the buyer or lessee has numerous remedies available under the UCC in addition to recovery of as much of the price as has been paid. Like the remedies available to sellers and lessors, the remedies of buyers and lessees depend on the circumstances existing at the time of the breach. (See the *Application* feature at the end of this chapter for some suggestions on what to do when a contract is breached.)

WHEN THE SELLER OR LESSOR REFUSES TO DELIVER THE GOODS

If the seller or lessor refuses to deliver the goods or the buyer or lessee has rejected the goods, the remedies available to the buyer or lessee include those discussed here.

The Right to Cancel the Contract   When a seller or lessor fails to make proper delivery or repudiates the contract, the buyer or lessee can cancel, or rescind, the contract. On notice of cancellation, the buyer or lessee is relieved of any further obligations under the contract but retains all rights to other remedies against the seller [UCC 2–711(1), 2A–508(1)(a)].

The Right to Recover the Goods   If a buyer or lessee has made a partial or full payment for goods that remain in the possession of the seller or lessor, the buyer or lessee can recover the goods if the seller or lessor is insolvent or becomes insolvent within ten days after receiving the first payment and if the goods are identified to the contract.[13] To exercise this right, the buyer or lessee must tender to the seller any unpaid balance of the purchase price [UCC 2–502, 2A–522].

NOTE A seller or lessor breaches a contract by wrongfully failing to deliver the goods, delivering nonconforming goods, making an improper tender of the goods, or repudiating the contract.

---

11. The 2003 amendments to UCC Article 2 omit the ten-day limitation and the three-month exception to the ten-day limitation, referring instead to "a reasonable time" [Amended UCC 2–702(2)].
12. A seller who has delivered goods to an insolvent buyer also receives preferential treatment if the buyer enters into bankruptcy proceedings (discussed in Chapter 16).
13. The 2003 amendments to UCC Articles 2 and 2A create a new right to recover goods identified to a contract when a consumer buyer or lessee makes a down payment and the seller or lessor then repudiates the contract or lease or fails to deliver the goods [Amended UCC 2–502, 2A–522].

The Right to Obtain Specific Performance A buyer or lessee can obtain specific performance when the goods are unique and the remedy at law is inadequate [UCC 2–716(1), 2A–521(1)]. Ordinarily, a successful suit for money damages is sufficient to place a buyer or lessee in the position he or she would have occupied if the seller or lessor had fully performed. When the contract is for the purchase of a particular work of art or a similarly unique item, however, money damages may not be sufficient. Under these circumstances, equity will require that the seller or lessor perform exactly by delivering the particular goods identified to the contract (a remedy of specific performance).

The Right of Cover In certain situations, buyers and lessees can protect themselves by obtaining **cover**—that is, by purchasing or leasing other goods to substitute for those due under the contract. This option is available when the seller or lessor repudiates the contract or fails to deliver the goods or when a buyer or lessee has rightfully rejected goods or revoked acceptance.

In obtaining cover, the buyer or lessee must act in good faith and without unreasonable delay [UCC 2–712, 2A–518]. After purchasing or leasing substitute goods, the buyer or lessee can recover from the seller or lessor the difference between the cost of cover and the contract price (or lease payments), plus incidental and consequential damages, less the expenses (such as delivery costs) that were saved as a result of the breach [UCC 2–712, 2–715, 2A–518]. Consequential damages are any losses suffered by the buyer or lessee that the seller or lessor could have foreseen (had reason to know about) at the time of contract formation and any injury to the buyer's or lessee's person or property proximately resulting from the contract's breach [UCC 2–715(2), 2A–520(2)].

Buyers and lessees are not required to cover, and failure to do so will not bar them from using any other remedies available under the UCC. A buyer or lessee who fails to cover, however, may *not* be able to collect consequential damages that could have been avoided by purchasing or leasing substitute goods.

The Right to Replevy Goods Buyers and lessees also have the right to replevy goods. **Replevin**[14] is an action to recover specific goods in the hands of a party who is wrongfully withholding them from the other party. Outside the UCC, the term *replevin* refers to a *prejudgment process* (a proceeding that takes place prior to a court's judgment) that permits the seizure of specific personal property in which a party claims a right or an interest. Under the UCC, the buyer or lessee can replevy goods subject to the contract if the seller or lessor has repudiated or breached the contract. To maintain an action to replevy goods, usually buyers and lessees must show that they are unable to cover for the goods after a reasonable effort [UCC 2–716(3), 2A–521(3)].

The Right to Recover Damages If a seller or lessor repudiates the sales contract or fails to deliver the goods, or the buyer or lessee has rightfully rejected or revoked acceptance of the goods, the buyer or lessee can sue for damages. The measure of recovery is the difference between the contract price (or lease payments) and the market price of (or lease payments that could be obtained for) the goods at the time the buyer (or lessee) *learned* of the breach.[15] The market price or market lease payments

---

COVER
Under the UCC, a remedy that allows the buyer or lessee, on the seller's or lessor's breach, to purchase the goods, in good faith and within a reasonable time, from another seller or lessor and substitute them for the goods due under the contract. If the cost of cover exceeds the cost of the contract goods, the breaching seller or lessor will be liable to the buyer or lessee for the difference, plus incidental and consequential damages.

REPLEVIN
An action to recover identified goods in the hands of a party who is wrongfully withholding them from the other party. Under the UCC, this remedy is usually available only if the buyer or lessee is unable to cover.

RECALL Consequential damages compensate for a loss (such as lost profits) that is not direct but was reasonably foreseeable at the time of the breach.

---

14. Pronounced ruh-*pleh*-vun.

15. The 2003 amendments to UCC Article 2 change the rule that the time for measuring damages is the time the buyer learned of the breach. Unless repudiation is involved, the buyer's damages will be based on the market price at the time for tender [Amended UCC 2–713(1)(a)].

Professor Cooper at the University of Missouri Law School posts a "quick and dirty" review of the remedies available under the UCC at **http://www1.law.umkc.edu/ faculty/cooper/listfaq. htm#UCC%20Remedies**.

are determined at the place where the seller or lessor was supposed to deliver the goods. The buyer or lessee can also recover incidental and consequential damages, less the expenses that were saved as a result of the breach [UCC 2–713, 2A–519].

■ **EXAMPLE 12.11** Schilling orders ten thousand bushels of wheat from Valdone for $5 a bushel, with delivery due on June 14 and payment due on June 20. Valdone does not deliver on June 14. On June 14, the market price of wheat is $5.50 per bushel. Schilling chooses to do without the wheat. He sues Valdone for damages for nondelivery. Schilling can recover $0.50 × 10,000, or $5,000, plus any expenses the breach may have caused him. The measure of damages is the market price less the contract price on the day Schilling was to have received delivery. Any expenses Schilling saved by the breach would be deducted from the damages. ■

WHEN THE SELLER OR LESSOR DELIVERS NONCONFORMING GOODS

When the seller or lessor delivers nonconforming goods, the buyer or lessee has several remedies available under the UCC.

The Right to Reject the Goods   If either the goods or the tender of the goods by the seller or lessor fails to conform to the contract *in any respect,* the buyer or lessee can reject the goods. If some of the goods conform to the contract, the buyer or lessee can keep the conforming goods and reject the rest [UCC 2–601, 2A–509]. If the buyer or lessee rejects the goods, she or he may then obtain cover, cancel the contract, or sue for damages for breach of contract, just as if the seller or lessor had refused to deliver the goods (see the earlier discussion of these remedies).

Timeliness and Reason for Rejection Required.   The buyer or lessee must reject the goods within a reasonable amount of time and must notify the seller or lessor seasonably—that is, in a timely fashion or at the proper time [UCC 2–602(1), 2A–509(2)]. If the buyer or lessee fails to reject the goods within a reasonable amount of time, acceptance will be presumed. Is there any way to keep the rejection period within more predictable limits than "a reasonable time"? See this chapter's *Letter of the Law* feature for a discussion of a case involving a contractually stipulated time period concerning the buyer's right of rejection.

Note that when rejecting goods, the buyer or lessee must designate defects that would have been apparent to the seller or lessor on reasonable inspection. Failure to do so precludes the buyer or lessee from using such defects to justify rejection or to establish breach when the seller could have cured the defects if they had been stated seasonably [UCC 2–605, 2A–514].[16]

Duties of Merchant Buyers and Lessees When Goods Are Rejected.   If a merchant buyer or lessee rightfully rejects goods, and the seller or lessor has no agent or business at the place of rejection, the buyer or lessee is required to follow any reasonable instructions received from the seller or lessor with respect to the goods controlled by the buyer or lessee. The buyer or lessee is entitled to reimbursement for the care and cost entailed in following the instructions [UCC 2–603, 2A–511]. The same requirements hold if the buyer or lessee rightfully revokes his or her acceptance of the goods at some later time [UCC 2–608(3), 2A–517(5)]. (Revocation of acceptance will be discussed shortly.)

Employees at a retail establishment sort through boxes of nonconforming goods that will be returned to the manufacturer. If the merchant buyer is following the seller's instructions for rejecting the goods, who should bear the cost of having the employees perform this task? (AP Photo/Douglas C. Pizac)

---

16. The 2003 amendments to UCC 2–605 and 2A–514 change this restriction. Under the amendments, a buyer's or lessee's failure to disclose the nature of the defect affects only the right to reject or revoke acceptance, not the right to establish a breach. The new sections expressly require that the seller or lessor has had a right to cure, as well as the ability to cure.

LETTER OF THE LAW Every Day Counts

As mentioned earlier, the term *reasonable* appears throughout the UCC. With respect to the right of rejection, the UCC provides that the buyer or lessee must reject goods within a "reasonable" time. The UCC makes it clear, however, that parties who desire more certainty can include a provision in their contract specifying the time period for rejection. UCC 1–204(1) states that "whenever this act requires any action to be taken within a reasonable time, any time which is not manifestly unreasonable may be fixed by agreement." Suppose, though, that a contract states that the buyer's right to reject the goods is limited to ten days. Even though "ten days" is more specific than "a reasonable time," there is still no guarantee that a dispute will not arise over the letter of the law in this instance.

In one case, for example, a question arose as to whether a ten-day period included holidays and weekends. If so, then the buyer's notification of rejection was just one day late. The court gave the buyer the benefit of the doubt on the inclusion of holidays and weekends but did not agree with the buyer that just one day late was acceptable. The letter of the law, as expressed in the parties' contract, had stated ten days, not eleven. Therefore, concluded the court, the buyer's failure to reject the goods within the ten-day period constituted an acceptance of the goods.[a]

THE BOTTOM LINE

This case underscores the importance of making sure that both parties (1) understand precisely what a certain contract term means and (2) take each contract term seriously.

a. *Northwest Airlines, Inc. v. Aeroservice, Inc.*, 168 F.Supp.2d 1052 (D.Minn. 2001).

If no instructions are forthcoming and the goods are perishable or threaten to decline in value quickly, the buyer can resell the goods in good faith, taking the appropriate reimbursement from the proceeds. In addition, the buyer is entitled to a selling commission (not to exceed 10 percent of the gross proceeds) [UCC 2–603(1), (2); 2A–511(1)]. If the goods are not perishable, the buyer or lessee may store them for the seller or lessor or reship them to the seller or lessor [UCC 2–604, 2A–512].

Buyers who rightfully reject goods that remain in their possession or control have a *security interest* in the goods (basically, a legal claim to the goods to the extent necessary to recover expenses, costs, and the like—see Chapter 16). The security interest encompasses any payments the buyer has made for the goods, as well as any expenses incurred with regard to inspection, receipt, transportation, care, and custody of the goods [UCC 2–711(3)]. A buyer with a security interest in the goods is a "person in the position of a seller." This gives the buyer the same rights as an unpaid seller. Thus, the buyer can resell, withhold delivery of, or stop delivery of the goods. A buyer who chooses to resell must account to the seller for any amounts received in excess of the security interest [UCC 2–706(6), 2–711].

Revocation of Acceptance   Acceptance of the goods precludes the buyer or lessee from exercising the right of rejection, but it does not necessarily preclude the buyer or lessee from pursuing other remedies. In certain circumstances, a buyer or lessee is permitted to *revoke* her or his acceptance of the goods. Acceptance of a lot or a commercial unit can be revoked if the nonconformity *substantially* impairs the value of the lot or unit and if one of the following factors is present:

1 If acceptance was predicated on the reasonable assumption that the nonconformity would be cured, and it has not been cured within a reasonable period of time [UCC 2–608(1)(a), 2A–517(1)(a)].[17]

---

17. Under the 2003 amendments to UCC 2–508 and 2A–513, after a justifiable revocation of acceptance, cure is not available as a matter of right in a consumer contract or lease.

2 If the buyer or lessee did not discover the nonconformity before acceptance, either because it was difficult to discover before acceptance or because assurances made by the seller or lessor that the goods were conforming kept the buyer or lessee from inspecting the goods [UCC 2–608(1)(b), 2A–517(1)(b)].

Revocation of acceptance is not effective until the seller or lessor is notified, which must occur within a reasonable time after the buyer or lessee either discovers *or should have discovered* the grounds for revocation. Additionally, revocation must occur before the goods have undergone any substantial change (such as spoilage) not caused by their own defects [UCC 2–608(2), 2A–517(4)].

The Right to Recover Damages for Accepted Goods A buyer or lessee who has accepted nonconforming goods may also keep the goods and recover damages caused by the breach. The buyer or lessee, however, must notify the seller or lessor of the breach within a reasonable time after the defect was or should have been discovered. Failure to give notice of the defects (breach) to the seller or lessor bars the buyer or lessee from pursuing any remedy [UCC 2–607(3), 2A–516(3)].[18] In addition, the parties to a sales or lease contract can insert a provision requiring that the buyer or lessee give notice of any defects in the goods within a set period.

When the goods delivered and accepted are not as promised, the measure of damages equals the difference between the value of the goods as accepted and their value if they had been delivered as warranted, plus incidental and consequential damages if appropriate [UCC 2–714(2), 2A–519(4)]. For this and other types of breaches in which the buyer or lessee has accepted the goods, the buyer or lessee is entitled to recover for any loss "resulting in the ordinary course of events . . . as determined in any manner which is reasonable" [UCC 2–714(1), 2A–519(3)]. The UCC also permits the buyer or lessee, with proper notice to the seller or lessor, to deduct all or any part of the damages from the price or lease payments still due and payable to the seller or lessor [UCC 2–717, 2A–516(1)].

Containers sit on ships as they wait to be unloaded at a port in the United States. If the buyer discovers that some of the goods are defective, what remedies under the UCC are available to the buyer? (Susan Goldman, Bloomberg News/Landov)

■ Limitation of Remedies

The parties to a sales or lease contract can vary their respective rights and obligations by contractual agreement. For example, a seller and buyer can expressly provide for remedies in addition to those provided in the UCC. They can also provide remedies in lieu of those provided in the UCC, or they can change the measure of damages. The seller can provide that the buyer's only remedy on breach of warranty will be repair or replacement of the item, or the seller can limit the buyer's remedy to return of the goods and refund of the purchase price. In sales and lease contracts, an agreed-on remedy is in addition to those provided in the UCC unless the parties expressly agree that the remedy is exclusive of all others [UCC 2–719(1), 2A–503(1)].

WHEN AN EXCLUSIVE REMEDY FAILS IN ITS ESSENTIAL PURPOSE

If the parties state that a remedy is exclusive, then it is the sole remedy. When circumstances cause an exclusive remedy to fail in its essential purpose, however, it is no longer considered exclusive, and the buyer or lessee may pursue other remedies

---

18. Under the 2003 amendments to UCC Articles 2 and 2A, a buyer or lessee who fails to give timely notice is barred from a remedy for the breach but *only* "to the extent that the seller is prejudiced by the failure." In other words, if the seller is not harmed by the buyer's failure to notify, the buyer may still recover. See Amended UCC 2–607(3)(a), 2A–516(3)(a).

For an example of a contract providing for an exclusive remedy, see the "Warranty and Limited Remedy" of 3M Company, which is online at

http://www.mmm.com/promote/warranty.htm.

available under the UCC [UCC 2–719(2), 2A–503(2)]. ■ **EXAMPLE 12.12** Suppose that a sales contract limits the buyer's remedy to repair or replacement. If the goods at issue cannot be repaired and no replacements are available, the exclusive remedy has failed in its essential purpose. In this situation, the buyer normally is entitled to seek other remedies provided to a buyer by the UCC. ■

LIMITATIONS ON CONSEQUENTIAL DAMAGES

A contract can limit or exclude consequential damages, provided the limitation is not unconscionable. When the buyer or lessee is a consumer, the limitation of consequential damages for personal injuries resulting from nonconforming goods is *prima facie* (on its face) unconscionable. The limitation of consequential damages is not necessarily unconscionable, however, when the loss is commercial in nature—for example, if the loss consists of lost profits and property damage [UCC 2–719(3), 2A–503(3)].

ETHICAL ISSUE 12.1

When an exclusive remedy fails in its essential purpose, should a clause limiting consequential damages be enforced? The UCC makes it clear that a contract clause providing for an exclusive remedy is enforceable—*unless* the exclusive remedy fails in its essential purpose. If the exclusive remedy fails in its essential purpose, then the buyer can pursue the full panoply of remedies available under the UCC. One of the remedies available to the buyer is to sue for damages, including consequential damages. Yet what if the contract, in addition to providing for an exclusive remedy, also excludes consequential damages? In this situation, does the failure of the exclusive remedy effectively eliminate the clause limiting consequential damages?

The courts have reached different conclusions on this issue, as noted by the U.S. Court of Appeals for the Eighth Circuit in a case involving just this question. In that court's eyes, however, it was clear that when an exclusive remedy fails of its essential purpose, the aggrieved buyer should be able to "invoke any remedies available under the Uniform Commercial Code"—including "provable consequential damages"—even though the contract had specifically excluded consequential damages. According to the court, "To find otherwise would, in our opinion, undermine the protections afforded to parties under Section 2–719(2) and deprive [the buyer] of the substantial value of the bargain."[19] ■

STATUTE OF LIMITATIONS

An action for breach of contract under the UCC must be commenced *within four years after the cause of action accrues*—that is, within four years after the breach occurs. In addition to filing suit within the four-year period, a buyer or lessee who has accepted nonconforming goods usually must notify the breaching party of the breach within a reasonable time, or the aggrieved party is barred from pursuing any remedy [UCC 2–607(3)(a), 2A–516(3)]. The parties can agree in their contract to reduce this period to not less than one year, but cannot extend it beyond four years [UCC 2–725(1), 2A–506(1)]. A cause of action accrues for breach of warranty when the seller or lessor tenders delivery. This is the rule even if the aggrieved party is unaware that the cause of action has accrued [UCC 2–725(2), 2A–506(2)].[20]

19. *Arabian Agriculture Services Co. v. Chief Industries, Inc.*, 309 F.3d 479 (8th Cir. 2002).
20. The 2003 amendments to UCC 2–725 adjusts this time limit. A cause of action may be brought within the later of four years after the right of action accrues or one year after a breach is, or should have been, discovered, but no later than five years after the time that the right has accrued. Specific rules are included for determining when rights of action accrue. In addition, the four-year limitation period cannot be reduced in a consumer contract or lease [Amended UCC 2–725, 2A–506(1)].

APPLICATION  What Can You Do When a Contract Is Breached?*

A contract for the sale of goods has been breached. Can the dispute be settled without a trip to court? The answer depends on the willingness of the parties to agree on an appropriate remedy.

CONTRACTUAL CLAUSES ON APPLICABLE REMEDIES

Often, the parties to sales and lease contracts agree in advance, in their contracts, on what remedies will be applicable in the event of a breach. This may take the form of a contract provision restricting or expanding remedies available under the Uniform Commercial Code [UCC 2–719]. Such clauses help to reduce uncertainty and the necessity for costly litigation.

WHEN THE CONTRACT IS SILENT ON APPLICABLE REMEDIES

If your agreement does not cover a breach of contract and you are the nonbreaching party, the UCC gives you a variety of alternatives. What you need to do is analyze the remedies that are available if you choose to go to court, put these remedies in order of priority, and then predict how successful you might be in pursuing each remedy. Next, look at the position of the breaching party to determine the basis for negotiating a settlement.

*This *Application* is not meant to substitute for the services of an attorney who is licensed to practice law in your state.

For example, when defective goods are delivered and accepted, usually it is preferable for the buyer and seller to reach an agreement on a reduced purchase price. Practically speaking, the buyer may be unable to obtain a partial refund from the seller. UCC 2–717 allows the buyer in such circumstances to give notice of the intention to deduct the damages from any part of the purchase price not yet paid. If you are a buyer who has accepted defective goods and has not yet paid in full, it may be appropriate for you to exercise your rights under UCC 2–717 and not pay in full when you make your final payment. Remember that most breaches of contract do not end up in court—they are settled beforehand.

CHECKLIST FOR THE NONBREACHING PARTY TO A CONTRACT

1. Ascertain if a remedy is explicitly written into your contract. Use that remedy, if possible, to avoid litigation.
2. If no specific remedy is available, look to the UCC.
3. Assess how successful you might be in pursuing a remedy if you go to court.
4. Analyze the position of the breaching party.
5. Determine whether a negotiated settlement is preferable to a lawsuit, which is best done by consulting your attorney.

■ KEY TERMS

CHAPTER SUMMARY ■ Sales and Leases: Performance and Breach

	REQUIREMENTS OF PERFORMANCE
Obligations of the Seller or Lessor (See pages 358–366.)	1. The seller or lessor must tender *conforming* goods to the buyer. Tender must take place at a *reasonable hour* and in a *reasonable manner*. Under the perfect tender doctrine, the seller or lessor must tender goods that conform exactly to the terms of the contract [UCC 2–503(1), 2A–508(1)].

CHAPTER SUMMARY Sales and Leases: Performance and Breach—Continued

Obligations of the Seller or Lessor—Continued	2. If the seller or lessor tenders nonconforming goods prior to the performance date and the buyer or lessee rejects them, the seller or lessor may *cure* (repair or replace the goods) within the contract time for performance [UCC 2–508(1), 2A–513(1)]. If the seller or lessor had reasonable grounds to believe the buyer or lessee would accept the tendered goods, on the buyer's or lessee's rejection the seller or lessor has a reasonable time to substitute conforming goods without liability [UCC 2–508(2), 2A–513(2)].
	3. If the agreed-on means of delivery becomes impracticable or unavailable, the seller must substitute an alternative means (such as a different carrier) if one is available [UCC 2–614(1)].
	4. If a seller or lessor tenders nonconforming goods in any one installment under an installment contract, the buyer or lessee may reject the installment only if its value is substantially impaired and cannot be cured. The entire installment contract is breached when one or more nonconforming installments *substantially* impair the value of the *whole* contract [UCC 2–612, 2A–510].
	5. When performance becomes commercially impracticable owing to circumstances that were not foreseeable when the contract was formed, the perfect tender rule no longer holds [UCC 2–615, 2A–405].
Obligations of the Buyer or Lessee (See pages 366–367.)	1. On tender of delivery by the seller or lessor, the buyer or lessee must pay for the goods at the time and place the buyer or lessee *receives* the goods, even if the place of shipment is the place of delivery, unless the sale is made on credit. Payment may be made by any method generally acceptable in the commercial world unless the seller demands cash [UCC 2–310, 2–511]. In lease contracts, the lessee must make lease payments in accordance with the contract [UCC 2A–516(1)].
	2. Unless otherwise agreed, the buyer or lessee has an absolute right to inspect the goods before acceptance [UCC 2–513(1), 2A–515(1)].
	3. The buyer or lessee can manifest acceptance of delivered goods expressly in words or by conduct or by failing to reject the goods after a reasonable period of time following inspection or after having had a reasonable opportunity to inspect them [UCC 2–606(1), 2A–515(1)]. A buyer will be deemed to have accepted goods if he or she performs any act inconsistent with the seller's ownership [UCC 2–606(1)(c)].
	4. Following the acceptance of delivered goods, the buyer or lessee may revoke acceptance only if the nonconformity *substantially* impairs the value of the unit or lot and if one of the following factors is present:
	a. Acceptance was predicated on the reasonable assumption that the nonconformity would be cured and it was not cured within a reasonable time [UCC 2–608(1)(a), 2A–517(1)(a)].
	b. The buyer or lessee did not discover the nonconformity before acceptance, either because it was difficult to discover before acceptance or because the seller's or lessor's assurance that the goods were conforming kept the buyer or lessee from inspecting the goods [UCC 2–608(1)(b), 2A–517(1)(b)].
Anticipatory Repudiation (See pages 367–368.)	If, before the time for performance, either party clearly indicates to the other an intention not to perform, under UCC 2–610 and 2A–402 the aggrieved party may do the following:
	1. Await performance by the repudiating party for a commercially reasonable time.
	2. Resort to any remedy for breach.
	3. In either situation, suspend performance.

(Continued)

CHAPTER SUMMARY Sales and Leases: Performance and Breach—Continued

REMEDIES FOR BREACH OF CONTRACT

Remedies of the Seller or Lessor (See pages 368–372.)	1. *When the goods are in the possession of the seller or lessor*—The seller or lessor may do the following: a. Cancel the contract [UCC 2–703(f), 2A–523(1)(a)]. b. Withhold delivery [UCC 2–703(a), 2A–523(1)(c)]. c. Resell or dispose of the goods [UCC 2–703(d), 2–706(1), 2A–523(1)(e), 2A–527(1)]. d. Sue to recover the purchase price or lease payments due [UCC 2–703(e), 2–709(1), 2A–529(1)]. e. Sue to recover damages [UCC 2–703(e), 2–708, 2A–528]. 2. *When the goods are in transit*—The seller or lessor may stop the carrier or bailee from delivering the goods [UCC 2–705, 2A–526]. 3. *When the goods are in the possession of the buyer or lessee*—The seller or lessor may do the following: a. Sue to recover the purchase price or lease payments due [UCC 2–709(1), 2A–529(1)]. b. Reclaim the goods. A seller may reclaim goods received by an insolvent buyer if the demand is made within ten days of receipt (reclaiming goods excludes all other remedies) [UCC 2–702]; a lessor may repossess goods if the lessee is in default [UCC 2A–525(2)].
Remedies of the Buyer or Lessee (See pages 372–376.)	1. *When the seller or lessor refuses to deliver the goods*—The buyer or lessee may do the following: a. Cancel the contract [UCC 2–711(1), 2A–508(1)(a)]. b. Recover the goods if the seller or lessor becomes insolvent within ten days after receiving the first payment and the goods are identified to the contract [UCC 2–502, 2A–522]. c. Obtain specific performance (when the goods are unique and when the remedy at law is inadequate) [UCC 2–716(1), 2A–521(1)]. d. Obtain cover [UCC 2–712, 2A–518]. e. Replevy the goods (if cover is unavailable) [UCC 2–716(3), 2A–521(3)]. f. Sue to recover damages [UCC 2–713, 2A–519]. 2. *When the seller or lessor delivers or tenders delivery of nonconforming goods*—The buyer or lessee may do the following: a. Reject the goods [UCC 2–601, 2A–509]. b. Revoke acceptance (in certain circumstances) [UCC 2–608, 2A–517]. c. Accept the goods and recover damages [UCC 2–607, 2–714, 2–717, 2A–519].
Limitation of Remedies (See pages 376–377.)	Remedies may be limited in sales or lease contracts by agreement of the parties. If the contract states that a remedy is exclusive, then that is the sole remedy unless the remedy fails in its essential purpose. Sellers and lessors can also limit the rights of buyers and lessees to consequential damages unless the limitation is unconscionable [UCC 2–719, 2A–503].
Statute of Limitations (See page 377.)	The UCC has a four-year statute of limitations for actions involving breach of contract. By agreement, the parties to a sales or lease contract can reduce this period to not less than one year, but they cannot extend it beyond four years [UCC 2–725(1), 2A–506(1)].

FOR REVIEW

Answers for the even-numbered questions in this For Review *section can be found in Appendix I at the end of this text.*

1 What are the respective obligations of the parties under a contract for the sale or lease of goods?

2 What is the perfect tender rule? What are some important exceptions to this rule that apply to sales and lease contracts?

3 What options are available to the nonbreaching party when the other party to a sales or lease contract repudiates the contract prior to the time for performance?

4 What remedies are available to a seller or lessor when the buyer or lessee breaches the contract? What remedies are available to a buyer or lessee if the seller or lessor breaches the contract?

5 In contracts subject to the UCC, are parties free to limit the remedies available to the nonbreaching party on a breach of contract? If so, in what ways?

QUESTIONS AND CASE PROBLEMS

12–1. Remedies. Genix, Inc., has contracted to sell Larson five hundred washing machines of a certain model at list price. Genix is to ship the goods on or before December 1. Genix produces one thousand washing machines of this model but has not yet prepared Larson's shipment. On November 1, Larson repudiates the contract. Discuss the remedies available to Genix in this situation.

12–2. Right of Inspection. Cummings ordered two model X Super Fidelity speakers from Jamestown Wholesale Electronics, Inc. Jamestown shipped the speakers via United Parcel Service, C.O.D. (collect on delivery), although Cummings had not requested or agreed to a C.O.D. shipment of the goods. When the speakers were delivered, Cummings refused to accept them because he would not be able to inspect them before payment. Jamestown claimed that it had shipped conforming goods and that Cummings had breached their contract. Had Cummings breached the contract? Explain.

12–3. Anticipatory Repudiation. Moore contracted in writing to sell her 1996 Ford Taurus to Hammer for $8,500. Moore agreed to deliver the car on Wednesday, and Hammer promised to pay the $8,500 on the following Friday. On Tuesday, Hammer informed Moore that he would not be buying the car after all. By Friday, Hammer had changed his mind again and tendered $8,500 to Moore. Moore, although she had not sold the car to another party, refused the tender and refused to deliver. Hammer claimed that Moore had breached their contract. Moore contended that Hammer's repudiation released her from her duty to perform under the contract. Who is correct, and why?

12–4. Remedies. Rodriguez is an antique car collector. He contracts to purchase spare parts for a 1938 engine from Gerrard. These parts are not made anymore and are scarce. To get the contract with Gerrard, Rodriguez has to pay 50 percent of the purchase price in advance. On May 1, Rodriguez sends the required payment, which is received on May 2. On May 3, Gerrard, having found another buyer willing to pay substantially more for the parts, informs Rodriguez that he will not deliver as

contracted. That same day, Rodriguez learns that Gerrard is insolvent. Gerrard has the parts, and Rodriguez wants them. Discuss fully any remedies available to Rodriguez.

12–5. Limitation of Remedies. Destileria Serralles, Inc., a distributor of rum and other products, operates a rum bottling plant in Puerto Rico. Figgie International, Inc., contracted with Serralles to provide bottle-labeling equipment capable of placing a clear label on a clear bottle of "Cristal" rum within a raised glass oval. The contract stated that Serralles's remedy, in case of a breach of contract, was limited to repair, replacement, or refund. When the equipment was installed in the Serralles plant, problems arose immediately. Figgie attempted to repair the equipment, but when it still did not work properly several months later, Figgie refunded the purchase price and Serralles returned the equipment. Serralles asked Figgie to pay for Serralles's losses caused by the failure of the equipment and by the delay in obtaining alternative machinery. Figgie filed a suit in a federal district court, asserting that it owed nothing to Serralles because the remedy for breach was limited to repair, replacement, or refund. Serralles responded that the limitation had failed in its essential purpose. In whose favor will the court resolve this dispute? Why? [*Figgie International, Inc. v. Destileria Serralles, Inc.*, 190 F.3d 252 (4th Cir. 1999)]

CASE PROBLEM WITH SAMPLE ANSWER

12–6. Metro-North Commuter Railroad Co. decided to install a fall-protection system for elevated walkways, roof areas, and interior catwalks in Grand Central Terminal, in New York City. The system was needed to ensure the safety of Metro-North employees when they worked at great heights on the interior and exterior of the terminal. Sinco, Inc., proposed a system called "Sayfglida," which involved a harness worn by the worker, a network of cables, and metal clips or sleeves called "Sayflinks" that connected the harness to the cables. Metro-North agreed to pay $197,325 for the installation of this system by June 26, 1999. Because the system's reliability was crucial, the contract required certain quality control processes. During a training session for Metro-North employees on June 29, the Sayflink sleeves fell apart. Within two days, Sinco manufactured and delivered two different types of replacement clips without subjecting them to the contract's quality control process, but Metro-North rejected them. Sinco suggested other possible solutions, which Metro-North did not accept. In September, Metro-North terminated its contract with Sinco and awarded the work to Surety, Inc., at a price of about $348,000. Sinco filed a suit in a federal district court, alleging breach of contract. Metro-North counterclaimed for its cost of cover. In whose favor should the court rule, and why? [*Sinco, Inc. v. Metro-North Commuter Railroad Co.,* 133 F.Supp.2d 308 (S.D.N.Y. 2001)]

After you have answered this problem, compare your answer with the sample answer given on the Web site that accompanies this text. Go to <u>http://blt.westbuslaw.com</u>, select "Chapter 12," and click on "Case Problem with Sample Answer."

12–7. Acceptance. In April 1996, Excalibur Oil Group, Inc., applied for credit and opened an account with Standard Distributors, Inc., to obtain snack foods and other items for Excalibur's convenience stores. For three months, Standard delivered the goods and Excalibur paid the invoices. In July, Standard was dissolved and its assets were distributed to J. F. Walker Co. Walker continued to deliver the goods to Excalibur, which continued to pay the invoices until November, when the firm began to experience financial difficulties. By January 1997, Excalibur owed Walker $54,241.77. Walker then dealt with Excalibur only on a collect-on-delivery basis until Excalibur's stores closed in 1998. Walker filed a suit in a Pennsylvania state court against Excalibur and its owner to recover amounts due on unpaid invoices. To successfully plead its case, Walker had to show that there was a contract between the parties. One question was whether Excalibur had manifested acceptance of the goods delivered by Walker. How does a buyer manifest acceptance? Was there an acceptance in this case? In whose favor should the court rule, and why? [*J. F. Walker Co. v. Excalibur Oil Group, Inc.,* 792 A.2d 1269 (Pa.Super. 2002)]

12–8. Right of Assurance. Advanced Polymer Sciences, Inc. (APS), based in Ohio, makes polymers and resins for use as protective coatings in industrial applications. APS also owns the technology for equipment used to make certain composite fibers. SAVA gumarska in kemijska industria d.d. (SAVA), based in Slovenia, makes rubber goods. In 1999, SAVA and APS contracted to form SAVA Advanced Polymers proizvodno podjetje d.o.o. (SAVA AP) to make and distribute APS products in Eastern Europe. Their contract provided for, among other things, the alteration of a facility to make the products using spe-

cially made equipment to be sold by APS to SAVA. Disputes arose between the parties, and in August 2000, SAVA stopped work on the new facility. APS then notified SAVA that it was stopping the manufacture of the equipment and "insist[ed] on knowing what is SAVA's intention towards this venture." In October, SAVA told APS that it was canceling their contract. In subsequent litigation, SAVA claimed that APS had repudiated the contract when it stopped making the equipment. What might APS assert in its defense? How should the court rule? Explain. [*SAVA gumarska in kemijska industria d.d. v. Advanced Polymer Sciences, Inc.,* 128 S.W.3d 304 (Tex.App.—Dallas 2004)]

A QUESTION OF ETHICS

12–9. Bobby Murray Chevrolet, Inc., contracted to supply 1,200 school bus chassis to local school boards. The contract stated that "products of any manufacturer may be offered," but Bobby Murray submitted its orders exclusively to General Motors Corp. (GMC). When a shortage in automatic transmissions occurred, GMC informed the dealer that it could not fill the orders. Bobby Murray told the school boards, which then bought the chassis from another dealer. The boards sued Bobby Murray for breach of contract. The dealer responded that its obligation to perform was excused under the doctrine of commercial impracticability, in part because of GMC's failure to fill its orders. Given these facts, answer the following questions. [*Alamance County Board of Education v. Bobby Murray Chevrolet, Inc.,* 121 N.C.App. 222, 465 S.E.2d 306 (1996)]

1. How will the court likely decide this issue? What factors will the court consider in making its decision? Discuss fully.
2. If the decision were yours to make, would you excuse Bobby Murray from its performance obligations in these circumstances? Would your decision be any different if Bobby Murray had specified in its contract that GMC would be the exclusive source of supply instead of stating that "products of any manufacturer may be offered"?
3. Generally, how does the doctrine of commercial impracticability attempt to balance the rights of both parties to a contract?

FOR CRITICAL ANALYSIS

12–10. Under what circumstances should courts not allow fully informed contracting parties to agree to limit remedies?

INTERNET EXERCISES

Go to the *Business Law Today: The Essentials* home page at <u>http://blt.westbuslaw.com</u>, select "Chapter 12," and click on "Internet Exercises." There you will find the following Internet research exercises that you can perform to learn more about topics covered in this chapter.

Activity 12–1: LEGAL PERSPECTIVE—The Right to Reject Goods

Activity 12–2: MANAGEMENT PERSPECTIVE—Good Faith and Fair Dealing

BEFORE THE TEST

Go to the *Business Law Today: The Essentials* home page at <u>http://blt.westbuslaw.com</u>, select "Chapter 12," and click on "Interactive Quizzes." You will find at least twenty interactive questions relating to this chapter.

CHAPTER 13

Warranties, Product Liability, and Consumer Law

"I'll warrant him heart-whole."
William Shakespeare, 1564–1616
(English dramatist and poet)

CHAPTER OUTLINE

■ **WARRANTIES**

■ **PRODUCT LIABILITY**

■ **STRICT PRODUCT LIABILITY**

■ **DEFENSES TO PRODUCT LIABILITY**

■ **CONSUMER PROTECTION LAWS**

▪▪ LEARNING OBJECTIVES

After reading this chapter, you should be able to answer the following questions:

1 What factors determine whether a seller's or lessor's statement constitutes an express warranty or mere "puffing"?

2 What implied warranties arise under the UCC?

3 Can a manufacturer be held liable to any person who suffers an injury proximately caused by the manufacturer's negligently made product?

4 What defenses to liability can be raised in a product liability lawsuit?

5 What are the major federal statutes providing for consumer protection?

Warranty is an age-old concept. In sales and lease law, a warranty is an assurance by one party of the existence of a fact on which the other party can rely. Just as William Shakespeare's character warranted his friend "heart-whole" in the play *As You Like It* in the quotation above, so sellers and lessors warrant to those who purchase or lease their goods that the goods are as represented or will be as promised.

The Uniform Commercial Code (UCC) has numerous rules governing product warranties as they occur in sales and lease contracts. That will be the subject matter of the first part of this chapter. A natural addition to the discussion is *product liability:* Who is liable to consumers, users, and bystanders for physical harm and property damage caused by a particular good or the use thereof? Product liability encompasses the contract theory of warranty, as well as the tort theories of negligence and strict liability (discussed in Chapter 4).

Consumer protection law consists of all statutes, agency rules, and common law judicial rulings that serve to protect the interest of consumers. State and federal laws regulate how businesses may advertise, engage in mail-order and telemarketing transactions, package and label their products, and so on. In addition, numerous local, state, and federal agencies now exist to aid the consumer in settling his or her grievances with sellers and producers. In the last part of this chapter, we examine some of the sources and some of the major issues of consumer protection.

◼ Warranties

Article 2 (on sales) and Article 2A (on leases) of the UCC designate several types of warranties that can arise in a sales or lease contract, including warranties of title, express warranties, and implied warranties.

WARRANTIES OF TITLE

Title warranty arises automatically in most sales contracts. The UCC imposes three types of warranties of title.

Good Title   In most cases, sellers warrant that they have good and valid title to the goods sold and that transfer of the title is rightful [UCC 2–312(1)(a)].[1]
◼ **EXAMPLE 13.1**   Sharon steals goods from Miguel and sells them to Carrie, who does not know that the goods are stolen. If Miguel reclaims the goods from Carrie, which he has a right to do, Carrie can then sue Sharon for breach of warranty. When Sharon sold Carrie the goods, Sharon *automatically* warranted to her that the title conveyed was valid and that its transfer was rightful. Because this was not in fact the case, Sharon breached the warranty of title imposed by UCC 2–312(1)(a) and became liable to the buyer for the appropriate damages. ◼

No Liens   A second warranty of title provided by the UCC protects buyers who are *unaware* of any encumbrances, or **liens** (see Chapter 16)—claims, charges, or liabilities against goods—at the time the contract is made [UCC 2–312(1)(b)]. This warranty protects buyers who, for example, unknowingly purchase goods that are subject to a creditor's security interest (see Chapter 16). If a creditor legally repossesses the goods from a buyer *who had no actual knowledge of the security interest,* the buyer can recover from the seller for breach of warranty.

Article 2A affords similar protection for lessees. Section 2A–211(1) provides that during the term of the lease, no claim of any third party will interfere with the lessee's enjoyment of the leasehold interest.

No Infringements   A merchant-seller is also deemed to warrant that the goods delivered are free from any copyright, trademark, or patent claims of a third person[2] [UCC 2–312(3), 2A–211(2)]. If this warranty is breached and the buyer is sued by the party holding copyright, trademark, or patent rights in the goods, the buyer must notify the seller of the litigation within a reasonable time to enable the seller

LIEN
An encumbrance on a property to satisfy a debt or protect a claim for payment of a debt.

---

1. Under the 2003 amendments to UCC 2–312(1)(a), good title also includes the warranty that the sale "shall not unreasonably expose the buyer to litigation because of any colorable [legitimate or reasonable] claim to or interest in the goods." Thus, the buyer is entitled not only to a good title but also to a marketable title that is free of "colorable claims."
2. Recall from Chapter 11 that a *merchant* is defined in UCC 2–104(1) as a person who deals in goods of the kind involved in the sales contract or who, by occupation, presents himself or herself as having knowledge or skill peculiar to the goods involved in the transaction.

to decide whether to defend the lawsuit. If the seller states in writing that she or he has decided to defend and agrees to bear all expenses, including that of an adverse judgment, then the buyer must let the seller undertake the litigation; otherwise, the buyer loses all rights against the seller if any infringement liability is established [UCC 2–607(3)(b), 2–607(5)(b)].

Article 2A provides for the same notice of litigation in situations that involve leases rather than sales [UCC 2A–516(3)(b), 2A–516(4)(b)]. There is an exception for leases to individual consumers for personal, family, or household purposes. A consumer who fails to notify the lessor within a reasonable time does not lose his or her remedy against the lessor for any liability established in the litigation [UCC 2A–516(3)(b)].

Disclaimer of Title Warranty   In an ordinary sales transaction, the title warranty can be disclaimed or modified only by *specific language* in the contract [UCC 2–312(2)]. For example, sellers can assert that they are transferring only such rights, title, and interest as they have in the goods. In a lease transaction, the disclaimer must "be specific, be by a writing, and be conspicuous" [UCC 2A–214(4)].

EXPRESS WARRANTIES

EXPRESS WARRANTY
A seller's or lessor's oral or written promise or affirmation of fact, ancillary to an underlying sales or lease agreement, as to the quality, description, or performance of the goods being sold or leased.

A seller or lessor can create an **express warranty** by making representations concerning the quality, condition, description, or performance potential of the goods. Under UCC 2–313 and 2A–210, express warranties arise when a seller or lessor indicates any of the following:

1 That the goods conform to any affirmation (declaration that something is true) or promise of fact that the seller or lessor makes to the buyer or lessee about the

A woman tries on a fur sweater in a New York furrier's shop. If the salesperson represents that the fur is mink, would that be enough to create an express warranty? Why or why not? (AP Photo/Tina Fineberg)

goods. Such affirmations or promises are usually made during the bargaining process. Statements such as "these drill bits will penetrate stainless steel—and without dulling" are express warranties.[3]

2 That the goods conform to any description of them. For example, a label that reads "Crate contains one 150-horsepower diesel engine" or a contract that calls for the delivery of a "camel's-hair coat" creates an express warranty.

3 That the goods conform to any sample or model of the goods shown to the buyer or lessee.[4]

The issue in the following case was whether the seller's statements constituted an express warranty.

---

3. The 2003 amendments to UCC Article 2 introduce the term *remedial promise,* which is "a promise by the seller to repair or replace the goods or to refund all or part of the price of the goods on the happening of a specified event" [Amended UCC 2–103(1)(n), 2–313(4)]. A remedial promise is not an express warranty, so a right of action for its breach accrues not at the time of tender, as with warranties, but if the promise is not performed when due [Amended UCC 2–725(2)(c)].

4. The 2003 amendments to the UCC distinguish between immediate buyers (those who enter into contracts with seller) and remote purchasers (those who buy or lease goods from immediate buyers) and extend sellers' obligations regarding new goods to remote purchasers. For example, suppose that a manufacturer sells packaged goods to a retailer, who resells the goods to a consumer. If a reasonable person in the position of the consumer would believe that a description on the package creates an obligation, the manufacturer is liable for its breach. [See Amended UCC 2–313, 2–313A, and 2–313B.]

CASE 13.1 Henley v. Philip Morris, Inc.

Court of Appeal of California,
First District, Division 4, 2004.
114 Cal.App.4th 1429,
9 Cal.Rptr.3d 29.

FACTS Patricia Henley began smoking cigarettes in 1961 or 1962, at the age of fifteen. She alleged that, at that time, nobody told her about the dangers of tobacco. There were no warnings on cigarette packages. She stated that she believed that cigarettes, which contained "[t]obacco, pure and simple," were "not a harmful product." Cigarette makers allegedly knew of a strong correlation between smoking and the incidence of serious illness, but they officially denied any link. Henley's first regular brand of cigarettes was "Marlboro Red," made by Philip Morris, Inc., which delivered relatively high amounts of tar and nicotine. It remained Henley's favorite brand throughout almost all of her thirty-five-year smoking history. Most of that time, she smoked one and a half to two packs a day. In the 1980s, she heard that "low-tar cigarettes were better. You wouldn't get as much tar and nicotine." She phoned Philip Morris and asked, "Is it really true? Is there less tar in this or less nicotine?" A representative assured her that if she was concerned, she could switch to Marlboro Lights. She did so and within a few weeks was smoking three and a half packs a day. In February 1998, she was diagnosed with carcinoma of the lung. She filed a

suit in a California state court against Philip Morris, alleging, among other things, breach of express warranty. A jury awarded her $1.5 million in compensatory damages and $50 million in punitive damages. The court reduced the punitive award to $25 million. Philip Morris appealed to a state intermediate appellate court.

ISSUE Did the Philip Morris representative's statements to Henley constitute an express warranty?

DECISION Yes. The court affirmed the lower court's decision on this question but reduced the punitive award to $9 million and remanded the case for a new trial on this amount if Henley did not consent to it.

REASON The court quoted Henley's testimony regarding her call to Philip Morris and its representative's assurance that if she was concerned, she could switch to Marlboro Lights. The court reasoned, "The least that the testimony reasonably could be understood to mean was that defendant represented to plaintiff that she would take in less tar and nicotine if she switched to Lights." This testimony "supported an inference that defendant's representative expressly assured plaintiff that Lights eliminated

(Continued)

CASE 13.1—Continued

or reduced whatever risks smoking might otherwise pose. That is, the assurance * * * was that switching to Lights would address some unspecified concerns. The jury could infer that the concerns discussed were related to what plaintiff said motivated the call, i.e., that she had

heard 'low-tar cigarettes were better.' By 'better,' the jury could infer, plaintiff meant 'healthier.' "

FOR CRITICAL ANALYSIS—Ethical Consideration
What ethical duty do manufacturers have to warn their customers of dangers associated with their products?

Basis of the Bargain   To create an express warranty, a seller or lessor does not have to use formal words such as *warrant* or *guarantee* [UCC 2–313(2), 2A–210(2)]. The UCC requires that for an express warranty to be created, the affirmation, promise, description, or sample must become part of the "basis of the bargain" [UCC 2–313(1), 2A–210(1)]. Just what constitutes the basis of the bargain is hard to say. The UCC does not define the concept, and it is a question of fact in each case whether a representation was made at such a time and in such a way that it induced the buyer or lessee to enter into the contract. (For more information on how sellers can create—or avoid creating—warranties, see the *Application* feature at the end of this chapter.)

Statements of Opinion   Statements of fact create express warranties. If the seller or lessor merely makes a statement that relates to the supposed value or worth of the goods, or makes a statement of opinion or recommendation about the goods, however, the seller or lessor is not creating an express warranty [UCC 2–313(2), 2A–210(2)].

■ **EXAMPLE 13.2** A seller claims that "this is the best used car to come along in years; it has four new tires and a 250-horsepower engine just rebuilt this year." The seller has made several *affirmations of fact* that can create a warranty: the automobile has an engine; it has a 250-horsepower engine; it was rebuilt this year; there are four tires on the automobile; and the tires are new. The seller's *opinion* that the vehicle is "the best used car to come along in years," however, is known as "puffing" and creates no warranty. (*Puffing* is an expression of opinion by a seller or lessor that is not made as a representation of fact.) ■

A statement relating to the value of the goods, such as "it's worth a fortune" or "anywhere else you'd pay $10,000 for it," usually does not create a warranty. If the

Cartons of Marlboro Light cigarettes, made by Philip Morris, sit on a shelf in a retail store. Suppose that the store clerk tells a customer that these cigarettes "are the best," and the customer buys three cartons. The customer later develops lung cancer from smoking and sues the seller. In this situation, would the seller's statements be enough to create an express warranty? Why or why not? (Nell Redmond/Bloomberg News)

seller or lessor is an expert and gives an opinion as an expert to a layperson, though, then a warranty may be created.

It is not always easy to determine whether a statement constitutes an express warranty or puffing. The reasonableness of the buyer's or lessee's reliance appears to be the controlling criterion in many cases. For example, a salesperson's statements that a ladder "will never break" and will "last a lifetime" are so clearly improbable that no reasonable buyer should rely on them. Additionally, the context in which a statement is made might be relevant in determining the reasonableness of the buyer's or lessee's reliance. For example, a reasonable person is more likely to rely on a written statement made in an advertisement than on a statement made orally by a salesperson.

ETHICAL ISSUE 13.1

Should sellers be held accountable for promises made to customers? The law assumes that most buyers know, or should know, that sellers commonly "huff and puff" their wares and that certain types of statements are not binding promises but mere puffery. Some customers, however, including persons who do not have a complete command of the English language, can easily be "taken in" by fast-talking salespersons. Also, even the courts have found it difficult at times to distinguish between statements that create guarantees and statements that amount to puffery. Because of the legal problems created by puffery, some scholars suggest that sellers should be held accountable for *all* of the promises that they make to customers, including the types of promises that traditionally have been regarded as puffery. Others, though, point out that changing the law relating to puffery could lead to further problems. Almost any innocent remark made by a sales representative could conceivably become the basis for litigation. For this reason, the National Conference of Commissioners on Uniform State Laws has not opted to change the UCC provisions on puffery. ■

IMPLIED WARRANTIES

IMPLIED WARRANTY
A warranty that arises by law because of the circumstances of a sale, rather than by the seller's express promise.

An **implied warranty** is one that *the law derives* by implication or inference because of the circumstances of a sale, rather than by the seller's express promise. In an action based on breach of implied warranty, it is necessary to show that an implied warranty existed and that the breach of the warranty proximately caused[5] the damage sustained. We look here at some of the implied warranties that arise under the UCC.

Implied Warranty of Merchantability   Every sale or lease of goods made *by a merchant* who deals in goods of the kind sold or leased automatically gives rise to an **implied warranty of merchantability** [UCC 2–314, 2A–212]. Thus, a merchant who is in the business of selling ski equipment makes an implied warranty of merchantability every time the merchant sells a pair of skis, but a neighbor selling his or her skis at a garage sale does not.

IMPLIED WARRANTY OF MERCHANTABILITY
A warranty that goods being sold or leased are reasonably fit for the general purpose for which they are sold or leased, are properly packaged and labeled, and are of proper quality. The warranty automatically arises in every sale or lease of goods made by a merchant who deals in goods of the kind sold or leased.

Merchantable Goods.   Goods that are *merchantable* are "reasonably fit for the ordinary purposes for which such goods are used." They must be of at least average, fair, or medium-grade quality. The quality must be comparable to a level that will pass without objection in the trade or market for goods of the same description. To be merchantable, the goods must also be adequately packaged and labeled as

---

5. Proximate cause, or legal cause, exists when the connection between an act and an injury is strong enough to justify imposing liability—see Chapter 4.

provided by the agreement, and they must conform to the promises or affirmations of fact made on the container or label, if any.

It makes no difference whether the merchant knew or could have discovered that a product was defective (not merchantable). Of course, merchants are not absolute insurers against all accidents arising in connection with the goods. For example, a bar of soap is not unmerchantable merely because a user could slip and fall by stepping on it.

Merchantable Food.   The UCC recognizes the serving of food or drink to be consumed on or off the premises as a sale of goods subject to the implied warranty of merchantability [UCC 2–314(1)]. "Merchantable" food means food that is fit to eat. Courts generally determine whether food is fit to eat on the basis of consumer expectations. For example, the courts assume that consumers should reasonably expect on occasion to find bones in fish fillets, cherry pits in cherry pie, a nutshell in a package of shelled nuts, and so on—because such substances are natural incidents of the food. In contrast, consumers would not reasonably expect to find an inchworm in a can of peas or a piece of glass in a soft drink—because these substances are not natural to the food product.[6] In the following classic case, the court had to determine whether a fish bone was a substance that one should reasonably expect to find in fish chowder.

---

6. See, for example, *Ruvolo v. Homovich,* 149 Ohio App.3d 701, 778 N.E.2d 661 (2002).

LANDMARK AND CLASSIC CASES
CASE 13.2   Webster v. Blue Ship Tea Room, Inc.

Supreme Judicial Court of Massachusetts, 1964.
347 Mass. 421,
198 N.E.2d 309.

HISTORICAL AND CULTURAL SETTING
Chowder, a soup or stew made with fresh fish, possibly originated in the fishing villages of Brittany (a French province to the west of Paris) and was probably carried to Canada and New England by Breton fishermen. In the nineteenth century and earlier, recipes for chowder did not call for the removal of the fish bones. Chowder recipes in the first half of the twentieth century were the same as in previous centuries, sometimes specifying that the fish head, tail, and backbone were to be broken in pieces and boiled, with the "liquor thus produced . . . added to the balance of the chowder."[a] By the middle of the twentieth century, there was a considerable body of case law concerning implied warranties and foreign and natural substances in food. It was perhaps inevitable that sooner or later, a consumer injured by a fish bone in chowder would challenge the merchantability of chowder containing fish bones.

FACTS   Blue Ship Tea Room, Inc., was located in Boston in an old building overlooking the ocean. Webster, who had been born and raised in New England, went to the restaurant and ordered fish chowder. The chowder was milky in color. After three or four spoonfuls, she felt something lodged in her throat. As a result, she underwent two esophagoscopies; in the second esophagoscopy, a fish bone was found and removed. Webster filed suit against the restaurant in a Massachusetts state court for breach of the implied warranty of merchantability. The jury rendered a verdict for Webster, and the restaurant appealed to the state's highest court.

ISSUE   Does serving fish chowder that contains a bone constitute a breach of an implied warranty of merchantability on the part of the restaurant?

DECISION   No. The Supreme Judicial Court of Massachusetts held that Webster could not recover against Blue Ship Tea Room because no breach of warranty had occurred.

REASON   The court, citing UCC Section 2–314, stated that "a warranty that goods shall be merchantable is implied in a

---

a. Fannie Farmer, *The Boston Cooking School Cook Book* (Boston: Little, Brown, 1937), p. 166.

CASE 13.2—Continued

contract for their sale if the seller is a merchant with respect to goods of that kind. Under this section the serving for value of food or drink to be consumed either on the premises or elsewhere is a sale. * * * Goods to be merchantable must at least be * * * fit for the ordinary purposes for which such goods are used." The question here is whether a fish bone made the chowder unfit for eating. In the judge's opinion, "the joys of life in New England include the ready availability of fresh fish chowder. We should be prepared to cope with the hazards of fish bones, the occasional presence of which in chowders is, it seems to us, to be anticipated, and which, in the light of a hallowed tradition, do not impair their fitness or merchantability."

COMMENTS *This classic case, phrased in memorable language, was an early application of the UCC's implied warranty of merchantability to food products. The case established the rule that consumers should expect to find, on occasion, elements of food products that are natural to the product (such as fish bones in fish chowder). In such cases, the food preparers or packagers will not normally be liable. This rule continues to be applied today in cases involving similar issues.*

RELEVANT WEB SITES *To locate information on the Web concerning* Webster v. Blue Ship Tea Room, Inc., *go to this text's Web site at* **http://blt.westbuslaw.com**, *select "Chapter 13," and click on "URLs for Landmarks."*

IMPLIED WARRANTY OF FITNESS FOR A PARTICULAR PURPOSE
A warranty that goods sold or leased are fit for a particular purpose. The warranty arises when any seller or lessor knows the particular purpose for which a buyer or lessee will use the goods and knows that the buyer or lessee is relying on the skill and judgment of the seller or lessor to select suitable goods.

Implied Warranty of Fitness for a Particular Purpose The **implied warranty of fitness for a particular purpose** arises when any seller or lessor (merchant or nonmerchant) knows the particular purpose for which a buyer or lessee will use the goods and knows that the buyer or lessee is relying on the skill and judgment of the seller or lessor to select suitable goods [UCC 2–315, 2A–213].

A "particular purpose" of the buyer or lessee differs from the "ordinary purpose for which goods are used" (merchantability). Goods can be merchantable but unfit for a particular purpose. ■ **EXAMPLE 13.3** Suppose that you need a gallon of paint to match the color of your living room walls—a light shade somewhere between coral and peach. You take a sample to your local hardware store and request a gallon of paint of that color. Instead, you are given a gallon of bright blue paint. Here, the salesperson has not breached any warranty of implied merchantability—the bright blue paint is of high quality and suitable for interior walls—but he or she has breached an implied warranty of fitness for a particular purpose. ■

A seller or lessor does not need to have actual knowledge of the buyer's or lessee's particular purpose. It is sufficient if a seller or lessor "has reason to know" the purpose. The buyer or lessee, however, must have *relied* on the skill or judgment of the seller or lessor in selecting or furnishing suitable goods for an implied warranty to be created.

■ **EXAMPLE 13.4** Bloomberg leases a computer from Future Tech, a lessor of technical business equipment. Bloomberg tells the clerk that she wants a computer that will run a complicated new engineering graphics program at a realistic speed. Future Tech leases Bloomberg an Architex One computer with a CPU speed of only 2 gigahertz, even though a speed of at least 3.2 gigahertz would be required to run Bloomberg's graphics program at a "realistic speed." Bloomberg, after discovering that it takes forever to run her program, wants her money back. Here, because Future Tech has breached the implied warranty of fitness for a particular purpose, Bloomberg normally will be able to recover. The clerk knew specifically that Bloomberg wanted a computer with enough speed to run certain software. Furthermore, Bloomberg relied on the clerk to furnish a computer that would fulfill this purpose. Because Future Tech did not do so, the warranty was breached. ■

Other Implied Warranties Implied warranties can also arise (or be excluded or modified) as a result of course of dealing or usage of trade [UCC 2–314(3),

2A–212(3)]. In the absence of evidence to the contrary, when both parties to a sales or lease contract have knowledge of a well-recognized trade custom, the courts will infer that both parties intended for that trade custom to apply to their contract. For example, if an industry-wide custom is to lubricate a new car before it is delivered and a dealer fails to do so, the dealer can be held liable to a buyer for damages resulting from the breach of an implied warranty. This, of course, would also be negligence on the part of the dealer.

WARRANTY DISCLAIMERS

Because each type of warranty is created in a special way, the manner in which warranties can be disclaimed or qualified by a seller or lessor varies depending on the type of warranty.

Express Warranties   As already stated, any affirmation of fact or promise, description of the goods, or use of samples or models by a seller or lessor creates an express warranty. Obviously, then, express warranties can be excluded if the seller or lessor carefully refrains from making any promise or affirmation of fact relating to the goods, describing the goods, or using a sample or model.

The UCC does permit express warranties to be negated or limited by specific and unambiguous language, provided that this is done in a manner that protects the buyer or lessee from surprise. Therefore, a written disclaimer in language that is clear and conspicuous, and called to a buyer's or lessee's attention, could negate all oral express warranties not included in the written sales contract [UCC 2–316(1), 2A–214(1)]. This allows the seller or lessor to avoid false allegations that oral warranties were made, and it ensures that only representations made by properly authorized individuals are included in the bargain.

Note, however, that a buyer or lessee must be made aware of any warranty disclaimers or modifications *at the time the contract is formed.* In other words, any oral or written warranties—or disclaimers—made during the bargaining process as part of a contract's formation cannot be modified at a later time by the seller or lessor.

Implied Warranties   Generally speaking, unless circumstances indicate otherwise, the implied warranties of merchantability and fitness are disclaimed by the expressions "as is," "with all faults," and other similar expressions that in common understanding call the buyer's or lessee's attention to the fact that there are no implied warranties [UCC 2–316(3)(a), 2A–214(3)(a)]. The UCC also permits a seller or lessor to specifically disclaim an implied warranty of either merchantability or fitness [UCC 2–316(2), 2A–214(2)].[7]

Disclaimer of the Implied Warranty of Merchantability.   A merchantability disclaimer must specifically mention the word *merchantability.* The disclaimer need not be written, but if it is, the writing must be conspicuous [UCC 2–316(2), 2A–214(4)].[8] According to UCC 1–201(10),

> [a] term or clause is conspicuous when it is so written that a reasonable person against
> whom it is to operate ought to have noticed it. A printed heading in capitals . . . is con-

WATCH OUT Courts generally view warranty disclaimers unfavorably, especially when consumers are involved.

For an example of a warranty disclaimer, go to

http://www. bizguardian.com/ terms.php.

---

7. The 2003 amendments to the UCC require more informative language for disclaimers of implied warranties [Amended UCC 2–316(2), 2A–214(2)].

8. Under the 2003 amendments to UCC Articles 2 and 2A, if a consumer contract or lease is set forth in a writing—physical or electronic—the implied warranty of merchantability can be disclaimed only by language also set forth in a writing [Amended UCC 2–316(3), 2A–214(3)].

spicuous. Language in the body of a form is conspicuous if it is in larger or other contrasting type or color.[9]

■ **EXAMPLE 13.5** Forbes, a merchant, sells Maves a particular lawn mower selected by Forbes with the characteristics clearly requested by Maves. At the time of the sale, Forbes orally tells Maves that he does not warrant the merchantability of the mower, as it is last year's model and has been used as a demonstrator. If the mower proves to be defective and does not work, Maves can hold Forbes liable for breach of the warranty of fitness for a particular purpose but not for breach of the warranty of merchantability. Forbes's oral disclaimer mentioning the word *merchantability* is a proper disclaimer. ■

Disclaimer of the Implied Warranty of Fitness.   To disclaim an implied warranty of fitness for a particular purpose, the disclaimer *must* be in writing and be conspicuous. The word *fitness* does not have to be mentioned in the writing; it is sufficient if, for example, the disclaimer states, "THERE ARE NO WARRANTIES THAT EXTEND BEYOND THE DESCRIPTION ON THE FACE HEREOF." Thus, in Example 13.5 above, for Forbes to have disclaimed the implied warranty of fitness for a particular purpose, a conspicuous writing would have been required. Although Forbes could not be held liable for breaching the implied warranty of merchantability, he could be held liable for breaching the warranty of fitness—because he made no *written* disclaimer with respect to that warranty.

Buyer's or Lessee's Examination or Refusal to Inspect   If a buyer or lessee actually examines the goods (or a sample or model) as fully as desired before entering into a contract, or if the buyer or lessee refuses to examine the goods on the seller's or lessor's demand that he or she do so, *there is no implied warranty with respect to defects that a reasonable examination would reveal or defects that are actually found* [UCC 2–316(3)(b), 2A–214(2)(b)].

■ **EXAMPLE 13.6** Suppose that Joplin buys an ax at Gershwin's Hardware Store. No express warranties are made. Gershwin requests that Joplin inspect the ax before buying it, but she refuses. Had she inspected the ax, she would have noticed that its handle was obviously cracked. If Joplin is later injured by the defective ax, she normally will not be able to hold Gershwin liable for breach of the warranty of merchantability because she would have spotted the defect during an inspection. ■

Warranty Disclaimers and Unconscionability   The UCC sections dealing with warranty disclaimers do not refer specifically to unconscionability as a factor. Ultimately, however, the courts will test warranty disclaimers with reference to the UCC's unconscionability standards [UCC 2–302, 2A–108]. Such things as lack of bargaining position, "take-it-or-leave-it" choices, and a buyer's or lessee's failure to understand or know of a warranty disclaimer will become relevant to the issue of unconscionability.

MAGNUSON-MOSS WARRANTY ACT

The Magnuson-Moss Warranty Act of 1975[10] was designed to prevent deception in warranties by making them easier to understand. The act is mainly enforced by the

---

9. The 2003 amendments to UCC Articles 2 and 2A expand the concept to include terms in electronic records [Amended UCC 2–103(1)(b), 2A–103(1)(d)]. These sections also add a special rule for the situation in which a sender of an electronic record intends to evoke a response from an e-agent.
10. 15 U.S.C. Sections 2301–2312.

Federal Trade Commission (FTC). Additionally, the attorney general or a consumer who has been injured can enforce the act if informal procedures for settling disputes prove to be ineffective. The act modifies UCC warranty rules to some extent when consumer transactions are involved. The UCC, however, remains the primary codification of warranty rules for industrial and commercial transactions.

Under the Magnuson-Moss Act, no seller or lessor is required to give an express written warranty for consumer goods sold. If a seller or lessor chooses to make an express written warranty, however, and the cost of the consumer goods is more than $10, the warranty must be labeled as "full" or "limited." In addition, if the cost of the goods is more than $15, by FTC regulation, the warrantor must make certain disclosures fully and conspicuously in a single document in "readily understood language." This disclosure must state the name and address of the warrantor, what specifically is warranted, procedures for enforcing the warranty, any limitations on warranty relief, and that the buyer has legal rights.

Full Warranty   Although a *full warranty* may not cover every aspect of the consumer product sold, what it does cover ensures some type of consumer satisfaction in the event that the product is defective. A full warranty requires free repair or replacement of any defective part; if the product cannot be repaired within a reasonable time, the consumer has the choice of a refund or a replacement without charge. A full warranty frequently does not have a time limit on it. Any limitation on consequential damages must be *conspicuously* stated. Additionally, the warrantor need not perform warranty services if the problem with the product was caused by the consumer's unreasonable use of the product.

Limited Warranty   A *limited warranty* arises when the written warranty fails to meet one of the minimum requirements of a full warranty. The fact that only a limited warranty is being given must be conspicuously stated. If the only distinction between a limited warranty and a full warranty is a time limitation, the Magnuson-Moss Warranty Act allows the warrantor to identify the warranty as a full warranty by such language as "full twelve-month warranty."

Implied Warranties   Implied warranties do not arise under the Magnuson-Moss Warranty Act; they continue to be created according to UCC provisions. Implied warranties may not be disclaimed under the Magnuson-Moss Warranty Act, however. Although a warrantor can impose a time limit on the duration of an implied warranty, it must correspond to the duration of the express warranty.[11]

> **REMEMBER** When a buyer or lessee is a consumer, a limitation on consequential damages for personal injuries resulting from nonconforming goods is *prima facie* unconscionable.

▟ Product Liability

Manufacturers, sellers, and lessors of goods can be held liable to consumers, users, and bystanders for physical harm or property damage that is caused by the goods. This is called **product liability**. Product liability may be based on the warranty theories just discussed, as well as on the theories of negligence, misrepresentation, and strict liability. We look here at product liability based on negligence and misrepresentation.

> **PRODUCT LIABILITY**
> The legal liability of manufacturers, sellers, and lessors of goods to consumers, users, and bystanders for injuries or damages that are caused by the goods.

---

11. The time limit on an implied warranty occurring by virtue of the warrantor's express warranty must, of course, be reasonable, conscionable, and set forth in clear and conspicuous language on the face of the warranty.

NEGLIGENCE

Chapter 4 defined *negligence* as the failure to exercise the degree of care that a reasonable, prudent person would have exercised under the circumstances. If a manufacturer fails to exercise "due care" to make a product safe, a person who is injured by the product may sue the manufacturer for negligence.

Due Care Must Be Exercised   The manufacturer must exercise due care in designing the product, selecting the materials, using the appropriate production process, assembling the product, and placing adequate warnings on the label informing the user of dangers of which an ordinary person might not be aware. The duty of care also extends to the inspection and testing of any purchased products that are used in the final product sold by the manufacturer.

RECALL The elements of negligence include a duty of care, a breach of the duty, and an injury to the plaintiff proximately caused by the breach.

Privity of Contract Not Required   A product liability action based on negligence does not require privity of contract between the injured plaintiff and the negligent defendant manufacturer. Section 395 of the *Restatement (Second) of Torts* states as follows:

> A manufacturer who fails to exercise reasonable care in the manufacture of a chattel [movable good] which, unless carefully made, he [or she] should recognize as involving an unreasonable risk of causing physical harm to those who lawfully use it for a purpose for which the manufacturer should expect it to be used and to those whom he [or she] should expect to be endangered by its probable use, is subject to liability for physical harm caused to them by its lawful use in a manner and for a purpose for which it is supplied.

In other words, a manufacturer is liable for its failure to exercise due care to any person who sustains an injury proximately caused by a negligently made (defective) product, regardless of whether the injured person is in privity of contract with the negligent defendant manufacturer or lessor. Relative to the long history of the common law, this exception to the privity requirement is a fairly recent development, dating to the early part of the twentieth century. A leading case in this respect is *MacPherson v. Buick Motor Co.*, which we present as this chapter's *Landmark in the Law* feature on the following page.

MISREPRESENTATION

When a fraudulent misrepresentation has been made to a user or consumer, and that misrepresentation ultimately results in an injury, the basis of liability may be the tort of fraud. For example, the intentional mislabeling of packaged cosmetics and the intentional concealment of a product's defects would constitute fraudulent misrepresentation.

▰ Strict Product Liability

Under the doctrine of strict liability (discussed in Chapter 4), people may be liable for the results of their acts regardless of their intentions or their exercise of reasonable care. Under this doctrine, liability does not depend on privity of contract. The injured party does not have to be the buyer or a third party beneficiary, as required under contract warranty theory. Indeed, the provisions of the UCC do not govern this type of liability in law because it is a tort doctrine, not a principle of the law relating to sales contracts.

LANDMARK IN THE LAW

MacPherson v. Buick Motor Co. (1916)

In the landmark case of *MacPherson v. Buick Motor Co.*,[a] the New York Court of Appeals—New York's highest court—dealt with the liability of a manufacturer that failed to exercise reasonable care in manufacturing a finished product.

CASE BACKGROUND   The case was brought by Donald MacPherson, who suffered injuries while riding in a Buick automobile that suddenly collapsed because one of the wheels was made of defective wood. The spokes crumbled into fragments, throwing MacPherson out of the vehicle and injuring him.

MacPherson had purchased the car from a Buick dealer, but he brought suit against the manufacturer, Buick Motor Company. The wheel itself had not been made by Buick; it had been bought from another manufacturer. There was evidence, though, that the defects could have been discovered by reasonable inspection by Buick and that no such inspection had taken place. MacPherson charged Buick with negligence for putting a human life in imminent danger.

THE ISSUE BEFORE THE COURT AND THE COURT'S RULING   The major issue before the court was whether Buick owed a duty of care to anyone except the immediate purchaser of the car (that is, the Buick dealer). In deciding the issue, Justice Benjamin Cardozo stated that "[i]f the nature of a thing is such that it is reasonably certain to place life and limb in peril when negligently made, it is then a thing of danger. . . . If to the element of danger there is added knowledge that the thing will be used by persons other than the purchaser, and used without new tests, then, irrespective of contract, the manufacturer of this thing of danger is under a duty to make it carefully."

The court concluded that "[b]eyond all question, the nature of an automobile gives warning of probable danger if its construction is defective. This automobile was designed to go 50 miles an hour. Unless its wheels were sound and strong, injury was almost certain." Although Buick had not manufactured the wheel itself, the court held that Buick had a duty to inspect the wheels and that Buick "was responsible for the finished product." Therefore, Buick was liable to MacPherson for the injuries he sustained when he was thrown from the car.

APPLICATION TO TODAY'S WORLD

This landmark decision was a significant step in creating the legal environment of the modern world. Today, it is common for an automobile manufacturer to be held liable when its negligence causes a product user to be injured. As is often the situation, technological developments necessitated changes in the law. Had the courts continued to require privity of contract in product liability cases, today's legal landscape would be quite different indeed. Certainly, fewer cases would be pending before the courts; and just as certainly, many purchasers of products, including automobiles, would have little recourse for obtaining legal redress for injuries caused by those products.

RELEVANT WEB SITES

To locate information on the Web concerning the MacPherson *decision, go to this text's Web site at* **http://blt.westbuslaw.com**, *select "Chapter 13," and click on "URLs for Landmarks."*

a. 217 N.Y. 382, 111 N.E. 1050 (1916).

STRICT PRODUCT LIABILITY AND PUBLIC POLICY

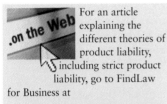

For an article explaining the different theories of product liability, including strict product liability, go to FindLaw for Business at

http://sv.biz.findlaw.com/ legal/prod_liability.html.

Strict product liability is imposed by law as a matter of public policy—the general principle of the law that prohibits actions that tend to be injurious to the public. With respect to strict liability, the policy rests on the threefold assumption that (1) consumers should be protected against unsafe products; (2) manufacturers and distributors should not escape liability for faulty products simply because they are not in privity of contract with the ultimate user of those products; and (3) manufacturers, sellers, and lessors of products are generally in a better position than consumers to bear the costs associated with injuries caused by their products—costs that they can ultimately pass on to all consumers in the form of higher prices.

California was the first state to impose strict product liability in tort on manufacturers. In a landmark 1962 decision, *Greenman v. Yuba Power Products, Inc.,*[12] the California Supreme Court set out the reason for applying tort law rather than contract law in cases involving consumers injured by defective products. According to the court, the "purpose of such liability is to [e]nsure that the costs of injuries resulting from defective products are borne by the manufacturers . . . rather than by the injured persons who are powerless to protect themselves."

REQUIREMENTS FOR STRICT LIABILITY

Section 402A of the *Restatement (Second) of Torts* indicates how the drafters envisioned that the doctrine of strict liability should be applied. It was issued in 1964, and during the next decade, it became a widely accepted statement of the liabilities of sellers of goods (including manufacturers, processors, assemblers, packagers,

12. 59 Cal.2d 57, 377 P.2d 897, 27 Cal.Rptr. 697 (1962).

Suppose that Ford Motor Company installs Firestone tires on all new Ford Explorers. The tires are defective and cause numerous accidents involving people driving new Explorers. Who should bear the costs of the resulting injuries—Ford, Firestone, or the drivers' insurance companies—and why? (AP Photo/ Eric Gay)

bottlers, wholesalers, distributors, retailers, and lessors). Section 402A states as follows:

(1) One who sells any product in a defective condition unreasonably dangerous to the user or consumer or to his [or her] property is subject to liability for physical harm thereby caused to the ultimate user or consumer or to his [or her] property, if
    (a) the seller is engaged in the business of selling such a product, and
    (b) it is expected to and does reach the user or consumer without substantial change in the condition in which it is sold.
(2) The rule stated in Subsection (1) applies although
    (a) the seller has exercised all possible care in the preparation and sale of his [or her] product, and
    (b) the user or consumer has not bought the product from or entered into any contractual relation with the seller.

The Six Requirements for Strict Liability   The bases for an action in strict liability as set forth in Section 402A of the *Restatement (Second) of Torts,* and as the doctrine came to be commonly applied, can be summarized as a series of six requirements, which are listed here. Depending on the jurisdiction, if these requirements are met, a manufacturer's liability to an injured party can be virtually unlimited.

1 The product must be in a defective condition when the defendant sells it.

2 The defendant must normally be engaged in the business of selling (or otherwise distributing) that product.

3 The product must be unreasonably dangerous to the user or consumer because of its defective condition (in most states).

4 The plaintiff must incur physical harm to self or property by use or consumption of the product.

5 The defective condition must be the proximate cause of the injury or damage.

6 The goods must not have been substantially changed from the time the product was sold to the time the injury was sustained.

Unreasonably Dangerous Products   Under the requirements just listed, in any action against a manufacturer, seller, or lessor, the plaintiff does not have to show why or in what manner the product became defective. To recover damages, however, the plaintiff must show that the product was so "defective" as to be "unreasonably dangerous"; that the product caused the plaintiff's injury; and that at the time the injury was sustained, the product was essentially in the same condition as when it left the hands of the defendant manufacturer, seller, or lessor.

A court may consider a product so defective as to be an **unreasonably dangerous product** if either (1) the product is dangerous beyond the expectation of the ordinary consumer or (2) a less dangerous alternative was economically feasible for the manufacturer, but the manufacturer failed to produce it. As will be discussed in the next section, a product may be unreasonably dangerous due to a flaw in the manufacturing process, a design defect, or an inadequate warning.

PRODUCT DEFECTS—RESTATEMENT (THIRD) OF TORTS

Because Section 402A of the *Restatement (Second) of Torts* did not clearly define such terms as "defective" and "unreasonably dangerous," they were interpreted differently by different courts. In 1997, to address these concerns, the American Law Institute issued the *Restatement (Third) of Torts: Products Liability.* The

UNREASONABLY DANGEROUS PRODUCT In product liability, a product that is defective to the point of threatening a consumer's health and safety. A product will be considered unreasonably dangerous if it is dangerous beyond the expectation of the ordinary consumer or if a less dangerous alternative was economically feasible for the manufacturer, but the manufacturer failed to produce it.

The Consumer Product Safety Commission has received complaints about the motor control circuits in this Fisher-Price minibike. If a child was injured by a malfunction of the circuits in the bike, what would the parents have to prove to establish that the bike has a design defect? (AP Photo/ Evan Vucci)

Restatement defines the three types of product defects that have traditionally been recognized in product liability law—manufacturing defects, design defects, and warning defects.

Manufacturing Defects   According to Section 2(a) of the *Restatement (Third) of Torts,* a product "contains a manufacturing defect when the product departs from its intended design even though all possible care was exercised in the preparation and marketing of the product." This statement imposes liability on the manufacturer (and on the wholesaler and retailer) whether or not the manufacturer acted "reasonably." This is strict liability, or liability without fault.

Design Defects   A design defect (or a warning defect, discussed later in this chapter), by nature, affects all of the units of a particular product. A product "is defective in design when the foreseeable risks of harm posed by the product could have been reduced or avoided by the adoption of a reasonable alternative design by the seller or other distributor, or a predecessor in the commercial chain of distribution, and the omission of the alternative design renders the product not reasonably safe."[13]

***Problems with the* Restatement (Second) of Torts.**   In the past, different states applied different tests to determine whether a product had a design defect under Section 402A of the *Restatement (Second) of Torts.* Some of the tests used were controversial, particularly one that focused on "consumer expectations" concerning a product.

***The Test for Design Defect under the* Restatement (Third) of Torts.**   The test prescribed by the *Restatement (Third) of Torts* focuses on a product's actual design and the reasonableness of that design. To succeed in a product liability suit alleging a design defect, a plaintiff has to show that there is a reasonable alternative design. In other words, a manufacturer or other defendant is liable only when the harm was reasonably preventable. According to the Official Comments accompanying the *Restatement (Third) of Torts,* factors that a court may consider on this point include

the magnitude and probability of the foreseeable risks of harm, the instructions and warnings accompanying the product, and the nature and strength of consumer expectations regarding the product, including expectations arising from product portrayal and marketing. The relative advantages and disadvantages of the product as designed and as it alternatively could have been designed may also be considered. Thus, the likely effects of the alternative design on production costs; the effects of the alternative design on product longevity, maintenance, repair, and esthetics; and the range of consumer choice among products are factors that may be taken into account.

Can videos, video games, and Internet transmissions that contain violence be deemed "defective products"? For a discussion of this question, see this chapter's *Adapting the Law to the Online Environment* feature on the next page.

Warning Defects   Product warnings and instructions alert consumers to the risks of using a product. A "reasonableness" test applies to this material. A product "is defective because of inadequate instructions or warnings when the foreseeable risks of harm posed by the product could have been reduced or avoided by the provision

---

13. *Restatement (Third) of Torts: Products Liability,* Section 2(b).

ADAPTING THE LAW TO THE ONLINE ENVIRONMENT

School Shootings and Strict Liability

Over the past decade, school shootings have led to lawsuits that pose a novel question for the courts: Can the producers and distributors of violence-laden media, such as video games and Internet transmissions, be held liable for the shootings? In one case, for example, the plaintiffs were the parents of several students who were killed by their classmate Michael Carneal in a 1997 high school shooting in Kentucky. The plaintiffs sued Meow Media, Inc., and other companies (the defendants), alleging that the defendants should be held liable for the shootings. The plaintiffs contended that the defendants' products—including videos, video games, and Internet transmissions—"desensitized" Carneal to violence. Carneal's indifference to violence, in turn, "caused" the shootings.

THE NEGLIGENCE CLAIM

One of the plaintiffs' claims was that the defendants had breached a duty of care by distributing such violent products and were thus negligent. The court, however, did not agree with the plaintiffs that the defendants owed a duty of care to the victims. Recall from Chapter 4 that a defendant's duty of care extends only to those who are injured as a result of a *foreseeable* risk. In the court's eyes, a school shooting was not a foreseeable risk for the defendants. Thus, the court dismissed the negligence claim.

WERE THE "PRODUCTS" DEFECTIVE?

The plaintiffs also alleged that the defendants should be held liable in strict product liability because the violence contained in their products rendered those products "defective." The court never reached the issue of whether the products were defective, however, because it concluded that the violence communicated by the videos, video games, and Internet transmissions was not a "product."

While videos and video games may be considered products for some purposes, the communications within those videos and games were not products for purposes of strict liability. The argument that an Internet transmission could constitute a product also failed. The plaintiffs had asserted that if electricity could be labeled a product, as it has been in some cases, then Internet transmissions, which can be characterized as a series of electrical impulses, should also be considered a product. The court pointed out, though, that the relevant state law defined the term *product* as something tangible—something that can be touched, felt, or otherwise perceived by the senses. The communicative element (ideas and images) of an Internet transmission was not a tangible object.

Furthermore, stated the court, even assuming that the videos, video games, and Internet transmissions were products, the plaintiffs could not succeed in a strict product liability action. For strict product liability to apply, the injuries complained of must have been caused by the products themselves. In this case, the injuries were caused not by the products but by Carneal's *reaction* to the products.[a]

FOR CRITICAL ANALYSIS

Another defense raised by the defendants in this case was that the expression in their videos, video games, and Internet transmissions was a protected form of speech under the First Amendment. Should such speech ever be restrained in the interests of protecting society against violence? Why or why not?

a. *James v. Meow Media, Inc.,* 300 F.3d 683 (6th Cir. 2002). For another case on this issue in which the court reached similar conclusions, see *Sanders v. Acclaim Entertainment, Inc.,* 188 F.Supp.2d 1264 (D.Colo. 2002).

of reasonable instructions or warnings by the seller or other distributor, or a predecessor in the commercial chain of distribution, and the omission of the instructions or warnings renders the product not reasonably safe."[14] Generally, a seller must warn those who purchase its product of the harm that can result from the *foreseeable misuse* of the product as well.

---

14. *Restatement (Third) of Torts: Products Liability,* Section 2(c).

Important factors for a court to consider under the *Restatement (Third) of Torts* include the risks of a product, the "content and comprehensibility" and "intensity of expression" of warnings and instructions, and the "characteristics of expected user groups."[15] For example, children will likely respond more readily to bright, bold, simple warning labels, while educated adults might need more detailed information.

There is no duty to warn about risks that are obvious or commonly known. Warnings about such risks do not add to the safety of a product and could even detract from it by making other warnings seem less significant. The obviousness of a risk and a user's decision to proceed in the face of that risk may be a defense in a product liability suit based on a warning defect. (This defense and other defenses in product liability suits are discussed later in this chapter.)

MARKET-SHARE LIABILITY

Generally, in all cases involving product liability, a plaintiff must prove that the defective product that caused her or his injury was the product of a specific defendant. Since the 1980s, however, some courts have dropped this requirement when a plaintiff cannot prove which of many distributors of a harmful product supplied the particular product that caused the injuries. Instead, under a theory of market-share liability, all firms that manufactured and distributed the product during the period in question are held liable for the plaintiff's injuries in proportion to the firms' respective shares of the market for that product during that period. ■ EXAMPLE 13.7 In one case, a plaintiff who was a hemophiliac received injections of a blood protein known as antihemophiliac factor (AHF) concentrate. The plaintiff later tested positive for the AIDS (acquired immune deficiency syndrome) virus. Because it was not known which manufacturer was responsible for the particular AHF received by the plaintiff, the court held that all of the manufacturers of AHF could be held liable under a theory of market-share liability.[16] ■ Many jurisdictions, however, do not apply this theory, believing that it deviates too significantly from traditional legal principles.[17]

OTHER APPLICATIONS OF STRICT LIABILITY

Although the drafters of Section 402A of the *Restatement (Second) of Torts* did not take a position on bystanders, virtually all courts extend the strict liability of manufacturers and other sellers to injured bystanders. ■ EXAMPLE 13.8 In one case, an automobile manufacturer was held liable for injuries caused by the explosion of a car's motor. A cloud of steam that resulted from the explosion caused multiple collisions because other drivers could not see well.[18] ■

The rule of strict liability is also applicable to suppliers of component parts. ■ EXAMPLE 13.9 General Motors buys brake pads from a subcontractor and puts them in Chevrolets without changing their composition. If those pads are defective, both the supplier of the brake pads and General Motors will be held strictly liable for the damages caused by the defects. ■

---

15. *Restatement (Third) of Torts: Products Liability,* Section 2, Comment h.
16. *Smith v. Cutter Biological, Inc.,* 72 Haw. 416, 823 P.2d 717 (1991). See also *Hymnowitz v. Eli Lilly and Co.,* 73 N.Y.2d 487, 539 N.E.2d 1069, 541 N.Y.S.2d 941 (1989).
17. For the Illinois Supreme Court's position on market-share liability, see *Smith v. Eli Lilly and Co.,* 137 Ill.2d 252, 560 N.E.2d 324, 148 Ill.Dec. 22 (1990).
18. *Giberson v. Ford Motor Co.,* 504 S.W.2d 8 (Mo. 1974).

STATUTE OF REPOSE
Basically, a statute of limitations that is not dependent on the happening of a cause of action. Statutes of repose generally begin to run at an earlier date and run for a longer period of time than statutes of limitations.

STATUTES OF REPOSE

As discussed in Chapter 1, *statutes of limitations* restrict the time within which an action may be brought. Many states have passed laws, called **statutes of repose,** placing outer time limits on some claims so that the defendant will not be left vulnerable to lawsuits indefinitely. These statutes may limit the time within which a plaintiff can file a product liability suit. Typically, a statute of repose begins to run at an earlier date and runs for a longer time than a statute of limitations. For example, a statute of repose may require that claims be brought within twelve years from the date of sale or manufacture of the defective product. It is immaterial that the product is defective or causes an injury if the injury occurs *after* this statutory period has lapsed. In addition, some of these legislative enactments limit the application of the doctrine of strict liability to new goods only.

◼ Defenses to Product Liability

Manufacturers, sellers, or lessors can raise several defenses to avoid liability for harms caused by their products. We look at some of these defenses in the following subsections.

ETHICAL ISSUE 13.2

Do pharmacists have a duty to warn customers about the side effects of drugs? Clearly, manufacturers of pharmaceuticals have a duty to disclose and warn users of any side effects associated with their products. Typically, these disclosures and warnings are given to physicians, and many pharmacies today include a list of possible side effects with the drugs that they dispense. Yet what if a pharmacist does not disclose the potential side effects of a drug being sold? Should the pharmacy be held liable if a purchaser suffers harms from a drug's side effects? This question, which has both legal and ethical implications, has come before several courts in recent years—and the courts have reached different conclusions.

In one case, for example, an Illinois court held that a pharmacist had a duty to warn his customer about a potentially fatal interaction with a prescribed medication. The court reasoned that the duty existed because the pharmacist knew of the customer's allergies, knew that the prescribed medication should not be taken by a person with those allergies, and knew that injury or death was substantially certain to result.[19] In another case, however, a Texas appellate court reached the opposite conclusion. The court held that imposing such a duty on pharmacists would necessarily interfere with the physician-patient relationship because pharmacies seeking to avoid liability would "question the propriety of every prescription they fill."[20] Clearly, the arguments put forth in both cases have merit, and as yet the courts have not reached a consensus on the issue. ◼

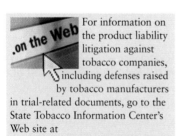

For information on the product liability litigation against tobacco companies, including defenses raised by tobacco manufacturers in trial-related documents, go to the State Tobacco Information Center's Web site at

**http://stic.neu.edu/
index.html**.

ASSUMPTION OF RISK

Assumption of risk can sometimes be used as a defense in a product liability action. For example, if a buyer fails to heed a product recall by the seller, a court might conclude that the buyer assumed the risk caused by the defect that led to the recall. To establish such a defense, the defendant must show that (1) the plaintiff knew and

---

19. *Happel v. Wal-Mart Stores, Inc.,* 193 Ill.2d 586, 744 N.E.2d 284, 253 Ill.Dec. 2 (2001).
20. *Morgan v. Wal-Mart Stores, Inc.,* 30 S.W.3d 455 (Tex.App.—Austin 2001).

appreciated the risk created by the product defect and (2) the plaintiff voluntarily assumed the risk, even though it was unreasonable to do so. (See Chapter 4 for a more detailed discussion of assumption of risk.)

PRODUCT MISUSE

Similar to the defense of voluntary assumption of risk is that of misuse of the product. Here, the injured party *does not know that the product is dangerous for a particular use* (contrast this with assumption of risk), but the use is not the one for which the product was designed. The courts have severely limited this defense, however. Even if the injured party does not know about the inherent danger of using the product in a wrong way, if the misuse is *foreseeable*, the seller must take measures to guard against it.

COMPARATIVE NEGLIGENCE

Developments in the area of comparative negligence, or fault (discussed in Chapter 4), have also affected the doctrine of strict liability—the most extreme theory of product liability. Whereas previously the plaintiff's conduct was not a defense to strict liability, today many jurisdictions, when apportioning liability and damages, consider the negligent or intentional actions of both the plaintiff and the defendant. This means that even if the plaintiff misused the products, she or he may nonetheless be able to recover at least some damages for injuries caused by the defendant's defective product.

COMMONLY KNOWN DANGERS

Is becoming overweight a commonly known danger of eating fast food on a regular basis? Why or why not? (Reuters/Joe Skipper/Landov)

The dangers associated with certain products (such as sharp knives and guns) are so commonly known that manufacturers need not warn users of those dangers. If a defendant succeeds in convincing the court that a plaintiff's injury resulted from a *commonly known danger,* the defendant normally will not be liable.

■ EXAMPLE 13.10 A classic case on this issue involved a plaintiff who was injured when an elastic exercise rope that she had purchased slipped off her foot and struck her in the eye, causing a detachment of the retina. The plaintiff claimed that the manufacturer should be liable because it had failed to warn users that the exerciser might slip off a foot in such a manner. The court stated that to hold the manufacturer liable in these circumstances "would go beyond the reasonable dictates of justice in fixing the liabilities of manufacturers." After all, stated the court, "[a]lmost every physical object can be inherently dangerous or potentially dangerous in a sense. . . . A manufacturer cannot manufacture a knife that will not cut or a hammer that will not mash a thumb or a stove that will not burn a finger. The law does not require [manufacturers] to warn of such common dangers." [21] ■

A related defense is the *knowledgeable user* defense. If a particular danger (such as electrical shock) is or should be commonly known by particular users of the product (such as electricians), the manufacturer of electrical equipment need not warn these users of the danger.

In the following case, the plaintiffs alleged that McDonald's, the well-known fast-food chain, should be held liable for failing to warn customers of the adverse health effects of eating its food products.

---

21. *Jamieson v. Woodward & Lothrop,* 247 F.2d 23, 101 D.C.App. 32 (1957).

CASE 13.3 ▪ Pelman v. McDonald's Corp.

United States District Court,
Southern District of New York, 2003.
237 F.Supp.2d 512.

FACTS McDonald's, with about 13,000 restaurants in the United States, has a 43 percent share of the U.S. fast-food market. Ashley Pelman, a New York resident, and other teenagers who often ate at McDonald's outlets, became overweight and developed adverse health effects. Their parents (the plaintiffs) filed a suit in a New York state court against McDonald's and others, alleging, among other things, that the defendants failed to warn of the quantities, qualities, and levels of cholesterol, fat, salt, sugar, and other ingredients in their products and that a diet high in fat, salt, sugar, and cholesterol could lead to obesity and health problems. The suit was transferred to a federal district court. The defendants filed a motion to dismiss the complaint.

ISSUE Were the products consumed by the plaintiffs dangerous in any way that was not open and obvious to a reasonable consumer?

DECISION No. The court dismissed the plaintiffs' complaint.

REASON The plaintiffs asserted in part that McDonald's failed to include nutritional labeling on its products. The court pointed out that "McDonald's has made its nutritional information available online and * * * upon request. Unless McDonald's has specifically promised to

provide nutritional information on all its products * * *, plaintiffs do not state a claim." The court added that the plaintiffs might have alleged that McDonald's products are so extraordinarily unhealthful that they are "outside the reasonable contemplation of the consuming public." Instead, they merely alleged that the foods "contain high levels of cholesterol, fat, salt, and sugar" and that the foods are therefore unhealthful. The court pointed out that it is well known that the products offered by McDonald's "contain high levels of cholesterol, fat, salt, and sugar, and that such attributes are bad for one." The court concluded, "If a person knows or should know that eating copious orders of supersized McDonald's products is unhealthful and may result in weight gain (and its con-comitant [related] problems) because of the high levels of cholesterol, fat, salt, and sugar, it is not the place of the law to protect them from their own excesses. Nobody is forced to eat at McDonald's."

WHY IS THIS CASE IMPORTANT? *The ruling in this case, which was the first of its kind, is important because, as the defendants argued and the court acknowledged, a ruling in the plaintiffs' favor "could spawn thousands of similar 'McLawsuits' against restaurants. Even if limited to that ilk of fare dubbed 'fast food,' the potential for lawsuits is great." On occasion, it is up to the courts to draw a line between individuals' responsibility to take care of themselves and society's responsibility to protect those individuals. This is one of those cases.*

OTHER DEFENSES

A defendant can also defend against product liability by showing that there is no basis for the plaintiff's claim. Suppose that a plaintiff alleges that a seller breached an implied warranty. If the seller can prove that he or she effectively disclaimed all implied warranties, the plaintiff cannot recover. Similarly, in a product liability case based on negligence, a defendant who can show that the plaintiff has not met the requirements (such as causation or the breach of a duty of care) for an action in negligence will not be liable. In regard to strict product liability, a defendant could claim that the plaintiff failed to meet one of the requirements for an action in strict liability. If, for example, the defendant establishes that the goods have been subsequently altered after they were sold, the defendant will not be held liable.

◨ Consumer Protection Laws

Sources of consumer protection exist at all levels of government. At the federal level, a number of laws have been passed to define the duties of sellers and the rights of consumers. Exhibit 13–1 indicates the areas of consumer law that are regulated by statutes. Federal administrative agencies, such as the Federal Trade Commission (FTC), also provide an important source of consumer protection. Nearly every agency and department of the federal government has an office of consumer affairs, and most states have one or more such offices, including the offices of state attorneys general, to assist consumers.

Because of the wide variation among state consumer protection laws, our primary focus here will be on federal legislation—specifically, on legislation governing deceptive advertising, telemarketing and electronic advertising, labeling and packaging, sales, health protection, product safety, and credit protection. Realize, though, that state laws often provide more sweeping and significant protections for the consumer than do federal laws. State consumer protection laws will be discussed later in this section.

Deceptive Advertising

One of the earliest—and still one of the most important—federal consumer protection laws is the Federal Trade Commission Act of 1914. The act created the Federal Trade Commission (FTC) to carry out the broadly stated goal of preventing unfair and deceptive trade practices, including deceptive advertising, within the meaning of Section 5 of the act.

DECEPTIVE ADVERTISING
Advertising that misleads consumers, either by unjustified claims concerning a product's performance or by the omission of a material fact concerning the product's composition or performance.

Defining Deceptive Advertising   Generally, **deceptive advertising** occurs if a reasonable consumer would be misled by the advertising claim. Vague generalities and obvious exaggerations are permissible. These claims are known as *puffing*. Recall

EXHIBIT 13–1 SELECTED AREAS OF CONSUMER LAW REGULATED BY STATUTES

These stuffed teddy bears were recalled because the plastic beads inside the toy could come out and create a choking hazard for young children. According to Exhibit 13–1 on the previous page, which area of consumer protection law governs such a recall? (Photo by the Consumer Product Safety Commission/Getty Images)

from earlier in this chapter that puffing, or puffery, consists of statements about a product that a reasonable person would not believe to be true. When a claim takes on the appearance of literal authenticity, however, it may create problems. Advertising that *appears* to be based on factual evidence but in fact is scientifically untrue will be deemed deceptive. A classic example occurred in a 1944 case in which the claim that a skin cream would restore youthful qualities to aged skin was deemed deceptive.[22]

Some advertisements contain "half-truths," meaning that the presented information is true but incomplete and, therefore, leads consumers to a false conclusion. ■ **EXAMPLE 13.11** The makers of Campbell's soups advertised that "most" Campbell's soups were low in fat and cholesterol and thus were helpful in fighting heart disease. What the ad did not say was that Campbell's soups were high in sodium, and high-sodium diets may increase the risk of heart disease. The FTC ruled that Campbell's claims were thus deceptive. ■ Advertising that contains an endorsement by a celebrity may be deemed deceptive if the celebrity does not actually use the product.

BAIT-AND-SWITCH ADVERTISING
Advertising a product at a very attractive price (the "bait") and then, once the consumer is in the store, saying that the advertised product is either not available or is of poor quality; the customer is then urged to purchase ("switched" to) a more expensive item.

Bait-and-Switch Advertising   The FTC has issued rules that govern specific advertising techniques. One of the most important rules is contained in the FTC's "Guides on Bait Advertising."[23] The rule is designed to prevent **bait-and-switch advertising—**that is, advertising a very low price for a particular item that will likely be unavailable to the consumer and then encouraging him or her to purchase a more expensive item. The low price is the "bait" to lure the consumer into the store. The salesperson is instructed to "switch" the consumer to a different, more expensive item. According to the FTC guidelines, bait-and-switch advertising occurs if the seller refuses to show the advertised item, fails to have reasonable quantities of it available, fails to promise to deliver the advertised item within a reasonable time, or discourages employees from selling the item.

Online Deceptive Advertising   Deceptive advertising may occur in the online environment as well. For several years, the FTC has actively monitored online advertising and has identified hundreds of Web sites that have made false or deceptive advertising claims for products ranging from medical treatments for various diseases to exercise equipment and weight loss aids.

---

22. *Charles of the Ritz Distributing Corp. v. Federal Trade Commission,* 143 F.2d 676 (2d Cir. 1944).
23. 16 C.F.R. Section 288.

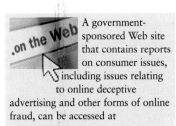 A government-sponsored Web site that contains reports on consumer issues, including issues relating to online deceptive advertising and other forms of online fraud, can be accessed at **http://www.consumer.gov**.

REMEMBER Changes in technology often require changes in the law.

In 2000, the FTC issued new guidelines to help online businesses comply with existing laws prohibiting deceptive advertising.[24] The guidelines did not set forth new rules but rather described how existing laws apply to online advertising. Generally, the rules emphasize that any ads—online or offline—must be truthful and not misleading and that any claims made in any ads must be substantiated. Additionally, ads cannot be unfair, defined in the guidelines as "caus[ing] or . . . likely to cause substantial consumer injury that consumers could not reasonably avoid and that is not outweighed by the benefit to consumers or competition."

The guidelines also call for "clear and conspicuous" disclosure of any qualifying or limiting information. The FTC suggests that advertisers should assume that consumers will not read an entire Web page. Therefore, to satisfy the "clear and conspicuous" requirement, advertisers should place the disclosure as close as possible to the claim being qualified or include the disclosure within the claim itself. If such placement is not feasible, the next-best placement is on a section of the page to which a consumer can easily scroll. Generally, hyperlinks to a disclosure are recommended only for lengthy disclosures or for disclosures that must be repeated in a variety of locations on the Web page.

FTC Actions against Deceptive Advertising The FTC receives complaints from many sources, including competitors of alleged violators, consumers, consumer organizations, trade associations, Better Business Bureaus, government organizations, and state and local officials. If enough consumers complain and the complaints are widespread, the FTC will investigate the problem. If the FTC concludes that a given advertisement is unfair or deceptive, it sends a formal complaint to the alleged offender. The company may agree to settle the complaint without further proceedings; if not, the FTC can conduct a hearing before an administrative law judge (discussed in Chapter 1) in which the company can present its defense.

If the FTC succeeds in proving that an advertisement is unfair or deceptive, it usually issues a **cease-and-desist order** requiring that the challenged advertising be stopped. It might also require **counteradvertising** in which the company advertises anew—in print, on radio, and on television—to inform the public about the earlier misinformation.

CEASE-AND-DESIST ORDER
An administrative or judicial order prohibiting a person or business firm from conducting activities that an agency or court has deemed illegal.

COUNTERADVERTISING
New advertising that is undertaken pursuant to a Federal Trade Commission order for the purpose of correcting earlier false claims that were made about a product.

TELEMARKETING AND ELECTRONIC ADVERTISING

The pervasive use of the telephone to market goods and services to homes and businesses led to the passage in 1991 of the Telephone Consumer Protection Act (TCPA).[25] The act prohibits telephone solicitation using an automatic telephone dialing system or a prerecorded voice. Most states also have laws regulating telephone solicitation. The TCPA also makes it illegal to transmit ads via fax without first obtaining the recipient's permission. (Similar issues have arisen with respect to junk e-mail, called "spam"—see Chapter 4.)

The act is enforced by the Federal Communications Commission and also provides for a private right of action. Consumers can recover any actual monetary loss resulting from a violation of the act or receive $500 in damages for each violation, whichever is greater. If a court finds that a defendant willfully or knowingly violated the act, the court has the discretion to treble (triple) the damages awarded.

---

24. *Advertising and Marketing on the Internet: Rules of the Road,* September 2000.
25. 47 U.S.C. Sections 227 *et seq.*

What federal act prohibits telemarketers from using an automatic telephone dialing system, and who enforces that act? (© Corbis. All rights reserved.)

The Telemarketing and Consumer Fraud and Abuse Prevention Act[26] of 1994 directed the FTC to establish rules governing telemarketing and to bring actions against fraudulent telemarketers. The FTC's Telemarketing Sales Rule[27] of 1995 requires a telemarketer, before making a sales pitch, to inform the recipient that the call is a sales call and to identify the seller's name and the product being sold. The rule makes it illegal for telemarketers to misrepresent information (including facts about their goods or services and earnings potential, for example). Additionally, telemarketers must inform the people they call of the total cost of the goods being sold, any restrictions on obtaining or using the goods, and whether a sale will be considered final and nonrefundable. A telemarketer must also remove a consumer's name from its list of potential contacts if the consumer so requests. A 2002 amendment to the Telemarketing Sales Rule established a national "Do Not Call" registry, which became effective in October 2003. Telemarketers must refrain from calling those consumers who have placed their names on the list.

LABELING AND PACKAGING

A number of federal and state laws deal specifically with the information given on labels and packages. The rules are designed to ensure that labels provide accurate information about the product and to warn about possible dangers from its use or misuse. In general, labels must be accurate and must use words that are understood by the ordinary consumer. For example, a box of cereal cannot be labeled "giant" if that would exaggerate the amount of cereal contained in the box. In some instances, labels must specify the raw materials used in the product, such as the percentage of cotton, nylon, or other fibers used in a garment. In other instances, the products must carry a warning. Cigarette packages and advertising, for example, must include one of several warnings about the health hazards associated with smoking.[28] Some cigar manufacturers have also agreed to voluntarily put similar warnings on cigar packages and labels.

Food Labeling   The Fair Packaging and Labeling Act requires that food product labels identify (1) the product; (2) the net quantity of the contents and, if the number of servings is stated, the size of a serving; (3) the manufacturer; and (4) the packager or distributor.[29] The act also provides for additional requirements concerning descriptions on packages, savings claims, components of nonfood products, and standards for the partial filling of packages.

Food products must bear labels detailing the food's nutrition content, including how much fat the food contains and what kind of fat it is. The Department of Health and Human Services, as well as the FTC, enforces these rules. The Nutrition Labeling and Education Act of 1990 requires standard nutrition facts (including fat content) on food labels; regulates the use of such terms as *fresh* and *low fat;* and, subject to the federal Food and Drug Administration's approval, authorizes certain health claims.

Other Federal Statutes   Federal laws regulating the labeling and packaging of products include the Wool Products Labeling Act of 1939,[30] the Fur Products

You can find current articles concerning consumer issues at the Alexander Law Firm's "Consumer Law Page." Go to **http://consumerlawpage. com/intro.html**.

---

26. 15 U.S.C. Sections 6101–6108.
27. 16 C.F.R. Sections 310.1–310.8.
28. 15 U.S.C. Sections 1331 *et seq.*
29. 15 U.S.C. Sections 4401–4408.
30. 15 U.S.C. Section 68.

Labeling Act of 1951,[31] the Flammable Fabrics Act of 1953,[32] the Fair Packaging and Labeling Act of 1966,[33] the Comprehensive Smokeless Tobacco Health Education Act of 1986,[34] and the Nutrition Labeling and Education Act of 1990.[35] The Comprehensive Smokeless Tobacco Health Education Act, for example, requires that producers, packagers, and importers of smokeless tobacco label their product with one of several warnings about the health hazards associated with the use of smokeless tobacco; the warnings are similar to those required on cigarette packages.

SALES

A number of statutes protect consumers by requiring the disclosure of certain terms in sales transactions and providing rules governing home or door-to-door sales, mail-order transactions, referral sales, and unsolicited merchandise. The Federal Reserve Board of Governors, for example, has issued **Regulation Z,** which governs credit provisions associated with sales contracts. Many states have also passed laws providing remedies to consumers in home sales. Furthermore, states have provided a number of consumer protection measures, such as implied warranties, through the adoption of the Uniform Commercial Code. In some states, the Uniform Consumer Credit Code's requirements, including disclosure requirements, also protect consumers in credit transactions.

REGULATION Z
A set of rules promulgated by the Federal Reserve Board of Governors to implement the provisions of the Truth-in-Lending Act.

Door-to-Door Sales   The laws of most states single out door-to-door sales for special treatment in part because of the nature of the sales transaction. Repeat purchases are less likely than in stores, so the seller has less incentive to cultivate the goodwill of the purchaser. Furthermore, the seller is unlikely to present alternative products and their prices. Thus, a number of states have passed **"cooling-off" laws** that permit the buyers of goods sold door-to-door to cancel their contracts within a specified period of time, usually two to three days after the sale.

An FTC regulation also requires sellers to give consumers three days to cancel any door-to-door sale. Because this rule applies in addition to the relevant state statutes, consumers are given the benefits of both the FTC rule and their own state statutes. In addition, the FTC rule requires that consumers be notified in Spanish of this right if the oral negotiations for the sale were in that language.

"COOLING-OFF" LAWS
Laws that allow buyers a period of time, such as three days, in which to cancel door-to-door sales contracts.

Telephone and Mail-Order Sales   The nation's Better Business Bureaus receive more complaints about sales made by telephone or mail order than about any other transactions. Many mail-order houses are far removed from the buyers who order from them, making it difficult for a consumer to bring a complaint against a seller. To a certain extent, consumers are protected under federal laws prohibiting mail fraud, which were discussed in Chapter 6, and under state consumer protection laws that parallel and supplement the federal laws.

The FTC's Mail or Telephone Order Merchandise Rule of 1993, which amended the FTC's Mail Order Rule of 1975,[36] provides specific protections for consumers

To learn more about the FTC's cooling-off rule, go to

http://www.ftc.gov/bcp/ conline/pubs/buying/ cooling.htm.

---

31. 15 U.S.C. Section 69.
32. 15 U.S.C. Section 1191.
33. 15 U.S.C. Sections 1451 *et seq.*
34. 15 U.S.C. Sections 4401–4408.
35. 21 U.S.C. Section 343–1.
36. 16 C.F.R. Sections 435.1–435.2.

who purchase goods via phone lines or through the mails. The 1993 rule extended the 1975 rule to include sales in which orders are transmitted using computers, fax machines, or any similar means involving telephone lines. Among other things, the rule requires mail-order merchants to ship orders within the time promised in their catalogues or advertisements, to notify consumers when orders cannot be shipped on time, and to issue a refund within a specified period of time when a consumer cancels an order.

In addition, the Postal Reorganization Act of 1970[37] provides that unsolicited merchandise sent by U.S. mail may be retained, used, discarded, or disposed of in any manner the recipient deems appropriate, without the recipient's incurring any obligation to the sender.

Online Sales   In recent years, the Internet has become a vehicle for a wide variety of business-to-consumer (B2C) sales transactions. Most mail-order houses now have a Web presence, and other Web sites offer consumers an increasing array of goods, ranging from airline tickets to books to xylophones. Protecting consumers from fraudulent and deceptive sales practices conducted via the Internet has proved to be a challenging task. Nonetheless, the FTC and other federal agencies have brought a number of enforcement actions against those who perpetrate online fraud. Additionally, the laws mentioned earlier, such as the federal statute prohibiting wire fraud, apply to online transactions.

Some states have amended their consumer protection statutes to cover Internet transactions as well. For example, the California legislature revised its Business and Professional Code to include transactions conducted over the Internet or by "any other electronic means of communication." Previously, that code covered only telephone, mail-order catalogue, radio, and television sales. Now any entity selling over the Internet in California must explicitly create an on-screen notice indicating its refund and return policies, where its business is physically located, its legal name, and a number of other details. Various states are also setting up information sites to help consumers protect themselves.

HEALTH AND SAFETY PROTECTION

The laws discussed earlier regarding the labeling and packaging of products go a long way toward promoting consumer health and safety. There is a significant distinction, however, between regulating the information dispensed about a product and regulating the actual content of the product. The classic example is tobacco products. Producers of tobacco products are required to warn consumers about the hazards associated with the use of their products. Yet the sale of tobacco products has not yet been subject to significant restrictions or banned outright despite their obvious hazards. We now examine various laws that regulate the actual products made available to consumers.

Food and Drugs   The first federal legislation regulating food and drugs was enacted in 1906 as the Pure Food and Drugs Act.[38] That law, as amended in 1938, exists now as the Federal Food, Drug and Cosmetic Act (FFDCA).[39] The act protects consumers against adulterated and misbranded foods and drugs. More recent

---

37. 39 U.S.C. Section 3009.
38. 21 U.S.C. Sections 1–5, 7–15.
39. 21 U.S.C. Section 301.

BE AWARE The Food and Drug Administration is authorized to obtain, among other things, orders for the recall and seizure of certain products.

amendments to the act added other substantive and procedural requirements. In its present form, the act establishes food standards, specifies safe levels of potentially hazardous food additives, and sets classifications of food and food advertising.

Most of these statutory requirements are monitored and enforced by the Food and Drug Administration (FDA). Under an extensive set of procedures established by the FDA, drugs must be shown to be effective as well as safe before they may be marketed to the public, and the use of some food additives suspected of being carcinogenic is prohibited. A 1976 amendment to the FFDCA[40] authorizes the FDA to regulate medical devices, such as pacemakers and other health devices or equipment, and to withdraw from the market any such device that is mislabeled.

Consumer Product Safety Legislation regulating the safety of consumer products began in 1953 with the enactment of the Flammable Fabrics Act, which prohibits the sale of highly flammable clothing or materials. Over the next two decades, Congress enacted legislation regarding the design or composition of specific classes of products. Then, in 1972, Congress enacted the Consumer Product Safety Act,[41] which created a comprehensive scheme of regulation over matters concerning consumer safety. The act also established the Consumer Product Safety Commission (CPSC) and gave it far-reaching authority over consumer safety.

The CPSC's Authority. The CPSC conducts research on the safety of individual products and maintains a clearinghouse on the risks associated with various products. The Consumer Product Safety Act authorizes the CPSC to set standards for consumer products and to ban the manufacture and sale of any product that the commission deems to be potentially hazardous to consumers. The CPSC also has authority to remove from the market any products it believes to be imminently hazardous and to require manufacturers to report on any products already sold or intended for sale if the products have proved to be hazardous. Additionally, the CPSC administers other product-safety legislation, such as the Child Protection and Toy Safety Act of 1969[42] and the Federal Hazardous Substances Act of 1960.[43]

The CPSC's authority is sufficiently broad to allow it to ban any product that the commission believes poses merely an "unreasonable risk" to the consumer. Products banned by the CPSC have included various types of fireworks, cribs, and toys, as well as many products containing asbestos or vinyl chloride.

Notification Requirements. The Consumer Product Safety Act imposes notification requirements on distributors of consumer products. Distributors must immediately notify the CPSC when they receive information that a product "contains a defect which . . . creates a substantial risk to the public" or "an unreasonable risk of serious injury or death."

CREDIT PROTECTION

Considering the extensive use of credit by U.S. consumers, credit protection is one of the most important aspects of consumer protection legislation. A key statute regulating the credit and credit-card industries is the Truth-in-Lending Act (TILA), the

---

40. 21 U.S.C. Sections 352(o), 360(j), 360(k), and 360c–360k.
41. 15 U.S.C. Section 2051.
42. 15 U.S.C. Section 1262(e).
43. 15 U.S.C. Sections 1261–1273.

name commonly given to Title 1 of the Consumer Credit Protection Act (CCPA),[44] which was passed by Congress in 1968.

Truth in Lending   The TILA is basically a *disclosure law*. It is administered by the Federal Reserve Board and requires sellers and lenders to disclose credit terms or loan terms so that individuals can shop around for the best financing arrangements. TILA requirements apply only to persons who, in the ordinary course of business, lend funds, sell on credit, or arrange for the extension of credit. Thus, sales or loans made between two consumers do not come under the protection of the act. Additionally, this law protects only debtors who are *natural* persons (as opposed to the artificial "person" of a corporation); it does not extend to other legal entities.

> **NOTE** The Federal Reserve Board is part of the Federal Reserve System, which influences the lending and investing activities of commercial banks and the cost and availability of credit.

The disclosure requirements are found in Regulation Z, which, as mentioned earlier in this chapter, was promulgated by the Federal Reserve Board. If the contracting parties are subject to the TILA, the requirements of Regulation Z apply to any transaction involving an installment sales contract that calls for payment to be made in more than four installments. Transactions subject to Regulation Z typically include installment loans, retail and installment sales, car loans, home-improvement loans, and certain real estate loans if the amount of financing is less than $25,000.

Under the provisions of the TILA, all of the terms of a credit instrument must be clearly and conspicuously disclosed. The TILA provides for contract rescission (cancellation) if a creditor fails to follow the exact procedures required by the act.[45]

Equal Credit Opportunity.   In 1974, Congress enacted, as an amendment to the TILA, the Equal Credit Opportunity Act (ECOA).[46] The ECOA prohibits the denial of credit solely on the basis of race, religion, national origin, color, gender, marital status, or age. The act also prohibits credit discrimination on the basis of whether an individual receives certain forms of income, such as public-assistance benefits.

Under the ECOA, a creditor may not require the signature of an applicant's spouse, or a cosigner, on a credit instrument if the applicant qualifies under the creditor's standards of creditworthiness for the amount requested. ■ **EXAMPLE 13.12** Tonja, an African American, applied for financing with a used-car dealer. The dealer looked at Tonja's credit report and, without submitting the application to the lender, decided that she would not qualify. Instead of informing Tonja that she did not qualify, the dealer told her that she needed a cosigner on the loan to purchase the car. According to a federal appellate court in 2004, the dealer qualified as a creditor in this situation because the dealer unilaterally denied the credit and thus could be held liable under the ECOA.[47]■

Credit-Card Rules.   The TILA also contains provisions regarding credit cards. One provision limits the liability of a cardholder to $50 per card for unauthorized charges made before the creditor is notified that the card has been lost. Another provision

---

44. 15 U.S.C. Sections 1601–1693r. The act was amended in 1980 by the Truth-in-Lending Simplification and Reform Act.

45. Note, though, that amendments to the TILA enacted in 1995 prevent borrowers from rescinding loans for minor clerical errors in closing documents [15 U.S.C. Sections 1605, 1631, 1635, 1640, and 1641].

46. 15 U.S.C. Section 1643.

47. *Treadway v. Gateway Chevrolet Oldsmobile, Inc.,* 362 F.3d 971 (7th Cir. 2004).

prohibits a credit-card company from billing a consumer for any unauthorized charges if the credit card was improperly issued by the company. ■ **EXAMPLE 13.13** Suppose that a consumer receives an unsolicited credit card in the mail and the card is later stolen and used by the thief to make purchases. In this situation, the consumer to whom the card was sent will not be liable for the unauthorized charges. ■

Further provisions of the act concern billing disputes related to credit-card purchases. If a debtor thinks that an error has occurred in billing or wishes to withhold payment for a faulty product purchased by credit card, the act outlines specific procedures for both the consumer and the credit-card company in settling the dispute.

Consumer Leases. The Consumer Leasing Act (CLA) of 1988[48] amended the TILA to provide protection for consumers who lease automobiles and other goods. The CLA applies to those who lease or arrange to lease consumer goods in the ordinary course of their business. The act applies only if the goods are priced at $25,000 or less and if the lease term exceeds four months. The CLA and its implementing regulation, Regulation M,[49] require lessors to disclose in writing all of the material terms of the lease.

Fair Credit Reporting In 1970, to protect consumers against inaccurate credit reporting, Congress enacted the Fair Credit Reporting Act (FCRA).[50] The act provides that consumer credit reporting agencies may issue credit reports to users only for specified purposes, including the extension of credit, the issuance of insurance policies, compliance with a court order, and compliance with a consumer's request for a copy of her or his own credit report. The act further provides that any time a consumer is denied credit or insurance on the basis of the consumer's credit report, or is charged more than others ordinarily would be for credit or insurance, the consumer must be notified of that fact and of the name and address of the credit reporting agency that issued the credit report.

Consumers Must Be Given Access to Information. Under the FCRA, consumers may request the source of any information being given out by a credit agency, as well as the identity of anyone who has received an agency's report. Consumers are also permitted to have access to the information contained about them in a credit reporting agency's files. If a consumer discovers that the agency's files contain inaccurate information about the consumer's credit standing, the agency, on the consumer's written request, must investigate the matter and delete any unverifiable or erroneous information within a reasonable period of time.

Reporting Agencies Must Investigate Disputed Information. An agency's investigation should include contacting the creditor whose information a consumer disputes. It would also seem clear that the creditor, after receiving notice of the dispute, should conduct a "reasonable investigation" of its records to determine whether the disputed information can be verified. The question in the following case was what exactly constitutes a "reasonable investigation" by the creditor.

---

48. 15 U.S.C. Sections 1667–1667e.
49. 12 C.F.R. Part 213.
50. 15 U.S.C. Sections 1681 *et seq.*

CASE 13.4 ■ Johnson v. MBNA America Bank, N.A.

United States Court of Appeals,
Fourth Circuit, 2004.
357 F.3d 426.

FACTS Edward Slater opened a MasterCard credit-card account with MBNA America Bank, N.A., in November 1987. Slater married Linda Johnson in March 1991. Almost ten years later, in December 2000, Slater filed for bankruptcy when the balance on the account was about $17,000. MBNA removed Slater's name from the account and told Johnson that she was responsible for paying the balance. Johnson disputed her responsibility and contacted consumer credit reporting agencies, which notified MBNA. MBNA confirmed that the disputed information matched the data in its computers, but it did not investigate further. The agencies continued to include the account on Johnson's credit report. Johnson filed a suit in a federal district court against MBNA and the agencies, claiming in part that MBNA had violated the FCRA by failing to conduct a "reasonable" investigation of her dispute. The court entered a judgment in Johnson's favor and awarded her $90,300 in damages. MBNA appealed to the U.S. Court of Appeals for the Fourth Circuit.

ISSUE Under the FCRA, does a creditor have to conduct more than a brief review of its records to verify disputed information?

DECISION Yes. The U.S. Court of Appeals for the Fourth Circuit affirmed the judgment of the lower court,

concluding that MBNA acted unreasonably in failing to verify the accuracy of the information in its database.

REASON The court noted that dictionaries define *investigation* as "a detailed inquiry," "a systematic examination," or "a searching inquiry." The FCRA uses *investigation* in specifying a creditor's duties in the consumer dispute process. "It would make little sense to conclude that, in creating a system intended to give consumers a means to dispute—and, ultimately, correct—inaccurate information on their credit reports, Congress used the term 'investigation' to include superficial, *un*reasonable inquiries by creditors." In any consumer dispute, MBNA never looked beyond the information in its database and never consulted underlying documents such as account applications. In fact, MBNA relied on the fact that the original application had been thrown out, so that it would not have to change the result of an investigation. The court added that MBNA should at least have told the agencies that the application was not available and thus it could not "conclusively verify" that Johnson was a co-obligor on the account.

FOR CRITICAL ANALYSIS—Social Consideration
Suppose that MBNA had done as the court suggested and reported to the agencies that it could not verify that Johnson's name was on the original account application because the application had been destroyed. Could Johnson still be held liable for the debt incurred in Slater's name? Why or why not?

Fair and Accurate Credit Transactions Act   In an effort to combat rampant identity theft (discussed in Chapter 6), Congress passed the Fair and Accurate Credit Transactions (FACT) Act of 2003.[51] The act established a national fraud alert system so that consumers who suspect that they have been or may be victimized by identity theft can place an alert in their credit files. The FACT Act also requires the major credit reporting agencies to provide consumers with a free copy of their credit reports every twelve months. Another provision requires account numbers on credit-card receipts to be shortened ("truncated") so that merchants, employees, and others who have access to the receipts cannot obtain a consumer's name and full credit-card numbers. The act also mandates that financial institutions work with the Federal Trade Commission to identify "red flag" indicators of identity theft and to develop rules on how to dispose of sensitive credit information.

The FACT Act also gives consumers who have been victimized by identity theft some assistance in rebuilding their credit reputations. For example, credit reporting agencies must stop reporting allegedly fraudulent account information once the consumer establishes that identify theft has occurred. Business owners and creditors are

---

51. Pub. L. No.108-159, 117 Stat. 1952 (December 4, 2003).

For information on the Fair and Accurate Credit Transactions Act, including transcripts of congressional testimony concerning the act, go to

http://www.ftc.gov/opa/ 2004/06/factaidt.htm.

required to provide a consumer with copies of any records that can help the consumer prove that a particular account or transaction is fraudulent (such as when an account was created by a fraudulent signature, for example). In addition, to help prevent the spread of erroneous credit information, the act allows consumers to report the accounts affected by identity theft directly to the creditors.

Fair Debt-Collection Practices   In 1977, Congress enacted the Fair Debt Collection Practices Act (FDCPA)[52] in an attempt to curb what were perceived to be abuses by collection agencies. The act applies only to specialized debt-collection agencies that regularly attempt to collect debts on behalf of someone else, usually for a percentage of the amount owed. Creditors attempting to collect debts are not covered by the act unless, by misrepresenting themselves, they cause the debtors to believe that they are collection agencies.

Requirements under the Act.   The act explicitly prohibits a collection agency from using any of the following tactics:

1 Contacting the debtor at the debtor's place of employment if the debtor's employer objects.

2 Contacting the debtor during inconvenient or unusual times (for example, calling the debtor at three o'clock in the morning) or at any time if the debtor is being represented by an attorney.

3 Contacting third parties other than the debtor's parents, spouse, or financial adviser about payment of a debt unless a court authorizes such action.

4 Using harassment or intimidation (for example, using abusive language or threatening violence) or employing false and misleading information (for example, posing as a police officer).

5 Communicating with the debtor at any time after receiving notice that the debtor is refusing to pay the debt, except to advise the debtor of further action to be taken by the collection agency.

The FDCPA also requires collection agencies to include a "validation notice" whenever they initially contact a debtor for payment of a debt or within five days of that initial contact. The notice must state that the debtor has thirty days within which to dispute the debt and to request a written verification of the debt from the collection agency. The debtor's request for debt validation must be in writing.

Enforcement of the Act.   The enforcement of the FDCPA is primarily the responsibility of the Federal Trade Commission. The FDCPA provides that a debt collector who fails to comply with the act is liable for actual damages, plus additional damages not to exceed $1,000 [53] and attorneys' fees.

Cases brought under the FDCPA often raise questions as to who qualifies as a debt collector or debt-collecting agency subject to the act. For example, for several years it was not clear whether attorneys who attempted to collect debts owed to their clients were subject to the FDCPA's provisions. In 1995, the United States Supreme Court addressed this issue to resolve conflicting opinions in the lower courts. The Court held that an attorney who regularly tries to obtain payment of consumer debts through legal proceedings meets the FDCPA's definition of "debt collector."[54]

---

52. 15 U.S.C. Section 1692.
53. According to the U.S. Court of Appeals for the Sixth Circuit, the $1,000 limit on damages applies to each lawsuit, not to each violation. See *Wright v. Finance Service of Norwalk, Inc.,* 22 F.3d 647 (6th Cir. 1994).
54. *Heintz v. Jenkins,* 514 U.S. 291, 115 S.Ct. 1489, 131 L.Ed.2d 395 (1995).

APPLICATION ▪ How Do Sellers Create Warranties?*

Warranties are important in both commercial and consumer purchase transactions. There are three types of product warranties: express warranties, implied warranties of merchantability, and implied warranties of fitness for a particular purpose. If you are a seller of products, you can make or create any one of these warranties, which are available to both consumers and commercial purchasers.

First and foremost, sellers and buyers need to know whether warranties have been created.

WARRANTY CREATION

Express warranties do not have to be labeled as such, but statements of simple opinion generally do not constitute express warranties. Express warranties can be made by descriptions of the goods. Express warranties can be found in a seller's advertisement, brochure, or promotional materials or can be made orally or in an express writing. A sales representative should use care in describing the merits of a product; otherwise, the seller could be held to an express warranty. If an express warranty is not intended, the sales pitch should not promise too much.

In most sales, because the seller is a merchant, the purchased goods carry the implied warranty of merchantability. If you are a seller, you must also be aware of the importance of the implied warranty of fitness for a particular purpose. Assume that a customer comes to your sales representative, describes the job to be done in detail, and says, "I really need something that can do the job." Your sales representative replies, "This product will do the job." An implied warranty that the product is fit for that particular purpose has been created.

*This *Application* is not meant to serve as a substitute for the services of an attorney who is licensed to practice law in your state.

WARRANTY DISCLAIMERS

Many sellers, particularly in commercial sales, try to limit or disclaim warranties. The Uniform Commercial Code permits all warranties, including express warranties, to be excluded or negated. Conspicuous statements—such as "THERE ARE NO WARRANTIES WHICH EXTEND BEYOND THE DESCRIPTION ON THE FACE HEREOF" or "THERE ARE NO IMPLIED WARRANTIES OF FITNESS FOR A PARTICULAR PURPOSE OR MERCHANTABILITY WHICH ACCOMPANY THIS SALE"—can be used to disclaim the implied warranties of fitness and merchantability. Used goods are sometimes sold "as is" or "with all faults" so that implied warranties of fitness and merchantability are disclaimed. Whenever these warranties are disclaimed, a purchaser should be aware that the product may not be of even average quality.

CHECKLIST FOR THE SELLER

1. If you wish to limit warranties, do so by means of a carefully worded and prominently placed written or printed provision that a reasonable person would understand and accept.
2. As a seller, you might wish to have the buyer sign a statement certifying that he or she has read all of your warranty disclaimer provisions.
3. If you do not intend to make an express warranty, do not make a promise or an affirmation of fact concerning the performance or quality of a product you are selling.

▪ KEY TERMS

CHAPTER SUMMARY ▦ Warranties, Product Liability, and Consumer Law

WARRANTIES	
Warranties of Title (See pages 385–386.)	The UCC provides for the following warranties of title [UCC 2–312, 2A–211]: 1. *Good title*—A seller warrants that he or she has the right to pass good and rightful title to the goods. 2. *No liens*—A seller warrants that the goods sold are free of any encumbrances (claims, charges, or liabilities—usually called liens). A lessor warrants that the lessee will not be disturbed in her or his possession of the goods by the claims of a third party. 3. *No infringements*—A merchant-seller warrants that the goods are free of infringement claims (claims that a patent, trademark, or copyright has been infringed) by third parties. Lessors make similar warranties.
Express Warranties (See pages 386–389.)	1. *Under the UCC*—An express warranty arises under the UCC when a seller or lessor indicates, as part of the basis of the bargain, any of the following: a. An affirmation or promise of fact. b. A description of the goods. c. A sample shown as conforming to the contract goods [UCC 2–313, 2A–210]. 2. Under the *Magnuson-Moss Warranty Act*—Express written warranties covering consumer goods priced at more than $10, *if made,* must be labeled as one of the following: a. Full warranty—Free repair or replacement of defective parts; refund or replacement for goods if they cannot be repaired in a reasonable time. b. Limited warranty—When less than a full warranty is being offered.
Implied Warranty of Merchantability (See pages 389–391.)	When a seller or lessor is a merchant who deals in goods of the kind sold or leased, the seller or lessor warrants that the goods sold or leased are properly packaged and labeled, are of proper quality, and are reasonably fit for the ordinary purposes for which such goods are used [UCC 2–314, 2A–212].
Implied Warranty of Fitness for a Particular Purpose (See page 391.)	Arises when the buyer's or lessee's purpose or use is expressly or impliedly known by the seller or lessor, and the buyer or lessee purchases or leases the goods in reliance on the seller's or lessor's selection [UCC 2–315, 2A–213].
Other Implied Warranties (See pages 391–392.)	Other implied warranties can arise as a result of course of dealing or usage of trade [UCC 2–314(3), 2A–212(3)].
PRODUCT LIABILITY	
Liability Based on Negligence (See page 395.)	1. The manufacturer must use due care in designing the product, selecting materials, using the appropriate production process, assembling and testing the product, and placing adequate warnings on the label or product. 2. Privity of contract is not required. A manufacturer is liable for failure to exercise due care to any person who sustains an injury proximately caused by a negligently made (defective) product.
Liability Based on Misrepresentation (See page 395.)	Fraudulent misrepresentation of a product may result in product liability based on the tort of fraud.
Strict Liability— Requirements (See pages 395–398.)	1. The defendant must sell the product in a defective condition. 2. The defendant must normally be engaged in the business of selling that product. 3. The product must be unreasonably dangerous to the user or consumer because of its defective condition (in most states).

(Continued)

CHAPTER SUMMARY ■ Warranties, Product Liability, and Consumer Law—Continued

Strict Liability— Requirements— Continued	4. The plaintiff must incur physical harm to self or property by use or consumption of the product. (Courts will also extend strict liability to include injured bystanders.) 5. The defective condition must be the proximate cause of the injury or damage. 6. The goods must not have been substantially changed from the time the product was sold to the time the injury was sustained.
Strict Liability— Product Defects (See pages 398–401.)	A product may be defective in three basic ways: 1. In its manufacture. 2. In its design. 3. In the instructions or warnings that come with it.
Market-Share Liability (See page 401.)	When plaintiffs cannot prove which of many distributors of a defective product supplied the particular product that caused the plaintiffs' injuries, some courts apply market-share liability. All firms that manufactured and distributed the harmful product during the period in question are then held liable for the plaintiffs' injuries in proportion to the firms' respective shares of the market, as directed by the court.
Other Applications of Strict Liability (See pages 401–402.)	1. Manufacturers and other sellers are liable for harms suffered by bystanders as a result of defective products. 2. Suppliers of component parts are strictly liable for defective parts that, when incorporated into a product, cause injuries to users.
Defenses to Product Liability (See pages 402–404.)	1. *Assumption of risk*—The user or consumer knew of the risk of harm and voluntarily assumed it. 2. *Product misuse*—The user or consumer misused the product in a way unforeseeable by the manufacturer. 3. *Comparative negligence and liability*—Liability may be distributed between the plaintiff and the defendant under the doctrine of comparative negligence if the plaintiff's misuse of the product contributed to the risk of injury. 4. *Commonly known dangers*—If a defendant succeeds in convincing the court that a plaintiff's injury resulted from a commonly known danger, such as the danger associated with using a sharp knife, the defendant will not be liable. 5. *Other defenses*—A defendant can also defend against a product liability claim by showing that there is no basis for the plaintiff's claim (that the plaintiff has not met the requirements for an action in negligence or strict liability, for example).
	CONSUMER PROTECTION LAW

Deceptive Advertising (See pages 405–407.)	1. *Definition of deceptive advertising*—Generally, an advertising claim will be deemed deceptive if it would mislead a reasonable consumer.
	
	2. *Bait-and-switch advertising*—Advertising a lower-priced product (the "bait") when the intention is not to sell the advertised product but to lure consumers into the store and convince them to buy a higher-priced product (the "switch") is prohibited by the FTC.
	
	3. *Online deceptive advertising*—The FTC has issued guidelines to help online businesses comply with existing laws prohibiting deceptive advertising. The guidelines do not set forth new rules but rather describe how existing laws apply to online advertising.
	
	4. *FTC actions against deceptive advertising*—
	  a. Cease-and-desist orders—Requiring the advertiser to stop the challenged advertising.
	  b. Counteradvertising—Requiring the advertiser to advertise to correct the earlier misinformation.

CHAPTER SUMMARY Warranties, Product Liability, and Consumer Law—Continued

Telemarketing and Electronic Advertising (See pages 407–408.)	The Telephone Consumer Protection Act of 1991 prohibits telephone solicitation using an automatic telephone dialing system or a prerecorded voice, as well as the transmission of advertising materials via fax without first obtaining the recipient's permission to do so.
Labeling and Packaging (See pages 408–409.)	Manufacturers must comply with labeling or packaging requirements for their specific products. In general, all labels must be accurate and not misleading.
Sales (See pages 409–410.)	1. *Door-to-door sales*—The FTC requires all door-to-door sellers to give consumers three days (a "cooling-off" period) to cancel any sale. States also provide for similar protection. 2. *Telephone and mail-order sales*—Federal and state statutes and regulations govern certain practices of sellers who solicit over the telephone or through the mails and prohibit the use of the mails to defraud individuals. 3. *Online sales*—Increasingly, the Internet is being used to conduct business-to-consumer (B2C) transactions. Both state and federal laws protect consumers to some extent against fraudulent and deceptive online sales practices.
Health and Safety Protection (See pages 410–411.)	1. *Food and drugs*—The Federal Food, Drug and Cosmetic Act of 1938, as amended, protects consumers against adulterated and misbranded foods and drugs. The act establishes food standards, specifies safe levels of potentially hazardous food additives, and sets classifications of food and food advertising. 2. *Consumer product safety*—The Consumer Product Safety Act of 1972 seeks to protect consumers from risk of injury from hazardous products. The Consumer Product Safety Commission has the power to remove products that are deemed imminently hazardous from the market and to ban the manufacture and sale of hazardous products.

Credit Protection (See pages 411–415.)	1. *Consumer Credit Protection Act, Title I (Truth-in-Lending Act, or TILA)*—A disclosure law that requires sellers and lenders to disclose credit terms or loan terms in certain transactions, including retail and installment sales and loans, car loans, home-improvement loans, and certain real estate loans. Additionally, the TILA provides for the following:
	
	    a. Equal credit opportunity—Creditors are prohibited from discriminating on the basis of race, religion, marital status, gender, and so on.
	
	    b. Credit-card protection—Credit-card users may withhold payment for a faulty product purchased by credit card, or for an error in billing, until the dispute is resolved; liability of cardholders for unauthorized charges is limited to $50, providing notice requirements are met; consumers are not liable for unauthorized charges made on unsolicited credit cards.
	
	    c. Consumer leases—The Consumer Leasing Act (CLA) of 1988 protects consumers who lease automobiles and other goods priced at $25,000 or less if the lease term exceeds four months.
	
	 2. *Fair Credit Reporting Act*—Entitles consumers to request verification of the accuracy of a credit report and to have unverified or false information removed from their files.
	
	 3. *Fair Debt Collection Practices Act*—Prohibits debt collectors from using unfair debt-collection practices, such as contacting the debtor at his or her place of employment if the employer objects or at unreasonable times, contacting third parties about the debt, and harassing the debtor, for example.

FOR REVIEW

Answers for the even-numbered questions in this For Review *section can be found in Appendix I at the end of this text.*

1 What factors determine whether a seller's or lessor's statement constitutes an express warranty or mere "puffing"?

2 What implied warranties arise under the UCC?

3 Can a manufacturer be held liable to any person who suffers an injury proximately caused by the manufacturer's negligently made product?

4 What defenses to liability can be raised in a product liability lawsuit?

5 What are the major federal statutes providing for consumer protection?

QUESTIONS AND CASE PROBLEMS

13–1. Product Liability. Under what contract theory can a seller be held liable to a consumer for physical harm or property damage that is caused by the goods sold? Under what tort theories can the seller be held liable?

13–2. Warranty Disclaimers. Tandy purchased a washing machine from Marshall Appliances. The sales contract included a provision explicitly disclaiming all express or implied warranties, including the implied warranty of merchantability. The disclaimer was printed in the same size and color as the rest of the contract. The machine turned out to be a "lemon" and never functioned properly. Tandy sought a refund of the purchase price, claiming that Marshall had breached the implied warranty of merchantability. Can Tandy recover her money, notwithstanding the warranty disclaimer in the contract? Explain.

13–3. Implied Warranties. Sam, a farmer, needs to install a two-thousand-pound piece of equipment in his barn. The equipment must be lifted thirty feet into a hayloft. Sam goes to Durham Hardware and tells Durham that he needs some heavy-duty rope to be used on his farm. Durham recommends a one-inch-thick nylon rope, and Sam purchases two hundred feet of it. Sam ties the rope around the piece of equipment, puts the rope through a pulley, and with the aid of a tractor lifts the equipment off the ground. Suddenly, the rope breaks. The equipment crashes to the ground and is extensively damaged. Sam files suit against Durham for breach of the implied warranty of fitness for a particular purpose. Discuss how successful Sam will be with his suit.

13–4. Credit Protection. Maria Ochoa receives two new credit cards on May 1. She had solicited one of them from Midtown Department Store, and the other arrived unsolicited from High-Flying Airlines. During the month of May, Ochoa makes numerous credit-card purchases from Midtown Department Store, but she does not use the High-Flying Airlines card. On May 31, a burglar breaks into Ochoa's home and steals both credit cards, along with other items. Ochoa notifies the Midtown Department Store of the theft on June 2, but she fails to notify High-Flying Airlines. Using the Midtown credit card, the burglar makes a $500 purchase on June 1 and a $200 purchase on June 3. The burglar then charges a vacation flight on the High-Flying Airlines card for $1,000 on June 5. Ochoa receives the bills for these charges and refuses to pay them. Discuss Ochoa's liability in these situations.

CASE PROBLEM WITH SAMPLE ANSWER

13–5. In May 1995, Ms. McCathern and her daughter, together with McCathern's cousin, Ms. Sanders, and her daughter, were riding in Sanders's 1994 Toyota 4Runner. Sanders was driving, McCathern was in the front passenger seat, and the children were in the back seat. Everyone was wearing a seat belt. While the group was traveling south on Oregon State Highway 395 at a speed of approximately 50 miles per hour, an oncoming vehicle veered into Sanders's lane of travel. When Sanders tried to steer clear, the 4Runner rolled over and landed upright on its four wheels. During the rollover, the roof over the front passenger seat collapsed, and as a result, McCathern sustained serious, permanent injuries. McCathern filed a suit in an Oregon state court against Toyota Motor Corp. and others, alleging in part that the 1994 4Runner "was dangerously defective and unreasonably dangerous in that the vehicle, as designed and sold, was unstable and prone to rollover." What is the test for product liability based on a design defect? What would McCathern have to prove to succeed under that test? [*McCathern v. Toyota Motor Corp.*, 332 Or. 59, 23 P.3d 320 (2001)]

After you have answered this problem, compare your answer with the sample answer given on the Web site that accompanies this text. Go to http://blt.westbuslaw.com, select "Chapter 13," and click on "Case Problem with Sample Answer."

13–6. Fair Credit Reporting Act. Source One Associates, Inc., is based in Poughquag, New York. Peter Easton, Source One's president, is responsible for its daily operations. Between 1995 and 1997, Source One received requests from persons in Massachusetts seeking financial information about individuals and businesses. To obtain this information, Easton first obtained the targeted individuals' credit reports through Equifax Consumer Information Services by claiming the reports would be used only in connection with credit transactions involving the consumers. From the reports, Easton identified financial institutions at which the targeted individuals held accounts and then called the institutions to learn the account balances by impersonating either officers of the institutions or the account holders. The information was then provided to Source One's customers for a fee. Easton did not know why the customers wanted the information. The state ("Commonwealth") of Massachusetts filed a suit in a Massachusetts state court against Source One and Easton, alleging, among other things, violations of the Fair Credit Reporting Act (FCRA). Did the defendants violate the FCRA? Explain. [*Commonwealth v. Source One Associates, Inc.*, 436 Mass. 118, 763 N.E.2d 42 (2002)]

13–7. Product Liability. In January 1999, John Clark of Clarksdale, Mississippi, bought a paintball gun. Clark practiced with the gun and knew how to screw in the carbon dioxide cartridge, pump the gun, and use its safety and trigger. He hunted and had taken a course in hunter safety education. He was aware that protective eyewear was available for purchase, but he chose not to buy it. Clark also understood that it was "common sense" not to shoot anyone in the face. Chris Rico, another Clarksdale resident, owned a paintball gun made by Brass Eagle, Inc. Rico was similarly familiar with the gun's use and its risks. Clark, Rico, and their friends played a game that involved shooting paintballs at cars whose occupants also had the guns. One night, while Clark and Rico were cruising with their guns, Rico shot at Clark's car but hit Clark in the eye. Clark filed a suit in a Mississippi state court against Brass Eagle to recover for the injury, alleging in part that its gun was defectively designed. During the trial, Rico testified that his gun "never malfunctioned." In whose favor should the court rule? Why? [*Clark v. Brass Eagle, Inc.*, 866 So.2d 456 (Miss. 2004)]

A QUESTION OF ETHICS

13–8. On July 1, 1993, Gian Luigi Ferri entered the offices of a law firm against which he had a grudge. Using two semiautomatic assault weapons (TEC-9 and TEC-DC9) manufactured and distributed by Navegar, Inc., he killed eight persons and wounded six others before killing himself. The survivors and the families of some of those who had died sued Navegar, based in part on negligence. They claimed that Navegar had a duty not to create risks to the public beyond those inherent in the lawful use of firearms. They offered evidence that Navegar knew or should have known

that the assault guns had "no legitimate sporting or self-defense purpose" and that the guns were "particularly well adapted to military-style assault on large numbers of people." They also claimed that the TEC-DC9 advertising "targets a criminal clientele," further increasing the risk of harm. A California trial court granted summary judgment in Navegar's favor. The appellate court reversed, ruling that the case should go to trial. The court stated that "the likelihood that a third person would make use of the TEC-DC9 in the kind of criminal rampage Ferri perpetrated is precisely the hazard that would support a determination that Navegar's conduct was negligent." Navegar appealed the decision to the California Supreme Court. In view of these facts, consider the following questions. [*Merrill v. Navegar, Inc.*, 26 Cal.4th 465, 28 P.3d 116, 110 Cal.Rptr.2d 370 (2001)]

1. Do you agree with the appellate court that Navegar could be held negligent in marketing the TEC-DC9? What should the California Supreme Court decide? (Before answering this question, you may wish to review the elements of negligence in Chapter 4.)
2. Should gun manufacturers ever be held liable for deaths caused by nondefective guns? Why or why not?
3. Generally, do you believe that policy decisions regarding the liability of gun manufacturers should be made by the courts, whose job is to interpret the law, or by Congress and state legislatures, whose job is to make the law?
4. In your opinion, have Congress and state legislatures gone far enough in regulating the use of firearms, or have they gone too far? Explain.

FOR CRITICAL ANALYSIS

13–9. The United States has the strictest product liability laws in the world today. Why do you think many other countries, particularly developing countries, are more lax with respect to holding manufacturers liable for product defects?

VIDEO QUESTION

13–10. Go to this text's Web site at **http://blt.westbuslaw.com** and select "Chapter 13." Click on "Video Questions" and view the video titled *Advertising Communication Law: Bait and Switch.* Then answer the following questions.

1. Is the auto dealership's advertisement for the truck in the video deceptive? Why or why not?
2. Is the advertisement for the truck an offer to which the dealership is bound? Does it matter if Betty detrimentally relied on the advertisement?
3. Is Tony committed to buying Betty's trade-in truck for $3,000 because that is what he told her over the phone?

INTERNET EXERCISES

Go to the *Business Law Today: The Essentials* home page at <u>**http://blt.westbuslaw.com**</u>, select "Chapter 13," and click on "Internet Exercises." There you will find the following Internet research exercises that you can perform to learn more about topics covered in this chapter.

Activity 13–1: LEGAL PERSPECTIVE—Remedial Promises

Activity 13–2: MANAGEMENT PERSPECTIVE—Warranties

Activity 13–3: LEGAL PERSPECTIVE—The Food and Drug Administration

BEFORE THE TEST

Go to the *Business Law Today: The Essentials* home page at <u>**http://blt.westbuslaw.com**</u>, select "Chapter 13," and click on "Interactive Quizzes." You will find at least twenty interactive questions relating to this chapter.

"It took many generations for people to feel comfortable accepting paper in lieu of gold or silver."

Alan Greenspan, 1926–
(Chairman of the Board of Governors of the Federal Reserve System, 1987–)

▦ LEARNING OBJECTIVES

After reading this chapter, you should be able to answer the following questions:

1 What are the four types of negotiable instruments with which Article 3 of the UCC is concerned? Which of these instruments are *orders* to pay, and which are *promises* to pay?

2 What requirements must an instrument meet to be negotiable?

3 What are the requirements for attaining HDC status?

4 What is the key to liability on a negotiable instrument? What is the difference between signature liability and warranty liability?

5 Certain defenses are valid against all holders, including HDCs. What are these defenses called? Name four defenses that fall within this category.

NEGOTIABLE INSTRUMENT
A signed writing (record) that contains an unconditional promise or order to pay an exact sum of money on demand or at an exact future time to a specific person or order, or to bearer.

Most modern commercial transactions would be inconceivable without negotiable instruments. A **negotiable instrument** is a signed writing (record) that contains an unconditional promise or order to pay an exact sum of money on demand or at a specified future time to a specific person or order, or to bearer. The checks you write to pay for groceries and other items are negotiable instruments.

A negotiable instrument can function as a substitute for money or as an extension of credit. For a negotiable instrument to operate *practically* as either a substitute for money or a credit device, or both, it is essential that the instrument be easily transferable without danger of being uncollectible. Each rule described in the following pages can be examined in light of this essential function of negotiable instruments.

The outcome of litigation concerning negotiable instruments usually turns on whether a holder is entitled to obtain payment on an instrument when it is due. Often, whether a holder is entitled to obtain payment will depend on whether the holder is a *holder in due course* (HDC), a concept we examine in this chapter. We also discuss the liability of the parties to negotiable instruments and the defenses available for avoiding liability on negotiable instruments.

Negotiable instruments must meet special requirements relating to form and content. These requirements, which are imposed by Article 3 of the Uniform Commercial Code (UCC), will be discussed in this chapter. Article 3 also governs the process of negotiation (transferring an instrument from one party to another), as will be discussed. Note that UCC 3–104(b) defines *instrument* as a "negotiable instrument." For that reason, whenever the term *instrument* is used in this book, it refers to a negotiable instrument.

■ Types of Negotiable Instruments

For an instrument to qualify as a *negotiable instrument,* it must meet the following requirements:

1 Be in writing.

2 Be signed by the maker or the drawer.

3 Be an unconditional promise or order to pay.

4 State a fixed amount of money.

5 Be payable on demand or at a definite time.

6 Be payable to order or to bearer, unless it is a check.

The UCC specifies four types of negotiable instruments: *drafts, checks, promissory notes,* and *certificates of deposit* (CDs). These instruments are frequently divided into the two classifications that we will discuss in the following subsections: *orders to pay* (drafts and checks) and *promises to pay* (promissory notes and CDs).

Negotiable instruments may also be classified as either demand instruments or time instruments. A *demand instrument* is payable on demand; that is, it is payable immediately after it is issued and thereafter for a reasonable period of time. All checks are demand instruments because, by definition, they must be payable on demand. A *time instrument* is payable at a future date.

DRAFTS AND CHECKS (ORDERS TO PAY)

A **draft** (bill of exchange) is an unconditional written order that involves three parties. The party creating the draft (the **drawer**) orders another party (the **drawee**) to pay funds, usually to a third party (the **payee**).

Time Drafts and Sight Drafts   A *time draft* is payable at a definite future time. A *sight draft* (or demand draft) is payable on sight—that is, when it is presented to the drawee (usually a bank or financial institution) for payment. A draft can be both a time and a sight draft; such a draft is payable at a stated time after sight. A sight draft may be payable on acceptance. **Acceptance** is the drawee's written promise to pay the draft when it comes due. The usual manner of accepting an instrument is by writing the word *accepted* across the face of the instrument, followed by the date of acceptance and the signature of the drawee.

DRAFT
Any instrument drawn on a drawee that orders the drawee to pay a certain sum of money, usually to a third party (the payee), on demand or at a definite future time.

DRAWER
The party that initiates a draft (such as a check), thereby ordering the drawee to pay.

DRAWEE
The party that is ordered to pay a draft or check. With a check, a bank or a financial institution is always the drawee.

PAYEE
A person to whom an instrument is made payable.

ACCEPTANCE
In negotiable instruments law, the drawee's signed agreement to pay a draft when presented.

Exhibit 14–1 shows a typical time draft. For the drawee to be obligated to honor the order, the drawee must be obligated to the drawer either by agreement or through a debtor-creditor relationship. ■ **EXAMPLE 14.1** On January 16, Ourtown Real Estate Company orders $1,000 worth of office supplies from Eastman Supply Company, with payment due April 16. Also on January 16, Ourtown sends Eastman a draft drawn on its account with the First National Bank of Whiteacre as payment. In this scenario, the drawer is Ourtown, the drawee is Ourtown's bank (First National Bank of Whiteacre), and the payee is Eastman Supply Company. ■

Trade Acceptances　A trade acceptance is a type of draft that is frequently used in the sale of goods. In a **trade acceptance,** the seller is both the drawer and the payee. Essentially, the draft orders the buyer to pay a specified sum of money to the seller, usually at a stated time in the future. (If the draft orders the buyer's bank to pay, it is called a *banker's acceptance.*)

■ **EXAMPLE 14.2** Each year Jackson River Fabrics sells fabric priced at $50,000 to Comfort Creations, Inc., on terms requiring payment to be made in ninety days. One year Jackson River needs cash, so it draws a *trade acceptance* (see Exhibit 14–2 on the following page) that orders Comfort Creations to pay $50,000 to the order of Jackson River Fabrics ninety days hence. Jackson River presents the paper to Comfort Creations. Comfort Creations *accepts* the draft, by signing the face of the draft, and returns it to Jackson River Fabrics. The acceptance by Comfort Creations gives rise to an enforceable obligation to pay the draft when it comes due in ninety days. Jackson River can then immediately sell the trade acceptance in the commercial money market for cash. ■

Checks　The most commonly used type of draft is a **check.** The writer of the check is the drawer, the bank on which the check is drawn is the drawee, and the person to whom the check is payable is the payee. As mentioned earlier, checks are demand instruments because they are payable on demand.

TRADE ACCEPTANCE
A draft that is drawn by a seller of goods ordering the buyer to pay a specified sum of money to the seller, usually at a stated time in the future. The buyer accepts the draft by signing the face of the draft, thus creating an enforceable obligation to pay the draft when it comes due. On a trade acceptance, the seller is both the drawer and the payee.

CHECK
A draft drawn by a drawer ordering the drawee bank or financial institution to pay a certain amount of money to the holder on demand.

EXHIBIT 14–1 A TYPICAL TIME DRAFT

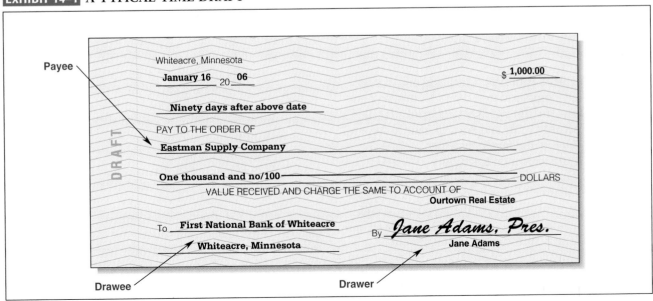

EXHIBIT 14–2 A TYPICAL TRADE ACCEPTANCE

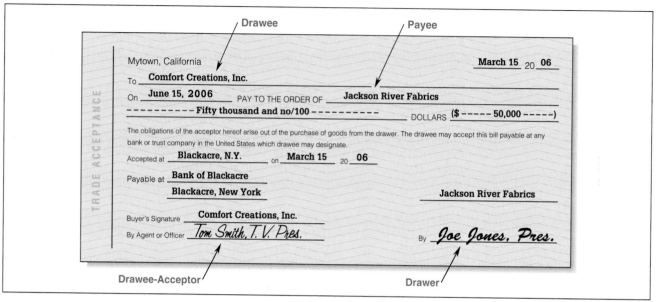

Checks will be discussed more fully in Chapter 15, but it should be noted here that with certain types of checks, such as *cashier's checks,* the bank is both the drawer and the drawee. The bank customer purchases a cashier's check from the bank—that is, pays the bank the amount of the check—and indicates to whom the check should be made payable. The bank, not the customer, is the drawer of the check—as well as the drawee. The idea behind a cashier's check is that it functions the same as cash, so there is no question about whether the check will be paid—the bank has committed itself to paying the stated amount on demand. The following case illustrates what this means to the payee of a cashier's check.

CASE 14.1 ■ Flatiron Linen, Inc. v. First American State Bank

Colorado Supreme Court, 2001.
23 P.3d 1209.

FACTS Fluffy Reed Foundation, Inc., and one of its officers, Bilgen Reed, promised to secure a $2 million loan for Flatiron Linen, Inc., for which Flatiron paid a fee. Flatiron later accused Fluffy and Reed of fraud in the deal. As a partial refund of the fee, Fluffy issued a check to Flatiron for $4,100, drawn on an account at First American State Bank. When Flatiron attempted to deposit the check, First American returned it due to insufficient funds in the account. Five months later, when the account had sufficient funds, Flatiron took the check to First American and exchanged it for a cashier's check in the amount of $4,100. In the meantime, however, Fluffy had asked First American not to pay the check. When the bank discovered its mistake, it refused to pay the cashier's check. Flatiron

filed a suit in a Colorado state court against a number of parties, including First American, from which Flatiron sought to recover the amount of the cashier's check. The court granted a summary judgment in favor of First American. The state intermediate appellate court affirmed this judgment, and Flatiron appealed to the Colorado Supreme Court.

ISSUE Should a cashier's check be treated as the equivalent of cash?

DECISION Yes. The Colorado Supreme Court reversed this part of the lower court's judgment and remanded the case for proceedings consistent with this opinion. Once a cashier's check has been issued, a bank may not legitimately refuse to pay it.

CASE 14.1—Continued

REASON The state supreme court pointed out that it agreed with the majority of courts, which "hold that a cashier's check is the equivalent of cash, accepted when issued." The court explained that UCC 3–104(g) "defines a cashier's check as 'a draft with respect to which the drawer and drawee are the same bank or branches of the same bank.' Because the bank serves as both the drawer and the drawee of the cashier's check, the check becomes a promise by the bank to draw the amount of the check from its own resources and to pay the check upon demand. * * * Once the bank issues and delivers the cashier's check to the payee, the transaction is com-

plete as far as the payee is concerned." The court also noted that "[t]he commercial world treats cashier's checks as the equivalent of cash. People accept cashier's checks as a substitute for cash because the bank, not an individual, stands behind it." To allow a bank not to pay a cashier's check "would be inconsistent with the representation it makes in issuing the check. Such a rule would undermine the public confidence in the bank and its checks and thereby deprive the cashier's check of the essential incident which makes it useful."

FOR CRITICAL ANALYSIS—Economic Consideration
What advantages might cashier's checks have over cash?

PROMISSORY NOTES AND CERTIFICATES OF DEPOSIT (PROMISES TO PAY)

PROMISSORY NOTE
A written promise made by one person (the maker) to pay a fixed amount of money to another person (the payee or a subsequent holder) on demand or on a specified date.

MAKER
One who promises to pay a fixed amount of money to the holder of a promissory note or a certificate of deposit (CD).

A **promissory note** is a written promise made by one person (the **maker** of the promise to pay) to another (usually a payee). A promissory note, which is often referred to simply as a *note*, can be made payable at a definite time or on demand. It can name a specific payee or merely be payable to bearer (bearer instruments are discussed later in this chapter). ■ EXAMPLE 14.3 On April 30, Laurence and Margaret Roberts sign a writing unconditionally promising to pay "to the order of" the First National Bank of Whiteacre $3,000 (with 8 percent interest) on or before June 29. This writing is a promissory note. ■ A typical promissory note is shown in Exhibit 14–3.

EXHIBIT 14–3 A TYPICAL PROMISSORY NOTE

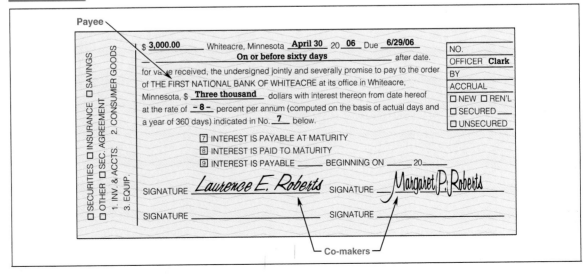

A customer fills out a form to purchase a CD. Who is the maker of a CD? Who is the payee? (Steven E. Frischling/Bloomberg News/Landov)

CERTIFICATE OF DEPOSIT (CD)
A note of a bank in which the bank acknowledges a receipt of money from a party and promises to repay the money, with interest, to the party on a certain date.

Types of Promissory Notes   Notes are used in a variety of credit transactions and often carry the name of the transaction involved. For example, a note that is secured by personal property, such as an automobile, is called a *collateral note* because the property pledged as security for the satisfaction of the debt is called collateral (see Chapter 16). A note payable in installments, such as for payment for a suite of furniture over a twelve-month period, is called an *installment note*.

Certificates of Deposit   A **certificate of deposit (CD)** is a type of note. A CD is issued when a party deposits funds with a bank that the bank promises to repay, with interest, on a certain date [UCC 3–104(j)]. The bank is the maker of the note, and the depositor is the payee. ■ **EXAMPLE 14.4** On February 15, Sara Levin deposits $5,000 with the First National Bank of Whiteacre. The bank issues a CD, in which it promises to repay the $5,000, plus 5 percent interest, on August 15. ■

Certificates of deposit in small denominations (for amounts up to $100,000) are often sold by savings and loan associations, savings banks, and commercial banks. Certificates of deposit for amounts over $100,000 are called large or jumbo CDs. Exhibit 14–4 shows a typical small CD.

■■ Transfer of Instruments

Once issued, a negotiable instrument can be transferred in one of two ways—by *assignment* or by *negotiation*.

TRANSFER BY ASSIGNMENT

Recall from Chapter 9 that an assignment is a transfer of rights under a contract. Under general contract principles, a transfer by assignment to an assignee gives the assignee only those rights that the assignor possessed. Any defenses that can be raised against an assignor can normally be raised against the assignee. This same

EXHIBIT 14–4 A TYPICAL SMALL CD

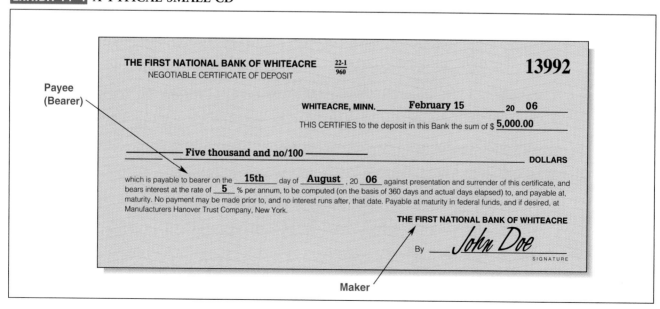

principle applies when an instrument, such as a promissory note, is transferred by assignment. The transferee is then an *assignee* rather than a *holder*. Sometimes, a transfer fails to qualify as a negotiation because it fails to meet one or more of the requirements of a negotiable instrument, discussed above. When this occurs, the transfer becomes an assignment.

TRANSFER BY NEGOTIATION

NEGOTIATION
The transfer of an instrument in such form that the transferee (the person to whom the instrument is transferred) becomes a holder.

HOLDER
Any person in possession of an instrument drawn, issued, or indorsed to him or her, to his or her order, to bearer, or in blank.

Negotiation is the transfer of an instrument in such form that the transferee (the person to whom the instrument is transferred) becomes a holder [UCC 3–201(a)]. The UCC defines a **holder** as any person in the possession of an instrument drawn, issued, or indorsed to him or her, to his or her order, to bearer, or in blank. The terms *indorse, bearer,* and *in blank* will be explained shortly. Under UCC principles, a transfer by negotiation creates a holder who, at the very least, receives the rights of the previous possessor [UCC 3–203(b)]. Unlike an assignment, a transfer by negotiation can make it possible for a holder to receive more rights in the instrument than the prior possessor had [UCC 3–202(b), 3–305, 3–306]. A holder who receives greater rights is known as a *holder in due course,* a concept that will be discussed shortly.

There are two methods of negotiating an instrument so that the receiver becomes a holder. The method used depends on whether the instrument is order paper or bearer paper.

ORDER INSTRUMENT
A negotiable instrument that is payable "to the order of an identified person" or "to an identified person or order."

INDORSEMENT
A signature placed on an instrument for the purpose of transferring one's ownership rights in the instrument.

Negotiating Order Instruments   An **order instrument** is a negotiable instrument that is payable to the order of a specific person. In other words, it contains the name of a payee capable of indorsing it, as in "Pay to the order of Lloyd Sorenson." An order instrument is negotiated by delivery with any necessary indorsements. (An **indorsement** is a signature placed on an instrument, such as on the back of a check, for the purpose of transferring one's ownership rights in the instrument. Exhibit 14–5 on the next page shows various types of indorsements and their consequences.)

■ **EXAMPLE 14.5** National Express Corporation issues a payroll check "to the order of Lloyd Sorenson." Sorenson takes the check to the supermarket, signs his name on the back (a blank indorsement), gives it to the cashier (a delivery), and receives cash. Sorenson has *negotiated* the check to the supermarket [UCC 3–201(b)]. ■

BEARER INSTRUMENT
Any instrument that is not payable to a specific person, including instruments payable to the bearer or to "cash."

Negotiating Bearer Instruments   A **bearer instrument** is a negotiable instrument that is not payable to a specific person, such as an instrument payable to "bearer" or to "cash." A bearer instrument is negotiated by delivery—that is, by transfer into another person's possession. Indorsement is not necessary [UCC 2–301(b)]. The use of bearer instruments thus involves more risk through loss or theft than the use of order instruments.

■ **EXAMPLE 14.6** Assume that Richard Kray writes a check "payable to cash" and hands it to Jessie Arnold (a delivery). Kray has issued the check (a bearer instrument) to Arnold. Arnold places the check in her wallet, which is subsequently stolen. The thief has possession of the check. At this point, the thief has no rights to the check. If the thief "delivers" the check to an innocent third person, however, negotiation will be complete. All rights to the check will be passed absolutely to that third person, and Arnold will lose all rights to recover the proceeds of the check from that person [UCC 3–306]. Of course, Arnold could attempt to recover the money from the thief if the thief can be found. ■

EXHIBIT 14–5 TYPES OF INDORSEMENTS AND THEIR CONSEQUENCES

WORDS CONSTITUTING THE INDORSEMENT	TYPE OF INDORSEMENT	INDORSER'S SIGNATURE LIABILITY[a]
"Mark Deitsch"	Blank	Unqualified signature liability on proper presentment and notice of dishonor.[b]
"Pay to William Hunter, Hal Cohen"	Special	Unqualified signature liability on proper presentment and notice of dishonor.
"Without recourse, Sarah Jacobs"	Qualified (blank for further negotiation)	No signature liability. Transfer warranty liability if breach occurs.[c]
"Pay to Allison Jong, without recourse, Sarah Jacobs"	Qualified (special for further negotiation)	No signature liability. Transfer warranty liability if breach occurs.
"For deposit only, Marcel Dumont"	Restrictive—for deposit (blank for further negotiation)	Signature liability only on Dumont's having amount deposited in his account. If deposit made, signature liability on proper presentment and notice of dishonor.
"Pay to Ellen Cook in trust for Roger Callahan, Roger Callahan"	Restrictive—trust (special for further negotiation)	Signature liability to original indorsee only on payment to Ellen Cook for Roger Callahan's benefit. Regardless of whether restriction is met, signature liability to subsequent indorsers on proper presentment and notice of dishonor.

a. Signature liability, discussed later in this chapter, refers to the liability of a party who signs an instrument.

b. When an instrument is dishonored—that is, when, for example, a drawer's bank refuses to cash the drawer's check on proper presentment—(see the discussion of dishonor later in this chapter) an indorser of the check may be liable on it if he or she is given proper notice of dishonor.

c. The transferor of an instrument makes certain warranties to the transferee and subsequent holders, and thus, even if the transferor's signature does not render him or her liable on the instrument, he or she may be liable for breach of a transfer warranty. Transfer warranties will be discussed in this chapter.

■■ Holder in Due Course

HOLDER IN DUE COURSE (HDC)
A holder who acquires a negotiable instrument for value; in good faith; and without notice that the instrument is overdue, that it has been dishonored, that any person has a defense against it or a claim to it, or that the instrument contains unauthorized signatures, has been altered, or is so irregular or incomplete as to call into question its authenticity.

An ordinary holder obtains only those rights that the transferor had in the instrument. In this respect, a holder has the same status as an assignee (see Chapter 9). Like an assignee, a holder normally is subject to the same defenses that could be asserted against the transferor.

In contrast, a **holder in due course (HDC)** is a holder who, by meeting certain acquisition requirements (to be discussed shortly), takes the instrument *free* of most of the defenses and claims that could be asserted against the transferor. Stated another way, an HDC can normally acquire a higher level of immunity than can an ordinary holder in regard to defenses against payment on the instrument or ownership claims to the instrument by other parties.

The basic requirements for attaining HDC status are set forth in UCC 3–302. A holder of a negotiable instrument is an HDC if she or he takes the instrument (1) for value; (2) in good faith; and (3) without notice that it is overdue, that it has been dishonored, that any person has a defense against it or a claim to it, or that the instrument contains unauthorized signatures, contains alterations, or is so irregular or incomplete as to call into question its authenticity. We now examine each of these requirements.

TAKING FOR VALUE

An HDC must have given *value* for the instrument [UCC 3–302(a)(2)(i)]. A person who receives an instrument as a gift or inherits it has not met the requirement of value. In these situations, the person becomes an ordinary holder and does not possess the rights of an HDC.

The concept of value in the law of negotiable instruments is not the same as the concept of *consideration* in the law of contracts. A promise to give value in the future is clearly sufficient consideration to support a contract [UCC 1–201(44)]. A promise to give value in the future, however, normally does not constitute value sufficient to make one an HDC. A holder takes an instrument for value only to the extent that the promise has been performed [UCC 3–303(a)(1)]. Therefore, if the holder plans to pay for the instrument later or plans to perform the required services at some future date, the holder has not yet given value. In that situation, the holder is not yet an HDC.

Under UCC 3–303(a), a holder can take an instrument for value in one of five ways:

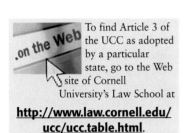

To find Article 3 of the UCC as adopted by a particular state, go to the Web site of Cornell University's Law School at **http://www.law.cornell.edu/ ucc/ucc.table.html**.

1 By performing the promise for which the instrument was issued or transferred.

2 By acquiring a security interest or other lien in the instrument, excluding a lien obtained by a judicial proceeding. (Security interests and liens will be discussed in Chapter 16.)

3 By taking an instrument in payment of, or as security for, a preexisting claim. ■ EXAMPLE 14.7 Zon owes Dwyer $2,000 on a past-due account. If Zon negotiates a $2,000 note signed by Gordon to Dwyer and Dwyer accepts it to discharge the overdue account balance, Dwyer has given value for the instrument. ■

4 By giving a negotiable instrument as payment. ■ EXAMPLE 14.8 Martin has issued a $500 negotiable promissory note to Paulene. The note is due six months from the date issued. Paulene needs money and does not want to wait for the maturity date to collect. She negotiates the note to her friend Kristen, who pays her $200 in cash and writes her a check—a negotiable instrument—for the balance of $300. Kristen has given full value for the note by paying $200 in cash and issuing Paulene the check for $300. ■

5 By giving an irrevocable commitment as payment.

TAKING IN GOOD FAITH

The second requirement for HDC status is that the holder take the instrument in *good faith* [UCC 3–302(a)(2)(ii)]. This means that the holder must have acted honestly in the process of acquiring the instrument. UCC 3–103(a)(4) defines *good faith* as "honesty in fact and the observance of reasonable commercial standards of fair dealing." The good faith requirement applies only to the *holder*. It is immaterial whether the transferor acted in good faith. Thus, even a person who takes a negotiable instrument from a thief may become an HDC if the person acquires the instrument in good faith.

Because of the good faith requirement, one must ask whether the purchaser, when acquiring the instrument, honestly believed that the instrument was not defective. If a person purchases a $10,000 note for $300 from a stranger on a street corner, the issue of good faith can be raised on the grounds of both the suspicious circumstances and the grossly inadequate consideration (value).

In the following case, the court considered whether a bank observed "reasonable commercial standards of fair dealing" to fulfill the good faith requirement and become an HDC.

CASE 14.2 Mid Wisconsin Bank v. Forsgard Trading, Inc.

Wisconsin Court of Appeals, 2003.
266 Wis.2d 685,
668 N.W.2d 830,
2003 WI App. 186.
http://www.wisbar.org/WisCtApp/index.html[a]

FACTS Forsgard Trading, Inc., opened an account at Mid Wisconsin Bank in July 1999. The account agreement stated, "Any items, other than cash, accepted for deposit . . . will be given provisional credit only until collection is final." Mid Wisconsin's practice is to give immediate credit on deposits, but an employee may place a hold on a check if, for example, there is reasonable doubt about it. On May 7, 2001, Lakeshore Truck and Equipment Sales, Inc., wrote a check payable to Forsgard in the amount of $18,500. On May 8, Forsgard deposited the check in its account at Mid Wisconsin, which gave Forsgard immediate credit. The same day, Lakeshore issued a stop-payment order (an order to its bank not to pay the check—see Chapter 15). When Mid Wisconsin received notice on May 16 that payment had been stopped, it deducted the $18,500 from Forsgard's account. Because of transfers from the account between May 8 and May 16, the deduction resulted in a negative balance. Before this incident, Forsgard had overdrawn the account twenty-four times but, on each occasion, had deposited money to cover the overdraft. Forsgard did not do so this time. Mid Wisconsin filed a suit in a Wisconsin state court against Forsgard, Lakeshore, and others, to recover the loss. The court issued a summary judgment in Mid Wisconsin's favor. Lakeshore appealed to a state intermediate appellate court.

a. In the "Court of Appeals 1995–2004" section, click on "2003 Opinions." In the result, in the "Index by Appellant's name" section, click on "July–September." On the next page, scroll to the name of the case and click on the docket number to access the opinion. The State Bar of Wisconsin maintains this Web site.

ISSUE Did Mid Wisconsin act in good faith?

DECISION Yes. The court affirmed the lower court's judgment on this issue, holding that Mid Wisconsin was an HDC of the check.

REASON The appellate court explained that under UCC 3–305, an HDC can recover from a drawer who places a stop-payment order on a check. Under UCC 3–302, an HDC is one who takes an instrument for value and in good faith. There was no dispute that Mid Wisconsin took the check for value. UCC 3–103(a)(4) defines good faith as "honesty in fact and the observance of reasonable commercial standards of fair dealing." Lakeshore conceded that Mid Wisconsin took the check with honesty in fact. Thus, the only question was whether Mid Wisconsin's granting Forsgard immediate credit was in line with "reasonable commercial standards of fair dealing." The court found that Mid Wisconsin's acts complied with its account agreement and that "Mid Wisconsin had no reason to suspect there would be any problem if immediate credit was extended for this check." Also, "extending immediate credit is consistent with reasonable banking standards." The court pointed out, "It would hinder commercial transactions if depository banks refused to permit the withdrawal prior to the clearance of checks. * * * [B]anking practice is to the contrary. It is clear that the Uniform Commercial Code was intended * * * to protect banks who have given credit on deposited items prior to notice of a stop payment order."

WHY IS THIS CASE IMPORTANT? *This case is important because it shows what constitutes "reasonable commercial standards of fair dealing" in banking transactions. It also illustrates that one of the functions of the UCC is to protect banks that give credit on deposited items, provided that those banks act in good faith.*

TAKING WITHOUT NOTICE

The final requirement for HDC status involves *notice* [UCC 3–302]. A person will not be afforded HDC protection if he or she acquires an instrument and is *on notice* (knows or has reason to know) that it is defective in any one of the following ways [UCC 3–302(a)]:

1. It is overdue.

2. It has been dishonored.

3 There is an uncured (uncorrected) default with respect to another instrument issued as part of the same series.

4 The instrument contains an unauthorized signature or has been altered.

5 There is a defense against the instrument or a claim to the instrument.

6 The instrument is so irregular or incomplete as to call into question its authenticity.

What Constitutes Notice? Notice of a defective instrument is given whenever the holder (1) has actual knowledge of the defect; (2) has received a notice of the defect (such as a bank's receipt of a letter listing the serial numbers of stolen bearer instruments); or (3) has reason to know that a defect exists, given all the facts and circumstances known at the time in question [UCC 1–201(25)]. The holder must also have received the notice "at a time and in a manner that gives a reasonable opportunity to act on it" [UCC 3–302(f)]. A purchaser's knowledge of certain facts, such as insolvency proceedings against the maker or drawer of the instrument, does not constitute notice that the instrument is defective [UCC 3–302(b)].

Overdue Instruments What constitutes notice that an instrument is overdue depends on whether it is a demand instrument (payable on demand) or a time instrument (payable at a definite time). As you will read in the *Application* feature at the end of this chapter, notice is one of the requirements to which you will need to pay close attention when purchasing negotiable instruments.

A purchaser has notice that a *demand instrument* is overdue if she or he either takes the instrument knowing that demand has been made or takes the instrument an unreasonable length of time after its issue. For a check, a "reasonable time" is ninety days after the date of the check. For all other demand instruments, what will be considered a reasonable time depends on the circumstances [UCC 3–304(a)].

A holder of a *time instrument* who takes the instrument at any time after its expressed due date is on notice that it is overdue [UCC 3–304(b)(2)]. Nonpayment by the due date should indicate to any purchaser that the instrument may be defective. Thus, a promissory note due on May 15 must be acquired before midnight on May 15. If it is purchased on May 16, the purchaser will be an ordinary holder, not an HDC. Sometimes, an instrument reads, "Payable in thirty days." To count thirty days, you exclude the first day and count the last day. Thus, a note dated December 1 that is payable in thirty days is due by midnight on December 31. If the payment date falls on a Sunday or holiday, the instrument is payable on the next business day.

REMEMBER Demand instruments are payable immediately. Time instruments are payable at a future date.

■ Holder through an HDC

A person who does not qualify as an HDC but who derives his or her title through an HDC can acquire the rights and privileges of an HDC. This rule is sometimes called the **shelter principle.** According to UCC 3–203(b),

> Transfer of an instrument, whether or not the transfer is a negotiation, vests in the transferee any right of the transferor to enforce the instrument, including any right as a holder in due course, but the transferee cannot acquire rights of a holder in due course by a transfer, directly or indirectly, from a holder in due course if the transferee engaged in fraud or illegality affecting the instrument.

Under this rule, anyone—no matter how far removed from an HDC—who can trace his or her title ultimately back to an HDC may acquire the rights of an HDC. By

SHELTER PRINCIPLE
The principle that the holder of a negotiable instrument who cannot qualify as a holder in due course (HDC), but who derives his or her title through an HDC, acquires the rights of an HDC.

extending the benefits of HDC status, the shelter principle promotes the marketability and free transferability of negotiable instruments.

There are some limitations on the shelter principle, however. Certain persons who formerly held instruments cannot improve their positions by later reacquiring the instruments from HDCs [UCC 3–203(b)]. If a holder participated in fraud or illegality affecting the instrument, or had notice of a claim or defense against an instrument, that holder is not allowed to improve her or his status by repurchasing from a later HDC.

■ **EXAMPLE 14.9** Matt and Carla collaborate to defraud Lorena. Lorena is induced to give Carla a negotiable note payable to Carla's order. Carla then specially indorses the note for value to Larry, an HDC. Matt and Carla split the proceeds. Larry negotiates the note to Stuart, another HDC. Stuart then negotiates the note for value to Matt. Even though Matt obtained the note through an HDC, he does not have the rights of an HDC—and can never acquire HDC rights in this note—because he participated in the original fraud. ■

▦ Signature Liability

The key to liability on a negotiable instrument is a *signature*. The general rule is as follows: Every party, except a qualified indorser,[1] who signs a negotiable instrument is either primarily or secondarily liable for payment of that instrument when it comes due. The following subsections discuss these two types of liability, as well as the conditions that must be met before liability can arise.

PRIMARY LIABILITY

A person who is primarily liable on a negotiable instrument is absolutely required to pay the instrument—unless, of course, he or she has a valid defense to payment [UCC 3–305]. Only *makers* and *acceptors* of instruments are primarily liable.

The maker of a promissory note promises to pay the note. It is the maker's promise to pay that makes the note a negotiable instrument. The words "I promise to pay" embody the maker's obligation to pay the instrument according to the terms as written at the time of the signing. If the instrument was incomplete when the maker signed it, the maker is obligated to pay it according to its stated terms or according to terms that were agreed on and later filled in to complete the instrument [UCC 3–115, 3–407(a), 3–412].

An **acceptor** is a drawee that promises to pay an instrument when it is presented for payment. Once a drawee indicates acceptance by signing the draft, the drawee becomes an acceptor and is obligated to pay the draft when it is presented for payment [UCC 3–409(a)]. A drawee that refuses to accept a draft that *requires* the drawee's acceptance (such as a trade acceptance) has dishonored the instrument. Acceptance of a check is called *certification* (certified checks will be discussed in Chapter 15). On certification, the drawee bank occupies the position of an acceptor and is primarily liable on the check to any holder [UCC 3–409(d)].

> **RECALL** A drawee is the party ordered to pay a draft or check, such as a bank or financial institution, for example.

ACCEPTOR
A drawee that is legally obligated to pay an instrument when the instrument is presented later for payment.

---

1. A qualified indorser—one who indorses "without recourse"—undertakes no contractual obligation to pay. A qualified indorser merely assumes warranty liability, which will be discussed later in this chapter.

SECONDARY LIABILITY

Drawers and *indorsers* are secondarily liable. On a negotiable instrument, secondary liability is similar to the liability of a guarantor in a simple contract (described in Chapter 9) in the sense that it is *contingent liability*. In other words, a drawer or an indorser will be liable only if the party that is responsible for paying the instrument refuses to do so (dishonors the instrument). In regard to drafts and checks, the drawer's secondary liability does not arise until the drawee fails to pay or to accept the instrument, whichever is required [UCC 3–412, 3–415].

RECALL A guarantor is liable on a contract to pay the debt of another only if the party who is primarily liable fails to pay.

Dishonor of an instrument thus triggers the liability of parties who are secondarily liable on the instrument—that is, the drawer and *unqualified* indorsers.
■ **EXAMPLE 14.10** Nina Lee writes a check on her account at Universal Bank payable to the order of Stephen Miller. Universal Bank refuses to pay the check when Miller presents it for payment, thus dishonoring the check. In this situation, Lee will be liable to Miller on the basis of her secondary liability. ■ Drawers are secondarily liable on drafts unless they disclaim their liability by drawing the instruments "without recourse" (if the draft is a check, however, a drawer cannot disclaim liability) [UCC 3–414(e)].

Parties who are secondarily liable on a negotiable instrument promise to pay on that instrument only if *all* of the following events occur:[2]

1 The instrument is properly and timely presented.

2 The instrument is dishonored.

3 Timely notice of dishonor is given to the secondarily liable party.

PRESENTMENT
The act of presenting an instrument to the party liable on the instrument to collect payment. Presentment also occurs when a person presents an instrument to a drawee for a required acceptance.

Proper and Timely Presentment   **Presentment** is the formal production of a negotiable instrument for acceptance or payment. The UCC requires that a holder present the instrument to the appropriate party, in a timely fashion, and give reasonable identification if demanded [UCC 3–414(f), 3–415(e), 3–501]. The party to whom the instrument must be presented depends on the type of instrument involved. A note or certificate of deposit (CD) must be presented to the maker for payment. A draft is presented to the drawee for acceptance, payment, or both. A check is presented to the drawee for payment [UCC 3–501(a), 3–502(b)].

Presentment can be made by any commercially reasonable means, including oral, written, or electronic communication [UCC 3–501(b)]. It is effective when the demand for payment or acceptance is received, although banks can treat a presentment that takes place after an established cutoff hour (such as 2 P.M.) as occurring the next business day.

One of the most crucial criteria for proper presentment is timeliness [UCC 3–414(f), 3–415(e), 3–501(b)(4)]. Failure to present an instrument on time is the most common reason that unqualified indorsers are discharged from secondary liability. The time for proper presentment for different types of instruments is shown in Exhibit 14–6 on the following page.

Dishonor   An instrument is dishonored when the required acceptance or payment is refused or cannot be obtained within the prescribed time. An instrument is also

---

2. These requirements are necessary for a secondarily liable party to have signature liability on a negotiable instrument, but they are not necessary for a secondarily liable party to have warranty liability (to be discussed later in the chapter).

EXHIBIT 14–6   TIME FOR PROPER PRESENTMENT

TYPE OF INSTRUMENT	FOR ACCEPTANCE	FOR PAYMENT
Time	On or before due date.	On due date.
Demand	Within a reasonable time (after date or issue or after secondary party becomes liable on the instrument).	
Check	Not applicable.	Within thirty days of its date, to hold drawer secondarily liable. Within thirty days of indorsement, to hold indorser secondarily liable.

dishonored when required presentment is excused (as it would be, for example, if the maker had died) and the instrument is not properly accepted or paid [UCC 3–502(e), 3–504].

In some situations, a postponement of payment or a refusal to pay an instrument will *not* dishonor the instrument. When presentment is made after an established cutoff hour, for instance, a bank can postpone payment until the following business day without dishonoring the instrument. In addition, when the holder refuses to exhibit the instrument, to give reasonable identification, or to sign a receipt on the instrument for payment, a bank's refusal to pay does not dishonor the instrument.

■ **EXAMPLE 14.11** Suppose that Deere, instead of depositing Lamar's check into his bank account, demands payment from Universal Bank in cash. The bank requests identification, which Deere refuses to provide. In this situation, the bank would be within its rights to refuse payment to Deere, and the bank's refusal to pay would not dishonor the check. ■

Some banks require a check holder who does not have an account at the bank to provide a thumbprint before the bank will honor the check. The issue in the following case was whether this practice was a reasonable identification requirement.

CASE 14.3 ■ **Messing v. Bank of America, N.A.**[a]

Maryland Court of Appeals, 2003.
373 Md. 672,
821 A.2d 22.

FACTS On August 3, 2000, Jeff Messing attempted to cash a check payable to his order for $976 at a branch office of Bank of America, N.A., in Baltimore City, Maryland. The check was drawn on a checking account of one of the bank's customers. A teller confirmed the availability of funds in the account and asked Messing if he was a bank customer. When he said "no," the teller asked Messing to place his "thumbprint signature" on the check in accord with the bank's policy for "non-account holders."[b] Messing refused, and the teller refused to cash

the check. Messing demanded to speak with the branch manager, who also refused to cash the check. Messing filed a suit in a Maryland state court against the bank, asking the court to declare, among other things, that requiring a thumbprint was not "reasonable identification" under Maryland Code Section 3–501(b)(2) of the state's Commercial Law Article [Maryland's version of UCC 3–501(b)(2)]. The bank filed a motion for summary judgment, which the court granted. Messing appealed to a state intermediate appellate court, which upheld the judgment. Messing appealed to the Maryland Court of Appeals, the state's highest court.

ISSUE Is it reasonable for a bank to require a thumbprint as a form of identification?

DECISION Yes. The Maryland Court of Appeals affirmed the lower court's decision, holding that the bank

a. *N.A.* stands for "National Association."
b. Here, as in most cases, Messing was asked to create a thumbprint signature by applying his right thumb to an inkless fingerprinting device, which leaves no ink stain or residue, and then placing his thumb on the face of the check between the memo and signature lines.

CASE 14.3—Continued

did not dishonor the check when it refused to accept it over the counter without Messing's thumbprint.

REASON The Maryland Court of Appeals agreed with the lower court that providing a thumbprint signature "assist[s] in the identification of the check holder should the check later prove to be bad. It therefore serves as a powerful deterrent to those who might otherwise attempt to pass a bad check." The state's highest court explained that "when a bank cashes a check over the counter, it assumes the risk that it may suffer losses for counterfeit documents, forged endorsements, or forged or altered checks." Nothing in the UCC "forces a bank to assume such risks. To the extent that banks are willing to cash checks over the counter, with reasonable identification, such willingness expands and facilitates * * * commercial activities." Reducing risk promotes the expansion of these activities, and "[p]rohibiting banks from taking reasonable steps to protect themselves from losses could result in banks refusing to cash checks of non-customers presented over the counter at all."

FOR CRITICAL ANALYSIS—Social Consideration
Why might a customer be reluctant to provide a thumbprint to a bank, even if he or she is presenting a valid check?

Proper Notice Once an instrument has been dishonored, proper notice must be given to secondary parties (drawers and indorsers) for them to be held contractually liable. Notice may be given in any reasonable manner, including an oral, written, or electronic communication, as well as notice written or stamped on the instrument itself. The bank must give any necessary notice before its midnight deadline (midnight of the next banking day after receipt). Notice by any party other than a bank must be given within thirty days following the day of dishonor or the day on which the person who is secondarily liable receives notice of dishonor [UCC 3–503].

UNAUTHORIZED SIGNATURES

People normally are not liable to pay on negotiable instruments unless their signatures appear on the instruments. As stated previously, the general rule is that an unauthorized signature is wholly inoperative and will not bind the person whose name is forged. There are two exceptions to this general rule:

1 An exception is made when the person whose name is signed ratifies (affirms) the signature [UCC 3–403(a)]. A principal can ratify an unauthorized signature made by an agent, either expressly, by affirming the validity of the signature, or impliedly, by other conduct, such as keeping any benefits received in the transaction or failing to repudiate the signature. The parties involved need not be principal and agent. ■ **EXAMPLE 14.12** Allison Malone steals several checks from her mother, Brenda Malone, makes them out to herself, and signs "Brenda Malone." Brenda, the mother, may ratify her daughter's forgery so that her daughter will not be prosecuted for forgery. ■

2 A person whose name is forged may be precluded from denying the effectiveness of an unauthorized signature if the person's own negligence substantially contributed to the forgery [UCC 3–115, 3–406, 4–401(d)(2)]. ■ **EXAMPLE 14.13** Suppose that the owner of a business, Rob, leaves his signature stamp and a blank check on an office counter. An employee, using the stamp, fills in and cashes the check. Rob can be estopped (prevented), on the basis of negligence, from denying liability for payment of the check. Whatever loss occurs may be allocated, however, between certain parties on the basis of comparative negligence [UCC 3–406(b)]. For example, if Rob can demonstrate that the bank was negligent in paying the check, the bank may bear a portion of the loss. ■

This woman was arrested for forging a series of checks. Seven of the checks were drawn on the account of Mary Smithson. If Smithson did not authorize the checks, can the bank debit her account for the amount of the checks? Why or why not? (AP Photo)

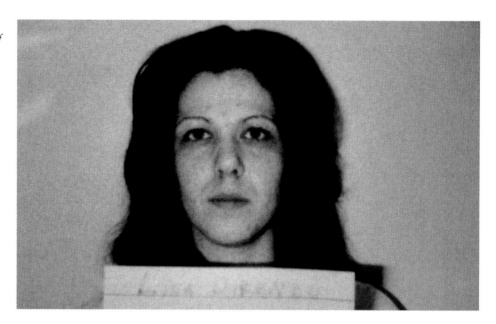

An unauthorized signature operates as the signature of the unauthorized signer in favor of an HDC. A person who forges a check, for instance, can be held personally liable for payment by an HDC [UCC 3–403(a)].

SPECIAL RULES FOR UNAUTHORIZED INDORSEMENTS

Generally, when an indorsement is forged or unauthorized, the burden of loss falls on the first party to take the instrument with the forged or unauthorized indorsement. If the indorsement was made by an imposter or by a fictitious payee, however, the loss falls on the maker or drawer. We look at these two situations here.

IMPOSTER
One who, by use of the mails, Internet, telephone, or personal appearance, induces a maker or drawer to issue an instrument in the name of an impersonated payee. Indorsements by imposters are treated as authorized indorsements under Article 3 of the UCC.

Imposters   An **imposter** is one who, by her or his personal appearance or use of the mails, Internet, telephone, or other communication, induces a maker or drawer to issue an instrument in the name of an impersonated payee. If the maker or drawer believes the imposter to be the named payee at the time of issue, the indorsement by the imposter is not treated as unauthorized when the instrument is transferred to an innocent party. This is because the maker or drawer intended the imposter to receive the instrument. In this situation, under the UCC's *imposter rule,* the imposter's indorsement will be effective—that is, not considered a forgery—insofar as the drawer or maker is concerned [UCC 3–404(a)]. ■ **EXAMPLE 14.14** Carol impersonates Donna and induces Edward to write a check payable to the order of Donna. Carol, continuing to impersonate Donna, negotiates the check to First National Bank as payment on her loan there. As the drawer of the check, Edward is liable for its amount to First National. ■

FICTITIOUS PAYEE
A payee on a negotiable instrument whom the maker or drawer does not intend to have an interest in the instrument. Indorsements by fictitious payees are treated as authorized indorsements under Article 3 of the UCC.

Fictitious Payees   An unauthorized indorsement will also be effective when a person causes an instrument to be issued to a payee who will have *no interest* in the instrument [UCC 3–404(b), 3–405]. In this situation, the payee is referred to as a **fictitious payee.** Situations involving fictitious payees most often arise when (1) a dishonest employee deceives the employer into signing an instrument payable to a party with no right to receive payment on the instrument or (2) a dishonest employee or agent has the authority to issue an instrument on behalf of the employer. Under the UCC's *fictitious payee rule,* the payee's indorsement is not treated as a forgery, and an innocent holder or an innocent party (such as a bank that pays the instrument in good faith) can hold the employer liable on the instrument.

How a Fictitious Payee Can Be Created—An Example. ■ EXAMPLE 14.15 Blair Industries, Inc., gives its bookkeeper, Axel Ford, general authority to issue checks in the company name drawn on First State Bank so that Ford can pay employees' wages and other corporate bills. Ford decides to cheat Blair Industries out of $10,000 by issuing a check payable to Erica Nied, an old acquaintance. Neither Blair nor Ford intends Nied to receive any of the money, and Nied is not an employee or creditor of the company. Ford indorses the check in Nied's name, naming himself as indorsee. He then cashes the check at a local bank, which collects payment from the drawee bank, First State Bank. First State Bank charges the Blair Industries account $10,000. Blair Industries discovers the fraud and demands that the account be recredited. ■

Who Bears the Loss? Who bears the loss? UCC 3–404(b)(2) provides the answer. Neither the local bank that first accepted the check nor First State Bank is liable. Because Ford's indorsement in the name of a payee with no interest in the instrument is "effective," there is no "forgery." Hence, the collecting bank is protected in paying on the check, and the drawee bank is protected in charging Blair's account. Thus, the employer-drawer, Blair Industries, will bear the loss. Of course, Blair Industries has recourse against Axel Ford, if Ford has not absconded with the funds.

Regardless of whether a dishonest employee actually signs the check or merely supplies his or her employer with names of fictitious creditors (or with true names of creditors having fictitious debts), the result is the same under the UCC. ■ EXAMPLE 14.16 Nathan Holtz draws up the payroll list from which employees' salary checks are written. He fraudulently adds the name Sally Vix (a fictitious person) to the payroll, and the employer signs checks to be issued to her. Again, it is the employer-drawer who bears the loss. ■

ETHICAL ISSUE 14.1

Should a bank that acts in "bad faith" be precluded from raising the fictitious payee rule as a defense? Remember from previous chapters that the requirement of good faith underlies all transactions governed by the UCC. Does this mean that a bank, to avoid liability for paying instruments with forged indorsements involving fictitious payees, must have acted in good faith when accepting the deposits? Yes, according to a number of courts. For example, a Pennsylvania appellate court held that to assert the rule "the bank must have acted in good faith when paying the instrument." The bank in this case had accepted 882 payroll checks generated and indorsed by Dorothy Heck, a payroll clerk employed by Pavex, Inc. The checks were made payable to various current and former Pavex employees, indorsed by Heck with the payees' names, and deposited into Heck's personal checking account at her bank.

In spite of the bank's policy that indorsements on checks must match exactly the names of the payees, the bank continued to accept Heck's deposited checks even when the indorsements did not match the payees' names. Furthermore, even though bank personnel discussed Heck's check-depositing activities on more than one occasion, they never contacted her employer to verify Heck's authority to deposit third party payroll checks. Given the bank's pattern of ignoring perceived irregularities in Heck's transactions, the trial court jury had concluded that the bank had acted in bad faith and was therefore liable for approximately $170,000 of the $250,000 loss suffered by Pavex. The appellate court affirmed the trial court's decision.[3] ■

---

3. *Pavex, Inc. v. York Federal Savings and Loan Association,* 716 A.2d 640 (Pa.Super.Ct. 1998).

Warranty Liability

In addition to the signature liability discussed in the preceding pages, transferors make certain implied warranties regarding the instruments that they are negotiating. Liability under these warranties is not subject to the conditions of proper presentment, dishonor, or notice of dishonor. These warranties arise even when a transferor does not indorse the instrument (as in the delivery of a bearer instrument) [UCC 3–416, 3–417]. Warranty liability is particularly important when a holder cannot hold a party liable on her or his signature.

Warranties fall into two categories: those that arise on the *transfer* of a negotiable instrument and those that arise on *presentment*. Both transfer and presentment warranties attempt to shift liability back to a wrongdoer or to the person who dealt face to face with the wrongdoer and thus was in the best position to prevent the wrongdoing.

TRANSFER WARRANTIES

TRANSFER WARRANTY
Implied warranties, made by any person who transfers an instrument for consideration to subsequent transferees and holders who take the instrument in good faith, that (1) the transferor is entitled to enforce the instrument; (2) all signatures are authentic and authorized; (3) the instrument has not been altered; (4) the instrument is not subject to a defense or claim of any party that can be asserted against the transferor; and (5) the transferor has no knowledge of any insolvency proceedings against the maker, the acceptor, or the drawer of the instrument.

The UCC describes five **transfer warranties** [UCC 3–416]. For transfer warranties to arise, an instrument must be transferred *for consideration*. One who transfers an instrument for consideration makes the following warranties to all subsequent transferees and holders who take the instrument in good faith (with some exceptions, as will be noted shortly):

1. The transferor is entitled to enforce the instrument.
2. All signatures are authentic and authorized.
3. The instrument has not been altered.
4. The instrument is not subject to a defense or claim of any party that can be asserted against the transferor.
5. The transferor has no knowledge of any insolvency proceedings against the maker, the acceptor, or the drawer of the instrument.[4]

The manner of transfer and the negotiation that is used determine how far and to whom a transfer warranty will run. Transfer of order paper, for consideration, by indorsement and delivery extends warranty liability to any subsequent holder who takes the instrument in good faith. The warranties of a person who transfers *without indorsement* (by the delivery of a bearer instrument), however, will extend the transferor's warranties only to the immediate transferee [UCC 3–416(a)].

PRESENTMENT WARRANTIES

PRESENTMENT WARRANTY
Implied warranties, made by any person who presents an instrument for payment or acceptance, that (1) the person obtaining payment or acceptance is entitled to enforce the instrument or is authorized to obtain payment or acceptance on behalf of a person who is entitled to enforce the instrument; (2) the instrument has not been altered; and (3) the person obtaining payment or acceptance has no knowledge that the signature of the drawer of the instrument is unauthorized.

Any person who presents an instrument for payment or acceptance makes the following **presentment warranties** to any other person who in good faith pays or accepts the instrument [UCC 3–417(a), 3–417(d)]:

1. The person obtaining payment or acceptance is entitled to enforce the instrument or is authorized to obtain payment or acceptance on behalf of a person

---

4. A 2002 amendment to UCC 3–416(a) adds a sixth warranty: "with respect to a remotely created consumer item, that the person on whose account the item is drawn authorized the issuance of the item in the amount for which the item is drawn." For example, a telemarketer submits an instrument to a bank for payment, claiming that the consumer on whose account the instrument purports to be drawn authorized it over the phone. Under this amendment, a bank that accepts and pays the instrument warrants to the next bank in the collection chain that the consumer authorized the item in that amount.

who is entitled to enforce the instrument. (This is, in effect, a warranty that there are no missing or unauthorized indorsements.)

2 The instrument has not been altered.

3 The person obtaining payment or acceptance has no knowledge that the signature of the issuer of the instrument is unauthorized.[5]

These warranties are referred to as presentment warranties because they protect the person to whom the instrument is presented. The second and third warranties do not apply to makers, acceptors, and drawers. It is assumed, for example, that a drawer or a maker will recognize his or her own signature and that a maker or an acceptor will recognize whether an instrument has been materially altered.

■ Defenses to Liability

Persons who would otherwise be liable on negotiable instruments may be able to avoid liability by raising certain defenses. There are two general categories of defenses—*universal defenses* and *personal defenses*.

UNIVERSAL DEFENSES

UNIVERSAL DEFENSES
Defenses that are valid against all holders of a negotiable instrument, including holders in due course (HDCs) and holders with the rights of HDCs.

Universal defenses (also called *real defenses*) are valid against *all* holders, including HDCs and holders who take through an HDC. Universal defenses include those described here.

Forgery   Forgery of a maker's or drawer's signature cannot bind the person whose name is used unless that person ratifies (approves or validates) the signature or is precluded from denying it (because the forgery was made possible by the maker's or drawer's negligence, for example) [UCC 3–403(a)]. Thus, when a person forges an instrument, the person whose name is forged normally has no liability to pay any holder or any HDC the value of the forged instrument.

Fraud in the Execution   If a person is deceived into signing a negotiable instrument, believing that she or he is signing something other than a negotiable instrument (such as a receipt), *fraud in the execution,* or fraud in the inception, is committed against the signer [UCC 3–305(a)(1)].

■ **EXAMPLE 14.17** Gerard, a salesperson, asks a customer to sign a paper, which Gerard says is a receipt for the delivery of goods that the customer is picking up from the store. In fact, the paper is a promissory note, but the customer, Javier, is unfamiliar with the English language and does not realize this. In this situation, even if the note is negotiated to an HDC, Javier has a valid defense against payment. ■

The defense of fraud in the execution cannot be raised, however, if a reasonable inquiry would have revealed the nature and terms of the instrument.[6] Thus, the signer's age, experience, and intelligence are relevant because they frequently determine whether the signer should have known the nature of the transaction before signing.

---

5. As discussed in footnote 4, the 2002 amendments to Article 3 of the UCC provide additional protection for "remotely created" consumer items [see Amended UCC 3–417(a)(4)].
6. *Burchett v. Allied Concord Financial Corp.,* 74 N.M. 575, 396 P.2d 186 (1964).

Material Alteration An alteration is material if it changes the contract terms between any two parties *in any way*. Examples of material alterations include completing an incomplete instrument, adding words or numbers to an instrument, or making any other change to an instrument in an unauthorized manner that affects the obligation of a party to the instrument [UCC 3–407(a)]. Thus, cutting off part of the paper of a negotiable instrument, adding clauses, or making any change in the amount, the date, or the rate of interest—even if the change is only one penny, one day, or 1 percent—is material.

It is not a material alteration, however, to correct the maker's address or to change the figures on a check so that they agree with the written amount. If the alteration is not material, any holder is entitled to enforce the instrument according to its terms.

Material alteration is a *complete defense* against an ordinary holder but only a partial defense against an HDC. An ordinary holder can recover nothing on an instrument if it has been materially altered [UCC 3–407(b)]. When the holder is an HDC, by contrast, if an original term, such as the monetary amount payable, has been *altered*, the HDC can enforce the instrument against the maker or drawer according to the original terms but not for the altered amount. If the instrument was originally incomplete and was later completed in an unauthorized manner, however, alteration no longer can be claimed as a defense against an HDC, and the HDC can enforce the instrument as completed [UCC 3–407(b)]. This is because the drawer or maker of the instrument, by issuing an incomplete instrument, will normally be held responsible for the alteration, which could have been avoided by the exercise of greater care. If the alteration is readily apparent, then obviously the holder has notice of some defect or defense and therefore cannot be an HDC [UCC 3–302(a)(1)].

Discharge in Bankruptcy Discharge in bankruptcy (see Chapter 16) is an absolute defense on any instrument, regardless of the status of the holder, because the purpose of bankruptcy is to settle finally all of the insolvent party's debts [UCC 3–305(a)(1)].

> **BE AWARE** Minority, illegality, mental incapacity, and duress can be universal defenses or personal defenses, depending in some circumstances on state law rather than the UCC.

Minority Minority, or infancy, is a universal defense only to the extent that state law recognizes it as a defense to a simple contract (see Chapter 8). Because state laws on minority vary, so do determinations of whether minority is a universal defense against an HDC [UCC 3–305(a)(1)(i)].

Illegality Certain types of illegality constitute universal defenses. Other types constitute personal defenses—that is, defenses that are effective against ordinary holders but not against HDCs. If a statute provides that an illegal transaction is void, then the defense is universal—that is, absolute against both an ordinary holder and an HDC. If the law merely makes the instrument voidable, then the illegality is still a personal defense against an ordinary holder but not against an HDC [UCC 3–305(a)(1)(ii)].

Mental Incapacity If a person has been declared mentally incompetent by state court proceedings, then any instrument issued thereafter by that person is void. The instrument is void *ab initio* (from the beginning) and unenforceable by any holder or HDC [UCC 3–305(a)(1)(ii)]. Mental incapacity in these circumstances is thus a universal defense. If a person has not been judged mentally incompetent by state proceedings, mental incapacity operates as a defense against an ordinary holder but not against an HDC.

Extreme Duress   When a person signs and issues a negotiable instrument under such extreme duress as an immediate threat of force or violence (for example, at gunpoint), the instrument is void and unenforceable by any holder or HDC [UCC 3–305(a)(1)(ii)]. (Ordinary duress is a defense against ordinary holders but not against HDCs.)

PERSONAL DEFENSES

Personal defenses (sometimes called *limited defenses*), such as those described here, can be used to avoid payment to an ordinary holder of a negotiable instrument but not to an HDC or a holder with the rights of an HDC.

Breach of Contract or Breach of Warranty   When there is a breach of the underlying contract for which the negotiable instrument was issued, the maker of a note can refuse to pay it, or the drawer of a check can order his or her bank to stop payment on the check. Breach of warranty can also be claimed as a defense to liability on the instrument.

   ■ EXAMPLE 14.18   Rhodes agrees to purchase several sets of imported china from Livingston. The china is to be delivered in four weeks. Rhodes gives Livingston a promissory note for $2,000, which is the price of the china. The china arrives, but many of the pieces are broken, and several others are chipped or cracked. Rhodes refuses to pay the note on the basis of breach of contract and breach of warranty. (Under sales law, a seller impliedly promises that the goods are at least merchantable—see Chapter 13.) Livingston cannot enforce payment on the note because of the breach of contract and breach of warranty. If Livingston has negotiated the note to a third party, however, and the third party is an HDC, Rhodes will not be able to use breach of contract or warranty as a defense against liability on the note. ■

Lack or Failure of Consideration   The absence of consideration (value) may be a successful personal defense in some instances [UCC 3–303(b), 3–305(a)(2)].
   ■ EXAMPLE 14.19   Tara gives Clem, as a gift, a note that states, "I promise to pay you $100,000." Clem accepts the note. Because there is no consideration for Tara's promise, a court will not enforce the promise. ■

Fraud in the Inducement (Ordinary Fraud)   A person who issues a negotiable instrument based on false statements by the other party will be able to avoid payment on that instrument, unless the holder is an HDC. ■ EXAMPLE 14.20   Jerry agrees to purchase Howard's used tractor for $24,500. Howard—knowing his statements to be false—tells Jerry that the tractor is in good working order, that it has been used for only one harvest, and that he owns the tractor free and clear of all claims. Jerry pays Howard $4,500 in cash and issues a negotiable promissory note for the balance. As it turns out, Howard still owes the original seller $10,000 on the purchase of the tractor. In addition, the tractor is three years old and has been used in three harvests. Jerry can refuse to pay the note if it is held by an ordinary holder. If Howard has negotiated the note to an HDC, however, Jerry must pay the HDC. (Of course, Jerry can then sue Howard to recover the funds paid.) ■

Illegality   As mentioned, if a statute provides that an illegal transaction is void, a universal defense exists. If, however, the statute provides that an illegal transaction is voidable, the defense is personal.

Mental Incapacity   As mentioned, if a maker or drawer has been declared by a court to be mentally incompetent, any instrument issued by the maker or drawer is void. Hence, mental incapacity can serve as a universal defense [UCC 3–305(a)(1)(ii)]. If a maker or drawer, in contrast, issues a negotiable instrument while mentally incompetent but before a formal court hearing has declared him or her to be so, the instrument is voidable. In this situation, mental incapacity can serve only as a personal defense.

Other Personal Defenses   Other personal defenses that can be used to avoid payment to an ordinary holder of a negotiable instrument include the following:

1. Discharge by payment or cancellation [UCC 3–601(b), 3–602(a), 3–603, 3–604].
2. Unauthorized completion of an incomplete instrument [UCC 3–115, 3–302, 3–407, 4–401(d)(2)].
3. Nondelivery of the instrument [UCC 1–201(14), 3–105(b), 3–305(a)(2)].
4. Ordinary duress or undue influence rendering the contract voidable [UCC 3–305(a)(1)(ii)].

APPLICATION ■ How to Purchase Negotiable Instruments*

Negotiable instruments are transferred every business day of the year. Most purchasers of negotiable instruments do not encounter any problems in further negotiating and transferring the instruments or in collecting payment on them if they are time instruments. Nevertheless, potential problems do exist, and purchasers should take precautions against them.

OVERDUE INSTRUMENTS

Suppose that you wish to purchase a demand instrument as a holder in due course (HDC). By definition, such an instrument has no stated time for payment and therefore may be overdue—that is, the payee may have demanded payment but not received it, or a reasonable amount of time may have passed. (With checks, a reasonable amount of time is presumed to be ninety days from the date on the check.) If you have any doubt about whether a demand instrument is overdue, you should investigate.

* This *Application* is not meant to substitute for the services of an attorney who is licensed to practice law in your state.

NOTICE OF DEFECTS

As a prospective holder, you cannot afford to ignore a defect in any negotiable instrument. A four-month-old date on a check, for example, constitutes notice that the instrument is overdue. Generally, whenever an instrument has a defect, you will not qualify as an HDC, and you may be unable to obtain payment. In other words, it is prudent to determine whether the instrument is complete and, in some situations, whether the transfer will qualify you for HDC status.

CHECKLIST FOR THE PURCHASER OF NEGOTIABLE INSTRUMENTS

1. Make sure that a demand instrument is not overdue before purchasing it.
2. Make sure that the negotiable instrument has no obvious defects—look for indications that the maker or drawer of the instrument might have a valid reason for refusing to pay.

▪ KEY TERMS

acceptance 424

acceptor 434

bearer instrument 429

certificate of deposit (CD) 428

check 425

draft 424

drawee 424

drawer 424

fictitious payee 438

holder 429

holder in due course (HDC) 430

imposter 438

indorsement 429

maker 427

negotiable instrument 423

negotiation 429

order instrument 429

payee 424

personal defenses 443

presentment 435

presentment warranty 440

promissory note 427

shelter principle 433

trade acceptance 425

transfer warranty 440

universal defenses 441

CHAPTER SUMMARY ▪ Negotiable Instruments

Types of Negotiable Instruments (See pages 424–428.)	To be negotiable, an instrument must meet the requirements stated below. 1. Be in writing. 2. Be signed by the maker or drawer. 3. Be an unconditional promise or order to pay. 4. State a fixed amount of money. 5. Be payable on demand or at a definite time. 6. Be payable to order or bearer. The UCC specifies four types of negotiable instruments: drafts, checks, promissory notes, and certificates of deposit (CDs). These instruments fall into two basic classifications: 1. *Demand instruments versus time instruments*—A demand instrument is payable on demand (when the holder presents it to the maker or drawer). A time instrument is payable at a future date. 2. *Orders to pay versus promises to pay*—Checks and drafts are *orders* to pay. Promissory notes and CDs are *promises* to pay.
Transfer of Instruments (See pages 428–430.)	1. *Transfer by assignment*—A transfer by assignment to an assignee gives the assignee only those rights that the assignor possessed. Any defenses against payment that can be raised against an assignor can normally be raised against the assignee. 2. *Transfer by negotiation*—An order instrument is negotiated by indorsement and delivery; a bearer instrument is negotiated by delivery only.

Holder in Due Course (HDC) (See pages 430–433.)	*Holder in due course (HDC)*—A holder who, by meeting certain acquisition requirements (summarized next), takes the instrument free of most defenses and claims to which the transferor was subject. To be an HDC, a holder must take the instrument:
	
	 1. *For value*—A holder can take an instrument for value in one of five ways [UCC 3–303]:
	
	    a. By the complete or partial performance of the promise for which the instrument was issued or transferred.
	
	    b. By acquiring a security interest or other lien in the instrument, excluding a lien obtained by a judicial proceeding.

(Continued)

CHAPTER SUMMARY ▦ Negotiable Instruments—Continued

Holder in Due Course (HDC)— Continued	c. By taking an instrument in payment of (or as security for) a preexisting debt.
	d. By giving a negotiable instrument as payment.
	e. By giving an irrevocable commitment as payment.
	2. *In good faith*—Good faith is defined as "honesty in fact and the observance of reasonable commercial standards of fair dealing" [UCC 3–103(a)(4)].
	3. *Without notice*—To be an HDC, a holder must not be on notice that the instrument is defective in any of the following ways [UCC 3–302, 3–304]:
	a. The instrument is overdue.
	b. The instrument has been dishonored.
	c. There is an uncured (uncorrected) default with respect to another instrument issued as part of the same series.
	d. The instrument contains an unauthorized signature or has been altered.
	e. There is a defense against the instrument or a claim to the instrument.
	f. The instrument is so irregular or incomplete as to call into question its authenticity.
Holder through an HDC (See pages 433–434.)	A holder who cannot qualify as an HDC has the *rights* of an HDC if he or she derives title through an HDC unless the holder engaged in fraud or illegality affecting the instrument [UCC 3–203(b)]. This is known as the shelter principle.
Signature Liability (See pages 434–439.)	Every party (except a qualified indorser) who signs a negotiable instrument is either primarily or secondarily liable for payment of the instrument when it comes due.
	1. *Primary liability*—Makers and acceptors are primarily liable (an acceptor is a drawee that promises in writing to pay an instrument when it is presented for payment at a later time) [UCC 3–115, 3–407, 3–409, 3–412].
	2. *Secondary liability*—Drawers and indorsers are secondarily liable [UCC 3–412, 3–414, 3–415, 3–501, 3–502, 3–503]. Parties who are secondarily liable on an instrument promise to pay on that instrument if the following events occur:
	a. The instrument is properly and timely presented.
	b. The instrument is dishonored.
	c. Timely notice of dishonor is given to the secondarily liable party.
	3. *Unauthorized signatures*—An unauthorized signature is wholly inoperative *unless:*
	a. The person whose name is signed ratifies (affirms) it or is precluded from denying it [UCC 3–115, 3–401, 3–403, 3–406].
	b. The instrument has been negotiated to an HDC [UCC 3–403].
	4. *Special rules for unauthorized indorsements*—An unauthorized indorsement will not bind the maker or drawer except in the following circumstances:
	a. When an imposter induces the maker or drawer of an instrument to issue it to the imposter (imposter rule) [UCC 3–404(a)].
	b. When a person signs as or on behalf of a maker or drawer, intending that the payee will have no interest in the instrument, or when an agent or employee of the maker or drawer has supplied him or her with the name of the payee, also intending the payee to have no such interest (fictitious payee rule) [UCC 3–404(b), 3–405].

CHAPTER SUMMARY Negotiable Instruments—Continued

Warranty Liability (See pages 440–441.)	1. *Transfer warranties*—Any person who transfers an instrument for consideration makes the following warranties to all subsequent transferees and holders who take the instrument in good faith (but when a bearer instrument is transferred by delivery only, the transferor's warranties extend only to the immediate transferee) [UCC 3–416]: a. The transferor is entitled to enforce the instrument. b. All signatures are authentic and authorized. c. The instrument has not been altered. d. The instrument is not subject to a defense or claim of any party that can be asserted against the transferor. e. The transferor has no knowledge of any insolvency proceedings against the maker, the acceptor, or the drawer of the instrument. 2. *Presentment warranties*—Any person who presents an instrument for payment or acceptance makes the following warranties to any other person who in good faith pays or accepts the instrument [UCC 3–417(a), 3–417(d)]: a. The person obtaining payment or acceptance is entitled to enforce the instrument or is authorized to obtain payment or acceptance on behalf of a person who is entitled to enforce the instrument. (This is, in effect, a warranty that there are no missing or unauthorized indorsements.) b. The instrument has not been altered. c. The person obtaining payment or acceptance has no knowledge that the signature of the drawer of the instrument is unauthorized.
Defenses to Liability (See pages 441–444.)	1. *Universal (real) defenses*—The following defenses are valid against all holders, including HDCs and holders with the rights of HDCs [UCC 3–305, 3–401, 3–403, 3–407]: a. Forgery. b. Fraud in the execution. c. Material alteration. d. Discharge in bankruptcy. e. Minority—if the contract is voidable under state law. f. Illegality, mental incapacity, or extreme duress—if the contract is void under state law. 2. *Personal (limited) defenses*—The following defenses are valid against ordinary holders but not against HDCs or holders with the rights of HDCs [UCC 3–105, 3–115, 3–302, 3–305, 3–306, 3–407, 3–601, 3–602, 3–603, 3–604, 4–401]: a. Breach of contract or breach of warranty. b. Lack or failure of consideration (value). c. Fraud in the inducement. d. Illegality and mental incapacity—if the contract is voidable. e. Previous payment of the instrument. f. Unauthorized completion of the instrument. g. Nondelivery of the instrument. h. Ordinary duress or undue influence that renders the contract voidable.

FOR REVIEW

Answers for the even-numbered questions in this For Review *section can be found in Appendix I at the end of this text.*

1 What are the four types of negotiable instruments with which Article 3 of the UCC is concerned? Which of these instruments are *orders* to pay, and which are *promises* to pay?

2 What requirements must an instrument meet to be negotiable?

3 What are the requirements for attaining HDC status?

4 What is the key to liability on a negotiable instrument? What is the difference between signature liability and warranty liability?

5 Certain defenses are valid against all holders, including HDCs. What are these defenses called? Name four defenses that fall within this category.

QUESTIONS AND CASE PROBLEMS

14–1. Requirements for Negotiability. Muriel Evans writes the following note on the back of an envelope: "I, Muriel Evans, promise to pay Karen Marvin or bearer $100 on demand." Is this a negotiable instrument? Discuss fully.

14–2. Unauthorized Indorsements. What are the exceptions to the rule that a bank will be liable for paying a check over an unauthorized indorsement?

14–3. Signature Liability. Marion makes a promissory note payable to the order of Perry. Perry indorses the note by writing "without recourse, Perry" and transfers the note for value to Steven. Steven, in need of cash, negotiates the note to Harriet by indorsing it with the words "Pay to Harriet, [signed] Steven." On the due date, Harriet presents the note to Marion for payment, only to learn that Marion has filed for bankruptcy and will have all debts (including the note) discharged in bankruptcy. Discuss fully whether Harriet can hold Marion, Perry, or Steven liable on the note.

14–4. Unauthorized Indorsements. Telemedia Publications, Inc., publishes *Cablecast Magazine*, a weekly guide for the listings of the cable television programming in Baton Rouge, Louisiana. Cablecast hired Jennifer Pennington as a temporary employee. Pennington's duties included indorsing subscription checks received in the mail with the Cablecast deposit stamp, preparing the deposit slip, and taking the checks to be deposited to City National Bank. John McGregor, the manager of Cablecast, soon noticed shortages in revenue coming into Cablecast. When he learned that Pennington had taken checks payable to Cablecast and deposited them in her personal account at Premier Bank, N.A., he confronted her. She admitted to taking $7,913.04 in Cablecast checks. Cablecast filed a suit in a Louisiana state court against Premier Bank. The bank responded in part that Cablecast was solely responsible for losses caused by the fraudulent indorsements of its employees. At trial, Cablecast failed to prove that Premier Bank had not acted in good faith or that it had not exercised ordinary care in its handling of the checks. What rule should the court apply here? Why? [*Cablecast Magazine v. Premier Bank, N.A.*, 729 So.2d 1165 (La.App. 1 Cir. 1999)]

CASE PROBLEM WITH SAMPLE ANSWER

14–5. In October 1998, Somerset Valley Bank notified Alfred Hauser, president of Hauser Co., that the bank had begun to receive what appeared to be Hauser Co. payroll checks. None of the payees were Hauser Co. employees, however, and Hauser had not written the checks or authorized anyone to sign them on his behalf. Automatic Data Processing, Inc., provided payroll services for Hauser Co. and used a facsimile signature on all its payroll checks. Hauser told the bank not to cash the checks. In early 1999, Robert Triffin, who deals in negotiable instruments, bought eighteen of the checks, totaling more than $8,800, from various check-cashing agencies. The agencies stated that they had cashed the checks expecting the bank to pay them. Each check was payable to a bearer for a fixed amount, on demand, and did not state any undertaking by the person promising payment other than the payment of money. Each check bore a facsimile drawer's signature stamp identical to Hauser Co.'s authorized stamp. Each check had been returned to an agency marked "stolen check" and stamped "do not present again." When the bank refused to cash the checks, Triffin filed a suit in a New Jersey state court against Hauser Co. Were the checks negotiable instruments? Why or why not? [*Triffin v. Somerset Valley Bank*, 777 A.2d 993 (N.J.Super.App.Div. 2001)]

After you have answered this problem, compare your answer with the sample answer given on the Web site that accompanies this text. Go to http://blt.westbuslaw.com, select "Chapter 14," and click on "Case Problem with Sample Answer."

14–6. Defenses. On September 13, 1979, Barbara Shearer and Barbara Couvion signed a note for $22,500, with interest at 11 percent, payable in monthly installments of $232.25 to Edgar House and Paul Cook. House and Cook assigned the note to Southside Bank in Kansas City, Missouri. In 1997, the note was assigned to Midstates Resources Corp., which assigned the note to The Cadle Co. in 2000. According to the payment history that Midstates gave to Cadle, the interest rate on the note was 12 percent. A Cadle employee noticed the discrepancy and recalculated the payments at 11 percent. When Shearer and Couvion refused to make further payments on the note, Cadle filed a suit in a Missouri state court against them to collect. Couvion and Shearer responded that they had made timely payments on the note, that Cadle and the previous holders had failed to accurately apply the payments to the reduction of principal and interest, and that the note "is either paid in full and satisfied or very close to being paid in full and satisfied." Is the makers' answer sufficient to support a verdict in their favor? If so, on what ground? If not, why not? [*The Cadle Co. v. Shearer,* 69 S.W.3d 122 (Mo.App. W.D. 2002)]

14–7. Holder in Due Course. The Brown family owns several companies, including J. H. Stevedoring Co. and Penn Warehousing and Distribution, Inc. Many aspects of the companies' operations and management are intertwined. Dennis Bishop began working for J. H. and Penn in 1984. By 1997, Bishop was financial controller at J. H., where he was responsible for approving invoices for payment and reconciling the corporate checkbook. In December, Bishop began stealing from Penn and J. H. by writing checks on their accounts and usually having one of the Browns sign the checks. Over the next two years, Bishop embezzled $1,209,436. He used $370,632 of the funds to buy horses from Fasig-Tipton Co. and Fasig-Tipton Midlantic, Inc., with Penn or J. H. checks made payable to those firms. When Bishop's fraud was revealed, J. H. and Penn filed a suit in a federal district court against the Fasig-Tipton firms to recover the amounts of the checks made payable to them. In whose favor should the court rule? Why? [*J. H. Stevedoring Co. v. Fasig-Tipton Co.,* 275 F.Supp.2d 644 (E.D.Pa. 2003)]

A QUESTION OF ETHICS

14–8. One day, while Ort, a farmer, was working alone in his field, a stranger approached him. The stranger said he was the state agent for a manufacturer of iron posts and wire fence. Eventually, the stranger persuaded Ort to accept a townshipwide agency for the same manufacturer. The stranger then asked Ort to sign a document that purportedly was an agency agreement. Because Ort did not have his glasses with him and could read only with great difficulty, he asked the stranger to read what the document said. The stranger then pretended to read the document to Ort, not mentioning that it was a promissory note. Both men signed the note,

and Ort assumed that he was signing a document of agency. The stranger later negotiated the note to a good faith purchaser for value. When that person sued Ort, Ort attempted to defend on the basis of fraud in the execution. In view of these facts, consider the following questions. [*Ort v. Fowler,* 31 Kan. 478, 2 P. 580 (1884)]

1. Although this classic case was decided long before the UCC was drafted, the court applied essentially the same rule that would apply under Article 3. What is this rule, and how would it be applied to Ort's attempted defense on the ground of fraud in the execution?

2. This case provides a clear example of a situation in which one of two innocent parties (Ort and the purchaser of the note) must bear the loss caused by a third party (the stranger, who was the perpetrator of the fraud). Under Article 3, which party should bear the loss, and why?

FOR CRITICAL ANALYSIS

14–9. How does the concept of holder in due course further Article 3's general goal of encouraging the negotiability of instruments? How does it further Article 3's goal of balancing the rights of parties to negotiable instruments?

VIDEO QUESTION

14–10. Go to this text's Web site at **http://blt. westbuslaw.com** and select "Chapter 14." Click on "Video Questions" and view the video titled *Negotiable Instruments.* Then answer the following questions.

1. Who is the maker of the promissory note discussed in the video?

2. Is the note in the video payable on demand or at a definite time?

3. Does the note contain an unconditional promise or order to pay?

4. If the note does not meet the requirements of negotiability, can Onyx assign the note (assignment was discussed in Chapter 9) to the bank in exchange for cash?

INTERNET EXERCISES

Go to the *Business Law Today: The Essentials* home page at **http://blt.westbuslaw.com**, select "Chapter 14," and click on "Internet Exercises." There you will find the following Internet research exercises that you can perform to learn more about topics covered in this chapter.

Activity 14–1: LEGAL PERSPECTIVE—Fictitious Payees

Activity 14–2: MANAGEMENT PERSPECTIVE—Holder in Due Course

Activity 14–3: TECHNOLOGICAL PERSPECTIVE—Electronic Negotiable Instruments

BEFORE THE TEST

Go to the *Business Law Today: The Essentials* home page at **http://blt.westbuslaw.com**, select "Chapter 14," and click on "Interactive Quizzes." You will find at least twenty interactive questions relating to this chapter.

CHAPTER 15

Checks, the Banking System, and E-Money

"Money is just what we use
to keep tally."

Henry Ford, 1863–1947
(American automobile manufacturer)

■ LEARNING OBJECTIVES

After reading this chapter, you should be able to answer the following questions:

1 On what types of checks does a bank serve as both the drawer and the drawee? What type of check does a bank agree in advance to accept when the check is presented for payment?

2 When may a bank properly dishonor a customer's check without liability to the customer? What happens if a bank wrongfully dishonors a customer's check?

3 What duties does the Uniform Commercial Code impose on the customers of a bank with regard to forged and altered checks? What are the consequences of a customer's negligence in performing those duties?

4 What are the four most common types of electronic fund transfers? What is the basic purpose of the Electronic Fund Transfer Act, and how does it benefit consumers?

5 What is e-money? How is e-money stored and used? What laws apply to e-money transactions and online banking services?

Checks are the most common type of negotiable instruments regulated by the Uniform Commercial Code (UCC). It is estimated that over sixty-five billion personal and commercial checks are written each year in the United States. Checks are more than a daily convenience; they are an integral part of the American economic system. They serve as substitutes for money and thus, as Henry Ford said in the chapter-opening quotation, help us to "keep tally."

Issues relating to checks are governed by Articles 3 and 4 of the UCC. Recall from Chapter 14 that Article 3 establishes the requirements that all negotiable instruments, including checks, must meet. Article 3 also sets forth the rights and liabilities of parties to negotiable instruments. Article 4 of the UCC governs bank deposits and collections as well as bank-customer relationships. Article 4 regulates the relationships of banks with one another as they process checks for payment, and it establishes a framework for deposit and checking agreements between a bank and its customers. A check therefore may fall within the scope of Article 3 and yet be subject to the provisions of Article 4 while in the course of collection. If a conflict between Article 3 and Article 4 arises, Article 4 controls [UCC 4–102(a)].

In this chapter, we first identify the legal characteristics of checks and the legal duties and liabilities that arise when a check is issued. Then we examine the collection process—that is, the actual procedure by which the checks deposited into bank accounts move through banking channels, causing the underlying funds to be shifted from one bank account to another. Increasingly, credit cards, debit cards, and other devices and methods to transfer funds electronically are being used to pay for goods and services. In the latter part of this chapter, we look at the law governing electronic fund transfers.

Checks

CHECK
A draft drawn by a drawer ordering the drawee bank or financial institution to pay a fixed amount of money to the holder on demand.

A **check** is a special type of draft that is drawn on a bank, ordering the bank to pay a fixed amount of money on demand [UCC 3–104(f)]. Article 4 defines a bank as "a person engaged in the business of banking, including a savings bank, savings and loan association, credit union or trust company" [UCC 4–105(1)]. If any other institution (such as a brokerage firm) handles a check for payment or for collection, the check is not covered by Article 4.

Recall from the discussion of negotiable instruments in Chapter 14 that a person who writes a check is called the *drawer*. The drawer is a depositor in the bank on which the check is drawn. The person to whom the check is payable is the *payee*. The bank or financial institution on which the check is drawn is the *drawee*. If Anita Cruzak writes a check from her checking account to pay her college tuition, she is the drawer, her bank is the drawee, and her college is the payee. We now look at some special types of checks.

CASHIER'S CHECKS

CASHIER'S CHECK
A check drawn by a bank on itself.

Checks are usually three-party instruments, but on certain types of checks, the bank can serve as both the drawer and the drawee. For example, when a bank draws a check on itself, the check is called a **cashier's check** and is a negotiable instrument on issue (see Exhibit 15–1) [UCC 3–104(g)]. Normally, a cashier's check indicates a specific payee. In effect, with a cashier's check, the bank assumes responsibility for paying the check, thus making the check more readily acceptable as a substitute for cash.

■ **EXAMPLE 15.1** Kramer needs to pay a moving company $8,000 for moving his household goods to a new home in another state. The moving company requests payment in the form of a cashier's check. Kramer goes to a bank (he need not have an account at the bank) and purchases a cashier's check, payable to the moving company, in the amount of $8,000. Kramer has to pay the bank the $8,000 for the check, plus a small service fee. He then gives the check to the moving company. ■

Cashier's checks are sometimes used in the business community as nearly the equivalent of cash. Except in very limited circumstances, the issuing bank must

EXHIBIT 15–1 A CASHIER'S CHECK

*The abbreviation *NT&SA* stands for National Trust and Savings Association. The Bank of America NT&SA is a subsidiary of BankAmerica Corporation, which is engaged in financial services, insurance, investment management, and other businesses.

honor its cashier's checks when they are presented for payment. If a bank wrongfully dishonors a cashier's check, a holder can recover from the bank all expenses incurred, interest, and consequential damages [UCC 3–411]. This same rule applies if a bank wrongfully dishonors a certified check (to be discussed shortly) or a teller's check. (A *teller's check* is a check drawn by a bank on another bank or, when drawn on a nonbank, payable at or through a bank [UCC 3–104(h)]).

TRAVELER'S CHECKS

TRAVELER'S CHECK
A check that is payable on demand, drawn on or payable through a financial institution (bank), and designated as a traveler's check.

A **traveler's check** is an instrument that is payable on demand, drawn on or payable at or through a financial institution (such as a bank), and designated as a traveler's check. The institution is directly obligated to accept and pay its traveler's check according to the check's terms. The purchaser is required to sign the check at the time it is bought and again at the time it is used [UCC 3–104(i)]. Exhibit 15–2 on the next page shows an example of a traveler's check.

CERTIFIED CHECKS

CERTIFIED CHECK
A check that has been accepted in writing by the bank on which it is drawn. Essentially, the bank, by certifying (accepting) the check, promises to pay the check at the time the check is presented.

A **certified check** is a check that has been *accepted* in writing by the bank on which it is drawn [UCC 3–409(d)]. When a drawee bank *certifies* (accepts) a check, it immediately charges the drawer's account with the amount of the check and transfers those funds to its own certified check account. In effect, the bank is agreeing in advance to accept that check when it is presented for payment and to make payment from those funds reserved in the certified check account. Essentially, certification prevents the bank from denying liability. It is a promise that sufficient funds are on deposit *and have been set aside* to cover the check.

A drawee bank is not obligated to certify a check, and failure to do so is not a dishonor of the check [UCC 3–409(d)]. If a bank does certify a check, however, the bank should write on the check the amount that it will pay. If the certification does

EXHIBIT 15-2 A TRAVELER'S CHECK

USD 20 • U.S. DOLLAR TRAVELERS CHEQUE • **USD 20**

U.S.$20 TWENTY U.S. DOLLARS

DB270·884·083

Purchaser

Richard Evans   JAN 3 2006

SIGN HERE IMMEDIATELY UPON RECEIPT OF THIS TRAVELERS CHEQUE   DATE

American Express® Travelers Cheque — Drawer/Drawee

ISSUED BY AMERICAN EXPRESS TRAVEL RELATED SERVICES COMPANY, INC. NEW YORK, N.Y.

PAY THIS CHEQUE
TO THE ORDER OF *SHANGHAI HOTEL*   Payee

Richard Evans   USD 20

COUNTERSIGN HERE IN PRESENCE OF PERSON CASHING

Purchaser's Countersignature

⑆800000051⑈42⑇270884083⑆

AMERICAN EXPRESS TRAVELERS CHEQUES NEVER EXPIRE **USD 20** ACCEPTANCE PROCEDURE ON REVERSE SIDE

not state an amount, and the amount is later increased and the instrument negotiated to a holder in due course (HDC), the obligation of the certifying bank is the amount of the instrument when it was taken by the HDC [UCC 3–413(b)].

Certification may be requested by a holder (to ensure that the check will not be dishonored for insufficient funds) or by the drawer. In either circumstance, once the check is certified, the drawer and any prior indorsers are completely discharged from liability [UCC 3–414(c), 3–415(d)].

◼ The Bank-Customer Relationship

The bank-customer relationship begins when the customer opens a checking account and deposits funds that the bank will use to pay for checks written by the customer. Essentially, three types of relationships come into being, as discussed next.

CREDITOR-DEBTOR RELATIONSHIP

A creditor-debtor relationship is created between a customer and a bank when, for example, the customer makes cash deposits into a checking account. When a customer makes a deposit, the customer becomes a creditor, and the bank a debtor, for the amount deposited.

AGENCY RELATIONSHIP

An agency relationship also arises between the customer and the bank when the customer writes a check on his or her account. In effect, the customer is ordering the bank to pay the amount specified on the check to the holder when the holder presents the check to the bank for payment. In this situation, the bank becomes the customer's agent and is obligated to honor the customer's request. Similarly, if the customer deposits a check into her or his account, the bank, as the customer's agent, is obligated to collect payment on the check from the bank on which the check was drawn. To transfer checkbook funds among different banks, each bank acts as the agent of collection for its customer [UCC 4–201(a)].

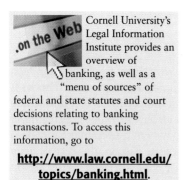

.on the Web

Cornell University's Legal Information Institute provides an overview of banking, as well as a "menu of sources" of federal and state statutes and court decisions relating to banking transactions. To access this information, go to

**http://www.law.cornell.edu/
topics/banking.html**.

CONTRACTUAL RELATIONSHIP

Whenever a bank-customer relationship is established, certain contractual rights and duties arise. The specific rights and duties of the bank and its customer depend on the nature of the transaction. The respective rights and duties of banks and their customers are discussed in detail in the following pages.

■ Bank's Duty to Honor Checks

When a banking institution provides checking services, it agrees to honor the checks written by its customers, with the usual stipulation that the account must have sufficient funds available to pay each check [UCC 4–401(a)]. When a drawee bank *wrongfully* fails to honor a check, it is liable to its customer for damages resulting from its refusal to pay. The UCC does not attempt to specify the theory under which the customer may recover for wrongful dishonor; it merely states that the drawee (bank) is liable. Thus, the customer does not have to prove that the bank breached its contractual commitment, slandered the customer's credit, or was negligent [UCC 4–402(b)].

The customer's agreement with the bank includes a general obligation to keep sufficient funds on deposit to cover all checks written. The customer is liable to the payee or to the holder of a check in a civil suit if a check is dishonored for insufficient funds. If intent to defraud can be proved, the customer can also be subject to criminal prosecution for writing a bad check.

When the bank properly dishonors a check for insufficient funds, it has no liability to the customer. The bank may rightfully refuse payment on a customer's check in other circumstances as well. We look here at the rights and duties of both the bank and its customers in relation to specific situations.

OVERDRAFTS

OVERDRAFT
A check that is paid by the bank when the checking account on which the check is written contains insufficient funds to cover the check.

When the bank receives an item properly payable from its customer's checking account but the account contains insufficient funds to cover the amount of the check, the bank has two options. It can either (1) dishonor the item or (2) pay the item and charge the customer's account, thus creating an **overdraft**, providing that the customer has authorized the payment and the payment does not violate any bank-customer agreement [UCC 4–401(a)].[1] The bank can subtract the difference (plus a service charge) from the customer's next deposit or other customer funds because the check carries with it an enforceable implied promise to reimburse the bank.

A bank can expressly agree with a customer to accept overdrafts through what is sometimes called an "overdraft protection agreement." If such an agreement is formed, any failure of the bank to honor a check because it would create an overdraft breaches this agreement and is treated as wrongful dishonor [UCC 4–402(a)].

When a check "bounces," a holder can resubmit the check, hoping that at a later date sufficient funds will be available to pay it. The holder must notify any indorsers on the check of the first dishonor, however; otherwise, they will be discharged from their signature liability.

---

1. With a joint account, the bank cannot hold the nonsigning customer liable for payment of an overdraft unless that person benefited from its proceeds [UCC 4–401(b)].

POSTDATED CHECKS

A bank may also charge a postdated check against a customer's account, unless the customer notifies the bank, in a timely manner, not to pay the check until the stated date. The notice of postdating must be given in time to allow the bank to act on the notice before committing itself to pay on the check. The UCC states that the bank should treat a notice of postdating the same as a stop-payment order (to be discussed shortly). If the bank fails to act on the customer's notice and charges the customer's account before the date on the postdated check, the bank may be liable for any damages incurred by the customer [UCC 4–401(c)].[2]

STALE CHECKS

Commercial banking practice regards a check that is presented for payment more than six months from its date as a **stale check**. A bank is not obligated to pay an uncertified check presented more than six months from its date [UCC 4–404]. When receiving a stale check for payment, the bank has the option of paying or not paying the check. The bank may consult the customer before paying the check. If a bank pays a stale check in good faith without consulting the customer, however, the bank has the right to charge the customer's account for the amount of the check.

STALE CHECK
A check, other than a certified check, that is presented for payment more than six months after its date.

STOP-PAYMENT ORDERS

A **stop-payment order** is an order by a customer to his or her bank not to pay or certify a certain check. Only a customer or a person authorized to draw on the account can order the bank not to pay the check when it is presented for payment [UCC 4–403(a)].[3] A customer has no right to stop payment on a check that has been certified or accepted by a bank, however. The customer must issue the stop-payment order within a reasonable time and in a reasonable manner to permit the bank to act on it [UCC 4–403(a)]. Although a stop-payment order can be given orally, usually by phone, it is binding on the bank for only fourteen calendar days unless confirmed in writing.[4] A written stop-payment order (see Exhibit 15–3) or an oral order confirmed in writing is effective for six months, at which time it must be renewed in writing [UCC 4–403(b)].

STOP-PAYMENT ORDER
An order by a bank customer to his or her bank not to pay or certify a certain check.

Bank's Liability for Wrongful Payment   If the bank pays the check over the customer's properly instituted stop-payment order, the bank will be obligated to recredit the customer's account—but only for the amount of the actual loss suffered by the drawer because of the wrongful payment [UCC 4–403(c)]. ■ **EXAMPLE 15.2** Toshio Murano orders six bamboo palms from a local nursery at $50 each and gives the nursery a check for $300. Later that day, the nursery tells Murano that it will not deliver the palms as arranged. Murano immediately calls his bank and stops payment on the check. If the bank nonetheless honors the check, the bank will be liable to Murano for the full $300. The result would be different, however, if the nursery had delivered five palms. In that situation, Murano would owe the nursery

---

2. Under the UCC, postdating does not affect the negotiability of a check. In the past, instead of treating postdated checks as checks payable on demand, some courts treated them as time drafts. Thus, regardless of whether the customer notified the bank of the postdating, a bank could not charge a customer's account for a postdated check without facing potential liability for the payment of later checks. Under the automated check-collection system currently in use, however, a check is usually paid without respect to its date. Thus, today the bank can ignore the postdate on the check (treat it as a demand instrument) unless it has received notice from the customer that the check was postdated.

3. For a deceased customer, any person claiming a legitimate interest in the account may issue a stop-payment order [UCC 4–405].

4. Some states do not recognize oral stop-payment orders; they must be in writing.

EXHIBIT 15–3 A STOP-PAYMENT ORDER

Bank of America

Checking Account
Stop Payment Order

To: Bank of America NT&SA
I want to stop payment on the following check(s).

ACCOUNT NUMBER:

SPECIFIC STOP

*ENTER DOLLAR AMOUNT:

*CHECK NUMBER:

THE CHECK WAS SIGNED BY: _____
THE CHECK IS PAYABLE TO: _____
THE REASON FOR THIS STOP PAYMENT IS: _____

STOP RANGE (Use for lost or stolen check(s) only.)

DOLLAR AMOUNT: 000

*ENTER STARTING CHECK NUMBER:

*END CHECK NUMBER:

THE REASON FOR THIS STOP PAYMENT IS: _____

I agree that this order (1) is effective only if the above check(s) has (have) not yet been cashed or paid against my account, (2) will end six months from the date it is delivered to you unless I renew it in writing, and (3) is not valid if the check(s) was (were) accepted on the strength of my Bank of America courtesy-check guarantee card by a merchant participating in that program. I also agree (1) to notify you immediately to cancel this order if the reason for the stop payment no longer exists or (2) that closing the account on which the check(s) is (are) drawn automatically cancels this order.

IF ANOTHER BRANCH OF THIS BANK OR ANOTHER PERSON OR ENTITY BECOMES A "HOLDER IN DUE COURSE" OF THE ABOVE CHECK, I UNDERSTAND THAT PAYMENT MAY BE ENFORCED AGINST THE CHECK'S MAKER (SIGNER).

*I CERTIFY THE AMOUNT AND CHECK NUMBER(S) ABOVE ARE CORRECT.
☐ I have written a replacement check (number and date of check).

(Optional—please circle one: Mr., Ms., Mrs., Miss) CUSTOMER'S SIGNATURE **X** _____ DATE _____

BANK USE ONLY

TRANCODE:
☐ 21—ENTER STOP PAYMENT (SEE OTHER SIDE TO REMOVE)

NON READS: _____
UNPROC. STMT HIST: _____
PRIOR STMT CYCLE: _____
HOLDS ON COOLS: _____
REJECTED CHKS: _____
LARGE ITEMS: _____
FEE COLLECTED: _____
DATE ACCEPTED: _____
TIME ACCEPTED: _____

$250 for the delivered palms, and his actual losses would be only $50. Consequently, the bank would be liable to Murano for only $50. ■

Customer's Liability for Wrongful Stop-Payment Order A stop-payment order has its risks for a customer. The customer-drawer must have a *valid legal ground* for issuing such an order; otherwise, the holder can sue the drawer for payment. Moreover, defenses sufficient to refuse payment against a payee may not be valid grounds to prevent payment against a subsequent holder in due course [UCC 3–305, 3–306]. A person who wrongfully stops payment on a check not only will be liable to the payee for the amount of the check but also may be liable for consequential damages incurred by the payee as a result of the wrongful stop-payment order. See the *Application* feature at the end of this chapter for guidelines on how and when to use stop-payment orders.

DEATH OR INCOMPETENCE OF A CUSTOMER

Neither the death nor the incompetence of a customer revokes a bank's authority to pay an item until the bank is informed of the situation and has had reasonable time to act on the notice. Thus, if, at the time a check is issued or its collection has been undertaken, a bank does not know of an adjudication of incompetence against the customer who wrote the check, the bank can pay the item without incurring liability [UCC 4–405]. Even when a bank knows of the death of its customer, for ten days after the *date of death,* it can pay or certify checks drawn on or before the date of death. An exception to this rule is made if a person claiming an interest in that account, such as an heir, orders the bank to stop payment. Without this provision, banks would constantly be required to verify the continued life and competence of their drawers.

CHECKS BEARING FORGED DRAWERS' SIGNATURES

When a bank pays a check on which the drawer's signature is forged, generally the bank is liable. A bank may be able to recover at least some of the loss, however, from the customer (if the customer's negligence contributed to the making of the forgery), from the forger of the check (if he or she can be found), or from the holder who presented the check for payment (if the holder knew that the signature was forged).

The General Rule   A forged signature on a check has no legal effect as the signature of a drawer [UCC 3–403(a)]. For this reason, banks require signature cards from each customer who opens a checking account. Signature cards allow the bank to verify whether the signatures on their customers' checks are genuine. The general rule is that the bank must recredit the customer's account when it pays a check with a forged signature. (Note that banks today normally verify signatures only on checks that exceed a certain threshold, such as $1,000, $2,500, or some higher amount. Even though a bank sometimes incurs liability costs when it has paid forged checks, the costs involved in verifying every check's signature would be much higher.)

Customer Negligence   When the customer's negligence substantially contributes to the forgery, the bank normally will not be obligated to recredit the customer's account for the amount of the check [UCC 3–406].[5] The customer's liability may be reduced, however, by the amount of loss caused by negligence on the part of the bank (or other "person") paying the instrument or taking it for value if the negligence substantially contributed to the loss [UCC 3–406(b)].

■ **EXAMPLE 15.3** Gemco Corporation uses special check-writing equipment to write its payroll and business checks. Gemco discovers that one of its employees used the equipment to write himself a check for $10,000 and that the bank subsequently honored it. Gemco asks the bank to recredit $10,000 to its account for improperly paying the forged check. If the bank can show that Gemco failed to take reasonable care in controlling access to the check-writing equipment, the bank will not be required to recredit Gemco's account for the amount of the forged check. If Gemco can show that negligence on the part of the bank contributed substantially to the loss, however, then Gemco's liability may be reduced proportionately. ■

Timely Examination of Bank Statements Required.   Banks typically send or make available to their customers monthly statements detailing activity in their checking accounts. Banks are not obligated to include the canceled checks themselves with the statement sent to the customer. If the bank does not send the canceled checks (or photocopies of the canceled checks), however, it must provide the customer with information (check number, amount, and date of payment) on the statement that will allow the customer to reasonably identify the checks that the bank has paid [UCC 4–406(a), (b)]. If the bank retains the canceled checks, it must keep the checks—or legible copies of the checks—for a period of seven years [UCC 4–406(b)]. The customer may obtain a canceled check (or a copy of the check) during this period of time.

The customer has a duty to examine bank statements (and canceled checks or photocopies, if they are included with the statements) promptly and with reasonable care, and to report any alterations or forged signatures promptly [UCC 4–406(c)].

---

5. Note that banks can shift some of the risk of forged checks to the customer by contract, such as the risk of forged signatures created by the use of facsimile or other nonmanual signature devices. See, for example, *Arkwright Mutual Insurance Co. v. Nations Bank,* 212 F.3d 1224 (11th Cir. 2000).

This includes forged signatures of indorsers, to be discussed later. If the customer fails to fulfill this duty and the bank suffers a loss as a result, the customer will be liable for the loss [UCC 4–406(d)]. Even if the customer can prove that she or he took reasonable care against forgeries, the UCC provides that the customer must discover the forgeries and notify the bank within a period of one year to require the bank to recredit her or his account.

Consequences of Failing to Detect Forgeries. When the same wrongdoer has committed a series of forgeries, the UCC provides that the customer, to recover for all the forged items, must discover and report the first forged check to the bank within thirty calendar days of the receipt of the bank statement (and canceled checks or copies, if they are included) [UCC 4–406(d)(2)]. Failure to notify the bank within this period of time discharges the bank's liability for all forged checks that it pays prior to notification. In the following case, the court was asked to apply this rule.

CASE 15.1 ■ Espresso Roma Corp. v. Bank of America, N.A.

Court of Appeal of California,
First District, Division 1, 2002.
100 Cal.App.4th 525,
124 Cal.Rptr.2d 549.

FACTS Espresso Roma Corporation owns a chain of coffee houses as well as a number of other businesses and real properties (including university dormitories). David Boyd is the president of Espresso Roma and runs Hillside Residence Hall on the Berkeley campus of the University of California. Espresso Roma and the other businesses had checking accounts with Bank of America, N.A. All of the businesses employed Joseph Montanez, whose duties included bookkeeping. As an employee, Montanez learned how to generate company checks on the computer and had access to blank company checks. In October 1997, Montanez began to steal blank checks and, using stolen company computer programs, printed company checks on his home computer. He forged the checks in amounts totaling more than $330,000. When the bank statements containing the forged checks arrived in the mail, Montanez sorted through the statements and removed the checks. Boyd discovered the forgeries and reported them to the bank in May 1999. Boyd and the businesses filed a suit in a California state court against the bank, alleging, among other things, unauthorized payment of the checks. The bank filed a motion for summary judgment in its favor, in part on the ground that UCC 4–406(d) precluded the claims. The court granted the motion, and the plaintiffs appealed to a state intermediate appellate court.

ISSUE Was the bank liable for payment of the checks?

DECISION No. The state intermediate appellate court affirmed the judgment of the lower court. Because the bank's customers did not report the first forged check to the bank within the thirty-day period of UCC 4–406(d), the bank's liability for payment of the checks was discharged.

REASON The court emphasized that a customer must notify "the bank no more than 30 days after the *first* forged item was included in the monthly statement or canceled checks and should have been discovered." The court explained that here "the forged checks were presented for payment between October 1997, and May 1999, but appellants [Boyd and the businesses] did not discover, or report them until on, or about, May 15, 1999," although they had received statements on a monthly basis, and the statements included canceled checks. "[T]he first monthly statement that would have reflected the forgery by Montanez would have been in November 1997. Yet, despite having the means to discover the forgeries, more than a year and a half elapsed before appellants discovered and reported any of them."

WHY IS THIS CASE IMPORTANT? *This case illustrates that the UCC's time period of thirty days to report forgeries is not flexible. Businesspersons need to be aware that the consequences can be harsh if they fail to examine bank statements promptly and notify the bank of any forged items.*

KEEP IN MIND If a bank is forced to recredit a customer's account, the bank may recover from the forger or from the party that cashed the check (usually a different customer or a collecting bank).

When the Bank Is Also Negligent.   In one situation, a bank customer can escape liability, at least in part, for failing to notify the bank of forged or altered checks promptly or within the required thirty-day period. If the customer can prove that the bank was also negligent—that is, that the bank failed to exercise ordinary care—then the bank will also be liable, and the loss will be allocated between the bank and the customer on the basis of comparative negligence [UCC 4–406(e)]. In other words, even though a customer may have been negligent, the bank may still have to recredit the customer's account for a portion of the loss if the bank failed to exercise ordinary care.

The UCC defines *ordinary care* to mean the "observance of reasonable commercial standards, prevailing in the area in which [a] person is located, with respect to the business in which that person is engaged" [UCC 3–103]. As mentioned earlier, it is customary in the banking industry to manually examine signatures only on checks over a certain amount (such as $1,000, $2,500, or some higher amount). Thus, if a bank, in accordance with prevailing banking standards, fails to examine a signature on a particular check, the bank has not necessarily breached its duty to exercise ordinary care.

Regardless of the degree of care exercised by the customer or the bank, the UCC places an absolute time limit on the liability of a bank for paying a check with a forged customer signature. A customer who fails to report a forged signature within one year from the date that the statement was made available for inspection loses the legal right to have the bank recredit his or her account [UCC 4–406(f)]. The court in the following case was asked to apply this rule.

CASE 15.2 ⊞ Halifax Corp. v. First Union National Bank

Supreme Court of Virginia, 2001.
262 Va. 91,
546 S.E.2d 696.

FACTS Between August 1995 and March 1999, Mary Adams served as Halifax Corporation's comptroller. Between August 1995 and January 1997, she wrote at least eighty-eight checks on Halifax's account at First Union National Bank. Adams used facsimile signatures on the checks, made them payable to herself or cash, and deposited them in her personal account at Wachovia Bank. First Union paid the checks and debited Halifax's account. Most of the checks were drawn in amounts exceeding $10,000, and about twenty were drawn in amounts of between $50,000 and $100,000 each. First Union knew Adams was an employee of Halifax. In January 1999, Halifax discovered accounting irregularities and, during an investigation, learned that Adams had embezzled more than $15 million from its checking account. Halifax filed a suit in a Virginia state court against First Union and others, seeking recovery on the ground of negligence under, in part, UCC 4–406. First Union filed a motion for summary judgment. The court granted the motion. Halifax appealed to the Virginia state supreme court.

ISSUE Were Halifax's claims against First Union barred by the one-year limit of UCC 4–406(f)?

DECISION Yes. The state supreme court affirmed the lower court's judgment.

REASON The state supreme court explained that UCC 4–406(f) "bars a customer, who received a statement or item from a bank but failed to discover or report the customer's unauthorized signature or alteration on the item to the bank within one year after the statement or item is made available to the customer, from asserting a claim against the bank for the unauthorized signature or alteration." UCC 4–406(f) "is devoid of any language which limits the customer's duty to discover and report unauthorized signatures and alterations to items paid in good faith by the bank." The court noted that the UCC includes the phrase "good faith" in other subsections of UCC 4–406. The court concluded that "the exclusion of the good faith requirement in [UCC 4–406(f)] was intentional, and the General Assembly [the Virginia state legislature] did not intend to impose that requirement upon a bank."

FOR CRITICAL ANALYSIS—Ethical Consideration
Why should a customer have to report a forged or unauthorized signature on a paid check within a certain time to recover the amount of the payment?

CHECKS BEARING FORGED INDORSEMENTS

A bank that pays a customer's check bearing a forged indorsement must recredit the customer's account or be liable to the customer-drawer for breach of contract. ■ **EXAMPLE 15.4** Suppose that Simon issues a $500 check "to the order of Antonio." Juan steals the check, forges Antonio's indorsement, and cashes the check. When the check reaches Simon's bank, the bank pays it and debits Simon's account. The bank must recredit the $500 to Simon's account because it failed to carry out Simon's order to pay "to the order of Antonio" [UCC 4–401(a)]. Of course, Simon's bank can in turn recover—for breach of warranty (see Chapter 14)—from the bank that cashed the check when Juan presented it [UCC 4–207(a)(2)]. ■

Eventually, the loss usually falls on the first party to take the instrument bearing the forged indorsement because, as discussed in Chapter 14, a forged indorsement does not transfer title. Thus, whoever takes an instrument with a forged indorsement cannot become a holder.

COMPARE Three years is also the limit for bringing actions for breach of warranty and to enforce other obligations, duties, and rights under Article 3.

The customer, in any event, has a duty to report forged indorsements promptly. Failure to report forged indorsements within a three-year period after the forged items have been made available to the customer relieves the bank of liability [UCC 4–111].

ALTERED CHECKS

The customer's instruction to the bank is to pay the exact amount on the face of the check to the holder. The bank has a duty to examine each check before making final payment. If it fails to detect an alteration, it is liable to its customer for the loss because it did not pay as the customer ordered. The loss is the difference between the original amount of the check and the amount actually paid [UCC 4–401(d)(1)]. ■ **EXAMPLE 15.5** Suppose that a check written for $11 is raised to $111. The customer's account will be charged $11 (the amount the customer ordered the bank to pay). The bank will normally be responsible for the $100. ■

A bank teller verifies a customer's signature. If a forged indorsement were part of this transaction, why should the bank suffer the loss? (Bob Daemmrich, Stock Boston)

Customer Negligence As in a situation involving a forged drawer's signature, a customer's negligence can shift the loss when payment is made on an altered check (unless the bank was also negligent). A common example occurs when a person carelessly writes a check and leaves large gaps around the numbers and words where additional numbers and words can be inserted (see Exhibit 15–4).

Similarly, a person who signs a check and leaves the dollar amount for someone else to fill in is barred from protesting when the bank unknowingly and in good faith pays whatever amount is shown [UCC 4–401(d)(2)]. Finally, if the bank can trace its loss on successive altered checks to the customer's failure to discover the initial alteration, then the bank can reduce its liability for reimbursing the customer's account [UCC 4–406]. The law governing the customer's duty to examine monthly statements and canceled checks, and to discover and report alterations to the bank, is the same as that applied to a forged drawer's signature.

In every situation involving a forged drawer's signature or an alteration, a bank must observe reasonable commercial standards of care in paying on a customer's checks [UCC 4–406(e)]. The customer's negligence can be used as a defense only if the bank has exercised ordinary care.

Other Parties from Whom the Bank May Recover The bank is entitled to recover the amount of loss from the transferor who, by presenting the check for payment, warrants that the check has not been materially altered. This rule has two exceptions, though. If the bank is the drawer (as it is on a cashier's check and a teller's check), it cannot recover from the presenting party if the party is an HDC acting in good faith [UCC 3–417(a)(2), 4–208(a)(2)]. The reason is that an instrument's drawer is in a better position than an HDC to know whether the instrument has been altered.

Similarly, an HDC, acting in good faith in presenting a certified check for payment, will not be held liable under warranty principles if the check was altered before the HDC acquired it [UCC 3–417(a)(2), 4–207(a)(2)]. ■ **EXAMPLE 15.6** Jordan draws a check for $500 payable to Deffen. Deffen alters the amount to

EXHIBIT 15–4 **A POORLY FILLED-OUT CHECK**

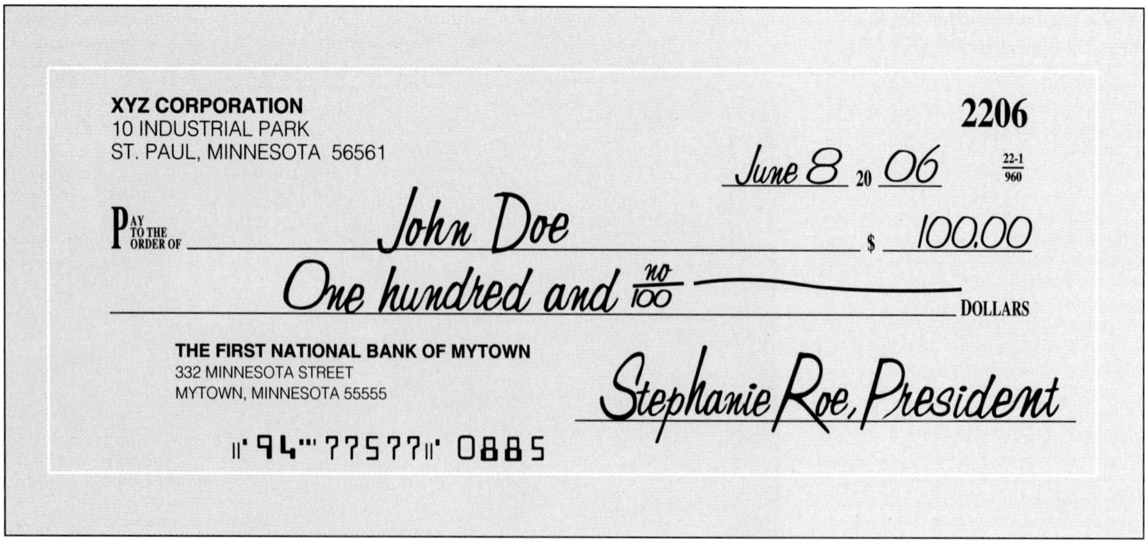

$5,000. The First National Bank of Whiteacre, the drawee bank, certifies the check for $5,000. Deffen negotiates the check to Evans, an HDC. The drawee bank pays Evans $5,000. On discovering the mistake, the bank cannot recover from Evans the $4,500 paid by mistake, even though the bank was not in a superior position to detect the alteration. This is in accord with the purpose of certification, which is to obtain the definite obligation of a bank to honor a definite instrument. ■

■ Bank's Duty to Accept Deposits

A bank has a duty to its customer to accept the customer's deposits of cash and checks. When checks are deposited, the bank must make the funds represented by those checks available within certain time frames. A bank also has a duty to collect payment on any checks payable or indorsed to its customers and deposited by them into their accounts. Cash deposits made in U.S. currency are received into customers' accounts without being subject to further collection procedures.

AVAILABILITY SCHEDULE FOR DEPOSITED CHECKS

The Expedited Funds Availability Act of 1987[6] and Regulation CC,[7] which was issued by the Federal Reserve Board of Governors (the Federal Reserve System will be discussed shortly) to implement the act, require that any local check deposited must be available for withdrawal by check or as cash within one business day from the date of deposit. A check is classified as a local check if the first bank to receive the check for payment and the bank on which the check is drawn are located in the same check-processing region (check-processing regions are designated by the Federal Reserve Board of Governors). For nonlocal checks, the funds must be available for withdrawal within not more than five business days.

Additional Requirements   In addition to the above requirements, the Expedited Funds Availability Act requires the following:

1 That funds be available on the next business day for cash deposits and wire transfers, government checks, the first $100 of a day's check deposits, cashier's checks, certified checks, and checks for which the depositary and payor banks are branches of the same institution.

2 That the first $100 of any deposit be available for cash withdrawal on the opening of the next business day after deposit. If a local check is deposited, the next $400 is to be available for withdrawal by no later than 5:00 P.M. the next business day. If, for example, you deposit a local check for $500 on Monday, you can withdraw $100 in cash at the opening of the business day on Tuesday, and an additional $400 must be available for withdrawal by no later than 5:00 P.M. on Wednesday.

Exceptions   A different availability schedule applies to deposits made at *nonproprietary* automated teller machines (ATMs). These are ATMs that are not owned or operated by the bank receiving the deposits. Basically, a five-day hold is permitted on all deposits, including cash deposits, made at nonproprietary ATMs.

A woman stands at the Vcom kiosk in a 7-Eleven. These machines can provide a number of services, including ATM transactions, check cashing, money orders, wire transfers, and even bill paying in some locations. How many days after a deposit do funds normally become available for withdrawal from this type of machine? (AP Photo/Jon Freilich)

---

6. 12 U.S.C. Sections 4001–4010.

7. 12 C.F.R. Sections 229.1–229.42.

Other exceptions also exist. A depository institution has eight days to make funds available in new accounts (those open less than thirty days). It has an extra four days on deposits over $5,000 (except deposits of government and cashier's checks), on accounts with repeated overdrafts, and on checks of questionable collectibility (if the institution tells the depositor it suspects fraud or insolvency).

THE COLLECTION PROCESS

Usually, deposited checks involve parties that do business at different banks, but sometimes checks are written between customers of the same bank. Either situation brings into play the bank collection process as it operates within the statutory framework of Article 4 of the UCC.[8]

Designations of Banks Involved in the Collection Process   The first bank to receive a check for payment is the **depository bank**.[9] For example, when a person deposits an IRS tax-refund check into a personal checking account at the local bank, that bank is the depository bank. The bank on which a check is drawn (the drawee bank) is called the **payor bank**. Any bank except the payor bank that handles a check during some phase of the collection process is a **collecting bank**. Any bank except the payor bank or the depository bank to which an item is transferred in the course of this collection process is called an **intermediary bank**.

During the collection process, any bank can take on one or more of the various roles of depositary, payor, collecting, and intermediary bank. ■ EXAMPLE 15.7 A buyer in New York writes a check on her New York bank and sends it to a seller in San Francisco. The seller deposits the check in her San Francisco bank account. The seller's bank is both a *depositary bank* and a *collecting bank*. The buyer's bank in New York is the *payor bank*. As the check travels from San Francisco to New York, any collecting bank handling the item in the collection process (other than the depositary bank and the payor bank) is also called an *intermediary bank*. Exhibit 15–5 illustrates how various banks function in the collection process in the context of this example. ■

Check Collection between Customers of the Same Bank   An item that is payable by the depositary bank (also the payor bank) that receives it is called an "on-us item." If the bank does not dishonor the check by the opening of the second banking day following its receipt, the check is considered paid [UCC 4–215(e)(2)]. ■ EXAMPLE 15.8 Williams and Merkowitz both have checking accounts at State Bank. On Monday morning, Merkowitz deposits into his own checking account a $300 check drawn by Williams. That same day, State Bank issues Merkowitz a "provisional credit" for $300. When the bank opens on Wednesday, Williams's check is considered honored, and Merkowitz's provisional credit becomes final. ■

Check Collection between Customers of Different Banks   Once a depositary bank receives a check, it must arrange to present it either directly or through intermedi-

You can find answers to "Frequently Asked Questions" about the banking industry at the American Bankers Association's Web site at

http://www.aba.com.

DEPOSITARY BANK
The first bank to receive a check for payment.

PAYOR BANK
The bank on which a check is drawn (the drawee bank).

COLLECTING BANK
Any bank handling an item for collection, except the payor bank.

INTERMEDIARY BANK
Any bank to which an item is transferred in the course of collection, except the depositary or payor bank.

---

8. The check-collection process discussed here will be modified in the future as the banking industry implements the Check Clearing in the 21st Century Act of 2003 (P.L. No. 108–100), also known as "Check21." This act, which went into effect in late 2004, makes an electronic copy of an original check a legal document, thus eliminating the need to physically transport and hand-process paper checks. Eventually, checks will be processed and cleared more quickly than described in this section.

9. All definitions in this section are found in UCC 4–105. The terms *depository* and *depository* have different meanings in the banking context. A depository bank refers to a *physical place* (a bank or other institution) in which deposits or funds are held or stored.

EXHIBIT 15–5 THE CHECK-COLLECTION PROCESS

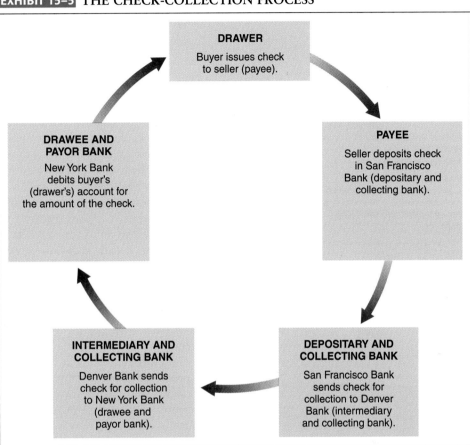

ary banks to the appropriate payor bank. Each bank in the collection chain must pass the check on before midnight of the next banking day following its receipt [UCC 4–202(b)].[10] A "banking day" is any part of a day that the bank is open to carry on substantially all of its banking functions. Thus, if a bank has only its drive-through facilities open, a check deposited on Saturday would not trigger a bank's midnight deadline until the following Monday. When the check reaches the payor bank, that bank is liable for the face amount of the check, unless the payor bank dishonors the check or returns it by midnight on the next banking day following receipt [UCC 4–302].[11]

Because of this deadline and because banks need to maintain an even work flow in the many items they handle daily, the UCC permits what is called *deferred posting*. According to UCC 4–108, "a bank may fix an afternoon hour of 2:00 P.M. or later as a cutoff hour for the handling of money and items and the making of entries

---

10. A bank may take a "reasonably longer time," such as when the bank's computer system is down due to a power failure, but the bank must show that its action is still timely [UCC 4–202(b)].

11. Most checks are cleared by a computerized process, and communication and computer facilities may fail because of weather, equipment malfunction, or other conditions. If such conditions arise and a bank fails to meet its midnight deadline, the bank is "excused" from liability if the bank has exercised "such diligence as the circumstances require" [UCC 4–109(d)].

on its books." Any checks received after that hour "may be treated as being received at the opening of the next banking day." Thus, if a bank's "cutoff hour" is 3:00 P.M., a check received by a payor bank at 4:00 P.M. on Monday would be deferred for posting until Tuesday. In this situation, the payor bank's deadline would be midnight Wednesday.

How the Federal Reserve System Clears Checks   The **Federal Reserve System** is our nation's central bank. It is a network of twelve district banks and related branches, which are located around the country and headed by the Federal Reserve Board of Governors. Most banks in the United States have Federal Reserve accounts. The Federal Reserve System has greatly simplified the check-collection process by acting as a **clearinghouse**—a system or a place where banks exchange checks and drafts drawn on each other and settle daily balances.

■ **EXAMPLE 15.9** Suppose that Pamela Moy of Philadelphia writes a check to Jeanne Sutton in San Francisco. When Sutton receives the check in the mail, she deposits it in her bank. Her bank then deposits the check in the Federal Reserve Bank of San Francisco, which transfers it to the Federal Reserve Bank of Philadelphia. That Federal Reserve bank then sends the check to Moy's bank, which deducts the amount of the check from Moy's account. Exhibit 15–6 illustrates this process. ■

Electronic Check Presentment   In the past, most checks were processed manually—the employees of each bank in the collection chain would physically handle each check that passed through the bank for collection or payment. Today, however, most checks are processed electronically. In contrast to manual check processing, which can take days, *electronic check presentment* can be done on the day of deposit. With electronic check presentment, items may be encoded with information (such as the amount of the check) that is read and processed by other banks' computers. In some situations, a check may be retained at its place of deposit, and only its image or description is presented for payment under an electronic presentment agreement [UCC 4–110].[12]

A person who encodes information on an item warrants to any subsequent bank or payor that the encoded information is correct [UCC 4–209]. This is also true for a person who retains an item while transmitting its image or information describing it as presentation for payment. This person warrants that the retention and presentment of the item comply with the electronic presentment agreement.

Regulation CC provides that a returned check must be encoded with the routing number of the depositary bank, the amount of the check, and other information and adds that this "does not affect a paying bank's responsibility to return a check within the deadlines required by the U.C.C." Under UCC 4–301(d)(2), an item is returned "when it is sent or delivered to the bank's customer or transferor or pursuant to his [or her] instructions." The question in the following case was whether an item that was not correctly encoded could be considered properly returned by its midnight deadline.

FEDERAL RESERVE SYSTEM
A network of twelve district banks and related branches located around the country and headed by the Federal Reserve Board of Governors. Most banks in the United States have Federal Reserve accounts.

CLEARINGHOUSE
A system or place where banks exchange checks and drafts drawn on each other and settle daily balances.

You can obtain extensive information about the Federal Reserve System by accessing "the Fed's" home page at **http://www. federalreserve.gov**.

---

12. This section of the UCC assumes that no bank will participate in an electronic presentment program without an agreement. See Comment 2 to UCC 4–110. For example, two banks that frequently do business with each other might enter an agreement allowing the depositary bank to retain the physical check and send an electronic image to the other bank for presentment.

EXHIBIT 15–6 HOW A CHECK IS CLEARED

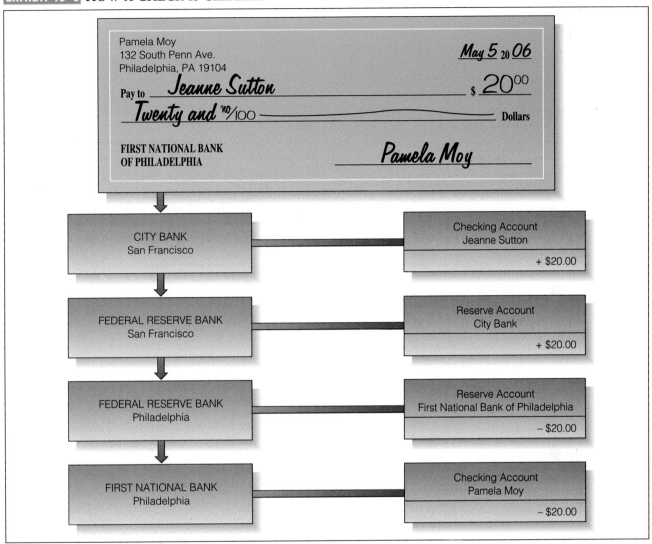

CASE 15.3 ■ **NBT Bank, N.A. v. First National Community Bank**

United States District Court,
Middle District of Pennsylvania, 2003.
287 F.Supp.2d 564.

FACTS Human Services Consultants, Inc. (HSC), had a checking account at First National Community Bank (FNCB) in Pennsylvania. A related firm, Human Services Consultants Management, Inc., had two checking accounts at NBT Bank, N.A., in New York, one of which was under the name PA Health. On March 8, 2001, PA Health pre-sented a check in the amount of $706,000 for deposit in its NBT account. The check was drawn on HSC's account at FNCB. NBT credited $706,000 to PA Health's account as a provisional credit and transmitted the check to the Federal Reserve Bank of Philadelphia for presentment to FNCB, which received the check on March 12. The next morning, FNCB dishonored the check because HSC's account con-tained insufficient funds, encoded the check for return to NBT, and sent it back to the Federal Reserve bank before

(Continued)

CASE 15.3—Continued

11:59 P.M. Later, on the morning of March 14, FNCB phoned NBT and also sent a letter by fax, informing it of the item's dishonor. The check's encoding was in error, however, and it was wrongly routed to another bank; as a result, NBT did not receive the physical check until March 16. Ultimately, the check was revealed to be part of a fraudulent scheme that caused NBT more than $1 million in losses. NBT filed a suit in a federal district court against FNCB, asserting that FNCB's encoding error rendered FNCB's "return" of the check ineffective. FNCB filed a motion for summary judgment.

ISSUE If a check is not correctly encoded but is physically transferred back to the Federal Reserve bank before the midnight deadline, can the item be considered properly returned?

DECISION Yes. The court issued a summary judgment in favor of FNCB, holding that the UCC's midnight deadline focuses on the physical return of a check, not encoding errors.

REASON The court reasoned that "the midnight deadline rule focuses on timing and a physical transfer; the requirements for delivering or sending an item are separate from encoding requirements. Accordingly, the return of a check under the midnight deadline rule does not encompass encoding requirements, which are not even specified in the U.C.C. The encoding requirement at issue in this case, regarding the routing number of a depositary bank, is found in Regulation CC." The encoding provisions "have nothing to do with the manner of sending or delivering a check * * *. 'Sending' or 'delivering,' on the other hand, is an applicable U.C.C. requirement, regardless of whether a check has been encoded." Besides, Regulation CC "explicitly states that the encoding requirements for routing numbers do not affect deadlines under the U.C.C. for a payor bank's return of a check."

FOR CRITICAL ANALYSIS—Social Consideration
How might the result in this case have been different if NBT had committed the encoding error and FNCB had suffered the loss?

▪ Electronic Fund Transfers

ELECTRONIC FUND TRANSFER (EFT)
A transfer of funds through the use of an electronic terminal, a telephone, a computer, or magnetic tape.

The application of computer technology to banking, in the form of electronic fund transfer systems, has helped to relieve banking institutions of the burden of having to move mountains of paperwork to process fund transfers. An **electronic fund transfer (EFT)** is a transfer of funds through the use of an electronic terminal, a telephone, a computer, or magnetic tape. The law governing EFTs depends on the type of transfer involved. Consumer fund transfers are governed by the Electronic Fund Transfer Act (EFTA) of 1978.[13] Commercial fund transfers are governed by Article 4A of the UCC.

The benefits of electronic banking are obvious. Automatic payments, direct deposits, and other fund transfers are now made electronically; no physical transfers of cash, checks, or other negotiable instruments are involved.

Not surprisingly, though, electronic banking also poses difficulties on occasion. It is difficult to issue stop-payment orders with electronic banking. Also, fewer records are available to prove or disprove that a transaction took place. The possibilities for tampering with a person's private banking information have increased. Finally, customers can no longer rely on having time between the writing of a check and its deduction from an account (float time).

TYPES OF EFT SYSTEMS

Most banks today offer EFT services to their customers. The four most common types of EFT systems used by bank customers are listed below.

1. *Automated teller machines* (ATMs)—Machines connected online to the bank's computers. Customers insert a plastic card issued by the bank and key in a per-

---

13. 15 U.S.C. Sections 1693–1693r. The EFTA amended Title IX of the Consumer Credit Protection Act.

sonal identification number (PIN) to access their accounts and conduct banking transactions.

2 *Point-of-sale systems*—Online terminals that allow consumers to transfer funds to merchants to pay for purchases using a debit card.

3 *Direct deposits and withdrawals*—Customers can authorize the bank to allow another party—such as the government or an employer—to make direct deposits into their accounts. Similarly, customers can request the bank to make automatic payments to a third party at regular, recurrent intervals from the customer's funds (insurance premiums or loan payments, for example).

4 *Pay-by-Internet systems*—Some financial institutions permit their customers to access the institution's computer system via the Internet and direct a transfer of funds between accounts or pay a particular bill, such as a utility bill, for example.

CONSUMER FUND TRANSFERS

REGULATION E
A set of rules issued by the Federal Reserve System's Board of Governors to protect users of elecronic fund transfer systems.

The Electronic Fund Transfer Act (EFTA) provides a basic framework for the rights, liabilities, and responsibilities of users of EFT systems. Additionally, the act gave the Federal Reserve Board authority to issue rules and regulations to help implement the act's provisions. The Federal Reserve Board's implemental regulation is called **Regulation E.**

The EFTA governs financial institutions that offer electronic fund transfers involving consumer accounts. The types of accounts covered include checking accounts, savings accounts, and any other asset accounts established for personal, family, or household purposes. Note that telephone transfers are covered by the EFTA only if they are made in accordance with a prearranged plan under which periodic or recurring transfers are contemplated.[14] What rights did the EFTA establish for consumers engaged in EFT transactions? This chapter's *Landmark in the Law* feature on the following pages describes the important benefits conferred by the Electronic Fund Transfer Act. In the subsections that follow, we look more closely at the act's provisions concerning two important issues: unauthorized transfers and error resolution.

Unauthorized Electronic Fund Transfers   Unauthorized electronic fund transfers are one of the hazards of electronic banking. A paper check leaves visible evidence of a transaction, and a customer can easily detect a forgery or an alteration on a check with ordinary vigilance. Evidence of an electronic transfer, however, is often only an entry in a computer printout of the various debits and credits made to a particular account during a specified time period.

BE CAREFUL The EFTA does not provide for the reversal of an electronic transfer of funds once it has occurred.

Because of the vulnerability of EFT systems to fraudulent activities, the EFTA of 1978 clearly defined what constitutes an unauthorized transfer. Under the act, a transfer is unauthorized if (1) it is initiated by a person other than the consumer who has no actual authority to initiate the transfer; (2) the consumer receives no benefit from it; and (3) the consumer did not furnish the person "with the card, code, or other means of access" to her or his account. Unauthorized access to an EFT system constitutes a federal felony, and those convicted may be sentenced to a fine of up to $10,000 and up to ten years' imprisonment.

Violations and Damages   Banks must strictly comply with the terms of the EFTA, as described in the *Landmark in the Law* feature, or they will be held liable. For a

---

14. *Kashanchi v. Texas Commerce Medical Bank, N.A.*, 703 F.2d 936 (5th Cir. 1983).

LANDMARK IN THE LAW

The Electronic Fund Transfer Act (1978)

Congress observed in 1978 that the use of electronic systems to transfer funds promised to provide substantial benefits for consumers. At the same time, Congress acknowledged that existing laws provided inadequate protection for consumers with respect to electronic fund transfers. Thus, Congress passed the Electronic Fund Transfer Act (EFTA).

THE PURPOSE OF THE EFTA Congress observed that the purpose of the EFTA was "to provide a basic framework establishing the rights, liabilities, and responsibilities of participants in electronic fund transfers." The EFTA is designed to protect consumers. It is not concerned with commercial electronic fund transfers—transfers between businesses or between businesses and financial institutions. (Commercial fund transfers are governed by Article 4A of the UCC.)

CONSUMER'S RIGHTS AND RESPONSIBILITIES UNDER THE EFTA The EFTA is essentially a disclosure law benefiting consumers. The act requires financial institutions to inform consumers of their rights and responsibilities, including those listed here, with respect to EFT systems.

1. If a customer's debit card is lost or stolen and used without his or her permission, the customer may be required to pay no more than $50. The customer, however, must notify the bank of the loss or theft within two days of learning about it. Otherwise, the liability increases to $500. The customer may be liable for more than $500 if he or she does not report the unauthorized use within sixty days after it appears on the customer's statement. (If a customer voluntarily gives her or his debit card to another, who then uses it improperly, the protections just mentioned do not apply.)

2. The customer must discover any error on the monthly statement within sixty days and must notify the bank. The bank then has ten days to investigate and

bank's violation of the EFTA, a consumer may recover both actual damages (including attorneys' fees and costs) and punitive damages of not less than $100 and not more than $1,000. (Unlike actual damages, punitive damages are assessed to punish a defendant or to set an example for similar wrongdoers.) Failure to investigate an error in good faith makes the bank liable for treble damages (three times the amount of damages). Even when a customer has sustained no actual damage, the bank may be liable for legal costs and punitive damages if it fails to follow the proper procedures outlined by the EFTA in regard to error resolution.

COMMERCIAL TRANSFERS

Funds are also transferred electronically "by wire" between commercial parties. In fact, the dollar volume of payments by wire transfer is more than $1 trillion a day—an amount that far exceeds the dollar volume of payments made by other means. The

---

LANDMARK IN THE LAW—Continued

must report its conclusions to the customer in writing. If the bank takes longer than ten days, it must return the disputed amount of money to the customer's account until it finds the error. If there is no error, the customer has to give the money back to the bank.

3 The bank must furnish receipts for transactions made through computer terminals, but it is not obligated to do so for telephone transfers.

4 The bank must provide a monthly statement for every month in which there is an electronic transfer of funds. Otherwise, the bank must provide statements every quarter. The statement must show the amount and date of the transfer, the names of the retailers or other third parties involved, the location or identification of the terminal, and the fees. Additionally, the statement must give an address and a phone number for inquiries and error notices.

5 Any authorized prepayment for utility bills and insurance premiums can be stopped three days before the scheduled transfer.

APPLICATION TO TODAY'S WORLD

Many credit-card issuers have voluntarily reduced the customer's liability for unauthorized use of his or her credit-card number to $50, or even to zero, for time periods longer than the EFTA's two days. These extended limits may also apply to transactions completed online. To further assure consumers of the security of e-commerce, some issuers provide a new card number for each online transaction.

RELEVANT WEB SITES

To locate information on the Web concerning the Electronic Fund Transfer Act, go to this text's Web site at <u>http://blt.westbuslaw.com</u>, *select "Chapter 15," and click on "URLs for Landmarks."*

NOTE If any part of an electronic fund transfer is covered by the EFTA, the entire transfer is excluded from UCC Article 4A.

two major wire payment systems are the Federal Reserve's wire transfer network (Fedwire) and the New York Clearing House Interbank Payments Systems (CHIPS).

Commercial wire transfers are governed by Article 4A of the UCC, which has been adopted by most states. The following example illustrates the type of fund transfer covered by Article 4A. ■ **EXAMPLE 15.10** Jellux, Inc., owes $5 million to Perot Corporation. Instead of sending Perot a check or some other instrument that would enable Perot to obtain payment, Jellux tells its bank, East Bank, to credit $5 million to Perot's account in West Bank. East Bank debits Jellux's East Bank account and wires $5 million to Perot's West Bank account. In more complex transactions, additional banks would be involved. ■

In these and similar circumstances, ordinarily a financial institution's instruction is transmitted electronically. Any means may be used, however, including first-class mail. To reflect this fact, Article 4A uses the term *funds transfer* rather than wire transfer to describe the overall payment transaction.

DIGITAL CASH
Funds contained on computer software, in the form of secure programs stored on microchips and other computer devices.

E-MONEY
Prepaid funds recorded on a computer or a card (such as a smart card or a stored-value card).

STORED-VALUE CARD
A card bearing magnetic strips that hold magnetically encoded data, providing access to stored funds.

SMART CARD
A card containing a microprocessor that permits storage of funds via security programming, can communicate with other computers, and does not require online authorization for fund transfers.

 You can find a series of articles on smart cards at the following Web site:

http://users.aol.com/ pjsmart/index.htm.

 Find out about the latest online banking options by going to

http://www. onlinebankingreport.com

and clicking on "Finding an Online Bank."

E-Money and Online Banking

New forms of electronic payments (e-payments) have the potential to replace *physical* cash—coins and paper currency—with *virtual* cash in the form of electronic impulses. This is the unique promise of **digital cash,** which consists of funds stored on microchips and other computer devices. Online banking has also become a reality in today's world. In a few minutes, anybody with the proper software can access his or her account, transfer funds, write "checks," pay bills, monitor investments, and often even buy and sell stocks.

Various forms of electronic money, or **e-money,** are emerging. The simplest kind of e-money system uses **stored-value cards.** These are plastic cards embossed with magnetic strips containing magnetically encoded data. A person can use a stored-value card to purchase specific goods and services offered by the card issuer. For example, university libraries typically have copy machines that students operate by inserting a stored-value card. Each time a student makes copies, the machine deducts the per-copy fee from the card.

Another form of e-money is the smart card. **Smart cards** are plastic cards containing computer microchips that can hold more information than a magnetic strip. A smart card carries and processes security programming. This capability gives smart cards a technical advantage over stored-value cards. The microprocessors on smart cards can also authenticate the validity of transactions. Retailers can program electronic cash registers to confirm the authenticity of a smart card by examining a unique digital signature stored on its microchip. (Digital signatures were discussed in Chapter 10.)

ONLINE BANKING SERVICES

Most online bank customers use three kinds of services. One of the most popular is bill consolidation and payment. Another is transferring funds among accounts. These online services are now offered via the Internet as well as by phone. The third is applying for loans, which many banks permit customers to do over the Internet. Customers typically have to appear in person to finalize the terms of a loan.

Two important banking activities generally are not yet available online: depositing and withdrawing funds. With smart cards, people could transfer funds on the Internet, thereby effectively transforming their personal computers into ATMs. Many observers believe that online banking is the way to introduce people to e-money and smart cards.

Since the late 1990s, several banks have operated exclusively on the Internet. These "virtual banks" have no physical branch offices. Because few people are equipped to send funds to virtual banks via smart-card technology, the virtual banks have accepted deposits through physical delivery systems, such as the U.S. Postal Service or FedEx.

REGULATORY COMPLIANCE

Banks have an interest in seeing the widespread use of online banking because of its significant potential for reducing costs and thus increasing profits. As in other areas of cyberspace, however, determining how laws apply to online banking activities can be difficult.

The Home Mortgage Disclosure Act[15] and the Community Reinvestment Act (CRA) of 1977,[16] for example, require a bank to define its market area and also to

---

15. 12 U.S.C. Sections 2801–2810.
16. 12 U.S.C. Sections 2901–2908.

provide information to regulators about its deposits and loans. Under the CRA, banks establish market areas in communities contiguous to their branch offices. The banks map these areas, using boundaries defined by counties or standard metropolitan areas, and annually review the maps. The purpose of these requirements is to prevent discrimination in lending practices.

But how does a successful "cyberbank" delineate its community? If, for instance, Bank of Internet becomes a tremendous success, does it really have a physical community? Will regulators simply allow a written description of a cybercommunity for Internet customers? Such regulatory issues are new, challenging, and certain to become more complicated as Internet banking widens its scope internationally.

PRIVACY PROTECTION

Currently, it is not clear which, if any, laws apply to the security of e-money payment information and e-money issuers' financial records. This is partly because it is not clear whether e-money issuers fit within the traditional definition of a financial institution.

E-Money Payment Information The Federal Reserve has decided not to impose Regulation E, which governs certain electronic fund transfers, on e-money transactions. Federal laws prohibiting unauthorized access to electronic communications might apply, however. For example, the Electronic Communications Privacy Act of 1986[17] prohibits any person from knowingly divulging to any other person the contents of an electronic communication while that communication is in transmission or in electronic storage.

A consumer uses a smart card to pay for lunch at a restaurant. Can the financial institution that issued the card disclose the consumer's personal information to a third party without the consumer's consent? Why or why not? (AP Photo/Eric Risberg)

E-Money Issuers' Financial Records Under the Right to Financial Privacy Act of 1978,[18] before a financial institution may give financial information about you to a federal agency, you must explicitly consent. If you do not, a federal agency wishing to obtain your financial records must obtain a warrant. A digital cash issuer may be subject to this act if that issuer is deemed to be (1) a bank by virtue of its holding customer funds or (2) any entity that issues a physical card similar to a credit or debit card.

Consumer Financial Data In 1999, Congress passed the Financial Services Modernization Act,[19] also known as the Gramm-Leach-Bliley Act, in an attempt to delineate how financial institutions can treat customer data. In general, the act and its rules[20] place restrictions and obligations on financial institutions to protect consumer data and privacy. Every financial institution must provide its customers with information on its privacy policies and practices. No financial institution can disclose nonpublic personal information about a consumer to an unaffiliated third party unless the act's disclosure and opt-out requirements are met.

17. 18 U.S.C. Sections 2510–2521.
18. 12 U.S.C. Sections 3401 *et seq.*
19. 12 U.S.C. Sections 24a, 248b, 1820a, 1828b, 1831v–1831y, 1848a, 2908, 4809; 15 U.S.C. Sections 80b-10a, 6701, 6711–6717, 6731–6735, 6751–6766, 6781, 6801–6809, 6821–6827, 6901–6910; and others.
20. 12 C.F.R. Part 40.

◼ The Uniform Money Services Act

Over the past few years, many states have enacted various regulations that apply to money services in a rather haphazard fashion. At the same time, e-money services that operate on the Internet—which, of course, cuts across jurisdictional lines—have been asking that these regulations be made more predictable.

In 2001, the National Conference of Commissioners on Uniform State Laws recommended to state legislatures a new law that would subject all money services businesses to the same regulations that apply to other, traditional financial service businesses. This law, which is known as the Uniform Money Services Act (UMSA), has been adopted in a few states.[21]

TRADITIONAL MONEY SERVICES

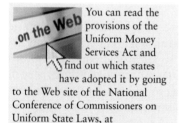

You can read the provisions of the Uniform Money Services Act and find out which states have adopted it by going to the Web site of the National Conference of Commissioners on Uniform State Laws, at

http://www.nccusl.org,

and selecting the "Money Services Act."

Money service businesses (MSBs) have not been subject to regulation to the same extent as other financial service businesses. Unlike banks, MSBs do not accept deposits. They do, however, issue money orders, traveler's checks, and stored-value cards; exchange foreign currency; and cash checks. Immigrants often use these businesses to send money to their relatives in other countries. Because MSBs often do not have continuing relationships with their customers, their customers have sometimes evaded federal law with respect to large currency transactions or used the services to launder money (see Chapter 6). This has been particularly true with respect to financing terrorist activities.

The UMSA applies to persons engaged in money transmission, check cashing, or currency exchange. The uniform act requires an MSB involved in these activities to obtain a license from a state, to be examined by state officials, to report on its activities to the state, and to comply with certain record-keeping requirements. Each of these subjects has its provisions and exceptions. Safety and soundness measures, such as annual examinations, surety bonds (to guarantee financial soundness), and permissible investments, are also mandated by the act.

INTERNET-BASED MONEY SERVICES

Under the UMSA, Internet-based money services, and other types of e-money services, would be treated the same as other money services.[22] The drafters of the UMSA ensured that it would cover these services by referring to *monetary value* instead of simply *money* [UMSA 1–102(c)(11)].

Internet-based monetary value systems subject to the new law may include:

1. *E-money and Internet payment mechanisms*—Money, or its substitute, that is stored as data on a chip or a personal computer so that it can be transferred over the Internet or an intranet.

2. *Internet scrip*—Monetary value that may be exchanged over the Internet but can also be redeemed for cash.

3. *Stored-value products*—Smart cards, prepaid cards, or value-added cards [UMSA 1–102(c)(21)].

---

21. To date, the UMSA has been adopted in Iowa, Vermont, and Washington State, and adoption legislation is currently pending in the U.S. Virgin Islands.
22. The UMSA does not apply to state governments, the federal government, securities dealers, banks, businesses that incidentally transport currency and instruments in the normal course of business, payday loan businesses, and others [UMSA 1–103].

APPLICATION ■■ How to Use Stop-Payment Orders*

For a variety of reasons, a drawer should not misuse stop-payment orders. We look at some of those reasons here.

MONETARY COSTS AND RISKS

One reason is monetary: banks usually charge between $15 and $25 for a stop-payment order, so stopping payment is not cost-effective for a check written for a small amount. Another reason is the risk attached to the issuing of a stop-payment order for any drawer-customer. The bank is entitled to take a reasonable amount of time to put your stop-payment order into effect before it has liability for improper payment. Hence, the payee or another holder may be able to cash the check despite your stop-payment order if he or she acts quickly. Indeed, you could be writing out a stop-payment order in the bank lobby while the payee or holder cashes the check in the drive-in facility outside. In addition, even if a bank pays over your proper stop-payment order, the bank will be liable to the drawer-customer only for the amount of loss the drawer suffers from the improper payment.

WHEN YOU CAN STOP PAYMENT

Remember that, to avoid liability, a drawer must have a legal reason for issuing a stop-payment order. You cannot stop payment on a check simply because you have had a change of heart about the wisdom of your purchase. Generally, you can safely stop payment if you clearly did not get what you paid for or were fraudulently induced to make a purchase. You can also stop payment if a "cooling-off" law governs the transaction—that is, if you legally have a few days in which to change your mind about a purchase. Any wrongful stop order subjects the *drawer* to liability to the payee or a holder, and this liability may include special damages that resulted from the order. When all is considered, it may be unwise to order a stop payment hastily on a check because of a minor dispute with the payee.

*This *Application* is not meant to substitute for the services of an attorney who is licensed to practice law in your state.

CHECKLIST FOR STOP-PAYMENT ORDERS

1. Compare the stop-payment fee with the disputed sum to make sure it is worthwhile to issue a stop-payment order.
2. Make sure that your bank will honor your stop-payment order before the payee cashes the check.
3. Make sure that you have a legal reason for issuing the stop-payment order.

■■ KEY TERMS

CHAPTER SUMMARY Checks, the Banking System, and E-Money

Checks (See pages 452–454.)	1. *Cashier's check*—A check drawn by a bank on itself (the bank is both the drawer and the drawee) and purchased by a customer. In effect, the bank lends its credit to the purchaser of the check, thus making the funds available for immediate use in banking circles.
	2. *Traveler's check*—An instrument on which a financial institution is both the drawer and the drawee. The purchaser must provide his or her signature as a countersignature for a traveler's check to become a negotiable instrument.
	3. *Certified check*—A check for which the drawee bank certifies in writing that it will set aside funds in the drawer's account to ensure payment of the check on presentation. On certification, the drawer and all prior indorsers are completely discharged from liability on the check.
The Bank-Customer Relationship (See pages 454–455.)	1. *Creditor-debtor relationship*—The bank and its customer have a creditor-debtor relationship (the bank is the debtor because it holds the customer's funds on deposit).
	2. *Agency relationship*—Because a bank must act in accordance with the customer's orders in regard to the customer's deposited money, an agency relationship also arises—the bank is the agent for the customer, who is the principal.
	3. *Contractual relationship*—The bank's relationship with its customer is also contractual; both the bank and the customer assume certain contractual duties when a customer opens a bank account.
Bank's Duty to Honor Checks (See pages 455–463.)	Generally, a bank has a duty to honor its customers' checks, provided that the customers have sufficient funds on deposit to cover the checks [UCC 4–401(a)]. The bank is liable to its customers for actual damages proved to be due to wrongful dishonor. The bank's duty to honor its customers' checks is not absolute.
Bank's Duty to Accept Deposits (See pages 463–468.)	A bank has a duty to accept deposits made by its customers into their accounts. Funds represented by checks deposited must be made available to customers according to a schedule mandated by the Expedited Funds Availability Act of 1987 and Regulation CC. A bank also has a duty to collect payment on any checks deposited by its customers. When checks deposited by customers are drawn on other banks, as they often are, the check-collection process comes into play (summarized next).
	1. *Definitions of banks*—UCC 4–105 provides the following definitions of banks involved in the collection process:
	a. Depositary bank—The first bank to accept a check for payment.
	b. Payor bank—The bank on which a check is drawn.
	c. Collecting bank—Any bank except the payor bank that handles a check during the collection process.
	d. Intermediary bank—Any bank except the payor bank or the depositary bank to which an item is transferred in the course of the collection process.
	2. *Check collection between customers of the same bank*—A check payable by the depositary bank that receives it is an "on-us item"; if the bank does not dishonor the check by the opening of the second banking day following its receipt, the check is considered paid [UCC 4–215(e)(2)].

CHAPTER SUMMARY ▦ Checks, the Banking System, and E-Money—Continued

Bank's Duty to Accept Deposits— Continued	3. *Check collection between customers of different banks*—Each bank in the collection process must pass the check on to the next appropriate bank before midnight of the next banking day following its receipt [UCC 4–108, 4–202(b), 4–302]. 4. *How the Federal Reserve System clears checks*—The Federal Reserve System facilitates the check-clearing process by serving as a clearinghouse for checks. 5. *Electronic check presentment*—When checks are presented electronically, items may be encoded with information (such as the amount of the check) that is read and processed by other banks' computers. In some situations, a check may be retained at its place of deposit, and only its image or information describing it is presented for payment under a Federal Reserve agreement, clearinghouse rule, or other agreement [UCC 4–110].

Electronic Fund Transfers (See pages 468–471.)	1. *Types of EFT systems*—
	  a. Automated teller machines (ATMs).
	  b. Point-of-sale systems.
	  c. Direct deposits and withdrawals.
	  d. Pay-by-telephone systems.
	
	2. *Consumer fund transfers*—Consumer fund transfers are governed by the Electronic Fund Transfer Act (EFTA) of 1978. The EFTA is basically a disclosure law that sets forth the rights and duties of the bank and the customer with respect to EFT systems. Banks must comply strictly with EFTA requirements.
	
	3. *Commercial transfers*—Disputes arising as a result of unauthorized or incorrectly made fund transfers between financial institutions are not covered under the EFTA. Article 4A of the UCC, which has been adopted by almost all of the states, governs fund transfers not subject to the EFTA or other federal or state statutes.

E-Money and Online Banking (See pages 472–473.)	1. *New forms of e-payments*—These include stored-value cards and smart cards.
	
	2. *Current online banking services*—
	  a. Bill consolidation and payment.
	  b. Transferring funds among accounts.
	  c. Applying for loans.
	
	3. *Regulatory compliance*—Banks must define their market areas, in communities contiguous to their branch offices, under the Home Mortgage Disclosure Act and the Community Reinvestment Act. It is not clear how an online bank would define its market area or its community.
	
	4. *Privacy protection*—It is not entirely clear which, if any, laws apply to e-money and online banking. The Financial Services Modernization Act (the Gramm-Leach-Bliley Act) outlines how financial institutions can treat consumer data and privacy in general. The Right to Financial Privacy Act may also apply.

The Uniform Money Services Act (See page 474.)	The National Conference of Commissioners on Uniform State Laws has recommended the Uniform Money Services Act to state legislatures. The purpose of the act is to subject online and e-money services to the same regulations that apply to traditional financial service businesses.

■ FOR REVIEW

Answers for the even-numbered questions in this For Review *section can be found in Appendix I at the end of this text.*

1 On what types of checks does a bank serve as both the drawer and the drawee? What type of check does a bank agree in advance to accept when the check is presented for payment?

2 When may a bank properly dishonor a customer's check without liability to the customer? What happens if a bank wrongfully dishonors a customer's check?

3 What duties does the Uniform Commercial Code impose on a bank's customers with regard to forged

and altered checks? What are the consequences of a customer's negligence in performing those duties?

4 What are the four most common types of electronic fund transfers? What is the basic purpose of the Electronic Fund Transfer Act, and how does it benefit consumers?

5 What is e-money? How is e-money stored and used? What laws apply to e-money transactions and online banking services?

■ QUESTIONS AND CASE PROBLEMS

15–1. Error Resolution. Sheridan has a checking account at Gulf Bank. She frequently uses her access card to obtain money from the automated teller machines. She always withdraws $50 when she makes a withdrawal, but she never withdraws more than $50 in any one day. When she received the April statement on her account, she noticed that on April 13 two withdrawals for $50 each had been made from the account. Believing this to be a mistake, she went to her bank on May 10 to inform the bank of the error. A bank officer told her that the bank would investigate and inform her of the result. On May 26, the bank officer called her and said that bank personnel were having trouble locating the error but would continue to try to find it. On June 20, the bank sent her a full written report advising her that no error had been made. Sheridan, unhappy with the bank's explanation, filed suit against the bank, alleging that it had violated the Electronic Fund Transfer Act. What was the outcome of the suit? Would it matter if the bank could show that on the day in question it had deducted $50 from Sheridan's account to cover a check that Sheridan had written to a local department store and that had cleared the bank on that day?

15–2. Online Banking. First Internet Bank operates exclusively on the Web with no physical branch offices. Although some of First Internet's business is transacted with smart-card technology, most of its business with its customers is conducted through the mail. First Internet offers free checking, no-fee money market accounts, mortgage refinancing, and other services. With what regulation covering banks might First Internet find it difficult to comply, and what is the difficulty?

15–3. Forged Checks. Roy Supply, Inc., and R. M. R. Drywall, Inc., had checking accounts at Wells Fargo Bank. Both accounts required all checks to carry two signatures—that of Edward Roy and that of Twila June Moore, both of whom were executive officers of both companies. Between January 1989 and March

1991, the bank honored hundreds of checks on which Roy's signature was forged by Moore. On January 31, 1992, Roy and the two corporations notified the bank of the forgeries and then filed a suit in a California state court against the bank, alleging negligence. Who is liable for the amounts of the forged checks? Why?

15–4. Stale Checks. On July 15, 1986, IBP, Inc., issued to Meyer Land & Cattle Co. a check for $135,234.18 payable to both Meyer and Sylvan State Bank for the purchase of cattle. IBP wrote the check on its account at Mercantile Bank of Topeka. Someone at the Meyer firm misplaced the check. In the fall of 1995, Meyer's president, Tim Meyer, found the check behind a desk drawer. Jana Huse, Meyer's office manager, presented the check for deposit at Sylvan, which accepted it. After Mercantile received the instrument and its computers noted the absence of any stop-payment order, it paid the check with funds from IBP's checking account. IBP insisted that Mercantile recredit IBP's account. Mercantile refused. IBP filed a suit in a federal district court against Mercantile and others, claiming, among other things, that Mercantile had not acted in good faith because it had processed the check by automated means without examining it manually. Mercantile responded that its check-processing procedures adhered to its own policies, as well as reasonable commercial standards of fair dealing in the banking industry. Mercantile filed a motion for summary judgment. Should the court grant the motion? Why or why not? [*IBP, Inc. v. Mercantile Bank of Topeka,* 6 F.Supp.2d 1258 (D.Kan. 1999)]

15–5. Debit Cards. On April 20, 1999, while visiting her daughter and son-in-law Michael Dowdell, Carol Farrow asked Dowdell to fix her car. She gave him her car keys, attached to which was a small wallet containing her debit card. Dowdell repaired her car and returned the keys. Two days later, Farrow noticed that her debit card was missing and contacted Auburn Bank, which had issued the card. Farrow reviewed her automated teller machine (ATM) transaction record and noticed that a large amount of cash had been withdrawn from her checking account on April 22 and April 23. When Farrow reviewed the photos taken by the ATM cameras at the time of the withdrawals, she recognized Dowdell as the person using her debit card. Dowdell was convicted in an Alabama state court of the crime of fraudulent use of a debit card. What procedures are involved in a debit-card transaction? What problems with debit-card transactions are apparent from the facts of this case? How might these problems be prevented? [*Dowdell v. State, 790 So.2d 359 (Ala.Crim.App. 2000)*]

CASE PROBLEM WITH SAMPLE ANSWER

15–6. Robert Santoro was the manager of City Check Cashing, Inc., a check-cashing service in New Jersey, and Peggyann Slansky was the clerk. On July 14, Misir Koci presented Santoro with a $290,000 check signed by Melvin Green and drawn on Manufacturers Hanover Trust Co. (a bank). The check was stamped with a Manufacturers certification stamp. The date on the check had clearly been changed from August 8 to July 7. Slansky called the bank to verify the check and was told that the serial number "did not sound like one belonging to the bank." Slansky faxed the check to the bank with a query about the date, but received no reply. Slansky also called Green, who stated that the date on the check was altered before it was certified. Check Cashing cashed and deposited the check within two hours. The drawee bank found the check to be invalid and timely returned it unpaid. Check Cashing filed a suit in a New Jersey state court against Manufacturers and others, asserting that the bank should have responded to the fax before the midnight deadline in UCC 4–302. Did the bank violate the midnight deadline rule? Explain. [*City Check Cashing, Inc. v. Manufacturers Hanover Trust Co., 166 N.J. 49, 764 A.2d 411 (2001)*]

After you have answered this problem, compare your answer with the sample answer given on the Web site that accompanies this text. Go to http://blt.westbuslaw.com, select "Chapter 15," and click on "Case Problem with Sample Answer."

15–7. Forged Indorsement. Visiting Nurses Association of Telfair County, Inc. (VNA), maintained a checking account at Security State Bank in Valdosta, Georgia. Wanda Williamson, a VNA clerk, was responsible for making VNA bank deposits, but she was not a signatory on the association's account. Over a four-year period, Williamson embezzled more than $250,000 from VNA by forging its indorsement on checks, cashing them at the bank, and keeping a portion of the proceeds. Williamson was arrested, convicted, sentenced to a prison term, and ordered to pay restitution. VNA filed a suit in a Georgia state court against the bank, alleging, among other things, negligence. The bank filed a motion for summary judgment on the ground that VNA was precluded by UCC 4–406(f) from recovering on checks with

forged indorsements. Should the court grant the motion? Explain. [*Security State Bank v. Visiting Nurses Association of Telfair County, Inc., 568 S.E.2d 491 (Ga.App. 2002)*]

15–8. Forged Signatures. Cynthia Stafford worked as an administrative professional at Gerber & Gerber, P.C. (professional corporation), a law firm, for more than two years. During that time, she stole ten checks payable to Gerber & Gerber (G&G), which she indorsed in blank by forging one of the attorney's signatures. She then indorsed the forged checks in her name and deposited them in her account at Regions Bank. Over the same period, G&G deposited in its accounts at Regions Bank thousands of checks amounting to $300 million to $400 million. Each G&G check was indorsed with a rubber stamp for deposit into the G&G account. The thefts were made possible in part because G&G kept unindorsed checks in an open file accessible to all employees and Stafford was sometimes the person assigned to stamp the checks. When the thefts were discovered, G&G filed a suit in a Georgia state court against Regions Bank to recover the stolen funds, alleging in part negligence. Regions Bank filed a motion for summary judgment. What principles apply to attribute liability between these parties? How should the court rule on the bank's motion? Explain. [*Gerber & Gerber, P.C. v. Regions Bank, 596 S.E.2d 174 (Ga.App. 2004)*]

A QUESTION OF ETHICS

15–9. Lorine Daniels worked as a bookkeeper for Wilder Binding Co., which had a checking account with Oak Park Trust and Savings Bank. Among Daniels's responsibilities was the reconciliation of the bank statements with the firm's checkbook each month. Daniels forged signatures on forty-two checks, each for an amount under $1,000, which she made payable to herself. Over a six-month period, she embezzled a total of $25,254.78 in this way. When the forgeries were discovered, Wilder demanded that the bank recredit Wilder's account with the $25,254.78. In the lawsuit that followed, a key issue was whether the bank's custom of manually verifying signatures only on checks drawn for more than $1,000 constituted a breach of its duty of ordinary care. The bank testified that such policies and procedures were customary and routine and, therefore, its adherence to these policies and procedures did not violate its duty of care. Given these facts, consider the following questions. [*Wilder Binding Co. v. Oak Park Trust and Savings Bank, 135 Ill.2d 121, 552 N.E.2d 783, 142 Ill.Dec. 1192 (1990)*]

1. This case was decided under Article 3 before it was revised in 1990. The court held that whether the bank had breached its duty of care was a question of fact for the jury. How would a court decide this issue under the revised Article 3?

2. Does the fact that a practice is "customary and routine" in a certain industry, such as the banking industry, mean that it is necessarily ethical?

FOR CRITICAL ANALYSIS

15–10. Under the 1990 revision of Article 4, a bank is not required to include the customer's canceled checks when it sends monthly statements to the customer. Banks may simply itemize the checks (by number, date, and amount) or, in addition to this itemization, also provide photocopies of the checks. What implications do the revised rules have for bank customers in terms of liability for unauthorized signatures and indorsements?

INTERNET EXERCISES

Go to the *Business Law Today: The Essentials* home page at <ins>http://blt.westbuslaw.com</ins>, select "Chapter 15," and click on "Internet Exercises." There you will find the following Internet research exercises that you can perform to learn more about topics covered in this chapter.

Activity 15–1: MANAGEMENT PERSPECTIVE—Check Fraud

Activity 15–2: LEGAL PERSPECTIVE—Smart Cards

BEFORE THE TEST

Go to the *Business Law Today: The Essentials* home page at <ins>http://blt.westbuslaw.com</ins>, select "Chapter 15," and click on "Interactive Quizzes." You will find at least twenty interactive questions relating to this chapter.

CHAPTER 16

Creditors' Rights and Bankruptcy

"Article 9 is clearly the most novel and probably the most important article of the Code . . . and covers the entire range of transactions in which the debts are secured by personal property."

Walter D. Malcolm, 1904–1979
(President of the National Conference of Commissioners on Uniform State Laws, 1963–1966)

CHAPTER OUTLINE

- ■ SECURED TRANSACTIONS
- ■ ADDITIONAL LAWS ASSISTING CREDITORS
- ■ ADDITIONAL LAWS ASSISTING DEBTORS
- ■ BANKRUPTCY AND REORGANIZATION

■■ LEARNING OBJECTIVES

After reading this chapter, you should be able to answer the following questions:

1 What is a security interest? What three requirements must be met to create an enforceable security interest?

2 What is a prejudgment attachment? What is a writ of execution? How does a creditor use these remedies?

3 What is garnishment? When might a creditor undertake a garnishment proceeding?

4 In a bankruptcy proceeding, what constitutes the debtor's estate in property? What property is exempt from the estate under federal bankruptcy law?

5 In a Chapter 11 reorganization, what is the role of the debtor in possession?

SECURED TRANSACTION
Any transaction in which the payment of a debt is guaranteed, or secured, by personal property owned by the debtor or in which the debtor has a legal interest.

Whenever the payment of a debt is guaranteed, or *secured,* by personal property owned by the debtor or in which the debtor has a legal interest, the transaction becomes known as a **secured transaction.** The concept of the secured transaction is as basic to modern business practice as the concept of credit. Logically, sellers and lenders do not want to risk nonpayment, so they usually will not sell goods or lend funds unless the payment is somehow guaranteed. Indeed, business as we know it could not exist without laws permitting and governing secured transactions.

Article 9 of the Uniform Commercial Code (UCC) governs secured transactions as applied to personal property, fixtures by contract, accounts, instruments, commercial assignments of $1,000 or more, *chattel paper* (any writing evidencing a debt secured by personal property), agricultural liens, and what are called general intangibles

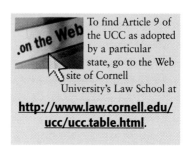
To find Article 9 of the UCC as adopted by a particular state, go to the Web site of Cornell University's Law School at **http://www.law.cornell.edu/ucc/ucc.table.html**.

(such as patents and copyrights). Article 9 does not cover other creditor devices, such as landlord's liens, mechanic's liens, real estate mortgages, and the like [UCC 9–109]. In 1999, the National Conference on Commissioners on Uniform State Laws promulgated a revised version of Article 9. Because the revised version, which was later amended, has now been adopted by all of the states, we base this chapter's discussion of secured transactions entirely on the provisions of the revised version.

In this chapter, after first examining the law governing secured transactions, we discuss other laws that assist creditors and debtors in resolving their disputes. In the last part of this chapter, we focus on bankruptcy as a last resort in resolving debtor-creditor disputes.

◨ Secured Transactions

The importance of being a secured creditor cannot be overemphasized. Secured creditors are generally not hampered by state laws favorable to debtors, and if their security interest meets certain requirements, they have a favored position should the debtor enter into bankruptcy.

THE TERMINOLOGY OF SECURED TRANSACTIONS

The UCC's terminology is now uniformly adopted in all documents used in situations involving secured transactions. A brief summary of the UCC's definitions of terms relating to secured transactions follows.

SECURED PARTY
A lender, seller, or any other person in whose favor there is a security interest, including a person to whom accounts or chattel paper has been sold.

DEBTOR
Under Article 9 of the UCC, a debtor is any party who owes payment or performance of a secured obligation, whether or not the party actually owns or has rights in the collateral.

SECURITY INTEREST
Any interest in personal property or fixtures that secures payment or performance of an obligation.

SECURITY AGREEMENT
An agreement that creates or provides for a security interest between the debtor and a secured party.

COLLATERAL
Under Article 9 of the UCC, the property subject to a security interest, including accounts and chattel paper that have been sold.

FINANCING STATEMENT
A document prepared by a secured creditor, and filed with the appropriate state or local official, to give notice to the public that the creditor has a security interest in collateral belonging to the debtor named in the statement.

DEFAULT
The failure to observe a promise or discharge an obligation. The term is commonly used to mean the failure to pay a debt when it is due.

1 A **secured party** is any creditor who has a *security interest* in the *debtor's collateral*. This creditor can be a seller, a lender, a cosigner, and even a buyer of accounts or chattel paper [UCC 9–102(a)(72)].

2 A **debtor** is the "person" who *owes payment* or other performance of a secured obligation [UCC 9–102(a)(28)].

3 A **security interest** is the *interest* in the collateral (personal property, fixtures, and so forth) that *secures payment or performance of an obligation* [UCC 1–201(37)].

4 A **security agreement** is an *agreement* that *creates* or provides for a *security interest* [UCC 9–102(a)(73)].

5 **Collateral** is the *subject* of the *security interest* [UCC 9–102(a)(12)].

6 A **financing statement**—referred to as the UCC-1 form—is the *instrument normally filed* to give *public notice* to *third parties* of the *secured party's security interest* [UCC 9–102(a)(39)].

These basic definitions form the concept under which a debtor-creditor relationship becomes a secured transaction relationship (see Exhibit 16–1).

A creditor has two main concerns if the debtor **defaults** (fails to pay the debt as promised): (1) satisfaction of the debt through the possession and (usually) sale of the collateral and (2) priority over any other creditors or buyers who may have rights in the same collateral. We look here at how these two concerns are met through the creation and perfection of a security interest.

CREATING A SECURITY INTEREST

To become a secured party, the creditor must obtain a security interest in the collateral of the debtor. Three requirements must be met for a creditor to have an enforceable security interest:

EXHIBIT 16-1 SECURED TRANSACTIONS—CONCEPT AND TERMINOLOGY

In a security agreement, a debtor and a creditor agree that the creditor will have a security interest in collateral in which the debtor has rights. In essence, the collateral secures the loan and ensures the creditor of payment should the debtor default.

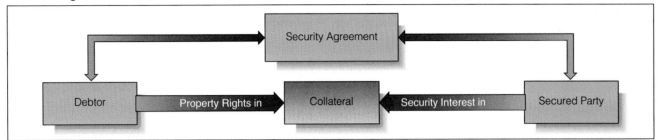

1 Either (a) the collateral must be in the possession of the secured party in accordance with an agreement, or (b) there must be a written or authenticated security agreement that describes the collateral subject to the security interest and is signed or authenticated by the debtor.

2 The secured party must give something of value to the debtor.

3 The debtor must have "rights" in the collateral.

Once these requirements have been met, the creditor's rights are said to attach to the collateral. **Attachment** gives the creditor an enforceable security interest in the collateral [UCC 9–203].[1]

ATTACHMENT
In a secured transaction, the process by which a secured creditor's interest "attaches" to the property of another (collateral) and the creditor's security interest becomes enforceable.

Written or Authenticated Security Agreement When the collateral is *not* in the possession of the secured party, the security agreement must be either written or authenticated, and it must describe the collateral. Note here that *authentication* includes any agreement or signature inscribed on a tangible medium or stored in an electronic or other medium (called a *record*) that is retrievable [UCC 9–102(a)(7)(69)]. If the security agreement is in writing or authenticated, only the debtor's signature or authentication is required to create the security interest. The reason electronic authentication is acceptable is to provide for electronic filing (the filing process will be discussed later).

A security agreement must contain a description of the collateral that reasonably identifies it. Generally, such words as "all the debtor's personal property" or "all the debtor's assets" would *not* constitute a sufficient description [UCC 9–108(c)].

Secured Party Must Give Value The secured party must give to the debtor something of value. Some examples would be a binding commitment to extend credit, as security for the satisfaction of a preexisting debt, or consideration to support a simple contract [UCC 1–201(44)]. Normally, the value given by a secured party is in the form of a direct loan or a commitment to sell goods on credit.

Debtor Must Have Rights in the Collateral The debtor must have rights in the collateral; that is, the debtor must have some ownership interest or right to obtain possession of that collateral. The debtor's rights can represent either a current or a

1. Note that in the context of judicial liens, which will be discussed later in this chapter, the term *attachment* has a different meaning. In that context, it refers to a court-ordered seizure and taking into custody of property prior to the securing of a court judgment for a past-due debt.

future legal interest in the collateral. For example, a retail seller-debtor can give a secured party a security interest not only in existing inventory owned by the retailer but also in *future* inventory to be acquired by the retailer.

PERFECTING A SECURITY INTEREST

Perfection is the legal process by which secured parties protect themselves against the claims of third parties who may wish to have their debts satisfied out of the same collateral. Usually, perfection is accomplished by filing a financing statement with the office of the appropriate government official. In some circumstances, however, a security interest becomes perfected without the filing of a financing statement.

Perfection by Filing   The most common means of perfection is by filing a *financing statement*—a document that gives public notice to third parties of the secured party's security interest—with the office of the appropriate government official. The security agreement itself can also be filed to perfect the security interest. The financing statement must provide the names of the debtor and the secured party and indicate the collateral covered by the financing statement. Once completed, filings are indexed in the name of the debtor so that they can be located by subsequent searchers.

In most states, a financing statement must be filed centrally in the appropriate state office, such as the office of the secretary of state, in the state where the debtor is located. Filing in the county where the collateral is located is required only when the collateral consists of timber to be cut, fixtures, or collateral to be extracted—such as oil, coal, gas, and minerals [UCC 9–301(3) and (4), 9–502(b)].

The Debtor's Name.   The UCC requires that a financing statement be filed under the name of the debtor [UCC 9–502(a)(1)]. Because most states use electronic filing systems, UCC 9–503 sets out some detailed rules for determining when the debtor's name as it appears on a financing statement is sufficient. For corporations, which are part of "registered organizations," the debtor's name on the financing statement must be "the name of the debtor indicated on the public record of the debtor's jurisdiction of organization" [UCC 9–503(a)(1)]. Slight variations in names normally will not be considered misleading if a search of the filing office's records, using a standard computer search engine routinely used by that office, would disclose the filings [UCC 9–506(c)]. Note that if the debtor is identified by the correct name at the time of the filing of a financing statement, the secured party's interest retains its priority even if the debtor later changes his or her name.

If the debtor is a trust or a trustee with respect to property held in trust, the filed financing statement must disclose this information and must provide the trust's name as specified in its official documents [UCC 9–503(a)(3)]. In other cases, the filed financing statement must disclose "the individual or organizational name of the debtor" [UCC 9–503(a)(4)(A)].

In general, providing only the debtor's trade name (or a fictitious name) in a financing statement is not sufficient for perfection [UCC 9–503(c)]. ■ **EXAMPLE 16.1** Assume that a loan is being made to a sole proprietorship owned by Peter Jones. The trade, or fictitious, name is Pete's Plumbing. A financing statement cannot use the trade name Pete's Plumbing; rather, it has to be filed under the name of the actual debtor—in this instance, Peter Jones. ■ The reason for this rule is that a sole proprietorship is not a legal entity distinct from the person who owns it. The rule also furthers an important goal of Article 9: to ensure that the debtor's name on a financing statement is one that prospective lenders can locate and recognize in future searches.

Description of the Collateral. The UCC requires that both the security agreement and the financing statement contain a description of the collateral in which the secured party has a security interest. The security agreement must describe the collateral because no security interest in goods can exist unless the parties agree on which goods are subject to the security interest. The financing statement must also describe the collateral because the purpose of filing the statement is to give public notice of the fact that certain goods of the debtor are subject to a security interest. Other parties who might later wish to lend money to the debtor or buy the collateral can thus learn of the security interest by checking with the state or local office in which a financing statement for that type of collateral would be filed. For land-related security interests, a legal description of the realty is also required [UCC 9–502(b)].

Consequences of an Improper Filing. Any improper filing renders the secured party unperfected and reduces the secured party's claim in bankruptcy to that of an unsecured creditor. For instance, if the debtor's name on the financing statement is inaccurate or if the collateral is not sufficiently described in the financing statement, the filing may not be effective.

Perfection without Filing In two types of situations, security interests can be perfected without filing a financing statement. The first occurs when the collateral is transferred into the possession of the secured party. The second occurs when the security interest is one of a limited number (thirteen) under the UCC that can be perfected on attachment (without a filing and without having to possess the goods) [UCC 9–309]. The phrase *perfected on attachment* means that these security interests are automatically perfected at the time of their creation. A common security interest that is perfected on attachment is a *purchase-money security interest* in consumer goods (defined and explained below).

PLEDGE
A common law security device (retained in Article 9 of the UCC) in which personal property is transferred into the possession of the creditor as security for the payment of a debt and retained by the creditor until the debt is paid.

Perfection by Possession. Under the common law, one of the most frequent means of obtaining financing was to **pledge** certain collateral as security for the debt and transfer the collateral into the creditor's possession. When the debt was paid, the collateral was returned to the debtor. Although the debtor usually entered into a written security agreement, an oral security agreement was also enforceable as long as the secured party possessed the collateral. Article 9 of the UCC retained the common law pledge and the principle that the security agreement need not be in writing to be enforceable if the collateral is transferred to the secured party [UCC 9–310, 9–312(b), 9–313].

PURCHASE-MONEY SECURITY INTEREST (PMSI)
A security interest that arises when a seller or lender extends credit for part or all of the purchase price of goods purchased by a buyer.

Perfection by Attachment—The Purchase-Money Security Interest in Consumer Goods. A **purchase-money security interest (PMSI)** in consumer goods is created when a person buys consumer goods (items bought primarily for personal, family, or household purposes) and the seller or lender agrees to extend credit for part or all of the purchase price of the goods. The entity that extends the credit and obtains the PMSI can be either the seller (a store, for example) or a financial institution that lends the buyer the funds with which to purchase the goods [UCC 9–102(a)(2)].

A PMSI in consumer goods is perfected automatically at the time of a credit sale—that is, at the time the PMSI is created. The seller in this situation need do nothing more to perfect her or his interest. ■ **EXAMPLE 16.2** Suppose that Jamie wants to purchase a new large-screen television from ABC Television, Inc. The purchase price is $2,500. Not being able to pay the entire amount in cash, Jamie signs

If a couple purchases a plasma TV on an installment plan, what kind of security interest would be created? (Digital Vision photo)

CONTINUATION STATEMENT
A statement that, if filed within six months prior to the expiration date of the original financing statement, continues the perfection of the original security interest for another five years. The perfection of a security interest can be continued in the same manner indefinitely.

PROCEEDS
Under Article 9 of the UCC, whatever is received when the collateral is sold or otherwise disposed of, such as by exchange.

AFTER-ACQUIRED PROPERTY
Property that is acquired by the debtor after the execution of a security agreement.

a purchase agreement to pay $1,000 down and $100 per month until the balance plus interest is fully paid. ABC is to retain a security interest in the purchased goods until full payment has been made. Because the security interest was created as part of the purchase agreement, it is a PMSI. ■

An important exception to this rule of automatic perfection under Article 9 deals with certain types of security interests that are subject to other federal or state laws, which may require additional steps to be perfected [UCC 9–311]. For example, if a consumer purchases an automobile, trailer, or boat, the secured party will need to file a certificate of title with the appropriate state authority to perfect the PMSI.

Effective Time Duration of Perfection   A financing statement is effective for five years from the date of filing [UCC 9–515]. If a **continuation statement** is filed within six months *prior to* the expiration date, the effectiveness of the original statement is continued for another five years, starting with the expiration date of the first five-year period [UCC 9–515(d) and (e)]. The effectiveness of the statement can be continued in the same manner indefinitely. Any attempt to file a continuation statement outside the six-month window will render the continuation ineffective, and the perfection will lapse at the end of the five-year period.

If a financing statement lapses, the security interest that had been perfected by the filing now becomes unperfected. A purchaser for value can acquire the collateral as if the security interest had never been perfected [UCC 9–515(c)].

THE SCOPE OF A SECURITY INTEREST

In addition to covering collateral already in the debtor's possession, a security agreement can cover various other types of property, including the proceeds of the sale of collateral, after-acquired property, and future advances. **Proceeds** include whatever is received when collateral is sold or disposed of in some other way [UCC 9–102(a)(64)]. A secured party's security interest in the collateral includes a security interest in the proceeds of the sale of that collateral. A security interest in proceeds perfects automatically on the *perfection* of the secured party's security interest in the original collateral and remains perfected for twenty days after receipt of the proceeds by the debtor. One way to extend the twenty-day automatic perfection period is to provide for such extended coverage in the original security agreement [UCC 9–315(c) and (d)]. This is typically done when the collateral is the type that is likely to be sold, such as a retailer's inventory—for example, of computers or DVD players. The UCC also permits a security interest in identifiable cash proceeds to remain perfected after twenty days [UCC 9–315(d)(2)].

After-acquired property is property that the debtor acquired after the execution of the security agreement. The security agreement may provide for a security interest in after-acquired property [UCC 9–204(1)]. This is particularly useful for inventory financing arrangements because a secured party whose security interest is in existing inventory knows that the debtor will sell that inventory, thereby reducing the collateral subject to the security interest. Generally, the debtor will purchase new inventory to replace the inventory sold. The secured party wants this newly acquired inventory to be subject to the original security interest. Thus, the after-acquired property clause continues the secured party's claim to any inventory acquired thereafter. This is not to say that the original security interest will be superior to the rights of all other creditors with regard to this after-acquired inventory, as will be discussed later.

Often, a debtor will arrange with a bank to have a *continuing line of credit* under which the debtor can borrow funds intermittently. Advances against lines of credit can be subject to a properly perfected security interest in certain collateral. The security agreement may provide that any future advances made against that line of credit are also subject to the security interest in the same collateral [UCC 9–204(c)].

A security agreement that provides for a security interest in proceeds, in after-acquired property, or in collateral subject to future advances by the secured party (or in all three) is often characterized as a **floating lien.** This type of security interest continues in the collateral or proceeds even if the collateral is sold, exchanged, or disposed of in some other way.

FLOATING LIEN
A security interest in proceeds, after-acquired property, or collateral subject to future advances by the secured party (or all three); a security interest in collateral that is retained even when the collateral changes in character, classification, or location.

PRIORITIES

The importance of perfection to a secured party cannot be overemphasized, particularly when another party is claiming an interest in the same collateral covered by the perfected secured party's security interest. The general rule is that a perfected secured party's interest has priority over the interests of the following parties [UCC 9–317, 9–322]:

1. An unsecured creditor.

2. An unperfected secured party.

3. A subsequent lien creditor, such as a judgment creditor who acquires a lien on the collateral by execution and levy—a process discussed later in this chapter.

4. A trustee in bankruptcy (discussed later in this chapter)—at least, the perfected secured party has priority to the proceeds from the sale of the collateral by the trustee.

5. Most buyers who *do not* purchase the collateral in the ordinary course of a seller's business.

In addition, whether a secured party's security interest is perfected or unperfected may have serious consequences for the secured party if the debtor defaults on the debt or files for bankruptcy. For example, what if the debtor has borrowed funds from two different creditors, using the same property as collateral for both loans? If the debtor defaults on both loans, which of the two creditors has first rights to the collateral? In this situation, the creditor with a perfected security interest will prevail.

Buyers of the Collateral   Sometimes, the conflict is between a perfected secured party and a buyer of the collateral. The question then arises as to which party has priority to the collateral. The UCC recognizes five types of buyers whose interest in purchased goods could conflict with those of a perfected secured party on the debtor's default. These five types are as follows (see Exhibit 16–2 on the next page for details):

1. Buyers in the ordinary course of business—this type of buyer will be discussed in detail shortly.

2. Buyers *not* in the ordinary course of business of consumer goods.

3. Buyers of chattel paper [UCC 9–330].

4. Buyers of instruments, documents, or securities [UCC 9–330(d), 9–331(a)].

5. Buyers of farm products.[2]

---

2. Under the Food Security Act of 1985, buyers in the ordinary course of business include buyers of farm products from a farmer. Under this act, these buyers are protected from prior perfected security interests unless the secured parties perfected centrally by a special form called an *effective financing statement* (EFS) or the buyers received proper notice of the secured party's security interest.

EXHIBIT 16-2 PRIORITY OF CLAIMS TO A DEBTOR'S COLLATERAL

PARTIES	PRIORITY
Unperfected Secured Party	An unperfected secured party prevails over unsecured creditors and creditors who have obtained judgments against the debtor but who have not begun the legal process to collect on those judgments [UCC 9–201(a)].

Purchaser of Debtor's Collateral	1. *Goods purchased in the ordinary course of the seller's business*—Buyer prevails over a secured party's security interest, even if perfected and even if the buyer knows of the security interest [UCC 9–320(a)].
	 2. *Consumer goods purchased outside the ordinary course of business*—Buyer prevails over a secured party's interest, even if perfected by attachment, providing buyer purchased as follows:
	   a. For value.
	   b. Without actual knowledge of the security interest.
	   c. For use as a consumer good.
	   d. Prior to secured party's perfection by *filing* [UCC 9–320(b)].
	 3. *Buyers of chattel paper*—Buyer prevails if the buyer:
	   a. Gave new value in making the purchase.
	   b. Took possession in the ordinary course of the buyer's business.
	   c. Took without knowledge of the security interest [UCC 9–330].
	 4. *Buyers of instruments, documents, or securities*—Buyers who are holders in due course, holders to whom negotiable documents have been duly negotiated, or bona fide purchasers of securities have priority over a previously perfected security interest [UCC 9–330(d), 9–331(a)].
	 5. *Buyers of farm products*—Buyers from a farmer take free and clear of perfected security interests unless, where permitted, a secured party files centrally an effective financing statement (EFS) or the buyer receives proper notice of the security interest before the sale.

Perfected Secured Parties to the Same Collateral	Between two perfected secured parties in the same collateral, the general rule is that first in time of perfection is first in right to the collateral [UCC 9–322(a)(1)].

Because buyers should not be required to find out if there is an outstanding security interest in, for example, a merchant's inventory, the UCC also provides that a person who buys "in the ordinary course of business" will take the goods free from any security interest created by the seller in the purchased collateral. The UCC defines a *buyer in the ordinary course of business* as any person who in good faith, and without knowledge that the sale is in violation of the ownership rights or security interest of a third party in the goods, buys in ordinary course from a person in the business of selling goods of that kind [UCC 1–201(9)].

■ EXAMPLE 16.3 On August 1, West Bank has a perfected security interest in all of ABC Television's existing inventory and any inventory thereafter acquired. On September 1, Carla, a student at Central University, purchases one of the television sets in ABC's inventory. On December 1, ABC goes into default. Can West Bank repossess the TV set sold to Carla? The answer is no, because Carla is a buyer in the ordinary course of business (ABC is in the business of selling goods of that kind) and takes free and clear of West Bank's perfected security interest. ■

Creditors or Secured Parties Generally, the following UCC rules apply when more than one creditor claims rights in the same collateral:

■ *Conflicting perfected security interests.* When two or more secured parties have perfected security interests in the same collateral, generally the first to perfect

KEEP IN MIND Secured creditors—perfected or not—have priority over unsecured creditors.

(file or take possession of the collateral) has priority, unless the state's statute provides otherwise [UCC 9–322(a)(1)].

2 *Conflicting unperfected security interests.* When two conflicting security interests are unperfected, the first to attach has priority [UCC 9–322(a)(3)].

3 *Conflicting perfected security interests in commingled or processed goods.* When goods to which two or more perfected security interests attach are so manufactured or commingled that they lose their identities into a product or mass, the perfected parties' security interests attach to the new product or mass "according to the ratio that the cost of goods to which each interest originally attached bears to the cost of the total product or mass" [UCC 9–336].

DEFAULT

Article 9 defines the rights, duties, and remedies of the secured party and of the debtor on the debtor's default. Should the secured party fail to comply with her or his duties, the debtor is afforded particular rights and remedies. Although any breach of the terms of the security agreement can constitute default, default occurs most commonly when the debtor fails to meet the scheduled payments that the parties have agreed on or when the debtor becomes bankrupt.

Basic Remedies   The rights and remedies under UCC 9–601(a)(b) are *cumulative* [UCC 9–601(c)]. Therefore, if a creditor is unsuccessful in enforcing rights by one method, he or she can pursue another method. Generally, a secured party's remedies can be divided into the two basic categories discussed next.

> **RECALL**   A trespass to land occurs when a person, without permission, enters onto another's land and is established as a trespasser.

Repossession of the Collateral—The Self-Help Remedy.   On the debtor's default, a secured party can take peaceful possession of the collateral without the use of judicial process [UCC 9–609(b)]. This provision is often referred to as the "self-help" provision of Article 9. The UCC does not define *peaceful possession,* however. The general rule is that the collateral has been taken peacefully if the secured party took possession without committing (1) trespass onto realty, (2) assault and/or battery, or (3) breaking and entering. On taking possession, the secured party may either want to retain the collateral for satisfaction of the debt [UCC 9–620] or resell the goods and apply the proceeds toward the debt [UCC 9–610].

Judicial Remedies.   A secured party can relinquish a security interest and use any judicial remedy available, such as proceeding to judgment on the underlying debt, followed by execution and levy. (**Execution** is the implementation of a court's decree or judgment. **Levy** is the obtaining of funds by legal process through the seizure and sale of nonsecured property, usually done after a writ of execution has been issued.) Execution and levy are rarely undertaken unless the collateral is no longer in existence or has declined so much in value that it is worth substantially less than the amount of the debt and the debtor has other assets available that may be legally seized to satisfy the debt [UCC 9–601(a)].[3]

> **EXECUTION**
> An action to carry into effect the directions in a court decree or judgment.
>
> **LEVY**
> The obtaining of money by legal process through the seizure and sale of nonsecured property, usually done after a writ of execution has been issued.

Disposition of Collateral   Once default has occurred and the secured party has obtained possession of the collateral, the secured party may either retain the collateral in full satisfaction of the debt or may sell, lease, or otherwise dispose of the collateral in any commercially reasonable manner and apply the proceeds toward satisfaction of

---

3. Some assets are exempt from creditors' claims, as will be discussed later in this chapter.

the debt [UCC 9–602(7), 9–603, 9–610(a), 9–620]. Any sale is always subject to procedures established by state law.

Proceeds from the Disposition. Proceeds from the disposition of collateral after default on the underlying debt are distributed in the following order:

1 Expenses incurred by the secured party in repossessing, storing, and reselling the collateral.

2 Balance of the debt owed to the secured party.

3 Junior (subordinate) lienholders who have made written or authenticated demands.

4 Unless the collateral consists of accounts, payment intangibles, promissory notes, or chattel paper, any surplus goes to the debtor [UCC 9–608(a), 9–615(a) and (e)].

Whenever the secured party receives noncash proceeds from the disposition of collateral after default, the secured party must make a value determination and apply this value in a commercially reasonable manner [UCC 9–608(a)(3), 9–615(c)].

Deficiency Judgment. Often, after proper disposition of the collateral, the secured party has not collected all that the debtor still owes. Unless otherwise agreed, the debtor is liable for any deficiency, and the creditor can obtain a **deficiency judgment** from a court to collect the deficiency. Note, however, that if the underlying transaction was, for example, a sale of accounts or of chattel paper, the debtor is entitled to any surplus or is liable for any deficiency only if the security agreement so provides [UCC 9–615(d) and (e)].

Whenever the secured party fails to conduct a disposition in a commercially reasonable manner or to give proper notice, the deficiency of the debtor is reduced to the extent that such failure affected the price received at the disposition [UCC 9–626(a)(3)].

DEFICIENCY JUDGMENT
A judgment against a debtor for the amount of a debt remaining unpaid after the collateral has been repossessed and sold.

ETHICAL ISSUE 16.1

How long should a secured party have to seek a deficiency judgment? Because of depreciation, the amount received from the sale of collateral is frequently less than the amount the debtor owes the secured party. As noted, the secured party can file suit against the debtor in an attempt to collect the balance due. Practically speaking, however, debtors who have defaulted on a loan rarely have the cash to pay any deficiency. Article 9 does not contain a statute of limitations provision, though. Thus, it is not clear how long secured parties have after default to file a deficiency suit against debtors. If a secured party waits until the debtor becomes solvent again, the court might not allow the suit. Is this fair?

Consider, for example, a case that came before the Vermont Supreme Court in 2003.[4] Duane Ouimette had bought a car with an extended warranty from a dealership under a retail installment sales contract. The contract was assigned to DaimlerChrysler. When Ouimette failed to make the payments, DaimlerChrysler repossessed the car and sold it at an auction. After the car was sold, Ouimette still owed more than $10,000 on the loan. Five and a half years later, DaimlerChrysler sued to collect the deficiency judgment, arguing that the company should have six years to file a deficiency action. The court noted that Vermont had never addressed the issue of what limitation period should apply to deficiency suits. Because the con-

---

4. *DaimlerChrysler Services North America, LLC v. Ouimette*, 830 A.2d 38 (Vt. 2003).

tract involved the sale of a car, however, the court held that the four-year limitation period stated in Article 2 applied, and thus the creditor's suit was too late. ■

Redemption Rights.   At any time before the secured party disposes of the collateral or enters into a contract for its disposition, or before the debtor's obligation has been discharged through the secured party's retention of the collateral, the debtor or any other secured party can exercise the right of *redemption* of the collateral. The debtor or other secured party can do this by tendering performance of all obligations secured by the collateral and by paying the expenses reasonably incurred by the secured party in retaking and maintaining the collateral [UCC 9–623].

■ Additional Laws Assisting Creditors

Both the common law and statutory laws other than Article 9 of the UCC create various rights and remedies for creditors. We discuss here some of these rights and remedies.

LIENS

As stated in Chapter 13, a *lien* is an encumbrance on (claim against) property to satisfy a debt or protect a claim for the payment of a debt. Creditors' liens may arise under the common law or under statutory law. Statutory liens include *mechanic's liens*. Liens created at common law include *artisan's liens* and *innkeeper's liens*. *Judicial liens* include those that represent a creditor's efforts to collect on a debt before or after a judgment is entered by a court.

Generally, a lien creditor has priority over an unperfected secured party but not over a perfected secured party. In other words, if a person becomes a lien creditor *before* another party perfects a security interest in the same property, the lienholder has priority. If a person obtains a lien *after* another's security interest in the property is perfected, the lienholder does not have priority. This is true for all liens except mechanic's and artisan's liens, which normally have priority over perfected security interests—unless a statute provides otherwise.

Mechanic's Lien   When a person contracts for labor, services, or materials to be furnished for the purpose of making improvements on real property (land and things attached to the land, such as buildings and trees—see Chapter 24) but does not immediately pay for the improvements, the creditor can file a **mechanic's lien** on the property. This creates a special type of debtor-creditor relationship in which the real estate itself becomes security for the debt. Note that state law governs the procedures that must be followed to create a mechanic's lien.

Artisan's Lien   An **artisan's lien** is a security device created at common law through which a creditor can recover payment from a debtor for labor and materials furnished for the repair or improvement of personal property. ■ **EXAMPLE 16.4** Tenetia leaves her diamond ring at the jeweler's to be repaired and to have her initials engraved on the band. In the absence of an agreement, the jeweler can keep the ring until Tenetia pays for the services. Should Tenetia fail to pay, the jeweler has a lien on Tenetia's ring for the amount of the bill and normally can sell the ring in satisfaction of the lien. ■

MECHANIC'S LIEN
A statutory lien on the real property of another, created to ensure payment for work performed and materials furnished in the repair or improvement of real property, such as a building.

ARTISAN'S LIEN
A possessory lien given to a person who has made improvements and added value to another person's personal property as security for payment for services performed.

Painters finish the trim on a house. If the homeowner does not pay for the work, what can the painters do to collect what they are owed? (© Myrleen Ferguson, PhotoEdit)

INNKEEPER'S LIEN
A possessory lien placed on the luggage of hotel guests for hotel charges that remain unpaid.

In contrast to a mechanic's lien, an artisan's lien is *possessory*. The lienholder ordinarily must have retained possession of the property and have expressly or impliedly agreed to provide the services on a cash, not a credit, basis. The lien remains in existence as long as the lienholder maintains possession, and the lien is terminated once possession is voluntarily surrendered—unless the surrender is only temporary. With a temporary surrender, there must be an agreement that the property will be returned to the lienholder. Even with such an agreement, if a third party obtains rights in that property while it is out of the possession of the lienholder, the lien is lost.

Modern statutes permit the holder of an artisan's lien to foreclose and sell the property subject to the lien to satisfy payment of the debt. As with the mechanic's lien, the holder of an artisan's lien is required to give notice to the owner of the property prior to foreclosure and sale. The sale proceeds are used to pay the debt and the costs of the legal proceedings, and the surplus, if any, is paid to the former owner.

Innkeeper's Lien   An **innkeeper's lien** is another security device created at common law. An innkeeper's lien is placed on the baggage of guests for any agreed-on hotel charges that remain unpaid. If no express agreement has been made concerning the amount of those charges, then the lien will be for the reasonable value of the accommodations furnished. The innkeeper's lien is terminated either by the guest's payment of the hotel charges or by the innkeeper's surrender of the baggage to the guest, unless the surrender is temporary. Most state statutes permit the innkeeper to satisfy the debt by means of a public sale of the guest's baggage.

Judicial Liens   When a debt is past due, a creditor can bring a legal action against the debtor to collect the debt. If the creditor is successful in the action, the court awards the creditor a judgment against the debtor (usually for the amount of the debt plus any interest and legal costs incurred in obtaining the judgment). Frequently, however, the creditor is unable to collect the awarded amount.

To ensure that a judgment in the creditor's favor will be collectible, creditors are permitted to request that certain nonexempt property of the debtor be seized to satisfy the debt. (As will be discussed later in this chapter, under state or federal statutes, certain property is exempt from attachment by creditors.) If the court orders the debtor's property to be seized prior to a judgment in the creditor's favor, the court's order is referred to as a *writ of attachment*. If the court orders the debtor's property to be seized following a judgment in the creditor's favor, the court's order is referred to as a *writ of execution*.

Attachment.   Recall from earlier in this chapter that *attachment*, in the context of secured transactions, refers to the process through which a security interest in a debtor's collateral becomes enforceable. In the context of judicial liens, this word has another meaning: *attachment* is a court-ordered seizure and taking into custody of property prior to the securing of a judgment for a past-due debt. Attachment rights are created by state statutes. Attachment is a *prejudgment* remedy because it occurs either at the time of or immediately after the commencement of a lawsuit and before the entry of a final judgment. By statute, to attach before judgment, a creditor must comply with specific restrictions and requirements. The due process clause of the Fourteenth Amendment to the U.S. Constitution limits the courts' power to authorize seizure of a debtor's property without notice to the debtor or a hearing on the facts.

To use attachment as a remedy, the creditor must have an enforceable right to payment of the debt under law and must follow certain procedures. Otherwise, the creditor can be liable for damages for wrongful attachment. She or he must file with the court an *affidavit* (a written or printed statement, made under oath or sworn to) stating that the debtor is in default and indicating the statutory grounds under which attachment is sought. The creditor must also post a bond to cover at least the court costs, the value of the loss of use of the good suffered by the debtor, and the value of the property attached. When the court is satisfied that all the requirements have been met, it issues a **writ of attachment,** which directs the sheriff or other public officer to seize nonexempt property. If the creditor prevails at trial, the seized property can be sold to satisfy the judgment.

Writ of Execution.   If the debtor will not or cannot pay the judgment, the creditor is entitled to go back to the court and obtain a court order directing the sheriff to seize (levy) and sell any of the debtor's nonexempt real or personal property that is within the court's geographic jurisdiction (usually the county in which the courthouse is located). This order is called a **writ of execution.** The proceeds of the sale are used to pay off the judgment, accrued interest, and the costs of the sale. Any excess is paid to the debtor. The debtor can pay the judgment and redeem the nonexempt property any time before the sale takes place. (Because of exemption laws and bankruptcy laws, however, many judgments are virtually uncollectible.)

GARNISHMENT

An order for **garnishment** permits a creditor to collect a debt by seizing property of the debtor that is being held by a third party. In a garnishment proceeding, the third party—the person or entity that the court is ordering to garnish an individual's property—is called the *garnishee.* Frequently, a garnishee is the debtor's employer. A creditor may seek a garnishment judgment against the debtor's employer so that part of the debtor's usual paycheck will be paid to the creditor. In some situations, however, the garnishee is a third party that holds funds belonging to the debtor (such as a bank) or a third party who has possession of, or exercises control over, funds or other types of property belonging to the debtor. Almost all types of property can be garnished, including tax refunds, pensions, and trust funds—as long as the property is not exempt from garnishment and is in the possession of a third party.

The legal proceeding for a garnishment action is governed by state law, and garnishment operates differently from state to state. As a result of a garnishment proceeding, as noted, the court orders a third party (such as the debtor's employer) to turn over property owned by the debtor (such as wages) to pay the debt. Garnishment can be a prejudgment remedy, requiring a hearing before a court, but is most often a postjudgment remedy. According to the laws in some states, the creditor needs to obtain only one order of garnishment, which will then apply continuously to the debtor's wages until the entire debt is paid. In other states, the judgment creditor must go back to court for a separate order of garnishment for each pay period.

Both federal and state laws limit the amount of funds that can be taken from a debtor's weekly take-home pay through garnishment proceedings.[5] Federal law provides a framework to protect debtors from suffering unduly when paying judgment debts.[6] State laws also provide dollar exemptions, and these amounts are often

WRIT OF ATTACHMENT
A court's order, issued prior to a trial to collect a debt, directing the sheriff or other officer to seize nonexempt property of the debtor. If the creditor prevails at trial, the seized property can be sold to satisfy the judgment.

WRIT OF EXECUTION
A court's order, issued after a judgment has been entered against the debtor, directing the sheriff to seize (levy) and sell any of the debtor's nonexempt real or personal property. The proceeds of the sale are used to pay off the judgment, accrued interest, and costs of the sale; any surplus is paid to the debtor.

GARNISHMENT
A legal process used by a creditor to collect a debt by seizing property of the debtor (such as wages) that is being held by a third party (such as the debtor's employer).

---

5. Some states (for example, Texas) do not permit garnishment of wages by private parties except under a child-support order.
6. For example, the federal Consumer Credit Protection Act of 1968, 15 U.S.C. Sections 1601–1693r, provides that a debtor can retain either 75 percent of the disposable earnings per week or a sum equivalent to thirty hours of work paid at federal minimum-wage rates, whichever is greater.

larger than those provided by federal law. Under federal law, an employer cannot dismiss an employee because his or her wages are being garnished.

Mortgage Foreclosure

Mortgage holders have the right to foreclose on mortgaged property in the event of a debtor's default. The usual method of foreclosure is by judicial sale of the property, although the statutory methods of foreclosure vary from state to state. If the proceeds of the foreclosure sale are sufficient to cover both the costs of the foreclosure and the mortgaged debt, the debtor receives any surplus. If the sale proceeds are insufficient to cover the foreclosure costs and the mortgaged debt, however, the **mortgagee** (the creditor-lender) can seek to recover the difference from the **mortgagor** (the debtor) by obtaining a deficiency judgment representing the difference between the mortgaged debt and the amount actually received from the proceeds of the foreclosure sale.

The mortgagee obtains a deficiency judgment in a separate legal action pursued subsequent to the foreclosure action. The deficiency judgment entitles the mortgagee to recover the amount of the deficiency from other property owned by the debtor.

Suretyship and Guaranty

When a third person promises to pay a debt owed by another in the event the debtor does not pay, either a *suretyship* or a *guaranty* relationship is created. Suretyship and guaranty have a long history under the common law and provide creditors with the right to seek payment from the third party if the primary debtor defaults on her or his obligations. Exhibit 16–3 illustrates the relationship between a suretyship or guaranty party and the creditor.

MORTGAGEE
Under a mortgage agreement, the creditor who takes a security interest in the debtor's property.

MORTGAGOR
Under a mortgage agreement, the debtor who gives the creditor a security interest in the debtor's property in return for a mortgage loan.

EXHIBIT 16–3 SURETYSHIP AND GUARANTY PARTIES

In a suretyship or guaranty arrangement, a third party promises to be responsible for a debtor's obligations. A third party who agrees to be responsible for the debt even if the primary debtor does not default is known as a surety; a third party who agrees to be *secondarily* responsible for the debt—that is, responsible only if the primary debtor defaults—is known as a guarantor. As noted in Chapter 9, normally a promise of guaranty (a collateral, or secondary, promise) must be in writing to be enforceable.

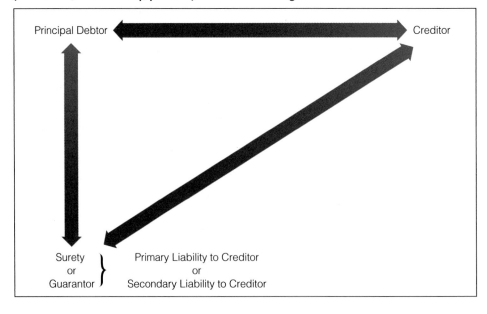

SURETYSHIP
An express contract in which a third party to a debtor-creditor relationship (the surety) promises to be primarily responsible for the debtor's obligation.

SURETY
A person, such as a cosigner on a note, who agrees to be primarily responsible for the debt of another.

GUARANTOR
A person who agrees to satisfy the debt of another (the debtor) only after the principal debtor defaults. Thus, a guarantor's liability is secondary.

Surety A contract of strict **suretyship** is a promise made by a third person to be responsible for the debtor's obligation. It is an express contract between the **surety** (the third party) and the creditor. The surety in the strictest sense is primarily liable for the debt of the principal. The creditor need not exhaust all legal remedies against the principal debtor before holding the surety responsible for payment. The creditor can demand payment from the surety from the moment the debt is due.

Guaranty With a suretyship arrangement, the surety is *primarily* liable for the debtor's obligation. With a guaranty arrangement, the **guarantor**—the third person making the guaranty—is *secondarily* liable. The guarantor can be required to pay the obligation *only after the principal debtor defaults*, and default usually takes place only after the creditor has made an attempt to collect from the debtor.

The Statute of Frauds requires that a guaranty contract between the guarantor and the creditor must be in writing to be enforceable unless the *main purpose* exception applies. (A suretyship agreement, by contrast, need not be in writing to be enforceable.) As discussed in Chapter 9, under this exception if the main purpose of the guaranty agreement is to benefit the guarantor, then the contract need not be in writing to be enforceable.

In the following case, the issue was whether a guaranty of a lease signed by the officer of a corporation was enforceable against the officer personally even though he claimed to have signed the guaranty only as a representative of the corporation.

CASE 16.1 **JSV, Inc. v. Hene Meat Co.**

Court of Appeals of Indiana, 2003.
794 N.E.2d 555.

FACTS On August 30, 1999, JSV, Inc., signed a lease to rent a portion of a building in Indianapolis, Indiana, from Hene Meat Company. Mark Kennedy signed the lease on behalf of JSV as one of its corporate officers. Kennedy also signed a document titled "GUARANTY," which stated that it was "an absolute and unconditional guaranty" of the lease's performance by JSV. Kennedy's printed name and signature on the document were not followed by any corporate officer designation. JSV stopped paying rent to Hene in September 2000. Hene filed a suit in an Indiana state court against JSV and Kennedy, alleging, among other things, that Kennedy was personally liable on the guaranty. He responded in part that he signed the guaranty only as an officer of JSV. The court issued a summary judgment against Kennedy for $75,041.07 in favor of Hene. Kennedy appealed to a state intermediate appellate court.

ISSUE Was Kennedy personally liable on the guaranty?

DECISION Yes. The state intermediate appellate court affirmed the judgment of the lower court, holding that the document Kennedy signed was "unambiguously a personal guaranty."

REASON The state intermediate appellate court explained that a guaranty agreement includes three parties: the obligor (the promisor or debtor), the obligee (the one to whom the debt or obligation is owed), and the guarantor. "Here, Hene as landlord under the lease was the obligee and JSV as the tenant was the obligor; the disputed issue is the identity of the guarantor." The court explained that there would have been no point in Hene's obtaining Kennedy's guaranty of the lease if he was doing so only in his official capacity as an officer of JSV. This would have been the same as JSV guaranteeing its own performance under the lease, which would have meant that JSV was both the obligor under the lease and the guarantor under the guaranty. The court felt that such a result would be "paradoxical and untenable," and concluded that the guaranty in this case is "clearly a personal one * * * because Kennedy's signature thereon is not followed by any corporate officer designation."

WHY IS THIS CASE IMPORTANT? *This case should be a warning to corporate officers and directors that to avoid personal liability when signing a guaranty, they need to clearly indicate that they are signing in their official capacity.*

Defenses of the Surety and the Guarantor The defenses of the surety and the guarantor are basically the same. Therefore, the following discussion applies to both, although it refers only to the surety.

Actions Releasing the Surety. Certain actions will release the surety from the obligation. For example, any binding material modification in the terms of the original contract made between the principal debtor and the creditor—including a binding agreement to extend the time for making payment—without first obtaining the consent of the surety will discharge a gratuitous surety completely and a compensated surety to the extent that the surety suffers a loss. (An example of a gratuitous surety is a father who agrees to assume responsibility for his daughter's obligation; an example of a compensated surety is a venture capitalist who will profit from a loan made to the principal debtor.)

Naturally, if the principal obligation is paid by the debtor or by another person on behalf of the debtor, the surety is discharged from the obligation. Similarly, if valid tender of payment is made, and the creditor rejects it with knowledge of the surety's existence, the surety is released from any obligation on the debt.

Defenses of the Principal Debtor. Generally, the surety can use any defenses available to a principal debtor to avoid liability on the obligation to the creditor. Defenses available to the principal debtor that the surety *cannot* use include the principal debtor's incapacity or bankruptcy and the statute of limitations. The ability of the surety to assert any defenses the debtor may have against the creditor is the most important concept in suretyship; it means that most of the defenses available to the surety are also those of the debtor.

Surrender or Impairment of Collateral. In addition, if a creditor surrenders the collateral to the debtor or impairs the collateral while knowing of the surety and without the surety's consent, the surety is released to the extent of any loss suffered from the creditor's actions. The primary reason for this requirement is to protect a surety who agreed to become obligated only because the debtor's collateral was in the possession of the creditor.

Other Defenses. Obviously, a surety may also have his or her own defenses—for example, incapacity or bankruptcy. If the creditor fraudulently induced the surety to guarantee the debt of the debtor, the surety can assert fraud as a defense. In most states, the creditor has a legal duty to inform the surety, prior to the formation of the suretyship contract, of material facts known by the creditor that would substantially increase the surety's risk. Failure to so inform may constitute fraud and makes the suretyship obligation voidable.

Rights of the Surety and the Guarantor Generally, when the surety or guarantor pays the debt owed to the creditor, the surety or guarantor is entitled to certain rights. Because the rights of the surety and guarantor are basically the same, the following discussion applies to both.

◼ Additional Laws Assisting Debtors

HOMESTEAD EXEMPTION
A law permitting a debtor to retain the family home, either in its entirety or up to a specified dollar amount, free from the claims of unsecured creditors or trustees in bankruptcy.

The law protects debtors as well as creditors. Certain property of the debtor, for example, is exempt from creditors' actions. Probably the most familiar exemption is the **homestead exemption.** Each state permits the debtor to retain the family

Livestock, such as the cattle shown here, is usually considered exempt property under laws that assist debtors. Why is this? (Photodisc)

home, either in its entirety or up to a specified dollar amount, free from the claims of unsecured creditors or trustees in bankruptcy (a bankruptcy trustee is appointed by the court to hold and protect estate property, as will be discussed later in this chapter). The purpose of the homestead exemption is to ensure that the debtor will retain some form of shelter.

■ **EXAMPLE 16.5** Suppose that Van Cleave owes Acosta $40,000. The debt is the subject of a lawsuit, and the court awards Acosta a judgment of $40,000 against Van Cleave. Van Cleave's home is valued at $50,000, and the state exemption on homesteads is $25,000. There are no outstanding mortgages or other liens. To satisfy the judgment debt, Van Cleave's family home is sold at public auction for $45,000. The proceeds of the sale are distributed as follows:

1 Van Cleave is given $25,000 as his homestead exemption.

2 Acosta is paid $20,000 toward the judgment debt, leaving a $20,000 deficiency judgment that can be satisfied from any other nonexempt property (personal or real) that Van Cleave may have, if allowed by state law. ■

Various types of personal property may also be exempt from satisfaction of judgment debts. Personal property that is most often exempt includes the following:

1 Household furniture up to a specified dollar amount.

2 Clothing and certain personal possessions, such as family pictures or a Bible or other religious text.

3 A vehicle (or vehicles) for transportation (at least up to a specified dollar amount).

4 Certain classified animals, usually livestock but including pets.

5 Equipment that the debtor uses in a business or trade, such as tools or professional instruments, up to a specified dollar amount.

■ Bankruptcy and Reorganization

Bankruptcy law in the United States has two goals—to protect a debtor by giving him or her a fresh start, free from creditors' claims, and to ensure equitable treatment to creditors who are competing for a debtor's assets. Bankruptcy law is federal law, but state laws on secured transactions, liens, judgments, and exemptions also play a role in federal bankruptcy proceedings.

Current bankruptcy law is based on the Bankruptcy Reform Act of 1978, as amended. In this chapter, we refer to this act, as amended, as the Bankruptcy Code (or, more simply, the Code). This chapter's *Landmark in the Law* feature on the following pages is unique in that it discusses *proposed* bankruptcy reform legislation, which is likely to significantly change existing law, rather than discussing legislation that has been adopted.

CHAPTER 7—LIQUIDATION

DISCHARGE
In bankruptcy proceedings, the extinction of the debtor's dischargeable debts.

Liquidation is the most familiar type of bankruptcy proceeding and is often referred to as an *ordinary*, or *straight, bankruptcy*. Put simply, debtors in straight bankruptcies state their debts and turn their assets over to trustees. The trustees sell the assets and distribute the proceeds to creditors. With certain exceptions, the remaining debts are then **discharged** (extinguished), and the debtors are relieved of the obligation to pay the debts.

LANDMARK IN THE LAW

Proposed Bankruptcy Reform Legislation

As mentioned elsewhere, the basis for bankruptcy law prior to 2005 was the Bankruptcy Reform Act of 1978, which has been amended several times since its passage. The 1978 act represented a major overhaul of U.S. bankruptcy law. If the proposed Bankruptcy Abuse Prevention and Consumer Protection Act of 2003[a] currently before Congress is enacted, as it may be by the time this book is in print, the Bankruptcy Code will undergo further significant changes.

THE NEED FOR REFORM   The proposed legislation is, in part, a response to businesses' concerns about the sharp rise in personal bankruptcy filings. Since 1980, bankruptcy filings have climbed from fewer than 300,000 per year to over 1.5 million. The perception has been that debtors who are by no means poor have been taking advantage of the bankruptcy system to erase debts that they legitimately owe. One of the major goals of the proposed act is to require consumers to pay as many of their debts as possible instead of having those debts discharged in Chapter 7 bankruptcy. (As discussed in this chapter, Chapter 7 of the Bankruptcy Code allows debtors to erase most of their debts and make a clean start.) Currently, about 70 percent of bankruptcy filings are Chapter 7 cases.

PREVENTING ABUSE   To discourage bankruptcy and prevent abuse, the act calls for a complicated system of "means testing." Persons whose incomes fall below the relevant state's median family income (in most states, about $50,000) will automatically qualify for Chapter 7 relief. Persons whose income is above the median may still qualify for Chapter 7 relief if they have as little as $166 a month left after making payments on their debts and after covering the cost of their living expenses. Debtors who do not qualify for Chapter 7 may be able to have some of their debts discharged under other chapters of the Bankruptcy Code. Relative to the existing Code, the terms of the payoff will be stricter, and more emphasis is given to paying off credit-card and auto-loan debts than in the past.

In a word, debtors who can afford to repay a certain percentage of their debts over a five-year period will not be able to take advantage of Chapter 7 but instead

a. The provisions of the act discussed in this feature are drawn from the congressional Joint Conference Committee's report on H.R. 333, issued on July 26, 2002; the same provisions are included in the reform act H.R. 975, which was proposed in 2003 and passed the House at the end of January 2004.

PETITION IN BANKRUPTCY
The document that is filed with a bankruptcy court to initiate bankruptcy proceedings. The official forms required for a petition in bankruptcy must be completed accurately, sworn to under oath, and signed by the debtor.

Any "person"—defined as including individuals, partnerships, and corporations—may be a debtor under Chapter 7. Railroads, insurance companies, banks, savings and loan associations, investment companies licensed by the Small Business Administration, and credit unions *cannot* be Chapter 7 debtors, however. Other chapters of the Code or other federal or state statutes apply to them. A husband and wife may file jointly for bankruptcy under a single petition.

Filing the Petition   A straight bankruptcy may be commenced by the filing of either a voluntary or an involuntary **petition in bankruptcy**—the document that is filed with a bankruptcy court to initiate bankruptcy proceedings.

LANDMARK IN THE LAW—Continued

will have to accept a Chapter 13 repayment plan. The act also requires debtors to participate in financial counseling before filing for bankruptcy.

THE HOMESTEAD EXEMPTION   One of the provisions of the reform legislation involves the homestead exemption. In six states, among them Florida and Texas, homestead exemptions allow debtors petitioning for bankruptcy to shield *unlimited* amounts of equity (which is the market value minus the outstanding mortgage owed) in their homes from creditors. The reform act leaves these exemptions in place but does put some limits on their use. Under the proposed act, a home must be owned for at least forty months before the exemption can be claimed. If the home is owned for less than forty months, a homeowner can claim only $125,000 as a homestead exemption.

OTHER PROVISIONS   The act also includes a number of other provisions. For example, one provision requires credit-card companies to make fuller disclosures about their interest rates and payment schedules. Another provision gives child-support obligations priority over other debts and allows enforcement agencies to continue efforts to collect child-support payments. Additionally, the act expands protections for family farmers and provides more protection for personal information about customers possessed by businesses undergoing bankruptcy.

APPLICATION TO TODAY'S WORLD

Clearly, the bankruptcy reform legislation will benefit lenders, particularly credit-card companies, which have often faced losses when a debtor runs up credit-card bills and then files for bankruptcy protection. Business debtors, though, may find it more daunting to file for bankruptcy because much more paperwork will be required than is needed under existing law. Inevitably, this will mean that the legal fees involved in filing for bankruptcy protection will increase—some estimate by more than 40 percent.

RELEVANT WEB SITES

To locate information on the Web concerning the proposed bankruptcy reform legislation, go to this text's Web site at http://blt.westbuslaw.com, *select "Chapter 16," and click on "URLs for Landmarks."*

CONSUMER-DEBTOR
An individual whose debts are primarily consumer debts (debts for purchases made primarily for personal or household use).

Voluntary Bankruptcy.   A voluntary petition is brought by the debtor, who files official forms designated for that purpose in the bankruptcy court. A **consumer-debtor** (defined as an individual whose debts are primarily consumer debts) who has selected Chapter 7 must state in the petition, at the time of filing, that he or she understands the relief available under other chapters and has chosen to proceed under Chapter 7. If the consumer-debtor is represented by an attorney, the attorney must file an affidavit stating that she or he has informed the debtor of the relief available under each chapter. Any debtor who is liable on a claim held by a creditor can file a voluntary petition. The debtor does not even have to be insolvent to file for bankruptcy relief.[7] Anyone liable to a creditor can declare bankruptcy. The voluntary petition contains the following schedules:

1 A list of both secured and unsecured creditors, their addresses, and the amount of debt owed to each.

2 A statement of the financial affairs of the debtor.

3 A list of all property owned by the debtor, including property claimed by the debtor to be exempt.

4 A listing of current income and expenses.

The official forms must be completed accurately, sworn to under oath, and signed by the debtor. To conceal assets or knowingly supply false information on these schedules is a crime under the bankruptcy laws. If the voluntary petition for bankruptcy is found to be proper, the filing of the petition will itself constitute an order for relief. An **order for relief** relieves the debtor of the immediate obligation to pay the debts listed in the petition. Once a debtor's voluntary petition has been filed, the clerk of the court (or person directed) must give the trustee and creditors mailed notice of the order for relief not more than twenty days after the entry of the order.

As mentioned previously, debtors do not have to be insolvent to file for voluntary bankruptcy. Debtors do not have unfettered access to Chapter 7 bankruptcy proceedings, however. Section 707(b) of the Bankruptcy Code allows a bankruptcy court to dismiss a petition for relief under Chapter 7 if the granting of relief would constitute "substantial abuse" of Chapter 7.

Involuntary Bankruptcy. An involuntary bankruptcy occurs when the debtor's creditors force the debtor into bankruptcy proceedings. An involuntary case cannot be commenced against a farmer[8] or a charitable institution, however. For an involuntary action to be filed against other debtors, the following requirements must be met: If the debtor has twelve or more creditors, three or more of those creditors having unsecured claims totaling at least $12,300 must join in the petition. If a debtor has fewer than twelve creditors, one or more creditors having a claim of $12,300 or more may file.

If the debtor challenges the involuntary petition, a hearing will be held, and the debtor's challenge will fail if the bankruptcy court finds either of the following:

1 That the debtor is generally not paying debts as they become due.

2 That a general receiver, custodian, or assignee took possession of, or was appointed to take charge of, substantially all of the debtor's property within 120 days before the filing of the involuntary petition.

If the court allows the bankruptcy to proceed, the debtor will be required to supply the same information in the bankruptcy schedules as in a voluntary bankruptcy.

An involuntary petition should not be used as an everyday debt-collection device, and the Code provides penalties for the filing of frivolous (unjustified) petitions

ORDER FOR RELIEF
A court's grant of assistance to a complainant. In bankruptcy proceedings, the order relieves the debtor of the immediate obligation to pay the debts listed in the bankruptcy petition.

---

7. The inability to pay debts as they become due is known as *equitable* insolvency. A *balance-sheet* insolvency, which exists when a debtor's liabilities exceed assets, is not the test. Thus, it is possible for debtors to petition voluntarily for bankruptcy even though their assets far exceed their liabilities. This situation may occur when a debtor's cash flow problems become severe.

8. Other than a *family farmer* (described later in this chapter). *Farmers* are defined as persons who receive more than 80 percent of their gross income from farming operations, such as tilling the soil; dairy farming; ranching; or the production or raising of crops, poultry, or livestock. Corporations and partnerships, as well as individuals, can be farmers.

against debtors. Judgment may be granted against the petitioning creditors for the costs and attorneys' fees incurred by the debtor in defending against an involuntary petition that is dismissed by the court. If the petition is filed in bad faith, damages can be awarded for injury to the debtor's reputation. Punitive damages may also be awarded.

Automatic Stay   The moment a petition, either voluntary or involuntary, is filed, an **automatic stay** on, or suspension of, virtually all actions by creditors against the debtor or the debtor's property goes into effect. In other words, once a petition has been filed, creditors cannot contact the debtor by phone or mail or start or finish any legal proceedings to recover debts or to repossess property. The Code provides that if a creditor knowingly violates the automatic stay (a willful violation), any party injured, including the debtor, is entitled to recover actual damages, costs, and attorneys' fees and may be entitled to recover punitive damages as well.

> **AUTOMATIC STAY**
> In bankruptcy proceedings, the suspension of virtually all litigation and other action by creditors against the debtor or the debtor's property. The stay is effective the moment the debtor files a petition in bankruptcy.

The automatic stay does not apply to paternity, alimony, or family maintenance and support debts. Creditors seeking payment on these debts can continue to contact the debtor and take appropriate actions to collect. In addition, a secured creditor can petition the bankruptcy court for relief from the automatic stay in certain circumstances.

Creditors' Meeting and Claims   Within a reasonable time after the order of relief is granted (not less than ten days or more than thirty days), the bankruptcy court must call a meeting of the creditors listed in the schedules filed by the debtor. The bankruptcy judge does not attend this meeting. The debtor must attend this meeting (unless excused by the court) and submit to an examination under oath. Failure to appear or the making of false statements under oath may result in the debtor's being denied a discharge of bankruptcy. At the meeting, the trustee ensures that the debtor is aware of the potential consequences of bankruptcy and of his or her ability to file under a different chapter of the Bankruptcy Code. If the debtor has sufficient assets available to be distributed to creditors, each creditor must normally file a *proof of claim* with the bankruptcy court clerk within ninety days of the creditors' meeting to be entitled to receive a portion of the debtor's estate.

> **BE AWARE**   A debtor who lies, commits bribery, conceals assets, uses a false name, or makes false claims at a creditors' meeting is subject to a $5,000 fine and up to five years in prison.

Property of the Estate   On the commencement of a liquidation proceeding under Chapter 7, an **estate in property** is created. The estate consists of all the debtor's interests in property currently held, wherever located, together with certain jointly owned property, property transferred in transactions voidable by the trustee, proceeds and profits from the property of the estate, and certain after-acquired property. Interests in certain property—such as gifts, inheritances, property settlements (resulting from divorce), or life insurance death proceeds—to which the debtor becomes entitled *within 180 days after filing* may also become part of the estate. Thus, the filing of a bankruptcy petition generally fixes a dividing line: property acquired prior to the filing becomes property of the estate, and property acquired after the filing, except as just noted, remains the debtor's.

> **ESTATE IN PROPERTY**
> In bankruptcy proceedings, all of the debtor's interests in property currently held, wherever located, together with certain jointly owned property, property transferred in transactions voidable by the trustee, proceeds and profits from the property of the estate, and certain property interests to which the debtor becomes entitled within 180 days after filing for bankruptcy.

Exempted Property   Any individual debtor is entitled to exempt certain property from the bankruptcy. The Bankruptcy Code establishes a federal exemption scheme under which the following property is exempt:

1 Up to $18,450 in equity in the debtor's residence and burial plot (the homestead exemption).

2 Interest in a motor vehicle up to $2,950.

A mother and her daughter look over a collection of antiques and collectibles on display at a public auction. The auction is part of a company's liquidation bankruptcy proceeding. What other types of property might be included in the debtor's estate in property? (AP Photo/The Charlotte Observer, Christopher Record)

U.S. TRUSTEE
A government official who performs certain administrative tasks that a bankruptcy judge would otherwise have to perform.

3 Interest in household goods and furnishings, wearing apparel, appliances, books, animals, crops, and musical instruments up to $475 in a particular item but limited to $9,850 in total.

4 Interest in jewelry up to $1,225.

5 Any other property worth up to $975, plus any unused part of the $18,450 homestead exemption up to an amount of $9,250.

6 Interest in any tools of the debtor's trade, up to $1,850.

7 Certain life insurance contracts owned by the debtor.

8 Certain interests in accrued dividends or interests in unmatured life insurance policies owned by the debtor, not to exceed $9,850.

9 Professionally prescribed health aids.

10 The right to receive Social Security and certain welfare benefits, alimony and support payments, and certain pension benefits.

11 The right to receive certain personal-injury and other awards, up to $18,450.[9]

Individual states have the power to pass legislation precluding debtors in their states from using the federal exemptions. At least thirty-five states have done this. In those states, debtors may use only state (not federal) exemptions. In the rest of the states, an individual debtor (or husband and wife who file jointly) may choose between the exemptions provided under state law and the federal exemptions.

The Trustee's Role   Promptly after the order for relief has been entered, an interim, or provisional, trustee is appointed by the **U.S. trustee** (a government official who performs certain administrative tasks that a bankruptcy judge would otherwise have to perform). The interim trustee administers the debtor's estate until the first meeting of the creditors, at which time either a permanent trustee is elected or the interim trustee becomes the permanent trustee. Trustees are entitled to compensation for services rendered, plus reimbursement for expenses.

The basic duty of the trustee is to collect the debtor's available estate and reduce it to money for distribution, preserving the interests of both the debtor and unsecured creditors. In other words, the trustee is accountable for administering the debtor's estate. To enable the trustee to accomplish this duty, the Code gives her or him certain powers, stated in both general and specific terms.

The powers of the trustee generally are described by the statement that the trustee occupies a position *equivalent* in rights to that of certain other parties. For example, the trustee has the same rights as a *lien creditor* who could have obtained a judicial lien on the debtor's property or who could have levied execution on the debtor's property. This means that a trustee's rights to the debtor's property have priority over those of an unperfected secured party (see the discussion earlier in this chapter). The trustee also has rights equivalent to those of the debtor. In addition, the trustee has the power to avoid (cancel) certain types of transactions, including those transactions that the debtor could rightfully avoid.

---

9. Most dollar amounts stated in the Bankruptcy Code are adjusted automatically every three years on April 1, based on changes in the Consumer Price Index. The new adjusted amounts are rounded to the nearest $25. The amounts stated in this chapter are in accordance with those computed on April 1, 2004.

Property Distribution   Creditors are either secured or unsecured. As discussed previously, a *secured* creditor has a security interest in collateral that secures the debt. An *unsecured* creditor does not have any security interest.

Secured Creditors.   The Code provides that a consumer-debtor, within thirty days of the filing of a Chapter 7 petition or before the date of the first meeting of the creditors (whichever is first), must file with the clerk a statement of intention with respect to the secured collateral. The statement must indicate whether the debtor will retain the collateral or surrender it to the secured party.[10] The trustee is obligated to enforce the debtor's statement within forty-five days after the statement is filed.

If the collateral is surrendered to the perfected secured party, the secured creditor can enforce the security interest either by accepting the property in full satisfaction of the debt or by foreclosing on the collateral and using the proceeds to pay off the debt. Thus, the secured party has priority over unsecured parties to the proceeds from the disposition of the secured collateral. Indeed, the Code provides that if the value of the secured collateral exceeds the secured party's claim, the secured party also has priority to the proceeds in an amount that will cover reasonable fees (including attorneys' fees, if provided for in the security agreement) and costs incurred because of the debtor's default. The trustee uses any excess over this amount to satisfy the claims of unsecured creditors. Should the secured collateral be insufficient to cover the secured debt owed, the secured creditor becomes an unsecured creditor for the remainder of the debt.

Unsecured Creditors.   Bankruptcy law establishes an order or priority for classes of debts owed to *unsecured* creditors, and they are paid in the order of their priority. Each class of debt must be fully paid before the next class is entitled to any of the proceeds—if there are sufficient funds to pay the entire class. If not, the proceeds are distributed *proportionately* to each creditor in the class, and all classes lower in priority on the list receive nothing. The order of priority among classes of unsecured creditors is as follows:

1 Administrative expenses—including court costs, trustee fees, and bankruptcy attorneys' fees.

2 In an involuntary bankruptcy, expenses incurred by the debtor in the ordinary course of business from the date of the filing of the petition up to the appointment of the trustee or the issuance by the court of an order for relief.

3 Unpaid wages, salaries, and commissions earned within ninety days of the filing of the petition, limited to $4,925 per claimant. Any claim in excess of $4,925 is treated as a claim of a general creditor (listed as number 9 below).

4 Unsecured claims for contributions to be made to employee benefit plans, limited to services performed during 180 days prior to the filing of the bankruptcy petition and $4,925 per employee.

5 Claims by farmers and fishers, up to $4,925, against debtor operators of grain storage or fish storage or processing facilities.

---

10. Also, if applicable, the debtor must specify whether the collateral will be claimed as exempt property and whether the debtor intends to redeem the property or reaffirm the debt secured by the collateral (reaffirmation will be discussed shortly).

6 Consumer deposits of up to $2,225 given to the debtor before the petition was filed in connection with the purchase, lease, or rental of property or the purchase of services that were not received or provided. Any claim in excess of $2,225 is treated as a claim of a general creditor (listed as number 9 below).

7 Paternity, alimony, maintenance, and support debts.

8 Certain taxes and penalties due to government units, such as income and property taxes.

9 Claims of general creditors.

Discharge   From the debtor's point of view, the purpose of a liquidation proceeding is to obtain a fresh start through the discharge of debts.[11] Certain debts, however, are not dischargeable in a liquidation proceeding. Also, certain debtors may not qualify—because of their conduct—to have all debts discharged in bankruptcy.

Exceptions to Discharge.   Claims that are not dischargeable under Chapter 7 include the following:

1 Claims for back taxes accruing within three years prior to bankruptcy.[12]

2 Claims for amounts borrowed by the debtor to pay federal taxes.

3 Claims against property or money obtained by the debtor under false pretenses or by false representations.

4 Claims by creditors who were not notified of the bankruptcy; these claims did not appear on the schedules the debtor was required to file.

5 Claims based on fraud or misuse of funds by the debtor while she or he was acting in a fiduciary capacity or claims involving the debtor's embezzlement or larceny.

6 Alimony, child support, and (with certain exceptions) property settlements.

7 Claims based on willful or malicious conduct by the debtor toward another or the property of another.

8 Certain government fines and penalties.

9 Certain student loans, unless payment of the loans imposes an undue hardship on the debtor and the debtor's dependents.

10 Consumer debts of more than $1,225 for luxury goods or services owed to a single creditor incurred within sixty days of the order for relief. This denial of discharge is a rebuttable presumption (that is, the denial may be challenged by the debtor), however, and any debts reasonably incurred to support the debtor or dependents are not classified as luxuries.

11 Cash advances totaling more than $1,225 that are extensions of open-end consumer credit obtained by the debtor within sixty days of the order for relief. A denial of discharge of these debts is also a rebuttable presumption.

12 Judgments or consent decrees against a debtor as a result of the debtor's operation of a motor vehicle while intoxicated.

BE AWARE   Often, a discharge in bankruptcy—even under Chapter 7—does not free a debtor of *all* of his or her debts.

---

11. Discharges are granted under Chapter 7 only to *individuals,* not to corporations or partnerships. The latter may use Chapter 11 (reorganization), or they may terminate their existence under state law.

12. This includes federal and state income taxes, employment taxes, taxes on gross receipts, property taxes, excise taxes, customs duties, and any other taxes for which the government claims the debtor is liable in some capacity. See 11 U.S.C. Sections 507(a)(8), 523(a)(1).

In the following case, an employer sought to have a debt to an ex-employee for unpaid commissions discharged in bankruptcy. The question before the court was whether the debt arose from "willful and malicious injury" caused by the debtor's tortious conduct, which would mean that it was not dischargeable.

CASE 16.2 ■ In re Jercich

United States Court of Appeals,
Ninth Circuit, 2001.
238 F.3d 1202.

FACTS In June 1981, James Petralia began to work for George Jercich, Inc., a mortgage company wholly owned and operated by George Jercich. Petralia's primary duty was to obtain investors to fund the home loans. Jercich agreed to pay Petralia a salary plus monthly commissions for loans that were funded through his efforts. When Jercich failed to pay the commissions, Petralia quit and filed a suit in a California state court against Jercich. The court found that Jercich had not paid Petralia; that Jercich had the clear ability to make the payments to Petralia, but chose not to do so; that instead of paying Petralia and other employees, Jercich used the funds for personal investments, including a horse ranch; and that Jercich's behavior was willful and deliberate and constituted "substantial oppression." The court ruled in Petralia's favor. Jercich appealed this ruling to a state intermediate appellate court and filed for bankruptcy in a federal bankruptcy court. The state court affirmed the judgment against Jercich, but the bankruptcy court held that the debt was dischargeable. A bankruptcy appellate panel affirmed this holding.[a] Petralia appealed to the U.S. Court of Appeals for the Ninth Circuit.

ISSUE Did Jercich's debt to Petralia arise from "willful and malicious injury" caused by the debtor's tortious (wrongful) conduct?

a. A *bankruptcy appellate panel,* with the consent of the parties, has jurisdiction to hear appeals from final judgments, orders, and decrees of bankruptcy judges.

DECISION Yes. The U.S. Court of Appeals for the Ninth Circuit reversed the decision of the bankruptcy appellate panel and held that Jercich's debt to Petralia was not dischargeable.

REASON The U.S. Court of Appeals for the Ninth Circuit recognized that "an intentional breach of contract *generally* will not give rise to a nondischargeable debt." The court held, however, that "where an intentional breach of contract is accompanied by tortious conduct which results in willful and malicious injury, the resulting debt is excepted from discharge." Based on the state court's findings, "Jercich's nonpayment of wages * * * constituted tortious conduct." Furthermore, "the injury to Petralia was willful. As the state court found, Jercich knew he owed the wages to Petralia and that injury to Petralia was substantially certain to occur if the wages were not paid; and Jercich had the clear ability to pay Petralia his wages, yet chose not to pay and instead used the money for his own personal benefit. He therefore inflicted willful injury on Petralia. * * * Jercich's deliberate and willful failure to pay was found by the state trial court to constitute substantial oppression, which by definition is 'despicable conduct that subjects a person to cruel and unjust hardship in conscious disregard of that person's rights.' We hold that these * * * findings are sufficient to show that the injury inflicted by Jercich was malicious."

FOR CRITICAL ANALYSIS—Social Consideration
A fundamental policy of bankruptcy law is to give a "fresh start" only to the "honest but unfortunate debtor." What corollary to this policy is the basis for some of the exceptions to discharge listed previously?

Objections to Discharge. In addition to the exceptions to discharge previously listed, the following circumstances (relating to the debtor's conduct and not the debt) will cause a discharge to be denied:

1. The debtor's concealment or destruction of property with the intent to hinder, delay, or defraud a creditor.

2. The debtor's fraudulent concealment or destruction of financial records.

3 The granting of a discharge to the debtor within six years of the filing of the petition.[13]

When a discharge is denied under these circumstances, the debtor's assets are still distributed to the creditors, but the debtor remains liable for the unpaid portions of all claims.

Reaffirmation of Debt. A debtor may voluntarily agree to pay off a debt—for example, a debt owed to a family member, close friend, or some other party—even though the debt could be discharged in bankruptcy. An agreement to pay a debt dischargeable in bankruptcy is referred to as a **reaffirmation agreement.**

To be enforceable, reaffirmation agreements must be made before a debtor is granted a discharge, and they must be filed with the court. Approval by the court is required unless the debtor's attorney files an affidavit stating that (1) the debtor has been fully informed of the consequences of the agreement (and a default under the agreement), (2) the agreement is made voluntarily, and (3) the agreement does not impose undue hardship on the debtor or the debtor's family. If the debtor is not represented by an attorney, court approval is required and a separate hearing is held. The court will approve the reaffirmation only if the court finds that the agreement will not result in undue hardship to the debtor and that the agreement is in the debtor's best interests.

The agreement must contain a clear and conspicuous statement advising the debtor that reaffirmation is not required. The debtor can rescind, or cancel, the agreement at any time prior to discharge or within sixty days of filing the agreement, whichever is later. This rescission period must be stated *clearly* and *conspicuously* in the reaffirmation agreement.

REAFFIRMATION AGREEMENT
An agreement between a debtor and a creditor in which the debtor voluntarily agrees to pay, or reaffirm, a debt dischargeable in bankruptcy. To be enforceable, the agreement must be made before the debtor is granted a discharge.

CHAPTER 11—REORGANIZATION

The type of bankruptcy proceeding used most commonly by corporate debtors is the Chapter 11 *reorganization.* In a reorganization, the creditors and the debtor formulate a plan under which the debtor pays a portion of its debts and the rest of the debts are discharged. The debtor is allowed to continue in business. Although this type of bankruptcy is commonly a corporate reorganization, any debtor (except a stockbroker or a commodities broker) who is eligible for Chapter 7 relief is eligible for relief under Chapter 11.[14] Railroads are also eligible.

The same principles that govern the filing of a liquidation petition apply to reorganization proceedings. The case may be brought either voluntarily or involuntarily. The same principles govern the entry of the order for relief. The automatic-stay provision is also applicable in reorganizations.

A bankruptcy court, after notice and a hearing, may dismiss or suspend all proceedings in a case at any time if dismissal or suspension would better serve the interests of the creditors. The Code also allows a court, after notice and a hearing, to dismiss a case under reorganization "for cause." Cause includes the absence of a reasonable likelihood of rehabilitation, the inability to effect a plan, and an unreasonable delay by the debtor that is prejudicial to (may harm the

A WorldCom executive discusses the company's filing for Chapter 11 bankruptcy protection in 2002. The company filed for bankruptcy after the disclosure that it had hidden almost $4 billion in expenses through deceptive accounting practices. What procedures are followed in a Chapter 11 reorganization? (AP Photo/Diane Bondareff)

---

13. A discharge under Chapter 13 of the Code within six years of the filing of the petition does not bar (prevent) a subsequent Chapter 7 discharge when a good faith Chapter 13 plan paid at least 70 percent of all allowed unsecured claims and was the debtor's "best effort."

14. *Toibb v. Radloff,* 501 U.S. 157, 111 S.Ct. 2197, 115 L.Ed.2d 145 (1991).

interests of) creditors.[15] A debtor need not be insolvent to be entitled to Chapter 11 protection.[16]

Workouts   In some instances, creditors may prefer private, negotiated debt-adjustment agreements, also known as **workouts,** to bankruptcy proceedings. Often, these out-of-court workouts are much more flexible and thus more conducive to a speedy settlement. Speed is critical because delay is one of the most costly elements in any bankruptcy proceeding. Another advantage of workouts is that they avoid the various administrative costs of bankruptcy proceedings. See the *Application* feature at the end of this chapter for suggestions for businesspersons who are contemplating reorganization under Chapter 11.

WORKOUT
An out-of-court agreement between a debtor and creditors in which the parties work out a payment plan or schedule under which the debtor's debts can be discharged.

Debtor in Possession   On entry of the order for relief, the debtor generally continues to operate the business as a **debtor in possession (DIP).** The court, however, may appoint a trustee (often referred to as a *receiver*) to operate the debtor's business if gross mismanagement of the business is shown or if appointing a trustee is in the best interests of the estate.

The DIP's role is similar to that of a trustee in a liquidation. The DIP is entitled to avoid preferential payments made to creditors and fraudulent transfers of assets. The DIP has the power to decide whether to cancel or assume obligations under executory contracts (contracts that have not yet been performed) that were made prior to the petition.

DEBTOR IN POSSESSION (DIP)
In Chapter 11 bankruptcy proceedings, a debtor who is allowed to continue in possession of the estate in property (the business) and to continue business operations.

ETHICAL ISSUE 16.2

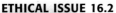

Should those who "bankrupt" a firm be allowed to continue to manage the firm as debtors in possession? Chapter 11 reorganizations have become the target of substantial criticism. One of the arguments against Chapter 11 is that it allows the very managers who "bankrupted" a firm to continue to manage it as debtors in possession while the firm is in Chapter 11 proceedings. According to some critics, the main beneficiaries of Chapter 11 corporate reorganizations are not the shareholder-owners of the corporations but rather attorneys and current management. Basically, these critics argue that reorganizations do not preserve companies' assets because large firms must pay millions of dollars for attorneys and accountants during the reorganization process, which can take years to complete. ▪

The Reorganization Plan   The purpose of a reorganization plan is to rehabilitate the debtor by conserving and administering the debtor's assets in the hope of an eventual return to successful operation and solvency. The plan must be fair and equitable and must do the following:

1 Designate classes of claims and interests.

2 Specify the treatment to be afforded the classes. (The plan must provide the same treatment for each claim in a particular class.)

3 Provide an adequate means for execution.

Filing the Plan.   Only the debtor may file a plan within the first 120 days after the date of the bankruptcy court's order for relief. If the debtor does not meet the 120-day deadline, however, or if the debtor fails to obtain the required creditor consent

---

15. See 11 U.S.C. Section 1112(b).
16. *In re Johns-Manville Corp.,* 36 Bankr. 727 (S.D.N.Y. 1984).

(see below) within 180 days, any party may propose a plan. The plan need not provide for full repayment to unsecured creditors. Instead, unsecured creditors receive a percentage of each dollar owed to them by the debtor. If a small-business debtor chooses to avoid creditors' committees, the time for the debtor's filing is shortened to 100 days, and any other party's plan must be filed within 160 days.

Acceptance and Confirmation of the Plan.   Once the plan has been developed, it is submitted to each class of creditors for acceptance. Each class must accept the plan unless the class is not adversely affected by the plan. A class has accepted the plan when a majority of the creditors, representing two-thirds of the amount of the total claim, vote to approve it. Even when all classes of claims accept the plan, the court may refuse to confirm it if it is not "in the best interests of the creditors." A spouse or child of the debtor can block the plan if it does not provide for payment of his or her claims in cash.

Even if only one class of claims has accepted the plan, the court may still confirm the plan under the Code's so-called **cram-down provision.** In other words, the court may confirm the plan over the objections of a class of creditors. Before the court can exercise this right of cram-down confirmation, it must be demonstrated that the plan "does not discriminate unfairly" against any creditors and that the plan is "fair and equitable."

Chapter 11 allows debtors considerable freedom to do business. But this freedom is not without limits, as the following case illustrates.

CRAM-DOWN PROVISION
A provision of the Bankruptcy Code that allows a court to confirm a debtor's Chapter 11 reorganization plan even though only one class of creditors has accepted it. To exercise the court's right under this provision, the court must demonstrate that the plan does not discriminate unfairly against any creditors and is fair and equitable.

Case 16.3 In re Beyond.com Corp.

United States Bankruptcy Court,
Northern District of California, 2003.
289 Bankr. 138.

COMPANY PROFILE *Founded in 1994, Beyond.com Corporation principally built, hosted, managed, and marketed online stores from its base in Santa Clara, California. Beyond.com's first venture was a retail Web site for computer products. In 2000, the firm began to focus on providing support for other Web merchants, showcasing its clients' e-Stores in an Internet mall. Despite the change in focus, however, Beyond.com was unable to pay its debts, and the company ceased operations.*

FACTS In 2002, Beyond.com filed a Chapter 11 petition and a reorganization plan in a federal bankruptcy court. The company also filed a disclosure statement, which set out the details underlying the plan. Among other things, the plan envisioned that the reorganized debtor would "retain all of the rights, powers, and duties of a trustee under the Bankruptcy Code." The plan appointed the debtor's former chief operating officer, John Barratt, "Liquidation Manager." In this capacity, Barratt could dispose of the debtor's property, enter into agreements on the debtor's behalf, file suits against unidentified

defendants, and retain and pay advisers and other "professionals." Under most circumstances, none of these actions would be subject to court supervision or limitation. The plan also limited Barratt's personal liability for acts performed in this capacity. The debtor asked the court to approve the disclosure statement, as required before a plan can be submitted to creditors.

ISSUE Did the plan comply with the notice requirements and court supervision provisions contained in Chapter 11 of the Bankruptcy Code?

DECISION No. The bankruptcy court refused to confirm Beyond.com's disclosure statement and reorganization plan.

REASON The court stated, "Conceptually, Beyond.com's plan and disclosure statement is as freewheeling with the Bankruptcy Code * * * as Enron's accountants were with the tax laws in the 1990s." The court found that "Beyond.com's proposed plan contains numerous provisions that modify the requirements of the Bankruptcy Code," including "provisions that dramatically reduce notice to creditors of matters that the drafters of the

CASE 16.3—Continued

Bankruptcy Code * * * considered fundamental." These modifications to the Code, in the court's view, "are not minor, ministerial or simply pragmatic. In effect, the plan affords the reorganized debtor the prerogative to comply selectively with the provisions of the Bankruptcy Code * * * without judicial supervision." The court concluded that these defects could not be cured and thus the plan did not comply with the notice requirements in the Code.

FOR CRITICAL ANALYSIS—Social Consideration
For the best interest of creditors, how much information should be revealed in a disclosure statement accompanying a reorganization plan?

Discharge. The plan is binding on confirmation. The debtor is given a reorganization discharge from all claims not protected under the plan. This discharge does not apply to any claims that would be denied discharge under liquidation.

INDIVIDUALS' REPAYMENT PLAN—CHAPTER 13

REMEMBER A secured debt is a debt in which a security interest in personal property or fixtures assures payment of the obligation.

Chapter 13 of the Bankruptcy Code provides for the "Adjustment of Debts of an Individual with Regular Income." Individuals (not partnerships or corporations) with regular income who owe fixed unsecured debts of less than $307,675 or fixed secured debts of less than $922,975 may take advantage of bankruptcy repayment plans. This includes salaried employees; sole proprietors; and individuals who live on welfare, Social Security, fixed pensions, or investment income. Many small-business debtors have a choice of filing under either Chapter 11 or Chapter 13. Repayment plans offer several advantages. One advantage is that they are less expensive and less complicated than reorganization proceedings or liquidation proceedings.

A Chapter 13 repayment plan can be initiated only by the filing of a voluntary petition by the debtor. Certain liquidation and reorganization cases may be converted to Chapter 13 with the consent of the debtor. A Chapter 13 repayment plan may be converted to a Chapter 7 liquidation at the request of either the debtor or, under certain circumstances, a creditor. A Chapter 13 repayment plan may also be converted to a Chapter 11 reorganization after a hearing. On the filing of a petition under Chapter 13, a trustee must be appointed. The automatic stay previously discussed also takes effect. Although the stay applies to all or part of a consumer debt, it does not apply to any business debt incurred by the debtor.

The Repayment Plan Shortly after the petition is filed, the debtor must file a repayment plan. This plan may provide either for payment of all obligations in full or for payment of a lesser amount. A plan of rehabilitation by repayment provides for the debtor's future earnings or income to be turned over to the trustee as necessary for execution of the plan.

Filing the Plan. The time for payment under the plan may not exceed three years unless the court approves an extension. The term, with extension, may not exceed five years.

The Code requires the debtor to make "timely" payments, and the trustee is required to ensure that the debtor commences these payments. The debtor must begin making payments under the proposed plan within thirty days after the plan has been filed with the court. If the plan has not been confirmed, the trustee is instructed to retain the payments until the plan is confirmed and then distribute them accordingly. If the plan is denied, the trustee will return the payments to the debtor less any costs. If the debtor fails to make timely payments or to begin payments within the thirty-day period, the court may convert the repayment plan to a liquidation bankruptcy or dismiss the petition.

Confirmation of the Plan.   After the plan is filed, the court holds a confirmation hearing, at which interested parties may object to the plan. The court will confirm a plan with respect to each claim of a secured creditor under any of the following circumstances:

1 If the secured creditors have accepted the plan.

2 If the plan provides that creditors retain their claims against the debtor's property, and the value of the property to be distributed to the creditors under the plan is not less than the secured portion of their claims.

3 If the debtor surrenders the property securing the claim to the creditors.

Objection to the Plan.   Unsecured creditors do not have a vote to confirm a repayment plan, but they can object to it. The court can approve a plan over the objection of the trustee or any unsecured creditor only in either of the following situations:

1 When the value of the property to be distributed under the plan is at least equal to the amount of the claims.

2 When all the debtor's projected disposable income to be received during the three-year plan period will be applied to making payments. Disposable income is all income received less amounts needed to support the debtor and dependents and/or amounts needed to meet ordinary expenses to continue the operation of a business.

Discharge   After the completion of all payments, the court grants a discharge of all debts provided for by the repayment plan. Except for allowed claims not provided for by the plan, certain long-term debts provided for by the plan, and claims for alimony and child support, all other debts are dischargeable. A discharge of debts under a Chapter 13 repayment plan is sometimes referred to as a "superdischarge." One of the reasons for this is that the law allows a Chapter 13 discharge to include fraudulently incurred debt and claims resulting from malicious or willful injury. Therefore, a discharge under Chapter 13 may be much more beneficial to some debtors than a liquidation discharge under Chapter 7 might be.

Even if the debtor does not complete the plan, a hardship discharge may be granted if failure to complete the plan was due to circumstances beyond the debtor's control and if the value of the property distributed under the plan was greater than creditors would have received in a liquidation proceeding. A discharge can be revoked within one year if it was obtained by fraud.

FAMILY FARMERS—CHAPTER 12

In 1986, to help relieve economic pressure on small farmers, Congress created Chapter 12 of the Bankruptcy Code. For purposes of Chapter 12, a *family farmer* is one whose gross income is at least 50 percent farm dependent and whose debts are at least 80 percent farm related.[17] The total debt must not exceed $1.5 million.

BE CAREFUL Courts, trustees, and creditors carefully monitor Chapter 13 debtors. If payments are not made, a court can require a debtor to explain why and may allow a creditor to take back her or his property.

---

17. Note that the Bankruptcy Code defines a *family farmer* differently than a *farmer*. To be a farmer, a person or business must receive 80 percent of his or her gross income from a farming operation that he or she owns or operates—see footnote 8.

A partnership or a closely held corporation (see Chapter 20) that is at least 50 percent owned by the farm family can also take advantage of Chapter 12. The procedure for filing a family-farmer bankruptcy plan is very similar to the procedure for filing a repayment plan under Chapter 13.

Court confirmation of the plan is the same as for a repayment plan. In summary, the plan must provide for payment of secured debts at the value of the collateral. If the secured debt exceeds the value of the collateral, the remaining debt is unsecured. For unsecured debtors, the plan must be confirmed if either the value of the property to be distributed under the plan equals the amount of the claim or the plan provides that all of the farmer-debtor's disposable income to be received in a three-year period (or longer, by court approval) will be applied to making payments. Completion of payments under the plan discharges all debts provided for by the plan.

APPLICATION ▪ What Can You Do to Prepare for a Chapter 11 Reorganization?*

Chapter 11 of the Bankruptcy Code expresses the broad public policy of encouraging commerce. To this end, Chapter 11 allows a financially troubled business firm to petition for reorganization in bankruptcy while it is still solvent so that the firm's business can continue. Small businesses, however, do not fare very well under Chapter 11. Although some corporations that enter Chapter 11 emerge as functioning entities, very few small companies survive the process. The reason is that Chapter 11 proceedings are prolonged and extremely costly, and whether a firm survives is largely a matter of size. The greater the firm's assets, the greater the likelihood it will emerge from Chapter 11 intact.

PLAN AHEAD

If you ever are a small-business owner contemplating Chapter 11 reorganization, you can improve your chances of being among the survivors by planning ahead. To ensure the greatest possibility of success, you should take action before, not after, entering bankruptcy proceedings. Your first step, of course, should be to do everything possible to avoid having to resort to Chapter 11. Discuss your financial troubles openly and cooperatively with creditors to see if you can agree on a workout or some other arrangement.

If you appear to have no choice but to file for Chapter 11 protection, try to interest a lender in loaning you funds

*This *Application* is not meant to substitute for the services of an attorney who is licensed to practice law in your state.

to see you through the bankruptcy. If your business is a small corporation, you might try to negotiate a favorable deal with a major investor. For example, you could offer to transfer ownership of stock to the investor in return for a loan to pay the costs of the bankruptcy proceedings and an option to repurchase the stock when the firm becomes profitable again.

CONSULT WITH CREDITORS

Most important, you should form a Chapter 11 plan prior to entering bankruptcy proceedings. Consult with creditors in advance to see what kind of a plan would be acceptable to them, and prepare your plan accordingly. Having an acceptable plan prepared before you file will expedite the proceedings and thus save substantially on costs.

CHECKLIST FOR THE SMALL-BUSINESS OWNER

1. Try to negotiate workouts with creditors to avoid costly Chapter 11 proceedings.
2. If your business is a small corporation, see if a major investor will loan you funds to help you pay bankruptcy costs in return for stock ownership.
3. Consult with creditors in advance, and have an acceptable Chapter 11 plan prepared before filing to expedite bankruptcy proceedings and save on costs.

■ KEY TERMS

after-acquired property   486
artisan's lien   491
attachment   483
automatic stay   501
collateral   482
consumer-debtor   499
continuation statement   486
cram-down provision   508
debtor   482
debtor in possession (DIP)   507
default   482
deficiency judgment   490
discharge   497
estate in property   501
execution   489

financing statement   482
floating lien   487
garnishment   493
guarantor   495
homestead exemption   496
innkeeper's lien   492
levy   489
mechanic's lien   491
mortgagee   494
mortgagor   494
order for relief   500
perfection   484
petition in bankruptcy   498
pledge   485
proceeds   486

purchase-money security
   interest (PMSI)   485
reaffirmation agreement   506
secured party   482
secured transaction   481
security agreement   482
security interest   482
surety   495
suretyship   495
U.S. trustee   502
workout   507
writ of attachment   493
writ of execution   493

CHAPTER SUMMARY ▪ Creditors' Rights and Bankruptcy

SECURED TRANSACTIONS

Creating a Security Interest (See pages 482–484.)	1. Unless the creditor has possession of the collateral, there must be a written or authenticated security agreement that is signed or authenticated by the debtor and describes the collateral subject to the security interest. 2. The secured party must give value to the debtor. 3. The debtor must have rights in the collateral—some ownership interest or right to obtain possession of the specified collateral.

Perfecting a Security Interest (See pages 484–486.)	1. *Perfection by filing*—The most common method of perfection is by filing a financing statement containing the names of the secured party and the debtor and indicating the collateral covered by the financing statement.
	
	    a. Communication of the financing statement to the appropriate filing office, together with the correct filing fee, constitutes a filing.
	
	    b. The financing statement must be filed under the name of the debtor; fictitious (trade) names normally are not accepted.
	
	    c. The classification of collateral determines whether filing is necessary and where to file.
	
	 2. *Perfection without filing—*
	
	    a. By transfer of collateral—The debtor can transfer possession of the collateral to the secured party. A *pledge* is an example of this type of transfer.
	
	    b. By attachment, such as the attachment of a purchase-money security interest (PMSI) in consumer goods—If the secured party has a PMSI in consumer goods (goods bought or used by the debtor for personal, family, or household purposes), the secured party's security interest is perfected automatically. In all, thirteen types of security interests can be perfected by attachment.

CHAPTER SUMMARY ▣ Creditors' Rights and Bankruptcy—Continued

The Scope of a Security Interest (See pages 486–487.)	A security agreement can cover collateral in the present possession or control of the debtor, proceeds from a disposition of secured collateral, property acquired after the execution of the security agreement, and future advances made against a line of credit.
Priority of Claims to a Debtor's Collateral (See pages 487–489.)	See Exhibit 16–2 on page 488.

Default (See pages 489–491.)	On the debtor's default, the secured party may do either of the following:
	
	1. Take possession (peacefully or by court order) of the collateral covered by the security agreement and then pursue one of two alternatives:
	
	  a. Retain the collateral (unless the secured party has a PMSI in consumer goods and the debtor has paid 60 percent or more of the selling price or loan).
	
	  b. Dispose of the collateral in accordance with the requirements of UCC 9–602(7), 9–603, 9–610(a), and 9–613.
	
	2. Relinquish the security interest and use any judicial remedy available, such as proceeding to judgment on the underlying debt, followed by execution and levy on the nonexempt assets of the debtor.

ADDITIONAL LAWS ASSISTING CREDITORS

Liens (See pages 491–493.)	1. *Mechanic's lien*—A nonpossessory, filed lien on an owner's real estate for labor, services, or materials furnished to or made on the realty.
	
	2. *Artisan's lien*—A possessory lien on an owner's personal property for labor performed or value added.
	
	3. *Innkeeper's lien*—A possessory lien on a hotel guest's baggage for hotel charges that remain unpaid.
	
	4. *Judicial liens*—
	
	  a. Attachment—A court-ordered seizure of property prior to a court's final determination of the creditor's rights to the property. Attachment is available only on the creditor's posting of a bond and strict compliance with the applicable state statutes.
	
	  b. Writ of execution—A court order directing the sheriff to seize (levy) and sell a debtor's nonexempt real or personal property to satisfy a court's judgment in the creditor's favor.

Garnishment (See pages 493–494.)	A collection remedy that allows the creditor to attach a debtor's money (such as wages owed or bank accounts) and property that are held by a third person.
Mortgage Foreclosure (See page 494.)	On the debtor's default, the entire mortgage debt is due and payable, allowing the creditor to foreclose on the realty by selling it to satisfy the debt.
Suretyship or Guaranty (See pages 494–496.)	Under contract, a third person agrees to be primarily or secondarily liable for the debt owed by the principal debtor. A creditor can turn to this third person for satisfaction of the debt.

ADDITIONAL LAWS ASSISTING DEBTORS

Exemptions (See pages 496–497.)	Numerous laws, including consumer protection statutes, assist debtors. Additionally, state laws exempt certain types of real and personal property from levy of execution or attachment. 1. *Real property*—Each state permits a debtor to retain the family home, either in its entirety or up to a specified dollar amount, free from the claims of unsecured creditors or trustees in bankruptcy (homestead exemption).

(Continued)

CHAPTER SUMMARY ▣ Creditors' Rights and Bankruptcy—Continued

Exemptions—Continued	2. *Personal property*—Personal property that is most often exempt from satisfaction of judgment debts includes the following: a. Household furniture up to a specified dollar amount. b. Clothing and certain personal possessions. c. Transportation vehicles up to a specified dollar amount. d. Certain classified animals, such as livestock and pets. e. Equipment used in a business or trade up to a specified dollar amount.

BANKRUPTCY—A COMPARISON OF CHAPTERS 7, 11, 12, AND 13

Issue	Chapter 7	Chapter 11	Chapters 12 and 13
Purpose	Liquidation.	Reorganization.	Adjustment.
Who Can Petition	Debtor (voluntary) or creditors (involuntary).	Debtor (voluntary) or creditors (involuntary).	Debtor (voluntary) only.
Who Can Be a Debtor	Any "person" (including partnerships and corporations) except railroads, insurance companies, banks, savings and loan institutions, investment companies licensed by the Small Business Administration, and credit unions. Farmers and charitable institutions cannot be involuntarily petitioned.	Any debtor eligible for Chapter 7 relief; railroads are also eligible.	*Chapter 12*—Any family farmer (one whose gross income is at least 50 percent farm dependent and whose debts are at least 80 percent farm related) or any partnership or closely held corporation at least 50 percent owned by a farm family, when total debt does not exceed $1.5 million. *Chapter 13*—Any individual (not partnerships or corporations) with regular income who owes fixed unsecured debts of less than $307,675 or fixed secured debts of less than $922,975.
Procedure Leading to Discharge	Nonexempt property is sold with proceeds to be distributed (in order) to priority groups. Dischargeable debts are terminated.	Plan is submitted; if it is approved and followed, debts are discharged.	Plan is submitted and must be approved if the debtor turns over disposable income for a three-year period; if the plan is followed, debts are discharged.
Advantages	On liquidation and distribution, most debts are discharged, and the debtor has an opportunity for a fresh start.	Debtor continues in business. Creditors can either accept the plan, or it can be "crammed down" on them. The plan allows for the reorganization and liquidation of debts over the plan period.	Debtor continues in business or possession of assets. If the plan is approved, most debts are discharged after a three-year period.

▪▪ FOR REVIEW

Answers for the even-numbered questions in this For Review *section can be found in Appendix I at the end of this text.*

1 What is a security interest? What three requirements must be met to create an enforceable security interest?

2 What is a prejudgment attachment? What is a writ of execution? How does a creditor use these remedies?

3 What is garnishment? When might a creditor undertake a garnishment proceeding?

4 In a bankruptcy proceeding, what constitutes the debtor's estate in property? What property is exempt from the estate under federal bankruptcy law?

5 In a Chapter 11 reorganization, what is the role of the debtor in possession?

▪▪ QUESTIONS AND CASE PROBLEMS

16–1. Oral Security Agreements. Marsh has a prize horse named Arabian Knight. Marsh is in need of working capital. She borrows $5,000 from Mendez, who takes possession of Arabian Knight as security for the loan. No written agreement is signed. Discuss whether, in the absence of a written agreement, Mendez has a security interest in Arabian Knight. If Mendez does have a security interest, is it a perfected security interest?

16–2. Artisan's Lien. Air Ruidoso, Ltd., operated a commuter airline and air charter service between Ruidoso, New Mexico, and airports in Albuquerque and El Paso. Executive Aviation Center, Inc., provided services for airlines at the Albuquerque International Airport. When Air Ruidoso failed to pay more than $10,000 that it owed for fuel, oil, and oxygen, Executive Aviation took possession of Air Ruidoso's plane. Executive Aviation claimed that it had a lien on the plane and filed a suit in a New Mexico state court to foreclose. Do supplies such as fuel, oil, and oxygen qualify as "materials" for the purpose of creating an artisan's lien? Why or why not?

16–3. Distribution of Property. Runyan voluntarily petitions for bankruptcy. He has three major claims against his estate. One is by Calvin, a friend who holds Runyan's negotiable promissory note for $2,500; one is by Kohak, an employee who is owed three months' back wages of $4,500; and one is by the First Bank of Sunny Acres on an unsecured loan of $5,000. In addition, Martinez, an accountant retained by the trustee, is owed $500, and property taxes of $1,000 are owed to Micanopa County. Runyan's nonexempt property has been liquidated, with the proceeds totaling $5,000. Discuss fully what amount each party will receive, and why.

16–4. Guaranty. In 1988, Jamieson-Chippewa Investment Co. entered into a five-year commercial lease with TDM Pharmacy, Inc., for certain premises in Ellisville, Missouri, on which TDM intended to operate a small drugstore. Dennis and Tereasa McClintock ran the pharmacy business. The lease granted TDM three additional five-year options to renew. The lease was signed by TDM and by the McClintocks individually as guarantors. The lease did not state that the guaranty was continuing. In fact, there were no words of guaranty in the lease other than the single word "Guarantors" on the signature page. In 1993, Dennis McClintock, acting as the president of TDM, exercised TDM's option to renew the lease for one term. Three years later, when the pharmacy failed, TDM defaulted on the lease. Jamieson-Chippewa filed a suit in a Missouri state court against the McClintocks for the rent for the rest of the term, based on their guaranty. The McClintocks filed a motion for summary judgment, contending that they had not guaranteed any rent payments beyond the initial five-year term. How should the court rule? Why? [*Jamieson-Chippewa Investment Co. v. McClintock*, 996 S.W.2d 84 (Mo.App.E.D. 1999)]

16–5. Pledge. On April 14, 1992, David and Myrna Grossman borrowed $10,000 from Brookfield Bank in Brookfield, Connecticut, and signed a note to repay the principal with interest. As collateral, the Grossmans gave the bank possession of stock certificates representing 123 shares in General Electric Co. The note was nonnegotiable and thus was not subject to UCC Article 3. On May 8, the bank closed its doors. The Grossmans did not make any payments on the note and refused to permit the sale of the stock to apply against the debt. The Grossmans' note and collateral were assigned to Premier Capital, Inc., which filed a suit in a Connecticut state court against them, seeking to collect the principal and interest due. The Grossmans responded in part that they were entitled to credit for the value of the stock that secured the note. By the time of the trial, the stock certificates had been lost. Should a creditor have a duty to preserve collateral that is transferred into the creditor's possession as security for a loan? How should the court rule, and why? [*Premier Capital, Inc. v. Grossman*, 68 Conn.App. 51, 789 A.2d 565 (2002)]

CASE PROBLEM WITH SAMPLE ANSWER

16–6. Jon Goulet attended the University of Wisconsin in Eau Claire and Regis University in Denver, Colorado, from which he earned a bachelor's degree in history in 1972. Over the next ten years, he worked as a bartender and a restaurant manager. In 1984, he became a life insurance agent, and his income ranged from $20,000 to $30,000. In 1989, however, his agent's license was revoked for insurance fraud, and he was arrested for cocaine possession. From 1991 to 1995, Goulet was again at the University of Wisconsin, working toward, but failing to obtain, a master's degree in psychology. To pay for his studies, he took out student loans totaling $76,000. Goulet then returned to bartending and restaurant management and tried real estate sales. His income for the year 2000 was $1,490, and his expenses, excluding a child-support obligation, were $5,904. When the student loans came due, Goulet filed a petition for bankruptcy. On what ground might the loans be dischargeable? Should the court grant a discharge on this ground? Why or why not? [*Goulet v. Educational Credit Management Corp.*, 284 F.3d 773 (7th Cir. 2002)]

After you have answered this problem, compare your answer with the sample answer given on the Web site that accompanies this text. Go to http://blt.westbuslaw.com, select "Chapter 16," and click on "Case Problem with Sample Answer."

16–7. Automatic Stay. On January 22, 2001, Marlene Moffett bought a used 1998 Honda Accord from Hendrick Honda in Woodbridge, Virginia. Moffett agreed to pay $20,024.25, with interest, in sixty monthly installments, and Hendrick retained a security interest in the car. Hendrick thus had the right to repossess the car in the event of default, subject to Moffett's right of redemption. Hendrick assigned its rights under the sales agreement to Tidewater Finance Co., which perfected its security interest. The car was Moffett's only means of traveling the forty miles from her home to her workplace. In March and April 2002, Moffett missed two monthly payments. On April 25, Tidewater repossessed the car. On the same day, Moffett filed a Chapter 13 plan in a federal bankruptcy court. Moffett asked that the car be returned to her, in part under the Bankruptcy Code's automatic-stay provision. Tidewater asked the court to terminate the automatic stay so that it could sell the car. How can the interests of both the debtor and the creditor be fully protected in this case? What should the court rule? Explain. [*In re Moffett*, 356 F.3d 518 (4th Cir. 2003)]

A QUESTION OF ETHICS

16–8. In September 1986, Edward and Debora Davenport pleaded guilty in a Pennsylvania court to welfare fraud and were sentenced to probation for one year. As a condition of their probation, the Davenports were ordered to make monthly restitution payments to the county probation department, which would forward the payments to the Pennsylvania Department of Public Welfare, the victim of the Davenports' fraud. In May 1987, the Davenports filed a petition for Chapter 13 relief and listed the restitution payments among their debts. The bankruptcy court held that the restitution obligation was a dischargeable debt. Ultimately, the United States Supreme Court reviewed the case. The Court noted that the Bankruptcy Code, defines a debt as a liability on a claim and defines a claim as a right to payment. Because the restitution obligations clearly constituted a right to payment, the Court held that the obligations were dischargeable in bankruptcy. [*Pennsylvania Department of Public Welfare v. Davenport*, 495 U.S. 552, 110 S.Ct. 2126, 109 L.Ed.2d 588 (1990)]

1. Critics of this decision contend that the Court adhered to the letter, but not the spirit, of bankruptcy law in arriving at its conclusion. In what way, if any, did the Court not abide by the "spirit" of bankruptcy law?
2. Do you think that Chapter 13 plans, which allow nearly all types of debts to be discharged, tip the scales of justice too far in favor of debtors?

FOR CRITICAL ANALYSIS

16–9. Has the Bankruptcy Code made it too easy for debtors to avoid their obligations by filing for bankruptcy? What are the implications of the increased number of bankruptcy filings for future potential debtors who seek to obtain credit?

VIDEO QUESTION

16–10. Go to this text's Web site at http://blt.westbuslaw.com and select "Chapter 16." Click on "Video Questions" and view the video titled *River*. Then answer the following questions.

1. In the video, a crowd (including Mel Gibson) is gathered at a farm auction in which a neighbor's (Jim Antonio's) farming goods are being sold. The people in the crowd, who are upset because they believe that the bank is selling out the farmer, begin chanting "no sale, no sale." In an effort the calm the group, the farmer tells the crowd that "they've already foreclosed" on his farm. What does he mean?
2. Assume that the auction is a result of Chapter 7 bankruptcy proceedings. Was the farmer's petition for bankruptcy voluntary or involuntary? Explain.
3. Compare the results of a Chapter 12 bankruptcy as opposed to a Chapter 7 bankruptcy for the farmer in the video.

INTERNET EXERCISES

Go to the *Business Law Today: The Essentials* home page at <u>http://blt.westbuslaw.com</u>, select "Chapter 16," and click on "Internet Exercises." There you will find the following Internet research exercises that you can perform to learn more about topics covered in this chapter.

Activity 16–1: LEGAL PERSPECTIVE—Repossession

Activity 16–2: LEGAL PERSPECTIVE—Bankruptcy

Activity 16–3: MANAGEMENT PERSPECTIVE—Bankruptcy Alternatives

BEFORE THE TEST

Go to the *Business Law Today: The Essentials* home page at <u>http://blt.westbuslaw.com</u>, select "Chapter 16," and click on "Interactive Quizzes." You will find at least twenty interactive questions relating to this chapter.

CHAPTER 17

Agency

> "[It] is a universal principle in the law of agency,
> that the powers of the agent are to be exercised for
> the benefit of the principal only, and not of the
> agent or of third parties."
>
> Joseph Story, 1779–1845
> (Associate justice of the United States Supreme Court, 1811–1844)

CHAPTER OUTLINE

■ AGENCY RELATIONSHIPS

■ HOW AGENCY
RELATIONSHIPS
ARE FORMED

■ DUTIES OF AGENTS
AND PRINCIPALS

■ AGENT'S AUTHORITY

■ LIABILITY IN AGENCY
RELATIONSHIPS

■ HOW AGENCY
RELATIONSHIPS
ARE TERMINATED

▦ LEARNING OBJECTIVES

After reading this chapter, you should be able to answer the following questions:

1 What is the difference between an employee and an independent contractor?

2 How do agency relationships arise?

3 What duties do agents and principals owe to each other?

4 When is a principal liable for the agent's actions with respect to third parties? When is the agent liable?

5 What are some of the ways in which an agency relationship can be terminated?

AGENCY
A relationship between two parties in which one party (the agent) agrees to represent or act for the other (the principal).

AGENT
A person who agrees to represent or act for another, called the principal.

PRINCIPAL
In agency law, a person who agrees to have another, called the agent, act on her or his behalf.

One of the most common, important, and pervasive legal relationships is that of **agency**. In an agency relationship between two parties, one of the parties, called the **agent**, agrees to represent or act for the other, called the **principal**. The principal has the right to control the agent's conduct in matters entrusted to the agent, and the agent must exercise his or her powers "for the benefit of the principal only," as Justice Joseph Story indicated in the above quotation. By using agents, a principal can conduct multiple business operations simultaneously in various locations. Thus, for example, contracts that bind the principal can be made at different places with different persons at the same time.

Agency relationships permeate the business world. Indeed, agency law is essential to the existence and operation of a corporate entity, because only through its agents can a corporation function and enter into contracts. A familiar example of an agent is a corporate officer who serves in a representative capacity for the owners of the corporation. In this capacity, the officer has the authority to bind the principal (the corporation) to a contract.

■ Agency Relationships

Section 1(1) of the *Restatement (Second) of Agency*[1] defines agency as "the fiduciary relation which results from the manifestation of consent by one person to another that the other shall act in his [or her] behalf and subject to his [or her] control, and consent by the other so to act." In other words, in a principal-agent relationship, the parties have agreed that the agent will act *on behalf and instead of* the principal in negotiating and transacting business with third parties.

The term **fiduciary** is at the heart of agency law. The term can be used both as a noun and as an adjective. When used as a noun, it refers to a person having a duty created by her or his undertaking to act primarily for another's benefit in matters connected with the undertaking. When used as an adjective, as in "fiduciary relationship," it means that the relationship involves trust and confidence.

Agency relationships commonly exist between employers and employees. Agency relationships may sometimes also exist between employers and independent contractors who are hired to perform special tasks or services.

EMPLOYER-EMPLOYEE RELATIONSHIPS

Normally, all employees who deal with third parties are deemed to be agents. A salesperson in a department store, for instance, is an agent of the store's owner (the principal) and acts on the owner's behalf. Any sale of goods made by the salesperson to a customer is binding on the principal. Similarly, most representations of fact made by the salesperson with respect to the goods sold are binding on the principal.

Because employees who deal with third parties are normally deemed to be agents of their employers, agency law and employment law overlap considerably. Agency relationships, though, as will become apparent, can exist outside an employer-employee relationship and thus have a broader reach than employment laws do. Additionally, bear in mind that agency law is based on the common law. In the employment realm, many common law doctrines have been displaced by statutory law and government regulations governing employment relationships.

Employment laws (state and federal) apply only to the employer-employee relationship. Statutes governing Social Security, withholding taxes, workers' compensation, unemployment compensation, workplace safety, employment discrimination, and the like (see Chapter 18) are applicable only if employer-employee status exists. *These laws do not apply to an independent contractor.*

EMPLOYER–INDEPENDENT CONTRACTOR RELATIONSHIPS

Independent contractors are not employees because, by definition, those who hire them have no control over the details of their physical performance. Section 2 of the *Restatement (Second) of Agency* defines an **independent contractor** as follows:

> [An independent contractor is] a person who contracts with another to do something for him [or her] but who is not controlled by the other nor subject to the other's right to

FIDUCIARY
As a noun, a person having a duty created by his or her undertaking to act primarily for another's benefit in matters connected with the undertaking. As an adjective, a relationship founded on trust and confidence.

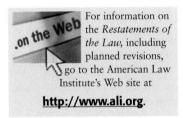
For information on the *Restatements of the Law,* including planned revisions, go to the American Law Institute's Web site at
http://www.ali.org.

INDEPENDENT CONTRACTOR
One who works for, and receives payment from, an employer but whose working conditions and methods are not controlled by the employer. An independent contractor is not an employee but may be an agent.

---

1. The *Restatement (Second) of Agency* is an authoritative summary of the law of agency and is often referred to by jurists in their decisions and opinions.

control with respect to his [or her] physical conduct in the performance of the undertaking. *He [or she] may or may not be an agent.* [Emphasis added.]

Building contractors and subcontractors are independent contractors; a property owner does not control the acts of either of these professionals. Truck drivers who own their equipment and hire themselves out on a per-job basis are independent contractors, but truck drivers who drive company trucks on a regular basis are usually employees.

The relationship between a person or firm and an independent contractor may or may not involve an agency relationship. To illustrate: An owner of real estate who hires a real estate broker to negotiate a sale of the property not only has contracted with an independent contractor (the real estate broker) but also has established an agency relationship for the specific purpose of assisting in the sale of the property. Another example is an insurance agent, who is both an independent contractor and an agent of the insurance company for which she or he sells policies. (Note that an insurance *broker*, in contrast, normally is an agent of the person obtaining insurance and not of the insurance company.)

DETERMINING EMPLOYEE STATUS

The courts are frequently asked to determine whether a particular worker is an employee or an independent contractor. How a court decides this issue can have a significant effect on the rights and liabilities of the parties.

A businessperson, an independent contractor, sits on the floor working on his laptop computer in a computer server facility. What are some significant differences between employees and independent contractors? (Thinkstock Photo)

Criteria Used by the Courts   In determining whether a worker has the status of an employee or an independent contractor, the courts often consider the following questions:

1. How much control can the employer exercise over the details of the work? (If an employer can exercise considerable control over the details of the work, this would indicate employee status. This is perhaps the most important factor weighed by the courts in determining employee status.)

2. Is the worker engaged in an occupation or business distinct from that of the employer? (If so, this points to independent-contractor status, not employee status.)

3. Is the work usually done under the employer's direction or by a specialist without supervision? (If the work is usually done under the employer's direction, this would indicate employee status.)

4. Does the employer supply the tools at the place of work? (If so, this would indicate employee status.)

5. For how long is the person employed? (If the person is employed for a long period of time, this would indicate employee status.)

6. What is the method of payment—by time period or at the completion of the job? (Payment by time period, such as once every two weeks or once a month, would indicate employee status.)

7. What degree of skill is required of the worker? (If little skill is required, this may indicate employee status.)

Sometimes, it is beneficial for workers to have employee status—to take advantage of laws protecting employees, for example. In contrast, independent-contractor status can sometimes be an advantage—for copyright ownership purposes, for example, as you will read shortly.

ETHICAL ISSUE 17.1

Why should it be left to the courts to determine who is or is not an independent contractor? Many employers prefer to designate certain workers as independent contractors rather than as employees. As long as an employee agrees to be classified as an independent contractor, why should a court interfere in this decision? The answer is, at least in part, that issues of fairness may be involved, and the common law of agency, as developed and applied by the courts, implicitly recognizes these issues. After all, if a worker is an independent contractor, the worker must pay all Social Security taxes, instead of sharing them with his or her employer. Additionally, the worker will not be entitled to employer-provided benefits—such as pension plans, stock option plans, and group insurance coverage—that are often available to employees. Furthermore, the worker will not receive the legal protections afforded to employees under such laws as those regulating safety in the workplace or those protecting employees from discrimination. But what can a worker do, if an employer states that the worker is being hired as an independent contractor? Generally, in this situation the worker has only two options: either accept the arrangement or forfeit the job.[2] ∎

Criteria Used by the IRS Often, the criteria for determining employee status are established by a statute or an administrative agency regulation. Businesspersons should be aware that the Internal Revenue Service (IRS) has established its own criteria for determining whether a worker is an independent contractor or an employee. Although the IRS once considered twenty factors in determining a worker's status, guidelines effective in 1997 encourage IRS examiners to focus on just one of those factors—the degree of control the business exercises over the worker.

The IRS tends to closely scrutinize a firm's classification of its workers because, as mentioned, employers can avoid certain tax liabilities by hiring independent contractors instead of employees. Even when a firm classifies a worker as an independent contractor, if the IRS decides that the worker is actually an employee, then the employer will be responsible for paying any applicable Social Security, withholding, and unemployment taxes.

In contrast, when a worker is a corporate officer, the exercise of control may be the opposite of the usual situation involving an employer and an employee. In that circumstance, the question may concern the degree of control that the officer (the employee) exercises over the corporation (the employer). In the following case, the issue was whether a corporate officer was an employee of the corporation.

---

2. See the *Question of Ethics* problem at the end of this chapter for a case brought by Microsoft Corporation's employees who were required to work as independent contractors instead of employees.

Case 17.1 ■ Nu-Look Design, Inc. v. Commissioner of Internal Revenue

United States Court of Appeals,
Third Circuit, 2004.
356 F.3d 290.

FACTS Nu-Look Design, Inc., is a home-improvement company that provides carpentry, siding installation, and general residential construction services. During 1996, 1997, and 1998, Ronald Stark was Nu-Look's president, manager, and sole shareholder. He solicited business for the company, performed the bookkeeping, handled the firm's finances, and hired and supervised its workers. Instead of paying Stark a salary or wages, Nu-Look distributed its income to him "as Mr. Stark's needs arose." Nu-Look reported on its tax returns for those years net

(Continued)

CASE 17.1—Continued

income of $10,866.14, $14,216.37, and $7,103.60, respectively. Stark reported the same amounts as income on his tax returns. In 2001, the Internal Revenue Service (IRS) classified Stark as Nu-Look's employee and assessed federal employment taxes for 1996, 1997, and 1998. Nu-Look filed a suit in the U.S. Tax Court against the commissioner of the IRS, seeking relief from this liability. Nu-Look contended in part that Stark was not an employee because Nu-Look did not control Stark—Stark controlled Nu-Look. The court ruled against the firm, which appealed to the U.S. Court of Appeals for the Third Circuit.

ISSUE   For federal tax purposes, was Stark an employee of Nu-Look?

DECISION   Yes. The U.S. Court of Appeals for the Third Circuit affirmed the ruling of the lower court.

REASON   The U.S. Court of Appeals for the Third Circuit focused on the nature of the services that Stark rendered and whether the income that Nu-Look distributed to Stark was payment for those services. The court pointed out that both the Federal Insurance Contributions Act and the Federal Unemployment Tax Act (see Chapter 18) impose taxes on employers based on the wages paid to individuals in their employ. Wages, as defined by both statutes, generally includes "all remuneration for employment." Employment is "any service of whatever nature, performed * * * by an employee for the person employing him." Both statutes define employee to include "any officer of a corporation." The court acknowledged that there is an exception for an "officer of a corporation who as such does not perform any services or performs only minor services and who neither receives nor is entitled to receive, directly or indirectly, any remuneration." In this case, however, "Stark performed more than minor services and the distributions Stark received were, in fact, remuneration for his services."

WHY IS THIS CASE IMPORTANT?   *Businesspersons should be aware that the mere designation of a person as either an independent contractor or a corporate officer does not mean the employer can avoid tax liability. The courts and the IRS look behind the label to ascertain the true relationship between the worker and the business entity.*

Employee Status and "Works for Hire"   Under the Copyright Act of 1976, any copyrighted work created by an employee within the scope of her or his employment at the request of the employer is a "work for hire," and the employer owns the copyright to the work. When an employer hires an independent contractor—a freelance artist, writer, or computer programmer, for example—the independent contractor owns the copyright *unless* the parties agree in writing that the work is a "work for hire" and the work falls into one of nine specific categories, including audiovisual and other works.

■ **EXAMPLE 17.1**   Graham marketed CD-ROM discs containing compilations of software programs that are available free to the public. Graham hired James to create a file-retrieval program that allowed users to access the software on the CDs. James built into the final version of the program a notice stating that he was the author of the program and owned the copyright. Graham removed the notice. When James sold the program to another CD-ROM publisher, Graham filed a suit claiming that James's program was "work for hire" and that Graham owned the copyright to the file-retrieval program. The court, however, decided that James—who was a skilled computer programmer who controlled the manner and method of his work—was an independent contractor and not an employee for hire. Thus, James owned the copyright to the file-retrieval program.[3] ■

---

3. *Graham v. James,* 144 F.3d 229 (2d Cir. 1998).

◧ How Agency Relationships Are Formed

Agency relationships normally are consensual; that is, they come about by voluntary consent and agreement between the parties. Generally, the agreement need not be in writing,[4] and consideration is not required.

A principal must have contractual capacity. A person who cannot legally enter into contracts directly should not be allowed to do so indirectly through an agent. Because an agent derives the authority to enter into contracts from the principal and because a contract made by an agent is legally viewed as a contract of the principal, it is immaterial whether the agent personally has the legal capacity to make that contract. Thus, a minor can be an agent but in some states cannot be a principal appointing an agent.[5] (When a minor is permitted to be a principal, however, any resulting contracts will be voidable by the minor principal but not by the adult third party.) In sum, any person can be an agent, regardless of whether he or she has the capacity to contract. Even a person who is legally incompetent can be appointed an agent.

An agency relationship can be created for any legal purpose. An agency relationship that is created for an illegal purpose or that is contrary to public policy is unenforceable. ◧ **EXAMPLE 17.2** Suppose that Sharp (as principal) contracts with Blesh (as agent) to sell illegal narcotics. This agency relationship is unenforceable because selling illegal narcotics is a felony and is contrary to public policy. ◧ It is also illegal for medical doctors and other licensed professionals to employ unlicensed agents to perform professional actions.

Generally, an agency relationship can arise in four ways: by agreement of the parties, by ratification, by estoppel, and by operation of law. We look here at each of these possibilities.

AGENCY BY AGREEMENT

Most agency relationships are based on an express or implied agreement that the agent will act for the principal and that the principal agrees to have the agent so act. An agency agreement can take the form of an express written contract. ◧ **EXAMPLE 17.3** Renato enters into a written agreement with Troy, a real estate agent, to sell Renato's house. An agency relationship exists between Renato and Troy for the sale of the house and is detailed in a document that both parties sign. ◧

Many express agency agreements are oral. ◧ **EXAMPLE 17.4** Suppose that Renato asks Cary, a gardener, to contract with others for the care of his lawn on a regular basis. Cary agrees. In this situation, an agency relationship exists between Renato and Cary for the lawn care. ◧

An agency agreement can also be implied by conduct. ◧ **EXAMPLE 17.5** A hotel expressly allows only Boris Koontz to park cars, but Boris has no employment contract there. The hotel's manager tells Boris when to work, as well as where and how to park the cars. The hotel's conduct amounts to a manifestation of its willingness

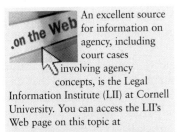

An excellent source for information on agency, including court cases involving agency concepts, is the Legal Information Institute (LII) at Cornell University. You can access the LII's Web page on this topic at

http://www.law.cornell.edu/ topics/agency.html.

---

4. There are two main exceptions to the statement that agency agreements need not be in writing: (1) Whenever agency authority empowers the agent to enter into a contract that the Statute of Frauds requires to be in writing, the agent's authority from the principal must likewise be in writing (this is called the *equal dignity rule,* to be discussed later in this chapter). (2) A power of attorney, which confers authority to an agent, must be in writing.

5. Some courts have granted exceptions to allow a minor to appoint an agent for the limited purpose of contracting for the minor's necessities of life. See *Casey v. Kastel,* 237 N.Y. 305, 142 N.E. 671 (1924).

to have Boris park its customers' cars, and Boris can infer from the hotel's conduct that he has authority to act as a parking valet. It can be inferred that Boris is an agent-employee for the hotel, his purpose being to provide valet parking services for hotel guests. ■

AGENCY BY RATIFICATION

RATIFICATION
The act of accepting and giving legal force to an obligation that previously was not enforceable.

On occasion, a person who is in fact not an agent (or who is an agent acting outside the scope of her or his authority) may make a contract on behalf of another (a principal). If the principal approves or affirms that contract by word or by action, an agency relationship is created by **ratification**. Ratification is a question of intent, and intent can be expressed by either words or conduct. The basic requirements for ratification are discussed later in this chapter.

AGENCY BY ESTOPPEL

When a principal causes a third person to believe that another person is his or her agent, and the third person deals with the supposed agent, the principal is "estopped to deny" the agency relationship. In such a situation, the principal's actions create the *appearance* of an agency that does not in fact exist. The third person must prove that she or he *reasonably* believed that an agency relationship existed, though.[6] Facts and circumstances must show that an ordinary, prudent person familiar with business practice and custom would have been justified in concluding that the agent had authority.

A restaurant offers valet parking services. Can it be inferred that the parking attendant shown here is an agent of the restaurant? Why or why not? (© Michael Newman, PhotoEdit—All rights reserved.)

■ **EXAMPLE 17.6** Suppose that Andrew accompanies Grant, a seed sales representative, to call on a customer, Steve, the proprietor of the General Seed Store. Andrew has done independent sales work but has never signed an employment agreement with Grant. Grant boasts to Steve that he wishes he had three more assistants "just like Andrew." By making this representation, Grant creates the impression that Andrew is his agent and has authority to solicit orders. Steve has reason to believe from Grant's statements that Andrew is an agent for Grant. Steve then places seed orders with Andrew. If Grant does not correct the impression that Andrew is an agent, Grant will be bound to fill the orders just as if Andrew were really his agent. Grant's representation to Steve created the impression that Andrew was Grant's agent and had authority to solicit orders. ■

The acts or declarations of a purported *agent* in and of themselves do not create an agency by estoppel. Rather, it is the deeds or statements *of the principal* that create an agency by estoppel. ■ **EXAMPLE 17.7** If Andrew walks into Steve's store and claims to be Grant's agent, when in fact he is not, and Grant has no knowledge of Andrew's representations, Grant will not be bound to any deal struck by Andrew and Steve. Andrew's acts and declarations alone do not create an agency by estoppel. ■

AGENCY BY OPERATION OF LAW

The courts may find an agency relationship in the absence of a formal agreement in other situations as well. This can occur in family relationships. For instance, suppose that one spouse purchases certain basic necessaries and charges them to the other spouse's charge account. The courts will often rule that the latter is liable for payment for the necessaries, either because of a social policy of promoting the gen-

---

6. These concepts also apply when a person who is in fact an agent undertakes an action that is beyond the scope of her or his authority, as will be discussed later in this chapter.

eral welfare of the spouse or because of a legal duty to supply necessaries to family members.

Agency by operation of law may also occur in emergency situations, when the agent's failure to act outside the scope of his or her authority would cause the principal substantial loss. If the agent is unable to contact the principal, the courts will often grant this emergency power. For instance, a railroad engineer may contract on behalf of her or his employer for medical care for an injured motorist hit by the train.

■ Duties of Agents and Principals

Once the principal-agent relationship has been created, both parties have duties that govern their conduct. As discussed previously, an agency relationship is *fiduciary*—one of trust. In a fiduciary relationship, each party owes the other the duty to act with the utmost good faith.

We now examine the various duties of agents and principals. In general, for every duty of the principal, the agent has a corresponding right, and vice versa. When one party to the agency relationship violates his or her duty to the other party, the remedies available to the nonbreaching party arise out of contract and tort law. These remedies include monetary damages, termination of the agency relationship, injunction, and required accountings.

AGENT'S DUTIES TO THE PRINCIPAL

Generally, the agent owes the principal five duties—performance, notification, loyalty, obedience, and accounting.

Performance   An implied condition in every agency contract is the agent's agreement to use reasonable diligence and skill in performing the work. When an agent fails to perform her or his duties entirely, liability for breach of contract normally will result. The degree of skill or care required of an agent is usually that expected of a reasonable person under similar circumstances. Generally, this is interpreted to mean ordinary care. If an agent has represented himself or herself as possessing special skills, however, the agent is expected to exercise the degree of skill or skills claimed. Failure to do so constitutes a breach of the agent's duty.

Not all agency relationships are based on contract. In some situations, an agent acts gratuitously—that is, not for money. A gratuitous agent cannot be liable for breach of contract, as there is no contract; he or she is subject only to tort liability. Once a gratuitous agent has begun to act in an agency capacity, he or she has the duty to continue to perform in that capacity in an acceptable manner and is subject to the same standards of care and duty to perform as other agents.

Notification   According to a maxim in agency law, notice to the agent is notice to the principal. An agent is thus required to notify the principal of all matters that come to her or his attention concerning the subject matter of the agency. This is the duty of notification, or the duty to inform.

■ **EXAMPLE 17.8** Suppose that Lang, an artist, is about to negotiate a contract to sell a series of paintings to Barber's Art Gallery for $15,000. Lang's agent learns that Barber is insolvent and will be unable to pay for the paintings. Lang's agent has a duty to inform Lang of this fact because it is relevant to the subject matter of the

BE AWARE   An agent's disclosure of confidential information could constitute the business tort of misappropriation of trade secrets.

agency—the sale of Lang's paintings. ■ Generally, the law assumes that the principal knows of any information acquired by the agent that is relevant to the agency—regardless of whether the agent actually passes on this information to the principal.

Loyalty   Loyalty is one of the most fundamental duties in a fiduciary relationship. Basically, the agent has the duty to act *solely for the benefit of his or her principal* and not in the interest of the agent or a third party. For example, an agent cannot represent two principals in the same transaction unless both know of the dual capacity and consent to it. The duty of loyalty also means that any information or knowledge acquired through the agency relationship is considered confidential. It would be a breach of loyalty to disclose such information either during the agency relationship or after its termination. Typical examples of confidential information are trade secrets and customer lists compiled by the principal.

In short, the agent's loyalty must be undivided. The agent's actions must be strictly for the benefit of the principal and must not result in any secret profit for the agent. ■ **EXAMPLE 17.9** Suppose that Ryder contracts with Alton, a real estate agent, to sell Ryder's property. Alton knows that she can find a buyer who will pay substantially more for the property than Ryder is asking. If Alton were to secretly purchase Ryder's property, however, and then resell it at a profit to another buyer, Alton would breach her duty of loyalty as Ryder's agent. Alton has a duty to act in Ryder's best interests and can only become the purchaser in this situation with Ryder's knowledge and approval. ■

Does an agent breach the duty of loyalty if, while working for a principal, the agent solicits the principal's customers for a new competing business? That was an issue in the following case.

CASE 17.2 ■ American Express Financial Advisors, Inc. v. Topel

United States District Court,
District of Colorado, 1999.
38 F.Supp.2d 1233.

FACTS Stephen Topel worked as a financial planner for American Express Financial Advisors, Inc. (AMEX), beginning in April 1992. More than four years later, Topel decided to resign to work for Multi-Financial Securities Corporation, an AMEX competitor. Before resigning, Topel encouraged his customers to liquidate their AMEX holdings and sent them new account forms for Multi-Financial. He ignored the request of customers James and Nancy Hemming to keep their investments with AMEX. In a letter on AMEX letterhead, Topel told Chris and Teresa Mammel to liquidate their AMEX holdings and invest in Multi-Financial's products. Another couple, Mr. and Ms. Rogers, changed their investments on Topel's advice. Before leaving AMEX, Topel sent a letter to all of his clients telling them that he was ending his relationship with AMEX and that their accounts would be assigned to another AMEX adviser. After Topel resigned in May 1997, he solicited the business of Theodore Benavidez, another AMEX customer.

AMEX filed a suit in a federal district court against Topel, alleging, among other things, breach of fiduciary duty (duty of loyalty) and seeking damages. AMEX filed a motion for summary judgment on this issue.

ISSUE Had Topel breached his fiduciary duty of loyalty?

DECISION Yes. The court granted AMEX's motion for summary judgment in its favor with respect to this claim.

REASON The court held that Topel breached his duty of loyalty when, while working for his principal, he solicited his principal's customers for his new competing business. The court cited the principle that an agent has a duty to act solely for the benefit of the principal in all matters connected with an agency. "While an agent is entitled to make some preparations to compete with his principal after the termination of their relationship," the court acknowledged, "an agent violates his duty of loyalty if he engages in pre-termination solicitation of customers for a new competing business." That Topel did not solicit Benavidez's business until after Topel left AMEX "does not

CASE 17.2—Continued

negate the testimony of other customers that he solicited their business for Multi-Financial while he was still affiliated with AMEX." As for the letter that Topel sent to all of his clients before resigning, "many customers had already signed new account forms with Multi-Financial by the time this neutral letter was purportedly sent."

FOR CRITICAL ANALYSIS—Ethical Consideration
Can you think of any situations in which the duty of loyalty to one's employer could come into conflict with other duties? Explain.

A real estate agent stands by a "For Sale" sign. If this agent knows a buyer who is willing to pay more than the asking price for this property, what duty would the agent breach if he bought the property from the seller and sold it at a profit to that buyer? (© Amy C. Etra, PhotoEdit)

Obedience   When acting on behalf of a principal, an agent has a duty to follow all lawful and clearly stated instructions of the principal. Any deviation from such instructions is a violation of this duty. During emergency situations, however, when the principal cannot be consulted, the agent may deviate from the instructions without violating this duty. Whenever instructions are not clearly stated, the agent can fulfill the duty of obedience by acting in good faith and in a manner reasonable under the circumstances.

Accounting   Unless an agent and a principal agree otherwise, the agent has the duty to keep and make available to the principal an account of all property and funds received and paid out on behalf of the principal. This includes gifts from third parties in connection with the agency. For example, a gift from a customer to a salesperson for prompt deliveries made by the salesperson's firm, in the absence of a company policy to the contrary, belongs to the firm. The agent has a duty to maintain separate accounts for the principal's funds and for the agent's personal funds, and no intermingling of these accounts is allowed.

PRINCIPAL'S DUTIES TO THE AGENT

The principal also owes certain duties to the agent. These duties relate to compensation, reimbursement and indemnification, cooperation, and safe working conditions.

Compensation   In general, when a principal requests certain services from an agent, the agent reasonably expects payment. The principal therefore has a duty to pay the agent for services rendered. For example, when an accountant or an attorney is asked to act as an agent, an agreement to compensate the agent for such service is implied. The principal also has a duty to pay that compensation in a timely manner. Except in a gratuitous agency relationship, in which an agent does not act for payment in return, the principal must pay the agreed-on value for an agent's services. If no amount has been expressly agreed on, the principal owes the agent the customary compensation for such services.

Reimbursement and Indemnification   Whenever an agent disburses funds to fulfill the request of the principal or to pay for necessary expenses in the course of a reasonable performance of his or her agency duties, the principal has the duty to reimburse the agent for these payments. Agents cannot recover for expenses incurred through their own misconduct or negligence, though.

Subject to the terms of the agency agreement, the principal has the duty to compensate, or *indemnify,* an agent for liabilities incurred because of authorized and lawful acts and transactions. For instance, if the principal fails to perform a contract formed by the agent with a third party and the third party then sues the agent, the

REMEMBER An agent who signs a negotiable instrument on behalf of a principal may be personally liable on the instrument. Liability depends in part on whether the identity of the principal is disclosed and whether the parties intend the agent to be bound by her or his signature.

principal is obligated to compensate the agent for any costs incurred in defending against the lawsuit.

Additionally, the principal must indemnify (pay) the agent for the value of benefits that the agent confers on the principal. The amount of indemnification is usually specified in the agency contract. If it is not, the courts will look to the nature of the business and the type of loss to determine the amount. Note that this rule applies to acts by gratuitous agents as well. If the finder of a dog that becomes sick takes the dog to a veterinarian and pays the required fees for the veterinarian's services, the agent is entitled to be reimbursed by the owner of the dog for those fees.

Cooperation   A principal has a duty to cooperate with the agent and to assist the agent in performing her or his duties. The principal must do nothing to prevent such performance.

■ **EXAMPLE 17.10** Suppose that Akers (the principal) grants Johnson (the agent) an exclusive territory within which Johnson may sell Akers's products, thus creating an exclusive agency. In this situation, Akers cannot compete with Johnson within that territory—or appoint or allow another agent to so compete—because this would violate the exclusive agency. If Akers did so, he would be exposed to liability for Johnson's lost sales or profits. ■

Safe Working Conditions   The common law requires the principal to provide safe working premises, equipment, and conditions for all agents and employees. The principal has a duty to inspect the working conditions and to warn agents and employees about any unsafe areas. When the agent is an employee, the employer's liability is frequently covered by state workers' compensation insurance, and federal and state statutes often require the employer to meet certain safety standards (see Chapter 18).

▨ Agent's Authority

An agent's authority to act can be either *actual* (express or implied) or *apparent*. If an agent contracts outside the scope of his or her authority, the principal may still become liable by ratifying the contract.

ACTUAL AUTHORITY

As indicated, an agent's actual authority can be express or implied. We look here at both of these forms of actual authority.

Express Authority   *Express authority* is authority declared in clear, direct, and definite terms. Express authority can be given orally or in writing.

EQUAL DIGNITY RULE
In most states, a rule stating that express authority given to an agent must be in writing if the contract to be made on behalf of the principal is required to be in writing.

The Equal Dignity Rule.   In most states, the **equal dignity rule** requires that if the contract being executed is or must be in writing, then the agent's authority must also be in writing. Failure to comply with the equal dignity rule can make a contract voidable *at the option of the principal.* The law regards the contract at that point as a mere offer. If the principal decides to accept the offer, acceptance must be ratified, or affirmed, in writing.

■ **EXAMPLE 17.11** Klee (the principal) orally asks Parkinson (the agent) to sell a ranch that Klee owns. Parkinson finds a buyer and signs a sales contract (a contract for an interest in realty must be in writing) on behalf of Klee to sell the ranch. The buyer cannot enforce the contract unless Klee subsequently ratifies Parkinson's agency status *in writing*. Once Parkinson's agency status is ratified, either party can enforce rights under the contract. ■

Exceptions to the Equal Dignity Rule. Modern business practice allows an exception to the equal dignity rule. The equal dignity rule does not apply when an agent acts in the presence of a principal or when the agent's act of signing is merely perfunctory. Thus, if Dickens (the principal) negotiates a contract but is called out of town the day it is to be signed and orally authorizes Santini to sign the contract, the oral authorization is sufficient.

POWER OF ATTORNEY
A written document, which is usually notarized, authorizing another to act as one's agent; can be special (permitting the agent to do specified acts only) or general (permitting the agent to transact all business for the principal).

NOTARY PUBLIC
A public official authorized to attest to the authenticity of signatures.

Power of Attorney. Giving an agent a **power of attorney** confers express authority.[7] The power of attorney normally is a written document and is usually notarized. (A document is notarized when a **notary public**—a public official authorized to attest to the authenticity of signatures—signs and dates the document and imprints it with his or her seal of authority.) A power of attorney can be special (permitting the agent to do specified acts only), or it can be general (permitting the agent to transact all business for the principal). A general power of attorney grants extensive authority to an agent to act on behalf of the principal in many ways (see Exhibit 17–1 on the following page). Because of this, a general power of attorney should be used with great caution and usually only in exceptional circumstances. Ordinarily, a power of attorney terminates on the incapacity or death of the person giving the power.[8]

Implied Authority *Implied authority* is conferred by custom, can be inferred from the position the agent occupies, or is implied by virtue of being reasonably necessary to carry out express authority. ■ EXAMPLE 17.12 Mueller is employed by Al's Supermarket to manage one of its stores. Al's has not expressly stated that Mueller has authority to contract with third persons. In this situation, though, authority to manage a business implies authority to do what is reasonably required (as is customary or can be inferred from a manager's position) to operate the business. This includes forming contracts to hire employees, to buy merchandise and equipment, and to advertise the products sold in the store. ■

ETHICAL ISSUE 17.2

Does an agent's breach of loyalty terminate the agent's authority? Suppose that an employee-agent who is authorized to access company trade secrets contained in computer files e-mails those secrets to a competitor for whom the employee is about to begin working. Clearly, in this situation the employee has violated the ethical—and legal—duty of loyalty to the employer. Does this breach of loyalty mean that the employee's act of accessing the trade secrets was unauthorized? The question has significant implications because if the act was unauthorized, the employee would be subject to state and federal laws prohibiting unauthorized access to computer information and data. If the act was authorized, the employee would not be subject to such laws. When this unusual question came before a federal district court, the court held that the moment the employee accessed trade secrets for the purpose of

---

7. An agent who holds the power of attorney is called an *attorney-in-fact* for the principal. The holder does not have to be an attorney-at-law (and often is not).

8. A *durable* power of attorney, however, continues to be effective despite the principal's incapacity. An elderly person, for example, might grant a durable power of attorney to provide for the handling of property and investments or specific health-care needs should she or he become incompetent.

EXHIBIT 17–1 A SAMPLE POWER OF ATTORNEY

GENERAL POWER OF ATTORNEY

Know All Men by These Presents:

That I, _____ , hereinafter referred to as PRINCIPAL, in the County of _____
State of _____ , do(es) appoint _____ as my true and lawful attorney.

In principal's name, and for principal's use and benefit, said attorney is authorized hereby;

(1) To demand, sue for, collect, and receive all money, debts, accounts, legacies, bequests, interest, dividends, annuities, and demands as are now or shall hereafter become due, payable, or belonging to principal, and take all lawful means, for the recovery thereof and to compromise the same and give discharges for the same;

(2) To buy and sell land, make contracts of every kind relative to land, any interest therein or the possession thereof, and to take possession and exercise control over the use thereof;

(3) To buy, sell, mortgage, hypothecate, assign, transfer, and in any manner deal with goods, wares and merchandise, choses in action, certificates or shares of capital stock, and other property in possession or in action, and to make, do, and transact all and every kind of business of whatever nature;

(4) To execute, acknowledge, and deliver contracts of sale, escrow instructions, deeds, leases including leases for minerals and hydrocarbon substances and assignments of leases, covenants, agreements and assignments of agreements, mortgages and assignments of mortgages, conveyances in trust, to secure indebtedness or other obligations, and assign the beneficial interest thereunder, subordinations of liens or encumbrances, bills of lading, receipts, evidences of debt, releases, bonds, notes, bills, requests to reconvey deeds of trust, partial or full judgments, satisfactions of mortgages, and other debts, and other written instruments of whatever kind and nature, all upon such terms and conditions as said attorney shall approve.

GIVING AND GRANTING to said attorney full power and authority to do all and every act and thing whatsoever requisite and necessary to be done relative to any of the foregoing as fully to all intents and purposes as principal might or could do if personally present.

All that said attorney shall lawfully do or cause to be done under the authority of this power of attorney is expressly approved.

Dated: _____   /s/_____

State of California
    County of _____ } SS.
On _____ , before me, the undersigned, a Notary Public in and for said
State, personally appeared _____

known to me to be the person _____ whose name _____ subscribed
to the within instrument and acknowledged that _____ executed the same.
Witness my hand and official seal.   (Seal) _____
                                              Notary Public in and for said State.

divulging them to a competitor, the employee's authority as an agent terminated. Thus, the employee could be subject to both criminal and civil sanctions under a federal law prohibiting unauthorized access to protected computer information. In reaching its decision, the court cited Section 112 of the *Restatement (Second) of Agency.* That section reads, in part, "Unless otherwise agreed, the authority of an agent terminates if, without knowledge of the principal, he acquires adverse interests or if he is otherwise guilty of a serious breach of loyalty to the principal."[9] ∎

---

9. *Shurgard Storage Centers, Inc. v. Safeguard Self Storage, Inc.,* 119 F.Supp.2d 1121 (W.D.Wash. 2000).

APPARENT AUTHORITY

Actual authority (express or implied) arises from what the principal manifests *to the agent. Apparent authority* exists when the principal, by either words or actions, causes a *third party* reasonably to believe that an agent has authority to act, even though the agent has no express or implied authority. If the third party changes her or his position in reliance on the principal's representations, the principal may be *estopped* (prevented) from denying that the agent had authority. Note that here, in contrast to agency formation by estoppel, the issue has to do with the apparent authority of an *agent,* not the apparent authority of a person who is in fact not an agent.

■ **EXAMPLE 17.13** Suppose that a traveling salesperson, Ling (the agent), is authorized to take customers' orders. Ling does not deliver the ordered goods and is not authorized to collect payments for the goods. A customer, Byron, pays Ling for a solicited order. Ling then takes the payment to the principal's accounting department, and an accountant accepts the payment and sends Byron a receipt. This procedure is thereafter followed for other orders solicited from and paid for by Byron. Later, Ling solicits an order, and Byron pays her as before. This time, however, Ling absconds with the money. Can Byron claim that the payment to the agent was authorized and was thus, in effect, a payment to the principal?

The answer is normally yes, because the principal's *repeated* acts of accepting Byron's payment led him reasonably to expect that Ling had authority to receive payments for goods solicited. Although Ling did not have express or implied authority, the principal's conduct gave Ling *apparent* authority to collect. In this situation, the principal would be estopped from denying that Ling had authority to collect payments. ■

RATIFICATION

As already mentioned, ratification occurs when the principal affirms an agent's *unauthorized* act. When ratification occurs, the principal is bound to the agent's act, and the act is treated as if it had been authorized by the principal *from the outset.* Ratification can be either express or implied.

If the principal does not ratify the contract, the principal is not bound, and the third party's agreement with the agent is viewed as merely an unaccepted offer. Because the third party's agreement is an unaccepted offer, the third party can revoke the offer at any time, without liability, before the principal ratifies the contract.

The requirements for ratification can be summarized as follows:

BE AWARE An agent who exceeds his or her authority and enters into a contract that the principal does not ratify may be liable to the third party on the ground of misrepresentation.

1 The agent must have acted on behalf of an identified principal who subsequently ratifies the action.

2 The principal must know of all material facts involved in the transaction. If a principal ratifies a contract without knowing all of the facts, the principal can rescind (cancel) the contract.

3 The principal must affirm the agent's act in its entirety.

4 The principal must have the legal capacity to authorize the transaction at the time the agent engages in the act and at the time the principal ratifies. The third party must also have the legal capacity to engage in the transaction.

5 The principal's affirmation must occur before the third party withdraws from the transaction.

6 The principal must observe the same formalities when approving the act done by the agent as would have been required to authorize it initially.

Liability in Agency Relationships

Frequently, a question arises as to which party, the principal or the agent, should be held liable for contracts formed by the agent or for torts or crimes committed by the agent. We look here at these aspects of agency law.

LIABILITY FOR CONTRACTS

Liability for contracts formed by an agent depends on how the principal is classified and on whether the actions of the agent were authorized or unauthorized. Principals are classified as disclosed, partially disclosed, or undisclosed.[10]

A **disclosed principal** is a principal whose identity is known by the third party at the time the contract is made by the agent. A **partially disclosed principal** is a principal whose identity is not known by the third party, but the third party knows that the agent is or may be acting for a principal at the time the contract is made. ■ **EXAMPLE 17.14** Sarah has contracted with a real estate agent to sell certain property. She wishes to keep her identity a secret, but the agent can make it perfectly clear to a purchaser of the real estate that the agent is acting in an agency capacity. In this situation, Sarah is a partially disclosed principal. ■ An **undisclosed principal** is a principal whose identity is totally unknown by the third party, and the third party has no knowledge that the agent is acting in an agency capacity at the time the contract is made.

Authorized Acts   If an agent acts within the scope of her or his authority, normally the principal is obligated to perform the contract regardless of whether the principal was disclosed, partially disclosed, or undisclosed. Whether the agent may also be held liable under the contract, however, depends on the disclosed, partially disclosed, or undisclosed status of the principal.

Disclosed or Partially Disclosed Principal.   A disclosed or partially disclosed principal is liable to a third party for a contract made by an agent who is acting within the scope of her or his authority. If the principal is disclosed, an agent has no contractual liability for the nonperformance of the principal or the third party. If the principal is partially disclosed, in most states the agent is also treated as a party to the contract, and the third party can hold the agent liable for contractual nonperformance.[11] The following case illustrates the rules that apply to contracts signed by agents on behalf of fully disclosed principals.

DISCLOSED PRINCIPAL
A principal whose identity is known to a third party at the time the agent makes a contract with the third party.

PARTIALLY DISCLOSED PRINCIPAL
A principal whose identity is unknown by a third party, but the third party knows that the agent is or may be acting for a principal at the time the agent and the third party form a contract.

UNDISCLOSED PRINCIPAL
A principal whose identity is unknown by a third person, and the third person has no knowledge that the agent is acting for a principal at the time the agent and the third person form a contract.

---

10. *Restatement (Second) of Agency,* Section 4.
11. *Restatement (Second) of Agency,* Section 321.

CASE 17.3 ■ McBride v. Taxman Corp.

Appellate Court of Illinois,
First District, 2002.
327 Ill.App.3d 992,
765 N.E.2d 51,
262 Ill.Dec. 225.
http://state.il.us/court/default.htm[a]

a. On this page, click on "Appellate Court of Illinois." On the next page, in the "Appellate Court Documents" section, click on "Appellate Court Opinions." In the result, in the "Appellate Court" section, click on "2002." On the next page, in the "First District" section, click on "January." Finally, scroll to the bottom of the chart and click on the case name to access the opinion. The state of Illinois maintains this Web site.

CASE 17.3—Continued

FACTS Walgreens Company entered into a lease with Taxman Corporation to operate a drugstore in Kedzie Plaza, a shopping center in Chicago, Illinois, owned by Kedzie Plaza Associates; Taxman was the center's property manager. The lease required the "Landlord" to promptly remove snow and ice from the center's sidewalks. Taxman also signed, on behalf of Kedzie Associates, an agreement with Arctic Snow and Ice Control, Inc., to remove ice and snow from the sidewalks surrounding the Walgreens store. On January 27, 1996, Grace McBride, a Walgreens employee, slipped and fell on snow and ice outside the entrance to the store. McBride filed a suit in an Illinois state court against Taxman and others, alleging, among other things, that Taxman had negligently failed to remove the accumulated ice and snow.[b] Taxman filed a motion for summary judgment in its favor, which the court granted. McBride appealed to a state intermediate appellate court.

ISSUE Could Taxman be held liable for McBride's injuries?

DECISION No. The state intermediate appellate court affirmed the judgment of the lower court. The appellate

b. McBride included complaints against Walgreens and Kedzie Associates in her suit but settled these complaints before trial.

court held that Taxman entered into the snow removal contracts only as the agent of the owner, whose identity was fully disclosed.

REASON The court reasoned that as the agent for a disclosed principal, Taxman had no liability for the non-performance of the principal or the third party to the contract. The court pointed out that "the Arctic proposal and contract was signed 'Kedzie Associates by the Taxman.' The Taxman-drafted portion of the contract contained a line above the signature of Taxman's director of property management stating 'The Taxman Corporation, agent for per contracts attached.' The latter document specifically stated that the contract was not an obligation of Taxman and that all liabilities were those of the owner and not Taxman. We conclude that Taxman was the management company for the property owner and entered into the two contracts for snow and ice removal only as the owner's agent. Taxman did not assume a contractual obligation to remove snow and ice; it merely retained Arctic as a contractor on behalf of the owner."

FOR CRITICAL ANALYSIS—Economic Consideration
Suppose that the Arctic contract had not identified Kedzie as the principal. Would the court's decision in this case have been different?

Undisclosed Principal. When neither the fact of agency nor the identity of the principal is disclosed, the undisclosed principal is fully bound to perform just as if the principal had been fully disclosed at the time the contract was made. The agent is also liable as a party to the contract.

When a principal's identity is undisclosed and the agent is forced to pay the third party, the agent is entitled to be indemnified (compensated) by the principal. The principal had a duty to perform, even though his or her identity was undisclosed,[12] and failure to do so will make the principal ultimately liable. Once the undisclosed principal's identity is revealed, the third party generally can elect to hold either the principal or the agent liable on the contract.

Conversely, the undisclosed principal can hold the third party to the contract, *unless* (1) the undisclosed principal was expressly excluded as a party in the contract, (2) the contract is a negotiable instrument signed by the agent with no indication of signing in a representative capacity, or (3) the performance of the agent is personal to the contract, allowing the third party to refuse the principal's performance.

Unauthorized Acts If an agent has no authority but nevertheless contracts with a third party, the principal cannot be held liable on the contract. It does not matter

---

12. If the agent is a gratuitous agent, and the principal accepts the benefits of the agent's contract with a third party, then the principal will be liable to the agent on the theory of *quasi contract* (see Chapter 7).

whether the principal was disclosed, partially disclosed, or undisclosed. The *agent* is liable, however. ■ **EXAMPLE 17.15** Scranton signs a contract for the purchase of a truck, purportedly acting as an agent under authority granted by Johnson. In fact, Johnson has not given Scranton any such authority. Johnson refuses to pay for the truck, claiming that Scranton had no authority to purchase it. The seller of the truck is entitled to hold Scranton liable for payment. ■

If the principal is disclosed or partially disclosed, the agent is liable to the third party as long as the third party relied on the agency status. The agent's liability here is based on the breach of an implied warranty that the agent had authority to enter the contract, not on breach of the contract itself.[13] If the third party knows at the time the contract is made that the agent is mistaken about the extent of her or his authority, though, the agent is not liable. Similarly, if the agent indicates to the third party *uncertainty* about the extent of the authority, the agent is not personally liable.

Liability for E-Agents   An electronic agent, or **e-agent,** is not a person but a semi-autonomous computer program that is capable of executing specific tasks. E-agents used in e-commerce include software that can search through many databases and retrieve only information that is relevant for the user.

Authorized versus Unauthorized Acts.   In the past, standard agency principles have applied only to *human* agents, who have express or implied authority to enter into specific contracts. The resolution of many disputes depends on whether the human agent acted within the scope of his or her authority. What does this concept mean when dealing with an intelligent e-agent?

Consider an example. E-agents searching the Internet may run into a wide variety of "click-on" agreements (see Chapter 10), which, by necessity, contain many different terms and conditions. If the e-agent ignores the terms and conditions of a licensing agreement outlined in the click-on setting, is the user of the agent nonetheless bound by the agreement? Conversely, many click-on agreements exempt third parties from any liability resulting from the underlying product or service. Is the user of the e-agent bound by this particular term? With respect to human agents, the courts have occasionally found that an agent could not agree to such a term without explicit authority. It remains to be seen, though, whether a court will ever conclude that an e-agent lacked the authority to enter such an agreement.

The Uniform Electronic Transactions Act.   The Uniform Electronic Transactions Act (UETA), which was discussed in detail in Chapter 10, contains several provisions relating to the principal's liability for the actions of e-agents. The majority of the states have adopted these provisions. Section 15 of the UETA states that e-agents may enter into binding agreements on behalf of their principals. Thus, if you place an order over the Internet, the company (principal) whose system took the order via an e-agent cannot claim that it did not receive your order.

The UETA also stipulates that if an e-agent does not provide an opportunity to prevent errors at the time of the transaction, the other party to the transaction can avoid the transaction. For instance, if an e-agent fails to provide an on-screen confirmation of a purchase or sale, the other party can avoid the effect of any errors.

E-AGENT
A computer program that by electronic or other automated means can independently initiate an action or respond to electronic messages or data without review by an individual.

Today, one can buy an array of products, including groceries, online. What steps have been taken to adapt traditional agency concepts to online transactions? (© Ed Bock/Corbis)

---

13. The agent is not liable on the contract because the agent was never intended personally to be a party to the contract.

The UETA establishes that e-agents generally have the authority to bind the principal in contract—at least in those states that have adopted the act. Presumably, this means that the principal would be bound by the terms in a contract entered into by an e-agent. Another significant issue today is whether the actions of an e-agent might create liability for other parties—a topic we treat in this chapter's *Adapting the Law to the Online Environment* feature.

ADAPTING THE LAW TO THE ONLINE ENVIRONMENT

Is Online Advertising Effective If Only an E-Agent "Views" It?

As mentioned in the text, e-agents are computer programs that are used in e-commerce to perform certain tasks. For example, an e-agent can be used to search the Web for the best price on a particular DVD and then offer links to the appropriate Web sites. Some e-agents can locate specific products in online catalogues and actually negotiate the acquisition and delivery of the product. E-agents used for shopping on the Web are commonly referred to as "bots" or "shopping bots." The fact that numerous e-agents are out there robotically shopping for people has caused problems in the online advertising industry.

INTERNET ADVERTISING AND "IMPRESSIONS"

The effectiveness of Internet advertising is dependent, of course, on how many people—that is, human beings—actually view an ad online. Internet advertising firms frequently charge for their services based on the number of "impressions" an ad generates. The advertising industry does not have a universal definition of the term *impression*, however. Consequently, Internet publishers use many different methods to measure ad impressions. Some companies define an impression as a single ad that appears on a Web page when the page is displayed on a (human) viewer's screen; thus, these companies filter out the times the ad is found by an e-agent. Other companies include visits by automated e-agents in their definition of impressions, even though no human consumer has actually viewed the ad.

THE *GO2NET* CASE

In the online environment, the actions of an e-agent can at times create liability (debt) for the business that hired an advertising firm. Consider, for example, the dispute in

Go2Net, Inc. v. CI Host, Inc.[a] A Web hosting company (Host) hired an Internet advertising company (Go2Net) to post a certain number of ads on the Internet. Payment for Go2Net's services was to be based on the number of "impressions." Host and Go2Net did not specify what they meant by "impressions" in the two contracts into which they entered, however. Host assumed that "impressions" referred to the number of times the ad was sent to a computer screen and viewed by a human. Go2Net counted as "impressions" all of the times that the ads were found by e-agents, such as Web crawlers or bots.

When the ads did not generate significant sales, Host canceled the advertising and refused to pay Go2Net for the number of "impressions" it claimed to have produced. Go2Net filed suit. Host argued that the term *impressions* was ambiguous and that the court should allow parol evidence to establish the parties' intent. Host wanted the court to rewrite the contract so that the term meant only the number of times the ad was actually sent to a computer screen. The trial court granted summary judgment for Go2Net, and the appellate court affirmed on appeal. The appellate court recognized that Host had presented "undisputed evidence in the record that there is no single industry-wide accepted definition of 'impressions.'" Nevertheless, a clause in the parties' contract stated that "all impressions billed are based on Go2Net's ad engine count." Thus, Go2Net was allowed to count as impressions the number of times that e-agents found the Internet ad.

FOR CRITICAL ANALYSIS

What might have been the result if the parties had not agreed that the number of impressions would be based on Go2Net's count? Would the court have allowed Host to reform the contract to exclude from the number of impressions the times that e-agents found the advertisement? Explain your answer.

a. 115 Wash.App. 73, 60 P.3d 1245 (2003).

LIABILITY FOR TORTS AND CRIMES

Obviously, any person, including an agent, is liable for her or his own torts and crimes. Whether a principal can also be held liable for an agent's torts and crimes depends on several factors, which we examine here. In some situations, a principal may be held liable not only for the torts of an agent but also for the torts committed by an independent contractor.

Liability for Agent's Negligence   As mentioned, an agent is liable for his or her own torts. A principal may also be liable for harm an agent caused to a third party under the doctrine of **respondeat superior**,[14] a Latin term meaning "let the master respond." This doctrine, which is discussed in this chapter's *Landmark in the Law* feature, is similar to the theory of strict liability discussed in Chapter 4 and again in Chapter 13 in the context of strict product liability. The doctrine imposes **vicarious liability**, or indirect liability, on the employer—that is, liability without regard to the personal fault of the employer for torts committed by an employee in the course or scope of employment.

Determining the Scope of Employment.   The key to determining whether a principal may be liable for the torts of an agent under the doctrine of *respondeat superior* is whether the torts are committed within the scope of the agency or employment. The *Restatement (Second) of Agency*, Section 229, indicates the factors that today's courts will consider in determining whether a particular act occurred within the course and scope of employment. These factors are as follows:

1 Whether the employee's act was authorized by the employer.

2 The time, place, and purpose of the act.

3 Whether the act was one commonly performed by employees on behalf of their employers.

4 The extent to which the employer's interest was advanced by the act.

5 The extent to which the private interests of the employee were involved.

6 Whether the employer furnished the means or instrumentality (for example, a truck or a machine) by which the injury was inflicted.

7 Whether the employer had reason to know that the employee would do the act in question and whether the employee had ever done it before.

8 Whether the act involved the commission of a serious crime.

The Distinction between a "Detour" and a "Frolic."   A useful insight into the "scope of employment" concept may be gained from the judge's classic distinction between a "detour" and a "frolic" in the case of *Joel v. Morison* (1834).[15] In this case, the English court held that if a servant merely took a detour from his master's business, the master will be responsible. If, however, the servant was on a "frolic of his own" and not in any way "on his master's business," the master will not be liable.

■ **EXAMPLE 17.16** Mandel, a traveling salesperson, while driving his employer's vehicle to call on a customer, decides to stop at the post office—which is one block off his route—to mail a personal letter. As Mandel approaches the post office, he negligently runs into a parked vehicle owned by Chan. In this situation, because

RESPONDEAT SUPERIOR
Latin for "let the master respond." A doctrine under which a principal or an employer is held liable for the wrongful acts committed by agents or employees while acting within the course and scope of their agency or employment.

VICARIOUS LIABILITY
Legal responsibility placed on one person for the acts of another; indirect liability imposed on a supervisory party (such as an employer) for the actions of a subordinate (such as an employee) because of the relationship between the two parties.

NOTE An agent-employee going to or from work or meals usually is not considered to be within the scope of employment. An agent-employee whose job requires travel, however, is considered to be within the scope of employment for the entire trip, including the return.

---

14. Pronounced ree-*spahn*-dee-uht soo-*peer*-ee-your.
15. 6 Car. & P. 501, 172 Eng. Reprint 1338 (1834).

LANDMARK IN THE LAW

The Doctrine of *Respondeat Superior*

The idea that a master (employer) must respond to third persons for losses negligently caused by the master's servant (employee) first appeared in Lord Holt's opinion in *Jones v. Hart* (1698).[a] By the early nineteenth century, this maxim had been adopted by most courts and was referred to as the doctrine of *respondeat superior.*

THEORIES OF LIABILITY The vicarious (indirect) liability of the master for the acts of the servant has been supported primarily by two theories. The first theory rests on the issue of *control*, or *fault*: the master has control over the acts of the servant and is thus responsible for injuries arising out of such service. The second theory is economic in nature: because the master takes the benefits or profits of the servant's service, he or she should also suffer the losses; moreover, the master is better able than the servant to absorb such losses.

The *control* theory is clearly recognized in the *Restatement (Second) of Agency,* which defines a master as "a principal who employs an agent to perform service in his [or her] affairs and who controls, or has the right to control, the physical conduct of the other in the performance of the service." Accordingly, a servant is defined as "an agent employed by a master to perform service in his [or her] affairs whose physical conduct in his [or her] performance of the service is controlled, or is subject to control, by the master."

LIMITATIONS ON THE EMPLOYER'S LIABILITY There are limitations on the master's liability for the acts of the servant, however. An employer (master) is only responsible for the wrongful conduct of an employee (servant) that occurs in "the scope of employment." The criteria used by the courts in determining whether an employee is acting within the scope of employment are set forth in the *Restatement (Second) of Agency* and will be discussed shortly. Generally, the act must be of a kind the servant was employed to do; must have occurred within "authorized time and space limits"; and must have been "activated, at least in part, by a purpose to serve the master."

APPLICATION TO TODAY'S WORLD

The courts have accepted the doctrine of respondeat superior *for nearly two centuries. This theory of vicarious liability is laden with practical implications in all situations in which a principal-agent (master-servant, employer-employee) relationship exists. Today, the small-town grocer with one clerk and the multinational corporation with thousands of employees are equally subject to the doctrinal demand of "let the master respond." (For a further discussion of employers' liability for wrongs committed by their employees, including wrongs committed in the online employment environment, see Chapter 18.)*

RELEVANT WEB SITES

To locate information on the Web concerning the doctrine of respondeat superior, *go to this text's Web site at* http://blt.westbuslaw.com, *select "Chapter 17," and click on "URLs for Landmarks."*

a. K.B. 642, 90 Eng. Reprint 1255 (1698).

Mandel's detour from the employer's business is not substantial, he is still acting within the scope of employment, and the employer is liable. The result would be different, though, if Mandel had decided to pick up a few friends for cocktails in another city and in the process had negligently run into Chan's vehicle. In that circumstance, the departure from the employer's business would be substantial, and the employer normally would not be liable to Chan for damages. Mandel would be considered to have been on a "frolic" of his own. ■

Notice of Dangerous Conditions. The employer is charged with knowledge of any dangerous conditions discovered by an employee and pertinent to the employment situation. ■ EXAMPLE 17.17 Chad, a maintenance employee in Martin's apartment building, notices a lead pipe protruding from the ground in the building's courtyard. The employee neglects either to fix the pipe or to inform the employer of the danger. John falls on the pipe and is injured. The employer is charged with knowledge of the dangerous condition regardless of whether or not Chad actually informed the employer. That knowledge is imputed to the employer by virtue of the employment relationship. ■

Liability for Agent's Intentional Torts Most intentional torts that employees commit have no relation to their employment; thus, their employers will not be held liable. Employers can face liability for an agent's intentional torts in some situations, though, including those discussed next.

Acts Committed within the Scope of Employment. The doctrine of *respondeat superior* applies to intentional torts as well as to negligence. Thus, an employer can be held indirectly liable for the intentional torts of an employee that are committed within the course and scope of employment. For instance, an employer is liable when an employee (such as a "bouncer" at a nightclub or a security guard at a department store) commits the tort of assault and battery or false imprisonment while acting within the scope of employment.

An employer may also be liable for permitting an employee to engage in reckless actions that can injure others. ■ EXAMPLE 17.18 An employer observes an employee smoking while filling containerized trucks with highly flammable liquids. Failure to stop the employee will cause the employer to be liable for any injuries that result if a truck explodes. ■

Acts of Misrepresentation by an Agent. A principal is exposed to tort liability whenever a third person sustains a loss due to an agent's misrepresentation. The principal's liability depends on whether the agent was actually or apparently authorized to make representations and whether such representations were made within the scope of the agency. The principal is always directly responsible for an agent's misrepresentation made within the scope of the agent's authority. When a principal has placed an agent in a position of apparent authority—making it possible for the agent to defraud a third party—the principal may also be liable for the agent's fraudulent acts.

■ EXAMPLE 17.19 Assume that Bassett is a demonstrator for Moore's products. Moore sends Bassett to a home show to demonstrate the products and to answer questions from consumers. Moore has given Bassett authority to make statements about the products. If Bassett makes only true representations, all is fine; but if she makes false claims, Moore will be liable for any injuries or damages sustained by third parties in reliance on Bassett's false representations. ■

A truck lies on its side following an accident. If the driver had stopped at a bar during working hours and become inebriated, and this accident was caused by the driver's inebriated state, who would be held responsible for the damage? (© Michael Newman, PhotoEdit)

Liability for Independent Contractor's Torts   Generally, an employer is not liable for physical harm caused to a third person by the negligent act of an independent contractor in the performance of the contract. This is because the employer does not have *the right to control* the details of an independent contractor's performance. Exceptions to this rule are made in certain situations, though, such as when unusually hazardous activities are involved. Typical examples of such activities include blasting operations, the transportation of highly volatile chemicals, or the use of poisonous gases. In these situations, an employer cannot be shielded from liability merely by using an independent contractor. Strict liability is imposed on the employer-principal as a matter of law. Also, in some states, strict liability may be imposed by statute.

Liability for Agent's Crimes   An agent is liable for his or her own crimes. A principal or employer is not liable for an agent's crime even if the crime was committed within the scope of authority or employment—unless the principal participated by conspiracy or other action. In some jurisdictions, under specific statutes, a principal may be liable for an agent's violation, in the course and scope of employment, of regulations, such as those governing sanitation, prices, weights, and the sale of liquor.

How Agency Relationships Are Terminated

Agency law is similar to contract law in that both an agency and a contract can be terminated by an act of the parties or by operation of law. Once the relationship between the principal and the agent has ended, the agent no longer has the right to bind the principal. For an agent's apparent authority to be terminated, though, third persons may also need to be notified that the agency has been terminated.

TERMINATION BY ACT OF THE PARTIES

An agency may be terminated by act of the parties in several ways, including those discussed here.

Lapse of Time   An agency agreement may specify the time period during which the agency relationship will exist. If so, the agency ends when that time period expires. For instance, if the parties agree that the agency will begin on January 1, 2005, and end on December 31, 2006, the agency is automatically terminated on December 31, 2006. If no definite time is stated, then the agency continues for a reasonable time and can be terminated at will by either party. What constitutes a "reasonable time" depends, of course, on the circumstances and the nature of the agency relationship.

Purpose Achieved   An agent can be employed to accomplish a particular objective, such as the purchase of stock for a cattle rancher. In that situation, the agency automatically ends after the cattle have been purchased. If more than one agent is employed to accomplish the same purpose, such as the sale of real estate, the first agent to complete the sale automatically terminates the agency relationship for all the others.

Occurrence of a Specific Event   An agency can be created to terminate on the happening of a certain event. If Posner appoints Rubik to handle her business affairs while she is away, the agency automatically terminates when Posner returns.

Mutual Agreement   Recall from the chapters on contract law that parties can cancel (rescind) a contract by mutually agreeing to terminate the contractual relationship. The same holds true in agency law regardless of whether the agency contract is in writing or whether it is for a specific duration.

Termination by One Party   As a general rule, either party can terminate the agency relationship. The agent's act is called a *renunciation of authority*. The principal's act is referred to as a *revocation of authority*. Although both parties have the *power* to terminate the agency, they may not possess the *right*.

Wrongful termination can subject the canceling party to a suit for damages. ▪ EXAMPLE 17.20 Rawlins has a one-year employment contract with Munro to act as an agent in return for $35,000. Munro can discharge Rawlins before the contract period expires (Munro has the *power* to breach the contract). Munro, though, will be liable to Rawlins for money damages because Munro has no *right* to breach the contract. ▪

A special rule applies in an *agency coupled with an interest*. This type of agency is not an agency in the usual sense because it is created for the agent's benefit instead of for the principal's benefit. ▪ EXAMPLE 17.21 Julie borrows $5,000 from Rob, giving Rob some of her jewelry and signing a letter giving Rob the power to sell the jewelry as her agent if she fails to repay the loan. After receiving the $5,000 from Rob, Julie attempts to revoke Rob's authority to sell the jewelry as her agent. Julie would not succeed in this attempt because a principal cannot revoke an agency created for the agent's benefit. ▪

Notice of Termination   When an agency has been terminated by act of the parties, it is the principal's duty to inform any third parties who know of the existence of the agency that it has been terminated (although notice of the termination may be given by others).

Agent's Authority Continues until Notified.   An agent's authority continues until the agent receives some notice of termination. Notice to third parties follows the general rule that an agent's *apparent authority* continues until the third party receives notice (from any source) that such authority has been terminated. If the principal knows that a third party has dealt with the agent, the principal should notify that person directly. For third parties who have heard about the agency but have not yet dealt with the agent, *constructive notice* is sufficient.[16]

Form of Notice.   No particular form is required for notice of agency termination to be effective. The principal can actually notify the agent, or the agent can learn of the termination through some other means. ▪ EXAMPLE 17.22 Manning bids on a shipment of steel, and Stone is hired as an agent to arrange transportation of the shipment. When Stone learns that Manning has lost the bid, Stone's authority to make the transportation arrangement terminates. ▪

If the agent's authority is written, it must be revoked in writing, and the writing must be shown to all people who saw the original writing that established the agency relationship. Sometimes, a written authorization (such as a power of attorney) contains an expiration date. The passage of the expiration date is sufficient notice of termination for third parties.

---

16. *Constructive notice* is information or knowledge of a fact imputed by law to a person if he or she could have discovered the fact by proper diligence. Constructive notice is often accomplished by newspaper publication.

TERMINATION BY OPERATION OF LAW

Termination of an agency by operation of law occurs in the circumstances discussed here. Note that when an agency terminates by operation of law, there is no duty to notify third persons.

Death or Insanity   The general rule is that the death or mental incompetence of either the principal or the agent automatically and immediately terminates the ordinary agency relationship. Knowledge of the death is not required. ■ **EXAMPLE 17.23** Suppose that Geer sends Pyron to China to purchase a rare painting. Before Pyron makes the purchase, Geer dies. Pyron's agent status is terminated at the moment of Geer's death, even though Pyron does not know that Geer has died. ■ Some states, however, have enacted statutes changing this common law rule to make knowledge of the principal's death a requirement for agency termination.

An agent's transactions that occur after the death of the principal are not binding on the principal's estate.[17] ■ **EXAMPLE 17.24** Assume that Carson is hired by Perry to collect a debt from Thomas (a third party). Perry dies, but Carson, not knowing of Perry's death, still collects the funds from Thomas. Thomas's payment to Carson is no longer legally sufficient to discharge the debt to Perry because Carson's authority to collect ended on Perry's death. If Carson absconds with the funds, Thomas is still liable for the debt to Perry's estate. ■

Impossibility   When the specific subject matter of an agency is destroyed or lost, the agency terminates. ■ **EXAMPLE 17.25** Bullard employs Gonzalez to sell Bullard's house. Prior to any sale, the house is destroyed by fire. In this situation, Gonzalez's agency and authority to sell Bullard's house terminate. ■ Similarly, when it is impossible for the agent to perform the agency lawfully because of war or a change in the law, the agency terminates.

Changed Circumstances   When an event occurs that has such an unusual effect on the subject matter of the agency that the agent can reasonably infer that the principal will not want the agency to continue, the agency terminates. ■ **EXAMPLE 17.26** Roberts hires Mullen to sell a tract of land for $20,000. Subsequently, Mullen learns that there is oil under the land and that the land is worth $1 million. The agency and Mullen's authority to sell the land for $20,000 are terminated. ■

Bankruptcy   If either the principal or the agent petitions for bankruptcy, the agency is *usually* terminated. In certain circumstances, as when the agent's financial status is irrelevant to the purpose of the agency, the agency relationship may continue. Insolvency (defined as the inability to pay debts when they become due or when liabilities exceed assets), as distinguished from bankruptcy, does not necessarily terminate the relationship.

War   When the principal's country and the agent's country are at war with each other, the agency is terminated. In this situation, the agency is automatically suspended or terminated because there is no way to enforce the legal rights and obligations of the parties.

---

17. There is an exception to this rule in banking under which the bank, as the agent of the customer, can continue to exercise specific types of authority even after the customer has died or become mentally incompetent unless it has knowledge of the death or incompetence [UCC 4–405]. Even with knowledge of the customer's death, the bank has authority for ten days following the customer's death to honor checks in the absence of a stop-payment order.

APPLICATION ▪▪ How Can an Employer Use Independent Contractors?*

As an employer, you may at some time consider hiring an independent contractor. Hiring workers as independent contractors instead of as employees may help you reduce both your potential tort liability and your tax liability.

MINIMIZING POTENTIAL TORT LIABILITY

One reason for using an independent contractor is that doing so may reduce your susceptibility to tort liability. If, however, an independent contractor's words or conduct leads another party to believe that the independent contractor is your employee, you may not escape liability for the contractor's tort.

To minimize the possibility of being legally liable for negligence on the part of an independent contractor, you should inquire about the contractor's qualifications before hiring him or her. The degree to which you should investigate depends, of course, on the nature of the work. A more thorough investigation is necessary when the contractor's activities present a potential danger to the public (as in delivering explosives).

Generally, it is a good idea to have the independent contractor assume, in a written contract, liability for harms caused to third parties by the contractor's negligence. You should also require the independent contractor to purchase liability insurance to cover the costs of potential lawsuits for harms caused to third persons by the independent contractor's hazardous activities or negligence.

REDUCING TAX LIABILITY

Another reason for hiring independent contractors is that you need not pay or deduct Social Security and unemployment taxes on their behalf. The independent contractor is the party responsible for paying these taxes. Additionally, the independent contractor is not eligible for any retirement or medical plans or other fringe benefits that you provide for yourself and your employees, and this is a cost saving to you.

A word of caution, though: simply designating a person as an independent contractor does not make her or him one. Under Internal Revenue Service (IRS) rules, individuals will be treated as employees if they are "in fact" employees, regardless of how you have classified them. For example, the IRS will not treat an office assistant as an independent contractor simply because you designate him or her as such. If the IRS determines that you exercise significant control over the assistant, the IRS may decide that the assistant is, in fact, an employee.

If you improperly designate an employee as an independent contractor, the penalty may be high. Usually, you will be liable for back Social Security and unemployment taxes, plus interest and penalties. When in doubt, seek professional assistance in such matters.

CHECKLIST FOR THE EMPLOYER

1. Check the qualifications of any independent contractor you plan to use to reduce the possibility that you might be legally liable for the contractor's negligence.
2. It is best to require in any contract with an independent contractor that the contractor assume liability for harm to a third person caused by the contractor's negligence.
3. Require that independent contractors working for you carry liability insurance. Examine the policy to make sure that it is current, particularly when the contractor will be undertaking actions that are more than normally hazardous to the public.
4. Make sure that independent contractors do not represent themselves as your employees to the rest of the world.
5. Regularly inspect the work of the independent contractor to make sure that it is being performed in accordance with contract specifications. Such supervision on your part will not change the worker's status as an independent contractor.

* This *Application* is not meant to substitute for the services of an attorney who is licensed to practice law in your state.

▪▪ KEY TERMS

CHAPTER SUMMARY ■ Agency

Agency Relationships (See pages 519–522.)	In a *principal-agent* relationship, an agent acts on behalf of and instead of the principal in dealing with third parties. An employee who deals with third parties is normally an agent. An independent contractor is not an employee, and the employer has no control over the details of physical performance. An independent contractor may or may not be an agent.
How Agency Relationships Are Formed (See pages 523–525.)	Agency relationships may be formed by agreement, by ratification, by estoppel, and by operation of law.
Duties of Agents and Principals (See pages 525–528.)	1. *Duties of the agent—* a. Performance—The agent must use reasonable diligence and skill in performing her or his duties or use the special skills that the agent has represented to the principal that the agent possesses. b. Notification—The agent is required to notify the principal of all matters that come to his or her attention concerning the subject matter of the agency. c. Loyalty—The agent has a duty to act solely for the benefit of the principal and not in the interest of the agent or a third party. d. Obedience—The agent must follow all lawful and clearly stated instructions of the principal. e. Accounting—The agent has a duty to make available to the principal records of all property and money received and paid out on behalf of the principal. 2. *Duties of the principal—* a. Compensation—Except in a gratuitous agency relationship, the principal must pay the agreed-on value (or reasonable value) for an agent's services. b. Reimbursement and indemnification—The principal must reimburse the agent for all sums of money disbursed at the request of the principal and for all sums of money the agent disburses for necessary expenses in the course of reasonable performance of his or her agency duties. c. Cooperation—A principal must cooperate with and assist an agent in performing her or his duties. d. Safe working conditions—A principal must provide safe working conditions for the agent-employee.
Agent's Authority (See pages 528–531.)	1. *Express authority*—Can be oral or in writing. Authorization must be in writing if the agent is to execute a contract that must be in writing. 2. *Implied authority*—Authority customarily associated with the position of the agent or authority that is deemed necessary for the agent to carry out expressly authorized tasks. 3. *Apparent authority*—Exists when the principal, by word or action, causes a third party reasonably to believe that an agent has authority to act, even though the agent has no express or implied authority. 4. *Ratification*—The affirmation by the principal of an agent's unauthorized action or promise. For the ratification to be effective, the principal must be aware of all material facts.
Liability in Agency Relationships (See pages 532–539.)	1. *Liability for contracts*—If the principal's identity is disclosed or partially disclosed at the time the agent forms a contract with a third party, the principal is liable to the third party under the contract if the agent acted within the scope of his or her authority. If the principal's identity is undisclosed at the time of contract formation, the agent is personally liable to the third party, but if the agent acted within the scope of his or her authority, the principal is also bound by the contract.

(Continued)

CHAPTER SUMMARY ▣ Agency—Continued

Liability in Agency Relationships— Continued	2. *Liability for agent's negligence*—Under the doctrine of *respondeat superior,* the principal is liable for any harm caused to another through the agent's torts if the agent was acting within the scope of her or his employment at the time the harmful act occurred.
	3. *Liability for agent's intentional torts*—Usually, employers are not liable for the intentional torts that their agents commit, *unless:*
	a. The acts are committed within the scope of employment and thus the doctrine of *respondeat superior* applies.
	b. The employer allowed an employee to engage in reckless acts that caused injury to another.
	c. The agent's misrepresentation causes a third party to sustain damage and the agent had either actual or apparent authority to act.
	4. *Liability for independent contractor's torts*—A principal is not liable for harm caused by an independent contractor's negligence, unless hazardous activities are involved (in which situation the principal is strictly liable for any resulting harm) or other exceptions apply.
	5. *Liability for agent's crimes*—An agent is responsible for his or her own crimes, even if the crimes were committed while the agent was acting within the scope of authority or employment. A principal will be liable for an agent's crime only if the principal participated by conspiracy or other action or (in some jurisdictions) if the agent violated certain government regulations in the course of employment.
How Agency Relationships Are Terminated (See pages 539–541.)	1. *By act of the parties*—
	a. Lapse of time (when the parties specified a definite time for the duration of the agency when it was established).
	b. Purpose achieved.
	c. Occurrence of a specific event.
	d. Mutual rescission (requires mutual consent of principal and agent).
	e. Termination by act of either the principal (revocation) or the agent (renunciation). (A principal cannot revoke an agency coupled with an interest.)
	f. Notice to third parties is required when an agency is terminated by act of the parties. Direct notice is required for those who have previously dealt with the agency; constructive notice will suffice for all other third parties.
	2. *By operation of law*—
	a. Death or mental incompetence of either the principal or the agent (except when an agency is coupled with an interest).
	b. Impossibility (when the purpose of the agency cannot be achieved because of an event beyond the parties' control).
	c. Changed circumstances (in which it would be inequitable to require that the agency be continued).
	d. Bankruptcy of the principal or the agent, or war between the principal's and agent's countries.
	e. Notice to third parties is not required when an agency is terminated by operation of law.

FOR REVIEW

Answers for the even-numbered questions in this For Review *section can be found in Appendix I at the end of this text.*

1 What is the difference between an employee and an independent contractor?

2 How do agency relationships arise?

3 What duties do agents and principals owe to each other?

4 When is a principal liable for the agent's actions with respect to third parties? When is the agent liable?

5 What are some of the ways in which an agency relationship can be terminated?

QUESTIONS AND CASE PROBLEMS

17–1. Ratification by Principal. Springer was a political candidate running for congressional office. He was operating on a tight budget and instructed his campaign staff not to purchase any campaign materials without his explicit authorization. In spite of these instructions, one of his campaign workers ordered Dubychek Printing Co. to print some promotional materials for Springer's campaign. When the printed materials were received, Springer did not return them but instead used them during his campaign. When Dubychek failed to obtain payment from Springer for the materials, he sued for recovery of the price. Springer contended that he was not liable on the sales contract because he had not authorized his agent to purchase the printing services. Dubychek argued that the campaign worker was Springer's agent and that the worker had authority to make the printing contract. Additionally, Dubychek claimed that even if the purchase was unauthorized, Springer's use of the materials constituted ratification of his agent's unauthorized purchase. Is Dubychek correct? Explain.

17–2. Employee versus Independent Contractor. Stephen Hemmerling was a driver for the Happy Cab Co. Hemmerling paid certain fixed expenses and abided by a variety of rules relating to the use of the cab, the hours that could be worked, and the solicitation of fares, among other things. Rates were set by the state. Happy Cab did not withhold taxes from Hemmerling's pay. While driving the cab, Hemmerling was injured in an accident and filed a claim against Happy Cab in a Nebraska state court for workers' compensation benefits. Such benefits are not available to independent contractors. On what basis might the court hold that Hemmerling is an employee? Explain.

17–3. Liability for Employee's Acts. Federated Financial Reserve Corp. leases consumer and business equipment. As part of its credit approval and debt-collection practices, Federated hires credit collectors, whom it authorizes to obtain credit reports on its customers. Janice Caylor, a Federated collector, used this authority to obtain a report on Karen Jones, who was not a Federated customer but who was the ex-wife of Caylor's roommate, Randy Lind. When Jones discovered that Lind had her address and how he had obtained it, she filed a suit in a federal district court against Federated and others. Jones claimed in part that they had violated the Fair Credit Reporting Act, the goal of which is to protect consumers from the improper use of credit reports. Under what theory might an employer be held liable for an agent-employee's violation of a statute? Does that theory apply in this case? Explain. [*Jones v. Federated Financial Reserve Corp.*, 144 F.3d 961 (6th Cir. 1998)]

17–4. Agent's Duties to Principal. Ana Barreto and Flavia Gugliuzzi asked Ruth Bennett, a real estate salesperson who worked for Smith Bell Real Estate, to list for sale their house in the Pleasant Valley area of Underhill, Vermont. Diana Carter, a California resident, visited the house as a potential buyer. Bennett worked under the supervision of David Crane, an officer of Smith Bell. Crane knew, but did not disclose to Bennett or Carter, that the house was subject to frequent and severe winds, that a window had blown in years earlier, and that other houses in the area had suffered wind damage. Crane knew of this because he lived in the Pleasant Valley area, had sold a number of nearby properties, and had been Underhill's zoning officer. Many valley residents, including Crane, had wind gauges on their homes to measure and compare wind speeds with their neighbors. Carter bought the house, and several months later, high winds blew in a number of windows and otherwise damaged the property. Carter filed a suit in a Vermont state court against Smith Bell and others, alleging fraud. She argued in part that Crane's knowledge of the winds was imputable to Smith Bell. Smith Bell responded that Crane's knowledge was obtained outside the scope of employment. What is the rule regarding how much of an agent's knowledge a principal is assumed to know? How should the court rule in this case? Why? [*Carter v. Gugliuzzi*, 716 A.2d 17 (Vt. 1998)]

CASE PROBLEM WITH SAMPLE ANSWER

17–5. Ford Motor Credit Co. is a subsidiary of Ford Motor Co. with its own offices, officers, and directors. Ford Credit buys contracts and leases of automobiles entered into by dealers and consumers. Ford Credit also provides inventory financing for dealers' purchases of Ford and non-Ford vehicles and makes loans to Ford and non-Ford dealers. Dealers and consumers are not required to finance their purchases or leases of Ford vehicles through

Ford Credit. Ford Motor is not a party to the agreements between Ford Credit and its customers and does not directly receive any payments under those agreements. Also, Ford Credit is not subject to any agreement with Ford Motor "restricting or conditioning" its ability to finance the dealers' inventories or the consumers' purchases or leases of vehicles. A number of plaintiffs filed a product liability suit in a Missouri state court against Ford Motor. Ford Motor claimed that the court did not have venue. The plaintiffs asserted that Ford Credit, which had an office in the jurisdiction, acted as Ford's "agent for the transaction of its usual and customary business" there. Is Ford Credit an agent of Ford Motor? Discuss. [*State ex rel. Ford Motor Co. v. Bacon*, 63 S.W.3d 641 (Mo. 2002)]

After you have answered this problem, compare your answer with the sample answer given on the Web site that accompanies this text. Go to http://blt.westbuslaw.com, select "Chapter 17," and click on "Case Problem with Sample Answer."

17–6. Liability for Independent Contractor's Torts. Greif Brothers Corp., a steel drum manufacturer, owned and operated a manufacturing plant in Youngstown, Ohio. In 1987, Lowell Wilson, the plant superintendent, hired Youngstown Security Patrol, Inc. (YSP), a security company, to guard Greif property and "deter thieves and vandals." Some YSP security guards, as Wilson knew, carried firearms. Eric Bator, a YSP security guard, was not certified as an armed guard but nevertheless took his gun, in a briefcase, to work. While working at the Greif plant on August 12, 1991, Bator fired his gun at Derrell Pusey, in the belief that Pusey was an intruder. The bullet struck and killed Pusey. Pusey's mother filed a suit in an Ohio state court against Greif and others, alleging in part that her son's death was the result of YSP's negligence, for which Greif was responsible. Greif filed a motion for a directed verdict. What is the plaintiff's best argument that Greif is responsible for YSP's actions? What is Greif's best defense? Explain. [*Pusey v. Bator*, 94 Ohio St.3d 275, 762 N.E.2d 968 (2002)]

17–7. Principal's Duties to Agent. Josef Boehm was an officer and the majority shareholder of Alaska Industrial Hardware, Inc. (AIH), in Anchorage, Alaska. In August 2001, Lincolnshire Management, Inc., in New York, created AIH Acquisition Corp. to buy AIH. The three firms signed a "commitment letter" to negotiate "a definitive stock purchase agreement" (SPA). In September, Harold Snow and Ronald Braley began to work, on Boehm's behalf, with Vincent Coyle, an agent for AIH Acquisition, to produce an SPA. They exchanged many drafts and dozens of e-mails. Finally, in February 2002, Braley told Coyle that Boehm would sign the SPA "early next week." That did not occur, however, and at the end of March, after more negotiations and drafts, Boehm demanded more money. AIH Acquisition agreed and, following more work by the agents, another SPA was drafted. In April, the parties met in Anchorage. Boehm still refused to sign. AIH Acquisition and others filed a suit in a federal district court against AIH. Did Boehm violate any of the

duties that principals owe to their agents? If so, which duty, and how was it violated? Explain. [*AIH Acquisition Corp. v. Alaska Industrial Hardware, Inc.,* __ F.Supp.2d __ (S.D.N.Y. 2004)]

A QUESTION OF ETHICS

17–8. In 1990, the Internal Revenue Service (IRS) determined that a number of independent contractors working for Microsoft Corp. were actually employees of the company for tax purposes. The IRS arrived at this conclusion based on the significant control that Microsoft exercised over the independent contractors' work performance. As a result of the IRS's findings, Microsoft was ordered to pay back payroll taxes for hundreds of independent contractors who should have been classified as employees. Rather than contest the ruling, Microsoft required most of the workers in question, as well as a number of its other independent contractors, to become associated with employment agencies and work for Microsoft as temporary workers ("temps") or lose the opportunity to work for Microsoft. Workers who refused to register with employment agencies, as well as some who did register, sued Microsoft. The workers alleged that they were actually employees of the company and, as such, entitled to participate in Microsoft's stock option plan for employees. Microsoft countered that it need not provide such benefits because each of the workers had signed an independent-contractor agreement specifically stating that the worker was responsible for his or her own benefits. In view of these facts, consider the following questions. [*Vizcaino v. U.S. District Court for the Western District of Washington*, 173 F.3d 713 (9th Cir. 1999)]

1. If the decision were up to you, how would you rule in this case? Why?
2. Normally, when a company hires temporary workers from an employment agency, the agency—not the employer—is responsible for paying Social Security taxes and other withholding taxes. Yet the U.S. Court of Appeals for the Ninth Circuit held that being an employee of a temporary employment agency did not preclude the employee from having the status of a common law employee of Microsoft at the same time. Is this fair to the employer? Why or why not?
3. Generally, do you believe that Microsoft was trying to "skirt the law"—and its ethical responsibilities—by requiring its employees to sign up as "temps"?
4. Each of the employees involved in this case had signed an independent-contractor agreement. In view of this fact, is this decision fair to Microsoft? Why or why not?

FOR CRITICAL ANALYSIS

17–9. What policy is served by the law that employers do not have copyright ownership in works created by independent contractors (unless there is a written "work for hire" agreement)?

VIDEO QUESTION

17–10. Go to this text's Web site at **http://blt.
westbuslaw.com** and select "Chapter 17." Click on
"Video Questions" and view the video titled *Fast
Times*. Then answer the following questions.

1. Recall from the video that Brad (Judge Reinhold) is
   told to deliver an order of Captain Hook Fish and
   Chips to IBM. Is Brad an employee or an independent
   contractor? Why?
2. Assume that Brad is an employee and agent of Captain
   Hook Fish and Chips. What duties does he owe Captain

Hook Fish and Chips? What duties does Captain Hook
Fish and Chips, as principal, owe to Brad?

3. In the video, Brad throws part of his uniform and several bags of the food that he is supposed to deliver out
   of his car window while driving. If Brad is an agent-
   employee and his actions cause injury to a person or
   property, can Captain Hook Fish and Chips be held
   liable? Why or why not? What should Captain Hook
   argue to avoid liability for Brad's actions?

INTERNET EXERCISES

Go to the *Business Law Today: The Essentials* home page at **http://blt.westbuslaw.com**,
select "Chapter 17," and click on "Internet Exercises." There you will find the following
Internet research exercises that you can perform to learn more about topics covered in this
chapter.

Activity 17–1: LEGAL PERSPECTIVE—Employees or Independent Contractors?

Activity 17–2: MANAGEMENT PERSPECTIVE—Liability in Agency Relationships

BEFORE THE TEST

Go to the *Business Law Today: The Essentials* home page at **http://blt.westbuslaw.com**,
select "Chapter 17," and click on "Interactive Quizzes." You will find at least twenty interactive questions relating to this chapter.

CHAPTER 18

Employment Law

"Show me the country in which there are no strikes, and I'll show you the country in which there is no liberty."

Samuel Gompers, 1850–1924
(American labor leader)

▦ LEARNING OBJECTIVES

After reading this chapter, you should be able to answer the following questions:

1 What is the employment-at-will doctrine? When and why are exceptions to this doctrine made?

2 What federal statute governs working hours and wages? What federal act was enacted to protect the health and safety of employees?

3 Under the Family and Medical Leave Act of 1993, under what circumstances may an employee take family or medical leave?

4 What federal acts prohibit discrimination in the workplace?

5 What are three defenses to claims of employment discrimination?

Until the early 1900s, most employer-employee relationships were governed by the common law. Today, the workplace is regulated extensively by statutes and administrative agency regulations. Recall from Chapter 1 that common law doctrines apply only to areas *not* covered by statutory law. Common law doctrines have thus been displaced to a large extent by statutory law.

In the 1930s, during the Great Depression, both state and federal governments began to regulate employment relationships. Legislation during the 1930s and subsequent decades established the right of employees to form labor unions. At the heart of labor rights is the right to unionize and bargain with management for improved working conditions, salaries, and benefits. The ultimate weapon of labor is, of course, the strike. As noted in the opening quotation, the labor leader Samuel Gompers concluded that without the right to strike, there could be no liberty. A succession of other laws during and since the 1930s provided further protection for employees. Today's employers must comply with a myriad of laws and regulations to ensure that employee rights are protected. In this chapter, we look at the most significant laws regulating employment relationships.

▪▪ Employment at Will

Traditionally, employment relationships have generally been governed by the common law doctrine of **employment at will**. Other common law rules governing employment relationships—including rules under contract, tort, and agency law—have already been discussed at length in previous chapters of this text.

Given that many employees (those who deal with third parties) are normally deemed agents of an employer, agency concepts are especially relevant in the employment context. The distinction under agency law between employee status and independent-contractor status is also relevant to employment relationships. Generally, the laws discussed in this chapter apply only to the employer-employee relationship; they do not apply to independent contractors.

Under the employment-at-will doctrine, either party may terminate the employment relationship at any time and for any reason, unless doing so would violate the provisions of an employment contract. The majority of U.S. workers continue to have the legal status of "employees at will." In other words, this common law doctrine is still in widespread use, and only one state (Montana) does not apply the doctrine. Nonetheless, as mentioned in the chapter introduction, federal and state statutes governing employment relationships prevent the doctrine from being applied in a number of circumstances. Today, an employer is not permitted to fire an employee if to do so would violate a federal or state employment statute, such as one prohibiting employment termination for discriminatory reasons.

EXCEPTIONS TO THE EMPLOYMENT-AT-WILL DOCTRINE

Under the employment-at-will doctrine, as mentioned, an employer may hire and fire employees at will (regardless of the employees' performance) without liability, unless doing so violates the terms of an employment contract or statutory law. Because of the harsh effects of the employment-at-will doctrine for employees, the courts have carved out various exceptions to the doctrine. These exceptions are based on contract theory, tort theory, and public policy.

Exceptions Based on Contract Theory   Some courts have held that an *implied* employment contract exists between an employer and an employee. If an employee is fired outside the terms of the implied contract, he or she may succeed in an action for breach of contract even though no written employment contract exists. ▪ EXAMPLE 18.1 Suppose that an employer's manual or personnel bulletin states that, as a matter of policy, workers will be dismissed only for good cause. If the employee is aware of this policy and continues to work for the employer, a court may find that there is an implied contract based on the terms stated in the manual or bulletin.[1] ▪ Generally, the key consideration in determining whether an employment manual creates an implied contractual obligation is the employee's reasonable expectations.

---

1. See, for example, *Pepe v. Rival Co.*, 85 F.Supp.2d 349 (D.N.J. 1999).

REMEMBER An implied contract may exist if a party furnishes a service expecting to be paid, and the other party, who knows (or should know) of this expectation, has a chance to reject the service and does not.

An employer's oral promises to employees regarding discharge policy may also be considered part of an implied contract. If the employer fires a worker in a manner contrary to what was promised, a court may hold that the employer has violated the implied contract and is liable for damages. Most state courts will judge a claimed breach of implied employment contract by traditional contract standards. In some cases, courts have held that an implied employment contract exists even though employees agreed in writing to be employees at will.[2]

Courts in a few states have gone further and held that all employment contracts contain an implied covenant of good faith. This means that both sides promise to abide by the contract in good faith. If an employer fires an employee for an arbitrary or unjustified reason, the employee can claim that the covenant of good faith was breached and the contract violated.

Exceptions Based on Tort Theory In a few situations, the discharge of an employee may give rise to an action for wrongful discharge under tort theories. Abusive discharge procedures may result in a suit for intentional infliction of emotional distress or defamation, and some courts have permitted workers to sue their employers under the tort theory of fraud. ■ **EXAMPLE 18.2** Suppose that an employer induces a prospective employee to leave a lucrative job and move to another state by offering "a long-term job with a thriving business." In fact, the employer is having significant financial problems. Also, the employer is planning a merger that will result in the elimination of the position offered to the prospective employee. If the employee takes the job in reliance on the employer's representations and is fired shortly thereafter, the employee may be able to bring an action against the employer for fraud.[3] ■

Exceptions Based on Public Policy The most widespread common law exception to the employment-at-will doctrine is made on the basis of public policy. Courts may apply this exception when an employer fires a worker for reasons that violate a fundamental public policy of the jurisdiction. Generally, the courts require that the public policy involved be expressed clearly in the statutory law governing the jurisdiction.

Sometimes, an employer will direct employees to perform an illegal act and fire them if they refuse to do so. At other times, employers will fire or discipline employees who "blow the whistle" on the employer's wrongdoing. **Whistleblowing** occurs when an employee tells government authorities, upper-level managers, or the press that her or his employer is engaged in some unsafe or illegal activity. Whistleblowers on occasion have been protected from wrongful discharge for reasons of public policy. For example, a bank was held to have wrongfully discharged an employee who pressured the employer to comply with state and federal consumer credit laws.[4]

Today, whistleblowers have some protection under statutory law. Most states have enacted so-called whistleblower statutes that protect a whistleblower from subsequent retaliation by the employer. On the federal level, the Whistleblower Protection Act of 1989[5] protects federal employees who blow the whistle on their employers from retaliatory actions. Whistleblower statutes may also offer an incentive to disclose information by providing the whistleblower with a monetary

WHISTLEBLOWING
An employee's disclosure to government authorities, upper-level managers, or the press that the employer is engaged in unsafe or illegal activities.

---

2. See, for example, *Kuest v. Regent Assisted Living, Inc.,* 111 Wash.App. 36, 43 P.3d 23 (2002).
3. See, for example, *Lazar v. Superior Court of Los Angeles County,* 12 Cal.4th 631, 909 P.2d 981, 49 Cal.Rptr.2d 377 (1996); and *McConkey v. Aon Corp.,* 804 A.2d 572 (N.J.Super.A.D. 2002).
4. *Harless v. First National Bank in Fairmont,* 162 W.Va. 116, 246 S.E.2d 270 (1978).
5. 5 U.S.C. Section 1201.

reward. For instance, under the federal False Claims Reform Act of 1986,[6] a whistleblower who has disclosed information relating to a fraud perpetrated against the U.S. government will receive between 15 and 25 percent of the proceeds if the government brings a suit against the wrongdoer.

ETHICAL ISSUE 18.1

Is it fair for whistleblowing statutes to reward employees who participated in the fraud? Many whistleblowing statutes reward employees who report their employer's wrongdoing with a percentage of the funds recovered after a lawsuit. In other words, employees have a strong financial incentive to disclose their employers' wrongful behavior. Is this practice fair? What happens if the employee was somehow involved in the employer's wrongdoing? Should the employee still receive a share of the proceeds?

Consider, for example, the largest Medicaid fraud settlement in U.S. history, involving a deal between Bayer Corporation and Kaiser Permanente, a health-care organization. As one of Bayer's biggest customers, Kaiser demanded a discount price on Cipro, an antibiotic manufactured by Bayer. By law, however, Bayer could not sell the antibiotic to Kaiser for less than it sold Cipro to the federal government for use in the Medicaid program. (Medicaid helps needy and low-income persons pay for necessary medical services.) If Bayer lowered the price of Cipro to Kaiser, it would have to refund millions of dollars to Medicaid. Therefore, Bayer "privately labeled" the antibiotic using a different name and sold it to Kaiser at a 40 percent discount. Ironically, the person who blew the whistle on the fraudulent scheme—George Couto—was the marketing manager who negotiated the private labeling deal with Kaiser. Although Couto did not initiate the labeling scheme and had suspected that it was illegal, he was instrumental in its success. Even though Couto had been a prime mover in the fraudulent scheme on behalf of Bayer, he was awarded 24 percent of the government's share of the $257 million settlement.[7] ■

WRONGFUL DISCHARGE

WRONGFUL DISCHARGE
An employer's termination of an employee's employment in violation of the law.

Whenever an employer discharges an employee in violation of an employment contract or a statute protecting employees, the employee may bring an action for **wrongful discharge**. Even if an employer's actions do not violate any provisions in an employment contract or a statute, the employer may still be subject to liability under a common law doctrine, such as a tort theory or agency.

■■ Wage-Hour Laws

In the 1930s, Congress enacted several laws regulating the wages and working hours of employees. In 1931, Congress passed the Davis-Bacon Act,[8] which requires contractors and subcontractors working on government construction projects to pay "prevailing wages" to their employees. In 1936, the Walsh-Healey Act[9] was passed. This act requires that a minimum wage, as well as overtime pay of time and a half, be paid to employees of manufacturers or suppliers entering into contracts with agencies of the federal government.

---

6. 31 U.S.C. Sections 3729–3733. This act amended the False Claims Act of 1863.
7. Peter Aronson, "A Rogue to Catch a Rogue," *The National Law Journal,* August 18–25, 2003.
8. 40 U.S.C. Sections 276a–276a-5.
9. 41 U.S.C. Sections 35–45.

In 1938, Congress passed the Fair Labor Standards Act[10] (FLSA). This act extended wage-hour requirements to cover all employers engaged in interstate commerce or in the production of goods for interstate commerce, plus selected types of other businesses. We examine here the FLSA's provisions in regard to child labor, maximum hours, and minimum wages.

CHILD LABOR

The FLSA prohibits oppressive child labor. Children under fourteen years of age are allowed to do certain types of work, such as deliver newspapers, work for their parents, and work in the entertainment and (with some exceptions) agricultural areas. Children who are fourteen or fifteen years of age are allowed to work, but not in hazardous occupations. There are also numerous restrictions on how many hours per day and per week they can work. ■ EXAMPLE 18.3 Children under the age of sixteen cannot work during school hours, for more than three hours on a school day (or eight hours on a nonschool day), for more than eighteen hours during a school week (or forty hours during a nonschool week), or before 7 A.M. or after 7 P.M. (9 P.M. during the summer). ■ Many states require persons under sixteen years of age to obtain work permits.

Working times and hours are not restricted for persons between the ages of sixteen and eighteen, but they cannot be employed in hazardous jobs or in jobs detrimental to their health and well-being. None of these restrictions apply to persons over the age of eighteen.

WAGES AND HOURS

MINIMUM WAGE
The lowest wage, either by government regulation or union contract, that an employer may pay an hourly worker.

The FLSA provides that a **minimum wage** of a specified amount (as of the writing of this edition, $5.15 per hour) must be paid to employees in covered industries. Congress periodically revises this minimum wage.[11] Under the FLSA, the term *wages* includes the reasonable cost of the employer in furnishing employees with board, lodging, and other facilities if they are customarily furnished by that employer.

Under the FLSA, employees who work more than forty hours per week normally must be paid one and a half times their regular pay for all hours over forty. Note that the FLSA overtime provisions apply only after an employee has worked more than forty hours per *week*. Thus, employees who work for ten hours a day, four days per week, are not entitled to overtime pay because they do not work more than forty hours a week.

OVERTIME EXEMPTIONS

Certain employees are exempt from the overtime provisions of the FLSA. These exemptions include employees whose jobs are categorized as executive, administrative, or professional, as well as outside salespersons and computer employees. In the past, to fall into one of these exemptions, an employee had to earn more than a specified salary threshold and devote a certain percentage of work time to the performance of specific types of duties. Because the salary limits were low and the duties tests were complex and confusing, some employers in the last few decades have been

---

10. 29 U.S.C. Sections 201–260.

11. Note that many state and local governments also have minimum-wage laws; these laws provide for higher minimum-wage rates than required by the federal government.

able to avoid paying overtime wages to their employees. This prompted the U.S. Department of Labor to substantially revise the regulations pertaining to overtime for the first time in over fifty years.

In August 2004, new rules were implemented that expand the number of workers eligible for overtime by nearly tripling the salary threshold.[12] Under the new provisions, workers earning less than $23,660 a year are guaranteed overtime pay for working more than forty hours per week (the previous ceiling was $8,060). The exemptions do not apply to manual laborers or other "blue-collar" workers who perform work involving repetitive operations with their hands (such as nonmanagement production-line employees, for example). The exemptions also do not apply to police, firefighters, licensed nurses, and other public safety workers. White-collar workers who earn more than $100,000 a year, computer programmers, dental hygienists, and insurance adjusters are typically exempt—though they must also meet certain other criteria. Employers can continue to pay overtime to ineligible employees if they want to do so, but cannot waive or reduce the overtime requirements of the FLSA.

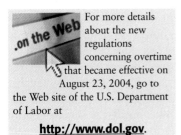

For more details about the new regulations concerning overtime that became effective on August 23, 2004, go to the Web site of the U.S. Department of Labor at

http://www.dol.gov.

■■ Worker Health and Safety

Under the common law, employees injured on the job had to rely on tort law or contract law theories in suits they brought against their employers. Additionally, workers had some recourse under the common law governing agency relationships (discussed in Chapter 17), which imposes a duty on a principal-employer to provide a safe workplace for an agent-employee. Today, numerous state and federal statutes protect employees and their families from the risk of accidental injury, death, or disease resulting from their employment. This section discusses the primary federal statute governing health and safety in the workplace, along with state workers' compensation laws.

THE OCCUPATIONAL SAFETY AND HEALTH ACT

At the federal level, the primary legislation protecting employees' health and safety is the Occupational Safety and Health Act of 1970.[13] Congress passed this act in an attempt to ensure safe and healthful working conditions for practically every employee in the country. The act requires employers to meet specific standards in addition to their general duty to keep workplaces safe.

Enforcement Agencies   Three federal agencies develop and enforce the standards set by the Occupational Safety and Health Act. The Occupational Safety and Health Administration (OSHA) is part of the Department of Labor and has the authority to promulgate standards, make inspections, and enforce the act. OSHA has developed safety standards governing many workplace details, such as the structural stability of ladders and the requirements for railings. OSHA also establishes standards that protect employees against exposure to substances that may be harmful to their health.

A good source for information relating to workplace health and safety is OSHA's Web site, which includes, among other things, the text of the Occupational Safety and Health Act of 1970, OSHA's regulatory standards and regulations, and instructions on how to file OSHA complaints. Go to

http://www.osha.gov.

The National Institute for Occupational Safety and Health is part of the Department of Health and Human Services. Its main duty is to conduct research on safety and health problems and to recommend standards for OSHA to adopt. Finally, the Occupational Safety and Health Review Commission is an independent agency set up to handle appeals from actions taken by OSHA administrators.

---

12. 29 C.F.R. Section 541.
13. 29 U.S.C. Sections 553, 651–678.

Procedures and Violations   OSHA compliance officers may enter and inspect facilities of any establishment covered by the Occupational Safety and Health Act.[14] Employees may also file complaints of violations. Under the act, an employer cannot discharge an employee who files a complaint or who, in good faith, refuses to work in a high-risk area if bodily harm or death might reasonably result.

Employers with eleven or more employees are required to keep occupational injury and illness records for each employee. Each record must be made available for inspection when requested by an OSHA inspector. Whenever a work-related injury or disease occurs, employers must make reports directly to OSHA. Whenever an employee is killed in a work-related accident or when five or more employees are hospitalized as a result of one accident, the employer must notify the Department of Labor within forty-eight hours. If the company fails to do so, it will be fined. Following the accident, a complete inspection of the premises is mandatory.

Criminal penalties for willful violation of the Occupational Safety and Health Act are limited. Employers may also be prosecuted under state laws, however. In other words, the act does not preempt state and local criminal laws.[15]

STATE WORKERS' COMPENSATION LAWS

State **workers' compensation laws** establish an administrative procedure for compensating workers injured on the job. Instead of suing, an injured worker files a claim with the administrative agency or board that administers local workers' compensation claims.

Employees Covered by Workers' Compensation   Most workers' compensation statutes are similar. No state covers all employees. Typically excluded are domestic workers, agricultural workers, temporary employees, and employees of common carriers (companies that provide transportation services to the public). Typically, the statutes cover minors. Usually, the statutes allow employers to purchase insurance from a private insurer or a state fund to pay workers' compensation benefits in the event of a claim. Most states also allow employers to be self-insured—that is, employers who show an ability to pay claims do not need to buy insurance.

Requirements for Receiving Workers' Compensation   In general, the right to recover benefits is predicated wholly on the existence of an employment relationship and the fact that the injury was *accidental* and *occurred on the job or in the course of employment*, regardless of fault. Intentionally inflicted self-injury, for example, would not be considered accidental and hence would not be covered. If an injury occurred while an employee was commuting to or from work, it usually would not be considered to have occurred on the job or in the course of employment and hence would not be covered.

An employee must notify her or his employer promptly (usually within thirty days) of an injury. Generally, an employee must also file a workers' compensation claim with the appropriate state agency or board within a certain period (sixty days to two years) from the time the injury is first noticed, rather than from the time of the accident.

BE AWARE   To check for compliance with safety standards without being cited for violations, an employer can often obtain advice from an insurer, a trade association, or a state agency.

WORKERS' COMPENSATION LAWS
State statutes establishing an administrative procedure for compensating workers' injuries that arise out of—or in the course of—their employment, regardless of fault.

---

14. In the past, warrantless inspections were conducted. In 1978, however, the United States Supreme Court held that warrantless inspections violated the warrant clause of the Fourth Amendment to the Constitution. See *Marshall v. Barlow's, Inc.,* 436 U.S. 307, 98 S.Ct. 1816, 56 L.Ed.2d 305 (1978).

15. *Pedraza v. Shell Oil Co.,* 942 F.2d 48 (1st Cir. 1991), *cert.* denied, *Shell Oil Co. v. Pedraza,* 502 U.S. 1082, 112 S.Ct. 993, 117 L.Ed.2d 154 (1992).

Workers' Compensation versus Litigation   An employee's acceptance of workers' compensation benefits bars the employee from suing for injuries caused by the employer's negligence. By barring lawsuits for negligence, workers' compensation laws also bar employers from raising common law defenses to negligence, such as contributory negligence, assumption of risk, or injury caused by a "fellow servant" (another employee). A worker may sue an employer who *intentionally* injures the worker, however.

▪▪ Income Security

Federal and state governments participate in insurance programs designed to protect employees and their families by covering the financial impact of retirement, disability, death, hospitalization, and unemployment. The key federal law on this subject is the Social Security Act of 1935.[16]

SOCIAL SECURITY

The Social Security Act provides for old-age (retirement), survivors, and disability insurance. The act is therefore often referred to as OASDI. Both employers and employees must "contribute" under the Federal Insurance Contributions Act (FICA)[17] to help pay for benefits that will partially make up for the employees' loss of income on retirement.

The basis for the employee's and the employer's contribution is the employee's annual wage base—the maximum amount of the employee's wages that are subject to the tax. The employer withholds the employee's FICA contribution from the employee's wages and then matches this contribution. (In 2005, employers were required to withhold 6.2 percent of each employee's wages, up to a maximum wage base of $90,000, and to match this contribution.)

Retired workers are then eligible to receive monthly payments from the Social Security Administration, which administers the Social Security Act. Social Security benefits are fixed by statute but increase automatically with increases in the cost of living.

NOTE   Social Security currently covers almost all jobs in the United States. Nine out of ten workers "contribute" to this protection for themselves and their families.

MEDICARE

Medicare, a federal government health-insurance program, is administered by the Social Security Administration for people sixty-five years of age and older and for some under the age of sixty-five who are disabled. It has two parts, one pertaining to hospital costs and the other to nonhospital medical costs, such as visits to physicians' offices. People who have Medicare hospital insurance can also obtain additional federal medical insurance if they pay small monthly premiums, which increase as the cost of medical care increases.

As with Social Security contributions, both the employer and the employee contribute to Medicare. As of this writing, both the employer and the employee pay 1.45 percent of the amount of *all* wages and salaries to finance Medicare. Unlike Social Security contributions, there is no cap on the amount of wages subject to the Medicare tax.

---

16. 42 U.S.C. Sections 301–1397e.
17. 26 U.S.C. Sections 3101–3125.

PRIVATE PENSION PLANS

Significant legislation has been enacted to regulate employee retirement plans set up by employers to supplement Social Security benefits. The major federal act covering these retirement plans is the Employee Retirement Income Security Act (ERISA) of 1974.[18] This act empowers the Labor Management Services Administration of the Department of Labor to enforce its provisions governing employers who have private pension funds for their employees. ERISA does not require an employer to establish a pension plan. When a plan exists, however, ERISA establishes standards for its management.

VESTING
The creation of an absolute or unconditional right or power.

A key provision of ERISA concerns vesting. **Vesting** gives an employee a legal right to receive pension benefits at some future date when he or she stops working. Before ERISA was enacted, some employees who had worked for companies for as long as thirty years received no pension benefits when their employment terminated, because those benefits had not vested. ERISA establishes complex vesting rules. Generally, however, all employee contributions to pension plans vest immediately, and employee rights to employer contributions to a plan vest after five years of employment.

In an attempt to prevent mismanagement of pension funds, ERISA has established rules on how they must be invested. Pension managers must be cautious in their investments and refrain from investing more than 10 percent of the fund in securities of the employer. ERISA also contains detailed record-keeping and reporting requirements.

UNEMPLOYMENT INSURANCE

To ease the financial impact of unemployment, the United States has a system of unemployment insurance. The Federal Unemployment Tax Act (FUTA) of 1935[19] created a state-administered system that provides unemployment compensation to eligible individuals. Under this system, employers pay into a fund, and the proceeds are paid out to qualified unemployed workers. The FUTA and state laws require employers that fall under the provisions of the act to pay unemployment taxes at regular intervals.

WATCH OUT If an employer does not pay unemployment taxes, a state government can place a lien (claim) on the employer's property to secure the debt. Liens were discussed in Chapter 16.

To be eligible for unemployment compensation, a worker must be willing and able to work and be actively seeking employment. Workers who have been fired for misconduct or who have voluntarily left their jobs are not eligible for benefits. To leave a job voluntarily is to leave it without good cause. In the following case, an unemployed worker left his job. The question was whether he left the job for good cause and was therefore eligible for unemployment benefits.

18. 29 U.S.C. Sections 1001 *et seq.*
19. 26 U.S.C. Sections 3301–3310.

CASE 18.1 ▪ **Lewis v. Director, Employment Security Department**

Court of Appeals of Arkansas,
Division I, 2004.
141 S.W.3d 896.
http://courts.state.ar.us/opinions/ca2004a.htm[a]

a. Click on "January 21, 2004." On the next page, scroll to the name of the case and click on the appropriate link to access the opinion. The Arkansas Judiciary maintains this Web site.

FACTS The jobs in the warehouse unit of Ace Hardware Corporation in Arkansas are divided between two departments: break order and full case. Break-order positions involve lifting no more than fifty pounds. The full-case department fills heavier orders (up to five thousand pounds). Employees who complete orders in less time than Ace allows earn incentive pay. Employees believe

CASE 18.1—Continued

that incentive pay is lower in the full-case department. Jobs are awarded on a seniority basis: new hires start in the full-case department but bid for other positions as soon as possible. Jimmy Lewis had worked for Ace since 1984, primarily in the break-order department. Ace had a high turnover in the full-case department, however, and whenever additional workers were needed, Ace reassigned Lewis. In 1998, Lewis began to complain regularly to his superiors about the reassignments. He offered to train others to fill the position, but his managers declined. In 2003, Lewis quit and applied for unemployment benefits. Ace questioned Lewis's entitlement. An Arkansas state employment tribunal ruled in Lewis's favor, a state review board reversed the ruling, and Lewis appealed to a state intermediate appellate court.

ISSUE   Was Lewis entitled to unemployment benefits?

DECISION   Yes. The state intermediate appellate court reversed the review board's decision and remanded the case for an order to award benefits. The court held that Lewis left his job for good cause.

REASON   The court emphasized that the only reason Ace did not train other workers to fill full-case positions

was that Lewis was already trained and it was easier to reassign him. The court reasoned that Ace's staffing problems were self-created and that its reassignment policy violated its seniority policy. Lewis quit his job when he realized that Ace was never going to permanently address the underlying situation that caused his reassignment to the full-case department. Although employees regularly bid out of the full-case department, causing staffing shortages, Ace refused to train other current employees to fill those positions. After five years of complaining to management about being reassigned to a position that Lewis felt caused him to lose pay, after offering to train other employees, and after seeing management violate its seniority policy and do virtually nothing to resolve the situation, Lewis quit. The court concluded, "We agree with appellant that his circumstances would reasonably impel an average, able-bodied, qualified worker to give up his or her employment."

FOR CRITICAL ANALYSIS—Social Consideration
The court in the Lewis *case based its decision in part on the employee's reaction to the situation on the job. What other factors should be considered in deciding whether a worker had "good cause" to quit?*

COBRA

Federal legislation also addresses the issue of health insurance for workers whose jobs have been terminated—and who are thus no longer eligible for group health-insurance plans. The Consolidated Omnibus Budget Reconciliation Act (COBRA) of 1985[20] prohibits the elimination of a worker's medical, optical, or dental insurance on the voluntary or involuntary termination of the worker's employment. The act applies to most workers who have either lost their jobs or had their hours decreased so that they are no longer eligible for coverage under the employer's health plan. Only workers fired for gross misconduct are excluded from protection.

Application of COBRA   The worker has sixty days (beginning with the date that the group coverage would stop) to decide whether to continue with the employer's group insurance plan. If the worker chooses to discontinue the coverage, the employer has no further obligation. If the worker chooses to continue coverage, though, the employer is obligated to keep the policy active for up to eighteen months. If the worker is disabled, the employer must extend coverage up to twenty-nine months. The coverage provided must be the same as that enjoyed by the worker prior to the termination or reduction of work. If family members were originally included,

---

20. 29 U.S.C. Sections 1161–1169.

for example, COBRA prohibits their exclusion. The worker does not receive the insurance coverage for free, however. To receive continued benefits, she or he may be required to pay all of the premiums, as well as a 2 percent administrative charge.

Employers' Obligations under COBRA Employers, with some exceptions, must comply with COBRA if they employ twenty or more workers and provide a benefit plan to those workers. An employer must inform an employee of COBRA's provisions when that worker faces termination or a reduction of hours that would affect his or her eligibility for coverage under the plan.

The employer is relieved of the responsibility to provide benefit coverage if the employer completely eliminates its group benefit plan. An employer is also relieved of responsibility when the worker becomes eligible for Medicare, becomes covered under a spouse's health plan, becomes insured under a different plan (with a new employer, for example), or fails to pay the premium. An employer that does not comply with COBRA risks substantial penalties, such as a tax of up to 10 percent of the annual cost of the group plan or $500,000, whichever is less.

FAMILY AND MEDICAL LEAVE

In 1993, Congress passed the Family and Medical Leave Act (FMLA)[21] to allow employees to take time off from work for family or medical reasons. A majority of the states also have legislation allowing for a leave from employment for family or medical reasons, and many employers maintain private family-leave plans for their workers.

Coverage and Applicability of the FMLA The FMLA requires employers who have fifty or more employees to provide employees with up to twelve weeks of unpaid family or medical leave during any twelve-month period. Generally, an employee may take family leave to care for a newborn baby, an adopted child, or a foster child and take medical leave when the employee or the employee's spouse, child, or parent has a "serious health condition" requiring care.[22] The employer must continue the worker's health-care coverage and guarantee employment in the same position or a comparable position when the employee returns to work. An important exception to the FMLA, however, allows the employer to avoid reinstating a *key employee*— defined as an employee whose pay falls within the top 10 percent of the firm's work force. Also, the act does not apply to part-time or newly hired employees (those who have worked for less than one year).

Employees suffering from certain chronic health conditions, such as asthma, diabetes, and pregnancy, may take FMLA leave for their own incapacities that require absences of less than three days. ■ **EXAMPLE 18.4** Estel, an employee who has asthma, suffers from periodic episodes of illness. According to regulations issued by the Department of Labor, employees with such conditions are covered by the FMLA. Thus, Estel may take a medical leave. ■

The FMLA expressly covers private and public (government) employees. Nevertheless, some states argued that public employees could not sue their state employers in federal courts to enforce their FMLA rights unless the states consented to be sued.[23] This argument came before the United States Supreme Court in the following case.

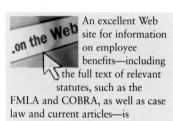

.on the Web An excellent Web site for information on employee benefits—including the full text of relevant statutes, such as the FMLA and COBRA, as well as case law and current articles—is BenefitsLink. Go to

http://www.benefitslink. com/index.shtml.

A boy leans against his pregnant mother's belly. The mother hopes to take time off from her full-time corporate job when the baby is born. What is required for the Family and Medical Leave Act (FMLA) to apply to her employer? If the employer is covered by the FMLA, how much family leave does the act authorize? (Photodisc Red)

---

21. 29 U.S.C. Sections 2601, 2611–2619, 2651–2654.

22. The foster care must be state sanctioned before such an arrangement falls within the coverage of the FMLA.

23. Under the Eleventh Amendment to the U.S. Constitution, a state is immune from suit in a federal court unless the state agrees to be sued.

CASE 18.2 Nevada Department of Human Resources v. Hibbs

Supreme Court of the United States, 2003.
538 U.S. 721,
123 S.Ct. 1972,
155 L.Ed.2d 953.
http://supct.law.cornell.edu/supct/cases/name.htm[a]

FACTS William Hibbs worked for the Nevada Department of Human Resources. In April 1997, Hibbs asked for time off under the FMLA to care for his sick wife, who was recovering from a car accident and neck surgery. The department granted Hibbs's request, allowing him to use the leave intermittently, as needed, beginning in May. Hibbs did this until August 5, after which he did not return to work. In October, the department told Hibbs that he had exhausted his FMLA leave, that no further leave would be granted, and that he must return to work by November 12. When he did not return, he was discharged. Hibbs filed a suit in a federal district court against the department. The court held that the Eleventh Amendment to the U.S. Constitution barred the suit. On Hibbs's appeal, the U.S. Court of Appeals for the Ninth Circuit reversed this holding. The department appealed to the United States Supreme Court.

ISSUE Can the FMLA, which expressly covers public employees, serve as the basis for a suit against a state employer whether or not the state consents to the suit?

a. Scroll to the name of the case and click on it to access the opinion.

DECISION Yes. The United States Supreme Court affirmed the appellate court's decision, concluding that the FMLA is "congruent and proportional" to the discrimination that Congress intended the FMLA to address.

REASON In deciding the case, the Supreme Court looked to the reason that Congress enacted the FMLA. The Court pointed out that when Congress enacted the FMLA, parental leave for fathers was rare. Even when family-leave policies did exist, men, *both in the public and private sectors,* "receive[d] notoriously discriminatory treatment in their requests for such leave." For example, the Court noted that fifteen states provided women with up to one year of extended maternity leave, while only four provided men with the same. This and other differential leave policies were not, according to the Court, attributable to any differential physical needs of men and women, but rather to the "pervasive sex-role stereotype that caring for family members is women's work. * * * By setting a minimum standard of family leave for *all* eligible employees, irrespective of gender, the FMLA attacks the formerly state-sanctioned stereotype that only women are responsible for family caregiving, thereby reducing employers' incentives to engage in discrimination by basing hiring and promotion decisions on stereotypes."

FOR CRITICAL ANALYSIS—Cultural Consideration *How might a law foster discrimination even when the law is not obviously discriminatory?*

Violations of the FMLA An employer who violates the FMLA may be held liable for damages to compensate an employee for unpaid wages (or salary), lost benefits, denied compensation, and actual monetary losses (such as the cost of providing for care of the family member) up to an amount equivalent to the employee's wages for twelve weeks. Supervisors may also be subject to personal liability, as employers, for violations of the act.[24] A court may require the employer to reinstate the employee in her or his job or to grant a promotion that had been denied. A successful plaintiff is entitled to court costs; attorneys' fees; and, in cases involving bad faith on the part of the employer, double damages.

Regulations issued by the Department of Labor (DOL) impose additional sanctions on employers who fail to notify employees when an absence will be counted against leave authorized under the act. Under one such rule, if an employer failed to provide notice, then the employee's absence would not count as a portion of the leave time available under the FMLA. ■ **EXAMPLE 18.5** An employee had been absent from work for thirty weeks while undergoing treatment for cancer. The employer had not designated any of the employee's time off as FMLA leave. ■ Thus, under

---

24. See, for example, *Rupnow v. TRC, Inc.,* 999 F.Supp. 1047 (N.D. Ohio 1998).

the DOL's regulation, the employee was entitled to an additional leave of twelve weeks. In 2002, however, the United States Supreme Court invalidated this rule. The Court reasoned that it would be unjust for an employee to obtain additional protected leave as a windfall.[25]

■ Employee Privacy Rights

In the last twenty-five years, concerns about the privacy rights of employees have arisen in response to the sometimes invasive tactics used by employers to monitor and screen workers. Perhaps the greatest privacy concern in today's employment arena has to do with electronic performance monitoring. Clearly, employers need to protect themselves from liability for their employees' online activities. They also have a legitimate interest in monitoring the productivity of their workers. At the same time, employees expect to have a certain zone of privacy in the workplace. Indeed, many lawsuits have involved allegations that employers' intrusive monitoring practices violate employees' privacy rights.

ELECTRONIC MONITORING IN THE WORKPLACE

According to a survey by the American Management Association, more than two-thirds of employers engage in some form of surveillance of their employees.[26] Types of monitoring include reviewing employees' e-mail and computer files, video recording of employee job performance, and recording and reviewing telephone conversations and voice mail. (See the *Application* feature at the end of this chapter for a discussion of how employers should develop an Internet policy for the workplace.)

A variety of specially designed software products have made it easier for an employer to track employees' Internet use. Software now allows an employer to track virtually every move made by an employee using the Internet, including the specific Web sites visited and the time spent surfing the Web. Filtering software, which was discussed in Chapter 1, can also be used to prevent employees from accessing certain Web sites, such as sites containing pornographic or sexually explicit images. Other filtering software may be used to screen incoming e-mail for viruses and block junk mail (spam).

Although the use of filtering software by public employers (government agencies) has led to charges that blocking access to Web sites violates employees' rights to free speech, this issue does not arise in private businesses. This is because the First Amendment's protection of free speech applies only to *government* restraints on speech, and not normally to restraints imposed in the private sector.

Laws Protecting Employee Privacy Rights   A number of laws protect privacy rights. We look here at laws that apply in the employment context.

Protection under Constitutional and Tort Law.   Recall from Chapter 1 that the U.S. Constitution does not contain a provision that explicitly guarantees a right to privacy. A personal right to privacy, however, has been inferred from other constitutional guarantees provided by the First, Third, Fourth, Fifth, and Ninth

---

25. *Ragsdale v. Wolverine World Wide, Inc.,* 535 U.S. 81, 122 S.Ct. 1155, 152 L.Ed.2d 167 (2002).
26. For a discussion of this survey and its results, see Allison R. Michael and Scott M. Lidman, "Monitoring of Employees Still Growing," *The National Law Journal,* January 29, 2001, p. B9.

Amendments to the Constitution. Tort law (see Chapter 4), state constitutions, and a number of state and federal statutes also provide for privacy rights.

The Electronic Communications Privacy Act. The major statute with which employers must comply is the Electronic Communications Privacy Act (ECPA) of 1986.[27] This act amended existing federal wiretapping law to cover electronic forms of communications, such as communications via cellular telephones or e-mail. The ECPA prohibits the intentional interception of any wire or electronic communication and the intentional disclosure or use of the information obtained by the interception. Excluded from coverage, however, are any electronic communications through devices that are "furnished to the subscriber or user by a provider of wire or electronic communication service" and that are being used by the subscriber or user, or by the provider of the service, "in the ordinary course of its business."

This "business-extension exception" to the ECPA permits employers to monitor employees' electronic communications made in the ordinary course of business. It does not, however, permit employers to monitor employees' personal communications. Under another exception to the ECPA, however, an employer may avoid liability under the act if the employees consent to having their electronic communications intercepted by the employer. Thus, an employer may be able to avoid liability under the ECPA by simply requiring employees to sign forms indicating that they consent to such monitoring.

Clearly, the law allows employers to engage in electronic monitoring in the workplace. In fact, cases in which courts have held that an employer's monitoring of electronic communications in the workplace violated employees' privacy rights are relatively rare. What if an employer monitors the e-mail of an independent contractor who works from a remote location? Does that violate the ECPA? See this chapter's *Adapting the Law to the Online Environment* feature on the next page for a case discussing this issue.

 The American Civil Liberties Union (ACLU) has a page on its Web site devoted to employee privacy rights with respect to electronic monitoring. Go to

http://www.aclu.org/ library/pbr2.html.

Factors Considered by the Courts in Employee Privacy Cases When determining whether an employer should be held liable for violating an employee's privacy rights, the courts generally weigh the employer's interests against the employee's reasonable expectation of privacy. Generally, if employees are informed that their communications are being monitored, they cannot reasonably expect those communications to be private. If employees are not informed that certain communications are being monitored, however, the employer may be held liable for invading their privacy.

■ EXAMPLE 18.6 In one case, an employer secretly recorded conversations among his four employees by placing a tape recorder in their common office. The conversations were of a highly personal nature and included harsh criticisms of the employer. The employer immediately fired two of the employees, informing them that their termination was due to their comments on the tape. In the ensuing suit, one of the issues was whether the employees, in these circumstances, had a reasonable expectation of privacy. The court held that they did and granted summary judgment in their favor. The employees clearly would not have criticized their boss if they had not assumed their conversations were private. Furthermore, the office was small, and the employees were careful that no third parties ever overheard their comments.[28]■

---

27. 18 U.S.C. Sections 2510–2521.
28. *Dorris v. Abscher,* 179 F.3d 420 (6th Cir. 1999).

ADAPTING THE LAW TO THE ONLINE ENVIRONMENT

Can an Employer Monitor an Independent Contractor's E-Mail?

Under the "business-extension exception" to the Electronic Communications Privacy Act (ECPA), an employer can monitor an employee's e-mail as long as the messages being monitored involve business rather than personal concerns. This exception is based on the assumption that when the employer furnishes e-mail services to an employee, that employee has no reasonable expectation of privacy. But what happens when the employer makes e-mail services available to an independent contractor who is working from a separate location? Does the independent contractor have a reasonable expectation of privacy in his or her e-mail, or can the employer legally monitor that person's e-mail? That was the issue before the U.S. Court of Appeals for the Third Circuit in *Fraser v. Nationwide Mutual Insurance Co.*[a]

THE PLAINTIFF WAS AN INDEPENDENT INSURANCE AGENT

The case involved Richard Fraser, an independent insurance agent who had entered an agreement to sell insurance policies exclusively for Nationwide Mutual Insurance Company. The agreement allowed either party to terminate the relationship at will. Recall from Chapter 24 that independent contractors are not employees (because the hiring party does not control their work performance), but they may be considered agents, as was the case with Fraser.

Fraser worked from his own office in Pennsylvania, but Nationwide provided him with an e-mail address and server. On learning that Fraser had written two letters to its competitors (inquiring about insurance poli-

cies), Nationwide became concerned about his loyalty. Nationwide then searched its main file server—on which all of Fraser's e-mail was logged—looking for any e-mail that demonstrated improper behavior. Nationwide concluded that Fraser had been disloyal and terminated his contract. An administrative review board affirmed the termination. Fraser then filed suit alleging, in part, violations of the ECPA. The trial court ruled that Nationwide had not violated the ECPA, and Fraser appealed.

THE E-MAIL WAS NOT "INTERCEPTED"

The appellate court affirmed the lower court's decision that Nationwide's search of Fraser's e-mail did not violate the ECPA. The court gave two reasons for its decision, neither of which was contingent on Fraser's status as an independent contractor. First, the court looked at the meaning of the word *intercept* in Title 1 of the act. Under the ECPA, the court concluded, an intercept must occur "contemporaneously with transmission"—that is, at the same time that it is sent. Because Nationwide had looked at Fraser's e-mail *after* it had already been sent, the court held that Nationwide had not intercepted the e-mail within the meaning of the act. Second, the court found that under Title 2 of the ECPA Nationwide was authorized to access the e-mail because it was the entity that provided the e-mail service. Fraser's independent-contractor status was irrelevant, in the court's view, because the employer provided the e-mail service and was authorized to access stored messages.

FOR CRITICAL ANALYSIS

Should the "business-extension exception" to the ECPA apply to independent contractors? Why or why not?

a. 352 F.3d 107 (3d Cir. 2004).

Privacy Expectations and E-Mail Systems   In cases brought by employees alleging that their privacy has been invaded by e-mail monitoring, the courts have tended to hold for the employers. This is true even when the employees were not informed that their e-mail would be monitored.

■ **EXAMPLE 18.7** In a leading case on this issue, the Pillsbury Company promised its employees that it would not read their e-mail or terminate or discipline them based on the content of their e-mail. Despite this promise, Pillsbury intercepted employee Michael Smyth's e-mail, decided that it was unprofessional and inappropriate, and fired him. In Pennsylvania, where the discharge occurred, it is against public policy for an employer to fire an employee based on a violation of the employee's right to privacy. In Smyth's suit against the company, he claimed that his termination was a violation of this policy. The court, however, found no "reasonable expectation of privacy in e-mail communications voluntarily made by an employee to his supervisor over the company e-mail system."[29] ■

OTHER TYPES OF MONITORING

In addition to monitoring their employees' online activities, employers also engage in other types of employee screening and monitoring practices. These practices, which have included lie-detector tests, drug tests, AIDS tests, and employment screening, have often been subject to challenge as violations of employee privacy rights.

Lie-Detector Tests   At one time, many employers required employees or job applicants to take polygraph examinations (lie-detector tests) in connection with their employment. To protect the privacy interests of employees and job applicants, in 1988 Congress passed the Employee Polygraph Protection Act.[30] The act prohibits employers from (1) requiring or causing employees or job applicants to take lie-detector tests or suggesting or requesting that they do so; (2) using, accepting, referring to, or asking about the results of lie-detector tests taken by employees or applicants; and (3) taking or threatening negative employment-related action against employees or applicants based on results of lie-detector tests or on their refusal to take the tests.

Employers excepted from these prohibitions include federal, state, and local government employers; certain security service firms; and companies manufacturing and distributing controlled substances. Other employers may use polygraph tests when investigating losses attributable to theft, including embezzlement and the theft of trade secrets.

Drug Testing   In the interests of public safety, many employers, including the government, require their employees to submit to drug testing. State laws relating to the privacy rights of private-sector employees vary from state to state. Some state constitutions may prohibit private employers from testing for drugs, and state statutes may restrict drug testing by private employers in any number of ways. A collective bargaining agreement may also provide protection against drug testing. In some instances, employees have brought an action against the employer for the tort of invasion of privacy (discussed in Chapter 4).

Constitutional limitations apply to the testing of certain employees. The Fourth Amendment provides that individuals have the right to be "secure in their persons" against "unreasonable searches and seizures" conducted by government agents. Nonetheless, drug tests have been held constitutional when there was a reasonable basis for suspecting government employees of using drugs. Additionally, when drug use in a particular job could threaten public safety, testing has been upheld. For example, a Department of Transportation rule that requires employees engaged in oil and gas pipeline operations to submit to random drug testing was upheld, even though the rule did not require that before being tested the individual must have been suspected of drug use.[31] The court held that the government's interest in promoting public safety in the pipeline industry outweighed the employees' privacy interests.

---

29. *Smyth v. Pillsbury Co.,* 914 F.Supp. 97 (E.D.Pa. 1996).
30. 29 U.S.C. Sections 2001 *et seq.*
31. *Electrical Workers Local 1245 v. Skinner,* 913 F.2d 1454 (9th Cir. 1990).

Workers at a toxicology lab place employees' urine samples in bar-coded test tubes before screening the samples for drugs. Many private employers today routinely require their employees to submit to drug testing. What recourse, if any, does an employee who does not consent to a drug test have against the employer? (U.S. Navy, Photo Jim Watson)

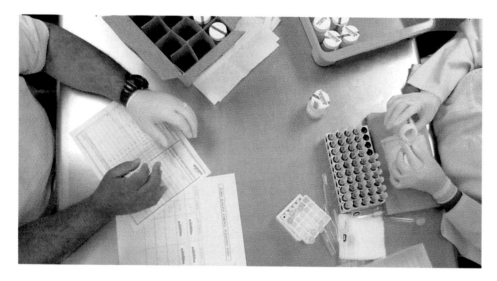

AIDS Testing   A number of employers test their workers for acquired immune deficiency syndrome (AIDS). Some state laws restrict AIDS testing, and federal statutes offer some protection to employees or job applicants who have AIDS or have tested positive for HIV, the virus that causes AIDS. The federal Americans with Disabilities Act of 1990[32] (discussed later in this chapter), for example, prohibits discrimination against persons with disabilities, and the term *disability* has been broadly defined to include those individuals with diseases such as AIDS. The law also requires employers to reasonably accommodate the needs of persons with disabilities. As a rule, although the law may not prohibit AIDS testing, it may prohibit the discharge of employees based on the results of those tests.

Genetic Testing   A serious privacy issue arose when some employers began conducting genetic testing of employees or prospective employees in an effort to identify individuals who might develop significant health problems in the future. To date, however, only a few cases involving this issue have come before the courts. In one case, the Lawrence Berkeley Laboratory screened prospective employees for the gene that causes sickle-cell anemia, although the applicants were not informed of this. In a lawsuit subsequently brought by the prospective employees, a federal appellate court held that they had a cause of action for violation of their privacy rights.[33] The case was later settled for $2.2 million.

In another case, the Equal Employment Opportunity Commission (EEOC), the federal agency in charge of administering laws prohibiting employment discrimination, brought an action against a railroad company that had genetically tested its employees. The EEOC contended that the genetic testing violated the Americans with Disabilities Act of 1990. In 2002, this case was settled out of court, also for $2.2 million.[34]

---

32. 42 U.S.C. Sections 12102–12118.

33. *Norman-Bloodsaw v. Lawrence Berkeley Laboratory,* 135 F.3d 1260 (9th Cir. 1998).

34. For a discussion of this settlement, see David Hechler, "Railroad to Pay $2.2 Million over Genetic Testing," *The National Law Journal,* May 13, 2002, p. A22.

Screening Procedures   Preemployment screening procedures are another area of concern to potential employees. What kinds of questions are permissible on an employment application or a preemployment test? What kinds of questions go too far in invading the applicant's privacy? Is it an invasion of privacy, for example, to ask questions about the prospective employee's sexual orientation or religious convictions? Although an employer may believe that such information is relevant to the job for which the individual has applied, the applicant may feel differently about the matter. Generally, questions on an employment application must have a reasonable nexus, or connection, with the job for which the person is applying.[35]

▪ Employment Discrimination

Out of the 1960s civil rights movement to end racial and other forms of discrimination grew a body of law protecting employees against discrimination in the workplace. This protective legislation further eroded the employment-at-will doctrine, which was discussed earlier in this chapter. In the past several decades, judicial decisions, administrative agency actions, and legislation have restricted the ability of employers, as well as unions, to discriminate against workers on the basis of race, color, religion, national origin, gender, age, or disability. A class of persons defined by one or more of these criteria is known as a **protected class.**

Several federal statutes prohibit **employment discrimination** against members of protected classes. The most important statute is Title VII of the Civil Rights Act of 1964.[36] Title VII prohibits discrimination on the basis of race, color, religion, national origin, or gender at any stage of employment. The Age Discrimination in Employment Act of 1967[37] and the Americans with Disabilities Act of 1990[38] prohibit discrimination on the basis of age and disability, respectively.

This chapter focuses on the kinds of discrimination prohibited by these federal statutes. Note, though, that discrimination against employees on the basis of any of these criteria may also violate state human rights statutes or other state laws or public policies prohibiting discrimination.

TITLE VII OF THE CIVIL RIGHTS ACT OF 1964

Title VII of the Civil Rights Act of 1964 and its amendments prohibit job discrimination against employees, applicants, and union members on the basis of race, color, national origin, religion, or gender at any stage of employment. Title VII applies to employers with fifteen or more employees, labor unions with fifteen or more members, labor unions that operate hiring halls (to which members go regularly to be rationed jobs as they become available), employment agencies, and state and local governing units or agencies. A special section of the act prohibits discrimination in most federal government employment.

The Equal Employment Opportunity Commission   Compliance with Title VII is monitored by the Equal Employment Opportunity Commission (EEOC). A victim of alleged discrimination, before bringing a suit against the employer, must first file

PROTECTED CLASS
A group of persons protected by specific laws because of the group's defining characteristics. Under laws prohibiting employment discrimination, these characteristics include race, color, religion, national origin, gender, age, and disability.

EMPLOYMENT DISCRIMINATION
Treating employees or job applicants unequally on the basis of race, color, national origin, religion, gender, age, or disability; prohibited by federal statutes.

---

35. See, for example, *Soroka v. Dayton Hudson Corp.,* 7 Cal.App.4th 203, 1 Cal.Rptr.2d 77 (1991).
36. 42 U.S.C. Sections 2000e–2000e-17.
37. 29 U.S.C. Sections 621–634.
38. 42 U.S.C. Sections 12102–12118.

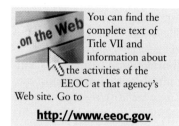

You can find the complete text of Title VII and information about the activities of the EEOC at that agency's Web site. Go to

http://www.eeoc.gov.

a claim with the EEOC. The EEOC may investigate the dispute and attempt to obtain the parties' voluntary consent to an out-of-court settlement. If voluntary agreement cannot be reached, the EEOC may then file a suit against the employer on the employee's behalf. If the EEOC decides not to investigate the claim, the victim may bring her or his own lawsuit against the employer.

The EEOC does not investigate every claim of employment discrimination, regardless of the merits of the claim. Generally, it investigates only "priority cases," such as cases involving retaliatory discharge (firing an employee in retaliation for submitting a claim to the EEOC) and cases involving types of discrimination that are of particular concern to the EEOC.

Intentional and Unintentional Discrimination   Title VII prohibits both intentional and unintentional discrimination.

Intentional Discrimination.   Intentional discrimination by an employer against an employee is known as **disparate-treatment discrimination.** Because intent may sometimes be difficult to prove, courts have established certain procedures for resolving disparate-treatment cases. Suppose that a woman applies for employment with a construction firm and is rejected. If she sues on the basis of disparate-treatment discrimination in hiring, she must show that (1) she is a member of a protected class, (2) she applied and was qualified for the job in question, (3) she was rejected by the employer, and (4) the employer continued to seek applicants for the position or filled the position with a person not in a protected class.

If the woman can meet these relatively easy requirements, she has made out a *prima facie* case of illegal discrimination. Making out a *prima facie* case of discrimination means that the plaintiff has met her initial burden of proof and will win in the absence of a legally acceptable employer defense (defenses to claims of employment discrimination will be discussed later in this chapter). The burden then shifts to the employer-defendant, who must articulate a legal reason for not hiring the plaintiff. To prevail, the plaintiff must then show that the employer's reason is a *pretext* (not the true reason) and that discriminatory intent actually motivated the employer's decision.

Unintentional Discrimination.   Employers often use interviews and testing procedures to choose from among a large number of applicants for job openings. Minimum educational requirements are also common. These practices and procedures may have an unintended discriminatory impact on a protected class. **Disparate-impact discrimination** occurs when, as a result of educational or other job requirements or hiring procedures, an employer's work force does not reflect the percentage of nonwhites, women, or members of other protected classes that characterizes qualified individuals in the local labor market. If a person challenging an employment practice having a discriminatory effect can show a connection between the practice and the disparity, he or she has made out a *prima facie* case, and no evidence of discriminatory intent needs to be shown.

Disparate-impact discrimination can also occur when an educational or other job requirement or hiring procedure excludes members of a protected class from an employer's work force at a substantially higher rate than nonmembers, regardless of the racial balance in the employer's work force. The EEOC has devised a test, called the "four-fifths rule," to determine whether an employment examination is discriminatory on its face. Under this rule, a selection rate for protected classes that is

DISPARATE-TREATMENT DISCRIMINATION
A form of employment discrimination that results when an employer intentionally discriminates against employees who are members of protected classes.

***PRIMA FACIE* CASE**
A case in which the plaintiff has produced sufficient evidence of his or her conclusion that the case can go to a jury; a case in which the evidence compels the plaintiff's conclusion if the defendant produces no affirmative defense or evidence to disprove it.

DISPARATE-IMPACT DISCRIMINATION
A form of employment discrimination that results from certain employer practices or procedures that, although not discriminatory on their face, have a discriminatory effect.

less than four-fifths, or 80 percent, of the rate for the group with the highest rate will generally be regarded as evidence of disparate impact.

■ EXAMPLE 18.8 One hundred white applicants take an employment test, and fifty pass the test and are hired. One hundred minority applicants take the test, and twenty pass the test and are hired. Because twenty is less than four-fifths (80 percent) of fifty, the test would be considered discriminatory under the EEOC guidelines. ■

Discrimination Based on Race, Color, and National Origin If a company's standards or policies for selecting or promoting employees have the effect of discriminating against employees or job applicants on the basis of race, color, or national origin, they are illegal—unless (except for race) they have a substantial, demonstrable relationship to realistic qualifications for the job in question. Discrimination against these protected classes in regard to employment conditions and benefits is also illegal.

■ EXAMPLE 18.9 In one case, Cynthia McCullough, an African American woman with a college degree, worked at a deli in a grocery store. More than a year later, the owner of the store promoted a white woman to the position of "deli manager." The white woman had worked in the deli for only three months, had only a sixth-grade education, and could not calculate prices or read recipes. Although the owner gave various reasons for promoting the white woman instead of McCullough, a federal appellate court held that these reasons were likely just excuses and that the real reason was discriminatory intent.[39] ■

ETHICAL ISSUE 18.2

Are English-only policies in the workplace a form of national-origin discrimination? As the U.S. population becomes more multilingual, so does the work force. In response to this development, many employers have instituted English-only policies in their workplaces, particularly in states with large immigrant populations, such as Texas and California. Are English-only policies fair to workers who do not speak English? Do they violate Title VII's prohibition against discrimination on the basis of race or national origin, as workers in a number of lawsuits have alleged? Generally, the courts have shown a fair degree of tolerance with respect to English-only rules, especially when an employer can show that there is a legitimate business reason for the rules, such as improved communication among employees or worker safety. Some courts, however, tend to regard with suspicion policies that require that English be spoken not only during work time but also on breaks, lunch hours, and the like. For example, one federal district court held that a Texas firm had engaged in disparate-treatment discrimination based on national origin by requiring that English be spoken exclusively in the workplace, including during breaks, except when employees were communicating with customers who could not speak English.[40] ■

Discrimination Based on Religion Title VII of the Civil Rights Act of 1964 also prohibits government employers, private employers, and unions from discriminating against persons because of their religion. An employer must "reasonably accommodate" the religious practices of its employees, unless to do so would cause undue

---

39. *McCullough v. Real Foods, Inc.,* 140 F.3d 1123 (8th Cir. 1998). The federal district court had granted summary judgment for the employer in this case. The Eighth Circuit Court of Appeals reversed the district court's decision and remanded the case for trial.
40. *EEOC v. Premier Operator Services, Inc.,* 113 F.Supp.2d 1066 (N.D.Tex. 2000).

A group of Muslims in prayer. As part of Islam, their religion, Muslims have five duties they must perform, including the duty to worship the One God in prayer five times each day. Suppose that several of these Muslim men work at a manufacturing plant. They have asked their employer for permission to take two brief breaks during work hours so that they can pray together. Can the employer prohibit its Muslim employees from praying in the workplace? Why or why not? (Reuters/Rebecca Cook, Landov)

hardship to the employer's business. For example, if an employee's religion prohibits him or her from working on a certain day of the week or at a certain type of job, the employer must make a reasonable attempt to accommodate these religious requirements. Employers must reasonably accommodate an employee's religious belief even if the belief is not based on the tenets or dogma of a particular church, sect, or denomination. The only requirement is that the belief be sincerely held by the employee.[41]

Discrimination Based on Gender   Under Title VII, as well as other federal acts, employers are forbidden to discriminate against employees on the basis of gender. Employers are prohibited from classifying jobs as male or female and from advertising in help-wanted columns that are designated male or female unless the employer can prove that the gender of the applicant is essential to the job. Furthermore, employers cannot have separate male and female seniority lists. Generally, to succeed in a suit for gender discrimination, a plaintiff must demonstrate that gender was a determining factor in the employer's decision to hire, fire, or promote her or him. Typically, this involves looking at all of the surrounding circumstances.

The Pregnancy Discrimination Act of 1978,[42] which amended Title VII, expanded the definition of gender discrimination to include discrimination based on pregnancy. Women affected by pregnancy, childbirth, or related medical conditions must be treated—for all employment-related purposes, including the receipt of benefits under employee benefit programs—the same as other persons not so affected but similar in ability to work.

---

41. *Frazee v. Illinois Department of Employment Security,* 489 U.S. 829, 109 S.Ct. 1514, 103 L.Ed.2d 914 (1989).
42. 42 U.S.C. Section 2000e(k).

CONSTRUCTIVE DISCHARGE
A termination of employment brought about by making the employee's working conditions so intolerable that the employee reasonably feels compelled to leave.

Sometimes employees claim that they were "constructively discharged" from their jobs. **Constructive discharge** occurs when the employer causes the employee's working conditions to be so intolerable that a reasonable person in the employee's position would feel compelled to quit. Title VII encompasses employer liability for constructive discharge.[43] In the case that follows, the question was whether the employer should have been aware of the employee's mistreatment and unbearable working conditions and done something about them.

---

43. *Pennsylvania State Police v. Suders,* ___U.S.___, 124 S.Ct. 2342, 159 L.Ed.2d 204 (2004).

CASE 18.3 ■ Conway-Jepsen v. Small Business Administration

United States District Court,
District of Montana, 2004.
303 F.Supp.2d 1155.

FACTS In August 1992, Jo Alice Mospan took charge of the Helena, Montana, office of the U.S. Small Business Administration (SBA) as the district director. At the time, there were no other females above a certain pay level in the Helena office, and most of the senior employees and supervisors were male. Mospan was an "in-your-face" micromanager, frequently disciplining employees. In Helena, her purportedly express purpose was to harass and ultimately rid the office of certain male employees so that they could be replaced by females. In 1993, Mospan recruited Mary Conway-Jepsen from the SBA office in Santa Ana, California. Conway-Jepsen soon learned what Mospan was doing, told her that it was wrong, and refused to cooperate. Mospan retaliated. Among other things, she overloaded Conway-Jepsen with irrelevant assignments, took counterproductive actions to her projects, and set her up to make mistakes. Conway-Jepsen's physician recommended that she quit. She applied for a transfer, but when none was forthcoming, she resigned in August 1997. By 2000, all of the targeted males were also gone. Conway-Jepsen filed a suit in a federal district court against the SBA, claiming a violation of Title VII.

ISSUE Was Conway-Jepsen constructively discharged in violation of Title VII?

DECISION Yes. The court concluded that the hostile working conditions at the Helena SBA office were created

by conduct in violation of Title VII, that Conway-Jepsen reasonably found the conditions intolerable, and that her resignation resulted from these conditions. On her behalf, the court ordered back pay, job reinstatement, compensatory damages, and attorneys' fees.

REASON The court emphasized that the retaliatory treatment spanned two and a half years. "No reasonable employee could be expected to put up with Mospan's harassment for a longer period of time." Conway-Jepsen "is an intelligent, knowledgeable, and aggressive program manager," whose "demeanor is that of a tough fighter, not a person who would easily wilt under pressure." She "was a diligent and competent SBA employee who was constructively discharged from her position by Mospan's lengthy, continuous, and pervasive pattern of retaliatory treatment." Further, Mospan ruined Conway-Jepsen's career, continuing to retaliate against her by interfering with her ability to obtain employment after her resignation. Because Mospan was the district director of the Helena SBA office, she was the SBA's agent, acting within the scope of her authority and the course of her employment. Thus, the SBA knew or should have known of the hostile working conditions but failed to remedy them.

WHY IS THIS CASE IMPORTANT? *Employers should be aware that if a manager or supervisor creates intolerable working conditions because of his or her own personal bias, the employer could be held liable under Title VII.*

SEXUAL HARASSMENT
In the employment context, the demanding of sexual favors in return for job promotions or other benefits, or language or conduct that is so sexually offensive that it creates a hostile working environment.

Sexual Harassment   Title VII also protects employees against **sexual harassment** in the workplace. Sexual harassment has often been classified as either *quid pro quo* harassment or hostile-environment harassment. *Quid pro quo* is a Latin phrase that is often translated to mean "something in exchange for something else." *Quid pro quo* harassment occurs when sexual favors are demanded in return for job opportunities, promotions, salary increases, and the like. According to the United States Supreme Court, hostile-environment harassment occurs when "the workplace is permeated with discriminatory intimidation, ridicule, and insult, that is sufficiently severe or pervasive to alter the conditions of the victim's employment and create an abusive working environment."[44]

Generally, the courts apply this Supreme Court guideline on a case-by-case basis. Some courts have held that just one incident of sexually offensive conduct—such as a sexist remark by a co-worker or a photo on an employer's desk of his bikini-clad wife—can create a hostile environment.[45] At least one court has held that a worker may recover damages under Title VII because *other* persons were sexually harassed in the workplace.[46] According to some employment specialists, employers should assume that hostile-environment harassment has occurred if an employee claims that it has. (For either type of harassment to be *sexual* harassment, it must involve gender-based discrimination—see this chapter's *Letter of the Law* feature.)

---

44. *Harris v. Forklift Systems*, 510 U.S. 17, 114 S.Ct. 367, 126 L.Ed.2d 295 (1993).
45. For other examples, see *Radtke v. Everett*, 442 Mich. 368, 501 N.W.2d 155 (1993); and *Nadeau v. Rainbow Rugs, Inc.*, 675 A.2d 973 (Me. 1996).
46. *Leibovitz v. New York City Transit Authority*, 4 F.Supp.2d 144 (E.D.N.Y. 1998).

LETTER OF THE LAW "Equal Opportunity" Harassment

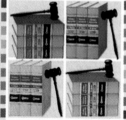

The prohibition against sexual harassment in the workplace is an extension of Title VII's prohibition against gender-based discrimination. This means that there can be no sexual harassment if no gender-based discrimination is involved. It also means, among other things, that Title VII does not protect employees from "equal opportunity" harassers—those who harass both sexes equally—because such persons are not discriminating on the basis of gender.

This point was made clear to Steven and Karen Holman, a married couple who worked for the Indiana Department of Transportation, when they sued their employer for sexual harassment. The Holmans alleged that their supervisor had sexually harassed each of them individually on separate occasions and that the supervisor retaliated against them—by denying them certain privileges and pay—when they rejected his advances. In evaluating their claim, the court looked at the letter of Title VII, which states, "It shall be an unlawful employment practice for an employer to . . . discriminate against any individual with respect to compensation, terms, conditions, or privileges of employment, because of such individual's . . . sex." The court observed that in the Holmans' case, there was no discrimination "because of . . . sex" because the supervisor harassed both of them. Thus, concluded the court, the Holmans could not maintain a Title VII action against their employer.[a]

THE BOTTOM LINE
Harassment in the workplace takes many forms, including harassment based on gender, race, national origin, religion, age, and disability. In cases alleging sexual harassment, however, the harassment must be on the basis of sex (gender), or Title VII will not apply.

a. *Holman v. Indiana*, 211 F.3d 399 (7th Cir. 2000).

Harassment by Supervisors.   What if an employee is harassed by a manager or supervisor of a large firm, and the firm itself (the "employer") is not aware of the harassment? Should the employer be held liable for the harassment nonetheless? For some time, the courts were in disagreement on this issue. Typically, employers were held liable for Title VII violations by the firm's managerial or supervisory personnel in *quid pro quo* harassment cases regardless of whether the employer knew about the harassment. In hostile-environment cases, the majority of courts tended to hold employers liable only if the employer knew or should have known of the harassment and failed to take prompt remedial action.

For an employer to be held liable for a supervisor's sexual harassment, the supervisor must have taken a tangible employment action against the employee. A *tangible employment action* is a significant change in employment status, such as firing or failing to promote an employee, reassigning the employee to a position with significantly different responsibilities, or effecting a significant change in employment benefits. Only a supervisor, or another person acting with the authority of the employer, can cause this sort of injury.

In 1998, in two separate cases,[47] the United States Supreme Court issued some significant guidelines relating to the liability of employers for their supervisors' harassment of employees in the workplace. On the one hand, employees benefit by the ruling that employers may be held liable for their supervisors' harassment even though the employers were unaware of the actions and even though the employees suffered no adverse job consequences. On the other hand, the Court made it clear in both decisions that employers have an affirmative defense against liability for their supervisors' harassment of employees if the employers can show the following:

1 That they have taken "reasonable care to prevent and correct promptly any sexually harassing behavior" (by establishing effective harassment policies and complaint procedures, for example).

2 That the employees suing for harassment failed to follow these policies and procedures.

Harassment by Co-Workers and Nonemployees.   Often, employees alleging harassment complain that the actions of co-workers, not supervisors, are responsible for creating a hostile working environment. In such cases, the employee may still have a cause of action against the employer. Normally, though, the employer will be held liable only if the employer knew, or should have known, about the harassment and failed to take immediate remedial action.

Employers may also be liable for harassment by *nonemployees* in certain circumstances.   ■ **EXAMPLE 18.10** If a restaurant owner or manager knows that a certain customer repeatedly harasses a waitress and permits the harassment to continue, the restaurant owner may be liable under Title VII even though the customer is not an employee of the restaurant. The issue turns on the control that the employer exerts over a nonemployee. In one case, an owner of a *Pizza Hut* franchise was held liable for the harassment of a waitress by two male customers because no steps were taken to prevent the harassment.[48]   ■

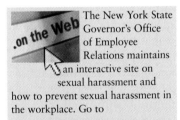

The New York State Governor's Office of Employee Relations maintains an interactive site on sexual harassment and how to prevent sexual harassment in the workplace. Go to

http://www.goer.state.ny.us/ Train/onlinelearning/SH/ intro.html.

---

47. *Faragher v. City of Boca Raton*, 524 U.S. 775, 118 S.Ct. 2275, 141 L.Ed.2d 662 (1998); and *Burlington Industries, Inc. v. Ellerth*, 524 U.S. 742, 118 S.Ct. 2257, 141 L.Ed.2d 633 (1998).
48. *Lockard v. Pizza Hut, Inc.*, 162 F.3d 1062 (10th Cir. 1998).

Same-Gender Harassment.   The courts have also had to address the issue of whether men who are harassed by other men, or women who are harassed by other women, are protected by laws that prohibit gender-based discrimination in the workplace. For example, what if the male president of a firm demands sexual favors from a male employee? Does this action qualify as sexual harassment? For some time, the courts were widely split on this issue. In 1998, in *Oncale v. Sundowner Offshore Services, Inc.*,[49] the Supreme Court resolved the issue by holding that Title VII protection extends to situations in which individuals are harassed by members of the same gender.

Nevertheless, it can be difficult to prove that the harassment in same-gender harassment cases is "based on sex." ■ **EXAMPLE 18.11** Suppose that a gay man is harassed by another man at the workplace. The harasser is not a homosexual and does not treat all men with hostility—just this one man. Does the victim in this situation have a cause of action under Title VII? A court may find that this does not qualify as sexual harassment under Title VII because the harasser's conduct was because of the employee's sexual orientation, not "because of sex."[50] ■

Remedies under Title VII   Employer liability under Title VII may be extensive. If the plaintiff successfully proves that unlawful discrimination occurred, he or she may be awarded reinstatement, back pay, retroactive promotions, and damages. Compensatory damages are available only in cases of intentional discrimination. Punitive damages may be recovered against a private employer only if the employer acted with malice or reckless indifference to an individual's rights. The statute limits the total amount of compensatory and punitive damages that the plaintiff can recover from specific employers—ranging from $50,000 against employers with one hundred or fewer employees to $300,000 against employers with more than five hundred employees.

.on the Web The Illinois state bar site provides information on remedies for employment discrimination at

http://www.illinoisbar.org/ LawEd/johnston.htm.

EQUAL PAY ACT OF 1963

The Equal Pay Act of 1963 was enacted as an amendment to the Fair Labor Standards Act of 1938. Basically, the act prohibits gender-based discrimination in the wages paid for similar work on jobs that require the same amount of skill, effort, and responsibility. For the act's equal pay requirements to apply, the male and female employees must work at the same establishment.

A person alleging wage discrimination in violation of the Equal Pay Act may sue her or his employer. To determine whether the Equal Pay Act has been violated, a court will look to the primary duties of the two jobs. It is job content rather than job description that controls in all cases. The jobs of a barber and a beautician, for example, are considered essentially "equal." So, too, are those of a tailor and a seamstress. Nevertheless, an employer will *not* be found liable for violating the act if it can show that the wage differential for equal work was based on (1) a seniority system, (2) a merit system, (3) a system that pays according to quality or quantity of production, or (4) any factor other than gender. Small differences in job content, however, do not justify higher pay for one gender. The Equal Pay Act is administered by the EEOC.

49. 523 U.S. 75, 118 S.Ct. 998, 140 L.Ed.2d 207 (1998).
50. See, for example, *McCown v. St. John's Health System,* 349 F.3d 540 (8th Cir. 2003); and *Rene v. MGM Grand Hotel, Inc.,* 305 F.3d 1061 (9th Cir. 2002).

DISCRIMINATION BASED ON AGE

Age discrimination is potentially the most widespread form of discrimination, because anyone—regardless of race, color, national origin, or gender—could be a victim at some point in life. The Age Discrimination in Employment Act (ADEA) of 1967, as amended, prohibits employment discrimination on the basis of age against individuals forty years of age or older. The act also prohibits mandatory retirement for nonmanagerial workers. For the act to apply, an employer must have twenty or more employees, and the employer's business activities must affect interstate commerce. The EEOC administers the ADEA, but the act also permits private causes of action against employers for age discrimination.

Procedures under the ADEA   The burden-shifting procedure under the ADEA is similar to that under Title VII. If a plaintiff can establish that she or he (1) was a member of the protected age group, (2) was qualified for the position from which she or he was discharged, and (3) was discharged under circumstances that give rise to an inference of discrimination, the plaintiff has established a *prima facie* case of unlawful age discrimination. The burden then shifts to the employer, who must articulate a legitimate reason for the discrimination. If the plaintiff can prove that the employer's reason is only a pretext (excuse) and that the plaintiff's age was a determining factor in the employer's decision, the employer will be held liable under the ADEA.

Replacing Older Workers with Younger Workers   Numerous age discrimination cases have been brought against employers who, to cut costs, replaced older, higher-salaried employees with younger, lower-salaried workers. Whether a firing is discriminatory or simply part of a rational business decision to prune the company's ranks is not always clear. Companies often defend a decision to discharge a worker by asserting that the worker could no longer perform his or her duties or that the worker's skills were no longer needed. The employee must prove that the discharge was motivated, at least in part, by age bias. Proof that qualified older employees are generally discharged before younger employees or that co-workers continually made unflattering age-related comments about the discharged worker may be enough.

   The plaintiff need not prove that he or she was replaced by a person outside the protected class—that is, by a person under the age of forty years.[51] Rather, the issue in all ADEA cases is whether age discrimination has, in fact, occurred, regardless of the age of the replacement worker.

State Employees Not Covered by the ADEA   The United States Supreme Court has generally held that the states are immune from lawsuits brought by private individuals in federal court—unless a state consents to the suit. This immunity stems from the Supreme Court's interpretation of the Eleventh Amendment (the text of this amendment is included in Appendix A). In a number of cases brought in the late 1990s, state agencies that were sued by state employees for age discrimination sought to have the suits dismissed on this ground.[52]

   State immunity under the Eleventh Amendment is not absolute, however, as the Supreme Court explained in 2004. A case was brought under the Americans with

REMEMBER   The Fourteenth Amendment prohibits any state from denying any person "the equal protection of the laws." This prohibition applies to the *federal* government through the due process clause of the Fifth Amendment.

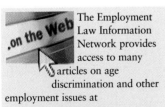

The Employment Law Information Network provides access to many articles on age discrimination and other employment issues at

http://www.elinfonet.com/ fedindex/2.

---

51. *O'Connor v. Consolidated Coin Caterers Corp.*, 517 U.S. 308, 116 S.Ct. 1307, 134 L.Ed.2d 433 (1996).
52. See, for example, *Kimel v. Florida Board of Regents*, 528 U.S. 62, 120 S.Ct. 631, 145 L.Ed.2d 522 (2000).

Disabilities Act, which will be discussed shortly, alleging that disabled individuals were denied access to the courts. The Court held that in some situations, such as when fundamental rights are at stake, Congress has the power to abrogate (abolish) state immunity to private suits through legislation that unequivocally shows Congress's intent to subject states to private suits.[53]

DISCRIMINATION BASED ON DISABILITY

The Americans with Disabilities Act (ADA) of 1990 is designed to eliminate discriminatory employment practices that prevent otherwise qualified workers with disabilities from fully participating in the national labor force. Prior to 1990, the major federal law providing protection to those with disabilities was the Rehabilitation Act of 1973. That act covered only federal government employees and those employed under federally funded programs. The ADA extends federal protection against disability-based discrimination to all workplaces with fifteen or more workers. Basically, the ADA requires that employers "reasonably accommodate" the needs of persons with disabilities unless to do so would cause the employer to suffer an "undue hardship." Note, though, that with the exception of the one 2004 case mentioned above, the Supreme Court has normally held that lawsuits under the ADA cannot be brought against state government employers.[54]

Co-workers discuss business matters. What is a disability under the Americans with Disabilities Act? (© Johnny Stockshooter, International Stock)

Procedures under the ADA   To prevail on a claim under the ADA, a plaintiff must show that he or she (1) has a disability, (2) is otherwise qualified for the employment in question, and (3) was excluded from the employment solely because of the disability. As in Title VII cases, a claim alleging a violation of the ADA may be commenced only after the plaintiff has pursued the claim through the EEOC. Plaintiffs may sue for many of the same remedies available under Title VII. The EEOC may decide to investigate and perhaps even sue the employer on behalf of the employee. If the EEOC decides not to sue, then the employee is entitled to sue.

Significantly, the United States Supreme Court held in 2002 that the EEOC could bring a suit against an employer for disability-based discrimination even though the employee had agreed to submit any job-related disputes to arbitration (see Chapter 3). The Court reasoned that because the EEOC was not a party to the arbitration agreement, the agreement was not binding on the EEOC.[55]

Plaintiffs in lawsuits brought under the ADA may seek many of the same remedies available under Title VII. These include reinstatement, back pay, a limited amount of compensatory and punitive damages (for intentional discrimination), and certain other forms of relief. Repeat violators may be ordered to pay fines of up to $100,000.

What Is a Disability?   The ADA is broadly drafted to cover persons with a wide range of disabilities. Specifically, the ADA defines *disability* as "(1) a physical or mental impairment that substantially limits one or more of the major life activities of such individuals; (2) a record of such impairment; or (3) being regarded as having such an impairment."

---

53. *Tennessee v. Lane,* ___ U.S. ___, 124 S.Ct. 1978, 158 L.Ed.2d 820 (2004).
54. *Board of Trustees of the University of Alabama v. Garrett,* 531 U.S. 356, 121 S.Ct. 955, 148 L.Ed.2d 866 (2001). The Supreme Court's ruling in *Tennessee v. Lane,* cited in footnote 53, did not expressly overrule this case. Thus, the Court has not held that private parties may always sue government employers under the ADA. Suits may be brought only for certain types of state ADA violations, such as denying a disabled person access to the courts.
55. *EEOC v. Waffle House, Inc.,* 534 U.S. 279, 122 S.Ct. 754, 151 L.Ed.2d 75 (2002).

Health conditions that have been considered disabilities under the federal law include blindness, alcoholism, heart disease, cancer, muscular dystrophy, cerebral palsy, paraplegia, diabetes, acquired immune deficiency syndrome (AIDS), testing positive for the human immunodeficiency virus (HIV), and morbid obesity (defined as existing when an individual's weight is two times that of a normal person).[56] The ADA excludes from coverage certain conditions, such as kleptomania (the obsessive desire to steal).

Although the ADA's definition of disability is broad, starting in 1999, the United States Supreme Court has issued a series of decisions narrowing the definition of what constitutes a disability under the act.

Correctable Conditions.   In 1999, in *Sutton v. United Airlines, Inc.,*[57] the Supreme Court reviewed a case raising the issue of whether severe myopia, or nearsightedness, which can be corrected with lenses, qualifies as a disability under the ADA. The Supreme Court ruled that it does not. The determination of whether a person is substantially limited in a major life activity is based on how the person functions when taking medication or using corrective devices, not on how the person functions without these measures.

In a similar case in 2002, a federal appellate court held that a pharmacist suffering from diabetes, which could be corrected by insulin, had no cause of action against his employer under the ADA.[58] In other cases decided in the early 2000s, the courts have held that plaintiffs with bipolar disorder, epilepsy, and other such conditions do *not* fall under the ADA's protections if the conditions can be corrected.

Repetitive-Stress Injuries.   For some time, the courts were divided on the issue of whether carpal tunnel syndrome (or other repetitive-stress injury) constituted a disability under the ADA. Carpal tunnel syndrome is a condition of pain and weakness in the hand caused by repetitive compression of a nerve in the wrist. In 2002, in a case involving this issue, the Supreme Court unanimously held that it did not. The Court stated that although the employee could not perform the manual tasks associated with her job, the condition did not constitute a disability under the ADA because it did not "substantially limit" the major life activity of performing manual tasks.[59]

Reasonable Accommodation   The ADA does not require that employers accommodate the needs of job applicants or employees with disabilities who are not otherwise qualified for the work. If a job applicant or an employee with a disability, with reasonable accommodation, can perform essential job functions, however, the employer must make the accommodation. Required modifications may include installing ramps for a wheelchair, establishing more flexible working hours, creating or modifying job assignments, and creating or improving training materials and procedures.

Considering Employees' Preferences.   Generally, employers should give primary consideration to employees' preferences in deciding what accommodations should be made. What happens if a job applicant or employee does not indicate to the

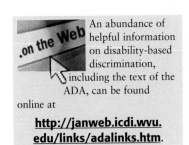

An abundance of helpful information on disability-based discrimination, including the text of the ADA, can be found online at **http://janweb.icdi.wvu. edu/links/adalinks.htm**.

---

56. *Cook v. Rhode Island Department of Mental Health,* 10 F.3d 17 (1st Cir. 1993).
57. 527 U.S. 471, 119 S.Ct. 2139, 144 L.Ed.2d 450 (1999).
58. *Orr v. Walmart Stores, Inc.,* 297 F.3d 720 (8th Cir. 2002).
59. *Toyota Motor Manufacturing, Kentucky, Inc. v. Williams,* 534 U.S. 184, 122 S.Ct. 681, 151 L.Ed.2d 615 (2002).

employer how her or his disability can be accommodated so that the employee can perform essential job functions? In this situation, the employer may avoid liability for failing to hire or retain the individual on the ground that the applicant or employee has failed to meet the "otherwise qualified" requirement.[60]

Undue Hardship. Employers who do not accommodate the needs of persons with disabilities must demonstrate that the accommodations will cause "undue hardship." Generally, the law offers no uniform standards for identifying what is an undue hardship other than the imposition of a "significant difficulty or expense" on the employer.

Usually, the courts decide whether an accommodation constitutes an undue hardship on a case-by-case basis. In one case, the court decided that paying for a parking space near the office for an employee with a disability was not an undue hardship.[61] In another case, the court held that accommodating the request of an employee with diabetes for indefinite leave until his disease was under control would create an undue hardship for the employer because the employer would not know when the employee was returning to work. The court stated that reasonable accommodation under the ADA means accommodation so that the employee can perform the job now or "in the immediate future" rather than at some unspecified distant time.[62]

Job Applications and Preemployment Physical Exams. Employers must modify their job-application process so that those with disabilities can compete for jobs with those who do not have disabilities. ■ **EXAMPLE 18.12** A job announcement that includes only a phone number would discriminate against potential job applicants with hearing impairments. Thus, the job announcement must also provide an address. ■

Employers are restricted in the kinds of questions they may ask on job-application forms and during preemployment interviews. Furthermore, they cannot require persons with disabilities to submit to preemployment physicals unless such exams are required of all other applicants. Employers can condition an offer of employment on the applicant's successfully passing a medical examination, but can disqualify the applicant only if the medical problems they discover would render the applicant unable to perform the job.

Dangerous Workers. Employers are not required to hire or retain workers who, because of their disabilities, pose a "direct threat to the health or safety" of their co-workers or the public.[63] This danger must be substantial and immediate; it cannot be speculative. In the wake of the AIDS epidemic, many employers have been concerned about hiring or continuing to employ a worker who has AIDS under the assumption that the worker might pose a direct threat to the health or safety of others in the workplace. Courts have generally held, however, that AIDS is not so contagious as to disqualify employees in most jobs. Therefore, employers must reasonably accommodate job applicants or employees who have AIDS or who test positive for HIV, the virus that causes AIDS.

DON'T FORGET Preemployment screening procedures must be applied equally in regard to all job applicants.

---

60. See, for example, *Beck v. University of Wisconsin Board of Regents,* 75 F.3d 1130 (7th Cir. 1996); and *White v. York International Corp.,* 45 F.3d 357 (10th Cir. 1995).

61. *Lyons v. Legal Aid Society,* 68 F.3d 1512 (2d Cir. 1995).

62. *Myers v. Hase,* 50 F.3d 278 (4th Cir. 1995).

63. Note that the United States Supreme Court has also upheld regulations that permit an employer to refuse to hire a worker when the job would pose a threat to that person's own health. *Chevron USA, Inc. v. Echazabal,* 536 U.S. 73, 122 S.Ct. 2045, 153 L.Ed.2d 82 (2002).

A discussion occurs at a meeting of Alcoholics Anonymous. Should employers be allowed to discriminate against persons suffering from alcoholism? Why or why not? (© John Boykin, PhotoEdit)

Substance Abusers. Drug addiction is a disability under the ADA because drug addiction is a substantially limiting impairment. Those who are currently using illegal drugs are not protected by the act, however. The ADA protects only persons with *former* drug addictions—those who have completed a supervised drug-rehabilitation program or are currently in a supervised rehabilitation program. Individuals who have used drugs casually in the past are not protected under the act. They are not considered addicts and therefore do not have a disability (addiction).

People suffering from alcoholism are protected by the ADA. Employers cannot legally discriminate against employees simply because they are suffering from alcoholism and must treat them in the same way they treat other employees. In other words, an employee with alcoholism who comes to work late because she or he was drinking the night before cannot be disciplined any differently than someone else who is late for another reason. Of course, employers have the right to prohibit the use of alcohol in the workplace and can require that employees not be under the influence of alcohol while working. Employers can also fire or refuse to hire a person with alcoholism if he or she poses a substantial risk of harm to either himself or herself or to others and the risk cannot be reduced by reasonable accommodation.

Health-Insurance Plans. Workers with disabilities must be given equal access to any health insurance provided to other employees. Employers can exclude from coverage preexisting health conditions and certain types of diagnostic or surgical procedures, though. An employer can also put a limit, or cap, on health-care payments under its particular group health policy—as long as such caps are "applied equally to all insured employees" and do not "discriminate on the basis of disability." Whenever a group health-care plan makes a disability-based distinction in its benefits, the plan violates the ADA. The employer must then be able to justify the distinction by proving one of the following:

1 That limiting coverage of certain ailments is required to keep the plan financially sound.

2 That coverage of certain ailments would cause such a significant increase in premium payments or their equivalent that the plan would be unappealing to a significant number of workers.

3 That the disparate treatment is justified by the risks and costs associated with a particular disability.

Hostile-Environment Claims under the ADA   As discussed earlier in this chapter, under Title VII of the Civil Rights Act of 1964, an employee may base certain types of employment-discrimination causes of action on a hostile-environment theory. Using this theory, a worker may successfully sue her or his employer, even if the worker was not fired or otherwise discriminated against.

Can a worker file a suit founded on a hostile-environment claim under the ADA? The ADA does not expressly provide for such suits, but some courts have allowed them. Others have assumed that the claim was possible without deciding whether the ADA allowed it.[64] To succeed, such a claim would likely have to be based on conduct that a reasonable person would find so offensive that it would change the conditions of the person's employment.

---

64. See, for example, *Steele v. Thiokol Corp.,* 241 F.3d 1248 (10th Cir. 2001).

▪▪ Defenses to Employment Discrimination

The first line of defense for an employer charged with employment discrimination is, of course, to assert that the plaintiff has failed to meet his or her initial burden of proving that discrimination occurred. As noted, plaintiffs bringing cases under the ADA sometimes find it difficult to meet this initial burden because they must prove that their alleged disabilities are disabilities covered by the ADA. Furthermore, plaintiffs in ADA cases must prove that they were otherwise qualified for the job and that their disabilities were the sole reason they were not hired or were fired.

Once a plaintiff succeeds in proving that discrimination occurred, the burden shifts to the employer to justify the discriminatory practice. Often, employers attempt to justify the discrimination by claiming that it was the result of a business necessity, a bona fide occupational qualification, or a seniority system. In some cases, as noted earlier, an effective antiharassment policy and prompt remedial action when harassment occurs may shield employers from liability under Title VII for sexual harassment.

BUSINESS NECESSITY

BUSINESS NECESSITY
A defense to allegations of employment discrimination in which the employer demonstrates that an employment practice that discriminates against members of a protected class is related to job performance.

An employer may defend against a claim of disparate-impact (unintentional) discrimination by asserting that a practice that has a discriminatory effect is a **business necessity**. ▪ EXAMPLE 18.13 If requiring a high school diploma is shown to have a discriminatory effect, an employer might argue that a high school education is necessary for workers to perform the job at a required level of competence. If the employer can demonstrate to the court's satisfaction that a definite connection exists between a high school education and job performance, the employer will normally succeed in this business necessity defense. ▪

BONA FIDE OCCUPATIONAL QUALIFICATION

BONA FIDE OCCUPATIONAL QUALIFICATION (BFOQ)
Identifiable characteristics reasonably necessary to the normal operation of a particular business. These characteristics can include gender, national origin, and religion, but not race.

Another defense applies when discrimination against a protected class is essential to a job—that is, when a particular trait is a **bona fide occupational qualification** (BFOQ). ▪ EXAMPLE 18.14 A women's clothing store might legitimately hire only female sales attendants if part of an attendant's job involves assisting clients in the store's dressing rooms. Similarly, the Federal Aviation Administration can legitimately impose age limits for airline pilots. ▪

Race, however, can never be a BFOQ. Generally, courts have restricted the BFOQ defense to instances in which the employee's gender is essential to the job. The United States Supreme Court has even held that a policy that was adopted to protect the unborn children of female employees from the harmful effects of exposure to lead was *not* an acceptable BFOQ.[65]

SENIORITY SYSTEMS

SENIORITY SYSTEM
In regard to employment relationships, a system in which those who have worked longest for the company are first in line for promotions, salary increases, and other benefits; they are also the last to be laid off if the workforce must be reduced.

An employer with a history of discrimination may have no members of protected classes in upper-level positions. Even if the employer now seeks to be unbiased, it may face a lawsuit in which the plaintiff asks a court to order that minorities be promoted ahead of schedule to compensate for past discrimination. If no present intent to discriminate is shown, however, and if promotions or other job benefits are distributed according to a fair **seniority system** (in which workers with more years of service are promoted first or laid off last), the employer has a good defense against the suit.

---

65. *United Auto Workers v. Johnson Controls, Inc.*, 499 U.S. 187, 111 S.Ct. 1196, 113 L.Ed.2d 158 (1991).

According to the Supreme Court in 2002, this defense may also apply to alleged discrimination under the ADA. If an employee with a disability requests an accommodation (such as an assignment to a particular position) that conflicts with an employer's seniority system, the accommodation will generally not be considered "reasonable" under the act.[66]

AFTER-ACQUIRED EVIDENCE OF EMPLOYEE MISCONDUCT

In some situations, employers have attempted to avoid liability for employment discrimination on the basis of "after-acquired evidence"—that is, evidence that the employer discovers after a lawsuit is filed—of an employee's misconduct. ■ EXAMPLE 18.15 Suppose that an employer fires a worker, who then sues the employer for employment discrimination. During pretrial investigation, the employer learns that the employee made material misrepresentations on his or her employment application—misrepresentations that, had the employer known about them, would have served as a ground to fire the individual. ■

According to the United States Supreme Court, after-acquired evidence of wrongdoing cannot be used to shield an employer entirely from liability for employment discrimination. It may, however, be used to limit the amount of damages for which the employer is liable.[67]

---

66. *U.S. Airways, Inc. v. Barnett*, 535 U.S. 391, 122 S.Ct. 1516, 152 L.E.2d 589 (2002).
67. *McKennon v. Nashville Banner Publishing Co.*, 513 U.S. 352, 115 S.Ct. 879, 130 L.Ed.2d 852 (1995).

APPLICATION ▪▪ How to Develop an Internet Policy*

Employers that make electronic communications systems (such as access to the Internet and e-mail) available to their employees face some obvious risks. One risk is that e-mail could be used to harass other employees. Another risk is that employees could subject the employer to liability by reproducing, without authorization, copyright-protected materials on the Internet. Still another risk is that some confidential information contained in e-mail messages transmitted via the Internet could be intercepted by an outside party. Finally, an employer that monitors employees' Internet use in an attempt to avoid these risks faces yet another risk: the risk of being held liable for violating the employees' privacy rights. If you are an employer and find it prudent to monitor employees' Internet use, you should take certain precautions.

Remember, a small company can be bankrupted by just one successful lawsuit against it. Even if your company

*This *Application* is not meant to substitute for the services of an attorney who is licensed to practice law in your state.*

wins the suit, the legal fees incurred to defend against the claim could be devastating for your profits.

INFORM YOUR EMPLOYEES OF THE MONITORING AND OBTAIN THEIR CONSENT

First of all, you should notify your employees that you will be monitoring their Internet communications, including their e-mail. Second, you should ask your employees to consent, in writing, to such actions. Generally, as discussed earlier in this chapter, if employees consent to employer monitoring, they cannot claim that their privacy rights have been invaded by such practices. You will find it easier to obtain employees' consent to monitoring if you explain why it is necessary or desirable and let them know what methods will be used to monitor Internet communications. As a rule, when employees are told the reasons for monitoring and clearly understand their rights and duties with respect to the company's communications system, they are less offended by the surveillance.

(Continued)

APPLICATION ▪ How to Develop an Internet Policy—Continued

SPELL OUT PERMISSIBLE AND IMPERMISSIBLE INTERNET USES

Employees should be told which uses of the firm's communications system are permissible and which uses are prohibited. To clarify Internet policy standards, develop a comprehensive policy setting forth your standards of Internet use and illustrate through specific examples what kinds of communications activities will constitute impermissible uses. It is also important to let employees know what will happen if they violate the policy. The policy might state, for example, that any employee who violates the policy will be subject to disciplinary actions, including termination.

CHECKLIST FOR THE EMPLOYER

1. Inform employees that their Internet communications will be monitored, why monitoring is necessary or desirable, and how it will be conducted.
2. Obtain employees' written consent to having their electronic communications monitored.
3. Develop a comprehensive policy statement explaining how Internet communications should and should not be used and indicating the consequences of misusing the firm's communications system.

▪ KEY TERMS

bona fide occupational qualification (BFOQ)   578
business necessity   578
constructive discharge   569
disparate-impact discrimination   566
disparate-treatment discrimination   566

employment at will   549
employment discrimination   565
minimum wage   552
prima facie case   566
protected class   565
seniority system   578
sexual harassment   570

vesting   556
whistleblowing   550
workers' compensation laws   554
wrongful discharge   551

CHAPTER SUMMARY ▪ Employment Law

Employment at Will
(See pages 549–551.)

1. *Employment-at-will doctrine*—Under this common law doctrine, either party may terminate the employment relationship at any time and for any reason ("at will"). This doctrine is still in widespread use throughout the United States, although federal and state statutes prevent the doctrine from being applied in certain circumstances.

2. *Exceptions to the employment-at-will doctrine*—To protect employees from some of the harsh results of the employment-at-will doctrine, courts have made exceptions to the doctrine on the basis of contract theory, tort theory, and public policy.

3. *Whistleblower statutes*—Most states have passed whistleblower statutes specifically to protect employees who "blow the whistle" on their employers from subsequent retaliation by those employers. The federal Whistleblower Protection Act of 1989 protects federal employees who report their employers' wrongdoing. The federal False Claims Reform Act of 1986 provides monetary rewards for whistleblowers who disclose information relating to fraud perpetrated against the U.S. government. Whistleblowers have occasionally received protection under the common law for reasons of public policy.

CHAPTER SUMMARY ▦ Employment Law—Continued

Employment at Will—Continued	4. *Wrongful discharge*—Whenever an employer discharges an employee in violation of an employment contract or statutory law protecting employees, the employee may bring a suit for wrongful discharge.
Wage-Hour Laws (See pages 551–553.)	1. *Davis-Bacon Act (1931)*—Requires contractors and subcontractors working on federal government construction projects to pay their employees "prevailing wages."
	2. *Walsh-Healey Act (1936)*—Requires that employees of firms that contract with federal agencies be paid a minimum wage and overtime pay.
	3. *Fair Labor Standards Act (1938)*—Extended wage-hour requirements to cover all employers whose activities affect interstate commerce plus certain other businesses. The act has specific requirements in regard to child labor, maximum hours, and minimum wages.
Worker Health and Safety (See pages 553–555.)	1. *Occupational Safety and Health Act (1970)*—Requires employers to meet specific safety and health standards that are established and enforced by the Occupational Safety and Health Administration (OSHA).
	2. *State workers' compensation laws*—Establish an administrative procedure for compensating workers who are injured in accidents that occur on the job, regardless of fault.
Income Security (See pages 555–558.)	1. *Social Security and Medicare*—The Social Security Act of 1935 provides for old-age (retirement), survivors, and disability insurance. Both employers and employees must make contributions under the Federal Insurance Contributions Act (FICA) to help pay for benefits that will partially make up for the employees' loss of income on retirement. The Social Security Administration also administers Medicare, a health-insurance program for older or disabled persons.
	2. *Private pension plans*—The federal Employee Retirement Income Security Act (ERISA) of 1974 establishes standards for the management of employer-provided pension plans.
	3. *Unemployment insurance*—The Federal Unemployment Tax Act of 1935 created a system that provides unemployment compensation to eligible individuals. Covered employers are taxed to help defray the costs of unemployment compensation.
	4. *COBRA*—The Consolidated Omnibus Budget Reconciliation Act (COBRA) of 1985 requires employers to give employees, on termination of employment, the option of continuing their medical, optical, or dental insurance coverage for a certain period.
Family and Medical Leave (See pages 558–560.)	The Family and Medical Leave Act (FMLA) of 1993 requires employers with fifty or more employees to provide their employees (except for key employees) with up to twelve weeks of unpaid family or medical leave during any twelve-month period for the following reasons:
	1. *Family leave*—May be taken to care for a newborn baby, an adopted child, or a foster child.
	2. *Medical leave*—May be taken when the employee or the employee's spouse, child, or parent has a serious health condition requiring care.
Employee Privacy Rights (See pages 560–565.)	A right to privacy has been inferred from guarantees provided by the First, Third, Fourth, Fifth, and Ninth Amendments to the U.S. Constitution. State laws may also provide for privacy rights. Employer practices that are often challenged by employees as invasive of their privacy rights include electronic performance monitoring, lie-detector tests, drug testing, AIDS testing, and screening procedures.
Title VII of the Civil Rights Act of 1964 (See pages 565–572.)	Title VII prohibits employment discrimination based on race, color, national origin, religion, or gender.
	1. *Procedures*—Employees must file a claim with the Equal Employment Opportunity Commission (EEOC). The EEOC may sue the employer on the employee's behalf; if not, the employee may sue the employer directly.

(Continued)

CHAPTER SUMMARY   ▦ Employment Law—Continued

Title VII of the Civil Rights Act of 1964—Continued	2. *Types of discrimination*—Title VII prohibits both intentional (disparate-treatment) and unintentional (disparate-impact) discrimination. Disparate-impact discrimination occurs when an employer's practice, such as hiring only persons with a certain level of education, has the effect of discriminating against a class of persons protected by Title VII. Title VII also extends to discriminatory practices, such as various forms of harassment, in the online environment.
	3. *Remedies for discrimination under Title VII*—If a plaintiff proves that unlawful discrimination occurred, he or she may be awarded reinstatement, back pay, and retroactive promotions. Damages (both compensatory and punitive) may be awarded for intentional discrimination.
Equal Pay Act of 1963 (See page 572.)	The Equal Pay Act of 1963 prohibits gender-based discrimination in the wages paid for equal work on jobs when their performance requires equal skill, effort, and responsibility under similar conditions.
Discrimination Based on Age (See pages 573–574.)	The Age Discrimination in Employment Act (ADEA) of 1967 prohibits employment discrimination on the basis of age against individuals forty years of age or older. Procedures for bringing a case under the ADEA are similar to those for bringing a case under Title VII.
Discrimination Based on Disability (See pages 574–577.)	The Americans with Disabilities Act (ADA) of 1990 prohibits employment discrimination against persons with disabilities who are otherwise qualified to perform the essential functions of the jobs for which they apply.
	1. *Procedures and remedies*—To prevail on a claim under the ADA, the plaintiff must show that she or he has a disability, is otherwise qualified for the employment in question, and was excluded from the employment solely because of the disability. Procedures under the ADA are similar to those required in Title VII cases; remedies are also similar to those under Title VII.
	2. *Definition of disability*—The ADA defines the term *disability* as a physical or mental impairment that substantially limits one or more major life activities, a record of such impairment, or being regarded as having such an impairment.
	3. *Reasonable accommodation*—Employers are required to reasonably accommodate the needs of persons with disabilities. Reasonable accommodations may include altering job-application procedures, modifying the physical work environment, and permitting more flexible work schedules. Employers are not required to accommodate the needs of all workers with disabilities. For example, employers need not accommodate workers who pose a definite threat to health and safety in the workplace or those who are not otherwise qualified for their jobs.
Defenses to Employment Discrimination (See pages 578–579.)	If a plaintiff proves that employment discrimination occurred, employers may avoid liability by successfully asserting certain defenses. Employers may assert that the discrimination was required for reasons of business necessity, to meet a bona fide occupational qualification, or to maintain a legitimate seniority system. Evidence of prior employee misconduct acquired after the employee has been fired is not a defense to discrimination.

FOR REVIEW

Answers for the even-numbered questions in this For Review *section can be found in Appendix I at the end of this text.*

1 What is the employment-at-will doctrine? When and why are exceptions to this doctrine made?

2 What federal statute governs working hours and wages? What federal act was enacted to protect the health and safety of employees?

3 Under the Family and Medical Leave Act of 1993, under what circumstances may an employee take family or medical leave?

4 What federal acts prohibit discrimination in the workplace?

5 What are three defenses to claims of employment discrimination?

QUESTIONS AND CASE PROBLEMS

18–1. Health and Safety Regulations. Denton and Carlo were employed at an appliance plant. Their job required them to do occasional maintenance work while standing on a wire mesh twenty feet above the plant floor. Other employees had fallen through the mesh; one was killed by the fall. When Denton and Carlo were asked by their supervisor to do work that would likely require them to walk on the mesh, they refused due to their fear of bodily harm or death. Because of their refusal to do the requested work, the two employees were fired from their jobs. Was their discharge wrongful? If so, under what federal employment law? To what federal agency or department should they turn for assistance?

18–2. Title VII Violations. Discuss fully whether any of the following actions would constitute a violation of Title VII of the 1964 Civil Rights Act, as amended.

(a) Tennington, Inc., is a consulting firm and has ten employees. These employees travel on consulting jobs in seven states. Tennington has an employment record of hiring only white males.

(b) Novo Films, Inc., is making a film about Africa and needs to employ approximately one hundred extras for this picture. Novo advertises in all major newspapers in southern California for the hiring of these extras. The ad states that only African Americans need apply.

18–3. Wrongful Discharge. Stephen Fredrick, a pilot for Simmons Airlines Corp., criticized the safety of the aircraft that Simmons used on many of its flights and warned the airline about possible safety problems. Simmons took no action. After one of the planes crashed, Fredrick appeared on the television program *Good Morning America* to discuss his safety concerns. The same day, Fredrick refused to allow employees of Simmons to search his personal bags before a flight that he was scheduled to work. Claiming insubordination, the airline terminated Fredrick. Fredrick filed a suit in a federal district court against Simmons, claiming, among other things, that he had been dis-

charged in retaliation for publicly expressing his concerns about the safety of the aircraft and that this discharge violated the public policy of providing for safe air travel. Simmons responded that an employee who "goes public" with his or her concerns should not be protected by the law. Will the court agree with Simmons? Explain. [*Fredrick v. Simmons Airlines Corp.*, 144 F.3d 500 (7th Cir. 1998)]

18–4. Hours and Wages. Richard Ackerman was an advance sales representative and account manager for Coca-Cola Enterprises, Inc. His primary responsibility was to sell Coca-Cola products to grocery stores, convenience stores, and other sales outlets. Coca-Cola also employed merchandisers, who did not sell Coca-Cola products but performed tasks associated with their distribution and promotion, including restocking shelves, filling vending machines, and setting up displays. The account managers, who serviced the smaller accounts themselves, regularly worked between fifty-five and seventy-two hours each week. Coca-Cola paid them a salary, bonuses, and commissions, but unlike the merchandisers, the account managers did not receive additional compensation for the overtime. Ackerman and the other account managers filed a suit in a federal district court against Coca-Cola, alleging that they were entitled to overtime compensation. Coca-Cola responded that because of an exemption under the Fair Labor Standards Act, it was not required to pay them overtime. Is Coca-Cola correct? Explain. [*Ackerman v. Coca-Cola Enterprises, Inc.*, 179 F.3d 1260 (10th Cir. 1999)]

CASE PROBLEM WITH SAMPLE ANSWER

18–5. Patience Oyoyo worked as a claims analyst in the claims management department of Baylor Healthcare Network, Inc. When questions arose about Oyoyo's performance on several occasions, department manager Debbie Outlaw met with Oyoyo to discuss, among other things, Oyoyo's personal use of a business phone.

Outlaw reminded Oyoyo that company policy prohibited excessive personal calls and that these would result in the termination of her employment. Outlaw began to monitor Oyoyo's phone usage, noting lengthy outgoing calls on several occasions, including some long-distance calls. Eventually, Outlaw terminated Oyoyo's employment, and Oyoyo filed a suit in a federal district court against Baylor. Oyoyo asserted in part that by monitoring her phone calls, the employer had invaded her privacy. Baylor asked the court to dismiss this claim. In whose favor should the court rule, and why? [*Oyoyo v. Baylor Healthcare Network, Inc.*, __ F.Supp.2d __ (N.D.Tex. 2000)]

After you have answered this problem, compare your answer with the sample answer given on the Web site that accompanies this text. Go to http://blt.westbuslaw.com, select "Chapter 18," and click on "Case Problem with Sample Answer."

18–6. Discrimination Based on Race. The hiring policy of Phillips Community College of the University of Arkansas (PCCUA) is to conduct an internal search for qualified applicants before advertising outside the college. Steven Jones, the university's chancellor, can determine the application and appointment process for vacant positions, however, and is the ultimate authority in hiring decisions. Howard Lockridge, an African American, was the chair of PCCUA's Technical and Industrial Department. Between 1988 and 1998, Lockridge applied for several different positions, some of which were unadvertised, some of which were unfilled for years, and some of which were filled with less qualified persons from outside the college. In 1998, when Jones advertised an opening for the position of dean of Industrial Technology and Workforce Development, Lockridge did not apply for the job. Jones hired Tracy McGraw, a white male. Lockridge filed a suit in a federal district court against the university under Title VII. The university filed a motion for summary judgment in its favor. What are the elements of a *prima facie* case of disparate-treatment discrimination? Can Lockridge pass this test, or should the court issue a judgment in the university's favor? Explain. [*Lockridge v. Board of Trustees of the University of Arkansas*, 294 F.3d 1010 (8th Cir. 2002)]

18–7. Discrimination Based on Age. The United Auto Workers (UAW) is the union that represents the employees of General Dynamics Land Systems, Inc. In 1997, a collective bargaining agreement between UAW and General Dynamics eliminated the company's obligation to provide health insurance to employees who retired after the date of the agreement, except for current workers at least fifty years old. Dennis Cline and 194 other employees, who were over forty years old but under fifty, objected to this term. They complained to the Equal Employment Opportunity Commission, claiming that the agreement violated the Age Discrimination in Employment Act (ADEA) of 1967. The ADEA forbids discriminatory preference for the "young" over the "old." Does the ADEA also prohibit favoring the old over the young? How should the court rule?

Explain. [*General Dynamics Land Systems, Inc. v. Cline*, 540 U.S. 581, 124 S.Ct. 1236, 157 L.Ed.2d 1094 (2004)]

A QUESTION OF ETHICS

18–8. Keith Cline worked for Wal-Mart Stores, Inc., as a night maintenance supervisor. When he suffered a recurrence of a brain tumor, he took a leave from work, which was covered by the Family and Medical Leave Act (FMLA) of 1993 and authorized by his employer. When he returned to work, his employer refused to allow him to continue his supervisory job and demoted him to the status of a regular maintenance worker. A few weeks later, the company fired him, ostensibly because he "stole" company time by clocking in thirteen minutes early for a company meeting. Cline sued Wal-Mart, alleging, among other things, that Wal-Mart had violated the FMLA by refusing to return him to his prior position when he returned to work. In view of these facts, answer the following questions. [*Cline v. Wal-Mart Stores, Inc.*, 144 F.3d 294 (4th Cir. 1998)]

1. Did Wal-Mart violate the FMLA by refusing to return Cline to his prior position when he returned to work?

2. From an ethical perspective, the FMLA has been viewed as a choice on the part of society to shift to the employer family burdens caused by changing economic and social needs. What "changing" needs does the act meet? In other words, why did Congress feel that workers should have the right to family and medical leave in 1993, but not in 1983, or 1973, or earlier?

3. "Congress should amend the FMLA, which currently applies to employers with fifty or more employees, so that it applies to employers with twenty-five or more employees." Do you agree with this statement? Why or why not?

FOR CRITICAL ANALYSIS

18–9. Why has the federal government limited the application of the statutes discussed in this chapter to firms with a specified number of employees, such as fifteen or twenty? Should these laws apply to all employers, regardless of size? Why or why not?

VIDEO QUESTION

18–10. Go to this text's Web site at **http://blt. westbuslaw.com** and select "Chapter 18." Click on "Video Questions" and view the video titled *Parenthood*. Then answer the following questions.

1. In the video, Gil (Steve Martin) threatens to leave his job when he discovers that his boss is promoting another person to partner instead of him. His boss (Dennis

Dugan) laughs and tells him that the threat is not realistic because if Gil leaves, he will be competing for positions with workers who are younger than he is and willing to accept lower salaries. If Gil takes his employer's advice and stays in his current position, can he sue his boss for age discrimination based on the boss's statements? Why or why not?

2. Suppose that Gil leaves his current position and applies for a job at another firm. The prospective employer refuses to hire him based on his age. What would Gil have to prove to establish a *prima facie* case of age discrimination? Explain your answer.

3. What defenses might Gil's current employer raise if Gil sues for age discrimination?

INTERNET EXERCISES

Go to the *Business Law Today: The Essentials* home page at <u>http://blt.westbuslaw.com</u>, select "Chapter 18," and click on "Internet Exercises." There you will find the following Internet research exercises that you can perform to learn more about topics covered in this chapter.

Activity 18–1: LEGAL PERSPECTIVE—Workers' Compensation

Activity 18–2: MANAGEMENT PERSPECTIVE—Workplace Monitoring and Surveillance

Activity 18–3: SOCIAL PERSPECTIVE—Religious and National-Origin Discrimination

BEFORE THE TEST

Go to the *Business Law Today: The Essentials* home page at <u>http://blt.westbuslaw.com</u>, select "Chapter 18," and click on "Interactive Quizzes." You will find at least twenty interactive questions relating to this chapter.

CHAPTER 19

The Entrepreneur's Options

"[E]veryone thirsteth after gaine."
Sir Edward Coke, 1552–1634
(English jurist and politician)

CHAPTER OUTLINE

■ MAJOR BUSINESS FORMS

■ SPECIAL BUSINESS FORMS

■ PRIVATE FRANCHISES

▦ LEARNING OBJECTIVES

After reading this chapter, you should be able to answer the following questions:

1 What are some of the major forms of business organization used by entrepreneurs in the United States?

2 What advantages and disadvantages are associated with each major business form?

3 Why have limited liability companies and limited liability partnerships come into widespread use in recent years?

4 What is a joint venture? What are some other special business organizational forms, and why are they used?

5 What is a franchise, and how does a franchising relationship arise?

ENTREPRENEUR
One who initiates and assumes the financial risks of a new enterprise and undertakes to provide or control its management.

Many Americans would agree with Sir Edward Coke that most people, at least, "thirsteth after gaine." Certainly, an entrepreneur's primary motive for undertaking a business enterprise is to make profits. An **entrepreneur** is by definition one who initiates and assumes the financial risks of a new enterprise and undertakes to provide or control its management.

One of the questions faced by any entrepreneur who wishes to start up a business is what form of business organization he or she should choose for the business endeavor. In this chapter, we first examine and compare the basic features of the several major business forms in use today. We then look at some special business forms that may be used to organize a business venture. A discussion of private franchises concludes the chapter.

◧ Major Business Forms

Traditionally, entrepreneurs have used three major forms to structure their business enterprises—the sole proprietorship; the partnership, including the limited partnership; and the corporation. In the last several years, two other business forms have come into widespread use—the limited liability company and the limited liability partnership. We examine each of these forms in this section.

SOLE PROPRIETORSHIPS

SOLE PROPRIETORSHIP
The simplest form of business, in which the owner is the business; the owner reports business income on his or her personal income tax return and is legally responsible for all debts and obligations incurred by the business.

The simplest form of business is a **sole proprietorship.** In this form, the owner is the business; thus, anyone who does business without creating a separate business organization has a sole proprietorship. Sole proprietorships constitute over two-thirds of all American businesses. They are also usually small enterprises—about 99 percent of the sole proprietorships existing in the United States have revenues of less than $1 million per year. Sole proprietors can own and manage any type of business from an informal, home-office undertaking to a large restaurant or construction firm.

Advantages of the Sole Proprietorship A major advantage of the sole proprietorship is that the proprietor receives all of the profits (because he or she assumes all of the risk). In addition, it is often easier and less costly to start a sole proprietorship than to start any other kind of business, as few legal forms are involved. This type of business organization also entails more flexibility than does a partnership or a corporation. The sole proprietor is free to make any decision he or she wishes concerning the business—whom to hire, when to take a vacation, what kind of business to pursue, and so on. A sole proprietor pays only personal income taxes on profits, which are reported as personal income on the proprietor's personal income tax return. Sole proprietors are also allowed to establish tax-exempt retirement accounts in the form of Keogh plans.[1]

Disadvantages of the Sole Proprietorship The major disadvantage of the sole proprietorship is that, as sole owner, the proprietor alone bears the burden of any losses or liabilities incurred by the business enterprise. In other words, the sole proprietor has unlimited liability, or legal responsibility, for all obligations incurred in doing business. This unlimited liability is a major factor to be considered in choosing a business form. The sole proprietorship also has the disadvantage of lacking continuity on the death of the proprietor. When the owner dies, so does the business—it is automatically dissolved. If the business is transferred to family members or other heirs, a new proprietorship is created.

Another disadvantage is that the proprietor's opportunity to raise capital is limited to personal funds and the funds of those who are willing to make loans. If the owner wishes to expand the business significantly, one way to raise more capital to finance the expansion is to join forces with another entrepreneur and establish a partnership or form a corporation. Note also that even though starting up a sole proprietorship involves relatively few legal formalities compared to other business organizational forms, even small sole proprietorships may need to comply with certain zoning requirements, obtain appropriate licenses, and the like.

What are the advantages of doing business as a sole proprietorship? (© James Schnepf, Getty Images)

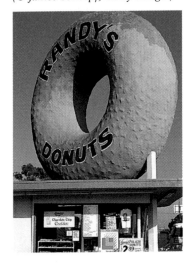

---

1. A *Keogh plan* is a retirement program designed for self-employed persons. A person can contribute a certain percentage of his or her income to the plan, and interest earnings will not be taxed until funds are withdrawn from the plan.

PARTNERSHIPS

PARTNERSHIP
An agreement by two or more persons to carry on, as co-owners, a business for profit.

A **partnership** arises from an agreement, express or implied, between two or more persons to carry on a business for profit. Partners are co-owners of a business and have joint control over its operation and the right to share in its profits. No particular form of partnership agreement is necessary for the creation of a partnership, but for practical reasons, the agreement should be in writing. Basically, the partners may agree to almost any terms when establishing the partnership so long as they are not illegal or countrary to public policy.

The Law Governing Partnerships The Uniform Partnership Act (UPA) governs the operation of partnerships *in the absence of express agreement* and has done much to reduce controversies in the law relating to partnerships. The UPA defines a *partnership* as "an association of two or more persons to carry on as co-owners a business for profit" [UPA 101(6)]. The *intent* to associate is a key element of a partnership, and one cannot join a partnership unless all other partners consent [UPA 401(i)].

Conflicts commonly arise over whether a business enterprise is legally a partnership, especially in the absence of a formal, written partnership agreement. In resolving disputes over whether partnership status exists, courts will usually look for the following three essential elements of partnership implicit in the UPA's definition of the term:

1 A sharing of profits and losses.

2 A joint ownership of the business.

3 An equal right in the management of the business.

Under the UPA, all partners have equal rights in managing the partnership [UPA 401(f)]. Each partner in an ordinary partnership has one vote in management matters *regardless of the proportional size of his or her interest in the firm*. Each partner is entitled to the proportion of business profits and losses designated in the partnership agreement. If the agreement does not apportion profits or losses, the UPA provides that *profits shall be shared equally* and *losses shall be shared in the same ratio as profits* [UPA 401(b)]. Each partner, however, can be held fully liable for all debts of the partnership.

When one of the parties disputes whether a partnership was created, the courts frequently look to other factors, such as the conduct of the parties, to determine partnership status. In the following case, the parties met and discussed buying and developing a commercial site. Using some of one party's funds, another party bought the site in the name of his business alone. The buyer refused to share ownership of the property, claiming that he had entered into only an unenforceable agreement to form a partnership and was not a partner.

CASE 19.1 ■ Cap Care Group, Inc. v. McDonald

North Carolina Court of Appeals, 2002.
149 N.C.App. 817,
561 S.E.2d 578.
**http://www.aoc.state.nc.us/www/public/html/
opinions.htm**[a]

a. In the "Court of Appeals Opinions" section, click on "2002." On the next page, scroll to the "16 April 2002" section and click on the name of the case to access the opinion.

FACTS Cap Care Group, Inc., PWPP Partners, and C & M Investments of High Point, Inc., buy and develop commercial real estate. Ronnel Parker is president of Cap Care and PWPP. Wayne McDonald owns and controls C & M. In November 1996, Parker and Daniel Greene, another Cap Care officer, met McDonald to discuss buying and renovating a commercial site in High Point, North Carolina. Cap Care later claimed that at the meeting the parties

CASE 19.1—Continued

(Parker on behalf of Cap Care and PWPP, and McDonald on behalf of C & M) agreed that they would be partners in the purchase and development of the property, and that McDonald would make an offer to the seller on the partnership's behalf. In February 1997, McDonald signed a contract to buy the site, using PWPP funds as half of the earnest money.[b] McDonald and Greene (of Cap Care) then discussed jointly owning the property as partners. In March, McDonald bought the property in the name of C & M only. Cap Care demanded that McDonald contribute the property to the partnership, but he refused. Cap Care filed a suit in a North Carolina state court against McDonald and C & M, alleging in part breach of contract. McDonald argued that he and Parker had merely entered into an unenforceable agreement to form a part-

b. *Earnest money* is a deposit of funds that usually accompanies an offer to buy real estate to show that the offer is earnest, or serious.

nership. The court awarded Cap Care $477,511, plus interest and fees. The defendants appealed to a state intermediate appellate court.

ISSUE   Was there a valid enforceable agreement among the parties to form a partnership to purchase property?

DECISION   Yes. The state intermediate appellate court affirmed the lower court's judgment. The defendants had entered into, and breached, an oral partnership contract to buy real estate, as evidenced by the parties' discussions, the defendants' acceptance of a partner's funds, and the defendants' acting according to the parties' plan until after the purchase of the property.

WHY IS THIS CASE IMPORTANT?   *This case illustrates that the acceptance by conduct of an offer to create a partnership results in the formation of the partnership, whether or not the "accepting" party subjectively intended to enter into a partnership.*

Advantages and Disadvantages of Partnerships   As with a sole proprietorship, one of the advantages of a partnership is that it can be organized fairly easily and inexpensively. Additionally, the partnership form of business offers important tax advantages. The partnership itself files only an informational tax return with the Internal Revenue Service. In other words, the firm itself pays no taxes. A partner's profit from the partnership (whether distributed or not) is taxed as individual income to the individual partner.

A partnership may also allow for greater capital contributions to the business than is possible in a sole proprietorship. Two or more persons can invest in the business, and lenders may be more willing to make loans to a partnership than they would be to a sole proprietorship.

The main disadvantage of the partnership form of business is that the partners are subject to personal liability for partnership obligations. If the partnership cannot pay its debts, the personal assets of the partners are subject to creditors' claims. Moreover, the acts of one partner in the ordinary course of business subject the other partners to personal liability [UPA 305].

LIMITED PARTNERSHIPS

A special form of partnership is the **limited partnership,** which consists of at least one general partner and one or more limited partners. A limited partnership is a creature of statute, because it does not come into existence until a *certificate of partnership* is filed with the appropriate state office. A **general partner** assumes responsibility for the management of the partnership and liability for all partnership debts. A **limited partner** has no right to participate in the general management or operation of the partnership and assumes no liability for partnership debts beyond the amount of capital that he or she has contributed. Thus, one of the major benefits of becoming a limited partner is this limitation on liability, both with respect to lawsuits brought against the partnership and the amount of money placed at risk.

LIMITED PARTNERSHIP
A partnership consisting of one or more general partners (who manage the business and are liable to the full extent of their personal assets for debts of the partnership) and one or more limited partners (who contribute only assets and are liable only up to the amount contributed by them).

GENERAL PARTNER
In a limited partnership, a partner who assumes responsibility for the management of the partnership and liability for all partnership debts.

LIMITED PARTNER
In a limited partnership, a partner who contributes capital to the partnership but has no right to participate in the management and operation of the business. The limited partner assumes no liability for partnership debts beyond the capital contributed.

ETHICAL ISSUE 19.1

Should a limited partner be able to sue a third party whose negligence caused the partnership to fail?   Limited partners in a limited partnership have a number of rights, yet these rights are limited. For example, a limited partner may not sue a third party with whom a limited partnership has contracted for causing the limited partnership to fail. Generally, the limited partnership itself must bring the suit—the limited partners have no standing to sue for losses that result in the failure of the enterprise. For example, in one case a limited partner invested $16 million in BCH Energy L.P. in reliance on BCH's representations that it would build and manage plants that convert waste products into energy. BCH hired Metric Constructors to construct an energy-generating project. Serious problems caused the project to lose all funds invested. The limited partner sued Metric Constructors, contending that Metric was negligent in its construction. The court, however, held that the limited partner did not have standing to sue the contractor (Metric). The court held that any complaint brought against the contractor had to be brought by the partnership, not by its limited partner or partners.[2] While this ruling may seem unfair to the limited partner, it is consistent with the principle that limited partners should not have a say in the management of limited partnerships. ■

CORPORATIONS

CORPORATION
A legal entity formed in compliance with statutory requirements. The entity is distinct from its shareholder-owners.

A third and widely used type of business organizational form is the **corporation.** The corporation, like the limited partnership, is a creature of statute. The corporation's existence as a legal entity, which can be perpetual, depends generally on state law.

Corporations are owned by *shareholders*—those who have purchased ownership shares in the business. A *board of directors,* elected by the shareholders, manages the business. The board of directors normally employs *officers* to oversee day-to-day operations.

One of the key advantages of the corporate form of business is that the liability of its owners (shareholders) is limited to their investments. The shareholders usually are not personally liable for the obligations of the corporation. A disadvantage of the corporate form is that profits are taxed twice. The corporation as an entity pays income taxes on corporate profits, and the shareholders pay income taxes on those profits that are distributed to them. The corporate business form will be discussed in detail in Chapter 20.

LIMITED LIABILITY COMPANIES

You can find information on how to form an LLC, including the fees charged in each state for filing LLC articles of organization, at the Web site of BIZCORP International, Inc. Go to

http://www.bizcorp.com.

Traditionally, the two most common forms of business organization selected by two or more persons entering into business together were the partnership and the corporation. As already explained, each form has distinct advantages and disadvantages. For partnerships, the advantage is that partnership income is taxed only once (all income is "passed through" the partnership entity to the partners themselves, who are taxed only as individuals); the disadvantage is the personal liability of the partners. For corporations, the advantage is the limited liability of shareholders; the disadvantage is the double taxation of corporate income. For many entrepreneurs and investors, the ideal business form would combine the tax advantages of the partnership form of business with the limited liability of the corporate enterprise.

---

2. *Energy Investors Fund, L.P. v. Metric Constructors, Inc.,* 351 N.C. 331, 525 S.E.2d 441 (2000).

LIMITED LIABILITY COMPANY (LLC)
A hybrid form of business enterprise that offers the limited liability of the corporation but the tax advantages of a partnership.

The Emergence of the LLC   A relatively new form of business organization, the **limited liability company (LLC)**, is a hybrid form of business enterprise that meets these needs by offering the limited liability of the corporation and the tax advantages of a partnership. Increasingly, LLCs are becoming an organizational form of choice among businesspersons, a trend encouraged by state statutes permitting their use. The origins and evolution of the LLC are discussed in this chapter's *Landmark in the Law* feature.

LANDMARK IN THE LAW

Limited Liability Company (LLC) Statutes

In 1977, Wyoming became the first state to pass legislation authorizing the creation of a limited liability company (LLC). Although LLCs emerged in the United States only in 1977, they have been in existence for over a century in other areas, including several European and South American nations. The South American *limitada*, for example, is a form of business organization that operates more or less as a partnership but provides limited liability for the owners.

TAXATION OF LLCs   In the United States, after Wyoming's adoption of an LLC statute, it still was not known how the Internal Revenue Service (IRS) would treat the LLC for tax purposes. In 1988, however, the IRS ruled that Wyoming LLCs would be taxed as partnerships instead of as corporations, providing that certain requirements were met. Prior to this ruling, only one other state—Florida, in 1982—had authorized LLCs. The 1988 ruling encouraged other states to enact LLC statutes, and in less than a decade, all states had done so.

New IRS rules that went into effect on January 1, 1997, encouraged even more widespread use of LLCs in the business world. These rules provide that any unincorporated business will automatically be taxed as a partnership unless it indicates otherwise on the tax form. The exceptions involve publicly traded companies, companies formed under a state incorporation statute, and certain foreign-owned companies. If a business chooses to be taxed as a corporation, it can indicate this choice by checking a box on the IRS form.

FOREIGN ENTITIES MAY BE LLC MEMBERS   Part of the impetus behind the creation of LLCs in this country is that foreign investors are allowed to become LLC members. Generally, in an era increasingly characterized by global business efforts and investments, the LLC offers U.S. firms and potential investors from other countries flexibility and opportunities greater than those available through partnerships or corporations.

APPLICATION TO TODAY'S WORLD

Once it became clear that LLCs could be taxed as partnerships, the LLC form of business organization was widely adopted. Members could avoid the personal liability associated with the partnership form of business as well as the "double taxation" of the corporate form of business. Today, LLCs, which only a few years ago were largely unknown in this country, are a widely used form of business organization.

RELEVANT WEB SITES

To locate information on the Web concerning limited liability company statutes, go to this text's Web site at **http://blt.westbuslaw.com**, *select "Chapter 19," and click on "URLs for Landmarks."*

Like corporations, LLCs must be formed and operated in compliance with state statutes. Statutes governing LLCs vary, of course, from state to state. In an attempt to create more uniformity among the states in this respect, in 1995 the National Conference of Commissioners on Uniform State Laws issued the Uniform Limited Liability Company Act (ULLCA). To date, less than one-fifth of the states have adopted the ULLCA, and thus the law governing LLCs remains far from uniform.

Operating an LLC   Some provisions are common to most state statutes, however. For example, in an LLC the owners (who are called *members*) themselves can normally decide how to operate the various aspects of the business by forming an **operating agreement**. Operating agreements typically contain provisions relating to management, how profits will be divided, the transfer of membership interests, whether the LLC will be dissolved on the death or departure of a member, and other important issues.

As with any business arrangement, disputes may arise over any number of issues. If there is no agreement covering the topic under dispute, such as how profits will be divided, the state LLC statute will govern the outcome. For example, most LLC statutes provide that if the members have not specified how profits will be divided, they will be divided equally among the members. Generally, when an issue is not covered by an operating agreement or by an LLC statute, the principles of partnership law are applied.

LIMITED LIABILITY PARTNERSHIPS

The **limited liability partnership (LLP)** is similar to the LLC but is designed more for professionals who normally do business as partners in a partnership. The major advantage of the LLP is that it allows a partnership to continue as a pass-through entity for tax purposes but limits the personal liability of the partners. For this reason, the LLP has become a widely preferred business organizational form for those who have traditionally conducted their business as a general partnership.

In 1991, Texas became the first state to enact an LLP statute. Other states quickly followed suit, and by 1997, virtually all of the states had enacted LLP statutes. LLPs must also be formed and operated in compliance with state statutes. In most states, it is relatively easy to convert a traditional partnership into an LLP because the firm's basic organizational structure remains the same. Additionally, all of the statutory and common law rules governing partnerships still apply (apart from those modified by the LLP statute). Normally, an LLP statute is simply an amendment to a state's already existing partnership law.

The LLP allows professionals to avoid personal liability for the malpractice of other partners. Remember that a major disadvantage of the partnership is the unlimited personal liability of its partners. ■ **EXAMPLE 19.1** A group of lawyers is operating as a partnership. A client sues one of the attorneys for malpractice and wins a large judgment, and the firm's malpractice insurance is insufficient to cover the obligation. When the attorney's personal assets are exhausted, the personal assets of the other, innocent partners can be used to satisfy the judgment. ■

Although LLP statutes vary from state to state, generally each state statute limits the liability of partners in some way. For example, Delaware law protects each innocent partner from the "debts and obligations of the partnership arising from negligence, wrongful acts, or misconduct." In North Carolina, Texas, and Washington, D.C., the statutes protect innocent partners from obligations arising from "errors, omissions, negligence, incompetence, or malfeasance." Although the language of these statutes

OPERATING AGREEMENT
In a limited liability company, an agreement in which the members set forth the details of how the business will be managed and operated. State statutes typically give the members wide latitude in deciding for themselves the rules that will govern their organization.

LIMITED LIABILITY PARTNERSHIP (LLP)
A business organizational form that is similar to the LLC but that is designed more for professionals who normally do business as partners in a partnership. The LLP is a pass-through entity for tax purposes, like the general partnership, but it limits the personal liability of the partners.

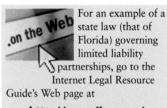

For an example of a state law (that of Florida) governing limited liability partnerships, go to the Internet Legal Resource Guide's Web page at

http://www.ilrg.com/ whatsnews/statute.html

and scroll down the page to "Registered Limited Liability Partnerships."

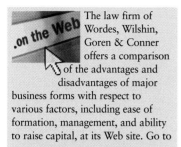

The law firm of Wordes, Wilshin, Goren & Conner offers a comparison of the advantages and disadvantages of major business forms with respect to various factors, including ease of formation, management, and ability to raise capital, at its Web site. Go to

http://www.wwgc.com/ wwgc-be1.htm.

may seem to apply specifically to attorneys, virtually any group of professionals can use the LLP.

MAJOR BUSINESS FORMS COMPARED

When deciding which form of business organization would be most appropriate, businesspersons normally consider several factors, including ease of creation, the liability of the owners, tax considerations, and the need for capital. Each major form of business organization offers distinct advantages and disadvantages with respect to these and other factors. Exhibit 19–1 on the following two pages summarizes the essential advantages and disadvantages of each of the forms of business organization discussed in this chapter.

■■ Special Business Forms

Besides the business forms discussed previously, there are several other forms that can be used to organize a business. For the most part, these other business forms are hybrid organizations—that is, they have characteristics similar to those of partnerships or corporations or combine features of both. These forms include joint ventures, syndicates, joint stock companies, business trusts, and cooperatives.

JOINT VENTURES

JOINT VENTURE
A joint undertaking of a specific commercial enterprise by an association of persons. A joint venture is normally not a legal entity and is treated like a partnership for federal income tax purposes.

A **joint venture** is an enterprise in which two or more persons or business entities combine their efforts or their property for a single transaction or project, or a related series of transactions or projects. ■ **EXAMPLE 19.2** When several contractors combine their resources to build and sell houses in a single development, their relationship is a joint venture. The joint venture is treated much like a partnership, but it differs in that it is created in contemplation of a limited activity or a single transaction. ■ Joint ventures are taxed like partnerships, and, unless otherwise agreed, joint venturers share profits and losses equally.

CONTRAST A partnership involves a continuing relationship of the partners. A joint venture is essentially a one-time association.

Members of a joint venture usually have limited powers to bind their co-venturers. A joint venture is normally not a legal entity and therefore cannot be sued as such, but its members can be sued individually. Joint ventures range in size from very small activities to huge, multimillion-dollar joint actions engaged in by some of the world's largest corporations.

SYNDICATES

SYNDICATE
An investment group of persons or firms brought together for the purpose of financing a project that they would not or could not undertake independently.

A group of individuals getting together to finance a particular project, such as the building of a shopping center or the purchase of a professional basketball franchise, is called a **syndicate** or an *investment group*. The form of such groups varies considerably. A syndicate may exist as a corporation or as a general or limited partnership. In some cases, the members merely purchase and own property jointly but have no legally recognized business arrangement.

JOINT STOCK COMPANIES

JOINT STOCK COMPANY
A hybrid form of business organization that combines characteristics of a corporation and a partnership. Usually, the joint stock company is regarded as a partnership for tax and other legally related purposes.

A **joint stock company** is a true hybrid of a partnership and a corporation. It has many characteristics of a corporation in that (1) its ownership is represented by transferable shares of stock, (2) it is usually managed by directors and officers of

EXHIBIT 19-1 MAJOR FORMS OF BUSINESS COMPARED

CHARACTERISTIC	SOLE PROPRIETORSHIP	PARTNERSHIP	CORPORATION
Method of Creation	Created at will by owner.	Created by agreement of the parties.	Charter issued by state—created by statutory authorization.
Legal Position	Not a separate entity; owner is the business.	Is a separate legal entity in most states.	Always a legal entity separate and distinct from its owners—a legal fiction for the purposes of owning property and being a party to litigation.
Liability	Unlimited liability.	Unlimited liability.	Limited liability of shareholders—shareholders are not liable for the debts of the corporation.
Duration	Determined by owner; automatically dissolved on owner's death.	Terminated by agreement of the partners, but can continue to do business even when a partner dissociates from the partnership.	Can have perpetual existence.
Transferability of Interest	Interest can be transferred, but individual's proprietorship then ends.	Although partnership interest can be assigned, assignee does not have full rights of a partner.	Shares of stock can be transferred.
Management	Completely at owner's discretion.	Each general partner has a direct and equal voice in management unless expressly agreed otherwise in the partnership agreement.	Shareholders elect directors, who set policy and appoint officers.
Taxation	Owner pays personal taxes on business income.	Each partner pays pro rata share of income taxes on net profits, whether or not they are distributed.	Double taxation—corporation pays income tax on net profits, with no deduction for dividends, and shareholders pay income tax on disbursed dividends they receive.
Organizational Fees, Annual License Fees, and Annual Reports	None.	None.	All required.
Transaction of Business in Other States	Generally no limitation.	Generally no limitation.[a]	Normally must qualify to do business and obtain certificate of authority.

a. A few states have enacted statutes requiring that foreign partnerships qualify to do business there.

EXHIBIT 19-1 MAJOR FORMS OF BUSINESS COMPARED—CONTINUED

CHARACTERISTIC	LIMITED PARTNERSHIP	LIMITED LIABILITY COMPANY	LIMITED LIABILITY PARTNERSHIP
Method of Creation	Created by agreement to carry on a business for a profit. At least one party must be a general partner and the other(s) limited partner(s). Certificate of limited partnership is filed. Charter must be issued by the state.	Created by an agreement of the owner-members of the company. Articles of organization are filed. Charter must be issued by the state.	Created by agreement of the partners. A statement of qualification for the limited liability partnership is filed.
Legal Position	Treated as a legal entity.	Treated as a legal entity.	Generally, treated same as a general partnership.
Liability	Unlimited liability of all general partners; limited partners are liable only to the extent of capital contributions.	Member-owners' liability is limited to the amount of capital contributions or investments.	Varies, but under the UPA, liability of a partner for acts committed by other partners is limited.
Duration	By agreement in certificate, or by termination of the last general partner (retirement, death, and the like) or last limited partner.	Unless a single-member LLC, can have perpetual existence (same as a corporation).	Remains in existence until cancellation or revocation.
Transferability of Interest	Interest can be assigned (same as general partnership), but if assignee becomes a member with consent of other partners, certificate must be amended.	Member interests are freely transferable.	Interest can be assigned same as in a general partnership.
Management	General partners have equal voice or by agreement. Limited partners may not retain limited liability if they actively participate in management.	Member-owners can fully participate in management, or management is selected by owner-members who manage on behalf of the members.	Same as a general partnership.
Taxation	Generally taxed as a partnership.	LLC is not taxed, and members are taxed personally on profits "passed through" the LLC.	Same as a general partnership.
Organizational Fees, Annual License Fees, and Annual Reports	Organizational fee required; usually not others.	Organizational fee required; others vary with states.	Fees are set by each state for filing statements of qualification, foreign qualification, and annual reports.
Transaction of Business in Other States	Generally, no limitations.	Generally, no limitation but may vary depending on state.	Must file a statement of foreign qualification before doing business in another state.

the company or association, and (3) it can have a perpetual existence. Most of its other features, however, are more characteristic of a partnership, and it is usually treated like a partnership. As with a partnership, it is formed by agreement (not statute), property is usually held in the names of the members, shareholders have personal liability, and generally the company is not treated as a legal entity for purposes of a lawsuit.

BUSINESS TRUSTS

BUSINESS TRUST
A form of business organization in which investors (trust beneficiaries) transfer cash or property to trustees in exchange for trust certificates that represent their investment shares. The certificate holders share in the trust's profits but have limited liability.

A **business trust** is created by a written trust agreement that sets forth the interests of the beneficiaries and the obligations and powers of the trustees. With a business trust, legal ownership and management of the property of the business stay with one or more of the trustees, and the profits are distributed to the beneficiaries.

The business trust was started in Massachusetts in an attempt to obtain the limited liability advantage of corporate status while avoiding certain restrictions on a corporation's ownership and development of real property. The business trust resembles a corporation in many respects. Beneficiaries of the trust, for example, are not personally responsible for the debts or obligations of the business trust. In fact, in a number of states, business trusts must pay corporate taxes.

COOPERATIVES

COOPERATIVE
An association, which may or may not be incorporated, that is organized to provide an economic service to its members.

A **cooperative** is an association, which may or may not be incorporated, that is organized to provide an economic service to its members (or shareholders). Most cooperatives are incorporated under either state statutes for cooperatives, general business incorporation statutes, or limited liability company (LLC) statutes. Generally, an incorporated cooperative will distribute dividends, or profits, to its owners on the basis of their transactions with the cooperative rather than on the basis of the amount of capital they contributed. Members of incorporated cooperatives have limited liability, as do shareholders of corporations or members of LLCs. Cooperatives that are unincorporated are often treated like partnerships. The members have joint liability for the cooperative's acts.

This form of business is generally adopted by groups of individuals who wish to pool their resources to gain some advantage in the marketplace. Consumer purchasing co-ops are formed to obtain lower prices through quantity discounts. Seller marketing co-ops are formed to control the market and thereby obtain higher sales prices from consumers. Co-ops range in size from small, local, consumer cooperatives to national businesses such as Ace Hardware and Land 'O Lakes, the well-known producer of dairy products.

◼ Private Franchises

FRANCHISE
Any arrangement in which the owner of a trademark, trade name, or copyright licenses another to use that trademark, trade name, or copyright in the selling of goods and services.

FRANCHISEE
One receiving a license to use another's (the franchisor's) trademark, trade name, or copyright in the sale of goods and services.

FRANCHISOR
One licensing another (the franchisee) to use his or her trademark, trade name, or copyright in the sale of goods or services.

Many entrepreneurs, instead of setting up a business form through which to market their own products or services, opt to purchase a franchise. A **franchise** is defined as any arrangement in which the owner of a trademark, a trade name, or a copyright licenses others to use the trademark, trade name, or copyright in the selling of goods or services. A **franchisee** (a purchaser of a franchise) is generally legally independent of the **franchisor** (the seller of the franchise). At the same time, the franchisee is economically dependent on the franchisor's integrated business system. In other words, a franchisee can operate as an independent businessperson but still obtain the advantages of a regional or national organization.

Today, close to 40 percent of all retail transactions and an increasing percentage of the total annual national output of the United States are generated by private franchises. Well-known franchises include McDonald's, 7-Eleven, and Burger King.

TYPES OF FRANCHISES

Because the franchising industry is so extensive and so many different types of businesses sell franchises, it is difficult to summarize the many types of franchises that now exist. Generally, though, the majority of franchises fall into one of the following three classifications: distributorships, chain-style business operations, or manufacturing or processing-plant arrangements. We briefly describe these types of franchises here.

Distributorship A *distributorship* arises when a manufacturer (franchisor) licenses a dealer (franchisee) to sell its product. Often, a distributorship covers an exclusive territory. An example of this type of franchise is an automobile dealership.

Chain-Style Business Operation A *chain-style business operation* exists when a franchise operates under a franchisor's trade name and is identified as a member of a select group of dealers that engages in the franchisor's business. Often, the franchisor requires that the franchisee maintain certain standards of operation. In addition, sometimes the franchisee is obligated to deal exclusively with the franchisor to obtain materials and supplies. Examples of this type of franchise are McDonald's and most other fast-food chains.

Manufacturing or Processing-Plant Arrangement A *manufacturing or processing-plant arrangement* exists when the franchisor transmits to the franchisee the essential ingredients or formula to make a particular product. The franchisee then markets the product either at wholesale or at retail in accordance with the franchisor's standards. Examples of this type of franchise are Coca-Cola and other soft-drink bottling companies.

THE FRANCHISE CONTRACT

The franchise relationship is defined by a contract between the franchisor and the franchisee. The franchise contract specifies the terms and conditions of the franchise and spells out the rights and duties of the franchisor and the franchisee. If either party fails to perform the contractual duties, that party may be subject to a lawsuit for breach of contract. Generally, the statutory and case law governing franchising tend to emphasize the importance of good faith and fair dealing in franchise relationships.

Because each type of franchise relationship has its own characteristics, it is difficult to describe the broad range of details a franchising contract may include. In the remaining pages of this chapter, we look at some of the major issues that typically are addressed in a franchise contract.

Payment for the Franchise The franchisee ordinarily pays an initial fee or lump-sum price for the franchise license (the privilege of being granted a franchise). This fee is separate from the various products that the franchisee purchases from or through the franchisor. In some industries, the franchisor relies heavily on the initial sale of the franchise for realizing a profit. In other industries, the continued dealing between the parties brings profit to both. In most situations, the franchisor will

KEEP IN MIND Because a franchise involves the licensing of a trademark, a trade name, or a copyright, the law governing intellectual property may apply in some cases.

A Ben & Jerry's franchise. Into which of the three basic classifications of franchises would this franchise fall? (Lon C. Diehl, PhotoEdit)

A good source of information on the purchase and sale of franchises is Franchising.org, which is online at **http://www.franchising.org**.

receive a stated percentage of the annual sales or annual volume of business done by the franchisee. The franchise agreement may also require the franchisee to pay a percentage of advertising costs and certain administrative expenses.

Business Premises The franchise agreement may specify whether the premises for the business must be leased or purchased outright. In some cases, construction of a building is necessary to meet the terms of the agreement. The agreement usually will specify whether the franchisor supplies equipment and furnishings for the premises or whether this is the responsibility of the franchisee.

Location of the Franchise Typically, the franchisor will determine the territory to be served. Some franchise contracts will give the franchisee exclusive rights, or "territorial rights," to a certain geographical area. Other franchise contracts, while they define the territory allotted to a particular franchise, either specifically state that the franchise is nonexclusive or are silent on the issue of territorial rights.

Many franchise cases involve disputes over territorial rights, and this is one area of franchising in which the implied covenant of good faith and fair dealing often comes into play. ■ EXAMPLE 19.3 Suppose that a franchisee is not given exclusive territorial rights in the franchise contract, or the contract is silent on the issue. If the franchisor allows a competing franchise to be established nearby, the franchisee may suffer a significant loss in profits. In this situation, a court may hold that the franchisor's actions breached an implied covenant of good faith and fair dealing. ■

A particular problem facing franchisees in today's online world is that franchisors may attempt to sell their own products via their Web sites. See, for example, the case discussed in this chapter's *Adapting the Law to the Online Environment* feature.

Business Organization of the Franchisee The business organization of the franchisee is of great concern to the franchisor. Depending on the terms of the franchise agreement, the franchisor may specify particular requirements for the form and capital structure of the business. The franchise agreement may also provide that standards of operation—relating to such aspects of the business as sales quotas, quality, and record keeping—be met by the franchisee. Furthermore, a franchisor may wish to retain stringent control over the training of personnel involved in the operation and over administrative aspects of the business.

Quality Control by the Franchisor Although the day-to-day operation of the franchise business is normally left up to the franchisee, the franchise agreement may provide for the amount of supervision and control agreed on by the parties. When the franchise is a service operation, such as a motel, the contract often provides that the franchisor will establish certain standards for the facility. Typically, the contract will provide that the franchisor is permitted to make periodic inspections to ensure that the standards are being maintained in order to protect the franchise's name and reputation.

As a general rule, the validity of a provision permitting the franchisor to establish and enforce certain quality standards is unquestioned. Because the franchisor has a legitimate interest in maintaining the quality of the product or service to protect its name and reputation, it can exercise greater control in this area than would otherwise be tolerated. Increasingly, however, franchisors are finding that if they exercise too much control over the operations of their franchisees, they may incur vicarious

RECALL Under agency law, an employer may be liable for the torts of his or her employees if they occur within the scope of employment, without regard to the personal fault of the employer.

ADAPTING THE LAW TO THE ONLINE ENVIRONMENT

What Happens to Exclusive Territorial Rights in the Online Environment?

With the growth of inexpensive and easy online marketing, it was inevitable that cyberturf conflicts would eventually arise between franchisors and franchisees. Suppose, for example, that a franchise contract grants to the franchisee exclusive rights to sell the franchised product within a certain territory. What happens if the franchisor then begins to sell the product from its Web site to anyone anywhere in the world, including in the franchisee's territory? Does this constitute a breach of the franchise contract?

This is a relatively new issue to come before the courts, and how the question is resolved has important implications for both franchisors and franchisees. From the franchisor's perspective, it would seem unfair to deprive it of the ability to market its goods, efficiently and inexpensively, from its Web site. From the franchisee's perspective, it would seem only fair (and consistent with the franchise contract's guarantee of exclusive territorial rights) to have the exclusive right to market the franchisor's product within its area.

DRUG EMPORIUM'S "ELECTRONIC ENCROACHMENT"

The issue of "electronic encroachment" came before a panel of arbitrators in an American Arbitration Association (AAA) proceeding. As you learned in Chapter 3, the AAA is a leading provider of arbitration services. The proceeding involved franchise contracts between the Drug Emporium, Inc., and several of its franchisees. The contracts provided that each franchisee had the exclusive right to conduct business in a specific geographic area. The franchisees claimed that the Drug Emporium breached its contractual obligation to honor their territo-

ries by using its Web site to sell directly to customers within the franchisees' territories.

WHAT, EXACTLY, IS A "VIRTUAL DRUGSTORE"?

One of the first questions the arbitrating panel had to decide was whether a "virtual drugstore" is a drugstore for purposes of a franchise agreement. The panel had little difficulty in answering the question, stating that "[i]t is not for this panel to divine whether a virtual reality is real or whether it is a phantom." The panel simply noted that the company marketed the site as "the full service online drugstore," that it called the site a "drugstore" in filings with the Securities and Exchange Commission, and that it advertised the site as "your neighborhood pharmacy."

Ultimately, in what is believed to be the first ruling by a court or arbitrating panel on the issue of electronic encroachment, the arbitrating panel decided in favor of the franchisees. The panel ordered the Drug Emporium to cease marketing its goods from its Web site to potential customers who were physically located within the franchisees' territories.[a]

FOR CRITICAL ANALYSIS

Conflicts such as the one involved in this case can occur not only between franchisors and franchisees but also among competing franchisees. What can franchisees do to protect themselves against electronic encroachment by their franchisors or other franchisees?

a. *Emporium Drug Mart, Inc. of Shreveport v. Drug Emporium, Inc.,* No. 71-114-0012600 (American Arbitration Association, September 2, 2000).

(indirect) liability under agency theory for the acts of their franchisees' employees. The actual exercise of control, or at least the right to control, is the key consideration. If the franchisee controls the day-to-day operations of the business to a significant degree, the franchisor may be able to avoid liability, as the following case illustrates.

CASE 19.2 Kerl v. Dennis Rasmussen, Inc.

Court of Appeals of Wisconsin, 2003.
267 Wis.App. 827,
672 N.W.2d 71,
2003 WI App 226.
http://www.wisbar.org/WisCtApp/index.html[a]

FACTS Arby's, Inc., is a national franchisor of fast-food restaurants. Dennis Rasmussen, Inc. (DRI), is an Arby's franchisee. Under the terms of their franchise contract, DRI agreed to follow Arby's specifications for several aspects of operating the business. DRI hired Cathy Propp as the manager for its Arby's restaurant in 1994. In early 1999, Propp hired Harvey Pierce, a local county jail inmate with work-release privileges after a conviction for sexual assault. On June 11, Pierce left his shift at the restaurant without permission, walked half a mile to a discount store parking lot, and shot his former girlfriend Robin Kerl, her fiancé David Jones, and himself. Pierce and Jones died. Kerl survived, but is permanently disabled. Kerl and others filed a suit in a Wisconsin state court against DRI and Arby's, claiming in part that Arby's was vicariously liable for DRI's allegedly negligent hiring and supervision of Pierce. Arby's filed a motion for summary judgment, which the court granted. The plaintiffs appealed this judgment to a state intermediate appellate court.

ISSUE Was Arby's vicariously liable for DRI's actions?

DECISION No. The state intermediate appellate court affirmed the lower court's summary judgment in Arby's

a. In the "Court of Appeals 1995–2004" section, click on "2003 Opinions." In the result, in the "Index by Appellant's name" section, click on "October–December." On the next page, scroll to the name of the case and click on the docket number to access the opinion.

favor, concluding that Arby's did not have a right of control, or actual control, over DRI's allegedly negligent actions.

REASON The court determined that in an action seeking to impose vicarious liability on a franchisor for the negligent actions of a franchisee, it is not enough that the franchisor has the general right to control certain aspects of a franchisee's operations. According to the court, "the decisive factor is whether the franchisor controls the daily operations of the franchisee such that it exercises a considerable degree of control over the instrumentality [the object or person that caused the injury] at issue." In this case, the franchise contract assigned responsibility for the employees to DRI, who "shall hire, train, maintain and properly supervise sufficient, qualified and courteous personnel." Under the contract, Arby's only remedy for DRI's failure to comply was to give DRI thirty days to cure the problem and then terminate the franchise agreement if DRI did not rectify the situation. "Nothing in the agreement gives Arby's the right to supervise directly how DRI handles personnel issues." Thus, the court held that Arby's was not vicariously liable for DRI's negligent hiring and supervision of Pierce.

WHY IS THIS CASE IMPORTANT? *This case addresses an important issue for franchisors—vicarious (indirect) liability for franchisees' actions. Many franchisors understandably want to exercise enough control over the franchisee to protect the identity and reputation of the franchise. Yet the more control a franchisor exercises, the more likely it is that a court will hold the franchisor liable for any injuries sustained at the franchise or as a result of the franchisee's conduct.*

Pricing Arrangements Franchises provide the franchisor with an outlet for the firm's goods and services. Depending on the nature of the business, the franchisor may require the franchisee to purchase certain supplies from the franchisor at an established price. A franchisor who sets the prices at which the franchisee will resell the goods may violate state or federal antitrust laws, or both, however.[3]

Termination of the Franchise The duration of the franchise is a matter to be determined between the parties. Generally, a franchise will start out for a short period,

---

3. Additionally, requiring a franchisee to purchase supplies *exclusively* from the franchisor may violate federal antitrust laws (see Chapter 22). For two landmark cases in these areas, see *United States v. Arnold, Schwinn & Co.,* 388 U.S. 365, 87 S.Ct. 1956, 18 L.Ed.2d (1967), and *Fortner Enterprises, Inc. v. U.S. Steel Corp.,* 394 U.S. 495, 89 S.Ct. 1252, 22 L.Ed.2d 495 (1969).

such as a year, so that the franchisee and the franchisor can determine whether they want to stay in business with one another. Usually, the franchise agreement will specify that termination must be "for cause," such as death or disability of the franchisee, insolvency of the franchisee, breach of the franchise agreement, or failure to meet specified sales quotas. Most franchise contracts provide that notice of termination must be given. If no set time for termination is specified, then a reasonable time, with notice, will be implied. A franchisee must be given reasonable time to wind up the business—that is, to do the accounting and return the copyright or trademark or any other property of the franchisor.

Wrongful Termination.   Because a franchisor's termination of a franchise often has adverse consequences for the franchisee, much franchise litigation involves claims of wrongful termination. Generally, the termination provisions of contracts are more favorable to the franchisor. This means that the franchisee, who normally invests a substantial amount of time and funds in the franchise operation to make it successful, may receive little or nothing for the business on termination. The franchisor owns the trademark and hence the business.

It is in this area that statutory and case law become important. Federal and state laws governing franchising attempt, among other things, to protect franchisees from the arbitrary or unfair termination of their franchises by the franchisors. Generally, both statutory and case law emphasize the importance of good faith and fair dealing in terminating a franchise relationship.

The Importance of Good Faith and Fair Dealing.   In determining whether a franchisor has acted in good faith when terminating a franchise agreement, the courts generally try to balance the rights of both parties. If a court perceives that a franchisor has arbitrarily or unfairly terminated a franchise, the franchisee will be provided with a remedy for wrongful termination. If a franchisor's decision to terminate a franchise was made in the normal course of the franchisor's business operations, however, and reasonable notice of termination was given to the franchisee, normally a court would not consider such a termination wrongful. At issue in the following case was whether General Motors Corporation, Chrysler Corporation, and Toyota Motor Sales, U.S.A., Inc., acted wrongfully in terminating their franchises with a motor vehicle dealer in Ohio.

CASE 19.3 ▦ General Motors Corp. v. Monte Zinn Chevrolet Co.

Ohio Court of Appeals,
Tenth District, 2000.
136 Ohio App.3d 157,
736 N.E.2d 62.

FACTS   Monte Zinn operated Ohio motor vehicle dealerships, as Monte Zinn Chevrolet Company and Monte Zinn Motor Company, under separate franchise agreements with General Motors Corporation (GMC), Chrysler Corporation, and Toyota Motor Sales, U.S.A., Inc. Each agreement permitted the franchisor to terminate the dealership if the dealer was convicted of a felony. In 1995, Zinn pleaded guilty to committing a felony by violating

federal statutes proscribing fraud and conspiracy to commit fraud in relation to his dealerships. He was sentenced to two years' probation and ordered to pay a fine and a special assessment. Each franchisor terminated its Zinn companies' franchise. The Zinn companies protested to the Ohio Motor Vehicle Dealers Board, a state agency that oversees motor vehicle franchises in Ohio. The board ruled in favor of the Zinn companies. The franchisors filed a suit in an Ohio state court against the Zinn companies, and the court reversed the board's order. The Zinn companies appealed to a state intermediate appellate court.

(Continued)

CASE 19.3—Continued

ISSUE Did the franchisors have good cause to terminate the Zinn companies' franchises?

DECISION Yes. The state intermediate appellate court affirmed the lower court's decision, citing Zinn's felony conviction and other circumstances that supported the franchisors' action.

REASON The state intermediate appellate court explained that the facts "all weigh in favor of finding good cause to terminate the franchise[s]." A "felony conviction for fraud committed by a dealer/operator undermines the trust between the manufacturer and the dealer, and between the public and the dealer." Discussing the GMC franchise, the court noted that between 1991 and 1995, the Zinn companies' "overall sales effectiveness had been in the bottom half of Chevrolet dealers in their service

area and consistently ranked in the bottom 20 percent of all dealers in customer service and satisfaction." As for the Chrysler franchise, the Zinn companies "had made few investments into the dealership" and had been seriously "undercapitalized every year from 1991." Between 1992 and 1996, "their new vehicle sales volume increased at less than half the rate" of other dealers "and actually decreased between 1995 and 1996." The Zinn companies also had "performed poorly in service-related areas" and their "scores on owner loyalty" were below average. Finally, concerning the Toyota franchise, the court pointed out that Toyota "uniformly terminated dealerships following felony convictions."

FOR CRITICAL ANALYSIS—Economic Consideration
Should franchisors conduct background checks on prospective franchisees, and, if so, would it have helped in this case?

APPLICATION ■ How Do You Choose between LLCs and LLPs?*

One of the most important decisions that an entrepreneur makes is the selection of the form in which to do business. To make the best decision, a businessperson should understand all of the aspects of the variety of forms, including legal, tax, licensing, and business considerations. It is also important that all of the participants in the business understand their actual relationship, regardless of the organizational structure.

NUMBER OF PARTICIPANTS

During the last decade or so, new forms of business organizations, including limited liability partnerships (LLPs) and limited liability companies (LLCs), have been added to the options for business entities. An initial consideration in choosing between these forms is the number of participants. An LLP must have two or more partners, but in many states, an LLC can have a single member (owner).

*This *Application* is not meant to substitute for the services of an attorney who is licensed to practice law in your state.

LIABILITY CONSIDERATIONS

The members of an LLC are not liable for the obligations of the organization. The liability of the partners in an LLP varies from state to state. About half of the states exempt the partners from liability for any obligation of the firm. In some states, the partners are individually liable for the contractual obligations of the firm but are not liable for obligations arising from the torts of others. In either situation, each partner may be on his or her own with respect to liability unless the other partners decide to help.

DISTRIBUTIONS FROM THE FIRM

Members and partners are generally paid by allowing them to withdraw funds from the firm against their share of the profits. In many states, a member of an LLC must repay so-called wrongful distributions even if she or he did not know that the distributions were wrongful. Under most LLP statutes, by contrast, the partners must repay only distributions that were fraudulent.

APPLICATION ■ How Do You Choose between LLCs and LLPs?—Continued

MANAGEMENT STRUCTURE

Both LLPs and LLCs can set up whatever management structure the participants desire to have. Also, all unincorporated business organizations, including LLPs and LLCs, are treated as partnerships for federal income tax purposes (unless an LLC elects to be treated as a corporation[a]). This means that the entities are not taxed at the firm level. Their income is passed through to the partners or members, who must report it on their individual income tax returns. Some states impose additional taxes on LLCs.

THE NATURE OF THE BUSINESS

The business in which a firm engages is another factor to consider in choosing a business form. For example, with a few exceptions, professionals—including accountants, attorneys, and physicians—may organize as either an LLP or an LLC in any state. In many states, however, the ownership of an entity that engages in a certain profession and the liability of the owners are prescribed by state law.

a. The chief benefits of electing corporate status for tax purposes are that the members generally are not subject to self-employment taxes, and fringe benefits may be provided to employee-members on a tax-reduced basis. The tax laws are complicated, however, and a professional should be consulted about the details.

FINANCIAL AND PERSONAL RELATIONSHIPS

Despite their importance, the legal consequences of choosing a business form are often secondary considerations to the financial and personal relationships among the participants. Work effort, motivation, ability, and other personal attributes can be significant factors, as may be fundamental business concerns, such as the expenses and debts of the firm. Other practical factors to consider include the willingness of others to do business with an LLP or an LLC. A supplier, for example, may not be willing to extend credit to a firm whose partners or members will not accept personal liability for the debt.

CHECKLIST FOR CHOOSING A LIMITED LIABILITY BUSINESS FORM

1. Determine the number of participants, which forms a state allows, and what limits on liability the state provides for the participants.
2. Evaluate the tax considerations.
3. Consider the business in which the firm engages, or will engage, and any restrictions that exist on that type of business.
4. Weigh such practical concerns as the financial and personal relationships among the participants, and among the participants and those with whom the firm will deal.

■ KEY TERMS

CHAPTER SUMMARY ▦ The Entrepreneur's Options

Major Business Forms (See pages 587–593.)	1. *Sole proprietorships*—The simplest form of business; used by anyone who does business without creating an organization. The owner is the business. The owner pays personal income taxes on all profits and is personally liable for all business debts.
	2. *Partnerships*—Created by agreement of the parties; not treated as an entity except for limited purposes. Partners have unlimited liability for partnership debts, and each partner normally has an equal voice in management. Income is "passed through" the partnership to the individual partners, who pay personal taxes on the income.
	3. *Limited partnerships*—Must be formed in compliance with statutory requirements. A limited partnership consists of one or more general partners, who have unlimited liability for partnership losses, and one or more limited partners, who are liable only to the extent of their contributions. Only general partners can participate in management.
	4. *Corporations*—A corporation is formed in compliance with statutory requirements, is a legal entity separate and distinct from its owners, and can have perpetual existence. The shareholder-owners elect directors, who set policy and hire officers to run the day-to-day business of the corporation. Shareholders normally are not personally liable for the debts of the corporation. The corporation pays income tax on net profits; shareholders pay income tax on disbursed dividends.
	5. *Limited liability companies (LLCs)*—The LLC is a hybrid form of business organization that offers the limited liability feature of corporations but the tax benefits of partnerships. LLC members participate in management. Members of LLCs may be corporations or partnerships, are not restricted in number, and may be residents of other countries.
	6. *Limited liability partnerships (LLPs)*—Typically, an LLP is formed by professionals who work together as partners in a partnership. Under most state LLP statutes, it is relatively easy to convert a traditional partnership into an LLP. LLP statutes vary, but generally they allow professionals to avoid personal liability for the malpractice of other partners.
Special Business Forms (See pages 593–596.)	1. *Joint venture*—An organization created by two or more persons in contemplation of a limited activity or a single transaction; otherwise, similar to a partnership.
	2. *Syndicate*—An investment group that undertakes to finance a particular project; may exist as a corporation or as a general or limited partnership.
	3. *Joint stock company*—A business form similar to a corporation in some respects (transferable shares of stock, management by directors and officers, perpetual existence) but otherwise resembling a partnership.
	4. *Business trust*—Created by a written trust agreement that sets forth the interests of the beneficiaries and obligations and powers of the trustee(s). Similar to a corporation in many respects. Beneficiaries are not personally liable for the debts or obligations of the business trust.
	5. *Cooperative*—An association organized to provide an economic service to its members. May be incorporated or unincorporated.
Private Franchises (See pages 596–602.)	1. *Types of franchises*—
	a. Distributorship (for example, automobile dealerships).
	b. Chain-style operation (for example, fast-food chains).
	c. Manufacturing/processing-plant arrangement (for example, soft-drink bottling companies, such as Coca-Cola).

CHAPTER SUMMARY ▦ The Entrepreneur's Options—Continued	
Private Franchises—Continued	2. *The franchise contract—* a. Ordinarily requires the franchisee (purchaser) to pay a price for the franchise license. b. Specifies the territory to be served by the franchisee's firm. c. May require the franchisee to purchase certain supplies from the franchisor at an established price. d. May require the franchisee to abide by certain standards of quality relating to the product or service offered but cannot set retail resale prices. e. Usually provides for the date and/or conditions of termination of the franchise arrangement. Both federal and state statutes attempt to protect certain franchisees from franchisors who unfairly or arbitrarily terminate franchises.

▦ FOR REVIEW

Answers for the even-numbered questions in this For Review *section can be found in Appendix I at the end of this text.*

1 What are some of the major forms of business organization used by entrepreneurs in the United States?

2 What advantages and disadvantages are associated with each major business form?

3 Why have limited liability companies and limited liability partnerships come into widespread use in recent years?

4 What is a joint venture? What are some other special business organizational forms, and why are they used?

5 What is a franchise, and how does a franchising relationship arise?

▦ QUESTIONS AND CASE PROBLEMS

19–1. Forms of Business Organization. In each of the following situations, determine whether Georgio's Fashions is a sole proprietorship, a partnership, a limited partnership, or a corporation.

(a) Georgio's defaults on a payment to supplier Dee Creations. Dee sues Georgio's and each of the owners of Georgio's personally for payment of the debt.

(b) Georgio's raises $200,000 through the sale of shares of its stock.

(c) At tax time, Georgio's files a tax return with the IRS and pays taxes on the firm's net profits.

(d) Georgio's is owned by three persons, two of whom are not allowed to participate in the firm's management.

19–2. Choice of Business Form. Jorge, Marta, and Jocelyn are college graduates, and Jorge has come up with an idea for a new product that he believes could make the three of them very rich. His idea is to manufacture soft-drink dispensers for home use and market them to consumers throughout the Midwest. Jorge's personal experience qualifies him to be both first-line supervisor and general manager of the new firm. Marta is a born salesperson. Jocelyn has little interest in sales or management but would like to invest a large sum of money that she has inherited from her aunt. What factors should Jorge, Marta, and Jocelyn consider in deciding which form of business organization to adopt?

19–3. Business Organizations. Alan, Jane, and Kyle organize a nonprofit business—AJK Markets, Inc.—to buy groceries from wholesalers and sell them to consumers who buy a membership in AJK. Because the firm is a nonprofit entity, it is able to sell the groceries for less than a commercial grocer could. What form of business organization is AJK Markets? Is it significant that AJK is incorporated?

19–4. Limited Liability Companies. John, Lesa, and Trevor form an LLC. John contributes 60 percent of the capital, and Lesa and Trevor each contribute 20 percent. Nothing is decided about how profits will be divided. John assumes that he will be entitled to 60 percent of the profits, in accordance with his contribution. Lesa and Trevor, however, assume that the profits will be divided equally. A dispute over the profits arises, and ultimately a court has to decide the issue. What law will the court apply? In most states, what will result? How could this dispute have been avoided in the first place? Discuss fully.

CASE PROBLEM WITH SAMPLE ANSWER

19–5. In 1985, Bruce Byrne, with his sons Scott and Gordon, opened Lone Star R.V. Sales, Inc., a motor home dealership in Houston, Texas. In 1994, Lone Star became a franchised dealer for Winnebago Industries, Inc., a manufacturer of recreational vehicles. The parties renewed the franchise in 1995, but during the next year, their relationship began to deteriorate. Lone Star did not maintain a current inventory, its sales did not meet goals agreed to between the parties, and Lone Star disparaged Winnebago products to consumers and otherwise failed to actively promote them. Several times, the Byrnes subjected Winnebago employees to verbal abuse. During one phone conversation, Bruce threatened to throw a certain Winnebago sales manager off Lone Star's lot if he appeared at the dealership. Bruce was physically incapable of carrying out the threat, however. In 1998, Winnebago terminated the franchise, claiming, among many other things, that it was concerned for the safety of its employees. Lone Star filed a protest with the Texas Motor Vehicle Board. Did Winnebago have good cause to terminate Lone Star's franchise? Discuss. [*Lone Star R.V. Sales, Inc. v. Motor Vehicle Board of the Texas Department of Transportation,* 49 S.W.3d 492 (Tex.App.—Austin, 2001)]

After you have answered this problem, compare your answer with the sample answer given on the Web site that accompanies this text. Go to http://blt.westbuslaw.com, select "Chapter 19," and click on "Case Problem with Sample Answer."

19–6. Franchise Termination. In the automobile industry, luxury-car customers are considered the most demanding segment of the market with respect to customer service. Jaguar Cars, a division of Ford Motor Co., is the exclusive U.S. distributor of Jaguar luxury cars. Jaguar Cars distributes its products through franchised dealers. In April 1999, Dave Ostrem Imports, Inc., an authorized Jaguar dealer in Des Moines, Iowa, contracted to sell its dealership to Midwest Automotive III, LLC. A Jaguar franchise generally cannot be sold without Jaguar Cars' permission. Jaguar Cars asked Midwest Auto to submit three years of customer satisfaction index (CSI) data for all franchises with which its owners had been associated. CSI data are intended to measure how well dealers treat their customers and satisfy their customers' needs. Jaguar Cars requires above-average CSI ratings for its dealers. Most of Midwest Auto's scores fell below the national average. Jaguar Cars rejected Midwest Auto's application and sought to terminate the franchise, claiming that a transfer of the dealership would be "substantially detrimental" to the distribution of Jaguar vehicles in the community. Is Jaguar Cars' attempt to terminate this franchise reasonable? Why or why not?

[*Midwest Automotive III, LLC v. Iowa Department of Transportation,* 646 N.W.2d 417 (Iowa 2002)]

19–7. The Franchise Contract. On August 23, 1995, Climaco Guzman entered into a commercial janitorial services franchise agreement with Jan-Pro Cleaning Systems, Inc., in Rhode Island for a franchise fee of $3,285. In the agreement, Jan-Pro promised to furnish Guzman with "one (1) or more customer account(s) . . . amounting to $8,000.00 gross volume per year. . . . No portion of the franchise fee is refundable except and to the extent that the Franchisor, within 120 business days following the date of execution of the Franchise Agreement, fails to provide accounts." By February 19, Guzman had not received any accounts and demanded a full refund. Jan-Pro then promised "two accounts grossing $12,000 per year in income." Despite the promises, Jan-Pro did not have the ability to furnish accounts that met the requirements. In September, Guzman filed a suit in a Rhode Island state court against Jan-Pro, alleging in part fraudulent misrepresentation. Should the court rule in Guzman's favor? Why or why not? [*Guzman v. Jan-Pro Cleaning Systems, Inc.,* 839 A.2d 504 (R.I. 2003)]

19–8. Partnership Status. Charlie Waugh owned and operated an auto parts junkyard in Georgia. Charlie's son, Mack, started working in the business part-time as a child and full-time when he left school at age sixteen. Mack oversaw the business's finances, depositing the profits in a bank. Charlie gave Mack a one-half interest in the business, telling him that if "something happened" to Charlie, the entire business would be his. In 1994, Charlie and his wife, Alene, transferred to Mack the land on which the junkyard was located. Two years later, however, Alene and her daughters, Gail and Jewel, falsely convinced Charlie, whose mental competence had deteriorated, that Mack had cheated him. Mack was ordered off the land. Shortly thereafter, Charlie died. Mack filed a suit in a Georgia state court against the rest of the family, asserting in part that he and Charlie had been partners and that he was entitled to Charlie's share of the business. Was the relationship between Charlie and Mack a partnership? Is Mack entitled to Charlie's "share"? Explain. [*Waugh v. Waugh,* 265 Ga.App. 799, 595 S.E.2d 647 (2004)]

A QUESTION OF ETHICS

19–9. Graham Oil Co. (Graham) had been a distributor of ARCO gasoline in Coos Bay, Oregon, for nearly forty years under successive distributorship agreements. ARCO notified Graham that it intended to terminate the franchise because Graham had not been purchasing the minimum amount of gasoline required under their most recent agreement. Graham sought a preliminary injunction against ARCO, arguing that ARCO had violated the Petroleum Marketing Practices Act (PMPA) by deliberately raising its prices so that Graham would be unable to meet the minimum gasoline requirements; thus, ARCO should not be allowed to terminate the agreement. The court ordered Graham to submit the claim to arbitration, in accordance with an arbitration clause in the distributorship agreement. Graham refused to do so, and the court granted summary judgment for ARCO. On appeal, Graham claimed that the arbitration clause was invalid because it forced him to forfeit rights given to franchisees under the PMPA, including the right to punitive damages and attorneys' fees. The appellate court agreed with Graham and remanded the case for trial. In view of these facts, answer the following questions. [*Graham Oil Co. v. Arco Products Co., A Division of Atlantic Richfield Co.*, 43 F.3d 1244 (9th Cir. 1994)]

1. Do you agree with Graham and the appellate court that statutory rights cannot be forfeited contractually, through an arbitration clause?
2. Review the discussion of arbitration in Chapter 3. Does the decision in the above case conflict with any estab-

lished public policy concerning arbitration? Is the decision in the case consistent with other court decisions on arbitration discussed in Chapter 3, including decisions of the United States Supreme Court?

FOR CRITICAL ANALYSIS

 19–10. The law permits individuals to exercise the option of organizing their business enterprises in many different forms. What policy interests are served by granting entrepreneurs these options? Would it be better if the law required that everyone organize his or her business in the same form? Discuss.

INTERNET EXERCISES

Go to the *Business Law Today: The Essentials* home page at **http://blt.westbuslaw.com**, select "Chapter 19," and click on "Internet Exercises." There you will find the following Internet research exercises that you can perform to learn more about topics covered in this chapter.

Activity 19–1: LEGAL PERSPECTIVE—Starting a Business

Activity 19–2: MANAGEMENT PERSPECTIVE—Franchises

Activity 19–3: MANAGEMENT PERSPECTIVE—Limited Partnerships and Limited Liability Partnerships

BEFORE THE TEST

Go to the *Business Law Today: The Essentials* home page at **http://blt.westbuslaw.com**, select "Chapter 19," and click on "Interactive Quizzes." You will find at least twenty interactive questions relating to this chapter.

CHAPTER 20

Corporations

"A corporation is an artificial being, invisible, intangible, and existing only in contemplation of law."

John Marshall, 1755–1835
(Chief justice of the United States
Supreme Court, 1801–1835)

LEARNING OBJECTIVES

After reading this chapter, you should be able to answer the following questions:

1 What are the express and implied powers of corporations? On what sources are these powers based?

2 What are the duties of corporate directors and officers?

3 What must directors do to avoid liability for honest mistakes of judgment and poor business decisions?

4 What role do corporate shareholders play in the corporate enterprise? What are some important rights of shareholders?

5 What is the difference between a corporate merger and a corporate consolidation? What steps are involved in the termination of a corporate enterprise?

In the previous chapter, we described several forms of business organizations. In this chapter, we look in more depth at corporations. The corporation is a creature of statute. As John Marshall indicated in the opening quotation, a corporation is an artificial being, existing only in law and neither tangible nor visible. Its existence generally depends on state law, although some corporations, especially public organizations, can be created under state or federal law.

Each state has its own body of corporate law, and these laws are not entirely uniform. The Model Business Corporation Act (MBCA) is a codification of modern corporation law that has been influential in the drafting and revision of state corporation statutes. Today, the majority of state statutes are guided by the revised version of the MBCA, which is often referred to as the Revised Model Business Corporation Act (RMBCA).

▚ The Nature of the Corporation

A corporation is a legal entity created and recognized by state law. It can consist of one or more *natural* persons (as opposed to the artificial "person" of the corporation) identified under a common name. A corporation can be owned by a single person, or it can have hundreds, thousands, or even millions of owners (shareholders). The corporation substitutes itself for its shareholders in conducting corporate business and in incurring liability, yet its authority to act and the liability for its actions are separate and apart from the individuals who own it.

In a corporation, the responsibility for the overall management of the firm is entrusted to a *board of directors,* which is elected by the shareholders. The board of directors hires *corporate officers* and other employees to run the daily business operations of the corporation. When an individual purchases a share of stock in a corporation, that person becomes a *shareholder* and an owner of the corporation. Unlike the members in a partnership, the body of shareholders can change constantly without affecting the continued existence of the corporation. A shareholder can sue the corporation, and the corporation can sue a shareholder. Also, under certain circumstances, a shareholder can sue on behalf of a corporation. The rights and duties of corporate personnel will be examined in detail later in this chapter.

The shareholder form of business organization developed in Europe at the end of the seventeenth century. Called *joint stock companies,* these organizations frequently collapsed because their organizers absconded with the funds or proved to be incompetent. Because of this history of fraud and collapse, organizations resembling corporations were regarded with suspicion in the United States during its early years. Although several business corporations were formed after the Revolutionary War, it was not until the nineteenth century that the corporation came into common use for private business. This chapter's *Landmark in the Law* feature on the next pages examines a leading case in the early development of private corporations in the United States.

THE CONSTITUTIONAL RIGHTS OF CORPORATIONS

A corporation is recognized under state and federal law as a "person," and it enjoys many of the same rights and privileges that U.S. citizens enjoy. The Bill of Rights guarantees a person, as a citizen, certain protections, and corporations are considered persons in most instances. Accordingly, a corporation has the same right as a natural person to equal protection of the laws under the Fourteenth Amendment. It has the right of access to the courts as an entity that can sue or be sued. It also has the right of due process before denial of life, liberty, or property, as well as freedom from unreasonable searches and seizures and from double jeopardy.

Under the First Amendment, corporations are entitled to freedom of speech. As we pointed out in Chapter 1, however, commercial speech (such as advertising) and political speech (such as contributions to political causes or candidates) receive significantly less protection than noncommercial speech.

Only the corporation's individual officers and employees possess the Fifth Amendment right against self-incrimination.[1] Additionally, the privileges and immunities clause of the Constitution (Article IV, Section 2) does not protect corporations, nor does it protect an unincorporated association.[2] This clause requires each state to treat citizens of other states equally with respect to access to courts, travel rights, and so forth.

The U.S. Constitution. Does it grant corporations the same rights as individuals? (Library of Congress)

---

1. *In re Grand Jury No. 86–3 (Will Roberts Corp.),* 816 F.2d 569 (11th Cir. 1987).
2. *W. C. M. Window Co. v. Bernardi,* 730 F.2d 486 (7th Cir. 1984).

LANDMARK IN THE LAW

The *Dartmouth College* Case (1819)

In 1819, the United States Supreme Court heard the case of *The Trustees of Dartmouth College v. Woodward*.[a] The decision focused on the continued private existence of the small college in New Hampshire but had a lasting impact on U.S. corporate law.

THE DISPUTE OVER THE STATUS OF DARTMOUTH COLLEGE Dartmouth College, named in honor of one of its wealthy patrons, the Earl of Dartmouth, had been founded by the Reverend Eleazar Wheelock, a young Connecticut minister who sought to establish a school to train both missionaries and Native Americans. In 1769, a corporate charter was obtained from the royal governor of New Hampshire. The charter made Wheelock and his English patrons who had donated capital to the college a self-perpetuating board of trustees for the project. When Wheelock died, his son became president of the college. Under the new, less experienced leadership, many disputes arose over the running of the institution, and the participants eventually divided along the prevailing political party lines of New Hampshire.

The Republican group[b] believed that the college ought to be under the control of the state and become a public rather than a sectarian institution. The Republicans persuaded the Republican-controlled New Hampshire Congress to pass legislation that significantly altered the composition of the board of trustees and added a board of overseers that had virtual authority to control the college.

The Federalist[c] board of trustees wanted to preserve the conservative, congregational character of the school and wished to continue to govern the college without interference. They brought suit against William Woodward, the secretary-treasurer of the state-appointed board of overseers, alleging that the legislation violated the college's original charter. The trustees argued that the original grant of the charter, with its self-perpetuating board of trustees, was effectively a contract between the king and the board. Thus, the U.S. Constitution, which in Article I, Section 10, forbids states from passing legislation that would impair the obligation of contracts, prohibited the state from legislating changes in the self-governing structure of the

a. 17 U.S. (4 Wheaton) 518, 4 L.Ed. 629 (1819).
b. The forerunner of the modern-day Democratic Party.
c. The Federalists were an early political group, or party, that advocated a strong national government.

THE LIMITED LIABILITY OF SHAREHOLDERS

One of the key advantages of the corporate form is the limited liability of its owners (shareholders). Corporate shareholders normally are not personally liable for the obligations of the corporation beyond the extent of their investments. In certain limited situations, however, the "corporate veil" can be pierced and liability for the corporation's obligations extended to shareholders—a concept that will be explained later in this chapter. Additionally, shareholders in small companies sometimes voluntarily assume personal liability, as guarantors, for corporate obligations in order to obtain credit.

LANDMARK IN THE LAW

The *Dartmouth College* Case (1819)—Continued

board. The New Hampshire legislature was, therefore, without power to add trustees to the board, to create a board of overseers, or to alter the original charter in any manner.

THE SUPREME COURT'S DECISION Chief Justice John Marshall delivered the opinion of the Court. He stated that the grant of the charter was a contract regarding private property within the meaning of Article I, Section 10, and that the legislative acts of New Hampshire, passed without the trustees' assent, were not binding on them.

Justice Joseph Story, in a separate opinion, distinguished between public and private corporations. He stated that if the shareholders of a corporation were municipal or other public officials, the corporation was a public corporation and therefore subject to continual public regulation. If the shareholders were private individuals, however, quite a contrary situation prevailed. The corporation was private, regardless of whether it consequently was bound only by the terms of its original charter. Had the state reserved regulatory rights in the original grant of the charter, the college would be subject to such control. In the absence of such reservations, the state of New Hampshire's legislative acts clearly impaired the original charter and thus violated the U.S. Constitution.

APPLICATION TO TODAY'S WORLD

This case is a landmark in corporate law because it allowed for the continued existence of private corporations in the United States. Story's opinion opened an avenue for the future regulation of new corporations, while at the same time creating vested rights in private corporations. Marshall and Story both made it clear that the United States Supreme Court would afford the property rights of private corporations the same protection afforded to other forms of property.

RELEVANT WEB SITES

To locate information on the Web concerning The Trustees of Dartmouth College v. Woodward, *go to this text's Web site at* **http://blt.westbuslaw.com,** *select "Chapter 20," and click on "URLs for Landmarks."*

CORPORATE TAXATION

DIVIDEND
A distribution to corporate shareholders of corporate profits or income, disbursed in proportion to the number of shares held.

RETAINED EARNINGS
The portion of a corporation's profits that has not been paid out as dividends to shareholders.

Corporate profits are taxed by state and federal governments. Corporations can do one of two things with corporate profits—retain them or pass them on to shareholders in the form of **dividends.** The corporation receives no tax deduction for dividends distributed to shareholders. Dividends are again taxable (except when they represent distributions of capital) as ordinary income to the shareholder receiving them. This double-taxation feature of the corporation is one of its major disadvantages.

Profits that are not distributed are retained by the corporation. These **retained earnings,** if invested properly, will yield higher corporate profits in the future and thus cause the price of the company's stock to rise. Individual shareholders can then reap the benefits of these retained earnings in the capital gains they receive when they sell their shares.

The consequences of a failure to pay corporate taxes can be severe. The state may dissolve a corporation for this reason. Alternatively, corporate status may be suspended until the taxes are paid. For example, a state may suspend a corporation's **corporate charter** (the document issued by a state agency or authority—usually the secretary of state—that grants a corporation legal existence and the right to function) because of the corporation's failure to pay certain taxes.

Another taxation issue of increasing importance to corporations today is whether corporations that sell goods or services to consumers via the Internet are required to collect state sales taxes. See this chapter's *Adapting the Law to the Online Environment* feature for a discussion of this issue.

Torts and Criminal Acts

A corporation is liable for the torts committed by its agents or officers within the course and scope of their employment. This principle applies to a corporation exactly as it applies to the ordinary agency relationships. We discussed agency law in Chapter 17.

As discussed in Chapter 6, under modern criminal law a corporation may be held liable for the criminal acts of its agents and employees, provided the punishment is one that can be applied to the corporation. Although corporations cannot be imprisoned, they can be fined. Of course, corporate directors and officers can be imprisoned, and in recent years, many have faced criminal penalties for their own actions or for the actions of employees under their supervision.

Recall from Chapter 6 that the U.S. Sentencing Commission, which was established by the Sentencing Reform Act of 1984, created standardized sentencing guidelines for federal crimes. These guidelines went into effect in 1987. The commission subsequently created specific sentencing guidelines for crimes committed by corporate employees (white-collar crimes). The net effect of the guidelines has been a fivefold to tenfold increase in criminal penalties for crimes committed by corporate personnel.

Corporate Powers

When a corporation is created, the express and implied powers necessary to achieve its purpose also come into existence. The express powers of a corporation are found in its **articles of incorporation** (a document containing information about the corporation, including its organization and functions), in the law of the state of incorporation, and in the state and federal constitutions. Corporate **bylaws** (rules of management adopted by the corporation at its first organizational meeting) and the resolutions of the corporation's board of directors also grant or restrict certain powers. The following order of priority is used when conflicts arise among documents involving corporations:

1. The U.S. Constitution.
2. State constitutions.
3. State statutes.
4. The articles of incorporation.

CORPORATE CHARTER
The document issued by a state agency or authority (usually the secretary of state) that grants a corporation legal existence and the right to function.

ARTICLES OF INCORPORATION
The document filed with the appropriate governmental agency, usually the secretary of state, when a business is incorporated. State statutes usually prescribe what kind of information must be contained in the articles of incorporation.

BYLAWS
A set of governing rules adopted by a corporation or other association.

ADAPTING THE LAW TO THE ONLINE ENVIRONMENT

 The Internet Taxation Debate

Since the advent of the Internet, governments at the state and federal levels have debated the following question: Should state governments be able to collect sales taxes on goods sold via the Internet? Many state governments claim that sales taxes should be imposed on such transactions. They argue that their inability to tax online sales of goods to in-state customers by out-of-state corporations has caused them to suffer significant losses in sales tax revenues. Opponents of Internet taxation argue that taxing online sales will impede the growth of e-commerce. They also claim that because online sellers do not benefit from the state services that are typically paid for by tax revenues (such as fire departments and road construction), they should not be required to collect sales taxes.

THE SUPREME COURT'S APPROACH

According to a United States Supreme Court ruling in 1992, no individual state can compel an out-of-state business that lacks a substantial physical presence within that state to collect and remit state taxes.[a] If the corporation has a warehouse, office, or retail store within the state, though, the state can compel the collection of state taxes. Nevertheless, as the Court recognized in that ruling, Congress has the power to pass legislation requiring out-of-state corporations to collect and remit state sales taxes. Congress so far has chosen not to tax Internet transactions. In fact, in 1998 Congress passed the Internet Tax Freedom Act, which temporarily prohibited states from taxing sales of products conducted over the Internet.[b] This ban expired in November 2003, but legislation has been proposed that would permanently prohibit state and local taxation of Internet sales. The law, called the Internet Tax Nondiscrimination Act, passed the Senate in April 2004 and is pending before the House.[c]

A STATE COURT'S DECISION

The issue of Internet taxation came before a Tennessee appellate court in *Prodigy Services Corp. v. Johnson*.[d] Prodigy, a Delaware corporation with its principal place of business in New York, is an Internet service provider (ISP) that offers two software programs for purchase online. A Tennessee statute imposes an obligation to collect sales taxes on anyone supplying "telecommunication services" to state residents. The Tennessee Department of Revenue determined that Prodigy's services constituted telecommunication services and assessed sales taxes. Prodigy appealed this tax assessment.

Ultimately, the state appellate court held that Prodigy did not have to charge its Tennessee customers the sales taxes. After looking closely at the wording of the statute and its legislative history, the court reasoned that the legislature had not intended the statute to apply to ISPs. The court also concluded that even if Prodigy had provided some telecommunications services, these services "were not the 'true object' of the Prodigy sale." The customer had to supply her or his own telephone services, and Prodigy had paid to use a telecommunications network to connect the customer to the main computer in New York. Thus, in the court's opinion, Prodigy was a consumer of telecommunication services rather than a provider.

FOR CRITICAL ANALYSIS

Although most states currently do not require corporations that sell goods and services online to collect state sales taxes, businesspersons should be aware that the law in this area is still developing. Thus, corporations may be required to collect state taxes on Internet sales in the future.

a. See *Quill Corp. v. North Dakota,* 504 U.S. 298, 112 S.Ct. 1904, 119 L.Ed.2d 91 (1992).
b. Public Law 105-277.

c. See Senate Bill 150 and House Resolution 49.
d. 125 S.W.3d 413 (Tenn.Ct.App. 2003).

⑤ Bylaws.

⑥ Resolutions of the board of directors.

Certain implied powers attach when a corporation is created. Barring express constitutional, statutory, or other prohibitions, the corporation has the implied power to perform all acts reasonably appropriate and necessary to accomplish its corporate purposes. For this reason, a corporation has the implied power to borrow funds within certain limits, to lend funds or to extend credit to those with whom it has a legal or contractual relationship, and to make charitable contributions.[3] To borrow money, the corporation acts through its board of directors to authorize the loan. Most often, the president or chief executive officer of the corporation will execute the necessary papers on behalf of the corporation. In so doing, corporate officers have the implied power to bind the corporation in matters directly connected with the *ordinary* business affairs of the enterprise.

Classification of Corporations

The classification of a corporation depends on its purpose, ownership characteristics, and location.

A **close corporation** is a corporation whose shareholders are limited to a small group of persons, often including only family members. The rights of shareholders of a close corporation usually are restricted regarding the transfer of shares to others. A *professional corporation* is a corporation formed by professional persons, such as physicians, lawyers, dentists, and accountants, to gain tax benefits. Subject to certain exceptions (when a court may treat a professional corporation as a partnership for liability purposes), the shareholders of a professional corporation have the limited liability characteristic of the corporate form of business. An **S corporation** is a close business corporation that has met certain requirements as set by the Internal Revenue Code and thus qualifies for special income tax treatment (all other corporations are C corporations). Essentially, an S corporation is taxed the same as a partnership, but its owners enjoy the privilege of limited liability.

A corporation is referred to as a **domestic corporation** by its home state (the state in which it incorporates). A corporation formed in one state but doing business in another is referred to in that other state as a **foreign corporation**. A corporation formed in another country—say, Mexico—but doing business in the United States is referred to in the United States as an **alien corporation.**

A corporation does not have an automatic right to do business in a state other than its state of incorporation. In some instances, it must obtain a *certificate of authority* in any state in which it plans to do business. Once the certificate has been issued, the powers conferred on a corporation by its home state generally can be exercised in the other state.

CLOSE CORPORATION
A corporation whose shareholders are limited to a small group of persons. The rights of shareholders of a close corporation usually are restricted regarding the transfer of shares to others.

S CORPORATION
A close business corporation that has met certain requirements as set out by the Internal Revenue Code and thus qualifies for special income tax treatment.

DOMESTIC CORPORATION
In a given state, a corporation that does business in, and is organized under the law of, that state.

FOREIGN CORPORATION
In a given state, a corporation that does business in the state without being incorporated therein.

ALIEN CORPORATION
A designation in the United States for a corporation formed in another country but doing business in the United States.

Corporate Formation

Up to this point, we have discussed some of the general characteristics of corporations. We now examine the process by which corporations come into existence. Generally, this process involves two steps: (1) preliminary organizational and promotional undertakings—particularly, obtaining capital for the future corporation; and (2) the legal process of incorporation.

---

3. Early law held that a corporation had no implied authority to make charitable contributions because charitable activities were contrary to the primary purpose of the corporation to make a profit. Modern law, by statutes and court decisions, holds that a corporation has such implied authority.

BMW automobiles are inspected at a plant in the United States. BMW is classified as an alien corporation. What is the difference between an alien corporation and a foreign corporation? (© McIntyre, Photo Researchers)

PROMOTIONAL ACTIVITIES

Before a corporation becomes a reality, **promoters**—those who, for themselves or others, take the preliminary steps in organizing a corporation—frequently make contracts with investors and others on behalf of the future corporation. One of the tasks of the promoter is to issue a prospectus. A **prospectus** is a document required by federal or state securities laws (to be discussed in Chapter 21) that describes the financial operations of the corporation, thus allowing investors to make informed decisions. The promoter also secures the corporate charter. In addition, a promoter may purchase or lease property with a view to selling or transferring it to the corporation when the corporation is formed. A promoter may also enter into contracts with attorneys, accountants, architects, or other professionals whose services will be needed in planning for the proposed corporation. Finally, a promoter induces people to purchase stock in the corporation.

INCORPORATION PROCEDURES

Exact procedures for incorporation differ among states, but the basic requirements are similar.

State Chartering   The first step in the incorporation procedure is to select a state in which to incorporate. Because state incorporation laws differ, individuals have found some advantage in looking for the states that offer the most advantageous tax or incorporation provisions. Delaware has historically had the least restrictive laws. Consequently, many corporations, including a number of the largest, have incorporated there. Delaware's statutes permit firms to incorporate in Delaware and carry out business and locate operating headquarters elsewhere. Most other states now permit this, as well. Note, though, that closely held corporations, particularly those of a professional nature, generally incorporate in the state in which their principal shareholders live and work.

PROMOTER
A person who takes the preliminary steps in organizing a corporation, including (usually) issuing a prospectus, procuring stock subscriptions, making contract purchases, securing a corporate charter, and the like.

PROSPECTUS
A document required by federal or state securities laws that describes the financial operations of the corporation, thus allowing investors to make informed decisions.

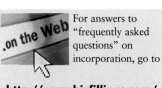

For answers to "frequently asked questions" on incorporation, go to **http://www.bizfillings.com/ learning/incfaq.htm.**

Articles of Incorporation The primary document needed to begin the incorporation process is called the *articles of incorporation*. The articles include basic information about the corporation and serve as a primary source of authority for its future organization and business functions. The person or persons who execute the articles are called *incorporators*.

◼ Corporate Management—Directors and Officers

A corporation typically is governed by a board of directors. A director occupies a position of responsibility unlike that of other corporate personnel. Directors are sometimes inappropriately characterized as *agents* because they act on behalf of the corporation. No *individual* director, however, can act as an agent to bind the corporation; and as a group, directors collectively control the corporation in a way that no agent is able to control a principal. Directors are often incorrectly characterized as *trustees* because they occupy positions of trust and control over the corporation. Unlike trustees, however, they do not own or hold title to property for the use and benefit of others.

ELECTION OF DIRECTORS

One of the best sources on the Web for information on corporations, including their directors, is the "EDGAR" database of the Securities and Exchange Commission (SEC) at

http://www.sec.gov/ edgar.shtml.

Subject to statutory limitations, the number of directors is set forth in the corporation's articles or bylaws. Historically, the minimum number of directors has been three, but today many states permit fewer. Indeed, the Revised Model Business Corporation Act (RMBCA), in Section 8.01, permits corporations with fewer than fifty shareholders to eliminate the board of directors.

The first board of directors is normally appointed by the incorporators on the creation of the corporation, or directors are named by the corporation itself in the articles. The first board serves until the first annual shareholders' meeting. Subsequent directors are elected by a majority vote of the shareholders.

The term of office for a director is usually one year—from annual meeting to annual meeting. Longer and staggered terms are permissible under most state statutes. A common practice is to elect one-third of the board members each year for a three-year term. In this way, there is greater management continuity.

BE AWARE The articles of incorporation may provide that a director can be removed only for cause.

A director can be removed *for cause* (that is, for failing to perform a required duty), either as specified in the articles or bylaws or by shareholder action. Even the board of directors itself may be given power to remove a director for cause, subject to shareholder review. In most states, unless the shareholders have reserved the right at the time of election, a director cannot be removed without cause.

Vacancies can occur on the board of directors because of death or resignation, or when a new position is created through amendment of the articles or bylaws. In these situations, either the shareholders or the board itself can fill the position, depending on state law or on the provisions of the bylaws.

DIRECTORS' QUALIFICATIONS AND COMPENSATION

Few legal requirements exist concerning directors' qualifications. Only a handful of states impose minimum age and residency requirements. A director is sometimes a shareholder, but this is not a necessary qualification—unless, of course, statutory provisions or corporate articles or bylaws require ownership.

Compensation for directors is ordinarily specified in the corporate articles or bylaws. Because directors have a fiduciary relationship to the shareholders and to the corporation, an express agreement or provision for compensation often is necessary for them to receive money income from the funds that they control and for which they have responsibilities.

BOARD OF DIRECTORS' MEETINGS

The board of directors conducts business by holding formal meetings with recorded minutes. The date on which regular meetings are held is usually established in the articles or bylaws or by board resolution, and no further notice is customarily required. Special meetings can be called, with notice sent to all directors.

QUORUM
The number of members of a decision-making body that must be present before business may be transacted.

Quorum requirements can vary among jurisdictions. (A **quorum** is the minimum number of members of a body of officials or other group that must be present in order for business to be validly transacted.) Many states leave the decision as to quorum requirements to the corporate articles or bylaws. In the absence of specific state statutes, most states provide that a quorum is a majority of the number of directors authorized in the articles or bylaws. Voting is done in person (unlike voting at shareholders' meetings, which can be done by proxy, as discussed later in this chapter).[4] The rule is one vote per director. Ordinary matters generally require a simple majority vote; certain extraordinary issues may require a greater-than-majority vote.

DIRECTORS' MANAGEMENT RESPONSIBILITIES

Directors have responsibility for all policymaking decisions necessary to the management of corporate affairs. Just as shareholders cannot act individually to bind the corporation, the directors must act as a body in carrying out routine corporate business. The general areas of responsibility of the board of directors include the following:

1. The declaration and payment of corporate dividends to shareholders.
2. The authorization for major corporate policy decisions—for example, the initiation of proceedings for the sale or lease of corporate assets outside the regular course of business, the determination of new product lines, and the overseeing of major contract negotiations and major management-labor negotiations.
3. The appointment, supervision, and removal of corporate officers and other managerial employees and the determination of their compensation.
4. Financial decisions, such as the decision to issue authorized shares and bonds.

The board of directors can delegate some of its functions to an executive committee or to corporate officers. In doing so, the board is not relieved of its overall responsibility for directing the affairs of the corporation, but corporate officers and managerial personnel are empowered to make decisions relating to ordinary, daily corporate affairs within well-defined guidelines.

IN CONTRAST Shareholders own a corporation and directors make policy decisions, but officers who run the daily business of the corporation often have significant decision-making power.

ROLE OF CORPORATE OFFICERS AND EXECUTIVES

The officers and other executive employees are hired by the board of directors or, in rare instances, by the shareholders. In addition to carrying out the duties articulated in the bylaws, corporate and managerial officers act as agents of the corporation,

---

4. Except in Louisiana, which allows a director to vote by proxy under certain circumstances.

You can find definitions for terms used in corporate law, as well as court decisions and articles on corporate law topics, at **http://www.law.com**.

and the ordinary rules of agency (discussed in Chapter 17) normally apply to their employment. The qualifications required of officers and executive employees are determined at the discretion of the corporation and are included in the articles or bylaws. In most states, a person can hold more than one office and can be both an officer and a director of the corporation.

The rights of corporate officers and other high-level managers are defined by employment contracts, because these persons are employees of the company. Corporate officers normally can be removed by the board of directors at any time with or without cause and regardless of the terms of the employment contracts—although in so doing, the corporation may be liable for breach of contract. The duties of corporate officers are the same as those of directors, because both groups are involved in decision making and are in similar positions of control. Hence, officers are viewed as having the same fiduciary duties of care and loyalty in their conduct of corporate affairs as directors have, a subject to which we now turn.

DUTIES OF DIRECTORS AND OFFICERS

Directors and officers are deemed *fiduciaries* of the corporation, because their relationship with the corporation and its shareholders is one of trust and confidence. The fiduciary duties of the directors and officers include the duty of care and the duty of loyalty.

Duty of Care   Directors and officers must exercise due care in performing their duties. The standard of *due care* has been variously described in judicial decisions and codified in many corporation codes. Generally, a director or officer is expected to act in good faith, to exercise the care that an ordinarily prudent person would exercise in similar circumstances, and to act in what he or she considers to be the best interests of the corporation.[5] Directors and officers who have not exercised the required duty of care can be held liable for the harms suffered by the corporation as a result of their negligence.

Duty to Make Informed and Reasonable Decisions.   Directors and officers are expected to be informed on corporate matters. To be informed, the director or officer must do what is necessary to become informed: attend presentations, ask for information from those who have it, read reports, review other written materials such as contracts—in other words, carefully study a situation and its alternatives. Depending on the nature of the business, directors and officers are often expected to act in accordance with their own knowledge and training. Most states (and Section 8.30 of the RMBCA), however, allow a director to make decisions in reliance on information furnished by competent officers or employees, professionals such as attorneys and accountants, or even an executive committee of the board without being accused of acting in bad faith or failing to exercise due care if such information turns out to be faulty.

Directors are also expected to make reasonable decisions. For example, a director should not accept a **tender offer** (an offer to purchase shares in the company that is made by another company directly to the shareholders, sometimes referred to as a "takeover" bid) with only a moment's consideration based solely on the market price of the corporation's shares.

TENDER OFFER
An offer to purchase shares made by one company directly to the shareholders of another (target) company; often referred to as a "takeover bid."

---

5. RMBCA 8.30.

Duty to Exercise Reasonable Supervision. Directors are also expected to exercise a reasonable amount of supervision when they delegate work to corporate officers and employees. ■ **EXAMPLE 20.1** Suppose that a corporate bank director fails to attend any board of directors' meetings for five years, never inspects any of the corporate books or records, and generally fails to supervise the efforts of the bank president and the loan committee. Meanwhile, a corporate officer, the bank president, makes various improper loans and permits large overdrafts. In this situation, the corporate director may be held liable to the corporation for losses resulting from the unsupervised actions of the bank president and the loan committee. ■

Duty of Loyalty *Loyalty* can be defined as faithfulness to one's obligations and duties. In the corporate context, the duty of loyalty requires directors and officers to subordinate their personal interests to the welfare of the corporation. This means, among other things, that directors may not use corporate funds or confidential corporate information for personal advantage. Similarly, they must refrain from self-dealing. For example, a director should not oppose a tender offer that is in the corporation's best interest simply because its acceptance may cost the director his or her position. Cases dealing with fiduciary duty typically involve one or more of the following:

1 Competing with the corporation.

2 Usurping (taking advantage of) a corporate opportunity.

3 Having an interest that conflicts with the interest of the corporation.

4 Engaging in insider trading (using information that is not public to make a profit trading securities, as will be discussed in Chapter 21).

5 Authorizing a corporate transaction that is detrimental to minority shareholders.

An officer or director usurps a corporate opportunity when she or he, for personal gain, takes advantage of a business opportunity that is financially within the corporation's reach and would be to the firm's practical advantage. The availability of cash to repay a corporation's debts can represent a "corporate opportunity." Does the use of that cash to repay a loan to a director constitute a "usurping" of that opportunity? That was the question in the following case.

Case 20.1 ■ In re Cumberland Farms, Inc.

United States Court of Appeals,
First Circuit, 2002.
284 F.3d 216.
http://www.ca1.uscourts.gov/opinions/main.php[a]

COMPANY PROFILE *In 1938, Vasilios and Aphrodite Haseotes bought a dairy farm in Rhode Island and began operating a successful dairy business. By 1990, the busi-* *ness had branched out and had become Cumberland Farms, Inc. (**http://www.cumberlandfarms.com**), a close corporation owned by their six children. In addition to conducting wholesale operations in dairy and other products, Cumberland Farms owned more than a thousand convenience stores and gas stations. It also delivered refined petroleum products to its own and other gas stations. Through these businesses, Cumberland enjoyed a gross annual income of more than $1 billion.*

FACTS Demetrios Haseotes became Cumberland's chief executive officer and chairman of its board of directors in

a. In the left column, click on "Search." In the "Opinion Number" box, type "01-1344.01A," and click on "Submit Query." In the result, click on the "Opinion" number to access the opinion. The U.S. Court of Appeals for the First Circuit maintains this Web site.

(Continued)

CASE 20.1—Continued

1960. In the 1970s, to provide Cumberland with a more secure gasoline supply, Haseotes acquired a refinery in Newfoundland, Canada. Because some states do not allow a company that operates a refinery to sell petroleum products retail, Haseotes chose to own the refinery through his own separate businesses, including Cumberland Crude Processing, Inc. (CCP). To operate the refinery, CCP borrowed more than $70 million from Cumberland, under an agreement that required the payment of that loan first. Haseotes also loaned money to CCP. When cash was available, Haseotes had CCP repay $5.75 million to him, without telling the Cumberland board. CCP defaulted on its debt to Cumberland, which filed a bankruptcy petition in 1992. Haseotes filed a claim for $3 million against the firm, which asserted a claim for $5.75 million against him. Cumberland argued that Haseotes breached his duty of loyalty when he had CCP pay its debt to him while ignoring its debt to Cumberland. The court disallowed Haseotes's claim. On appeal, a federal district court affirmed this ruling. Haseotes appealed to the U.S. Court of Appeals for the First Circuit.

ISSUE Did Haseotes breach his duty of loyalty to Cumberland by having CCP pay its debt to him while ignoring its debt to Cumberland?

DECISION Yes. the U.S. Court of Appeals for the First Circuit affirmed the lower court's judgment. The appellate court held that Haseotes breached his duty of loyalty to Cumberland when, without informing Cumberland's board that money had become available in CCP, he had CCP apply the money toward its debt to himself rather than to its debt to Cumberland.

REASON The court explained that as a member of Cumberland's board of directors, Haseotes owed the corporation a fiduciary duty of loyalty and fair dealing. A director is required to act with "absolute fidelity" to the corporation and to put his or her duties to the corporation above all personal financial and business obligations. According to the court, "The fiduciary duty is especially exacting where the corporation is closely held." Thus, when a corporate director learns of an opportunity that could benefit the corporation, the director must inform the shareholders of all the material details of the opportunity. The shareholders then are able to decide whether the corporation can and should take advantage of it. In the court's view, "[I]t is inherently unfair for the director to deny the corporation that choice and instead take the opportunity for herself [or himself]." Here, "any funds that became available in CCP provided an opportunity to pay down CCP's * * * debt to Cumberland" and the loan agreement "explicitly required Haseotes to apply any available money toward Cumberland's loan before paying down CCP's debt to himself." In these circumstances, "Haseotes was obligated to seek approval from Cumberland's board before acting."

WHY IS THIS CASE IMPORTANT? *As the judge in this case explained, the duty of loyalty is often considered to be more demanding for the directors and officers of a closely held corporation.*

Conflicts of Interest The duty of loyalty also requires officers and directors to disclose fully to the board of directors any possible conflict of interest that might occur in conducting corporate transactions. The various state statutes contain different standards, but a contract will generally *not* be voidable if it was fair and reasonable to the corporation at the time it was made, if there was a full disclosure of the interest of the officers or directors involved in the transaction, and if the contract was approved by a majority of the disinterested directors or shareholders.

■ EXAMPLE 20.2 Southwood Corporation needs office space. Lambert Alden, one of its five directors, owns the building adjoining the corporation's main office building. He negotiates a lease with Southwood for the space, making a full disclosure to Southwood and the other four board directors. The lease arrangement is fair and reasonable, and it is unanimously approved by the corporation's board of directors. In this situation, Alden has not breached his duty of loyalty to the corporation, and the contract is thus valid. If it were otherwise, directors would be prevented from ever giving financial assistance to the corporations they serve. ■

ETHICAL ISSUE 20.1

What happens to the duty of loyalty when a director sits on the boards of two corporations?   Corporate directors often have many business affiliations, and they may even sit on the board of more than one corporation. (Of course, directors generally are precluded from sitting on the boards of directors of competing companies.) The duty of loyalty can become cloudy when corporate directors sit on the board of more than one corporation. Because of the potential for abuse in transactions negotiated between corporations whose boards have some members in common, courts tend to scrutinize such actions closely.

For example, suppose that four individuals own a total of 70 percent of the shares of Company A and 100 percent of the shares of Company B. All four of these shareholders sit on the boards of directors of both corporations. Company A decides to purchase all of Company B's stock for $6 million, when in fact it is worth only $3 million. The shareholder-directors of both firms have not breached their duty to Company B because the $6 million price is beneficial to that company. A court would likely hold that the directors breached their duty to the other shareholders of Company A (who owned the remaining 30 percent of Company A's shares), however, because these other shareholders had nothing to gain by the transaction and much to lose by Company A's purchase of Company B at an inflated price.[6] ■

The Business Judgment Rule   Directors and officers are expected to exercise due care and to use their best judgment in guiding corporate management, but they are not insurers of business success. Honest mistakes of judgment and poor business decisions on their part do not make them liable to the corporation for resulting damages. Under the **business judgment rule,** a corporate director or officer may be able to avoid liability to the corporation or to its shareholders for poor business judgments. The business judgment rule generally immunizes directors and officers from liability for the consequences of a decision that is within managerial authority, as long as the decision complies with management's fiduciary duties, and as long as acting on the decision is within the powers of the corporation. Consequently, if there is a reasonable basis for a business decision, it is unlikely that the court will interfere with that decision, even if the corporation suffers as a result.

To benefit from the rule, directors and officers must act in good faith, in what they consider to be the best interests of the corporation, and with the care that an ordinarily prudent person in a similar position would exercise in similar circumstances. This requires an informed decision, with a rational basis, and with no conflict between the decision maker's personal interest and the interest of the corporation.

BUSINESS JUDGMENT RULE
A rule that immunizes corporate management from liability for actions that result in corporate losses or damages if the actions are undertaken in good faith and are within both the power of the corporation and the authority of management to make.

■ Corporate Ownership—Shareholders

The acquisition of a share of stock makes a person an owner and shareholder in a corporation. Shareholders thus own the corporation. Although they have no legal title to corporate property, such as buildings and equipment, they do have an equitable (ownership) interest in the firm.

As a general rule, shareholders have no responsibility for the daily management of the corporation, although they are ultimately responsible for choosing the board of directors, which does have such control. Ordinarily, corporate officers and other

---

6. See, for example, *Gries Sports Enterprises, Inc. v. Cleveland Browns Football Co.,* 26 Ohio St.3d 15, 496 N.E.2d 959 (1986).

employees owe no direct duty to individual shareholders. Their duty is to the corporation as a whole. A director, however, is in a fiduciary relationship to the corporation and therefore serves the interests of the shareholders. Generally, there is no legal relationship between shareholders and creditors of the corporation. Shareholders can, in fact, be creditors of the corporation and thus have the same rights of recovery against the corporation as any other creditor.

In this section, we look at the powers and voting rights of shareholders, which are generally established in the articles of incorporation and under the state's general incorporation law.

Shareholders' Powers

Shareholders must approve fundamental corporate changes before the changes can be effected. Hence, shareholders are empowered to amend the articles of incorporation (charter) and bylaws, approve a merger or the dissolution of the corporation, and approve the sale of all or substantially all of the corporation's assets. Some of these powers are subject to prior board approval.

Directors are elected to (and removed from) the board of directors by a vote of the shareholders. The first board of directors is either named in the articles of incorporation or chosen by the incorporators to serve until the first shareholders' meeting. From that time on, the selection and retention of directors are exclusively shareholder functions.

Directors usually serve their full terms; if they are unsatisfactory, they are simply not reelected. Shareholders have the inherent power, however, to remove a director from office *for cause* (breach of duty or misconduct) by a majority vote.[7] Some state statutes (and some corporate charters) even permit removal of directors without cause by the vote of a majority of the holders of outstanding shares entitled to vote.

Shareholders' Meetings

Shareholders' meetings must occur at least annually, and additional, special meetings can be called as needed to take care of urgent matters. Because it is usually not practical for owners of only a few shares of stock of publicly traded corporations to attend shareholders' meetings, such stockholders normally give third parties written authorization to vote their shares at the meeting. This authorization is called a **proxy** (from the Latin *procurare*, "to manage, take care of "). Proxies are often solicited by management, but any person can solicit proxies to concentrate voting power.

Shareholder Voting

Shareholders exercise ownership control through the power of their votes. Each shareholder is entitled to one vote per share, although the voting techniques that will be discussed shortly all enhance the power of the shareholder's vote. The articles of incorporation can exclude or limit voting rights, particularly for certain classes of shares, such as preferred shares (see Chapter 21).

Quorum Requirements   For shareholders to act during a meeting, a quorum must be present. Generally, a quorum exists when shareholders holding more than 50 per-

PROXY
In corporation law, a written agreement between a stockholder and another under which the stockholder authorizes the other to vote the stockholder's shares in a certain manner.

BE CAREFUL Once a quorum is present, a vote can be taken even if some shareholders leave without casting their votes.

---

7. A director can often demand court review of removal for cause.

Shareholders meet to vote on corporate issues. Must shareholders attend such meetings in person? Explain. (Bill Stryker)

For an example of one state's (Minnesota's) statute governing corporations, go to **http://www.revisor.leg.state.mn.us/stats/302A.**

cent of the outstanding shares are present. Corporate business matters are presented in the form of *resolutions,* which shareholders vote to approve or disapprove. Some state statutes have set forth specific voting requirements, and corporations' articles or bylaws must abide by these statutory requirements. Some states provide that the unanimous written consent of shareholders is a permissible alternative to holding a shareholders' meeting. Once a quorum is present, a majority vote of the shares represented at the meeting is usually required to pass resolutions.

■ EXAMPLE 20.3 Assume that Novo Pictures, Inc., has 10,000 outstanding shares of voting stock. Its articles of incorporation set the quorum at 50 percent of outstanding shares and provide that a majority vote of the shares present is necessary to pass resolutions concerning ordinary matters. Therefore, for this firm, a quorum of shareholders representing 5,000 outstanding shares must be present at a shareholders' meeting to conduct business. If exactly 5,000 shares are represented at the meeting, a vote of at least 2,501 of those shares is needed to pass a resolution. If 6,000 shares are represented, a vote of 3,001 will be required, and so on. ■

At times, a larger-than-majority vote will be required either by a statute or by the corporate charter. Extraordinary corporate matters, such as a merger, consolidation, or dissolution of the corporation, require a higher percentage of the representatives of all corporate shares entitled to vote, not just a majority of those present at that particular meeting.

Cumulative Voting Most states permit or even require shareholders to elect directors by *cumulative voting,* a method of voting designed to allow minority shareholders representation on the board of directors.[8] When cumulative voting is allowed or required, the number of members of the board to be elected is multiplied by the total number of voting shares. The result equals the number of votes a shareholder has, and this total can be cast for one or more nominees for director. All nominees stand for election at the same time. When cumulative voting is not required either by statute or under the articles, the entire board can be elected by a simple majority of shares at a shareholders' meeting.

Cumulative voting can best be understood by an example. ■ EXAMPLE 20.4 Suppose that a corporation has 10,000 shares issued and outstanding. One group of shareholders (the minority shareholders) holds only 3,000 shares, and the other group of shareholders (the majority shareholders) holds the other 7,000 shares. Three members of the board are to be elected. The majority shareholders' nominees are Acevedo, Barkley, and Craycik. The minority shareholders' nominee is Drake. Can Drake be elected by the minority shareholders?

If cumulative voting is allowed, the answer is yes. The minority shareholders have 9,000 votes among them (the number of directors to be elected times the number of shares held by the minority shareholders equals 3 times 3,000, which equals 9,000 votes). All of these votes can be cast to elect Drake. The majority shareholders have 21,000 votes (3 times 7,000 equals 21,000 votes), but these votes have to be distributed among their three nominees. The principle of cumulative voting is that no matter how the majority shareholders cast their 21,000 votes, they will not be able to elect all three directors if the minority shareholders cast all of their 9,000 votes for Drake, as illustrated in Exhibit 20–1 on the following page. ■

---

8. See, for example, California Corporate Code Section 708. Under RMBCA 7.28, however, no cumulative voting rights exist unless the articles of incorporation so provide.

EXHIBIT 20-1 RESULTS OF CUMULATIVE VOTING

This exhibit illustrates how cumulative voting gives minority shareholders a greater chance of electing a director of their choice. By casting all of their 9,000 votes for one candidate (Drake), the minority shareholders will succeed in electing Drake to the board of directors.

BALLOT	MAJORITY SHAREHOLDERS' VOTES			MINORITY SHAREHOLDERS' VOTES	DIRECTORS ELECTED
	Acevedo	Barkley	Craycik	Drake	
1	10,000	10,000	1,000	9,000	Acevedo/Barkley/Drake
2	9,001	9,000	2,999	9,000	Acevedo/Barkley/Drake
3	6,000	7,000	8,000	9,000	Barkley/Craycik/Drake

SHAREHOLDERS' RIGHTS

Shareholders possess numerous rights. A significant right—the right to vote their shares—has already been discussed. We now look at some additional rights of shareholders.

STOCK CERTIFICATE
A certificate issued by a corporation evidencing the ownership of a specified number of shares in the corporation.

Stock Certificates   A **stock certificate** is a certificate issued by a corporation that evidences ownership of a specified number of shares in the corporation. In jurisdictions that require the issuance of stock certificates, shareholders have the right to demand that the corporation issue certificates. In most states and under RMBCA 6.26, boards of directors may provide that shares of stock be uncertificated—that is, that physical stock certificates need not be issued. In that circumstance, the corporation may be required to send the holders of uncertificated shares letters or some other form of notice containing the same information as that included on stock certificates.

Stock is intangible personal property, and the ownership right exists independently of the certificate itself. A stock certificate may be lost or destroyed, but ownership is not destroyed with it. A new certificate can be issued to replace one that has been lost or destroyed.[9] Notice of shareholders' meetings, dividends, and operational and financial reports are all distributed according to the recorded ownership listed in the corporation's books, not on the basis of possession of the certificate.

PREEMPTIVE RIGHTS
Rights held by shareholders that entitle them to purchase newly issued shares of a corporation's stock, equal in percentage to shares currently held, before the stock is offered to any outside buyers. Preemptive rights enable shareholders to maintain their proportionate ownership and voice in the corporation.

Preemptive Rights   A **preemptive right** is a common law concept under which a preference is given to shareholders over all other purchasers to subscribe to or purchase shares of a new issue of stock in proportion to the percentage of total shares they already hold. This allows each shareholder to maintain his or her portion of control, voting power, or financial interest in the corporation. Most statutes either (1) grant preemptive rights but allow them to be negated in the corporation's articles or (2) deny preemptive rights except to the extent that they are granted in the articles. The result is that the articles of incorporation determine the existence and scope of preemptive rights. Generally, preemptive rights apply only to additional, newly issued stock sold for cash, and the preemptive rights must be exercised within a specified time period, which is usually thirty days.

---

9. For a lost or destroyed certificate to be reissued, a shareholder normally must furnish an indemnity bond to protect the corporation against potential loss should the original certificate reappear at some future time in the hands of a bona fide purchaser [UCC 8–302, 8–405(2)].

Stock certificates are displayed. To be a shareholder, is it necessary to have physical possession of a certificate? Why or why not? (© Amy C. Etra, PhotoEdit)

Dividends As mentioned earlier in this chapter, a *dividend* is a distribution of corporate profits or income *ordered by the directors* and paid to the shareholders in proportion to their respective shares in the corporation. Dividends can be paid in cash, property, stock of the corporation that is paying the dividends, or stock of other corporations.[10]

State laws vary, but each state determines the general circumstances and legal requirements under which dividends are paid. State laws also control the sources of revenue to be used; only certain funds are legally available for paying dividends. Depending on state law, dividends may be paid from the following sources:

1 *Retained earnings.* All state statutes allow dividends to be paid from the undistributed net profits earned by the corporation, including capital gains from the sale of fixed assets. The undistributed net profits are called retained earnings.

2 *Net profits.* A few state statutes allow dividends to be issued from current net profits without regard to deficits in prior years.

3 *Surplus.* A number of statutes allow dividends to be paid out of any surplus.

Illegal Dividends. A dividend paid while the corporation is insolvent is automatically an illegal dividend, and shareholders may be liable for returning the payment to the corporation or its creditors. Furthermore, as just discussed, dividends are generally required by statute to be distributed only from certain authorized corporate accounts. Sometimes dividends are improperly paid from an unauthorized account, or their payment causes the corporation to become insolvent. Generally, in such cases, shareholders must return illegal dividends only if they knew that the dividends were illegal when they received them. Whenever dividends are illegal or improper, the board of directors can be held personally liable for the amount of the payment. When directors can show that a shareholder knew that a dividend was illegal when it was received, however, the directors are entitled to reimbursement from the shareholder.

Directors' Failure to Declare a Dividend. When directors fail to declare a dividend, shareholders can ask a court to compel the directors to meet and to declare a dividend. For the shareholders to succeed, they must show that the directors have acted so unreasonably in withholding the dividend that the directors' conduct is an abuse of their discretion.

Often, large cash reserves are accumulated for a bona fide purpose, such as expansion, research, or other legitimate corporate goals. The mere fact that sufficient corporate earnings or surplus is available to pay a dividend is not enough to compel directors to distribute funds that, in the board's opinion, should not be paid. The courts are circumspect about interfering with corporate operations and will not compel directors to declare dividends unless abuse of discretion is clearly shown.

Inspection Rights Shareholders in a corporation enjoy both common law and statutory inspection rights.[11] The shareholder's right of inspection is limited, however, to the inspection and copying of corporate books and records for a *proper purpose*, provided the request is made in advance. The shareholder can inspect in person, or an attorney, agent, accountant, or other type of assistant can do so. The RMBCA requires the corporation to maintain an alphabetical voting list of shareholders with

---

10. Technically, dividends paid in stock are not dividends. They maintain each shareholder's proportional interest in the corporation. On one occasion, a distillery declared and paid a "dividend" in bonded whiskey.
11. See, for example, *Schwartzman v. Schwartzman Packing Co.,* 99 N.M. 436, 659 P.2d 888 (1983).

addresses and number of shares owned; this list must be kept open at the annual meeting for inspection by any shareholder of record [RMBCA 7.20].

Transfer of Shares   Stock certificates generally are negotiable and freely transferable by indorsement and delivery. Transfer of stock in closely held corporations, however, usually is restricted by the bylaws, by a restriction stamped on the stock certificate, or by a shareholder agreement. The existence of any restrictions on transferability must always be noted on the face of the stock certificate, and these restrictions must be reasonable.

Sometimes, corporations or their shareholders restrict transferability by reserving the option to purchase any shares offered for resale by a shareholder. This **right of first refusal** remains with the corporation or the shareholders for only a specified time or a reasonable time. Variations on the purchase option are possible. For example, a shareholder might be required to offer the shares to other shareholders first or to the corporation first.

When shares are transferred, a new entry is made in the corporate stock book to indicate the new owner. Until the corporation is notified and the entry is complete, the current record owner has the right to be notified of (and attend) shareholders' meetings, the right to vote the shares, the right to receive dividends, and all other shareholder rights.

Rights on Dissolution   When a corporation is dissolved and its outstanding debts and the claims of its creditors have been satisfied, the remaining assets are distributed to the shareholders in proportion to the percentage of shares owned by each shareholder. Certain classes of preferred stock can be given priority. If no preferences to distribution of assets on liquidation are given to any class of stock, then the shareholders are entitled to the remaining assets.

In some circumstances, shareholders may petition a court to have the corporation dissolved. Suppose, for example, that a minority shareholder knows that the board of directors is mishandling corporate assets. The minority shareholder is not powerless to intervene. He or she can petition a court to appoint a **receiver**—who will wind up corporate affairs and liquidate the business assets of the corporation.

The RMBCA permits any shareholder to initiate such an action in any of the following circumstances [RMBCA 14.30]:

1. The directors are deadlocked in the management of corporate affairs. The shareholders are unable to break that deadlock, and irreparable injury to the corporation is being suffered or threatened.
2. The acts of the directors or those in control of the corporation are illegal, oppressive, or fraudulent.
3. Corporate assets are being misapplied or wasted.
4. The shareholders are deadlocked in voting power and have failed, for a specified period (usually two annual meetings), to elect successors to directors whose terms have expired or would have expired with the election of successors.

The Shareholder's Derivative Suit   When those in control of a corporation—the corporate directors—fail to sue in the corporate name to redress a wrong suffered by the corporation, shareholders are permitted to do so "derivatively" in what is known as a **shareholder's derivative suit.** Some wrong must have been done to the corporation, and before a derivative suit can be brought, the shareholders must first

---

RIGHT OF FIRST REFUSAL
The right to purchase personal or real property—such as corporate shares or real estate—before the property is offered for sale to others.

RECEIVER
In a corporate dissolution, a court-appointed person who winds up corporate affairs and liquidates corporate assets.

SHAREHOLDER'S DERIVATIVE SUIT
A suit brought by a shareholder to enforce a corporate cause of action against a third person.

state their complaint to the board of directors. Only if the directors fail to solve the problem or take appropriate action can the derivative suit go forward.

The right of shareholders to bring a derivative action is especially important when the wrong suffered by the corporation results from the actions of corporate directors or officers. This is because the directors and officers would probably want to prevent any action against themselves.

The shareholder's derivative suit is unusual in that those suing are not pursuing rights or benefits for themselves personally but are acting as guardians of the corporate entity. Therefore, any damages recovered by the suit normally go into the corporation's treasury, not to the shareholders personally.

DUTIES OF MAJORITY SHAREHOLDERS

In some cases, a majority shareholder is regarded as having a fiduciary duty to the corporation and to the minority shareholders. This occurs when a single shareholder (or a few shareholders acting in concert) owns a sufficient number of shares to exercise *de facto* control over the corporation. In these situations, when the majority shareholder sells her or his shares, the shareholder owes a fiduciary duty to the minority shareholders because such a sale is, in fact, a transfer of control of the corporation.

A breach of fiduciary duty also occurs when the majority shareholders of a closely held corporation use their control to their own advantage and exclude the minority from the benefits of participating in the firm unless, of course, there is a genuine business purpose for the exercise of control. ■ **EXAMPLE 20.5** In one case, a family member who was a minority shareholder in a family-owned corporation was fired after working for the business for forty-five years. The court concluded that the majority shareholders had breached their fiduciary duty to the minority shareholder by firing him, even though state law allowed employees to be hired and fired "at will" (the employment-at-will doctrine was discussed in Chapter 18).[12] ■

Such a breach of fiduciary duties by those who control a closely held corporation normally constitutes what is known as *oppressive conduct*. The court in the following case was asked to review a pattern of oppressive conduct by the person in control and determine whether that conduct fell within a two-year statute of limitations.

---

12. *Pedro v. Pedro,* 489 N.W.2d 798 (Minn.App. 1992).

CASE 20.2 ■ Robbins v. Sanders

Supreme Court of Alabama, 2004.
__ So.2d __.

FACTS James and Mary Bailey owned fifty-three acres of land, subject to mortgages totaling $450,000, in Birmingham, Alabama. The Baileys rented buildings on the property and used part of the land as a landfill. In 1988, an underground fire broke out in the landfill. Pete Robbins offered to extinguish the fire and to pay the mortgages. The parties formed Corridor Enterprises, Inc., to which the Baileys contributed the land. Half of the stock—one thousand shares—was issued to Robbins. In 1991, the Baileys agreed to sell their thousand shares to Robbins at the rate of two

shares per month. The Baileys both died in 1997. Terrill Sanders was appointed administrator of their estates. Over the next twelve months, Sanders had problems obtaining information from Robbins and uncovered discrepancies in Corridor's corporate records. On the estates' behalf, Sanders filed a suit in an Alabama state court, alleging, among other things, oppression of minority shareholders. The court assessed more than $4 million in damages against Robbins, who appealed to the Alabama Supreme Court, arguing in part that a two-year statute of limitations barred the suit.

ISSUE Were the minority shareholders entitled to recover for their claim of oppression?

(Continued)

CASE 20.2—Continued

DECISION Yes. The Alabama Supreme Court held that Sanders's claims on behalf of the Baileys' estates were timely. The court remanded the case, though, so that the lower court could clearly state how the damages should be apportioned among the estates and Corridor.[a]

REASON The state supreme court rejected Robbins's statute-of-limitations argument. The court explained that the Baileys' estates became minority shareholders after the Baileys died in 1997. The court pointed out that Robbins engaged in oppressive conduct after this event. "For example, in 1998, Robbins used funds of Corridor Enterprises to purchase real estate in his own name, to invest in other businesses in his own name, and to pur-

a. The lower court's decision on remand was not available at the time this book went to press, but it may be by the time you read this. If you have purchased access to Westlaw Campus, you may be able to locate the remanded decision using that database. Alternatively, you might be able to find the case online at some other site. (See this text's inside front cover for information on Westlaw Campus and URLs for online court decisions.)

chase personal property for himself; he refused to provide an accounting of the corporate finances when he was requested to do so; he failed to pay the corporate property and income taxes, failed to have tax returns prepared and filed, and failed to maintain proper corporate records; he entered into a contract to sell property belonging to Corridor Enterprises without notice to or approval of the minority shareholders; and he failed to declare dividends during the entire time the estates were shareholders while he paid himself an exorbitant salary and drained the corporate funds." Sanders initiated this suit on the estates' behalf in the same year that many of these activities occurred. "Therefore, the estates' claims of * * * oppression were not time-barred to the extent those claims sought to recover damages for injuries occurring to the estates."

FOR CRITICAL ANALYSIS—Economic Consideration
What should be the basis for determining the specific amount of damages to be awarded to the minority shareholders in this case?

■ Merger and Consolidation

Corporations increase the size of their operations for a number of reasons. They may wish to enlarge their physical plants, for example, or to increase their property or investment holdings. They may wish to acquire the assets, know-how, or goodwill of another corporation. Sometimes, the acquisition of another company is motivated by a desire to eliminate a competitor, to accomplish diversification, or to ensure adequate resources and markets for the acquiring corporation's product. A corporation typically extends its operations by combining with another corporation through a merger, a consolidation, a purchase of assets, or a purchase of a controlling interest in the other corporation.

The terms *merger* and *consolidation* often are used interchangeably, but they refer to two legally distinct proceedings. The rights and liabilities of the corporation, its shareholders, and its creditors are the same for both, however.

MERGER

MERGER
A contractual and statutory process in which one corporation (the surviving corporation) acquires all of the assets and liabilities of another corporation (the merged corporation). The shareholders of the merged corporation receive either payment for their shares or shares in the surviving corporation.

A **merger** involves the legal combination of two or more corporations in such a way that only one of the corporations continues to exist. ■ **EXAMPLE 20.6** Corporation A and Corporation B decide to merge. It is agreed that A will absorb B, so on merging, B ceases to exist as a separate entity, and A continues as the *surviving corporation.* Exhibit 20–2 graphically illustrates this process. ■

After the merger, A is recognized as a single corporation, possessing all the rights, privileges, and powers of itself and B. It automatically acquires all of B's property and assets without the necessity of formal transfer. Additionally, A becomes liable for all of B's debts and obligations. Finally, A's articles of incorporation are deemed amended to include any changes that are stated in the *articles of merger* (a docu-

EXHIBIT 20–2 MERGER

In this illustration, Corporation A and Corporation B decide to merge. They agree that A will absorb B, so after the merger, B no longer exists as a separate entity, and A continues as the surviving corporation.

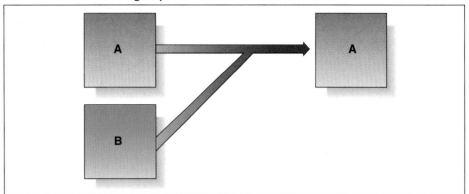

ment setting forth the terms and conditions of the merger that is filed with the secretary of state).

In a merger, the surviving corporation inherits the disappearing corporation's preexisting legal rights and obligations. For example, if the disappearing corporation had a right of action against a third party, the surviving corporation can bring suit after the merger to recover the disappearing corporation's damages. The corporation statutes of many states provide that a successor (surviving) corporation inherits a **chose**[13] **in action** (a right to sue for a debt or sum of money) from a merging corporation as a matter of law. The common law similarly recognizes that, following a merger, a chose in action to enforce a property right will vest with the successor (surviving) corporation, and no right of action will remain with the disappearing corporation.

CHOSE IN ACTION
A right that can be enforced in court to recover a debt or to obtain damages.

ETHICAL ISSUE 20.2

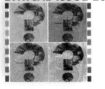

Should corporate law apply to a merger of labor unions? Suppose that two labor unions, both of which are unincorporated associations, merge into one union. Does the successor (surviving) union inherit the obligations of the disappearing union, just as a corporate successor inherits the obligations of the disappearing corporation in a corporate merger? This question, which has both legal and ethical implications, arose in a case involving a merger of two Teamsters local unions. When Teamsters Local 513 merged into Teamsters Local 115, an older employee of Local 513 quit and applied for a pension. The pension was denied because Local 513 had not made any contributions to the pension fund on his behalf, as was required by its rules. Local 115, the successor union, denied any liability for Local 513's failure to contribute to the fund. In the lawsuit that followed, the court had to decide whether corporate law governing mergers should apply to the merger of two unincorporated associations. The court ruled that it should, stating that "when two unincorporated local unions merge, the survivor assumes the liabilities of the extinct constituent even if it does not have pre-merger notice of the debt." The court explained that this is a nearly universal principle for corporations and that the same logic applies to unions. Employees of unincorporated associations deserve the same protection as employees of corporations.[14] ■

13. The word *chose* is French for "thing."
14. *Teamsters Pension Trust Fund of Philadelphia & Vicinity v. Littlejohn,* 155 F.3d 206 (3d Cir. 1998).

CONSOLIDATION

CONSOLIDATION
A contractual and statutory process in which two or more corporations join to become a completely new corporation. The original corporations cease to exist, and the new corporation acquires all their assets and liabilities.

In a **consolidation**, two or more corporations combine in such a way that each corporation ceases to exist and a new one emerges. ■ **EXAMPLE 20.7** Corporation A and Corporation B consolidate to form an entirely new organization, Corporation C. In the process, A and B both terminate, and C comes into existence as an entirely new entity. ■ Exhibit 20–3 graphically illustrates this process.

As a result of the consolidation, C is recognized as a new corporation and a single entity; A and B cease to exist. C inherits all of the rights, privileges, and powers that A and B previously held. Title to any property and assets owned by A and B passes to C without formal transfer. C assumes liability for all of the debts and obligations owed by A and B. The terms and conditions of the consolidation are set forth in the *articles of consolidation,* which are filed with the secretary of state. These articles *take the place of* A's and B's original corporate articles and are thereafter regarded as C's corporate articles.

▉ Purchase of Assets

RECALL In a merger or consolidation, the surviving corporation inherits the disappearing corporation's rights *and* obligations.

When a corporation acquires all or substantially all of the assets of another corporation by direct purchase, the purchasing, or *acquiring,* corporation simply extends its ownership and control over more physical assets. Because no change in the legal entity occurs, the acquiring corporation is not required to obtain shareholder approval for the purchase.[15]

Although the acquiring corporation may not be required to obtain shareholder approval for such an acquisition, the U.S. Department of Justice and the Federal Trade Commission have issued guidelines that significantly constrain and often prohibit

---

15. If the acquiring corporation plans to pay for the assets with its own corporate stock and not enough authorized unissued shares are available, the shareholders must vote to approve issuance of additional shares by amendment of the corporate articles. Additionally, acquiring corporations whose stock is traded in a national stock exchange can be required to obtain their own shareholders' approval if they plan to issue a significant number of shares, such as a number equal to 20 percent or more of the outstanding shares.

EXHIBIT 20–3 CONSOLIDATION

In this illustration, Corporation A and Corporation B consolidate to form an entirely new corporation, Corporation C. In the process, A and B terminate, and C comes into existence as an entirely new entity.

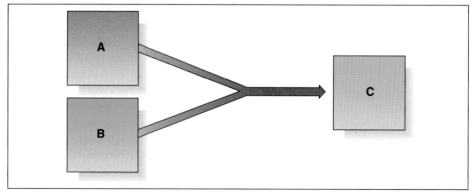

mergers that could result from a purchase of assets, including takeover bids. These guidelines will be discussed in Chapter 22, in the context of federal antitrust laws.

Note that the corporation that is selling all its assets is substantially changing its business position and perhaps its ability to carry out its corporate purposes. For that reason, the corporation whose assets are acquired must obtain the approval of both the board of directors and the shareholders. In most states and under RMBCA 13.02, a dissenting shareholder of the selling corporation can demand **appraisal rights.**

Generally, a corporation that purchases the assets of another corporation is not responsible for the liabilities of the selling corporation. Exceptions to this rule are made in the following circumstances:

1 When the purchasing corporation impliedly or expressly assumes the seller's liabilities.

2 When the sale amounts to what in fact is a merger or consolidation.

3 When the purchaser continues the seller's business and retains the same personnel (same shareholders, directors, and officers).

4 When the sale is fraudulently executed to escape liability.

In any of these situations, the acquiring corporation will be held to have assumed both the assets and the liabilities of the selling corporation.

Purchase of Stock

An alternative to the purchase of another corporation's assets is the purchase of a substantial number of the voting shares of its stock. This enables the acquiring corporation to control the acquired corporation. The acquiring corporation deals directly with the target company's shareholders in seeking to purchase the shares they hold. It does this by making a *tender offer* to all of the shareholders of the corporation to be acquired, or the **target corporation.** The tender offer is publicly advertised and addressed to all shareholders of the target company. The price of the stock in the tender offer is generally higher than the market price of the target stock prior to the announcement of the tender offer. The higher price induces shareholders to tender their shares to the acquiring firm.

The tender offer can be conditioned on the receipt of a specified number of outstanding shares by a specified date. The offering corporation can make an *exchange tender offer* in which it offers target stockholders its own securities in exchange for their target stock. In a *cash tender offer,* the offering corporation offers the target stockholders cash in exchange for their target stock.

Federal securities laws strictly control the terms, duration, and circumstances under which most tender offers are made. In addition, a majority of states have passed takeover statutes that impose additional regulations on tender offers.

A firm may respond to a tender offer in numerous ways. Sometimes, a target firm's board of directors will see a tender offer as favorable and will recommend to the shareholders that they accept it. To resist a takeover, a target company may make a *self-tender,* which is an offer to acquire stock from its own shareholders and thereby retain corporate control. Alternatively, a target corporation might resort to one of several other tactics to resist a takeover. One commonly used tactic is known as the "poison pill"—a target company gives its shareholders rights to purchase additional shares at low prices when there is a takeover attempt. The use of poison pills often prevents takeovers by making them prohibitively expensive.

APPRAISAL RIGHTS
The rights of dissenting shareholders, if they object to an extraordinary transaction of the corporation (such as a merger or a consolidation), to have their shares appraised and to be paid the fair value of their shares by the corporation.

A searchable database of court cases dealing with corporate litigation, including lawsuits stemming from purchases of corporate assets, is available at **http://corporate-law. widener.edu.**

TARGET CORPORATION
The corporation to be acquired in a corporate takeover; a corporation to whose shareholders a tender offer is submitted.

DISSOLUTION
The formal disbanding of a partnership or a corporation. Dissolution of a corporation can take place by (1) an act of the state legislature, (2) agreement of the shareholders and the board of directors, (3) the expiration of a time period stated in the certificate of incorporation, or (4) court order.

LIQUIDATION
In regard to corporations, the process by which corporate assets are converted into cash and distributed among creditors and shareholders according to specific rules of preference.

◼️ Termination

The termination of a corporation's existence has two phases. **Dissolution** is the legal death of the artificial "person" of the corporation. **Liquidation** is the process by which corporate assets are converted into cash and distributed among creditors and shareholders according to specific rules of preference.

DISSOLUTION

Dissolution of a corporation can be brought about in any of the following ways:

1. An act of a legislature in the state of incorporation.
2. Expiration of the time provided in the certificate of incorporation.
3. Voluntary approval of the shareholders and the board of directors.
4. Unanimous action by all shareholders.[16]
5. A court decree brought about by the attorney general of the state of incorporation for any of the following reasons: (a) the failure to comply with administrative requirements (for example, failure to pay annual franchise taxes, to submit an annual report, or to have a designated registered agent), (b) the procurement of a corporation charter through fraud or misrepresentation on the state, (c) the abuse of corporate powers, (d) the violation of the state criminal code after the demand to discontinue has been made by the secretary of state, (e) the failure to commence business operations, or (f) the abandonment of operations before starting up [RMBCA 14.20].

As discussed earlier in this chapter, sometimes a shareholder or a group of shareholders petitions a court for corporate dissolution. For example, the board of directors may be deadlocked. Courts hesitate to order involuntary dissolution in such circumstances unless there is specific statutory authorization to do so. If the deadlock cannot be resolved by the shareholders and if it will irreparably injure the cor-

---

16. This is permitted under Delaware law—see Delaware Code Section 275(c)—but not under the RMBCA.

A store advertises a liquidation sale. What is the difference between corporate dissolution and corporate liquidation? (© Robert Brenner, PhotoEdit)

poration, however, the court will proceed with an involuntary dissolution. Courts can also dissolve a corporation in other circumstances, such as when the controlling shareholders or directors are committing fraudulent or oppressive acts or when management is misapplying or wasting corporate assets [RMBCA 14.30].

In the following case, a shareholder sued to have a corporation dissolved on the basis of allegedly illegal, oppressive, and fraudulent conduct.

CASE 20.3 ■ Colt v. Mt. Princeton Trout Club, Inc.

Colorado Court of Appeals,
Division I, 2003.
78 P.3d 1115.
http://www.findlaw.com/11stategov/co/coca.html[a]

FACTS ...lub, Inc. (MPTC), was formed ...do and provide fishing and ... s shareholders. MPTC's capi- ...t shares of stock with voting rights. The ...d the board of directors under the ...ohibited MPTC from sell- ...i assets of the corpo- ...directors. Despite ...into leases—including ...h some of the share- ...ell corporate property ...e directors. MPTC ...urns and did not timely ...ting in at least $10,000 in ... Among other things, ...t accounted for, and min- utes ... ...gs were withheld from the shareholders. ... of the original eight share- holders, filed a suit in a Colorado state court against MPTC and others, seeking to dissolve the corporation in part on the basis of illegal, oppressive, and fraudulent activities. The court ordered dissolution. MPTC appealed to a state intermediate appellate court.

ISSUE Was it proper to dissolve the corporation on the basis of illegal, oppressive, and fraudulent activities?

a. In the "Search Title or Docket Number" box, type in the name of the case and click on "submit query." On the next page, click on "HTML" to access the opinion.

DECISION Yes. The state intermediate appellate court affirmed the order of the lower court.

REASON The appellate court explained that under a state statute, a corporation may be dissolved if "[t]hose in control of the corporation have acted, are acting, or will act in a manner that is illegal, oppressive, or fraudulent." Oppressive conduct is "burdensome, harsh and wrongful conduct; a lack of probity [honesty] and fair dealing in the affairs of the company to the prejudice of some of its members; or a * * * departure from the standards of fair dealing, and a violation of fair play on which every shareholder who entrusts his money to a company is entitled to rely." In this case, the court noted that there had been a consistent undercurrent of dealing corporate interests without notice to the shareholders and all directors. These acts, according to the court, are "properly characterized as illegal, oppressive, or fraudulent." The court added that "implicit in the formation of MPTC was the idea that the shareholders could pursue their fishing hobby with reasonable and unfettered access to the land and reap the rewards of appreciation when the land was ultimately sold. * * * Here, the primary reason for corporate existence has disappeared. MPTC no longer serves the interests of all the shareholders."

WHY IS THIS CASE IMPORTANT? *As this case illustrates, the breach of the fiduciary duty of a corporate director or officer can affect the judge's decision as to whether a corporation should be dissolved on the basis of oppression.*

LIQUIDATION

When dissolution takes place by voluntary action, the members of the board of directors act as trustees of the corporate assets. As trustees, they are responsible for winding up the affairs of the corporation for the benefit of corporate creditors and shareholders. This makes the board members personally liable for any breach of their fiduciary trustee duties.

Liquidation can be accomplished without court supervision unless the members of the board do not wish to act as trustees of the corporate assets, or unless shareholders or creditors can show cause to the court why the board should not be permitted to assume the trustee function. In either situation, the court will appoint a receiver to wind up the corporate affairs and liquidate corporate assets. A receiver is always appointed by the court if the dissolution is involuntary.

APPLICATION ▪ Creating an E-Document-Retention Policy*

If a corporation becomes the target of a civil lawsuit or criminal investigation, the company may be required to turn over any documents in its files relating to the matter during the discovery stage of litigation. These documents may include legal documents, contracts, e-mail, faxes, letters, interoffice memorandums, notebooks, diaries, and other materials, even if they are kept in personal files in the homes of directors or officers. Under the current Federal Rules of Civil Procedure, which govern civil litigation procedures (see Chapter 3), a defendant in a lawsuit must disclose all relevant electronic data compilations and documents, as well as all relevant paper documents.

Although certain documents or data might free a company of any liability arising from a claim, others might serve to substantiate a civil claim or criminal charge. It is also possible that information contained in a document—an interoffice e-mail memo, for example (or even a memo referring to that memo)—could be used to convince a jury that the company or its directors or officers had condoned a certain action that they later denied condoning.

WHICH E-DOCUMENTS SHOULD BE RETAINED?

How does a company decide which e-documents should be retained and which should be destroyed? By law, corporations are required to keep certain types of documents, such as those specified in the *Code of Federal Regulations* and in regulations issued by government agencies, such as the Occupational Safety and Health Administration. Generally, any records that the company is not legally required to keep or that the company is sure it will have no legal need for should be removed from the files and destroyed. A partnership agreement, for example, should be kept. A memo about last year's company picnic, however, should be

removed from the files and destroyed; obviously, it is just taking up storage space.

MODIFICATIONS MAY BE NECESSARY DURING AN INVESTIGATION

If the company becomes the target of an investigation, it usually must modify its document-retention policy until the investigation has been completed. Company officers, after receiving a subpoena to produce specific types of documents, should instruct the appropriate employees not to destroy relevant papers or e-documents that would otherwise be disposed of as part of the company's normal document-retention program.

Generally, to avoid being charged with obstruction of justice, company officials must always exercise good faith in deciding which documents should or should not be destroyed when attempting to comply with a subpoena. The specter of criminal prosecution would appear to encourage the retention of even those documents that are only remotely related to the dispute—at least until it has been resolved.

CHECKLIST FOR AN E-DOCUMENT-RETENTION POLICY

1. Let employees know not only which e-documents should be retained and deleted but also which types of documents should not be created in the first place.
2. Find out which documents must be retained under the *Code of Federal Regulations* and under other government agency regulations to which your corporation is subject.
3. Retain other e-documents only if their retention is in the corporation's interest.
4. If certain corporate documents are subpoenaed, modify your document-retention policy to retain any document that is even remotely related to the dispute until the legal action has been resolved.

---

* This *Application* is not meant to substitute for the services of an attorney who is licensed to practice law in your state.

KEY TERMS

CHAPTER SUMMARY Corporations

The Nature of the Corporation (See pages 609–614.)	A corporation is a legal entity distinct from its owners. Formal statutory requirements, which vary somewhat from state to state, must be followed in forming a corporation. The corporation can have perpetual existence or be chartered for a specific period of time.
	
	1. *Corporate parties*—The shareholders own the corporation. They elect a board of directors to govern the corporation. The board of directors hires corporate officers and other employees to run the daily business of the firm.
	
	2. *Corporate taxation*—The corporation pays income tax on net profits; shareholders pay income tax on the disbursed dividends that they receive from the corporation (double-taxation feature).
	
	3. *Torts and criminal acts*—The corporation is liable for the torts committed by its agents or officers within the course and scope of their employment (under the doctrine of *respondeat superior*). In some circumstances, a corporation can be held liable (and be fined) for the criminal acts of its agents and employees. In certain situations, corporate officers may be held personally liable for corporate crimes.
	
	4. *Corporate powers*—
	
	  a. Express powers—The express powers of a corporation are granted by the following laws and documents (listed according to their priority): federal constitution, state constitutions, state statutes, articles of incorporation, bylaws, and resolutions of the board of directors.
	
	  b. Implied powers—Barring express constitutional, statutory, or other prohibitions, the corporation has the implied power to do all acts reasonably appropriate and necessary to accomplish its corporate purposes.

Classification of Corporations (See page 614.)	1. *Domestic, foreign, and alien corporations*—A corporation is referred to as a *domestic corporation* within its home state (the state in which it incorporates). A corporation is referred to as a *foreign corporation* by any state that is not its home state. A corporation is referred to as an *alien corporation* if it originates in another country but does business in the United States. 2. *Close corporations*—Corporations owned by a family or a relatively small number of individuals; transfer of shares is usually restricted, and the corporation cannot make a public offering of its securities.

(Continued)

CHAPTER SUMMARY Corporations—Continued

Classification of Corporations— Continued	3. *S corporations*—Small domestic corporations (must have seventy-five or fewer shareholders as members) that under Subchapter S of the Internal Revenue Code are given special tax treatment. These corporations allow shareholders to enjoy the limited legal liability of the corporate form but avoid its double-taxation feature (taxes are paid by shareholders as personal income, and the S corporation is not taxed separately).
	4. *Professional corporations*—Corporations formed by professionals (for example, doctors and lawyers) to obtain the benefits of incorporation (such as tax benefits and limited liability). In most situations, the professional corporation is treated as other corporations, but sometimes the courts will disregard the corporate form and treat the shareholders as partners.
Corporate Formation (See pages 614–616.)	1. *Promotional activities*—A corporate promoter is one who takes the preliminary steps in organizing a corporation (issues a prospectus, secures the charter, interests investors in the purchase of corporate stock, forms subscription agreements, makes contracts with third parties so that the corporation can immediately begin doing business, and so on).
	2. *Incorporation procedures*—
	a. A state in which to incorporate is selected.
	b. The articles of incorporation are prepared and filed.
	c. The certificate of incorporation (or charter), which authorizes the corporation to conduct business, is received from the appropriate state office (usually the secretary of state) after the articles of incorporation have been filed.
Corporate Management— Directors and Officers (See pages 616–621.)	1. *Election of directors*—The first board of directors is usually appointed by the incorporators; thereafter, directors are elected by the shareholders. Directors usually serve a one-year term, although the term can be longer and staggered terms are permitted under most state statutes.
	2. *Directors' qualifications and compensation*—Few qualifications are required; a director can be a shareholder but is not required to be. Compensation is usually specified in the corporate articles or bylaws.
	3. *Board of directors' meetings*—The board of directors conducts business by holding formal meetings with recorded minutes. The date of regular meetings is usually established in the corporate articles or bylaws; special meetings can be called, with notice sent to all directors. Quorum requirements vary from state to state; usually, a quorum is a majority of the corporate directors. Voting must usually be done in person, and in ordinary matters only a majority vote is required.
	4. *Directors' management responsibilities*—Directors are responsible for declaring and paying corporate dividends to shareholders; authorizing major corporate decisions; appointing, supervising, and removing corporate officers and other managerial employees; determining employees' compensation; making financial decisions necessary to the management of corporate affairs; and issuing authorized shares and bonds. Directors may delegate some of their responsibilities to executive committees and corporate officers and executives.
	5. *Role of corporate officers and executives*—Corporate officers and other executive employees are normally hired by the board of directors. In most states, a person can hold more than one office and can be both an officer and a director of a corporation. The rights of corporate officers and executives are defined by employment contracts. The duties of corporate officers are the same as those of directors.
	6. *Duties of directors and officers*—
	a. Duty of care—Directors are obligated to act in good faith, to use prudent business judgment in the conduct of corporate affairs, and to act in the corporation's best interests. If a director fails to exercise this duty of care, he or she can be answerable to the corporation and to the shareholders for breaching the duty.

CHAPTER SUMMARY ▦ Corporations—Continued

Corporate Management—Directors and Officers—Continued	b. Duty of loyalty—Directors have a fiduciary duty to subordinate their own interests to those of the corporation in matters relating to the corporation. c. Conflicts of interest—To fulfill their duty of loyalty, directors and officers must make a full disclosure of any potential conflicts of interest between their personal interests and those of the corporation. d. Business judgment rule—This rule immunizes a director from liability for a corporate decision as long as the decision was within the powers of the corporation and the authority of the director to make, and was an informed, reasonable, and loyal decision.

Corporate Ownership—Shareholders (See pages 621–628.)	1. *Shareholders' powers*—Shareholders' powers include the approval of all fundamental changes affecting the corporation and the election of the board of directors.
	
	2. *Shareholders' meetings*—Shareholders' meetings must occur at least annually; special meetings can be called when necessary. Notice of the date, time, and place of the meeting (and its purpose, if it is specially called) must be sent to shareholders. Shareholders may vote by proxy (authorizing someone else to vote their shares) and may submit proposals to be included in the company's proxy materials sent to shareholders before meetings.
	
	3. *Shareholder voting*—Shareholder voting requirements and procedures are as follows:
	  a. A minimum number of shareholders (a quorum—generally, more than 50 percent of shares held) must be present at a meeting for business to be conducted; resolutions are passed (usually) by simple majority vote.
	  b. The corporation must prepare voting lists of shareholders on record prior to each shareholders' meeting.
	  c. Cumulative voting may or may not be required or permitted. Cumulative voting gives minority shareholders a better chance to be represented on the board of directors.
	  d. A shareholder may appoint a proxy (substitute) to vote her or his shares.

Merger and Consolidation (See pages 628–630.)	1. *Merger*—The legal combination of two or more corporations, the result of which is that the surviving corporation acquires all the assets and obligations of the other corporation, which then ceases to exist. 2. *Consolidation*—The legal combination of two or more corporations, the result of which is that each corporation ceases to exist and a new one emerges. The new corporation assumes all the assets and obligations of the former corporations.
Purchase of Assets (See pages 630–631.)	A purchase of assets occurs when one corporation acquires all or substantially all of the assets of another corporation. 1. *Acquiring corporation*—The acquiring (purchasing) corporation is not required to obtain shareholder approval; the corporation is merely increasing its assets, and no fundamental business change occurs. 2. *Acquired corporation*—The acquired (purchased) corporation is required to obtain the approval of both its directors and its shareholders for the sale of its assets, because this creates a substantial change in the corporation's business position.
Purchase of Stock (See page 631.)	A purchase of stock occurs when one corporation acquires a substantial number of the voting shares of the stock of another (target) corporation. 1. *Tender offer*—A public offer to all shareholders of the target corporation to purchase its stock at a price that is generally higher than the market price of the target stock prior to the announcement of the tender offer. Federal and state securities laws strictly control the terms, duration, and circumstances under which most tender offers are made.

(Continued)

CHAPTER SUMMARY ▪ Corporations—Continued

Purchase of Stock—Continued	2. *Target responses*—Ways in which target corporations respond to takeover bids. These include self-tenders, poison pills, and numerous other strategies.
Termination (See pages 632–634.)	The termination of a corporation involves the following two phases:
	1. *Dissolution*—The legal death of the artificial "person" of the corporation. Dissolution can be brought about in any of the following ways:
	a. An act of a legislature in the state of incorporation.
	b. Expiration of the time provided in the certificate of incorporation (corporate charter).
	c. Voluntary approval of the shareholders and the board of directors.
	d. Unanimous action by all shareholders.
	e. Court decree.
	2. *Liquidation*—The process by which corporate assets are converted into cash and distributed to creditors and shareholders according to specified rules of preference. May be supervised by members of the board of directors (when dissolution is voluntary) or by a receiver appointed by the court to wind up corporate affairs.

▪ FOR REVIEW

Answers for the even-numbered questions in this For Review *section can be found in Appendix I at the end of this text.*

1 What are the express and implied powers of corporations? On what sources are these powers based?

2 What are the duties of corporate directors and officers?

3 What must directors do to avoid liability for honest mistakes of judgment and poor business decisions?

4 What role do corporate shareholders play in the corporate enterprise? What are some important rights of shareholders?

5 What is the difference between a corporate merger and a corporate consolidation? What steps are involved in the termination of a corporate enterprise?

▪ QUESTIONS AND CASE PROBLEMS

20–1. Rights of Shareholders. Dmitri has acquired one share of common stock of a multimillion-dollar corporation with over 500,000 shareholders. Dmitri's ownership is so small that he is questioning what his rights are as a shareholder. For example, he wants to know whether this one share entitles him to attend and vote at shareholders' meetings, inspect the corporate books, and receive periodic dividends. Discuss Dmitri's rights in these matters.

20–2. Voting Techniques. Algonquin Corp. has issued and has outstanding 100,000 shares of common stock. Four stockholders own 60,000 of these shares, and for the past six years they have nominated a slate of people for membership on the board, all of whom have been elected. Sergio and twenty other shareholders, owning 20,000 shares, are dissatisfied with corporate management and want a representative on the board who shares their views. Explain under what circumstances Sergio and the minority shareholders can elect their representative to the board.

20–3. Duties of Directors. Overland Corp. is negotiating with Wharton Construction Co. for the renovation of Overland's corporate headquarters. Wharton, the owner of Wharton Construction, is also one of the five members of the board of directors of Overland. The contract terms are standard for this type of contract. Wharton has previously informed two of the other Overland directors of his interest in the construction company. Overland's board approves the contract on a three-to-two vote, with Wharton voting with the majority. Discuss whether this contract is binding on the corporation.

20–4. Corporate Combinations. Jolson is chairman of the board of directors of Artel, Inc., and Douglas is chairman of the board of directors of Fox Express, Inc. Artel is a manufacturing corporation, and Fox Express is a transportation corporation. Jolson and Douglas meet to consider the possibility of combining their corporations and activities into a single corporate entity. They consider two alternative courses of action: Artel could acquire all of the stock and assets of Fox Express, or the corporations could combine to form a new corporation, called A&F Enterprises, Inc. Both chairmen are concerned about the necessity of a formal transfer of property, liability for existing debts, and the problem of amending the articles of incorporation. Discuss what the two proposed combinations are called and the legal effect each has on the transfer of property, the liabilities of the combined corporations, and the need to amend the articles of incorporation.

20–5. Duties of Majority Shareholders. Atlas Food Systems & Services, Inc., based in South Carolina, was a food vending service that provided refreshments to factories and other businesses. Atlas was a closely held corporation. John Kiriakides was a minority shareholder of Atlas. Alex Kiriakides was the majority shareholder. Throughout most of Atlas's history, Alex was the chairman of the board, which included John as a director. In 1995, while John was the president of the firm, the board and shareholders decided to convert Atlas to an S corporation. A few months later, however, Alex, without calling a vote, decided that the firm would not convert. In 1996, a dispute arose over Atlas's contract to buy certain property. John and others decided not to buy it. Without consulting anyone, Alex elected to go through with the sale. Within a few days, Alex refused to allow John to stay on as president. Two months later, Atlas offered to buy John's interest in the firm for almost $2 million. John refused, believing the offer was too low. John filed a suit in a South Carolina state court against Atlas and Alex, seeking, among other things, to force a buyout of John's shares. On what basis might the court grant John's request? Discuss. [*Kiriakides v. Atlas Food Systems & Services, Inc.*, 541 S.E.2d 257 (S.C. 2001)]

CASE PROBLEM WITH SAMPLE ANSWER

20–6. In 1996, Robert McClellan, a licensed contractor doing business as McClellan Design and Construction, entered into a contract with Peppertree North Condominium Association, Inc., to do earthquake repair work on Peppertree's seventy-six-unit condominium complex in Northridge, California. McClellan completed the work, but Peppertree failed to pay. In an arbitration proceeding against Peppertree to collect the amount due, McClellan was awarded $141,000, plus 10 percent interest, attorneys' fees, and costs. McClellan filed a suit in a California state court against Peppertree to confirm the award. Meanwhile, the Peppertree board of directors filed articles of incorporation for Northridge Park Townhome Owners Association, Inc., and immediately transferred Peppertree's authority, responsibilities, and assets to the new association. Two weeks later, the court issued a judgment against Peppertree. When McClellan learned about the new association, he filed a motion asking the court to add Northridge as a debtor to the judgment. Should the court grant the motion? Why or why not? [*McClellan v. Northridge Park Townhome Owners Association, Inc.*, 89 Cal.App.4th 746, 107 Cal.Rptr.2d 702 (2 Dist. 2001)]

After you have answered this problem, compare your answer with the sample answer given on the Web site that accompanies this text. Go to http://blt.westbuslaw.com, select "Chapter 20," and click on "Case Problem with Sample Answer."

20–7. Purchase of Assets. Paradise Pools, Inc. (PPI), also known as "Paradise Pools and Spas," was incorporated in 1981. In 1994, PPI entered into a contract with Bromanco, Inc., to build a pool in Vicksburg, Mississippi, as part of a Days Inn Hotel project being developed by Amerihost Development, Inc. PPI built the pool, but Bromanco, the general contractor, defaulted on other parts of the project, so Amerihost completed the construction itself. Litigation ensued in Mississippi state courts, and Amerihost was awarded $12,656.46 against PPI. Meanwhile, Paradise Corp. (PC) was incorporated in 1995 with the same management as PPI, but different shareholders. PC acquired PPI's assets in 1996, without assuming its liabilities, and soon became known as "Paradise Pools and Spas." Amerihost obtained a writ of garnishment against PC to enforce the judgment against PPI. PC filed a motion to dismiss the writ on the basis that it was "not a party to the proceeding." Should the court dismiss the case? Why or why not? [*Paradise Corp. v. Amerihost Development, Inc.*, 848 So.2d 177 (Miss. 2003)]

20–8. Duty of Loyalty. Digital Commerce, Ltd., designed software to enable its clients to sell their products or services over the Internet. Kevin Sullivan served as a Digital vice president until 2000, when he became president. Sullivan was dissatisfied that his compensation did not include stock in Digital, but he was unable to negotiate a deal that included equity (referring to shares of ownership in the company). In May, Sullivan solicited ASR Corp.'s business for Digital while he investigated employment opportunities with ASR for himself. When ASR would not include an "equity component" in a job offer, Sullivan refused to negotiate further on Digital's behalf. A few months later, Sullivan began to form his own firm to compete with Digital, conducting organizational and marketing activities on Digital's time, including soliciting ASR's business. In August, Sullivan resigned after first having all e-mail pertaining to the new firm deleted from Digital's computers. ASR signed a contract with Sullivan's new firm and paid it $400,000 for work through October 2001. Digital filed a suit in a federal district court against Sullivan, claiming that he had usurped a corporate opportunity. Did Sullivan breach his fiduciary duty to Digital? Explain. [*In re Sullivan*, 305 Bankr. 809 (W.D.Mich. 2004)]

A QUESTION OF ETHICS

20–9. McQuade was the manager of the New York Giants baseball team. McQuade and John McGraw purchased shares in the National Exhibition Co., the corporation that owned the Giants, from Charles Stoneham, who owned a majority of National Exhibition's stock. As part of the transaction, each of the three agreed to use his best efforts to ensure that the others continued as directors and officers of the organization. Stoneham and McGraw, however, subsequently failed to use their best efforts to ensure that McQuade continued as the treasurer and a director of the corporation, and McQuade sued to compel specific performance of the agreement. A court reviewing the matter noted that McQuade had been "shabbily" treated by the others but refused to grant specific performance on the ground that the agreement was void because it interfered with the duty of the others as directors to do what was best for all the shareholders. Although shareholders may join to elect corporate directors, they may not join to limit the directors' discretion in managing the business affairs of an organization; the directors must retain their independent judgment. Consider the implications of the case, and address the following questions. [*McQuade v. Stoneham*, 263 N.Y. 323, 189 N.E. 234 (1934)]

1. Given that even the court sympathized with McQuade, was it ethical to put the business judgment of the directors ahead of an otherwise valid promise they had made?
2. Are there practical considerations that support the court's decision? How can directors perform the tasks dictated to them if their judgment is constrained by earlier agreements with some of the shareholders?

FOR CRITICAL ANALYSIS

20–10. What are some of the ways in which the limited liability of corporate shareholders serves the public interest? Can you think of any ways in which this limited liability is harmful to the public interest? Explain.

ONLINE ACTIVITIES

INTERNET EXERCISES

Go to the *Business Law Today: The Essentials* home page at <u>http://blt.westbuslaw.com</u>, select "Chapter 20," and click on "Internet Exercises." There you will find the following Internet research exercises that you can perform to learn more about topics covered in this chapter.

Activity 20–1: LEGAL PERSPECTIVE—Corporate Law

Activity 20–2: LEGAL PERSPECTIVE—Liability of Directors and Officers

Activity 20–3: MANAGEMENT PERSPECTIVE—D&O Insurance

Activity 20–4: LEGAL PERSPECTIVE—Mergers

BEFORE THE TEST

Go to the *Business Law Today: The Essentials* home page at <u>http://blt.westbuslaw.com</u>, select "Chapter 20," and click on "Interactive Quizzes." You will find at least twenty interactive questions relating to this chapter.

CHAPTER 21

Financing, Investor Protection, and Online Securities Offerings

"It shall be unlawful for any person in the offer or sale of any security . . . to engage in any transaction, practice, or course of business which operates or would operate as a fraud or deceit upon the purchaser."

Securities Act of 1933, Section 17

CHAPTER OUTLINE

SECURITY
Generally, a stock certificate, bond, note, debenture, warrant, or other document given as evidence of an ownership interest in a corporation or as a promise of repayment by a corporation.

■ LEARNING OBJECTIVES

After reading this chapter, you should be able to answer the following questions:

1 What is meant by the term *securities*?

2 What are the two major statutes regulating the securities industry? When was the Securities and Exchange Commission created, and what are its major purposes and functions?

3 What is insider trading? Why is it prohibited?

4 What are some of the features of state securities laws?

5 How are securities laws being applied in the online environment?

A corporation is financed by the issuance of **securities**—generally defined as any documents evidencing corporate ownership (stock) or debts (bonds). After the stock market crash of 1929, many members of Congress argued in favor of regulating securities markets. Basically, legislation for such regulation was enacted to provide investors with more information to help them make buying and selling decisions about securities and to prohibit deceptive, unfair, and manipulative practices. Today, the sale and transfer of securities are heavily regulated by federal and state statutes and by government agencies.

In this chapter, after discussing how corporations are financed, we look at the nature of federal securities regulation and its effect on the business world. We discuss the Sarbanes-Oxley Act of 2002,[1] which significantly affects certain types of securities transactions. We then examine the major traditional laws governing securities offerings and trading. The online world has brought some dramatic changes

---

1. 15 U.S.C. Sections 7201 *et seq.*

641

to securities offerings and regulation. In the concluding pages of this chapter, we look at how securities laws are being adapted to the online environment. Before we begin, though, the important role played by the Securities and Exchange Commission (SEC) in the regulation of federal securities laws requires some attention. We examine the origin and functions of the SEC in this chapter's *Landmark in the Law* feature.

LANDMARK IN THE LAW

The Securities and Exchange Commission

In 1931, the Senate passed a resolution calling for an extensive investigation of securities trading. The investigation led, ultimately, to the passage by Congress of the Securities Act of 1933, which is also known as the *truth-in-securities* bill. In the following year, Congress passed the Securities Exchange Act. This 1934 act created the Securities and Exchange Commission (SEC).

MAJOR RESPONSIBILITIES OF THE SEC   The SEC was created as an independent regulatory agency with the function of administering the 1933 and 1934 acts. Its major responsibilities in this respect are as follows:

1. Requiring disclosure of facts concerning offerings of securities listed on national securities exchanges and of certain securities traded over the counter (OTC).

2. Regulating the trade in securities on national and regional securities exchanges and in the OTC markets.

3. Investigating securities fraud.

4. Regulating the activities of securities brokers, dealers, and investment advisers and requiring their registration.

5. Supervising the activities of mutual funds.

6. Recommending administrative sanctions, injunctive remedies, and criminal prosecution against those who violate securities laws. (The SEC can bring enforcement actions for civil violations of federal securities laws. The Fraud Section of the Criminal Division of the Department of Justice prosecutes criminal violations.)

THE SEC'S EXPANDING REGULATORY POWERS   Since its creation, the SEC's regulatory functions have gradually been increased by legislation granting it authority in different areas. For example, to further curb securities fraud, the Securities Enforcement Remedies and Penny Stock Reform Act of 1990[a] amended existing securities laws to allow SEC administrative law judges to hear many more types of securities violation cases; the SEC's enforcement options were also greatly expanded. The act also provides that courts can prevent persons who have engaged in securities fraud from serving as officers and directors of publicly held corporations. The Securities Acts Amendments of 1990 authorized the SEC to seek sanctions against those who violate foreign securities laws.[b]

a. 15 U.S.C. Section 77g.
b. 15 U.S.C. Section 78a.

(Continued)

LANDMARK IN THE LAW   The Securities and Exchange Commission—Continued

The National Securities Markets Improvement Act of 1996 expanded the power of the SEC to exempt persons, securities, and transactions from the requirements of the securities laws.[c] (This part of the act is also known as the Capital Markets Efficiency Act.) The act also limited the authority of the states to regulate certain securities transactions and particular investment advisory firms.[d] The Sarbanes-Oxley Act of 2002,[e] which you will read about shortly, further expanded the authority of the SEC by directing the agency to issue new rules relating to corporate disclosure requirements and by creating an SEC oversight board.

APPLICATION TO TODAY'S WORLD

Congress and the SEC have been attempting to update the regulatory process to make it more relevant to today's securities trading practices, including those occurring in the online environment. Another goal is to establish more oversight over securities transactions and accounting practices. Additionally, as the number and types of online securities frauds increase, the SEC is trying to keep pace by expanding its online fraud division.

RELEVANT WEB SITES

To locate information on the Web concerning the SEC, go to this text's Web site at **http://blt.westbuslaw.com,** *select "Chapter 21," and click on "URLs for Landmarks."*

c. 15 U.S.C. Sections 77z-3, 78mm.
d. 15 U.S.C. Section 80b-3a.
e. 15 U.S.C. Sections 7201 *et seq.*

Corporate Financing

Part of the process of corporate formation involves corporate financing. Corporations are financed by the issuance and sale of corporate securities. Securities (stocks and bonds) evidence the right to participate in earnings and the distribution of corporate property or the obligation to pay funds.

STOCK
An equity (ownership) interest in a corporation, measured in units of shares.

BOND
A certificate that evidences a corporate (or government) debt. It is a security that involves no ownership interest in the issuing entity.

   Stocks, or *equity securities,* represent the purchase of ownership in the business firm. **Bonds** (debentures), or *debt securities,* represent the borrowing of funds by firms (and governments). Of course, not all debt is in the form of debt securities. For example, some debt is in the form of accounts payable and notes payable. Accounts and notes payable are typically short-term debts. Bonds are simply a way for the corporation to split up its long-term debt so that it can market it more easily.

BONDS

Bonds are issued by business firms and by governments at all levels as evidence of the funds they are borrowing from investors. Bonds normally have a designated *maturity date*—the date when the principal, or face, amount of the bond is returned to the investor. They are sometimes referred to as *fixed-income securities* because their owners (that is, the creditors) receive fixed-dollar interest payments, usually semiannually, during the period of time prior to maturity.

BOND INDENTURE
A contract between the issuer of a bond and the bondholder.

Because debt financing represents a legal obligation on the part of the corporation, various features and terms of a particular bond issue are specified in a lending agreement called a **bond indenture.** A corporate trustee, often a commercial bank trust department, represents the collective well-being of all bondholders in ensuring that the corporation meets the terms of the bond issue. The bond indenture specifies the maturity date of the bond and the pattern of interest payments until maturity. The different types of corporate bonds are described in Exhibit 21–1.

STOCKS

Issuing stocks is another way that corporations can obtain financing. The ways in which stocks differ from bonds are summarized in Exhibit 21–2. Basically, as mentioned, stocks represent ownership in a business firm, whereas bonds represent borrowing by the firm.

Exhibit 21–3 on page 646 summarizes the types of stocks issued by corporations. We look now at the two major types of stock—*common stock* and *preferred stock.*

COMMON STOCK
Shares of ownership in a corporation that give the owner of the stock a proportionate interest in the corporation with regard to control, earnings, and net assets. Shares of common stock are lowest in priority with respect to payment of dividends and distribution of the corporation's assets on dissolution.

Common Stock   The true ownership of a corporation is represented by **common stock.** Common stock provides a proportionate interest in the corporation with regard to (1) control, (2) earnings, and (3) net assets. A shareholder's interest is generally in proportion to the number of shares he or she owns out of the total number of shares issued.

Voting rights in a corporation apply to the election of the firm's board of directors and to any proposed changes in the ownership structure of the firm. For example, a holder of common stock generally has the right to vote in a decision on a proposed merger, as mergers can change the proportion of ownership. State corporation law specifies the types of actions for which shareholder approval must be obtained.

Firms are not obligated to return a principal amount per share to each holder of common stock because no firm can ensure that the market price per share of its common stock will not decline over time. The issuing firm also does not have to guarantee a dividend; indeed, some corporations never pay dividends.

EXHIBIT 21–1 **TYPES OF CORPORATE BONDS**

Debenture Bonds	Bonds for which no specific assets of the corporation are pledged as backing. Rather, they are backed by the general credit rating of the corporation, plus any assets that can be seized if the corporation allows the debentures to go into default.
Mortgage Bonds	Bonds that pledge specific property. If the corporation defaults on the bonds, the bondholders can take the property.
Convertible Bonds	Bonds that can be exchanged for a specified number of shares of common stock under certain conditions.
Callable Bonds	Bonds that may be called in and the principal repaid at specified times or under conditions specified in the bond when it is issued.

EXHIBIT 21–2   HOW DO STOCKS AND BONDS DIFFER?

STOCKS	BONDS
1. Stocks represent ownership.	1. Bonds represent debt.
2. Stocks (common) do not have a fixed dividend rate.	2. Interest on bonds must always be paid, whether or not any profit is earned.
3. Stockholders can elect the board of directors, which controls the corporation.	3. Bondholders usually have no voice in, or control over, management of the corporation.
4. Stocks do not have a maturity date; the corporation usually does not repay the stockholder.	4. Bonds have a maturity date, when the corporation is to repay the bondholder the face value of the bond.
5. All corporations issue or offer to sell stocks. This is the usual definition of a corporation.	5. Corporations do not necessarily issue bonds.
6. Stockholders have a claim against the property and income of a corporation after all creditors' claims have been met.	6. Bondholders have a claim against the property and income of a corporation that must be met before the claims of stockholders.

Holders of common stock are investors who assume a *residual* position in the overall financial structure of a business. In terms of receiving payment for their investments, they are last in line. They are entitled to the earnings that are left after preferred stockholders, bondholders, suppliers, employees, and other groups have been paid. Once those groups are paid, however, the owners of common stock may be entitled to *all* the remaining earnings as dividends. (Note, though, that the board of directors normally is not under any duty to declare the remaining earnings as dividends.)

PREFERRED STOCK
Classes of stock that have priority over common stock as to both payment of dividends and distribution of assets on the corporation's dissolution.

Preferred Stock   Preferred stock is stock with *preferences*. Usually, this means that holders of preferred stock have priority over holders of common stock as to dividends and as to payment on dissolution of the corporation. Holders of preferred stock may or may not have the right to vote.

Preferred stock is not included among the liabilities of a business because it is equity. Like other equity securities, preferred shares have no fixed maturity date on which the firm must pay them off. Although firms occasionally buy back preferred stock, they are not legally obligated to do so.

Holders of preferred stock are investors who have assumed a rather cautious position in their relationship to the corporation. They have a stronger position than common shareholders with respect to dividends and claims on assets, but as a result, they will not share in the full prosperity of the firm if it grows successfully over time. This is because the value of preferred shares will not rise as rapidly as that of common shares during a period of financial success. Preferred stockholders receive fixed dividends periodically.

EXHIBIT 21–3 TYPES OF STOCKS

Common Stock	Voting shares that represent ownership interest in a corporation. Common stock has the lowest priority with respect to payment of dividends and distribution of assets on the corporation's dissolution.
Preferred Stock	Shares of stock that have priority over common-stock shares as to payment of dividends and distribution of assets on dissolution. Dividend payments are usually a fixed percentage of the face value of the share.
Cumulative Preferred Stock	Required dividends not paid in a given year must be paid in a subsequent year before any common-stock dividends are paid.
Participating Preferred Stock	Stock entitling the owner to receive the preferred-stock dividend and additional dividends if the corporation has paid dividends on common stock.
Convertible Preferred Stock	Stock entitling the owners to convert their shares into a specified number of common shares either in the issuing corporation or, sometimes, in another corporation.
Redeemable, or Callable, Preferred Stock	Preferred shares issued with the express condition that the issuing corporation has the right to repurchase the shares as specified.

The return and the risk for preferred stock lie somewhere between those for bonds and those for common stock. Preferred stock is more similar to bonds than to common stock, even though preferred stock appears in the ownership section of the firm's balance sheet. As a result, preferred stock is often categorized with corporate bonds as a fixed-income security, even though the legal status is not the same.

■ Sarbanes-Oxley Act of 2002

As discussed in Chapter 2, in 2002, following a series of corporate scandals, Congress passed the Sarbanes-Oxley Act. Some regard this act as one of the most significant modifications of securities regulation since the 1930s. Generally, the act attempts to increase corporate accountability by imposing stricter disclosure requirements and harsher penalties for violations of securities laws. Among other things, the act requires chief corporate executives to take responsibility for the accuracy of financial statements and reports that are filed with the SEC. Chief executive officers and chief financial officers must personally certify that the statements and reports are accurate and complete.

Additionally, the new rules require that certain financial and stock-transaction reports be filed with the SEC earlier than was required under the previous rules. The act also mandates SEC oversight over a new entity, called the Public Company Accounting Oversight Board, which now regulates and oversees public accounting firms. Other provisions of the act created new private civil actions and expanded the SEC's remedies in administrative and civil actions.

Because of the importance of this act for corporate leaders and for those dealing with securities transactions, we present some of its key provisions relating to corporate accountability in Exhibit 21–4. (Provisions of the act that relate to public accounting firms and accounting practices were discussed in Chapter 2.)

ETHICAL ISSUE 21.1

Should lawyers be required to withdraw as counsel and notify the SEC if a corporate client is violating securities laws? The attorney-client privilege generally prevents lawyers from disclosing confidential client information—even when the client has committed an unlawful act. The idea is to encourage clients to be open and honest with their attorneys to ensure competent representation. The Sarbanes-Oxley Act of 2002 requires an attorney to report any material violations of securities laws to the corporation's highest authority.[2] The act does not require that the lawyer break client confidences, though, because the lawyer is still reporting to officials within the corporation.

2. See Section 307 of the Sarbanes-Oxley Act.

EXHIBIT 21–4 SOME KEY PROVISIONS OF THE SARBANES-OXLEY ACT OF 2002 RELATING TO CORPORATE ACCOUNTABILITY

Certification Requirements—Under Section 906 of the Sarbanes-Oxley Act, the chief executive officers (CEOs) and chief financial officers (CFOs) of most major companies listed on public stock exchanges must now certify the financial statements that are filed with the SEC. For virtually all filed financial reports, CEOs and CFOs have to certify that the reports "fully comply" with SEC requirements and that all of the information reported "fairly represents in all material respects, the financial conditions and results of operations of the issuer."

Under Section 302 of the act, for each quarterly and annual filing with the SEC, CEOs and CFOs of reporting companies are required to certify that a signing officer reviewed the report, and that to the best of the signing officer's knowledge, the report contains no untrue statements of material fact. Also, the signing officer or officers must certify that they have established an internal control system to identify all material information and that any deficiencies in the system were disclosed to the auditors.

Loans to Directors and Officers—Section 402 prohibits any reporting company, as well as any private company that is filing an initial public offering, from making personal loans to directors and executive officers, with a few limited exceptions.

Protection for Whistleblowers—Section 806 protects "whistleblowers"—those employees who report ("blow the whistle" on) securities violations by their employers—from being fired or in any way discriminated against by their employers.

Blackout Periods—Section 306 prohibits certain types of securities transactions during "blackout periods"—periods during which the issuer's ability to purchase, sell, or otherwise transfer funds in individual account plans (such as pension funds) is suspended.

Enhanced Penalties for—

• *Violations of Section 906 Certification Requirements*—Willful violators of the certification requirements may be subject to a maximum of $5 million in fines, twenty years in prison, or both.

• *Violations of the Securities Exchange Act of 1934*—Penalties for violating the 1934 act were also increased (as discussed later in this chapter).

• *Destruction or Alteration of Documents*—Anyone who alters, destroys, or conceals documents or otherwise obstructs any official proceeding may be subject to fines, imprisonment, or both.

• *Other Forms of White-Collar Crime*—The act stiffened penalties for certain criminal offenses, such as violations of the federal mail and wire fraud laws.

Statute of Limitations for Securities Fraud—Section 804 of the act provides that a private right of action for securities fraud may be brought no later than two years after the discovery of the violation or five years after the violation, whichever is earlier.

The SEC now wants to go one step further than the Sarbanes-Oxley Act and mandate a "noisy withdrawal." Under the SEC's proposal, attorneys whose corporate clients are violating securities laws would have to withdraw publicly from representing the corporation and notify the SEC. This proposal is controversial and has been the subject of much debate. Should the SEC be able to force lawyers to disclose privileged client information? Would this be fair to the corporation? In 2003, the American Bar Association (ABA) modified its ethics rules to allow attorneys to break confidence with a client to report possible corporate fraud. The ABA rules do not *require* attorneys to do so, however. Nonetheless, the SEC wants to make the disclosure mandatory. In the SEC's view, lawyers owe a duty to the corporation and its investors, not to the individual officers and directors. ∎

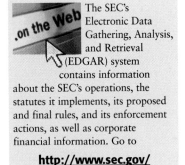

The SEC's Electronic Data Gathering, Analysis, and Retrieval (EDGAR) system contains information about the SEC's operations, the statutes it implements, its proposed and final rules, and its enforcement actions, as well as corporate financial information. Go to

http://www.sec.gov/ edgar.shtml.

▦ Securities Act of 1933

The Securities Act of 1933[3] governs initial sales of stock by businesses. The act was designed to prohibit various forms of fraud and to stabilize the securities industry by requiring that all essential information concerning the issuance of securities be made available to the investing public. Basically, the purpose of this act is to require disclosure.

WHAT IS A SECURITY?

Section 2(1) of the Securities Act states that securities include the following:

> [A]ny note, stock, treasury stock, bond, debenture, evidence of indebtedness, certificate of interest or participation in any profit-sharing agreement, collateral-trust certificate, preorganization certificate or subscription, transferable share, investment contract, voting-trust certificate, certificate of deposit for a security, fractional undivided interest in oil, gas, or other mineral rights, or, in general, any interest or instrument commonly known as a "security," or any certificate of interest or participation in, temporary or interim certificate for, receipt for, guarantee of, or warrant or right to subscribe to or purchase, any of the foregoing.[4]

The New York Stock Exchange. (Photo courtesy of NYSE)

The courts have interpreted the act's definition of what constitutes a security[5] to include investment contracts. An investment contract is any transaction in which a person (1) invests (2) in a common enterprise (3) reasonably expecting profits (4) derived *primarily* or *substantially* from others' managerial or entrepreneurial efforts.[6]

For our purposes, it is probably convenient to think of securities in their most common forms—stocks and bonds issued by corporations. Bear in mind, though, that securities can take many forms and have been held to include whiskey, cosmetics,

---

3. 15 U.S.C. Sections 77–77aa.
4. 15 U.S.C. Section 77b(1). Amendments in 1982 added stock options.
5. See 15 U.S.C. Section 77b(a)(1).
6. *SEC v. W. J. Howey Co.,* 328 U.S. 293, 66 S.Ct. 1100, 90 L.Ed. 1244 (1946).

worms, beavers, boats, vacuum cleaners, muskrats, and cemetery lots, as well as investment contracts in condominiums, franchises, limited partnerships, oil or gas or other mineral rights, and farm animals accompanied by care agreements.

In the following case, the question was whether sales of pay phones and agreements to service the phones constituted sales of securities.

CASE 21.1 ■ SEC v. Alpha Telcom, Inc.

United States District Court,
District of Oregon, 2002.
187 F.Supp.2d 1250.

FACTS Paul Rubera started Alpha Telcom, Inc., in 1986 to sell, install, and maintain phones and business systems in Grants Pass, Oregon. In 1997, Alpha began to sell pay phones to buyers, most of whom also entered into service agreements with Alpha. Most of these buyers selected a "Level Four Service Agreement," which required Alpha to select a location for a phone, install it, obtain all licenses, maintain and clean the phone, pay the bills, and collect the revenue. Buyers were guaranteed—and were paid—a 14 percent return on the amount of their purchase. The pay-phone program was presented and promoted through American Telecommunications Company (ATC), Alpha's marketing subsidiary. From July 1998 through June 2001, Alpha's expenses for the program were $21,798,000, while revenues were $21,698,000. Despite the loss, Alpha paid investors approximately $17.9 million. To make these payments, Alpha borrowed money from ATC. Alpha filed for bankruptcy in August 2001. The Securities and Exchange Commission (SEC) filed a suit in a federal district court against Alpha and Rubera, alleging violations of the Securities Act of 1933. The defendants argued that the pay-phone program did not involve sales of securities.

ISSUE Was the pay-phone program a security?

DECISION Yes. The court concluded that the pay-phone program was a security because it involved an investment contract, which is a contract that is "(1) an investment of money; (2) in a common enterprise; (3) with the expectation of profits to be derived from the efforts of others." The court issued an injunction to prohibit further violations of the Securities Act of 1933 and ordered Rubera to disgorge profits of more than $3.7 million, plus interest.

REASON As for the individual elements of the definition of "an investment contract," the court reasoned that investors make cash investments with the expectation of receiving profits. Here, investors relied on the expertise of Alpha, as a common enterprise, to do all of the work, including making all of the business decisions with regard to the phones. Also, "ATC's only source of revenue was money from new investors. As a result, new investor money was being used to pay returns to existing investors," and "[i]nvestors would receive their 14 percent return * * * regardless of whether their particular phone actually generated that much money." Finally, "Alpha was ultimately responsible for those essential managerial efforts [that] affect the failure or success of the enterprise, and the investors retained no control over the business."

WHY IS THIS CASE IMPORTANT? *This case demonstrates that securities are not solely limited to simple stocks and bonds but can encompass a wide variety of materials. The analysis hinges on the nature of the transaction rather than the substances involved.*

REGISTRATION STATEMENT

Section 5 of the Securities Act of 1933 broadly provides that unless a security qualifies for an exemption, that security must be *registered* before it is offered to the public either through the mails or through any facility of interstate commerce, including securities exchanges. Issuing corporations must file a *registration statement* with the SEC. Investors must be provided with a prospectus that describes the security being

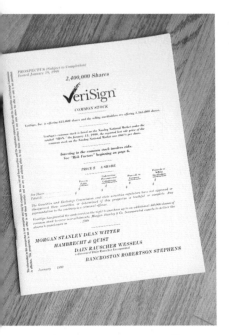

A registration statement discusses a security that is being offered to the public. What are the major contents of a registration statement? (© David Young-Wolff, PhotoEdit)

RED HERRING
A preliminary prospectus that can be distributed to potential investors after the registration statement (for a securities offering) has been filed with the Securities and Exchange Commission. The name derives from the red legend printed across the prospectus stating that the registration has been filed but has not become effective.

TOMBSTONE AD
An advertisement, historically in a format resembling a tombstone, of a securities offering. The ad tells potential investors where and how they may obtain a prospectus.

DON'T FORGET   The purpose of the Securities Act of 1933 is disclosure—the SEC does not consider whether a security is worth the investment price.

sold, the issuing corporation, and the investment or risk attaching to the security. In principle, the registration statement and the prospectus supply sufficient information to enable unsophisticated investors to evaluate the financial risk involved.

Contents of the Registration Statement   The registration statement must be written in plain English and include the following:

1 A description of the significant provisions of the security offered for sale, including the relationship between that security and the other securities of the registrant. Also, the corporation must disclose how it intends to use the proceeds of the sale.

2 A description of the corporation's properties and business.

3 A description of the management of the corporation and its security holdings; remuneration; and other benefits, including pensions and stock options. Any interests of directors or officers in any material transactions with the corporation must be disclosed.

4 A financial statement certified by an independent public accounting firm.

5 A description of pending lawsuits.

Other Requirements   Before filing the registration statement and the prospectus with the SEC, the corporation is allowed to obtain an *underwriter*—a company that agrees to purchase the new issue of securities for resale to the public. There is a twenty-day waiting period (which can be accelerated by the SEC) after registration before the securities can be sold. During this period, oral offers between interested investors and the issuing corporation concerning the purchase and sale of the proposed securities may take place, and very limited written advertising is allowed. At this time, the so-called **red herring** prospectus may be distributed. The name comes from the red legend printed across the prospectus stating that the registration has been filed but has not become effective.

After the waiting period, the registered securities can be legally bought and sold. Written advertising is allowed in the form of a **tombstone ad,** so named because historically the format resembled a tombstone. Such ads simply tell the investor where and how to obtain a prospectus. Normally, any other type of advertising is prohibited until the registration becomes effective.

EXEMPT SECURITIES

A number of specific securities are exempt from the registration requirements of the Securities Act of 1933. These securities—which can also generally be resold without being registered—include the following:[7]

1 All bank securities sold prior to July 27, 1933.

2 Commercial paper (such as negotiable instruments), if the maturity date does not exceed nine months.

3 Securities of charitable organizations.

4 Securities resulting from a corporate reorganization that are issued for exchange with the issuer's existing security holders and certificates that are

---

7. 15 U.S.C. Section 77c.

The Center for Corporate Law at the University of Cincinnati College of Law examines all of the acts discussed in this chapter. Go to **http://www.law.uc.edu/CCL**.

BE AWARE The issuer of an exempt security does not have to disclose the same information that other issuers do.

issued by trustees, receivers, or debtors in possession under the bankruptcy laws (bankruptcy laws were discussed in Chapter 16).

5 Securities issued exclusively for exchange with the issuer's existing security holders, provided no commission is paid (for example, stock dividends and stock splits).

6 Securities issued to finance the acquisition of railroad equipment.

7 Any insurance, endowment, or annuity contract issued by a state-regulated insurance company.

8 Government-issued securities.

9 Securities issued by banks, savings and loan associations, farmers' cooperatives, and similar institutions subject to supervision by governmental authorities.

10 In consideration of the "small amount involved,"[8] an issuer's offer of up to $5 million in securities in any twelve-month period.

For the last exemption, under Regulation A,[9] the issuer must file with the SEC a notice of the issue and an offering circular, which must also be provided to investors before the sale. This is a much simpler and less expensive process than the procedures associated with full registration. Companies are allowed to "test the waters" for potential interest before preparing the offering circular. To *test the waters* means to determine potential interest without actually selling any securities or requiring any commitment on the part of those who express interest. Small-business issuers (companies with annual revenues of less than $25 million) can also use an integrated registration and reporting system that uses simpler forms than the full registration system.

Exhibit 21–5 on the following page summarizes the securities and transactions that are exempt (discussed next) from the registration requirements under the Securities Act of 1933 and SEC regulations.

EXEMPT TRANSACTIONS

An issuer of securities that are not exempt under one of the ten categories listed in the previous subsection can avoid the high cost and complicated procedures associated with registration by taking advantage of certain transaction exemptions. These exemptions are very broad, and thus many sales occur without registration. Because the coverage of the exemptions overlaps somewhat, an offering may qualify for more than one.

Small Offerings—Regulation D   The SEC's Regulation D contains four separate exemptions from registration requirements for limited offers (offers that either involve a small amount or are made in a limited manner). Regulation D provides that any of these offerings made during any twelve-month period are exempt from the registration requirements.

Rule 504.   Noninvestment company offerings up to $1 million in any twelve-month period are exempt.[10] In contrast to investment companies (discussed later in

---

8. 15 U.S.C. Section 77c(b).

9. 17 C.F.R. Sections 230.251–230.263.

10. 17 C.F.R. Section 230.504. Rule 504 is the exemption used by most small businesses, but that could change under new SEC Rule 1001. This rule permits, under certain circumstances, "testing the waters" for offerings of up to $5 million *per transaction*. These offerings can be made only to "qualified purchasers" (knowledgeable, sophisticated investors), though.

EXHIBIT 21–5 EXEMPTIONS UNDER THE 1933 SECURITIES ACT

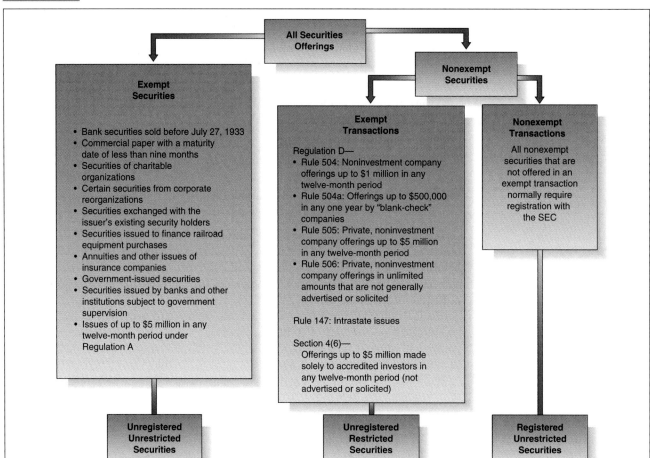

this chapter), noninvestment companies are firms that are not engaged primarily in the business of investing or trading in securities.

Rule 504a. Offerings up to $500,000 in any one year by so-called blank-check companies—companies with no specific business plans except to locate and acquire currently unknown businesses or opportunities—are exempt if no general solicitation or advertising is used; the SEC is notified of the sales; and precaution is taken against nonexempt, unregistered resales.[11] The limits on advertising and unregistered resales do not apply if the offering is made solely in states that provide for registration and disclosure and the securities are sold in compliance with those provisions.[12]

---

11. Precautions to be taken against nonexempt, unregistered resales include asking the investor whether he or she is buying the securities for others; before the sale, disclosing to each purchaser in writing that the securities are unregistered and thus cannot be resold, except in an exempt transaction, without first being registered; and indicating on the certificates that the securities are unregistered and restricted.
12. 17 C.F.R. Section 230.504a.

ACCREDITED INVESTOR
In the context of securities offerings, "sophisticated" investors, such as banks, insurance companies, investment companies, the issuer's executive officers and directors, and persons whose income or net worth exceeds certain limits.

Rule 505. Private, noninvestment company offerings up to $5 million in any twelve-month period are exempt, regardless of the number of **accredited investors** (banks, insurance companies, investment companies, the issuer's executive officers and directors, and persons whose income or net worth exceeds a certain threshold), so long as there are no more than thirty-five unaccredited investors; no general solicitation or advertising is used; the SEC is notified of the sales; and precaution is taken against nonexempt, unregistered resales. If the sale involves *any* unaccredited investors, *all* investors must be given material information about the offering company, its business, and the securities before the sale. Unlike Rule 506 (discussed next), Rule 505 includes no requirement that the issuer believe each unaccredited investor "has such knowledge and experience in financial and business matters that he [or she] is capable of evaluating the merits and the risks of the prospective investment."[13]

Rule 506. Private offerings in unlimited amounts that are not generally solicited or advertised are exempt if the SEC is notified of the sales; precaution is taken against nonexempt, unregistered resales; and the issuer believes that each unaccredited investor has sufficient knowledge or experience in financial matters to be capable of evaluating the investment's merits and risks. There may be no more than thirty-five unaccredited investors, but there are no limits on the number of accredited investors. If there are *any* unaccredited investors, the issuer must provide to *all* purchasers material information about itself, its business, and the securities before the sale.[14]

This exemption is perhaps most important to those firms that want to raise funds through the sale of securities without registering them. It is often referred to as the *private placement* exemption because it exempts "transactions not involving any public offering."[15] This provision applies to private offerings to a limited number of persons who are sufficiently sophisticated and able to assume the risk of the investment (and who thus have no need for federal registration protection). It also applies to private offerings to similarly situated institutional investors.

KEEP IN MIND An investor can be "sophisticated" by virtue of his or her education and experience or by investing through a knowledgeable, experienced representative.

Small Offerings—Section 4(6) Under Section 4(6) of the Securities Act of 1933, an offer made *solely* to accredited investors is exempt if its amount is not more than $5 million. Any number of accredited investors may participate, but no unaccredited investors may do so. No general solicitation or advertising may be used; the SEC must be notified of all sales; and precaution must be taken against nonexempt, unregistered resales. Precaution is necessary because these are *restricted* securities and may be resold only by registration or in an exempt transaction.[16] (The securities purchased and sold by most people who deal in stock are called, in contrast, *unrestricted* securities.)

Intrastate Issues—Rule 147 Also exempt are intrastate transactions involving purely local offerings.[17] This exemption applies to most offerings that are restricted to residents of the state in which the issuing company is organized and doing business. For nine months after the last sale, virtually no resales may be made to nonresidents, and precautions must be taken against this possibility. These offerings remain subject to applicable laws in the state of issue.

---

13. 17 C.F.R. Section 230.505.
14. 17 C.F.R. Section 230.506.
15. 15 U.S.C. Section 77d(2).
16. 15 U.S.C. Section 77d(6).
17. 15 U.S.C. Section 77c(a)(11); 17 C.F.R. Section 230.147.

Resales   Most securities can be resold without registration (although some resales may be subject to restrictions, as discussed above in connection with specific exemptions). The Securities Act of 1933 provides exemptions for resales by most persons other than issuers or underwriters. The average investor who sells shares of stock does not have to file a registration statement with the SEC. Resales of restricted securities acquired under Rule 504a, Rule 505, Rule 506, or Section 4(6), however, trigger the registration requirements unless the party selling them complies with Rule 144 or Rule 144A. These rules are sometimes referred to as "safe harbors."

Rule 144.   Rule 144 exempts restricted securities from registration on resale if there is adequate current public information about the issuer, the person selling the securities has owned them for at least one year, they are sold in certain limited amounts in unsolicited brokers' transactions, and the SEC is given notice of the resale.[18] "Adequate current public information" refers to the reports that certain companies are required to file under the Securities Exchange Act of 1934. A person who has owned the securities for at least three years is subject to none of these requirements, unless the person is an affiliate. An *affiliate* is one who controls, is controlled by, or is in common control with the issuer. Sales of *nonrestricted* securities by an affiliate are also subject to the requirements for an exemption under Rule 144 (except that the affiliate need not have owned the securities for at least two years).

Rule 144A.   Securities that at the time of issue are not of the same class as securities listed on a national securities exchange or quoted in a U.S. automated interdealer quotation system may be resold under Rule 144A.[19] They may be sold only to a qualified institutional buyer (an institution, such as an insurance company, an investment company, or a bank, that owns and invests at least $100 million in securities). The seller must take reasonable steps to ensure that the buyer knows that the seller is relying on the exemption under Rule 144A. A sample restricted stock certificate is shown in Exhibit 21–6.

CONTRAST   Securities do not have to be held for two years to be exempt from registration on a resale under Rule 144A, as they do under Rule 144.

VIOLATIONS OF THE 1933 ACT

As mentioned, the SEC has the power to investigate and bring civil enforcement actions against companies that violate federal securities laws. It is a violation of the Securities Act of 1933 to intentionally defraud investors by misrepresenting or omitting facts in a registration statement or prospectus. Liability is also imposed on those who are negligent for not discovering the fraud. Selling securities before the effective date of the registration statement or under an exemption for which the securities do not qualify results in liability.

Criminal violations are prosecuted by the Department of Justice. Violators may be fined up to $10,000, imprisoned for up to five years, or both. The SEC is authorized to seek civil sanctions against those who willfully violate the 1933 act. It can request an injunction to prevent further sales of the securities involved or ask the court to grant other relief, such as an order to a violator to refund profits. Those parties who purchase securities and suffer harm as a result of false or omitted statements may also bring suits in a federal court to recover their losses and other damages.

---

18. 17 C.F.R. Section 230.144.
19. 17 C.F.R. Section 230.144A.

EXHIBIT 21–6 A SAMPLE RESTRICTED STOCK CERTIFICATE

Securities Exchange Act of 1934

The Securities Exchange Act of 1934 provides for the regulation and registration of securities exchanges, brokers, dealers, and national securities associations such as the National Association of Securities Dealers (NASD). The SEC regulates the markets in which securities are traded by maintaining a continuous disclosure system for all corporations with securities on the securities exchanges and for those companies that have assets in excess of $10 million and five hundred or more shareholders. These corporations are referred to as Section 12 companies because they are required to register their securities under Section 12 of the 1934 act.

The act also authorizes the SEC to regulate proxy solicitations for voting and to engage in market surveillance to deter undesirable market practices such as fraud, market manipulation, and misrepresentation.

SECTION 10(b), SEC RULE 10b-5, AND INSIDER TRADING

SEC RULE 10b-5
A rule of the Securities and Exchange Commission that makes it unlawful, in connection with the purchase or sale of any security, to make any untrue statement of a material fact or to omit a material fact if such omission causes the statement to be misleading.

Section 10(b) is one of the most important sections of the Securities Exchange Act of 1934. This section proscribes the use of any manipulative or deceptive device in violation of SEC rules and regulations. Among the rules that the SEC has promulgated pursuant to the 1934 act is **SEC Rule 10b-5,** which prohibits the commission of fraud in connection with the purchase or sale of any security.

A former executive of Enron Corporation leaves the federal courthouse in Houston in May 2004 after pleading guilty to an insider-trading charge. What is the reasoning behind laws that make insider trading illegal? (AP Photo/ Pat Sullivan)

INSIDER TRADING
The purchase or sale of securities on the basis of information that has not been made available to the public.

One of the major goals of Section 10(b) and SEC Rule 10b-5 is to prevent so-called **insider trading.** Because of their positions, corporate directors and officers often obtain advance inside information that can affect the future market value of the corporate stock. Obviously, their positions give them a trading advantage over the general public and shareholders. The 1934 Securities Exchange Act defines inside information and extends liability to officers and directors for taking advantage of such information in their personal transactions when they know that it is unavailable to the persons with whom they are dealing.

Section 10(b) of the 1934 act and SEC Rule 10b-5 cover not only corporate officers, directors, and majority shareholders but also any persons having access to or receiving information of a nonpublic nature on which trading is based.

Disclosure under SEC Rule 10b-5   Any material omission or misrepresentation of material facts in connection with the purchase or sale of a security may violate not only the Securities Act of 1933 but also the antifraud provisions of Section 10(b) and SEC Rule 10b-5 of the 1934 act. The key to liability (which can be civil or criminal) under Section 10(b) and SEC Rule 10b-5 is whether the insider's information is *material.*

Examples of Material Facts Calling for Disclosure.   The following are some examples of material facts calling for disclosure under the rule:

1. Fraudulent trading in the company stock by a broker-dealer.
2. A dividend change (whether up or down).
3. A contract for the sale of corporate assets.
4. A new discovery, a new process, or a new product.
5. A significant change in the firm's financial condition.
6. Potential litigation against the company.

Note that any one of these facts, by itself, will not automatically be considered a material fact. Rather, it will be regarded as a material fact if it is significant enough that it will likely affect an investor's decision as to whether to purchase or sell certain securities.

The following is one of the landmark cases interpreting SEC Rule 10b-5. The SEC sued Texas Gulf Sulphur Company for issuing a misleading press release. The release underestimated the magnitude and value of a mineral discovery. The SEC also sued several of Texas Gulf Sulphur's directors, officers, and employees under SEC Rule 10b-5 for purchasing large amounts of the corporate stock prior to the announcement of the corporation's rich ore discovery.

LANDMARK AND CLASSIC CASES

CASE 21.2 ◼ SEC v. Texas Gulf Sulphur Co.

United States Court of Appeals,
Second Circuit, 1968.
401 F.2d 833.

HISTORICAL AND ENVIRONMENTAL SETTING
No court has ever held that every buyer or seller is entitled to all of the information relating to all of the circumstances in every stock transaction. By the mid-1950s,

however, significant understatement of the value of the assets of a company had been held to be materially misleading.[a] *In 1957, the Texas Gulf Sulphur Company (TGS) began exploring for minerals in eastern Canada. In March 1959, aerial geophysical surveys were conducted over more than fifteen thousand square miles of the area.*

a. *Speed v. Transamerica Corp.,* 99 F.Supp. 808 (D.Del. 1951).

CASE 21.2—Continued

The operations revealed numerous and extraordinary variations in the conductivity of the rock, which indicated a remarkable concentration of commercially exploitable minerals. One site of such variations was near Timmins, Ontario. On October 29 and 30, 1963, a ground survey of the site near Timmins indicated a need to drill for further evaluation.

FACTS On November 12, 1963, the Texas Gulf Sulphur Company drilled a hole that appeared to yield a core with an exceedingly high mineral content, although further drilling would be necessary to establish whether there was enough ore to be mined commercially. TGS kept secret the results of the core sample. After learning of the ore discovery, officers and employees of the company made substantial purchases of TGS's stock or accepted stock options. On April 11, 1964, an unauthorized report of the mineral find appeared in the newspapers. On the following day, April 12, TGS issued a press release that played down the discovery and stated that it was too early to tell whether the ore finding would be a significant one. Later on, TGS announced a strike of at least twenty-five million tons of ore. The news led to a substantial increase in the price of TGS stock. The Securities and Exchange Commission (SEC) brought suit in a federal district court against the officers and employees of TGS for violating the insider-trading prohibition of SEC Rule 10b-5. The officers and employees argued that the prohibition did not apply. They reasoned that the information on which they had traded was not material, as the mine had not been commercially proved. The court held that most of the defendants had not violated SEC Rule 10b-5, and the SEC appealed.

ISSUE Had the officers and employees of TGS violated SEC Rule 10b-5 by purchasing the stock, even though they did not know the full extent and profit potential of the mine at the time they purchased the stock?

DECISION Yes. The federal appellate court reversed the lower court's decision and remanded the case to the trial court, holding that the employees and officers had violated SEC Rule 10b-5's prohibition against insider trading.

REASON For SEC Rule 10b-5 purposes, the test of materiality is whether the information would affect the judgment of reasonable investors. Reasonable investors include speculative as well as conservative investors. "[A] major factor in determining whether the *   *   * discovery [of the ore] was a material fact is the importance attached to the drilling results by those who knew about it. *   *   * [T]he timing by those who knew of it of their stock purchases and their purchases of short-term calls [rights to buy shares at a specified price within a specified time period]—purchases in some cases by individuals who had never before purchased calls or even TGS stock—virtually compels the inference that the insiders were influenced by the drilling results. *   *   * We hold, therefore, that all transactions in TGS stock or calls by individuals apprised of the drilling results *   *   * were made in violation of Rule 10b-5."

COMMENTS *This landmark case affirmed the principle that the test of whether information is "material," for SEC Rule 10b-5 purposes, is whether it would affect the judgment of reasonable investors. The corporate insiders' purchases of stock and stock options (rights to purchase stock) indicated that they were influenced by the drilling results and that the information about the drilling results was material. The courts continue to cite this case when applying SEC Rule 10b-5 to cases of alleged insider trading.*

RELEVANT WEB SITES *To locate information on the Web concerning the SEC v. Texas Gulf Suphur Co. decision, go to this text's Web site at* **http://blt. westbuslaw.com**, *select "Chapter 21," and click on "URLs for Landmarks."*

The Private Securities Litigation Reform Act of 1995. One of the unintended effects of SEC Rule 10b-5 was to deter the disclosure of some material information, such as financial forecasts. To understand why, consider an example. ■ EXAMPLE 21.1 A company announces that its projected earnings in a certain time period will be X amount. It turns out that the forecast is wrong. The earnings are in fact much lower, and the price of the company's stock is affected—negatively. The shareholders then bring a class-action suit against the company, alleging that the directors violated SEC Rule 10b-5 by disclosing misleading financial information. ■

Wall Street in New York has become nearly synonymous with securities trading. What federal laws regulate the purchase and sale of securities? Why is such regulation necessary? (Brand X Pictures)

In an attempt to rectify this problem and promote disclosure, Congress passed the Private Securities Litigation Reform Act of 1995. Among other things, the act provides a "safe harbor" for publicly held companies that make forward-looking statements, such as financial forecasts. Those who make such statements are protected against liability for securities fraud as long as the statements are accompanied by "meaningful cautionary statements identifying important factors that could cause actual results to differ materially from those in the forward-looking statement."[20]

After the 1995 act was passed, a number of securities class-action suits were filed in state courts to skirt the requirements of the 1995 federal act. In response to this problem, Congress passed the Securities Litigation Uniform Standards Act of 1998. The act placed stringent limits on the ability of plaintiffs to bring class-action suits in state courts against firms whose securities are traded on national stock exchanges.

Applicability of SEC Rule 10b-5   SEC Rule 10b-5 applies in virtually all cases concerning the trading of securities, whether on organized exchanges, in over-the-counter markets, or in private transactions. The rule covers, among other things, notes, bonds, agreements to form a corporation, and joint-venture agreements. Generally, it covers just about any form of security. It is immaterial whether a firm has securities registered under the 1933 act for the 1934 act to apply.

Although SEC Rule 10b-5 is applicable only when the requisites of federal jurisdiction—such as the use of the mails, of stock exchange facilities, or of any instrumentality of interstate commerce—are present, virtually no commercial transaction can be completed without such contact. In addition, the states have corporate securities laws, many of which include provisions similar to SEC Rule 10b-5.

ETHICAL ISSUE 21.2

Should insider trading be legal? SEC Rule 10b-5 has broad applicability. As will be discussed shortly, the rule covers not only corporate insiders but even "outsiders"—those who receive and trade on tips received from insiders. Investigating and prosecuting violations of SEC Rule 10b-5 is costly, both for the government and for those accused of insider trading. Some people doubt that such extensive regulation is necessary and even contend that insider trading should be legal. Would there be any benefit from legalizing insider trading? To evaluate this question, review the facts in *SEC v. Texas Gulf Sulphur Co.* (Case 21.2 in this chapter). If insider trading had been legal, the discovery of the ore sample would probably have caused many more company insiders to purchase stock. Consequently, the price of Texas Gulf's stock would have increased fairly quickly. These increases presumably would have attracted the attention of outside investors, who would have learned sooner that something positive had happened to the company and would thus have had the opportunity to purchase the stock. The higher demand for the stock would have more quickly translated into higher prices for the stock and hence, perhaps, have resulted in a more efficient capital market. ■

Outsiders and SEC Rule 10b-5   The traditional insider-trading case involves true insiders—corporate officers, directors, and majority shareholders who have access to (and trade on) inside information. Increasingly, liability under Section 10(b) of the 1934 act and SEC Rule 10b-5 is being extended to include certain "outsiders"—those persons who trade on inside information acquired indirectly. Two theories have been developed under which outsiders may be held liable for insider trading: the *tipper/tippee theory* and the *misappropriation theory*.

---

20. 15 U.S.C. Sections 77z-2, 78u-5.

TIPPEE
A person who receives inside information.

Tipper/Tippee Theory.   Anyone who acquires inside information as a result of a corporate insider's breach of his or her fiduciary duty can be liable under SEC Rule 10b-5. This liability extends to **tippees** (those who receive "tips" from insiders) and even remote tippees (tippees of tippees).

The key to liability under this theory is that the inside information must be obtained as a result of someone's breach of a fiduciary duty to the corporation whose shares are involved in the trading. The tippee is liable under this theory only if there is a breach of a duty not to disclose inside information, the disclosure is in exchange for personal benefit, and the tippee knows (or should know) of this breach and benefits from it.[21]

Misappropriation Theory.   Liability for insider trading may also be established under the misappropriation theory. This theory holds that if an individual wrongfully obtains (misappropriates) inside information and trades on it for her or his personal gain, then the individual should be held liable because, in essence, the individual stole information rightfully belonging to another.

The misappropriation theory has been controversial because it significantly extends the reach of SEC Rule 10b-5 to outsiders who would not ordinarily be deemed fiduciaries of the corporations in whose stock they trade. The United States Supreme Court, however, has held that liability under SEC Rule 10b-5 can be based on the misappropriation theory.[22]

INSIDER REPORTING AND TRADING—SECTION 16(b)

For information on investor protection, including answers to frequently asked questions on the topic of securities fraud, go to **http://www.securitieslaw.com**.

Officers, directors, and certain large stockholders[23] of Section 12 corporations (corporations that are required to register their securities under Section 12 of the 1934 act) must file reports with the SEC concerning their ownership and trading of the corporations' securities.[24] To discourage such insiders from using nonpublic information about their companies for their personal benefit in the stock market, Section 16(b) of the 1934 act provides for the recapture by the corporation of all profits realized by an insider on any purchase and sale or sale and purchase of the corporation's stock within any six-month period.[25] It is irrelevant whether the insider actually uses inside information; *all such short-swing profits must be returned to the corporation.*

Section 16(b) applies not only to stock but also to warrants, options, and securities convertible into stock. In addition, the courts have fashioned complex rules for determining profits. Note that the SEC exempts a number of transactions under Rule 16b-3.[26] For all of these reasons, corporate insiders are wise to seek specialized counsel prior to trading in the corporation's stock. Exhibit 21–7 on the following page compares the effects of SEC Rule 10b-5 and Section 16(b).

---

21. See, for example, *Chiarella v. United States,* 445 U.S. 222, 100 S.Ct. 1108, 63 L.Ed.2d 348 (1980); and *Dirks v. SEC,* 463 U.S. 646, 103 S.Ct. 3255, 77 L.Ed.2d 911 (1983).
22. *United States v. O'Hagan,* 521 U.S. 642, 117 S.Ct. 2199, 138 L.Ed.2d 724 (1997).
23. Those stockholders owning 10 percent of the class of equity securities registered under Section 12 of the 1934 act.
24. 15 U.S.C. Section 78*l*.
25. A person who expects the price of a particular stock to decline can realize profits by "selling short"—selling at a high price and repurchasing later at a lower price to cover the "short sale."
26. 17 C.F.R. Section 240.16b-3.

EXHIBIT 21–7 COMPARISON OF COVERAGE, APPLICATION, AND
LIABILITIES UNDER SEC RULE 10b-5 AND SECTION 16(b)

AREA OF COMPARISON	SEC RULE 10b-5	SECTION 16(b)
What is the subject matter of the transaction?	Any security (does not have to be registered).	Any security (does not have to be registered).
What transactions are covered?	Purchase or sale.	Short-swing purchase and sale or short-swing sale and purchase.
Who is subject to liability?	Virtually anyone with inside information under a duty to disclose—including officers, directors, controlling stockholders, and tippees.	Officers, directors, and certain 10-percent stockholders.
Is omission or misrepresentation necessary for liability?	Yes.	No.
Are there any exempt transactions?	No.	Yes, there are a variety of exemptions.
Is direct dealing with the party necessary?	No.	No.
Who may bring an action?	A person transacting with an insider, the SEC, or a purchaser or seller damaged by a wrongful act.	A corporation or a shareholder by derivative action.

PROXY STATEMENTS

A proxy statement. Who regulates the content of proxy statements, and how? (Courtesy of Prudential Financial)

Section 14(a) of the Securities Exchange Act of 1934 regulates the solicitation of proxies from shareholders of Section 12 companies. The SEC regulates the content of proxy statements (proxies were discussed in Chapter 20). A proxy statement is sent to shareholders when corporate officials are requesting authority to vote on behalf of the shareholders in a particular election on specified issues. Whoever solicits a proxy must fully and accurately disclose in the proxy statement all of the facts that are pertinent to the matter on which the shareholders are to vote. SEC Rule 14a-9 is similar to the antifraud provisions of SEC Rule 10b-5. Remedies for violations are extensive; they range from injunctions that prevent a vote from being taken to monetary damages.

VIOLATIONS OF THE 1934 ACT

Violations of Section 10(b) of the Securities Exchange Act of 1934 and SEC Rule 10b-5 include insider trading. This is a criminal offense, with criminal penalties. Violators of these laws may also be subject to civil liability. For any sanctions to be imposed, however, there must be *scienter*—the violator must have had an intent to defraud or knowledge of her or his misconduct (see Chapter 8). *Scienter* can be proved by showing that a defendant made false statements or wrongfully failed to disclose material facts.

Violations of Section 16(b) include the sale by insiders of stock acquired less than six months before the sale. These violations are subject to civil sanctions. Liability under Section 16(b) is strict liability. Thus, liability is imposed regardless of whether *scienter* or negligence existed.

Criminal Penalties   For violations of Section 10(b) and Rule 10b-5, an individual may be fined up to $5 million, imprisoned for up to twenty years, or both.[27] A partnership or a corporation may be fined up to $25 million. Under Section 807 of the Sarbanes-Oxley Act of 2002, for a willful violation of the 1934 act the violator may, in addition to being subject to a fine, be imprisoned for up to twenty-five years.

In a criminal prosecution under the securities laws, a jury is not allowed to speculate on whether a defendant acted willfully—there can be no reasonable doubt that the defendant knew he or she was acting wrongfully. The issue in the following case was whether, in light of this principle, there was enough evidence that Martha Stewart, founder of a well-known media and homemaking empire, intended to deceive investors to present the matter to a jury.

---

27. These numbers reflect the increased penalties imposed by the Sarbanes-Oxley Act of 2002.

CASE 21.3 ▦ **United States v. Stewart**

United States District Court,
Southern District of New York, 2004.
305 F.Supp.2d 368.

FACTS Samuel Waksal, the chief executive officer of ImClone Systems, Inc., a biotechnology company, was a client of stockbroker Peter Bacanovic. Bacanovic's other clients included Martha Stewart, then the chief executive officer of Martha Stewart Living Omnimedia (MSLO). On December 27, 2001, Waksal began selling his ImClone stock. Bacanovic allegedly had Stewart informed of Waksal's sales, and she also sold her ImClone shares. The next day, ImClone announced that the Food and Drug Administration had rejected the company's application for approval of its leading product, a medication called Erbitux. The government began to investigate Stewart's ImClone trades, the media began to report on the investigation, and the value of MSLO stock began to drop. In June 2002, at a "Mid-Year Media Review" conference attended by investment professionals and investors, Stewart said that she had previously agreed with Bacanovic to sell her ImClone stock if the price fell to $60 per share. "I have nothing to add on this matter today. And I'm here to talk about our terrific company." Her statements were followed by a forty-minute presentation on MSLO. Subsequently, Stewart was charged with, among other things, fraud in connection with the purchase and sale of MSLO securities in violation of the Securities Exchange Act of 1934. She filed a motion for a judgment of acquittal on this charge.

ISSUE Could a reasonable juror find beyond a reasonable doubt that Stewart lied to influence the market for the securities of her company?

DECISION No. The court concluded that in Stewart's case, "to find the essential element of criminal intent beyond a reasonable doubt, a rational juror would have to speculate."[a]

REASON The government argued that Stewart was aware that the negative publicity about her ImClone trade was having an impact on the market value of MSLO securities and that she deliberately directed her statement to investors. The government pointed out that Stewart was aware that she was speaking to analysts and investors at the conference and began by saying that she was embarking on a topic about which her audience was "probably interested." According to the government, Stewart's awareness of her audience (investors and analysts) and the timing of her statement as the price of MSLO stock was falling were sufficient to permit a jury to infer that she intended to deceive the investors when she made the statement. The court reasoned, however, that

---

a. Stewart was later convicted on other charges related to her ImClone trades and was sentenced to five months in prison and five months under house arrest.

(Continued)

CASE 21.3—Continued

"any inference to be drawn from the makeup of the audience must also take into account the fact that Stewart was only one of several representatives of MSLO, and that MSLO was only one of several corporations making presentations at the conference. * * * There is no evidence that the negative publicity about ImClone influenced Stewart's decision to attend and take advantage of a platform from which to reach investors directly. To the contrary, her statement—a very brief portion of a much longer presentation—indicates otherwise."

FOR CRITICAL ANALYSIS—Social Consideration
How does the scienter, *or intent, requirement in the context of criminal securities fraud differ from its counterpart in the context of civil securities fraud?*

Civil Sanctions   The SEC can bring suit in a federal district court against anyone violating or aiding in a violation of the 1934 act or SEC rules by purchasing or selling a security while in the possession of material nonpublic information.[28] The violation must occur on or through the facilities of a national securities exchange or from or through a broker or dealer. Transactions pursuant to a public offering by an issuer of securities are excepted. The court may assess as a penalty as much as triple the profits gained or the loss avoided by the guilty party. Profit or loss is defined as "the difference between the purchase or sale price of the security and the value of that security as measured by the trading price of the security at a reasonable period of time after public dissemination of the nonpublic information."[29]

The Insider Trading and Securities Fraud Enforcement Act of 1988 enlarged the class of persons who may be subject to civil liability for insider-trading violations. This act also gave the SEC authority to award **bounty payments** (rewards given by government officials for acts beneficial to the state) to persons providing information leading to the prosecution of insider-trading violations.[30]

Private parties may also sue violators of Section 10(b) and Rule 10b-5. A private party may obtain rescission (cancellation) of a contract to buy securities or damages to the extent of the violator's illegal profits. Those found liable have a right to seek contribution from those who share responsibility for the violations, including accountants, attorneys, and corporations.[31] For violations of Section 16(b), a corporation can bring an action to recover the short-swing profits.

BOUNTY PAYMENT
A reward (payment) given to a person or persons who perform a certain service, such as informing legal authorities of illegal actions.

▦ The Regulation of Investment Companies

Investment companies, and mutual funds in particular, grew rapidly after World War II. **Investment companies** act on behalf of many smaller shareholders by buying a large portfolio of securities and professionally managing that portfolio. A **mutual fund** is a specific type of investment company that continually buys or sells to investors shares of ownership in a portfolio. Such companies are regulated by the Investment Company Act of 1940,[32] which provides for SEC regulation of their

INVESTMENT COMPANY
A company that acts on behalf of many smaller shareholders/owners by buying a large portfolio of securities and professionally managing that portfolio.

MUTUAL FUND
A specific type of investment company that continually buys or sells to investors shares of ownership in a portfolio.

---

28. The Insider Trading Sanctions Act of 1984. 15 U.S.C. Section 78u(d)(2)(A).
29. 15 U.S.C. Section 78u(d)(2)(C).
30. 15 U.S.C. Section 78u-1.
31. Note that a private cause of action under Section 10(b) and SEC Rule 10b-5 cannot be brought against accountants, attorneys, and others who "aid and abet" violations of the act. Only the SEC can bring actions against so-called aiders and abettors. See *SEC v. Fehn,* 97 F.3d 1276 (9th Cir. 1996).
32. 15 U.S.C. Sections 80a-1 to 64.

activities. The act was expanded by the 1970 amendments to the Investment Company Act. Further minor changes were made in the Securities Act Amendments of 1975 and in later years.

DEFINITION OF AN INVESTMENT COMPANY

For the purposes of the act, an *investment company* is any entity that (1) is engaged primarily "in the business of investing, reinvesting, or trading in securities" or (2) is engaged in such business and has more than 40 percent of its assets in investment securities. Excluded from coverage by the act are banks, insurance companies, savings and loan associations, finance companies, oil and gas drilling firms, charitable foundations, tax-exempt pension funds, and other special types of institutions, such as closely held corporations.

REGISTRATION AND REPORTING REQUIREMENTS

The 1940 act requires that every investment company register with the SEC by filing a notification of registration. Each year, registered investment companies must file reports with the SEC. To safeguard company assets, all securities must be held in the custody of a bank or stock exchange member, which must follow strict procedures established by the SEC.

RESTRICTIONS ON INVESTMENT COMPANIES

The 1940 act also imposes restrictions on the activities of investment companies and persons connected with them. For example, investment companies are not allowed to purchase securities on the margin (pay only part of the total price, borrowing the rest), sell short (sell shares not yet owned), or participate in joint trading accounts. In addition, no dividends may be paid from any source other than accumulated, undistributed net income.

■■ State Securities Laws

BE AWARE Federal securities laws do not take priority over state securities laws.

Today, all states have their own corporate securities laws, or "blue sky laws," that regulate the offer and sale of securities within individual state borders. (As mentioned in Chapter 8, the phrase *blue sky laws* dates to a 1917 decision by the United States Supreme Court in which the Court declared that the purpose of such laws was to prevent "speculative schemes which have no more basis than so many feet of 'blue sky.'"[33]) Article 8 of the Uniform Commercial Code, which has been adopted by all of the states, also imposes various requirements relating to the purchase and sale of securities.

REQUIREMENTS UNDER STATE SECURITIES LAWS

Despite some differences in philosophy, all state blue sky laws have certain features. Typically, state laws have disclosure requirements and antifraud provisions, many of which are patterned after Section 10(b) of the Securities Exchange Act of 1934 and SEC Rule 10b-5. State laws also provide for the registration or qualification of securities offered or issued for sale within the state and impose disclosure

---

33. *Hall v. Geiger-Jones Co.*, 242 U.S. 539, 37 S.Ct. 217, 61 L.Ed. 480 (1917).

requirements. Unless an exemption from registration is applicable, issuers must register or qualify their stock with the appropriate state official, often called a *corporations commissioner.* Additionally, most state securities laws regulate securities brokers and dealers.

CONCURRENT REGULATION

State securities laws apply mainly to intrastate transactions. Since the adoption of the 1933 and 1934 federal securities acts, the state and federal governments have regulated securities concurrently. Issuers must comply with both federal and state securities laws, and exemptions from federal law are not exemptions from state laws.

The dual federal and state system has not always worked well, particularly during the early 1990s, when the securities markets underwent considerable expansion. In response, Congress passed the National Securities Markets Improvement Act of 1996, which eliminated some of the duplicate regulations and gave the SEC exclusive power to regulate most national securities activities. The National Conference of Commissioners on Uniform State Laws then substantially revised the Uniform Securities Act and recommended it to the states for adoption in 2002. Unlike the previous version of this law, the new act is designed to coordinate state and federal securities regulation and enforcement efforts. Since 2002, six states have adopted the Uniform Securities Act, and a number of other states are considering adoption.[34]

◼ Online Securities Offerings and Disclosures

The Spring Street Brewing Company, headquartered in New York, made history when it became the first company to attempt to sell securities via the Internet. Through its online initial public offering (IPO), which ended in early 1996, Spring Street raised about $1.6 million—without having to pay any commissions to brokers or underwriters. The offering was made pursuant to Regulation A, which, as mentioned earlier in this chapter, allows small-business issuers to use a simplified registration procedure.

Such online IPOs are particularly attractive to small companies and start-up ventures that may find it difficult to raise capital from institutional investors or through underwriters. By making the offering online under Regulation A, the company can avoid both commissions and the costly and time-consuming filings required for a traditional IPO under federal and state law.

REGULATIONS GOVERNING ONLINE SECURITIES OFFERINGS

One of the early questions posed by online offerings was whether the delivery of securities *information* via the Internet met the requirements of the 1933 Securities Act, which traditionally were applied to the delivery of paper documents. In an interpretive release issued in 1995, the SEC stated that "[t]he use of electronic media should be at least an equal alternative

The home page of E*Trade. Online trading through a firm such as E*Trade does not involve personal contact with a broker. (Courtesy of E-Trade Financial Group)

---

34. At the time this book went to press, the 2002 Uniform Securities Act had been adopted in Idaho, Iowa, Kansas, Missouri, Oklahoma, and South Dakota. Adoption legislation was pending in Alabama, Alaska, Nebraska, the U.S. Virgin Islands, Vermont, and Virginia. You can find current information on state adoptions at **http://www.nccusl.org**.

to the use of paper-based media" and that anything that can be delivered in paper form under the current securities laws might also be delivered in electronic form.[35]

Basically, there has been no change in the substantive law of disclosure; only the delivery vehicle has changed. When the Internet is used for delivery of a prospectus, the same rules apply as for the delivery of a paper prospectus. Once the three requirements listed below have been satisfied, the prospectus has been successfully delivered.

1 *Timely and adequate notice of the delivery of information is required.* Hosting a prospectus on a Web site does not constitute adequate notice, but separate e-mails or even postcards will satisfy the SEC's notice requirements.

2 *The online communication system must be easily accessible.* This is very simple to do today because virtually anyone interested in purchasing securities has access to the Web.

3 *Some evidence of delivery must be created.* This requirement is relatively easy to satisfy. Those making online offerings can require an e-mail return receipt verification of any materials sent electronically.

POTENTIAL LIABILITY CREATED BY ONLINE OFFERING MATERIALS

Every printed prospectus indicates that only the information given in the prospectus can be used in conjunction with making an investment decision in the securities offered. The same wording, of course, appears on Web-based offerings. What happens if an electronic prospectus contains information that conflicts with the information provided in a printed prospectus? Will such an error render the registration statement ineffective? See this chapter's *Adapting the Law to the Online Environment* feature on the following page for a discussion of a case involving this issue.

Hyperlinks to Other Web Pages   Those who create such Web-based offerings may be tempted to insert hyperlinks to other Web pages. They may include links to other sites that have analyzed the future prospects of the company, the products and services sold by the company, or the offering itself. To avoid potential liability, however, online offerors (the entities making the offerings) need to exercise caution when including such hyperlinks.

 EXAMPLE 21.2 Suppose that a hyperlink goes to an analyst's Web page that makes optimistic statements concerning the financial outlook of the offering company. Further suppose that after the IPO, the stock price falls. By including the hyperlink on its Web site, the offering company is impliedly supporting the information presented on the linked page. If it turns out that the company knew the statements made on the analyst's Web page were false or misleading, the company may be liable for violating sections of the Securities Exchange Act of 1934.[36]

Regulation D Offerings   Potential problems may also occur with some Regulation D offerings, if the offeror places the offering circular on its Web site for general consumption by anybody on the Internet. Because Regulation D offerings are private placements, general solicitation is restricted. If anyone can have access to the offering circular on the Web, the Regulation D exemption may be disqualified.

---

35. "Use of Electronic Media for Delivery Purposes," Securities Act Release No. 33-7233 (October 6, 1995). The rules governing the use of electronic transmissions for delivery purposes were subsequently confirmed in Securities Act Release No. 33-7289 (May 9, 1996) and expanded in Securities Act Release No. 33-7856 (April 28, 2000).

36. See, for example, *In re Syntex Corp. Securities Litigation,* 95 F.3d. 922 (9th Cir. 1996), involving alleged violations of Sections 10(b) and 20(a) of the 1934 act.

ADAPTING THE LAW TO THE ONLINE ENVIRONMENT

Will Inaccurate Information in an Electronic Prospectus Invalidate the Registration?

Many companies now submit registration statements, prospectuses, and other information to the Securities and Exchange Commission (SEC) via the Internet. The SEC's Electronic Data Gathering, Analysis and Retrieval (EDGAR) system then posts much of this information online to inform investors about the corporation, the security being sold, and the risk of investing in that security. Some corporations also send investors a printed prospectus. Theoretically, a corporation should provide the same information in electronic form as it does in a printed prospectus, but practical difficulties can arise in transmitting digital information.

THE PROBLEM WITH GRAPHICS

As anyone who is familiar with the Internet knows, the graphics, images, and audio files created by one computer are not always readable by another computer when they are exchanged online. The SEC has created Rule 304 to deal with this situation.[a] The first part of the rule states that if graphic, image, or audio material in a prospectus cannot be reproduced in an electronic form on EDGAR, the electronic prospectus must include a fair and accurate narrative description of the omitted data. The second part of Rule 304 provides that the graphic, image, and audio material contained in the version of a document delivered to investors is *deemed to be part of the electronic document* filed with the SEC.

As a result, a corporation can have two versions of a prospectus—a print version that contains graphics and an electronic version that describes the information shown in the graphics. What if the summary describing the graphics in an electronic prospectus is inaccurate but the investors received an accurate print version? That was the issue before a federal appellate court in *DeMaria v. Andersen.*[b]

a. 17 C.F.R. Section 232.304.
b. 318 F.3d 170 (2d Cir. 2003).

THE ELECTRONIC PROSPECTUS CONTAINED INACCURACIES

In anticipation of an initial public offering (IPO), ILife.com, Inc., filed a registration statement and a prospectus with the SEC via the EDGAR database. ILife.com also distributed a printed version of the prospectus to the public. The printed prospectus contained a bar graph that provided historical financial information about the company, while the EDGAR prospectus contained a table that summarized the bar graph inaccurately (without mentioning losses). Brian DeMaria and other investors filed a suit against officers of ILife.com. The investors claimed that because of the inaccurate summary, the securities in the IPO were "unregistered" and thus were sold in violation of the Securities Act of 1933. The lower court dismissed the case, and DeMaria appealed.

THE REGISTRATION HELD VALID

Despite the inaccurate summary of the bar graph in the electronic prospectus, the appellate court had no trouble deciding that the securities sold were still registered as required by the Securities Act of 1933. Federal courts are bound to follow the SEC's interpretation of its own regulations unless the interpretations are plainly erroneous. Here, the SEC had filed a brief explaining that because the graphics in the printed prospectus are deemed to be part of the electronic registration statement, it did not matter that the narrative description was inaccurate.

FOR CRITICAL ANALYSIS

Does the part of Rule 304 that deems a printed prospectus to be part of a registration statement completely eliminate liability for any inaccuracies in the electronic materials filed? Why or why not?

ONLINE SECURITIES OFFERINGS BY FOREIGN COMPANIES

Another question raised by Internet transactions has to do with securities offerings by foreign companies. Traditionally, foreign companies have not been able to offer new shares to the U.S. public without first registering them with the SEC. Today, however, anybody in the world can offer shares of stock worldwide via the Web.

The SEC asks that foreign issuers on the Internet implement measures to warn U.S. investors. For example, a foreign company offering shares of stock on the Internet must add a disclaimer on its Web site stating that it has not gone through the registration procedure in the United States. If the SEC believes that a Web site's offering of foreign securities is targeting U.S. residents, it will pursue that company in an attempt to require it to register in the United States.[37]

Online Securities Fraud

A major problem facing the SEC today is how to enforce the antifraud provisions of the securities laws in the online environment. In 1999, in the first cases involving illegal online securities offerings, the SEC filed suit against three individuals for illegally offering securities on an Internet auction site.[38] In essence, all three indicated that their companies would go public soon and attempted to sell unregistered securities via the Web auction site. All of these actions were in violation of Sections 5, 17(a)(1), and 17(a)(3) of the 1933 Securities Act. Since then, the SEC has brought a variety of Internet-related fraud cases, including cases involving investment scams and the manipulation of stock prices in Internet chat rooms.

INVESTMENT SCAMS

An ongoing problem is how to curb online investment scams. One fraudulent investment scheme involved twenty thousand investors, who lost, in all, more than $3 million. Some cases have involved false claims about the earnings potential of home-business programs, such as the claim that one could "earn $4,000 or more each month." Others have concerned claims of "guaranteed credit repair."

USING CHAT ROOMS TO MANIPULATE STOCK PRICES

"Pumping and dumping" occurs when a person who has purchased a particular stock heavily promotes ("pumps up") that stock—thereby creating a great demand for it and driving up its price—and then sells ("dumps") it. The practice of pumping up a stock and then dumping it is quite old. In the online world, however, the process can occur much more quickly and efficiently.

■ **EXAMPLE 21.3** The most famous case in this area involved Jonathan Lebed, a fifteen-year-old stock trader and Internet user from New Jersey. Lebed was the first minor ever charged with securities fraud by the SEC, but it is unlikely that he will be the last. The SEC charged that Lebed bought thinly traded stocks. After purchasing a stock, he would flood stock-related chat rooms, particularly at Yahoo's finance boards, with messages touting the stock's virtues. He used numerous false names so that no one would know that a single person was posting the messages. He would say that the stock was the most "undervalued stock in history" and that its price would jump by 1,000 percent "very soon." When other investors would then buy the stock, the price would go up quickly, and Lebed would sell out. The SEC forced the teenager to repay almost $300,000 in gains plus interest. He was

---

37. International Series Release No. 1125 (March 23, 1998).

38. *In re Davis,* SEC Administrative File No. 3-10080 (October 20, 1999); *In re Haas,* SEC Administrative File No. 3-10081 (October 20, 1999); *In re Sitaras,* SEC Administrative File No. 3-10082 (October 20, 1999).

allowed, however, to keep about $500,000 of the profits he made by trading small-company stocks that he also touted on the Internet. ■

The SEC has been bringing an increasing number of cases against those who manipulate stock prices in this way. Consider that in 1995, such fraud resulted in only six SEC cases. By 2004, the SEC had brought over two hundred actions against online perpetrators of fraudulent stock-price manipulation.

■■ KEY TERMS

accredited investor 653	insider trading 656	SEC Rule 10b-5 655
bond 643	investment company 662	security 641
bond indenture 644	mutual fund 662	stock 643
bounty payment 662	preferred stock 645	tippee 659
common stock 644	red herring 650	tombstone ad 650

CHAPTER SUMMARY ■ Financing, Investor Protection, and Online Securities Offerings

Corporate Financing—Bonds (See pages 643–644.)	Corporate bonds are securities representing *corporate debt*—money borrowed by a corporation. See Exhibit 21–1 for a description of the various types of corporate bonds.

Corporate Financing—Stocks (See pages 644–646.)	Stocks are equity securities issued by a corporation that represent the purchase of ownership in the business firm.
	
	1. *Important characteristics of stockholders—*
	  a. They need not be paid back.
	  b. The stockholder receives dividends only when so voted by the directors.
	  c. Stockholders are the last investors to be paid on dissolution.
	  d. Stockholders vote for management and on major issues.
	
	2. *Types of stock* (see Exhibit 21–3)—
	  a. Common stock—Represents the true ownership of the firm. Holders of common stock share in the control, earning capacity, and net assets of the corporation. Common stockholders carry more risk than preferred stockholders but, if the corporation is successful, are compensated for this risk by greater returns on their investments.
	  b. Preferred stock—Stock whose holders have a preferred status. Preferred stockholders have a stronger position than common shareholders with respect to dividends and claims on assets, but as a result, they will not share in the full prosperity of the firm if it grows successfully over time. The return and risk for preferred stock lie somewhere between those for bonds and those for common stock.

Sarbanes-Oxley Act of 2002 (See pages 646–648.)	Attempts to increase corporate accountability by imposing stricter disclosure requirements and harsher penalties for violations of securities laws.
Securities Act of 1933 (See pages 648–655.)	Prohibits fraud and stabilizes the securities industry by requiring disclosure of all essential information relating to the issuance of stocks to the investing public. 1. *Registration requirements*—Securities, unless exempt, must be registered with the SEC before being offered to the public through the mails or any facility of interstate commerce (including securities exchanges). The *registration statement* must include detailed financial information about the issuing corporation; the intended use of the proceeds of the securities being issued; and certain disclosures, such as interests of directors or officers and pending lawsuits.

CHAPTER SUMMARY	Financing, Investor Protection, and Online Securities Offerings—Continued
Securities Act of 1933—Continued	2. *Prospectus*—A *prospectus* must be provided to investors, describing the security being sold, the issuing corporation, and the risk attaching to the security. 3. *Exemptions*—The SEC has exempted certain offerings from the requirements of the Securities Act of 1933. Exemptions may be determined on the basis of the size of the issue, whether the offering is private or public, and whether advertising is involved. Exemptions are summarized in Exhibit 21–5.

Securities Exchange Act of 1934 (See pages 655–662.)	Provides for the regulation and registration of securities exchanges, brokers, dealers, and national securities associations (such as the NASD). Maintains a continuous disclosure system for all corporations with securities on the securities exchanges and for those companies that have assets in excess of $10 million and five hundred or more shareholders (Section 12 companies).
	
	1. *SEC Rule 10b-5 [under Section 10(b) of the 1934 act]*—
	  a. Applies to insider trading by corporate officers, directors, majority shareholders, and any persons receiving information not available to the public who base their trading on this information.
	  b. Liability for violations can be civil or criminal.
	  c. May be violated by failing to disclose "material facts" that must be disclosed under this rule.
	  d. Applies in virtually all cases concerning the trading of securities—a firm's securities do not have to be registered under the 1933 act for the 1934 act to apply.
	  e. Liability may be based on the tipper/tippee theory or the misappropriation theory.
	  f. Applies only when the requisites of federal jurisdiction (such as use of the mails, stock exchange facilities, or any facility of interstate commerce) are present.
	
	2. *Insider trading [under Section 16(b) of the 1934 act]*—To prevent corporate officers and directors from taking advantage of inside information (information not available to the investing public), the 1934 act requires officers, directors, and shareholders owning 10 percent or more of the issued stock of a corporation to turn over to the corporation all short-term profits (called short-swing profits) realized from the purchase and sale or sale and purchase of corporate stock within any six-month period.
	
	3. *Proxies [under Section 14(a) of the 1934 act]*—The SEC regulates the content of proxy statements sent to shareholders by corporate managers of Section 12 companies who are requesting authority to vote on behalf of the shareholders in a particular election on specified issues. Section 14(a) is essentially a disclosure law, with provisions similar to the antifraud provisions of SEC Rule 10b-5.

The Regulation of Investment Companies (See pages 662–663.)	The Investment Company Act of 1940 provides for SEC regulation of investment company activities. It was altered and expanded by the amendments of 1970 and 1975.
State Securities Laws (See pages 663–664.)	All states have corporate securities laws *(blue sky laws)* that regulate the offer and sale of securities within state borders; these laws are designed to prevent "speculative schemes which have no more basis than so many feet of 'blue sky.'" States regulate securities concurrently with the federal government. The Uniform Securities Act of 2002, which is being considered by a number of states, is designed to promote coordination and reduce duplication between state and federal securities regulation.

(Continued)

CHAPTER SUMMARY ■ Financing, Investor Protection, and Online Securities Offerings—Continued

Online Securities Offerings and Disclosures (See pages 664–667.)	In 1995, the SEC announced that anything that can be delivered in paper form under current securities laws may also be delivered in electronic form. Generally, when the Internet is used for the delivery of a prospectus, the same rules apply as for the delivery of a paper prospectus. When securities offerings are made online, the offerors should be careful that any hyperlinked materials do not mislead investors. Caution should also be used when making Regulation D offerings (private placements), because general solicitation is restricted with these offerings.
Online Securities Fraud (See pages 667–668.)	A major problem facing the SEC today is how to enforce the antifraud provisions of the securities laws in the online environment. Internet-related forms of securities fraud include investment scams and the manipulation of stock prices in online chat rooms.

■ FOR REVIEW

Answers for the even-numbered questions in this For Review *section can be found in Appendix I at the end of this text.*

1 What is meant by the term *securities?*

2 What are the two major statutes regulating the securities industry? When was the Securities and Exchange Commission created, and what are its major purposes and functions?

3 What is insider trading? Why is it prohibited?

4 What are some of the features of state securities laws?

5 How are securities laws being applied in the online environment?

■ QUESTIONS AND CASE PROBLEMS

21–1. Registration Requirements. Langley Brothers, Inc., a corporation incorporated and doing business in Kansas, decides to sell no-par common stock worth $1 million to the public. The stock will be sold only within the state of Kansas. Joseph Langley, the chairman of the board, says the offering need not be registered with the Securities and Exchange Commission. His brother, Harry, disagrees. Who is right? Explain.

21–2. Definition of a Security. The W. J. Howey Co. owned large tracts of citrus acreage in Lake County, Florida. For several years, it planted about five hundred acres annually, keeping half of the groves itself and offering the other half to the public to help finance additional development. Howey-in-the-Hills Service, Inc., was a service company engaged in cultivating and developing these groves, including harvesting and marketing the crops. Each prospective customer was offered both a land sales contract and a service contract, after being told that it was not feasible to invest in a grove unless service arrangements were made. Of the acreage sold by Howey, 85 percent was sold with a service contract with Howey-in-the-Hills Service. Howey did not register with the Securities and Exchange Commission (SEC) or meet the other administrative requirements that issuers of securities must fulfill. The SEC sued to enjoin Howey from continuing to offer the land sales and service contracts. Howey responded that no SEC violation existed because no securities had been issued. Evaluate the definition of a security given in this chapter, and then determine whether Howey or the SEC should prevail in court. [*SEC v. W. J. Howey Co.*, 328 U.S. 293, 66 S.Ct. 1100, 90 L.Ed. 1244 (1946)]

21–3. SEC Rule 10b-5. Grand Metropolitan PLC (Grand Met) planned to make a tender offer as part of an attempted takeover of the Pillsbury Co. Grand Met hired Robert Falbo, an independent contractor, to complete electrical work as part of security renovations to its offices to prevent leaks of information concerning the planned tender offer. Falbo was given a master key to access the executive offices. When an executive secretary told Falbo that a takeover was brewing, he used his key to access the offices and eavesdrop on conversations; in this way, he learned that Pillsbury was the target. Falbo bought thousands of shares of Pillsbury stock for less than $40 per share. Within two months, Grand Met made an offer for all outstanding Pillsbury stock at $60 per share and ultimately paid up to $66 per share. Falbo made over $165,000 in profit. The Securities and Exchange Commission (SEC) filed a suit in a federal district court against Falbo and others for alleged violations of, among other things, SEC Rule 10b-5. Under what theory might Falbo be liable? Do the circumstances of this case meet all of the requirements for liability under that theory? Explain. [*SEC v. Falbo*, 14 F.Supp.2d 508 (S.D.N.Y. 1998)]

21–4. Definition of a Security. In 1997, Scott and Sabrina Levine formed Friendly Power Co. (FPC) and Friendly Power Franchise Co. (FPC-Franchise). FPC obtained a license to operate as a utility company in California. FPC granted FPC-Franchise the right to pay commissions to "operators" who converted residential customers to FPC. Each operator paid for a "franchise"—a geographic area, determined by such factors as the number of households and competition from other utilities. In exchange for 50 percent of FPC's net profits on sales to residential customers in its territory, each franchise was required to maintain a 5 percent market share of power customers in that territory. Franchises were sold to telemarketing firms, which solicited customers. The telemarketers sold interests in each franchise to between fifty and ninety-four "partners," each of whom invested money. FPC began supplying electricity to its customers in May 1998. Less than three months later, the Securities and Exchange Commission (SEC) filed a suit in a federal district court against the Levines and others, alleging that the "franchises" were unregistered securities offered for sale to the public in violation of the Securities Act of 1933. What is the definition of a security? Should the court rule in favor of the SEC? Why or why not? [*SEC v. Friendly Power Co., LLC,* 49 F.Supp.2d 1363 (S.D.Fla. 1999)]

CASE PROBLEM WITH SAMPLE ANSWER

21–5. 2TheMart.com, Inc., was conceived in January 1999 to launch an auction Web site to compete with eBay, Inc. On January 19, 2TheMart announced that its Web site was in its "final development" stages and was expected to be active by the end of July as a "preeminent" auction site. The company also said that it had "retained the services of leading Web site design and architecture consultants to design and construct" the site. Based on the announcement, investors rushed to buy 2TheMart's stock, causing a rapid increase in the price. On February 3, 2TheMart entered into an agreement with IBM to take preliminary steps to plan the site. Three weeks later, 2TheMart announced that the site was "currently in final development." On June 1, 2TheMart signed a contract with IBM to design, build, and test the site, with a target delivery date of October 8. When 2TheMart's site did not debut as announced, Mary Harrington and others who had bought the stock filed a suit in a federal district court against the firm's officers, alleging violations of the Securities Exchange Act of 1934. The defendants responded, in part, that any alleged misrepresentations were not material and asked the court to dismiss the suit. How should the court rule, and why? [*In re 2TheMart.com, Inc. Securities Litigation,* 114 F.Supp.2d 955 (C.D.Ca. 2000)]

After you have answered this problem, compare your answer with the sample answer given on the Web site that accompanies this text. Go to http://blt.westbuslaw.com, select "Chapter 21," and click on "Case Problem with Sample Answer."

21–6. Insider Reporting and Trading. Ronald Bleakney, an officer at Natural Microsystems Corp. (NMC), a Section 12 corporation, directed NMC sales in North America, South America, and Europe. In November 1998, Bleakney sold more than 7,500 shares of NMC stock. The following March, Bleakney resigned from the firm, and the next month, he bought more than 20,000 shares of its stock. NMC provided some guidance to employees concerning the rules of insider trading, but with regard to Bleakney's transactions, the corporation said nothing about potential liability. Richard Morales, an NMC shareholder, filed a suit against NMC and Bleakney to compel recovery, under Section 16(b) of the Securities Exchange Act of 1934, of Bleakney's profits from the sale and purchase of his shares. (When Morales died, his executor Deborah Donoghue became the plaintiff.) Bleakney argued that he should not be liable because he relied on NMC's advice. Should the court order Bleakney to disgorge his profits? Explain. [*Donoghue v. Natural Microsystems Corp.,* 198 F.Supp.2d 487 (S.D.N.Y. 2002)]

21–7. SEC Rule 10b-5. Scott Ginsburg was chief executive officer (CEO) of Evergreen Media Corp. In 1996, Evergreen became interested in acquiring EZ Communications, Inc. Ginsburg met with EZ's CEO, Alan Box, on July 12. Evergreen and EZ executives began negotiating confidentially for the purchase of EZ at the specific price of $50 a share. Ginsburg called his brother, Mark, who spoke to their father, Jordan, about the deal. Mark and Jordan bought almost 75,000 shares of EZ stock. Evergreen's bid for EZ fell through, but in August, EZ announced its merger with another company. The price of EZ stock rose 30 percent, increasing the value of Mark and Jordan's shares by more than $1.76 million. The Securities and Exchange Commission (SEC) filed a suit in a federal district court against Ginsburg, alleging, among other things, violations of SEC Rule 10b-5 for communicating material nonpublic information to Mark and Jordan, who traded on the basis of that information. Ginsburg contended in part that the information was not material and filed a motion for a judgment as a matter of law. What is the test for materiality in this context? Does the information in this case meet the test, or should the court grant the motion? Explain. [*SEC v. Ginsburg,* 362 F.3d 1292 (11th Cir. 2004)]

A QUESTION OF ETHICS

21–8. Susan Waldbaum was a niece of the president and controlling shareholder of Waldbaum, Inc. Susan's mother (the president's sister) told Susan that the company was going to be sold at a favorable price and that a tender offer was soon to be made. She told Susan not to tell anyone except her husband, Keith Loeb, about the sale. (Loeb did not work for the company and was never brought into the family's inner circle, in which family members discussed confidential business information.) The next day, Susan told her husband of the sale and cautioned him not to tell anyone because "it could possibly ruin the sale." The day after he learned of the sale, Loeb told Robert Chestman, his broker, about the sale, and Chestman purchased shares of the company for both Loeb and himself. Chestman was later convicted by a jury of, among other things, trading on misappropriated inside information in violation of SEC Rule 10b-5. [*United States v. Chestman*, 947 F.2d 551 (2d Cir. 1991)]

1. On appeal, the central question was whether Chestman had acquired the inside information about the tender offer as a result of an insider's breach of a fiduciary duty. Could Loeb—the "tipper" in this case—be considered an insider?

2. If Loeb was not an insider, did he owe any fiduciary (legal) duty to his wife or his wife's family to keep the information confidential? Would it be fair of the court to impose such a legal duty on Loeb?

FOR CRITICAL ANALYSIS

21–9. Do you think that the tipper/tippee and misappropriation theories extend liability under SEC Rule 10b-5 too far? Why or why not?

VIDEO QUESTION

21–10. Go to this text's Web site at **http://blt. westbuslaw.com** and select "Chapter 21." Click on "Video Questions" and view the video titled *Mergers and Acquisitions*. Then answer the following questions.

1. Analyze whether the purchase of Onyx Advertising is a material fact that the Quigley Co. had a duty to disclose under SEC Rule 10b-5.

2. Does it matter whether Quigley personally knew about or authorized the company spokesperson's statements? Why or why not?

3. Which case discussed in the chapter presented issues that are very similar to those raised in the video? Under the holding of that case, would Onyx Advertising be able to maintain a suit against the Quigley Co. for violation of SEC Rule 10b-5?

4. Who else might be able to bring a suit against the Quigley Co. for insider trading under SEC Rule 10b-5?

INTERNET EXERCISES

Go to the *Business Law Today: The Essentials* home page at **http://blt.westbuslaw.com,** select "Chapter 21," and click on "Internet Exercises." There you will find the following Internet research exercises that you can perform to learn more about topics covered in this chapter.

Activity 21–1: LEGAL PERSPECTIVE—Electronic Delivery

Activity 21–2: MANAGEMENT PERSPECTIVE—The SEC's Role

BEFORE THE TEST

Go to the *Business Law Today: The Essentials* home page at **http://blt.westbuslaw.com,** select "Chapter 21," and click on "Interactive Quizzes." You will find at least twenty interactive questions relating to this chapter.

CHAPTER 22

Antitrust Law

"Free competition is worth more to
society than it costs."
Oliver Wendell Holmes, Jr., 1841–1935
(Associate justice of the United States Supreme Court,
1902–1932)

CHAPTER OUTLINE

- **THE SHERMAN ANTITRUST ACT**

- **SECTION 1 OF THE SHERMAN ACT**

- **SECTION 2 OF THE SHERMAN ACT**

- **THE CLAYTON ACT**

- **ENFORCEMENT OF ANTITRUST LAWS**

- **EXEMPTIONS FROM ANTITRUST LAWS**

⬛ LEARNING OBJECTIVES

After reading this chapter, you should be able to answer the following questions:

1 What is a monopoly? What is market power? How do these concepts relate to each other?

2 What type of activity is prohibited by Section 1 of the Sherman Act? What type of activity is prohibited by Section 2 of the Sherman Act?

3 What are the four major provisions of the Clayton Act, and what types of activities do these provisions prohibit?

4 What agencies of the federal government enforce the federal antitrust laws?

5 What are four activities that are exempt from the antitrust laws?

Today's antitrust laws are the direct descendants of common law actions intended to limit *restraints on trade* (agreements between firms that have the effect of reducing competition in the marketplace). Such actions date to the fifteenth century in England. In the United States, concern over monopolistic practices arose following the Civil War with the growth of large corporate enterprises and their attempts to reduce or eliminate competition. In an effort to thwart competition, they legally tied themselves together in business trusts. As discussed in Chapter 19, a *business trust* is a form of business organization in which trustees hold title to property for the benefit of others. The most powerful of these trusts, the Standard Oil trust, is examined in this chapter's *Landmark in the Law* feature on the next page.

Many states tried to curb such monopolistic behavior by enacting statutes outlawing the use of trusts. That is why all the laws regulating economic competition

LANDMARK IN THE LAW

The Sherman Antitrust Act of 1890

The author of the Sherman Antitrust Act of 1890, Senator John Sherman, was the brother of the famed Civil War general William Tecumseh Sherman and a recognized financial authority. Sherman had been concerned for years with the diminishing competition within U.S. industry and the emergence of monopolies, such as the Standard Oil trust.

THE STANDARD OIL TRUST By 1890, the Standard Oil trust had become the foremost petroleum refining and marketing combination in the United States. Streamlined, integrated, and centrally and efficiently controlled, its monopoly over the industry could not be disputed. Standard Oil controlled 90 percent of the U.S. market for refined petroleum products, and small manufacturers were incapable of competing with such an industrial leviathan.

The increasing consolidation occurring in U.S. industry, and particularly the Standard Oil trust, came to the attention of the public for the first time in March 1881. Henry Demarest Lloyd, a young journalist from Chicago, published an article in the *Atlantic Monthly* entitled "The Story of a Great Monopoly." The article discussed the success of the Standard Oil Company and clearly demonstrated that the petroleum industry in the United States was dominated by one firm—Standard Oil. Lloyd's article, which was so popular that the issue was reprinted six times, marked the beginning of the U.S. public's growing awareness of, and concern over, the growth of monopolies.

THE PASSAGE OF THE SHERMAN ANTITRUST ACT The common law regarding trade regulation was not always consistent. Certainly, it was not very familiar to the members of Congress. The public concern over large business integrations and trusts was familiar, however. In 1888, 1889, and again in 1890, Senator Sherman introduced in Congress bills designed to destroy the large combinations of capital that, he felt, were creating a lack of balance within the nation's economy. Sherman told Congress that the Sherman Act "does not announce a new principle of law, but applies old and well-recognized principles of the common law."[a] In 1890, the Fifty-first Congress enacted the bill into law.

In the pages that follow, we look closely at the major provisions of this act. Generally, the act prohibits business combinations and conspiracies that restrain trade and commerce, as well as certain monopolistic practices.

APPLICATION TO TODAY'S WORLD

The Sherman Antitrust Act remains very relevant to today's world. The widely publicized monopolization case brought in 2001 by the U.S. Department of Justice and a number of state attorneys general against Microsoft Corporation is just one example of the relevance of the Sherman Act to modern business developments and practices. (This case is presented later in this chapter as Case 22.2.)

RELEVANT WEB SITES

To locate information on the Web concerning the Sherman Antitrust Act, go to this text's Web site at **http://blt.westbuslaw.com,** *select "Chapter 22," and click on "URLs for Landmarks."*

a. 21 Congressional Record 2456 (1890).

ANTITRUST LAW
Laws protecting commerce from
unlawful restraints.

today are referred to as **antitrust laws.** At the national level, Congress passed the Sherman Antitrust Act in 1890. In 1914, Congress passed the Clayton Act and the Federal Trade Commission Act in an attempt to further curb anticompetitive or unfair business practices. Congress later amended the 1914 acts to broaden and strengthen their coverage.

This chapter examines these major antitrust statutes, focusing particularly on the Sherman Act and the Clayton Act, as amended, and the types of activities they prohibit. Remember in reading this chapter that the basis of antitrust legislation is the desire to foster competition. Antitrust legislation was initially created—and continues to be enforced—because of our belief that competition leads to lower prices, generates more product information, and results in a more equitable distribution of wealth between consumers and producers. As Oliver Wendell Holmes, Jr., indicated in the chapter-opening quotation, free competition is worth more to our society than the cost we pay for it. The cost is, of course, government regulation of business behavior.

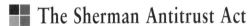 **The Sherman Antitrust Act**

In 1890, Congress passed "An Act to Protect Trade and Commerce against Unlawful Restraints and Monopolies"—commonly known as the Sherman Antitrust Act or, more simply, as the Sherman Act. The Sherman Act was and remains one of the government's most powerful weapons in the effort to maintain a competitive economy. Because of the act's significance, we examine its passage more closely in this chapter's *Landmark in the Law* feature on the facing page.

The Web site of Cornell University's Legal Information Institute contains the text of federal statutes relating to commerce and trade, including the Sherman Antitrust Act, at

http://www4.law.cornell.edu/ uscode/15/1.html.

MAJOR PROVISIONS OF THE SHERMAN ACT

Sections 1 and 2 contain the main provisions of the Sherman Act:

> **1:** Every contract, combination in the form of trust or otherwise, or conspiracy, in restraint of trade or commerce among the several States, or with foreign nations, is hereby declared to be illegal [and is a felony punishable by fine and/or imprisonment].
>
> **2:** Every person who shall monopolize, or attempt to monopolize, or combine or conspire with any other person or persons, to monopolize any part of the trade or commerce among the several States, or with foreign nations, shall be deemed guilty of a felony [and is similarly punishable].

DIFFERENCES BETWEEN SECTION 1 AND SECTION 2

These two sections of the Sherman Act are quite different. Violation of Section 1 requires two or more persons, as a person cannot contract or combine or conspire alone. Thus, the essence of the illegal activity is *the act of joining together.* Section 2, though, can apply either to one person or to two or more persons because it refers to "[e]very person." Thus, unilateral conduct can result in a violation of Section 2.

The cases brought to court under Section 1 of the Sherman Act differ from those brought under Section 2. Section 1 cases are often concerned with finding an agreement (written or oral) that leads to a restraint of trade. Section 2 cases deal with the structure of a monopoly that already exists in the marketplace. The term **monopoly** is generally used to describe a market in which there is a single seller or a limited number of sellers. Whereas Section 1 focuses on agreements that are restrictive— that is, agreements that have a wrongful purpose—Section 2 looks at the so-called misuse of **monopoly power** in the marketplace.

MONOPOLY
A term generally used to describe a market in which there is a single seller or a limited number of sellers.

MONOPOLY POWER
The ability of a monopoly to dictate what takes place in a given market.

MARKET POWER
The power of a firm to control the market price of its product. A monopoly has the greatest degree of market power.

Monopoly power exists when a firm has an extremely great amount of **market power**—the power to affect the market price of its product. Both Section 1 and Section 2 seek to curtail market practices that result in undesired monopoly pricing and output behavior. For a case to be brought under Section 2, however, the "threshold" or "necessary" amount of monopoly power must already exist. We will return to a discussion of these two sections of the Sherman Act after we look at the act's jurisdictional requirements.

JURISDICTIONAL REQUIREMENTS

The Sherman Act applies only to restraints that have a significant impact on interstate commerce. The Sherman Act also extends to U.S. nationals abroad who are engaged in activities that have an effect on U.S. foreign commerce. (The extraterritorial application of U.S. antitrust laws will be discussed in Chapter 25.) State laws regulate local restraints on competition.

Courts have generally held that any activity that substantially affects interstate commerce falls within the scope of the Sherman Act. As discussed in Chapter 1, courts have construed the meaning of *interstate commerce* broadly, bringing even local activities within the regulatory power of the national government.

◼ Section 1 of the Sherman Act

You can find a discussion of the *per se* rule and the rule of reason, as well as an extensive summary of antitrust laws, at

**http:// profs.lp.findlaw.com/
antitrust/antitrust_2.html**.

The underlying assumption of Section 1 of the Sherman Act is that society's welfare is harmed if rival firms are permitted to join in an agreement that consolidates their market power or otherwise restrains competition. The types of trade restraints that Section 1 of the Sherman Act prohibits generally fall into two broad categories: *horizontal restraints* and *vertical restraints*, both of which will be discussed shortly. First, though, we look at the rules that the courts may apply when assessing the anticompetitive impact of alleged restraints on trade.

PER SE VIOLATIONS VERSUS THE RULE OF REASON

PER SE VIOLATION
A type of anticompetitive agreement that is considered to be so injurious to the public that there is no need to determine whether it actually injures market competition; rather, it is in itself *(per se)* a violation of the Sherman Act.

RULE OF REASON
A test by which a court balances the positive effects (such as economic efficiency) of an agreement against its potentially anticompetitive effects. In antitrust litigation, many practices are analyzed under the rule of reason.

Some restraints are so blatantly and substantially anticompetitive that they are deemed *per se* violations—illegal *per se* (on their face, or inherently)—under Section 1. Other agreements, however, even though they result in enhanced market power, do not *unreasonably* restrain trade. Using what is called the **rule of reason,** the courts analyze anticompetitive agreements that allegedly violate Section 1 of the Sherman Act to determine whether they may, in fact, constitute reasonable restraints on trade.

The need for a rule-of-reason analysis of some agreements in restraint of trade is obvious—if the rule of reason had not been developed, virtually any business agreement could conceivably be held to violate the Sherman Act. Justice Louis Brandeis effectively phrased this sentiment in *Chicago Board of Trade v. United States*, a case decided in 1918:

> Every agreement concerning trade, every regulation of trade, restrains. To bind, to restrain, is of their very essence. The true test of legality is whether the restraint imposed is such as merely regulates and perhaps thereby promotes competition or whether it is such as may suppress or even destroy competition.[1]

---

1. 246 U.S. 231, 38 S.Ct. 242, 62 L.Ed. 683 (1918).

When analyzing an alleged Section 1 violation under the rule of reason, a court will consider several factors. These factors include the purpose of the agreement, the parties' power to implement the agreement to achieve that purpose, and the effect or potential effect of the agreement on competition. Yet another factor that a court might consider is whether the parties could have relied on less restrictive means to achieve their purpose.

HORIZONTAL RESTRAINTS

HORIZONTAL RESTRAINT
Any agreement that in some way restrains competition between rival firms competing in the same market.

The term **horizontal restraint** is encountered frequently in antitrust law. A horizontal restraint is any agreement that in some way restrains competition between rival firms competing in the same market. In the following subsections, we look at several types of horizontal restraints.

PRICE-FIXING AGREEMENT
An agreement between competitors to fix the prices of products or services at a certain level.

Price Fixing Any **price-fixing agreement**—an agreement among competitors to fix prices—constitutes a *per se* violation of Section 1. Perhaps the definitive case regarding price-fixing agreements is still the 1940 case of *United States v. Socony-Vacuum Oil Co.*[2] In that case, a group of independent oil producers in Texas and Louisiana were caught between falling demand due to the Great Depression of the 1930s and increasing supply from newly discovered oil fields in the region. In response to these conditions, a group of major refining companies agreed to buy "distress" gasoline (excess supplies) from the independents so as to dispose of it in an "orderly manner." Although there was no explicit agreement as to price, it was clear that the purpose of the agreement was to limit the supply of gasoline on the market and thereby raise prices.

There may have been good reasons for the agreement. Nonetheless, the United States Supreme Court recognized the dangerous effects that such an agreement could have on open and free competition. The Court held that the reasonableness of a price-fixing agreement is never a defense; any agreement that restricts output or artificially fixes price is a *per se* violation of Section 1. The rationale of the *per se* rule was best stated in what is now the most famous portion of the Court's opinion—footnote 59. In that footnote, Justice William O. Douglas compared a freely functioning price system to a body's central nervous system, condemning price-fixing agreements as threats to "the central nervous system of the economy."

At issue in the following case was whether an agreement between two pharmaceutical manufacturers violated the Sherman Act.

2. 310 U.S. 150, 60 S.Ct. 811, 84 L.Ed. 1129 (1940).

CASE 22.1 ■ **In re Cardizem CD Antitrust Litigation**

United States Court of Appeals,
Sixth Circuit, 2003.
332 F.3d 896.

FACTS Hoescht Marion Roussel, Inc. (HMR), is the manufacturer of the prescription drug Cardizem CD, which is used to treat angina and hypertension and to prevent heart attacks and strokes. HMR's patent for the drug expired in November 1992. Andrx Pharmaceuticals, Inc.,

developed a generic version. On receiving the approval of the Food and Drug Administration (FDA), Andrx would have 180 days within which to sell the generic without competition from other drugmakers. HMR and Andrx became involved in litigation over the patent, however, which delayed FDA approval. In 1997, after the FDA tentatively approved the generic, Andrx agreed not to market it in exchange for $40 million per year from HMR until their

(Continued)

CASE 22.1—Continued

dispute was resolved in an "unappealable determination." Louisiana Wholesale Drug Company and other buyers of Cardizem CD filed a suit in a federal district court against the two firms, challenging their agreement as a violation of antitrust law. The court issued a summary judgment in the plaintiffs' favor. The defendants appealed to the U.S. Court of Appeals for the Sixth Circuit.

ISSUE Was the agreement between HMR and Andrx an illegal restraint of trade under Section 1 of the Sherman Act?

DECISION Yes. The U.S. Court of Appeals for the Sixth Circuit held that the agreement was illegal *per se* under the Sherman Act. The appellate court affirmed the lower court's summary judgment on this issue.

REASON The U.S. Court of Appeals for the Sixth Circuit explained that by delaying the entry into the market of Andrx's generic version of Cardizem CD, the agreement between HMR and Andrx also delayed the entry of the generic versions of other competitors, which could not place their products in the market until the expiration of Andrx's 180-day period of marketing exclusivity. The court stated, "There is simply no escaping the conclusion that the Agreement * * * was, at its core, a horizontal agreement to eliminate competition in the market for Cardizem CD throughout the entire United States, a classic example of a *per se* illegal restraint of trade." In the court's view, the agreement was not merely an attempt to enforce patent rights or a settlement of the patent litigation, as the defendants claimed.

FOR CRITICAL ANALYSIS—Social Consideration
If the defendants had argued that their agreement had pro-competitive benefits, what effect might their argument have had on the outcome in this case?

GROUP BOYCOTT
The refusal by a group of competitors to deal with a particular person or firm; prohibited by the Sherman Act.

Group Boycotts   A **group boycott** is an agreement by two or more sellers to refuse to deal with (boycott) a particular person or firm. Such group boycotts have been held to constitute *per se* violations of Section 1 of the Sherman Act. Section 1 has been violated if it can be demonstrated that the boycott or joint refusal to deal was undertaken with the intention of eliminating competition or preventing entry into a given market. Some boycotts, such as group boycotts against a supplier for political reasons, may be protected under the First Amendment right to freedom of expression, however.

The rule of *per se* illegality does not apply to college and professional league sports. In that context, the validity of an allegedly illegal agreement is analyzed under the rule of reason. ■ EXAMPLE 22.1 The National Football League (NFL) has a rule that limits eligibility to players three seasons removed from their high school graduation. Dwayne, a star football player, has led his team to an undefeated season in his freshman year at college. He wants to play for the NFL, but he is only one year out of high school, so he is not eligible under the rule. He files suit claiming the NFL teams' agreement to exclude a broad class of players from the NFL labor market constitutes a group boycott in violation of the Sherman Act. In this situation, the court would evaluate his claim under the rule of reason, balancing Dwayne's right to compete for a job against the NFL's right to exclude players whom it deems are not ready to play.[3] ■

Horizontal Market Division   It is a *per se* violation of Section 1 of the Sherman Act for competitors to divide up territories or customers. ■ EXAMPLE 22.2 Manufacturers A, B, and C compete against each other in the states of Kansas, Nebraska, and Iowa. By agreement, A sells products only in Kansas; B sells only in Nebraska; and C sells

---

3. For another example, see *Clarett v. National Football League*, 369 F.3d 124 (2d Cir. 2004).

A quarterback for the Miami Dolphins prepares to throw the football to a teammate. If the teams in the National Football League (NFL) agree that players are not eligible for the NFL until three years after their high school graduation, is this a group boycott? How would a court evaluate the legality of this agreement? (Reuters/Pierre DuCharme/Landov)

VERTICAL RESTRAINT
Any restraint on trade created by agreements between firms at different levels in the manufacturing and distribution process.

VERTICALLY INTEGRATED FIRM
A firm that carries out two or more functional phases (manufacture, distribution, and retailing, for example) of the chain of production.

only in Iowa. This concerted action not only reduces marketing costs but also allows all three (assuming there is no other competition) to raise the price of the goods sold in their respective states. The same violation would take place if A, B, and C simply agreed that A would sell only to institutional purchasers (such as school districts, universities, state agencies and departments, and cities) in all three states, B only to wholesalers, and C only to retailers. ■

Trade Associations   Businesses in the same general industry or profession frequently organize trade associations to pursue common interests. The joint activities of the trade association may include exchanges of information, representation of the members' business interests before governmental bodies, advertising campaigns, and the setting of regulatory standards to govern the industry or profession.

Generally, the rule of reason is applied to many of these horizontal actions. If a court finds that a trade association practice or agreement that restrains trade is sufficiently beneficial both to the association and to the public, it may deem the restraint reasonable.

Other trade association agreements may have such substantially anticompetitive effects that the court will consider them to be in violation of Section 1 of the Sherman Act. ■ **EXAMPLE 22.3** A professional engineering society's code of ethics prohibited members from discussing prices with a potential customer until after the customer had chosen an engineer. When this ban on competitive bidding was challenged as a violation of Section 1, the United States Supreme Court held that it was "nothing less than a frontal assault on the basic policy of the Sherman Act."[4] ■

VERTICAL RESTRAINTS

A **vertical restraint** of trade results from an agreement between firms at different levels in the manufacturing and distribution process. In contrast to horizontal relationships, which occur at the same level of operation, vertical relationships encompass the entire chain of production. The chain of production normally includes the purchase of inventory, basic manufacturing, distribution to wholesalers, and eventual sale of a product at the retail level. For some products, these distinct phases may be carried out by different firms. In other instances, a single firm carries out two or more of the separate functional phases. Such enterprises are considered to be **vertically integrated firms.**

Even though firms operating at different functional levels are not in direct competition with one another, they are in competition with other firms. Thus, agreements between firms standing in a vertical relationship may affect competition. Some vertical restraints are *per se* violations of Section 1; others are judged under the rule of reason.

Territorial or Customer Restrictions   In arranging for the distribution of its products, a manufacturing firm often wishes to insulate dealers from direct competition with other dealers selling the product. To this end, it may institute territorial restrictions or attempt to prohibit wholesalers or retailers from reselling the product to certain classes of buyers, such as competing retailers.

A firm may have legitimate reasons for imposing such territorial or customer restrictions. ■ **EXAMPLE 22.4** A computer manufacturer may wish to prevent a dealer

---

4. *National Society of Professional Engineers v. United States,* 435 U.S. 679, 98 S.Ct. 1355, 55 L.Ed.2d 637 (1978).

The Federal Trade Commission (FTC) offers an abundance of information on antitrust law, including "A Plain English Guide to Antitrust Laws," at its Web site. Go to

http://www.ftc.gov/ftc/ antitrust.htm.

RESALE PRICE MAINTENANCE AGREEMENT
An agreement between a manufacturer and a retailer in which the manufacturer specifies what the retail prices of its products must be.

A retail store displays a well-known designer's clothing. Is an agreement between the manufacturer and an independent retailer to sell the clothing at a certain price considered a violation of the Sherman Act? Why or why not? (© John Coletti, Stock Boston)

from cutting costs and undercutting rivals by selling computers without promotion or customer service, while relying on nearby dealers to provide these services. In this situation, the cost-cutting dealer reaps the benefits (sales of the product) paid for by other dealers who undertake promotion and arrange for customer service. By not providing customer service, the cost-cutting dealer may also harm the manufacturer's reputation. ◼

Territorial and customer restrictions are judged under the rule of reason. In *United States v. Arnold, Schwinn & Co.,*[5] a case decided in 1967, the Supreme Court had held that vertical territorial and customer restrictions were *per se* violations of Section 1 of the Sherman Act. Ten years later, however, in *Continental T.V., Inc. v. GTE Sylvania, Inc.,*[6] the Court overturned the *Schwinn* decision and held that such vertical restrictions should be judged under the rule of reason. The *Continental* case marked a definite shift from rigid characterization of these kinds of vertical restraints to a more flexible, economic analysis of the restraints under the rule of reason.

Resale Price Maintenance Agreements   An agreement between a manufacturer and a distributor or retailer in which the manufacturer specifies what the retail prices of its products must be is referred to as a **resale price maintenance agreement.** This type of agreement may violate Section 1 of the Sherman Act. As with territorial restrictions, the Supreme Court originally held that resale price maintenance agreements were *per se* violations.[7] Subsequently, however, in 1997 the Court reversed this decision.[8] Today, such price-fixing arrangements are evaluated under the rule of reason.

Refusals to Deal   As discussed previously, joint refusals to deal (group boycotts) are subject to close scrutiny under Section 1 of the Sherman Act. A single manufacturer acting unilaterally, though, is generally free to deal, or not to deal, with whomever it wishes. In vertical arrangements, even though a manufacturer cannot set retail prices for its products, it can refuse to deal with retailers or dealers that cut prices to levels substantially below the manufacturer's suggested retail prices. In *United States v. Colgate & Co.,*[9] for example, the United States Supreme Court held that a manufacturer's advance announcement that it would not sell to price cutters was not a violation of the Sherman Act.

Nevertheless, in some instances, a unilateral refusal to deal will violate antitrust laws. These instances involve offenses proscribed under Section 2 of the Sherman Act and occur only if (1) the firm refusing to deal has—or is likely to acquire—monopoly power and (2) the refusal is likely to have an anticompetitive effect on a particular market.

◼ Section 2 of the Sherman Act

Section 1 of the Sherman Act proscribes certain concerted, or joint, activities that restrain trade. In contrast, Section 2 condemns "every person who shall monopolize, or attempt to monopolize." Thus, two distinct types of behavior are subject to sanction under Section 2: *monopolization* and *attempts to monopolize*. One tactic

5. 388 U.S. 365, 87 S.Ct. 1856, 18 L.Ed.2d 1249 (1967).
6. 433 U.S. 36, 97 S.Ct. 2549, 53 L.Ed.2d 568 (1977).
7. *Albrecht v. Herald Co.,* 390 U.S. 145, 88 S.Ct. 869, 19 L.Ed.2d 998 (1968).
8. *State Oil Co. v. Khan,* 522 U.S. 3, 118 S.Ct. 275, 139 L.Ed.2d 199 (1997).
9. 250 U.S. 300, 39 S.Ct. 465, 63 L.Ed. 992 (1919).

PREDATORY PRICING
The pricing of a product below cost with the intent to drive competitors out of the market.

that may be involved in either offense is **predatory pricing.** Predatory pricing involves an attempt by one firm to drive its competitors from the market by selling its product at prices substantially *below* the normal costs of production. Once the competitors are eliminated, the firm will attempt to recapture its losses and go on to earn higher profits by driving prices up far above their competitive levels.

MONOPOLIZATION

MONOPOLIZATION
The possession of monopoly power in the relevant market and the willful acquisition or maintenance of that power, as distinguished from growth or development as a consequence of a superior product, business acumen, or historic accident.

In *United States v. Grinnell Corp.*,[10] the United States Supreme Court defined the offense of **monopolization** as involving the following two elements: "(1) the possession of monopoly power in the relevant market and (2) the willful acquisition or maintenance of [that] power as distinguished from growth or development as a consequence of a superior product, business acumen, or historic accident." A violation of Section 2 requires that both these elements—monopoly power and an intent to monopolize—be established.

Monopoly Power   The Sherman Act does not define *monopoly.* In economic parlance, monopoly refers to control by a single entity. It is well established in antitrust law, however, that a firm may be deemed a monopolist even though it is not the sole seller in a market. Additionally, size alone does not determine whether a firm is a monopoly. For example, a "mom and pop" grocery located in an isolated desert town is a monopolist if it is the only grocery serving that particular market. Size in relation to the market is what matters because monopoly involves the power to affect prices.

Market Power.   *Monopoly power,* as mentioned earlier in this chapter, exists when a firm has an extremely large amount of market power. If a firm has sufficient market power to control prices and exclude competition, that firm has monopoly power. As difficult as it is to define market power precisely, it is even more difficult to measure it. In determining the extent of a firm's market power, courts often use the so-called **market-share test,**[11] which measures the firm's percentage share of the "relevant market." A firm may be considered to have monopoly power if its share of the relevant market is 70 percent or more. This is merely a rule of thumb, though; it is not a binding principle of law. In some cases, a smaller share may be held to constitute monopoly power.[12]

MARKET-SHARE TEST
The primary measure of monopoly power. A firm's market share is the percentage of a market that the firm controls.

Relevant Market.   The relevant market consists of two elements: (1) a relevant product market and (2) a relevant geographic market. What should the relevant product market include? No doubt, it must include all products that, although produced by different firms, have identical attributes, such as sugar. Products that are not identical, however, may sometimes be substituted for one another. Coffee may be substituted for tea, for example. In defining the relevant product market, the key issue is the degree of interchangeability between products. If one product is a sufficient substitute for another, the two products are considered to be part of the same product market. (For a case discussing the "relevant market" for domain names, see this chapter's *Adapting the Law to the Online Environment* feature on the next page.)

 The American Antitrust Institute maintains a Web site that is devoted entirely to the topic of antitrust law. The site includes news, articles, and a very detailed archive on antitrust topics. To access this site, go to

http://www. antitrustinstitute.org.

---

10. 384 U.S. 563, 86 S.Ct. 1698, 16 L.Ed.2d 778 (1966).

11. Other measures of market power have been devised, but the market-share test is the most widely used.

12. This standard was first articulated by Judge Learned Hand in *United States v. Aluminum Co. of America,* 148 F.2d 416 (2d Cir. 1945). A 90 percent share was held to be clear evidence of monopoly power. Anything less than 64 percent, said Judge Hand, made monopoly power doubtful, and anything less than 30 percent was clearly not monopoly power.

ADAPTING THE LAW TO THE ONLINE ENVIRONMENT

What Is the Relevant Product Market for Domain Names?

Most attempts to measure monopoly power involve quantifying the degree of concentration in a relevant market and/or the extent of a particular firm's ability to control that market. Accordingly, defining the relevant market is a necessary step in any monopolization case brought under Section 2 of the Sherman Act. Thus, when Stan Smith brought a monopolization case against Network Solutions, Inc. (NSI), a domain name registrar (see Chapter 5), for not allowing Smith and others to register for expired domain names, a threshold question before the court was the following: What is the relevant product market for domain names?

THE REGISTRY

At one time, NSI was the only registrar for domain names in this country. In 1998, however, the federal government opened domain name registration to competition and set up a nonprofit corporation, the Internet Corporation for Assigned Names and Numbers (ICANN), to oversee the distribution of domain names. At that time, NSI's domain name registration service was divided into two separate units: a registrar and a registry (the Registry).[a]

The registrar unit continues to register domain names, although it is now only one of eighty or so accredited registrars in operation. The Registry, in contrast, is the only entity of its kind. It maintains a centralized "WHOIS" database of all domain names using the ".com," ".org," and ".net" top level domains, regardless of whether the names have been registered by NSI or one of the other accredited registrars. The Registry's WHOIS database allows all registrars to determine almost instan-

taneously which domain names are already registered and therefore unavailable. The public can also access the Registry's WHOIS database.

At the time Smith brought his suit, the WHOIS database included approximately 163,000 expired domain names—names that had been registered but belonged to registrants who had failed to pay the required registration renewal fees. NSI's policy was to give registrants a "grace period" of two to three months in which they could renew their expired registrations. In the meantime, the names remained on the WHOIS database and were unavailable for others.

WHAT IS THE RELEVANT PRODUCT MARKET?

Smith claimed that by failing to make expired domain names available to himself and others, NSI had intentionally maintained an unlawful monopoly over expired domain names in violation of Section 2 of the Sherman Act. The court, however, concluded that the relevant product market was not expired domain names but all domain names—and NSI did not have monopoly power over all domain names. The court reasoned that "the relevant market includes those commodities or services that are reasonably interchangeable." Because of the "virtually limitless" supply of domain names, said the court, "there will always be reasonable substitute names available for any given name kept out of circulation."[b]

FOR CRITICAL ANALYSIS

Do you agree that the relevant market for domain names should include all domain names and not just those that have expired? Why or why not?

a. In 2000, NSI became a wholly owned subsidiary of VeriSign, Inc., and the Registry was subsequently renamed VeriSign Global Registry Services. Both NSI and VeriSign were defendants in this case.

b. *Smith v. Network Solutions, Inc.,* 135 F.Supp.2d 1159 (N.D.Ala. 2001).

The second component of the relevant market is the geographic boundaries of the market. For products that are sold nationwide, the geographic boundaries of the market encompass the entire United States. If a producer and its competitors sell in only a limited area (one in which customers have no access to other sources of the product), the geographic market is limited to that area. A national firm may thus compete in several distinct areas and have monopoly power in one area but not in another.

The Intent Requirement Monopoly power, in and of itself, does not constitute the offense of monopolization under Section 2 of the Sherman Act. The offense also requires an *intent* to monopolize. A dominant market share may be the result of business acumen or the development of a superior product. It may simply be the result of historic accident. In these situations, the acquisition of monopoly power is not an antitrust violation. Indeed, it would be contrary to society's interest to condemn every firm that acquired a position of power because it was well managed and efficient and marketed a product desired by consumers.

If a firm possesses market power as a result of carrying out some purposeful act to acquire or maintain that power through anticompetitive means, then it is in violation of Section 2. In most monopolization cases, intent may be inferred from evidence that the firm had monopoly power and engaged in anticompetitive behavior.

The following case included an allegation of a violation of Section 2 of the Sherman Act.

> **KEEP IN MIND** Section 2 of the Sherman Act essentially condemns the act of monopolizing, not the possession of monopoly power.

CASE 22.2 United States v. Microsoft Corp.

United States Court of Appeals,
District of Columbia Circuit, 2001.
253 F.3d 34.
http://www.cadc.uscourts.gov[a]

HISTORICAL AND TECHNOLOGICAL SETTING
In 1981, Microsoft Corporation released the first version of its Microsoft Disk Operating System (MS-DOS). When International Business Machines Corporation (IBM) selected MS-DOS for preinstallation on its first generation of personal computers (PCs), Microsoft's product became the dominant operating system for Intel-compatible PCs.[b] *In 1985, Microsoft began shipping a software package called Windows. Although originally a user interface on top of MS-DOS, Windows took on more operating-system functionality over time. Throughout the 1990s, Microsoft's share of the market for Intel-compatible operating systems was more than 90 percent.*

FACTS In 1994, Netscape Communications Corporation began marketing Navigator, the first popular graphical Internet browser. Navigator worked with Java, a technology developed by Sun Microsystems, Inc. Java enabled applications to run on a variety of platforms, which meant

that users did not need Windows. Microsoft perceived a threat to its dominance of the operating-system market and developed a competing browser, Internet Explorer (Explorer). Microsoft then began to require computer makers who wanted to install Windows to also install Explorer and exclude Navigator. Meanwhile, Microsoft commingled browser code and other code in Windows so that deleting files containing Explorer would cripple the operating system. Microsoft offered to promote and pay Internet service providers to distribute Explorer and exclude Navigator. Microsoft also developed its own Java code and deceived many independent software sellers into believing that this code would help in designing cross-platform applications when, in fact, it would run only on Windows. The U.S. Department of Justice and a number of state attorneys general filed a suit in a federal district court against Microsoft, alleging, in part, monopolization in violation of Section 2 of the Sherman Act. The court ruled against Microsoft.[c] Microsoft appealed to the U.S. Court of Appeals for the District of Columbia Circuit.

ISSUE Did Microsoft possess and maintain monopoly power in the market for Intel-compatible operating systems?

DECISION Yes. The U.S. Court of Appeals for the District of Columbia Circuit affirmed this part of the lower court's opinion. The appellate court reversed other

a. On this page, under "Opinions," click on "All Opinions." Then, in the section headed "Please select from the following menu to find opinions by date of issue," choose "June" from the "Month" menu, select "2001" from the "Year" menu, and click on "Go!" From the result, scroll to the name of the case and click on the docket number to access the opinion. The U.S. Court of Appeals for the District of Columbia Circuit maintains this Web site.
b. An *Intel-compatible PC* is designed to function with Intel Corporation's 80×86/Pentium families of microprocessors or with compatible microprocessors.

c. The district court ordered, among other things, a structural reorganization of Microsoft, including a separation of its operating-system and applications businesses. See *United States v. Microsoft,* 97 F.Supp.2d 59 (D.D.C. 2000).

(Continued)

CASE 22.2—Continued

holdings of the lower court, however, and remanded the case for a reconsideration of the appropriate remedy.

REASON The U.S. Court of Appeals for the District of Columbia Circuit rejected Microsoft's arguments, including its contention that in the "uniquely dynamic" software market, intent should not be inferred but rather must be proved. The court responded, "Microsoft's pattern of exclusionary conduct could only be rational if the firm knew that it possessed monopoly power." This conduct included Microsoft's restrictions on the computer makers' Windows licenses. "Microsoft's efforts to gain market share in one market (browsers) served to meet the threat to Microsoft's monopoly in another market (operating systems) by keeping rival browsers from gaining the critical mass of users necessary to attract developer attention away from Windows as the platform for software development." The exclusionary conduct also included Microsoft's other actions welding Explorer to Windows. In part, the court reasoned, the commingling of the browsing and other code deterred computer makers "from pre-installing rival browsers, thereby reducing the rivals' usage share and, hence, developers' interest in rivals' [operating systems]." The court also concluded that Microsoft's agreements with the Internet service providers were "exclusionary devices" and that Microsoft's dealings with the independent software sellers constituted "exclusionary conduct."

FOR CRITICAL ANALYSIS—Technological Consideration *What effect does the passage of time between certain conduct and the outcome of litigation concerning that conduct have on judicial rulings that apply to technological product markets?*

COMMENTS *Ultimately, the Department of Justice and several of the state attorneys general who brought the suit agreed with Microsoft to settle the case. In November 2002, a federal trial judge approved the settlement. Generally, the settlement gave consumers more choices and allowed Microsoft's rivals more flexibility to offer competing software features on computers running Windows. Although Microsoft has settled a number of antitrust suits, it is still involved in litigating numerous private antitrust claims. Moreover, in 2004 the European Union imposed a $613 million fine on Microsoft for its Windows software monopoly, which could result in another lengthy court battle. Microsoft appealed the fine.*

ATTEMPTS TO MONOPOLIZE

ATTEMPTED MONOPOLIZATION
Any actions by a firm to eliminate competition and gain monopoly power.

Section 2 also prohibits **attempted monopolization** of a market. Any action challenged as an attempt to monopolize must have been specifically intended to exclude competitors and garner monopoly power. In addition, the attempt must have had a "dangerous" probability of success—only *serious* threats of monopolization are condemned as violations. The probability cannot be dangerous unless the alleged offender possesses some degree of market power.

ETHICAL ISSUE 22.1

Are we destined for more monopolies in the future? Knowledge and information form the building blocks of the so-called new economy. Some observers believe that the nature of this new economy means that we will see an increasing number of monopolies similar to Microsoft. Consider that the justification for all antitrust law is that monopoly leads to restricted output and hence higher prices for consumers. That is how a monopolist maximizes profits relative to a competitive firm. In the knowledge-based sector, however, firms face *economies of scale* (defined as decreases in long-run average costs resulting from increases in output), so they will do the exact opposite of a traditional monopolist—they will increase output and reduce prices. That is exactly what Microsoft has done over the years—the prices of its operating system and applications have fallen, particularly when corrected for inflation.

This characteristic of knowledge-based monopolies may mean that antitrust authorities will have to have greater tolerance for these monopolies to allow them to benefit from full economies of scale. After all, consumers are the ultimate beneficiaries of such economies of scale. In the early 1900s, economist Joseph Schumpeter argued in favor of allowing monopolies. According to his theory of "creative destruction," monopolies stimulate innovation and economic growth because firms that capture monopoly profits have a greater incentive to innovate. Those that do not survive—the firms that are "destroyed"—leave room for the more efficient firms that will survive. ■

■■ The Clayton Act

In 1914, Congress attempted to strengthen federal antitrust laws by enacting the Clayton Act. The Clayton Act was aimed at specific anticompetitive or monopolistic practices that the Sherman Act did not cover. The substantive provisions of the act deal with four distinct forms of business behavior, which are declared illegal but not criminal. With regard to each of the four provisions, the act's prohibitions are qualified by the general condition that the behavior is illegal only if it substantially tends to lessen competition or create monopoly power. The major offenses under the Clayton Act are set out in Sections 2, 3, 7, and 8 of the act.

SECTION 2—PRICE DISCRIMINATION

Section 2 of the Clayton Act prohibits **price discrimination,** which occurs when a seller charges different prices to competitive buyers for identical goods. Because businesses frequently circumvented Section 2 of the act, Congress strengthened this section by amending it with the passage of the Robinson-Patman Act in 1936.

As amended, Section 2 prohibits price discrimination that cannot be justified by differences in production costs or transportation costs, or cost differences due to other reasons. To violate Section 2, the seller must be engaged in interstate commerce, and the effect of the price discrimination must be to substantially lessen competition or create a competitive injury. Under Section 2, as amended, a seller is prohibited from reducing a price to one buyer below the price charged to that buyer's competitor. Even offering goods to different customers at the same price but with different delivery arrangements may violate Section 2 in some circumstances.[13]

An exception is made if the seller can justify the price reduction by demonstrating that the lower price was charged temporarily and in good faith to meet another seller's equally low price to the buyer's competitor. To be predatory, a seller's pricing policies must also include a reasonable prospect that the seller will recoup its losses.[14]

SECTION 3—EXCLUSIONARY PRACTICES

Under Section 3 of the Clayton Act, sellers or lessors cannot sell or lease goods "on the condition, agreement or understanding that the . . . purchaser or lessee thereof shall not use or deal in the goods . . . of a competitor or competitors of the seller."

PRICE DISCRIMINATION
Setting prices in such a way that two competing buyers pay two different prices for an identical product or service.

Microsoft's chairman and chief software architect, Bill Gates, demonstrates the future of Windows computing at an industry conference. Suppose that Microsoft stops requiring computer makers who want to install Windows to also install Microsoft's browser (Explorer) and exclude competing browsers. Also suppose that despite this change, Microsoft continues to maintain monopoly power in the relevant operating-system market. Can Microsoft still be guilty of the offense of monopolization? Why or why not? How might a rival firm prove the required intent? (EPA/Jeff Christensen/Landov)

---

13. *Bell v. Fur Breeders Agricultural Cooperative,* 3 F.Supp.2d 1241 (D. Utah 1998).

14. See, for example, *Brooke Group, Ltd. v. Brown & Williamson Tobacco Corp.,* 509 U.S. 209, 113 S.Ct. 2578, 125 L.Ed.2d 168 (1993), in which the Supreme Court held that a seller's price-cutting policies could not be predatory "[g]iven the market's realities"—the size of the seller's market share and the expanding output by other sellers, as well as additional factors.

In effect, this section prohibits two types of vertical agreements involving exclusionary practices—exclusive-dealing contracts and tying arrangements.

Exclusive-Dealing Contracts   A contract under which a seller forbids a buyer to purchase products from the seller's competitors is called an **exclusive-dealing contract.** A seller is prohibited from making an exclusive-dealing contract under Section 3 if the effect of the contract is "to substantially lessen competition or tend to create a monopoly."

■ **EXAMPLE 22.5** In *Standard Oil Co. of California v. United States,*[15] a leading case decided by the United States Supreme Court in 1949, the then-largest gasoline seller in the nation made exclusive-dealing contracts with independent stations in seven western states. The contracts involved 16 percent of all retail outlets, with sales amounting to approximately 7 percent of all retail sales in that market. The Court noted that the market was substantially concentrated because the seven largest gasoline suppliers all used exclusive-dealing contracts with their independent retailers and together controlled 65 percent of the market. Looking at market conditions after the arrangements were instituted, the Court found that market shares were extremely stable and that entry into the market was apparently restricted. Thus, the Court held that Section 3 of the Clayton Act had been violated because competition was "foreclosed in a substantial share" of the relevant market. ■

Tying Arrangements   When a seller conditions the sale of a product (the tying product) on the buyer's agreement to purchase another product (the tied product) produced or distributed by the same seller, a **tying arrangement,** or *tie-in sales agreement,* results. The legality of a tie-in agreement depends on many factors, particularly the purpose of the agreement and its likely effect on competition in the relevant markets (the market for the tying product and the market for the tied product).

■ **EXAMPLE 22.6** In 1936, the United States Supreme Court held that International Business Machines and Remington Rand had violated Section 3 of the Clayton Act by requiring the purchase of their own machine cards (the tied product) as a condition for leasing their tabulation machines (the tying product). Because only these two firms sold completely automated tabulation machines, the Court concluded that each possessed market power sufficient to "substantially lessen competition" through the tying arrangements.[16] ■

Section 3 of the Clayton Act has been held to apply only to commodities, not to services. Tying arrangements, however, can also be considered agreements that restrain trade in violation of Section 1 of the Sherman Act. Thus, cases involving tying arrangements of services have been brought under Section 1 of the Sherman Act. Traditionally, the courts have held tying arrangements challenged under the Sherman Act to be illegal *per se.* In recent years, however, courts have shown a willingness to look at factors that are important in a rule-of-reason analysis.

SECTION 7—MERGERS

Under Section 7 of the Clayton Act, a person or business organization cannot hold stock and/or assets in another entity "where the effect . . . may be to substantially lessen competition." Section 7 is the statutory authority for preventing mergers or acquisitions that could result in monopoly power or a substantial lessening of

---

EXCLUSIVE-DEALING CONTRACT
An agreement under which a seller forbids a buyer to purchase products from the seller's competitors.

TYING ARRANGEMENT
An agreement between a buyer and a seller in which the buyer of a specific product or service becomes obligated to purchase additional products or services from the seller.

Suppose that the owner of this gas station agrees to buy gas only from Shell Oil Company. Does this agreement necessarily violate the Clayton Act? Why or why not? (Noah Berger/Bloomberg News/Landov)

---

15. 337 U.S. 293, 69 S.Ct. 1051, 93 L.Ed. 1371 (1949).
16. *International Business Machines Corp. v. United States,* 298 U.S. 131, 56 S.Ct. 701, 80 L.Ed. 1085 (1936).

MARKET CONCENTRATION
The degree to which a small number of firms control a large percentage share of a relevant market; determined by calculating the percentages held by the largest firms in that market.

HORIZONTAL MERGER
A merger between two firms that are competing in the same marketplace.

VERTICAL MERGER
The acquisition by a company at one level in a marketing chain of a company at a higher or lower level in the chain (such as a company merging with one of its suppliers or retailers).

competition in the marketplace. Section 7 applies to horizontal mergers and vertical mergers, both of which we discuss in the following subsections.

A crucial consideration in most merger cases is the **market concentration** of a product or business. Determining market concentration involves allocating percentage market shares among the various companies in the relevant market. When a small number of companies control a large share of the market, the market is concentrated. For example, if the four largest grocery stores in Chicago accounted for 80 percent of all retail food sales, the market clearly would be concentrated in those four firms. Competition, however, is not necessarily diminished solely as a result of market concentration, and other factors will be considered in determining whether a merger will violate Section 7. One factor of particular importance in evaluating the effects of a merger is whether the merger will make it more difficult for potential competitors to enter the relevant market.

Horizontal Mergers Mergers between firms that compete with each other in the same market are called **horizontal mergers.** If a horizontal merger creates an entity with anything other than a small percentage market share, the merger will be presumed illegal. This is because the United States Supreme Court has held that Congress, in amending Section 7 of the Clayton Act in 1950, intended to prevent mergers that increase market concentration.[17] When analyzing the legality of a horizontal merger, the courts also consider three other factors: overall concentration of the relevant product market, the relevant market's history of tending toward concentration, and whether the apparent design of the merger is to establish market power or to restrict competition.

The Federal Trade Commission and the U.S. Department of Justice have established guidelines indicating which mergers will be challenged. Under the guidelines, the first factor to be considered is the degree of concentration in the relevant market. Other factors to be considered include the ease of entry into the relevant market, economic efficiency, the financial condition of the merging firms, the nature and price of the product or products involved, and so on. If a firm is a leading one—having at least a 35 percent share and twice that of the next leading firm—any merger with a firm having as little as a 1 percent share will probably be challenged.

Vertical Mergers A **vertical merger** occurs when a company at one stage of production acquires a company at a higher or lower stage of production. An example of a vertical merger is a company merging with one of its suppliers or retailers. In the past, courts focused almost exclusively on "foreclosure" in assessing vertical mergers. Foreclosure occurs because competitors of the merging firms lose opportunities to sell or buy products from the merging firms.

■ **EXAMPLE 22.7** In *United States v. E. I. du Pont de Nemours & Co.,*[18] du Pont was challenged for acquiring a considerable amount of General Motors (GM) stock. In holding that the transaction was illegal, the United States Supreme Court noted that the stock acquisition would enable du Pont to prevent other sellers of fabrics and finishes from selling to GM, which then accounted for 50 percent of all auto fabric and finishes purchases. ■

Today, whether a vertical merger will be deemed illegal generally depends on several factors, including market concentration, barriers to entry into the market, and the apparent intent of the merging parties. Mergers that do not prevent competitors

17. *Brown Shoe v. United States,* 370 U.S. 294, 82 S.Ct. 1502, 8 L.Ed.2d 510 (1962).
18. 353 U.S. 586, 77 S.Ct. 872, 1 L.Ed.2d 1057 (1957).

of either merging firm from competing in a segment of the market will not be condemned as "foreclosing" competition and are legal.

SECTION 8—INTERLOCKING DIRECTORATES

Section 8 of the Clayton Act deals with *interlocking directorates*—that is, the practice of having individuals serve as directors on the boards of two or more competing companies simultaneously. Specifically, no person may be a director in two or more competing corporations at the same time if either of the corporations has capital, surplus, or undivided profits aggregating more than $20,090,000 or competitive sales of $2,009,000 or more. The Federal Trade Commission (FTC) adjusts the threshold amounts each year. (The amounts given here are those announced by the FTC in 2004.)

CONTRAST Section 5 of the Federal Trade Commission Act is broader than the other antitrust laws. It covers virtually all anticompetitive behavior, including conduct that does not violate either the Sherman Act or the Clayton Act.

Enforcement of Antitrust Laws

The federal agencies that enforce the federal antitrust laws are the U.S. Department of Justice (DOJ) and the Federal Trade Commission (FTC). The FTC was established by the Federal Trade Commission Act of 1914. Section 5 of that act condemns all forms of anticompetitive behavior that are not covered under other federal antitrust laws.

Only the DOJ can prosecute violations of the Sherman Act, which can be either criminal or civil offenses. Either the DOJ or the FTC can enforce the Clayton Act, but violations of that statute are not crimes and can be pursued only through civil proceedings. The DOJ or the FTC may ask the courts to impose various remedies, including **divestiture** (making a company give up one or more of its operating functions) and dissolution. A group of meatpackers, for example, might be forced to divest itself of control or ownership of butcher shops. (To find out how you can avoid antitrust problems, see the *Application* feature at the end of this chapter.)

The FTC has the sole authority to enforce violations of Section 5 of the Federal Trade Commission Act. FTC actions are effected through administrative orders, but if a firm violates an FTC order, the FTC can seek court sanctions for the violation.

DIVESTITURE
The act of selling one or more of a company's divisions or parts, such as a subsidiary or plant; often mandated by the courts in merger or monopolization cases.

You can find links to the home pages for federal government agencies, including the Department of Justice and the Federal Trade Commission, at **http://www.firstgov.gov**.

PRIVATE ACTIONS

A private party who has been injured as a result of a violation of the Sherman Act or the Clayton Act can sue for damages and attorneys' fees. In some instances, private parties may also seek injunctive relief to prevent antitrust violations. The courts have determined that the ability to sue depends on the directness of the injury suffered by the would-be plaintiff. Thus, a person wishing to sue under the Sherman Act must prove (1) that the antitrust violation either caused or was a substantial factor in causing the injury that was suffered and (2) that the unlawful actions of the accused party affected business activities of the plaintiff that were protected by the antitrust laws.

TREBLE DAMAGES

TREBLE DAMAGES
Damages that, by statute, are three times the amount that the fact finder determines is owed.

In recent years, more than 90 percent of all antitrust actions have been brought by private plaintiffs. One reason for this is that successful plaintiffs may recover **treble damages**—three times the damages that they have suffered as a result of the violation. Such recoveries by private plaintiffs for antitrust violations have been rationalized as encouraging people to act as "private attorneys general" who will vigorously pursue antitrust violators on their own initiative.

In a situation involving a price-fixing agreement, normally each competitor is jointly and severally liable for the total amount of any damages, including treble damages if they are imposed. Should the presence of multiple wholesalers, retailers, and other intermediaries affect this assessment of damages? That was the question before the court in the following case.

CASE 22.3 ■ Paper Systems Inc. v. Nippon Paper Industries Co.

United States Court of Appeals,
Seventh Circuit, 2002.
281 F.3d 629.
http://www.ca7.uscourts.gov[a]

FACTS In the 1990s, the five major producers of thermal fax paper used different distribution systems. Kanzaki Specialty Papers, Inc., and Appleton Papers, Inc., sold directly to firms such as Paper Systems, Inc., which resold the paper to its own customers. Two other manufacturers, Oji Paper Company and Mitsubishi Paper Mills Limited, sold exclusively to distributors that resold the paper to firms such as Paper Systems. The fifth manufacturer, the predecessor of Nippon Paper Industries Company, sold its output in Japan to Japanese firms, which resold the paper through subsidiaries around the world. Paper Systems and two other buyers filed a suit in a federal district court against Nippon and the other paper producers, alleging violations of the antitrust laws. Four of the defendants reached a settlement with the plaintiffs, and the court dismissed the claim against Nippon. The plaintiffs appealed this dismissal to the U.S. Court of Appeals for the Seventh Circuit. Nippon argued that even if it was liable, the presence of so many wholesalers, retailers, and others in the chain of distribution created complications, including possible double recovery, too great to impose joint liability.

ISSUE Was Nippon jointly and severally (separately) liable for the total amount of damages, even though there were multiple parties in the chain of distribution?

DECISION Yes. The U.S. Court of Appeals for the Seventh Circuit reversed the lower court's decision and

remanded the case for a determination as to whether Nippon had been a member of the cartel. If Nippon had been a member, the court held that Nippon was jointly and severally liable for the cartel's entire overcharge.

REASON The appellate court held that if Nippon had been a member of the cartel, it was jointly and severally liable for the cartel's entire overcharge to any direct purchaser from any conspirator, to the extent of the damages attributable to that buyer's direct purchases. The court pointed out that under the rule of joint and several liability, "each member of a conspiracy is liable for all damages caused by the conspiracy's entire output. * * * If Nippon Paper was among those conspirators, then it is responsible for the entire overcharge of all five manufacturers—and any direct purchaser from any conspirator can collect its own portion of damages (that is, the damages attributable to its direct purchases) from any conspirator. This makes it impossible to dismiss Nippon Paper outright." As for the "overcharges" and "duplicative recovery," the court found that "tracing overcharges through the chain of distribution * * * is unimportant [and] duplicative recovery has been blocked at the outset." The court explained that regardless of the number of parties in the chain of distribution, no direct purchaser could recover more than the amount the purchaser paid in overcharges (multiplied by three because of the trebling of damages).

WHY IS THIS CASE IMPORTANT? *This case illustrates that the consequences of violating antitrust laws can be harsh, particularly when several businesses are involved in a conspiracy. Each violator can be forced to pay an injured party the entire amount of that party's damages times three (treble damages), even if that violator was not responsible for all of those damages.*

a. In the left column, click on "Opinions." On the next page, in the "Last Name or Corporation" box, enter "Nippon," select "Begins," and click on "Search for Person." Click on the number next to the name of the case in the result to access the opinion.

▦ Exemptions from Antitrust Laws

There are many legislative and constitutional limitations on antitrust enforcement. Most statutory and judicially created exemptions to the antitrust laws apply to the following areas or activities:

1 *Labor.* Section 6 of the Clayton Act generally permits labor unions to organize and bargain without violating antitrust laws. Section 20 of the Clayton Act specifies that strikes and other labor activities are not violations of any law of the United States. A union can lose its exemption, however, if it combines with a nonlabor group rather than acting simply in its own self-interest.

2 *Agricultural associations and fisheries.* Section 6 of the Clayton Act (along with the Capper-Volstead Act of 1922) exempts agricultural cooperatives from the antitrust laws. The Fisheries Cooperative Marketing Act of 1976 exempts from antitrust legislation individuals in the fishing industry who collectively catch, produce, and prepare for market their products. Both exemptions allow members of such co-ops to combine and set prices for a particular product, but do not allow them to engage in exclusionary practices or restraints of trade directed at competitors.

3 *Insurance.* The McCarran-Ferguson Act of 1945 exempts the insurance business from the antitrust laws whenever state regulation exists. This exemption does not cover boycotts, coercion, or intimidation on the part of insurance companies.

4 *Foreign trade.* Under the provisions of the Webb-Pomerene Act of 1918, U.S. exporters may engage in cooperative activity to compete with similar foreign associations. This type of cooperative activity may not, however, restrain trade within the United States or injure other U.S. exporters. The Export Trading Company Act of 1982 broadened the Webb-Pomerene Act by permitting the Department of Justice to certify properly qualified export trading companies. Any activity within the scope described by the certificate is exempt from public prosecution under the antitrust laws.

5 *Professional baseball.* In 1922, the United States Supreme Court held that professional baseball was not within the reach of federal antitrust laws because it did not involve "interstate commerce."[19] Some of the effects of this decision, however, were modified by the Curt Flood Act of 1998. Essentially, the act allows players the option of suing team owners for anticompetitive practices if, for example, the owners collude to "blacklist" players, hold down players' salaries, or force players to play for specific teams.[20]

6 *Oil marketing.* The Interstate Oil Compact of 1935 allows states to determine quotas on oil that will be marketed in interstate commerce.

7 *Cooperative research and production.* Cooperative research among small-business firms is exempt under the Small Business Act of 1958, as amended. Research or production of a product, process, or service by joint ventures con-

---

19. *Federal Baseball Club of Baltimore, Inc. v. National League of Professional Baseball Clubs,* 259 U.S. 200, 42 S.Ct. 465, 66 L.Ed. 898 (1922).

20. In 2003, a federal appellate court held that because baseball was exempt from federal antitrust laws, it was also exempt from the reach of state antitrust laws due to the supremacy clause. *Major League Baseball v. Crist,* 331 F.3d 1177 (11th Cir. 2003).

sisting of competitors is exempt under special federal legislation, including the National Cooperative Research Act of 1984 and the National Cooperative Production Amendments of 1993.

8 *Joint efforts by businesspersons to obtain legislative or executive action.* This is often referred to as the *Noerr-Pennington* doctrine.[21] For example, DVD producers may jointly lobby Congress to change the copyright laws without being held liable for attempting to restrain trade. Though selfish rather than purely public-minded conduct is permitted, there is an exception: an action will not be protected if it is clear that the action is "objectively baseless in the sense that no reasonable [person] could reasonably expect success on the merits" and it is an attempt to make anticompetitive use of government processes.[22]

9 *Other exemptions.* Other activities exempt from antitrust laws include activities approved by the president in furtherance of the defense of our nation (under the Defense Production Act of 1950, as amended); state actions, when the state policy is clearly articulated and the policy is actively supervised by the state;[23] and activities of regulated industries (such as the communication and banking industries) when federal commissions, boards, or agencies (such as the Federal Communications Commission and the Federal Maritime Commission) have primary regulatory authority.

> **NOTE** State actions include the regulation of public utilities, whose rates may be set by the states in which they do business.

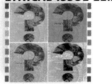

ETHICAL ISSUE 22.2

Should the U.S. Postal Service, which can "sue or be sued" for violating other laws, be exempt from antitrust laws? In 2004, the United States Supreme Court decided *United States Postal Service v. Flamingo.*[24] The case had both legal and ethical ramifications: Should the federal government be able to engage in activities that are forbidden to private businesses by antitrust laws? The lawsuit was brought by Flamingo Industries, which produces mailbags. Flamingo claimed that the Postal Service had adopted outdated requirements for mailbags that could not be met by U.S. producers using modern manufacturing methods so that it could buy cheaper, lower-quality mailbags made in Mexico. According to Flamingo, these activities suppressed competition and created a monopoly in violation of federal laws.

Under the Postal Reorganization Act (PRA) of 1970, the Postal Service is "an independent establishment" that has the power to "sue and be sued in its official name."[25] Flamingo argued that by using the phrase "sue and be sued," Congress had intended to waive the Postal Service's immunity to suits for violating federal antitrust laws. The federal appellate court agreed, but the Supreme Court reversed, holding that the Sherman Act does not apply to the Postal Service because it is a government-run operation and differs from private businesses. The Postal Service is not a profit-seeking enterprise, and the government granted its monopoly on mail delivery. Therefore, the Court concluded that antitrust laws do not apply. ▪

---

21. See *United Mine Workers of America v. Pennington,* 381 U.S. 657, 89 S.Ct. 1585, 14 L.Ed.2d 626 (1965); and *Eastern Railroad Presidents Conference v. Noerr Motor Freight, Inc.,* 365 U.S. 127, 81 S.Ct. 523, 5 L.Ed.2d 464 (1961).
22. *Professional Real Estate Investors, Inc. v. Columbia Pictures Industries, Inc.,* 508 U.S. 49, 113 S.Ct. 1920, 123 L.Ed.2d 611 (1993).
23. See *Parker v. Brown,* 317 U.S. 341, 63 S.Ct. 307, 87 L.Ed. 315 (1943).
24. 540 U.S. 736, 124 S.Ct. 1321, 158 L.Ed.2d 19 (2004).
25. 39 U.S.C. Section 401(1).

APPLICATION ■■ How Can You Avoid Antitrust Problems?*

Business managers need to be aware of how antitrust legislation may affect their activities. In addition to the federal antitrust laws covered in this chapter, numerous state antitrust laws also exist. States also now have the power to bring civil suits to enforce federal antitrust laws. Additionally, antitrust law is subject to various interpretations by the courts. Unless a businessperson exercises caution, a court may decide that his or her actions are in violation of a federal or state statute.

If you are a business manager or owner, you should be careful when communicating with a direct competitor that offers products or services that are similar to those of your own company. If you know that such communications might cause problems in your line of business, you should probably arrange for the appropriate employees to attend

a seminar given by professionals who will explain what is legal and what is not in dealing with competitors. Generally, any businessperson who is worried about potential antitrust violations should seek counsel from a competent attorney specializing in antitrust law.

** This *Application* is not meant to substitute for the services of an attorney who is licensed to practice law in your state.*

CHECKLIST FOR AVOIDING ANTITRUST PROBLEMS

1. Exercise caution when communicating and dealing with competitors.
2. Seek the advice of an attorney specializing in antitrust law to ensure that your business practices and agreements do not violate antitrust laws.
3. If you conduct business ventures in other countries, obtain the advice of an attorney who is familiar with the antitrust laws of those nations.

■■ KEY TERMS

CHAPTER SUMMARY ■■ Antitrust Law

The Sherman Antitrust Act (1890) (See pages 674–685.)	1. *Major provisions—*
	
	a. Section 1—Prohibits contracts, combinations, and conspiracies in restraint of trade.
	
	   (1) Horizontal restraints subject to Section 1 include price-fixing agreements, group boycotts (joint refusals to deal), horizontal market divisions, and trade association agreements.
	
	   (2) Vertical restraints subject to Section 1 include territorial or customer restrictions, resale price maintenance agreements, and refusals to deal.
	
	b. Section 2—Prohibits monopolies and attempts to monopolize.
	
	2. *Jurisdictional requirements—*The Sherman Act applies only to activities that have a significant impact on interstate commerce.

CHAPTER SUMMARY ▦ Antitrust Law—Continued

The Sherman Antitrust Act (1890)—Continued	3. *Interpretative rules—* a. *Per se* rule—Applied to restraints on trade that are so inherently anticompetitive that they cannot be justified and are deemed illegal as a matter of law. b. Rule of reason—Applied when an anticompetitive agreement may be justified by legitimate benefits. Under the rule of reason, the lawfulness of a trade restraint will be determined by the purpose and effects of the restraint.
The Clayton Act (1914) (See pages 685–688.)	The major provisions are as follows: 1. *Section 2*—As amended in 1936 by the Robinson-Patman Act, prohibits price discrimination that substantially lessens competition and prohibits a seller engaged in interstate commerce from selling to two or more buyers goods of similar grade and quality at different prices when the result is a substantial lessening of competition or the creation of a competitive injury. 2. *Section 3*—Prohibits exclusionary practices, such as exclusive-dealing contracts and tying arrangements, when the effect may be to substantially lessen competition. 3. *Section 7*—Prohibits mergers when the effect may be to substantially lessen competition or to tend to create a monopoly. a. Horizontal mergers—The acquisition by merger or consolidation of a competing firm engaged in the same relevant market. Will be unlawful only if the merger results in the merging firms' holding a disproportionate share of the market, resulting in a substantial lessening of competition, and if the merger does not enhance consumer welfare by increasing efficiency of production or marketing. b. Vertical mergers—The acquisition by a seller of one of its buyers or vice versa. Will be unlawful if the merger prevents competitors of either merging firm from competing in a segment of the market that otherwise would be open to them, resulting in a substantial lessening of competition. 4. *Section 8*—Prohibits interlocking directorates.
Enforcement of Antitrust Laws (See pages 688–689.)	Federal agencies that enforce antitrust laws are the Department of Justice and the Federal Trade Commission, which was established by the Federal Trade Commission Act of 1914. Private parties who have been injured as a result of violations of the Sherman Act or Clayton Act may also bring civil suits. In recent years, many private parties have filed such suits largely because, if successful, they may be awarded treble damages and attorneys' fees.
Exemptions from Antitrust Laws (See pages 690–691.)	1. Labor unions (under Section 6 of the Clayton Act of 1914). 2. Agricultural associations and fisheries (under Section 6 of the Clayton Act of 1914, the Capper-Volstead Act of 1922, and the Fisheries Cooperative Marketing Act of 1976). 3. Insurance when state regulation exists (under the McCarran-Ferguson Act of 1945). 4. Export trading companies (under the Webb-Pomerene Act of 1918 and the Export Trading Company Act of 1982). 5. Professional baseball (by a 1922 judicial decision, although modified by a 1998 federal statute). 6. Oil marketing (under the Interstate Oil Compact of 1935). 7. Cooperative research and production (under various acts, including the Small Business Act of 1958, as amended, the National Cooperative Research Act of 1984, and the National Cooperative Production Amendments of 1993). 8. Joint efforts by businesspersons to obtain legislative or executive action (under the *Noerr-Pennington* doctrine). 9. Other activities, including certain national defense activities, state actions, and activities of certain regulated industries.

FOR REVIEW

Answers for the even-numbered questions in this For Review *section can be found in Appendix I at the end of this text.*

1 What is a monopoly? What is market power? How do these concepts relate to each other?

2 What type of activity is prohibited by Section 1 of the Sherman Act? What type of activity is prohibited by Section 2 of the Sherman Act?

3 What are the four major provisions of the Clayton Act, and what types of activities do these provisions prohibit?

4 What agencies of the federal government enforce the federal antitrust laws?

5 What are four activities that are exempt from the antitrust laws?

QUESTIONS AND CASE PROBLEMS

22–1. Sherman Act. An agreement that is blatantly and substantially anticompetitive is deemed a *per se* violation of Section 1 of the Sherman Act. Under what rule is an agreement analyzed if it appears to be anticompetitive but is not a *per se* violation? In making this analysis, what factors will a court consider?

22–2. Antitrust Laws. Allitron, Inc., and Donovan, Ltd., are interstate competitors selling similar appliances, principally in the states of Illinois, Indiana, Kentucky, and Ohio. Allitron and Donovan agree that Allitron will no longer sell in Ohio and Indiana and that Donovan will no longer sell in Kentucky and Illinois. Have Allitron and Donovan violated any antitrust laws? If so, which law? Explain.

22–3. Horizontal Restraints. Jorge's Appliance Corp. was a new retail seller of appliances in Sunrise City. Because of its innovative sales techniques and financing, Jorge's caused the appliance department of No-Glow Department Store, a large chain store with a great deal of buying power, to lose a substantial amount of sales. No-Glow told a number of appliance manufacturers that if they continued to sell to Jorge's, No-Glow would discontinue its large volume of purchases from them. The manufacturers immediately stopped selling appliances to Jorge's. Jorge's filed suit against No-Glow and the manufacturers, claiming that their actions constituted an antitrust violation. No-Glow and the manufacturers were able to prove that Jorge's was a small retailer with a small portion of the market. They claimed that because the relevant market was not substantially affected, they were not guilty of restraint of trade. Discuss fully whether there was an antitrust violation.

22–4. Exclusionary Practices. Instant Foto Corp. is a manufacturer of photography film. At the present time, Instant Foto has approximately 50 percent of the market. Instant Foto advertises that the purchase price for its film includes photo processing by Instant Foto Corp. Instant Foto claims that its film processing is specially designed to improve the quality of photos taken with Instant Foto film. Is Instant Foto's combination of film and film processing an antitrust violation? Explain.

22–5. Tying Arrangement. Public Interest Corp. (PIC) owned and operated the television station WTMV-TV in Lakeland, Florida. MCA Television, Ltd., owns and licenses syndicated television programs. The parties entered into a licensing contract with respect to several television shows. MCA conditioned the license on PIC's agreeing to take another show, *Harry and the Hendersons*. PIC agreed to this arrangement, although it would not have chosen to license *Harry* if it had not had to do so to secure the licenses for the other shows. More than two years into the contract, a dispute arose over PIC's payments, and negotiations failed to resolve the dispute. In a letter, MCA suspended PIC's broadcast rights for all of its shows and stated that "[a]ny telecasts of MCA programming by WTMV-TV . . . will be deemed unauthorized and shall constitute an infringement of MCA's copyrights." PIC nonetheless continued broadcasting MCA's programs, with the exception of *Harry*. MCA filed a suit in a federal district court against PIC, alleging breach of contract and copyright infringement. PIC filed a counterclaim, contending in part that MCA's deal was an illegal tying arrangement. Is PIC correct? Explain. [*MCA Television, Ltd. v. Public Interest Corp.*, 171 F.3d 1265 (11th Cir. 1999)]

CASE PROBLEM WITH SAMPLE ANSWER

22–6. In 1995, to make personal computers (PCs) easier to use, Intel Corp. and other companies developed a standard, called the Universal Serial Bus (USB) specification, to enable peripherals (printers and other hardware) to be easily attached to PCs. Intel and others formed the Universal Serial Bus Implementers Forum (USB-IF) to promote USB technology and products. Intel, however, makes relatively few USB products and does not make any USB interconnect devices. Multivideo Labs, Inc. (MVL), designed and distributed Active Extension Cables (AECs) to connect peripheral devices to each other or to a PC. The AECs were not USB compliant, a fact that Intel employees told other USB-IF members. Asserting that this caused a "general cooling of the market" for AECs, MVL filed a suit in a federal district court against Intel, claiming in part attempted monopolization in violation of the Sherman Act. Intel filed a motion for summary judgment. How should the court rule, and why? [*Multivideo Labs, Inc. v. Intel Corp.*, __ F.Supp.2d __ (S.D.N.Y. 2000)]

After you have answered this problem, compare your answer with the sample answer given on the Web site that accompanies this text. Go to http://blt.westbuslaw.com, select "Chapter 22," and click on "Case Problem with Sample Answer."

22–7. Monopolization. Moist snuff is a smokeless tobacco product sold in small round cans from racks, which include point-of-sale (POS) ads. POS ads are critical because tobacco advertising is restricted and the number of people who use smokeless tobacco products is relatively small. In the moist snuff market in the United States, there are only four competitors, including U.S. Tobacco Co. and its affiliates (USTC) and Conwood Co. In 1990, USTC, which held 87 percent of the market, began to convince major retailers, including Wal-Mart Stores, Inc., to use USTC's "exclusive racks" to display its products and those of all other snuff makers. USTC agents would then destroy competitors' racks. USTC also began to provide retailers with false sales data to convince them to maintain its poor-selling items and drop competitors' less expensive products. Conwood's Wal-Mart market share fell from 12 percent to 6.5 percent. In stores in which USTC did not have rack exclusivity, however, Conwood's market share increased to 25 percent. Conwood filed a suit in a federal district court against USTC, alleging in part that USTC used its monopoly power to exclude competitors from the moist snuff market. Should the court rule in Conwood's favor? What is USTC's best defense? Discuss. [*Conwood Co., L.P. v. U.S. Tobacco Co.*, 290 F.3d 768 (6th Cir. 2002)]

22–8. Restraint of Trade. Visa U.S.A., Inc., MasterCard International, Inc., American Express (Amex), and Discover are the four major credit- and charge-card networks in the United States. Visa and MasterCard are joint ventures, owned by the thousands of banks that are their members. The banks issue the cards, clear transactions, and collect fees from the merchants that accept the cards. By contrast, Amex and Discover themselves issue cards to customers, process transactions, and collect fees. Since 1995, Amex has asked banks to issue its cards. No bank has been willing to do so, however, because it would have to stop issuing Visa and MasterCard cards under those networks' rules barring member banks from issuing cards on rival networks. The U.S. Department of Justice filed a suit in a federal district court against Visa and MasterCard, alleging in part that the rules were illegal restraints of trade under the Sherman Act. Do the rules harm competition? If so, how? What relief might the court order to stop any anticompetitiveness? [*United States v. Visa U.S.A., Inc.*, 344 F.3d 229 (2d Cir. 2003)]

A QUESTION OF ETHICS

22–9. A group of lawyers in the District of Columbia regularly acted as court-appointed attorneys for indigent defendants in District of Columbia criminal cases. At a meeting of the Superior Court Trial Lawyers Association (SCTLA), the attorneys agreed to stop providing this representation until the district increased their compensation. Their subsequent boycott had a severe impact on the district's criminal justice system, and the District of Columbia gave in to the lawyers' demands for higher pay. After the lawyers had returned to work, the Federal Trade Commission filed a complaint against the SCTLA and four of its officers and, after an investigation, ruled that the SCTLA's activities constituted an illegal group boycott in violation of antitrust laws. [*Federal Trade Commission v. Superior Court Trial Lawyers Association*, 493 U.S. 411, 110 S.Ct. 768, 107 L.Ed.2d 851 (1990)]

1. The SCTLA obviously was aware of the negative impact its decision would have on the district's criminal justice system. Given this fact, do you think the lawyers behaved ethically?

2. On appeal, the SCTLA claimed that its boycott was undertaken to publicize that the attorneys were underpaid and that the boycott thus constituted an expression protected by the First Amendment. Do you agree with this argument?

3. Labor unions have the right to strike when negotiations between labor and management fail to result in agreement. Is it fair to prohibit members of the SCTLA from "striking" against their employer, the District of Columbia, simply because the SCTLA is a professional organization and not a labor union?

FOR CRITICAL ANALYSIS

22–10. Critics of antitrust law claim that in the long run, competitive market forces will eliminate private monopolies unless they are fostered by government regulation. Do you agree? Why or why not?

INTERNET EXERCISES

Go to the *Business Law Today: The Essentials* home page at **http://blt.westbuslaw.com,** select "Chapter 22," and click on "Internet Exercises." There you will find the following Internet research exercises that you can perform to learn more about topics covered in this chapter.

Activity 22–1: LEGAL PERSPECTIVE—The Standard Oil Trust

Activity 22–2: MANAGEMENT PERSPECTIVE—Avoiding Antitrust Problems

BEFORE THE TEST

Go to the *Business Law Today: The Essentials* home page at **http://blt.westbuslaw.com,** select "Chapter 22," and click on "Interactive Quizzes." You will find at least twenty interactive questions relating to this chapter.

CHAPTER 23

Personal Property, Bailments, and Insurance

"The great . . . end . . . of men united into commonwealths, and putting themselves under government, is the preservation of their property."

John Locke, 1632–1704
(English political philosopher)

CHAPTER OUTLINE

■ PROPERTY OWNERSHIP

■ ACQUIRING OWNERSHIP
  OF PERSONAL PROPERTY

■ MISLAID, LOST, AND
  ABANDONED PROPERTY

■ BAILMENTS

■ INSURANCE

▦ LEARNING OBJECTIVES

After reading this chapter, you should be able to answer the following questions:

1 What is real property? What is personal property?

2 What are the three elements necessary for an effective gift? How else can property be acquired?

3 What are the three elements of a bailment? What are the basic rights and duties of a bailee? What are the rights and duties of a bailor?

4 What is an insurable interest? When must an insurable interest exist—at the time the insurance policy is obtained, at the time the loss occurs, or both?

5 What clauses are typically included in insurance contracts?

PROPERTY
Legally protected rights and interests in anything with an ascertainable value that is subject to ownership.

REAL PROPERTY
Land and everything attached to it, such as trees and buildings.

PERSONAL PROPERTY
Property that is movable; any property that is not real property.

CHATTEL
All forms of personal property.

Property consists of the legally protected rights and interests a person has in anything with an ascertainable value that is subject to ownership. Property would have little value (and the word would have little meaning) if the law did not define the right to use it, to sell or dispose of it, and to prevent trespass on it. Indeed, John Locke, as indicated in the opening quotation, considered the preservation of property to be the primary reason for the establishment of government.

Property is divided into real property and personal property. **Real property** (sometimes called *realty* or *real estate*) means the land and everything permanently attached to it. Everything else is **personal property**, or *personalty*. Attorneys sometimes refer to personal property as **chattel**, a term used under the common law to denote all forms of personal property. Personal property can be tangible or intangible. *Tangible* personal property, such as a television set or a car, has physical substance. *Intangible* personal property represents some set of rights and interests but has no real physical existence. Stocks and bonds, patents, and copyrights are examples of intangible personal property.

In the first part of this chapter, we look at the ways in which title to property is held; the methods of acquiring ownership of personal property; and issues relating to mislaid, lost, and abandoned personal property. In the second part of the chapter, we examine bailment relationships. A *bailment* is created when personal property is temporarily delivered into the care of another without a transfer of title. This is the distinguishing characteristic of a bailment compared with a sale or a gift—there is no passage of title and no intent to transfer title. In the last part of this chapter, we consider insurance, which is a foremost concern of property owners and others. By insuring our property, and our lives, we protect ourselves against damage and loss.

■ Property Ownership

Property ownership[1] can be viewed as a bundle of rights, including the right to possess property and to dispose of it—by sale, gift, lease, or other means.

FEE SIMPLE

A person who holds the entire bundle of rights to property is said to be the owner in **fee simple.** The owner in fee simple is entitled to use, possess, or dispose of the property as he or she chooses during his or her lifetime, and on this owner's death, the interests in the property descend to his or her heirs. We will return to this form of property ownership in Chapter 24, in the context of ownership rights in real property.

CONCURRENT OWNERSHIP

Persons who share ownership rights simultaneously in a particular piece of property are said to be *concurrent* owners. There are two principal types of **concurrent ownership:** *tenancy in common* and *joint tenancy.* Other types of concurrent ownership include tenancy by the entirety and community property.

Tenancy in Common   The term **tenancy in common** refers to a form of co-ownership in which each of two or more persons owns an *undivided* interest in the property. The interest is undivided because each tenant has rights in the *whole* property. ■ **EXAMPLE 23.1** Rosa and Chad own a rare stamp collection together as tenants in common. This does not mean that Rosa owns some particular stamps and Chad others. Rather, it means that Rosa and Chad each have rights in the *entire* collection. (If Rosa owned some of the stamps and Chad owned others, then the interest would be *divided*.) ■

On the death of a tenant in common, that tenant's interest in the property passes to her or his heirs. ■ **EXAMPLE 23.2** Should Rosa die before Chad, a one-half interest in the stamp collection will become the property of Rosa's heirs. If Rosa sells her interest to Fred before she dies, Fred and Chad will be co-owners as tenants in common. If Fred dies, his interest in the personal property will pass to his heirs, and they in turn will own the property with Chad as tenants in common. ■

FEE SIMPLE
An absolute form of property ownership entitling the property owner to use, possess, or dispose of the property as he or she chooses during his or her lifetime. On death, the interest in the property descends to the owner's heirs.

CONCURRENT OWNERSHIP
Joint ownership.

TENANCY IN COMMON
Co-ownership of property in which each party owns an undivided interest that passes to her or his heirs at death.

---

1. The principles discussed in this section apply equally to real property ownership, discussed in Chapter 24.

How should the value of the property owned by two tenants in common be apportioned when neither tenant has died but both agree that their interests should be divided? This was the question in the following case.

CASE 23.1 ▪ Clark v. Dady

Missouri Court of Appeals,
Western District, 2004.
131 S.W.3d 382.
http://www.findlaw.com/11stategov/mo/moca.html[a]

FACTS In 1998, John Dady and Mary Clark bought a mobile home in Missouri for $35,848. Clark made a $4,000 down payment. Greentree Financial financed the $31,848 balance through a promissory note signed by both parties, in whose names title was issued. They lived together until August 2001 when Dady moved out. Clark made the subsequent payments on the note and for the lot rental and utilities. Less than six months later, Clark filed a petition in a Missouri state court against Dady, asking in part that she be adjudged "the rightful owner of [the] personal property due to the care and amount of money that she has contributed to the purchase." A balance of $31,964.19, including interest, was due on the note. John Dady asked to be reimbursed for the cost of adding a $10,000 deck, a $1,500 barn, and $2,000 worth of landscaping, plus "hours of painting" and his portion of the rental value of the mobile home after he had moved out. The court awarded the mobile home to Clark and ordered Dady to pay her $3,050 for his half of the lot and loan payments that she made after he had left. Dady appealed to a state intermediate appellate court.

ISSUE Did the trial court properly determine the respective interests of the owners of the property?

DECISION No. The state intermediate appellate court reversed the judgment of the lower court and remanded

the case for a decision as to which expenses should be credited to the parties.[b]

REASON The court held that tenants in common own property in equal shares if the transfer that created their interests does not state otherwise, or if there is no other evidence showing the contributions of the owners toward the acquisition of the property to be unequal. Contributions toward acquisition include liability incurred in financing any part of the purchase price. Here, Clark made the down payment, but the parties jointly obligated themselves for the payment of the balance by signing a promissory note. The court explained, "As a result of the appellant's [Dady's] being jointly obligated on the note, he is considered to have contributed $15,924 to the acquisition of the mobile home ($31,848/2)." In other words, he owned "a 44.42% ($15,924/$35,848) share." The court acknowledged its responsibility to make a final determination of the parties' interests, but remanded the case because "the record is insufficient to allow us to determine what, if any, expenditures should be reimbursed to the parties."

WHY IS THIS CASE IMPORTANT? *As this case illustrates, how property is held can have a significant impact on the respective rights of the parties. In the absence of conflicting evidence, courts will presume that tenants in common own equal shares of the property, even if the parties' contributions to the property were unequal.*

b. The lower court's decision on remand was not available at the time this book went to press, but it may be by the time you read this. If you have purchased access to Westlaw Campus, you may be able to locate the remanded decision using that database. Alternatively, you might be able to find the case online at some other site. (See this text's inside front cover for information on Westlaw Campus and URLs for online court decisions.)

a. In the "Court of Appeals" section, in the "2004" row, click on "April." On the next page, in the "04/06/2004" section, click on the docket number beside the name of the case to access the opinion.

JOINT TENANCY
The joint ownership of property by two or more co-owners in which each co-owner owns an undivided portion of the property. On the death of one of the joint tenants, his or her interest automatically passes to the surviving joint tenant(s).

Joint Tenancy In a **joint tenancy,** each of two or more persons owns an undivided interest in the property, and a deceased joint tenant's interest passes to the surviving joint tenant or tenants. The rights of a surviving joint tenant to inherit a deceased joint tenant's ownership interest—which are referred to as *survivorship rights*—distinguish the joint tenancy from the tenancy in common. A joint tenancy can be terminated before a joint tenant's death by gift or by sale; in this situation, the person who receives the property as a gift or who purchases the property becomes a tenant in common, not a joint tenant.

■ **EXAMPLE 23.3** If, in the preceding example, Rosa and Chad held their stamp collection in a joint tenancy and if Rosa died before Chad, the entire collection would become the property of Chad; Rosa's heirs would receive absolutely no interest in the collection. If Rosa, while living, sold her interest to Fred, however, the sale would terminate the joint tenancy, and Fred and Chad would become owners as tenants in common. ■

Generally, it is presumed that a co-tenancy is a tenancy in common unless there is a clear intention to establish a joint tenancy. Thus, language such as "to Jerrold and Eva as joint tenants with right of survivorship, and not as tenants in common" would be necessary to create a joint tenancy.

Tenancy by the Entirety   A **tenancy by the entirety** is a less common form of ownership that can be created by a conveyance (transfer) of real property to a husband and wife. It differs from a joint tenancy only by the fact that neither spouse can make a separate lifetime transfer of his or her interest without the consent of the other spouse. In some states where statutes give the wife the right to convey her property, this form of concurrent ownership has been effectively abolished. A divorce, either spouse's death, or mutual agreement will terminate a tenancy by the entirety.

Community Property   A married couple is allowed to own property as **community property** in only a limited number of states.[2] If property is held as community property, each spouse technically owns an undivided one-half interest in property acquired during the marriage. Generally, community property does not include property acquired prior to the marriage or property acquired by gift or inheritance as separate property during the marriage. After a divorce, community property is divided equally in some states and according to the discretion of the court in other states.

■ Acquiring Ownership of Personal Property

The most common way of acquiring personal property is by purchasing it. We have already discussed the purchase and sale of personal property (goods) in Chapters 11 and 12. Often, property is acquired by will or inheritance. Here we look at additional ways in which ownership of personal property can be acquired, including acquisition by possession, production, gift, accession, and confusion.

POSSESSION

One example of acquiring ownership by possession is the capture of wild animals. Wild animals belong to no one in their natural state, and the first person to take possession of a wild animal normally owns it. The killing of a wild animal amounts to assuming ownership of it. Merely being in hot pursuit does not give title, however. This basic rule has two exceptions. First, any wild animals captured by a trespasser are the property of the landowner, not the trespasser. Second, if wild animals are captured or killed in violation of wild-game statutes, the state, and not the capturer,

---

TENANCY BY THE ENTIRETY
The joint ownership of property by a husband and wife. Neither party can transfer her or his interest in the property without the consent of the other.

COMMUNITY PROPERTY
A form of concurrent ownership of property in which each spouse technically owns an undivided one-half interest in property acquired during the marriage. This form of joint ownership occurs in only ten states and Puerto Rico.

---

2. These states include Alaska, Arizona, California, Idaho, Louisiana, Nevada, New Mexico, Texas, Washington, and Wisconsin. Puerto Rico allows property to be owned as community property as well.

obtains title to the animals. (Sometimes, a question arises as to what is a wild animal—see this chapter's *Letter of the Law* feature.)

Those who find lost or abandoned property can also acquire ownership rights through mere possession of the property, as will be discussed later in the chapter. (Ownership rights in real property can also be acquired through possession, such as adverse possession—see Chapter 24.)

PRODUCTION

Production—the fruits of labor—is another means of acquiring ownership of personal property. For instance, writers, inventors, and manufacturers all produce personal property and thereby acquire title to it. (In some situations, though, as when a researcher is hired to invent a new product or technique, the researcher-producer may not own what is produced—see Chapter 17.)

GIFTS

GIFT
Any voluntary transfer of property made without consideration, past or present.

A **gift** is another fairly common means of acquiring and transferring ownership of real and personal property. A gift is essentially a voluntary transfer of property ownership for which no consideration is given. As discussed in Chapter 7, the presence of consideration is what distinguishes a contract from a gift.

To be an effective gift, three requirements must be met—donative intent on the part of the *donor* (the one giving the gift), delivery, and acceptance by the *donee* (the one receiving the gift). We examine each of these requirements here, as well as the requirements of a gift made in contemplation of imminent death. Until these three requirements are met, no effective gift has been made. ■ **EXAMPLE 23.4** Suppose that your aunt tells you that she *intends* to give you a new Mercedes-Benz for your next birthday. This is simply a promise to make a gift. It is not considered a gift until the Mercedes-Benz is delivered and accepted. ■

LETTER OF THE LAW Are Clams "Wild Animals"?

Timothy Longshore was arrested and convicted for stealing clams from a private beach near Puget Sound, Washington. On appeal to the Supreme Court of Washington, Longshore argued that he had not committed theft because the landowner did not own the clams. He asserted that because clams are wild animals, or *ferae naturae*, they are not owned by anyone until someone takes possession of them. The court, however, viewed the matter differently. The court emphasized that clams "ordinarily live in the soil under the waters" and belong with the land. "When taken, they must be wrenched from their beds, made well down in the soil itself." Therefore, said the court, it

must follow that a private landowner "has the right to exercise dominion [control] and ownership over what is upon the land, and especially over things so closely related to the soil as clams." The court also had the letter of Washington law on its side: the Washington legislature had enacted a statute that, among other things, stated that the term *wildlife* "does not include . . . fish, shellfish, and marine invertebrates classified as food fish or shellfish."[a]

THE BOTTOM LINE
In the state of Washington, an individual who privately owns tidelands also owns any naturally occurring clams embedded in the soil.

a. *State v. Longshore,* 141 Wash.2d 414, 5 P.3d 1256 (2000).

Who owns the engagement ring? Often, when a couple decides to marry, one party gives the other an engagement ring. What if the engagement is called off? Etiquette authorities routinely counsel that if the woman breaks the engagement, she should return the ring, but if the man calls the wedding off, the woman is entitled to keep the ring. Interestingly, the courts are coming up with a different approach. Courts in Kansas, Michigan, New York, Ohio, and a number of other states have held that an engagement ring is not a real gift. Rather, it is a "conditional gift" that becomes final only if the marriage occurs. If the marriage does not take place, the ring is returned to the donor regardless of who broke the engagement.[3] This so-called modern trend among the courts is actually similar to the law of ancient Rome, which mandated that when an engagement was broken, the woman had to return the ring, as a penalty, regardless of who was at fault. Some judges, however, disagree with the conditional-gift theory and contend that an engagement ring is a gift, and, as such, it belongs to the donee, even if the engagement is broken. As one judge stated, "Those jurisdictions that rely on the analysis that an engagement ring is a conditional gift ignore general gift law, which holds that a gift is complete if there is intent, delivery, and acceptance."[4] ■

Donative Intent   When a gift is challenged in court, the court will determine whether donative intent exists by looking at the language of the donor and the surrounding circumstances. ■ EXAMPLE 23.5 A court may look at the relationship between the parties and the size of the gift in relation to the donor's other assets. A gift to a mortal enemy is viewed with suspicion. Similarly, when a gift represents a large portion of a person's assets, the court will scrutinize the transaction closely to determine the mental capacity of the donor and ascertain whether any element of fraud or duress is present. ■

Delivery   The gift must be delivered to the donee. Delivery is obvious in most cases, but some objects cannot be relinquished physically. Then the question of delivery depends on the surrounding circumstances.

Constructive Delivery.   When the object itself cannot be physically delivered, a symbolic, or constructive, delivery will be sufficient. **Constructive delivery** does not confer actual possession of the object in question, only the right to take actual possession. Thus, constructive delivery is a general term used to describe an action that the law holds to be the equivalent of real delivery. ■ EXAMPLE 23.6 Suppose that you want to make a gift of various old rare coins that you have stored in a safe-deposit box at your bank. You certainly cannot deliver the box itself to the donee, and you do not want to take the coins out of the bank. In this situation, you can simply deliver the key to the box to the donee and authorize the donee's access to the box and its contents. This action constitutes a constructive delivery of the contents of the box. ■

The delivery of intangible property—such as stocks, bonds, insurance policies, and contracts, for example—must always be accomplished by symbolic, or constructive, delivery. This is because the documents represent rights and are not, in themselves, the true property.

Delivery by Agents.   Delivery may be accomplished by means of a third person who is the agent of either the donor or the donee. If the third person is the agent of the donor, the delivery is effective when the agent delivers the gift to the donee. If the third person is the agent of the donee, the gift is effectively delivered when the donor deliv-

CONSTRUCTIVE DELIVERY
An act equivalent to the actual, physical delivery of property that cannot be physically delivered because of difficulty or impossibility. For example, the transfer of a key to a safe constructively delivers the contents of the safe.

---

3. See, for example, *Meyer v. Mitnick,* 244 Mich.App. 697, 625 N.W.2d 136 (2001).
4. See the dissenting opinion in *Heiman v. Parrish,* 262 Kan. 926, 942 P.2d 631 (1997).

ers the property to the donee's agent.[5] Naturally, no delivery is necessary if the gift is already in the hands of the donee. All that is necessary to complete the gift in such a situation is that the donor had the required intent and the donee accepted the gift.

DOMINION
Ownership rights in property, including the right to possess and control the property.

Relinquishing Dominion and Control. An effective delivery also requires giving up complete control and **dominion** (ownership rights) over the subject matter of the gift. The outcome of disputes often turns on whether control has actually been relinquished. The Internal Revenue Service scrutinizes transactions between relatives when one claims to have given income-producing property to the other. A relative who does not relinquish complete control over a piece of property will have to pay taxes on the income from that property, as opposed to the family member who received the "gift."

In the following case, the court focused on the requirement that a donor must relinquish complete control and dominion over property given to the donee before a gift can be effectively delivered.

5. *Bickford v. Mattocks,* 95 Me. 547, 50 A. 894 (1901).

LANDMARK AND CLASSIC CASES
CASE 23.2 ■ In re Estate of Piper

Missouri Court of Appeals, 1984.
676 S.W.2d 897.

FACTS Gladys Piper died intestate (without a will) in 1982. At her death, she owned miscellaneous personal property worth $5,000 and had in her purse $200 in cash and two diamond rings, known as the Andy Piper rings. The contents of her purse were taken by her niece Wanda Brown, allegedly to preserve them for the estate. Clara Kaufmann, a friend of Piper's, filed a claim against the estate for $4,800. From October 1974 until Piper's death, Kaufmann had taken Piper to the doctor, beauty shop, and grocery store; had written her checks to pay her bills; and had helped her care for her home. Kaufmann maintained that Piper had promised to pay her for these services and had given her the diamond rings as a gift. A Missouri state trial court denied her request for payment; the court found that her services had been voluntary. Kaufmann then filed a petition for delivery of personal property—the rings— which was granted by the trial court. Brown, other heirs, and the administrator of Piper's estate appealed.

ISSUE Had Gladys Piper made an effective gift of the rings to Clara Kaufmann?

DECISION No. The state appellate court reversed the judgment of the trial court on the ground that Piper had never delivered the rings to Kaufmann.

REASON Kaufmann claimed that the rings belonged to her by reason of a "consummated gift long prior to the death of Gladys Piper." Two witnesses testified for Kaufmann at the trial that Piper had told them the rings

belonged to Kaufmann but that she was going to wear them until she died. The appellate court found "no evidence of any actual delivery." The court held that the essentials of a gift are (1) a present intention to make a gift on the part of the donor, (2) a delivery of the property by the donor to the donee, and (3) an acceptance by the donee. The evidence in the case showed only an intent to make a gift. Because there was no delivery—either actual or constructive—a valid gift was not made. For Piper to have made a gift, her intention would have to have been executed by the complete and unconditional delivery of the property or the delivery of a proper written instrument evidencing the gift. As this did not occur, the court found that there had been no gift.

COMMENTS *Although this case is relatively recent in the long span of the law governing gifts, we present it here as a classic case because it so clearly illustrates the delivery requirement when making a gift. Assuming that Piper did, indeed, intend for Kaufmann to have the rings, it was unfortunate that Kaufmann had no right to receive them after Piper's death. Yet the alternative could lead to perhaps even more unfairness. The policy behind the delivery requirement is to protect alleged donors and their heirs from fraudulent claims based solely on parol evidence. If not for this policy, an alleged donee could easily claim that a gift was made when, in fact, it was not.*

RELEVANT WEB SITES *To locate information on the Web concerning* In re Estate of Piper, *go to this text's Web site at* **http://blt.westbuslaw.com**, *select "Chapter 23," and click on "URLs for Landmarks."*

Acceptance   The final requirement of a valid gift is acceptance by the donee. This rarely presents any problem, as most donees readily accept their gifts. The courts generally assume acceptance unless the circumstances indicate otherwise.

GIFT *INTER VIVOS*
A gift made during one's lifetime and not in contemplation of imminent death, in contrast to a gift *causa mortis*.

GIFT *CAUSA MORTIS*
A gift made in contemplation of death. If the donor does not die of that ailment, the gift is revoked.

Gifts *Inter Vivos* and Gifts *Causa Mortis*   A gift made during one's lifetime is termed a **gift *inter vivos*.** Gifts *causa mortis* (so-called *deathbed gifts*), in contrast, are made in contemplation of imminent death. A gift *causa mortis* does not become absolute until the donor dies from the contemplated illness, and it is automatically revoked if the donor recovers from the illness. Moreover, the donee must survive to take the gift. To be effective, a gift *causa mortis* must also meet the three requirements discussed earlier—donative intent, delivery, and acceptance by the donee.

■ EXAMPLE 23.7 Suppose that Yang is to be operated on for a cancerous tumor. Before the operation, he delivers an envelope to a close business associate. The envelope contains a letter saying, "I realize my days are numbered, and I want to give you this check for $1 million in the event of my death from this operation." The business associate cashes the check. The surgeon performs the operation and removes the tumor. Yang recovers fully. Several months later, Yang dies from a heart attack that is totally unrelated to the operation. If Yang's personal representative (the party charged with administering Yang's estate) tries to recover the $1 million, normally she will succeed. The gift *causa mortis* is automatically revoked if the donor recovers. The *specific event* that was contemplated in making the gift was death from a particular operation. Because Yang's death was not the result of this event, the gift is revoked, and the $1 million passes to Yang's estate. ■

ACCESSION

ACCESSION
Occurs when an individual adds value to personal property by either labor or materials. In some situations, a person may acquire ownership rights in another's property through accession.

Accession means "something added." Accession occurs when someone adds value to an item of personal property by use of either labor or materials. Generally, there is no dispute about who owns the property after the accession occurs, especially when the accession is accomplished with the owner's consent. ■ EXAMPLE 23.8 A Corvette-customizing specialist comes to Hoshi's house. Hoshi has all the materials necessary to customize the car. The customizing specialist uses them to add a unique bumper to Hoshi's Corvette. Hoshi simply pays the customizer for the value of the labor, obviously retaining title to the property. ■

When a Party Wrongfully Causes the Accession   When accession occurs without the permission of the owner, the courts will tend to favor the owner over the improver—the one who improves the property—provided that the accession was wrongful and undertaken in bad faith. This is true even if the accession increased the value of the property substantially. In addition, many courts will deny the improver (wrongdoer) any compensation for the value added. ■ EXAMPLE 23.9 Patti steals a car and puts new tires on it. Obviously, a car thief will not be compensated for the value of the new tires if the rightful owner recovers the car. ■

Increased Property Value Due to a Good Faith Accession   If the accession is performed in good faith, however, even without the owner's consent, ownership of the improved item most often depends on whether the accession has increased the value of the property or changed its identity. The greater the increase in value, the more likely that ownership will pass to the improver. If ownership does pass, the improver must compensate the original owner for the value of the property prior to the accession. If the increase in value is not sufficient for ownership to pass to the improver, most courts will require the owner to compensate the improver for the value added.

CONFUSION

CONFUSION
The mixing together of goods belonging to two or more owners so that the separately owned goods cannot be identified.

Confusion is the commingling (mixing together) of goods so that one person's personal property cannot be distinguished from another's. Confusion frequently occurs when the goods are *fungible*. *Fungible goods* are goods consisting of identical particles, such as grain or oil. For instance, if two farmers put their number 2–grade winter wheat into the same storage bin, confusion will occur and the farmers become tenants in common.

When goods are confused due to a wrongful and willful act and the wrongdoer is unable to prove what percentage of the confused goods belongs to him or her, then the innocent party ordinarily acquires title to the whole. If confusion occurs as a result of agreement, an honest mistake, or the act of some third party, the owners share ownership as tenants in common and will share any loss in proportion to their ownership interests in the property.

■ EXAMPLE 23.10 Five farmers in a small Iowa community enter a cooperative arrangement. Each fall, the farmers harvest the same amount of number 2–grade yellow corn and store it in silos that are held by the cooperative. Each farmer thus owns one-fifth of the total corn in the silos. If, however, one farmer harvests and stores more corn than the others in the cooperative silos and wants to claim a greater ownership interest, that farmer must keep careful records. Otherwise, the courts will presume that each farmer has an equal interest in the corn. ■

■■ Mislaid, Lost, and Abandoned Property

As already mentioned, one of the methods of acquiring ownership of property is to possess it. Simply finding something and holding on to it, however, does not necessarily give the finder any legal rights in the property. Different rules apply, depending on whether the property was mislaid, lost, or abandoned.

MISLAID PROPERTY

MISLAID PROPERTY
Property with which the owner has voluntarily parted and then cannot find or recover.

Property that has voluntarily been placed somewhere by the owner and then inadvertently forgotten is **mislaid property.** ■ EXAMPLE 23.11 Suppose that you go to the theater. You leave your gloves on the concession stand and then forget about them. The gloves are mislaid property, and the theater owner is entrusted with the duty of reasonable care for them. ■ When mislaid property is found, the finder does not obtain title to the goods. Instead, the owner of the place where the property was mislaid becomes the caretaker of the property because it is highly likely that the true owner will return.[6]

LOST PROPERTY

LOST PROPERTY
Property with which the owner has involuntarily parted and then cannot find or recover.

Property that is involuntarily left and forgotten is **lost property.** A finder of the property can claim title to the property against the whole world *except the true owner.*[7] If the true owner demands that the lost property be returned, the finder must return

---

6. The finder of mislaid property is an involuntary bailee (to be discussed later in this chapter).
7. See *Armory v. Delamirie,* discussed in this chapter's *Landmark in the Law* feature on the following pages.

it. If a third party attempts to take possession of lost property from a finder, the third party cannot assert a better title than the finder.

■ **EXAMPLE 23.12** Suppose that Kamul works in a large library at night. In the courtyard on her way home, she finds a piece of gold jewelry set with stones that look like precious stones to her. She takes it to a jeweler to have it appraised. While pretending to weigh the jewelry, an employee of the jeweler removes several of the stones. If Kamul brings an action to recover the stones from the jeweler, she normally will win because she found lost property and holds valid title against everyone *except the true owner*. Because the property was lost, rather than mislaid, the finder is the caretaker of the jewelry, and the finder acquires title good against the whole world (except the true owner). ■

Relativity of Title   The law that finders of lost property may obtain good title to the property has a long history. The cases discussed in this chapter's *Landmark in the Law* feature on the origin of the law of finders illustrate the doctrine of *relativity of title*. Under this doctrine, if two contestants are before the court, neither of whom can claim absolute title to the property, the one who can claim prior possession will likely have established sufficient rights to the property to win the case.

Some states and government agencies now post online a list of unclaimed property. For an example of the various types of property that may go unclaimed, go to the following Web page, which is part of the state of Delaware's Web site:

http://www.state.de.us/ revenue/information/ Escheat.shtml.

LANDMARK IN THE LAW   The Law of Finders

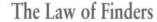

The well-known children's adage, "Finders keepers, losers weepers," is actually written into law—provided that the loser (the rightful owner) cannot be found. A finder of lost personal property may acquire good title to the property *against everyone except the true owner*. A number of landmark cases have made this principle clear. An early English case, *Armory v. Delamirie*,[a] is considered a landmark in Anglo-American jurisprudence concerning finders' rights in property.

FINDERS' RIGHTS   The plaintiff in the case was Armory, a chimney sweep who found a jewel in its setting during the course of his work. He took the jewel to a goldsmith to have it appraised. The goldsmith refused to return the jewel to Armory, claiming that Armory was not the rightful owner of the property. The court held that the finder, as prior possessor of the item, had rights to the jewel superior to those of all others except the rightful owner. The court stated, "The finder of a jewel, though he does not by such finding acquire an absolute property or ownership, yet . . . has such a property as will enable him to keep it against all but the rightful owner."

WHO HAS RIGHTS TO WRONGFULLY OBTAINED GOODS?   A curious situation arises when goods wrongfully obtained by one person are in turn wrongfully obtained by another, and the two parties contest each other's rights to possession. In such a situation, does the *Armory* rule still apply—that is, does the first (illegal) possessor have more rights in the property than the second (illegal)

a. 93 Eng.Rep. 664 (K.B. [King's Bench] 1722).

Conversion of Lost Property   When a finder knows who the true owner of the property is and fails to return it to that person, the finder is guilty of the tort of *conversion* (the wrongful taking of another's property—see Chapter 4). Many states require the finder to make a reasonably diligent search to locate the true owner of lost property.

ESTRAY STATUTE
A statute defining finders' rights in property when the true owners are unknown.

Estray Statutes   Many states have **estray statutes,** which encourage and facilitate the return of property to its true owner and then reward a finder for honesty if the property remains unclaimed. These laws provide an incentive for finders to report their discoveries by making it possible for them, after the passage of a specified period of time, to acquire legal title to the property they have found. Such statutes usually require the county clerk to advertise the property in an attempt to help the owner recover what has been lost. Some preliminary questions must always be resolved before the estray statute can be employed. The item must be lost property, not merely mislaid property. When the circumstances indicate that the property was probably lost and not mislaid or abandoned, loss is presumed as a matter of public policy, and the estray statute applies.

LANDMARK IN THE LAW   The Law of Finders—Continued

BE AWARE   A finder who appropriates the personal property of another, knowing who the true owner is, can be guilty of conversion.

possessor? In a case that came before the Minnesota Supreme Court in 1892, *Anderson v. Gouldberg,*[b] the court said yes.

In the *Anderson* case, the plaintiffs had trespassed on another's land and wrongfully cut timber. The defendants later took the logs from the mill site, allegedly in the name of the owner of the property on which the timber had been cut. The evidence at trial indicated that both parties had illegally acquired the property. The court instructed the jury that even if the plaintiffs were trespassers when they cut the logs, they were entitled to recover them from later possessors—except the true owner or an agent of the true owner. The jury found for the plaintiffs, a decision affirmed later by the Minnesota Supreme Court. The latter court held that the plaintiffs' possession, "though wrongfully obtained," justified an action to repossess the property from another who took it from them.

APPLICATION TO TODAY'S WORLD

Although the Armory *case was decided nearly three hundred years ago, the principle enunciated by the court in that case remains applicable today. Finders of lost property continue to acquire good title to the property against all but the true owner.*

RELEVANT WEB SITES

To locate information on the Web concerning Armory v. Delamirie, *go to this text's Web site at* http://blt.westbuslaw.com, *select "Chapter 23," and click on "URLs for Landmarks."*

b. 51 Minn. 294, 53 N.W. 636 (1892).

A man found the Super Bowl ring of a Chicago Bears football player under a couch that the player had once owned. Is the ring mislaid, lost, or abandoned property? Did the finder acquire valid title to the ring? Why or why not? What, if anything, might the finder be required to do? (AP Photo/ The Journal and Courier, Kevin Howell)

ABANDONED PROPERTY
Property with which the owner has voluntarily parted, with no intention of recovering it.

BAILMENT
A situation in which the personal property of one person (a bailor) is entrusted to another (a bailee), who is obligated to return the bailed property to the bailor or dispose of it as directed.

BAILOR
One who entrusts goods to a bailee.

BAILEE
One to whom goods are entrusted by a bailor.

ABANDONED PROPERTY

Property that has been discarded by the true owner, with no intention of reclaiming title to it, is **abandoned property.** Someone who finds abandoned property acquires title to it, and such title is good against the whole world, *including the original owner.* The owner of lost property who eventually gives up any further attempt to find it is frequently held to have abandoned the property. If a person finds abandoned property while trespassing on the property of another, title vests in the owner of the land, not in the finder.

■ **EXAMPLE 23.13** Aleka is driving with the windows down in her car. Somewhere along her route, a valuable scarf blows out the window. She retraces her route and searches for the scarf but cannot find it. She finally gives up her search and proceeds to her destination five hundred miles away. Six months later, Frye, a hitchhiker, finds the scarf. Frye has acquired title, which is good even against Aleka. By completely giving up her search, Aleka abandoned the scarf just as effectively as if she had intentionally discarded it. ■

▦ Bailments

A **bailment** is formed by the delivery of personal property, without transfer of title, by one person, called a **bailor,** to another, called a **bailee,** usually under an agreement for a particular purpose—for example, to loan, lease, store, repair, or transport the property. On completion of the purpose, the bailee is obligated to return the bailed property in the same or better condition to the bailor or a third person or to dispose of it as directed.

Bailments are usually created by agreement, but not necessarily by contract, because in many bailments not all of the elements of a contract (such as mutual assent and consideration) are present. ■ **EXAMPLE 23.14** If you lend your bicycle to a friend, a bailment is created, but not by contract, because there is no consideration. Many commercial bailments, such as the delivery of clothing to the cleaners for dry cleaning, are based on contract, though. ■

The law of bailments applies to many routine personal and business transactions. When individuals deal with bailments, whether they realize it or not, they are subject to the obligations and duties that arise from the bailment relationship. The number, scope, and importance of bailments created daily in the business community and in everyday life make it desirable for every person to understand the elements necessary for the creation of a bailment and to know what rights, duties, and liabilities flow from bailments.

ELEMENTS OF A BAILMENT

Not all transactions involving the delivery of property from one person to another create a bailment. For such a transfer to become a bailment, three conditions must be met. We look here at each of these conditions.

Personal Property   Only personal property is bailable; there can be no bailment of persons. Although a bailment of your luggage is created when it is transported by an airline, as a passenger you are not the subject of a bailment. Additionally, you cannot bail realty; thus, leasing your house to a tenant does not create a bailment. Although bailments commonly involve *tangible* items—jewelry, cattle, automobiles,

erty or to obtain damages is important because, as you will read shortly, a bailee is liable to the bailor for any loss or damage to bailed property resulting from the bailee's negligence.

Right to Use Bailed Property.   Depending on the type of bailment and the terms of the bailment agreement, a bailee may also have a right to use the bailed property. When no provision is made, the extent of use depends on how necessary it is for the goods to be at the bailee's disposal for the ordinary purpose of the bailment to be carried out. ■ EXAMPLE 23.20 If you borrow a friend's car to drive to the airport, you, as the bailee, would obviously be expected to use the car. In a bailment involving the long-term storage of a car, however, the bailee is not expected to use the car because the ordinary purpose of a storage bailment does not include use of the property. ■

Right of Compensation.   Except in a gratuitous bailment, a bailee has a right to be compensated as provided for in the bailment agreement, to be reimbursed for costs and services rendered in the keeping of the bailed property, or both. Even in a gratuitous bailment, a bailee has a right to be reimbursed or compensated for costs incurred in the keeping of the bailed property. ■ EXAMPLE 23.21 Margo loses her pet dog, and Justine finds it. Justine takes Margo's dog to her home and feeds it. Even though she takes good care of the dog, it becomes ill, and she takes it to a veterinarian. Justine pays the bill for the veterinarian's services and the medicine. Justine normally will be entitled to be reimbursed by Margo for all reasonable costs incurred in the keeping of Margo's dog. ■

To enforce the right of compensation, the bailee has a right to place a *possessory lien* (which entitles a creditor to retain possession of the debtor's goods until a debt is paid) on the specific bailed property until he or she has been fully compensated. This type of lien, sometimes referred to as an artisan's lien or a *bailee's lien,* was discussed in Chapter 16.

Right to Limit Liability.   In ordinary bailments, bailees have the right to limit their liability as long as the limitations are called to the attention of the bailor and are not against public policy. It is essential that the bailor be informed of the limitation in some way. Even when the bailor knows of the limitation, certain types of disclaimers of liability have been considered to be against public policy and therefore illegal. The courts carefully scrutinize *exculpatory clauses,* or clauses that limit a person's liability for her or his own wrongful acts, and in bailments they are often held to be illegal. This is particularly true in bailments for the mutual benefit of the bailor and the bailee. ■ EXAMPLE 23.22 A receipt from a parking garage expressly disclaims liability for any damage to parked cars, regardless of the cause. Because the bailee has attempted to exclude liability for the bailee's own negligence, including the parking attendant's negligence, the clause will likely be deemed unenforceable because it is against public policy. ■

Duties of the Bailee   The bailee has two basic responsibilities: (1) to take appropriate care of the property and (2) to surrender the property to the bailor or dispose of it in accordance with the bailor's instructions at the end of the bailment.

The Duty of Care.   The bailee must exercise reasonable care in preserving the bailed property. What constitutes reasonable care in a bailment situation normally depends on the nature and specific circumstances of the bailment. Traditionally, the courts have determined the appropriate standard of care on the basis of the type of bailment involved. In a bailment for the sole benefit of the bailor, for example, the bailee need exercise only a slight degree of care. In a bailment for the sole benefit of the bailee, however, the bailee must exercise great care. In a mutual-benefit bailment, courts normally impose a reasonable standard of care—that is, the bailee must exercise the degree of care that a reasonable and prudent person would exercise in the same circumstances. Exhibit 23–1 illustrates these concepts. A bailee's failure to exercise appropriate care in handling the bailor's property results in tort liability.

Duty to Return Bailed Property. At the end of the bailment, the bailee normally must hand over the original property to either the bailor or someone the bailor designates or must otherwise dispose of it as directed This is usually a *contractual* duty arising from the bailment agreement (contract). Failure to give up possession at the time the bailment ends is a breach of contract and could result in the tort of conversion or an action based on bailee negligence. If the bailed property has been lost or is returned damaged, a court will presume that the bailee was negligent. The exception is when the obligation is excused because the goods or chattels have been destroyed, lost, or stolen through no fault of the bailee (or claimed by a third party with a superior claim).

Because the bailee has a duty to return the bailed goods to the bailor, a bailee may be liable if the goods being held or delivered are given to the wrong person. Hence, a bailee must be satisfied that a person (other than the bailor) to whom the goods are being delivered is the actual owner or has authority from the owner to take possession of the goods. Should the bailee deliver in error, then the bailee may be liable for conversion or misdelivery.

Duties of the Bailor   It goes without saying that the duties of a bailor are essentially the same as the rights of a bailee. Obviously, a bailor has a duty to compensate the bailee either as agreed or as reimbursement for costs incurred by the bailee in keeping the bailed property. A bailor also has an all-encompassing duty to provide the bailee with goods or chattels that are free from known defects that could cause injury to the bailee.

Bailor's Duty to Reveal Defects. The bailor's duty to reveal defects to the bailee translates into two rules:

1 In a *mutual-benefit bailment,* the bailor must notify the bailee of all known defects and any hidden defects that the bailor knows of or could have discovered with reasonable diligence and proper inspection.

2 In a *bailment for the sole benefit of the bailee,* the bailor must notify the bailee of any known defects.

EXHIBIT 23–1 DEGREE OF CARE REQUIRED OF A BAILEE

Bailment for the Sole Benefit of the Bailor	Mutual-Benefit Bailment	Bailment for the Sole Benefit of the Bailee
	DEGREE OF CARE →	
SLIGHT	REASONABLE	GREAT

The bailor's duty to reveal defects is based on a negligence theory of tort law. A bailor who fails to give the appropriate notice is liable to the bailee and to any other person who might reasonably be expected to come into contact with the defective article.

■ EXAMPLE 23.23 Rentco (the bailor) rents a tractor to Hal Iverson. Unknown to Rentco (but *discoverable* by reasonable inspection), the brake mechanism on the tractor is defective at the time the bailment is made. Iverson uses the defective tractor without knowledge of the brake problem and is injured along with two other field workers when the tractor rolls out of control. Because this is a mutual-benefit bailment, Rentco has a *duty* to notify Iverson of the discoverable brake defect. Rentco's failure to fulfill this duty is the *proximate cause* (discussed in Chapter 4) of injuries to farm workers who might be expected to use, or have contact with, the tractor. Therefore, Rentco is liable under a negligence theory for the injuries sustained by Iverson and the two others. ■

Warranty Liability for Defective Goods.   A bailor can also incur *warranty liability* based on contract law (see Chapter 13) for injuries resulting from the bailment of defective articles. Property leased by a bailor must be *fit for the intended purpose of the bailment*. Warranties of fitness arise by law in sales contracts and leases, and judges have extended these warranties to situations in which the bailees are compensated for the bailment (such as when one leaves a car with a parking attendant). Article 2A of the Uniform Commercial Code (UCC) extends the implied warranties of merchantability and fitness for a particular purpose to bailments whenever the bailments include rights to use the bailed goods.[10]

SPECIAL TYPES OF BAILMENTS

Up to this point, our discussion of bailments has been concerned with ordinary bailments—bailments in which bailees are expected to exercise ordinary care in the handling of bailed property. Some bailment transactions warrant special consideration. These include bailments in which the bailee's duty of care is *extraordinary*—that is, the bailee's liability for loss or damage to the property is absolute—as is generally true in bailments involving common carriers and innkeepers. Warehouse companies have the same duty of care as ordinary bailees; but, like carriers, they are subject to extensive regulation under federal and state laws, including Article 7 of the UCC.

Common Carriers   Transportation providers that are publicly licensed to provide transportation services to the general public are referred to as **common carriers.** They are distinguished from private carriers, which operate transportation facilities for a select clientele. A private carrier is not required to provide service to every person or company making a request. A common carrier, however, must arrange carriage for all who apply, within certain limitations.[11]

The delivery of goods to a common carrier creates a bailment relationship between the shipper (bailor) and the common carrier (bailee). Unlike ordinary bailees, the common carrier is held to a standard of care based on *strict liability*, rather than reasonable care, in protecting the bailed personal property. This means

COMMON CARRIER
An owner of a truck, railroad, airline, ship, or other vehicle that is licensed to offer transportation services to the public, generally in return for compensation or a payment.

---

10. UCC 2A–212, 2A–213.
11. A common carrier is not required to take any and all property anywhere in all instances. Public regulatory agencies govern common carriers, and carriers can be restricted to geographic areas. They can also be limited to carrying certain kinds of goods or to providing only special types of transportation equipment.

A truck travels a highway.
To what standard of care are
common carriers subject?
(© Peter Vadnai, Getty Images)

that the common carrier is absolutely liable, regardless of due care, for all loss or damage to goods except damage caused by one of the following common law exceptions: (1) an act of God, (2) an act of a public enemy, (3) an order of a public authority, (4) an act of the shipper, or (5) the inherent nature of the goods.

Common carriers cannot contract away their liability for damaged goods. Subject to government regulations, however, they are permitted to limit their dollar liability to an amount stated on the shipment contract or rate filing.[12]

Warehouse Companies   *Warehousing* is the business of providing storage of property for compensation.[13] Like ordinary bailees, warehouse companies are liable for loss or damage to property resulting from *negligence*. A warehouse company, however, is a professional bailee and is therefore expected to exercise a high degree of care to protect and preserve the goods. A warehouse company can limit the dollar amount of its liability, but the bailor must be given the option of paying a higher rate to the bailee to increase the amount of liability.

Unlike ordinary bailees, a warehouse company can issue *documents of title*—in particular, *warehouse receipts*—and is subject to extensive government regulation, including Article 7 of the UCC.[14] A warehouse receipt describes the bailed property and the terms of the bailment contract. It can be negotiable or nonnegotiable, depending on how it is written. It is negotiable if its terms provide that the warehouse company will deliver the goods "to the bearer" of the receipt or "to the order of" a person named on the receipt.[15] The warehouse receipt represents the goods (that is, it indicates title) and hence has value and utility in financing commercial transactions.

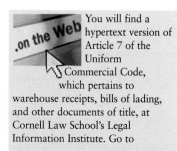

You will find a hypertext version of Article 7 of the Uniform Commercial Code, which pertains to warehouse receipts, bills of lading, and other documents of title, at Cornell Law School's Legal Information Institute. Go to

http://www.law.cornell.edu/ ucc/7/overview.html.

---

12. Federal laws require common carriers to offer shippers the opportunity to obtain higher dollar limits for loss by paying a higher fee for the transport.
13. UCC 7–102(h) defines the person engaged in the storing of goods for hire as a "warehouseman."
14. A *document of title* is defined in UCC 1–201(15) as any "document which in the regular course of business or financing is treated as adequately evidencing that the person in possession of it is entitled to receive, hold, and dispose of the document and the goods it covers. To be a document of title, a document must purport to be issued by or addressed to a bailee and purport to cover goods in the bailee's possession." A *warehouse receipt* is a receipt issued by a person engaged in the business of storing goods for hire.
15. UCC 7–104.

INSURANCE
A contract in which, for a stipulated consideration, one party agrees to compensate the other for loss on a specific subject by a specified peril.

RISK
A prediction concerning potential loss based on known and unknown factors.

RISK MANAGEMENT
Planning that is undertaken to protect one's interest should some event threaten to undermine its security. In the context of insurance, risk management involves transferring certain risks from the insured to the insurance company.

■ **EXAMPLE 23.24** Ossip delivers 6,500 cases of canned corn to Chaney, the owner of a warehouse. Chaney issues a negotiable warehouse receipt payable "to bearer" and gives it to Ossip. Ossip sells and delivers the warehouse receipt to Better Foods, Inc. Better Foods is now the owner of the corn and has the right to obtain the cases by simply presenting the warehouse receipt to Chaney. ■

Innkeepers At common law, innkeepers, hotel owners, and similar operators were held to the same strict liability as common carriers with respect to property brought into the rooms by guests. Today, only those who provide lodging to the public for compensation as a *regular* business are covered under this rule of strict liability. Moreover, the rule applies only to those who are guests, as opposed to lodgers. A lodger is a permanent resident of the hotel or inn, whereas a guest is a transient traveler.

In many states, innkeepers can avoid strict liability for loss of guests' valuables and funds by providing a safe in which to keep them. Each guest must be clearly notified of the availability of such a safe. Statutes often limit the liability of innkeepers with regard to articles that are not kept in the safe or are of such a nature that they normally are not kept in a safe. These statutes may limit the amount of monetary damages or even provide for no liability in the absence of innkeeper negligence.

Normally, the innkeeper (a motel keeper, for example) assumes no responsibility for the safety of a guest's automobile because the guest usually retains possession and control over it. If, however, the innkeeper provides parking facilities and the guest's car is entrusted to the innkeeper or to an employee, the innkeeper will be liable under the rules that pertain to parking-lot bailments (which are ordinary bailments).

A New York building was damaged by debris from the collapse of the World Trade Center in 2001. What impact has the risk of terrorist acts had on insurance? (Michael Rieger, FEMA News Photo)

Insurance

Many precautions may be taken to protect against the hazards of life. For instance, an individual may wear a seat belt to protect against injuries from automobile accidents or install smoke detectors to guard against injury from fire. Of course, no one can predict whether an accident or a fire will ever occur, but individuals and businesses must establish plans to protect their personal and financial interests should some event threaten to undermine their security.

Insurance is a contract by which the insurance company (the insurer) promises to pay a sum of money or give something of value to another (either the insured or the beneficiary) in the event that the insured is injured, dies, or sustains damage to her or his property as a result of particular, stated contingencies. Basically, insurance is an arrangement for *transferring and allocating risk*. In many cases, **risk** can be described as a prediction concerning potential loss based on known and unknown factors. Insurance, however, involves much more than a game of chance.

Risk management normally involves the transfer of certain risks from the individual to the insurance company by a contractual agreement. The insurance contract and its provisions will be examined shortly. First, however, we look at the different types of insurance that can be obtained, insurance terminology, and the concept of insurable interest.

CLASSIFICATIONS OF INSURANCE

Insurance is classified according to the nature of the risk involved. For instance, fire insurance, casualty insurance, life insurance, and title insurance apply to different types of risk. Furthermore, policies of these types protect different persons and interests. This is reasonable because the types of losses that are expected and that are foreseeable or unforeseeable vary with the nature of the activity. Exhibit 23–2 on pages 718–719 presents a list of insurance classifications. (For a discussion of insurance policies designed to cover the special kinds of risks faced by online businesses, see the *Application* feature at the end of this chapter.)

All-risk insurance is property insurance that covers damage resulting from all risks not specifically excluded. Typical exclusions are war, pollution, earthquakes, and floods. After September 11, 2001, insurance companies commonly added acts of terrorism to the list of exclusions. Separate terrorism insurance is available, though. The question in the following case was whether an agreement that required a business to carry all-risk insurance and "other reasonable insurance" included coverage against terrorism.

CASE 23.3 ▪ Omni Berkshire Corp. v. Wells Fargo Bank, N.A.

United States District Court,
Southern District of New York, 2004.
307 F.Supp.2d 534.

FACTS Omni Berkshire Corporation and its business affiliates own or operate hotels in the United States, Canada, and Mexico. In 1998, Omni borrowed $250 million from Secore Financial Corporation. The loan was secured by five of Omni's hotels, worth collectively about $349 million. The loan agreement required Omni to obtain and maintain certain insurance, including "all risk insurance" on the hotels and "such other reasonable insurance" as the lender might request. In 1998, Omni's all-risk policy provided that "damage done by terrorists * * * is insured." When Omni renewed the policy in 2002, however, it excluded coverage for acts of terrorism. Wells Fargo Bank, N.A., which collected the payments on the loan, told Omni that insurance against terrorist acts was required to comply with the agreement. Omni learned that $60 million in terrorism coverage for the five hotels for one year could be purchased for $316,000—63 percent of the cost of an all-risk policy. Omni filed a suit in a federal district court against Wells Fargo, seeking an order that it was *not* required to obtain insurance against terrorism.

ISSUE Is a business required to carry terrorism insurance under an agreement that requires "all risk insurance" and "such other reasonable insurance" as the lender might request?

DECISION Yes. The court dismissed Omni's complaint and ordered it to obtain terrorism insurance. If Omni failed to do so, the court authorized Wells Fargo to obtain a policy and charge the expense to Omni.

REASON The court concluded that Omni was not required to buy insurance against terrorist acts under the "all risk" clause, but that Wells Fargo acted reasonably in requesting the coverage under the "other reasonable insurance" clause. When the parties negotiated the loan, if they had intended to require Omni to maintain "all risk" insurance that included coverage against terrorism, "they surely would have said so." The parties did not discuss the issue at the time, and the agreement did not define "all risk" to include terrorist acts. Nevertheless, the court concluded that Wells Fargo's concern for the risk was reasonable and noted that several recent terrorist attacks had involved hotels. For example, "[i]n the World Trade Center attacks on 9/11, one hotel was destroyed and two others were damaged." Other hotel operators and commercial property owners have bought terrorism insurance. The cost appeared to be "reasonable." Also, Omni, as well as Wells Fargo, would benefit from the coverage.

WHY IS THIS CASE IMPORTANT? *The decision in this case is the first time that terrorism insurance has been classified and required as "other reasonable insurance."*

INSURANCE TERMINOLOGY

POLICY
In insurance law, a contract between the insurer and the insured in which, for a stipulated consideration, the insurer agrees to compensate the insured for loss on a specific subject by a specified peril.

PREMIUM
In insurance law, the price paid by the insured for insurance protection for a specified period of time.

UNDERWRITER
In insurance law, the insurer, or the one assuming a risk in return for the payment of a premium.

An insurance contract is called a **policy;** the consideration paid to the insurer is called a **premium;** and the insurance company is sometimes called an **underwriter.** The parties to an insurance policy are the *insurer* (the insurance company) and the *insured* (the person covered by its provisions or the holder of the policy).

Insurance contracts are usually obtained through an *agent,* who ordinarily works for the insurance company, or through a *broker,* who is ordinarily an *independent contractor.* When a broker deals with an applicant for insurance, the broker is, in effect, the applicant's agent and not an agent of the insurance company. In contrast, an insurance agent is an agent of the insurance company, not of the applicant. As a general rule, the insurance company is bound by the acts of its insurance agents when they act within the agency relationship (discussed in Chapter 17). In most situations, state law determines the status of all parties writing or obtaining insurance.

ETHICAL ISSUE 23.2

Does an insurance agent have a duty to advise insurance applicants about coverage? When a person applies for insurance coverage through an insurance company's agent, is the agent obligated to advise that person as to what coverage he or she should obtain? If the agent does not advise a client about certain types of coverage, has the agent breached a duty to the applicant? For example, suppose that a couple applies for auto insurance, and the insurance agent does not advise them that they should sign up for uninsured motorist coverage. Later, the couple is involved in an accident with an uninsured motorist, and the insurance company refuses to compensate them for their injuries and losses. The couple claims that the insurance agent was negligent in not advising them to sign up for uninsured motorist coverage. Was the agent negligent? No. As mentioned earlier, an insurance agent is an agent of the insurer, not the insured. As such, the agent owes fiduciary duties to the insurer (the insurance company), but not to the insured. The agent's only duties to the insured are contractual in nature.

While some may think that this rule is unfair to insurance applicants, who may know less about the need for certain types of insurance coverage than the agent does, a contrary rule might create even more unfairness. An insurance agent could be held liable for failure to advise a client of every possible insurance option, and the insured would be relieved of any burden to take care of his or her own financial needs and expectations. Also, as one court noted, if the state legislature does not require such coverage, why should the courts require insurance companies to offer or explain available optional coverage?[16] ■

INSURABLE INTEREST

INSURABLE INTEREST
An interest either in a person's life or well-being or in property that is sufficiently substantial that insuring against injury to (or the death of) the person or against damage to the property does not amount to a mere wagering (betting) contract.

A person can insure anything in which she or he has an **insurable interest.** Without this insurable interest, there is no enforceable contract, and a transaction to purchase insurance coverage would have to be treated as a wager. In regard to real and personal property, an insurable interest exists when the insured derives a pecuniary benefit (a benefit consisting of or relating to money) from the preservation and continued existence of the property. Put another way, one has an insurable interest in property when one would sustain a financial loss from its destruction. In regard to life insurance, a person must have a reasonable expectation of benefit from the continued life

---

16. *Jones v. Kennedy,* 108 S.W.3d 203 (Mo.App. 2003).

EXHIBIT 23–2 INSURANCE CLASSIFICATIONS

TYPE OF INSURANCE	COVERAGE
Accident	Covers expenses, losses, and suffering incurred by the insured because of accidents causing physical injury and any consequent disability; sometimes includes a specified payment to heirs of the insured if death results from an accident.
All-risk	Covers all losses that the insured may incur except those resulting from fraud on the part of the insured.
Automobile	May cover damage to automobiles resulting from specified hazards or occurrences (such as fire, vandalism, theft, or collision); normally provides protection against liability for personal injuries and property damage resulting from the operation of the vehicle.
Casualty	Protects against losses incurred by the insured as a result of being held liable for personal injuries or property damage sustained by others.
Credit	Pays to a creditor the balance of a debt on the disability, death, insolvency, or bankruptcy of the debtor; often offered by lending institutions.
Decreasing-term life	Provides life insurance; requires uniform payments over the life (term) of the policy, but with a decreasing face value (amount of coverage).
Employer's liability	Insures employers against liability for injuries or losses sustained by employees during the course of their employment; covers claims not covered under workers' compensation insurance.
Fidelity or guaranty	Provides indemnity against losses in trade or losses caused by the dishonesty of employees, the insolvency of debtors, or breaches of contract.
Fire	Covers losses incurred by the insured as a result of fire.
Floater	Covers movable property, as long as the property is within the territorial boundaries specified in the contract.
Group	Provides individual life, medical, or disability insurance coverage but is obtainable through a group of persons, usually employees; the policy premium is paid either entirely by the employer or partially by the employer and partially by the employee.

of another in order to have an insurable interest in that person's life. The benefit may be pecuniary (as with so-called *key-person insurance,* which insures the lives of important employees, usually in small companies), or it may be founded on the relationship between the parties (by blood or affinity).

For property insurance, the insurable interest must exist at the time the loss occurs but need not exist when the policy is purchased. In contrast, for life insurance, the insurable interest must exist at the time the policy is obtained. The existence of an insurable interest is a primary concern in determining liability under an insurance policy.

THE INSURANCE CONTRACT

NOTE The federal government has the power to regulate the insurance industry under the commerce clause of the U.S. Constitution. Instead of exercising this power itself, Congress allows the states to regulate insurance.

An insurance contract is governed by the general principles of contract law, although the insurance industry is heavily regulated by each state. Several aspects of the insurance contract will be treated here, including the application for insurance, the date when the contract takes effect, and some of the important provisions typically found in insurance contracts. In addition, we will also discuss the cancellation of an insurance policy and defenses that insurance companies can raise against payment on a policy.

EXHIBIT 23–2 INSURANCE CLASSIFICATIONS—CONTINUED

TYPE OF INSURANCE	COVERAGE
Health	Covers expenses incurred by the insured as a result of physical injury or illness and other expenses relating to health and life maintenance.
Homeowners'	Protects homeowners against some or all risks of loss to their residences and the residences' contents or liability arising from the use of the property.
Key-person	Protects a business in the event of the death or disability of a key employee.
Liability	Protects against liability imposed on the insured as a result of injuries to the person or property of another.
Life	Covers the death of the policyholder. On the death of the insured, an amount specified in the policy is paid by the insurer to the insured's beneficiary.
Major medical	Protects the insured against major hospital, medical, or surgical expenses.
Malpractice	Protects professionals (physicians, lawyers, and others) against malpractice claims brought against them by their patients or clients; a form of liability insurance.
Marine	Covers movable property (including ships, freight, and cargo) against certain perils or navigation risks during a specific voyage or time period.
Mortgage	Covers a mortgage loan; the insurer pays the balance of the mortgage to the creditor on the death or disability of the debtor.
No-fault auto	Covers personal injuries and (sometimes) property damage resulting from automobile accidents. The insured submits his or her claims to his or her own insurance company, regardless of who was at fault. A person may sue the party at fault or that party's insurer only when an accident results in serious medical injury and consequent high medical costs. Governed by state "no-fault" statutes.
Term life	Provides life insurance for a specified period of time (term) with no cash surrender value; usually renewable.
Title	Protects against any defects in title to real property and any losses incurred as a result of existing claims against or liens on the property at the time of purchase.

Application   The filled-in application form for insurance is usually attached to the policy and made a part of the insurance contract. Thus, an insurance applicant is bound by any false statements that appear in the application (subject to certain exceptions). Because the insurance company evaluates the risk factors based on the information included in the insurance application, misstatements or misrepresentations can void a policy, especially if the insurance company can show that it would not have extended insurance if it had known the true facts.

Effective Date   The effective date of an insurance contract—that is, the date on which the insurance coverage begins—is important. In some instances, the insurance applicant is not protected until a formal written policy is issued. In other situations, the applicant is protected between the time the application is received and the time the insurance company either accepts or rejects it. Four facts should be kept in mind:

1 A broker is merely the agent of an applicant. Therefore, until the broker obtains a policy, the applicant normally is not insured.

2 A person who seeks insurance from an insurance company's agent will usually be protected from the moment the application is made, provided that some form

BINDER
A written, temporary insurance policy.

of premium has been paid. Between the time the application is received and either rejected or accepted, the applicant is covered (possibly subject to a medical examination). Usually, the agent will write a memorandum, or **binder,** indicating that a policy is pending and stating its essential terms.

3 If the parties agree that the policy will be issued and delivered at a later time, the contract is not effective until the policy is issued and delivered or sent to the applicant, depending on the agreement. Thus, any loss sustained between the time of application and the delivery of the policy is not covered.

4 The parties may agree that a life insurance policy will be binding at the time the insured pays the first premium, or the policy may be expressly contingent on the applicant's passing a physical examination. If the applicant pays the premium and passes the examination, the policy coverage is continuously in effect. If the applicant pays the premium but dies before having the physical examination, then in order to collect, the applicant's estate must show that the applicant *would have passed* the examination had he or she not died.

Coinsurance Clauses   Often, when taking out fire insurance policies, property owners insure their property for less than full value because most fires do not result in a total loss. To encourage owners to insure their property for an amount as close to full value as possible, fire insurance policies commonly include a coinsurance clause. Typically, a *coinsurance clause* provides that if the owner insures the property up to a specified percentage—usually 80 percent—of its value, she or he will recover any loss up to the face amount of the policy. If the insurance is for less than the fixed percentage, the owner is responsible for a proportionate share of the loss.

Coinsurance applies only in instances of partial loss. ■ EXAMPLE 23.25 If the owner of property valued at $100,000 takes out a policy in the amount of $40,000 and suffers a loss of $30,000, the recovery will be $15,000. The formula for calculating the recovery amount is as follows:

$$\frac{\text{amount of insurance (\$40,000)}}{\text{coinsurance percentage (80\%)} \times \text{property value (\$100,000)}} = \frac{\text{recovery percentage}}{(50\%)}$$

recovery percentage (50%) × amount of loss ($30,000) = recovery amount ($15,000)

If the owner had taken out a policy in the amount of $80,000, then, according to the same formula, the full loss would have been recovered up to the face value of the policy. ■

Other Provisions and Clauses   Some other important provisions and clauses contained in insurance contracts are listed and defined in Exhibit 23–3. The courts are aware that most people do not have the special training necessary to understand the intricate terminology used in insurance policies. Thus, the words used in an insurance contract have their ordinary meanings. They are interpreted by the courts in light of the nature of the coverage involved—see, for example, this chapter's *Adapting the Law to the Online Environment* feature on page 722.

When there is an ambiguity in the policy, the provision generally is interpreted against the insurance company. Also when it is unclear whether an insurance contract actually exists because the written policy has not been delivered, the uncertainty normally is resolved against the insurance company. The court presumes that the policy is in effect unless the company can show otherwise. Similarly, an insurer must make sure that the insured is adequately notified of any change in coverage under an existing policy.

EXHIBIT 23-3 INSURANCE CONTRACT PROVISIONS AND CLAUSES

Incontestability clause	An incontestability clause provides that after a policy has been in force for a specified length of time—usually two or three years—the insurer cannot contest statements made in the application.
Appraisal clause	Insurance policies frequently provide that if the parties cannot agree on the amount of a loss covered under the policy or the value of the property lost, an appraisal, or estimate, by an impartial and qualified third party can be demanded.
Arbitration clause	Many insurance policies include clauses that call for arbitration of disputes that may arise between the insurer and the insured concerning the settlement of claims.
Antilapse clause	An antilapse clause provides that the policy will not automatically lapse if no payment is made on the date due. Ordinarily, under such a provision, the insured has a *grace period* of thirty or thirty-one days within which to pay an overdue premium before the policy is canceled.
Multiple insurance	Many insurance policies include a clause providing that if the insured has multiple insurance policies that cover the same property and the amount of coverage exceeds the loss, the loss will be shared proportionately by the insurance companies.

Cancellation The insured can cancel a policy at any time, and the insurer can cancel under certain circumstances. When an insurance company can cancel its insurance contract, the policy or a state statute usually requires that the insurer give advance written notice of the cancellation to the insured.[17] The same requirement applies when only part of a policy is canceled. Any premium paid in advance may be refundable on the policy's cancellation. The insured may also be entitled to a life insurance policy's cash surrender value.

The insurer may cancel an insurance policy for various reasons, depending on the type of insurance. For example, automobile insurance can be canceled for nonpayment of premiums or suspension of the insured's driver's license. Property insurance can be canceled for nonpayment of premiums or for other reasons, including the insured's fraud or misrepresentation, conviction for a crime that increases the hazard insured against, or gross negligence that increases the hazard insured against. Life and health policies can be canceled because of false statements made by the insured in the application, but cancellation can only take place before the effective date of an incontestability clause. An insurer cannot cancel—or refuse to renew—a policy for discriminatory reasons or other reasons that violate public policy, or because the insured has appeared as a witness in a case against the company.

Good Faith Obligations Both parties to an insurance contract are responsible for the obligation they assume under the contract (contract law was discussed in

The Web site of the Insurance Information Institute provides a wealth of news and information on insurance-related issues, including statistical data, a glossary of insurance terms, and various PowerPoint presentations. Go to **http://www.iii.org**.

---

17. In at least one case, the court held that a diskette containing a computerized document, which could be printed out as "hard copy," was sufficient to constitute "written notice" of cancellation. See *Clyburn v. Allstate Insurance Co.,* 826 F.Supp. 955 (D.S.C. 1993).

ADAPTING THE LAW TO THE ONLINE ENVIRONMENT

Recovering for the Loss of Computer Data

Over the past decade, hackers have spread numerous viruses that can cause computer systems to fail and stored data to be lost. When a business's computer system comes under attack, often the damage is extensive. Yet traditional business insurance policies usually do not specifically cover the risks associated with the loss of computer information. Typically, business insurance covers only "physical loss," and a number of courts have held that computer information is not physical.[a] Only in rare circumstances have courts held that general business insurance policies cover the loss of computerized information.

A COMPUTER VIRUS CAUSED SIGNIFICANT DAMAGE

In one case, the operating system of an employment agency, Lambrecht & Associates, Inc., was attacked by a computer virus. All of Lambrecht's employees were networked into a large central server that was equipped with certain prepackaged software programs, such as Microsoft Office and Norton AntiVirus™. One day when the employees came to work, they discovered the computers were having difficulty booting up and were performing strange operations. Ultimately, the entire system froze up, and all of the information that had previously been stored on the system was deleted. As a result, Lambrecht's employees were unable to use their computers to communicate with prospective employers and employees, and the business lost income. In addition, Lambrecht had to replace its server, buy a new operating system and new software, and manually reenter a large amount of data. When Lambrecht filed a claim with its insurer, State Farm Lloyd's, State Farm denied coverage. Lambrecht filed suit, but the trial court agreed with the insurer that the loss was not covered. Lambrecht appealed.

THE EXACT LANGUAGE OF THE INSURANCE POLICY

Lambrecht had a business insurance policy that provided coverage for "accidental direct physical loss to business personal property." In addition, Lambrecht had purchased $100,000 of additional coverage for replacement of valuable "papers or records, including those which exist on electronic or magnetic media," provided that the loss is not "caused by an error in programming." State Farm contended that the damage to Lambrecht's computer system was neither "accidental" nor "physical," as the insurance policy required for coverage.

THE MEANING OF "ACCIDENTAL" AND "PHYSICAL" LOSS

According to State Farm, the damage was not accidental because the hacker's act of infecting Lambrecht's computer system with a virus was voluntary and intentional. The state appellate court, however, held that the question of whether an occurrence was "accidental" should be determined by looking at the incident from the perspective of the insured. Here, there was no evidence to indicate "that Lambrecht was involved in any voluntary or intentional conduct or took any action which caused the damage Lambrecht suffered." Thus, the court held that the damage was unexpected and accidental.

The court also rejected State Farm's argument that the data loss was not "physical" because data are not tangible (capable of being touched). Although the court recognized that other judges have focused on this distinction, in this case, the plain terms of the policy expressly covered electronic records and storage media. Hence, the court held that the language of the policy dictated a finding that the data losses Lambrecht suffered were "physical" as a matter of law.[b]

FOR CRITICAL ANALYSIS

If the policy in this case had not expressly mentioned loss of electronic records, would the court have found that the loss was "physical"? Why or why not?

---

a. See, for example, *America Online, Inc. v. St. Paul Mercury Insurance Co.*, 207 F.Supp.2d 459 (E.D.Va. 2002).

b. *Lambrecht & Associates, Inc. v. State Farm Lloyd's,* 119 S.W.3d 16 (Tex.App. 2003).

Chapters 7 through 10). In addition, both the insured and the insurer have an implied duty to act in good faith.

Good faith requires the party who is applying for insurance to reveal everything necessary for the insurer to evaluate the risk. In other words, the applicant must disclose all material facts, including all facts that an insurer would consider in determining whether to charge a higher premium or to refuse to issue a policy altogether.

Once the insurer has accepted the risk, and some event occurs that gives rise to a claim, the insurer has a duty to investigate to determine the facts. When a policy provides insurance against third party claims, the insurer is obligated to make reasonable efforts to settle such a claim. If a settlement cannot be reached, then regardless of the claim's merit, the insurer must defend any suit against the insured. Usually, a policy provides that in this situation the insured must cooperate. A policy provision may expressly require the insured to attend hearings and trials, to help in obtaining evidence and witnesses, and to assist in reaching a settlement.

Defenses against Payment An insurance company can raise any of the defenses that would be valid in any ordinary action on a contract, as well as some defenses that do not apply in ordinary contract actions. If the insurance company can show that the policy was procured by fraud or misrepresentation, it may have a valid defense for not paying on a claim. (The insurance company may also have the right to disaffirm or rescind an insurance contract.) An absolute defense exists if the insurer can show that the insured lacked an insurable interest—thus rendering the policy void from the beginning. Improper actions, such as those that are against public policy or are otherwise illegal, can also give the insurance company a defense against the payment of a claim or allow it to rescind the contract.

An insurance company can be prevented from asserting some defenses that are normally available, however. ■ EXAMPLE 23.26 Suppose that a company tells an insured that information requested on a form is optional, and the insured provides it anyway. The company cannot use the information to avoid its contractual obligation under the insurance contract. Similarly, an insurance company normally cannot escape payment on the death of an insured on the ground that the person's age was stated incorrectly on the application. ■

APPLICATION ▪ How Can You Manage Risk in Cyberspace?*

As mentioned elsewhere, companies doing business online face many risks that are not covered by traditional types of insurance (see Exhibit 23–2). Not surprisingly, a growing number of companies are now offering policies designed to cover Web-related risks.

INSURANCE COVERAGE FOR WEB-RELATED RISKS

Consider the types of coverage that are offered by Net Secure, a venture undertaken by IBM, several insurance

* This *Application* is not meant to substitute for the services of an attorney who is licensed to practice law in your state.

companies, and a New York broker. Net Secure provides insurance protection against losses resulting from programming errors; network and Web site disruptions; the theft of electronic data and assets, including intellectual property; Web-related defamation, copyright infringement, and false advertising; and the violation of users' privacy rights.

InsureTrust.com, an insurer affiliated with three leading insurance companies—American International Group, Lloyd's of London, and Reliance National—offers similar coverage. Existing insurers, such as Lloyd's of London, Hartford Insurance, and the Chubb Group of Insurance

(Continued)

APPLICATION ▦ How Can You Manage Risk in Cyberspace?—Continued

Companies, are also adding insurance for Web-related perils to their offerings. Clearly, the market for these new types of insurance coverage is rapidly evolving, and new policies will continue to appear.

CUSTOMIZED POLICIES

Unlike traditional insurance policies, which are generally drafted by insurance companies and presented to insurance applicants on a "take-it-or-leave-it" basis, Internet-particular policies are usually customized to provide protection against specific risks faced by a particular type of business. For example, an Internet service provider will face different risks than an online merchant, and a banking institution will face different risks than a law firm. The specific business-related risks are taken into consideration when determining the policy premium.

QUALIFYING CRITERIA

Many companies that offer cyberinsurance require applicants to meet high security standards. In other words, to qualify for a policy under the insurance companies' risk management processes, a business must have Web-related security measures in place. Several of the companies assess

the applicant's security system before underwriting a policy. For example, Net Secure assesses the applicant's security measures and will not provide coverage unless the business scores better than 60 percent. If the business does not score that high, it can contract with Net Secure to improve its Web-related security.

CHECKLIST FOR THE BUSINESSPERSON

1. Determine the types of risks to which your Web business is exposed and try to obtain an insurance policy that protects you against those specific risks.
2. As when procuring any type of insurance coverage, read the policy carefully, including any exclusions contained in the fine print, before committing to it.
3. Do not be "penny wise and pound foolish" when it comes to insurance protection. Though insurance coverage may seem expensive, it may be much less costly than defending against a lawsuit. Often, the cost of coverage can be reduced by purchasing a policy with a high deductible.
4. Find out what the company's underwriting standards are and determine whether your Web security measures meet its standards.

▦ KEY TERMS

CHAPTER SUMMARY Personal Property, Bailments, and Insurance

PERSONAL PROPERTY

Definition of Personal Property (See pages 697–698.)	Personal property (personalty) includes all property not classified as real property (realty). Personal property can be tangible (such as a TV set or a car) or intangible (such as stocks or bonds). Personal property may be referred to legally as *chattel*—a term used under the common law to denote all forms of personal property.
Property Ownership (See pages 698–700.)	Having the fullest ownership rights in property is called *fee simple* ownership. There are various ways of co-owning property, including *tenancy in common, joint tenancy, tenancy by the entirety,* and *community property.*
Acquiring Ownership of Personal Property (See pages 700–705.)	The most common means of acquiring ownership in personal property is by purchasing it (see Chapters 11 through 13). Another way in which personal property is often acquired is by will or inheritance. The following are additional methods of acquiring personal property: 1. *Possession*—Ownership may be acquired by possession if no other person has ownership title (for example, capturing wild animals or finding abandoned property). 2. *Production*—Any product or item produced by an individual (with minor exceptions) becomes the property of that individual. 3. *Gift*—An effective gift exists when the following conditions exist: a. There is evidence of *intent* to make a gift of the property in question. b. The gift is *delivered* (physically or constructively) to the donee or the donee's agent. c. The gift is *accepted* by the donee or the donee's agent. 4. *Accession*—When someone adds value to an item of personal property by labor or materials, the added value generally becomes the property of the owner of the original property (includes accessions made in bad faith or wrongfully). Good faith accessions that substantially increase the property's value or change the identity of the property may cause title to pass to the improver. 5. *Confusion*—In the case of fungible goods, if a person wrongfully and willfully commingles goods with those of another in order to render them indistinguishable, the innocent party acquires title to the whole. Otherwise, the owners become tenants in common of the commingled goods.
Mislaid, Lost, and Abandoned Property (See pages 705–708.)	1. *Mislaid property*—Property that is placed somewhere voluntarily by the owner and then inadvertently forgotten. A finder of mislaid property will not acquire title to the goods, and the owner of the place where the property was mislaid becomes a caretaker of the mislaid property. 2. *Lost property*—Property that is involuntarily left and forgotten. A finder of lost property can claim title to the property against the whole world *except the true owner.* 3. *Abandoned property*—Property that has been discarded by the true owner, who has no intention of claiming title to the property in the future. A finder of abandoned property can claim title to it against the whole world, *including the original owner.*

BAILMENTS

Elements of a Bailment (See pages 708–710.)	1. *Personal property*—Bailments involve only personal property. 2. *Delivery of possession*—For an effective bailment to exist, the bailee (the one receiving the property) must be given exclusive possession and control over the property, and in a voluntary bailment, the bailee must knowingly accept the personal property. 3. *The bailment agreement*—Expressly or impliedly provides for the return of the bailed property to the bailor or a third party, or for the disposal of the bailed property by the bailee.

(Continued)

CHAPTER SUMMARY Personal Property, Bailments, and Insurance—Continued

Ordinary Bailments
(See pages 710–713.)
	1. *Types of bailments—*
	
	  a. Bailment for the sole benefit of the bailor—A gratuitous bailment undertaken for the sole benefit of the bailor (for example, as a favor to the bailor).
	
	  b. Bailment for the sole benefit of the bailee—A gratuitous loan of an article to a person (the bailee) solely for the bailee's benefit.
	
	  c. Mutual-benefit (contractual) bailment—The most common kind of bailment; involves compensation between the bailee and bailor for the service provided.
	
	2. *Rights of a bailee (duties of a bailor)—*
	
	  a. The right of possession—Allows actions against third persons who damage or convert the bailed property and allows actions against the bailor for wrongful breach of the bailment.
	
	  b. The right to be compensated and reimbursed for expenses—In the event of nonpayment, the bailee has the right to place a possessory (bailee's) lien on the bailed property.
	
	  c. The right to limit liability—An ordinary bailee can limit his or her liability for loss or damage, provided proper notice is given and the limitation is not against public policy. In special bailments, limitations on liability for negligence or on types of losses usually are not allowed, but limitations on the monetary amount of liability are permitted.
	
	3. *Duties of a bailee (rights of a bailor)—*
	
	  a. A bailee must exercise appropriate care over property entrusted to her or him. What constitutes appropriate care normally depends on the nature and circumstances of the bailment.
	
	  b. Bailed goods in a bailee's possession must be either returned to the bailor or disposed of according to the bailor's directions. A bailee's failure to return the bailed property creates a presumption of negligence and constitutes a breach of contract or the tort of conversion of goods.

Special Types of Bailments (See pages 713–715.)	1. *Common carriers*—Carriers that are publicly licensed to provide transportation services to the general public. A common carrier is held to a standard of care based on *strict liability* unless the bailed property is lost or destroyed due to (a) an act of God, (b) an act of a public enemy, (c) an order of a public authority, (d) an act of the shipper, or (e) the inherent nature of the goods. 2. *Warehouse companies*—Professional bailees that differ from ordinary bailees in that they (a) can issue documents of title (warehouse receipts) and (b) are subject to state and federal statutes, including Article 7 of the UCC (as are common carriers). They must exercise a high degree of care over the bailed property and are liable for loss of or damage to property if they fail to do so. 3. *Innkeepers (hotel operators)*—Those who provide lodging to the public for compensation as a *regular* business. The common law strict liability standard to which innkeepers were once held is limited today by state statutes, which vary from state to state.
<div align="center">**INSURANCE**</div>	
Classifications (See pages 715–716.)	See Exhibit 23–2 on pages 718 and 719.
Terminology (See page 717.)	1. *Policy*—The insurance contract. 2. *Premium*—The consideration paid to the insurer for a policy. 3. *Underwriter*—The insurance company. 4. *Parties*—Include the insurer (the insurance company), the insured (the person covered by insurance), an agent (a representative of the insurance company) or a broker (ordinarily an independent contractor), and a beneficiary (a person to receive proceeds under the policy).

CHAPTER SUMMARY Personal Property, Bailments, and Insurance—Continued

Insurable Interest (See pages 717–718.)	An insurable interest exists whenever an individual or entity benefits from the preservation of the health or life of the insured or the property to be insured. For life insurance, an insurable interest must exist at the time the policy is issued. For property insurance, an insurable interest must exist at the time of the loss.
The Insurance Contract (See pages 718–723.)	1. *Laws governing*—The general principles of contract law are applied; the insurance industry is also heavily regulated by the states. 2. *Application*—An insurance applicant is bound by any false statements that appear in the application (subject to certain exceptions), which is part of the insurance contract. Misstatements or misrepresentations may be grounds for voiding the policy. 3. *Effective date*—Coverage on an insurance policy can begin when a *binder* (a written memorandum indicating that a formal policy is pending and stating its essential terms) is written; when the policy is issued; at the time of contract formation; or depending on the terms of the contract, when certain conditions are met. 4. *Provisions and clauses*—See Exhibit 23–3 on page 721. Words will be given their ordinary meanings, and any ambiguity in the policy will be interpreted against the insurance company. When the written policy has not been delivered and it is unclear whether an insurance contract actually exists, the uncertainty will be resolved against the insurance company. The court will presume that the policy is in effect unless the company can show otherwise. 5. *Defenses against payment to the insured*—Defenses include misrepresentation, fraud, or violation of warranties by the applicant.

▉ FOR REVIEW

Answers for the even-numbered questions in this For Review *section can be found in Appendix I at the end of this text.*

1 What is real property? What is personal property?

2 What are the three elements necessary for an effective gift? How else can property be acquired?

3 What are the three elements of a bailment? What are the basic rights and duties of a bailee? What are the rights and duties of a bailor?

4 What is an insurable interest? When must an insurable interest exist—at the time the insurance policy is obtained, at the time the loss occurs, or both?

5 What clauses are typically included in insurance contracts?

▉ QUESTIONS AND CASE PROBLEMS

23–1. Duties of the Bailee. Discuss the standard of care traditionally required of the bailee for the bailed property in each of the following situations, and determine whether the bailee breached that duty.

(a) Ricardo borrows Steve's lawn mower because his own lawn mower needs repair. Ricardo mows his front yard. To mow the backyard, he needs to move some hoses and lawn furniture. He leaves the mower in front of his house while doing so. When he returns to the front yard, he discovers that the mower has been stolen.

(b) Alicia owns a valuable speedboat. She is going on vacation and asks her neighbor, Maureen, to store the boat in one stall of Maureen's double garage. Maureen consents, and the boat is moved into the garage. Maureen needs some grocery items for dinner and drives to the store. She leaves the garage door open while she is gone, as is her custom, and the speedboat is stolen during that time.

23–2. Gifts. Reineken, very old and ill, wanted to make a gift to his nephew, Gerald. He had a friend obtain $2,500 in cash for him from his bank account, placed this cash in an envelope, and wrote on the envelope, "This is for my nephew, Gerald." Reineken then placed the envelope in his dresser drawer. When Reineken died a month later, his family found the envelope, and Gerald got word of the intended gift. Gerald then demanded that Reineken's daughter, the executor of Reineken's estate (the person who was appointed by Reineken to handle his affairs after his death), turn over the gift to him. The daughter refused to do so. Discuss fully whether Gerald can successfully claim ownership rights to the $2,500.

23–3. Timing of Insurance Coverage. On October 10, Joleen Vora applied for a $50,000 life insurance policy with Magnum Life Insurance Co.; she named her husband, Jay, as the beneficiary. Joleen paid the insurance company the first year's policy premium on making the application. Two days later, before she had a chance to take the physical examination required by the insurance company and before the policy was issued, Joleen was killed in an automobile accident. Jay submitted a claim to the insurance company for the $50,000. Can Jay collect? Explain.

23–4. Insurer's Defenses. In 1990, the city of Worcester, Massachusetts, adopted an ordinance that required rooming houses to be equipped with automatic sprinkler systems no later than September 25, 1995. In Worcester, James and Mark Duffy owned a forty-eight-room lodging house with two retail stores on the first floor. In 1994, the Duffys applied with General Star Indemnity Co. for an insurance policy to cover the premises. The application indicated that the premises had a sprinkler system. General issued a policy that required, among other safety features, a sprinkler system. Within a month, the premises were inspected on behalf of General. On the inspection form forwarded to the insurer, the inspector inserted only a hyphen next to the word *sprinkler* in the list of safety systems. In July 1995, when the premises sustained over $100,000 in fire damage, General learned that there was no sprinkler system. The insurer filed a suit in a federal district court against the Duffys to rescind the policy, alleging misrepresentation in their insurance application about the presence of sprinklers. How should the court rule, and why? [*General Star Indemnity Co. v. Duffy,* 191 F.3d 55 (1st Cir. 1999)]

23–5. Interpretation of an Insurance Policy's Terms. Valley Furniture & Interiors, Inc., bought an insurance policy from Transportation Insurance Co. (TIC). The policy provided coverage of $50,000 for each occurrence of property loss caused by employee dishonesty. An "occurrence" was defined as "a single act or series of related acts." Valley allowed its employees to take pay advances and to buy discounted merchandise, with the advances and the cost of the merchandise deducted from their paychecks. The payroll manager was to notify the payroll company to make the deductions. Over a period of six years, without notifying the payroll company, the payroll manager issued advances to other employees and herself and bought merchandise for herself, in amounts totaling more than $200,000. Valley filed claims with TIC for three "occurrences" of employee theft. TIC considered the acts a "series of related acts" and paid only $50,000. Valley filed a suit in a Washington state court against TIC, alleging, in part, breach of contract. What is the standard

for interpreting an insurance clause? How should this court interpret "series of related acts"? Why? [*Valley Furniture & Interiors, Inc. v. Transportation Insurance Co.,* 107 Wash.App. 104, 26 P.3d 952 (Div. 1 2001)]

CASE PROBLEM WITH SAMPLE ANSWER

23–6. A. D. Lock owned Lock Hospitality, Inc., which in turn owned the Best Western Motel in Conway, Arkansas. Joe Terry and David Stocks were preparing the motel for renovation. As they were removing the ceiling tiles in room 118, with Lock present in the room, they noticed a dusty cardboard box near the heating and air-supply vent where it had apparently been concealed. Terry climbed a ladder to reach the box, opened it, and handed it to Stocks. The box was filled with more than $38,000 in old currency. Lock took possession of the box and its contents. Terry and Stocks filed a suit in an Arkansas state court against Lock and his corporation to obtain the money. Should the money be characterized as lost, mislaid, or abandoned property? To whom should the court award it? Explain. [*Terry v. Lock,* 37 S.W.3d 202 (Ark. 2001)]

After you have answered this problem, compare your answer with the sample answer given on the Web site that accompanies this text. Go to http://blt.westbuslaw.com, select "Chapter 23," and click on "Case Problem with Sample Answer."

23–7. Concurrent Ownership. Vincent Slavin was a partner at Cantor Fitzgerald Securities in the World Trade Center (WTC) in New York City. In 1998, Slavin and Anna Baez became engaged and began living together. They placed both of their names on three accounts at Chase Manhattan Bank according to the bank's terms, which provided that "accounts with multiple owners are joint, payable to either owner or the survivor." Slavin arranged for the direct deposit of his salary and commissions into one of the accounts. On September 11, 2001, Slavin died when two planes piloted by terrorists crashed into the WTC towers, causing their collapse. At the time, the balance in the three accounts was $656,944.36. On September 14, Cantor Fitzgerald deposited an additional $58,264.73 into the direct-deposit account. Baez soon withdrew the entire amount from all of the accounts. Mary Jelnek, Slavin's mother, filed a suit in a New York state court against Baez to determine the ownership of the funds that had been in the accounts. In what form of ownership were the accounts held? Who is entitled to which of the funds, and why? [*In re Jelnek,* 3 Misc.3d 725, 777 N.Y.S.2d 871 (Sur. 2004)]

A QUESTION OF ETHICS

23–8. George Cook stayed at a Day's Inn motel in Nashville, Tennessee, while attending a trade show. At the trade show, Cook received orders for 225 cases of his firm's product, representing $17,336.25 in profits to the company. On the third day of his stay, Cook's room was burglarized while he was gone from the room. The burglar took Cook's order lists, as well as $174 in cash and medicine worth about $10. Cook sued the owner of the motel, Columbia Sussex Corp., alleging negligence. The motel defended by stating that it had posted a notice on the door of Cook's room informing guests of the fact that the motel would not be liable for any valuable property not placed in the motel safe for safekeeping. Given these circumstances, evaluate and answer the following questions. [*Cook v. Columbia Sussex Corp.*, 807 S.W.2d 567 (Tenn.App. 1990)]

1. The relevant state statute governing the liability of innkeepers allowed motels to disclaim their liability by posting a notice such as the one posted by Day's Inn, but the statute also required that the notice be posted "in a conspicuous manner." The notice posted by Day's Inn on the inside of the door to Cook's room was six-by-three inches in size. In your opinion, is the notice sufficiently conspicuous? If you were the guest, would you have seen the disclaimer? Is it fair to guests to assume that they will notice such disclaimers? Discuss fully.

2. Should hotels or motels ever be allowed to disclaim liability by posting such notices? From a policy point of view, evaluate the implications of your answer.

FOR CRITICAL ANALYSIS

23–9. Suppose that a certificate of deposit (CD) owned by two joint tenants (with the right of survivorship) is given by one of the joint tenants as security for a loan (without the other joint tenant's knowledge). Further suppose that the joint tenant dies after defaulting on the loan. Who has superior rights in the CD, the creditor or the other surviving joint tenant?

VIDEO QUESTION

23–10. Go to this text's Web site at **http://blt. westbuslaw.com** and select "Chapter 23." Click on "Video Questions" and view the video titled *Personal Property and Bailments*. Then answer the following questions.

1. What type of bailment is discussed in the video?
2. What were Vinny's duties with regard to the rug-cleaning machine? What standard of care should apply?
3. Did Vinny exercise the appropriate degree of care? Why or why not? How would a court decide this issue?

INTERNET EXERCISES

Go to the *Business Law Today: The Essentials* home page at **http://blt.westbuslaw.com**, select "Chapter 23," and click on "Internet Exercises." There you will find the following Internet research exercises that you can perform to learn more about topics covered in this chapter.

Activity 23–1: LEGAL PERSPECTIVE—Lost Property

Activity 23–2: MANAGEMENT PERSPECTIVE—Bailments

Activity 23–3: MANAGEMENT PERSPECTIVE—Risk Management in Cyberspace

BEFORE THE TEST

Go to the *Business Law Today: The Essentials* home page at **http://blt.westbuslaw.com**, select "Chapter 23," and click on "Interactive Quizzes." You will find at least twenty interactive questions relating to this chapter.

CHAPTER 24

Real Property and Environmental Law

"The right of property is the most sacred of all the rights of citizenship."

Jean-Jacques Rousseau, 1712–1778
(French writer and philosopher)

CHAPTER OUTLINE

■ **THE NATURE OF REAL PROPERTY**

■ **OWNERSHIP INTERESTS IN REAL PROPERTY**

■ **TRANSFER OF OWNERSHIP**

■ **LEASEHOLD ESTATES**

■ **LANDLORD-TENANT RELATIONSHIPS**

■ **ENVIRONMENTAL LAW**

■■ LEARNING OBJECTIVES

After reading this chapter, you should be able to answer the following questions:

1 What can a person who holds property in fee simple absolute do with the property? Can a person who holds property as a life estate do the same?

2 How can ownership rights in real property be transferred?

3 What are the respective duties of the landlord and tenant concerning the use and maintenance of leased property? Is the tenant responsible for all damages that he or she causes?

4 What is contained in an environmental impact statement, and who must file one?

5 What major federal statutes regulate air and water pollution? What is Superfund, and who is potentially liable under Superfund?

From earliest times, property has provided a means for survival. Primitive peoples lived off the fruits of the land, eating the vegetation and wildlife. Later, as the wildlife was domesticated and the vegetation cultivated, property provided pasturage and farmland. In the twelfth and thirteenth centuries in Europe, the power of feudal lords was determined by the amount of land they held; the more land, the more powerful they were. After the age of feudalism passed, property continued to be an indicator of family wealth and social position. In the Western world, an individual's right to his or her property has become, in the words of Jean-Jacques Rousseau, one of the "most sacred of all the rights of citizenship."

In this chapter, we first examine the nature of real property. We then look at the various ways in which real property can be owned and at how ownership rights in real property are transferred from one person to another. Finally, we look at some of the major statutes that help to protect our environment.

■ The Nature of Real Property

Real property consists of land and the buildings, plants, and trees that are on it. Real property also includes subsurface and air rights, as well as personal property that has become permanently attached to real property. Whereas personal property is movable, real property—also called *real estate* or *realty*—is immovable.

LAND

Land includes the soil on the surface of the earth and the natural or artificial structures that are attached to it. It further includes all the waters contained on or under the surface and much, but not necessarily all, of the airspace above it. The exterior boundaries of land extend down to the center of the earth and up to the farthest reaches of the atmosphere (subject to certain qualifications).

AIR AND SUBSURFACE RIGHTS

The owner of real property has rights to the airspace above the land, as well as to the soil and minerals underneath it. Limitations on either air rights or subsurface rights normally have to be indicated on the document that transfers title at the time of purchase. When no such limitations, or *encumbrances*, are noted, a purchaser can normally expect to have an unlimited right to possession of the property.

Air Rights Early cases involving air rights dealt with such matters as whether a telephone wire could be run across a person's property when the wire did not touch any of the property[1] and whether a bullet shot over a person's land constituted trespass.[2] Today, disputes concerning air rights may involve the right of commercial and private planes to fly over property and the right of individuals and governments to seed clouds and produce rain artificially. Flights over private land normally do not violate the property owners' rights unless the flights are low and frequent enough to cause a direct interference with the enjoyment and use of the land.[3] Leaning walls or buildings and projecting eave spouts or roofs may also violate the air rights of an adjoining property owner.

For links to numerous online legal sources relating to real property, go to

http://www.findlaw.com/ 01topics/index.html

and click on "Property Law & Real Estate."

A plane flies low over a residential area. Are the property owners' rights violated by such a low-flying plane? Why or why not? (© Jonathan Nourok, PhotoEdit)

---

1. *Butler v. Frontier Telephone Co.*, 186 N.Y. 486, 79 N.E. 716 (1906).
2. *Herrin v. Sutherland*, 74 Mont. 587, 241 P. 328 (1925). Shooting over a person's land constitutes trespass.
3. *United States v. Causby*, 328 U.S. 256, 66 S.Ct. 1062, 90 L.Ed. 1206 (1946).

Subsurface Rights   In many states, land ownership may be separated, in that the surface of a piece of land and the subsurface may have different owners. Subsurface rights can be extremely valuable, as these rights include the ownership of minerals, oil, and natural gas. But subsurface rights would be of little value if the owner could not use the surface to exercise those rights. Hence, a subsurface owner will have a right (called a *profit*, discussed later in this chapter) to go onto the surface of the land to, for example, discover and mine minerals.

When the ownership is separated into surface and subsurface rights, each owner can pass title to what she or he owns without the consent of the other owner. Of course, conflicts can arise between a surface owner's use and the subsurface owner's need to extract minerals, oil, or natural gas. One party's interest may become subservient (secondary) to the other party's interest either by statute or case law. At common law and generally today if the owners of the subsurface rights excavate (dig), they are absolutely liable if their excavation causes the surface to collapse. Depending on the circumstances, the excavators may also be liable for any damage to structures on the land. Many states have statutes that extend excavators' liability to include damage to structures on the property. Typically, these statutes provide precise requirements for excavations of various depths.

Plant Life and Vegetation

Plant life, both natural and cultivated, is also considered to be real property. In many instances, the natural vegetation, such as trees, adds greatly to the value of the realty. When a parcel of land is sold and the land has growing crops on it, the sale includes the crops, unless otherwise specified in the sales contract. When crops are sold by themselves, however, they are considered to be personal property or goods. Consequently, the sale of crops is a sale of goods and thus is governed by the Uniform Commercial Code (UCC) rather than by real property law.[4]

Fixtures

Certain personal property can become so closely associated with the real property to which it is attached that the law views it as real property. Such property is known as a **fixture**—a thing *affixed* to realty, meaning that it is attached to the real property by roots; embedded in it; permanently situated on it; or permanently attached by means of cement, plaster, bolts, nails, or screws. The fixture can be physically attached to real property, be attached to another fixture, or even be without any actual physical attachment to the land (such as a statue). As long as the owner intends the property to be a fixture, normally it will be a fixture.

> **FIXTURE**
> A thing that was once personal property but has become attached to real property in such a way that it takes on the characteristics of real property and becomes part of that real property.

Fixtures are included in the sale of land if the sales contract does not provide otherwise. The sale of a house includes the land and the house and the garage on the land, as well as the cabinets, plumbing, and windows. Because these are permanently affixed to the property, they are considered to be a part of it. Certain items, such as drapes and window-unit air conditioners, are difficult to classify. Thus, a contract for the sale of a house or commercial realty should indicate which items of this sort are included in the sale.

At issue in the following case was whether an agricultural irrigation system qualified as a fixture.

---

4. See UCC 2–107(2).

CASE 24.1 ▪ In re Sand & Sage Farm & Ranch, Inc.

United States Bankruptcy Court,
District of Kansas, 2001.
266 Bankr. 507.

FACTS In 1988, Randolf and Sandra Ardery bought an eighty-acre tract in Edwards County, Kansas. On the land was an eight-tower center-pivot irrigation system. The system consisted of an underground well and pump connected to a pipe that ran to the pivot where the water line was attached to a further system of pipes and sprinklers suspended from the towers, extending over the land in a circular fashion. The system's engine and gearhead were bolted to a concrete slab above the pump and well and were attached to the pipe. To secure a loan to buy the land, the Arderys granted to Farmers State Bank a mortgage that covered "all buildings, improvements, and fixtures." In 1996, the Arderys, and their firm Sand & Sage Farm & Ranch, Inc., granted Ag Services of America a security interest in the farm's "equipment." Nothing in the security agreement or financing statement referred to fixtures.[a] In 2000, the Arderys and Sand & Sage filed for bankruptcy in a federal bankruptcy court and asked for permission to sell the land, with the irrigation system, to Bohn Enterprises, Limited Partnership. Ag Services claimed that it had priority to the proceeds covering the value of the irrigation system. The bank responded that it had priority because the system was a "fixture."

ISSUE Was this irrigation system a "fixture"?

a. Security agreements and financing statements were discussed in Chapter 16.

DECISION Yes. The court concluded that the system was a fixture. The bank was entitled to the proceeds from its sale.

REASON The court explained that whether personal property attached to land is a fixture depends on "(i) how firmly the goods are attached or the ease of their removal (annexation); (ii) the relationship of the parties involved (intent); and (iii) how operation of the goods is related to the use of the land (adaptation). Of the three factors, intent is the controlling factor and is deduced largely from the property-owner's acts and the surrounding circumstances." Here, the irrigation system was firmly attached to the realty. Disassembly and removal would be time consuming and expensive. As for intent, in each transaction all of the parties—except Ag Services, whose security agreement and financing statement did not refer to the irrigation system—"share[d] the intent that the system in question should pass with the land." Furthermore, the system "is suitably adapted to the land. There can be little dispute concerning the need for pivot irrigation in the semi-arid conditions of southwestern Kansas. *   *   * This alone demonstrates the relation between the operation of the goods and use of the land."

WHY IS THIS CASE IMPORTANT? *When dealing with real property, it is crucial that the parties to a contract specifically list which fixtures they intend to be subjected to a security interest or included in a sale or transfer. In the end, it is far simpler and less expensive to itemize fixtures in a contract than to engage in litigation.*

▪ Ownership Interests in Real Property

Ownership of property is an abstract concept that cannot exist independently of the legal system. No one can actually possess or *hold* a piece of land, the air above it, the earth below it, and all the water contained on it. The legal system therefore recognizes certain rights and duties that constitute ownership interests in real property.

Recall from Chapter 23 that property ownership is often viewed as a bundle of rights. One who possesses the entire bundle of rights is said to hold the property in *fee simple*, which is the most complete form of ownership. When only some of the rights in the bundle are transferred to another person, the effect is to limit the ownership rights of both the transferor of the rights and the recipient.

OWNERSHIP IN FEE SIMPLE

FEE SIMPLE ABSOLUTE
An ownership interest in land in which the owner has the greatest possible aggregation of rights, privileges, and power. Ownership in fee simple absolute is limited absolutely to a person and her or his heirs.

In a **fee simple absolute,** the owner has the greatest aggregation of rights, privileges, and power possible. The owner can give the property away, sell the property, or transfer the property by will to another. Also, the owner has the rights of *exclusive* possession and use of the property. The fee simple is limited to a person and his or her heirs and is assigned forever without limitation or condition.

The rights that accompany a fee simple include the right to use the land for whatever purpose the owner sees fit. Of course, other laws, including laws that prevent the owner from unreasonably interfering with another person's land and applicable zoning and environmental laws, may limit the owner's ability to use the property in certain ways. A fee simple is potentially infinite in duration and can be disposed of by deed (the instrument used to transfer property, which will be discussed later in this chapter) or by will. When there is no will, the fee simple passes to the owner's legal heirs.

LIFE ESTATES

LIFE ESTATE
An interest in land that exists only for the duration of the life of some person, usually the holder of the estate.

CONVEYANCE
The transfer of a title to land from one person to another by deed; a document (such as a deed) by which an interest in land is transferred from one person to another.

A **life estate** is an estate that lasts for the life of some specified individual. A **conveyance,** or transfer of real property, "to A for his life" creates a life estate.[5] In a life estate, the life tenant's ownership rights cease to exist on the life tenant's death. The life tenant has the right to use the land, provided that he or she commits no waste (injury to the land). In other words, the life tenant cannot use the land in a manner that would adversely affect its value. The life tenant is entitled to any rents generated by the land and can harvest crops from the land. If mines and oil wells are already on the land, the life tenant is entitled to any royalties and can extract minerals and oil from it, but he or she cannot exploit the land by creating new wells or mines.

The life tenant has the right to mortgage the life estate and can create liens, *easements* (discussed below), and leases, but none can extend beyond the life of the tenant. In addition, with few exceptions, the owner of a life estate has an exclusive right to possession during her or his life.

Along with these rights, the life tenant also has some duties—to keep the property in repair and to pay property taxes. In short, the owner of the life estate has the same rights as a fee simple owner except that the life tenant must maintain the value of the property during her or his tenancy.

NONPOSSESSORY INTERESTS

In contrast to the types of property interests just described, some interests in land do not include any rights to possess the property. These interests, known as *nonpossessory interests,* include easements, profits, and licenses.

EASEMENT
A nonpossessory right to use another's property in a manner established by either express or implied agreement.

PROFIT
In real property law, the right to enter on and remove things from the property of another (for example, the right to enter onto a person's land and remove sand and gravel therefrom).

Easements and Profits   An **easement** is the right of a person to make limited use of another person's real property without taking anything from the property. An easement, for instance, can be the right to walk or drive across another's property. In contrast, a **profit**[6] is the right to go onto land in possession of another and take away some part of the land itself or some product of the land. ■ **EXAMPLE 24.1**

---

5. A less common type of life estate is created by the conveyance "to A for the life of B." This is known as an estate *pur autre vie,* or an estate for the duration of the life of another.

6. The term *profit,* as used here, does not refer to the "profits" made by a business firm. Rather, it means a gain or an advantage.

Akmed owns Sandy View. Akmed gives Carmen the right to go there to remove all the sand and gravel that she needs for her cement business. Carmen has a profit. ■

Licenses A **license** is the revocable right of a person to come onto another person's land. It is a personal privilege that arises from the consent of the owner of the land and can be revoked by the owner. A ticket to attend a movie at a theater is an example of a license. ■ EXAMPLE 24.2 The owner of a Broadway theater issues Alena a ticket to see a play. If Alena is refused entry into the theater because she is improperly dressed, she has no right to force her way into the theater. The ticket is only a revocable license, not a conveyance of an interest in property. ■

LICENSE
A revocable right or privilege of a person to come onto another person's land.

Transfer of Ownership

Ownership of real property can pass from one person to another in several ways. Commonly, ownership interests in land are transferred by sale, and the terms of the transfer are specified in a real estate sales contract. Often, real estate brokers or agents who are licensed by the state assist the buyers and sellers during the sales transaction. (For a discussion of some issues involving online advertising by real estate professionals, see this chapter's *Adapting the Law to the Online Environment* feature on page 736). Real property ownership can also be transferred by gift, by will or inheritance, by possession, or by *eminent domain*. When ownership rights in real property are transferred, the type of interest being transferred and the conditions of the transfer normally are set forth in a *deed* executed by the person who is conveying the property.

DEEDS

Possession and title to land are passed from person to person by means of a **deed**—the instrument of conveyance of real property. A deed is a writing signed by an owner of real property that transfers title to another. Deeds must meet certain requirements. Unlike a contract, a deed does not have to be supported by legally sufficient consideration. Gifts of real property are common, and they require deeds even though there is no consideration for the gift. The necessary components of a valid deed are the following:

DEED
A document by which title to property (usually real property) is passed.

1. The names of the *grantor* (the giver or seller) and the *grantee* (donee or buyer).
2. Words evidencing an intent to convey the property (for example, "I hereby bargain, sell, grant, or give").
3. A legally sufficient description of the land.
4. The grantor's (and usually her or his spouse's) signature.
5. Delivery of the deed.

Warranty Deeds Different types of deeds provide different degrees of protection against defects of title. A **warranty deed** makes the greatest number of warranties and thus provides the greatest protection against defects of title.

WARRANTY DEED
A deed in which the grantor assures (warrants to) the grantee that the grantor has title to the property conveyed in the deed, that there are no encumbrances on the property other than what the grantor has represented, and that the grantee will enjoy quiet possession of the property; a deed that provides the greatest amount of protection for the grantee.

Creation of a Warranty Deed. In most states, special language is required to create a general warranty deed. Typically, the deed must include a written promise to protect the buyer against all claims of ownership of the property. A general warranty deed makes the grantor liable for all defects of title occurring while he or she (the grantor) and the previous titleholders held the property.

ADAPTING THE LAW TO THE ONLINE ENVIRONMENT

Potential Problems When Real Estate Is Advertised Online

The Internet has transformed the real estate business, just as it has transformed other industries. Today's real estate professionals market properties—and themselves—online. Given that the Internet knows no physical borders, what happens when an online advertisement reaches people outside the state in which the real estate professional is licensed? Is this illegal? Can the agent be sued for fraud if the ad contains misrepresentations? Such questions are likely to arise in the future as more and more people use the Internet to search for properties.

STATE LICENSING STATUTES AND ADVERTISING

Every state requires anyone who sells or offers to sell real property in that state to obtain a license. To be licensed, a person normally must pass a state examination and pay a fee and then must take a minimum number of continuing education courses periodically (every year or two) to maintain the license. The purpose of requiring real estate licenses is to protect the public and to maintain quality standards for real property transactions in that state. Usually, a person must also be licensed to list real property for sale or to negotiate the purchase, sale, lease, or exchange of real property or a business opportunity involving real property.[a] Often, a state agency, such as a real estate commission, is in charge of granting licenses and enforcing the laws and regulations governing real estate professionals.

Although some states have rules regarding the advertising of real property, these regulations usually do not specifically address Internet advertising, which necessarily reaches consumers beyond the state's borders. At least one state, California, flatly prohibits Internet advertising of real estate by individuals not licensed in the state.[b] But how can a state enforce such a law or check the credentials of Web advertisers? California's Department of Real Estate *suggests* that anyone who advertises real property online and is not licensed in California should include a disclaimer on the ad—but this is not required.

ACTIONS FOR MISREPRESENTATIONS (FRAUD)

Suppose that a real estate agent, either inadvertently or intentionally, makes a misstatement online about some important aspect of real property that is for sale. Someone, relying on the statements, responds to the ad and eventually contracts to buy the property, only to discover later that the ad misrepresented it. What remedies does the buyer have? In this situation, the buyer can complain to the state authority that granted the agent's license, and the state may even revoke the license for such conduct. If the buyer wants to obtain damages or cancel the contract, however, he or she will have to sue the agent for fraud (see Chapters 4 and 8). At this point, jurisdiction problems may arise.

If the real estate agent and the buyer are located in different states and the Internet ad was the agent's only contact with the buyer's state, the buyer may have to travel to the agent's state to file the suit. Courts have reached different conclusions on the type of Internet advertising that permits a court to have jurisdiction over an out-of-state advertiser. In many states, a court will not have jurisdiction unless the Web site advertisement is *interactive*. In other states, the courts have held that a passive Web site that solicited business in the state,[c] or a passive Web site coupled with a toll-free phone number or downloadable forms,[d] provided the minimum contacts necessary for jurisdiction. Thus, people who are deceived when buying real property from an online ad and wish to sue the perpetrator of the fraud may be in a precarious position depending on the state where they live.

FOR CRITICAL ANALYSIS

Do you think that the federal government should regulate the advertising of real property on the Internet to protect consumers from potential fraud? If so, what kind of regulations would be appropriate, and how might they be enforced?

c. *Telco Communications v. An Apple A Day,* 977 F.Supp. 404 (E.D.Va. 1997); *Inset Systems, Inc. v. Instruction Set, Inc.,* 937 F.Supp. 161 (D.Conn. 1996).

d. *State by Humphrey v. Granite Gate Resorts, Inc.,* 1996 WL 767431 (Minn.Dist.Ct. 1996), aff'd, 568 N.W.2d 715 (Minn.App. 1997), aff'd again, 576 N.W.2d 747 (Minn. 1998); *Hasbro, Inc. v. Clue Computing, Inc.,* 994 F.Supp. 34 (D.Mass. 1997).

a. See, for example, Section 10131 of the Cal. Bus. & Prof. Code and Vermont's 26 V.S.A. Sections 2211–2212.

b. 9 Cal. Code of Regs. Section 2770.

The Usual Covenants. Warranty deeds commonly include a number of *covenants,* or promises, that the grantor makes to the grantee. A *covenant of seisin*[7] and a *covenant of the right to convey* warrant that the seller has title to, and the power to convey, the property described in the deed. A *covenant against encumbrances* is a promise that the property being sold or conveyed is not subject to any outstanding rights or interests of third parties, except as explicitly stated. Examples of common encumbrances include mortgages, liens, profits, easements, and private deed restrictions on the use of the land. (For an example of how an owner's use of the land might be restricted, see this chapter's *Letter of the Law* feature.)

A *covenant of quiet enjoyment* guarantees that the buyer will not be disturbed in her or his possession of the land by the seller or any third persons. ■ EXAMPLE 24.3 Assume that Julio sells a two-acre lot and office building by warranty deed. Subsequently, a third person shows up who has better title than Julio had and forces the buyer off the property. Here, the covenant of quiet enjoyment has been breached, and the buyer can sue Julio to recover the purchase price of the land plus any other damages incurred as a result. ■

If a contract calls for a "warranty deed" without specifying the covenants to be included in the deed, or if a deed states that the seller is providing the "usual covenants," most courts will infer that all of the covenants mentioned above are included.

Special Warranty Deeds. In contrast to a warranty deed, a **special warranty deed,** which is frequently referred to as a *limited warranty deed,* warrants only that the

SPECIAL WARRANTY DEED
A deed in which the grantor only warrants that the grantor or seller held good title during his or her ownership of the property and does not warrant that there were no defects of title when the property was held by previous owners.

---

7. Pronounced *see-zuhn.*

LETTER OF THE LAW A Shed Is One Thing, a Garage Quite Another

Shortly after Richard and Laura Dufrane purchased a home with an attached garage in a subdivision in Greenfield, Wisconsin, they began constructing a detached garage on the edge of their property. Their neighbor, Mary Pietrowski, told the Dufranes "multiple times" that the garage violated a restrictive covenant that prevented property owners in the subdivision from erecting any buildings other than one house and one garage on their land. After the garage had been built, Pietrowski asked a court to issue an order that the garage be razed (destroyed).

The Dufranes argued that Pietrowski herself had violated the covenant because she had built a shed on her property. Thus, by violating the covenant herself, she had waived her equitable right to enforce it. After all, a fundamental principle of equity is that a person seeking equitable relief must come to the court with clean

hands. Further, claimed the Dufranes, enforcing the covenant would lead to unjust results because Pietrowski would be allowed to maintain a violation of the restrictions on her property while enforcing the restrictions on her neighbors. The Dufranes' arguments were in vain, however. The court interpreted the letter of the law in this case to mean that building a shed constituted only a "minor violation" of the covenant, whereas building a garage was a "major violation" that materially breached the covenant. According to the court, "enforcement against a major violation of the restrictive covenant by a party who committed a minor violation does not result in an injustice." The court ordered that the garage be razed.[a]

THE BOTTOM LINE
Those who purchase real estate should check carefully to determine what restrictive covenants, if any, apply to the property.

a. *Pietrowski v. Dufrane,* 634 N.W.2d 109 (Wis.App. 2001).

grantor or seller held good title during his or her ownership of the property. In other words, the grantor is not warranting that there were no defects of title when the property was held by previous owners.

If the special warranty deed discloses all liens or other encumbrances, the seller will not be liable to the buyer if a third person subsequently interferes with the buyer's ownership. If the third person's claim arises out of, or is related to, some act of the seller, however, the seller will be liable to the buyer for damages.

Quitclaim Deeds   A **quitclaim deed** offers the least amount of protection against defects in the title. Basically, a quitclaim deed conveys to the grantee whatever interest the grantor had; so, if the grantor had no interest, then the grantee receives no interest. Naturally, if the grantor had a defective title or no title at all, a conveyance by warranty deed or special warranty deed would not cure the defects. Such deeds, however, will give the buyer a cause of action to sue the seller.

A quitclaim deed can and often does serve as a release of the grantor's interest in a particular parcel of property. ■ EXAMPLE 24.4 Sandi and Jim were married for ten years and are now getting a divorce. During the marriage, Sandi purchased a parcel of waterfront property next to her grandparents' home in Louisiana. Jim helped make some improvements to the property, but he is not sure what ownership interests, if any, he has in the property because Sandi used her own funds to purchase the lot. Jim agrees to quitclaim the property to Sandi as part of the divorce settlement, releasing any interest he might have in that piece of property. ■

Recording Statutes   Every jurisdiction has **recording statutes,** which allow deeds to be recorded for a fee. The grantee normally pays this fee because he or she is the one who will be protected by recording the deed.

Recording a deed gives notice to the public that a certain person is now the owner of a particular parcel of real estate. Thus, prospective buyers can check the public records to see whether there have been earlier transactions creating interests or rights in specific parcels of real property. Placing everyone on notice as to the identity of the true owner is intended to prevent the previous owners from fraudulently conveying the land to other purchasers. Deeds are recorded in the county where the property is located. Many state statutes require that the grantor sign the deed in the presence of two witnesses before it can be recorded.

WILL OR INHERITANCE

Property that is transferred on an owner's death is passed either by will or by state inheritance laws. If the owner of land dies with a will, the land passes in accordance with the terms of the will. If the owner dies without a will, state inheritance statutes prescribe how and to whom the property will pass.

ADVERSE POSSESSION

Adverse possession is a means of obtaining title to land without delivery of a deed. Essentially, when one person possesses the property of another for a certain statutory period of time (three to thirty years, with ten years being most common), that person, called the *adverse possessor*, acquires title to the land and cannot be removed from it by the original owner. The adverse possessor may ultimately obtain a perfect title just as if there had been a conveyance by deed.

For property to be held adversely, four elements must be satisfied:

QUITCLAIM DEED
A deed intended to pass any title, interest, or claim that the grantor may have in the property without warranting that such title is valid. A quitclaim deed offers the least amount of protection against defects in the title.

RECORDING STATUTES
Statutes that allow deeds, mortgages, and other real property transactions to be recorded so as to provide notice to future purchasers or creditors of an existing claim on the property.

ADVERSE POSSESSION
The acquisition of title to real property by occupying it openly, without the consent of the owner, for a period of time specified by a state statute. The occupation must be actual, open, notorious, exclusive, and in opposition to all others, including the owner.

Should the government be permitted to take undeveloped coastal property from private citizens for public use without compensation? Why or why not? (©Vic Bider, PhotoEdit)

1 Possession must be actual and exclusive—that is, the possessor must take sole physical occupancy of the property.

2 The possession must be open, visible, and notorious, not secret or clandestine. The possessor must occupy the land for all the world to see.

3 Possession must be continuous and peaceable for the required period of time. This requirement means that the possessor must not be interrupted in the occupancy by the true owner or by the courts.

4 Possession must be hostile and adverse. In other words, the possessor must claim the property as against the whole world. He or she cannot be living on the property with the permission of the owner.

EMINENT DOMAIN

EMINENT DOMAIN
The power of a government to take land for public use from private citizens for just compensation.

Even ownership in real property in fee simple absolute is limited by a superior ownership. Just as in medieval England the king was the ultimate landowner, so in the United States the government has an ultimate ownership right in all land. This right is called **eminent domain,** and it allows the government to take land for public use. Eminent domain gives the government the right to acquire possession of real property in the manner directed by the U.S. Constitution and the laws of the state whenever the public interest requires it. Property may be taken only for public use, not for private benefit.

CONDEMNATION
The process of taking private property for public use through the government's power of eminent domain.

The power of eminent domain is generally invoked through **condemnation** proceedings (and the power of eminent domain is sometimes referred to as the *condemnation power* of government). When a new public highway is to be built, for instance, the government must decide where to build it and how much land to condemn. After the government determines that a particular parcel of land is necessary for public use, it will first offer to buy the property. If the owner refuses the offer, the government brings a judicial (condemnation) proceeding to obtain title to the land. Then, in another proceeding, the court determines the *fair value* of the land, which is usually approximately equal to its market value.

TAKING
The taking of private property by the government for public use. The government may not take private property for public use without "just compensation."

When the government takes land owned by a private party for public use, it is referred to as a **taking,** and the government must compensate the private party. Under the so-called *takings clause* of the Fifth Amendment to the U.S. Constitution, the government may not take private property for public use without "just compensation." State constitutions contain similar provisions.

ETHICAL ISSUE 24.1

Should eminent domain be used to promote private developments? Issues of fairness often arise when the government takes private property for public use. One issue is whether it is fair for property taken by eminent domain to then be conveyed to private developers. For example, suppose that a city government decides that it is in the public interest to have a larger parking lot for a local, privately owned sports stadium or to have a manufacturing plant locate in the city to create more jobs. The government may condemn certain tracts of existing housing or business property and then, later, convey the land to the privately owned stadium or to the owner of the manufacturing plant. The increasingly widespread use of eminent domain for such purposes has generated substantial controversy. Government officials claim that this use of eminent domain helps bring in private developers and businesses that provide jobs and increase tax revenues, thus revitalizing communities. Critics of this trend, however, contend that when eminent domain is used in this way, essentially one group of private owners simply replaces another group of private owners. In other words, the land is not being taken for "public" use, as required by the Fifth Amendment to the U.S. Constitution. Although the courts, by and large, have supported the government agencies in cases challenging such takings of private property, the tide may be turning. In recent years, some courts have held for the landowners in these cases.[8] ■

■ Leasehold Estates

LEASEHOLD ESTATE
An estate in realty held by a tenant under a lease. In every leasehold estate, the tenant has a qualified right to possess and/or use the land.

A **leasehold estate** is created when a real property owner or lessor (landlord) agrees to convey the right to possess and use the property to a lessee (tenant) for a certain period of time. In every leasehold estate, the tenant has a *qualified* right to exclusive possession (qualified by the right of the landlord to enter on the premises to assure that waste is not being committed). The tenant can use the land—for example, by harvesting crops—but cannot injure it by such activities as cutting down timber for sale or extracting oil.

The respective rights and duties of the landlord and tenant that arise under a lease agreement will be discussed shortly. Here we look at the types of leasehold estates, or tenancies, that can be created when real property is leased.

TENANCY FOR YEARS

TENANCY FOR YEARS
A type of tenancy under which property is leased for a specified period of time, such as a month, a year, or a period of years.

A **tenancy for years** is created by an express contract by which property is leased for a specified period of time, such as a day, a month, a year, or a period of years. Signing a one-year lease to occupy an apartment, for instance, creates a tenancy for years. At the end of the period specified in the lease, the lease ends (without notice), and possession of the apartment returns to the lessor. If the tenant dies during the period of the lease, the lease interest passes to the tenant's heirs as personal property. Often, leases include renewal or extension provisions.

PERIODIC TENANCY

PERIODIC TENANCY
A lease interest in land for an indefinite period involving payment of rent at fixed intervals, such as week to week, month to month, or year to year.

A **periodic tenancy** is created by a lease that does not specify how long it is to last but does specify that rent is to be paid at certain intervals. This type of tenancy is automatically renewed for another rental period unless properly terminated. ■ **EXAMPLE 24.5** Kayla enters a lease with Capital Properties. The lease states, "Rent is due on the tenth day of every month." This provision creates a periodic tenancy from month to month. ■ This type of tenancy can also extend from week to week or from year to year.

---

8. See, for example, *Southwestern Illinois Development Authority v. National City Environmental, L.L.C.,* 199 Ill.2d 225, 798 N.E.2d 1, 263 Ill.Dec. 241 (2002); *In re Condemnation of 110 Washington St.,* 767 A.2d 1154 (Pa. Cmwlth. 2001); and *99 Cents Only Stores v. Lancaster Redevelopment Agency,* 237 F.Supp.2d 1123 (C.D.Cal. 2001).

Under the common law, to terminate a periodic tenancy, the landlord or tenant must give at least one period's notice to the other party. If the tenancy extends from month to month, for example, one month's notice must be given prior to the last month's rent payment. State statutes may require a different period for notice of termination in a periodic tenancy, however.

TENANCY AT WILL

TENANCY AT WILL
A type of tenancy that either party can terminate without notice; usually arises when a tenant who has been under a tenancy for years retains possession, with the landlord's consent, after the tenancy for years has terminated.

Suppose that a landlord rents an apartment to a tenant "for as long as both agree." In such a situation, the tenant receives a leasehold estate known as a **tenancy at will.** Under the common law, either party can terminate the tenancy without notice (that is, "at will"). This type of estate usually arises when a tenant who has been under a tenancy for years retains possession after the termination date of that tenancy with the landlord's consent. Before the tenancy has been converted into a periodic tenancy—by the periodic payment of rent—it is a tenancy at will, terminable by either party without notice. Once the tenancy is treated as a periodic tenancy, notice of termination must conform to the requirements already discussed for that type of tenancy. The death of either party or the voluntary commission of waste by the tenant will terminate a tenancy at will.

TENANCY AT SUFFERANCE

TENANCY AT SUFFERANCE
A type of tenancy under which a tenant who, after rightfully being in possession of leased premises, continues (wrongfully) to occupy the property after the lease has been terminated. The tenant has no rights to possess the property and occupies it only because the person entitled to evict the tenant has not done so.

The mere possession of land without right is called a **tenancy at sufferance.** A tenancy at sufferance is not a true tenancy because it is created when a tenant *wrongfully* retains possession of property. Whenever a tenancy for years or a periodic tenancy ends and the tenant continues to retain possession of the premises without the owner's permission, a tenancy at sufferance is created.

You can find online links to most uniform laws, including the URLTA, at **http://www.lawsource.com.**

■■ Landlord-Tenant Relationships

In the past several decades, landlord-tenant relationships have become much more complex, as has the law governing them. Generally, the law has come to apply contract doctrines, such as those relating to implied warranties and unconscionability, to the landlord-tenant relationship. Increasingly, landlord-tenant relationships have become subject to specific state and local statutes and ordinances as well. In 1972, in an effort to create more uniformity in the law governing landlord-tenant relationships, the National Conference of Commissioners on Uniform State Laws issued the Uniform Residential Landlord and Tenant Act (URLTA). More than one-third of the states have adopted variations of the URLTA. We look now at how a landlord-tenant relationship is created and at the respective rights and duties of landlords and tenants.

CREATING THE LANDLORD-TENANT RELATIONSHIP

A landlord-tenant relationship is established by a lease contract. As mentioned, a lease contract arises when a property owner (landlord) agrees to give another party (the tenant) the exclusive right to possess the property—usually for a price and for a specified term.

Form of the Lease A lease contract may be oral or written. Under the common law, an oral lease is valid. As with most oral contracts, however, a party who seeks to enforce an oral lease may have difficulty proving its existence. In most states, statutes mandate that leases be in writing for some tenancies (such as those exceeding one year). Therefore, to ensure the validity of a lease agreement, it should be in writing and do the following:

1 Express an intent to establish the relationship.

2 Provide for the transfer of the property's possession to the tenant at the beginning of the term.

3 Provide for the landlord's *reversionary* (future) interest, which entitles the property owner to retake possession at the end of the term.

4 Describe the property—for example, give its street address.

5 Indicate the length of the term, the amount of the rent, and how and when it is to be paid.

In drafting commercial leases, sound business practice dictates that the leases be written carefully and that the parties' rights and obligations be clearly defined in the lease agreements. (The *Application* feature at the end of this chapter provides suggestions to businesspersons on how to negotiate a favorable lease contract.)

Illegality   State or local law often dictates permissible lease terms. For example, a statute or ordinance might prohibit the leasing of a structure that is in a certain physical condition or is not in compliance with local building codes. Similarly, a statute may prohibit the leasing of property for a particular purpose. For instance, a state law might prohibit gambling houses. Thus, if a landlord and tenant intend that the leased premises be used only to house an illegal betting operation, their lease is unenforceable.

A property owner cannot legally discriminate against prospective tenants on the basis of race, color, national origin, religion, gender, or disability. In addition, a tenant cannot legally promise to do something counter to laws prohibiting discrimination. A commercial tenant, for example, cannot legally promise to do business only with members of a particular race. The public policy underlying these prohibitions is to treat all people equally. In the following case, a rental housing applicant claimed that her rental application had been denied because of her live-in boyfriend's race.

CASE 24.2 ▪ Osborn v. Kellogg

Court of Appeals of Nebraska, 1996.
4 Neb.App. 594,
547 N.W.2d 504.

FACTS Kristi Kellogg, her daughter Mindy, and her boyfriend James Greene attempted to lease half of a house. The house was owned by Keith Osborn and Pam Lyman and managed, as rental property, by Keith's mother, Barbara Osborn. Kellogg was white. Greene was African American. The owners refused to rent to them, claiming, among other things, that three people were too many, Greene's income was too low, and Greene had not

provided credit references. They later rented half of the house to the Li family, which had five members, and the other half to the Suggett family, which numbered three. Both the Li family and the Suggett family had less income than Kellogg and Greene. Kellogg had provided extensive credit references, but the Lis and the Suggetts had provided none. Kellogg filed a complaint with the Nebraska Equal Opportunity Commission (NEOC) against the Osborns and Lyman. The NEOC concluded that the defendants had discriminated against Kellogg in violation of state fair housing laws. A Nebraska state trial court

CASE 24.2—Continued

adopted the NEOC's conclusion. The defendants appealed to an intermediate state appellate court.

ISSUE Had the defendants discriminated against Kellogg in violation of state fair housing laws?

DECISION Yes. The intermediate state appellate court affirmed the judgment of the lower court.

REASON The appellate court reasoned that while Kellogg was not a member of a racial minority, Greene was, and Kellogg thus qualified as a person who had been injured by a discriminatory housing practice. The

court stated, "The NEOC hearing examiner found that Kellogg proved by a preponderance of the evidence that the Osborns' seemingly legitimate reasons for rejecting Kellogg were, in fact, a pretext for intentional discrimination. * * * [W]e conclude that competent evidence supports the NEOC hearing examiner's factual findings."

FOR CRITICAL ANALYSIS—Ethical Consideration
What if the Osborns and Lyman discriminated against Kellogg not because her boyfriend was African American but because they disapproved of cohabitation by unmarried couples? Should this form of discrimination be permissible?

RIGHTS AND DUTIES

The rights and duties of landlords and tenants generally pertain to four broad areas of concern—the possession, use, maintenance, and, of course, rent of leased property.

Possession A landlord is obligated to give a tenant possession of the property that the tenant has agreed to lease. Many states follow the "English" rule, which requires the landlord to provide actual *physical possession* to the tenant (making sure that the previous tenant has vacated). Other states follow the "American" rule, which requires the landlord to transfer only the *legal right to possession* (thus, the new tenant is responsible for removing a previous tenant). After obtaining possession, the tenant retains the property exclusively until the lease expires, unless the lease states otherwise.

Many Web sites now provide information on laws and other information relating to landlord-tenant relationships. One of them is TenantNet™ at

http://www.tenant.net.

The covenant of quiet enjoyment mentioned previously also applies to leased premises. Under this covenant, the landlord promises that during the lease term, neither the landlord nor anyone having a superior title to the property will disturb the tenant's use and enjoyment of the property. This covenant forms the essence of the landlord-tenant relationship, and if it is breached, the tenant can terminate the lease and sue for damages.

If the landlord deprives the tenant of possession of the leased property or interferes with the tenant's use or enjoyment of it, an **eviction** occurs. An eviction occurs, for instance, when the landlord changes the lock and refuses to give the tenant a new key. A **constructive eviction** occurs when the landlord wrongfully performs or fails to perform any of the duties the lease requires, thereby making the tenant's further use and enjoyment of the property exceedingly difficult or impossible. Examples of constructive eviction include a landlord's failure to provide heat in the winter, light, or other essential utilities.

EVICTION
A landlord's act of depriving a tenant of possession of the leased premises.

CONSTRUCTIVE EVICTION
A form of eviction that occurs when a landlord fails to perform adequately any of the undertakings (such as providing heat in the winter) required by the lease, thereby making the tenant's further use and enjoyment of the property exceedingly difficult or impossible.

Use and Maintenance of the Premises If the parties do not limit by agreement the uses to which the property may be put, the tenant may make any use of it, as long as the use is legal and reasonably relates to the purpose for which the property is adapted or ordinarily used and does not injure the landlord's interest.

The tenant is responsible for any damages to the premises that he or she causes, intentionally or negligently, and may be held liable for the cost of returning the property to the physical condition it was in at the lease's inception. Also, the tenant is not entitled to substantially interfere with others' quiet enjoyment of their property rights. Unless the parties have agreed otherwise, the tenant is not responsible for ordinary wear and tear and the property's consequent depreciation in value.

In some jurisdictions, landlords of residential property are required by statute to maintain the premises in good repair. Landlords must also comply with any applicable state statutes and city ordinances regarding maintenance and repair of buildings.

IMPLIED WARRANTY OF HABITABILITY
An implied promise by a landlord that rented residential premises are fit for human habitation—that is, in a condition that is safe and suitable for people to live in.

Implied Warranty of Habitability   The **implied warranty of habitability** requires a landlord who leases residential property to furnish premises that are in a habitable condition—that is, in a condition that is safe and suitable for people to live. Also, the landlord must make repairs to maintain the premises in that condition for the lease's duration. Some state legislatures have enacted this warranty into law. In other jurisdictions, courts have based the warranty on the existence of a landlord's statutory duty to keep leased premises in good repair, or they have simply applied it as a matter of public policy.

Generally, this warranty applies to major, or *substantial,* physical defects that the landlord knows or should know about and has had a reasonable time to repair—for example, a large hole in the roof. An unattractive or annoying feature, such as a crack in the wall, may be unpleasant, but unless the crack is a structural defect or affects the residence's heating capabilities, it is probably not sufficiently substantial to make the place uninhabitable.

Rent   *Rent* is the tenant's payment to the landlord for the tenant's occupancy or use of the landlord's real property. Usually, the tenant must pay the rent even if she or he refuses to occupy the property or moves out, as long as the refusal or the move is unjustified and the lease is in force. Under the common law, if the leased premises were destroyed by fire or flood, the tenant still had to pay rent. Today, however, most state's statutes provide that if an apartment building burns down, tenants are not required to continue to pay rent.

NOTE   Options that may be available to a tenant on a landlord's breach of the implied warranty of habitability include repairing the defect and deducting the amount from the rent, canceling the lease, and suing for damages.

In some situations, such as when a landlord breaches the implied warranty of habitability, a tenant may be allowed to withhold rent as a remedy. When rent withholding is authorized under a statute, the tenant must usually put the amount withheld into an *escrow account.* This account is held in the name of the depositor (the tenant) and an *escrow agent* (usually the court or a government agency), and the funds are returnable to the depositor if the third person (the landlord) fails to make the premises habitable. Generally, the tenant may withhold an amount equal to the amount by which the defect rendering the premises unlivable reduces the property's rental value. How much that is may be determined in different ways, and a tenant who withholds more than is legally permissible is liable to the landlord for the excessive amount withheld.

TRANSFERRING RIGHTS TO LEASED PROPERTY

Either the landlord or the tenant may wish to transfer her or his rights to the leased property during the term of the lease.

Transferring the Landlord's Interest   Just as any other real property owner can sell, give away, or otherwise transfer his or her property, so can a landlord—who is, of course, the leased property's owner. If complete title to the leased property is

Under what conditions can this lessee sublease the premises? (Scott Saltzman, Bloomberg News/Landov)

SUBLEASE
A lease executed by the lessee of real estate to a third person, conveying the same interest that the lessee enjoys but for a shorter term than that held by the lessee.

transferred, the tenant becomes the tenant of the new owner. The new owner may collect subsequent rent but must abide by the terms of the existing lease agreement.

Transferring the Tenant's Interest   The tenant's transfer of his or her entire interest in the leased property to a third person is an *assignment of the lease.* The tenant's transfer of all or part of the premises for a period shorter than the lease term is a *sublease.*

A lease assignment is an agreement to transfer all rights, title, and interest in the lease to the assignee. It is a complete transfer. Many leases require that the assignment have the landlord's written consent. An assignment that lacks consent can be avoided (nullified) by the landlord. State statutes may specify that the landlord may not unreasonably withhold such consent, though. Also, a landlord who knowingly accepts rent from the assignee may be held to have waived the consent requirement.

When an assignment is valid, the assignee acquires all of the tenant's rights under the lease. But an assignment does not release the assigning tenant from the obligation to pay rent should the assignee default. Also, if the assignee exercises an option under the original lease to extend the term, the assigning tenant remains liable for the rent during the extension, unless the landlord agrees otherwise.

The tenant's transfer of all or part of the premises for a period shorter than the lease term is a **sublease.** The same restrictions that apply to an assignment of the tenant's interest in leased property apply to a sublease. If the landlord's consent is required, a sublease without such permission is ineffective. Also, a sublease does not release the tenant from her or his obligations under the lease any more than an assignment does. ■ **EXAMPLE 24.6** Derek, a student, leases an apartment for a two-year period. Although Derek had planned on attending summer school, he is offered a job in Europe for the summer months, and he accepts. Because he does not wish to pay three months' rent for an unoccupied apartment, Derek subleases the apartment to Adva, who becomes a sublessee. (Derek may have to obtain his landlord's consent for this sublease if the lease requires it.) Adva is bound by the same terms of the lease as Derek. As in a lease assignment, the landlord can hold Derek liable if Adva violates the lease terms. ■

◼ Environmental Law

We now turn to a discussion of the various ways in which businesses are regulated by the government in the interest of protecting the environment. To a great extent, environmental law consists of statutes passed by federal, state, or local governments and regulations issued by administrative agencies.

STATE AND LOCAL REGULATION

Many states regulate the degree to which the environment may be polluted. Thus, for example, even when state zoning laws permit a business's proposed development, the proposal may have to be altered to lessen the development's impact on the environment. State laws may restrict a business's discharge of chemicals into the air or water or regulate its disposal of toxic wastes. States may also regulate the disposal or recycling of other wastes, including glass, metal, and plastic containers and paper. Additionally, states may restrict the emissions from motor vehicles.

City, county, and other local governments control some aspects of the environment. For instance, local zoning laws control some land use. These laws may be designed to inhibit or regulate the growth of cities and suburbs or to protect the natural environment. Other aspects of the environment may be subject to local regulation for other reasons. Methods of waste and garbage removal and disposal, for example, can have a substantial impact on a community. The appearance of buildings and other structures, including advertising signs and billboards, may affect traffic safety, property values, or local aesthetics. Noise generated by a business or its customers may be annoying, disruptive, or damaging to neighbors. The location and condition of parks, streets, and other publicly used land subject to local control affect the environment and can also affect business.

In recent years, many state and local governments have passed what are referred to as *brownfields redevelopment laws*. These laws are designed to provide incentives to buyers to purchase and clean up contaminated land ("brownfields") or old buildings containing asbestos. Incentives may be in the form of tax credits, government grants, or other assistance. In 2004, the Environmental Protection Agency gave a record $75.4 million in brownfields grants to communities in forty-two states and Puerto Rico.

FEDERAL REGULATION

Congress has enacted a number of statutes to control the impact of human activities on the environment. Some of these laws have been passed to improve the quality of air and water. Some of them specifically regulate toxic chemicals, including pesticides, herbicides, and hazardous wastes.

Environmental Regulatory Agencies   Much of the body of federal law governing business activities consists of the regulations issued and enforced by administrative agencies. The most well known of the agencies regulating environmental law is, of course, the Environmental Protection Agency (EPA), which was created in 1970 to coordinate federal environmental responsibilities. Other federal agencies with authority to regulate specific environmental matters include the Department of the Interior, the Department of Defense, the Department of Labor, the Food and Drug Administration, and the Nuclear Regulatory Commission. These regulatory agencies—and all other agencies of the federal government—must take environmental factors into consideration when making significant decisions.

Most federal environmental laws provide that citizens can sue to enforce environmental regulations if government agencies fail to do so—or if agencies go too far in their enforcement actions. Typically, a threshold hurdle in such suits is meeting the requirements for standing to sue.

State and local regulatory agencies also play a significant role in implementing federal environmental legislation. Typically, the federal government relies on state and local governments to enforce federal environmental statutes and regulations such as those regulating air quality.

Environmental Impact Statements   The National Environmental Policy Act (NEPA) of 1969[9] requires that an **environmental impact statement (EIS)** be pre-

ENVIRONMENTAL IMPACT STATEMENT (EIS)
A statement required by the National Environmental Policy Act for any major federal action that will significantly affect the quality of the environment. The statement must analyze the action's impact on the environment and explore alternative actions that might be taken.

---

9. 42 U.S.C. Sections 4321–4370d.

pared for every major federal action that significantly affects the quality of the environment. An EIS must analyze (1) the impact on the environment that the action will have, (2) any adverse effects on the environment and alternative actions that might be taken, and (3) irreversible effects the action might generate.

An action qualifies as "major" if it involves a substantial commitment of resources (monetary or otherwise). An action is "federal" if a federal agency has the power to control it. Construction by a private developer of a ski resort on federal land, for example, may require an EIS.[10] Building or operating a nuclear plant, which requires a federal permit,[11] would require an EIS, as would constructing a dam as part of a federal project.[12] If an agency decides that an EIS is unnecessary, it must issue a statement supporting this conclusion. EISs have become instruments for private citizens, consumer interest groups, businesses, and others to challenge federal agency actions on the basis that the actions improperly threaten the environment.

AIR POLLUTION

Federal involvement with air pollution goes back to the 1950s, when Congress authorized funds for air-pollution research. In 1963, the federal government passed the Clean Air Act,[13] which focused on multistate air pollution and provided assistance to states. Various amendments, particularly in 1970, 1977, and 1990, have strengthened the government's authority to regulate the quality of air. These laws provide the basis for issuing regulations to control pollution coming primarily from mobile sources (such as automobiles) and stationary sources (such as electric utilities and industrial plants).

For information on EPA standards, guidelines, and regulations, go to the EPA's Web site at **http://www.epa.gov**.

Mobile Sources of Pollution   Regulations governing air pollution from automobiles and other mobile sources specify pollution standards and establish time schedules for meeting the standards. For example, under the 1990 amendments to the Clean Air Act, automobile manufacturers were required to cut new automobiles' exhaust emissions of nitrogen oxide by 60 percent and of other pollutants by 35 percent by 1998. Regulations that became effective beginning with 2004 model cars call for nitrogen oxide tailpipe emissions to be cut by nearly 10 percent by 2007. For the first time, sport utility vehicles (SUVs) and light trucks are required to meet the same standards as automobiles.

Service stations are also subject to environmental regulations. The 1990 amendments require service stations to sell gasoline with a higher oxygen content in forty-one cities that experience carbon monoxide pollution in the winter. Service stations are required to sell even cleaner burning gasoline in the most polluted urban areas.

The EPA attempts to update pollution-control standards when new scientific information becomes available. For example, studies conducted in the 1990s purportedly showed that very small particles (2.5 microns, or about one-thirtieth the size of a human hair) of soot affect our health as significantly as larger particles. Based on this evidence, the EPA issued new particulate standards for motor vehicle exhaust systems and other sources of pollution. The EPA also instituted a more rigorous standard for ozone (the basic ingredient of smog), which is formed when sunlight combines with pollutants from cars and other sources.

10. *Robertson v. Methow Valley Citizens' Council,* 490 U.S. 332, 109 S.Ct. 1835, 104 L.Ed.2d 351 (1989).
11. *Calvert Cliffs Coordinating Committee v. Atomic Energy Commission,* 449 F.2d 1109 (D.C. Cir. 1971).
12. *Marsh v. Oregon Natural Resources Council,* 490 U.S. 360, 109 S.Ct. 1851, 104 L.Ed.2d 377 (1989).
13. 42 U.S.C. Sections 7401 *et seq.*

ETHICAL ISSUE 24.2

Should the costs of EPA regulations be weighed against their prospective benefits? In setting standards governing air quality, traditionally the EPA has not been required to take costs into account. Rather, the emphasis is on the benefits. For example, when the EPA issued its new rules on particulate matter and ozone, the head of the EPA claimed that the new standards would save 15,000 lives a year. Given that the EPA values a human life at $5 million, the agency calculated that the lives saved and medical expenses avoided by the strict standards would amount to $100 billion a year in benefits. Nothing was said about the costs of implementing these rules, though. Environmental groups tend to downplay these costs and to value potential lives saved very highly. In contrast, business groups, particularly those that are affected adversely by strict air standards, think that the EPA should factor in these costs.

In 2001, the United States Supreme Court resolved the debate over this issue after years of litigation. A number of business groups had challenged the EPA's stricter air-quality standards, claiming that the EPA had exceeded its authority under the Clean Air Act by issuing the regulations. The groups also claimed that the EPA had to take economic costs into account when developing new regulations. The Court, however, held that the EPA had not exceeded its authority under the Clean Air Act and confirmed that the EPA does not have to take economic costs into account when creating new rules.[14] ■

Stationary Sources of Pollution   The Clean Air Act authorizes the EPA to establish air-quality standards for stationary sources (such as manufacturing plants) but recognizes that the primary responsibility for preventing and controlling air pollution rests with state and local governments. The EPA sets primary and secondary levels of ambient standards—that is, the maximum levels of certain pollutants—and the states formulate plans to achieve those standards. Different standards apply depending on whether the sources of pollution are in clean areas or polluted areas and whether they are already existing sources or major new sources. Generally, major sources are required to use the *maximum achievable control technology,* or MACT, to reduce emissions. The EPA issues guidelines as to what equipment meets this standard.

Under the 1990 amendments to the Clean Air Act, 110 of the oldest coal-burning power plants in the United States had to cut their emissions by 40 percent by the year 2001 to reduce acid rain. Utilities were granted "credits" to emit certain amounts of sulfur dioxide, and those that emit less than the allowed amounts can sell their credits to other polluters. The amendments also required an end to the production of chlorofluorocarbons, carbon tetrachloride, and methyl chloroform, which are used in air-conditioning, refrigeration, and insulation and have been linked to depletion of the ozone layer. The relationship between the Clean Air Act's 1990 amendments and a New York state law was at issue in the following case.

---

14. *Whitman v. American Trucking Associations,* 531 U.S. 457, 121 S.Ct. 903, 149 L.Ed.2d 1 (2001).

CASE 24.3 ■ Clean Air Markets Group v. Pataki

United States District Court,
Northern District of New York, 2002.
194 F.Supp.2d 147.

HISTORICAL AND ENVIRONMENTAL SETTING *Acid rain allegedly has negative effects on*

water, forests, human health, and buildings and other structures. Acid rain consists of atmospheric sulfates and nitrates, which are formed from sulfur dioxide (SO_2) and nitrogen oxides (NO_x). These substances are emitted as by-products of the combustion of fossil fuels, most notably

CASE 24.3—Continued

during the generation of electricity. Emissions originating in fourteen midwestern, eastern, and southern states, referred to as "upwind states," contribute significantly to acid rain in New York.

FACTS By 1999, it was clear to some scientists that SO_2 emissions at the rates permitted by the Clean Air Act would not permit the environmental restoration of parts of the state of New York. Additional reductions in SO_2 emissions would be required. George Pataki, the governor of New York, ordered New York utilities to cut SO_2 emissions to half of the amount permitted by the Clean Air Act by January 2, 2007. By doing this, the New York utilities would have additional SO_2 credits to sell. In May 2000, the New York state legislature enacted the Air Pollution Mitigation Law (APML), which stipulated that most sums received for the sale or trade of SO_2 allowances to a polluter in an upwind state would be forfeited to the New York Public Service Commission (PSC), which regulates New York utilities. This effectively lowered the market value of credits originating with New York utilities. Clean Air Markets Group (CAMG) filed a suit in a federal district court against Pataki and others, claiming in part that the APML was preempted under the U.S. Constitution's supremacy clause.[a] All parties filed motions for summary judgment.

a. As explained in Chapter 1, if federal law has not supplanted a whole field of state law, state law is preempted to the extent that it actually conflicts with federal law. A conflict between state and federal law occurs when compliance with both is physically impossible or when the state law is an obstacle to accomplishing the objective of federal law.

ISSUE Is New York's Air Pollution Mitigation Law preempted, under the supremacy clause, by the federal Clean Air Act?

DECISION Yes. The court granted CAMG's motion for summary judgment, holding that New York's Air Pollution Mitigation Law is preempted by the Clean Air Act.

REASON The court held that under the supremacy clause, the Clean Air Act preempts the APML because the state law interferes with the Clean Air Act's methods for achieving air-pollution control. The court enjoined (prevented) the enforcement of the APML. The court noted that the Clean Air Act provides that SO_2 allowances "may be transferred among designated representatives of the owners or operators of covered units (utilities) and *any* other person who holds such allowances." Thus, the APML's "restriction on transferring allowances to units in the Upwind States is contrary to the federal provision that allowances be tradeable to any other person," the court reasoned. Additionally, both Congress and the EPA had considered geographically restricted allowance transfers at some time and rejected them. In the court's view, "[t]he rejection of a regionally restricted allowance trading system illustrates the Congressional objective of having a nationwide trading market for SO_2 allowances. New York's regional restriction on SO_2 allowance trading by New York units is an obstacle to the execution of that objective."

FOR CRITICAL ANALYSIS—Environmental Consideration *Suppose that the APML also provided for a subsidy to those who claimed that the value of their pollution credits had been reduced. Would this have affected the outcome of the case? Why or why not?*

Hazardous Air Pollutants Hazardous air pollutants are those likely to cause death or serious irreversible or incapacitating illness. In all, there are 189 of these pollutants, including asbestos, benzene, beryllium, cadmium, mercury, and vinyl chloride. These pollutants may cause cancer as well as neurological and reproductive damage. They are emitted from stationary sources by a variety of business activities, including smelting (melting ore to produce metal), dry cleaning, house painting, and commercial baking. Instead of establishing specific emissions standards for each hazardous air pollutant, the 1990 amendments to the Clean Air Act require industry to use pollution-control equipment that represents the maximum achievable control technology to limit emissions. The EPA issues guidelines as to what equipment meets this standard.

In 1996, the EPA issued a rule to regulate hazardous air pollutants emitted by landfills. The rule required landfills constructed after May 30, 1991, that emit more than a specified amount of pollutants to install landfill gas collection and control systems.

This worker is cleaning asbestos, a hazardous air pollutant, from the interior of an old building. Does the Clean Air Act establish specific emission standards for hazardous air pollutants? Why or why not? What is the EPA's role in controlling hazardous air pollutants? (© Corbis)

The rule also required the states to impose the same requirements on landfills constructed before May 30, 1991, if they accepted waste after November 8, 1987.[15]

Violations of the Clean Air Act   For violations of emission limits under the Clean Air Act, the EPA can assess civil penalties of up to $25,000 per day. Additional fines of up to $5,000 per day can be assessed for other violations, such as failing to maintain the required records. To penalize those who find it more cost-effective to violate the act than to comply with it, the EPA is authorized to obtain a penalty equal to the violator's economic benefits from noncompliance. Persons who provide information about violators may be paid up to $10,000. Private citizens can also sue violators.

Those who knowingly violate the act may be subject to criminal penalties, including fines of up to $1 million and imprisonment for up to two years (for false statements or failures to report violations). Corporate officers are among those who may be subject to these penalties.

WATER POLLUTION

Water pollution stems mostly from industrial, municipal, and agricultural sources. Pollutants entering streams, lakes, and oceans include organic wastes, heated water, sediments from soil runoff, nutrients (including detergents, fertilizers, and human and animal wastes), and toxic chemicals and other hazardous substances. We look here at laws and regulations governing water pollution.

Navigable Waters   Federal regulations governing the pollution of water can be traced back to the Rivers and Harbors Appropriations Act of 1899.[16] These regulations prohibited ships and manufacturers from discharging or depositing refuse in navigable waterways without a permit. In 1948, Congress passed the Federal Water Pollution Control Act (FWPCA),[17] but its regulatory system and enforcement powers proved to be inadequate.

In 1972, amendments to the FWPCA—known as the Clean Water Act—established the following goals: (1) make waters safe for swimming, (2) protect fish and wildlife, and (3) eliminate the discharge of pollutants into the water. The amendments set specific time schedules, which were extended by amendment in 1977 and by the Water Quality Act of 1987.[18] Under these schedules, the EPA limits the discharge of various types of pollutants based on the technology available for controlling them. The 1972 act also requires municipal and industrial polluters to apply for permits before discharging wastes into navigable waters.

Under the act, violators are subject to a variety of civil and criminal penalties. Depending on the violation, civil penalties range from $10,000 per day to as much as $25,000 per day, but not more than $25,000 per violation. Criminal penalties, which apply only if a violation was intentional, range from a fine of $2,500 per day and imprisonment for up to one year to a fine of $1 million and fifteen years' imprisonment. Injunctive relief and damages can also be imposed. The polluting party can be required to clean up the pollution or pay for the cost of doing so.

Wetlands   The Clean Water Act prohibits the filling or dredging of **wetlands** unless a permit is obtained from the Army Corps of Engineers. The EPA defines *wetlands* as

WETLANDS
Water-saturated areas of land that are designated by government agencies (such as the Army Corps of Engineers or the Environmental Protection Agency) as protected areas that support wildlife and therefore cannot be filled in or dredged by private contractors or parties without a permit.

15. 40 C.F.R. Sections 60.750–759.

16. 33 U.S.C. Sections 401–418.

17. 33 U.S.C. Sections 1251–1387.

18. This act amended 33 U.S.C. Section 1251.

"those areas that are inundated or saturated by surface or ground water at a frequency and duration sufficient to support, and that under normal circumstances do support, a prevalence of vegetation typically adapted for life in saturated soil conditions." In recent years, the broad interpretation of what constitutes a wetland subject to the regulatory authority of the federal government has generated substantial controversy.

■ **EXAMPLE 24.7** Perhaps one of the most controversial regulations was the "migratory-bird rule" issued by the Army Corps of Engineers. Under this rule, any bodies of water that could affect interstate commerce, including seasonal ponds or waters "used or suitable for use by migratory birds" that fly over state borders, were "navigable waters" subject to federal regulation as wetlands under the Clean Water Act. The rule was challenged in a case brought by a group of communities in the Chicago suburbs that wanted to build a landfill in a tract of land northwest of Chicago that had once been used as a strip mine. Over time, areas that were once pits in the mine became ponds used by a variety of migratory birds. The Army Corps of Engineers, claiming that the shallow ponds formed a habitat for migratory birds, refused to grant a permit for the landfill. Ultimately, the United States Supreme Court held that the Army Corps of Engineers had exceeded its authority under the Clean Water Act. The Court stated that it was not prepared to hold that isolated and seasonable ponds, puddles, and "prairie potholes" become "navigable waters of the United States" simply because they serve as a habitat for migratory birds.[19] ■

Drinking Water   Another statute governing water pollution is the Safe Drinking Water Act of 1974.[20] This act requires the EPA to set maximum levels for pollutants in public water systems. Public water system operators must come as close as possible to meeting the EPA's standards by using the best available technology that is economically and technologically feasible. The EPA is particularly concerned about contamination from underground sources. Pesticides and wastes leaked from landfills or disposed of in underground injection wells are among the more than two hundred pollutants known to exist in groundwater used for drinking in at least thirty-four states. Many of these substances may be associated with cancer and may cause damage to the central nervous system, liver, and kidneys. The act was amended in 1996 to give the EPA more flexibility in setting regulatory standards.

Ocean Dumping   The Marine Protection, Research, and Sanctuaries Act of 1972[21] (popularly known as the Ocean Dumping Act), as amended in 1983, regulates the transportation and dumping of material into ocean waters. It prohibits entirely the ocean dumping of radiological, chemical, and biological warfare agents and high-level radioactive waste. Each violation of any provision may result in a civil penalty of up to $50,000, and a knowing violation is a criminal offense that may result in a $50,000 fine, imprisonment for not more than a year, or both. The court may also grant an injunction to prevent an imminent or continuing violation of the Ocean Dumping Act.

Oil Spills   In 1989, the supertanker *Exxon Valdez* caused the worst oil spill in North American history in the waters of Alaska's Prince William Sound. A quarter of a million barrels of crude oil—more than ten million gallons—leaked out of the ship's broken hull. In response to the *Exxon Valdez* disaster, Congress passed the Oil

19. *Solid Waste Agency of Northern Cook County v. U.S. Army Corps of Engineers,* 531 U.S. 159, 121 S.Ct. 675, 148 L.Ed.2d 576 (2001).
20. 42 U.S.C. Sections 300f to 300j-25.
21. 16 U.S.C. Sections 1401–1445.

Pollution Act of 1990.[22] Any onshore or offshore oil facility, oil shipper, vessel owner, or vessel operator that discharges oil into navigable waters or onto an adjoining shore may be liable for clean-up costs, as well as damages.

Under the act, damage to natural resources, private property, and the local economy, including the increased cost of providing public services, is compensable. The act provides for civil penalties of $1,000 per barrel spilled or $25,000 for each day of the violation. The party held responsible for the clean-up costs can bring a civil suit for contribution from other potentially liable parties. The act also decreed that by the year 2011, oil tankers using U.S. ports must be double hulled to limit the severity of accidental spills.

NOISE POLLUTION

Regulations concerning noise pollution include the Noise Control Act of 1972.[23] This act directed the EPA to establish standards for noise emissions—for example, for railroad noise emissions. The standards must be achievable by the best available technology, and they must be economically within reason. The act prohibits, among other things, distributing products manufactured in violation of the standards and tampering with noise-control devices. Violations of the Noise Control Act can result in penalties of not more than $50,000 per day and imprisonment for not more than two years.

TOXIC CHEMICALS

Originally, most environmental clean-up efforts were directed toward reducing smog and making water safe for fishing and swimming. Over time, however, control of toxic chemicals has become an important part of environmental law.

Pesticides and Herbicides   The Federal Insecticide, Fungicide, and Rodenticide Act (FIFRA) of 1947 regulates pesticides and herbicides.[24] Under FIFRA, pesticides and herbicides must be (1) registered before they can be sold, (2) certified and used only for approved applications, and (3) used in limited quantities when applied to food crops. The EPA can cancel or suspend registration of substances that are identified as harmful and may also inspect factories where the chemicals are made. Under 1996 amendments to FIFRA, there must be no more than a one-in-a-million risk to people of developing cancer from any kind of exposure to the substance, including eating food that contains pesticide residues.[25] Also, the EPA must distribute brochures to grocery stores on the high-risk pesticides that are in or on food, and the stores must display these brochures for consumers.

It is a violation of FIFRA to sell a pesticide or herbicide that is unregistered or has had its registration canceled or suspended. It is also a violation to sell a pesticide or herbicide with a false or misleading label or to destroy or deface any labeling required under the act. Penalties for commercial dealers include imprisonment for up to one year and a fine of no more than $25,000. Farmers and

Clean-up efforts in Alaska's Prince William Sound following the Exxon Valdez *oil spill. How did this disaster change the law regarding oil spills? Who can be held responsible for clean-up costs? (Photo Courtesy of* Exxon Valdez *Oil Spill Trustee Council and National Oceanic & Atmospheric Administration)*

22. 33 U.S.C. Sections 2701–2761.
23. 42 U.S.C. Sections 4901–4918.
24. 7 U.S.C. Sections 135–136y.
25. 21 U.S.C. Section 346a.

other private users of pesticides or herbicides who violate the act are subject to a $1,000 fine and incarceration for up to thirty days.

Toxic Substances The first comprehensive law covering toxic substances was the Toxic Substances Control Act of 1976.[26] The act was passed to regulate chemicals and chemical compounds that are known to be toxic—such as asbestos and polychlorinated biphenyls, popularly known as PCBs—and to institute investigation of any possible harmful effects from new chemical compounds. The regulations authorize the EPA to require that manufacturers, processors, and other organizations planning to use chemicals first determine their effects on human health and the environment. The EPA can regulate substances that potentially pose an imminent hazard or an unreasonable risk of injury to health or the environment. The EPA may require special labeling, limit the use of a substance, set production quotas, or prohibit the use of a substance altogether.

HAZARDOUS WASTE DISPOSAL

Some industrial, agricultural, and household wastes pose more serious threats than others. If not properly disposed of, these toxic chemicals may present a substantial danger to human health and the environment. If released into the environment, they may contaminate public drinking water resources.

Resource Conservation and Recovery Act In 1976, Congress passed the Resource Conservation and Recovery Act (RCRA)[27] in reaction to the growing concern over the effects of hazardous waste materials on the environment. The RCRA required the EPA to determine which forms of solid waste should be considered hazardous and to establish regulations to monitor and control hazardous waste disposal. The act also requires all producers of hazardous waste materials to label and package properly any hazardous waste to be transported. The RCRA was amended in 1984 and 1986 to decrease the use of land containment in the disposal of hazardous waste and to require smaller generators of hazardous waste to comply with the act.

Under the RCRA, a company may be assessed a civil penalty of up to $25,000 for each violation.[28] Penalties are based on the seriousness of the violation, the probability of harm, and the extent to which the violation deviates from RCRA requirements. Criminal penalties include fines of up to $50,000 for each day of violation, imprisonment for up to two years (in most instances), or both.[29] Criminal fines and the period of imprisonment can be doubled for certain repeat offenders.

Superfund In 1980, Congress passed the Comprehensive Environmental Response, Compensation, and Liability Act (CERCLA),[30] commonly known as Superfund, to regulate the clean-up of leaking hazardous waste–disposal sites. A special federal fund was created for that purpose. Because of its impact on the business community, the act is presented as this chapter's *Landmark in the Law* feature on the following page.

A hazardous waste–disposal team cleans up toxic chemicals that spilled from a truck onto a public highway. If the substance was not properly labeled in violation of the RCRA, what civil penalty might a court impose on the company that operated the vehicle? (Courtesy of Minnesota Pollution Control Agency)

26. 15 U.S.C. Sections 2601–2692.
27. 42 U.S.C. Sections 6901 *et seq.*
28. 42 U.S.C. Section 6928(a).
29. 42 U.S.C. Section 6928(d).
30. 42 U.S.C. Sections 9601–9675.

LANDMARK IN THE LAW ## Superfund

The origins of the Comprehensive Environmental Response, Compensation, and Liability Act (CERCLA) of 1980, commonly referred to as Superfund, can be traced to drafts that the Environmental Protection Agency (EPA) started to circulate in 1978.

DUMP SITES CHARACTERIZED AS "TICKING TIME BOMBS"   EPA officials emphasized the necessity of new legislation by pointing to what they characterized as "ticking time bombs"—dump sites around the country that were ready to explode and injure the public with toxic fumes.

The popular press was also running prominent stories about hazardous waste–dump sites at the time. The New York Love Canal disaster first made headlines in 1978 when residents in the area complained about health problems, contaminated sludge oozing into their basements, and chemical "volcanoes" erupting in their yards. These problems were the result of approximately 21,000 tons of chemicals that Hooker Chemical had dumped into the canal from 1942 to 1953. By the middle of May 1980, the Love Canal situation was making the national news virtually every day, and it remained in the headlines for a month.

CERCLA—ITS PURPOSE AND PRIMARY ELEMENTS   The basic purpose of CERCLA, which was amended in 1986, is to regulate the clean-up of leaking hazardous waste–disposal sites. The act has four primary elements:

1 It established an information-gathering and analysis system that enables the government to identify chemical dump sites and determine the appropriate action.

2 It authorized the EPA to respond to hazardous substance emergencies and to arrange for the clean-up of a leaking site directly if the persons responsible for the problem fail to clean up the site.

3 It created a Hazardous Substance Response Trust Fund (Superfund) to pay for the clean-up of hazardous sites using funds obtained through taxes on certain businesses.

4 It allowed the government to recover the cost of clean-up from the persons who were (even remotely) responsible for hazardous substance releases.

APPLICATION TO TODAY'S WORLD

The provisions of CERCLA profoundly affect today's businesses. Virtually any business decision relating to the purchase and sale of property, for example, requires an analysis of previous activities on the property to determine whether they resulted in contamination. Additionally, to avoid violating CERCLA, owners and managers of manufacturing plants must be extremely careful in arranging for the removal and disposal of any hazardous waste materials. Unless Congress significantly changes CERCLA and the way that it is implemented, businesses will continue to face potentially extensive liability for violations under this act.

RELEVANT WEB SITES

To locate information on the Web concerning Superfund, go to this text's Web site at **http://blt.westbuslaw.com,** *select "Chapter 24," and click on "URLs for Landmarks."*

Potentially Responsible Parties under Superfund. Superfund provides that when a release or a threatened release of hazardous chemicals from a site occurs, the EPA can clean up the site and recover the cost of the clean-up from the following persons: (1) the person who generated the wastes disposed of at the site, (2) the person who transported the wastes to the site, (3) the person who owned or operated the site at the time of the disposal, or (4) the current owner or operator. A person falling within one of these categories is referred to as a **potentially responsible party (PRP)**.

POTENTIALLY RESPONSIBLE PARTY (PRP)
A party liable for the costs of cleaning up a hazardous waste–disposal site under the Comprehensive Environmental Response, Compensation, and Liability Act (CERCLA). Any person who generated the hazardous waste, transported it, owned or operated the waste site at the time of disposal, or currently owns or operates the site may be responsible for some or all of the clean-up costs.

Joint and Several Liability under Superfund. Liability under Superfund is usually joint and several (separate)—that is, a person who generated *only a fraction of the hazardous waste* disposed of at the site may nevertheless be liable for *all* of the clean-up costs. CERCLA authorizes a party who has incurred clean-up costs to bring a "contribution action" against any other person who is liable or potentially liable for a percentage of the costs.

APPLICATION ■ How to Negotiate a Favorable Business Lease*

Generally, an entrepreneur starting a business is well advised to lease rather than buy property because the future success of the business is uncertain. By leasing instead of purchasing property, persons just starting out in business allow themselves some time to determine whether business profits will warrant the outright purchase of property.

FACTORS TO CONSIDER

One thing to keep in mind when leasing property is that lease contracts are usually form contracts that favor the landlord. Thus, as a prospective tenant, you need to think about negotiating terms more favorable to you. Before negotiating the terms of the lease, do some comparison shopping to find out the rent for other similar properties in the area. Usually, rental prices for business property are stated as so many dollars per square foot (per month or per year). In commercial leases to retail stores, part or all of the rent commonly consists of a percentage of the tenant's sales made on the premises during the term of the lease. Bear in mind, too, that the nature of your business should determine, to a great extent, the location of the leased premises. If you are involved in a mail-order business, for example, you need not pay the extra price for a prime location that might be required for a restaurant business.

NEGOTIATING LEASE TERMS

When negotiating a lease, you must also determine who will pay the property taxes, insurance premiums, and utility bills and who will be responsible for repairs to the property. These terms are generally negotiable, and depending on who takes responsibility, the rent payment may be adjusted accordingly. Generally, your success in negotiating favorable lease terms will depend on the market. If the rental market is weak (that is, if you have numerous other rental options at favorable rates), you may be able to convince the landlord to be responsible for taxes, insurance, maintenance, and the like, and possibly for improvements to the property necessary for your business. Therefore, it is important to investigate the status of the market before you begin negotiations with a potential landlord.

CHECKLIST FOR THE LESSEE OF BUSINESS PROPERTY

1. When you are starting a business, leasing can be beneficial because it reduces your liability in the event that your business is unsuccessful.
2. Realize that although lease contracts normally favor the landlord, you usually can negotiate advantageous terms for your lease of the premises.
3. Make sure that the lease clearly indicates whether the landlord or the tenant is to be responsible for taxes on the property, expenses relating to necessary maintenance and repairs, and utility costs. By comparison shopping, you should be able to judge which lease terms are favorable and which are not.
4. To protect yourself in the event your business is unsuccessful, start with a short-term initial lease, perhaps with an option to renew the lease in the future.

* This *Application* is not meant to substitute for the services of an attorney who is licensed to practice law in your state.

KEY TERMS

adverse possession 738
condemnation 739
constructive eviction 743
conveyance 734
deed 735
easement 734
eminent domain 739
environmental impact
   statement (EIS) 746
eviction 743
fee simple absolute 734

fixture 732
implied warranty of
   habitability 744
leasehold estate 740
license 735
life estate 734
periodic tenancy 740
potentially responsible party
   (PRP) 755
profit 734
quitclaim deed 738

recording statutes 738
special warranty deed 737
sublease 745
taking 739
tenancy at sufferance 741
tenancy at will 741
tenancy for years 740
warranty deed 735
wetlands 750

CHAPTER SUMMARY Real Property and Environmental Law

REAL PROPERTY

The Nature of Real Property (See pages 731–733.)	Real property (also called real estate or realty) is immovable. It includes land, subsurface and air rights, plant life and vegetation, and fixtures.
Ownership Interests in Real Property (See pages 733–735.)	1. *Fee simple absolute*—The most complete form of ownership. 2. *Life estate*—An estate that lasts for the life of a specified individual during which time the individual is entitled to possess, use, and benefit from the estate; ownership rights in a life estate are subject to the rights of the future-interest holder. 3. *Nonpossessory interest*—An interest that involves the right to use real property but not to possess it. Easements, profits, and licenses are nonpossessory interests.
Transfer of Ownership (See pages 735–740.)	1. *By deed*—When real property is sold or transferred as a gift, title to the property is conveyed by means of a deed. A deed must meet specific legal requirements. A *warranty deed* warrants the most extensive protection against defects of title. A *quitclaim deed* conveys to the grantee only whatever interest the grantor had in the property. A deed may be recorded in the manner prescribed by *recording statutes* in the appropriate jurisdiction to give third parties notice of the owner's interest. 2. *By will or inheritance*—If the owner dies after having made a valid will, the land passes as specified in the will. If the owner dies without having made a will, the heirs inherit according to state inheritance statutes. 3. *By adverse possession*—When a person possesses the property of another for a statutory period of time (three to thirty years, with ten years being the most common), that person acquires title to the property, provided the possession is actual and exclusive, open and visible, continuous and peaceable, and hostile and adverse (without the permission of the owner). 4. *By eminent domain*—The government can take land for public use, with just compensation, when the public interest requires the taking.
Leasehold Estates (See pages 740–741.)	A leasehold estate is an interest in real property that is held for only a limited period of time, as specified in the lease agreement. Types of tenancies relating to leased property include the following:

CHAPTER SUMMARY ▦ Real Property and Environmental Law—Continued

Leasehold Estates— Continued	1. *Tenancy for years*—Tenancy for a period of time stated by express contract.
	2. *Periodic tenancy*—Tenancy for a period determined by the frequency of rent payments; automatically renewed unless proper notice is given.
	3. *Tenancy at will*—Tenancy for as long as both parties agree; no notice of termination is required.
	4. *Tenancy at sufferance*—Possession of land without legal right.
Landlord-Tenant Relationships (See pages 741–745.)	1. *Lease agreement*—The landlord-tenant relationship is created by a lease agreement. State or local laws may dictate whether the lease must be in writing and what lease terms are permissible.
	2. *Rights and duties*—The rights and duties that arise under a lease agreement generally pertain to the following areas:
	a. Possession—The tenant has an exclusive right to possess the leased premises, which must be available to the tenant at the agreed-on time. Under the covenant of quiet enjoyment, the landlord promises that during the lease term neither the landlord nor anyone having superior title to the property will disturb the tenant's use and enjoyment of the property.
	b. Use and maintenance of the premises—Unless the parties agree otherwise, the tenant may make any legal use of the property. The tenant is responsible for any damage that he or she causes. The landlord must comply with laws that set specific standards for the maintenance of real property. The implied warranty of habitability requires that a landlord furnish and maintain residential premises in a habitable condition (that is, in a condition safe and suitable for human life).
	c. Rent—The tenant must pay the rent as long as the lease is in force, unless the tenant justifiably refuses to occupy the property or withholds the rent because of the landlord's failure to maintain the premises properly.
	3. *Transferring rights to leased property*—
	a. If the landlord transfers complete title to the leased property, the tenant becomes the tenant of the new owner. The new owner may then collect the rent but must abide by the existing lease.
	b. Generally, in the absence of an agreement to the contrary, tenants may assign their rights (but not their duties) under a lease contract to a third person. Tenants may also sublease leased property to a third person, but the original tenant is not relieved of any obligations to the landlord under the lease. In either situation, the landlord's consent may be required, but statutes may prohibit the landlord from unreasonably withholding such consent.

ENVIRONMENTAL LAW

State and Local Regulation (See pages 745–746.)	Activities affecting the environment are controlled at the local and state levels through regulations relating to land use, the disposal and recycling of garbage and waste, and pollution-causing activities in general.
Federal Regulation (See pages 746–755.)	1. *Environmental protection agencies*—The most well known of the agencies regulating environmental law is the federal Environmental Protection Agency (EPA), which was created in 1970 to coordinate federal environmental programs. The EPA administers most federal environmental policies and statutes.
	2. *Assessing environmental impact*—The National Environmental Policy Act of 1969 imposes environmental responsibilities on all federal agencies and requires the preparation of an environmental impact statement (EIS) for every major federal action. An EIS must analyze the action's impact on the environment, its adverse effects and possible alternatives, and its irreversible effects on environmental quality.

(Continued)

CHAPTER SUMMARY ▦ Real Property and Environmental Law—Continued

Federal Regulation—Continued	3. *Important areas regulated by the federal government*—Important areas regulated by the federal government include the following:
	a. Air pollution—Regulated under the authority of the Clean Air Act of 1963 and its amendments, particularly those of 1970, 1977, and 1990.
	b. Water pollution—Regulated under the authority of the Rivers and Harbors Appropriation Act of 1899, as amended, and the Federal Water Pollution Control Act of 1948, as amended by the Clean Water Act of 1972.
	c. Noise pollution—Regulated by the Noise Control Act of 1972.
	d. Toxic chemicals and hazardous waste—Pesticides and herbicides, toxic substances, and hazardous waste are regulated under the authority of the Federal Insecticide, Fungicide, and Rodenticide Act of 1947, the Toxic Substances Control Act of 1976, and the Resource Conservation and Recovery Act of 1976, respectively. The Comprehensive Environmental Response, Compensation, and Liability Act (CERCLA) of 1980, as amended, regulates the clean-up of hazardous waste–disposal sites.

▦ FOR REVIEW

Answers for the even-numbered questions in this For Review *section can be found in Appendix I at the end of this text.*

1 What can a person who holds property in fee simple absolute do with the property? Can a person who holds property as a life estate do the same?

2 How can ownership rights in real property be transferred?

3 What are the respective duties of the landlord and tenant concerning the use and maintenance of leased property? Is the tenant responsible for all damages that he or she causes?

4 What is contained in an environmental impact statement, and who must file one?

5 What major federal statutes regulate air and water pollution? What is Superfund, and who is potentially liable under Superfund?

▦ QUESTIONS AND CASE PROBLEMS

24–1. Clean Air Act. Current scientific knowledge indicates that there is no safe level of exposure to a cancer-causing agent. In theory, even one molecule of such a substance has the potential for causing cancer. Section 112 of the Clean Air Act requires that all cancer-causing substances be regulated to ensure a margin of safety. Some environmental groups have argued that all emissions of such substances must be eliminated if a margin of safety is to be reached. Such a total elimination would likely shut down many major U.S. industries. Should the Environmental Protection Agency totally eliminate all emissions of cancer-causing chemicals? Discuss.

24–2. Property Ownership. Twenty-two years ago Lorenz was a wanderer. At that time, he decided to settle down on an unoccupied, three-acre parcel of land that he did not own. People in the area told him that they had no idea who owned the property. Lorenz built a house on the land, got married, and raised three children while living there. He fenced in the land, installed a gate with a sign above it that read "Lorenz's Homestead," and had trespassers removed. Lorenz is now confronted by Joe Reese, who has a deed in his name as owner of the property. Reese, claiming ownership of the land, orders Lorenz and his family off the property. Discuss who has the better "title" to the property.

24–3. Deeds. Wiley and Gemma are neighbors. Wiley's lot is extremely large, and his present and future use of it will not involve the entire area. Gemma wants to build a single-car garage and driveway along the present lot boundary. Because of ordinances requiring buildings to be set back fifteen feet from an adjoining property line, and because of the placement of her existing structures, Gemma cannot build the garage. Gemma contracts to purchase ten feet of Wiley's property along their boundary line for $3,000. Wiley is willing to sell but will give Gemma only a quitclaim deed, whereas Gemma wants a warranty deed. Discuss the differences between these deeds as they would affect the rights of the parties if the title to this ten feet of land later proves to be defective.

24–4. Adverse Possession. In 1972, Ted Pafundi bought a quarry in West Pawlet, Vermont, from his neighbor, Marguerite Scott. The deed vaguely described the eastern boundary of the quarry as "the westerly boundary of the lands of" the neighboring property owners. Pafundi quarried green slate from the west wall until his death in 1979, when his son Gary began to work the east wall until *his* death in 1989. Gary's daughter Connie then took over operations. All of the Pafundis used the floor of the quarry as their base of operations. In 1992, N.A.S. Holdings, Inc., bought the neighboring property. A survey revealed that virtually the entire quarry was within the boundaries of N.A.S.'s property and that twenty years earlier, Ted had actually bought only a small strip of land on the west side. When N.A.S. attempted to begin quarrying, Connie blocked the access. N.A.S. filed a suit in a Vermont state court against Connie, seeking to establish title. Connie argued that she had title to the quarry through adverse possession under a state statute with a possessory period of fifteen years. What are the elements to acquire title by adverse possession? Are they satisfied in this case? In whose favor should the court rule, and why? [*N.A.S. Holdings, Inc. v. Pafundi,* 736 A.2d 780 (Vt. 1999)]

CASE PROBLEM WITH SAMPLE ANSWER

24–5. Jennifer Tribble leased an apartment from Spring Isle II, a limited partnership. The written lease agreement provided that if Tribble was forced to move because of a job transfer or because she accepted a new job, she could vacate on sixty days' notice and owe only an extra two months' rent plus no more than a $650 rerenting fee. The initial term was for one year, and the parties renewed the lease for a second one-year term. The security deposit was $900. State law allowed a landlord to withhold a security deposit for the nonpayment of rent but required timely notice stating valid reasons for the withholding or the tenant would be entitled to twice the amount of the deposit as damages. One month into the second term, Tribble notified Spring Isle in writing that she had accepted a new job and would move out within a week. She paid the extra rent required by the lease, but not the rerental fee, and vacated the apartment. Spring Isle wrote her a letter, stating that it was keeping the entire security deposit until the apartment was rerented or the lease term ended, whichever came first. Spring Isle later filed a suit in a Wisconsin state court against Tribble, claiming that she owed, among other things, the rest of the rent until the apartment had been rented again and the costs of rerenting. Tribble responded that withholding the security deposit was improper and that she was enti-

tled to "any penalties." Does Tribble owe Spring Isle anything? Does Spring Isle owe Tribble anything? Explain. [*Spring Isle II v. Tribble,* 610 N.W.2d 229 (Wis.App. 2000)]

After you have answered this problem, compare your answer with the sample answer given on the Web site that accompanies this text. Go to http://blt.westbuslaw.com, select "Chapter 24," and click on "Case Problem with Sample Answer."

24–6. Commercial Lease Terms. Metropolitan Life Insurance Co. leased space in its Trail Plaza Shopping Center in Florida to Winn-Dixie Stores, Inc., to operate a supermarket. Under the lease, the landlord agreed not to permit "any [other] property located within the shopping center to be used for or occupied by any business dealing in or which shall keep in stock or sell for off-premises consumption any staple or fancy groceries" in more than "500 square feet of sales area." In 1999, Metropolitan leased 22,000 square feet of space in Trail Plaza to 99 Cent Stuff-Trail Plaza, LLC, under a lease that prohibited it from selling "groceries" in more than 500 square feet of "sales area." Shortly after 99 Cent Stuff opened, it began selling food and other products, including soap, matches, and paper napkins. Alleging that these sales violated the parties' leases, Winn-Dixie filed a suit in a Florida state court against 99 Cent Stuff and others. The defendants argued in part that the groceries provision covered only food and the 500-square-foot restriction included only shelf space, not store aisles. How should these lease terms be interpreted? Should the court grant an injunction in Winn-Dixie's favor? Explain. [*Winn-Dixie Stores, Inc. v. 99 Cent Stuff-Trail Plaza, LLC,* 811 So.2d 719 (Fla.App. 3 Dist. 2002)]

24–7. Environmental Impact Statement. Greers Ferry Lake is in Arkansas, and its shoreline is under the management of the U.S. Army Corps of Engineers, which is part of the U.S. Department of Defense (DOD). The Corps's 2000 Shoreline Management Plan (SMP) rezoned numerous areas along the lake, authorized the Corps to issue permits for the construction of new boat docks in the rezoned areas, increased by 300 percent the area around habitable structures that could be cleared of vegetation, and instituted a Wildlife Enhancement Permit to allow limited modifications of the shoreline. In relation to the SMP's adoption, the Corps issued a Finding of No Significant Impact, which declared that no environmental impact statement (EIS) was necessary. The Corps issued thirty-two boat dock construction permits under the SMP before Save Greers Ferry Lake, Inc., filed a suit in a federal district court against the DOD, asking the court to, among other things, stop the Corps from acting under the SMP and order it to prepare an EIS. What are the requirements for an EIS? Is an EIS needed in this case? Explain. [*Save Greers Ferry Lake, Inc. v. Department of Defense,* 255 F.3d 498 (8th Cir. 2001)]

24–8. CERCLA. Beginning in 1926, Marietta Dyestuffs Co. operated an industrial facility in Marietta, Ohio, to make dyes and other chemicals. In 1944, Dyestuffs became part of American Home Products Corp. (AHP), which sold the Marietta facility to American Cyanamid Co. in 1946. In 1950, AHP sold the rest of the Dyestuffs assets and all of its stock to B. F. Goodrich Co., which immediately liquidated the acquired corporation. Goodrich continued to operate the dissolved corporation's business, however. Cyanamid continued to make chemicals at the Marietta facility, and in 1993, it created Cytec Industries, Inc., which expressly assumed all environmental liabilities associated with Cyanamid's ownership and operation of the facility. Cytec spent nearly $25 million in clean-up costs and filed a suit in a federal district court against Goodrich to recover, under the Comprehensive Environmental Response, Compensation, and Liability Act (CERCLA), a portion of the costs attributable to the clean-up of hazardous wastes that may have been discarded at the site between 1926 and 1946. Cytec filed a motion for summary judgment in its favor. Should the court grant Cytec's motion? Explain. [*Cytec Industries, Inc. v. B. F. Goodrich Co.*, 196 F.Supp.2d 644 (S.D. Ohio 2002)]

A QUESTION OF ETHICS

 24–9. The Endangered Species Act of 1973 makes it unlawful for any person to "take" endangered or threatened species. The act defines *take* to mean to "harass, harm, pursue," "wound," or "kill." The secretary of the interior (Bruce Babbitt) issued a regulation that further defined *harm* to include "significant habitat modification or degradation where it actually kills or injures wildlife." A group of businesses and individuals involved in the timber industry brought an action against the secretary of the interior and others. The group complained that the application of the "harm" regulation to the red-cockaded woodpecker and the northern spotted owl had injured the group economically because it prevented logging operations (habitat modification) in Pacific Northwest forests containing these species. The group challenged the regulation's validity, contending that Congress

did not intend the word *take* to include habitat modification. The case ultimately reached the United States Supreme Court, which held that the secretary reasonably construed Congress's intent when he defined *harm* to include habitat modification. [*Babbitt v. Sweet Home Chapter of Communities for a Great Oregon*, 515 U.S. 687, 115 S.Ct. 2407, 132 L.Ed.2d 597 (1995)]

1. Traditionally, the term *take* has been used to refer to the capture or killing of wildlife, usually for private gain. Is the secretary's regulation prohibiting habitat modification consistent with this definition?
2. One of the issues in this case was whether Congress intended to protect existing generations of species or future generations. How do the terms *take* and *habitat modification* relate to this issue?
3. Three dissenting Supreme Court justices contended that construing the act as prohibiting habitat modification "imposes unfairness to the point of financial ruin—not just upon the rich, but upon the simplest farmer who finds his land conscripted to national zoological use." Should private parties be required to bear the burden of preserving habitats for wildlife?
4. Generally, should the economic welfare of private parties be taken into consideration when creating and applying environmental statutes and regulations?

FOR CRITICAL ANALYSIS

 24–10. Real property law dates back hundreds of years. What changes have occurred in society, including business and technological changes, that have affected the development and application of real property law? (Hint: Was airspace an issue three hundred years ago?)

 **ONLINE ACTIVITIES**

INTERNET EXERCISES

Go to the *Business Law Today: The Essentials* home page at <u>http://blt.westbuslaw.com</u>, select "Chapter 24," and click on "Internet Exercises." There you will find the following Internet research exercises that you can perform to learn more about topics covered in this chapter.

Activity 24–1: LEGAL PERSPECTIVE—Eminent Domain

Activity 24–2: MANAGEMENT PERSPECTIVE—Fair Housing

Activity 24–3: MANAGEMENT PERSPECTIVE—Complying with Environmental Regulation

BEFORE THE TEST

Go to the *Business Law Today: The Essentials* home page at <u>http://blt.westbuslaw.com</u>, select "Chapter 24," and click on "Interactive Quizzes." You will find at least twenty interactive questions relating to this chapter.

CHAPTER 25

International Law in a Global Economy

> "Our interests are those of the open door—a door of friendship and mutual advantage. This is the only door we care to enter."
>
> Woodrow Wilson, 1856–1924
> (Twenty-eighth president of the United States, 1913–1921)

CHAPTER OUTLINE

- **INTERNATIONAL PRINCIPLES AND DOCTRINES**

- **DOING BUSINESS INTERNATIONALLY**

- **COMMERCIAL CONTRACTS IN AN INTERNATIONAL SETTING**

- **MAKING PAYMENT ON INTERNATIONAL TRANSACTIONS**

- **REGULATION OF SPECIFIC BUSINESS ACTIVITIES**

- **U.S. LAWS IN A GLOBAL CONTEXT**

■■ LEARNING OBJECTIVES

After reading this chapter, you should be able to answer the following questions:

1 What is the principle of comity, and why do courts deciding disputes involving a foreign law or judicial decree apply this principle?

2 What is the act of state doctrine? In what circumstances is this doctrine applied?

3 Under the Foreign Sovereign Immunities Act of 1976, on what bases might a foreign state be considered subject to the jurisdiction of U.S. courts?

4 In what circumstances will U.S. antitrust laws be applied extraterritorially?

5 Do U.S. laws prohibiting employment discrimination apply in all circumstances to U.S. employees working for U.S. employers abroad?

International business transactions are not unique to the modern world. Indeed, as suggested by President Woodrow Wilson's statement in the opening quotation, people have always found that they can benefit from exchanging goods with others. What is new in our day is the dramatic growth in world trade and the emergence of a global business community. Because the exchange of goods, services, and ideas on a global level is now routine, students of business law should be familiar with the laws pertaining to international business transactions. In this chapter, we first examine the legal context of international business transactions. We then look at some selected areas relating to business activities in a global context, including international sales contracts, civil dispute resolution, letters of credit, and investment protection. We conclude the chapter with a discussion of the application of certain U.S. laws in a transnational setting.

International Principles and Doctrines

International law can be defined as a body of law—formed as a result of international customs, treaties, and organizations—that governs relations among or between nations. **National law,** in contrast, is the law of a particular nation, such as the United States, Japan, Germany, or Brazil. Here, we look at some legal principles and doctrines of international law that have evolved over time and that the courts of various nations have employed—to a greater or lesser extent—to resolve or reduce conflicts that involve a foreign element. The three important legal principles and doctrines discussed in the following subsections are based primarily on courtesy and respect and are applied in the interests of maintaining harmonious relations among nations.

THE PRINCIPLE OF COMITY

Under what is known as the principle of **comity,** one nation will defer and give effect to the laws and judicial decrees of another country, as long as those laws and judicial decrees are consistent with the law and public policy of the accommodating nation.

■ **EXAMPLE 25.1** Assume that a Swedish seller and a U.S. buyer have formed a contract, which the buyer breaches. The seller sues the buyer in a Swedish court, which awards damages. The buyer's assets, however, are in the United States and cannot be reached unless the judgment is enforced by a U.S. court of law. In this situation, if a U.S. court determines that the procedures and laws applied in the Swedish court were consistent with U.S. national law and policy, that court will likely defer to (and enforce) the foreign court's judgment. ■

One way to understand the principle of comity (and the *act of state doctrine,* which will be discussed shortly) is to consider the relationships among the states in our federal form of government. Each state honors (gives "full faith and credit" to) the contracts, property deeds, wills, and other legal obligations formed in other states, as well as judicial decisions with respect to such obligations. On a worldwide basis, nations similarly attempt to honor judgments rendered in other countries when it is feasible to do so. Of course, in the United States the states are constitutionally required to honor other states' actions, whereas, internationally, nations are not *required* to honor the actions of other nations.

Normally, the principle of comity is extended to foreign bankruptcy proceedings. The question in the following case was whether a U.S. court is required to determine the ownership of a disputed asset before a bankruptcy case goes forward in a foreign court.

CASE 25.1 ■ JP Morgan Chase Bank v. Altos Hornos de Mexico, S.A. de C.V.

United States District Court,
Southern District of New York, 2004.
__ F.Supp.2d __.

FACTS In April 1997, Altos Hornos de Mexico, S.A. de C.V., Mexico's largest liquid steel producer, borrowed $330 million from twenty-eight banks, including JP Morgan Chase Bank (JPMCB). JPMCB was the loan's "facility agent," distributing payments among the lenders through a "collection account" set up in the loan documents. As a term of the loan, Altos Hornos told three of its customers to pay into the collection account. The loan documents contained forum-selection and choice-of-law clauses in favor of New York. In May 1999, after significant losses in the global steel market, Altos Hornos filed a petition with a Mexican court to be declared in *suspensión de pagos* (suspension of payments, or SOP, which, under Mexican

CASE 25.1—Continued

bankruptcy law, is similar to a Chapter 11 reorganization under U.S. bankruptcy law—see Chapter 16). The court granted the petition. In June and August, Altos Hornos's three customers paid $4.7 million into JPMCB's collection account. Altos Hornos asked the SOP court to order JPMCB to reimburse the funds for distribution in the SOP proceeding. Meanwhile, JPMCB filed a suit in a federal district court against Altos Hornos, seeking a declaration that these funds did not belong to the borrower. Altos Hornos filed a motion to dismiss this suit.

ISSUE Is a U.S. court required to resolve the question of the ownership of a bank account before its possible owner's bankruptcy proceeding in a Mexican court?

DECISION No. The court held that it was not required to determine the ownership of the funds in the account and dismissed JPMCB's complaint on the basis of comity.

REASON The court stated that "comity is especially appropriate for foreign bankruptcy proceedings." The court

acknowledged that under Mexican law, the SOP court was not required to resolve the question of ownership. But under Mexican law, the SOP court had jurisdiction to rule on JPMCB's claim to the funds in the SOP proceedings, which, the U.S. court noted, were fundamentally fair and did not violate public policy in the United States. The U.S. court also reasoned that the loan's forum-selection and choice-of-law clauses did not proscribe comity if it was otherwise warranted. Under most contracts, "the considerations associated with comity trump [take precedence over] the parties' express wishes. * * * [T]here are important considerations that may not have concerned the parties" when they entered into their contract, but with which the court must be concerned, such as "Altos Hornos's other creditors and the importance of a unified administration rather than a piecemeal administration of its estate in the SOP proceeding."

FOR CRITICAL ANALYSIS—Social Consideration
Why might a Mexican court be better able to determine the ownership of the funds in the collection account in this case?

THE ACT OF STATE DOCTRINE

ACT OF STATE DOCTRINE
A doctrine providing that the judicial branch of one country will not examine the validity of public acts committed by a recognized foreign government within its own territory.

The **act of state doctrine** is a judicially created doctrine that provides that the judicial branch of one country will not examine the validity of public acts committed by a recognized foreign government within its own territory. This doctrine is premised on the theory that the judicial branch should not "pass upon the validity of foreign acts when to do so would vex the harmony of our international relations with that foreign nation."[1]

EXPROPRIATION
The seizure by a government of a privately owned business or personal property for a proper public purpose and with just compensation.

CONFISCATION
A government's taking of a privately owned business or personal property without a proper public purpose or an award of just compensation.

When a Foreign Government Takes Private Property The act of state doctrine can have important consequences for individuals and firms doing business with, and investing in, other countries. For example, this doctrine is frequently employed in situations involving expropriation or confiscation. **Expropriation** occurs when a government seizes a privately owned business or privately owned goods for a proper public purpose and awards just compensation. When a government seizes private property for an illegal purpose or without just compensation, the taking is referred to as a **confiscation**. The line between these two forms of taking is sometimes blurred because of differing interpretations of what is illegal and what constitutes just compensation.

■ **EXAMPLE 25.2** Flaherty, Inc., a U.S. company, owns a mine in Brazil. The government of Brazil seizes the mine for public use and claims that the profits that Flaherty realized from the mine in preceding years constitute just compensation.

---

1. *Libra Bank, Ltd. v. Banco Nacional de Costa Rica, S.A.*, 570 F.Supp. 870 (S.D.N.Y. 1983).

Flaherty disagrees, but the act of state doctrine may prevent the company's recovery in a U.S. court. ■

Immunity from U.S. Jurisdiction   When applicable, both the act of state doctrine and the doctrine of *sovereign immunity* (to be discussed next) tend to immunize (protect) foreign governments from the jurisdiction of U.S. courts. This means that firms or individuals who own property overseas often have diminished legal protection against government actions in the countries in which they operate.

THE DOCTRINE OF SOVEREIGN IMMUNITY

SOVEREIGN IMMUNITY
A doctrine that immunizes foreign nations from the jurisdiction of U.S. courts when certain conditions are satisfied.

When certain conditions are satisfied, the doctrine of **sovereign immunity** immunizes foreign nations from the jurisdiction of U.S. courts. In 1976, Congress codified this rule in the Foreign Sovereign Immunities Act (FSIA).[2] The FSIA exclusively governs the circumstances in which an action may be brought in the United States against a foreign nation, including attempts to attach a foreign nation's property.

Section 1605 of the FSIA sets forth the major exceptions to the jurisdictional immunity of a foreign state or country. A foreign state is not immune from the jurisdiction of U.S. courts when the state has "waived its immunity either explicitly or by implication" or when the action is taken "in connection with a commercial activity carried on in the United States by the foreign state" or having "a direct effect in the United States."[3]

The question frequently arises as to whether an entity falls within the category of a foreign state. The question of what is a commercial activity has also been the subject of dispute. Under Section 1603 of the FSIA, a *foreign state* includes both a political subdivision of a foreign state and an instrumentality of a foreign state. Section 1603 broadly defines a *commercial activity* as a commercial activity that is carried out by a foreign state within the United States, but it does not describe the particulars of what constitutes a commercial activity. Thus, the courts are left to decide whether a particular activity is governmental or commercial in nature.

FindLaw's Web site includes an extensive array of links to international doctrines, treaties, and other nations' laws. Go to

http://www.findlaw.com

and select "International Law."

■■ Doing Business Internationally

A U.S. domestic firm can engage in international business transactions in a number of ways. The simplest way is to seek out foreign markets for domestically produced products or services. In other words, U.S. firms can look abroad for **export** markets for their goods and services.

EXPORT
To sell products to buyers located in other countries.

Alternatively, a U.S. firm can establish foreign production facilities so as to be closer to the foreign market or markets in which its products are sold. The advantages may include lower labor costs, fewer government regulations, and lower taxes and trade barriers. A domestic firm can also obtain revenues by licensing its technology to an existing foreign company. Yet another way to expand abroad is by selling franchises to overseas entities. The presence of McDonald's, Burger King, and KFC franchises throughout the world attests to the popularity of franchising.

---

2. 28 U.S.C. Sections 1602–1611.
3. See, for example, *Keller v. Central Bank of Nigeria,* 277 F.3d 811 (6th Cir. 2002), in which the court held that failure to pay promised funds to a Cleveland account was an action having a direct effect in the United States.

EXPORTING

Most U.S. companies make their initial foray into international business through exporting. Exporting can take two forms: direct exporting and indirect exporting. In *direct exporting*, a U.S. company signs a sales contract with a foreign purchaser that provides for the conditions of shipment and payment for the goods. (How payments are made in international transactions is discussed later in this chapter.) If sufficient business develops in a foreign country, a U.S. corporation may set up a specialized marketing organization in that foreign market by appointing a foreign agent or a foreign distributor. This is called *indirect exporting*.

Foreign Agent   When a U.S. firm desires to limit its involvement in an international market, it will typically establish an *agency relationship* with a foreign firm. In an agency relationship (discussed in Chapter 17), one person (the agent) agrees to act on behalf of another (the principal). The foreign agent is thereby empowered to enter into contracts in the agent's country on behalf of the U.S. principal.

Foreign Distributor   When a substantial market exists in a foreign country, a U.S. firm may wish to appoint a distributor located in that country. The U.S. firm and the distributor enter into a **distribution agreement,** which is a contract between the seller and the distributor setting out the terms and conditions of the distributorship—for example, price, currency of payment, availability of supplies, and method of payment. The terms and conditions primarily involve contract law. Disputes concerning distribution agreements may involve jurisdictional or other issues (discussed in detail later in this chapter). In addition, some **exclusive distributorships**—in which distributors agree to distribute only the sellers' goods—have raised antitrust problems.

MANUFACTURING ABROAD

An alternative to direct or indirect exporting is the establishment of foreign manufacturing facilities. Typically, U.S. firms establish manufacturing plants abroad if they believe that doing so will reduce their costs—particularly for labor, shipping, and raw materials—and enable them to compete more effectively in foreign markets. Apple Computer, IBM, General Motors, and Ford are some of the many U.S. companies that have established manufacturing facilities abroad. Foreign firms have done the same in the United States. Sony, Nissan, and other Japanese manufacturers have established U.S. plants to avoid import duties that the U.S. Congress may impose on Japanese products entering this country.

A U.S. firm can manufacture goods in other countries in several ways. They include licensing and franchising, as well as investing in a wholly owned subsidiary or a joint venture.

Licensing   A U.S. firm can obtain business from abroad by licensing a foreign manufacturing company to use its copyrighted, patented, or trademarked intellectual property or trade secrets. Like any other licensing agreement (see Chapters 5 and 10), a licensing agreement with a foreign-based firm calls for a payment of royalties on some basis—such as so many cents per unit produced or a certain percentage of profits from units sold in a particular geographic territory.

In some circumstances, even in the absence of a patent, a firm may be able to license the "know-how" associated with a particular manufacturing process—for example, a plant design or a secret formula. The foreign firm that agrees to sign the

If you are interested in learning more about what is involved in exporting goods to other countries, go to the state of New Mexico's Web page on "How to Export" at

http://www.edd.state.nm.us/ TRADE/HOWTO/howto.html.

DISTRIBUTION AGREEMENT
A contract between a seller and a distributor of the seller's products setting out the terms and conditions of the distributorship.

EXCLUSIVE DISTRIBUTORSHIP
A distributorship in which the seller and the distributor of the seller's products agree that the distributor has the exclusive right to distribute the seller's products in a certain geographic area.

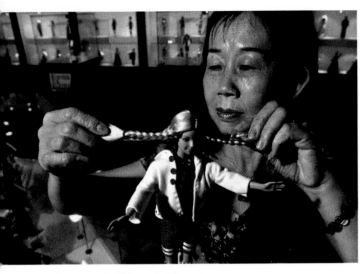

A woman in Taiwan holds a Barbie doll that was manufactured in Taiwan. Why would a U.S. corporation, such as Mattel, Inc., outsource its manufacturing jobs to a foreign firm? (AP Photo/ Wally Santana)

licensing agreement further agrees to keep the know-how confidential and to pay royalties. ■ **EXAMPLE 25.3** Coca-Cola licenses firms worldwide to use (and keep confidential) its secret formula for the syrup used in its soft drink. In return, the foreign firms licensed to make the syrup pay Coca-Cola a percentage of the income earned from the sale of the soft drink. ■

The licensing of intellectual property rights benefits all parties to the transaction. The firm that receives the license can take advantage of an established reputation for quality. The firm that grants the license receives income from the foreign sales of its products and also establishes a global reputation. Additionally, once a firm's trademark is known worldwide, the firm may see increased demand for other products it manufactures or sells—obviously an important consideration.

Franchising   Franchising is a well-known form of licensing. Recall from Chapter 19 that in a franchise arrangement the owner of a trademark, trade name, or copyright (the franchisor) licenses another (the franchisee) to use the trademark, trade name, or copyright under certain conditions or limitations in the selling of goods or services. In return, the franchisee pays a fee, which is usually based on a percentage of gross or net sales. Examples of international franchises include McDonald's, Holiday Inn, Avis, and Hertz.

Investing in a Wholly Owned Subsidiary or a Joint Venture   Another way to expand into a foreign market is to establish a wholly owned subsidiary firm in a foreign country. In many European countries, a subsidiary would take the form of what is called in French a *société anonyme* (S.A.), which is similar to a U.S. corporation. In German-speaking nations, it would be called an *Aktiengesellschaft* (A.G.). When a wholly owned subsidiary is established, the parent company, which remains in the United States, retains complete ownership of all the facilities in the foreign country, as well as complete authority and control over all phases of the operation.

A U.S. firm can also expand into international markets through a joint venture. In a joint venture, the U.S. company owns only part of the operation; the rest is owned either by local owners in the foreign country or by another foreign entity. All of the firms involved in a joint venture share responsibilities, as well as profits and liabilities.

.on the Web   For information on the legal requirements of doing business abroad, a good source is the Internet Law Library's collection of laws of other nations. Go to

http://www.lawguru.com/ ilawlib/index.html.

◼ Commercial Contracts in an International Setting

Like all commercial contracts, an international contract should be in writing. For an example of an actual international sales contract, see this chapter's foldout contract.

Language and legal differences among nations can create special problems for parties to international contracts when disputes arise. It is possible to avoid these problems by including in a contract special provisions designating the official language of the contract, the legal forum (court or place) in which disputes under the contract will be settled, and the substantive law that will be applied in settling any disputes. Parties to international contracts should also indicate in their contracts what acts or events will excuse the parties from performance under the contract and whether disputes under the contract will be arbitrated or litigated.

RECALL   The interpretation of the words in a contract can be a matter of dispute even when both parties communicate in the same language.

CHOICE OF LANGUAGE

A deal struck between a U.S. company and a company in another country normally involves two languages. Typically, many phrases in one language are not readily translatable into another. Consequently, the complex contractual terms involved may not be understood by one party in the other party's language. To make sure that no disputes arise out of this language problem, an international sales contract should have a **choice-of-language clause** designating the official language by which the contract will be interpreted in the event of disagreement.

CHOICE-OF-LANGUAGE CLAUSE
A clause in a contract designating the official language by which the contract will be interpreted in the event of a future disagreement over the contract's terms.

CHOICE OF FORUM

When parties from several countries are involved, litigation may be pursued in courts in different nations. There are no universally accepted rules as to which court has jurisdiction over particular subject matter or parties to a dispute. Consequently, parties to an international transaction should always include in the contract a **forum-selection clause** indicating what court, jurisdiction, or tribunal will decide any disputes arising under the contract. It is especially important to indicate the specific court that will have jurisdiction. The forum does not necessarily have to be within the geographic boundaries of the home nation of either party. The following case involved a question about the application of a forum-selection clause.

FORUM-SELECTION CLAUSE
A provision in a contract designating the court, jurisdiction, or tribunal that will decide any disputes arising under the contract.

CASE 25.2 ◼ Garware Polyester, Ltd. v. Intermax Trading Corp.

United States District Court,
Southern District of New York, 2001.
__ F.Supp.2d __.

FACTS Garware Polyester, Ltd., based in Mumbai, India, develops and makes plastics and high-tech polyester film. In 1987, Intermax Trading Corporation, based in New York, became Garware's North American sales agent. Over the next decade, the parties executed four written agreements, collectively referred to as the "Agency Agreements." Each agreement provided, "The courts at Bombay [India] alone will have jurisdiction to try out suits in respect of any claim or dispute arising out of or under this agreement or in any way relating to the same." Intermax sold Garware products on a commission basis. In some transactions, Intermax arranged for customers to order products directly from Garware. In other transactions, Intermax sold Garware products through warehouse sales by which Intermax bought products from Garware, warehoused them in the United States, and resold them. When Intermax fell behind in its payments, Garware filed a suit in a U.S. district court to collect on the unpaid invoices. Garware argued that the forum-selection clause did not apply to the invoices in dispute because they involved the warehouse sales, which, Garware claimed, were not part of, and did not relate to, the Agency Agreements.

ISSUE Did the forum-selection clause require the dismissal of this suit?

DECISION Yes. The court held that each of the Agency Agreements contained a valid and enforceable forum-selection clause, which applied to this suit. The court dismissed the case for improper venue.

REASON The court recognized that forum-selection clauses "eliminate uncertainty in international commerce and insure that the parties are not unexpectedly subjected to hostile forums and laws. Moreover, international comity dictates that American courts enforce these sorts of clauses out of respect for the integrity and respect of foreign tribunals." The court stated that a forum-selection clause applies when "claims grow out of the contractual relationship, or if the gist of those claims is a breach of that relationship." Here, "the 'gist' of Garware's claim is a breach of the Agency Agreements. The warehouse sales in question were made by Intermax for the purpose of selling Garware products in the contractually defined territory. The Agency Agreements specifically relate to Intermax's role as Garware's 'selling agent * * * in the United States of America * * * '. Thus, if these sales are not squarely within the scope of the Agency

(Continued)

CASE 25.2—Continued

Agreements, they are, at the very least, related to the Agreements. Further, the parties' course of dealing supports the conclusion that the parties themselves believed the Agency Agreements included warehouse sales: as required by the Agreements, Garware paid commissions to Intermax on these sales."

WHY IS THIS CASE IMPORTANT? *As this case illustrates, when the underlying transaction is international, courts generally presume that forum-selection clauses are valid because such clauses eliminate uncertainty in international commerce. It takes a strong showing that the clause was unreasonable under the circumstances to overcome this presumptive validity.*

CHOICE OF LAW

CHOICE-OF-LAW CLAUSE
A clause in a contract designating the law (such as the law of a particular state or nation) that will govern the contract.

A contractual provision designating the applicable law—such as the law of Germany or England or California—is called a **choice-of-law clause**. Every international contract typically includes a choice-of-law clause. At common law (and in European civil law systems), parties are allowed to choose the law that will govern their contractual relationship, provided that the law chosen is the law of a jurisdiction that has a substantial relationship to the parties and to the international business transaction.

Under Section 1–105 of the Uniform Commercial Code, parties may choose the law that will govern the contract as long as the choice is "reasonable." Article 6 of the United Nations Convention on Contracts for the International Sale of Goods, however, imposes no limitation on the parties' choice of what law will govern the contract. The 1986 Hague Convention on the Law Applicable to Contracts for the International Sale of Goods—often referred to as the Choice-of-Law Convention—allows unlimited autonomy in the choice of law. The Hague Convention indicates that whenever a contract does not specify a choice of law, the governing law is that of the country in which the *seller's* place of business is located.

FORCE MAJEURE CLAUSE

FORCE MAJEURE CLAUSE
A provision in a contract stipulating that certain unforeseen events—such as war, political upheavals, or acts of God—will excuse a party from liability for nonperformance of contractual obligations.

Every contract, particularly those involving international transactions, should have a *force majeure* clause. *Force majeure* is a French term meaning "impossible or irresistible force"—sometimes loosely identified as "an act of God." In international business contracts, *force majeure* clauses commonly stipulate that in addition to acts of God, a number of other eventualities (such as government orders or embargoes, for example) may excuse a party from liability for nonperformance.

CIVIL DISPUTE RESOLUTION

International contracts frequently include arbitration clauses. By means of such clauses, the parties agree in advance to be bound by the decision of a specified third party in the event of a dispute, as discussed in Chapter 3. The third party may be a neutral entity (such as the International Chamber of Commerce), a panel of individuals representing both parties' interests, or some other group or organization. (For an example of an arbitration clause in an international contract, refer to the foldout exhibit in this chapter.) The United Nations Convention on the Recognition and Enforcement of Foreign Arbitral Awards (often referred to as the New York Convention) assists in the enforcement of arbitration clauses, as do provisions in specific treaties among nations. The New York Convention has been implemented in nearly one hundred countries, including the United States.

If a sales contract does not include an arbitration clause, litigation may occur. If the contract contains forum-selection and choice-of-law clauses, the lawsuit will be heard by a court in the specified forum and decided according to that forum's law. If no

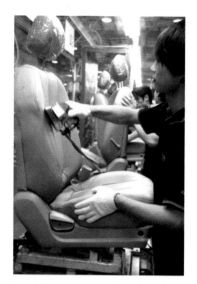

Workers at a manufacturing plant owned by a U.S. company in Beijing, China. What contract clauses would affect where and how these foreign workers are able to resolve disputes with their U.S. employer? (Ricky Wong, Bloomberg News/Landov)

FOREIGN EXCHANGE MARKET
A worldwide system in which foreign currencies are bought and sold.

CORRESPONDENT BANK
A bank in which another bank has an account (and vice versa) for the purpose of facilitating fund transfers.

forum and choice of law have been specified, however, legal proceedings will be more complex and attended by much more uncertainty. For instance, litigation may take place in two or more countries, with each country applying its own choice-of-law rules to determine the substantive law that will be applied to the particular transactions.

Even if a plaintiff wins a favorable judgment in a lawsuit litigated in the plaintiff's country, there is no way to predict whether courts in the defendant's country will enforce the judgment. As discussed earlier in this chapter, courts in the defendant's country may enforce the judgment under the principle of comity, particularly if the defendant's country is the United States and the foreign court's decision is consistent with U.S. national law and policy. Other nations, though, may not be as accommodating as the United States in this respect.

▣ Making Payment on International Transactions

Currency differences between nations and the geographic distance between parties to international sales contracts add a degree of complexity to international sales that does not exist in the domestic market. Because international contracts involve greater financial risks, special care should be taken in drafting these contracts to specify both the currency in which payment is to be made and the method of payment.

MONETARY SYSTEMS

Although our national currency, the U.S. dollar, is one of the primary forms of international currency, any U.S. firm undertaking business transactions abroad must be prepared to deal with one or more other currencies. After all, just as a U.S. firm wants to be paid in U.S. dollars for goods and services sold abroad, so, too, does a Japanese firm want to be paid in Japanese yen for goods and services sold outside Japan. Both firms therefore must rely on the convertibility of currencies.

Foreign Exchange Markets   Currencies are convertible when they can be freely exchanged one for the other at some specified market rate in a **foreign exchange market.** Foreign exchange markets comprise a worldwide system for the buying and selling of foreign currencies. At any point in time, the foreign exchange rate is set by the forces of supply and demand in unrestricted foreign exchange markets. The foreign exchange rate is simply the price of a unit of one country's currency in terms of another country's currency. For example, if today's exchange rate is one hundred Japanese yen for one dollar, that means that anybody with one hundred yen can obtain one dollar, and vice versa.

Correspondent Banking   Frequently, a U.S. company can rely on its domestic bank to take care of all international transfers of funds. Commercial banks often transfer funds internationally through their **correspondent banks** in other countries.

■ **EXAMPLE 25.4** Suppose that a customer of Citibank wishes to pay a bill in euros to a company in Paris. Citibank can draw a bank check payable in euros on its account in Crédit Lyonnais, a Paris correspondent bank, and then send the check to the French company to which its customer owes the funds. Alternatively, Citibank's customer can request a wire transfer of the funds to the French company. Citibank instructs Crédit Lyonnais by wire to pay the necessary amount in euros. ■

The Clearinghouse Interbank Payment System (CHIPS) handles about 90 percent of both national and international interbank transfers of U.S. funds. In addition, the Society for Worldwide International Financial Telecommunications (SWIFT) is a communication system that provides banks with messages concerning international transactions.

LETTERS OF CREDIT

LETTER OF CREDIT
A written instrument, usually issued by a bank on behalf of a customer or other person, in which the issuer promises to honor drafts or other demands for payment by third persons in accordance with the terms of the instrument.

Because buyers and sellers engaged in international business transactions are frequently separated by thousands of miles, special precautions are often taken to ensure performance under the contract. Sellers want to avoid delivering goods for which they might not be paid. Buyers desire the assurance that sellers will not be paid until there is evidence that the goods have been shipped. Thus, **letters of credit** are frequently used to facilitate international business transactions.

In a simple letter-of-credit transaction, the *issuer* (a bank) agrees to issue a letter of credit and to ascertain whether the *beneficiary* (seller) performs certain acts. In return, the *account party* (buyer) promises to reimburse the issuer for the amount paid to the beneficiary. The transaction may also involve an *advising bank* that transmits information and a *paying bank* that expedites payment under the letter of credit. See Exhibit 25–1 for an illustration of a letter-of-credit transaction.

Under a letter of credit, the issuer is bound to pay the beneficiary (seller) when the beneficiary has complied with the terms and conditions of the letter of credit.

EXHIBIT 25–1 **A LETTER-OF-CREDIT TRANSACTION**

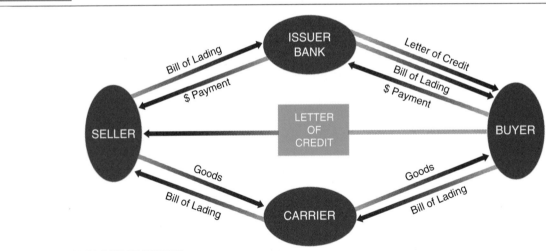

CHRONOLOGY OF EVENTS

1. Buyer contracts with issuer bank to issue a letter of credit; this sets forth the bank's obligation to pay on the letter of credit and buyer's obligation to pay the bank.

2. Letter of credit is sent to seller informing seller that on compliance with the terms of the letter of credit (such as presentment of necessary documents—in this example, a bill of lading), the bank will issue payment for the goods.

3. Seller delivers goods to carrier and receives a bill of lading.

4. Seller delivers the bill of lading to issuer bank and, if the document is proper, receives payment.

5. Issuer bank delivers the bill of lading to buyer.

6. Buyer delivers the bill of lading to carrier.

7. Carrier delivers the goods to buyer.

8. Buyer settles with issuer bank.

The beneficiary looks to the issuer, not to the account party (buyer), when it presents the documents required by the letter of credit. Typically, the letter of credit will require that the beneficiary deliver a *bill of lading* to the issuing bank to prove that shipment has been made. A letter of credit assures the beneficiary (seller) of payment and at the same time assures the account party (buyer) that payment will not be made until the beneficiary has complied with the terms and conditions of the letter of credit.

The Value of a Letter of Credit The basic principle behind letters of credit is that payment is made against the documents presented by the beneficiary and not against the facts that the documents purport to reflect. Thus, in a letter-of-credit transaction, the issuer does not police the underlying contract; a letter of credit is independent of the underlying contract between the buyer and the seller. Eliminating the need for banks (issuers) to inquire into whether actual contractual conditions have been satisfied greatly reduces the costs of letters of credit. Moreover, the use of a letter of credit protects both buyers and sellers.

DON'T FORGET A letter of credit is independent of the underlying contract between the buyer and the seller.

Compliance with a Letter of Credit A letter-of-credit transaction generally involves at least three separate and distinct contracts: the contract between the account party (buyer) and the beneficiary (seller); the contract between the issuer (bank) and the account party (buyer); and, finally, the letter of credit itself, which involves the issuer (bank) and the beneficiary (seller). These contracts are separate and distinct, and the issuer's obligations under the letter of credit do not concern the underlying contract between the buyer and the seller. Rather, it is the issuer's duty to ascertain whether the documents presented by the beneficiary (seller) comply with the terms of the letter of credit.

If the documents presented by the beneficiary comply with the terms of the letter of credit, the issuer (bank) must honor the letter of credit. If the issuing bank refuses to pay the beneficiary (seller) even though the beneficiary has complied with all the requirements, the beneficiary can bring an action to enforce payment. Sometimes, however, it can be difficult to determine exactly what a letter of credit requires. Traditionally, courts required strict compliance with the terms of a letter of credit, but in recent years, some courts have moved to a standard of *reasonable* compliance.

■ Regulation of Specific Business Activities

Doing business abroad can affect the economies, foreign policies, domestic policies, and other national interests of the countries involved. For this reason, nations impose laws to restrict or facilitate international business. Controls may also be imposed by international agreements. We discuss here how different types of international activities are regulated.

INVESTING

Firms that invest in foreign nations face the risk that the foreign government may take possession of the investment property. Expropriation, as already mentioned, occurs when property is taken and the owner is paid just compensation for what is taken. Expropriation does not violate generally observed principles of international law. Such principles are normally violated, however, when a government confiscates property without compensation (or without adequate compensation). Few remedies are available for confiscation of property by a foreign government. Claims are often resolved by lump-sum settlements after negotiations between the United States and the taking nation.

To counter the deterrent effect that the possibility of confiscation may have on potential investors, many countries guarantee that foreign investors will be compensated if their property is taken. A guaranty can take the form of national constitutional or statutory laws or provisions in international treaties. As further protection for foreign investments, some countries provide insurance for their citizens' investments abroad.

EXPORT CONTROLS

The U.S. Constitution provides in Article I, Section 9, that "No Tax or Duty shall be laid on Articles exported from any State." Thus, Congress cannot impose any export taxes. Congress can, however, use a variety of other devices to control exports. Congress may set export quotas on various items, such as grain being sold abroad. Under the Export Administration Act of 1979,[4] the flow of technologically advanced products and technical data can be restricted. In recent years, the U.S. Department of Commerce has made a controversial attempt to restrict the export of encryption software.

While restricting certain exports, the United States (and other nations) also use devices such as export incentives and subsidies to stimulate other exports and thereby aid domestic businesses. The Revenue Act of 1971,[5] for instance, gave tax benefits to firms marketing their products overseas through certain foreign sales corporations by exempting income produced by the exports. Under the Export Trading Company Act of 1982,[6] U.S. banks are encouraged to invest in export trading companies, which are formed when exporting firms join together to export a line of goods. The Export-Import Bank of the United States provides financial assistance, consisting primarily of credit guaranties given to commercial banks that in turn lend funds to U.S. exporting companies.

IMPORT CONTROLS

All nations have restrictions on imports, and the United States is no exception. Restrictions include strict prohibitions, quotas, and tariffs. Under the Trading with the Enemy Act of 1917,[7] for instance, no goods may be imported from nations that have been designated enemies of the United States. Other laws prohibit the importation of illegal drugs, books that urge insurrection against the United States, and agricultural products that pose dangers to domestic crops or animals.

Quotas and Tariffs Limits on the amounts of goods that can be imported are known as **quotas**. At one time, the United States had legal quotas on the number of automobiles that could be imported from Japan. Today, Japan "voluntarily" restricts the number of automobiles exported to the United States. **Tariffs** are taxes on imports. A tariff is usually a percentage of the value of the import, but it can be a flat rate per unit (for example, per barrel of oil). Tariffs raise the prices of goods, causing some consumers to purchase less expensive, domestically manufactured goods.

NOTE Most countries restrict exports for the same reasons: to protect national security, to further foreign policy objectives, to prevent the spread of nuclear weapons, and to preserve scarce commodities.

QUOTA
  A set limit on the amount of goods that can be imported.

TARIFF
  A tax on imported goods.

---

4. 50 U.S.C. Sections 2401–2420.
5. 26 U.S.C. Sections 991–994.
6. 15 U.S.C. Sections 4001, 4003.
7. 12 U.S.C. Section 95a.

DUMPING
The selling of goods in a foreign country at a price below the price charged for the same goods in the domestic market.

Dumping   The United States has specific laws directed at what it sees as unfair international trade practices. **Dumping,** for example, is the sale of imported goods at "less than fair value." "Fair value" is usually determined by the price of those goods in the exporting country. Foreign firms that engage in dumping in the United States hope to undersell U.S. businesses to obtain a larger share of the U.S. market. To prevent this, an extra tariff—known as an *antidumping duty*—may be assessed on the imports.

Minimizing Trade Barriers   Restrictions on imports are also known as *trade barriers*. The elimination of trade barriers is sometimes seen as essential to the world's economic well-being. Most of the world's leading trading nations are members of the World Trade Organization (WTO), which was established in 1995. To minimize trade barriers among nations, each member country of the WTO is required to grant **normal trade relations (NTR) status** (formerly known as *most-favored-nation status*) to other member countries. This means each member is obligated to treat other members at least as well as it treats the country that receives its most favorable treatment with regard to imports or exports.

NORMAL TRADE RELATIONS (NTR) STATUS
A status granted in an international treaty by a provision stating that the citizens of the contracting nations may enjoy the privileges accorded by either party to citizens of its NTR nations. Generally, this status is designed to establish equality of international treatment.

Various regional trade agreements and associations also help to minimize trade barriers between nations. The European Union (EU), for example, is working to minimize or remove barriers to trade among its member countries. The EU is a single integrated trading unit made up of twenty-five European nations. Another important regional trade agreement is the North American Free Trade Agreement (NAFTA). NAFTA, which became effective on January 1, 1994, created a regional trading unit consisting of Mexico, the United States, and Canada. The primary goal of NAFTA is to eliminate tariffs among these three countries on substantially all goods over a period of fifteen to twenty years.

BRIBING FOREIGN OFFICIALS

Giving cash or in-kind benefits to foreign government officials to obtain business contracts and other favors is often considered normal practice. To reduce such bribery by representatives of U.S. corporations, Congress enacted the Foreign Corrupt Practices Act in 1977.[8] This act and its implications for American businesspersons engaged in international business transactions were discussed in Chapter 2.

▦ U.S. Laws in a Global Context

The internationalization of business raises questions about the extraterritorial application of a nation's laws—that is, the effect of the country's laws outside its boundaries. To what extent do U.S. domestic laws apply to other nations' businesses? To what extent do U.S. domestic laws apply to U.S. firms doing business abroad? Here, we discuss these questions in the context of U.S. antitrust law. We also look at the extraterritorial application of U.S. laws prohibiting employment discrimination.

U.S. ANTITRUST LAWS

U.S. antitrust laws (discussed in Chapter 22) have a wide application. They may *subject* persons in foreign nations to their provisions, as well as *protect* foreign consumers and competitors from violations committed by U.S. citizens. Consequently, *foreign persons*, a term that by definition includes foreign governments, may sue under U.S. antitrust laws in U.S. courts.

---

8. 15 U.S.C. Sections 78m–78ff.

Section 1 of the Sherman Act provides for the extraterritorial effect of the U.S. antitrust laws. The United States is a major proponent of free competition in the global economy. Thus, any conspiracy that has a *substantial effect* on U.S. commerce is within the reach of the Sherman Act. The law applies even if the violation occurs outside the United States, and foreign governments as well as persons can be sued for violations.

Before U.S. courts will exercise jurisdiction and apply antitrust laws, however, it must be shown that the alleged violation had a substantial effect on U.S. commerce. U.S. jurisdiction is automatically invoked when a *per se* violation occurs.[9] An example of a *per se* violation is a price-fixing contract. ■ **EXAMPLE 25.5** If a domestic firm joins a foreign cartel to control the production, price, or distribution of goods, and this cartel has a *substantial restraining effect* on U.S. commerce, a *per se* violation may exist. Hence, both the domestic firm and the foreign cartel may be sued for violation of the U.S. antitrust laws. Likewise, if foreign firms doing business in the United States enter into a price-fixing or other anticompetitive agreement to control a portion of U.S. markets, a *per se* violation may exist. ■

In the following case, the court considered whether a *criminal* prosecution under the Sherman Act could be based on price-fixing activities that took place entirely outside the United States but had a substantial effect in this country.

---

9. Certain types of restrictive contracts, such as price-fixing agreements, are deemed inherently anticompetitive and thus in restraint of trade as a matter of law. Such a restrictive contract constitutes a *per se* violation of the antitrust laws. See Chapter 22.

CASE 25.3 ■ United States v. Nippon Paper Industries Co.

United States Court of Appeals,
First Circuit, 1997.
109 F.3d 1.

FACTS Nippon Paper Industries Company (NPI) makes paper and paper products, including thermal fax paper for use in fax machines and medical printing equipment. A federal grand jury issued a criminal indictment against NPI and others, charging the defendants with agreeing to fix the price of thermal fax paper throughout North America. The indictment alleged that the meetings to reach the agreement had occurred entirely in Japan but that the defendants had sold the paper through subsidiaries in the United States at above-normal prices. The indictment stated that these activities had had a substantial adverse effect on commerce in the United States and had unreasonably restrained trade in violation of Section 1 of the Sherman Act. NPI filed a motion to dismiss the indictment. The court granted the motion, declaring that a criminal antitrust prosecution could not be based on wholly extraterritorial conduct. The government appealed.

ISSUE May a criminal antitrust prosecution in the United States be based on wholly extraterritorial conduct?

DECISION Yes. The U.S. Court of Appeals for the First Circuit reversed the decision of the lower court.

REASON The appellate court stated that the criminal indictment under the Sherman Act should not be dismissed simply because the actions on which it was based occurred outside the United States. The court reasoned that "in both criminal and civil cases, the claim that Section One applies extraterritorially is based on the same language in the same section of the same statute." The court noted that "civil antitrust actions predicated on wholly foreign conduct which has an intended and substantial effect in the United States come within Section One's jurisdictional reach." The court concluded that because "the text under consideration is not merely a duplicate appearing somewhere else in the statute, but is the original phrase in the original setting," Section 1 applies.

FOR CRITICAL ANALYSIS—Economic Consideration
Why should the United States apply its antitrust laws to business firms owned by citizens or the government of another nation?

DISCRIMINATION LAWS

As explained in Chapter 18, federal laws in the United States prohibit discrimination on the basis of race, color, national origin, religion, gender, age, and disability. These laws, as they affect employment relationships, generally apply extraterritorially. Since 1984, for example, the Age Discrimination in Employment Act of 1967 has covered U.S. employees working abroad for U.S. employers. The Americans with Disabilities Act of 1990, which requires employers to accommodate the needs of workers with disabilities, also applies to U.S. nationals working abroad for U.S. firms.

For some time, it was uncertain whether the major U.S. law regulating discriminatory practices in the workplace, Title VII of the Civil Rights Act of 1964, applied extraterritorially. The Civil Rights Act of 1991 addressed this issue. The act provides that Title VII applies extraterritorially to all U.S. employees working for U.S. employers abroad. Generally, U.S. employers must abide by U.S. discrimination laws unless to do so would violate the laws of the country where their workplaces are located. This "foreign laws exception" allows employers to avoid being subjected to conflicting laws.

■ KEY TERMS

act of state doctrine 763

choice-of-language clause 767

choice-of-law clause 768

comity 762

confiscation 763

correspondent bank 769

distribution agreement 765

dumping 773

exclusive distributorship 765

export 764

expropriation 763

force majeure clause 768

foreign exchange market 769

forum-selection clause 767

international law 762

letter of credit 770

national law 762

normal trade relations (NTR) status 773

quota 772

sovereign immunity 764

tariff 772

CHAPTER SUMMARY ■ International Law in a Global Economy

International Principles and Doctrines (See pages 762–764.)	1. *The principle of comity*—Under this principle, nations give effect to the laws and judicial decrees of other nations for reasons of courtesy and international harmony.
	2. *The act of state doctrine*—A doctrine under which U.S. courts avoid passing judgment on the validity of public acts committed by a recognized foreign government within its own territory.
	3. *The doctrine of sovereign immunity*—When certain conditions are satisfied, foreign nations are immune from U.S. jurisdiction under the Foreign Sovereign Immunities Act of 1976. Exceptions are made (a) when a foreign state has "waived its immunity either explicitly or by implication" or (b) when the action is "based upon a commercial activity carried on in the United States by the foreign state."
Doing Business Internationally (See pages 764–766.)	Ways in which U.S. domestic firms engage in international business transactions include (a) exporting, which may involve foreign agents or distributors, and (b) manufacturing abroad through licensing arrangements, franchising operations, wholly owned subsidiaries, or joint ventures.

(Continued)

CHAPTER SUMMARY ▣ International Law in a Global Economy—Continued

Commercial Contracts in an International Setting (See pages 766–769.)	International business contracts often include choice-of-language, forum-selection, and choice-of-law clauses to reduce the uncertainties associated with interpreting the language of the agreement and dealing with legal differences. Most domestic and international contracts include *force majeure* clauses. They commonly stipulate that certain events, such as floods, fires, accidents, labor strikes, and government orders, may excuse a party from liability for nonperformance of the contract. Arbitration clauses are also frequently found in international contracts.
Making Payment on International Transactions (See pages 769–771.)	1. *Currency conversion*—Because nations have different monetary systems, payment on international contracts requires currency conversion at a rate specified in a foreign exchange market. 2. *Correspondent banking*—Correspondent banks facilitate the transfer of funds from a buyer in one country to a seller in another. 3. *Letters of credit*—Letters of credit facilitate international transactions by ensuring payment to sellers and assuring buyers that payment will not be made until the sellers have complied with the terms of the letters of credit. Typically, compliance occurs when a bill of lading is delivered to the issuing bank.
Regulation of Specific Business Activities (See pages 771–773.)	In the interests of their economies, foreign policies, domestic policies, or other national priorities, nations impose laws that restrict or facilitate international business. Such laws regulate foreign investments, exporting, and importing. The World Trade Organization attempts to minimize trade barriers among nations, as do regional trade agreements and associations, including the European Union and the North American Free Trade Agreement.
U.S. Laws in a Global Context (See pages 773–775.)	1. *Antitrust laws*—U.S. antitrust laws may be applied beyond the borders of the United States. Any conspiracy that has a substantial effect on commerce within the United States may be subject to the Sherman Act, even if the violation occurs outside the United States. 2. *Discrimination laws*—The major U.S. laws prohibiting employment discrimination, including Title VII of the Civil Rights Act of 1964, the Age Discrimination in Employment Act of 1967, and the Americans with Disabilities Act of 1990, cover U.S. employees working abroad for U.S. firms—*unless* to apply the U.S. laws would violate the laws of the host country.

▦ FOR REVIEW

Answers for the even-numbered questions in this For Review *section can be found in Appendix I at the end of this text.*

1 What is the principle of comity, and why do courts deciding disputes involving a foreign law or judicial decree apply this principle?

2 What is the act of state doctrine? In what circumstances is this doctrine applied?

3 Under the Foreign Sovereign Immunities Act of 1976, on what bases might a foreign state be considered subject to the jurisdiction of U.S. courts?

4 In what circumstances will U.S. antitrust laws be applied extraterritorially?

5 Do U.S. laws prohibiting employment discrimination apply in all circumstances to U.S. employees working for U.S. employers abroad?

▦ QUESTIONS AND CASE PROBLEMS

25–1. Letters of Credit. The Swiss Credit Bank issued a letter of credit in favor of Antex Industries to cover the sale of 92,000 electronic integrated circuits manufactured by Electronic Arrays. The letter of credit specified that the chips would be transported to Tokyo by ship. Antex shipped the circuits by air. Payment on the letter of credit was dishonored because the shipment by air did not fulfill the precise terms of the letter of credit. Should a court compel payment? Explain.

25–2. Antitrust Claims. Billy Lamb and Carmon Willis (the plaintiffs) were tobacco growers in Kentucky. Phillip Morris, Inc., and B.A.T. Industries, PLC, routinely purchased tobacco not only from Kentucky growers but also from producers in several foreign countries. In 1982, subsidiaries of Phillip Morris and B.A.T. (the defendants) entered into an agreement with La Fundacion Del Niño (the Children's Foundation) of Caracas, Venezuela, headed by the wife of the president of Venezuela. The agreement provided that the two subsidiaries would donate a total of approximately $12.5 million to the Children's Foundation, and in exchange, the subsidiaries would obtain price controls on Venezuelan tobacco, elimination of controls on retail cigarette prices in Venezuela, tax deductions for the donations, and assurances that existing tax rates applicable to tobacco companies would not be increased. The plaintiffs brought an action, alleging that the Venezuelan arrangement was an inducement designed to restrain trade in violation of U.S. antitrust laws. Such an arrangement, the plaintiffs contended, would result in the artificial depression of tobacco prices to the detriment of domestic tobacco growers, while ensuring lucrative retail prices for tobacco products sold abroad. The trial court held that the plaintiffs' claim was barred by the act of state doctrine. What will result on appeal? Discuss. [*Lamb v. Phillip Morris, Inc.,* 915 F.2d 1024 (6th Cir. 1990)]

25–3. Discrimination Claims. Radio Free Europe and Radio Liberty (RFE/RL), a U.S. corporation doing business in Germany, employs more than three hundred U.S. citizens at its principal place of business in Munich, Germany. The concept of mandatory retirement is deeply embedded in German labor policy, and a contract formed in 1982 between RFE/RL and a German labor union contained a clause that required workers to be retired when they reach the age of sixty-five. When William Mahoney and other U.S. employees (the plaintiffs) reached the age of sixty-five, RFE/RL terminated their employment as required under its contract with the labor union. The plaintiffs sued RFE/RL for discriminating against them on the basis of age, in violation of the Age Discrimination in Employment Act of 1967. Will the plaintiffs succeed in their suit? Discuss fully. [*Mahoney v. RFE/RL, Inc.,* 47 F.3d 447 (D.C. Cir. 1995)]

25–4. Sovereign Immunity. Nuovo Pignone, Inc., is an Italian company that designs and manufactures turbine systems. Nuovo sold a turbine system to Cabinda Gulf Oil Co. (CABGOC). The system was manufactured, tested, and inspected in Italy; then it was sent to Louisiana for mounting on a platform by CABGOC's contractor. Nuovo sent a representative to consult on the mounting. The platform went to a CABGOC site off the coast of West Africa. Marcus Pere, an instrument technician at the site, was killed when a turbine within the system exploded. Pere's widow filed a suit in a U.S. district court against Nuovo and others. Nuovo claimed sovereign immunity on the ground that its majority shareholder at the time of the explosion was Ente Nazionale Idrocaburi, which was created by the government of Italy to lead its oil and gas exploration and development. Is Nuovo exempt from suit under the doctrine of sovereign immunity? Is it subject to suit under the "commercial activity" exception? Why or why not? [*Pere v. Nuovo Pignone, Inc.,* 150 F.3d 477 (5th Cir. 1998)]

25–5. Dumping. In response to a petition filed on behalf of the U.S. pineapple industry, the U.S. Commerce Department initiated an investigation of canned pineapple imported from Thailand. The investigation concerned Thai producers of the canned fruit, including the Thai Pineapple Public Co. The Thai producers also turned out products, such as pineapple juice and juice concentrate, outside the scope of the investigation. These products use separate parts of the same fresh pineapple, so they share raw material costs. To determine fair value and antidumping duties, the Commerce Department had to calculate the Thai producers' cost of production and, in so doing, had to allocate a portion of the shared fruit costs to the canned fruit. These allocations were based on the producers' own financial records, which were consistent with Thai generally accepted accounting principles. The result was a determination that more than 90 percent of the canned fruit sales were below the cost of production. The producers filed a suit in the U.S. Court of International Trade against the federal government, challenging this allocation. The producers argued that their records did not reflect actual production costs, which instead should be based on the weight of fresh fruit used to make the products. Did the Commerce Department act reasonably in determining the cost of production? Why or why not? [*Thai Pineapple Public Co. v. United States,* 187 F.3d 1362 (Fed.Cir. 1999)]

CASE PROBLEM WITH SAMPLE ANSWER

25–6. Tonoga, Ltd., doing business as Taconic Plastics, Ltd., is a manufacturer incorporated in Ireland with its principal place of business in New York. In 1997, Taconic entered into a contract with a German construction company to supply special material for a tent project designed to shelter religious pilgrims visiting holy sites in Saudi Arabia. Most of the material was made in, and shipped from, New York. The company did not pay Taconic and eventually filed for bankruptcy. Another German firm, Werner Voss Architects and Engineers, acting as an agent for the government of Saudi Arabia, guaranteed the payments due Taconic to induce it to complete the project. When it did not receive the final payment, Taconic filed a suit in a U.S. district court against the government of Saudi Arabia, claiming a breach of the guaranty and seeking to collect, in part, about $3 million. The defendant filed a motion to dismiss based, in part, on the doctrine of sovereign immunity. Under what circumstances does this doctrine apply? What are its exceptions? Should this suit be dismissed under the "commercial activity" exception? Explain. [*Tonoga, Ltd. v. Ministry of Public Works and Housing of Kingdom of Saudi Arabia,* 135 F.Supp.2d 350 (N.D.N.Y. 2001)]

After you have answered this problem, compare your answer with the sample answer given on the Web site that accompanies this text. Go to http://blt.westbuslaw.com, select "Chapter 25," and click on "Case Problem with Sample Answer."

25–7. Imports. DaimlerChrysler Corp. makes and markets motor vehicles. DaimlerChrysler assembled the 1993 and 1994 model years of its trucks at plants in Mexico. Assembly involved sheet metal components sent from the United States. DaimlerChrysler subjected some of the parts to a complicated treatment process, which included applying coats of paint to prevent corrosion, impart color, and protect the finish. Under U.S. law, goods that are assembled abroad using U.S.–made parts can be imported tariff free. A U.S. *statute* provides that painting is "incidental" to assembly and does not affect the status of the goods. A U.S. *regulation*, however, states that "painting primarily intended to enhance the appearance of an article or to impart distinctive features or characteristics" is not incidental. The U.S. Customs Service levied a tariff on the trucks. DaimlerChrysler filed a suit in the U.S. Court of International Trade, challenging the levy. Should the court rule in DaimlerChrysler's favor? Why or why not? [*DaimlerChrysler Corp. v. United States*, 361 F.3d 1378 (Fed.Cir. 2004)]

A QUESTION OF ETHICS

25–8. Ronald Riley, a U.S. citizen, and Council of Lloyd's, a British insurance corporation with its principal place of business in London, entered into an agreement in 1980 that allowed Riley to underwrite insurance through Lloyd's. The agreement provided that if any dispute arose between Lloyd's and Riley, the courts of England would have exclusive jurisdiction, and the laws of England would apply. Over the next decade, some of the parties insured under policies that Riley underwrote experienced large losses, for which they filed claims. Instead of paying his share of the claims, Riley filed a lawsuit in a U.S. district court against Lloyd's and its managers and directors (all British citizens or entities), seeking, among other things, rescission of the 1980 agreement. Riley alleged that the defendants had violated the Securities Act of 1933, the Securities Exchange Act of 1934, and Rule 10b-5. The defendants asked the court to enforce the forum-selection clause in the agreement. Riley argued that if the clause was enforced, he would be deprived of his rights under the U.S. securities laws. The court held that the parties were to resolve their dispute in England. [*Riley v. Kingsley Underwriting Agencies, Ltd.*, 969 F.2d 953 (10th Cir. 1992)]

1. Did the court's decision fairly balance the rights of the parties? How would you argue in support of the court's decision in this case? How would you argue against it?

2. Should the fact that an international transaction may be subject to laws and remedies different from or less favorable than those of the United States be a valid basis for denying enforcement of forum-selection and choice-of-law clauses?

3. All parties to this litigation other than Riley were British. Should the court consider this fact in deciding this case?

FOR CRITICAL ANALYSIS

25–9. Business cartels and monopolies that are legal in some countries may engage in practices that violate U.S. antitrust laws. In view of this fact, what are some of the implications of applying U.S. antitrust laws extraterritorially?

VIDEO QUESTION

25–10. Go to this text's Web site at **http://blt. westbuslaw.com** and select "Chapter 25." Click on "Video Questions" and view the video titled *International Letter of Credit.* Then answer the following questions.

1. Do banks always require the same documents to be presented in letter-of-credit transactions? If not, who dictates what documents will be required in the letter of credit?

2. At what point does the seller receive payment in a letter-of-credit transaction?

3. What assurances does a letter of credit provide to the buyer and the seller involved in the transaction?

INTERNET EXERCISES

Go to the *Business Law Today: The Essentials* home page at **http://blt.westbuslaw.com,** select "Chapter 25," and click on "Internet Exercises." There you will find the following Internet research exercises that you can perform to learn more about topics covered in this chapter.

Activity 25–1: LEGAL PERSPECTIVE—The World Trade Organization

Activity 25–2: MANAGEMENT PERSPECTIVE—Overseas Business Opportunities

BEFORE THE TEST

Go to the *Business Law Today: The Essentials* home page at **http://blt.westbuslaw.com,** select "Chapter 25," and click on "Interactive Quizzes." You will find at least twenty interactive questions relating to this chapter.

APPENDIX A

The Constitution of the United States

We the People of the United States, in Order to form a more perfect Union, establish Justice, insure domestic Tranquility, provide for the common defence, promote the general Welfare, and secure the Blessings of Liberty to ourselves and our Posterity, do ordain and establish this Constitution for the United States of America.

ARTICLE I

Section 1. All legislative Powers herein granted shall be vested in a Congress of the United States, which shall consist of a Senate and House of Representatives.

Section 2. The House of Representatives shall be composed of Members chosen every second Year by the People of the several States, and the Electors in each State shall have the Qualifications requisite for Electors of the most numerous Branch of the State Legislature.

No Person shall be a Representative who shall not have attained to the Age of twenty five Years, and been seven Years a Citizen of the United States, and who shall not, when elected, be an Inhabitant of that State in which he shall be chosen.

Representatives and direct Taxes shall be apportioned among the several States which may be included within this Union, according to their respective Numbers, which shall be determined by adding to the whole Number of free Persons, including those bound to Service for a Term of Years, and excluding Indians not taxed, three fifths of all other Persons. The actual Enumeration shall be made within three Years after the first Meeting of the Congress of the United States, and within every subsequent Term of ten Years, in such Manner as they shall by Law direct. The Number of Representatives shall not exceed one for every thirty Thousand, but each State shall have at Least one Representative; and until such enumeration shall be made, the State of New Hampshire shall be entitled to chuse three, Massachusetts eight, Rhode Island and Providence Plantations one, Connecticut five, New York six, New Jersey four, Pennsylvania eight, Delaware one, Maryland six, Virginia ten, North Carolina five, South Carolina five, and Georgia three.

When vacancies happen in the Representation from any State, the Executive Authority thereof shall issue Writs of Election to fill such Vacancies.

The House of Representatives shall chuse their Speaker and other Officers; and shall have the sole Power of Impeachment.

Section 3. The Senate of the United States shall be composed of two Senators from each State, chosen by the Legislature thereof, for six Years; and each Senator shall have one Vote.

Immediately after they shall be assembled in Consequence of the first Election, they shall be divided as equally as may be into three Classes. The Seats of the Senators of the first Class shall be vacated at the Expiration of the second Year, of the second Class at the Expiration of the fourth Year, and of the third Class at the Expiration of the sixth Year, so that one third may be chosen every second Year; and if Vacancies happen by Resignation, or otherwise, during the Recess of the Legislature of any State, the Executive thereof may make temporary Appointments until the next Meeting of the Legislature, which shall then fill such Vacancies.

No Person shall be a Senator who shall not have attained to the Age of thirty Years, and been nine Years a Citizen of the United States, and who shall not, when elected, be an Inhabitant of that State for which he shall be chosen.

The Vice President of the United States shall be President of the Senate, but shall have no Vote, unless they be equally divided.

The Senate shall chuse their other Officers, and also a President pro tempore, in the Absence of the Vice President, or when he shall exercise the Office of President of the United States.

The Senate shall have the sole Power to try all Impeachments. When sitting for that Purpose, they shall be on Oath or Affirmation. When the President of the United States is tried, the Chief Justice shall preside: And no Person shall be convicted without the Concurrence of two thirds of the Members present.

Judgment in Cases of Impeachment shall not extend further than to removal from Office, and disqualification to hold and enjoy any Office of honor, Trust, or Profit under the United States: but the Party convicted shall nevertheless be liable and subject to Indictment, Trial, Judgment, and Punishment, according to Law.

Section 4. The Times, Places and Manner of holding Elections for Senators and Representatives, shall be prescribed in each State by the Legislature thereof; but the Congress may at any time by Law make or alter such Regulations, except as to the Places of chusing Senators.

The Congress shall assemble at least once in every Year, and such Meeting shall be on the first Monday in December, unless they shall by Law appoint a different Day.

Section 5. Each House shall be the Judge of the Elections, Returns, and Qualifications of its own Members, and a Majority of each shall constitute a Quorum to do Business; but a smaller Number may adjourn from day to day, and may be authorized to compel the Attendance of absent Members, in such Manner, and under such Penalties as each House may provide.

Each House may determine the Rules of its Proceedings, punish its Members for disorderly Behavior, and, with the Concurrence of two thirds, expel a Member.

Each House shall keep a Journal of its Proceedings, and from time to time publish the same, excepting such Parts as may in their Judgment require Secrecy; and the Yeas and Nays of the Members of either House on any question shall, at the Desire of one fifth of those Present, be entered on the Journal.

Neither House, during the Session of Congress, shall, without the Consent of the other, adjourn for more than three days, nor to any other Place than that in which the two Houses shall be sitting.

Section 6. The Senators and Representatives shall receive a Compensation for their Services, to be ascertained by Law, and paid out of the Treasury of the United States. They shall in all Cases, except Treason, Felony and Breach of the Peace, be privileged from Arrest during their Attendance at the Session of their respective Houses, and in going to and returning from the same; and for any Speech or Debate in either House, they shall not be questioned in any other Place.

No Senator or Representative shall, during the Time for which he was elected, be appointed to any civil Office under the Authority of the United States, which shall have been created, or the Emoluments whereof shall have been increased during such time; and no Person holding any Office under the United States, shall be a Member of either House during his Continuance in Office.

Section 7. All Bills for raising Revenue shall originate in the House of Representatives; but the Senate may propose or concur with Amendments as on other Bills.

Every Bill which shall have passed the House of Representatives and the Senate, shall, before it become a Law, be presented to the President of the United States; If he approve he shall sign it, but if not he shall return it, with his Objections to the House in which it shall have originated, who shall enter the Objections at large on their Journal, and proceed to reconsider it. If after such Reconsideration two thirds of that House shall agree to pass the Bill, it shall be sent together with the Objections, to the other House, by which it shall likewise be reconsidered, and if approved by two thirds of that House, it shall become a Law. But in all such Cases the Votes of both Houses shall be determined by Yeas and Nays, and the Names of the Persons voting for and against the Bill shall be entered on the Journal of each House respectively. If any Bill shall not be returned by the President within ten Days (Sundays excepted) after it shall have been presented to him, the Same shall be a Law, in like Manner as if he had signed it, unless the Congress by their Adjournment prevent its Return in which Case it shall not be a Law.

Every Order, Resolution, or Vote, to which the Concurrence of the Senate and House of Representatives may be necessary (except on a question of Adjournment) shall be presented to the President of the United States; and before the Same shall take Effect, shall be approved by him, or being disapproved by him, shall be repassed by two thirds of the Senate and House of Representatives, according to the Rules and Limitations prescribed in the Case of a Bill.

Section 8. The Congress shall have Power To lay and collect Taxes, Duties, Imposts and Excises, to pay the Debts and provide for the common Defence and general Welfare of the United States; but all Duties, Imposts and Excises shall be uniform throughout the United States;

To borrow Money on the credit of the United States;

To regulate Commerce with foreign Nations, and among the several States, and with the Indian Tribes;

To establish an uniform Rule of Naturalization, and uniform Laws on the subject of Bankruptcies throughout the United States;

To coin Money, regulate the Value thereof, and of foreign Coin, and fix the Standard of Weights and Measures;

To provide for the Punishment of counterfeiting the Securities and current Coin of the United States;

To establish Post Offices and post Roads;

To promote the Progress of Science and useful Arts, by securing for limited Times to Authors and Inventors the exclusive Right to their respective Writings and Discoveries;

To constitute Tribunals inferior to the supreme Court;

To define and punish Piracies and Felonies committed on the high Seas, and Offenses against the Law of Nations;

To declare War, grant Letters of Marque and Reprisal, and make Rules concerning Captures on Land and Water;

To raise and support Armies, but no Appropriation of Money to that Use shall be for a longer Term than two Years;

To provide and maintain a Navy;

To make Rules for the Government and Regulation of the land and naval Forces;

To provide for calling forth the Militia to execute the Laws of the Union, suppress Insurrections and repel Invasions;

To provide for organizing, arming, and disciplining, the Militia, and for governing such Part of them as may be employed in the Service of the United States, reserving to the States respectively, the Appointment of the Officers, and the Authority of training the Militia according to the discipline prescribed by Congress;

To exercise exclusive Legislation in all Cases whatsoever, over such District (not exceeding ten Miles square) as may, by Cession of particular States, and the Acceptance of Congress, become the Seat of the Government of the United States, and to exercise like Authority over all Places purchased by the Consent of the Legislature of the State in which the Same shall be, for the Erection of Forts, Magazines, Arsenals, dock-Yards, and other needful Buildings;—And

To make all Laws which shall be necessary and proper for carrying into Execution the foregoing Powers, and all other Powers vested by this Constitution in the Government of the United States, or in any Department or Officer thereof.

Section 9. The Migration or Importation of such Persons as any of the States now existing shall think proper to admit, shall not be prohibited by the Congress prior to the Year one thousand eight hundred and eight, but a Tax or duty may be imposed on such Importation, not exceeding ten dollars for each Person.

The privilege of the Writ of Habeas Corpus shall not be suspended, unless when in Cases of Rebellion or Invasion the public Safety may require it.

No Bill of Attainder or ex post facto Law shall be passed.

No Capitation, or other direct, Tax shall be laid, unless in Proportion to the Census or Enumeration herein before directed to be taken.

No Tax or Duty shall be laid on Articles exported from any State.

No Preference shall be given by any Regulation of Commerce or Revenue to the Ports of one State over those of another: nor shall Vessels bound to, or from, one State be obliged to enter, clear, or pay Duties in another.

No Money shall be drawn from the Treasury, but in Consequence of Appropriations made by Law; and a regular Statement and Account of the Receipts and Expenditures of all public Money shall be published from time to time.

No Title of Nobility shall be granted by the United States: And no Person holding any Office of Profit or Trust under them, shall, without the Consent of the Congress, accept of any present, Emolument, Office, or Title, of any kind whatever, from any King, Prince, or foreign State.

Section 10. No State shall enter into any Treaty, Alliance, or Confederation; grant Letters of Marque and Reprisal; coin Money; emit Bills of Credit; make any Thing but gold and silver Coin a Tender in Payment of Debts; pass any Bill of Attainder, ex post facto Law, or Law impairing the Obligation of Contracts, or grant any Title of Nobility.

No State shall, without the Consent of the Congress, lay any Imposts or Duties on Imports or Exports, except what may be absolutely necessary for executing its inspection Laws: and the net Produce of all Duties and Imposts, laid by any State on Imports or Exports, shall be for the Use of the Treasury of the United States; and all such Laws shall be subject to the Revision and Controul of the Congress.

No State shall, without the Consent of Congress, lay any Duty of Tonnage, keep Troops, or Ships of War in time of Peace, enter into any Agreement or Compact with another State, or with a foreign Power, or engage in War, unless actually invaded, or in such imminent Danger as will not admit of delay.

ARTICLE II

Section 1. The executive Power shall be vested in a President of the United States of America. He shall hold his Office during the Term of four Years, and, together with the Vice President, chosen for the same Term, be elected, as follows:

Each State shall appoint, in such Manner as the Legislature thereof may direct, a Number of Electors, equal to the whole Number of Senators and Representatives to which the State may be entitled in the Congress; but no Senator or Representative, or Person holding an Office of Trust or Profit under the United States, shall be appointed an Elector.

The Electors shall meet in their respective States, and vote by Ballot for two Persons, of whom one at least shall not be an Inhabitant of the same State with themselves. And they shall make a List of all the Persons voted for, and of the Number of Votes for each; which List they shall sign and certify, and transmit sealed to the Seat of the Government of the United States, directed to the President of the Senate. The President of the Senate shall, in the Presence of the Senate and House of Representatives, open all the Certificates, and the Votes shall then be counted. The Person having the greatest Number of Votes shall be the President, if such Number be a Majority of the whole Number of Electors appointed; and if there be more than one who have such Majority, and have an equal Number of Votes, then the House of Representatives shall immediately chuse by Ballot one of them for President; and if no Person have a Majority, then from the five highest on the List the said House shall in like Manner chuse the President. But in chusing the President, the Votes shall be taken by States, the Representation from each State having one Vote; A quorum for this Purpose shall consist of a Member or Members from two thirds of the States, and a Majority of all the States shall be necessary to a Choice. In every Case, after the Choice of the President, the Person having the greater Number of Votes of the Electors shall be the Vice President. But if there should remain two or more who have equal Votes, the Senate shall chuse from them by Ballot the Vice President.

The Congress may determine the Time of chusing the Electors, and the Day on which they shall give their Votes; which Day shall be the same throughout the United States.

No person except a natural born Citizen, or a Citizen of the United States, at the time of the Adoption of this Constitution, shall be eligible to the Office of President; neither shall any Person be eligible to that Office who shall not have attained to the Age of thirty five Years, and been fourteen Years a Resident within the United States.

In Case of the Removal of the President from Office, or of his Death, Resignation or Inability to discharge the Powers and Duties of the said Office, the same shall devolve on the Vice President, and the Congress may by Law provide for the Case of Removal, Death, Resignation or Inability, both of the President and Vice President, declaring what Officer shall then act as President, and such Officer shall act accordingly, until the Disability be removed, or a President shall be elected.

The President shall, at stated Times, receive for his Services, a Compensation, which shall neither be increased nor diminished during the Period for which he shall have been elected, and he shall not receive within that Period any other Emolument from the United States, or any of them.

Before he enter on the Execution of his Office, he shall take the following Oath or Affirmation: "I do solemnly swear (or affirm) that I will faithfully execute the Office of President of the United States, and will to the best of my Ability, preserve, protect and defend the Constitution of the United States."

Section 2. The President shall be Commander in Chief of the Army and Navy of the United States, and of the Militia of the several States, when called into the actual Service of the United States; he may require the Opinion, in writing, of the principal Officer in each of the executive Departments, upon any Subject relating to the Duties of their respective Offices, and he shall have Power to grant Reprieves and Pardons for Offenses against the United States, except in Cases of Impeachment.

He shall have Power, by and with the Advice and Consent of the Senate to make Treaties, provided two thirds of the Senators present concur; and he shall nominate, and by and with the Advice and Consent of the Senate, shall appoint Ambassadors, other public Ministers and Consuls, Judges of the supreme Court, and all other Officers of the United States, whose Appointments are not herein otherwise provided for, and which shall be established by Law; but the Congress may by Law vest the Appointment of such inferior Officers, as they think proper, in the President alone, in the Courts of Law, or in the Heads of Departments.

The President shall have Power to fill up all Vacancies that may happen during the Recess of the Senate, by granting Commissions which shall expire at the End of their next Session.

Section 3. He shall from time to time give to the Congress Information of the State of the Union, and recommend to their Consideration such Measures as he shall judge necessary and expedient; he may, on extraordinary Occasions, convene both Houses, or either of them, and in Case of Disagreement between them, with Respect to the Time of Adjournment, he may adjourn them to such Time as he shall think proper; he shall receive Ambassadors and other public Ministers; he shall take Care that the Laws be faithfully executed, and shall Commission all the Officers of the United States.

Section 4. The President, Vice President and all civil Officers of the United States, shall be removed from Office on Impeachment for, and Conviction of, Treason, Bribery, or other high Crimes and Misdemeanors.

ARTICLE III

Section 1. The judicial Power of the United States, shall be vested in one supreme Court, and in such inferior Courts as the Congress may from time to time ordain and establish. The Judges, both of the supreme and inferior Courts, shall hold their Offices during good Behaviour, and shall, at stated Times, receive for their Services a Compensation, which shall not be diminished during their Continuance in Office.

Section 2. The judicial Power shall extend to all Cases, in Law and Equity, arising under this Constitution, the Laws of the United States, and Treaties made, or which shall be made, under their Authority;—to all Cases affecting Ambassadors, other public Ministers and Consuls;—to all Cases of admiralty and maritime Jurisdiction;—to Controversies to which the United States shall be a Party;—to Controversies between two or more States;—between a State and Citizens of another State;—between Citizens of different States;—between Citizens of the same State claiming Lands under Grants of different States, and between a State, or the Citizens thereof, and foreign States, Citizens or Subjects.

In all Cases affecting Ambassadors, other public Ministers and Consuls, and those in which a State shall be a Party, the supreme Court shall have original Jurisdiction. In all the other Cases before mentioned, the supreme Court shall have appellate Jurisdiction, both as to Law and Fact, with such Exceptions, and under such Regulations as the Congress shall make.

The Trial of all Crimes, except in Cases of Impeachment, shall be by Jury; and such Trial shall be held in the State where the said Crimes shall have been committed; but when not committed within any State, the Trial shall be at such Place or Places as the Congress may by Law have directed.

Section 3. Treason against the United States, shall consist only in levying War against them, or, in adhering to their Enemies, giving them Aid and Comfort. No Person shall be convicted of Treason unless on the Testimony of two Witnesses to the same overt Act, or on Confession in open Court.

The Congress shall have Power to declare the Punishment of Treason, but no Attainder of Treason shall work Corruption of Blood, or Forfeiture except during the Life of the Person attainted.

ARTICLE IV

Section 1. Full Faith and Credit shall be given in each State to the public Acts, Records, and judicial Proceedings of every other State. And the Congress may by general Laws prescribe the Manner in which such Acts, Records and Proceedings shall be proved, and the Effect thereof.

Section 2. The Citizens of each State shall be entitled to all Privileges and Immunities of Citizens in the several States.

A Person charged in any State with Treason, Felony, or other Crime, who shall flee from Justice, and be found in another State, shall on Demand of the executive Authority of the State from which he fled, be delivered up, to be removed to the State having Jurisdiction of the Crime.

No Person held to Service or Labour in one State, under the Laws thereof, escaping into another, shall, in Consequence of any Law or Regulation therein, be discharged from such Service or Labour, but shall be delivered up on Claim of the Party to whom such Service or Labour may be due.

Section 3. New States may be admitted by the Congress into this Union; but no new State shall be formed or erected within the Jurisdiction of any other State; nor any State be formed by the Junction of two or more States, or Parts of States, without the Consent of the Legislatures of the States concerned as well as of the Congress.

The Congress shall have Power to dispose of and make all needful Rules and Regulations respecting the Territory or other Property belonging to the United States; and nothing in this Constitution shall be so construed as to Prejudice any Claims of the United States, or of any particular State.

Section 4. The United States shall guarantee to every State in this Union a Republican Form of Government, and shall protect each of them against Invasion; and on Application of the Legislature, or of the Executive (when the Legislature cannot be convened) against domestic Violence.

ARTICLE V

The Congress, whenever two thirds of both Houses shall deem it necessary, shall propose Amendments to this Constitution, or, on the Application of the Legislatures of two thirds of the several States, shall call a Convention for proposing Amendments, which, in either Case, shall be valid to all Intents and Purposes, as part of this Constitution, when ratified by the Legislatures of three fourths of the several States, or by Conventions in three fourths thereof, as the one or the other Mode of Ratification may be proposed by the Congress; Provided that no Amendment which may be made prior to the Year One thousand eight hundred and eight shall in any Manner affect the first and fourth Clauses in the Ninth Section of the first Article; and that no State, without its Consent, shall be deprived of its equal Suffrage in the Senate.

ARTICLE VI

All Debts contracted and Engagements entered into, before the Adoption of this Constitution shall be as valid against the United States under this Constitution, as under the Confederation.

This Constitution, and the Laws of the United States which shall be made in Pursuance thereof; and all Treaties made, or which shall be made, under the Authority of the United States, shall be the supreme Law of the Land; and the Judges in every

State shall be bound thereby, any Thing in the Constitution or Laws of any State to the Contrary notwithstanding.

The Senators and Representatives before mentioned, and the Members of the several State Legislatures, and all executive and judicial Officers, both of the United States and of the several States, shall be bound by Oath or Affirmation, to support this Constitution; but no religious Test shall ever be required as a Qualification to any Office or public Trust under the United States.

ARTICLE VII

The Ratification of the Conventions of nine States shall be sufficient for the Establishment of this Constitution between the States so ratifying the Same.

AMENDMENT I [1791]

Congress shall make no law respecting an establishment of religion, or prohibiting the free exercise thereof; or abridging the freedom of speech, or of the press; or the right of the people peaceably to assembly, and to petition the Government for a redress of grievances.

AMENDMENT II [1791]

A well regulated Militia, being necessary to the security of a free State, the right of the people to keep and bear Arms, shall not be infringed.

AMENDMENT III [1791]

No Soldier shall, in time of peace be quartered in any house, without the consent of the Owner, nor in time of war, but in a manner to be prescribed by law.

AMENDMENT IV [1791]

The right of the people to be secure in their persons, houses, papers, and effects, against unreasonable searches and seizures, shall not be violated, and no Warrants shall issue, but upon probable cause, supported by Oath or affirmation, and particularly describing the place to be searched, and the persons or things to be seized.

AMENDMENT V [1791]

No person shall be held to answer for a capital, or otherwise infamous crime, unless on a presentment or indictment of a Grand Jury, except in cases arising in the land or naval forces, or in the Militia, when in actual service in time of War or public danger; nor shall any person be subject for the same offence to be twice put in jeopardy of life or limb; nor shall be compelled in any criminal case to be a witness against himself, nor be deprived of life, liberty, or property, without due process of law; nor shall private property be taken for public use, without just compensation.

AMENDMENT VI [1791]

In all criminal prosecutions, the accused shall enjoy the right to a speedy and public trial, by an impartial jury of the State and district wherein the crime shall have been committed, which district shall have been previously ascertained by law, and to be informed of the nature and cause of the accusation; to be confronted with the witnesses against him; to have compulsory process for obtaining witnesses in his favor, and to have the Assistance of Counsel for his defence.

AMENDMENT VII [1791]

In Suits at common law, where the value in controversy shall exceed twenty dollars, the right of trial by jury shall be preserved, and no fact tried by jury, shall be otherwise re-examined in any Court of the United States, than according to the rules of the common law.

AMENDMENT VIII [1791]

Excessive bail shall not be required, nor excessive fines imposed, nor cruel and unusual punishments inflicted.

AMENDMENT IX [1791]

The enumeration in the Constitution, of certain rights, shall not be construed to deny or disparage others retained by the people.

AMENDMENT X [1791]

The powers not delegated to the United States by the Constitution, nor prohibited by it to the States, are reserved to the States respectively, or to the people.

AMENDMENT XI [1798]

The Judicial power of the United States shall not be construed to extend to any suit in law or equity, commenced or prosecuted against one of the United States by Citizens of another State, or by Citizens or Subjects of any Foreign State.

AMENDMENT XII [1804]

The Electors shall meet in their respective states, and vote by ballot for President and Vice-President, one of whom, at least, shall not be an inhabitant of the same state with themselves; they shall name in their ballots the person voted for as President, and in distinct ballots the person voted for as Vice-President, and they shall make distinct lists of all persons voted for as President, and of all persons voted for as Vice-President, and of the number of votes for each, which lists they shall sign and certify, and transmit sealed to the seat of the government of the United States, directed to the President of the Senate;—The President of the Senate shall, in the presence of the Senate and House of Representatives, open all the certificates and the votes shall then be counted;—The person having the greatest number of votes for President, shall be the President, if such number be a majority of the whole number of Electors appointed; and if no person have such majority, then from the persons having the highest numbers not exceeding three on the list of those voted for as President, the House of Representatives shall choose immediately, by ballot, the President. But in choosing the President, the votes shall be taken by states, the representation from each state

having one vote; a quorum for this purpose shall consist of a member or members from two-thirds of the states, and a majority of all states shall be necessary to a choice. And if the House of Representatives shall not choose a President whenever the right of choice shall devolve upon them, before the fourth day of March next following, then the Vice-President shall act as President, as in the case of the death or other constitutional disability of the President.—The person having the greatest number of votes as Vice-President, shall be the Vice-President, if such number be a majority of the whole number of Electors appointed, and if no person have a majority, then from the two highest numbers on the list, the Senate shall choose the Vice-President; a quorum for the purpose shall consist of two-thirds of the whole number of Senators, and a majority of the whole number shall be necessary to a choice. But no person constitutionally ineligible to the office of President shall be eligible to that of Vice-President of the United States.

AMENDMENT XIII [1865]

Section 1. Neither slavery nor involuntary servitude, except as a punishment for crime whereof the party shall have been duly convicted, shall exist within the United States, or any place subject to their jurisdiction.

Section 2. Congress shall have power to enforce this article by appropriate legislation.

AMENDMENT XIV [1868]

Section 1. All persons born or naturalized in the United States, and subject to the jurisdiction thereof, are citizens of the United States and of the State wherein they reside. No State shall make or enforce any law which shall abridge the privileges or immunities of citizens of the United States; nor shall any State deprive any person of life, liberty, or property, without due process of law; nor deny to any person within its jurisdiction the equal protection of the laws.

Section 2. Representatives shall be apportioned among the several States according to their respective numbers, counting the whole number of persons in each State, excluding Indians not taxed. But when the right to vote at any election for the choice of electors for President and Vice President of the United States, Representatives in Congress, the Executive and Judicial officers of a State, or the members of the Legislature thereof, is denied to any of the male inhabitants of such State, being twenty-one years of age, and citizens of the United States, or in any way abridged, except for participation in rebellion, or other crime, the basis of representation therein shall be reduced in the proportion which the number of such male citizens shall bear to the whole number of male citizens twenty-one years of age in such State.

Section 3. No person shall be a Senator or Representative in Congress, or elector of President and Vice President, or hold any office, civil or military, under the United States, or under any State, who having previously taken an oath, as a member of Congress, or as an officer of the United States, or as a member of any State legislature, or as an executive or judicial officer of any State, to support the Constitution of the United States, shall have engaged in insurrection or rebellion against the same, or given aid or comfort to the enemies thereof. But Congress may by a vote of two-thirds of each House, remove such disability.

Section 4. The validity of the public debt of the United States, authorized by law, including debts incurred for payment of pensions and bounties for services in suppressing insurrection or rebellion, shall not be questioned. But neither the United States nor any State shall assume or pay any debt or obligation incurred in aid of insurrection or rebellion against the United States, or any claim for the loss or emancipation of any slave; but all such debts, obligations and claims shall be held illegal and void.

Section 5. The Congress shall have power to enforce, by appropriate legislation, the provisions of this article.

AMENDMENT XV [1870]

Section 1. The right of citizens of the United States to vote shall not be denied or abridged by the United States or by any State on account of race, color, or previous condition of servitude.

Section 2. The Congress shall have power to enforce this article by appropriate legislation.

AMENDMENT XVI [1913]

The Congress shall have power to lay and collect taxes on incomes, from whatever source derived, without apportionment among the several States, and without regard to any census or enumeration.

AMENDMENT XVII [1913]

Section 1. The Senate of the United States shall be composed of two Senators from each State, elected by the people thereof, for six years; and each Senator shall have one vote. The electors in each State shall have the qualifications requisite for electors of the most numerous branch of the State legislatures.

Section 2. When vacancies happen in the representation of any State in the Senate, the executive authority of such State shall issue writs of election to fill such vacancies: *Provided,* That the legislature of any State may empower the executive thereof to make temporary appointments until the people fill the vacancies by election as the legislature may direct.

Section 3. This amendment shall not be so construed as to affect the election or term of any Senator chosen before it becomes valid as part of the Constitution.

AMENDMENT XVIII [1919]

Section 1. After one year from the ratification of this article the manufacture, sale, or transportation of intoxicating liquors within, the importation thereof into, or the exportation thereof from the United States and all territory subject to the jurisdiction thereof for beverage purposes is hereby prohibited.

Section 2. The Congress and the several States shall have concurrent power to enforce this article by appropriate legislation.

Section 3. This article shall be inoperative unless it shall have been ratified as an amendment to the Constitution by the

legislatures of the several States, as provided in the Constitution, within seven years from the date of the submission hereof to the States by the Congress.

AMENDMENT XIX [1920]

Section 1. The right of citizens of the United States to vote shall not be denied or abridged by the United States or by any State on account of sex.

Section 2. Congress shall have power to enforce this article by appropriate legislation.

AMENDMENT XX [1933]

Section 1. The terms of the President and Vice President shall end at noon on the 20th day of January, and the terms of Senators and Representatives at noon on the 3d day of January, of the years in which such terms would have ended if this article had not been ratified; and the terms of their successors shall then begin.

Section 2. The Congress shall assemble at least once in every year, and such meeting shall begin at noon on the 3d day of January, unless they shall by law appoint a different day.

Section 3. If, at the time fixed for the beginning of the term of the President, the President elect shall have died, the Vice President elect shall become President. If the President shall not have been chosen before the time fixed for the beginning of his term, or if the President elect shall have failed to qualify, then the Vice President elect shall act as President until a President shall have qualified; and the Congress may by law provide for the case wherein neither a President elect nor a Vice President elect shall have qualified, declaring who shall then act as President, or the manner in which one who is to act shall be selected, and such person shall act accordingly until a President or Vice President shall have qualified.

Section 4. The Congress may by law provide for the case of the death of any of the persons from whom the House of Representatives may choose a President whenever the right of choice shall have devolved upon them, and for the case of the death of any of the persons from whom the Senate may choose a Vice President whenever the right of choice shall have devolved upon them.

Section 5. Sections 1 and 2 shall take effect on the 15th day of October following the ratification of this article.

Section 6. This article shall be inoperative unless it shall have been ratified as an amendment to the Constitution by the legislatures of three-fourths of the several States within seven years from the date of its submission.

AMENDMENT XXI [1933]

Section 1. The eighteenth article of amendment to the Constitution of the United States is hereby repealed.

Section 2. The transportation or importation into any State, Territory, or possession of the United States for delivery or use therein of intoxicating liquors, in violation of the laws thereof, is hereby prohibited.

Section 3. This article shall be inoperative unless it shall have been ratified as an amendment to the Constitution by conventions in the several States, as provided in the Constitution, within seven years from the date of the submission hereof to the States by the Congress.

AMENDMENT XXII [1951]

Section 1. No person shall be elected to the office of the President more than twice, and no person who has held the office of President, or acted as President, for more than two years of a term to which some other person was elected President shall be elected to the office of President more than once. But this Article shall not apply to any person holding the office of President when this Article was proposed by the Congress, and shall not prevent any person who may be holding the office of President, or acting as President, during the term within which this Article becomes operative from holding the office of President or acting as President during the remainder of such term.

Section 2. This article shall be inoperative unless it shall have been ratified as an amendment to the Constitution by the legislatures of three-fourths of the several States within seven years from the date of its submission to the States by the Congress.

AMENDMENT XXIII [1961]

Section 1. The District constituting the seat of Government of the United States shall appoint in such manner as the Congress may direct:

A number of electors of President and Vice President equal to the whole number of Senators and Representatives in Congress to which the District would be entitled if it were a State, but in no event more than the least populous state; they shall be in addition to those appointed by the states, but they shall be considered, for the purposes of the election of President and Vice President, to be electors appointed by a state; and they shall meet in the District and perform such duties as provided by the twelfth article of amendment.

Section 2. The Congress shall have power to enforce this article by appropriate legislation.

AMENDMENT XXIV [1964]

Section 1. The right of citizens of the United States to vote in any primary or other election for President or Vice President, for electors for President or Vice President, or for Senator or Representative in Congress, shall not be denied or abridged by the United States, or any State by reason of failure to pay any poll tax or other tax.

Section 2. The Congress shall have power to enforce this article by appropriate legislation.

AMENDMENT XXV [1967]

Section 1. In case of the removal of the President from office or of his death or resignation, the Vice President shall become President.

Section 2. Whenever there is a vacancy in the office of the Vice President, the President shall nominate a Vice President who shall take office upon confirmation by a majority vote of both Houses of Congress.

Section 3. Whenever the President transmits to the President pro tempore of the Senate and the Speaker of the House of Representatives his written declaration that he is unable to discharge the powers and duties of his office, and until he transmits to them a written declaration to the contrary, such powers and duties shall be discharged by the Vice President as Acting President.

Section 4. Whenever the Vice President and a majority of either the principal officers of the executive departments or of such other body as Congress may by law provide, transmit to the President pro tempore of the Senate and the Speaker of the House of Representatives their written declaration that the President is unable to discharge the powers and duties of his office, the Vice President shall immediately assume the powers and duties of the office as Acting President.

Thereafter, when the President transmits to the President pro tempore of the Senate and the Speaker of the House of Representatives his written declaration that no inability exists, he shall resume the powers and duties of his office unless the Vice President and a majority of either the principal officers of the executive department or of such other body as Congress may by law provide, transmit within four days to the President pro tempore of the Senate and the Speaker of the House of Representatives their written declaration that the President is unable to discharge the powers and duties of his office. Thereupon Congress shall decide the issue, assembling within forty-eight hours for that purpose if not in session. If the Congress, within twenty-one days after receipt of the latter written declaration, or, if Congress is not in session, within twenty-one days after Congress is required to assemble, determines by two-thirds vote of both Houses that the President is unable to discharge the powers and duties of his office, the Vice President shall continue to discharge the same as Acting President; otherwise, the President shall resume the powers and duties of his office.

AMENDMENT XXVI [1971]

Section 1. The right of citizens of the United States, who are eighteen years of age or older, to vote shall not be denied or abridged by the United States or by any State on account of age.

Section 2. The Congress shall have power to enforce this article by appropriate legislation.

AMENDMENT XXVII [1992]

No law, varying the compensation for the services of the Senators and Representatives, shall take effect, until an election of Representatives shall have intervened.

APPENDIX B

Articles 2 and 2A of the Uniform Commercial Code

Article 2
SALES

Part 1 Short Title, General Construction and Subject Matter

§ 2–101. Short Title.

This Article shall be known and may be cited as Uniform Commercial Code—Sales.

§ 2–102. Scope; Certain Security and Other Transactions Excluded From This Article.

Unless the context otherwise requires, this Article applies to transactions in goods; it does not apply to any transaction which although in the form of an unconditional contract to sell or present sale is intended to operate only as a security transaction nor does this Article impair or repeal any statute regulating sales to consumers, farmers or other specified classes of buyers.

§ 2–103. Definitions and Index of Definitions.

(1) In this Article unless the context otherwise requires

(a) "Buyer" means a person who buys or contracts to buy goods.

(b) "Good faith" in the case of a merchant means honesty in fact and the observance of reasonable commercial standards of fair dealing in the trade.

(c) "Receipt" of goods means taking physical possession of them.

(d) "Seller" means a person who sells or contracts to sell goods.

(2) Other definitions applying to this Article or to specified Parts thereof, and the sections in which they appear are:

"Acceptance". Section 2–606.
"Banker's credit". Section 2–325.
"Between merchants". Section 2–104.
"Cancellation". Section 2–106(4).
"Commercial unit". Section 2–105.
"Confirmed credit". Section 2–325.
"Conforming to contract". Section 2–106.
"Contract for sale". Section 2–106.
"Cover". Section 2–712.
"Entrusting". Section 2–403.
"Financing agency". Section 2–104.
"Future goods". Section 2–105.
"Goods". Section 2–105.
"Identification". Section 2–501.
"Installment contract". Section 2–612.
"Letter of Credit". Section 2–325.
"Lot". Section 2–105.
"Merchant". Section 2–104.
"Overseas". Section 2–323.
"Person in position of seller". Section 2–707.
"Present sale". Section 2–106.
"Sale". Section 2–106.
"Sale on approval". Section 2–326.
"Sale or return". Section 2–326.
"Termination". Section 2–106.

(3) The following definitions in other Articles apply to this Article:

"Check". Section 3–104.

"Consignee". Section 7–102.

"Consignor". Section 7–102.

"Consumer goods". Section 9–109.

"Dishonor". Section 3–507.

"Draft". Section 3–104.

(4) In addition Article 1 contains general definitions and principles of construction and interpretation applicable throughout this Article.

As amended in 1994 and 1999.

§ 2–104. Definitions: "Merchant"; "Between Merchants"; "Financing Agency".

(1) "Merchant" means a person who deals in goods of the kind or otherwise by his occupation holds himself out as having knowledge or skill peculiar to the practices or goods involved in the transaction or to whom such knowledge or skill may be attributed by his employment of an agent or broker or other intermediary who by his occupation holds himself out as having such knowledge or skill.

(2) "Financing agency" means a bank, finance company or other person who in the ordinary course of business makes advances against goods or documents of title or who by arrangement with either the seller or the buyer intervenes in ordinary course to make or collect payment due or claimed under the contract for sale, as by purchasing or paying the seller's draft or making advances against it or by merely taking it for collection whether or not documents of title accompany the draft. "Financing agency" includes also a bank or other person who similarly intervenes between persons who are in the position of seller and buyer in respect to the goods (Section 2–707).

(3) "Between merchants" means in any transaction with respect to which both parties are chargeable with the knowledge or skill of merchants.

§ 2–105. Definitions: Transferability; "Goods"; "Future" Goods; "Lot"; "Commercial Unit".

(1) "Goods" means all things (including specially manufactured goods) which are movable at the time of identification to the contract for sale other than the money in which the price is to be paid, investment securities (Article 8) and things in action. "Goods" also includes the unborn young of animals and growing crops and other identified things attached to realty as described in the section on goods to be severed from realty (Section 2–107).

(2) Goods must be both existing and identified before any interest in them can pass. Goods which are not both existing and identified are "future" goods. A purported present sale of future goods or of any interest therein operates as a contract to sell.

(3) There may be a sale of a part interest in existing identified goods.

(4) An undivided share in an identified bulk of fungible goods is sufficiently identified to be sold although the quantity of the bulk is not determined. Any agreed proportion of such a bulk or any quantity thereof agreed upon by number, weight or other measure may to the extent of the seller's interest in the bulk be sold to the buyer who then becomes an owner in common.

(5) "Lot" means a parcel or a single article which is the subject matter of a separate sale or delivery, whether or not it is sufficient to perform the contract.

(6) "Commercial unit" means such a unit of goods as by commercial usage is a single whole for purposes of sale and division of which materially impairs its character or value on the market or in use. A commercial unit may be a single article (as a machine) or a set of articles (as a suite of furniture or an assortment of sizes) or a quantity (as a bale, gross, or carload) or any other unit treated in use or in the relevant market as a single whole.

§ 2–106. Definitions: "Contract"; "Agreement"; "Contract for Sale"; "Sale"; "Present Sale"; "Conforming" to Contract; "Termination"; "Cancellation".

(1) In this Article unless the context otherwise requires "contract" and "agreement" are limited to those relating to the present or future sale of goods. "Contract for sale" includes both a present sale of goods and a contract to sell goods at a future time. A "sale" consists in the passing of title from the seller to the buyer for a price (Section 2–401). A "present sale" means a sale which is accomplished by the making of the contract.

(2) Goods or conduct including any part of a performance are "conforming" or conform to the contract when they are in accordance with the obligations under the contract.

(3) "Termination" occurs when either party pursuant to a power created by agreement or law puts an end to the contract otherwise than for its breach. On "termination" all obligations which are still executory on both sides are discharged but any right based on prior breach or performance survives.

(4) "Cancellation" occurs when either party puts an end to the contract for breach by the other and its effect is the same as that of "termination" except that the cancelling party also retains any remedy for breach of the whole contract or any unperformed balance.

§ 2–107. Goods to Be Severed From Realty: Recording.

(1) A contract for the sale of minerals or the like (including oil and gas) or a structure or its materials to be removed from realty is a contract for the sale of goods within this Article if they are to be severed by the seller but until severance a purported present sale thereof which is not effective as a transfer of an interest in land is effective only as a contract to sell.

(2) A contract for the sale apart from the land of growing crops or other things attached to realty and capable of severance without material harm thereto but not described in subsection (1) or of timber to be cut is a contract for the sale of goods within this Article whether the subject matter is to be severed by the buyer or by the seller even though it forms part of the realty at the time of contracting, and the parties can by identification effect a present sale before severance.

(3) The provisions of this section are subject to any third party rights provided by the law relating to realty records, and the contract for sale may be executed and recorded as a document transferring an interest in land and shall then constitute notice to third parties of the buyer's rights under the contract for sale.

As amended in 1972.

Part 2 Form, Formation and Readjustment of Contract

§ 2–201. Formal Requirements; Statute of Frauds.

(1) Except as otherwise provided in this section a contract for the sale of goods for the price of $500 or more is not enforceable by way of action or defense unless there is some writing sufficient to indicate that a contract for sale has been made between the parties and signed by the party against whom enforcement is sought or by his authorized agent or broker. A writing is not insufficient because it omits or incorrectly states a term agreed upon but the contract is not enforceable under this paragraph beyond the quantity of goods shown in such writing.

(2) Between merchants if within a reasonable time a writing in confirmation of the contract and sufficient against the sender is received and the party receiving it has reason to know its contents, its satisfies the requirements of subsection (1) against such party unless written notice of objection to its contents is given within ten days after it is received.

(3) A contract which does not satisfy the requirements of subsection (1) but which is valid in other respects is enforceable

(a) if the goods are to be specially manufactured for the buyer and are not suitable for sale to others in the ordinary course of the seller's business and the seller, before notice of repudiation is received and under circumstances which reasonably indicate that the goods are for the buyer, has made either a substantial beginning of their manufacture or commitments for their procurement; or

(b) if the party against whom enforcement is sought admits in his pleading, testimony or otherwise in court that a contract for sale was made, but the contract is not enforceable under this provision beyond the quantity of goods admitted; or

(c) with respect to goods for which payment has been made and accepted or which have been received and accepted (Sec. 2–606).

§ 2–202. Final Written Expression: Parol or Extrinsic Evidence.

Terms with respect to which the confirmatory memoranda of the parties agree or which are otherwise set forth in a writing intended by the parties as a final expression of their agreement with respect to such terms as are included therein may not be contradicted by evidence of any prior agreement or of a contemporaneous oral agreement but may be explained or supplemented

(a) by course of dealing or usage of trade (Section 1–205) or by course of performance (Section 2–208); and

(b) by evidence of consistent additional terms unless the court finds the writing to have been intended also as a complete and exclusive statement of the terms of the agreement.

§ 2–203. Seals Inoperative.

The affixing of a seal to a writing evidencing a contract for sale or an offer to buy or sell goods does not constitute the writing a sealed instrument and the law with respect to sealed instruments does not apply to such a contract or offer.

§ 2–204. Formation in General.

(1) A contract for sale of goods may be made in any manner sufficient to show agreement, including conduct by both parties which recognizes the existence of such a contract.

(2) An agreement sufficient to constitute a contract for sale may be found even though the moment of its making is undetermined.

(3) Even though one or more terms are left open a contract for sale does not fail for indefiniteness if the parties have intended to make a contract and there is a reasonably certain basis for giving an appropriate remedy.

§ 2–205. Firm Offers.

An offer by a merchant to buy or sell goods in a signed writing which by its terms gives assurance that it will be held open is not revocable, for lack of consideration, during the time stated or if no time is stated for a reasonable time, but in no event may such period of irrevocability exceed three months; but any such term of assurance on a form supplied by the offeree must be separately signed by the offeror.

§ 2–206. Offer and Acceptance in Formation of Contract.

(1) Unless other unambiguously indicated by the language or circumstances

(a) an offer to make a contract shall be construed as inviting acceptance in any manner and by any medium reasonable in the circumstances;

(b) an order or other offer to buy goods for prompt or current shipment shall be construed as inviting acceptance either by a prompt promise to ship or by the prompt or current shipment of conforming or nonconforming goods, but such a shipment of non-conforming goods does not constitute an acceptance if the seller seasonably notifies the buyer that the shipment is offered only as an accommodation to the buyer.

(2) Where the beginning of a requested performance is a reasonable mode of acceptance an offeror who is not notified of acceptance within a reasonable time may treat the offer as having lapsed before acceptance.

§ 2–207. Additional Terms in Acceptance or Confirmation.

(1) A definite and seasonable expression of acceptance or a written confirmation which is sent within a reasonable time

operates as an acceptance even though it states terms additional to or different from those offered or agreed upon, unless acceptance is expressly made conditional on assent to the additional or different terms.

(2) The additional terms are to be construed as proposals for addition to the contract. Between merchants such terms become part of the contract unless:

(a) the offer expressly limits acceptance to the terms of the offer;

(b) they materially alter it; or

(c) notification of objection to them has already been given or is given within a reasonable time after notice of them is received.

(3) Conduct by both parties which recognizes the existence of a contract is sufficient to establish a contract for sale although the writings of the parties do not otherwise establish a contract. In such case the terms of the particular contract consist of those terms on which the writings of the parties agree, together with any supplementary terms incorporated under any other provisions of this Act.

§ 2–208. Course of Performance or Practical Construction.

(1) Where the contract for sale involves repeated occasions for performance by either party with knowledge of the nature of the performance and opportunity for objection to it by the other, any course of performance accepted or acquiesced in without objection shall be relevant to determine the meaning of the agreement.

(2) The express terms of the agreement and any such course of performance, as well as any course of dealing and usage of trade, shall be construed whenever reasonable as consistent with each other; but when such construction is unreasonable, express terms shall control course of performance and course of performance shall control both course of dealing and usage of trade (Section 1–205).

(3) Subject to the provisions of the next section on modification and waiver, such course of performance shall be relevant to show a waiver or modification of any term inconsistent with such course of performance.

§ 2–209. Modification, Rescission and Waiver.

(1) An agreement modifying a contract within this Article needs no consideration to be binding.

(2) A signed agreement which excludes modification or rescission except by a signed writing cannot be otherwise modified or rescinded, but except as between merchants such a requirement on a form supplied by the merchant must be separately signed by the other party.

(3) The requirements of the statute of frauds section of this Article (Section 2–201) must be satisfied if the contract as modified is within its provisions.

(4) Although an attempt at modification or rescission does not satisfy the requirements of subsection (2) or (3) it can operate as a waiver.

(5) A party who has made a waiver affecting an executory portion of the contract may retract the waiver by reasonable notification received by the other party that strict performance will be required of any term waived, unless the retraction would be unjust in view of a material change of position in reliance on the waiver.

§ 2–210. Delegation of Performance; Assignment of Rights.

(1) A party may perform his duty through a delegate unless otherwise agreed or unless the other party has a substantial interest in having his original promisor perform or control the acts required by the contract. No delegation of performance relieves the party delegating of any duty to perform or any liability for breach.

(2) Except as otherwise provided in Section 9–406, unless otherwise agreed, all rights of either seller or buyer can be assigned except where the assignment would materially change the duty of the other party, or increase materially the burden or risk imposed on him by his contract, or impair materially his chance of obtaining return performance. A right to damages for breach of the whole contract or a right arising out of the assignor's due performance of his entire obligation can be assigned despite agreement otherwise.

(3) The creation, attachment, perfection, or enforcement of a security interest in the seller's interest under a contract is not a transfer that materially changes the duty of or increases materially the burden or risk imposed on the buyer or impairs materially the buyer's chance of obtaining return performance within the purview of subsection (2) unless, and then only to the extent that, enforcement actually results in a delegation of material performance of the seller. Even in that event, the creation, attachment, perfection, and enforcement of the security interest remain effective, but (i) the seller is liable to the buyer for damages caused by the delegation to the extent that the damages could not reasonably by prevented by the buyer, and (ii) a court having jurisdiction may grant other appropriate relief, including cancellation of the contract for sale or an injunction against enforcement of the security interest or consummation of the enforcement.

(4) Unless the circumstnaces indicate the contrary a prohibition of assignment of "the contract" is to be construed as barring only the delegation to the assignee of the assignor's performance.

(5) An assignment of "the contract" or of "all my rights under the contract" or an assignment in similar general terms is an assignment of rights and unless the language or the circumstances (as in an assignment for security) indicate the contrary, it is a delegation of performance of the duties of the assignor and its acceptance by the assignee constitutes a promise by him to perform those duties. This promise is enforceable by either the assignor or the other party to the original contract.

(6) The other party may treat any assignment which delegates performance as creating reasonable grounds for insecurity and may without prejudice to his rights against the assignor demand assurances from the assignee (Section 2–609).

As amended in 1999.

Part 3 General Obligation and Construction of Contract

§ 2–301. General Obligations of Parties.

The obligation of the seller is to transfer and deliver and that of the buyer is to accept and pay in accordance with the contract.

§ 2–302. Unconscionable Contract or Clause.

(1) If the court as a matter of law finds the contract or any clause of the contract to have been unconscionable at the time it was made the court may refuse to enforce the contract, or it may enforce the remainder of the contract without the unconscionable clause, or it may so limit the application of any unconscionable clause as to avoid any unconscionable result.

(2) When it is claimed or appears to the court that the contract or any clause thereof may be unconscionable the parties shall be afforded a reasonable opportunity to present evidence as to its commercial setting, purpose and effect to aid the court in making the determination.

§ 2–303. Allocations or Division of Risks.

Where this Article allocates a risk or a burden as between the parties "unless otherwise agreed", the agreement may not only shift the allocation but may also divide the risk or burden.

§ 2–304. Price Payable in Money, Goods, Realty, or Otherwise.

(1) The price can be made payable in money or otherwise. If it is payable in whole or in part in goods each party is a seller of the goods which he is to transfer.

(2) Even though all or part of the price is payable in an interest in realty the transfer of the goods and the seller's obligations with reference to them are subject to this Article, but not the transfer of the interest in realty or the transferor's obligations in connection therewith.

§ 2–305. Open Price Term.

(1) The parties if they so intend can conclude a contract for sale even though the price is not settled. In such a case the price is a reasonable price at the time for delivery if

(a) nothing is said as to price; or

(b) the price is left to be agreed by the parties and they fail to agree; or

(c) the price is to be fixed in terms of some agreed market or other standard as set or recorded by a third person or agency and it is not so set or recorded.

(2) A price to be fixed by the seller or by the buyer means a price for him to fix in good faith.

(3) When a price left to be fixed otherwise than by agreement of the parties fails to be fixed through fault of one party the other may at his option treat the contract as cancelled or himself fix a reasonable price.

(4) Where, however, the parties intend not to be bound unless the price be fixed or agreed and it is not fixed or agreed there is

no contract. In such a case the buyer must return any goods already received or if unable so to do must pay their reasonable value at the time of delivery and the seller must return any portion of the price paid on account.

§ 2–306. Output, Requirements and Exclusive Dealings.

(1) A term which measures the quantity by the output of the seller or the requirements of the buyer means such actual output or requirements as may occur in good faith, except that no quantity unreasonably disproportionate to any stated estimate or in the absence of a stated estimate to any normal or otherwise comparable prior output or requirements may be tendered or demanded.

(2) A lawful agreement by either the seller or the buyer for exclusive dealing in the kind of goods concerned imposes unless otherwise agreed an obligation by the seller to use best efforts to supply the goods and by the buyer to use best efforts to promote their sale.

§ 2–307. Delivery in Single Lot or Several Lots.

Unless otherwise agreed all goods called for by a contract for sale must be tendered in a single delivery and payment is due only on such tender but where the circumstances give either party the right to make or demand delivery in lots the price if it can be apportioned may be demanded for each lot.

§ 2–308. Absence of Specified Place for Delivery.

Unless otherwise agreed

(a) the place for delivery of goods is the seller's place of business or if he has none his residence; but

(b) in a contract for sale of identified goods which to the knowledge of the parties at the time of contracting are in some other place, that place is the place for their delivery; and

(c) documents of title may be delivered through customary banking channels.

§ 2–309. Absence of Specific Time Provisions; Notice of Termination.

(1) The time for shipment or delivery or any other action under a contract if not provided in this Article or agreed upon shall be a reasonable time.

(2) Where the contract provides for successive performances but is indefinite in duration it is valid for a reasonable time but unless otherwise agreed may be terminated at any time by either party.

(3) Termination of a contract by one party except on the happening of an agreed event requires that reasonable notification be received by the other party and an agreement dispensing with notification is invalid if its operation would be unconscionable.

§ 2–310. Open Time for Payment or Running of Credit; Authority to Ship Under Reservation.

Unless otherwise agreed

(a) payment is due at the time and place at which the buyer is to receive the goods even though the place of shipment is the place of delivery; and

(b) if the seller is authorized to send the goods he may ship them under reservation, and may tender the documents of title, but the buyer may inspect the goods after their arrival before payment is due unless such inspection is inconsistent with the terms of the contract (Section 2–513); and

(c) if delivery is authorized and made by way of documents of title otherwise than by subsection (b) then payment is due at the time and place at which the buyer is to receive the documents regardless of where the goods are to be received; and

(d) where the seller is required or authorized to ship the goods on credit the credit period runs from the time of shipment but post-dating the invoice or delaying its dispatch will correspondingly delay the starting of the credit period.

§ 2–311. Options and Cooperation Respecting Performance.

(1) An agreement for sale which is otherwise sufficiently definite (subsection (3) of Section 2–204) to be a contract is not made invalid by the fact that it leaves particulars of performance to be specified by one of the parties. Any such specification must be made in good faith and within limits set by commercial reasonableness.

(2) Unless otherwise agreed specifications relating to assortment of the goods are at the buyer's option and except as otherwise provided in subsections (1)(c) and (3) of Section 2–319 specifications or arrangements relating to shipment are at the seller's option.

(3) Where such specification would materially affect the other party's performance but is not seasonably made or where one party's cooperation is necessary to the agreed performance of the other but is not seasonably forthcoming, the other party in addition to all other remedies

(a) is excused for any resulting delay in his own performance; and

(b) may also either proceed to perform in any reasonable manner or after the time for a material part of his own performance treat the failure to specify or to cooperate as a breach by failure to deliver or accept the goods.

§ 2–312. Warranty of Title and Against Infringement; Buyer's Obligation Against Infringement.

(1) Subject to subsection (2) there is in a contract for sale a warranty by the seller that

(a) the title conveyed shall be good, and its transfer rightful; and

(b) the goods shall be delivered free from any security interest or other lien or encumbrance of which the buyer at the time of contracting has no knowledge.

(2) A warranty under subsection (1) will be excluded or modified only by specific language or by circumstances which give the buyer reason to know that the person selling does not claim title in himself or that he is purporting to sell only such right or title as he or a third person may have.

(3) Unless otherwise agreed a seller who is a merchant regularly dealing in goods of the kind warrants that the goods shall be delivered free of the rightful claim of any third person by way of infringement or the like but a buyer who furnishes specifications to the seller must hold the seller harmless against any such claim which arises out of compliance with the specifications.

§ 2–313. Express Warranties by Affirmation, Promise, Description, Sample.

(1) Express warranties by the seller are created as follows:

(a) Any affirmation of fact or promise made by the seller to the buyer which relates to the goods and becomes part of the basis of the bargain creates an express warranty that the goods shall conform to the affirmation or promise.

(b) Any description of the goods which is made part of the basis of the bargain creates an express warranty that the goods shall conform to the description.

(c) Any sample or model which is made part of the basis of the bargain creates an express warranty that the whole of the goods shall conform to the sample or model.

(2) It is not necessary to the creation of an express warranty that the seller use formal words such as "warrant" or "guarantee" or that he have a specific intention to make a warranty, but an affirmation merely of the value of the goods or a statement purporting to be merely the seller's opinion or commendation of the goods does not create a warranty.

§ 2–314. Implied Warranty: Merchantability; Usage of Trade.

(1) Unless excluded or modified (Section 2–316), a warranty that the goods shall be merchantable is implied in a contract for their sale if the seller is a merchant with respect to goods of that kind. Under this section the serving for value of food or drink to be consumed either on the premises or elsewhere is a sale.

(2) Goods to be merchantable must be at least such as

(a) pass without objection in the trade under the contract description; and

(b) in the case of fungible goods, are of fair average quality within the description; and

(c) are fit for the ordinary purposes for which such goods are used; and

(d) run, within the variations permitted by the agreement, of even kind, quality and quantity within each unit and among all units involved; and

(e) are adequately contained, packaged, and labeled as the agreement may require; and

(f) conform to the promises or affirmations of fact made on the container or label if any.

(3) Unless excluded or modified (Section 2–316) other implied warranties may arise from course of dealing or usage of trade.

§ 2–315. Implied Warranty: Fitness for Particular Purpose.

Where the seller at the time of contracting has reason to know any particular purpose for which the goods are required and that the buyer is relying on the seller's skill or judgment to select or furnish suitable goods, there is unless excluded or modified under the next section an implied warranty that the goods shall be fit for such purpose.

§ 2–316. Exclusion or Modification of Warranties.

(1) Words or conduct relevant to the creation of an express warranty and words or conduct tending to negate or limit warranty shall be construed wherever reasonable as consistent with each other; but subject to the provisions of this Article on parol or extrinsic evidence (Section 2–202) negation or limitation is inoperative to the extent that such construction is unreasonable.

(2) Subject to subsection (3), to exclude or modify the implied warranty of merchantability or any part of it the language must mention merchantability and in case of a writing must be conspicuous, and to exclude or modify any implied warranty of fitness the exclusion must be by a writing and conspicuous. Language to exclude all implied warranties of fitness is sufficient if it states, for example, that "There are no warranties which extend beyond the description on the face hereof."

(3) Notwithstanding subsection (2)

(a) unless the circumstances indicate otherwise, all implied warranties are excluded by expressions like "as is", "with all faults" or other language which in common understanding calls the buyer's attention to the exclusion of warranties and makes plain that there is no implied warranty; and

(b) when the buyer before entering into the contract has examined the goods or the sample or model as fully as he desired or has refused to examine the goods there is no implied warranty with regard to defects which an examination ought in the circumstances to have revealed to him; and

(c) an implied warranty can also be excluded or modified by course of dealing or course of performance or usage of trade.

(4) Remedies for breach of warranty can be limited in accordance with the provisions of this Article on liquidation or limitation of damages and on contractual modification of remedy (Sections 2–718 and 2–719).

§ 2–317. Cumulation and Conflict of Warranties Express or Implied.

Warranties whether express or implied shall be construed as consistent with each other and as cumulative, but if such construction is unreasonable the intention of the parties shall determine which warranty is dominant. In ascertaining that intention the following rules apply:

(a) Exact or technical specifications displace an inconsistent sample or model or general language of description.

(b) A sample from an existing bulk displaces inconsistent general language of description.

(c) Express warranties displace inconsistent implied warranties other than an implied warranty of fitness for a particular purpose.

§ 2–318. Third Party Beneficiaries of Warranties Express or Implied.

Note: If this Act is introduced in the Congress of the United States this section should be omitted. (States to select one alternative.)

Alternative A

A seller's warranty whether express or implied extends to any natural person who is in the family or household of his buyer or who is a guest in his home if it is reasonable to expect that such person may use, consume or be affected by the goods and who is injured in person by breach of the warranty. A seller may not exclude or limit the operation of this section.

Alternative B

A seller's warranty whether express or implied extends to any natural person who may reasonably be expected to use, consume or be affected by the goods and who is injured in person by breach of the warranty. A seller may not exclude or limit the operation of this section.

Alternative C

A seller's warranty whether express or implied extends to any person who may reasonably be expected to use, consume or be affected by the goods and who is injured by breach of the warranty. A seller may not exclude or limit the operation of this section with respect to injury to the person of an individual to whom the warranty extends.

As amended 1966.

§ 2–319. F.O.B. and F.A.S. Terms.

(1) Unless otherwise agreed the term F.O.B. (which means "free on board") at a named place, even though used only in connection with the stated price, is a delivery term under which

(a) when the term is F.O.B. the place of shipment, the seller must at that place ship the goods in the manner provided in this Article (Section 2–504) and bear the expense and risk of putting them into the possession of the carrier; or

(b) when the term is F.O.B. the place of destination, the seller must at his own expense and risk transport the goods to that place and there tender delivery of them in the manner provided in this Article (Section 2–503);

(c) when under either (a) or (b) the term is also F.O.B. vessel, car or other vehicle, the seller must in addition at his own expense and risk load the goods on board. If the term is F.O.B. vessel the buyer must name the vessel and in an appropriate case the seller must comply with the provisions of this Article on the form of bill of lading (Section 2–323).

(2) Unless otherwise agreed the term F.A.S. vessel (which means "free alongside") at a named port, even though used

only in connection with the stated price, is a delivery term under which the seller must

(a) at his own expense and risk deliver the goods alongside the vessel in the manner usual in that port or on a dock designated and provided by the buyer; and

(b) obtain and tender a receipt for the goods in exchange for which the carrier is under a duty to issue a bill of lading.

(3) Unless otherwise agreed in any case falling within subsection (1)(a) or (c) or subsection (2) the buyer must seasonably give any needed instructions for making delivery, including when the term is F.A.S. or F.O.B. the loading berth of the vessel and in an appropriate case its name and sailing date. The seller may treat the failure of needed instructions as a failure of cooperation under this Article (Section 2–311). He may also at his option move the goods in any reasonable manner preparatory to delivery or shipment.

(4) Under the term F.O.B. vessel or F.A.S. unless otherwise agreed the buyer must make payment against tender of the required documents and the seller may not tender nor the buyer demand delivery of the goods in substitution for the documents.

§ 2–320. C.I.F. and C. & F. Terms.

(1) The term C.I.F. means that the price includes in a lump sum the cost of the goods and the insurance and freight to the named destination. The term C. & F. or C.F. means that the price so includes cost and freight to the named destination.

(2) Unless otherwise agreed and even though used only in connection with the stated price and destination, the term C.I.F. destination or its equivalent requires the seller at his own expense and risk to

(a) put the goods into the possession of a carrier at the port for shipment and obtain a negotiable bill or bills of lading covering the entire transportation to the named destination; and

(b) load the goods and obtain a receipt from the carrier (which may be contained in the bill of lading) showing that the freight has been paid or provided for; and

(c) obtain a policy or certificate of insurance, including any war risk insurance, of a kind and on terms then current at the port of shipment in the usual amount, in the currency of the contract, shown to cover the same goods covered by the bill of lading and providing for payment of loss to the order of the buyer or for the account of whom it may concern; but the seller may add to the price the amount of the premium for any such war risk insurance; and

(d) prepare an invoice of the goods and procure any other documents required to effect shipment or to comply with the contract; and

(e) forward and tender with commercial promptness all the documents in due form and with any indorsement necessary to perfect the buyer's rights.

(3) Unless otherwise agreed the term C. & F. or its equivalent has the same effect and imposes upon the seller the same obligations and risks as a C.I.F. term except the obligation as to insurance.

(4) Under the term C.I.F. or C. & F. unless otherwise agreed the buyer must make payment against tender of the required documents and the seller may not tender nor the buyer demand delivery of the goods in substitution for the documents.

§ 2–321. C.I.F. or C. & F.: "Net Landed Weights"; "Payment on Arrival"; Warranty of Condition on Arrival.

Under a contract containing a term C.I.F. or C. & F.

(1) Where the price is based on or is to be adjusted according to "net landed weights", "delivered weights", "out turn" quantity or quality or the like, unless otherwise agreed the seller must reasonably estimate the price. The payment due on tender of the documents called for by the contract is the amount so estimated, but after final adjustment of the price a settlement must be made with commercial promptness.

(2) An agreement described in subsection (1) or any warranty of quality or condition of the goods on arrival places upon the seller the risk of ordinary deterioration, shrinkage and the like in transportation but has no effect on the place or time of identification to the contract for sale or delivery or on the passing of the risk of loss.

(3) Unless otherwise agreed where the contract provides for payment on or after arrival of the goods the seller must before payment allow such preliminary inspection as is feasible; but if the goods are lost delivery of the documents and payment are due when the goods should have arrived.

§ 2–322. Delivery "Ex-Ship".

(1) Unless otherwise agreed a term for delivery of goods "ex-ship" (which means from the carrying vessel) or in equivalent language is not restricted to a particular ship and requires delivery from a ship which has reached a place at the named port of destination where goods of the kind are usually discharged.

(2) Under such a term unless otherwise agreed

(a) the seller must discharge all liens arising out of the carriage and furnish the buyer with a direction which puts the carrier under a duty to deliver the goods; and

(b) the risk of loss does not pass to the buyer until the goods leave the ship's tackle or are otherwise properly unloaded.

§ 2–323. Form of Bill of Lading Required in Overseas Shipment; "Overseas".

(1) Where the contract contemplates overseas shipment and contains a term C.I.F. or C. & F. or F.O.B. vessel, the seller unless otherwise agreed must obtain a negotiable bill of lading stating that the goods have been loaded on board or, in the case of a term C.I.F. or C. & F., received for shipment.

(2) Where in a case within subsection (1) a bill of lading has been issued in a set of parts, unless otherwise agreed if the documents

are not to be sent from abroad the buyer may demand tender of the full set; otherwise only one part of the bill of lading need be tendered. Even if the agreement expressly requires a full set

(a) due tender of a single part is acceptable within the provisions of this Article on cure of improper delivery (subsection (1) of Section 2–508); and

(b) even though the full set is demanded, if the documents are sent from abroad the person tendering an incomplete set may nevertheless require payment upon furnishing an indemnity which the buyer in good faith deems adequate.

(3) A shipment by water or by air or a contract contemplating such shipment is "overseas" insofar as by usage of trade or agreement it is subject to the commercial, financing or shipping practices characteristic of international deep water commerce.

§ 2–324. "No Arrival, No Sale" Term.

Under a term "no arrival, no sale" or terms of like meaning, unless otherwise agreed,

(a) the seller must properly ship conforming goods and if they arrive by any means he must tender them on arrival but he assumes no obligation that the goods will arrive unless he has caused the non-arrival; and

(b) where without fault of the seller the goods are in part lost or have so deteriorated as no longer to conform to the contract or arrive after the contract time, the buyer may proceed as if there had been casualty to identified goods (Section 2–613).

§ 2–325. "Letter of Credit" Term; "Confirmed Credit".

(1) Failure of the buyer seasonably to furnish an agreed letter of credit is a breach of the contract for sale.

(2) The delivery to seller of a proper letter of credit suspends the buyer's obligation to pay. If the letter of credit is dishonored, the seller may on seasonable notification to the buyer require payment directly from him.

(3) Unless otherwise agreed the term "letter of credit" or "banker's credit" in a contract for sale means an irrevocable credit issued by a financing agency of good repute and, where the shipment is overseas, of good international repute. The term "confirmed credit" means that the credit must also carry the direct obligation of such an agency which does business in the seller's financial market.

§ 2–326. Sale on Approval and Sale or Return; Rights of Creditors.

(1) Unless otherwise agreed, if delivered goods may be returned by the buyer even though they conform to the contract, the transaction is

(a) a "sale on approval" if the goods are delivered primarily for use, and

(b) a "sale or return" if the goods are delivered primarily for resale.

(2) Goods held on approval are not subject to the claims of the buyer's creditors until acceptance; goods held on sale or return are subject to such claims while in the buyer's possession.

(3) Any "or return" term of a contract for sale is to be treated as a separate contract for sale within the statute of frauds section of this Article (Section 2–201) and as contradicting the sale aspect of the contract within the provisions of this Article or on parol or extrinsic evidence (Section 2–202).

As amended in 1999.

§ 2–327. Special Incidents of Sale on Approval and Sale or Return.

(1) Under a sale on approval unless otherwise agreed

(a) although the goods are identified to the contract the risk of loss and the title do not pass to the buyer until acceptance; and

(b) use of the goods consistent with the purpose of trial is not acceptance but failure seasonably to notify the seller of election to return the goods is acceptance, and if the goods conform to the contract acceptance of any part is acceptance of the whole; and

(c) after due notification of election to return, the return is at the seller's risk and expense but a merchant buyer must follow any reasonable instructions.

(2) Under a sale or return unless otherwise agreed

(a) the option to return extends to the whole or any commercial unit of the goods while in substantially their original condition, but must be exercised seasonably; and

(b) the return is at the buyer's risk and expense.

§ 2–328. Sale by Auction.

(1) In a sale by auction if goods are put up in lots each lot is the subject of a separate sale.

(2) A sale by auction is complete when the auctioneer so announces by the fall of the hammer or in other customary manner. Where a bid is made while the hammer is falling in acceptance of a prior bid the auctioneer may in his discretion reopen the bidding or declare the goods sold under the bid on which the hammer was falling.

(3) Such a sale is with reserve unless the goods are in explicit terms put up without reserve. In an auction with reserve the auctioneer may withdraw the goods at any time until he announces completion of the sale. In an auction without reserve, after the auctioneer calls for bids on an article or lot, that article or lot cannot be withdrawn unless no bid is made within a reasonable time. In either case a bidder may retract his bid until the auctioneer's announcement of completion of the sale, but a bidder's retraction does not revive any previous bid.

(4) If the auctioneer knowingly receives a bid on the seller's behalf or the seller makes or procures such as bid, and notice has not been given that liberty for such bidding is reserved, the buyer may at his option avoid the sale or take the goods at the

price of the last good faith bid prior to the completion of the sale. This subsection shall not apply to any bid at a forced sale.

Part 4 Title, Creditors and Good Faith Purchasers

§ 2–401. Passing of Title; Reservation for Security; Limited Application of This Section.

Each provision of this Article with regard to the rights, obligations and remedies of the seller, the buyer, purchasers or other third parties applies irrespective of title to the goods except where the provision refers to such title. Insofar as situations are not covered by the other provisions of this Article and matters concerning title became material the following rules apply:

(1) Title to goods cannot pass under a contract for sale prior to their identification to the contract (Section 2–501), and unless otherwise explicitly agreed the buyer acquires by their identification a special property as limited by this Act. Any retention or reservation by the seller of the title (property) in goods shipped or delivered to the buyer is limited in effect to a reservation of a security interest. Subject to these provisions and to the provisions of the Article on Secured Transactions (Article 9), title to goods passes from the seller to the buyer in any manner and on any conditions explicitly agreed on by the parties.

(2) Unless otherwise explicitly agreed title passes to the buyer at the time and place at which the seller completes his performance with reference to the physical delivery of the goods, despite any reservation of a security interest and even though a document of title is to be delivered at a different time or place; and in particular and despite any reservation of a security interest by the bill of lading

(a) if the contract requires or authorizes the seller to send the goods to the buyer but does not require him to deliver them at destination, title passes to the buyer at the time and place of shipment; but

(b) if the contract requires delivery at destination, title passes on tender there.

(3) Unless otherwise explicitly agreed where delivery is to be made without moving the goods,

(a) if the seller is to deliver a document of title, title passes at the time when and the place where he delivers such documents; or

(b) if the goods are at the time of contracting already identified and no documents are to be delivered, title passes at the time and place of contracting.

(4) A rejection or other refusal by the buyer to receive or retain the goods, whether or not justified, or a justified revocation of acceptance revests title to the goods in the seller. Such revesting occurs by operation of law and is not a "sale".

§ 2–402. Rights of Seller's Creditors Against Sold Goods.

(1) Except as provided in subsections (2) and (3), rights of unsecured creditors of the seller with respect to goods which have been identified to a contract for sale are subject to the buyer's rights to recover the goods under this Article (Sections 2–502 and 2–716).

(2) A creditor of the seller may treat a sale or an identification of goods to a contract for sale as void if as against him a retention of possession by the seller is fraudulent under any rule of law of the state where the goods are situated, except that retention of possession in good faith and current course of trade by a merchant-seller for a commercially reasonable time after a sale or identification is not fraudulent.

(3) Nothing in this Article shall be deemed to impair the rights of creditors of the seller

(a) under the provisions of the Article on Secured Transactions (Article 9); or

(b) where identification to the contract or delivery is made not in current course of trade but in satisfaction of or as security for a pre-existing claim for money, security or the like and is made under circumstances which under any rule of law of the state where the goods are situated would apart from this Article constitute the transaction a fraudulent transfer or voidable preference.

§ 2–403. Power to Transfer; Good Faith Purchase of Goods; "Entrusting".

(1) A purchaser of goods acquires all title which his transferor had or had power to transfer except that a purchaser of a limited interest acquires rights only to the extent of the interest purchased. A person with voidable title has power to transfer a good title to a good faith purchaser for value. When goods have been delivered under a transaction of purchase the purchaser has such power even though

(a) the transferor was deceived as to the identity of the purchaser, or

(b) the delivery was in exchange for a check which is later dishonored, or

(c) it was agreed that the transaction was to be a "cash sale", or

(d) the delivery was procured through fraud punishable as larcenous under the criminal law.

(2) Any entrusting of possession of goods to a merchant who deals in goods of that kind gives him power to transfer all rights of the entruster to a buyer in ordinary course of business.

(3) "Entrusting" includes any delivery and any acquiescence in retention of possession regardless of any condition expressed between the parties to the delivery or acquiescence and regardless of whether the procurement of the entrusting or the possessor's disposition of the goods have been such as to be larcenous under the criminal law.

(4) The rights of other purchasers of goods and of lien creditors are governed by the Articles on Secured Transactions (Article 9), Bulk Transfers (Article 6) and Documents of Title (Article 7).

As amended in 1988.

Part 5 Performance

§ 2–501. Insurable Interest in Goods; Manner of Identification of Goods.

(1) The buyer obtains a special property and an insurable interest in goods by identification of existing goods as goods to which the contract refers even though the goods so identified are nonconforming and he has an option to return or reject them. Such identification can be made at any time and in any manner explicitly agreed to by the parties. In the absence of explicit agreement identification occurs

(a) when the contract is made if it is for the sale of goods already existing and identified;

(b) if the contract is for the sale of future goods other than those described in paragraph (c), when goods are shipped, marked or otherwise designated by the seller as goods to which the contract refers;

(c) when the crops are planted or otherwise become growing crops or the young are conceived if the contract is for the sale of unborn young to be born within twelve months after contracting or for the sale of crops to be harvested within twelve months or the next normal harvest season after contracting whichever is longer.

(2) The seller retains an insurable interest in goods so long as title to or any security interest in the goods remains in him and where the identification is by the seller alone he may until default or insolvency or notification to the buyer that the identification is final substitute other goods for those identified.

(3) Nothing in this section impairs any insurable interest recognized under any other statute or rule of law.

§ 2–502. Buyer's Right to Goods on Seller's Insolvency.

(1) Subject to subsections (2) and (3) and even though the goods have not been shipped a buyer who has paid a part or all of the price of goods in which he has a special property under the provisions of the immediately preceding section may on making and keeping good a tender of any unpaid portion of their price recover them from the seller if:

(a) in the case of goods bought for personal, family, or household purposes, the seller repudiates or fails to deliver as required by the contract; or

(b) in all cases, the seller becomes insolvent within ten days after receipt of the first installment on their price.

(2) The buyer's right to recover the goods under subsection (1)(a) vests upon acquisition of a special property, even if the seller had not then repudiated or failed to deliver.

(3) If the identification creating his special property has been made by the buyer he acquires the right to recover the goods only if they conform to the contract for sale.

As amended in 1999.

§ 2–503. Manner of Seller's Tender of Delivery.

(1) Tender of delivery requires that the seller put and hold conforming goods at the buyer's disposition and give the buyer any notification reasonably necessary to enable him to take delivery. The manner, time and place for tender are determined by the agreement and this Article, and in particular

(a) tender must be at a reasonable hour, and if it is of goods they must be kept available for the period reasonably necessary to enable the buyer to take possession; but

(b) unless otherwise agreed the buyer must furnish facilities reasonably suited to the receipt of the goods.

(2) Where the case is within the next section respecting shipment tender requires that the seller comply with its provisions.

(3) Where the seller is required to deliver at a particular destination tender requires that he comply with subsection (1) and also in any appropriate case tender documents as described in subsections (4) and (5) of this section.

(4) Where goods are in the possession of a bailee and are to be delivered without being moved

(a) tender requires that the seller either tender a negotiable document of title covering such goods or procure acknowledgment by the bailee of the buyer's right to possession of the goods; but

(b) tender to the buyer of a non-negotiable document of title or of a written direction to the bailee to deliver is sufficient tender unless the buyer seasonably objects, and receipt by the bailee of notification of the buyer's rights fixes those rights as against the bailee and all third persons; but risk of loss of the goods and of any failure by the bailee to honor the non-negotiable document of title or to obey the direction remains on the seller until the buyer has had a reasonable time to present the document or direction, and a refusal by the bailee to honor the document or to obey the direction defeats the tender.

(5) Where the contract requires the seller to deliver documents

(a) he must tender all such documents in correct form, except as provided in this Article with respect to bills of lading in a set (subsection (2) of Section 2–323); and

(b) tender through customary banking channels is sufficient and dishonor of a draft accompanying the documents constitutes non-acceptance or rejection.

§ 2–504. Shipment by Seller.

Where the seller is required or authorized to send the goods to the buyer and the contract does not require him to deliver them at a particular destination, then unless otherwise agreed he must

(a) put the goods in the possession of such a carrier and make such a contract for their transportation as may be reasonable having regard to the nature of the goods and other circumstances of the case; and

(b) obtain and promptly deliver or tender in due form any document necessary to enable the buyer to obtain possession of the goods or otherwise required by the agreement or by usage of trade; and

(c) promptly notify the buyer of the shipment.

Failure to notify the buyer under paragraph (c) or to make a proper contract under paragraph (a) is a ground for rejection only if material delay or loss ensues.

§ 2–505. Seller's Shipment under Reservation.

(1) Where the seller has identified goods to the contract by or before shipment:

(a) his procurement of a negotiable bill of lading to his own order or otherwise reserves in him a security interest in the goods. His procurement of the bill to the order of a financing agency or of the buyer indicates in addition only the seller's expectation of transferring that interest to the person named.

(b) a non-negotiable bill of lading to himself or his nominee reserves possession of the goods as security but except in a case of conditional delivery (subsection (2) of Section 2–507) a non-negotiable bill of lading naming the buyer as consignee reserves no security interest even though the seller retains possession of the bill of lading.

(2) When shipment by the seller with reservation of a security interest is in violation of the contract for sale it constitutes an improper contract for transportation within the preceding section but impairs neither the rights given to the buyer by shipment and identification of the goods to the contract nor the seller's powers as a holder of a negotiable document.

§ 2–506. Rights of Financing Agency.

(1) A financing agency by paying or purchasing for value a draft which relates to a shipment of goods acquires to the extent of the payment or purchase and in addition to its own rights under the draft and any document of title securing it any rights of the shipper in the goods including the right to stop delivery and the shipper's right to have the draft honored by the buyer.

(2) The right to reimbursement of a financing agency which has in good faith honored or purchased the draft under commitment to or authority from the buyer is not impaired by subsequent discovery of defects with reference to any relevant document which was apparently regular on its face.

§ 2–507. Effect of Seller's Tender; Delivery on Condition.

(1) Tender of delivery is a condition to the buyer's duty to accept the goods and, unless otherwise agreed, to his duty to pay for them. Tender entitles the seller to acceptance of the goods and to payment according to the contract.

(2) Where payment is due and demanded on the delivery to the buyer of goods or documents of title, his right as against the seller to retain or dispose of them is conditional upon his making the payment due.

§ 2–508. Cure by Seller of Improper Tender or Delivery; Replacement.

(1) Where any tender or delivery by the seller is rejected because non-conforming and the time for performance has not yet expired, the seller may seasonably notify the buyer of his intention to cure and may then within the contract time make a conforming delivery.

(2) Where the buyer rejects a non-conforming tender which the seller had reasonable grounds to believe would be acceptable with or without money allowance the seller may if he seasonably notifies the buyer have a further reasonable time to substitute a conforming tender.

§ 2–509. Risk of Loss in the Absence of Breach.

(1) Where the contract requires or authorizes the seller to ship the goods by carrier

(a) if it does not require him to deliver them at a particular destination, the risk of loss passes to the buyer when the goods are duly delivered to the carrier even though the shipment is under reservation (Section 2–505); but

(b) if it does require him to deliver them at a particular destination and the goods are there duly tendered while in the possession of the carrier, the risk of loss passes to the buyer when the goods are there duly so tendered as to enable the buyer to take delivery.

(2) Where the goods are held by a bailee to be delivered without being moved, the risk of loss passes to the buyer

(a) on his receipt of a negotiable document of title covering the goods; or

(b) on acknowledgment by the bailee of the buyer's right to possession of the goods; or

(c) after his receipt of a non-negotiable document of title or other written direction to deliver, as provided in subsection (4)(b) of Section 2–503.

(3) In any case not within subsection (1) or (2), the risk of loss passes to the buyer on his receipt of the goods if the seller is a merchant; otherwise the risk passes to the buyer on tender of delivery.

(4) The provisions of this section are subject to contrary agreement of the parties and to the provisions of this Article on sale on approval (Section 2–327) and on effect of breach on risk of loss (Section 2–510).

§ 2–510. Effect of Breach on Risk of Loss.

(1) Where a tender or delivery of goods so fails to conform to the contract as to give a right of rejection the risk of their loss remains on the seller until cure or acceptance.

(2) Where the buyer rightfully revokes acceptance he may to the extent of any deficiency in his effective insurance coverage treat the risk of loss as having rested on the seller from the beginning.

(3) Where the buyer as to conforming goods already identified to the contract for sale repudiates or is otherwise in breach before risk of their loss has passed to him, the seller may to the extent of any deficiency in his effective insurance coverage treat the risk of loss as resting on the buyer for a commercially reasonable time.

§ 2–511. Tender of Payment by Buyer; Payment by Check.

(1) Unless otherwise agreed tender of payment is a condition to the seller's duty to tender and complete any delivery.

(2) Tender of payment is sufficient when made by any means or in any manner current in the ordinary course of business unless the seller demands payment in legal tender and gives any extension of time reasonably necessary to procure it.

(3) Subject to the provisions of this Act on the effect of an instrument on an obligation (Section 3–310), payment by check is conditional and is defeated as between the parties by dishonor of the check on due presentment.

As amended in 1994.

§ 2–512. Payment by Buyer Before Inspection.

(1) Where the contract requires payment before inspection non-conformity of the goods does not excuse the buyer from so making payment unless

(a) the non-conformity appears without inspection; or

(b) despite tender of the required documents the circumstances would justify injunction against honor under this Act (Section 5–109(b)).

(2) Payment pursuant to subsection (1) does not constitute an acceptance of goods or impair the buyer's right to inspect or any of his remedies.

As amended in 1995.

§ 2–513. Buyer's Right to Inspection of Goods.

(1) Unless otherwise agreed and subject to subsection (3), where goods are tendered or delivered or identified to the contract for sale, the buyer has a right before payment or acceptance to inspect them at any reasonable place and time and in any reasonable manner. When the seller is required or authorized to send the goods to the buyer, the inspection may be after their arrival.

(2) Expenses of inspection must be borne by the buyer but may be recovered from the seller if the goods do not conform and are rejected.

(3) Unless otherwise agreed and subject to the provisions of this Article on C.I.F. contracts (subsection (3) of Section 2–321), the buyer is not entitled to inspect the goods before payment of the price when the contract provides

(a) for delivery "C.O.D." or on other like terms; or

(b) for payment against documents of title, except where such payment is due only after the goods are to become available for inspection.

(4) A place or method of inspection fixed by the parties is presumed to be exclusive but unless otherwise expressly agreed it does not postpone identification or shift the place for delivery or for passing the risk of loss. If compliance becomes impossible, inspection shall be as provided in this section unless the place or method fixed was clearly intended as an indispensable condition failure of which avoids the contract.

§ 2–514. When Documents Deliverable on Acceptance; When on Payment.

Unless otherwise agreed documents against which a draft is drawn are to be delivered to the drawee on acceptance of the draft if it is payable more than three days after presentment; otherwise, only on payment.

§ 2–515. Preserving Evidence of Goods in Dispute.

In furtherance of the adjustment of any claim or dispute

(a) either party on reasonable notification to the other and for the purpose of ascertaining the facts and preserving evidence has the right to inspect, test and sample the goods including such of them as may be in the possession or control of the other; and

(b) the parties may agree to a third party inspection or survey to determine the conformity or condition of the goods and may agree that the findings shall be binding upon them in any subsequent litigation or adjustment.

Part 6 Breach, Repudiation and Excuse

§ 2–601. Buyer's Rights on Improper Delivery.

Subject to the provisions of this Article on breach in installment contracts (Section 2–612) and unless otherwise agreed under the sections on contractual limitations of remedy (Sections 2–718 and 2–719), if the goods or the tender of delivery fail in any respect to conform to the contract, the buyer may

(a) reject the whole; or

(b) accept the whole; or

(c) accept any commercial unit or units and reject the rest.

§ 2–602. Manner and Effect of Rightful Rejection.

(1) Rejection of goods must be within a reasonable time after their delivery or tender. It is ineffective unless the buyer seasonably notifies the seller.

(2) Subject to the provisions of the two following sections on rejected goods (Sections 2–603 and 2–604),

(a) after rejection any exercise of ownership by the buyer with respect to any commercial unit is wrongful as against the seller; and

(b) if the buyer has before rejection taken physical possession of goods in which he does not have a security interest under the provisions of this Article (subsection (3) of Section 2–711), he is under a duty after rejection to hold them with reasonable care at the seller's disposition for a time sufficient to permit the seller to remove them; but

(c) the buyer has no further obligations with regard to goods rightfully rejected.

(3) The seller's rights with respect to goods wrongfully rejected are governed by the provisions of this Article on Seller's remedies in general (Section 2–703).

§ 2–603. Merchant Buyer's Duties as to Rightfully Rejected Goods.

(1) Subject to any security interest in the buyer (subsection (3) of Section 2–711), when the seller has no agent or place of business at the market of rejection a merchant buyer is under a duty after rejection of goods in his possession or control to follow any reasonable instructions received from the seller with respect to the goods and in the absence of such instructions to make reasonable efforts to sell them for the seller's account if they are perishable or threaten to decline in value speedily. Instructions are not reasonable if on demand indemnity for expenses is not forthcoming.

(2) When the buyer sells goods under subsection (1), he is entitled to reimbursement from the seller or out of the proceeds for reasonable expenses of caring for and selling them, and if the expenses include no selling commission then to such commission as is usual in the trade or if there is none to a reasonable sum not exceeding ten per cent on the gross proceeds.

(3) In complying with this section the buyer is held only to good faith and good faith conduct hereunder is neither acceptance nor conversion nor the basis of an action for damages.

§ 2–604. Buyer's Options as to Salvage of Rightfully Rejected Goods.

Subject to the provisions of the immediately preceding section on perishables if the seller gives no instructions within a reasonable time after notification of rejection the buyer may store the rejected goods for the seller's account or reship them to him or resell them for the seller's account with reimbursement as provided in the preceding section. Such action is not acceptance or conversion.

§ 2–605. Waiver of Buyer's Objections by Failure to Particularize.

(1) The buyer's failure to state in connection with rejection a particular defect which is ascertainable by reasonable inspection precludes him from relying on the unstated defect to justify rejection or to establish breach

   (a) where the seller could have cured it if stated seasonably; or

   (b) between merchants when the seller has after rejection made a request in writing for a full and final written statement of all defects on which the buyer proposes to rely.

(2) Payment against documents made without reservation of rights precludes recovery of the payment for defects apparent on the face of the documents.

§ 2–606. What Constitutes Acceptance of Goods.

(1) Acceptance of goods occurs when the buyer

   (a) after a reasonable opportunity to inspect the goods signifies to the seller that the goods are conforming or that he will take or retain them in spite of their nonconformity; or

   (b) fails to make an effective rejection (subsection (1) of Section 2–602), but such acceptance does not occur until the buyer has had a reasonable opportunity to inspect them; or

   (c) does any act inconsistent with the seller's ownership; but if such act is wrongful as against the seller it is an acceptance only if ratified by him.

(2) Acceptance of a part of any commercial unit is acceptance of that entire unit.

§ 2–607. Effect of Acceptance; Notice of Breach; Burden of Establishing Breach After Acceptance; Notice of Claim or Litigation to Person Answerable Over.

(1) The buyer must pay at the contract rate for any goods accepted.

(2) Acceptance of goods by the buyer precludes rejection of the goods accepted and if made with knowledge of a non-conformity cannot be revoked because of it unless the acceptance was on the reasonable assumption that the non-conformity would be seasonably cured but acceptance does not of itself impair any other remedy provided by this Article for non-conformity.

(3) Where a tender has been accepted

   (a) the buyer must within a reasonable time after he discovers or should have discovered any breach notify the seller of breach or be barred from any remedy; and

   (b) if the claim is one for infringement or the like (subsection (3) of Section 2–312) and the buyer is sued as a result of such a breach he must so notify the seller within a reasonable time after he receives notice of the litigation or be barred from any remedy over for liability established by the litigation.

(4) The burden is on the buyer to establish any breach with respect to the goods accepted.

(5) Where the buyer is sued for breach of a warranty or other obligation for which his seller is answerable over

   (a) he may give his seller written notice of the litigation. If the notice states that the seller may come in and defend and that if the seller does not do so he will be bound in any action against him by his buyer by any determination of fact common to the two litigations, then unless the seller after seasonable receipt of the notice does come in and defend he is so bound.

   (b) if the claim is one for infringement or the like (subsection (3) of Section 2–312) the original seller may demand in writing that his buyer turn over to him control of the litigation including settlement or else be barred from any remedy over and if he also agrees to bear all expense and to satisfy any adverse judgment, then unless the buyer after seasonable receipt of the demand does turn over control the buyer is so barred.

(6) The provisions of subsections (3), (4) and (5) apply to any obligation of a buyer to hold the seller harmless against infringement or the like (subsection (3) of Section 2–312).

§ 2–608. Revocation of Acceptance in Whole or in Part.

(1) The buyer may revoke his acceptance of a lot or commercial unit whose non-conformity substantially impairs its value to him if he has accepted it

(a) on the reasonable assumption that its nonconformity would be cured and it has not been seasonably cured; or

(b) without discovery of such non-conformity if his acceptance was reasonably induced either by the difficulty of discovery before acceptance or by the seller's assurances.

(2) Revocation of acceptance must occur within a reasonable time after the buyer discovers or should have discovered the ground for it and before any substantial change in condition of the goods which is not caused by their own defects. It is not effective until the buyer notifies the seller of it.

(3) A buyer who so revokes has the same rights and duties with regard to the goods involved as if he had rejected them.

§ 2–609. Right to Adequate Assurance of Performance.

(1) A contract for sale imposes an obligation on each party that the other's expectation of receiving due performance will not be impaired. When reasonable grounds for insecurity arise with respect to the performance of either party the other may in writing demand adequate assurance of due performance and until he receives such assurance may if commercially reasonable suspend any performance for which he has not already received the agreed return.

(2) Between merchants the reasonableness of grounds for insecurity and the adequacy of any assurance offered shall be determined according to commercial standards.

(3) Acceptance of any improper delivery or payment does not prejudice the party's right to demand adequate assurance of future performance.

(4) After receipt of a justified demand failure to provide within a reasonable time not exceeding thirty days such assurance of due performance as is adequate under the circumstances of the particular case is a repudiation of the contract.

§ 2–610. Anticipatory Repudiation.

When either party repudiates the contract with respect to a performance not yet due the loss of which will substantially impair the value of the contract to the other, the aggrieved party may

(a) for a commercially reasonable time await performance by the repudiating party; or

(b) resort to any remedy for breach (Section 2–703 or Section 2–711), even though he has notified the repudiating party that he would await the latter's performance and has urged retraction; and

(c) in either case suspend his own performance or proceed in accordance with the provisions of this Article on the seller's right to identify goods to the contract notwithstanding breach or to salvage unfinished goods (Section 2–704).

§ 2–611. Retraction of Anticipatory Repudiation.

(1) Until the repudiating party's next performance is due he can retract his repudiation unless the aggrieved party has since the repudiation cancelled or materially changed his position or otherwise indicated that he considers the repudiation final.

(2) Retraction may be by any method which clearly indicates to the aggrieved party that the repudiating party intends to perform, but must include any assurance justifiably demanded under the provisions of this Article (Section 2–609).

(3) Retraction reinstates the repudiating party's rights under the contract with due excuse and allowance to the aggrieved party for any delay occasioned by the repudiation.

§ 2–612. "Installment Contract"; Breach.

(1) An "installment contract" is one which requires or authorizes the delivery of goods in separate lots to be separately accepted, even though the contract contains a clause "each delivery is a separate contract" or its equivalent.

(2) The buyer may reject any installment which is non-conforming if the non-conformity substantially impairs the value of that installment and cannot be cured or if the non-conformity is a defect in the required documents; but if the non-conformity does not fall within subsection (3) and the seller gives adequate assurance of its cure the buyer must accept that installment.

(3) Whenever non-conformity or default with respect to one or more installments substantially impairs the value of the whole contract there is a breach of the whole. But the aggrieved party reinstates the contract if he accepts a non-conforming installment without seasonably notifying of cancellation or if he brings an action with respect only to past installments or demands performance as to future installments.

§ 2–613. Casualty to Identified Goods.

Where the contract requires for its performance goods identified when the contract is made, and the goods suffer casualty without fault of either party before the risk of loss passes to the buyer, or in a proper case under a "no arrival, no sale" term (Section 2–324) then

(a) if the loss is total the contract is avoided; and

(b) if the loss is partial or the goods have so deteriorated as no longer to conform to the contract the buyer may nevertheless demand inspection and at his option either treat the contract as voided or accept the goods with due allowance from the contract price for the deterioration or the deficiency in quantity but without further right against the seller.

§ 2–614. Substituted Performance.

(1) Where without fault of either party the agreed berthing, loading, or unloading facilities fail or an agreed type of carrier becomes unavailable or the agreed manner of delivery otherwise becomes commercially impracticable but a commercially reasonable substitute is available, such substitute performance must be tendered and accepted.

(2) If the agreed means or manner of payment fails because of domestic or foreign governmental regulation, the seller may withhold or stop delivery unless the buyer provides a means or manner of payment which is commercially a substantial equivalent. If delivery has already been taken, payment by the means or in the manner provided by the regulation discharges the buyer's obligation unless the regulation is discriminatory, oppressive or predatory.

§ 2–615. Excuse by Failure of Presupposed Conditions.

Except so far as a seller may have assumed a greater obligation and subject to the preceding section on substituted performance:

(a) Delay in delivery or non-delivery in whole or in part by a seller who complies with paragraphs (b) and (c) is not a breach of his duty under a contract for sale if performance as agreed has been made impracticable by the occurrence of a contingency the nonoccurrence of which was a basic assumption on which the contract was made or by compliance in good faith with any applicable foreign or domestic governmental regulation or order whether or not it later proves to be invalid.

(b) Where the causes mentioned in paragraph (a) affect only a part of the seller's capacity to perform, he must allocate production and deliveries among his customers but may at his option include regular customers not then under contract as well as his own requirements for further manufacture. He may so allocate in any manner which is fair and reasonable.

(c) The seller must notify the buyer seasonably that there will be delay or non-delivery and, when allocation is required under paragraph (b), of the estimated quota thus made available for the buyer.

§ 2–616. Procedure on Notice Claiming Excuse.

(1) Where the buyer receives notification of a material or indefinite delay or an allocation justified under the preceding section he may by written notification to the seller as to any delivery concerned, and where the prospective deficiency substantially impairs the value of the whole contract under the provisions of this Article relating to breach of installment contracts (Section 2–612), then also as to the whole,

   (a) terminate and thereby discharge any unexecuted portion of the contract; or

   (b) modify the contract by agreeing to take his available quota in substitution.

(2) If after receipt of such notification from the seller the buyer fails so to modify the contract within a reasonable time not exceeding thirty days the contract lapses with respect to any deliveries affected.

(3) The provisions of this section may not be negated by agreement except in so far as the seller has assumed a greater obligation under the preceding section.

Part 7 Remedies

§ 2–701. Remedies for Breach of Collateral Contracts Not Impaired.

Remedies for breach of any obligation or promise collateral or ancillary to a contract for sale are not impaired by the provisions of this Article.

§ 2–702. Seller's Remedies on Discovery of Buyer's Insolvency.

(1) Where the seller discovers the buyer to be insolvent he may refuse delivery except for cash including payment for all goods theretofore delivered under the contract, and stop delivery under this Article (Section 2–705).

(2) Where the seller discovers that the buyer has received goods on credit while insolvent he may reclaim the goods upon demand made within ten days after the receipt, but if misrepresentation of solvency has been made to the particular seller in writing within three months before delivery the ten day limitation does not apply. Except as provided in this subsection the seller may not base a right to reclaim goods on the buyer's fraudulent or innocent misrepresentation of solvency or of intent to pay.

(3) The seller's right to reclaim under subsection (2) is subject to the rights of a buyer in ordinary course or other good faith purchaser under this Article (Section 2–403). Successful reclamation of goods excludes all other remedies with respect to them.

§ 2–703. Seller's Remedies in General.

Where the buyer wrongfully rejects or revokes acceptance of goods or fails to make a payment due on or before delivery or repudiates with respect to a part or the whole, then with respect to any goods directly affected and, if the breach is of the whole contract (Section 2–612), then also with respect to the whole undelivered balance, the aggrieved seller may

(a) withhold delivery of such goods;

(b) stop delivery by any bailee as hereafter provided (Section 2–705);

(c) proceed under the next section respecting goods still unidentified to the contract;

(d) resell and recover damages as hereafter provided (Section 2–706);

(e) recover damages for non-acceptance (Section 2–708) or in a proper case the price (Section 2–709);

(f) cancel.

§ 2–704. Seller's Right to Identify Goods to the Contract Notwithstanding Breach or to Salvage Unfinished Goods.

(1) An aggrieved seller under the preceding section may

   (a) identify to the contract conforming goods not already identified if at the time he learned of the breach they are in his possession or control;

(b) treat as the subject of resale goods which have demonstrably been intended for the particular contract even though those goods are unfinished.

(2) Where the goods are unfinished an aggrieved seller may in the exercise of reasonable commercial judgment for the purposes of avoiding loss and of effective realization either complete the manufacture and wholly identify the goods to the contract or cease manufacture and resell for scrap or salvage value or proceed in any other reasonable manner.

§ 2–705. Seller's Stoppage of Delivery in Transit or Otherwise.

(1) The seller may stop delivery of goods in the possession of a carrier or other bailee when he discovers the buyer to be insolvent (Section 2–702) and may stop delivery of carload, truckload, planeload or larger shipments of express or freight when the buyer repudiates or fails to make a payment due before delivery or if for any other reason the seller has a right to withhold or reclaim the goods.

(2) As against such buyer the seller may stop delivery until

(a) receipt of the goods by the buyer; or

(b) acknowledgment to the buyer by any bailee of the goods except a carrier that the bailee holds the goods for the buyer; or

(c) such acknowledgment to the buyer by a carrier by reshipment or as warehouseman; or

(d) negotiation to the buyer of any negotiable document of title covering the goods.

(3) (a) To stop delivery the seller must so notify as to enable the bailee by reasonable diligence to prevent delivery of the goods.

(b) After such notification the bailee must hold and deliver the goods according to the directions of the seller but the seller is liable to the bailee for any ensuing charges or damages.

(c) If a negotiable document of title has been issued for goods the bailee is not obliged to obey a notification to stop until surrender of the document.

(d) A carrier who has issued a non-negotiable bill of lading is not obliged to obey a notification to stop received from a person other than the consignor.

§ 2–706. Seller's Resale Including Contract for Resale.

(1) Under the conditions stated in Section 2–703 on seller's remedies, the seller may resell the goods concerned or the undelivered balance thereof. Where the resale is made in good faith and in a commercially reasonable manner the seller may recover the difference between the resale price and the contract price together with any incidental damages allowed under the provisions of this Article (Section 2–710), but less expenses saved in consequence of the buyer's breach.

(2) Except as otherwise provided in subsection (3) or unless otherwise agreed resale may be at public or private sale including sale by way of one or more contracts to sell or of identification to an existing contract of the seller. Sale may be as a unit or in parcels and at any time and place and on any terms but every aspect of the sale including the method, manner, time, place and terms must be commercially reasonable. The resale must be reasonably identified as referring to the broken contract, but it is not necessary that the goods be in existence or that any or all of them have been identified to the contract before the breach.

(3) Where the resale is at private sale the seller must give the buyer reasonable notification of his intention to resell.

(4) Where the resale is at public sale

(a) only identified goods can be sold except where there is a recognized market for a public sale of futures in goods of the kind; and

(b) it must be made at a usual place or market for public sale if one is reasonably available and except in the case of goods which are perishable or threaten to decline in value speedily the seller must give the buyer reasonable notice of the time and place of the resale; and

(c) if the goods are not to be within the view of those attending the sale the notification of sale must state the place where the goods are located and provide for their reasonable inspection by prospective bidders; and

(d) the seller may buy.

(5) A purchaser who buys in good faith at a resale takes the goods free of any rights of the original buyer even though the seller fails to comply with one or more of the requirements of this section.

(6) The seller is not accountable to the buyer for any profit made on any resale. A person in the position of a seller (Section 2–707) or a buyer who has rightfully rejected or justifiably revoked acceptance must account for any excess over the amount of his security interest, as hereinafter defined (subsection (3) of Section 2–711).

§ 2–707. "Person in the Position of a Seller".

(1) A "person in the position of a seller" includes as against a principal an agent who has paid or become responsible for the price of goods on behalf of his principal or anyone who otherwise holds a security interest or other right in goods similar to that of a seller.

(2) A person in the position of a seller may as provided in this Article withhold or stop delivery (Section 2–705) and resell (Section 2–706) and recover incidental damages (Section 2–710).

§ 2–708. Seller's Damages for Non-Acceptance or Repudiation.

(1) Subject to subsection (2) and to the provisions of this Article with respect to proof of market price (Section 2–723),

the measure of damages for non-acceptance or repudiation by the buyer is the difference between the market price at the time and place for tender and the unpaid contract price together with any incidental damages provided in this Article (Section 2–710), but less expenses saved in consequence of the buyer's breach.

(2) If the measure of damages provided in subsection (1) is inadequate to put the seller in as good a position as performance would have done then the measure of damages is the profit (including reasonable overhead) which the seller would have made from full performance by the buyer, together with any incidental damages provided in this Article (Section 2–710), due allowance for costs reasonably incurred and due credit for payments or proceeds of resale.

§ 2–709. Action for the Price.

(1) When the buyer fails to pay the price as it becomes due the seller may recover, together with any incidental damages under the next section, the price

    (a) of goods accepted or of conforming goods lost or damaged within a commercially reasonable time after risk of their loss has passed to the buyer; and

    (b) of goods identified to the contract if the seller is unable after reasonable effort to resell them at a reasonable price or the circumstances reasonably indicate that such effort will be unavailing.

(2) Where the seller sues for the price he must hold for the buyer any goods which have been identified to the contract and are still in his control except that if resale becomes possible he may resell them at any time prior to the collection of the judgment. The net proceeds of any such resale must be credited to the buyer and payment of the judgment entitles him to any goods not resold.

(3) After the buyer has wrongfully rejected or revoked acceptance of the goods or has failed to make a payment due or has repudiated (Section 2–610), a seller who is held not entitled to the price under this section shall nevertheless be awarded damages for non-acceptance under the preceding section.

§ 2–710. Seller's Incidental Damages.

Incidental damages to an aggrieved seller include any commercially reasonable charges, expenses or commissions incurred in stopping delivery, in the transportation, care and custody of goods after the buyer's breach, in connection with return or resale of the goods or otherwise resulting from the breach.

§ 2–711. Buyer's Remedies in General; Buyer's Security Interest in Rejected Goods.

(1) Where the seller fails to make delivery or repudiates or the buyer rightfully rejects or justifiably revokes acceptance then with respect to any goods involved, and with respect to the whole if the breach goes to the whole contract (Section 2–612), the buyer may cancel and whether or not he has done so may in addition to recovering so much of the price as has been paid

    (a) "cover" and have damages under the next section as to all the goods affected whether or not they have been identified to the contract; or

    (b) recover damages for non-delivery as provided in this Article (Section 2–713).

(2) Where the seller fails to deliver or repudiates the buyer may also

    (a) if the goods have been identified recover them as provided in this Article (Section 2–502); or

    (b) in a proper case obtain specific performance or replevy the goods as provided in this Article (Section 2–716).

(3) On rightful rejection or justifiable revocation of acceptance a buyer has a security interest in goods in his possession or control for any payments made on their price and any expenses reasonably incurred in their inspection, receipt, transportation, care and custody and may hold such goods and resell them in like manner as an aggrieved seller (Section 2–706).

§ 2–712. "Cover"; Buyer's Procurement of Substitute Goods.

(1) After a breach within the preceding section the buyer may "cover" by making in good faith and without unreasonable delay any reasonable purchase of or contract to purchase goods in substitution for those due from the seller.

(2) The buyer may recover from the seller as damages the difference between the cost of cover and the contract price together with any incidental or consequential damages as hereinafter defined (Section 2–715), but less expenses saved in consequence of the seller's breach.

(3) Failure of the buyer to effect cover within this section does not bar him from any other remedy.

§ 2–713. Buyer's Damages for Non-Delivery or Repudiation.

(1) Subject to the provisions of this Article with respect to proof of market price (Section 2–723), the measure of damages for non-delivery or repudiation by the seller is the difference between the market price at the time when the buyer learned of the breach and the contract price together with any incidental and consequential damages provided in this Article (Section 2–715), but less expenses saved in consequence of the seller's breach.

(2) Market price is to be determined as of the place for tender or, in cases of rejection after arrival or revocation of acceptance, as of the place of arrival.

§ 2–714. Buyer's Damages for Breach in Regard to Accepted Goods.

(1) Where the buyer has accepted goods and given notification (subsection (3) of Section 2–607) he may recover as damages for any non-conformity of tender the loss resulting in the ordinary course of events from the seller's breach as determined in any manner which is reasonable.

(2) The measure of damages for breach of warranty is the difference at the time and place of acceptance between the value of

the goods accepted and the value they would have had if they had been as warranted, unless special circumstances show proximate damages of a different amount.

(3) In a proper case any incidental and consequential damages under the next section may also be recovered.

§ 2–715. Buyer's Incidental and Consequential Damages.

(1) Incidental damages resulting from the seller's breach include expenses reasonably incurred in inspection, receipt, transportation and care and custody of goods rightfully rejected, any commercially reasonable charges, expenses or commissions in connection with effecting cover and any other reasonable expense incident to the delay or other breach.

(2) Consequential damages resulting from the seller's breach include

(a) any loss resulting from general or particular requirements and needs of which the seller at the time of contracting had reason to know and which could not reasonably be prevented by cover or otherwise; and

(b) injury to person or property proximately resulting from any breach of warranty.

§ 2–716. Buyer's Right to Specific Performance or Replevin.

(1) Specific performance may be decreed where the goods are unique or in other proper circumstances.

(2) The decree for specific performance may include such terms and conditions as to payment of the price, damages, or other relief as the court may deem just.

(3) The buyer has a right of replevin for goods identified to the contract if after reasonable effort he is unable to effect cover for such goods or the circumstances reasonably indicate that such effort will be unavailing or if the goods have been shipped under reservation and satisfaction of the security interest in them has been made or tendered. In the case of goods bought for personal, family, or household purposes, the buyer's right of replevin vests upon acquisition of a special property, even if the seller had not then repudiated or failed to deliver.

As amended in 1999.

§ 2–717. Deduction of Damages From the Price.

The buyer on notifying the seller of his intention to do so may deduct all or any part of the damages resulting from any breach of the contract from any part of the price still due under the same contract.

§ 2–718. Liquidation or Limitation of Damages; Deposits.

(1) Damages for breach by either party may be liquidated in the agreement but only at an amount which is reasonable in the light of the anticipated or actual harm caused by the breach, the difficulties of proof of loss, and the inconvenience or nonfeasibility of otherwise obtaining an adequate remedy. A term fixing unreasonably large liquidated damages is void as a penalty.

(2) Where the seller justifiably withholds delivery of goods because of the buyer's breach, the buyer is entitled to restitution of any amount by which the sum of his payments exceeds

(a) the amount to which the seller is entitled by virtue of terms liquidating the seller's damages in accordance with subsection (1), or

(b) in the absence of such terms, twenty per cent of the value of the total performance for which the buyer is obligated under the contract or $500, whichever is smaller.

(3) The buyer's right to restitution under subsection (2) is subject to offset to the extent that the seller establishes

(a) a right to recover damages under the provisions of this Article other than subsection (1), and

(b) the amount or value of any benefits received by the buyer directly or indirectly by reason of the contract.

(4) Where a seller has received payment in goods their reasonable value or the proceeds of their resale shall be treated as payments for the purposes of subsection (2); but if the seller has notice of the buyer's breach before reselling goods received in part performance, his resale is subject to the conditions laid down in this Article on resale by an aggrieved seller (Section 2–706).

§ 2–719. Contractual Modification or Limitation of Remedy.

(1) Subject to the provisions of subsections (2) and (3) of this section and of the preceding section on liquidation and limitation of damages,

(a) the agreement may provide for remedies in addition to or in substitution for those provided in this Article and may limit or alter the measure of damages recoverable under this Article, as by limiting the buyer's remedies to return of the goods and repayment of the price or to repair and replacement of nonconforming goods or parts; and

(b) resort to a remedy as provided is optional unless the remedy is expressly agreed to be exclusive, in which case it is the sole remedy.

(2) Where circumstances cause an exclusive or limited remedy to fail of its essential purpose, remedy may be had as provided in this Act.

(3) Consequential damages may be limited or excluded unless the limitation or exclusion is unconscionable. Limitation of consequential damages for injury to the person in the case of consumer goods is prima facie unconscionable but limitation of damages where the loss is commercial is not.

§ 2–720. Effect of "Cancellation" or "Rescission" on Claims for Antecedent Breach.

Unless the contrary intention clearly appears, expressions of "cancellation" or "rescission" of the contract or the like shall not be construed as a renunciation or discharge of any claim in damages for an antecedent breach.

§ 2–721. Remedies for Fraud.

Remedies for material misrepresentation or fraud include all remedies available under this Article for non-fraudulent breach.

Neither rescission or a claim for rescission of the contract for sale nor rejection or return of the goods shall bar or be deemed inconsistent with a claim for damages or other remedy.

§ 2–722. Who Can Sue Third Parties for Injury to Goods.

Where a third party so deals with goods which have been identified to a contract for sale as to cause actionable injury to a party to that contract

(a) a right of action against the third party is in either party to the contract for sale who has title to or a security interest or a special property or an insurable interest in the goods; and if the goods have been destroyed or converted a right of action is also in the party who either bore the risk of loss under the contract for sale or has since the injury assumed that risk as against the other;

(b) if at the time of the injury the party plaintiff did not bear the risk of loss as against the other party to the contract for sale and there is no arrangement between them for disposition of the recovery, his suit or settlement is, subject to his own interest, as a fiduciary for the other party to the contract;

(c) either party may with the consent of the other sue for the benefit of whom it may concern.

§ 2–723. Proof of Market Price: Time and Place.

(1) If an action based on anticipatory repudiation comes to trial before the time for performance with respect to some or all of the goods, any damages based on market price (Section 2–708 or Section 2–713) shall be determined according to the price of such goods prevailing at the time when the aggrieved party learned of the repudiation.

(2) If evidence of a price prevailing at the times or places described in this Article is not readily available the price prevailing within any reasonable time before or after the time described or at any other place which in commercial judgment or under usage of trade would serve as a reasonable substitute for the one described may be used, making any proper allowance for the cost of transporting the goods to or from such other place.

(3) Evidence of a relevant price prevailing at a time or place other than the one described in this Article offered by one party is not admissible unless and until he has given the other party such notice as the court finds sufficient to prevent unfair surprise.

§ 2–724. Admissibility of Market Quotations.

Whenever the prevailing price or value of any goods regularly bought and sold in any established commodity market is in issue, reports in official publications or trade journals or in newspapers or periodicals of general circulation published as the reports of such market shall be admissible in evidence. The circumstances of the preparation of such a report may be shown to affect its weight but not its admissibility.

§ 2–725. Statute of Limitations in Contracts for Sale.

(1) An action for breach of any contract for sale must be commenced within four years after the cause of action has accrued.

By the original agreement the parties may reduce the period of limitation to not less than one year but may not extend it.

(2) A cause of action accrues when the breach occurs, regardless of the aggrieved party's lack of knowledge of the breach. A breach of warranty occurs when tender of delivery is made, except that where a warranty explicitly extends to future performance of the goods and discovery of the breach must await the time of such performance the cause of action accrues when the breach is or should have been discovered.

(3) Where an action commenced within the time limited by subsection (1) is so terminated as to leave available a remedy by another action for the same breach such other action may be commenced after the expiration of the time limited and within six months after the termination of the first action unless the termination resulted from voluntary discontinuance or from dismissal for failure or neglect to prosecute.

(4) This section does not alter the law on tolling of the statute of limitations nor does it apply to causes of action which have accrued before this Act becomes effective.

Article 2 Amendments (Excerpts)[1]

Part 1 Short Title, General Construction and Subject Matter

* * * *

§ 2–103. Definitions and Index of Definitions.

(1) In this article unless the context otherwise requires

* * * *

(b) "Conspicuous", with reference to a term, means so written, displayed, or presented that a reasonable person against which it is to operate ought to have noticed it. A term in an electronic record intended to evoke a response by an electronic agent is conspicuous if it is presented in a form that would enable a reasonably configured electronic agent to take it into account or react to it without review of the record by an individual. Whether a term is "conspicuous" or not is a decision for the court. Conspicuous terms include the following:

(i) for a person:

(A) a heading in capitals equal to or greater in size than the surrounding text, or in contrasting type, font, or color to the surrounding text of the same or lesser size and;

(B) language in the body of a record or display in larger type than the surrounding text, or in contrasting type, font, or color to the surrounding text of the

---

1. Additions and new wording are underlined. What follows represents only selected changes made by the 2003 amendments. Although the National Conference of Commissioners on Uniform State Laws and the American Law Institute approved the amendments in May of 2003, as of this writing, they have not as yet been adopted by any state.

same size, or set off from surrounding text of the same size by symbols or other marks that call attention to the language; and

(ii) for a person or an electronic agent, a term that is so placed in a record or display that the person or electronic agent cannot proceed without taking action with respect to the particular term.

(c) "Consumer" means an individual who buys or contracts to buy goods that, at the time of contracting, are intended by the individual to be used primarily for personal, family, or household purposes.

(d) "Consumer contract" means a contract between a merchant seller and a consumer.

*   *   *   *

(j) "Good faith" means honesty in fact and the observance of reasonable commercial standards of fair dealing.

(k) "Goods" means all things that are movable at the time of identification to a contract for sale. The term includes future goods, specially manufactured goods, the unborn young of animals, growing crops, and other identified things attached to realty as described in Section 2–107. The term does not include information, the money in which the price is to be paid, investment securities under Article 8, the subject matter of foreign exchange transactions, and choses in action.

*   *   *   *

(m) "Record" means information that is inscribed on a tangible medium or that is stored in an electronic or other medium and is retrievable in perceivable form.

(n) "Remedial promise" means a promise by the seller to repair or replace the goods or to refund all or part of the price upon the happening of a specified event.

*   *   *   *

(p) "Sign" means, with present intent to authenticate or adopt a record,

(i) to execute or adopt a tangible symbol; or

(ii) to attach to or logically associate with the record an electronic sound, symbol, or process.

*   *   *   *

Part 2 Form, Formation, Terms and Readjustment of Contract; Electronic Contracting

§ 2–201. Formal Requirements; Statute of Frauds.

(1) A contract for the sale of goods for the price of $5,000 or more is not enforceable by way of action or defense unless there is some record sufficient to indicate that a contract for sale has been made between the parties and signed by the party against which enforcement is sought or by the party's authorized agent or broker. A record is not insufficient because it omits or incorrectly states a term agreed upon but the contract is not enforceable under this subsection beyond the quantity of goods shown in the record.

(2) Between merchants if within a reasonable time a record in confirmation of the contract and sufficient against the sender is received and the party receiving it has reason to know its contents, it satisfies the requirements of subsection (1) against the recipient unless notice of objection to its contents is given in a record within 10 days after it is received.

(3) A contract which does not satisfy the requirements of subsection (1) but which is valid in other respects is enforceable

(a) if the goods are to be specially manufactured for the buyer and are not suitable for sale to others in the ordinary course of the seller's business and the seller, before notice of repudiation is received and under circumstances which reasonably indicate that the goods are for the buyer, has made either a substantial beginning of their manufacture or commitments for their procurement; or

(b) if the party against which enforcement is sought admits in the party's pleading, or in the party's testimony or otherwise under oath that a contract for sale was made, but the contract is not enforceable under this paragraph beyond the quantity of goods admitted; or

(c) with respect to goods for which payment has been made and accepted or which have been received and accepted (Sec. 2–606).

(4) A contract that is enforceable under this section is not rendered unenforceable merely because it is not capable of being performed within one year or any other applicable period after its making.

*   *   *   *

§ 2–207. Terms of Contract; Effect of Confirmation.

Subject to Section 2–202, if (i) conduct by both parties recognizes the existence of a contract although their records do not otherwise establish a contract, (ii) a contract is formed by an offer and acceptance, or (iii) a contract formed in any manner is confirmed by a record that contains terms additional to or different from those in the contract being confirmed, the terms of the contract, are:

(a) terms that appear in the records of both parties;

(b) terms, whether in a record or not, to which both parties agree; and

(c) terms supplied or incorporated under any provision of this Act.

*   *   *   *

Part 3 General Obligation and Construction of Contract

*   *   *   *

§ 2–312. Warranty of Title and Against Infringement; Buyer's Obligation Against Infringement.

(1) Subject to subsection (3) there is in a contract for sale a warranty by the seller that

(a) the title conveyed shall be, <u>good</u> and its transfer rightful and shall not, unreasonably expose the buyer to litigation because of any colorable claim to or interest in the goods; and

(b) the goods shall be delivered free from any security interest or other lien or encumbrance of which the buyer at the time of contracting has no knowledge.

(2) Unless otherwise agreed a seller that is a merchant regularly dealing in goods of the kind warrants that the goods shall be delivered free of the rightful claim of any third person by way of infringement or the like but a buyer that furnishes specifications to the seller must hold the seller harmless against any such claim that arises out of compliance with the specifications.

(3) A warranty under this section may be disclaimed or modified only by specific language or by circumstances that give the buyer reason to know that the seller does not claim title, that the seller is purporting to sell only the right or title as the seller or a third person may have, or that the seller is selling subject to any claims of infringement or the like.

§ 2–313. Express Warranties by Affirmation, Promise, Description, Sample; Remedial Promise.

(1) In this section, "immediate buyer" means a buyer that enters into a contract with the seller.

*   *   *   *

(4) Any remedial promise made by the seller to the immediate buyer creates an obligation that the promise will be performed upon the happening of the specified event.

§ 2–313A. Obligation to Remote Purchaser Created by Record Packaged with or Accompanying Goods.

(1) In this section:

(a) "Immediate buyer" means a buyer that enters into a contract with the seller.

(b) "Remote purchaser" means a person that buys or leases goods from an immediate buyer or other person in the normal chain of distribution.

(2) This section applies only to new goods and goods sold or leased as new goods in a transaction of purchase in the normal chain of distribution.

(3) If in a record packaged with or accompanying the goods the seller makes an affirmation of fact or promise that relates to the goods, provides a description that relates to the goods, or makes a remedial promise, and the seller reasonably expects the record to be, and the record is, furnished to the remote purchaser, the seller has an obligation to the remote purchaser that:

(a) the goods will conform to the affirmation of fact, promise or description unless a reasonable person in the position of the remote purchaser would not believe that the affirmation of fact, promise or description created an obligation; and

(b) the seller will perform the remedial promise.

(4) It is not necessary to the creation of an obligation under this section that the seller use formal words such as "warrant" or "guarantee" or that the seller have a specific intention to undertake an obligation, but an affirmation merely of the value of the goods or a statement purporting to be merely the seller's opinion or commendation of the goods does not create an obligation.

(5) The following rules apply to the remedies for breach of an obligation created under this section:

(a) The seller may modify or limit the remedies available to the remote purchaser if the modification or limitation is furnished to the remote purchaser no later than the time of purchase or if the modification or limitation is contained in the record that contains the affirmation of fact, promise or description.

(b) Subject to a modification or limitation of remedy, a seller in breach is liable for incidental or consequential damages under Section 2–715, but not for lost profits.

(c) The remote purchaser may recover as damages for breach of a seller's obligation arising under subsection (2) the loss resulting in the ordinary course of events as determined in any reasonable manner.

(5) An obligation that is not a remedial promise is breached if the goods did not conform to the affirmation of fact, promise or description creating the obligation when the goods left the seller's control.

§ 2–313B. Obligation to Remote Purchaser Created by Communication to the Public.

(1) In this section:

(a) "Immediate buyer" means a buyer that enters into a contract with the seller.

(b) "Remote purchaser" means a person that buys or leases goods from an immediate buyer or other person in the normal chain of distribution.

(2) This section applies only to new goods and goods sold or leased as new goods in a transaction of purchase in the normal chain of distribution.

(3) If in an advertisement or a similar communication to the public a seller makes an affirmation of fact or promise that relates to the goods, provides a description that relates to the goods, or makes a remedial promise, and the remote purchaser enters into a transaction of purchase with knowledge of and with the expectation that the goods will conform to the affirmation of fact, promise, or description, or that the seller will perform the remedial promise, the seller has an obligation to the remote purchaser that:

(a) the goods will conform to the affirmation of fact, promise or description unless a reasonable person in the position of the remote purchaser would not believe that the affirmation of fact, promise or description created an obligation; and

(b) the seller will perform the remedial promise.

(4) It is not necessary to the creation of an obligation under this section that the seller use formal words such as "warrant" or "guarantee" or that the seller have a specific intention to undertake an obligation, but an affirmation merely of the value of the goods or a statement purporting to be merely the seller's opinion or commendation of the goods does not create an obligation.

(5) The following rules apply to the remedies for breach of an obligation created under this section:

(a) The seller may modify or limit the remedies available to the remote purchaser if the modification or limitation is furnished to the remote purchaser no later than the time of purchase. The modification or limitation may be furnished as part of the communication that contains the affirmation of fact, promise or description.

(b) Subject to a modification or limitation of remedy, a seller in breach is liable for incidental or consequential damages under Section 2–715, but not for lost profits.

(c) The remote purchaser may recover as damages for breach of a seller's obligation arising under subsection (2) the loss resulting in the ordinary course of events as determined in any reasonable manner.

(6) An obligation that is not a remedial promise is breached if the goods did not conform to the affirmation of fact, promise or description creating the obligation when the goods left the seller's control.

* * * *

§ 2–316. Exclusion or Modification of Warranties.

* * * *

(2) Subject to subsection (3), to exclude or modify the implied warranty of merchantability or any part of it in a consumer contract the language must be in a record, be conspicuous, and state "The seller undertakes no responsibility for the quality of the goods except as otherwise provided in this contract," and in any other contract the language must mention merchantability and in case of a record must be conspicuous. Subject to subsection (3), to exclude or modify the implied warranty of fitness the exclusion must be in a record and be conspicuous. Language to exclude all implied warranties of fitness in a consumer contract must state "The seller assumes no responsibility that the goods will be fit for any particular purpose for which you may be buying these goods, except as otherwise provided in the contract," and in any other contract the language is sufficient if it states, for example, that "There are no warranties that extend beyond the description on the face hereof." Language that satisfies the requirements of this subsection for the exclusion and modification of a warranty in a consumer contract also satisfies the requirements for any other contract.

(3) Notwithstanding subsection (2):

(a) unless the circumstances indicate otherwise, all implied warranties are excluded by expressions like "as is", "with all faults" or other language which in common understanding calls the buyer's attention to the exclusion of warranties, makes plain that there is no implied warranty, and in a consumer contract evidenced by a record is set forth conspicuously in the record; and

(b) when the buyer before entering into the contract has examined the goods or the sample or model as fully as desired or has refused to examine the goods after a demand by the seller there is no implied warranty with regard to defects which an examination ought in the circumstances to have revealed to the buyer; and

(c) an implied warranty can also be excluded or modified by course of dealing or course of performance or usage of trade.

* * * *

§ 2–318. Third Party Beneficiaries of Warranties and Obligations.

(1) In this section:

(a) "Immediate buyer" means a buyer that enters into a contract with the seller.

(b) "Remote purchaser" means a person that buys or leases goods from an immediate buyer or other person in the normal chain of distribution.

Alternative A to subsection (2)

(2) A seller's warranty to an immediate buyer, whether express or implied, a seller's remedial promise to an immediate buyer, or a seller's obligation to a remote purchaser under Section 2–313A or 2–313B extends to any natural person who is in the family or household of the immediate buyer or the remote purchaser or who is a guest in the home of either if it is reasonable to expect that the person may use, consume or be affected by the goods and who is injured in person by breach of the warranty, remedial promise or obligation. A seller may not exclude or limit the operation of this section.

Alternative B to subsection (2)

(2) A seller's warranty to an immediate buyer, whether express or implied, a seller's remedial promise to an immediate buyer, or a seller's obligation to a remote purchaser under Section 2–313A or 2–313B extends to any natural person who may reasonably be expected to use, consume or be affected by the goods and who is injured in person by breach of the warranty, remedial promise or obligation. A seller may not exclude or limit the operation of this section.

Alternative C to subsection (2)

(2) A seller's warranty to an immediate buyer, whether express or implied, a seller's remedial promise to an immediate buyer, or a seller's obligation to a remote purchaser under Section

2–313A or 2–313B extends to any person that may reasonably be expected to use, consume or be affected by the goods and that is injured by breach of the warranty, remedial promise or obligation. A seller may not exclude or limit the operation of this section with respect to injury to the person of an individual to whom the warranty, remedial promise or obligation extends.

*   *   *   *

Part 5 Performance

*   *   *   *

§ 2–502. Buyer's Right to Goods on Seller's Insolvency.

(1) Subject to subsections (2) and (3) and even though the goods have not been shipped a buyer that has paid a part or all of the price of goods in which the buyer has a special property under the provisions of the immediately preceding section may on making and keeping good a tender of any unpaid portion of their price recover them from the seller if:

(a) in the case of goods bought by a consumer, the seller repudiates or fails to deliver as required by the contract; or

(b) in all cases, the seller becomes insolvent within ten days after receipt of the first installment on their price.

(2) The buyer's right to recover the goods under subsection (1) vests upon acquisition of a special property, even if the seller had not then repudiated or failed to deliver.

(3) If the identification creating the special property has been made by the buyer, the buyer acquires the right to recover the goods only if they conform to the contract for sale.

*   *   *   *

§ 2–508. Cure by Seller of Improper Tender or Delivery; Replacement.

(1) Where the buyer rejects goods or a tender of delivery under Section 2–601 or 2–612 or, except in a consumer contract, justifiably revokes acceptance under Section 2–608(1)(b) and the agreed time for performance has not expired, a seller that has performed in good faith, upon seasonable notice to the buyer and at the seller's own expense, may cure the breach of contract by making a conforming tender of delivery within the agreed time. The seller shall compensate the buyer for all of the buyer's reasonable expenses caused by the seller's breach of contract and subsequent cure.

(2) Where the buyer rejects goods or a tender of delivery under Section 2–601 or 2–612 or except in a consumer contract justifiably revokes acceptance under Section 2–608(1)(b) and the agreed time for performance has expired, a seller that has performed in good faith, upon seasonable notice to the buyer and at the seller's own expense, may cure the breach of contract, if the cure is appropriate and timely under the circumstances, by making a tender of conforming goods. The seller shall compensate the buyer for all of the buyer's reasonable expenses caused by the seller's breach of contract and subsequent cure.

§ 2–509. Risk of Loss in the Absence of Breach.

(1) Where the contract requires or authorizes the seller to ship the goods by carrier

(a) if it does not require the seller to deliver them at a particular destination, the risk of loss passes to the buyer when the goods are delivered to the carrier even though the shipment is under reservation (Section 2–505); but

(b) if it does require the seller to deliver them at a particular destination and the goods are there tendered while in the possession of the carrier, the risk of loss passes to the buyer when the goods are there so tendered as to enable the buyer to take delivery.

(2) Where the goods are held by a bailee to be delivered without being moved, the risk of loss passes to the buyer

(a) on the buyer's receipt of a negotiable document of title covering the goods; or

(b) on acknowledgment by the bailee to the buyer of the buyer's right to possession of the goods; or

(c) after the buyer's receipt of a non-negotiable document of title or other direction to deliver in a record, as provided in subsection (4)(b) of Section 2–503.

(3) In any case not within subsection (1) or (2), the risk of loss passes to the buyer on the buyer's receipt of the goods.

(4) The provisions of this section are subject to contrary agreement of the parties and to the provisions of this Article on sale on approval (Section 2–327) and on effect of breach on risk of loss (Section 2–510).

*   *   *   *

§ 2–513. Buyer's Right to Inspection of Goods.

*   *   *   *

(3) Unless otherwise agreed, the buyer is not entitled to inspect the goods before payment of the price when the contract provides

(a) for delivery on terms that under applicable course of performance, course of dealing, or usage of trade are interpreted to preclude inspection before payment; or

(b) for payment against documents of title, except where such payment is due only after the goods are to become available for inspection.

*   *   *   *

Part 6 Breach, Repudiation and Excuse

*   *   *   *

§ 2–605. Waiver of Buyer's Objections by Failure to Particularize.

(1) The buyer's failure to state in connection with rejection a particular defect or in connection with revocation of acceptance a defect that justifies revocation precludes the buyer from relying

on the unstated defect to justify rejection or revocation of acceptance if the defect is ascertainable by reasonable inspection

(a) where the seller had a right to cure the defect and could have cured it if stated seasonally; or

(b) between merchants when the seller has after rejection made a request in a record for a full and final statement in record form of all defects on which the buyer proposes to rely.

(2) A buyer's payment against documents tendered to the buyer made without reservation of rights precludes recovery of the payment for defects apparent on the face of the documents.

*   *   *   *

§ 2–607. Effect of Acceptance; Notice of Breach; Burden of Establishing Breach After Acceptance; Notice of Claim or Litigation to Person Answerable Over.

*   *   *   *

(3) Where a tender has been accepted

(a) the buyer must within a reasonable time after the buyer discovers or should have discovered any breach notify the seller. However, failure to give timely notice bars the buyer from a remedy only to the extent that the seller is prejudiced by the failure and

(b) if the claim is one for infringement or the like (subsection (3) of Section 2–312) and the buyer is sued as a result of such a breach the buyer must so notify the seller within a reasonable time after the buyer receives notice of the litigation or be barred from any remedy over for liability established by the litigation.

*   *   *   *

§ 2–608. Revocation of Acceptance in Whole or in Part.

*   *   *   *

(4) If a buyer uses the goods after a rightful rejection or justifiable revocation of acceptance, the following rules apply:

(a) Any use by the buyer which is unreasonable under the circumstances is wrongful as against the seller and is an acceptance only if ratified by the seller.

(b) Any use of the goods which is reasonable under the circumstances is not wrongful as against the seller and is not an acceptance, but in an appropriate case the buyer shall be obligated to the seller for the value of the use to the buyer.

*   *   *   *

§ 2–612. "Installment Contract"; Breach.

*   *   *   *

(2) The buyer may reject any installment which is nonconforming if the non-conformity substantially impairs the value of that installment to the buyer or if the non-conformity is a defect in the required documents; but if the non-conformity

does not fall within subsection (3) and the seller gives adequate assurance of its cure the buyer must accept that installment.

(3) Whenever non-conformity or default with respect to one or more installments substantially impairs the value of the whole contract there is a breach of the whole. But the aggrieved party reinstates the contract if the party accepts a non-conforming installment without seasonably notifying of cancellation or if the party brings an action with respect only to past installments or demands performance as to future installments.

*   *   *   *

Part 7 Remedies

§ 2–702. Seller's Remedies on Discovery of Buyer's Insolvency.

*   *   *   *

(2) Where the seller discovers that the buyer has received goods on credit while insolvent the seller may reclaim the goods upon demand made within a reasonable time after the buyer's receipt of the goods. Except as provided in this subsection the seller may not base a right to reclaim goods on the buyer's fraudulent or innocent misrepresentation of solvency or of intent to pay.

*   *   *   *

§ 2–703. Seller's Remedies in General.

(1) A breach of contract by the buyer includes the buyer's wrongful rejection or wrongful attempt to revoke acceptance of goods, wrongful failure to perform a contractual obligation, failure to make a payment when due, and repudiation.

(2) If the buyer is in breach of contract the seller, to the extent provided for by this Act or other law, may:

(a) withhold delivery of the goods:

(b) stop delivery of the goods under Section 2–705;

(c) proceed under Section 2–704 with respect to goods unidentified to the contract or unfinished;

(d) reclaim the goods under Section 2–507(2) or 2–702(2);

(e) require payment directly from the buyer under Section 2–325(c);

(f) cancel;

(g) resell and recover damages under Section 2–706;

(h) recover damages for nonacceptance or repudiation under Section 2–708(1);

(i) recover lost profits under Section 2–708(2);

(j) recover the price under Section 2–709;

(k) obtain specific performance under Section 2–716;

(l) recover liquidated damages under Section 2–718;

(m) in other cases, recover damages in any manner that is reasonable under the circumstances.

(3) If a buyer becomes insolvent, the seller may:

(a) withhold delivery under Section 2–702(1);

(b) stop delivery of the goods under Section 2–705;

(c) reclaim the goods under Section 2–702(2).

* * * *

§ 2–705. Seller's Stoppage of Delivery in Transit or Otherwise.

(1) The seller may stop delivery of goods in the possession of a carrier or other bailee when the seller discovers the buyer to be insolvent (Section 2–702) or when the buyer repudiates or fails to make a payment due before delivery or if for any other reason the seller has a right to withhold or reclaim the goods.

* * * *

§ 2–706. Seller's Resale Including Contract for Resale.

(1) In an appropriate case involving breach by the buyer, the seller may resell the goods concerned or the undelivered balance thereof. Where the resale is made in good faith and in a commercially reasonable manner the seller may recover the difference between the contract price and the resale price together with any incidental or consequential damages allowed under the provisions of this Article (Section 2–710), but less expenses saved in consequence of the buyer's breach.

* * * *

§ 2–708. Seller's Damages for Non-Acceptance or Repudiation.

(1) Subject to subsection (2) and to the provisions of this Article with respect to proof of market price (Section 2–723)

(a) the measure of damages for non-acceptance by the buyer is the difference between the contract price and the market price at the time and place for tender together with any incidental or consequential damages provided in this Article (Section 2–710), but less expenses saved in consequence of the buyer's breach; and

(b) the measure of damages for repudiation by the buyer is the difference between the contract price and the market price at the place for tender at the expiration of a commercially reasonable time after the seller learned of the repudiation, but no later than the time stated in paragraph (a), together with any incidental or consequential damages provided in this Article (Section 2–710), but less expenses saved in consequence of the buyer's breach.

(2) If the measure of damages provided in subsection (1) or in Section 2–706 is inadequate to put the seller in as good a position as performance would have done then the measure of damages is the profit (including reasonable overhead) which the seller would have made from full performance by the buyer, together with any incidental or consequential damages provided in this Article (Section 2–710).

§ 2–709. Action for the Price.

(1) When the buyer fails to pay the price as it becomes due the seller may recover, together with any incidental or consequential damages under the next section, the price

(a) of goods accepted or of conforming goods lost or damaged within a commercially reasonable time after risk of their loss has passed to the buyer; and

(b) of goods identified to the contract if the seller is unable after reasonable effort to resell them at a reasonable price or the circumstances reasonably indicate that such effort will be unavailing.

* * * *

§ 2–710. Seller's Incidental and Consequential Damages.

(1) Incidental damages to an aggrieved seller include any commercially reasonable charges, expenses or commissions incurred in stopping delivery, in the transportation, care and custody of goods after the buyer's breach, in connection with return or resale of the goods or otherwise resulting from the breach.

(2) Consequential damages resulting from the buyer's breach include any loss resulting from general or particular requirements and needs of which the buyer at the time of contracting had reason to know and which could not reasonably be prevented by resale or otherwise.

(3) In a consumer contract, a seller may not recover consequential damages from a consumer.

* * * *

§ 2–711. Buyer's Remedies in General; Buyer's Security Interest in Rejected Goods.

(1) A breach of contract by the seller includes the seller's wrongful failure to deliver or to perform a contractual obligation, making of a nonconforming tender of delivery or performance, and repudiation.

(2) If a seller is in breach of contract under subsection (1) the buyer, to the extent provided for by this Act or other law, may:

(a) in the case of rightful cancellation, rightful rejection or justifiable revocation of acceptance recover so much of the price as has been paid;

(b) deduct damages from any part of the price still due under Section 2–717;

(c) cancel;

(d) cover and have damages under Section 2–712 as to all goods affected whether or not they have been identified to the contract;

(e) recover damages for non-delivery or repudiation under Section 2–713;

(f) recover damages for breach with regard to accepted goods or breach with regard to a remedial promise under Section 2–714;

(g) recover identified goods under Section 2–502;

(h) obtain specific performance or obtain the goods by replevin or similar remedy under Section 7–716;

(i) recover liquidated damages under Section 2–718;

(j) in other cases, recover damages in any manner that is reasonable under the circumstances.

(3) On rightful rejection or justifiable revocation of acceptance a buyer has a security interest in goods in the buyer's possession or control for any payments made on their price and any expenses reasonably incurred in their inspection, receipt, transportation, care and custody and may hold such goods and resell them in like manner as an aggrieved seller (Section 2–706).

* * * *

§ 2–713. Buyer's Damages for Non-Delivery or Repudiation.

(1) Subject to the provisions of this Article with respect to proof of market price (Section 2–723), if the seller wrongfully fails to deliver or repudiates or the buyer rightfully rejects or justifiably revokes acceptance

(a) the measure of damages in the case of wrongful failure to deliver by the seller or rightful rejection or justifiable revocation of acceptance by the buyer is the difference between the market price at the time for tender under the contract and the contract price together with any incidental or consequential damages provided in this Article (Section 2–715), but less expenses saved in consequence of the seller's breach; and

(b) the measure of damages for repudiation by the seller is the difference between the market price at the expiration of a commercially reasonable time after the buyer learned of the repudiation, but no later than the time stated in paragraph (a), and the contract price together with any incidental or consequential damages provided in this Article (Section 2–715), less expenses saved in consequence of the seller's breach.

* * * *

§ 2–725. Statute of Limitations in Contracts for Sale.

(1) Except as otherwise provided in this section, an action for breach of any contract for sale must be commenced within the later of four years after the right of action has accrued under subsection (2) or (3) or one year after the breach was or should have been discovered, but no longer than five years after the right of action accrued. By the original agreement the parties may reduce the period of limitation to not less than one year but may not extend it. However, in a consumer contract, the period of limitation may not be reduced.

(2) Except as otherwise provided in subsection (3), the following rules apply:

(a) Except as otherwise provided in this subsection, a right of action for breach of a contract accrues when the breach occurs, even if the aggrieved party did not have knowledge of the breach.

(b) For breach of a contract by repudiation, a right of action accrues at the earlier of when the aggrieved party elects to treat the repudiation as a breach or when a commercially reasonable time for awaiting performance has expired.

(c) For breach of a remedial promise, a right of action accrues when the remedial promise is not performed when performance is due.

(d) In an action by a buyer against a person that is answerable over to the buyer for a claim asserted against the buyer, the buyer's right of action against the person answerable over accrues at the time the claim was originally asserted against the buyer.

(3) If a breach of a warranty arising under Section 2–312, 2–313(2), 2–314, or 2–315, or a breach of an obligation, other than a remedial promise, arising under Section 2–313A or 2–313B, is claimed the following rules apply:

(a) Except as otherwise provided in paragraph (c), a right of action for breach of a warranty arising under Section 2–313(2), 2–314 or 2–315 accrues when the seller has tendered delivery to the immediate buyer, as defined in Section 2–313, and has completed performance of any agreed installation or assembly of the goods.

(b) Except as otherwise provided in paragraph (c), a right of action for breach of an obligation other than a remedial promise arising under Section 2–313A or 2–313B accrues when the remote purchaser, as defined in sections 2–313A and 2–313B, receives the goods.

(c) Where a warranty arising under Section 2–313(2) or an obligation, other than a remedial promise, arising under 2–313A or 2–313B explicitly extends to future performance of the goods and discovery of the breach must await the time for performance the right of action accrues when the immediate buyer as defined in Section 2–313 or the remote purchaser as defined in Sections 2–313A and 2–313B discovers or should have discovered the breach.

(d) A right of action for breach of warranty arising under Section 2–312 accrues when the aggrieved party discovers or should have discovered the breach. However, an action for breach of the warranty of non-infringement may not be commenced more than six years after tender of delivery of the goods to the aggrieved party.

* * * *

Article 2A
LEASES

Part 1 General Provisions

§ 2A–101. Short Title.

This Article shall be known and may be cited as the Uniform Commercial Code—Leases.

§ 2A–102. Scope.

This Article applies to any transaction, regardless of form, that creates a lease.

§ 2A–103. Definitions and Index of Definitions.

(1) In this Article unless the context otherwise requires:

(a) "Buyer in ordinary course of business" means a person who in good faith and without knowledge that the sale to him [or her] is in violation of the ownership rights or security interest or leasehold interest of a third party in the goods buys in ordinary course from a person in the business of selling goods of that kind but does not include a pawnbroker. "Buying" may be for cash or by exchange of other property or on secured or unsecured credit and includes receiving goods or documents of title under a pre-existing contract for sale but does not include a transfer in bulk or as security for or in total or partial satisfaction of a money debt.

(b) "Cancellation" occurs when either party puts an end to the lease contract for default by the other party.

(c) "Commercial unit" means such a unit of goods as by commercial usage is a single whole for purposes of lease and division of which materially impairs its character or value on the market or in use. A commercial unit may be a single article, as a machine, or a set of articles, as a suite of furniture or a line of machinery, or a quantity, as a gross or carload, or any other unit treated in use or in the relevant market as a single whole.

(d) "Conforming" goods or performance under a lease contract means goods or performance that are in accordance with the obligations under the lease contract.

(e) "Consumer lease" means a lease that a lessor regularly engaged in the business of leasing or selling makes to a lessee who is an individual and who takes under the lease primarily for a personal, family, or household purpose [, if the total payments to be made under the lease contract, excluding payments for options to renew or buy, do not exceed $_____].

(f) "Fault" means wrongful act, omission, breach, or default.

(g) "Finance lease" means a lease with respect to which:

(i) the lessor does not select, manufacture or supply the goods;

(ii) the lessor acquires the goods or the right to possession and use of the goods in connection with the lease; and

(iii) one of the following occurs:

(A) the lessee receives a copy of the contract by which the lessor acquired the goods or the right to possession and use of the goods before signing the lease contract;

(B) the lessee's approval of the contract by which the lessor acquired the goods or the right to possession and use of the goods is a condition to effectiveness of the lease contract;

(C) the lessee, before signing the lease contract, receives an accurate and complete statement designating the promises and warranties, and any disclaimers of warranties, limitations or modifications of remedies, or liquidated damages, including those of a third party, such as the manufacturer of the goods, provided to the lessor by the person supplying the goods in connection with or as part of the contract by which the lessor acquired the goods or the right to possession and use of the goods; or

(D) if the lease is not a consumer lease, the lessor, before the lessee signs the lease contract, informs the lessee in writing (a) of the identity of the person supplying the goods to the lessor, unless the lessee has selected that person and directed the lessor to acquire the goods or the right to possession and use of the goods from that person, (b) that the lessee is entitled under this Article to any promises and warranties, including those of any third party, provided to the lessor by the person supplying the goods in connection with or as part of the contract by which the lessor acquired the goods or the right to possession and use of the goods, and (c) that the lessee may communicate with the person supplying the goods to the lessor and receive an accurate and complete statement of those promises and warranties, including any disclaimers and limitations of them or of remedies.

(h) "Goods" means all things that are movable at the time of identification to the lease contract, or are fixtures (Section 2A–309), but the term does not include money, documents, instruments, accounts, chattel paper, general intangibles, or minerals or the like, including oil and gas, before extraction. The term also includes the unborn young of animals.

(i) "Installment lease contract" means a lease contract that authorizes or requires the delivery of goods in separate lots to be separately accepted, even though the lease contract contains a clause "each delivery is a separate lease" or its equivalent.

(j) "Lease" means a transfer of the right to possession and use of goods for a term in return for consideration, but a sale, including a sale on approval or a sale or return, or retention or creation of a security interest is not a lease. Unless the context clearly indicates otherwise, the term includes a sublease.

(k) "Lease agreement" means the bargain, with respect to the lease, of the lessor and the lessee in fact as found in their language or by implication from other circumstances including course of dealing or usage of trade or course of performance as provided in this Article. Unless the context clearly indicates otherwise, the term includes a sublease agreement.

(l) "Lease contract" means the total legal obligation that results from the lease agreement as affected by this Article and any other applicable rules of law. Unless the context clearly indicates otherwise, the term includes a sublease contract.

(m) "Leasehold interest" means the interest of the lessor or the lessee under a lease contract.

(n) "Lessee" means a person who acquires the right to possession and use of goods under a lease. Unless the context clearly indicates otherwise, the term includes a sublessee.

(o) "Lessee in ordinary course of business" means a person who in good faith and without knowledge that the lease to him [or her] is in violation of the ownership rights or security interest or leasehold interest of a third party in the goods, leases in ordinary course from a person in the business of selling or leasing goods of that kind but does not include a pawnbroker. "Leasing" may be for cash or by exchange of other property or on secured or unsecured credit and includes receiving goods or documents of title under a pre-existing lease contract but does not include a transfer in bulk or as security for or in total or partial satisfaction of a money debt.

(p) "Lessor" means a person who transfers the right to possession and use of goods under a lease. Unless the context clearly indicates otherwise, the term includes a sublessor.

(q) "Lessor's residual interest" means the lessor's interest in the goods after expiration, termination, or cancellation of the lease contract.

(r) "Lien" means a charge against or interest in goods to secure payment of a debt or performance of an obligation, but the term does not include a security interest.

(s) "Lot" means a parcel or a single article that is the subject matter of a separate lease or delivery, whether or not it is sufficient to perform the lease contract.

(t) "Merchant lessee" means a lessee that is a merchant with respect to goods of the kind subject to the lease.

(u) "Present value" means the amount as of a date certain of one or more sums payable in the future, discounted to the date certain. The discount is determined by the interest rate specified by the parties if the rate was not manifestly unreasonable at the time the transaction was entered into; otherwise, the discount is determined by a commercially reasonable rate that takes into account the facts and circumstances of each case at the time the transaction was entered into.

(v) "Purchase" includes taking by sale, lease, mortgage, security interest, pledge, gift, or any other voluntary transaction creating an interest in goods.

(w) "Sublease" means a lease of goods the right to possession and use of which was acquired by the lessor as a lessee under an existing lease.

(x) "Supplier" means a person from whom a lessor buys or leases goods to be leased under a finance lease.

(y) "Supply contract" means a contract under which a lessor buys or leases goods to be leased.

(z) "Termination" occurs when either party pursuant to a power created by agreement or law puts an end to the lease contract otherwise than for default.

(2) Other definitions applying to this Article and the sections in which they appear are:

"Accessions". Section 2A–310(1).

"Construction mortgage". Section 2A–309(1)(d).

"Encumbrance". Section 2A–309(1)(e).

"Fixtures". Section 2A–309(1)(a).

"Fixture filing". Section 2A–309(1)(b).

"Purchase money lease". Section 2A–309(1)(c).

(3) The following definitions in other Articles apply to this Article:

"Accounts". Section 9–106.

"Between merchants". Section 2–104(3).

"Buyer". Section 2–103(1)(a).

"Chattel paper". Section 9–105(1)(b).

"Consumer goods". Section 9–109(1).

"Document". Section 9–105(1)(f).

"Entrusting". Section 2–403(3).

"General intangibles". Section 9–106.

"Good faith". Section 2–103(1)(b).

"Instrument". Section 9–105(1)(i).

"Merchant". Section 2–104(1).

"Mortgage". Section 9–105(1)(j).

"Pursuant to commitment". Section 9–105(1)(k).

"Receipt". Section 2–103(1)(c).

"Sale". Section 2–106(1).

"Sale on approval". Section 2–326.

"Sale or return". Section 2–326.

"Seller". Section 2–103(1)(d).

(4) In addition Article 1 contains general definitions and principles of construction and interpretation applicable throughout this Article.

As amended in 1990 and 1999.

§ 2A–104. Leases Subject to Other Law.

(1) A lease, although subject to this Article, is also subject to any applicable:

(a) certificate of title statute of this State: (list any certificate of title statutes covering automobiles, trailers, mobile homes, boats, farm tractors, and the like);

(b) certificate of title statute of another jurisdiction (Section 2A–105); or

(c) consumer protection statute of this State, or final consumer protection decision of a court of this State existing on the effective date of this Article.

(2) In case of conflict between this Article, other than Sections 2A–105, 2A–304(3), and 2A–305(3), and a statute or decision referred to in subsection (1), the statute or decision controls.

(3) Failure to comply with an applicable law has only the effect specified therein.

As amended in 1990.

§ 2A–105. Territorial Application of Article to Goods Covered by Certificate of Title.

Subject to the provisions of Sections 2A–304(3) and 2A–305(3), with respect to goods covered by a certificate of title issued under a statute of this State or of another jurisdiction, compliance and the effect of compliance or noncompliance with a certificate of title statute are governed by the law (including the conflict of laws rules) of the jurisdiction issuing the certificate until the earlier of (a) surrender of the certificate, or (b) four months after the goods are removed from that jurisdiction and thereafter until a new certificate of title is issued by another jurisdiction.

§ 2A–106. Limitation on Power of Parties to Consumer Lease to Choose Applicable Law and Judicial Forum.

(1) If the law chosen by the parties to a consumer lease is that of a jurisdiction other than a jurisdiction in which the lessee resides at the time the lease agreement becomes enforceable or within 30 days thereafter or in which the goods are to be used, the choice is not enforceable.

(2) If the judicial forum chosen by the parties to a consumer lease is a forum that would not otherwise have jurisdiction over the lessee, the choice is not enforceable.

§ 2A–107. Waiver or Renunciation of Claim or Right After Default.

Any claim or right arising out of an alleged default or breach of warranty may be discharged in whole or in part without consideration by a written waiver or renunciation signed and delivered by the aggrieved party.

§ 2A–108. Unconscionability.

(1) If the court as a matter of law finds a lease contract or any clause of a lease contract to have been unconscionable at the time it was made the court may refuse to enforce the lease contract, or it may enforce the remainder of the lease contract without the unconscionable clause, or it may so limit the application of any unconscionable clause as to avoid any unconscionable result.

(2) With respect to a consumer lease, if the court as a matter of law finds that a lease contract or any clause of a lease contract has been induced by unconscionable conduct or that unconscionable conduct has occurred in the collection of a claim arising from a lease contract, the court may grant appropriate relief.

(3) Before making a finding of unconscionability under subsection (1) or (2), the court, on its own motion or that of a party, shall afford the parties a reasonable opportunity to present evidence as to the setting, purpose, and effect of the lease contract or clause thereof, or of the conduct.

(4) In an action in which the lessee claims unconscionability with respect to a consumer lease:

  (a) If the court finds unconscionability under subsection (1) or (2), the court shall award reasonable attorney's fees to the lessee.

  (b) If the court does not find unconscionability and the lessee claiming unconscionability has brought or maintained an action he [or she] knew to be groundless, the court shall award reasonable attorney's fees to the party against whom the claim is made.

  (c) In determining attorney's fees, the amount of the recovery on behalf of the claimant under subsections (1) and (2) is not controlling.

§ 2A–109. Option to Accelerate at Will.

(1) A term providing that one party or his [or her] successor in interest may accelerate payment or performance or require collateral or additional collateral "at will" or "when he [or she] deems himself [or herself] insecure" or in words of similar import must be construed to mean that he [or she] has power to do so only if he [or she] in good faith believes that the prospect of payment or performance is impaired.

(2) With respect to a consumer lease, the burden of establishing good faith under subsection (1) is on the party who exercised the power; otherwise the burden of establishing lack of good faith is on the party against whom the power has been exercised.

Part 2 Formation and Construction of Lease Contract

§ 2A–201. Statute of Frauds.

(1) A lease contract is not enforceable by way of action or defense unless:

  (a) the total payments to be made under the lease contract, excluding payments for options to renew or buy, are less than $1,000; or

  (b) there is a writing, signed by the party against whom enforcement is sought or by that party's authorized agent, sufficient to indicate that a lease contract has been made between the parties and to describe the goods leased and the lease term.

(2) Any description of leased goods or of the lease term is sufficient and satisfies subsection (1)(b), whether or not it is specific, if it reasonably identifies what is described.

(3) A writing is not insufficient because it omits or incorrectly states a term agreed upon, but the lease contract is not enforceable under subsection (1)(b) beyond the lease term and the quantity of goods shown in the writing.

(4) A lease contract that does not satisfy the requirements of subsection (1), but which is valid in other respects, is enforceable:

  (a) if the goods are to be specially manufactured or obtained for the lessee and are not suitable for lease or sale to others in the ordinary course of the lessor's business, and the lessor, before notice of repudiation is received and under circumstances that reasonably indicate that the goods are for the lessee, has made either a substantial beginning of their manufacture or commitments for their procurement;

(b) if the party against whom enforcement is sought admits in that party's pleading, testimony or otherwise in court that a lease contract was made, but the lease contract is not enforceable under this provision beyond the quantity of goods admitted; or

(c) with respect to goods that have been received and accepted by the lessee.

(5) The lease term under a lease contract referred to in subsection (4) is:

(a) if there is a writing signed by the party against whom enforcement is sought or by that party's authorized agent specifying the lease term, the term so specified;

(b) if the party against whom enforcement is sought admits in that party's pleading, testimony, or otherwise in court a lease term, the term so admitted; or

(c) a reasonable lease term.

§ 2A–202. Final Written Expression: Parol or Extrinsic Evidence.

Terms with respect to which the confirmatory memoranda of the parties agree or which are otherwise set forth in a writing intended by the parties as a final expression of their agreement with respect to such terms as are included therein may not be contradicted by evidence of any prior agreement or of a contemporaneous oral agreement but may be explained or supplemented:

(a) by course of dealing or usage of trade or by course of performance; and

(b) by evidence of consistent additional terms unless the court finds the writing to have been intended also as a complete and exclusive statement of the terms of the agreement.

§ 2A–203. Seals Inoperative.

The affixing of a seal to a writing evidencing a lease contract or an offer to enter into a lease contract does not render the writing a sealed instrument and the law with respect to sealed instruments does not apply to the lease contract or offer.

§ 2A–204. Formation in General.

(1) A lease contract may be made in any manner sufficient to show agreement, including conduct by both parties which recognizes the existence of a lease contract.

(2) An agreement sufficient to constitute a lease contract may be found although the moment of its making is undetermined.

(3) Although one or more terms are left open, a lease contract does not fail for indefiniteness if the parties have intended to make a lease contract and there is a reasonably certain basis for giving an appropriate remedy.

§ 2A–205. Firm Offers.

An offer by a merchant to lease goods to or from another person in a signed writing that by its terms gives assurance it will be held open is not revocable, for lack of consideration, during the time stated or, if no time is stated, for a reasonable time, but in no event may the period of irrevocability exceed 3 months. Any such term of assurance on a form supplied by the offeree must be separately signed by the offeror.

§ 2A–206. Offer and Acceptance in Formation of Lease Contract.

(1) Unless otherwise unambiguously indicated by the language or circumstances, an offer to make a lease contract must be construed as inviting acceptance in any manner and by any medium reasonable in the circumstances.

(2) If the beginning of a requested performance is a reasonable mode of acceptance, an offeror who is not notified of acceptance within a reasonable time may treat the offer as having lapsed before acceptance.

§ 2A–207. Course of Performance or Practical Construction.

(1) If a lease contract involves repeated occasions for performance by either party with knowledge of the nature of the performance and opportunity for objection to it by the other, any course of performance accepted or acquiesced in without objection is relevant to determine the meaning of the lease agreement.

(2) The express terms of a lease agreement and any course of performance, as well as any course of dealing and usage of trade, must be construed whenever reasonable as consistent with each other; but if that construction is unreasonable, express terms control course of performance, course of performance controls both course of dealing and usage of trade, and course of dealing controls usage of trade.

(3) Subject to the provisions of Section 2A–208 on modification and waiver, course of performance is relevant to show a waiver or modification of any term inconsistent with the course of performance.

§ 2A–208. Modification, Rescission and Waiver.

(1) An agreement modifying a lease contract needs no consideration to be binding.

(2) A signed lease agreement that excludes modification or rescission except by a signed writing may not be otherwise modified or rescinded, but, except as between merchants, such a requirement on a form supplied by a merchant must be separately signed by the other party.

(3) Although an attempt at modification or rescission does not satisfy the requirements of subsection (2), it may operate as a waiver.

(4) A party who has made a waiver affecting an executory portion of a lease contract may retract the waiver by reasonable notification received by the other party that strict performance will be required of any term waived, unless the retraction would be unjust in view of a material change of position in reliance on the waiver.

§ 2A–209. Lessee under Finance Lease as Beneficiary of Supply Contract.

(1) The benefit of the supplier's promises to the lessor under the supply contract and of all warranties, whether express or implied, including those of any third party provided in connection with or as part of the supply contract, extends to the lessee to the extent of the lessee's leasehold interest under a finance lease related to the supply contract, but is subject to the terms warranty and of the supply contract and all defenses or claims arising therefrom.

(2) The extension of the benefit of supplier's promises and of warranties to the lessee (Section 2A–209(1)) does not: (i) modify the rights and obligations of the parties to the supply contract, whether arising therefrom or otherwise, or (ii) impose any duty or liability under the supply contract on the lessee.

(3) Any modification or rescission of the supply contract by the supplier and the lessor is effective between the supplier and the lessee unless, before the modification or rescission, the supplier has received notice that the lessee has entered into a finance lease related to the supply contract. If the modification or rescission is effective between the supplier and the lessee, the lessor is deemed to have assumed, in addition to the obligations of the lessor to the lessee under the lease contract, promises of the supplier to the lessor and warranties that were so modified or rescinded as they existed and were available to the lessee before modification or rescission.

(4) In addition to the extension of the benefit of the supplier's promises and of warranties to the lessee under subsection (1), the lessee retains all rights that the lessee may have against the supplier which arise from an agreement between the lessee and the supplier or under other law.
As amended in 1990.

§ 2A–210. Express Warranties.

(1) Express warranties by the lessor are created as follows:

(a) Any affirmation of fact or promise made by the lessor to the lessee which relates to the goods and becomes part of the basis of the bargain creates an express warranty that the goods will conform to the affirmation or promise.

(b) Any description of the goods which is made part of the basis of the bargain creates an express warranty that the goods will conform to the description.

(c) Any sample or model that is made part of the basis of the bargain creates an express warranty that the whole of the goods will conform to the sample or model.

(2) It is not necessary to the creation of an express warranty that the lessor use formal words, such as "warrant" or "guarantee," or that the lessor have a specific intention to make a warranty, but an affirmation merely of the value of the goods or a statement purporting to be merely the lessor's opinion or commendation of the goods does not create a warranty.

§ 2A–211. Warranties Against Interference and Against Infringement; Lessee's Obligation Against Infringement.

(1) There is in a lease contract a warranty that for the lease term no person holds a claim to or interest in the goods that arose from an act or omission of the lessor, other than a claim by way of infringement or the like, which will interfere with the lessee's enjoyment of its leasehold interest.

(2) Except in a finance lease there is in a lease contract by a lessor who is a merchant regularly dealing in goods of the kind a warranty that the goods are delivered free of the rightful claim of any person by way of infringement or the like.

(3) A lessee who furnishes specifications to a lessor or a supplier shall hold the lessor and the supplier harmless against any claim by way of infringement or the like that arises out of compliance with the specifications.

§ 2A–212. Implied Warranty of Merchantability.

(1) Except in a finance lease, a warranty that the goods will be merchantable is implied in a lease contract if the lessor is a merchant with respect to goods of that kind.

(2) Goods to be merchantable must be at least such as

(a) pass without objection in the trade under the description in the lease agreement;

(b) in the case of fungible goods, are of fair average quality within the description;

(c) are fit for the ordinary purposes for which goods of that type are used;

(d) run, within the variation permitted by the lease agreement, of even kind, quality, and quantity within each unit and among all units involved;

(e) are adequately contained, packaged, and labeled as the lease agreement may require; and

(f) conform to any promises or affirmations of fact made on the container or label.

(3) Other implied warranties may arise from course of dealing or usage of trade.

§ 2A–213. Implied Warranty of Fitness for Particular Purpose.

Except in a finance of lease, if the lessor at the time the lease contract is made has reason to know of any particular purpose for which the goods are required and that the lessee is relying on the lessor's skill or judgment to select or furnish suitable goods, there is in the lease contract an implied warranty that the goods will be fit for that purpose.

§ 2A–214. Exclusion or Modification of Warranties.

(1) Words or conduct relevant to the creation of an express warranty and words or conduct tending to negate or limit a warranty must be construed wherever reasonable as consistent with each other; but, subject to the provisions of Section 2A–202 on parol or extrinsic evidence, negation or limitation is inoperative to the extent that the construction is unreasonable.

(2) Subject to subsection (3), to exclude or modify the implied warranty of merchantability or any part of it the language must mention "merchantability", be by a writing, and be conspicuous. Subject to subsection (3), to exclude or modify any implied

warranty of fitness the exclusion must be by a writing and be conspicuous. Language to exclude all implied warranties of fitness is sufficient if it is in writing, is conspicuous and states, for example, "There is no warranty that the goods will be fit for a particular purpose".

(3) Notwithstanding subsection (2), but subject to subsection (4),

(a) unless the circumstances indicate otherwise, all implied warranties are excluded by expressions like "as is" or "with all faults" or by other language that in common understanding calls the lessee's attention to the exclusion of warranties and makes plain that there is no implied warranty, if in writing and conspicuous;

(b) if the lessee before entering into the lease contract has examined the goods or the sample or model as fully as desired or has refused to examine the goods, there is no implied warranty with regard to defects that an examination ought in the circumstances to have revealed; and

(c) an implied warranty may also be excluded or modified by course of dealing, course of performance, or usage of trade.

(4) To exclude or modify a warranty against interference or against infringement (Section 2A–211) or any part of it, the language must be specific, be by a writing, and be conspicuous, unless the circumstances, including course of performance, course of dealing, or usage of trade, give the lessee reason to know that the goods are being leased subject to a claim or interest of any person.

§ 2A–215. Cumulation and Conflict of Warranties Express or Implied.

Warranties, whether express or implied, must be construed as consistent with each other and as cumulative, but if that construction is unreasonable, the intention of the parties determines which warranty is dominant. In ascertaining that intention the following rules apply:

(a) Exact or technical specifications displace an inconsistent sample or model or general language of description.

(b) A sample from an existing bulk displaces inconsistent general language of description.

(c) Express warranties displace inconsistent implied warranties other than an implied warranty of fitness for a particular purpose.

§ 2A–216. Third-Party Beneficiaries of Express and Implied Warranties.

Alternative A

A warranty to or for the benefit of a lessee under this Article, whether express or implied, extends to any natural person who is in the family or household of the lessee or who is a guest in the lessee's home if it is reasonable to expect that such person may use, consume, or be affected by the goods and who is injured in person by breach of the warranty. This section does not displace principles of law and equity that extend a warranty to or for the benefit of a lessee to other persons. The operation of this section may not be excluded, modified, or limited, but an exclusion, modification, or limitation of the warranty, including any with respect to rights and remedies, effective against the lessee is also effective against any beneficiary designated under this section.

Alternative B

A warranty to or for the benefit of a lessee under this Article, whether express or implied, extends to any natural person who may reasonably be expected to use, consume, or be affected by the goods and who is injured in person by breach of the warranty. This section does not displace principles of law and equity that extend a warranty to or for the benefit of a lessee to other persons. The operation of this section may not be excluded, modified, or limited, but an exclusion, modification, or limitation of the warranty, including any with respect to rights and remedies, effective against the lessee is also effective against the beneficiary designated under this section.

Alternative C

A warranty to or for the benefit of a lessee under this Article, whether express or implied, extends to any person who may reasonably be expected to use, consume, or be affected by the goods and who is injured by breach of the warranty. The operation of this section may not be excluded, modified, or limited with respect to injury to the person of an individual to whom the warranty extends, but an exclusion, modification, or limitation of the warranty, including any with respect to rights and remedies, effective against the lessee is also effective against the beneficiary designated under this section.

§ 2A–217. Identification.

Identification of goods as goods to which a lease contract refers may be made at any time and in any manner explicitly agreed to by the parties. In the absence of explicit agreement, identification occurs:

(a) when the lease contract is made if the lease contract is for a lease of goods that are existing and identified;

(b) when the goods are shipped, marked, or otherwise designated by the lessor as goods to which the lease contract refers, if the lease contract is for a lease of goods that are not existing and identified; or

(c) when the young are conceived, if the lease contract is for a lease of unborn young of animals.

§ 2A–218. Insurance and Proceeds.

(1) A lessee obtains an insurable interest when existing goods are identified to the lease contract even though the goods identified are nonconforming and the lessee has an option to reject them.

(2) If a lessee has an insurable interest only by reason of the lessor's identification of the goods, the lessor, until default or insolvency or notification to the lessee that identification is final, may substitute other goods for those identified.

(3) Notwithstanding a lessee's insurable interest under subsections (1) and (2), the lessor retains an insurable interest until an option to buy has been exercised by the lessee and risk of loss has passed to the lessee.

(4) Nothing in this section impairs any insurable interest recognized under any other statute or rule of law.

(5) The parties by agreement may determine that one or more parties have an obligation to obtain and pay for insurance covering the goods and by agreement may determine the beneficiary of the proceeds of the insurance.

§ 2A–219. Risk of Loss.

(1) Except in the case of a finance lease, risk of loss is retained by the lessor and does not pass to the lessee. In the case of a finance lease, risk of loss passes to the lessee.

(2) Subject to the provisions of this Article on the effect of default on risk of loss (Section 2A–220), if risk of loss is to pass to the lessee and the time of passage is not stated, the following rules apply:

(a) If the lease contract requires or authorizes the goods to be shipped by carrier

(i) and it does not require delivery at a particular destination, the risk of loss passes to the lessee when the goods are duly delivered to the carrier; but

(ii) if it does require delivery at a particular destination and the goods are there duly tendered while in the possession of the carrier, the risk of loss passes to the lessee when the goods are there duly so tendered as to enable the lessee to take delivery.

(b) If the goods are held by a bailee to be delivered without being moved, the risk of loss passes to the lessee on acknowledgment by the bailee of the lessee's right to possession of the goods.

(c) In any case not within subsection (a) or (b), the risk of loss passes to the lessee on the lessee's receipt of the goods if the lessor, or, in the case of a finance lease, the supplier, is a merchant; otherwise the risk passes to the lessee on tender of delivery.

§ 2A–220. Effect of Default on Risk of Loss.

(1) Where risk of loss is to pass to the lessee and the time of passage is not stated:

(a) If a tender or delivery of goods so fails to conform to the lease contract as to give a right of rejection, the risk of their loss remains with the lessor, or, in the case of a finance lease, the supplier, until cure or acceptance.

(b) If the lessee rightfully revokes acceptance, he [or she], to the extent of any deficiency in his [or her] effective insurance coverage, may treat the risk of loss as having remained with the lessor from the beginning.

(2) Whether or not risk of loss is to pass to the lessee, if the lessee as to conforming goods already identified to a lease contract repudiates or is otherwise in default under the lease contract, the lessor, or, in the case of a finance lease, the supplier, to the extent of any deficiency in his [or her] effective insurance coverage may treat the risk of loss as resting on the lessee for a commercially reasonable time.

§ 2A–221. Casualty to Identified Goods.

If a lease contract requires goods identified when the lease contract is made, and the goods suffer casualty without fault of the lessee, the lessor or the supplier before delivery, or the goods suffer casualty before risk of loss passes to the lessee pursuant to the lease agreement or Section 2A–219, then:

(a) if the loss is total, the lease contract is avoided; and

(b) if the loss is partial or the goods have so deteriorated as to no longer conform to the lease contract, the lessee may nevertheless demand inspection and at his [or her] option either treat the lease contract as avoided or, except in a finance lease that is not a consumer lease, accept the goods with due allowance from the rent payable for the balance of the lease term for the deterioration or the deficiency in quantity but without further right against the lessor.

Part 3 Effect of Lease Contract

§ 2A–301. Enforceability of Lease Contract.

Except as otherwise provided in this Article, a lease contract is effective and enforceable according to its terms between the parties, against purchasers of the goods and against creditors of the parties.

§ 2A–302. Title to and Possession of Goods.

Except as otherwise provided in this Article, each provision of this Article applies whether the lessor or a third party has title to the goods, and whether the lessor, the lessee, or a third party has possession of the goods, notwithstanding any statute or rule of law that possession or the absence of possession is fraudulent.

§ 2A–303. Alienability of Party's Interest Under Lease Contract or of Lessor's Residual Interest in Goods; Delegation of Performance; Transfer of Rights.

(1) As used in this section, "creation of a security interest" includes the sale of a lease contract that is subject to Article 9, Secured Transactions, by reason of Section 9–109(a)(3).

(2) Except as provided in subsections (3) and Section 9–407, a provision in a lease agreement which (i) prohibits the voluntary or involuntary transfer, including a transfer by sale, sublease, creation or enforcement of a security interest, or attachment, levy, or other judicial process, of an interest of a party under the lease contract or of the lessor's residual interest in the goods, or (ii) makes such a transfer an event of default, gives rise to the rights and remedies provided in subsection (4), but a transfer that is prohibited or is an event of default under the lease agreement is otherwise effective.

(3) A provision in a lease agreement which (i) prohibits a transfer of a right to damages for default with respect to the whole lease contract or of a right to payment arising out of the transferor's due performance of the transferor's entire obligation, or (ii) makes such a transfer an event of default, is not enforceable, and such a transfer is not a transfer that materially impairs the propsect of obtaining return performance by, materially changes the duty of, or materially increases the burden or risk imposed on, the other party to the lease contract within the purview of subsection (4).

(4) Subject to subsection (3) and Section 9–407:

(a) if a transfer is made which is made an event of default under a lease agreement, the party to the lease contract not making the transfer, unless that party waives the default or otherwise agrees, has the rights and remedies described in Section 2A–501(2);

(b) if paragraph (a) is not applicable and if a transfer is made that (i) is prohibited under a lease agreement or (ii) materially impairs the prospect of obtaining return performance by, materially changes the duty of, or materially increases the burden or risk imposed on, the other party to the lease contract, unless the party not making the transfer agrees at any time to the transfer in the lease contract or otherwise, then, except as limited by contract, (i) the transferor is liable to the party not making the transfer for damages caused by the transfer to the extent that the damages could not reasonably be prevented by the party not making the transfer and (ii) a court having jurisdiction may grant other appropriate relief, including cancellation of the lease contract or an injunction against the transfer.

(5) A transfer of "the lease" or of "all my rights under the lease", or a transfer in similar general terms, is a transfer of rights and, unless the language or the circumstances, as in a transfer for security, indicate the contrary, the transfer is a delegation of duties by the transferor to the transferee. Acceptance by the transferee constitutes a promise by the transferee to perform those duties. The promise is enforceable by either the transferor or the other party to the lease contract.

(6) Unless otherwise agreed by the lessor and the lessee, a delegation of performance does not relieve the transferor as against the other party of any duty to perform or of any liability for default.

(7) In a consumer lease, to prohibit the transfer of an interest of a party under the lease contract or to make a transfer an event of default, the language must be specific, by a writing, and conspicuous.

As amended in 1990 and 1999.

§ 2A–304. Subsequent Lease of Goods by Lessor.

(1) Subject to Section 2A–303, a subsequent lessee from a lessor of goods under an existing lease contract obtains, to the extent of the leasehold interest transferred, the leasehold interest in the goods that the lessor had or had power to transfer, and except as provided in subsection (2) and Section 2A–527(4), takes subject to the existing lease contract. A lessor with voidable title has power to transfer a good leasehold inter-

est to a good faith subsequent lessee for value, but only to the extent set forth in the preceding sentence. If goods have been delivered under a transaction of purchase the lessor has that power even though:

(a) the lessor's transferor was deceived as to the identity of the lessor;

(b) the delivery was in exchange for a check which is later dishonored;

(c) it was agreed that the transaction was to be a "cash sale"; or

(d) the delivery was procured through fraud punishable as larcenous under the criminal law.

(2) A subsequent lessee in the ordinary course of business from a lessor who is a merchant dealing in goods of that kind to whom the goods were entrusted by the existing lessee of that lessor before the interest of the subsequent lessee became enforceable against that lessor obtains, to the extent of the leasehold interest transferred, all of that lessor's and the existing lessee's rights to the goods, and takes free of the existing lease contract.

(3) A subsequent lessee from the lessor of goods that are subject to an existing lease contract and are covered by a certificate of title issued under a statute of this State or of another jurisdiction takes no greater rights than those provided both by this section and by the certificate of title statute.

As amended in 1990.

§ 2A–305. Sale or Sublease of Goods by Lessee.

(1) Subject to the provisions of Section 2A–303, a buyer or sublessee from the lessee of goods under an existing lease contract obtains, to the extent of the interest transferred, the leasehold interest in the goods that the lessee had or had power to transfer, and except as provided in subsection (2) and Section 2A–511(4), takes subject to the existing lease contract. A lessee with a voidable leasehold interest has power to transfer a good leasehold interest to a good faith buyer for value or a good faith sublessee for value, but only to the extent set forth in the preceding sentence. When goods have been delivered under a transaction of lease the lessee has that power even though:

(a) the lessor was deceived as to the identity of the lessee;

(b) the delivery was in exchange for a check which is later dishonored; or

(c) the delivery was procured through fraud punishable as larcenous under the criminal law.

(2) A buyer in the ordinary course of business or a sublessee in the ordinary course of business from a lessee who is a merchant dealing in goods of that kind to whom the goods were entrusted by the lessor obtains, to the extent of the interest transferred, all of the lessor's and lessee's rights to the goods, and takes free of the existing lease contract.

(3) A buyer or sublessee from the lessee of goods that are subject to an existing lease contract and are covered by a certificate of title issued under a statute of this State or of another jurisdiction

takes no greater rights than those provided both by this section and by the certificate of title statute.

§ 2A–306. Priority of Certain Liens Arising by Operation of Law.

If a person in the ordinary course of his [or her] business furnishes services or materials with respect to goods subject to a lease contract, a lien upon those goods in the possession of that person given by statute or rule of law for those materials or services takes priority over any interest of the lessor or lessee under the lease contract or this Article unless the lien is created by statute and the statute provides otherwise or unless the lien is created by rule of law and the rule of law provides otherwise.

§ 2A–307. Priority of Liens Arising by Attachment or Levy on, Security Interests in, and Other Claims to Goods.

(1) Except as otherwise provided in Section 2A–306, a creditor of a lessee takes subject to the lease contract.

(2) Except as otherwise provided in subsection (3) and in Sections 2A–306 and 2A–308, a creditor of a lessor takes subject to the lease contract unless the creditor holds a lien that attached to the goods before the lease contract became enforceable.

(3) Except as otherwise provided in Sections 9–317, 9–321, and 9–323, a lessee takes a leasehold interest subject to a security interest held by a creditor of the lessor.

As amended in 1990 and 1999.

§ 2A–308. Special Rights of Creditors.

(1) A creditor of a lessor in possession of goods subject to a lease contract may treat the lease contract as void if as against the creditor retention of possession by the lessor is fraudulent under any statute or rule of law, but retention of possession in good faith and current course of trade by the lessor for a commercially reasonable time after the lease contract becomes enforceable is not fraudulent.

(2) Nothing in this Article impairs the rights of creditors of a lessor if the lease contract (a) becomes enforceable, not in current course of trade but in satisfaction of or as security for a pre-existing claim for money, security, or the like, and (b) is made under circumstances which under any statute or rule of law apart from this Article would constitute the transaction a fraudulent transfer or voidable preference.

(3) A creditor of a seller may treat a sale or an identification of goods to a contract for sale as void if as against the creditor retention of possession by the seller is fraudulent under any statute or rule of law, but retention of possession of the goods pursuant to a lease contract entered into by the seller as lessee and the buyer as lessor in connection with the sale or identification of the goods is not fraudulent if the buyer bought for value and in good faith.

§ 2A–309. Lessor's and Lessee's Rights When Goods Become Fixtures.

(1) In this section:

(a) goods are "fixtures" when they become so related to particular real estate that an interest in them arises under real estate law;

(b) a "fixture filing" is the filing, in the office where a mortgage on the real estate would be filed or recorded, of a financing statement covering goods that are or are to become fixtures and conforming to the requirements of Section 9–502(a) and (b);

(c) a lease is a "purchase money lease" unless the lessee has possession or use of the goods or the right to possession or use of the goods before the lease agreement is enforceable;

(d) a mortgage is a "construction mortgage" to the extent it secures an obligation incurred for the construction of an improvement on land including the acquisition cost of the land, if the recorded writing so indicates; and

(e) "encumbrance" includes real estate mortgages and other liens on real estate and all other rights in real estate that are not ownership interests.

(2) Under this Article a lease may be of goods that are fixtures or may continue in goods that become fixtures, but no lease exists under this Article of ordinary building materials incorporated into an improvement on land.

(3) This Article does not prevent creation of a lease of fixtures pursuant to real estate law.

(4) The perfected interest of a lessor of fixtures has priority over a conflicting interest of an encumbrancer or owner of the real estate if:

(a) the lease is a purchase money lease, the conflicting interest of the encumbrancer or owner arises before the goods become fixtures, the interest of the lessor is perfected by a fixture filing before the goods become fixtures or within ten days thereafter, and the lessee has an interest of record in the real estate or is in possession of the real estate; or

(b) the interest of the lessor is perfected by a fixture filing before the interest of the encumbrancer or owner is of record, the lessor's interest has priority over any conflicting interest of a predecessor in title of the encumbrancer or owner, and the lessee has an interest of record in the real estate or is in possession of the real estate.

(5) The interest of a lessor of fixtures, whether or not perfected, has priority over the conflicting interest of an encumbrancer or owner of the real estate if:

(a) the fixtures are readily removable factory or office machines, readily removable equipment that is not primarily used or leased for use in the operation of the real estate, or readily removable replacements of domestic appliances that are goods subject to a consumer lease, and before the goods become fixtures the lease contract is enforceable; or

(b) the conflicting interest is a lien on the real estate obtained by legal or equitable proceedings after the lease contract is enforceable; or

(c) the encumbrancer or owner has consented in writing to the lease or has disclaimed an interest in the goods as fixtures; or

(d) the lessee has a right to remove the goods as against the encumbrancer or owner. If the lessee's right to remove terminates, the priority of the interest of the lessor continues for a reasonable time.

(6) Notwithstanding paragraph (4)(a) but otherwise subject to subsections (4) and (5), the interest of a lessor of fixtures, including the lessor's residual interest, is subordinate to the conflicting interest of an encumbrancer of the real estate under a construction mortgage recorded before the goods become fixtures if the goods become fixtures before the completion of the construction. To the extent given to refinance a construction mortgage, the conflicting interest of an encumbrancer of the real estate under a mortgage has this priority to the same extent as the encumbrancer of the real estate under the construction mortgage.

(7) In cases not within the preceding subsections, priority between the interest of a lessor of fixtures, including the lessor's residual interest, and the conflicting interest of an encumbrancer or owner of the real estate who is not the lessee is determined by the priority rules governing conflicting interests in real estate.

(8) If the interest of a lessor of fixtures, including the lessor's residual interest, has priority over all conflicting interests of all owners and encumbrancers of the real estate, the lessor or the lessee may (i) on default, expiration, termination, or cancellation of the lease agreement but subject to the agreement and this Article, or (ii) if necessary to enforce other rights and remedies of the lessor or lessee under this Article, remove the goods from the real estate, free and clear of all conflicting interests of all owners and encumbrancers of the real estate, but the lessor or lessee must reimburse any encumbrancer or owner of the real estate who is not the lessee and who has not otherwise agreed for the cost of repair of any physical injury, but not for any diminution in value of the real estate caused by the absence of the goods removed or by any necessity of replacing them. A person entitled to reimbursement may refuse permission to remove until the party seeking removal gives adequate security for the performance of this obligation.

(9) Even though the lease agreement does not create a security interest, the interest of a lessor of fixtures, including the lessor's residual interest, is perfected by filing a financing statement as a fixture filing for leased goods that are or are to become fixtures in accordance with the relevant provisions of the Article on Secured Transactions (Article 9).

As amended in 1990 and 1999.

§ 2A–310. **Lessor's and Lessee's Rights When Goods Become Accessions.**

(1) Goods are "accessions" when they are installed in or affixed to other goods.

(2) The interest of a lessor or a lessee under a lease contract entered into before the goods became accessions is superior to all interests in the whole except as stated in subsection (4).

(3) The interest of a lessor or a lessee under a lease contract entered into at the time or after the goods became accessions is superior to all subsequently acquired interests in the whole except as stated in subsection (4) but is subordinate to interests in the whole existing at the time the lease contract was made unless the holders of such interests in the whole have in writing consented to the lease or disclaimed an interest in the goods as part of the whole.

(4) The interest of a lessor or a lessee under a lease contract described in subsection (2) or (3) is subordinate to the interest of

(a) a buyer in the ordinary course of business or a lessee in the ordinary course of business of any interest in the whole acquired after the goods became accessions; or

(b) a creditor with a security interest in the whole perfected before the lease contract was made to the extent that the creditor makes subsequent advances without knowledge of the lease contract.

(5) When under subsections (2) or (3) and (4) a lessor or a lessee of accessions holds an interest that is superior to all interests in the whole, the lessor or the lessee may (a) on default, expiration, termination, or cancellation of the lease contract by the other party but subject to the provisions of the lease contract and this Article, or (b) if necessary to enforce his [or her] other rights and remedies under this Article, remove the goods from the whole, free and clear of all interests in the whole, but he [or she] must reimburse any holder of an interest in the whole who is not the lessee and who has not otherwise agreed for the cost of repair of any physical injury but not for any diminution in value of the whole caused by the absence of the goods removed or by any necessity for replacing them. A person entitled to reimbursement may refuse permission to remove until the party seeking removal gives adequate security for the performance of this obligation.

§ 2A–311. **Priority Subject to Subordination.**

Nothing in this Article prevents subordination by agreement by any person entitled to priority.

As added in 1990.

Part 4 Performance of Lease Contract: Repudiated, Substituted and Excused

§ 2A–401. **Insecurity: Adequate Assurance of Performance.**

(1) A lease contract imposes an obligation on each party that the other's expectation of receiving due performance will not be impaired.

(2) If reasonable grounds for insecurity arise with respect to the performance of either party, the insecure party may demand in writing adequate assurance of due performance. Until the insecure party receives that assurance, if commercially reasonable the insecure party may suspend any performance for which he [or she] has not already received the agreed return.

(3) A repudiation of the lease contract occurs if assurance of due performance adequate under the circumstances of the particular case is not provided to the insecure party within a reasonable time, not to exceed 30 days after receipt of a demand by the other party.

(4) Between merchants, the reasonableness of grounds for insecurity and the adequacy of any assurance offered must be determined according to commercial standards.

(5) Acceptance of any nonconforming delivery or payment does not prejudice the aggrieved party's right to demand adequate assurance of future performance.

§ 2A–402. Anticipatory Repudiation.

If either party repudiates a lease contract with respect to a performance not yet due under the lease contract, the loss of which performance will substantially impair the value of the lease contract to the other, the aggrieved party may:

(a) for a commercially reasonable time, await retraction of repudiation and performance by the repudiating party;

(b) make demand pursuant to Section 2A–401 and await assurance of future performance adequate under the circumstances of the particular case; or

(c) resort to any right or remedy upon default under the lease contract or this Article, even though the aggrieved party has notified the repudiating party that the aggrieved party would await the repudiating party's performance and assurance and has urged retraction. In addition, whether or not the aggrieved party is pursuing one of the foregoing remedies, the aggrieved party may suspend performance or, if the aggrieved party is the lessor, proceed in accordance with the provisions of this Article on the lessor's right to identify goods to the lease contract notwithstanding default or to salvage unfinished goods (Section 2A–524).

§ 2A–403. Retraction of Anticipatory Repudiation.

(1) Until the repudiating party's next performance is due, the repudiating party can retract the repudiation unless, since the repudiation, the aggrieved party has cancelled the lease contract or materially changed the aggrieved party's position or otherwise indicated that the aggrieved party considers the repudiation final.

(2) Retraction may be by any method that clearly indicates to the aggrieved party that the repudiating party intends to perform under the lease contract and includes any assurance demanded under Section 2A–401.

(3) Retraction reinstates a repudiating party's rights under a lease contract with due excuse and allowance to the aggrieved party for any delay occasioned by the repudiation.

§ 2A–404. Substituted Performance.

(1) If without fault of the lessee, the lessor and the supplier, the agreed berthing, loading, or unloading facilities fail or the agreed type of carrier becomes unavailable or the agreed manner of delivery otherwise becomes commercially impracticable, but a commercially reasonable substitute is available, the substitute performance must be tendered and accepted.

(2) If the agreed means or manner of payment fails because of domestic or foreign governmental regulation:

(a) the lessor may withhold or stop delivery or cause the supplier to withhold or stop delivery unless the lessee provides a means or manner of payment that is commercially a substantial equivalent; and

(b) if delivery has already been taken, payment by the means or in the manner provided by the regulation discharges the lessee's obligation unless the regulation is discriminatory, oppressive, or predatory.

§ 2A–405. Excused Performance.

Subject to Section 2A–404 on substituted performance, the following rules apply:

(a) Delay in delivery or nondelivery in whole or in part by a lessor or a supplier who complies with paragraphs (b) and (c) is not a default under the lease contract if performance as agreed has been made impracticable by the occurrence of a contingency the nonoccurrence of which was a basic assumption on which the lease contract was made or by compliance in good faith with any applicable foreign or domestic governmental regulation or order, whether or not the regulation or order later proves to be invalid.

(b) If the causes mentioned in paragraph (a) affect only part of the lessor's or the supplier's capacity to perform, he [or she] shall allocate production and deliveries among his [or her] customers but at his [or her] option may include regular customers not then under contract for sale or lease as well as his [or her] own requirements for further manufacture. He [or she] may so allocate in any manner that is fair and reasonable.

(c) The lessor seasonably shall notify the lessee and in the case of a finance lease the supplier seasonably shall notify the lessor and the lessee, if known, that there will be delay or nondelivery and, if allocation is required under paragraph (b), of the estimated quota thus made available for the lessee.

§ 2A–406. Procedure on Excused Performance.

(1) If the lessee receives notification of a material or indefinite delay or an allocation justified under Section 2A–405, the lessee may by written notification to the lessor as to any goods involved, and with respect to all of the goods if under an installment lease contract the value of the whole lease contract is substantially impaired (Section 2A–510):

(a) terminate the lease contract (Section 2A–505(2)); or

(b) except in a finance lease that is not a consumer lease, modify the lease contract by accepting the available quota in substitution, with due allowance from the rent payable for the balance of the lease term for the deficiency but without further right against the lessor.

(2) If, after receipt of a notification from the lessor under Section 2A–405, the lessee fails so to modify the lease agreement within a reasonable time not exceeding 30 days, the lease contract lapses with respect to any deliveries affected.

§ 2A–407. Irrevocable Promises: Finance Leases.

(1) In the case of a finance lease that is not a consumer lease the lessee's promises under the lease contract become irrevocable and independent upon the lessee's acceptance of the goods.

(2) A promise that has become irrevocable and independent under subsection (1):

(a) is effective and enforceable between the parties, and by or against third parties including assignees of the parties, and

(b) is not subject to cancellation, termination, modification, repudiation, excuse, or substitution without the consent of the party to whom the promise runs.

(3) This section does not affect the validity under any other law of a covenant in any lease contract making the lessee's promises irrevocable and independent upon the lessee's acceptance of the goods.

As amended in 1990.

Part 5 Default

A. In General

§ 2A–501. Default: Procedure.

(1) Whether the lessor or the lessee is in default under a lease contract is determined by the lease agreement and this Article.

(2) If the lessor or the lessee is in default under the lease contract, the party seeking enforcement has rights and remedies as provided in this Article and, except as limited by this Article, as provided in the lease agreement.

(3) If the lessor or the lessee is in default under the lease contract, the party seeking enforcement may reduce the party's claim to judgment, or otherwise enforce the lease contract by self-help or any available judicial procedure or nonjudicial procedure, including administrative proceeding, arbitration, or the like, in accordance with this Article.

(4) Except as otherwise provided in Section 1–106(1) or this Article or the lease agreement, the rights and remedies referred to in subsections (2) and (3) are cumulative.

(5) If the lease agreement covers both real property and goods, the party seeking enforcement may proceed under this Part as to the goods, or under other applicable law as to both the real property and the goods in accordance with that party's rights and remedies in respect of the real property, in which case this Part does not apply.

As amended in 1990.

§ 2A–502. Notice After Default.

Except as otherwise provided in this Article or the lease agreement, the lessor or lessee in default under the lease contract is not entitled to notice of default or notice of enforcement from the other party to the lease agreement.

§ 2A–503. Modification or Impairment of Rights and Remedies.

(1) Except as otherwise provided in this Article, the lease agreement may include rights and remedies for default in addition to or in substitution for those provided in this Article and may limit or alter the measure of damages recoverable under this Article.

(2) Resort to a remedy provided under this Article or in the lease agreement is optional unless the remedy is expressly agreed to be exclusive. If circumstances cause an exclusive or limited remedy to fail of its essential purpose, or provision for an exclusive remedy is unconscionable, remedy may be had as provided in this Article.

(3) Consequential damages may be liquidated under Section 2A–504, or may otherwise be limited, altered, or excluded unless the limitation, alteration, or exclusion is unconscionable. Limitation, alteration, or exclusion of consequential damages for injury to the person in the case of consumer goods is prima facie unconscionable but limitation, alteration, or exclusion of damages where the loss is commercial is not prima facie unconscionable.

(4) Rights and remedies on default by the lessor or the lessee with respect to any obligation or promise collateral or ancillary to the lease contract are not impaired by this Article.

As amended in 1990.

§ 2A–504. Liquidation of Damages.

(1) Damages payable by either party for default, or any other act or omission, including indemnity for loss or diminution of anticipated tax benefits or loss or damage to lessor's residual interest, may be liquidated in the lease agreement but only at an amount or by a formula that is reasonable in light of the then anticipated harm caused by the default or other act or omission.

(2) If the lease agreement provides for liquidation of damages, and such provision does not comply with subsection (1), or such provision is an exclusive or limited remedy that circumstances cause to fail of its essential purpose, remedy may be had as provided in this Article.

(3) If the lessor justifiably withholds or stops delivery of goods because of the lessee's default or insolvency (Section 2A–525 or 2A–526), the lessee is entitled to restitution of any amount by which the sum of his [or her] payments exceeds:

(a) the amount to which the lessor is entitled by virtue of terms liquidating the lessor's damages in accordance with subsection (1); or

(b) in the absence of those terms, 20 percent of the then present value of the total rent the lessee was obligated to pay for the balance of the lease term, or, in the case of a consumer lease, the lesser of such amount or $500.

(4) A lessee's right to restitution under subsection (3) is subject to offset to the extent the lessor establishes:

(a) a right to recover damages under the provisions of this Article other than subsection (1); and

(b) the amount or value of any benefits received by the lessee directly or indirectly by reason of the lease contract.

§ 2A–505. Cancellation and Termination and Effect of Cancellation, Termination, Rescission, or Fraud on Rights and Remedies.

(1) On cancellation of the lease contract, all obligations that are still executory on both sides are discharged, but any right based on prior default or performance survives, and the cancelling party also retains any remedy for default of the whole lease contract or any unperformed balance.

(2) On termination of the lease contract, all obligations that are still executory on both sides are discharged but any right based on prior default or performance survives.

(3) Unless the contrary intention clearly appears, expressions of "cancellation," "rescission," or the like of the lease contract may not be construed as a renunciation or discharge of any claim in damages for an antecedent default.

(4) Rights and remedies for material misrepresentation or fraud include all rights and remedies available under this Article for default.

(5) Neither rescission nor a claim for rescission of the lease contract nor rejection or return of the goods may bar or be deemed inconsistent with a claim for damages or other right or remedy.

§ 2A–506. Statute of Limitations.

(1) An action for default under a lease contract, including breach of warranty or indemnity, must be commenced within 4 years after the cause of action accrued. By the original lease contract the parties may reduce the period of limitation to not less than one year.

(2) A cause of action for default accrues when the act or omission on which the default or breach of warranty is based is or should have been discovered by the aggrieved party, or when the default occurs, whichever is later. A cause of action for indemnity accrues when the act or omission on which the claim for indemnity is based is or should have been discovered by the indemnified party, whichever is later.

(3) If an action commenced within the time limited by subsection (1) is so terminated as to leave available a remedy by another action for the same default or breach of warranty or indemnity, the other action may be commenced after the expiration of the time limited and within 6 months after the termination of the first action unless the termination resulted from voluntary discontinuance or from dismissal for failure or neglect to prosecute.

(4) This section does not alter the law on tolling of the statute of limitations nor does it apply to causes of action that have accrued before this Article becomes effective.

§ 2A–507. Proof of Market Rent: Time and Place.

(1) Damages based on market rent (Section 2A–519 or 2A–528) are determined according to the rent for the use of the goods concerned for a lease term identical to the remaining lease term of the original lease agreement and prevailing at the times specified in Sections 2A–519 and 2A–528.

(2) If evidence of rent for the use of the goods concerned for a lease term identical to the remaining lease term of the original lease agreement and prevailing at the times or places described in this Article is not readily available, the rent prevailing within any reasonable time before or after the time described or at any other place or for a different lease term which in commercial judgment or under usage of trade would serve as a reasonable substitute for the one described may be used, making any proper allowance for the difference, including the cost of transporting the goods to or from the other place.

(3) Evidence of a relevant rent prevailing at a time or place or for a lease term other than the one described in this Article offered by one party is not admissible unless and until he [or she] has given the other party notice the court finds sufficient to prevent unfair surprise.

(4) If the prevailing rent or value of any goods regularly leased in any established market is in issue, reports in official publications or trade journals or in newspapers or periodicals of general circulation published as the reports of that market are admissible in evidence. The circumstances of the preparation of the report may be shown to affect its weight but not its admissibility.

As amended in 1990.

B. Default by Lessor

§ 2A–508. Lessee's Remedies.

(1) If a lessor fails to deliver the goods in conformity to the lease contract (Section 2A–509) or repudiates the lease contract (Section 2A–402), or a lessee rightfully rejects the goods (Section 2A–509) or justifiably revokes acceptance of the goods (Section 2A–517), then with respect to any goods involved, and with respect to all of the goods if under an installment lease contract the value of the whole lease contract is substantially impaired (Section 2A–510), the lessor is in default under the lease contract and the lessee may:

    (a) cancel the lease contract (Section 2A–505(1));

    (b) recover so much of the rent and security as has been paid and is just under the circumstances;

    (c) cover and recover damages as to all goods affected whether or not they have been identified to the lease contract (Sections 2A–518 and 2A–520), or recover damages for non-delivery (Sections 2A–519 and 2A–520);

    (d) exercise any other rights or pursue any other remedies provided in the lease contract.

(2) If a lessor fails to deliver the goods in conformity to the lease contract or repudiates the lease contract, the lessee may also:

    (a) if the goods have been identified, recover them (Section 2A–522); or

    (b) in a proper case, obtain specific performance or replevy the goods (Section 2A–521).

(3) If a lessor is otherwise in default under a lease contract, the lessee may exercise the rights and pursue the remedies provided in the lease contract, which may include a right to cancel the lease, and in Section 2A–519(3).

(4) If a lessor has breached a warranty, whether express or implied, the lessee may recover damages (Section 2A–519(4)).

(5) On rightful rejection or justifiable revocation of acceptance, a lessee has a security interest in goods in the lessee's possession or control for any rent and security that has been paid and any expenses reasonably incurred in their inspection, receipt, transportation, and care and custody and may hold those goods and dispose of them in good faith and in a commercially reasonable manner, subject to Section 2A–527(5).

(6) Subject to the provisions of Section 2A–407, a lessee, on notifying the lessor of the lessee's intention to do so, may deduct all or any part of the damages resulting from any default under the lease contract from any part of the rent still due under the same lease contract.

As amended in 1990.

§ 2A–509. Lessee's Rights on Improper Delivery; Rightful Rejection.

(1) Subject to the provisions of Section 2A–510 on default in installment lease contracts, if the goods or the tender or delivery fail in any respect to conform to the lease contract, the lessee may reject or accept the goods or accept any commercial unit or units and reject the rest of the goods.

(2) Rejection of goods is ineffective unless it is within a reasonable time after tender or delivery of the goods and the lessee seasonably notifies the lessor.

§ 2A–510. Installment Lease Contracts: Rejection and Default.

(1) Under an installment lease contract a lessee may reject any delivery that is nonconforming if the nonconformity substantially impairs the value of that delivery and cannot be cured or the nonconformity is a defect in the required documents; but if the nonconformity does not fall within subsection (2) and the lessor or the supplier gives adequate assurance of its cure, the lessee must accept that delivery.

(2) Whenever nonconformity or default with respect to one or more deliveries substantially impairs the value of the installment lease contract as a whole there is a default with respect to the whole. But, the aggrieved party reinstates the installment lease contract as a whole if the aggrieved party accepts a nonconforming delivery without seasonably notifying of cancellation or brings an action with respect only to past deliveries or demands performance as to future deliveries.

§ 2A–511. Merchant Lessee's Duties as to Rightfully Rejected Goods.

(1) Subject to any security interest of a lessee (Section 2A–508(5)), if a lessor or a supplier has no agent or place of business at the market of rejection, a merchant lessee, after rejection of goods in his [or her] possession or control, shall follow any reasonable instructions received from the lessor or the supplier with respect to the goods. In the absence of those instructions, a merchant lessee shall make reasonable efforts to sell, lease, or otherwise dispose of the goods for the lessor's account if they threaten to decline in value speedily. Instructions are not reasonable if on demand indemnity for expenses is not forthcoming.

(2) If a merchant lessee (subsection (1)) or any other lessee (Section 2A–512) disposes of goods, he [or she] is entitled to reimbursement either from the lessor or the supplier or out of the proceeds for reasonable expenses of caring for and disposing of the goods and, if the expenses include no disposition commission, to such commission as is usual in the trade, or if there is none, to a reasonable sum not exceeding 10 percent of the gross proceeds.

(3) In complying with this section or Section 2A–512, the lessee is held only to good faith. Good faith conduct hereunder is neither acceptance or conversion nor the basis of an action for damages.

(4) A purchaser who purchases in good faith from a lessee pursuant to this section or Section 2A–512 takes the goods free of any rights of the lessor and the supplier even though the lessee fails to comply with one or more of the requirements of this Article.

§ 2A–512. Lessee's Duties as to Rightfully Rejected Goods.

(1) Except as otherwise provided with respect to goods that threaten to decline in value speedily (Section 2A–511) and subject to any security interest of a lessee (Section 2A–508(5)):

   (a) the lessee, after rejection of goods in the lessee's possession, shall hold them with reasonable care at the lessor's or the supplier's disposition for a reasonable time after the lessee's seasonable notification of rejection;

   (b) if the lessor or the supplier gives no instructions within a reasonable time after notification of rejection, the lessee may store the rejected goods for the lessor's or the supplier's account or ship them to the lessor or the supplier or dispose of them for the lessor's or the supplier's account with reimbursement in the manner provided in Section 2A–511; but

   (c) the lessee has no further obligations with regard to goods rightfully rejected.

(2) Action by the lessee pursuant to subsection (1) is not acceptance or conversion.

§ 2A–513. Cure by Lessor of Improper Tender or Delivery; Replacement.

(1) If any tender or delivery by the lessor or the supplier is rejected because nonconforming and the time for performance has not yet expired, the lessor or the supplier may seasonably notify the lessee of the lessor's or the supplier's intention to cure and may then make a conforming delivery within the time provided in the lease contract.

(2) If the lessee rejects a nonconforming tender that the lessor or the supplier had reasonable grounds to believe would be

acceptable with or without money allowance, the lessor or the supplier may have a further reasonable time to substitute a conforming tender if he [or she] seasonably notifies the lessee.

§ 2A–514. Waiver of Lessee's Objections.

(1) In rejecting goods, a lessee's failure to state a particular defect that is ascertainable by reasonable inspection precludes the lessee from relying on the defect to justify rejection or to establish default:

(a) if, stated seasonably, the lessor or the supplier could have cured it (Section 2A–513); or

(b) between merchants if the lessor or the supplier after rejection has made a request in writing for a full and final written statement of all defects on which the lessee proposes to rely.

(2) A lessee's failure to reserve rights when paying rent or other consideration against documents precludes recovery of the payment for defects apparent on the face of the documents.

§ 2A–515. Acceptance of Goods.

(1) Acceptance of goods occurs after the lessee has had a reasonable opportunity to inspect the goods and

(a) the lessee signifies or acts with respect to the goods in a manner that signifies to the lessor or the supplier that the goods are conforming or that the lessee will take or retain them in spite of their nonconformity; or

(b) the lessee fails to make an effective rejection of the goods (Section 2A–509(2)).

(2) Acceptance of a part of any commercial unit is acceptance of that entire unit.

§ 2A–516. Effect of Acceptance of Goods; Notice of Default; Burden of Establishing Default after Acceptance; Notice of Claim or Litigation to Person Answerable Over.

(1) A lessee must pay rent for any goods accepted in accordance with the lease contract, with due allowance for goods rightfully rejected or not delivered.

(2) A lessee's acceptance of goods precludes rejection of the goods accepted. In the case of a finance lease, if made with knowledge of a nonconformity, acceptance cannot be revoked because of it. In any other case, if made with knowledge of a nonconformity, acceptance cannot be revoked because of it unless the acceptance was on the reasonable assumption that the nonconformity would be seasonably cured. Acceptance does not of itself impair any other remedy provided by this Article or the lease agreement for nonconformity.

(3) If a tender has been accepted:

(a) within a reasonable time after the lessee discovers or should have discovered any default, the lessee shall notify the lessor and the supplier, if any, or be barred from any remedy against the party notified;

(b) except in the case of a consumer lease, within a reasonable time after the lessee receives notice of litigation for infringement or the like (Section 2A–211) the lessee shall notify the lessor or be barred from any remedy over for liability established by the litigation; and

(c) the burden is on the lessee to establish any default.

(4) If a lessee is sued for breach of a warranty or other obligation for which a lessor or a supplier is answerable over the following apply:

(a) The lessee may give the lessor or the supplier, or both, written notice of the litigation. If the notice states that the person notified may come in and defend and that if the person notified does not do so that person will be bound in any action against that person by the lessee by any determination of fact common to the two litigations, then unless the person notified after seasonable receipt of the notice does come in and defend that person is so bound.

(b) The lessor or the supplier may demand in writing that the lessee turn over control of the litigation including settlement if the claim is one for infringement or the like (Section 2A–211) or else be barred from any remedy over. If the demand states that the lessor or the supplier agrees to bear all expense and to satisfy any adverse judgment, then unless the lessee after seasonable receipt of the demand does turn over control the lessee is so barred.

(5) Subsections (3) and (4) apply to any obligation of a lessee to hold the lessor or the supplier harmless against infringement or the like (Section 2A–211).

As amended in 1990.

§ 2A–517. Revocation of Acceptance of Goods.

(1) A lessee may revoke acceptance of a lot or commercial unit whose nonconformity substantially impairs its value to the lessee if the lessee has accepted it:

(a) except in the case of a finance lease, on the reasonable assumption that its nonconformity would be cured and it has not been seasonably cured; or

(b) without discovery of the nonconformity if the lessee's acceptance was reasonably induced either by the lessor's assurances or, except in the case of a finance lease, by the difficulty of discovery before acceptance.

(2) Except in the case of a finance lease that is not a consumer lease, a lessee may revoke acceptance of a lot or commercial unit if the lessor defaults under the lease contract and the default substantially impairs the value of that lot or commercial unit to the lessee.

(3) If the lease agreement so provides, the lessee may revoke acceptance of a lot or commercial unit because of other defaults by the lessor.

(4) Revocation of acceptance must occur within a reasonable time after the lessee discovers or should have discovered the ground for it and before any substantial change in condition of the goods which is not caused by the nonconformity. Revocation is not effective until the lessee notifies the lessor.

(5) A lessee who so revokes has the same rights and duties with regard to the goods involved as if the lessee had rejected them.

As amended in 1990.

§ 2A–518. Cover; Substitute Goods.

(1) After a default by a lessor under the lease contract of the type described in Section 2A–508(1), or, if agreed, after other default by the lessor, the lessee may cover by making any purchase or lease of or contract to purchase or lease goods in substitution for those due from the lessor.

(2) Except as otherwise provided with respect to damages liquidated in the lease agreement (Section 2A–504) or otherwise determined pursuant to agreement of the parties (Sections 1–102(3) and 2A–503), if a lessee's cover is by lease agreement substantially similar to the original lease agreement and the new lease agreement is made in good faith and in a commercially reasonable manner, the lessee may recover from the lessor as damages (i) the present value, as of the date of the commencement of the term of the new lease agreement, of the rent under the new lease agreement applicable to that period of the new lease term which is comparable to the then remaining term of the original lease agreement minus the present value as of the same date of the total rent for the then remaining lease term of the original lease agreement, and (ii) any incidental or consequential damages, less expenses saved in consequence of the lessor's default.

(3) If a lessee's cover is by lease agreement that for any reason does not qualify for treatment under subsection (2), or is by purchase or otherwise, the lessee may recover from the lessor as if the lessee had elected not to cover and Section 2A–519 governs.

As amended in 1990.

§ 2A–519. Lessee's Damages for Non-Delivery, Repudiation, Default, and Breach of Warranty in Regard to Accepted Goods.

(1) Except as otherwise provided with respect to damages liquidated in the lease agreement (Section 2A–504) or otherwise determined pursuant to agreement of the parties (Sections 1–102(3) and 2A–503), if a lessee elects not to cover or a lessee elects to cover and the cover is by lease agreement that for any reason does not qualify for treatment under Section 2A–518(2), or is by purchase or otherwise, the measure of damages for non-delivery or repudiation by the lessor or for rejection or revocation of acceptance by the lessee is the present value, as of the date of the default, of the then market rent minus the present value as of the same date of the original rent, computed for the remaining lease term of the original lease agreement, together with incidental and consequential damages, less expenses saved in consequence of the lessor's default.

(2) Market rent is to be determined as of the place for tender or, in cases of rejection after arrival or revocation of acceptance, as of the place of arrival.

(3) Except as otherwise agreed, if the lessee has accepted goods and given notification (Section 2A–516(3)), the measure of damages for non-conforming tender or delivery or other default by a lessor is the loss resulting in the ordinary course of events from the lessor's default as determined in any manner that is

reasonable together with incidental and consequential damages, less expenses saved in consequence of the lessor's default.

(4) Except as otherwise agreed, the measure of damages for breach of warranty is the present value at the time and place of acceptance of the difference between the value of the use of the goods accepted and the value if they had been as warranted for the lease term, unless special circumstances show proximate damages of a different amount, together with incidental and consequential damages, less expenses saved in consequence of the lessor's default or breach of warranty.

As amended in 1990.

§ 2A–520. Lessee's Incidental and Consequential Damages.

(1) Incidental damages resulting from a lessor's default include expenses reasonably incurred in inspection, receipt, transportation, and care and custody of goods rightfully rejected or goods the acceptance of which is justifiably revoked, any commercially reasonable charges, expenses or commissions in connection with effecting cover, and any other reasonable expense incident to the default.

(2) Consequential damages resulting from a lessor's default include:

(a) any loss resulting from general or particular requirements and needs of which the lessor at the time of contracting had reason to know and which could not reasonably be prevented by cover or otherwise; and

(b) injury to person or property proximately resulting from any breach of warranty.

§ 2A–521. Lessee's Right to Specific Performance or Replevin.

(1) Specific performance may be decreed if the goods are unique or in other proper circumstances.

(2) A decree for specific performance may include any terms and conditions as to payment of the rent, damages, or other relief that the court deems just.

(3) A lessee has a right of replevin, detinue, sequestration, claim and delivery, or the like for goods identified to the lease contract if after reasonable effort the lessee is unable to effect cover for those goods or the circumstances reasonably indicate that the effort will be unavailing.

§ 2A–522. Lessee's Right to Goods on Lessor's Insolvency.

(1) Subject to subsection (2) and even though the goods have not been shipped, a lessee who has paid a part or all of the rent and security for goods identified to a lease contract (Section 2A–217) on making and keeping good a tender of any unpaid portion of the rent and security due under the lease contract may recover the goods identified from the lessor if the lessor becomes insolvent within 10 days after receipt of the first installment of rent and security.

(2) A lessee acquires the right to recover goods identified to a lease contract only if they conform to the lease contract.

C. Default by Lessee

§ 2A–523. Lessor's Remedies.

(1) If a lessee wrongfully rejects or revokes acceptance of goods or fails to make a payment when due or repudiates with respect to a part or the whole, then, with respect to any goods involved, and with respect to all of the goods if under an installment lease contract the value of the whole lease contract is substantially impaired (Section 2A–510), the lessee is in default under the lease contract and the lessor may:

(a) cancel the lease contract (Section 2A–505(1));

(b) proceed respecting goods not identified to the lease contract (Section 2A–524);

(c) withhold delivery of the goods and take possession of goods previously delivered (Section 2A–525);

(d) stop delivery of the goods by any bailee (Section 2A–526);

(e) dispose of the goods and recover damages (Section 2A–527), or retain the goods and recover damages (Section 2A–528), or in a proper case recover rent (Section 2A–529)

(f) exercise any other rights or pursue any other remedies provided in the lease contract.

(2) If a lessor does not fully exercise a right or obtain a remedy to which the lessor is entitled under subsection (1), the lessor may recover the loss resulting in the ordinary course of events from the lessee's default as determined in any reasonable manner, together with incidental damages, less expenses saved in consequence of the lessee's default.

(3) If a lessee is otherwise in default under a lease contract, the lessor may exercise the rights and pursue the remedies provided in the lease contract, which may include a right to cancel the lease. In addition, unless otherwise provided in the lease contract:

(a) if the default substantially impairs the value of the lease contract to the lessor, the lessor may exercise the rights and pursue the remedies provided in subsections (1) or (2); or

(b) if the default does not substantially impair the value of the lease contract to the lessor, the lessor may recover as provided in subsection (2).

As amended in 1990.

§ 2A–524. Lessor's Right to Identify Goods to Lease Contract.

(1) After default by the lessee under the lease contract of the type described in Section 2A–523(1) or 2A–523(3)(a) or, if agreed, after other default by the lessee, the lessor may:

(a) identify to the lease contract conforming goods not already identified if at the time the lessor learned of the default they were in the lessor's or the supplier's possession or control; and

(b) dispose of goods (Section 2A–527(1)) that demonstrably have been intended for the particular lease contract even though those goods are unfinished.

(2) If the goods are unfinished, in the exercise of reasonable commercial judgment for the purposes of avoiding loss and of effective realization, an aggrieved lessor or the supplier may either complete manufacture and wholly identify the goods to the lease contract or cease manufacture and lease, sell, or otherwise dispose of the goods for scrap or salvage value or proceed in any other reasonable manner.

As amended in 1990.

§ 2A–525. Lessor's Right to Possession of Goods.

(1) If a lessor discovers the lessee to be insolvent, the lessor may refuse to deliver the goods.

(2) After a default by the lessee under the lease contract of the type described in Section 2A–523(1) or 2A–523(3)(a) or, if agreed, after other default by the lessee, the lessor has the right to take possession of the goods. If the lease contract so provides, the lessor may require the lessee to assemble the goods and make them available to the lessor at a place to be designated by the lessor which is reasonably convenient to both parties. Without removal, the lessor may render unusable any goods employed in trade or business, and may dispose of goods on the lessee's premises (Section 2A–527).

(3) The lessor may proceed under subsection (2) without judicial process if that can be done without breach of the peace or the lessor may proceed by action.

As amended in 1990.

§ 2A–526. Lessor's Stoppage of Delivery in Transit or Otherwise.

(1) A lessor may stop delivery of goods in the possession of a carrier or other bailee if the lessor discovers the lessee to be insolvent and may stop delivery of carload, truckload, planeload, or larger shipments of express or freight if the lessee repudiates or fails to make a payment due before delivery, whether for rent, security or otherwise under the lease contract, or for any other reason the lessor has a right to withhold or take possession of the goods.

(2) In pursuing its remedies under subsection (1), the lessor may stop delivery until

(a) receipt of the goods by the lessee;

(b) acknowledgment to the lessee by any bailee of the goods, except a carrier, that the bailee holds the goods for the lessee; or

(c) such an acknowledgment to the lessee by a carrier via reshipment or as warehouseman.

(3) (a) To stop delivery, a lessor shall so notify as to enable the bailee by reasonable diligence to prevent delivery of the goods.

(b) After notification, the bailee shall hold and deliver the goods according to the directions of the lessor, but the lessor is liable to the bailee for any ensuing charges or damages.

(c) A carrier who has issued a nonnegotiable bill of lading is not obliged to obey a notification to stop received from a person other than the consignor.

§ 2A–527. Lessor's Rights to Dispose of Goods.

(1) After a default by a lessee under the lease contract of the type described in Section 2A–523(1) or 2A–523(3)(a) or after the lessor refuses to deliver or takes possession of goods (Section 2A–525 or 2A–526), or, if agreed, after other default by a lessee, the lessor may dispose of the goods concerned or the undelivered balance thereof by lease, sale, or otherwise.

(2) Except as otherwise provided with respect to damages liquidated in the lease agreement (Section 2A–504) or otherwise determined pursuant to agreement of the parties (Sections 1–102(3) and 2A–503), if the disposition is by lease agreement substantially similar to the original lease agreement and the new lease agreement is made in good faith and in a commercially reasonable manner, the lessor may recover from the lessee as damages (i) accrued and unpaid rent as of the date of the commencement of the term of the new lease agreement, (ii) the present value, as of the same date, of the total rent for the then remaining lease term of the original lease agreement minus the present value, as of the same date, of the rent under the new lease agreement applicable to that period of the new lease term which is comparable to the then remaining term of the original lease agreement, and (iii) any incidental damages allowed under Section 2A–530, less expenses saved in consequence of the lessee's default.

(3) If the lessor's disposition is by lease agreement that for any reason does not qualify for treatment under subsection (2), or is by sale or otherwise, the lessor may recover from the lessee as if the lessor had elected not to dispose of the goods and Section 2A–528 governs.

(4) A subsequent buyer or lessee who buys or leases from the lessor in good faith for value as a result of a disposition under this section takes the goods free of the original lease contract and any rights of the original lessee even though the lessor fails to comply with one or more of the requirements of this Article.

(5) The lessor is not accountable to the lessee for any profit made on any disposition. A lessee who has rightfully rejected or justifiably revoked acceptance shall account to the lessor for any excess over the amount of the lessee's security interest (Section 2A–508(5)).

As amended in 1990.

§ 2A–528. Lessor's Damages for Non-acceptance, Failure to Pay, Repudiation, or Other Default.

(1) Except as otherwise provided with respect to damages liquidated in the lease agreement (Section 2A–504) or otherwise determined pursuant to agreement of the parties (Section 1–102(3) and 2A–503), if a lessor elects to retain the goods or a lessor elects to dispose of the goods and the disposition is by lease agreement that for any reason does not qualify for treatment under Section 2A–527(2), or is by sale or otherwise, the lessor may recover from the lessee as damages for a default of the type described in Section 2A–523(1) or 2A–523(3)(a), or if

agreed, for other default of the lessee, (i) accrued and unpaid rent as of the date of the default if the lessee has never taken possession of the goods, or, if the lessee has taken possession of the goods, as of the date the lessor repossesses the goods or an earlier date on which the lessee makes a tender of the goods to the lessor, (ii) the present value as of the date determined under clause (i) of the total rent for the then remaining lease term of the original lease agreement minus the present value as of the same date of the market rent at the place where the goods are located computed for the same lease term, and (iii) any incidental damages allowed under Section 2A–530, less expenses saved in consequence of the lessee's default.

(2) If the measure of damages provided in subsection (1) is inadequate to put a lessor in as good a position as performance would have, the measure of damages is the present value of the profit, including reasonable overhead, the lessor would have made from full performance by the lessee, together with any incidental damages allowed under Section 2A–530, due allowance for costs reasonably incurred and due credit for payments or proceeds of disposition.

As amended in 1990.

§ 2A–529. Lessor's Action for the Rent.

(1) After default by the lessee under the lease contract of the type described in Section 2A–523(1) or 2A–523(3)(a) or, if agreed, after other default by the lessee, if the lessor complies with subsection (2), the lessor may recover from the lessee as damages:

(a) for goods accepted by the lessee and not repossessed by or tendered to the lessor, and for conforming goods lost or damaged within a commercially reasonable time after risk of loss passes to the lessee (Section 2A–219), (i) accrued and unpaid rent as of the date of entry of judgment in favor of the lessor (ii) the present value as of the same date of the rent for the then remaining lease term of the lease agreement, and (iii) any incidental damages allowed under Section 2A–530, less expenses saved in consequence of the lessee's default; and

(b) for goods identified to the lease contract if the lessor is unable after reasonable effort to dispose of them at a reasonable price or the circumstances reasonably indicate that effort will be unavailing, (i) accrued and unpaid rent as of the date of entry of judgment in favor of the lessor, (ii) the present value as of the same date of the rent for the then remaining lease term of the lease agreement, and (iii) any incidental damages allowed under Section 2A–530, less expenses saved in consequence of the lessee's default.

(2) Except as provided in subsection (3), the lessor shall hold for the lessee for the remaining lease term of the lease agreement any goods that have been identified to the lease contract and are in the lessor's control.

(3) The lessor may dispose of the goods at any time before collection of the judgment for damages obtained pursuant to subsection (1). If the disposition is before the end of the remaining

lease term of the lease agreement, the lessor's recovery against the lessee for damages is governed by Section 2A–527 or Section 2A–528, and the lessor will cause an appropriate credit to be provided against a judgment for damages to the extent that the amount of the judgment exceeds the recovery available pursuant to Section 2A–527 or 2A–528.

(4) Payment of the judgment for damages obtained pursuant to subsection (1) entitles the lessee to the use and possession of the goods not then disposed of for the remaining lease term of and in accordance with the lease agreement.

(5) After default by the lessee under the lease contract of the type described in Section 2A–523(1) or Section 2A–523(3)(a) or, if agreed, after other default by the lessee, a lessor who is held not entitled to rent under this section must nevertheless be awarded damages for non-acceptance under Sections 2A–527 and 2A–528.

As amended in 1990.

§ 2A–530. Lessor's Incidental Damages.

Incidental damages to an aggrieved lessor include any commercially reasonable charges, expenses, or commissions incurred in stopping delivery, in the transportation, care and custody of goods after the lessee's default, in connection with return or disposition of the goods, or otherwise resulting from the default.

§ 2A–531. Standing to Sue Third Parties for Injury to Goods.

(1) If a third party so deals with goods that have been identified to a lease contract as to cause actionable injury to a party to the lease contract (a) the lessor has a right of action against the third party, and (b) the lessee also has a right of action against the third party if the lessee:

  (i) has a security interest in the goods;

  (ii) has an insurable interest in the goods; or

  (iii) bears the risk of loss under the lease contract or has since the injury assumed that risk as against the lessor and the goods have been converted or destroyed.

(2) If at the time of the injury the party plaintiff did not bear the risk of loss as against the other party to the lease contract and there is no arrangement between them for disposition of the recovery, his [or her] suit or settlement, subject to his [or her] own interest, is as a fiduciary for the other party to the lease contract.

(3) Either party with the consent of the other may sue for the benefit of whom it may concern.

§ 2A–532. Lessor's Rights to Residual Interest.

In addition to any other recovery permitted by this Article or other law, the lessor may recover from the lessee an amount that will fully compensate the lessor for any loss of or damage to the lessor's residual interest in the goods caused by the default of the lessee.

As added in 1990.

APPENDIX C

Securities Act of 1933 (Excerpts)

Definitions

Section 2. When used in this title, unless the context requires—

(1) The term "security" means any note, stock, treasury stock, bond, debenture, evidence of indebtedness, certificate of interest or participation in any profit-sharing agreement, collateral-trust certificate, preorganization certificate or subscription, transferable share, investment contract, voting-trust certificate, certificate of deposit for a security, fractional undivided interest in oil, gas, or other mineral rights, any put, call, straddle, option, or privilege on any security, certificate of deposit, or group or index of securities (including any interest therein or based on the value thereof), or any put, call, straddle, option, or privilege entered into on a national securities exchange relating to foreign currency, or, in general, any interest or participation in, temporary or interim certificate for, receipt for, guarantee of, or warrant or right to subscribe to or purchase, any of the foregoing.

Exempted Securities

Section 3. (a) Except as hereinafter expressly provided the provisions of this title shall not apply to any of the following classes of securities:

* * * *

(2) Any security issued or guaranteed by the United States or any territory thereof, or by the District of Columbia, or by any State of the United States, or by any political subdivision of a State or Territory, or by any public instrumentality of one or more States or Territories, or by any person controlled or supervised by and acting as an instrumentality of the Government of the United States pursuant to authority granted by the Congress of the United States; or any certificate of deposit for any of the foregoing; or any security issued or guaranteed by any bank; or any security issued by or representing an interest in or a direct obligation of a Federal Reserve Bank. * * *

(3) Any note, draft, bill of exchange, or banker's acceptance which arises out of a current transaction or the proceeds of which have been or are to be used for current transactions, and which has a maturity at the time of issuance of not exceeding nine months, exclusive of days of grace, or any renewal thereof the maturity of which is likewise limited;

(4) Any security issued by a person organized and operated exclusively for religious, educational, benevolent, fraternal, charitable, or reformatory purposes and not for pecuniary profit, and no part of the net earnings of which inures to the benefit of any person, private stockholder, or individual;

* * * *

(11) Any security which is a part of an issue offered and sold only to persons resident within a single State or Territory, where the issuer of such security is a person resident and doing business within, or, if a corporation, incorporated by and doing business within, such State or Territory.

(b) The Commission may from time to time by its rules and regulations and subject to such terms and conditions as may be described therein, add any class of securities to the securities exempted as provided in this section, if it finds that the enforcement of this title with respect to such securities is not necessary in the public interest and for the protection of investors by reason of the small amount involved or the limited character of the public offering; but no issue of securities shall be exempted under this subsection where the aggregate amount at which such issue is offered to the public exceeds $5,000,000.

Exempted Transactions

Section 4. The provisions of section 5 shall not apply to—

(1) transactions by any person other than an issuer, underwriter, or dealer.

(2) transactions by an issuer not involving any public offering.

(3) transactions by a dealer (including an underwriter no longer acting as an underwriter in respect of the security involved in such transactions), except—

(A) transactions taking place prior to the expiration of forty days after the first date upon which the security was bona fide offered to the public by the issuer or by or through an underwriter.

(B) transactions in a security as to which a registration statement has been filed taking place prior to the expiration of forty days after the effective date of such registration statement or prior to the expiration of forty days after the first date upon which the security was bona fide offered to the public by the issuer or by or through an underwriter after such effective date, whichever is later (excluding in the computation of such forty days any time during which a stop order issued under section 8 is in effect as to the security), or such shorter period as the Commission may specify by rules and regulations or order, and

(C) transactions as to the securities constituting the whole or a part of an unsold allotment to or subscription by such dealer as a participant in the distribution of such securities by the issuer or by or through an underwriter.

With respect to transactions referred to in clause (B), if securities of the issuer have not previously been sold pursuant to an earlier effective registration statement the applicable period, instead of forty days, shall be ninety days, or such shorter period as the Commission may specify by rules and regulations or order.

(4) brokers' transactions, executed upon customers' orders on any exchange or in the over-the-counter market but not the solicitation of such orders.

*   *   *   *

(6) transactions involving offers or sales by an issuer solely to one or more accredited investors, if the aggregate offering price of an issue of securities offered in reliance on this paragraph does not exceed the amount allowed under Section 3(b) of this title, if there is no advertising or public solicitation in connection with the transaction by the issuer or anyone acting on the issuer's behalf, and if the issuer files such notice with the Commission as the Commission shall prescribe.

Prohibitions Relating to Interstate Commerce and the Mails

Section 5. (a) Unless a registration statement is in effect as to a security, it shall be unlawful for any person, directly or indirectly—

(1) to make use of any means or instruments of transportation or communication in interstate commerce or of the mails to sell such security through the use or medium of any prospectus or otherwise; or

(2) to carry or cause to be carried through the mails or in interstate commerce, by any means or instruments of transportation, any such security for the purpose of sale or for delivery after sale.

(b) It shall be unlawful for any person, directly or indirectly—

(1) to make use of any means or instruments of transportation or communication in interstate commerce or of the mails to carry or transmit any prospectus relating to any security with respect to which a registration statement has been filed under this title, unless such prospectus meets the requirements of section 10, or

(2) to carry or to cause to be carried through the mails or in interstate commerce any such security for the purpose of sale or for delivery after sale, unless accompanied or preceded by a prospectus that meets the requirements of subsection (a) of section 10.

(c) It shall be unlawful for any person, directly, or indirectly, to make use of any means or instruments of transportation or communication in interstate commerce or of the mails to offer to sell or offer to buy through the use or medium of any prospectus or otherwise any security, unless a registration statement has been filed as to such security, or while the registration statement is the subject of a refusal order or stop order or (prior to the effective date of the registration statement) any public proceeding of examination under section 8.

APPENDIX D

Securities Exchange Act of 1934 (Excerpts)

Definitions and Application of Title

Section 3. (a) When used in this title, unless the context otherwise requires—

*   *   *   *

(4) The term "broker" means any person engaged in the business of effecting transactions in securities for the account of others, but does not include a bank.

(5) The term "dealer" means any person engaged in the business of buying and selling securities for his own account, through a broker or otherwise, but does not include a bank, or any person insofar as he buys or sells securities for his own account, either individually or in some fiduciary capacity, but not as part of a regular business.

*   *   *   *

(7) The term "director" means any director of a corporation or any person performing similar functions with respect to any organization, whether incorporated or unincorporated.

(8) The term "issuer" means any person who issues or proposes to issue any security; except that with respect to certificates of deposit for securities, voting-trust certificates, or collateral-trust certificates, or with respect to certificates of interest or shares in an unincorporated investment trust not having a board of directors or the fixed, restricted management, or unit type, the term "issuer" means the person or persons performing the acts and assuming the duties of depositor or manager pursuant to the provisions of the trust or other agreement or instrument under which such securities are issued; and except that with respect to equipment-trust certificates or like securities, the term "issuer" means the person by whom the equipment or property is, or is to be, used.

(9) The term "person" means a natural person, company, government, or political subdivision, agency, or instrumentality of a government.

Regulation of the Use of Manipulative and Deceptive Devices

Section 10. It shall be unlawful for any person, directly or indirectly, by the use of any means or instrumentality of interstate commerce or of the mails, or of any facility of any national securities exchange—

(a) To effect a short sale, or to use or employ any stop-loss order in connection with the purchase or sale, of any security registered on a national securities exchange, in contravention of such rules and regulations as the Commission may prescribe as necessary or appropriate in the public interest or for the protection of investors.

(b) To use or employ, in connection with the purchase or sale of any security registered on a national securities exchange or any security not so registered, any manipulative or deceptive device or contrivance in contravention of such rules and regulations as the Commission may prescribe as necessary or appropriate in the public interest or for the protection of investors.

APPENDIX E

Title VII of the Civil Rights Act of 1964 (Excerpts)

Section 703. **Unlawful Employment Practices.** (a) It shall be an unlawful employment practice for an employer—

(1) to fail or refuse to hire or to discharge any individual, or otherwise to discriminate against any individual with respect to his compensation, terms, conditions, or privileges of employment, because of such individual's race, color, religion, sex, or national origin; or

(2) to limit, segregate, or classify his employees or applicants for employment in any way which would deprive or tend to deprive any individual of employment opportunities or otherwise adversely affect his status as an employee, because of such individual's race, color, religion, sex, or national origin.

(b) It shall be an unlawful employment practice for an employment agency to fail or refuse to refer for employment, or otherwise to discriminate against, any individual because of his race, color, religion, sex, or national origin, or to classify or refer for employment any individual on the basis or his race, color, religion, sex, or national origin.

(c) It shall be an unlawful employment practice for a labor organization—

(1) to exclude or to expel from its membership, or otherwise to discriminate against, any individual because of his race, color, religion, sex, or national origin;

(2) to limit, segregate, or classify its membership or applicants for membership, or to classify or fail or refuse to refer for employment any individual, in any way which would deprive or tend to deprive any individual of employment opportunities, or would limit such employment opportunities or otherwise adversely affect his status as an employee or as an applicant for employment, because of such individual's race, color, religion, sex, or national origin; or

(3) to cause or attempt to cause an employer to discriminate against an individual in violation of this section.

(d) It shall be an unlawful employment practice for any employer, labor organization, or joint labor-management committee controlling apprenticeship or other training or retraining, including on-the-job training programs to discriminate against any individual because of his race, color, religion, sex, or national origin in admission to, or employment in, any program established to provide apprenticeship or other training.

(e) Notwithstanding any other provision of this subchapter—

(1) it shall not be an unlawful employment practice for an employer to hire and employ employees, for an employment agency to classify, or refer for employment any individual, for a labor organization to classify its membership or to classify or refer for employment any individual, or for an employer, labor organization, or joint labor-management committee controlling apprenticeship or other training or retraining programs to admit or employ any individual in any such program, on the basis of his religion, sex, or national origin in those certain instances where religion, sex, or national origin is a bona fide occupational qualification reasonably necessary to the normal operation of that particular business or enterprise, and

(2) it shall not be an unlawful employment practice for a school, college, university, or other educational institution or institution of learning to hire and employ employees of a particular religion if such school, college, university, or other educational institution or institution of learning is, in whole or in substantial part,

owned, supported, controlled, or managed by a particular religion or by a particular religious corporation, association, or society, or if the curriculum of such school, college, university, or other educational institution or institution of learning is directed toward the propagation of a particular religion.

(f) As used in this subchapter, the phrase "unlawful employment practice" shall not be deemed to include any action or measure taken by an employer, labor organization, joint labor-management committee, or employment agency with respect to an individual who is a member of the Communist Party of the United States or of any other organization required to register as a Communist-action or Communist-front organization. * * *

(g) Notwithstanding any other provision of this subchapter, it shall not be an unlawful employment practice for an employer to fail or refuse to hire and employ any individual for any position, for an employer to discharge any individual from any position, or for an employment agency to fail or refuse to refer any individual for employment in any position, or for a labor organization to fail or refuse to refer any individual for employment in any position, if—

(1) the occupancy of such position, or access to the premises in or upon which any part of the duties of such position is performed or is to be performed, is subject to any requirement imposed in the interest of the national security of the United States * * * and

(2) such individual has not fulfilled or has ceased to fulfill that requirement.

(h) Notwithstanding any other provision of this subchapter, it shall not be an unlawful employment practice for an employer to apply different standards of compensation, or different terms, conditions, or privileges of employment pursuant to a bona fide seniority or merit system, or a system which measures earnings by quantity or quality of production or to employees who work in different locations, provided that such differences are not the result of an intention to discriminate because of race, color, religion, sex, or national origin, nor shall it be an unlawful employment practice for an employer to give and act upon the results of any professionally developed ability test provided that such test, its administration or action upon the results is not designed, intended or used to discriminate because of race, color, religion, sex, or national origin. * * *

(j) Nothing contained in this subchapter shall be interpreted to require any employer, employment agency, labor organization, or joint labor-management committee subject to this subchapter to grant preferential treatment to any individual or to any group because of the race, color, religion, sex, or national origin of such individual or group on account of an imbalance which may exist with respect to the total number or percentage of persons of any race, color, religion, sex, or national origin employed by any employer, referred or classified for employment by any employment agency or labor organization, or admitted to, or employed in, any apprenticeship or other training program, in comparison with the total number or percentage of persons of such race, color, religion, sex, or national origin in any community, State, section, or other area, or in the available work force in any community, State, section, or other area.

* * * *

Section 704. Other Unlawful Employment Practices.

(a) It shall be an unlawful employment practice for an employer to discriminate against any of his employees or applicants for employment, for an employment agency, or joint labor-management committee controlling apprenticeship or other training or retraining, including on-the-job training programs, to discriminate against any individual, or for a labor organization to discriminate against any member thereof or applicant for membership, because he has opposed any practice made an unlawful employment practice by this subchapter, or because he has made a charge, testified, assisted, or participated in any manner in an investigation, proceeding, or hearing under this subchapter.

(b) It shall be an unlawful employment practice for an employer, labor organization, employment agency, or joint labor-management committee controlling apprenticeship or other training or retraining, including on-the-job training programs, to print or publish or cause to be printed or published any notice or advertisement relating to employment by such an employer or membership or any classification or referral for employment by such a labor organization, or relating to any classification or referral for employment by such an employment agency, or relating to admission to, or employment in, any program established to provide apprenticeship or other training by such a joint-labor-management committee, indicating any preference, limitation, specification, or discrimination, based on race, color, religion, sex, or national origin, except that such a notice or advertisement may indicate a preference, limitation, specification, or discrimination based on religion, sex or national origin when religion, sex, or national origin is a bona fide occupational qualification for employment.

APPENDIX F

Digital Millennium Copyright Act of 1998 (Excerpts)

Sec. 1201. Circumvention of copyright protection systems

(a) VIOLATIONS REGARDING CIRCUMVENTION OF TECHNOLOGICAL MEASURES—(1)(A) No person shall circumvent a technological measure that effectively controls access to a work protected under this title. * * *

* * * *

(b) ADDITIONAL VIOLATIONS—(1) No person shall manufacture, import, offer to the public, provide, or otherwise traffic in any technology, product, service, device, component, or part thereof, that—

(A) is primarily designed or produced for the purpose of circumventing protection afforded by a technological measure that effectively protects a right of a copyright owner under this title in a work or a portion thereof;

(B) has only limited commercially significant purpose or use other than to circumvent protection afforded by a technological measure that effectively protects a right of a copyright owner under this title in a work or a portion thereof; or

(C) is marketed by that person or another acting in concert with that person with that person's knowledge for use in circumventing protection afforded by a technological measure that effectively protects a right of a copyright owner under this title in a work or a portion thereof.

* * * *

Sec. 1202. Integrity of copyright management information

(a) FALSE COPYRIGHT MANAGEMENT INFORMATION—No person shall knowingly and with the intent to induce, enable, facilitate, or conceal infringement—

(1) provide copyright management information that is false, or

(2) distribute or import for distribution copyright management information that is false.

(b) REMOVAL OR ALTERATION OF COPYRIGHT MANAGEMENT INFORMATION—No person shall, without the authority of the copyright owner or the law—

(1) intentionally remove or alter any copyright management information,

(2) distribute or import for distribution copyright management information knowing that the copyright management information has been removed or altered without authority of the copyright owner or the law, or

(3) distribute, import for distribution, or publicly perform works, copies of works, or phonorecords, knowing that copyright management information has been removed or altered without authority of the copyright owner or the law, knowing, or, with respect to civil remedies under section 1203, having reasonable grounds to know, that it will induce, enable, facilitate, or conceal an infringement of any right under this title.

(c) DEFINITION—As used in this section, the term "copyright management information" means any of the following information conveyed in connection with copies or phonorecords of a work or performances or displays of a work, including in digital form, except that such term does not include any personally identifying information about a user of a work or of a copy, phonorecord, performance, or display of a work:

(1) The title and other information identifying the work, including the information set forth on a notice of copyright.

(2) The name of, and other identifying information about, the author of a work.

(3) The name of, and other identifying information about, the copyright owner of the work, including the information set forth in a notice of copyright.

(4) With the exception of public performances of works by radio and television broadcast stations, the name of, and other identifying information about, a performer whose performance is fixed in a work other than an audiovisual work.

(5) With the exception of public performances of works by radio and television broadcast stations, in the case of an audiovisual work, the name of, and other identifying information about, a writer, performer, or director who is credited in the audiovisual work.

(6) Terms and conditions for use of the work.

(7) Identifying numbers or symbols referring to such information or links to such information.

(8) Such other information as the Register of Copyrights may prescribe by regulation, except that the Register of Copyrights may not require the provision of any information concerning the user of a copyrighted work.

* * * *

Sec. 512. Limitations on liability relating to material online

(a) TRANSITORY DIGITAL NETWORK COMMUNICA-TIONS—A service provider shall not be liable for monetary relief, or, except as provided in subsection (j), for injunctive or other equitable relief, for infringement of copyright by reason of the provider's transmitting, routing, or providing connections for, material through a system or network controlled or operated by or for the service provider, or by reason of the intermediate and transient storage of that material in the course of such transmitting, routing, or providing connections, if—

(1) the transmission of the material was initiated by or at the direction of a person other than the service provider;

(2) the transmission, routing, provision of connections, or storage is carried out through an automatic technical process without selection of the material by the service provider;

(3) the service provider does not select the recipients of the material except as an automatic response to the request of another person;

(4) no copy of the material made by the service provider in the course of such intermediate or transient storage is maintained on the system or network in a manner ordinarily accessible to anyone other than anticipated recipients, and no such copy is maintained on the system or network in a manner ordinarily accessible to such anticipated recipients for a longer period than is reasonably necessary for the transmission, routing, or provision of connections; and

(5) the material is transmitted through the system or network without modification of its content.

APPENDIX G

Uniform Electronic Transactions Act (Excerpts)

* * * *

Section 5. USE OF ELECTRONIC RECORDS AND ELECTRONIC SIGNATURES; VARIATION BY AGREEMENT.

(a) This [Act] does not require a record or signature to be created, generated, sent, communicated, received, stored, or otherwise processed or used by electronic means or in electronic form.

(b) This [Act] applies only to transactions between parties each of which has agreed to conduct transactions by electronic means. Whether the parties agree to conduct a transaction by electronic means is determined from the context and surrounding circumstances, including the parties' conduct.

(c) A party that agrees to conduct a transaction by electronic means may refuse to conduct other transactions by electronic means. The right granted by this subsection may not be waived by agreement.

(d) Except as otherwise provided in this [Act], the effect of any of its provisions may be varied by agreement. The presence in certain provisions of this [Act] of the words "unless otherwise agreed," or words of similar import, does not imply that the effect of other provisions may not be varied by agreement.

(e) Whether an electronic record or electronic signature has legal consequences is determined by this [Act] and other applicable law.

Section 6. CONSTRUCTION AND APPLICATION. This [Act] must be construed and applied:

(1) to facilitate electronic transactions consistent with other applicable law;

(2) to be consistent with reasonable practices concerning electronic transactions and with the continued expansion of those practices; and

(3) to effectuate its general purpose to make uniform the law with respect to the subject of this [Act] among States enacting it.

Section 7. LEGAL RECOGNITION OF ELECTRONIC RECORDS, ELECTRONIC SIGNATURES, AND ELECTRONIC CONTRACTS.

(a) A record or signature may not be denied legal effect or enforceability solely because it is in electronic form.

(b) A contract may not be denied legal effect or enforceability solely because an electronic record was used in its formation.

(c) If a law requires a record to be in writing, an electronic record satisfies the law.

(d) If a law requires a signature, an electronic signature satisfies the law.

* * * *

Section 10. EFFECT OF CHANGE OR ERROR. If a change or error in an electronic record occurs in a transmission between parties to a transaction, the following rules apply:

(1) If the parties have agreed to use a security procedure to detect changes or errors and one party has conformed to the procedure, but the other party has not, and the nonconforming party would have detected the change or error had that party also conformed, the conforming party may avoid the effect of the changed or erroneous electronic record.

A-62

(2) In an automated transaction involving an individual, the individual may avoid the effect of an electronic record that resulted from an error made by the individual in dealing with the electronic agent of another person if the electronic agent did not provide an opportunity for the prevention or correction of the error and, at the time the individual learns of the error, the individual:

   (A) promptly notifies the other person of the error and that the individual did not intend to be bound by the electronic record received by the other person;

   (B) takes reasonable steps, including steps that conform to the other person's reasonable instructions, to return to the other person or, if instructed by the other person, to destroy the consideration received, if any, as a result of the erroneous electronic record; and

   (C) has not used or received any benefit or value from the consideration, if any, received from the other person.

(3) If neither paragraph (1) nor paragraph (2) applies, the change or error has the effect provided by other law, including the law of mistake, and the parties' contract, if any.

(4) Paragraphs (2) and (3) may not be varied by agreement.

APPENDIX H

Electronic Signatures in Global and National Commerce Act of 2000 (Excerpts)

SEC. 101. GENERAL RULE OF VALIDITY.

(a) IN GENERAL—Notwithstanding any statute, regulation, or other rule of law (other than this title and title II), with respect to any transaction in or affecting interstate or foreign commerce—

(1) a signature, contract, or other record relating to such transaction may not be denied legal effect, validity, or enforceability solely because it is in electronic form; and

(2) a contract relating to such transaction may not be denied legal effect, validity, or enforceability solely because an electronic signature or electronic record was used in its formation.

* * * *

(d) RETENTION OF CONTRACTS AND RECORDS—

(1) ACCURACY AND ACCESSIBILITY—If a statute, regulation, or other rule of law requires that a contract or other record relating to a transaction in or affecting interstate or foreign commerce be retained, that requirement is met by retaining an electronic record of the information in the contract or other record that—

(A) accurately reflects the information set forth in the contract or other record; and

(B) remains accessible to all persons who are entitled to access by statute, regulation, or rule of law, for the period required by such statute, regulation, or rule of law, in a form that is capable of being accurately reproduced for later reference, whether by transmission, printing, or otherwise.

(2) EXCEPTION—A requirement to retain a contract or other record in accordance with paragraph (1) does not apply to any information whose sole purpose is to enable the contract or other record to be sent, communicated, or received.

(3) ORIGINALS—If a statute, regulation, or other rule of law requires a contract or other record relating to a transaction in or affecting interstate or foreign commerce to be provided, available, or retained in its original form, or provides consequences if the contract or other record is not provided, available, or retained in its original form, that statute, regulation, or rule of law is satisfied by an electronic record that complies with paragraph (1).

(4) CHECKS—If a statute, regulation, or other rule of law requires the retention of a check, that requirement is satisfied by retention of an electronic record of the information on the front and back of the check in accordance with paragraph (1).

* * * *

(g) NOTARIZATION AND ACKNOWLEDGMENT—If a statute, regulation, or other rule of law requires a signature or record relating to a transaction in or affecting interstate or foreign commerce to be notarized, acknowledged, verified, or made under oath, that requirement is satisfied if the electronic signature of the person authorized to perform those acts, together with all other information required to be included by other applicable statute, regulation, or rule of law, is attached to or logically associated with the signature or record.

(h) ELECTRONIC AGENTS—A contract or other record relating to a transaction in or affecting interstate or foreign commerce may not be denied legal effect, validity, or enforceability solely because its formation, creation, or delivery involved the action of one or more electronic agents so long as the action of any such electronic agent is legally attributable to the person to be bound.

(i) INSURANCE—It is the specific intent of the Congress that this title and title II apply to the business of insurance.

(j) INSURANCE AGENTS AND BROKERS—An insurance agent or broker acting under the direction of a party that enters into a contract by means of an electronic record or electronic signature may not be held liable for any deficiency in the electronic procedures agreed to by the parties under that contract if—

(1) the agent or broker has not engaged in negligent, reckless, or intentional tortious conduct;

(2) the agent or broker was not involved in the development or establishment of such electronic procedures; and

(3) the agent or broker did not deviate from such procedures.

*   *   *   *

SEC. 103. SPECIFIC EXCEPTIONS.

(a) EXCEPTED REQUIREMENTS—The provisions of section 101 shall not apply to a contract or other record to the extent it is governed by—

(1) a statute, regulation, or other rule of law governing the creation and execution of wills, codicils, or testamentary trusts;

(2) a State statute, regulation, or other rule of law governing adoption, divorce, or other matters of family law; or

(3) the Uniform Commercial Code, as in effect in any State, other than sections 1–107 and 1–206 and Articles 2 and 2A.

(b) ADDITIONAL EXCEPTIONS—The provisions of section 101 shall not apply to—

(1) court orders or notices, or official court documents (including briefs, pleadings, and other writings) required to be executed in connection with court proceedings;

(2) any notice of—

(A) the cancellation or termination of utility services (including water, heat, and power);

(B) default, acceleration, repossession, foreclosure, or eviction, or the right to cure, under a credit agreement secured by, or a rental agreement for, a primary residence of an individual;

(C) the cancellation or termination of health insurance or benefits or life insurance benefits (excluding annuities); or

(D) recall of a product, or material failure of a product, that risks endangering health or safety; or

(3) any document required to accompany any transportation or handling of hazardous materials, pesticides, or other toxic or dangerous materials.

APPENDIX I

Answers to Even-Numbered *For Review* Questions

CHAPTER 1

2A. *Precedent*
Judges attempt to be consistent, and when possible, they base their decisions on the principles suggested by earlier cases. They seek to decide similar cases in a similar way and consider new cases with care, because they know that their conflicting decisions make new law. Each interpretation becomes part of the law on the subject and serves as a legal precedent—a decision that furnishes an example or authority for deciding subsequent cases involving similar legal principles or facts. A court will depart from the rule of a precedent when it decides that the rule should no longer be followed. If a court decides that a precedent is simply incorrect or that technological or social changes have rendered the precedent inapplicable, the court might rule contrary to the precedent.

4A. *Commercial activities*
To prevent states from establishing laws and regulations that would interfere with trade and commerce among the states, the Constitution expressly delegated to the national government the power to regulate interstate commerce. The commerce clause (Article I, Section 8, of the U.S. Constitution) expressly permits Congress "[t]o regulate Commerce with foreign Nations, and among the several States, and with the Indian Tribes."

CHAPTER 2

2A. *Ensuring legal and ethical behavior*
Ethical leadership is important to create and maintain an ethical workplace. Management can set standards, and apply those standards to themselves and their firm's employees.

4A. *Professionals' duties*
Generally, professionals are subject to standards of conduct established by codes of professional ethics, as well as the law. To those who rely on their services, professionals owe duties that include compliance with the standards of care, knowledge, and judgment set by these sources.

CHAPTER 3

2A. *Jurisdiction*
To hear a case, a court must have jurisdiction over the person against whom the suit is brought or over the property involved in the suit. The court must also have jurisdiction over the subject matter. Generally, courts apply a "sliding-scale" standard to determine when it is proper to exercise jurisdiction over a defendant whose only connection with the jurisdiction is the Internet.

4A. *Pleadings, discovery, and electronic filing*
The pleadings include a plaintiff's complaint and a defendant's answer (and the counterclaim and reply). The pleadings inform each party of the other's claims and specify the issues involved in a case. Discovery is the process of obtaining information and evidence about a case from the other party or third parties. Discovery entails gaining access to witnesses, documents, records, and other types of evidence. Electronic discovery differs in its subject (e-media rather than traditional sources of information). Electronic filing involves the filing of court documents in electronic media, typically over the Internet.

CHAPTER 4

2A. *Purpose and categories of torts*
Generally, the purpose of tort law is to provide remedies for the invasion of legally recognized and protected interests (personal

safety, freedom of movement, property, and some intangibles, including privacy and reputation). The two broad categories of torts are intentional and unintentional.

4A. *Strict liability*

Strict liability is liability without fault. Strict liability for damages proximately caused by an abnormally dangerous or exceptional activity, or the keeping of dangerous animals is an application of this doctrine. Another significant application of strict liability is in the area of product liability.

CHAPTER 5

2A. *Trademarks and patents*

As stated in Article I, Section 8, of the Constitution, Congress is authorized "[t]o promote the Progress of Science and useful Arts, by securing for limited Times to Authors and Inventors the exclusive Right to their respective Writings and Discoveries." Laws protecting patents and trademarks, as well copyrights, are designed to protect and reward inventive and artistic creativity.

4A. *Trade secrets*

Trade secrets are business processes and information that are not or cannot be patented, copyrighted, or trademarked. Trade secrets consist of generally anything that makes an individual company unique and that would have value to a competitor. The Uniform Trade Secrets Act, the Economic Espionage Act, and the common law offer trade secrets protection.

CHAPTER 6

2A. *Types of crime and white-collar crime*

Traditionally, crimes have been grouped into the following categories: violent crime (crimes against persons), property crime, public order crime, white-collar crime, and organized crime. White-collar crime is an illegal act or series of acts committed by an individual or business entity using some nonviolent means, usually in the course of a legitimate occupation.

4A. *Constitutional safeguards and criminal process*

Under the Fourth Amendment, before searching or seizing private property, law enforcement officers must obtain a search warrant, which requires probable cause. Under the Fifth Amendment, no one can be deprived of "life, liberty, or property without due process of law." The Fifth Amendment also protects persons against double jeopardy and self-incrimination. The Sixth Amendment guarantees the right to a speedy trial, the right to a jury trial, the right to a public trial, the right to confront witnesses, and the right to counsel. All evidence obtained in violation of the Fourth, Fifth, and Sixth Amendments must be excluded from the trial, as well as all evidence derived from the illegally obtained evidence. Individuals who are arrested must be informed of certain constitutional rights, including their Fifth Amendment right to remain silent and their Sixth Amendment right to counsel. The Eighth Amendment prohibits excessive bails and fines, and cruel and unusual punishment. The basic steps in the criminal process include an arrest, the booking, the initial appearance, a preliminary hearing, a grand jury or magistrate's review, the arraignment, a plea bargain (if any), and the trial or guilty plea.

CHAPTER 7

2A. *Types of contracts*

The various types of contracts include bilateral, unilateral, express, implied, formal, informal, quasi, valid, void, voidable, and unenforceable.

4A. *Acceptance of an offer*

An acceptance is a voluntary act on the part of the offeree that shows assent, or agreement, to the terms of an offer. The acceptance must be unequivocal and must be timely communicated to the offeror.

CHAPTER 8

2A. *Intoxication*

If a person who is sufficiently intoxicated to lack mental capacity enters into a contract, the contract is voidable at the option of that person. It must be proved that the person's reason and judgment were impaired to the extent that he or she did not comprehend the legal consequences of entering into the contract.

4A. *Elements of fraudulent misrepresentation*

Fraudulent misrepresentation has three elements: (1) misrepresentation of a material fact must occur, (2) there must be an intent to deceive, and (3) the innocent party must justifiably rely on the misrepresentation. Also, to collect damages, a party must have been injured as a result of the misrepresentation.

CHAPTER 9

2A. *Intended beneficiary*

A beneficiary will be considered an intended beneficiary if a reasonable person in the position of the beneficiary would believe that the promisee intended to confer on the beneficiary the right to bring suit to enforce the contract. Other factors include whether performance is rendered directly to the third party, whether the third party has the right to control the details of performance, and whether the third party is expressly designated as a beneficiary in the contract.

4A. *Equitable remedies*

When fraud, mistake, duress, or failure of consideration is present, rescission is available. The failure of one party to perform under a contract entitles the other party to rescind the contract. Specific performance might be granted as a remedy when damages is an inadequate remedy and the subject matter of the contract is unique. Reformation allows a contract to be rewritten to reflect the parties' true intentions. It applies most often when fraud or mutual mistake occurs.

CHAPTER 10

2A. *Shrink-wrap and click-on agreements*

A shrink-wrap agreement is an agreement whose terms are expressed inside a box in which the goods are packaged.

Generally, courts have enforced the terms of shrink-wrap agreements the same as the terms of other contracts, applying the traditional common law of contracts.

4A. *Partnering agreement*
A partnering agreement is an agreement between a seller and a buyer who often do business on the terms and conditions that apply to all of their transactions conducted electronically. Such an agreement reduces the likelihood of a dispute and provides for the resolution of any dispute that does arise.

CHAPTER 11

2A. *Additional terms*
Under the UCC, a contract can be formed even if the acceptance includes an offeree's additional or different terms. If one of the parties is a nonmerchant, the contract does not include the additional terms. If both parties are merchants, the additional terms automatically become part of the contract unless (1) the original offer expressly limits acceptance to the terms of the offer, (2) the new or changed terms *materially* alter the contract, or (3) the offeror objects to the new or changed terms within a reasonable period of time. (If the additional terms expressly require the offeror's assent, the offeree's expression is not an acceptance, but a counteroffer.) Under some circumstances, a court might strike the additional terms.

4A. *Passage of risk without movement of goods*
If the goods are held by a seller, and the seller is a merchant, the risk of loss passes to the buyer when the buyer actually takes physical possession of the goods. If the seller is not a merchant, the risk of loss to goods held by the seller passes to the buyer on tender of delivery. When a bailee is holding the goods, the risk of loss passes to the buyer when (1) the buyer receives a negotiable document of title for the goods, (2) the bailee acknowledges the buyer's right to possess the goods, or (3) the buyer receives a nonnegotiable document of title and has had a reasonable time to present the document to the bailee and demand the goods.

CHAPTER 12

2A. *Perfect tender rule*
Under the perfect tender rule, the seller or lessor has an obligation to ship or tender conforming goods, and if goods or tender of delivery fail in any respect, the buyer or lessee has the right to accept the goods, reject the entire shipment, or accept part and reject part. Exceptions to the perfect tender rule may be established by agreement. When tender is rejected because of nonconforming goods and the time for performance has not yet expired, the seller or lessor can notify the buyer or lessee promptly of the intention to cure and can then do so within the contract time for performance. Once the time for performance has expired, the seller or lessor can, for a reasonable time, exercise the right to cure if he or she had, at the time of delivery, reasonable grounds to believe that the nonconforming tender would be acceptable to the buyer or lessee. When an agreed-on manner of delivery becomes impracticable or unavailable through no fault of either party, a seller may choose a commercially reasonable substitute. In an installment contract, a buyer or lessee can reject an installment only if the nonconformity substantially impairs the value of the installment and cannot be cured. Delay in delivery or nondelivery in whole or in part is not a breach when performance is commercially impracticable. If an unexpected event totally destroys goods identified at the time the contract is formed through no fault of either party and before risk passes to the buyer or lessee, the parties are excused from performance. If a party has reasonable grounds to believe that the other party will not perform, he or she may in writing demand assurance of performance from the other party. Until such assurance is received, he or she may suspend further performance. Finally, when required cooperation is not forthcoming, the cooperative party can suspend her or his own performance without liability.

4A. *Remedies for breach*
Depending on the circumstances at the time of a buyer's breach, a seller may have the right to cancel the contract, withhold delivery, resell or dispose of the goods subject to the contract, recover the purchase price (or lease payments), recover damages, stop delivery in transit, or reclaim the goods. Similarly, on a seller's breach, a buyer may have the right to cancel the contract, recover the goods, obtain specific performance, obtain cover, replevy the goods, recover damages, reject the goods, withhold delivery, resell or dispose of the goods, stop delivery, or revoke acceptance.

CHAPTER 13

2A. *Implied warranties*
Implied warranties that arise under the UCC include the implied warranty of merchantability, the implied warranty of fitness for a particular purpose, and implied warranties that may arise from, or be excluded or modified by, course of dealing, course of performance, or usage of trade.

4A. *Defenses*
Defenses to product liability include plaintiff's assumption of risk, product misuse, and comparative negligence, as well as the attribution of injuries to commonly known dangers. Also, as in any suit, a defendant can avoid liability by showing that the elements of the cause of action have not been properly pleaded or proved.

CHAPTER 14

2A. *Requirements for negotiability*
For an instrument to be negotiable, it must (1) be in writing, (2) be signed by the maker or the drawer, (3) be an unconditional promise or order to pay, (4) state a fixed amount of money, (5) be payable on demand or at a definite time, and (6) be payable to order or to bearer, unless it is a check.

4A. *Liability*
The key to liability on a negotiable instrument is a signature. Every party, except a qualified indorser, who signs a negotiable instrument is primarily or secondarily liable for payment of that instrument when it comes due. Signature liability arises from indorsing an instrument. Warranty liability arises from transferring an instrument, whether or not the transferor also indorses it.

CHAPTER 15

2A. *Dishonor*

A bank may dishonor a customer's check without liability to the customer when the customer's account contains insufficient funds to pay the check, providing the bank did not agree to cover overdrafts. A bank may also properly dishonor a stale check, a timely check subject to a valid stop-payment order, a check drawn after the customer's death, and forged or altered checks.

4A. *EFTs and consumers*

The four most common types of EFT systems used by bank customers are automated teller machines, point-of-sale systems, systems handling direct deposits and withdrawals of funds, and pay-by-telephone systems. The EFTA provides a basic framework for the rights, liabilities, and responsibilities of users of these EFT systems. For consumers, the terms and conditions of EFTs must be disclosed in readily understandable language, a receipt must be provided at an e-terminal at the time of a transfer, periodic statements must describe transfers for each account through which an EFT system provides access, and some preauthorized payments can be stopped within three days before they are made.

CHAPTER 16

2A. *Attachment and writs of execution*

Attachment is a court-ordered seizure and taking into custody of property prior to the securing of a judgment for a past-due debt. To use attachment as a remedy, a creditor (1) files with a court an affidavit, stating that a debtor is in default and the grounds on which attachment is sought, and (2) posts a bond to cover costs, the value of the loss of use of the good by the debtor, and the value of the property. The court directs the sheriff or other officer to seize nonexempt property, which can be sold to satisfy a judgment. A *writ of execution* is a court order directing a sheriff to seize and sell any of the debtor's nonexempt real or personal property within the court's jurisdiction. This is used when a debtor will not or cannot pay a judgment.

4A. *Debtor's estate in bankruptcy and debtor in possession*

In a bankruptcy proceeding, a *debtor's estate in property* consists of all the debtor's legal and equitable interests in property currently held, wherever located, together with certain jointly owned property, property transferred in transactions voidable by the trustee, proceeds and profits from the property of the estate, and certain after-acquired property. Federal law exempts (1) up to $18,450 in equity in the debtor's residence and burial plot; (2) interest in a motor vehicle up to $2,950; (3) interest in household goods and furnishings, wearing apparel, appliances, books, animals, crops, and musical instruments up to $475 in a particular item but limited to $9,850 in total; (4) interest in jewelry up to $1,225; (5) any other property worth up to $975, plus any unused part of the $18,450 homestead exemption up to an amount of $9,250; (6) interest in any tools of the debtor's trade, up to $1,850; (7) certain life insurance contracts owned by the debtor; (8) certain interests in accrued dividends or interests under life insurance contracts owned by the debtor; (9) professionally prescribed health aids;

(10) the right to receive Social Security and certain welfare benefits, alimony and support payments, and certain pension benefits; and (11) the right to receive certain personal injury and other awards, up to $18,450.

CHAPTER 17

2A. *Agency relationships*

Agency relationships normally are consensual: they arise by voluntary consent and agreement between the parties.

4A. *Liability to third parties*

A disclosed or partially disclosed principal is liable to a third party for a contract made by an agent who is acting within the scope of her or his authority. If the agent exceeds the scope of authority and the principal fails to ratify the contract, the agent may be liable (and the principal may not). When neither the fact of agency nor the identity of the principal is disclosed, the agent is liable, and if an agent has acted within the scope of his or her authority, the undisclosed principal is also liable. Each party is liable for his or her own torts and crimes. A principal may also be liable for an agent's torts committed within the course or scope of employment. A principal is liable for an agent's crime if the principal participated by conspiracy or other action.

CHAPTER 18

2A. *Hours, wages, health, and safety*

The Fair Labor Standards Act is the most significant federal statute governing working hours and wages. To protect the health and safety of workers, Congress passed the Occupational Safety and Health Act.

4A. *Federal employment discrimination acts*

Title VII of the Civil Rights Act of 1964 and its amendments prohibit job discrimination against employees, applicants, and union members on the basis of race, color, national origin, religion, and gender at any stage of employment. The Age Discrimination in Employment Act of 1967 and the Americans with Disabilities Act of 1990 prohibit discrimination on the basis of age and disability, respectively.

CHAPTER 19

2A. *Advantages and disadvantages of business forms*

Advantages of the sole proprietorship include the proprietor receiving all of the profits and the ease and inexpensiveness to start the business. Disadvantages of the sole proprietorship include the exclusive burden on the owner of any losses or liabilities incurred by the business enterprise and the limitation on capital to personal funds and the funds of those who are willing to make loans. One of the advantages of a partnership is that it can be organized fairly easily and inexpensively. Additionally, the partnership itself files only an informational tax return. The main disadvantage of the partnership form of business is that partners are subject to personal liability for partnership obligations. One of the key advantages of a corporation is that the liability of its owners is limited to their investments. A disadvantage of the corporate form is that profits are taxed twice.

4A. *Joint ventures and other business organizational forms*

A *joint venture* is an enterprise in which two or more persons or business entities combine their efforts or their property for a single transaction or project, or a related series of transactions or projects. Other special business organizational forms include a joint stock company, syndicate, and cooperative. A *joint stock company* has many characteristics of a corporation (its ownership is represented by transferable shares of stock, it is usually managed by directors and officers of the company or association, and it can have a perpetual existence), but most of its other features are more characteristic of a partnership, and it is usually treated like a partnership. A *syndicate* is a group of individuals getting together to finance a particular project, such as the building of a shopping center. A *business trust* is created by a written trust agreement that sets forth the interests of the beneficiaries, who receive the profits, and the obligations and powers of the trustees, with whom legal ownership and management of the property of the business rests. A *cooperative* is an association, which may not or may be incorporated, that is organized to provide an economic service to its members (or shareholders), who have limited liability. Cooperatives that are unincorporated are often treated like partnerships, and the members have joint liability for the cooperative's acts.

CHAPTER 20

2A. *Duties of directors and officers*

Directors and officers are fiduciaries of the corporation. The fiduciary duties of the directors and officers include the duty of care and the duty of loyalty.

4A. *Shareholders*

Shareholders have an equitable interest in the firm. They are ultimately responsible for choosing the board of directors. Shareholders must approve fundamental corporate changes before the changes can be effected. Shareholders possess numerous rights, including preemptive rights in the purchase of new stock, dividends from corporate profits, and the right to inspection of corporate books and records. Shareholders also have the right to act on behalf of the firm by filing a shareholder's derivative suit to compel the directors to act to redress a wrong suffered by the corporation.

CHAPTER 21

2A. *Major statutes and Securities and Exchange Commission*

The major statutes regulating the securities industry are the Securities Act of 1933 and the Securities Exchange Act of 1934, which created the Securities and Exchange Commission (SEC). The SEC's major functions are to (1) require the disclosure of facts concerning offerings of securities listed on national securities exchanges and of certain securities traded over the counter; (2) regulate the trade in securities on the national and regional securities exchanges and in the over-the-counter markets; (3) investigate securities fraud; (4) regulate the activities of securities brokers, dealers, and investment advisers and requiring their registration; (5) supervise the activities of mutual funds; and (6) recommend administrative sanctions, injunctive reme-

dies, and criminal prosecution against those who violate securities laws.

4A. *State securities laws*

Typically, state laws have disclosure requirements and antifraud provisions patterned after Section 10(b) of the Securities Exchange Act of 1934 and SEC Rule 10b-5. State laws provide for the registration or qualification of securities offered or issued for sale within the state with the appropriate state official. Also, most state securities laws regulate securities brokers and dealers.

CHAPTER 22

2A. *Sherman Act*

Section 1 prohibits agreements that are anticompetitively restrictive—that is, agreements that have the wrongful purpose of restraining competition. Section 2 prohibits the misuse, and attempted misuse, of monopoly power in the marketplace.

4A. *Enforcing agencies*

The federal agencies that enforce the federal antitrust laws are the U.S. Department of Justice and the Federal Trade Commission.

CHAPTER 23

2A. *Gifts and other means of acquisition*

To make an effective gift, the donor must intend to make the gift, the gift must be delivered to the donee, and the donee must accept the gift. Property can also be acquired by purchase, possession, production, accession, and confusion.

4A. *Insurable interest*

For real and personal property, an insurable interest exists when the insured derives a pecuniary benefit from the existence of the property and would sustain a pecuniary loss from its destruction. For a life, an insurable interest exists when a person has a reasonable expectation of benefit from the continued life of another. The benefit may be pecuniary, or it may be founded on the relationship between the parties (by blood or affinity). For property insurance, the interest must exist at the time the loss occurs but need not exist when the policy is purchased. For life insurance, the interest must exist at the time the policy is obtained.

CHAPTER 24

2A. *Transfers*

Ownership of real property can pass from one person to another by sale, gift, will, inheritance laws, adverse possession, or eminent domain. In the case of sale or gift, title to the property is conveyed by means of a deed—the instrument of conveyance of real property. On an owner's death, real property can be transferred by will or by state inheritance laws. An adverse possessor can acquire title to land and cannot be removed from it by the original owner if he or she possesses the property for a certain statutory period of time. The government has the power, called eminent domain, to take land for public use.

4A. *Environmental impact statements*

An environmental impact statement (EIS) analyzes (1) the impact on the environment that an action will have, (2) any adverse effects on the environment and alternative actions that might be taken, and (3) irreversible effects the action might generate. For every major federal action that significantly affects the quality of the environment, an EIS must be prepared. An action is "major" if it involves a substantial commitment of resources (monetary or otherwise). An action is "federal" if a federal agency has the power to control it.

CHAPTER 25

2A. *Act of state doctrine*

The *act of state doctrine* is a judicially created doctrine that provides that the judicial branch of one country will not examine the validity of public acts committed by a recognized foreign government within its own territory. This doctrine is often employed in cases involving expropriation or confiscation.

4A. *Antitrust laws*

U.S. courts will apply U.S. antitrust laws extraterritorially when it is shown that an alleged violation has a substantial effect on U.S. commerce.

■ GLOSSARY

A

ABANDONED PROPERTY ■ Property with which the owner has voluntarily parted, with no intention of recovering it.

ACCELERATION CLAUSE ■ A clause that allows a payee or other holder of a time instrument to demand payment of the entire amount due, with interest, if a certain event occurs, such as a default in the payment of an installment when due.

ACCEPTANCE ■ In contract law, a voluntary act by the offeree that shows assent, or agreement, to the terms of an offer; may consist of words or conduct. In negotiable instruments law, the drawee's signed agreement to pay a draft when presented.

ACCEPTOR ■ A drawee that is legally obligated to pay an instrument when the instrument is presented later for payment.

ACCESSION ■ Occurs when an individual adds value to personal property by either labor or materials. In some situations, a person may acquire ownership rights in another's property through accession.

ACCOMMODATION PARTY ■ A person who signs an instrument for the purpose of lending his or her name as credit to another party on the instrument.

ACCORD AND SATISFACTION ■ A common means of settling a disputed claim, in which a debtor offers to pay a lesser amount than the creditor purports to be owed. The creditor's acceptance of the offer creates an accord (agreement), and when the accord is executed, satisfaction occurs.

ACCREDITED INVESTORS ■ In the context of securities offerings, "sophisticated" investors, such as banks, insurance companies, investment companies, the issuer's executive officers and directors, and persons whose income or net worth exceeds certain limits.

ACT OF STATE DOCTRINE ■ A doctrine providing that the judicial branch of one country will not examine the validity of public acts committed by a recognized foreign government within its own territory.

ACTIONABLE ■ Capable of serving as the basis of a lawsuit. An actionable claim can be pursued in a lawsuit or other court action.

ACTUAL MALICE ■ In a defamation suit, a statement made about a public figure normally must be made with actual malice (with either knowledge of its falsity or a reckless disregard of the truth) for liability to be incurred.

ADEQUATE PROTECTION DOCTRINE ■ In bankruptcy law, a doctrine that protects secured creditors from losing the value of their security as a result of the automatic stay on legal proceedings. The bankruptcy court can provide adequate protection by requiring the debtor or trustee to make cash payments to the creditor or to provide additional collateral or replacement liens in case the stay causes the property to lose value.

ADHESION CONTRACT ■ A "standard-form" contract, such as that between a large retailer and a consumer, in which the stronger party dictates the terms.

ADJUDICATE ■ To render a judicial decision. In the administrative process, the proceeding in which an administrative law judge hears and decides issues that arise when an administrative agency charges a person or a firm with violating a law or regulation enforced by the agency.

ADMINISTRATIVE AGENCY ■ A federal or state government agency established to perform a specific function. Administrative agencies are authorized by legislative acts to make and enforce rules to administer and enforce the acts.

ADMINISTRATIVE LAW ■ The body of law created by administrative agencies (in the form of rules, regulations, orders, and decisions) in order to carry out their duties and responsibilities.

ADMINISTRATIVE LAW JUDGE (ALJ) ■ One who presides over an administrative agency hearing and has the power to administer oaths, take testimony, rule on questions of evidence, and make determinations of fact.

ADMINISTRATIVE PROCESS ■ The procedure used by administrative agencies in the administration of law.

ADMINISTRATOR ■ One who is appointed by a court to handle the probate (disposition) of a person's estate if that person dies intestate (without a valid will) or if the executor named in the will cannot serve.

ADVERSE POSSESSION ■ The acquisition of title to real property by occupying it openly, without the consent of the owner, for a period of time specified by a state statute. The occupation must be actual, open, notorious, exclusive, and in opposition to all others, including the owner.

AFFIRMATIVE ACTION ■ Job-hiring policies that give special consideration to members of protected classes in an effort to overcome present effects of past discrimination.

AFTER-ACQUIRED PROPERTY ■ Property that is acquired by the debtor after the execution of a security agreement.

AGENCY ■ A relationship between two parties in which one party (the agent) agrees to represent or act for the other (the principal).

AGENT A person who agrees to represent or act for another, called the principal.

AGREEMENT ■ A meeting of two or more minds in regard to the terms of a contract; usually broken down into two events—an offer by one party to form a contract, and an acceptance of the offer by the person to whom the offer is made.

ALIEN CORPORATION ■ A designation in the United States for a corporation formed in another country but doing business in the United States.

ALIENATION ■ The process of transferring land out of one's possession (thus "alienating" the land from oneself).

ALLONGE ■ A piece of paper firmly attached to a negotiable instrument, on which transferees can make indorsements if there is no room left on the instrument itself.

ALTERNATIVE DISPUTE RESOLUTION (ADR) ■ The resolution of disputes in ways other than those involved in the traditional judicial process. Negotiation, mediation, and arbitration are forms of ADR.

ANSWER ■ Procedurally, a defendant's response to the plaintiff's complaint.

ANTICIPATORY REPUDIATION ■ An assertion or action by a party indicating that he or she will not perform an obligation that the party is contractually obligated to perform at a future time.

ANTITRUST LAWS ■ Laws protecting commerce from unlawful restraints.

APPRAISAL RIGHT ■ The right of a dissenting shareholder, who objects to an extraordinary transaction of the corporation (such as a merger or a consolidation), to have his or her shares appraised and to be paid the fair value of those shares by the corporation.

APPROPRIATION ■ In tort law, the use by one person of another person's name, likeness, or other identifying characteristic without permission and for the benefit of the user.

ARBITRATION ■ The settling of a dispute by submitting it to a disinterested third party (other than a court), who renders a decision that is (most often) legally binding.

ARBITRATION CLAUSE ■ A clause in a contract that provides that, in the event of a dispute, the parties will submit the dispute to arbitration rather than litigate the dispute in court.

ARSON ■ The intentional burning of another's dwelling. Some statutes have expanded this to include any real property regardless of ownership and the destruction of property by other means—for example, by explosion.

ARTICLES OF INCORPORATION ■ The document filed with the appropriate governmental agency, usually the secretary of state, when a business is incorporated. State statutes usually prescribe what kind of information must be contained in the articles of incorporation.

ARTICLES OF ORGANIZATION ■ The document filed with a designated state official by which a limited liability company is formed.

ARTICLES OF PARTNERSHIP ■ A written agreement that sets forth each partner's rights and obligations with respect to the partnership.

ARTISAN'S LIEN ■ A possessory lien given to a person who has made improvements and added value to another person's personal property as security for payment for services performed.

ASSAULT ■ Any word or action intended to make another person fearful of immediate physical harm; a reasonably believable threat.

ASSIGNEE ■ A party to whom the rights under a contract are transferred, or assigned.

ASSIGNMENT ■ The act of transferring to another all or part of one's rights arising under a contract.

ASSIGNOR ■ A party who transfers (assigns) his or her rights under a contract to another party (called the assignee).

ASSUMPTION OF RISK ■ A doctrine under which a plaintiff may not recover for injuries or damages suffered from risks he or she knows of and has voluntarily assumed.

ATTACHMENT ■ In a secured transaction, the process by which a secured creditor's interest "attaches" to the property of another (collateral) and the creditor's security interest becomes enforceable. In the context of judicial liens, a court-ordered seizure and taking into custody of property prior to the securing of a judgment for a past-due debt.

ATTEMPTED MONOPOLIZATION ■ Any actions by a firm to eliminate competition and gain monopoly power.

AUTOMATIC STAY ■ In bankruptcy proceedings, the suspension of virtually all litigation and other action by creditors against the debtor or the debtor's property. The stay is effective the moment the debtor files a petition in bankruptcy.

AWARD ■ In litigation, the amount of money awarded to a plaintiff in a civil lawsuit as damages. In the context of alternative dispute resolution, the decision rendered by an arbitrator.

B

BAILEE ■ One to whom goods are entrusted by a bailor. Under the UCC, a party who, by a bill of lading, warehouse receipt, or other document of title, acknowledges possession of goods and/or contracts to deliver them.

BAILMENT ■ A situation in which the personal property of one person (a bailor) is entrusted to another (a bailee), who is obligated to return the bailed property to the bailor or dispose of it as directed.

BAILOR ■ One who entrusts goods to a bailee.

BAIT-AND-SWITCH ADVERTISING ■ Advertising a product at a very attractive price (the "bait") and then, once the consumer is in the store, saying that the advertised product is either not available or is of poor quality; the customer is then urged to purchase ("switched" to) a more expensive item.

BANKRUPTCY COURT ■ A federal court of limited jurisdiction that handles only bankruptcy proceedings. Bankruptcy proceedings are governed by federal bankruptcy law.

BATTERY ■ The unprivileged, intentional touching of another.

BEARER INSTRUMENT ■ Any instrument that is not payable to a specific person, including instruments payable to the bearer or to "cash."

BEARER ■ A person in possession of an instrument payable to bearer or indorsed in blank.

BEQUEST ■ A gift by will of personal property (from the verb *to bequeath*).

BEYOND A REASONABLE DOUBT ■ The burden of proof used in criminal cases. If there is any reasonable doubt that a criminal defendant did not commit the crime with which she or he has been charged, then the verdict must be "not guilty."

BILATERAL CONTRACT ■ A type of contract that arises when a promise is given in exchange for a return promise.

BILL OF RIGHTS ■ The first ten amendments to the U.S. Constitution.

BINDER ■ A written, temporary insurance policy.

BINDING AUTHORITY ■ Any source of law that a court must follow when deciding a case. Binding authorities include constitutions, statutes, and regulations that govern the issue being decided, as well as court decisions that are controlling precedents within the jurisdiction.

BLANK INDORSEMENT ■ An indorsement that specifies no particular indorsee and can consist of a mere signature. An order instrument that is indorsed in blank becomes a bearer instrument.

BLUE LAWS ■ State or local laws that prohibit the performance of certain types of commercial activities on Sunday.

BLUE SKY LAWS ■ State laws that regulate the offer and sale of securities.

BONA FIDE OCCUPATIONAL QUALIFICATION (BFOQ) ■ Identifiable characteristics reasonably necessary to the normal operation of a particular business. These characteristics can include gender, national origin, and religion, but not race.

BOND ■ A certificate that evidences a corporate (or government) debt. It is a security that involves no ownership interest in the issuing entity.

BOND INDENTURE ■ A contract between the issuer of a bond and the bondholder.

BOUNTY PAYMENT ■ A reward (payment) given to a person or persons who perform a certain service, such as informing legal authorities of illegal actions.

BREACH ■ The failure to perform a legal obligation.

BREACH OF CONTRACT ■ The failure, without legal excuse, of a promisor to perform the obligations of a contract.

BRIEF ■ A formal legal document submitted by the attorney for the appellant or the appellee (in answer to the appellant's brief) to an appellate court when a case is appealed. The appellant's brief outlines the facts and issues of the case, the judge's rulings or jury's findings that should be reversed or modified, the applicable law, and the arguments on the client's behalf.

BROWSE-WRAP TERMS ■ Terms and conditions of use that are presented to an Internet user at the time certain products, such as software, are being downloaded but that need not be agreed to (by clicking "I agree," for example) before the user is able to install or use the product.

BURGLARY ■ The unlawful entry or breaking into a building with the intent to commit a felony. (Some state statutes expand this to include the intent to commit any crime.)

BUSINESS ETHICS ■ Ethics in a business context; a consensus of what constitutes right or wrong behavior in the world of business and the application of moral principles to situations that arise in a business setting.

BUSINESS INVITEE ■ A person, such as a customer or a client, who is invited onto business premises by the owner of those premises for business purposes.

BUSINESS JUDGMENT RULE ■ A rule that immunizes corporate management from liability for actions that result in corporate losses or damages if the actions are undertaken in good faith and are within both the power of the corporation and the authority of management to make.

BUSINESS NECESSITY ■ A defense to allegations of employment discrimination in which the employer demonstrates that an employment practice that discriminates against members of a protected class is related to job performance.

BUSINESS TORT ■ Wrongful interference with another's business rights.

BUSINESS TRUST ■ A form of business organization in which investors (trust beneficiaries) transfer cash or property to trustees in exchange for trust certificates that represent their investment shares. The certificate holders share in the trust's profits but have limited liability.

BUYOUT PRICE ■ The amount payable to a partner on his or her dissociation from a partnership, based on the amount distributable to that partner if the firm were wound up on that date, and offset by any damages for wrongful dissociation.

BYLAWS ■ A set of governing rules adopted by a corporation or other association.

C

CASE LAW ■ The rules of law announced in court decisions. Case law includes the aggregate of reported cases that interpret judicial precedents, statutes, regulations, and constitutional provisions.

CASHIER'S CHECK ■ A check drawn by a bank on itself.

CATEGORICAL IMPERATIVE ■ A concept developed by the philosopher Immanuel Kant as an ethical guideline for behavior. In deciding whether an action is right or wrong, or desirable or undesirable, a person should evaluate the action in terms of what would happen if everybody else in the same situation, or category, acted the same way.

CAUSATION IN FACT ■ An act or omission without which an event would not have occurred.

CEASE-AND-DESIST ORDER ■ An administrative or judicial order prohibiting a person or business firm from conducting activities that an agency or court has deemed illegal.

CERTIFICATE OF DEPOSIT (CD) ■ A note of a bank in which the bank acknowledges a receipt of money from a party and promises to repay the money, with interest, to the party on a certain date.

CERTIFICATE OF INCORPORATION ■ The primary document that evidences corporate existence (often referred to as the *corporate charter*).

CERTIFICATE OF LIMITED PARTNERSHIP ■ The basic document filed with a designated state official by which a limited partnership is formed.

CERTIFIED CHECK ■ A check that has been accepted in writing by the bank on which it is drawn. Essentially, the bank, by certifying (accepting) the check, promises to pay the check at the time the check is presented.

CHARGING ORDER ■ In partnership law, an order granted by a court to a judgment creditor that entitles the creditor to attach profits or assets of a partner on the dissolution of the partnership.

CHARITABLE TRUST ■ A trust in which the property held by the trustee must be used for a charitable purpose, such as the advancement of health, education, or religion.

CHATTEL ■ All forms of personal property.

CHECK ■ A draft drawn by a drawer ordering the drawee bank or financial institution to pay a fixed amount of money to the holder on demand.

CHECKS AND BALANCES ■ The principle under which the powers of the national government are divided among three separate branches—the executive, legislative, and judicial branches—each of which exercises a check on the actions of the others.

CHOICE-OF-LANGUAGE CLAUSE ■ A clause in a contract designating the official language by which the contract will be interpreted in the event of a future disagreement over the contract's terms.

CHOICE-OF-LAW CLAUSE ■ A clause in a contract designating the law (such as the law of a particular state or nation) that will govern the contract.

CHOSE IN ACTION ■ A right that can be enforced in court to recover a debt or to obtain damages.

CITATION ■ A reference to a publication in which a legal authority—such as a statute or a court decision—or other source can be found.

CIVIL LAW ■ The branch of law dealing with the definition and enforcement of all private or public rights, as opposed to criminal matters.

CIVIL LAW SYSTEM ■ A system of law derived from that of the Roman Empire and based on a code rather than case law; the predominant system of law in the nations of continental Europe and the nations that were once their colonies. In the United States, Louisiana, because of its historical ties to France, has in part a civil law system.

CLEARINGHOUSE ■ A system or place where banks exchange checks and drafts drawn on each other and settle daily balances.

CLICK-ON AGREEMENT ■ An agreement that arises when a buyer, engaging in a transaction on a computer, indicates his or her assent to be bound by the terms of an offer by clicking on a button that says, for example, "I agree"; sometimes referred to as a *click-on license* or a *click-wrap agreement*.

CLOSE CORPORATION ■ A corporation whose shareholders are limited to a small group of persons, often including only family members. In a close corporation, the shareholders' rights to transfer shares to others are usually restricted.

CLOSED SHOP ■ A firm that requires union membership by its workers as a condition of employment. The closed shop was made illegal by the Labor-Management Relations Act of 1947.

CODICIL ■ A written supplement or modification to a will. A codicil must be executed with the same formalities as a will.

COLLATERAL ■ Under Article 9 of the UCC, the property subject to a security interest, including accounts and chattel paper that have been sold.

COLLATERAL PROMISE ■ A secondary promise that is ancillary (subsidiary) to a principal transaction or primary contractual relationship, such as a promise made by one person to pay the debts of another if the latter fails to perform. A collateral promise normally must be in writing to be enforceable.

COLLECTING BANK ■ Any bank handling an item for collection, except the payor bank.

COLLECTIVE BARGAINING ■ The process by which labor and management negotiate the terms and conditions of employment, including working hours and workplace conditions.

COMITY ■ The principle by which one nation defers and gives effect to the laws and judicial decrees of another nation. This recognition is based primarily on respect.

COMMERCE CLAUSE ■ The provision in Article I, Section 8, of the U.S. Constitution that gives Congress the power to regulate interstate commerce.

COMMINGLE ■ To mix together; to put funds or goods together into one mass so that they are so mixed that they no longer have separate identities. In corporate law, if personal and corporate interests are commingled to the extent that the corporation has no separate identity, a court may "pierce the corporate veil" and expose the shareholders to personal liability.

COMMON CARRIER ■ An owner of a truck, railroad, airline, ship, or other vehicle that is licensed to offer transportation services to the public, generally in return for compensation or a payment.

COMMON LAW ■ That body of law developed from custom or judicial decisions in English and U.S. courts, not attributable to a legislature.

COMMON STOCK ■ Shares of ownership in a corporation that give the owner of the stock a proportionate interest in the corporation with regard to control, earnings, and net assets. Shares of common stock are lowest in priority with respect to payment of dividends and distribution of the corporation's assets on dissolution.

COMMUNITY PROPERTY ■ A form of concurrent ownership of property in which each spouse technically owns an undivided one-half interest in property acquired during the marriage. This form of joint ownership occurs in only ten states and Puerto Rico.

COMPARATIVE NEGLIGENCE ■ A rule in tort law that reduces the plaintiff's recovery in proportion to the plaintiff's degree of fault, rather than barring recovery completely; used in the majority of states.

COMPENSATORY DAMAGES ■ A money award equivalent to the actual value of injuries or damages sustained by the aggrieved party.

COMPLAINT ■ The pleading made by a plaintiff alleging wrongdoing on the part of the defendant; the document that, when filed with a court, initiates a lawsuit.

COMPUTER CRIME ■ Any act that is directed against computers and computer parts, that uses computers as instruments of crime, or that involves computers and constitutes abuse.

COMPUTER INFORMATION ■ As defined by the Uniform Computer Information Transactions Act, "information in an electronic form obtained from or through use of a computer, or that is in digital or an equivalent form capable of being processed by a computer."

CONCURRENT CONDITIONS ■ Conditions that must occur or be performed at the same time; they are mutually dependent. No obligations arise until these conditions are simultaneously performed.

CONCURRENT JURISDICTION ■ Jurisdiction that exists when two different courts have the power to hear a case. For example, some cases can be heard in a federal or a state court.

CONCURRENT OWNERSHIP ■ Joint ownership.

CONDEMNATION ■ The process of taking private property for public use through the government's power of eminent domain.

CONDITION ■ A qualification, provision, or clause in a contractual agreement, the occurrence or nonoccurrence of which creates, suspends, or terminates the obligations of the contracting parties.

CONDITION PRECEDENT ■ In a contractual agreement, a condition that must be met before a party's promise becomes absolute.

CONDITION SUBSEQUENT ■ A condition in a contract that, if not fulfilled, operates to terminate a party's absolute promise to perform.

CONFESSION OF JUDGMENT ■ The act or agreement of a debtor in permitting a judgment to be entered against him or her by a creditor, for an agreed sum, without the institution of legal proceedings.

CONFISCATION ■ A government's taking of a privately owned business or personal property without a proper public purpose or an award of just compensation.

CONFUSION ■ The mixing together of goods belonging to two or more owners so that the separately owned goods cannot be identified.

CONSENT ■ The voluntary agreement to a proposition or an act of another; a concurrence of wills.

CONSEQUENTIAL DAMAGES ■ Special damages that compensate for a loss that does not directly or immediately result from the breach (for example, lost profits). For the plaintiff to collect consequential damages, they must have been reasonably foreseeable at the time the breach or injury occurred.

CONSIDERATION ■ Generally, the value given in return for a promise. The consideration must result in a detriment to the promisee (something of legally sufficient value and bargained for) or a benefit to the promisor.

CONSIGNMENT ■ A transaction in which an owner of goods (the consignor) delivers the goods to another (the consignee) for the consignee to sell. The consignee pays the consignor only for the goods that are sold by the consignee.

CONSOLIDATION ■ A contractual and statutory process in which two or more corporations join to become a completely new corporation. The original corporations cease to exist, and the new corporation acquires all their assets and liabilities.

CONSTITUTIONAL LAW ■ The body of law derived from the U.S. Constitution and the constitutions of the various states.

CONSTRUCTIVE DELIVERY ■ An act equivalent to the actual, physical delivery of property that cannot be physically delivered because of difficulty or impossibility. For example, the transfer of a key to a safe constructively delivers the contents of the safe.

CONSTRUCTIVE DISCHARGE ■ A termination of employment brought about by making the employee's working conditions so intolerable that the employee reasonably feels compelled to leave.

CONSTRUCTIVE EVICTION ■ A form of eviction that occurs when a landlord fails to perform adequately any of the undertakings (such as providing heat in the winter) required by the lease, thereby making the tenant's further use and enjoyment of the property exceedingly difficult or impossible.

CONSTRUCTIVE TRUST ■ An equitable trust that is imposed in the interests of fairness and justice when someone wrongfully holds legal title to property. A court may require the owner to hold the property in trust for the person or persons who rightfully should own the property.

CONSUMER-DEBTOR ■ An individual whose debts are primarily consumer debts (debts for purchases made primarily for personal or household use).

CONTINUATION STATEMENT ■ A statement that, if filed within six months prior to the expiration date of the original financing statement, continues the perfection of the original security interest for another five years. The perfection of a security interest can be continued in the same manner indefinitely.

CONTRACT ■ An agreement that can be enforced in court; formed by two or more competent parties who agree, for consideration, to perform or to refrain from performing some legal act now or in the future.

CONTRACTUAL CAPACITY ■ The threshold mental capacity required by law for a party who enters into a contract to be bound by that contract.

CONTRIBUTORY NEGLIGENCE ■ A rule in tort law that completely bars the plaintiff from recovering any damages if the damage suffered is partly the plaintiff's own fault; used in a minority of states.

CONVERSION ■ Wrongfully taking or retaining possession of an individual's personal property and placing it in the service of another.

CONVEYANCE ■ The transfer of a title to land from one person to another by deed; a document (such as a deed) by which an interest in land is transferred from one person to another.

"COOLING-OFF" LAWS ■ Laws that allow buyers a period of time, such as three days, in which to cancel door-to-door sales contracts.

COOPERATIVE ■ An association, which may or may not be incorporated, that is organized to provide an economic service to its members. Unincorporated cooperatives are often treated like partnerships for tax and other legal purposes. Examples of cooperatives include consumer purchasing cooperatives, credit cooperatives, and farmers' cooperatives.

COPYRIGHT ■ The exclusive right of "authors" to publish, print, or sell an intellectual production for a statutory period of time. A copyright has the same monopolistic nature as a patent or trademark, but it differs in that it applies exclusively to works of art, literature, and other works of authorship (including computer programs).

CORPORATE CHARTER ■ The document issued by a state agency or authority (usually the secretary of state) that grants a corporation legal existence and the right to function.

CORPORATION ■ A legal entity formed in compliance with statutory requirements that is distinct from its shareholder-owners.

CORRESPONDENT BANK ■ A bank in which another bank has an account (and vice versa) for the purpose of facilitating fund transfers.

COST-BENEFIT ANALYSIS ■ A decision-making technique that involves weighing the costs of a given action against the benefits of that action.

CO-SURETY ■ A joint surety; a person who assumes liability jointly with another surety for the payment of an obligation.

COUNTERADVERTISING ■ New advertising that is undertaken pursuant to a Federal Trade Commission order for the purpose of correcting earlier false claims that were made about a product.

COUNTERCLAIM ■ A claim made by a defendant in a civil lawsuit against the plaintiff. In effect, the defendant is suing the plaintiff.

COUNTEROFFER ■ An offeree's response to an offer in which the offeree rejects the original offer and at the same time makes a new offer.

COURSE OF DEALING ■ Prior conduct between the parties to a contract that establishes a common basis for their understanding.

COURSE OF PERFORMANCE ■ The conduct that occurs under the terms of a particular agreement. Such conduct indicates what the parties to an agreement intended it to mean.

COVENANT NOT TO COMPETE ■ A contractual promise of one party to refrain from conducting business similar to that of another party for a certain period of time and within a specified geographic area. Courts commonly enforce such covenants if they are reasonable in terms of time and geographic area and part of, or supplemental to, an employment contract or a contract for the sale of a business.

COVENANT NOT TO SUE ■ An agreement to substitute a contractual obligation for some other type of legal action based on a valid claim.

COVER ■ Under the UCC, a remedy that allows the buyer or lessee, on the seller's or lessor's breach, to purchase the goods, in good faith and within a reasonable time, from another seller or lessor and substitute them for the goods due under the contract. If the cost of cover exceeds the cost of the contract goods, the breaching seller or lessor will be liable to the buyer or lessee for the difference, plus incidental and consequential damages.

CRAM-DOWN PROVISION ■ A provision of the Bankruptcy Code that allows a court to confirm a debtor's Chapter 11 reorganization plan even though only one class of creditors has accepted it. To exercise the court's right under this provision, the court must demonstrate that the plan does not discriminate unfairly against any creditors and is fair and equitable.

CREDITORS' COMPOSITION AGREEMENT ■ An agreement formed between a debtor and his or her creditors in which the creditors agree to accept a lesser sum than that owed by the debtor in full satisfaction of the debt.

CRIME ■ A wrong against society proclaimed in a statute and, if committed, punishable by society through fines and/or imprisonment—and, in some cases, death.

CRIMINAL LAW ■ Law that defines and governs actions that constitute crimes. Generally, criminal law has to do with wrongful actions committed against society for which society demands redress.

CURE ■ The right of a party who tenders nonconforming performance to correct that performance within the contract period [UCC 2–508(1)].

CYBER CRIME ■ A crime that occurs online, in the virtual community of the Internet, as opposed to the physical world.

CYBER MARK ■ A trademark in cyberspace.

CYBER STALKER ■ A person who commits the crime of stalking in cyberspace. Generally, stalking consists of harassing a person and putting that person in reasonable fear for his or her safety or the safety of the person's immediate family.

CYBER TERRORIST ■ A hacker whose purpose is to exploit a target computer for a serious impact, such as corrupting a program to sabotage a business.

CYBER TORT ■ A tort committed in cyberspace.

CYBERLAW ■ An informal term used to refer to all laws governing electronic communications and transactions, particularly those conducted via the Internet.

CYBERNOTARY ■ A legally recognized authority that can certify the validity of digital signatures.

CYBERSQUATTING ■ The act of registering a domain name that is the same as, or confusingly similar to, the trademark of another and then offering to sell that domain name back to the trademark owner.

 D

DAMAGES ■ Money sought as a remedy for a breach of contract or a tortious action.

DEBTOR ■ Under Article 9 of the UCC, a debtor is any party who owes payment or performance of a secured obligation, whether or not the party actually owns or has rights in the collateral.

DEBTOR IN POSSESSION (DIP) ■ In Chapter 11 bankruptcy proceedings, a debtor who is allowed to continue in possession of the estate in property (the business) and to continue business operations.

DECEPTIVE ADVERTISING ■ Advertising that misleads consumers, either by unjustified claims concerning a product's performance or by the omission of a material fact concerning the product's composition or performance.

DEED ■ A document by which title to property (usually real property) is passed.

DEFAMATION ■ Anything published or publicly spoken that causes injury to another's good name, reputation, or character.

DEFAULT ■ The failure to observe a promise or discharge an obligation. The term is commonly used to mean the failure to pay a debt when it is due.

DEFAULT JUDGMENT ■ A judgment entered by a court against a defendant who has failed to appear in court to answer or defend against the plaintiff's claim.

DEFENDANT ■ One against whom a lawsuit is brought; the accused person in a criminal proceeding.

DEFENSE ■ A reason offered and alleged by a defendant in an action or suit as to why the plaintiff should not recover or establish what she or he seeks.

DEFICIENCY JUDGMENT ■ A judgment against a debtor for the amount of a debt remaining unpaid after the collateral has been repossessed and sold.

DELEGATEE ■ A party to whom contractual obligations are transferred, or delegated.

DELEGATION OF DUTIES ■ The act of transferring to another all or part of one's duties arising under a contract.

DELEGATOR ■ A party who transfers (delegates) her or his obligations under a contract to another party (called the delegatee).

DEPOSITARY BANK ■ The first bank to receive a check for payment.

DEPOSITION ■ The testimony of a party to a lawsuit or a witness taken under oath before a trial.

DESTINATION CONTRACT ■ A contract for the sale of goods in which the seller is required or authorized to ship the goods by carrier and tender delivery of the goods at a particular destination. The seller assumes liability for any losses or damage to the goods until they are tendered at the destination specified in the contract.

DEVISE ■ To make a gift of real property by will.

DEVISEE ■ One designated in a will to receive a gift of real property.

DIGITAL CASH ■ Funds contained on computer software, in the form of secure programs stored on microchips and other computer devices.

DISAFFIRMANCE ■ The legal avoidance, or setting aside, of a contractual obligation.

DISCHARGE ■ The termination of an obligation. In bankruptcy proceedings, the extinction of the debtor's dischargeable debts. In contract law, discharge occurs when the parties have fully performed their contractual obligations or when events, conduct of the parties, or operation of law releases the parties from performance.

DISCLOSED PRINCIPAL ■ A principal whose identity is known to a third party at the time the agent makes a contract with the third party.

DISCOVERY ■ A phase in the litigation process during which the opposing parties may obtain information from each other and from third parties prior to trial.

DISPARAGEMENT OF PROPERTY ■ An economically injurious falsehood made about another's product or property. A general term for torts that are more specifically referred to as slander of quality or slander of title.

DISPARATE-IMPACT DISCRIMINATION ■ A form of employment discrimination that results from certain employer practices or procedures that, although not discriminatory on their face, have a discriminatory effect.

DISPARATE-TREATMENT DISCRIMINATION ■ A form of employment discrimination that results when an employer intentionally discriminates against employees who are members of protected classes.

DISSOCIATION ■ The severance of the relationship between a partner and a partnership when the partner ceases to be associated with the carrying on of the partnership business.

DISSOLUTION ■ The formal disbanding of a partnership or a corporation. It can take place by (1) acts of the partners or, in a corporation, of the shareholders and board of directors; (2) the subsequent illegality of the partnership business; (3) the expiration of a time period stated in a partnership agreement or a certificate of incorporation; or (4) judicial decree.

DISTRIBUTED NETWORK ■ A network that can be used by persons located (distributed) around the country or the globe to share computer files.

DISTRIBUTION AGREEMENT ■ A contract between a seller and a distributor of the seller's products setting out the terms and conditions of the distributorship.

DIVERSITY OF CITIZENSHIP ■ Under Article III, Section 2, of the Constitution, a basis for federal district court jurisdiction over a lawsuit between (1) citizens of different states, (2) a foreign country and citizens of a state or of different states, or (3) citizens of a state and citizens or subjects of a foreign country. The amount in controversy must be more than $75,000 before a federal district court can take jurisdiction in such cases.

DIVESTITURE ■ The act of selling one or more of a company's divisions or parts, such as a subsidiary or plant; often mandated by the courts in merger or monopolization cases.

DIVIDEND ■ A distribution to corporate shareholders of corporate profits or income, disbursed in proportion to the number of shares held.

DOCKET ■ The list of cases entered on a court's calendar and thus scheduled to be heard by the court.

DOCUMENT OF TITLE ■ Paper exchanged in the regular course of business that evidences the right to possession of goods (for example, a bill of lading or a warehouse receipt).

DOMAIN NAME ■ The last part of an Internet address, such as "westlaw.com." The top level (the part of the name to the right of the period) indicates the type of entity that operates the site ("com" is an abbreviation for "commercial"). The second level (the part of the name to the left of the period) is chosen by the entity.

DOMESTIC CORPORATION ■ In a given state, a corporation that does business in, and is organized under the law of, that state.

DOMINION ■ Ownership rights in property, including the right to possess and control the property.

DOUBLE JEOPARDY ■ A situation occurring when a person is tried twice for the same criminal offense; prohibited by the Fifth Amendment to the Constitution.

DRAFT ■ Any instrument drawn on a drawee that orders the drawee to pay a certain sum of money, usually to a third party (the payee), on demand or at a definite future time.

DRAM SHOP ACT ■ A state statute that imposes liability on the owners of bars and taverns, as well as those who serve alcoholic drinks to the public, for injuries resulting from accidents caused by intoxicated persons when the sellers or servers of alcoholic drinks contributed to the intoxication.

DRAWEE ■ The party that is ordered to pay a draft or check. With a check, a bank or a financial institution is always the drawee.

DRAWER ■ The party that initiates a draft (such as a check), thereby ordering the drawee to pay.

DUE PROCESS CLAUSE ■ The provisions in the Fifth and Fourteenth Amendments to the Constitution that guarantee that no person shall be deprived of life, liberty, or property without due process of law. Similar clauses are found in most state constitutions.

DUMPING ■ The selling of goods in a foreign country at a price below the price charged for the same goods in the domestic market.

DURESS ■ Unlawful pressure brought to bear on a person, causing the person to perform an act that she or he would not otherwise perform.

DUTY OF CARE ■ The duty of all persons, as established by tort law, to exercise a reasonable amount of care in their dealings with others. Failure to exercise due care, which is normally determined by the "reasonable person standard," constitutes the tort of negligence.

E

E-AGENT ■ A computer program that by electronic or other automated means can independently initiate an action or respond to electronic messages or data without review by an individual.

EARLY NEUTRAL CASE EVALUATION ■ A form of alternative dispute resolution in which a neutral third party evaluates the strengths and weaknesses of the disputing parties' positions. The evaluator's opinion then forms the basis for negotiating a settlement.

EASEMENT ■ A nonpossessory right to use another's property in a manner established by either express or implied agreement.

E-CONTRACT ■ A contract that is formed electronically.

E-EVIDENCE ■ A type of evidence that consists of computer-generated or electronically recorded information, including e-mail, voice mail, spreadsheets, word processing documents, and other data.

ELECTRONIC FUND TRANSFER (EFT) ■ A transfer of funds through the use of an electronic terminal, a telephone, a computer, or magnetic tape.

EMANCIPATION ■ In regard to minors, the act of being freed from parental control; occurs when a child's parent or legal guardian relinquishes the legal right to exercise control over the child. Normally, a minor who leaves home to support himself or herself is considered emancipated.

EMBEZZLEMENT ■ The fraudulent appropriation of funds or other property by a person to whom the funds or property has been entrusted.

EMINENT DOMAIN ■ The power of a government to take land for public use from private citizens for just compensation.

E-MONEY ■ Prepaid funds recorded on a computer or a card (such as a smart card or a stored-value card).

EMPLOYMENT AT WILL ■ A common law doctrine under which either party may terminate an employment relationship at any time for any reason, unless a contract specifies otherwise.

EMPLOYMENT CONTRACT ■ A contract between an employer and an employee in which the terms and conditions of employment are stated.

EMPLOYMENT DISCRIMINATION ■ Treating employees or job applicants unequally on the basis of race, color, national origin, religion, gender, age, or disability; prohibited by federal statutes.

ENABLING LEGISLATION ■ A statute enacted by Congress that authorizes the creation of an administrative agency and specifies the name, composition, purpose, and powers of the agency being created.

ENTRAPMENT ■ In criminal law, a defense in which the defendant claims that he or she was induced by a public official—usually an undercover agent or police officer—to commit a crime that he or she would otherwise not have committed.

ENTREPRENEUR ■ One who initiates and assumes the financial risk of a new business enterprise and undertakes to provide or control its management.

ENVIRONMENTAL IMPACT STATEMENT (EIS) ■ A statement required by the National Environmental Policy Act for any major federal action that will significantly affect the quality of the environment. The statement must analyze the action's impact on the environment and explore alternative actions that might be taken.

EQUAL DIGNITY RULE ■ In most states, a rule stating that express authority given to an agent must be in writing if the contract to be made on behalf of the principal is required to be in writing.

EQUAL PROTECTION CLAUSE ■ The provision in the Fourteenth Amendment to the Constitution that guarantees that no state will "deny to any person within its jurisdiction the equal protection of the laws." This clause mandates that the state governments treat similarly situated individuals in a similar manner.

EQUITABLE PRINCIPLES AND MAXIMS ■ General propositions or principles of law that have to do with fairness (equity).

E-SIGNATURE ■ As defined by the Uniform Electronic Transactions Act, "an electronic sound, symbol, or process attached to or logically associated with a record and executed or adopted by a person with the intent to sign the record."

ESTABLISHMENT CLAUSE ■ The provision in the First Amendment to the Constitution that prohibits the government from establishing any state-sponsored religion or enacting any law that promotes religion or favors one religion over another.

ESTATE IN PROPERTY ■ In bankruptcy proceedings, all of the debtor's interests in property currently held, wherever located, together with certain jointly owned property, property transferred in transactions voidable by the trustee, proceeds and profits from the property of the estate, and certain property interests to which the debtor becomes entitled within 180 days after filing for bankruptcy.

ESTOPPED ■ Barred, impeded, or precluded.

ESTRAY STATUTE ■ A statute defining finders' rights in property when the true owners are unknown.

ETHICAL REASONING ■ A reasoning process in which an individual links his or her moral convictions or ethical standards to the particular situation at hand.

ETHICS ■ Moral principles and values applied to social behavior.

EVICTION ■ A landlord's act of depriving a tenant of possession of the leased premises.

EXCLUSIONARY RULE ■ In criminal procedure, a rule under which any evidence that is obtained in violation of the accused's constitutional rights guaranteed by the Fourth, Fifth, and Sixth Amendments, as well as any evidence derived from illegally obtained evidence, will not be admissible in court.

EXCLUSIVE DISTRIBUTORSHIP ■ A distributorship in which the seller and the distributor of the seller's products agree that the distributor has the exclusive right to distribute the seller's products in a certain geographic area.

EXCLUSIVE JURISDICTION ■ Jurisdiction that exists when a case can be heard only in a particular court or type of court.

EXCLUSIVE-DEALING CONTRACT ■ An agreement under which a seller forbids a buyer to purchase products from the seller's competitors.

EXCULPATORY CLAUSE ■ A clause that releases a contractual party from liability in the event of monetary or physical injury, no matter who is at fault.

EXECUTED CONTRACT ■ A contract that has been completely performed by both parties.

EXECUTION ■ An action to carry into effect the directions in a court decree or judgment.

EXECUTIVE AGENCY ■ An administrative agency within the executive branch of government. At the federal level, executive agencies are those within the cabinet departments.

EXECUTOR ■ A person appointed by a testator in a will to see that her or his will is administered appropriately.

EXECUTORY CONTRACT ■ A contract that has not as yet been fully performed.

EXPORT ■ To sell products to buyers located in other countries.

EXPRESS CONTRACT ■ A contract in which the terms of the agreement are stated in words, oral or written.

EXPRESS WARRANTY ■ A seller's or lessor's oral or written promise or affirmation of fact ancillary to an underlying sales or lease agreement, as to the quality, description, or performance of the goods being sold or leased.

EXPROPRIATION ■ The seizure by a government of a privately owned business or personal property for a proper public purpose and with just compensation.

EXTENSION CLAUSE ■ A clause in a time instrument that allows the instrument's date of maturity to be extended into the future.

FAMILY LIMITED LIABILITY PARTNERSHIP (FLLP) ■ A type of limited liability partnership owned by family members or fiduciaries of family members.

FEDERAL FORM OF GOVERNMENT ■ A system of government in which the states form a union and the sovereign power is divided between the central government and the member states.

FEDERAL QUESTION ■ A question that pertains to the U.S. Constitution, acts of Congress, or treaties. A federal question provides a basis for federal jurisdiction.

FEDERAL RESERVE SYSTEM ■ A network of twelve district banks and related branches located around the country and headed by the Federal Reserve Board of Governors. Most banks in the United States have Federal Reserve accounts.

FEE SIMPLE ■ An absolute form of property ownership entitling the property owner to use, possess, or dispose of the property as he or she chooses during his or her lifetime. On death, the interest in the property descends to the owner's heirs.

FEE SIMPLE ABSOLUTE ■ An ownership interest in land in which the owner has the greatest possible aggregation of rights, privileges, and power. Ownership in fee simple absolute is limited absolutely to a person and her or his heirs.

FELONY ■ A crime—such as arson, murder, rape, or robbery—that carries the most severe sanctions, which range from more than one year in a state or federal prison to the death penalty.

FICTITIOUS PAYEE ■ A payee on a negotiable instrument whom the maker or drawer does not intend to have an interest in the instrument. Indorsements by fictitious payees are treated as authorized indorsements under Article 3 of the UCC.

FIDUCIARY ■ As a noun, a person having a duty created by his or her undertaking to act primarily for another's benefit in matters connected with the undertaking. As an adjective, a relationship founded on trust and confidence.

FILTERING SOFTWARE ■ A computer program that includes a pattern through which data are passed. When designed to block access to certain Web sites, the pattern blocks the retrieval of a site whose URL or key words are on a list within the program.

FINANCING STATEMENT ■ A document prepared by a secured creditor, and filed with the appropriate state or local official, to give notice to the public that the creditor has a security interest in collateral belonging to the debtor named in the statement.

FIRM OFFER ■ An offer (by a merchant) that is irrevocable without consideration for a stated period of time or, if no definite period is stated, for a reasonable time (neither period to exceed three months). A firm offer by a merchant must be in writing and must be signed by the offeror.

FIXTURE ■ A thing that was once personal property but has become attached to real property in such a way that it takes on the characteristics of real property and becomes part of that real property.

FLOATING LIEN ■ A security interest in proceeds, after-acquired property, or collateral subject to future advances by the secured party (or all three); a security interest in collateral that is retained even when the collateral changes in character, classification, or location.

FORBEARANCE ■ The act of refraining from an action that one has a legal right to undertake.

***FORCE MAJEURE* CLAUSE** ■ A provision in a contract stipulating that certain unforeseen events—such as war, political upheavals, or acts of God—will excuse a party from liability for nonperformance of contractual obligations.

FOREIGN CORPORATION ■ In a given state, a corporation that does business in the state without being incorporated therein.

FOREIGN EXCHANGE MARKET ■ A worldwide system in which foreign currencies are bought and sold.

FORGERY ■ The fraudulent making or altering of any writing in a way that changes the legal rights and liabilities of another.

FORMAL CONTRACT ■ A contract that by law requires a specific form, such as being executed under seal, for its validity.

FORUM-SELECTION CLAUSE ■ A provision in a contract designating the court, jurisdiction, or tribunal that will decide any disputes arising under the contract.

FRANCHISE ■ Any arrangement in which the owner of a trademark, trade name, or copyright licenses another to use that trademark, trade name, or copyright in the selling of goods and services.

FRANCHISEE ■ One receiving a license to use another's (the franchisor's) trademark, trade name, or copyright in the sale of goods and services.

FRANCHISOR ■ One licensing another (the franchisee) to use the owner's trademark, trade name, or copyright in the sale of goods or services.

FRAUDULENT MISREPRESENTATION ■ Any misrepresentation, either by misstatement or omission of a material fact, knowingly made with the intention of deceiving another and on which a reasonable person would and does rely to his or her detriment.

FREE EXERCISE CLAUSE ■ The provision in the First Amendment to the Constitution that prohibits the government from interfering with people's religious practices or forms of worship.

FUNGIBLE GOODS ■ Goods that are alike by physical nature, by agreement, or by trade usage. Examples of fungible goods are wheat, oil, and wine that are identical in type and quality. When owners of fungible goods hold the goods as tenants in common, title and risk can pass without actually separating the goods being sold from the mass of fungible goods.

G

GARNISHMENT ■ A legal process used by a creditor to collect a debt by seizing property of the debtor (such as wages) that is being held by a third party (such as the debtor's employer).

GENERAL PARTNER ■ In a limited partnership, a partner who assumes responsibility for the management of the partnership and liability for all partnership debts.

GENERALLY ACCEPTED ACCOUNTING PRINCIPLES (GAAP) ■ The conventions, rules, and procedures necessary to define accepted accounting practices at a particular time. The source of the principles is the Financial Accounting Standards Board (FASB).

GENERALLY ACCEPTED AUDITING STANDARDS (GAAS) ■ Standards concerning an auditor's professional qualities and the judgment exercised by him or her in the performance of an examination and report. The source of the standards is the American Institute of Certified Public Accountants.

GIFT ■ Any voluntary transfer of property made without consideration, past or present.

GIFT *CAUSA MORTIS* ■ A gift made in contemplation of death. If the donor does not die of that ailment, the gift is revoked.

GIFT *INTER VIVOS* ■ A gift made during one's lifetime and not in contemplation of imminent death, in contrast to a gift *causa mortis*.

GOOD FAITH PURCHASER ■ A purchaser who buys without notice of any circumstance that would put a person of ordinary prudence on inquiry as to whether the seller has valid title to the goods being sold.

GOOD SAMARITAN STATUTE ■ A state statute stipulating that persons who provide emergency services to, or rescue, someone in peril cannot be sued for negligence, unless they act recklessly, thereby causing further harm.

GRAND JURY ■ A group of citizens called to decide, after hearing the state's evidence, whether a reasonable basis (probable cause) exists for believing that a crime has been committed and whether a trial ought to be held.

GROUP BOYCOTT ■ The refusal by a group of competitors to deal with a particular person or firm; prohibited by the Sherman Act.

GUARANTOR ■ A person who agrees to satisfy the debt of another (the debtor) only after the principal debtor defaults. Thus, a guarantor's liability is secondary.

H

HACKER ■ A person who uses one computer to break into another. Professional computer programmers refer to such persons as "crackers."

HISTORICAL SCHOOL ■ A school of legal thought that emphasizes the evolutionary process of law and that looks to the past to discover what the principles of contemporary law should be.

HOLDER ■ Any person in possession of an instrument drawn, issued, or indorsed to him or her, to his or her order, to bearer, or in blank.

HOLDER IN DUE COURSE (HDC) ■ A holder who acquires a negotiable instrument for value; in good faith; and without notice that the instrument is overdue, that it has been dishonored, that any person has a defense against it or a claim to it, or that the instrument contains unauthorized signatures, has been altered, or is so irregular or incomplete as to call into question its authenticity.

HOLOGRAPHIC WILL ■ A will written entirely in the signer's handwriting and usually not witnessed.

HOMESTEAD EXEMPTION ■ A law permitting a debtor to retain the family home, either in its entirety or up to a specified dollar amount, free from the claims of unsecured creditors or trustees in bankruptcy.

HORIZONTAL MERGER ■ A merger between two firms that are competing in the same marketplace.

HORIZONTAL RESTRAINT ■ Any agreement that in some way restrains competition between rival firms competing in the same market.

HOT-CARGO AGREEMENT ■ An agreement in which employers voluntarily agree with unions not to handle, use, or deal in other employers' goods that were not produced by union employees; a type of secondary boycott explicitly prohibited by the Labor-Management Reporting and Disclosure Act of 1959.

I

IDENTIFICATION ■ In a sale of goods, the express designation of the goods provided for in the contract.

IDENTITY THEFT ■ The act of stealing another's identifying information—such as a name, date of birth, or Social Security number—and using that information to access the victim's financial resources.

IMPLIED-IN-FACT CONTRACT ■ A contract formed in whole or in part from the conduct of the parties (as opposed to an express contract).

IMPLIED WARRANTY ■ A warranty that arises by law because of the circumstances of a sale, rather than by the seller's express promise.

IMPLIED WARRANTY OF FITNESS FOR A PARTICULAR PURPOSE ■ A warranty that goods sold or leased are fit for a particular purpose. The warranty arises when any seller or lessor knows the particular purpose for which a buyer or lessee will use the goods and knows that the buyer or lessee is relying on the skill and judgment of the seller or lessor to select suitable goods.

IMPLIED WARRANTY OF HABITABILITY ■ An implied promise by a landlord that rented residential premises are fit for human habitation—that is, in a condition that is safe and suitable for people to live in.

IMPLIED WARRANTY OF MERCHANTABILITY ■ A warranty that goods being sold or leased are reasonably fit for the general purpose for which they are sold or leased, are properly packaged and labeled, and are of proper quality. The warranty automatically arises in every sale or lease of goods made by a merchant who deals in goods of the kind sold or leased.

IMPOSSIBILITY OF PERFORMANCE ■ A doctrine under which a party to a contract is relieved of his or her duty to perform when performance becomes objectively impossible or totally impracticable (through no fault of either party).

IMPOSTER ■ One who, by use of the mails, Internet, telephone, or personal appearance, induces a maker or drawer to issue an instrument in the name of an impersonated payee. Indorsements by imposters are treated as authorized indorsements under Article 3 of the UCC.

INCIDENTAL BENEFICIARY ■ A third party who incidentally benefits from a contract but whose benefit was not the reason the contract was formed. An incidental beneficiary has no rights in a contract and cannot sue to have the contract enforced.

INCIDENTAL DAMAGES ■ All costs resulting from a breach of contract, including all reasonable expenses incurred because of the breach.

INDEPENDENT CONTRACTOR ■ One who works for, and receives payment from, an employer but whose working conditions and methods are not controlled by the employer. An independent contractor is not an employee but may be an agent.

INDEPENDENT REGULATORY AGENCY ■ An administrative agency that is not considered part of the government's executive branch and is not subject to the authority of the president. Independent agency officials cannot be removed without cause.

INDICTMENT ■ A charge by a grand jury that a named person has committed a crime.

INDORSEE ■ The person to whom a negotiable instrument is transferred by indorsement.

INDORSEMENT ■ A signature placed on an instrument for the purpose of transferring one's ownership rights in the instrument.

INDORSER ■ A person who transfers an instrument by signing (indorsing) it and delivering it to another person.

INFORMAL CONTRACT ■ A contract that does not require a specified form or formality to be valid.

INFORMATION ■ A formal accusation or complaint (without an indictment) issued in certain types of actions (usually criminal actions involving lesser crimes) by a law officer, such as a magistrate.

INFORMATION RETURN ■ A tax return submitted by a partnership that only reports the income and losses earned by the business. The partnership as an entity does not pay taxes on the income received by the partnership. A partner's profit from the partnership (whether distributed or not) is taxed as individual income to the individual partner.

INNKEEPER'S LIEN ■ A possessory lien placed on the luggage of hotel guests for hotel charges that remain unpaid.

INSIDER TRADING ■ The purchase or sale of securities on the basis of "inside information" (information that has not been made available to the public).

INSOLVENT ■ Under the UCC, a term describing a person who ceases to pay "his [or her] debts in the ordinary course of business or cannot pay his [or her] debts as they become due or is insolvent within the meaning of federal bankruptcy law" [UCC 1–201(23)].

INSTALLMENT CONTRACT ■ Under the UCC, a contract that requires or authorizes delivery in two or more separate lots to be accepted and paid for separately.

INSURABLE INTEREST ■ An interest either in a person's life or well-being or in property that is sufficiently substantial that insuring against injury to (or the death of) the person or against damage to the property does not amount to a mere wagering (betting) contract.

INSURANCE ■ A contract in which, for a stipulated consideration, one party agrees to compensate the other for loss on a specific subject by a specified peril.

INTANGIBLE PROPERTY ■ Property that cannot be seen or touched but exists only conceptually, such as corporate stocks and bonds, patents and copyrights, and ordinary contract rights. Article 2 of the UCC does not govern intangible property.

INTEGRATED CONTRACT ■ A written contract that constitutes the final expression of the parties' agreement. If a contract is integrated, evidence extraneous to the contract that contradicts or alters the meaning of the contract in any way is inadmissible.

INTELLECTUAL PROPERTY ■ Property resulting from intellectual, creative processes.

INTENDED BENEFICIARY ■ A third party for whose benefit a contract is formed. An intended beneficiary can sue the promisor if such a contract is breached.

INTENTIONAL TORT ■ A wrongful act knowingly committed.

INTER VIVOS TRUST ■ A trust created by the grantor (settlor) and effective during the grantor's lifetime; a trust not established by a will.

INTERMEDIARY BANK ■ Any bank to which an item is transferred in the course of collection, except the depositary or payor bank.

INTERNATIONAL LAW ■ The law that governs relations among nations. National laws, customs, treaties, and international conferences and organizations are generally considered to be the most important sources of international law.

INTERROGATORIES ■ A series of written questions for which written answers are prepared, usually with the assistance of the party's attorney, and then signed under oath by a party to a lawsuit.

INTESTACY LAWS ■ State statutes that specify how property will be distributed when a person dies intestate (without a valid will); also called statutes of descent and distribution.

INTESTATE ■ As a noun, one who has died without having created a valid will; as an adjective, the state of having died without a will.

INVESTMENT COMPANY ■ A company that acts on behalf of many smaller shareholders/owners by buying a large portfolio of securities and professionally managing that portfolio.

 J

JOINT AND SEVERAL LIABILITY ■ In partnership law, a doctrine under which a plaintiff may sue, and collect a judgment from all of the partners together (jointly), or one or more of the partners separately (severally, or individually). This is true even if one of the partners sued did not participate in, ratify, or know about whatever it was that gave rise to the cause of action.

JOINT STOCK COMPANY ■ A hybrid form of business organization that combines characteristics of a corporation and a partnership. Usually, a joint stock company is regarded as a partnership for tax and other legal purposes.

JOINT TENANCY ■ The joint ownership of property by two or more co-owners in which each co-owner owns an undivided portion of the property. On the death of one of the joint tenants, his or her interest automatically passes to the surviving joint tenant(s).

JOINT VENTURE ■ A joint undertaking of a specific commercial enterprise by an association of persons. A joint venture normally is not a legal entity and is treated like a partnership for federal income tax purposes.

JUDICIAL REVIEW ■ The process by which a court decides on the constitutionality of legislative enactments and actions of the executive branch.

JURISDICTION ■ The authority of a court to hear and decide a specific action.

JURISPRUDENCE ■ The science or philosophy of law.

JUSTICIABLE CONTROVERSY ■ A controversy that is not hypothetical or academic but real and substantial; a requirement that must be satisfied before a court will hear a case.

LARCENY ■ The wrongful taking and carrying away of another person's personal property with the intent to permanently deprive the owner of the property. Some states classify larceny as either grand or petit, depending on the property's value.

LAW ■ A body of enforceable rules governing relationships among individuals and between individuals and their society.

LEASE AGREEMENT ■ In regard to the lease of goods, an agreement in which one person (the lessor) agrees to transfer the right to the possession and use of property to another person (the lessee) in exchange for rental payments.

LEASEHOLD ESTATE ■ An estate in realty held by a tenant under a lease. In every leasehold estate, the tenant has a qualified right to possess and/or use the land.

LEGACY ■ A gift of personal property under a will.

LEGAL POSITIVISM ■ A school of legal thought centered on the assumption that there is no law higher than the laws created by a national government. Laws must be obeyed, even if they are unjust, to prevent anarchy.

LEGAL REALISM ■ A school of legal thought of the 1920s and 1930s that generally advocated a less abstract and more realistic approach to the law, an approach that takes into account customary practices and the circumstances in which transactions take place. This school left a lasting imprint on American jurisprudence.

LEGATEE ■ One designated in a will to receive a gift of personal property.

LESSEE ■ A person who acquires the right to the possession and use of another's goods in exchange for rental payments.

LESSOR ■ A person who sells the right to the possession and use of goods to another in exchange for rental payments.

LETTER OF CREDIT ■ A written instrument, usually issued by a bank on behalf of a customer or other person, in which the issuer promises to honor drafts or other demands for payment by third persons in accordance with the terms of the instrument.

LEVY ■ The obtaining of money by legal process through the seizure and sale of nonsecured property, usually done after a writ of execution has been issued.

LIBEL ■ Defamation in writing or other permanent form (such as a digital recording) having the quality of permanence.

LICENSE ■ A revocable right or privilege of a person to come onto another person's land.

LIEN ■ An encumbrance on a property to satisfy a debt or protect a claim for payment of a debt.

LIFE ESTATE ■ An interest in land that exists only for the duration of the life of some person, usually the holder of the estate.

LIMITED LIABILITY COMPANY (LLC) ■ A hybrid form of business enterprise that offers the limited liability of a corporation and the tax advantages of a partnership.

LIMITED LIABILITY LIMITED PARTNERSHIP (LLLP) ■ A type of limited partnership in which the liability of all of the partners, including general partners, is limited to the amount of their investments.

LIMITED LIABILITY PARTNERSHIP (LLP) ■ A hybrid form of business organization that is used mainly by professionals who normally do business in a partnership. Like a partnership, an LLP is a pass-through entity for tax purposes, but the personal liability of the partners is limited.

LIMITED PARTNER ■ In a limited partnership, a partner who contributes capital to the partnership but has no right to participate in the management and operation of the business. The limited partner assumes no liability for partnership debts beyond the capital contributed.

LIMITED PARTNERSHIP ■ A partnership consisting of one or more general partners (who manage the business and are liable to the full extent of their personal assets for debts of the partnership) and one or more limited partners (who contribute only assets and are liable only up to the extent of their contributions).

LIQUIDATED DAMAGES ■ An amount, stipulated in a contract, that the parties to the contract believe to be a reasonable estimation of the damages that will occur in the event of a breach.

LIQUIDATION ■ In regard to corporations, the process by which corporate assets are converted into cash and distributed among creditors and shareholders according to specific rules of preference. In bankruptcy proceedings, the sale of all of the nonexempt assets of a debtor and the distribution of the proceeds to the debtor's creditors. Chapter 7 of the Bankruptcy Code provides for liquidation bankruptcy proceedings.

LITIGATION ■ The process of resolving a dispute through the court system.

LONG ARM STATUTE ■ A state statute that permits a state to obtain personal jurisdiction over nonresident defendants. A defendant must have certain "minimum contacts" with that state for the statute to apply.

LOST PROPERTY ■ Property with which the owner has involuntarily parted and then cannot find or recover.

M

MAILBOX RULE ■ A rule providing that an acceptance of an offer becomes effective on dispatch (on being placed in an official mailbox), if mail is, expressly or impliedly, an authorized means of communication of acceptance to the offeror.

MAKER ■ One who promises to pay a fixed amount of money to the holder of a promissory note or a certificate of deposit (CD).

MALPRACTICE ■ Professional misconduct or the lack of the requisite degree of skill as a professional. Negligence—the failure to exercise due care—on the part of a professional, such as a physician, is commonly referred to as malpractice.

MARKET CONCENTRATION ■ The degree to which a small number of firms control a large percentage share of a relevant market; determined by calculating the percentages held by the largest firms in that market.

MARKET POWER ■ The power of a firm to control the market price of its product. A monopoly has the greatest degree of market power.

MARKET-SHARE TEST ■ The primary measure of monopoly power. A firm's market share is the percentage of a market that the firm controls.

MECHANIC'S LIEN ■ A statutory lien on the real property of another, created to ensure payment for work performed and materials furnished in the repair or improvement of real property, such as a building.

MEDIATION ■ A method of settling disputes outside of court by using the services of a neutral third party, who acts as a communicating agent between the parties and assists them in negotiating a settlement.

MEMBER ■ The term used to designate a person who has an ownership interest in a limited liability company.

MERCHANT ■ A person who is engaged in the purchase and sale of goods. Under the UCC, a person who deals in goods of the kind involved in the sales contract or who holds herself or himself out as having skill or knowledge peculiar to the practices or use of the goods being purchased or sold. For definitions, see UCC 2–104.

MERGER ■ A contractual and statutory process in which one corporation (the surviving corporation) acquires all of the assets and liabilities of another corporation (the merged corporation). The shareholders of the merged corporation either are paid for their shares or receive shares in the surviving corporation.

META TAG ■ A key word in a document that can serve as an index reference to the document. On the Web, search engines return results based, in part, on the tags in Web documents. Words inserted into a Web site's key-word field to increase the site's inclusion in search engine results.

MINIMUM WAGE ■ The lowest wage, either by government regulation or union contract, that an employer may pay an hourly worker.

MINI-TRIAL ■ A private proceeding in which each party to a dispute argues its position before the other side and vice versa. A neutral third party may be present as an adviser and may render an opinion if the parties fail to reach an agreement.

MIRROR IMAGE RULE ■ A common law rule that requires that the terms of the offeree's acceptance adhere exactly to the terms of the offeror's offer for a valid contract to be formed.

MISDEMEANOR ■ A lesser crime than a felony, punishable by a fine or incarceration in jail for up to one year.

MISLAID PROPERTY ■ Property with which the owner has voluntarily parted and then cannot find or recover.

MITIGATION OF DAMAGES ■ A rule requiring a plaintiff to do whatever is reasonable to minimize the damages caused by the defendant.

MONEY LAUNDERING ■ Falsely reporting income that has been obtained through criminal activity as income obtained through a legitimate business enterprise—in effect, "laundering" the "dirty money."

MONOPOLIZATION ■ The possession of monopoly power in the relevant market and the willful acquisition or maintenance of that power, as distinguished from growth or development as a consequence of a superior product, business acumen, or historic accident.

MONOPOLY ■ A term generally used to describe a market in which there is a single seller or a limited number of sellers.

MONOPOLY POWER ■ The ability of a monopoly to dictate what takes place in a given market.

MORAL MINIMUM ■ The minimum degree of ethical behavior expected of a business firm, which is usually defined as compliance with the law.

MORTGAGEE ■ Under a mortgage agreement, the creditor who takes a security interest in the debtor's property.

MORTGAGOR ■ Under a mortgage agreement, the debtor who gives the creditor a security interest in the debtor's property in return for a mortgage loan.

MOTION FOR A DIRECTED VERDICT ■ In a jury trial, a motion for the judge to take the decision out of the hands of the jury and to direct a verdict for the party who filed the motion on the ground that the other party has not produced sufficient evidence to support her or his claim.

MOTION FOR A NEW TRIAL ■ A motion asserting that the trial was so fundamentally flawed (because of error, newly discovered evidence, prejudice, or other reason) that a new trial is necessary to prevent a miscarriage of justice.

MOTION FOR JUDGMENT *N.O.V.* ■ A motion requesting the court to grant judgment in favor of the party making the motion on the ground that the jury's verdict against him or her was unreasonable and erroneous.

MOTION FOR JUDGMENT ON THE PLEADINGS ■ A motion by either party to a lawsuit at the close of the pleadings requesting the court to decide the issue solely on the pleadings without proceeding to trial. The motion will be granted only if no facts are in dispute.

MOTION FOR SUMMARY JUDGMENT ■ A motion requesting the court to enter a judgment without proceeding to trial. The motion can be based on evidence outside the pleadings and will be granted only if no facts are in dispute.

MOTION TO DISMISS ■ A pleading in which a defendant asserts that the plaintiff's claim fails to state a cause of action (that is, has no basis in law) or that there are other grounds on which a suit should be dismissed.

MUTUAL FUND ■ A specific type of investment company that continually buys or sells to investors shares of ownership in a portfolio.

N

NATIONAL LAW ■ Law that pertains to a particular nation (as opposed to international law).

NATURAL LAW ■ The belief that government and the legal system should reflect universal moral and ethical principles that are inherent in human nature. The natural law school is the oldest and one of the most significant schools of legal thought.

NECESSARIES ■ Necessities required for life, such as food, shelter, clothing, and medical attention; may include whatever is believed to be necessary to maintain a person's standard of living or financial and social status.

NEGLIGENCE ■ The failure to exercise the standard of care that a reasonable person would exercise in similar circumstances.

NEGLIGENCE *PER SE* ■ An action or failure to act in violation of a statutory requirement.

NEGOTIABLE INSTRUMENT ■ A signed writing (record) that contains an unconditional promise or order to pay an exact sum of money on demand or at an exact future time to a specific person or order, or to bearer.

NEGOTIATION ■ In alternative dispute resolution, a process in which parties attempt to settle their dispute informally, with or without attorneys to represent them. In negotiable instruments law, the transfer of an instrument in such form that the transferee (the person to whom the instrument is transferred) becomes a holder.

NOMINAL DAMAGES ■ A small monetary award (often one dollar) granted to a plaintiff when no actual damage was suffered.

NO-PAR SHARES ■ Corporate shares that have no face value; that is, no specific dollar amount is printed on their face.

NORMAL TRADE RELATIONS (NTR) STATUS ■ A status granted in an international treaty by a provision stating that the citizens of the contracting nations may enjoy the privileges accorded by either party to citizens of its NTR nations. Generally, this status is designed to establish equality of international treatment.

NOTARY PUBLIC ■ A public official authorized to attest to the authenticity of signatures.

NOVATION ■ The substitution, by agreement, of a new contract for an old one, with the rights under the old one being terminated. Typically, novation involves the substitution of a new person who is responsible for the contract and the removal of the original party's rights and duties under the contract.

NUISANCE ■ A common law doctrine under which persons may be held liable for using their property in a manner that unreasonably interferes with others' rights to use or enjoy their own property.

NUNCUPATIVE WILL ■ An oral will (often called a deathbed will) made before witnesses; usually limited to transfers of personal property.

O

OBJECTIVE THEORY OF CONTRACTS ■ A theory under which the intent to form a contract will be judged by outward, objective facts (what the party said when entering into the contract, how the party acted or appeared, and the circumstances surrounding the transaction) as interpreted by a reasonable person, rather than by the party's own secret, subjective intentions.

OBLIGEE ■ One to whom an obligation is owed.

OBLIGOR ■ One who owes an obligation to another.

OFFER ■ A promise or commitment to perform or refrain from performing some specified act in the future.

OFFEREE ■ A person to whom an offer is made.

OFFEROR ■ A person who makes an offer.

ONLINE DISPUTE RESOLUTION (ODR) ■ The resolution of disputes with the assistance of organizations that offer dispute-resolution services via the Internet.

OPERATING AGREEMENT ■ In a limited liability company, an agreement in which the members set forth the details of how the business will be managed and operated. State statutes typically give the members wide latitude in deciding for themselves the rules that will govern their organization.

OPTION CONTRACT ■ A contract under which the offeror cannot revoke his or her offer for a stipulated time period, and the offeree can accept or reject the offer during this period without fear that the offer will be made to another person. The offeree must give consideration for the option (the irrevocable offer) to be enforceable.

ORDER FOR RELIEF ■ A court's grant of assistance to a complainant. In bankruptcy proceedings, the order relieves the debtor of the immediate obligation to pay the debts listed in the bankruptcy petition.

ORDER INSTRUMENT ■ A negotiable instrument that is payable "to the order of an identified person" or "to an identified person or order."

ORDINANCE ■ A regulation enacted by a city or county legislative body that becomes part of that state's statutory law.

OUTPUT CONTRACT ■ An agreement in which a seller agrees to sell and a buyer agrees to buy all or up to a stated amount of what the seller produces.

OVERDRAFT ■ A check that is paid by the bank when the checking account on which the check is written contains insufficient funds to cover the check.

P

PARENT-SUBSIDIARY MERGER ■ A merger of companies in which one company (the parent corporation) owns most of the stock of the other corporation (the subsidiary corporation). A parent-subsidiary merger (short-form merger) can use a simplified procedure when the parent corporation owns at least 90 percent of the outstanding shares of each class of stock of the subsidiary corporation.

PARTIALLY DISCLOSED PRINCIPAL ■ A principal whose identity is unknown by a third party, but the third party knows that the agent is or may be acting for a principal at the time the agent and the third party form a contract.

PARTNERING AGREEMENT ■ An agreement between a seller and a buyer who frequently do business with each other concerning the terms and conditions that will apply to all subsequently formed electronic contracts.

PARTNERSHIP ■ An agreement by two or more persons to carry on, as co-owners, a business for profit.

PAR-VALUE SHARES ■ Corporate shares that have a specific face value, or formal cash-in value, written on them, such as one dollar.

PASS-THROUGH ENTITY ■ A business entity that has no tax liability; the entity's income is passed through to the owners, and the owners pay taxes on the income.

PAST CONSIDERATION ■ An act that takes place before the contract is made and that ordinarily, by itself, cannot be consideration for a later promise to pay for the act.

PATENT ■ A government grant that gives an inventor the exclusive right or privilege to make, use, or sell his or her invention for a limited time period.

PAYEE ■ A person to whom an instrument is made payable.

PAYOR BANK ■ The bank on which a check is drawn (the drawee bank).

PEER-TO-PEER (P2P) NETWORKING ■ The sharing of resources (such as files, hard drives, and processing styles) among multiple computers without necessarily requiring a central network server.

PENALTY ■ A contractual clause that states that a certain amount of money damages will be paid in the event of a future default or breach of contract. The damages are not a measure of compensation for the contract's breach but rather a punishment for a default. The agreement as to the amount will not be enforced, and recovery will be limited to actual damages.

PER CAPITA ■ A Latin term meaning "per person." In the law governing estate distribution, a method of distributing the property of an intestate's estate so that each heir in a certain class (such as grandchildren) receives an equal share.

PER SE VIOLATION ■ A type of anticompetitive agreement that is considered to be so injurious to the public that there is no need to determine whether it actually injures market competition; rather, it is in itself (per se) a violation of the Sherman Act.

PER STIRPES ■ A Latin term meaning "by the roots." In the law governing estate distribution, a method of distributing an intestate's estate so that each heir in a certain class (such as grandchildren) takes the share to which her or his deceased ancestor (such as a mother or father) would have been entitled.

PERFECTION ■ The legal process by which secured parties protect themselves against the claims of third parties who may wish to have their debts satisfied out of the same collateral; usually accomplished by filing a financing statement with the appropriate government official.

PERFORMANCE ■ In contract law, the fulfillment of one's duties arising under a contract with another; the normal way of discharging one's contractual obligations.

PERIODIC TENANCY ■ A lease interest in land for an indefinite period involving payment of rent at fixed intervals, such as week to week, month to month, or year to year.

PERSONAL DEFENSES ■ Defenses that can be used to avoid payment to an ordinary holder of a negotiable instrument but not a holder in due course (HDC) or a holder with the rights of an HDC.

PERSONAL PROPERTY ■ Property that is movable; any property that is not real property.

PERSUASIVE AUTHORITY ■ Any legal authority or source of law that a court may look to for guidance but on which it need not rely in making its decision. Persuasive authorities include cases from other jurisdictions and secondary sources of law.

PETITION IN BANKRUPTCY ■ The document that is filed with a bankruptcy court to initiate bankruptcy proceedings. The official forms required for a petition in bankruptcy must be completed accurately, sworn to under oath, and signed by the debtor.

PETTY OFFENSE ■ In criminal law, the least serious kind of criminal offense, such as a traffic or building-code violation.

PIERCING THE CORPORATE VEIL ■ An action in which a court disregards the corporate entity and holds the shareholders personally liable for corporate debts and obligations.

PLAINTIFF ■ One who initiates a lawsuit.

PLEA BARGAINING ■ The process by which a defendant and the prosecutor in a criminal case work out a mutually satisfactory disposition of the case, subject to court approval; usually involves the defendant's pleading guilty to a lesser offense in return for a lighter sentence.

PLEADINGS ■ Statements made by the plaintiff and the defendant in a lawsuit that detail the facts, charges, and defenses involved in the litigation. The complaint and answer are part of the pleadings.

PLEDGE ■ A common law security device (retained in Article 9 of the UCC) in which personal property is transferred into the possession of the creditor as security for the payment of a debt and retained by the creditor until the debt is paid.

POLICE POWERS ■ Powers possessed by the states as part of their inherent sovereignty. These powers may be exercised to protect or promote the public order, health, safety, morals, and general welfare.

POLICY ■ In insurance law, a contract between the insurer and the insured in which, for a stipulated consideration, the insurer agrees to compensate the insured for loss on a specific subject by a specified peril.

POSITIVE LAW ■ The body of conventional, or written, law of a particular society at a particular point in time.

POTENTIALLY RESPONSIBLE PARTY (PRP) ■ A party liable for the costs of cleaning up a hazardous waste–disposal site under the Comprehensive Environmental Response, Compensation, and Liability Act (CERCLA). Any person who generated the hazardous waste, transported it, owned or operated the waste site at the time of disposal, or currently owns or operates the site may be responsible for some or all of the clean-up costs.

POWER OF ATTORNEY ■ A written document, which is usually notarized, authorizing another to act as one's agent; can be special (permitting the agent to do specified acts only) or general (permitting the agent to transact all business for the principal).

PRECEDENT ■ A court decision that furnishes an example or authority for deciding subsequent cases involving identical or similar facts.

PREDATORY BEHAVIOR ■ Business behavior that is undertaken with the intention of unlawfully driving competitors out of the market.

PREDATORY PRICING ■ The pricing of a product below cost with the intent to drive competitors out of the market.

PREDOMINANT-FACTOR TEST ■ A test courts use to determine whether a contract is primarily for the sale of goods or for the sale of services.

PREEMPTION ■ A doctrine under which certain federal laws preempt, or take precedence over, conflicting state or local laws.

PREEMPTIVE RIGHTS ■ Rights held by shareholders that entitle them to purchase newly issued shares of a corporation's stock, equal in percentage to shares currently held, before the stock is offered to any outside buyers. Preemptive rights enable shareholders to maintain their proportionate ownership and voice in the corporation.

PREFERENCE ■ In bankruptcy proceedings, property transfers or payments made by the debtor that favor (give preference to) one creditor over others. The bankruptcy trustee is allowed to recover payments made both voluntarily and involuntarily to one creditor in preference over another.

PREFERRED STOCK ■ Classes of stock that have priority over common stock as to both payment of dividends and distribution of assets on the corporation's dissolution.

PREMIUM ■ In insurance law, the price paid by the insured for insurance protection for a specified period of time.

PRENUPTIAL AGREEMENT ■ An agreement made before marriage that defines each partner's ownership rights in the other partner's property. Prenuptial agreements must be in writing to be enforceable.

PRESENTMENT ■ The act of presenting an instrument to the party liable on the instrument to collect payment. Presentment also occurs when a person presents an instrument to a drawee for a required acceptance.

PRESENTMENT WARRANTIES ■ Implied warranties, made by any person who presents an instrument for payment or acceptance, that (1) the person obtaining payment or acceptance is entitled to enforce the instrument or is authorized to obtain payment or acceptance on behalf of a person who is entitled to enforce the instrument, (2) the instrument has not been altered, and (3) the person obtaining payment or acceptance has no knowledge that the signature of the drawer of the instrument is unauthorized.

PRICE DISCRIMINATION ■ Setting prices in such a way that two competing buyers pay two different prices for an identical product or service.

PRICE-FIXING AGREEMENT ■ An agreement between competitors to fix the prices of products or services at a certain level.

PRIMA FACIE CASE ■ A case in which the plaintiff has produced sufficient evidence of his or her conclusion that the case can go to a jury; a case in which the evidence compels the plaintiff's conclusion if the defendant produces no affirmative defense or evidence to disprove it.

PRIMARY SOURCE OF LAW ■ A document that establishes the law on a particular issue, such as a constitution, a statute, an administrative rule, or a court decision.

PRINCIPAL ■ In agency law, a person who agrees to have another, called the agent, act on her or his behalf.

PRINCIPLE OF RIGHTS ■ The principle that human beings have certain fundamental rights (to life, freedom, and the pursuit of happiness, for example). Those who adhere to this "rights theory" believe that a key factor in determining whether a business decision is ethical is how that decision affects the rights of various groups. These groups include the firm's owners, its employees, the consumers of its products or services, its suppliers, the community in which it does business, and society as a whole.

PRIVILEGE ■ A legal right, exemption, or immunity granted to a person or a class of persons. In the context of defamation, an absolute privilege immunizes the actor from suit, regardless of whether the actor's statements were malicious. A qualified privilege immunizes an actor from suit only when the privilege is properly exercised in the performance of a legal or moral duty.

PRIVITY OF CONTRACT ■ The relationship that exists between the promisor and the promisee of a contract.

PROBABLE CAUSE ■ Reasonable grounds for believing that a person should be arrested or searched.

PROBATE ■ The process of proving and validating a will and settling all matters pertaining to an estate.

PROBATE COURT ■ A state court of limited jurisdiction that conducts proceedings relating to the settlement of a deceased person's estate.

PROCEDURAL LAW ■ Law that establishes the methods of enforcing the rights established by substantive law.

PROCEEDS ■ Under Article 9 of the UCC, whatever is received when the collateral is sold or otherwise disposed of, such as by exchange.

PRODUCT LIABILITY ■ The legal liability of manufacturers, sellers, and lessors of goods to consumers, users, and bystanders for injuries or damages that are caused by the goods.

PROFIT ■ In real property law, the right to enter upon and remove things from the property of another (for example, the right to enter onto a person's land and remove sand and gravel therefrom).

PROMISE ■ An assertion that something either will or will not happen in the future.

PROMISEE ■ A person to whom a promise is made.

PROMISOR ■ A person who makes a promise.

PROMISSORY ESTOPPEL ■ A doctrine that applies when a promisor makes a clear and definite promise on which the promisee justifiably relies; such a promise is binding if justice will be better served by the enforcement of the promise.

PROMISSORY NOTE ■ A written promise made by one person (the maker) to pay a fixed amount of money to another person (the payee or a subsequent holder) on demand or on a specified date.

PROMOTER ■ A person who takes the preliminary steps in organizing a corporation, including (usually) issuing a prospectus, procuring stock subscriptions, making contracts for necessary purchases and services, securing a corporate charter, and the like.

PROPERTY ■ Legally protected rights and interests in anything with an ascertainable value that is subject to ownership.

PROSPECTUS ■ A document required by federal or state securities laws that describes the financial operations of the corporation, thus allowing investors to make informed decisions.

PROTECTED CLASS ■ A group of persons protected by specific laws because of the group's defining characteristics. Under laws prohibiting employment discrimination, these characteristics include race, color, religion, national origin, gender, age, and disability.

PROXIMATE CAUSE ■ Legal cause; exists when the connection between an act and an injury is strong enough to justify imposing liability.

PROXY ■ In corporation law, a written agreement between a stockholder and another party under which the stockholder authorizes the other party to vote the stockholder's shares in a certain manner.

PUFFERY ■ A salesperson's often exaggerated claims concerning the quality of property offered for sale. Such claims involve opinions rather than facts and are not considered to be legally binding promises or warranties.

PUNITIVE DAMAGES ■ Money damages that may be awarded to a plaintiff to punish the defendant and deter future similar conduct.

PURCHASE-MONEY SECURITY INTEREST (PMSI) ■ A security interest that arises when a seller or lender extends credit for part or all of the purchase price of goods purchased by a buyer.

 Q

QUALIFIED INDORSEMENT ■ An indorsement on a negotiable instrument in which the indorser disclaims any contract liability on the instrument. The notation "without recourse" is commonly used to create a qualified indorsement.

QUASI CONTRACT ■ A fictional contract imposed on parties by a court in the interests of fairness and justice; usually imposed to avoid the unjust enrichment of one party at the expense of another.

QUITCLAIM DEED ■ A deed intended to pass any title, interest, or claim that the grantor may have in the property without warranting that such title is valid. A quitclaim deed offers the least amount of protection against defects in the title.

QUORUM ■ The number of members of a decision-making body that must be present before business may be transacted.

QUOTA ■ A set limit on the amount of goods that can be imported.

 R

RATIFICATION ■ The act of accepting and giving legal force to an obligation that previously was not enforceable.

REAFFIRMATION AGREEMENT ■ An agreement between a debtor and a creditor in which the debtor voluntarily agrees to pay, or reaffirm, a debt dischargeable in bankruptcy. To be enforceable, the agreement must be made before the debtor is granted a discharge.

REAL PROPERTY ■ Land and everything attached to it, such as trees and buildings.

REASONABLE PERSON STANDARD ■ The standard of behavior expected of a hypothetical "reasonable person"; the standard against which negligence is measured and that must be observed to avoid liability for negligence.

RECEIVER ■ In a corporate dissolution, a court-appointed person who winds up corporate affairs and liquidates corporate assets.

RECORD ■ According to the Uniform Electronic Transactions Act, information that is either inscribed on a tangible medium or stored in an electronic or other medium and that is retrievable. The Uniform Computer Information Transactions Act also uses the term *record* instead of *writing*.

RECORDING STATUTES ■ Statutes that allow deeds, mortgages, and other real property transactions to be recorded so as to provide notice to future purchasers or creditors of an existing claim on the property.

RED HERRING ■ A preliminary prospectus that can be distributed to potential investors after the registration statement (for a securities offering) has been filed with the Securities and Exchange Commission. The name derives from the red legend printed across the prospectus stating that the registration has been filed but has not become effective.

REFORMATION ■ A court-ordered correction of a written contract so that it reflects the true intentions of the parties.

REGULATION E ■ A set of rules issued by the Federal Reserve System's Board of Governors to protect users of elecronic fund transfer systems.

REGULATION Z ■ A set of rules promulgated by the Federal Reserve Board of Governors to implement the provisions of the Truth-in-Lending Act.

RELEASE ■ A contract in which one party forfeits the right to pursue a legal claim against the other party.

REMEDY ■ The relief given to an innocent party to enforce a right or compensate for the violation of a right.

REPLEVIN ■ An action to recover identified goods in the hands of a party who is wrongfully withholding them from the other party. Under the UCC, this remedy is usually available only if the buyer or lessee is unable to cover.

REPLY ■ Procedurally, a plaintiff's response to a defendant's answer.

REQUIREMENTS CONTRACT ■ An agreement in which a buyer agrees to purchase and the seller agrees to sell all or up to a stated amount of what the buyer needs or requires.

RES IPSA LOQUITUR ■ A doctrine under which negligence may be inferred simply because an event occurred, if it is the type of event that would never occur in the absence of negligence. Literally, the term means "the facts speak for themselves."

RESALE PRICE MAINTENANCE AGREEMENT ■ An agreement between a manufacturer and a retailer in which the manufacturer specifies what the retail prices of its products must be.

RESCISSION ■ A remedy whereby a contract is canceled and the parties are returned to the positions they occupied before the contract was made; may be effected through the mutual consent of the parties, by the parties' conduct, or by court decree.

RESPONDEAT SUPERIOR ■ Latin for "let the master respond." A doctrine under which a principal or an employer is held liable for the wrongful acts committed by agents or employees while acting within the course and scope of their agency or employment.

RESTITUTION ■ An equitable remedy under which a person is restored to his or her original position prior to loss or injury, or placed in the position he or she would have been in had the breach not occurred.

RESTRICTIVE INDORSEMENT ■ Any indorsement on a negotiable instrument that requires the indorsee to comply with certain instructions regarding the funds involved. A restrictive indorsement does not prohibit the further negotiation of the instrument.

RESULTING TRUST ■ An implied trust arising from the conduct of the parties. A trust in which a party holds the actual legal title to another's property but only for that person's benefit.

RETAINED EARNINGS ■ The portion of a corporation's profits that has not been paid out as dividends to shareholders.

REVOCATION ■ In contract law, the withdrawal of an offer by an offeror. Unless the offer is irrevocable, it can be revoked at any time prior to acceptance without liability.

RIGHT OF CONTRIBUTION ■ The right of a co-surety who pays more than his or her proportionate share on a debtor's default to recover the excess paid from other co-sureties.

RIGHT OF FIRST REFUSAL ■ The right to purchase personal or real property—such as corporate shares or real estate—before the property is offered for sale to others.

RIGHT OF REIMBURSEMENT ■ The legal right of a person to be restored, repaid, or indemnified for costs, expenses, or losses incurred or expended on behalf of another.

RIGHT OF SUBROGATION ■ The right of a person to stand in the place of (be substituted for) another, giving the substituted party the same legal rights that the original party had.

RIGHT-TO-WORK LAW ■ A state law providing that employees may not be required to join a union as a condition of retaining employment.

RISK ■ A prediction concerning potential loss based on known and unknown factors.

RISK MANAGEMENT ■ Planning that is undertaken to protect one's interest should some event threaten to undermine its security. In the context of insurance, risk management involves transferring certain risks from the insured to the insurance company.

ROBBERY ■ The act of forcefully and unlawfully taking personal property of any value from another. Force or intimidation is usually necessary for an act of theft to be considered a robbery.

RULE OF FOUR ■ A rule of the United States Supreme Court under which the Court will not issue a *writ of certiorari* unless at least four justices approve of the decision to issue the writ.

RULE OF REASON ■ A test by which a court balances the positive effects (such as economic efficiency) of an agreement against its potentially anticompetitive effects. In antitrust litigation, many practices are analyzed under the rule of reason.

RULEMAKING ■ The process undertaken by an administrative agency when formally adopting a new regulation or amending an old one. Rulemaking involves notifying the public of a proposed rule or change and receiving and considering the public's comments.

S

S CORPORATION ■ A close business corporation that has met certain requirements set out in the Internal Revenue Code and thus qualifies for special income tax treatment. Essentially, an S corporation is taxed the same as a partnership, but its owners enjoy the privilege of limited liability.

SALE ■ The passing of title to property from the seller to the buyer for a price.

SALE ON APPROVAL ■ A type of conditional sale in which the buyer may take the goods on a trial basis. The sale becomes absolute only when the buyer approves of (or is satisfied with) the goods being sold.

SALE OR RETURN ■ A type of conditional sale in which title and possession pass from the seller to the buyer, but the buyer retains the option to return the goods during a specified period even though the goods conform to the contract.

SALES CONTRACT ■ A contract for the sale of goods under which the ownership of goods is transferred from a seller to a buyer for a price.

SCIENTER ■ Knowledge by the misrepresenting party that material facts have been falsely represented or omitted with an intent to deceive.

SEARCH WARRANT ■ An order granted by a public authority, such as a judge, that authorizes law enforcement personnel to search particular premises or property.

SEASONABLY ■ Within a specified time period or, if no period is specified, within a reasonable time.

SEC RULE 10b-5 ■ A rule of the Securities and Exchange Commission (SEC) that makes it unlawful, in connection with the purchase or sale of any security, to make any untrue statement of a material fact or to omit a material fact if such omission causes the statement to be misleading.

SECONDARY BOYCOTT ■ A union's refusal to work for, purchase from, or handle the products of a secondary employer, with whom the union has no dispute, in order to force that employer to stop doing business with the primary employer, with whom the union has a labor dispute.

SECONDARY SOURCE OF LAW ■ A publication that summarizes or interprets the law, such as a legal encyclopedia, a legal treatise, or an article in a law review.

SECURED PARTY ■ A lender, seller, or any other person in whose favor there is a security interest, including a person to whom accounts or chattel paper has been sold.

SECURED TRANSACTION ■ Any transaction in which the payment of a debt is guaranteed, or secured, by personal property owned by the debtor or in which the debtor has a legal interest.

SECURITIES ■ Generally, stock certificates, bonds, notes, debentures, warrants, or other documents given as evidence of an ownership interest in a corporation or as a promise of repayment by a corporation.

SECURITY ■ Generally, a stock certificate, bond, note, debenture, warrant, or other document given as evidence of an ownership interest in a corporation or as a promise of repayment by a corporation.

SECURITY AGREEMENT ■ An agreement that creates or provides for a security interest between the debtor and a secured party.

SECURITY INTEREST ■ Any interest in personal property or fixtures that secures payment or performance of an obligation.

SELF-DEFENSE ■ The legally recognized privilege to protect oneself or one's property against injury by another. The privilege of self-defense protects only acts that are reasonably necessary to protect oneself, one's property, or another person.

SELF-INCRIMINATION ■ The giving of testimony that may subject the testifier to criminal prosecution. The Fifth Amendment to the Constitution protects against self-incrimination by providing that no person "shall be compelled in any criminal case to be a witness against himself."

SENIORITY SYSTEM ■ In regard to employment relationships, a system in which those who have worked longest for the company are first in line for promotions, salary increases, and other benefits; they are also the last to be laid off if the work force must be reduced.

SERVICE MARK ■ A mark used in the sale or the advertising of services to distinguish the services of one person from those of others. Titles, character names, and other distinctive features of radio and television programs may be registered as service marks.

SEXUAL HARASSMENT ■ In the employment context, the demanding of sexual favors in return for job promotions or other benefits, or language or conduct that is so sexually offensive that it creates a hostile working environment.

SHAREHOLDER'S DERIVATIVE SUIT ■ A suit brought by a shareholder to enforce a corporate cause of action against a third person.

SHELTER PRINCIPLE ■ The principle that the holder of a negotiable instrument who cannot qualify as a holder in due course (HDC), but who derives his or her title through an HDC, acquires the rights of an HDC.

SHIPMENT CONTRACT ■ A contract for the sale of goods in which the seller is required or authorized to ship the goods by carrier. The seller assumes liability for any losses or damage to the goods until they are delivered to the carrier.

SHORT-FORM MERGER ■ A merger between a subsidiary corporation and a parent corporation that owns at least 90 percent of the outstanding shares of each class of stock issued by the subsidiary corporation. Short-form mergers can be accomplished without the approval of the shareholders of either corporation.

SHRINK-WRAP AGREEMENT ■ An agreement whose terms are expressed in a document located inside a box in which goods (usually software) are packaged; sometimes called a *shrink-wrap license*.

SIGNATURE ■ Under the UCC, "any symbol executed or adopted by a party with a present intention to authenticate a writing."

SLANDER ■ Defamation in oral form.

SLANDER OF QUALITY (TRADE LIBEL) ■ The publication of false information about another's product, alleging that it is not what its seller claims.

SLANDER OF TITLE ■ The publication of a statement that denies or casts doubt on another's legal ownership of any property, causing financial loss to that property's owner.

SMALL CLAIMS COURT ■ A special court in which parties may litigate small claims (such as $5,000 or less). Attorneys are not required in small claims courts and, in some states, are not allowed to represent the parties.

SMART CARD ■ A card containing a microprocessor that permits storage of funds via security programming, can communicate with other computers, and does not require online authorization for fund transfers.

SOCIOLOGICAL SCHOOL ■ A school of legal thought that views the law as a tool for promoting justice in society.

SOLE PROPRIETORSHIP ■ The simplest form of business organization, in which the owner is the business. The owner reports business income on his or her personal income tax return and is legally responsible for all debts and obligations incurred by the business.

SOVEREIGN IMMUNITY ■ A doctrine that immunizes foreign nations from the jurisdiction of U.S. courts when certain conditions are satisfied.

SPAM ■ Bulk, unsolicited ("junk") e-mail.

SPECIAL INDORSEMENT ■ An indorsement on an instrument that indicates the specific person to whom the indorser intends to make the instrument payable; that is, it names the indorsee.

SPECIAL WARRANTY DEED ■ A deed in which the grantor only warrants that the grantor or seller held good title during his or her ownership of the property and does not warrant that there were no defects of title when the property was held by previous owners.

SPECIFIC PERFORMANCE ■ An equitable remedy requiring exactly the performance that was specified in a contract; usually granted only when money damages would be an inadequate remedy and the subject matter of the contract is unique (for example, real property).

SPENDTHRIFT TRUST ■ A trust created to protect the beneficiary from spending all the funds to which she or he is entitled. Only a certain portion of the total amount is given to the beneficiary at any one time, and most states prohibit creditors from attaching assets of the trust.

STALE CHECK ■ A check, other than a certified check, that is presented for payment more than six months after its date.

STANDING TO SUE ■ The requirement that an individual must have a sufficient stake in a controversy before he or she can bring a lawsuit. The plaintiff must demonstrate that he or she has been either injured or threatened with injury.

STARE DECISIS ■ A common law doctrine under which judges are obligated to follow the precedents established in prior decisions.

STATUTE OF FRAUDS ■ A state statute under which certain types of contracts must be in writing to be enforceable.

STATUTE OF LIMITATIONS ■ A federal or state statute setting the maximum time period during which a certain action can be brought or certain rights enforced.

STATUTE OF REPOSE ■ Basically, a statute of limitations that is not dependent on the happening of a cause of action. Statutes of repose generally begin to run at an earlier date and run for a longer period of time than statutes of limitations.

STATUTORY LAW ■ The body of law enacted by legislative bodies (as opposed to constitutional law, administrative law, or case law).

STOCK ■ An equity (ownership) interest in a corporation, measured in units of shares.

STOCK CERTIFICATE ■ A certificate issued by a corporation evidencing the ownership of a specified number of shares in the corporation.

STOCK WARRANT ■ A certificate that grants the owner the option to buy a given number of shares of stock, usually within a set time period.

STOP-PAYMENT ORDER ■ An order by a bank customer to his or her bank not to pay or certify a certain check.

STORED-VALUE CARD ■ A card bearing magnetic strips that hold magnetically encoded data, providing access to stored funds.

STRICT LIABILITY ■ Liability regardless of fault. In tort law, strict liability is imposed on a manufacturer or seller that introduces into commerce a good that is unreasonably dangerous when in a defective condition.

STRIKE ■ An action undertaken by unionized workers when collective bargaining fails; the workers leave their jobs, refuse to work, and (typically) picket the employer's workplace.

SUBLEASE ■ A lease executed by the lessee of real estate to a third person, conveying the same interest that the lessee enjoys but for a shorter term than that held by the lessee.

SUBSTANTIVE LAW ■ Law that defines, describes, regulates, and creates legal rights and obligations.

SUMMARY JURY TRIAL (SJT) ■ A method of settling disputes, used in many federal courts, in which a trial is held, but the jury's verdict is not binding. The verdict acts only as a guide to both sides in reaching an agreement during the mandatory negotiations that immediately follow the summary jury trial.

SUMMONS ■ A document informing a defendant that a legal action has been commenced against him or her and that the defendant must appear in court on a certain date to answer the plaintiff's complaint. The document is delivered by a sheriff or any other person so authorized.

SUPREMACY CLAUSE ■ The provision in Article VI of the Constitution that provides that the Constitution, laws, and treaties of the United States are "the supreme Law of the Land." Under this clause, state and local laws that directly conflict with federal law will be rendered invalid.

SURETY ■ A person, such as a cosigner on a note, who agrees to be primarily responsible for the debt of another.

SURETYSHIP ■ An express contract in which a third party to a debtor-creditor relationship (the surety) promises to be primarily responsible for the debtor's obligation.

SYMBOLIC SPEECH ■ Nonverbal expressions of beliefs. Symbolic speech, which includes gestures, movements, and articles of clothing, is given substantial protection by the courts.

SYNDICATE ■ An investment group of persons or firms brought together for the purpose of financing a project that they would not or could not undertake independently.

T

TAKEOVER ■ The acquisition of control over a corporation through the purchase of a substantial number of the voting shares of the corporation.

TAKING ■ The taking of private property by the government for public use. The government may not take private property for public use without "just compensation."

TANGIBLE PROPERTY ■ Property that has physical existence and can be distinguished by the senses of touch, sight, and so on. A car is tangible property; a patent right is intangible property.

TARGET CORPORATION ■ The corporation to be acquired in a corporate takeover; a corporation to whose shareholders a tender offer is submitted.

TARIFF ■ A tax on imported goods.

TENANCY AT SUFFERANCE ■ A type of tenancy under which a tenant who, after rightfully being in possession of leased premises, continues (wrongfully) to occupy the property after the lease has been terminated. The tenant has no rights to possess the property and occupies it only because the person entitled to evict the tenant has not done so.

TENANCY AT WILL ■ A type of tenancy that either party can terminate without notice; usually arises when a tenant who has been under a tenancy for years retains possession, with the landlord's consent, after the tenancy for years has terminated.

TENANCY BY THE ENTIRETY ■ The joint ownership of property by a husband and wife. Neither party can transfer her or his interest in the property without the consent of the other.

TENANCY FOR YEARS ■ A type of tenancy under which property is leased for a specified period of time, such as a month, a year, or a period of years.

TENANCY IN COMMON ■ Co-ownership of property in which each party owns an undivided interest that passes to her or his heirs at death.

TENDER ■ An unconditional offer to perform an obligation by a person who is ready, willing, and able to do so.

TENDER OFFER ■ An offer to purchase shares made by one company directly to the shareholders of another (target) company; often referred to as a "takeover bid."

TESTAMENTARY TRUST ■ A trust that is created by will and therefore does not take effect until the death of the testator.

TESTATE ■ Having left a will at death.

TESTATOR ■ One who makes and executes a will.

THIRD PARTY BENEFICIARY ■ One for whose benefit a promise is made in a contract but who is not a party to the contract.

TIPPEE ■ A person who receives inside information.

TOMBSTONE AD ■ An advertisement, historically in a format resembling a tombstone, of a securities offering. The ad tells potential investors where and how they may obtain a prospectus.

TORT ■ A civil wrong not arising from a breach of contract. A breach of a legal duty that proximately causes harm or injury to another.

TORTFEASOR ■ One who commits a tort.

TOTTEN TRUST ■ A trust created by the deposit of a person's own funds in his or her own name as a trustee for another. It is a tentative trust, revocable at will until the depositor dies or completes the gift in his or her lifetime by some unequivocal act or declaration.

TOXIC TORT ■ A civil wrong arising from exposure to a toxic substance, such as asbestos, radiation, or hazardous waste.

TRADE ACCEPTANCE ■ A draft that is drawn by a seller of goods ordering the buyer to pay a specified sum of money to the seller, usually at a stated time in the future. The buyer accepts the draft by signing the face of the draft, thus creating an enforceable obligation to pay the draft when it comes due. On a trade acceptance, the seller is both the drawer and the payee.

TRADE DRESS ■ The image and overall appearance of a product—for example, the distinctive decor, menu, layout, and style of service of a particular restaurant. Basically, trade dress is subject to the same protection as trademarks.

TRADE NAME ■ A term that is used to indicate part or all of a business's name and that is directly related to the business's reputation and goodwill. Trade names are protected under the common law (and under trademark law, if the name is the same as the firm's trademarked property).

TRADE SECRETS ■ Information or processes that give a business an advantage over competitors that do not know the information or processes.

TRADEMARK ■ A distinctive mark, motto, device, or emblem that a manufacturer stamps, prints, or otherwise affixes to the goods it produces so that they may be identified on the market and their origins made known. Once a trademark is established (under the common law or through registration), the owner is entitled to its exclusive use.

TRANSFER WARRANTIES ■ Implied warranties, made by any person who transfers an instrument for consideration to subsequent transferees and holders who take the instrument in good faith, that (1) the transferor is entitled to enforce the instrument; (2) all signatures are authentic and authorized; (3) the instrument has not been altered; (4) the instrument is not subject to a defense or claim of any party that can be asserted against the transferor; and (5) the transferor has no knowledge of any insolvency proceedings against the maker, the acceptor, or the drawer of the instrument.

TRAVELER'S CHECK ■ A check that is payable on demand, drawn on or payable through a financial institution (bank), and designated as a traveler's check.

TREBLE DAMAGES ■ Damages that, by statute, are three times the amount that the fact finder determines is owed.

TRESPASS TO LAND ■ The entry onto, above, or below the surface of land owned by another without the owner's permission or legal authorization.

TRESPASS TO PERSONAL PROPERTY ■ The unlawful taking or harming of another's personal property; interference with another's right to the exclusive possession of his or her personal property.

TRUST ■ An arrangement in which title to property is held by one person (a trustee) for the benefit of another (a beneficiary).

TRUST INDORSEMENT ■ An indorsement for the benefit of the indorser or a third person; also known as an agency indorsement. The indorsement results in legal title vesting in the original indorsee.

TYING ARRANGEMENT ■ An agreement between a buyer and a seller in which the buyer of a specific product or service becomes obligated to purchase additional products or services from the seller.

U.S. TRUSTEE ■ A government official who performs certain administrative tasks that a bankruptcy judge would otherwise have to perform.

ULTRA VIRES ■ A Latin term meaning "beyond the powers"; in corporate law, acts of a corporation that are beyond its express and implied powers to undertake.

UNCONSCIONABLE CONTRACT (OR UNCONSCIONABLE CLAUSE) ■ A contract or clause that is void on the basis of public policy because one party, as a result of disproportionate bargaining power, is forced to accept terms that are unfairly burdensome and that unfairly benefit the dominating party.

UNDERWRITER ■ In insurance law, the insurer, or the one assuming a risk in return for the payment of a premium.

UNDISCLOSED PRINCIPAL ■ A principal whose identity is unknown by a third person, and the third person has no knowledge that the agent is acting for a principal at the time the agent and the third person form a contract.

UNENFORCEABLE CONTRACT ■ A valid contract rendered unenforceable by some statute or law.

UNILATERAL CONTRACT ■ A contract that results when an offer can be accepted only by the offeree's performance.

UNION SHOP ■ A place of employment where all workers, once employed, must become union members within a specified period of time as a condition of their continued employment.

UNIVERSAL DEFENSES ■ Defenses that are valid against all holders of a negotiable instrument, including holders in due course (HDCs) and holders with the rights of HDCs.

UNREASONABLY DANGEROUS PRODUCT ■ In product liability, a product that is defective to the point of threatening a consumer's health and safety. A product will be considered unreasonably dangerous if it is dangerous beyond the expectation of the ordinary consumer or if a less dangerous alternative was economically feasible for the manufacturer, but the manufacturer failed to produce it.

USAGE OF TRADE ■ Any practice or method of dealing having such regularity of observance in a place, vocation, or trade as to justify an expectation that it will be observed with respect to the transaction in question.

USURY ■ Charging an illegal rate of interest.

UTILITARIANISM ■ An approach to ethical reasoning that evaluates behavior not on the basis of any absolute ethical or moral values but on the consequences of that behavior for those who will be affected by it. In utilitarian reasoning, a "good" decision is one that results in the greatest good for the greatest number of people affected by the decision.

VALID CONTRACT ■ A contract that results when the elements necessary for contract formation (agreement, consideration, legal purpose, and contractual capacity) are present.

VENUE ■ The geographic district in which an action is tried and from which the jury is selected.

VERTICAL MERGER ■ The acquisition by a company at one level in a marketing chain of a company at a higher or lower level in the chain (such as a company merging with one of its suppliers or retailers).

VERTICAL RESTRAINT ■ Any restraint on trade created by agreements between firms at different levels in the manufacturing and distribution process.

VERTICALLY INTEGRATED FIRM ■ A firm that carries out two or more functional phases (manufacture, distribution, and retailing, for example) of the chain of production.

VESTING ■ The creation of an absolute or unconditional right or power.

VICARIOUS LIABILITY ■ Legal responsibility placed on one person for the acts of another; indirect liability imposed on a supervisory party (such as an employer) for the actions of a subordinate (such as an employee) because of the relationship between the two parties.

VOID CONTRACT ■ A contract having no legal force or binding effect.

VOIDABLE CONTRACT ■ A contract that may be legally avoided (canceled, or annulled) at the option of one or both of the parties.

VOIR DIRE ■ An old French phrase meaning "to speak the truth." In legal language, the phrase refers to the process in which the attorneys question prospective jurors to learn about their backgrounds, attitudes, biases, and other characteristics that may affect their ability to serve as impartial jurors.

VOTING TRUST ■ An agreement (trust contract) under which legal title to shares of corporate stock is transferred to a trustee who is authorized by the shareholders to vote the shares on their behalf.

WARRANTY DEED ■ A deed in which the grantor assures (warrants to) the grantee that the grantor has title to the property conveyed in the deed, that there are no encumbrances on the property other than what the grantor has represented, and that the grantee will enjoy quiet possession of the property; a deed that provides the greatest amount of protection for the grantee.

WATERED STOCK ■ Shares of stock issued by a corporation for which the corporation receives, as payment, less than the stated value of the shares.

WETLANDS ■ Water-saturated areas of land that are designated by government agencies (such as the Army Corps of Engineers or the Environmental Protection Agency) as protected areas that support wildlife and therefore cannot be filled in or dredged by private contractors or parties without a permit.

WHISTLEBLOWING ■ An employee's disclosure to government authorities, upper-level managers, or the press that the employer is engaged in unsafe or illegal activities.

WHITE-COLLAR CRIME ■ Nonviolent crime committed by individuals or corporations to obtain a personal or business advantage.

WILL ■ An instrument directing what is to be done with the testator's property on his or her death, made by the testator and revocable during his or her lifetime. No interests in the testator's property pass until the testator dies.

WILL SUBSTITUTES ■ Various documents that attempt to dispose of an estate in the same or similar manner as a will, such as trusts or life insurance plans.

WINDING UP ■ The second of two stages in the termination of a partnership or corporation. Once the firm is dissolved, it continues to exist legally until the process of winding up all business affairs (collecting and distributing the firm's assets) is complete.

WORKERS' COMPENSATION LAWS ■ State statutes establishing an administrative procedure for compensating workers' injuries that arise out of—or in the course of—their employment, regardless of fault.

WORKOUT ■ An out-of-court agreement between a debtor and creditors in which the parties work out a payment plan or schedule under which the debtor's debts can be discharged.

WRIT OF ATTACHMENT ■ A court's order, issued prior to a trial to collect a debt, directing the sheriff or other officer to seize nonexempt property of the debtor. If the creditor prevails at trial, the seized property can be sold to satisfy the judgment.

WRIT OF CERTIORARI ■ A writ from a higher court asking the lower court for the record of a case.

WRIT OF EXECUTION ■ A court's order, issued after a judgment has been entered against the debtor, directing the sheriff to seize (levy) and sell any of the debtor's nonexempt real or personal property. The proceeds of the sale are used to pay off the judgment, accrued interest, and costs of the sale; any surplus is paid to the debtor.

WRONGFUL DISCHARGE ■ An employer's termination of an employee's employment in violation of the law.

■ TABLE OF CASES

■ INDEX